1,000,000 Books

are available to read at

www.ForgottenBooks.com

Read online
Download PDF
Purchase in print

ISBN 978-1-333-97866-2
PIBN 10624352

This book is a reproduction of an important historical work. Forgotten Books uses state-of-the-art technology to digitally reconstruct the work, preserving the original format whilst repairing imperfections present in the aged copy. In rare cases, an imperfection in the original, such as a blemish or missing page, may be replicated in our edition. We do, however, repair the vast majority of imperfections successfully; any imperfections that remain are intentionally left to preserve the state of such historical works.

Forgotten Books is a registered trademark of FB &c Ltd.
Copyright © 2018 FB &c Ltd.
FB &c Ltd, Dalton House, 60 Windsor Avenue, London, SW19 2RR.
Company number 08720141. Registered in England and Wales.

For support please visit www.forgottenbooks.com

1 MONTH OF FREE READING

at
www.ForgottenBooks.com

By purchasing this book you are eligible for one month membership to ForgottenBooks.com, giving you unlimited access to our entire collection of over 1,000,000 titles via our web site and mobile apps.

To claim your free month visit:
www.forgottenbooks.com/free624352

* Offer is valid for 45 days from date of purchase. Terms and conditions apply.

English
Français
Deutsche
Italiano
Español
Português

www.forgottenbooks.com

Mythology Photography **Fiction** Fishing Christianity **Art** Cooking Essays Buddhism Freemasonry Medicine **Biology** Music **Ancient Egypt** Evolution Carpentry Physics Dance Geology **Mathematics** Fitness Shakespeare **Folklore** Yoga Marketing **Confidence** Immortality Biographies Poetry **Psychology** Witchcraft Electronics Chemistry History **Law** Accounting **Philosophy** Anthropology Alchemy Drama Quantum Mechanics Atheism Sexual Health **Ancient History** **Entrepreneurship** Languages Sport Paleontology Needlework Islam **Metaphysics** Investment Archaeology Parenting Statistics Criminology **Motivational**

THE
Christian Remembrancer:

ONTHLY MAGAZINE

AND

REVIEW.

VOL. III.

JANUARY——JUNE.

LONDON:
JAMES BURNS, 17, PORTMAN STREET,
PORTMAN SQUARE.

1842.

LONDON:
R. CLAY, PRINTER, BREAD STREET HILL.

THE
CHRISTIAN REMEMBRANCER.

JANUARY, 1842.

The Theology of the Early Christian Church, exhibited in Quotations from the Writers of the first three Centuries, with Reflections. By JAMES BENNETT, D.D. London: Jackson & Walford. 1841. Pp. 463.

IT is evident that the study of the early christian writers is spreading, even amongst dissenters, and that some are beginning to feel the force of the evidence to be found in them, in support of the discipline and doctrine of the Church. This is the result in part of a feeling that the learning of the clergy gives them a real advantage; in part of the darling principle of modern dissent, that inquiry should be free and unrestricted, and that every one should form his creed for himself. For amidst incalculable evil, this is one result, that some will take the liberty of seeing what the Church has to say for herself, and what side has the best support from christian antiquity. For after all the special pleading that can be brought to bear upon the subject, an ingenuous mind cannot fail to see that what is nearest to the foundation of the religion has the best chance of being true. The consequence has been already, not merely that such dubious converts as Mr. Isaac Taylor have chosen to range themselves under the banners of the Church, but that other more valuable converts have been made; and amongst the most recent, one of their best scholars, a principal tutor in one of their colleges, has been so wrought upon by the force of overwhelming evidence, that upon mature conviction he has quitted an honourable office and respectable emolument, and sat down to live or starve, as he can, in one of the lowest and most laborious stations in the Church,—poor in this world, but rich in the possession of an upright mind and approving conscience, and certainty to rest his soul upon, rather than everchanging opinion. And thus we see that even the leading principle of dissent can work its own cure.

But this can be the case only where the mind is *really* candid and unprejudiced, and seeks for truth with the intention of following it whithersoever it may lead; and seeks, likewise, in humility and without self-conceit. It is far otherwise where there is a host of evil prejudices, barring up access to truth; far otherwise where the mind is vain and self-conceited; far otherwise where the inquiry is entered into in an official and party spirit, with the view of seeing what can be said to hinder younger and inquiring minds from pursuing the track to which they are tending. And something of this sort, we are constrained to say, seems to be the case with the writer of the book whose title is to be found at the head of this article. He *speaks* indeed of the " simple honest course" by which the cause of *truth* is to be maintained and advanced; but we think it will appear, before we have done, that something or other has so perverted his mental vision, that he has not been able to *follow* it. He speaks of " the reflections which are interspersed" with his quotations from the early writers "as mere helps to the formation of just conclusions," which " may be adopted or rejected according to the degree of evidence they present :" and well it is that he says so; for these reflections are so contradictory to each other, that it would be impossible to follow them all. The only astonishing thing is, that any one should be found who could bring himself to *print* such contradictions.

But our readers shall judge for themselves. We will not garble his words, but give a lengthened extract from his account of St. Clement of Rome, (pp. 12—16,) which we doubt not will be so satisfactory, that we shall be excused if we do not repeat the infliction.

" The letter itself is not that of Clement, but of the whole church at Rome, though doubtless written by their pastor,—[Dr. Bennett, although he strenuously contends that all dissenting teachers 'are presbyter-bishops,' is very much afraid of the consequences of calling Clement a *bishop*,]— in answer to an epistle from the church at Corinth, brought by a deputation of its members, on account of a disturbance in which some pastors had been deposed. In calling this the epistle of Clement, therefore, we sacrifice strict accuracy to convenient popular usage; and when we pronounce it valuable, we refer to its historic worth, and its superiority to other writings of an early age. It is distinguished by that kind of simplicity which arises, from what may be called, in a good sense, an affected imitation of the inspired writings, which renders it utterly unlike the native classical style of the epistle to Diognetus."

Why may not the similarity have arisen more naturally from Clement having, by long association, acquired the same tone of thought and expression with some of the apostles, as well as from the circumstance that to both parties Greek was not the native language?

" Clement is a preacher rather than an epistolator; rambling over the whole Bible, on which he gives comments, usually pious, but sometimes foolish, and seldom very instructive."

What a passage is this! What a pleasant idea does it give one of dissenting *sermons*, of which of course Dr. Bennett must be a good judge ! " Rambling over the whole Bible, usually pious, sometimes foolish, and seldom very instructive!" And what can be the tone of mind of a person who can read in the original an epistle, almost worthy to stand by the side of the inspired writings, and euter so little into its apostolical spirit, as to pen such a character of it?

"The worst consequence of this injudicious course is, that we are left to guess at the exact question in dispute, and to wish that we could give away the well-meant sermonizing declamation for a strict letter of business."

Surely Clement knew how to address himself to the persons he was writing to, rather better than a person who lives in a different country, age, and state of civilization. What need of explaining the business of the letter to persons who knew it before-hand? It was their *spirit* and *temper* which needed rectifying, and to that St. Clement addressed himself, and, as should seem from the result, very effectually. What folly then to complain that it has not qualities suitable to us, for whom it was not designed!

" Of its fifty-nine chapters, or short sections, some contain nothing but quotations from Scripture, which, however, are valuable as testimonies to the Divine writings, and proofs of the exclusive authority attached to them, as well as of their abundant and familiar use in the earliest churches of Christ. Clement appeals almost exclusively to the Old Testament, which he knew only in the Greek version called the Septuagint. He sometimes founds his arguments on words which have no prototype in the original, to say nothing of hints at apocryphal authority."

What then becomes of his assertion as to St. Clement's attaching " exclusive *authority*" to the present Scriptures, which is of course what the dissenting Doctor would contend for?

" He allegorizes so egregiously, that his arguments must often have fallen as pointless darts at the feet of those who had any superior knowledge of the word of God."

Is Dr. Bennett aware that some people of his school have said the same of St. Paul?

" His strange comments on the resurrection seem to be an unwise attempt to imitate an apostle. Because Paul had written the 15th chapter of the First Epistle to the Corinthians, Clement, though writing on a totally different question, *must do something in the same line*, [!!!] and thus has left on his letter a blot of folly, which will for ever sink the reputation of the apostolical fathers. He gravely adduces as a fact, the fable of the phœnix, to show that God has given in nature proofs of the resurrection of the body."

So that a mistake in a point of *natural history*, in which the whole age was mistaken, (as every age must be in some matters, till knowledge is perfect,) is to ruin the credit of a set of writers as witnesses to matters of *fact* which came under their own knowledge, and points of *doctrine* which they were constantly employed in teaching! What security can Dr. Bennett give, that if he had lived at the time, he would not have employed the self-same argument? And again, we ask, does he not know that the very reasoning he uses has been employed by infidels " to sink the reputation" of the inspired writers?

" For this conceit, in which he is followed by other fathers, *who are sure to adopt the worst thoughts of their predecessors*, [surely the man is insane!] Clement runs the tremendous risk of sanctioning idolatry; for the phœnix comes to a heathen temple to deposit the bones of its progenitor; and the Egyptian priests are the mystagogues to calculate the times, [what have 'mystagogues' to do with the special office of calculating times?] and ascertain that it was exactly five hundred years since the prodigy last occurred."

Now supposing the facts to have been as the people of that age believed, what had St. Clement to do with any possible inferences persons might choose to draw from them? The oracles delivered in heathen temples were a much stronger argument for idolatry than this phœnix; but does any well-informed person think he is " running the tremendous risk of sanctioning idolatry," by stating his belief that prophecies, which were verified by the result, were really delivered in those temples?

" But when he is wise enough to speak of what he understands, his aim is so pure, that his spirit is excellent, and the tendency of his exhortation is to promote the peace and holiness and prosperity of the church."

That is, this poor, silly driveller, who is " sometimes foolish, and seldom very instructive;" whose " arguments fall as pointless darts at the feet of those who have any superior knowledge of the word of God;" who, " though writing on a different subject, must *do something in the line*" of St. Paul; *he* is to " promote the peace, the holiness and prosperity of the church."!!

" He, unlike Ignatius, keeps himself out of sight, assuming no priestly airs, [*i. e.* writing to a factious set of people, he does not defeat his object by asserting an authority which would only arouse their pride,] but claiming authority for the word of God alone, and exhibiting Christ as the Redeemer, example, and sovereign Lord. The fear of God ever before his eyes, and the love of the brethren burning in his breast, often raise him above his numerous disadvantages, and exert over the conscience of the reader an autho ty, which far superior learning, reason, or eloquence, could never rival." ri

Here is a spark of good feeling; but how is it reconcilable with what has gone before?

" The importance of this epistle, in various points of view, it would be difficult to overrate. This is the link of connexion between the inspired and uninspired writings of the christian church. [viz., doing something in the line of St. Paul.] Here centers [*sic*] almost the whole of the real value of the testimony of the fathers, and the sincere lover of them should deposit this letter in his bosom as a jewel. [*i. e.* because it " will ever sink the reputation of the apostolical fathers."] For, if Clement was the first pastor [why not bishop?] of the church at Rome, and especially if he was the man eulogized by Paul, he the more clearly shows what was apostolical but if he was the third in succession, then it is demonstrated, that, even so low down in the descending scale towards the divinely predicted apostasy, the christian church was still at antipodes from the hierarchy of modern times. This letter from the church at Rome shows that the body of the faithful lost their liberties, not merely by the ambition of pastors, but by popular turbulence; for Clement, though an humble man, fearlessly declares, that the presbyters whom the Corinthians had displaced, were made the innocent victims of three or four factious men. This naturally induced the more modest and devout Christians to yield to the pastors the sole government of the church, just as the peaceable members of society suffer the horrors of a bloody revolution to terminate in military despotism."

This is, of course, Dr. Bennett's theory to account for the prevalence of episcopacy. We need scarcely say that, as to the church at large, it is entirely gratuitous and destitute of foundation. In regard to that of Corinth, it would only account for the clergy being allowed to govern the laity, but not for one bishop being set up over the rest. And it goes not a single step towards accounting for the settled, universal, pre-eminence of one presbyter above the rest, and the stamping a permanent official character upon him distinct from ordinary presbyters.

" The epistle of Clement became the innocent occasion of hastening this consummation so much to be deplored. [This is mere assertion, without the slightest proof.] That it was publicly read in the churches, though *after* the inspired Scriptures, was a disgrace to the early Christians, [1] and leads us to regret that Clement ever wrote :"

i. e. a letter " whose tendency is to promote the peace and holiness and prosperity of the church," which " exerts over the conscience of the reader an authority which far superior learning, reason, or eloquence, could never rival," and which " every sincere lover of the fathers should deposit in his bosom as a jewel." Truly this is an admirable specimen of " well-meant sermonizing declamation !"

" He would have acted more wisely if he had sent the messengers back to their church with Paul's epistles written to themselves, [he does, as we shall see by and by, refer them to those very epistles, which there was no need of sending, because they had them already,] for his own makes no really valuable addition, [though in it 'centers almost the whole of the real value of the testimony of the fathers,' and 'it would be difficult to overrate the importance of this epistle in various points of view;'] and the reading of it gave a pernicious example of setting up the authority of the fathers as a rival to that of prophets and apostles. To this letter may be traced the mania for allegory, which at length Judaized or paganized the christian church."

Every person acquainted with the subject knows that this passion existed amongst both Jews and pagans anterior to Christianity, and poured into the church from the mass of converts from philosophical Judaism or paganism. In Clement we find scarcely more of it than in the sacred writers.

" The comparison Clement forms between the Jewish temple and the christian church; the Aaronic priesthood and the evangelical ministry; [here is the secret of Dr. Bennett's wish to lower Clement;] the abolished sacrificial rites and our spiritual worship; though innocently, if not wisely intended, proved the box of Pandora. What was with him mere figure and illustration, was converted by his successors into argument and authority."

If Dr. Bennett means that Clement's epistle had any definite weight in setting up episcopacy universally, the assertion is contrary to evidence. Every thing shows that there was some universally acknowledged authority at the bottom of it.

" Still, however, too pure to be suffered to continue and repeat its testimony, this first and best document of the fathers, after being read in the churches, was consigned to oblivion, and has but recently returned to testify against the general corruption of our age."

Now, considering that Dr. Bennett regards episcopacy as one of the corruptions of the church, and thinks that this epistle is valuable as showing that in Clement's time " the christian church was still at antipodes from the hierarchy of modern times," it is rather remarkable that this carefully-neglected document should have been "brought to light" in this country by Patrick Young, librarian to that devoted upholder of episcopacy, King Charles the First, and, we believe, under the patronage of that arch-hierarch, Archbishop Laud. How judicially blinded they must have been!

" Clement, the oldest known writer, never pretends to have seen the apostles, [why should he, when the Corinthians must have been fully aware of it?] nor tells us a word that was heard to drop from their lips; [Dr. Bennett has already told us that Clement scarcely quotes any *written* document of the apostles, and he was not very likely to quote what only rested upon memory;] but arguing from Scripture, just as we may, he exhorts the Corinthians to 'take up the epistle of the blessed Paul, written to them.' [He had been blaming Clement for not *sending* them copies of St. Paul's epistle.] Would that the fathers had confined themselves to such advice! for one inspired book is worth more than all their ponderous tomes."

But does Dr. Bennett pretend to understand the inspired books without help? And of all help, why should we throw away what can be gathered from those who lived nearer to apostolical times?

We trust there is none of our readers who will not admire the modesty, the consistency, the good taste, the deep wisdom, with which this account of Clement of Rome is drawn up. After this, no one can be surprised at his speaking of "vanity" as the great fault of Ignatius, characterising him as "a weak old man," likely to " prove an apostate instead of a martyr," "a vain prelate," "a child parading a new toy, of which he thinks he can never make enough." He says that "the rash expression, 'I am your expiation,' $\pi\epsilon\rho\iota\psi\eta\mu\alpha$, however favourably interpreted, stands in singular contrast with the words of him who said, 'Was Paul crucified for you?'" It is however rather remarkable that St. Paul speaks of himself and the other apostles as "the $\pi\epsilon\rho\iota\psi\eta\mu\alpha$ of all things." 1 Cor. iv. 13. He rails at him for showing " eagerness for martyrdom," and therein "evincing no small conceit of the glory, if not the merit of the sacrifice, as the price of heaven." God forgive the man whose hatred of "prelacy" could so far blind him, as to cause him to rise from the perusal of the writings and martyrdom of the blessed Ignatius with such feelings towards him!

Irenæus does not meet with much better treatment. He is "a wearisome writer," who "has said many strange things, and in a work so large, few good ones;" who "bewildered himself with his researches, and sometimes raises more dust than he lays;" who "gives many foolish reasons for believing wise doctrines."

The "morality" of Clement of Alexandria, "is like that of Socinian writers, a substitute for the merits of Christ;" and he "generally displays knowledge without wisdom, mortification without holiness, and zeal without truth." Dr. Bennett thinks "he may not have believed" one of his statements, "but thought it a good device to stop the mouths of the Gnostics."

Cyprian "might have been much better employed" than in his contests with Pope Stephen; and "no important use can be made of one who was so little of a theologian." The simple meaning of which is, that he gives the strongest possible testimony against schism of all kinds, and modern independency in particular.

Did our space allow, we might cull, in the richest abundance, flowers of equal elegance and beauty with those we have selected; but it is time to give some account of the book as a whole, and to expose some of its misstatements and false reasonings, especially on the subject of church government.

The volume comprises eight lectures and an appendix. The first lecture, viz., that from which we have already quoted, is on the "Sources of Information;" the succeeding ones severally on "the Scriptures and the Divine Nature;" "the Purposes and Works of God;" "the Church, its Officers and Worship;" "the Sacraments, and Christian Ethics;" "Death, Future State, Resurrection, the Millennium, and Antichrist;" "Causes of the peculiar Characteristics of early Theology;" and a concluding lecture against those who in our own times appeal to the authority of the fathers.

The least objectionable portions of these lectures are those on the Divine Nature, the Divinity of Christ, the Trinity, the Redemption of Christ, Election and Grace, Justification, and Infant Baptism; but even in these there is a larger mixture of misapprehension and slip-slop writing than we should have expected. For instance, he is apparently perplexed by the language of the fathers, where they speak of God the Son as being subordinate to God the Father, not understanding (what Bishop Pearson has so well shown) that there may be *subordination* without *inferiority* of nature. So, again, we are told that Irenæus, "by the Word and Wisdom, *seems* to mean the Son and Spirit;" whereas that father himself expressly *tells*[*] us

---

[*] Adv. Hæreses, IV. vii. 4.

that he does mean this. He concludes his account of Christ's divinity with the following lucid and purpose-like sentence:—

"Of Dr. Priestley's Ebionites and Nazarenes, it is not necessary to speak, except to refer to the controversy between him and Horseley, [*sic*] which was too personal to yield the most valuable fruit."

On the subject of "election and predestination," Dr. Bennett's quotations, and many of his remarks, are really just and valuable, although possibly not in the sense in which he intended them. He says, very truly,

"That Christians spoke of themselves and their brethren as elect so freely and constantly, that the heathens knew it, and supposed the church deemed her converts not spontaneous, is manifest. Whether we call this the knowledge or error of the heathen, it proves both the practice of the ancient church, which gave rise to the one or the other, and the nonconformity of the ancients to many in the present day who speak (or rather do not speak) of election, so that the world would never learn from them that Christians are elect persons."

It is too true that a doctrine which the Church teaches in her Baptismal Service, and hints at in her Catechism, is too much, as Dr. Bennett says, "abandoned to those who are termed high Calvinists;" as though because there is a false doctrine on the subject, the true was to be eschewed, or not so much as sought for, or even used, where the Church leads us to use it. But it is quite uncertain what is Dr. Bennett's doctrine on the subject, as he gives us nothing but the vaguest hints.

But let us come to the Fourth Lecture, "Of the Church, its Officers and Worship," on which it may be supposed that the lecturer, being a teacher of a sect which has separated from the Church on the express ground of supposed corruption in its constitution and government, is more full and studied than on other subjects.

Dr. Bennett's object is first to show that there are only two ideas of *a church* to be found in the early fathers; viz. a congregation assembling in one place under one pastor, and the whole body of Christians; and, consequently, that the idea of a diocesan or national church is unsanctioned by primitive antiquity. Now supposing it were granted, that down to the middle of the third century the word *church* had only two meanings, what would it prove, but that a word had afterwards obtained a new meaning by change of circumstances? Of what consequence can it be, whether a diocese is called a diocese, a parish, or a church? or, whether the united churches of a nation be *called* a church or not? Does Dr. Bennett mean to say, that because the fathers used a word in only two senses, therefore it is wrong to use it in any other sense? If so, he will condemn St. Paul himself, who certainly used the word in a third sense in his Epistle to the Corinthians: for he addresses the epistle to "the *church* of Christ which is at Corinth;" and ch. xiv. 34, says, "Let your women keep silence in the *churches*." Here we find a plurality of churches in the one church of Corinth; so that unless Dr. Bennett means to " set up the authority of the fathers as a rival to that of prophets and apostles," he must agree that *we may* use the word in more senses than two, whatever the fathers do. If he means to say, that because all separate congregations were called churches, therefore they were all independent of each other,—he may as well assert that because the charges of all bishops are now called dioceses, therefore they are all independent of each other. The two ideas have no connexion. They might be both true, but they have no connexion. We know that the several congregations of which St. Paul speaks at Corinth were not independent of each other, because he addresses them as one church; and so the congregations which, from the nature of the case, must have been in the one church of Jerusalem, could not have been independent of each other.

Ἐκκλησία, which we call *church*, means *assembly*, or *congregation*. Dr. Bennett has no scruple to take it from its literal meaning, and apply it to the whole body of christian people, who are in no *proper* sense an assembly or congregation, but only figuratively. Indeed, if St. Paul used it to signify all the congregations in the city of Corinth, considered as one body, what reason can be given why it may not be applied figuratively to all Christians in one country, bound together by certain rules? It was not so applied in the first ages, because, from the nature of the case, there were no such territorial unions; because, in fact, no *nation* had received Christianity. But in the dispute about Easter, we find collections of churches acting together, and exhibiting a habit of union,—as for instance, those of France, those of proconsular Asia; and in Cyprian's time matters had undergone so considerable a change, that we find him speaking of "the *church* of God in the province of Africa and Numidia."*

He finds great fault with archbishop Wake, for translating τὴν ἐν Συρίᾳ ἐκκλησίαν "the church of Syria." It certainly is better to translate with strict correctness; but it is of no *practical* consequence in this case, for St. Ignatius distinctly calls himself "bishop *of* Syria;" and if there was a *bishop* of Syria, there is no reason why there should not be a *church* of Syria.† But so long as the mass of the population were heathens, it was certainly more natural to speak of the church *in* a place or country; and accordingly Bishop Pearson, and all our writers, point out that such was the case. Change of circumstances produces change of language. Under what category of primitive instruction does Dr. Bennett rank his "Lectures?" Or what primitive authority has he for his degree of D.D.? Such reasoning can only deceive.

In order to show that in the primitive ages, every church consisted of only one congregation, Dr. Bennett quotes passages of Ignatius, which in his rendering speaks of the Christians of Ephesus and Philadelphia as meeting together "in one place;" apparently quite

---

* Epist. 71. s. 4. p. 214. "In provincia Africa et Numidia Ecclesiam Domini."
† Ad Roman. 2. Τὸν ἐπίσκοπον Συρίας κατηξίωσεν ὁ Θεὸς εὑρεθῆναι.

unaware of the fact, which he may ascertain by consulting the biblical critics upon Acts ii. 1, and similar passages, that ἐπὶ τὸ αὐτὸ is a phrase of ambiguous meaning, and that it signifies nothing more definite than our English word *together*. This we suppose is a specimen of his "literal translation" to maintain "the cause of truth." Any one who will examine the passages will see that, even taking them in this sense, they only prove that the churches of Ephesus and Philadelphia were not individually very numerous ; and that the stress of the argument lies not in the duty of meeting *at the same place*, but of meeting in communion with the bishop.

What Dr. Bennett can mean by asserting that Clement wrote his letter from the church at Rome, "as from one assembly ;" and that Justin Martyr, Minucius Felix, Tertullian, and Cyprian, all know of no more than one assembly at Rome ; likewise that there was no more than one congregation at Antioch, down to the time of Paul of Samosata; or at Carthage in Cyprian's time ; or at Alexandria in Origen's ; we are at a loss to say, as in most cases he gives us no proof or reference : and when he does, it is to show on what slender foundation he builds his argument. For instance, he proves that there was only one assembly at Antioch, by the fact that Paul of Samosata "refused to resign the church's house, not houses, ἐκκλησίας οἶκου ;" whereas this phrase is ambiguous, and was undoubtedly used to signify the bishop's residence, the property of the church. (See the second council of Toledo, can. i. quoted in Bingham, VIII. i. 4.) As then his proof fails, when he attempts it, whatever rests upon his bare assertion we deny. Supposing, however, it were so, it cannot avail the congregationalist divine, for there were undoubtedly more presbyters than one, both at Rome, and at several of the churches to which Ignatius wrote ; and if at the same time there was only one congregation, that is contrary to the independent scheme, which divides the Christians of a town into as many congregations, or churches, as there are pastors, or presbyter-bishops, (see these Lectures, p. 207 :) so that what rational object he can have in contending for only one congregation in each church we cannot divine. If he had been merely contending that episcopacy had *no more* ground to stand upon than congregationalism, and, consequently, that either may be adopted without blame, his course would be more intelligible. But even then he would be wrong in separating from the church upon the mere matter of opinion that independency was more expedient. But that is not his view. He calls upon the members of his sect, to " pursue with redoubled zeal their high vocation, to restore the scriptural polity, which, while it continued in purity and vigour, promised to fill the world with 'the churches of the saints.'" We do not know what may be the working of this " scriptural polity" under Dr. Bennett's "pastorate," but we could tell a few things about it in a western county, which would go to show that it can be as bad even as dissenters depict a " corrupt establishment." Those who know dissenters well are satisfied that the whole tone of feeling amongst them is absolutely awful.

But Dr. Bennett not only condemns the *term*, "a national church;" he also contends that the *thing* is schismatical. We are perfectly willing to grant not only that a national church *may* be schismatical, but that our own church *has* in some instances acted schismatically. But that is no more than what Dr. Bennett must grant that many so called congregational churches have done; and how a national church is more schismatical than a "congregational union," we are at a loss to understand. It is curious that Dr. Bennett and the Romish Dr. Wiseman should both agree in denouncing national churches as "schismatical." How often extremes meet! Let Dr. Bennett show that a national church must *necessarily* exclude other churches from communion, and he will have done something to the purpose. To prove that they have *acted* schismatically, is only proving that a thing may be abused.

But it is time to pass from the church itself to its *officers*; of which Dr. Bennett contends there are only two orders, presbyter-bishops and deacons.

Respecting the second he asserts—what we have no intention to contravene—that they "were in the first instance appointed to serve tables, not only those where money was counted out to the poor, but that of the Lord's supper;" and we should be rejoiced to see the day when deacons should be *more* distinctly marked out from presbyters, by being more markedly employed in inferior offices, and by not being so uniformly raised to the priesthood. But when he goes on to add, "that the deacons soon became ecclesiastics, or teachers of religion, is a curious fact, that shows how quickly men contravene the designs of God;" we wonder that he has no suspicion that he is speaking any thing like blasphemy. The case of the *deacon* Philip, whose *teaching* was *expressly sanctioned by the Holy Ghost*, and whose *baptizing* was confirmed by two apostles, adding *the gift of the Holy Ghost* to his converts, one should have supposed might have given him some misgivings; but it is disposed of in this exquisite bit of slip-slop:

"But it is said, 'the first deacons preached.' [He forgets *baptized*.] The Acts show that any Christian who is able may preach. [How then can 'teachers of religion' mean 'ecclesiastics?' And where is the harm of deacons becoming 'teachers of religion?'] And the fathers prove that this right was not at first denied."

The fathers prove that a layman of extraordinary qualifications was *sometimes requested by the bishop* to preach; but they say nothing of any *right* to preach inherent in laymen.

"Besides, the deacons are exhorted, by using their office well, to purchase to themselves a good degree, which is supposed to mean promotion to the ministry of the word, which the deacons frequently obtained."

That is, they obtained promotion to an office, which every layman had a right to exercise! What a promotion! But this is said to make things in *some* degree tally with congregational practice, which very seldom admits deacons to the "pastorate."

"It is not improbable that the first deacons, improved by their office, afterwards became pastors, or ministers of the word [which 'every christian who is able may preach,'] as we read of Philip the evangelist."

That of course in regard to him remains to be proved. For all that appears, he preached as a deacon; and not only preached, but baptized. This we find in Scripture, and it is confirmed by the practice of the early church. But it would not have suited the "independent" view, where the deacon is a mere layman, only permitted to preach occasionally instead of the pastor, and never, we believe, baptizing.

It is curious to see the extent of information, or the hardihood of assertion, betrayed in the following sentence. "The bishops early took from the deacons the administration of the ecclesiastical funds; and as these were at Rome immensely large, they at length created a pope."!! Every tyro in church history knows that the deacons were but the bishop's deputies in the administration of church funds, as they were of the apostles, and that the bishops in general were, *like the apostles*, the treasurers, and distributed the funds by the ministry of the deacons. Where then was the change, excepting that any particular bishop might abuse his trust, and some did? Again, every tyro knows that *so late as St. Jerome's time*, the deacons of Rome (who were then only seven in number) became so powerful, through having the administration of the church alms in their hands, that they bore a considerable resemblance to certain "lord deacons" we have heard of, and appeared to regard themselves as superior to the presbyters. Lastly, every tyro knows that the pope of Rome is nothing more than the lineal descendant of Linus, the first bishop, (appointed by St. Peter and St. Paul,) and that no time can be fixed on when any one of these bishops has been either more or less *created pope* than another.

We have done with *deacons*, and proceed to *presbyter-bishops*. Dr. Bennett takes a great deal of unnecessary pains to prove, (what even the most extreme "high-church" writers would have granted him at once,) that the *names* "presbyter" and "bishop" were at first applied indifferently to the same persons; and he argues thence most inconsequently, that *therefore* there were no presbyters or bishops (call them which you will) placed permanently above the rest, with powers (like those of Timothy and Titus) which *mere* presbyters did not possess. For that is the real question. What person is there, who, because St. John the apostle calls himself an *elder*, and some, such as Barnabas and Epaphroditus, were called *apostles*, concludes that therefore all elders had the same powers and functions as the twelve and St. Paul? Or to come to something nearer home, what sane person would contend, that, because the Queen's cabinet ministers are called *servants*, therefore they are on a par with her *household servants?* Or that they were originally nothing but household servants, and their present eminence a usurpation on their part? The very writers Dr. Bennett quotes to show what no one disputes, viz. Tertullian, and

Clement of Alexandria, to say nothing of Ignatius, distinctly recount the *three* orders of bishops, presbyters, and deacons.* Could they have counted three orders, if they had not been three? What then becomes of the ambiguity of a name?

But Dr. Bennett relies greatly upon Clement of Rome, and his mention of only two orders in his first epistle to the Corinthians; it may be worth while, therefore, to go into this case more particularly, especially as it is the case most relied upon by those who contend that the distinction between the two superior orders of the ministry is un-apostolical. Not that we can say any thing new upon the subject, but because it is the only part of the evidence which can present the least difficulty.

Now, in the first place, supposing it to have been the fact that there had been *at Corinth* no presbyter placed permanently above the rest, can a person acquainted with the Scriptures, and with St. Clement's epistle, suggest no reason why this arrangement had not yet been made in that particular place? Is there nothing in the spirit and temper of the Corinthians to account for it? Were they not a factious, quarrelsome, insubordinate set of people, even under the government of an apostle? Did it not require all his powers of persuasion, backed by irresistible miraculous powers of punishment, to obtain obedience from them? And although he did, in some degree, conquer this spirit, is it not evident from St. Clement's epistle that it had sprung up again, and was in full action when he wrote? Would it not be quite in keeping with their conduct, if the discovery of the lost history of Hegesippus should bring to light that these Corinthians, who had resisted an apostle in the plenitude of his power, and had expelled a number of presbyters in a body, had resisted the appointment of one chief? Or that a portion of the presbyters had been expelled for the very fact of siding with and upholding a bishop actually appointed, he being one of the banished presbyters? All this would be in perfect consistency with the epistle, and would account for Clement's introducing the *threefold* order of the Jewish priesthood, *with one chief*, to reconcile them to submission. Be that as it may, Clement's making the *names* of presbyter and bishop synonymous, no more proves that there was no one presbyter or bishop who had powers greater than any other, than the similar use of words by his namesake of Alexandria. He, we are aware, sometimes mentions only two orders; but in *his* case we *know* that it proves no such thing, because (as we have shown) he more than once mentions bishops and presbyters as distinct from each

---

* Tertull. *de Baptismo*, 17. Dandi quidem (sc. baptismum) habet jus summus sacerdos, qui est episcopus: dehinc presbyteri et diaconi. *De fuga in persecutione*, 11. Sed quam ipsi auctores, id est, ipsi diaconi, presbyteri et episcopi fugiunt, quomodo laicus intelligere poterit, &c. Clem. Alex. *Pædag*. iii. 12. s. 97. Μυρίαι δὲ ὅσαι ὑποθῆκαι εἰς πρόσωπα ἐκλεκτὰ διατείνουσαι ἐγγεγράφαται ταῖς βίβλοις ταῖς ἁγίαις, αἱ μὲν πρεσβυτέροις, αἱ δὲ ἐπισκόποις, αἱ δὲ διακόνοις, ἄλλαι χήραις. *Strom*. vi. 13, s. 107. Ἐπεὶ καὶ αἱ ἐνταῦθα κατὰ τὴν ἐκκλησίαν προκοπαὶ ἐπισκόπων, πρεσβυτέρων, διακόνων, μιμήματα οἶμαι ἀγγελικῆς δόξης κἀκείνης τῆς οἰκονομίας τυγχάνουσιν.

other, equally with presbyters and deacons. Now if the mention of two orders *only*, in some passages of Clement of Alexandria, does not prove that he recognised only two orders, no more can it in Clement of Rome; so that the argument attempted to be drawn from him falls to the ground. And his introduction of the analogy of the Jewish priesthood is so evident a *hint* of the threefold order of the christian ministry, that Dr. Bennett thinks it a reproach to Clement to have introduced such an analogy. This, indeed, shows that he feels the force of the argument, whilst he refuses to be governed by it.

It is curious to see how he gets over the clear and overwhelming testimony of Ignatius. At one time he speaks of him as that "vain prelate, parading a new toy;" at another, he will have the epistles which pass under his name to be interpolated when they speak of the *three* orders; but he cannot trust himself to either hypothesis, and so he writes, in a see-saw way, sometimes on one theory, sometimes on the other. We need not tell our readers that *we* have not to vindicate the genuineness of the present epistles of St. Ignatius: that has been done long ago by Archbishop Usher and Bishop Pearson. But it may be as well to give the heads of the argument in proof of their genuineness.

We have, then, two sets of epistles, one much longer than the other, and containing more epistles. The shorter copies correspond *in number* with those known in the time of Eusebius, and they contain *the same text* as that quoted by ancient authors; and the longer are evidently built upon them, only paraphrased and added to. Now, would not any fair-minded person say, upon the face of the matter, —when we have two sets of letters, one a paraphrase of the other, with the addition of some other letters, and when the shorter correspond in number and in readings with those most anciently known,— that these are the genuine and original epistles? If a person calls them in question, should we not say that he must have some end to serve?

But Dr. Bennett objects to the style, so different from that of St. Clement of Rome, so pompous in parts, as we think, and inflated; so different again from that of Polycarp. To our mind, this so much the more clearly proves the genuineness of the epistles; for to what countries did Clement, Polycarp, and Ignatius respectively belong? Is not the name of Clement Roman, of Polycarp Greek, and of Ignatius neither, but probably Syrian? Do we not find them settled respectively in a Roman, Greek, and Syrian church? Is it not notorious that the style of the East is generally inflated, according to our ideas? Are we to expect that religion is to annihilate such distinctions? Is it not the distinction of the inspired writings, that their style, although differing in different writers, is more chastened than that of any others of their age? To us, then, the apparently turgid and untranslatable style is one of the proofs of the genuineness of the epistles.

The other objection of Dr. Bennett, that Ignatius appears, when speaking of episcopacy, to be like a child, parading a new toy, cannot of course stand with the previous fancy, that the strong language about episcopacy has been introduced by interpolation; for if it was interpolation, it would bring the writing down to a time when even Dr. Bennett would be obliged to grant that episcopacy was not new. If, on the contrary, it was written by Ignatius, we have at least the testimony of a contemporary of the apostles to the general prevalence of episcopacy in Asia Minor at that time. And that is all we actually *want* his testimony for. Let Ignatius be ever so vain and foolish (which, however, we by no means grant), his language is at least competent evidence of matter of fact. We do not find him *instituting* episcopacy, but *speaking of it as already established,* and in action, although not willingly submitted to, as it never has been, by factious men. It is useless to try to get rid of the fact by blaming the tone of the writer's language. There it stands, and has to be accounted for. It is no great matter whether dioceses existed then or not. There might be no occasion for them; but the *three* orders existed over a considerable tract of country, fresh from the residence and superintendence of St. John and St. Philip; and the single bishop had presbyters and deacons under him. We have store of other facts of the same description, to apply to other parts of the world. But first let Dr. Bennett account for this *fact* upon the principles of independency, or upon any other principle than that of the Church, that the three orders were appointed by the apostles, and he will have done something to the purpose. But to play fast and loose with evidence, and shuffle off inconvenient testimony, in the way which he has done, is nothing short of discreditable, and can never serve his cause with those who know any thing of the matter.

We doubt whether our readers will not think that we have bestowed unnecessary space upon Dr. Bennett and his Lectures; but we know in what way dissenters are apt to puff off their books as unanswerable (even if they contain nothing but the stalest arguments, ten times before refuted), if no notice is taken of them by churchmen. We know, too, that there is no probability that any independent author will take the trouble to dissect such a book, for his labour would be remunerated in no quarter; not by churchmen, because few of them would have read the "Lectures;" not by dissenters, for the greater part of them would not buy a book in opposition to themselves. We thought it proper, therefore, to give such a notice of them, as should suffice to show our readers that the judgment of the writer was worthless, and his arguments no better, and to be appealed to as showing it sufficiently. We trust we have succeeded.

There are abundance of other points we might have taken up (as, for instance, the apostolical succession and the use of the fathers), for the book abounds everywhere with error, contradiction, and loose, aimless remarks, mixed up, it is true, with facts and true doctrines; but so incorrectly treating them, as to make them worthless, or worse than worthless. And this is the sort of rubbish which is to stand to dissenters in the place of the "Boyle," the "Warburton," and the

"Bampton" Lectures, in the National Church! and in upholding the delivery and publication of which, "the liberal and opulent friends of evangelical and congregational nonconformity," are called upon to "evince, by their generous support, the sincerity of their attachment to the great principles of their christian profession!"

Our chief fear, however, is that our friends, with the right feeling which we trust always animates them, will think that our language is unnecessarily harsh towards Dr. Bennett. It certainly was not meant to be so. We opened his book with the resolution to give his arguments fair and candid attention, and to reply to them calmly; not doubting that we should be able to detect error, but still expecting a fair and scholar-like way of stating things. But we had not proceeded far before the absurdity of the mistakes and the perpetual self-contradictions fairly compelled us to lay down the book and laugh outright. The only course then appeared to be to expose the book without scruple, but still without virulence. We know nothing of Dr. Bennett *personally*, and but for his book, should not have known of his existence; we only know him as a writer, who, with a considerable mass of facts, ill-digested and distorted in his brain, has undertaken the task of instructing others, when he stands in great need of instruction himself; for he would evidently be much benefited by a less confined range of reading, and still more by time and patience to digest what he reads, and a single-minded pursuit of truth, without reference to party. This, perhaps, is quite as much the fault of his position as of himself personally. We repeat, then, that we are in perfect charity with the individual; but his book had no claims at our hands. All the harm we wish him is, that he may escape from the mill-horse round and illiberal feelings of a sectarian partizan, and learn to look at things like a liberal-minded scholar and fair-judging man. He would then find that there are writers of the Church of England and of the Romish Church, aye, and Fathers too, who would disabuse him of many an error, and bring him to clear, consistent views; and if this could be, and he is an honest man, we doubt not of the result.

So far, however, it is satisfactory to find that the dissenters are going to the Fathers, and reading them for themselves. Men full of irrational and uncatholic prejudice, and who, whilst residing within reach of magnificent libraries, do not even avail themselves of the helps which such collections afford, may not be able to derive much benefit from them; but we cannot avoid hoping and believing that there are amongst dissenters men of another spirit, who will search with more unbiassed minds, and will not refuse those aids in their search which the divines of the Church can render them; and we doubt not that such an investigation will convince them that catholic consent is of more weight than modern opinion, and the judgment even of the "vain, weak, and impious" Ignatius more to be regarded in some things than that of the strong-minded, and consistent, and reverent Congregational Lecturer.

The English Hexapla, exhibiting the six important English Translations of the New Testament Scriptures, Wiclif, Tyndale, Cranmer, the Genevan, Anglo-Rhemish, and Authorized, the original Greek Text after Scholz, with the various Readings of the Textus Receptus and the principal Constantinopolitan and Alexandrine Manuscripts, and a complete Collation of Scholz's Text with Griesbach's Edition of 1805, *preceded by an Historical Account of the English Translations.* London: Bagster & Sons. 1841.

WE are not surprised at the success which has already attended the circulation of this very handsome volume. The beauty of its Greek typography, recalling to our minds the best days of printing, has had no slight share in contributing to this success; but there are other causes which have led to its so frequently adorning the table or the study of the man of taste and the antiquarian. It is only necessary to open the book to see what these causes are. On the top of each page, in large and beautiful characters, appears the Greek text of Scholz, the rival of the immortal Griesbach, and ranged in six parallel columns below, are the six English versions which have been most in repute for the last four centuries. The first in order, as being the earliest translation, although the latest printed, is that of Wiclif, bearing the date of 1380, (which was printed for the first time in 1731,) and the others following the order in which they were printed, bearing the respective dates of 1534, 1539, 1557, 1582, and 1611. These are Tyndale's, Cranmer's, or the Great Bible, the Geneva, the Rhemish or Roman Catholic version, and the present Authorized translation. We shall speak of these in order.

The reprint of Scholz, now for the first time issuing from an English press, naturally leads us to take a brief view of the history of the text of the New Testament.

The first published edition was that of the celebrated Erasmus, which issued from the press of Basle, in 1516, in folio. The manuscripts used by Erasmus appear to have been few, and not very ancient; but his text has formed the basis of that which has been commonly received since the days of Elzevir, and his manuscripts were partly of the Constantinopolitan and partly of the Western recension.* His single manuscript of the Apocalypse was ancient, but mutilated, and he filled up the chasms with translations made by himself from the Vulgate. These he corrected, in his fourth edition, from the Complutensian.

---

* Of the four manuscripts used by Erasmus, one of the tenth century contained the whole New Testament except the Apocalypse. In this MS. the Gospels were of the Alexandrine, and the Acts and Epistles of the Constantinopolitan recensions; in another, of the fifteenth century, the Gospels were of the Constantinopolitan recension. He had no manuscript of a date more ancient than the tenth century.

We shall briefly trace from this period the history of the text from Erasmus to Scholz, the editor of the text before us, which is chiefly derived from manuscripts of the last eight centuries. Of the history of this text the editor has given us no account, having confined his observations to the English versions.

The publication of Erasmus's text was followed by that of the Complutensian edition in the beautiful folio Polyglott Bible, printed at Complutum, or Alcala, at the munificent cost of Cardinal Ximenes, in 1514, but not published before the year 1522. We are not acquainted with the manuscripts upon which this edition was founded, but if the story be correct of their having been disposed of to a rocket maker, the world has probably been no great loser by the transaction, as they appear to have been selected rather for their beauty than their antiquity. They were no doubt modern, and of the Western recension. Their existence, however, would have determined one point, in which the honesty of the editors is open to great suspicion; viz.—whether they had any Greek authority for the celebrated clause 1 John v. 7, respecting the heavenly witnesses, and which it is most probable they themselves translated from the Latin, and from one of their own incorrect manuscripts of the same, which omits the final clause of the eighth verse, and which they, on the authority of Thomas of Aquin, charge the Arians with forging in order to neutralize the argument in favour of the unity of essence of the persons of the blessed Trinity, derived from the final clause of the supposed seventh verse. But as we shall have an opportunity of reverting to this subject, we shall at once proceed with our account of the editions of the Greek Testament.

The edition of Elzevir, printed in 1624, was little more than a reprint of Beza's edition of 1565, which was chiefly derived from the beautiful and justly celebrated folio edition printed by Robert Stephens, in 1550. Stephens's was a mixed text, founded partly on Erasmus's, and partly on the Complutensian, with the aid of a few manuscripts not previously made use of. The paper and typography of this edition have never been surpassed for beauty; but it does not deserve the name of a critical edition. Our Authorized version was made from Beza's text.

The first person who collected an apparatus for forming a critical edition of the text was Dr. Mill of Oxford, who did not, however, attempt to form a new text, but republished the third edition of Stephens. His collection of various readings was so great, that some persons ignorantly accused him of an attempt to undermine the authority of the sacred volume. Bengel, in 1734, published his edition of the New Testament at Tubingen. This was the first attempt to amend the received text. But such was the superstitious attachment entertained at this time for a printed text, that Bengel himself laid it down as a rule not to alter or introduce a word which had not been already printed. Although the common text was prepared from a few comparatively modern and random materials, intermixed with arbitrary and questionable insertions, it soon acquired such a degree of sanctity as to be regarded as infallible, and any attempt to alter it was looked upon as almost sacrilegious. Bengel, however, did not in every instance adhere to his rule, having introduced into the Apocalypse some alterations derived from manuscript authority.

Bengel was followed by the illustrious Wetstein in 1757. He also followed the received text, but noted such omissions and alterations as he approved of. He first gave names to the various manuscripts, designating uncial manuscripts by capital letters. He was a man of unwearied energy, and never suffered himself to be biassed in his judgment by his religious opinions, which were Unitarian. He added largely to the collection of texts, which had been already prepared with such amazing industry by Dr. Mill. We shall not stop to recount the various labours in the same department of Matthæi, Alter and Birch, the latter of whom collated some of the most valuable manuscripts, including B, or the celebrated uncial manuscript in the Vatican, which contains, except in the Gospel of St. Matthew, the text of Alexandria.

But the person who first made a practical use of these materials, and who actively devoted his unmatched talents to the construction of a pure text of the New Testament, was the celebrated J. J. Griesbach, of whom it is sufficient to say, in the words of Bishop Marsh, that "his scrupulous integrity, as a man and a scholar, is sufficient guarantee for the honest application of them;" that "his diligence was unremitted, his erudition was profound, his caution was extreme, and his judgment was directed by a sole regard to the evidence before him;"* and as the question is now narrowed by an approach to the rival system of Scholz, it will be necessary, in order to form a correct judgment on this subject, to give a more extended view of Griesbach's system, which that of Scholz is designed to supersede.

To Griesbach we are indebted for the classification of manuscripts into Recensions, or Families, the idea of which was first suggested by Bengel, and approved by Semler. In the middle of the third century, the text seems to have been uncertain and arbitrary. About this period, critical labours appear to have been applied, in different countries, to its correction. From the period of the third century, Griesbach distinguishes three principal families, or editions as we should now call them; viz. the Asiatic or Constantinopolitan, the African or Alexandrian, and the European or Western. These have been, upon very solid grounds, reduced by Scholz to two—the Asiatic and the African. He considers the European to be but a subdivision of the African.

The grand problem is to ascertain the most accurate text, or that text which was contained in the autographs of the sacred writers. These original writings, and doubtless the oldest copies of them, existed in Asia. After the fifth century the Asiatic recension became

---

* Lecture vi.

the source of the text commonly received in the Eastern church. But the copies were, notwithstanding, far from being so pure as the transcripts found in Alexandria, these having been corrected by the critical labours of Origen and other eminent scholars. It is to these very critical labours that Scholz ascribes the corruptions of the African text, to which he prefers the Asiatic, as being in his opinion faithfully transcribed without any attempt at critical alteration, and as presenting on this account a genuine and faithful transcript of the autographs of the apostles. Griesbach, however, had made similar charges against the transcribers of Asiatic manuscripts, whom he accuses of altering the text without exhibiting that judgment which the African transcribers brought to the subject. Neither was the number of copies transcribed nearly as great as in Greece and Asia; the most ancient manuscripts were most highly prized, and consequently the same liberties of alteration in the text were not taken here as in Asia, where the transcribers laboured to render the Greek text as pure as possible, especially in such passages as seemed to them to savour of Hebrew phraseology. Griesbach, therefore, conceives that the most ancient readings may be restored from the text of the Alexandrian fathers, or even of Origen alone. The ancient Latin version, (which was made in the first and second centuries,) may be referred to this class. Jerome, in his edition of the Latin version, made use of very ancient Palestine manuscripts, which were closely allied to the African recension. The uncial manuscripts B, C, L, in the Gospels, and A, B, C, in the Epistles, contain this text, a text remarkable for its grammatical purity.

Such was Griesbach's theory, and well and faithfully did he apply the greater part of his valuable life to reduce his system to practice, in his admirable edition of the New Testament, which presents to the reader at a glance, not only all the variations from the received printed text, but the evidences on which every single alteration was made, and which enable the reader to test and correct the learned editor himself, whenever he has introduced a reading at variance with the principles which he has laid down, as it has been shown that he has done in more than one instance, by the learned Dr. Lawrence, and others.

The system as well as the text of Griesbach, has been that generally adopted, with some few modifications, by subsequent editors. It remained for the distinguished editor of the text before us to give the first critical edition of the Asiatic, or Constantinopolitan text, in which, while he duly appreciates the labour and skill of Griesbach, and adopts his celebrated edition as the model of his own, making use of all his materials, he labours to supersede Griesbach's Alexandrian text, and to substitute in its room the Constantinopolitan, or Asiatic.

Dr. John Martin Scholz is a priest of the church of Rome, and one of the distinguished professors belonging to that communion in the University of Bonn, on the Rhine. Without ascribing to him the patience, the acumen, or even the coolness in discrimination for which Griesbach was so justly celebrated, it is only common justice to say that Dr. Scholz has applied himself with laborious and indefatigable industry to the work which he has undertaken. While Griesbach generally made use of the labours of Mill, Wetstein, Matthæi, Birch, and others, it was part of Dr. Scholz's labour to visit the libraries which contained the most rare manuscripts of the New Testament in various parts of the world, and there collate them himself. He visited, with this view, Paris, Vienna, Landshut, Munich, Berlin, Treves, London, Geneva, Turin, Florence, Venice, Parma, Rome, Naples, Jerusalem, St. Saba, and the Isle of Patmos. And the result of his labours has been the critical edition of the text, of which Mr. Bagster has presented a transcript, without, however, those critical materials, and references to the various authorities, which constitute the principal value of Scholz's edition.

Notwithstanding the value which we justly ascribe to Scholz's indefatigable industry, it does not appear that much has been added to those materials which Griesbach had already collected. Great as the labour has been which this eminent critic has undertaken, the additional materials to which he has had access appear to have been but scanty. This will be evident to any one who compares the two editions; for there is very little indeed to be found in Scholz which we had not already in the more original work of his precursor. The only part of the work which can be considered as new is his text, and this, no doubt, is the most important in its consideration to the Biblical scholar and the critic. The text then before us, is that of the Constantinopolitan or Asiatic recension, which Dr. Scholz prefers to the Alexandrian or Western, on grounds which we have already referred to. These, however, we shall more fully recapitulate.

Dr. Scholz recognises, after Bengel, only two recensions—the Asiatic and the African. The Western, or European recension, he includes in the latter, with which it has evidently a close alliance. The Asiatic he conceives to contain a faithful transcript of the autographs of the apostles and evangelists; and could he prove this point, the question as to superiority would be settled at once. But this is not quite so easy a matter; and although Scholz labours hard to prove this most important fact, we confess that the mystery requires some further elucidation before it can command our unqualified assent. Dr. Scholz acquaints us that, after the first autographs were lost or worn out, the numerous copyists who were engaged in multiplying manuscripts of them, did not imitate the audacity of the Alexandrian grammarians. Such audacity the Doctor conceives to be improbable, if the question related to profane authors; and utterly incredible as regards the New Testament. He assures us that the venerable bishops of Greece and Asia laboured to preserve the text pure and unmolested, whence it remained unaltered until the times of Constantine and Constans. Such is Scholz's primary reason (and an excellent one it is if founded on good evidence), for preferring the Asiatic recension.

Dr. Scholz further appeals to six Palestine manuscripts, to prove its agreement with the text of that country, as well as to the two Syrian versions—the Peschito and the Philoxenian—both executed in Palestine. To this class he also refers the Gothic, Georgian, and Sclavonic versions, and the quotations of the Greek, Asiatic, and Syrian ecclesiastical writers. The text of this recension he maintains to have been equally fixed with the canon of the New Testament in the fourth century; any alteration, he conceives, must have taken place before this period, and such alteration he ascribes, as we have said, to the learned grammarians of Alexandria. This pure Asiatic text, found in the manuscripts destined for liturgical use, and made principally in Constantinople, under the eyes of the superiors, from the fifth to the middle of the fifteenth century, is what Dr. Scholz has, with praiseworthy diligence, endeavoured to restore to something like apostolic purity.

The corruptions of the Alexandrian text, Dr. Scholz believes, commenced in the very first, most of them, he thinks, were made in the two first, centuries. As a proof of this, he adduces the most ancient muniments which we possess—the Vatican, the Alexandrine, and the Ephrem codices—which, though transcribed in the fifth or sixth centuries, are copies of more ancient exemplars, exhibiting Egyptian tamperings with the text. The Coptic and Latin versions also, in his estimate, afford evidences of these corruptions, inasmuch as they agree with the text of Alexandria; as do also the quotations of the ecclesiastical writers, Clement, Origen, and Dionysius. Jerome, he says, made use of manuscripts of both families. The text of Alexandria was thus diffused in the West, in Greek manuscripts and Latin versions, and is that constantly used by the Italian and African fathers, as well as in the early Gallican church.

Dr. Scholz also considers the remarkable and scrupulously exact uniformity of the Asiatic manuscripts as almost a proof of the legitimacy of this text, which he contrasts with the peculiar discrepancies and variations of the Egyptian exemplars. The manuscripts of the Alexandrian text confessedly exceed all others in antiquity; but notwithstanding this, Dr. Scholz appeals for the superiority of the Alexandrian text to Dr. Griesbach himself; for although in the estimation of that cautious critic the authority of a few manuscripts of the Alexandrian class outweighed that of a multitude of the Constantinopolitan, he never adopted a reading from this class of manuscripts into the text, unless it was confirmed by a variety of collateral testimony,—another instance of the unshaken impartiality of that critic, who would not allow his predilections to interfere with the solemn and sacred task which he had undertaken. Scholz's notes are taken verbatim from Griesbach, with which he has intermixed his own additions.

Mr. Bagster has enriched his work with a tabular list of the variations between the printed texts of Scholz and Griesbach, as well as a reference to the passages in which the printed received text, including both Elzevir's and Beza's, differs from both. The number of variations between Scholz and Griesbach is four hundred and thirty-four; the number of passages in which the received text agrees with Scholz and differs from Griesbach, is one hundred and seventy-six; and that of those in which the received text agrees with that of Griesbach, is two hundred and eleven. Upon the whole, therefore, the "Textus Receptus," (from which our Authorized version is taken,) is more conformable to Griesbach than it is to Scholz. But the resemblance is much stronger in the Epistles and Apocalypse than it is in the Gospels, where the text harmonizes more with Scholz. This arises from the fact, that the first editors of the New Testament used for the Gospels and Acts manuscripts of the Asiatic, and for the rest of the New Testament manuscripts of the Alexandrine recension. This took place, however, more by accident than design.

Some of our readers may, perhaps, be under the impression that these four hundred and thirty-four variations between the rival texts may be of great consequence, as affecting points of real importance. Quite the contrary. In nearly all important matters, the two texts harmonize. The discrepancies are seldom even verbal. They often consist in a different orthography, such as $\Gamma\epsilon\theta\sigma\eta\mu\alpha\nu\epsilon\iota$ for $\Gamma\epsilon\theta\sigma\eta\mu\alpha\nu\eta$; or of appellation, as Cephas for Peter; frequently of transposition merely. There are not half a dozen that affect either a matter of fact, or a point of doctrine. It may appear to some that much labour has been thus thrown away, in the preparation of such editions, and the collection of materials for such a purpose. But the slightest consideration will serve to dissipate a delusion of this kind. But for labours of this kind, we should not have been certain of the correctness of a single phrase in the written word, nor should we be now in possession of the invaluable treasure of the sacred records. And if no expense or labour is considered too much to procure an accurate edition of a profane author, how much more should we appreciate the pious labours of the sacred critic, who devotes his whole mind to ascertaining, and giving to the world, a pure text of the records of our salvation, where every word and every letter is of inestimable importance. Not that we are such worshippers of the mere letter of Scripture, as to consider our faith endangered by every variety which may occur even in matters of vital importance. Our faith in the blessed Trinity, for instance, is not shaken by the consideration whether an *omicron* (O) or a *theta* (Θ) formed the first letter of a contraction in the Alexandrine manuscript now in the British Museum.*
We do not here wish to be misunderstood. We do not mean to deny the vital importance of a word, or of a letter, in what regards the salvation of man and the cause of eternal truth. But we mean to say, that the Catholic Christian has a security for his faith which

---

* 1 Tim, iii. 16. 'ΟΣ or ΘΣ, ὅs or Θεὸs. Griesbach gives the preference to the former reading; Scholz to the latter. Some officious orthodox scribe has rendered the reading in this manuscript still more doubtful, by retracing the line across the Θ; that is, if the line ever existed.

cannot be shaken by the transposition or loss of a letter, a word, a clause, or of whole books of the sacred volume. We do not forget that our holy religion was taught and believed for years before a word of the New Testament existed:—that it was written for the instruction of individuals and of churches which had already been taught the christian faith by those who had received it from Christ himself, and that this teaching, rather than the sacred volume, was the foundation of their faith. When the world, with this sacred volume in their hands, was divided into many contending factions, each interpreting it in his own way, the doctrines which had been taught by the apostles were collected from Scripture and from the teaching of the apostles, then fresh in the minds of men, and embodied in those creeds which we now receive on their authority as containing divine and apostolic truths; and thus believing that, in addition to the letter of Scripture, or the written word, there is a living testimony in the Church of God to all Catholic truth, we are not at all alarmed at the change of a word, or the loss of any portion of the sacred volume which we might have once mistakenly reverenced as part of the written word. Thus, whether we read with Griesbach, in 1 Tim. iii. 16, ὃς; or with Scholz, Θεὸς; or with the Latin Vulgate *quod;* this does not in the least shake our faith in the doctrine of the true and proper deity of our Lord, as taught by the voice of the universal church.

There seems to us, indeed, to have been a good deal of tampering by the orthodox, as well as by heretics, with some of the most remarkable texts relating to this very subject. To say nothing of the text just alluded to, which appears to have been tampered with more than once, even by some pious hand—or, of the other remarkable text in Acts xx. 28, where Griesbach, with the Alexandrine recension, reads Ἐκκλησίαν τοῦ κυρίου, and Scholz with the Constantinopolitan, Ἐκκλησίαν τοῦ Θεοῦ, if we had been superstitiously attached, as some have been, to a corrupt printed text, or to a particular manuscript, or set of manuscripts, of the Vulgate, or even to what we might have considered a pure Greek manuscript, how staggered we should be at Scholz's omission of the celebrated text, 1 John v. 7, the text of the heavenly witnesses! But we have not so learned our faith. We believe that the church of the living God is the depositary and the keeper of divine truth. Although all its temples be destroyed, and all its material records should be lost, its faith will not fail. It is founded on an immoveable rock, and the gates of hell will never prevail against it.

And here we shall make a passing observation on the fate of this remarkable clause. It found no place in the Editio Princeps—the first printed edition of the Greek Testament, the edition of Erasmus, although, to appease the clamours of the divines of his church, he inserted it in his third edition. With anxious and eager curiosity we turned to the place which this clause ought to occupy in the last critical edition, that of Scholz, himself a divine of the Church of

Rome. The clause was not there! We had been just reading Dr. Wiseman's able treatise in vindication of the genuineness of this clause, as it exists in the printed editions of the "authentic" Vulgate,* which most Roman-catholic divines place above any existing Greek text, and we confess that we scarcely expected to see the clause so unceremoniously treated by a faithful son of the Roman see. But anxious to know whether Scholz, more honest than the Complutensian editors, merely rejected it from his *Greek* text, as not having found it in the manuscripts of his favourite recension, we turned to his note, and there found that he had indignantly rejected the clause as having never come from the pen of the apostle John, but been a direct interpolation. Thus, after three centuries, Erasmus has been vindicated, and this celebrated and much contested clause has disappeared from the sacred volume. *Requiescat in pace.*†

We now come to consider the value of the English translations which enrich Mr. Bagster's volume, and which have led to its being called the Hexapla.

The first printed translation of the Bible appeared in Germany, and in the language of that country. This was nearly a century before the Bible was printed in England. It must in candour be admitted that, notwithstanding the difficulties which have been thrown by the Church of Rome in the way of the general and indiscriminate circulation of the sacred volume, it was from members of that church that the first translations of the Bible emanated, as well as the first editions of the original Hebrew and Greek. The first German Bible appeared in the year 1466; a Spanish translation appeared in 1478, and an Italian in 1471. The first edition of the English New Testament did not appear before the year 1526, and even this was not printed in England. But although we had not the honour of being among the first nations which printed the Bible, we have had manuscript translations from a very early period. We have had the Gospels in our vernacular tongue from the seventh century. In the beginning of the eighth, the venerable Bede translated the entire Bible.

At the close of the thirteenth century it was again translated, but we know not the name of the pious individual who completed this difficult task. About a century later, Wiclif's translation, which bears the date 1380, and which occupied in the first column in the volume before us, appeared.

But as all these early translations were made from the Latin Vulgate, it may be useful to consider for a moment the nature of this

---

* We say, *printed editions,* for the oldest manuscripts of the Vulgate know nothing of this clause.

† There are many other passages of minor importance in which Scholz agrees with Griesbach, such as the omission of the doxology in the Lord's Prayer, and the omission of the final clause in the Lord's Prayer, as given by St. Luke. There are many others, and those some of the most controverted, in which Scholz agrees with Elzevir's edition, or the received text, such as 1 Tim. iii. 16; Acts xx. 28, &c.

work. There were many Latin translations as early as the second century; but their variations were such, that the celebrated Jerome, the translator of the Old Testament from the Hebrew, undertook to revise them, and publish a corrected version by a comparison with Greek manuscripts. This being at the close of the fourth century, and it being probable that Jerome, who was a sound critic, procured very ancient manuscripts for this important task, we might be assured that if we were in possession of Jerome's original work, it would, although a translation, be of more value than probably any existing manuscript, as he translated from manuscripts centuries older than any now extant. But the manuscripts of the Vulgate which have come down to us are far from being authentic. The present Vulgate has been properly shown to be a mixed text, consisting partly of Jerome's revision, partly of an admixture with the earlier Latin translations. Even this mixed version has been corrupted in its transmission by various readings. We do not know what manuscripts were used in forming the present printed Vulgate; although we have no doubt that it was honestly collated, and that it may be in general relied on. A critical edition of the Latin Vulgate, with a collection of various readings on the model of Griesbach's Greek Testament, is, however, at present a desideratum, and the materials for it are abundant. It would probably, however, exceed the powers of any individual. Even our own happy islands afford a large stock of materials for so valuable and important a task. Few manuscripts of the entire New Testament are known to exist which are more ancient than the close of the eighth century. There is one in Ireland—the Codex Armachanus—which bears the date of the early part of the seventh.* There are also manuscripts of the four Gospels of the Latin version, which appear to be of as ancient a date as the fifth century. One of these, which has been lately discovered, has been supposed, by a judicious antiquary,† to be the identical book of the Gospels brought into Ireland by St. Patrick or Palladius, whom he considers to be the same person on no improbable grounds. This manuscript, in some phrases, agrees with Jerome's Vulgate, in others, with the old Italian; only a few pages have been collated. It is now the property of the University of Dublin.

Wiclif's manuscript is translated immediately from the Vulgate; and it is the opinion of Mr. Bagster's editor, that it would have been impossible to have procured a copy of the Greek at this time, as it was not until the year 1453, after the taking of Constantinople by the Turks, that the Greek Scriptures found their way into the western

---

* Mr. Davidson, in his Lectures on Biblical Criticism, classes this among *Greek* MSS., which is the more surprising, as it is correctly placed among Latin MSS. in the Appendix to Dr. Wright's Translation of Seiler's Biblical Hermeneutics, whose very words have been adopted by Mr. Davidson, in this and many other instances, without any recognition of the existence of the work from whence he has derived his information. See Lecture XIII.

† Mr. Petrie. Transactions of the Royal Irish Academy.

parts of Europe. The Greek literature was first introduced into England by Dr. Linacre at the close of the fifteenth century.

Wiclif appears to have judiciously chosen a correct text of the Vulgate, and to have faithfully executed his translation; but of this we leave the reader to judge, as he has got the work in his hands. The editor truly asserts that Wiclif possessed no peculiar powers of detecting such glosses as had crept into the text of the Vulgate, and he gives as a specimen of one of these glosses, the verse, 2 Peter i. 10, "Wherfor, brethren, be ye more bisie that (bi good werkis) ye make youre cleping and chesynge certeyn;" or, as it is in the Rhemish version, "Wherefore, brethren, labour more, that by good works you may make sure your calling and election." The words, "by good works," the editor, with justice, considers a gloss. Yet this gloss is supported not only by the Benedictine editors of Jerome's works, but by the Alexandrian manuscript in the British Museum, with six others, and also by the Syriac and several other ancient versions. We shall dismiss this version with referring the reader for further particulars to the editor's dissertation, fully agreeing with him, that it is indeed wonderful that the language of four hundred and sixty years since should be so intelligible to us as is the version of John Wiclif.

Our limits will not allow us to enter at present into the merits of the other translations of the Bible presented to us in this volume; the character of these has been frequently discussed. The first is the earliest printed English version, that of Tindale, which is translated from the Greek. This point, we know, has been contested, but we think on insufficient grounds, although there can be little doubt that Tindale was aided by Luther's German translation. Nor can we here follow the translator through his eventful history, as affectingly described by the author of the Preliminary Dissertation, to the period of the cruel execution of this excellent man by order of the Emperor, which took place near Brussels, in 1536. And it gives us pleasure to add the following testimony from the pen of a distinguished Roman-catholic divine:—" Few first translations will be found preferable to Tindale's. In point of perspicuity and noble simplicity, propriety of idiom, and purity of style, no English version has yet surpassed it."

The first edition of Tindale's Greek Testament, first published in 1526, has been also reprinted by Mr. Bagster in 1836. The present is a reprint of the second edition, revised by Tindale himself, and published in 1534.

The next in order is the Great Bible, or Cranmer's, so called, probably, from his Prologue prefixed to it, although no part of it was translated by him. The New Testament is the same which Cranmer had caused to be executed, and this continued to be the authorized Bible, until it was superseded by Archbishop Parker's, or the Bishops' Bible, in 1568.

The version of the Psalms of David from this Bible, "pointed as they are to be sung or said in churches," is that still retained in our church service. So that we have two authorized versions of the Psalms, one sanctioned by liturgical usage, and the other by the last Authorized version. It is singular that a similar circumstance has taken place in the Roman church, which still uses the Gallican Psalter in her church services, although there is a different version in the Vulgate, executed by St. Jerome.

We add a specimen of Tindale's translation, compared with Cranmer's, taken from the 3d chapter of St. John's Gospel.

TINDALE.	CRANMER.
"Ther was a man of the pharises, named Nicodemus, a ruler amonge the Jewes. The same cam to Jesus by nyght, and saide unto him: Rabbi, we knowe that thou art a teacher whiche arte come from God; for no man coulde do suche miracles as thou doest, except God were with him. Jesus answered and sayde unto him, Verely, verely, I saye unto the: Except a man be boren anewe, he cannot se the kyngdom of God."	"Ther was a man of the Pharises, named Nycodemus, a ruler of the Jewes. The same cam to Jesus by nyght, and sayde unto him: Rabbi, we know that thou arte a teacher come from God: for no man coulde do suche myracles as thou doest, except God were with him. Jesus answered & sayd unto him, Verely, verely, I saye unto the: except a man be boren from above, he cannot se the kyngdom of God."

The same is thus rendered by Wiclif.

"There was a man of the fariseis, nicodeme bi name, a prince of the jewis, and he cam to ihesus bi nygt, and seide to him, rabi, we witen that thou art comen fro god, maister, for no man mai do these signes that thou doist, but god be with hym. ihesus answerid: and seide to hym, truli truli I seie to thee, but a man be borun agen, he mai not se the kyngdom of god."

A very superior work is the Geneva translation of the New Testament, which was first printed in 1557. This was the work of the exiles who fled from Queen Mary's persecution, and sought refuge in Switzerland. It contains several notes in the margin, some of which seeming to inculcate limits to the doctrine of passive obedience, gave dire offence to King James, who pronounced it to be the worst of all translations. This translation is further remarkable as being the first English edition which contains the division of verses, with the notation of figures vulgarly attributed to Robert Stephens. According to the work before us, "In Robert Stephens's fourth edition of the Greek Testament (1551) the notation of the verses had been for the first time appended; and in this edition the numbers were put in the margin, while the text went on continuously. These numbers were found so convenient for purposes of reference, that they soon became universally adopted; the Geneva translation being the first to break the text into little paragraphs." We believe that the writer is quite mistaken in adopting the common notion that this notation was first adopted by Robert Stephens, although there can be no doubt that it first flowed into the subsequent editions of the Bible from Stephens's edition of the New Testament, printed in 1551, and of the Latin Bible, printed in 1555, in which latter the numerals are incorporated with the text. The notation by figures in our printed Bibles is much more ancient than any of Robert Stephens's editions. It had been adapted to parts of the Bible as early as the year 1509. But as we hope to have another opportunity of correcting the erroneous ideas which are current on this subject, we shall here only remark that if it were true that the Geneva translators were the first who divided our Bibles into these paragraphs, which, to use the words of a learned writer, "appear to the eyes of the learned, and to the minds of the unlearned, as so many detached sentences," they have given currency to a practice more honoured in the breach than the observance, and which we regret to see still so much followed in the editions of the Bible. We believe that much misunderstanding and misinterpretation of the holy Scriptures has followed from the practice. But we must here observe that Mr. Bagster's editor is evidently mistaken in supposing that the text "went on continuously" in Stephens's edition of 1551, for it contains this identical division into broken sentences, or *paragraphs*, corresponding to the notation of the verses, and commencing each verse with the line.

Next in order follows the Rhemish Testament, which has been the subject of much angry controversy. Like Wiclif's and Coverdale's, it is made, not from the Greek, but from the Latin Vulgate, and it appears to be an honest and faithful, although inelegant translation. It is entitled, "The New Testament of Jesus Christ, translated faithfully into English, out of the authentical Latin, according to the best corrected copies of the same, diligently conferred with the Greeke, and other editions in divers languages, with arguments of bookes and chapters, annotations, and other necessarie helpes, for the better understanding of the text, and specially for the discoverie of the corruptions of divers late translations, and for cleering the controversies in religion in these daies. In the English College of Rhemes. Printed at Rhemes, by Iohn Fogny. 1582." The present editor acquaints us, that the Protestants were disposed to depreciate the Latin Vulgate, and the Papists to extol it, as though it surpassed in authority even the original texts themselves. But we venture to assert that the writer is mistaken in the latter charge, and that they only meant to consider its authority as superior to the modern or existing Greek texts, not to the autographs of the apostles. We believe him to be more correct in his next assertion, that they took their idea of adding controversial notes from the Geneva translators. With these notes, however, we have at present nothing to do. The principal in this work was the celebrated Cardinal Allen, aided by Gregory Master, Richard Bristow, and Thomas Worthington.

The author of the "Historical Account" gives a fair and impartial view of the reasons which induced the Rhemish translators to defend the Vulgate, from which they made their translation. "They defend it thus: first, that it commonly agrees with the Greek text; secondly;

that when it differs from the common Greek text, it frequently accords with some of the various readings of Stephens's third edition; thirdly, they say, that even Protestants do not unfrequently prefer the marginal reading to that in the text; fourthly, that in the passages in which the printed Greek authority does not agree with the Latin, there is sometimes to be found a manuscript Greek copy which does accord with the Latin; fifthly, they allege that where no Greek copy accords with the Latin text, not unfrequently the citation of some ancient Greek 'father' supplies a confirmation; sixthly, they suppose in passages where some variation is found which cannot otherwise be accounted for, that the Latin interpreter followed some other Greek copy; seventhly, they bring forward the Latin fathers as witnesses of what the reading of the Greek text was in their days; lastly, they account for variations in the citations made by the Latin 'fathers,' by the fact that the Latin versions were in the early days very numerous; and thus when their quotations vary from the Vulgate, they suppose that they may have cited some other of these versions. This last reason is merely apologetic; the rest contain, on the whole, a great deal of truth. One thing, however, they ought to have stated; namely, that the Vulgate contains not a few passages which are clearly the corruptions of copyists. Candour on the part of the Rhemish translators would have acknowledged this; but as that version had been declared 'authentic' they were willing fully to carry out this Tridentine decree.

"It is quite true, that they do acknowledge some faults to have crept in, but merely such as would, in a printed book, be regarded as typographical errata; those to which I have just referred are such as have a more serious character.

"They strenuously deny that they prefer the Latin to the Greek text because of its being more favourable to their views and opinions; alleging that the Greek text makes for them more than the Latin. This they endeavour to prove by examples which they bring forward; and I think that it must be admitted, by any one who dispassionately considers the subject, that very few of the variations of the Latin from the Greek text, bear the mark of having been made to serve a purpose. They almost all must have crept in, just like various readings in Greek copies, through the negligence or oversight of transcribers."

"This account of portions of the preface will serve to give some idea of the plan pursued by these translators. They had their minds fully bent upon preserving, untouched, the whole of what they deemed 'Catholic verity,' and their minds recoiled from whatever seemed to oppose this. In a previous part of their preface, they had spoken thus of their version:—

"'How well we have done it, we must not be iudges, but referre all to Gods church and our superiours in the same,—to them we submit ourselues, and this, and all other our labours, to be in part or in the whole, reformed, corrected, altered, or quite abolished: most humbly desiring pardon, if through our ignorance, temeritie, or other humane infirmitie, we haue anywhere mistaken the sense of the Holy Ghost,—further promising that if hereafter we espie any of our owne errors, or of any other, either frende of good will, or adversarie for desire of reprehension, shal open unto us the same: we will not (as Protestants doe) for defense of our estimation, or of pride and contention by wrangling wordes wilfully persist in them, but be most glad to heare of them, and in the next edition or otherwise to correct them; for it is truth that we seek for, and God's honour: which being had either by good intention or by occasion al is well. This we professe onely, that we haue done our endevour, with praier, much fear and trembling, lest we should dangerously erre in so sacred, high, and diuine a worke: that we haue done it with all faith, diligence, and sinceritie: that we haue used no partialitie for the disadvantage of our adversaries, nor no more license than is sufferable in translating of holy Scriptures: continually keeping ourselues as neere as is possible, to our text, and to the very words and phrases which by long use are made venerable, though to some prophane or delicate eares they may seeme more hard or barbarous, as the whole style of Scripture doth lightly to such at the beginning: acknowledging with S. Hierome, that in other writings it is ynough to give in translation, sense for sense, but that in Scriptures lest we misse the sense we must keepe the very wordes.'

" They thus invite criticism as to their labours, and the invitation has been very fully responded to. They attacked all previous versions, and in their turn were attacked, both as it regards their text and their notes. It may, I believe, be said, as an impartial judgment on this version, that the translators were fully competent to execute the task before them, so far as learning and ability could go; but their minds were so imbued with the same feelings which had led, but fifty years before, to persecution in England for the word of God, that they desired any thing rather than to give the rendering of the text simply and fairly. Very few passages, however, show in their rendering a really dishonest perversion, but very many exhibit a desire of expressing the sense obscurely; or at least, in such a way that a common reader may find not a little difficulty in gathering from the words a definite meaning. If we take the whole version, we shall however find a very large portion well translated, and truly exhibiting the sense of the Latin Vulgate such as they had it. I say such as they had it; for although the Council of Trent had defined the Latin Vulgate to be the authentic version, it remained a considerable question what copy was to be regarded as such."

An observation of the editor, "that in enlarging on the subjection with which the Scripture should be read, they mean subjection to the authority of the Church, and not subjection to what God has seen fit to reveal," leads us to make a few remarks on the limits of church authority.

It seems to us that if God has really commanded us in his word to respect the authority of his Church, we are not acting in opposition to his revelation in submitting ourselves to this authority.

We believe that there are many who speak of subjection to God's word, meaning subjection to their own fallible interpretations. In fact, the general idea that the Scriptures are so easily understood, that no honest-minded man can mistake their meaning, was once the prevailing opinion amongst Protestants. If these sentiments were true, what a beautiful picture of uniformity should we not reasonably expect that Protestanism would have presented.—Instead of which we see Trinitarians, Arians, Socinians, Calvinists, Arminians, Quakers, Baptists and Pœdobaptists, &c. &c. all deriving their diversified and clashing opinions from the same source. Some degree of modesty, some degree of diffidence in one's own private judgment, seems then a necessary qualification for entering upon the perusal of a work which good and learned men have so variously misunderstood.

It appears to us also to be inconsistent with the nature of a church to allow of any appeal from its decisions. Even what are called national churches, such as the Presbyterian communities of Holland, Geneva, or Scotland, claim some such degree of authority, rejecting or excommunicating any of their members who do not interpret the Scriptures in subjection to their teaching. It would not be received as a sufficient plea, before these tribunals, were an Arian or Socinian to appeal from their decisions to the word of God. The reply would be, "We found our opinion also in the word of God, but we object to your interpretation of it. This interpretation, resting on your own private judgment, we look upon as false, and, therefore, we excommunicate you." The editor has, no doubt upon the exercise of his own judgment, pronounced Arianism and Socinianism to be "blasphemous," and our own private interpretation leads us to the same conclusion, which has been further confirmed by the judgment of our own Church, derived from that of the church catholic,—but we cannot bring ourselves to adopt the uncharitable inference, that Socinians are necessarily cowards and hypocrites, because, as he asserts, "they do not avow themselves to be infidels at once." To name one instance among many, we believe that the celebrated Socinian, Dr. Nathaniel Lardner, was as far from being an infidel as any man breathing; and that the poor Arian, who was burned at Smithfield by the Reformers under Edward VI., (some of whom had narrowly escaped the same fate in the former reign,) had as perfect a right to exercise his judgment on the sense of Scripture as any of his executioners. It was unfortunately the case that when the infallibility of the church of Rome was rejected, an individual infallibility succeeded to its place; each believing that his own interpretation must necessarily be the right one, concluded that every individual who differed from his notion of the sense of the divine word, was a blasphemer, and an enemy of God, reserved for the eternal fires of a future judgment, and considered as a fit subject for such temporal inflictions, amounting to burning at the stake, as the State thought fit to adjudge to those whom it pronounced heretics. We shall give an example of this assertion of individual infallibility which came within our own experience.

A French Protestant minister, a man highly respected for his piety, boldly maintained his own opinions against his Roman antagonist in the south of France. He quoted the Hebrew Bible to his audience; asking if there was any one present who could read it in the original. "Oh, yes," said a Roman-catholic layman, pulling out his Hebrew Bible;—" but I cannot receive your interpretation of that particular text, nor is it that of some of the best commentators."—The other replied that he preferred the word of God to all human authority. " But, sir, you surely do not consider yourself infallible?" "But I do, sir," was the reply ;—" I am infallible: so far as I quote from this book, I *am* infallible." Such is the natural tendency of the uncontrolled exercise of private judgment. Decrying all church authority as human, the Protestant is often led to forget that his own judgment is that of a human being, or to fancy that he is inspired by God, when he is only under the influence of a warm imagination. The church of Rome, however—in denying the moral right of her members to interpret the Scriptures in a sense different from that of the church catholic—asserts herself to be that church—and thus assumes that she has the authority of the universal church of Christ for the propagation of her comparatively modern dogmas and practices—some of which are as unscriptural as they are uncatholic, though blended with all that is sound and orthodox in doctrine, and with much that is derived from the purest ages of the church in practice, intermixed with what one of the articles of the church of England, founded on Scripture, and the voice of the primitive church, designates as "blasphemous fables, and dangerous deceits." From these errors the Anglican church has freed herself. Declaring that the particular churches of Rome, Antioch, and Jerusalem have erred, she has maintained the duty of confiding in the church catholic, " the witness and keeper of holy writ." She obliges her sons to acknowledge the full " authority " of the universal church, not in rites and ceremonies only, (which every *particular* or *national* church has a right to change, if ordained only by man's authority,) but in "controversies of faith." Individuals may err, synods may err, general councils may err, but the catholic church of Christ, that " congregation of faithful men, in which the pure word of God is preached, and the sacraments are duly administered," is promised that Spirit which is to guide her into all truth; and the only limitation to her authority is, that nothing is to be ordained by her " contrary to God's word written." The church of England, while, after the example of the purest ages, she has placed no restriction on the liberty of reading the sacred volume, has enjoined subjection to the authority of the universal church; and herein she differs essentially from the Roman, which places such restrictions on the perusal of the Scriptures, as are calculated effectually to prevent her members from even judging whether she has the true marks and characters which alone ought to give her a claim to universal obedience, as being guided by the Spirit of God; and robs her children of some of their highest consolations and most delightful privileges,—while she arrogates for that portion of the visible church which happens to be in external communion with the see of Peter, those attributes which can only belong to the church universal,—that church which is built not on Peter only, but on the "foundation of the apostles and prophets, Jesus Christ himself being the chief corner-stone."

We have been partly led to make these observations on the responsibility which attends too great confidence in our own judgment, from a consideration of some of the errors of the learned and pious Wiclif, who published notions which are as opposed to the principles of our own church as they are to those of the church of Rome, and which have been animadverted on as they deserved by the mild Melancthon and by our own Bishop Fell, although unnoticed by the present editor. Among these notions were the following—that no obedience is due to any of the authorities in church or state who are living in mortal sin, from the pope to the deacon, and from the king to the constable; and that the wickedness of the minister invalidates the sacraments—that the clergy have no right to tithes, or other church property, &c. &c.

Before leaving the Rhemish version we shall remark, that it has been repeatedly improved and modernised in its language, and sometimes altered in conformity with the Authorized version, even in passages which had once been the subject of acrimonious animadversion, and charged as wilful mistranslations by Roman Catholic writers. There are, however, some alterations in which modern editors have departed from the sounder principles of the Rhemish translation—of these we shall give a specimen from John ii. 2, adduced by the Rhemish editors as an example of their manner of translating.

"Moreover, we presume not in hard places to mollifie the speaches or phrases, but religiously keep them word for word, and point for point, for fear of missing or restraining the sense of the Holy Ghost to our fantasie," as Eph. vi., 'against the spirituals of wickedness in the celestials,' and 'what to me and thee, woman.'" It is thus that it literally translates the Greek idiomatic phrase, τί ἐμοὶ καί σοι, γύναι, which is nearly identical with Wiclif's "what to me and to thee, womman." The Rhemish translation no doubt conveys no idea to an English ear, but as the real meaning might be a matter of controversy, it appears to us that the translators acted consistently with their principle in giving the literal phrase, rather than the interpretation of the words. It is scarcely necessary to add, that all the other English translations, including our Authorized version, render this phrase, "What have I to do with thee?" which, or rather, "What hast thou to do with me?" (the sense adopted in the note to the Rhemish version,) is no doubt the true interpretation. But in some of the modern editions of the Rhemish Testament, by interpolating the word *it*, the "sense of the Holy Ghost" is "restrained," and the phrase is thus altered into, *What is* IT *to me and thee?* an interpretation being thus forced on the passage, which the words will not bear, and which is at variance with the truth and with the whole context. In the parallel passage in Luke viii. 28, where the demoniac addresses our Lord in the same words, τί ἐμοὶ καί σοι, and which, in our translation, is rendered, "What have I to do with thee?" the Rhemish has consistently rendered the phrase, "What is to me and thee?"*

It is not uncommon with Roman Catholic divines in this country to contrast the various readings of the Greek text (of which Mill's edition contains thirty thousand) with the uniformity of their own *authentic Vulgate*. They forget that the *manuscripts* of the Vulgate are liable to the same charge of a variety of readings. Of these, Michaelis enumerates no less than eighty thousand.

We have but a few words to add, respecting the Authorized version, which completes this work. It is printed from the first edition, that of Barker, of 1611. As to its character, it would be superfluous in us to speak. It has already commanded the respect and admiration of all parties. Should the wants of the age, or the improved state of criticism, call for a revision of this version, we only trust that the task may be accomplished with an equal degree of beauty, dignity, and fidelity.

The Greek of this edition is given in a continued text, as are the various translations, which are divided, not into verses, but longer paragraphs, according to the sense. The numeral figures, as in the edition of Stephens of 1555, are incorporated into the text.

We should have wished that the editor had been less prolix in his Historical Dissertation, which exhibits much industry, and many interesting and affecting particulars respecting the lives and characters of the translators.

Journals of Two Expeditions of Discovery in North-West and Western Australia, during the years 1837, 38, *and* 39, *under the Authority of her Majesty's Government. Describing many newly-discovered, important, and fertile Districts, with Observations on the Moral and Physical Condition of the Aboriginal Inhabitants, &c. &c.* By GEORGE GREY, *Esq., Governor of South Australia; late Captain of the* 83d *Regiment.* 2 vols. 8vo. Pp. 894. Maps and Plates. London: Boone, 1841.

THIS is a delightful book; a simple, modest, unvarnished history of the perilous adventures of a good and brave man, to whose courage, ability, and sound discretion it was (under Providence) mainly owing, that those adventures were not brought to a fatal termination. A more agreeable work for family reading we never fell in with; and if those to whom we are about to introduce it, should happen to peruse

---

* Luke vii. 28. It is but fair to add, that Schott renders the passage in John ii. 2, "Quid hoc, inquit, ad me atque te, mulier," which he explains by, aliorum est curare. He gives us another translation, Quid mihi tecum rei est. But in the parallel passage in Luke, the only translation which Schott gives, is, "Quid mihi tecum." " Missum me fac," is the rendering of Titmann.

it, as we ourselves did, by the side of a brightly burning fire, when the wind is howling, and the rain is driving against the windows, they will hardly fail before they lay their heads upon their pillows to offer one additional petition for those who travel by land or water, one additional thanksgiving for the warm roof that covers them, while many of their fellow-countrymen are tossing upon the deep, or wandering amid deserts and mountains, or sheltering themselves as best they can from the stormy blast "in dens and caves of the earth."

Every thing connected with Australia,—that country, which so sadly witnesses against us for those " penal settlements, founded on a selfish policy, which has made them more like hell, than, as they should have been, a place for christian penitents,"—that country which we are filling with our emigrants, over which our commerce and our enterprize are rapidly extending themselves, and for which we grudge nothing but the cheap means of making men wise unto salvation,—every thing connected with Australia is full of interest; almost every thing is anomalous, and unlike what is to be found elsewhere. To the natural philosopher, especially, it is the very land of paradox. Mammals, birds and reptiles, insects and molluscs,—the whole animal creation, in short, vertebrate and invertebrate,—no less than the treasures of the vegetable kingdom, either present new forms, (and those devised by nature in her most fantastic mood,) or (if the genera are known elsewhere), species entirely peculiar to that region of the world. And what is very remarkable is, that in many respects the productions of Australia seem to form the link between extinct and existing races of animals,—between the ante and post-diluvian world. The only recent types of many fossil shells are to be found upon the shores of that vast insular continent; and we believe that the same remark is applicable to the higher classes of organized beings. But Australia is not a land of wonder only, it is a land of promise; every fresh expedition of discovery along its coasts, or into its interior, seems to develop more and more advantages to emigrants, and to give sure and certain hope that in a few centuries (if the world should last so long) it will become a far more important country than America is now. God grant that when such is the case, Australia may be to her colonies, what *we might* have been, and *ought* to have been, but have *not been* to her!

Mr. Grey informs his readers at the outset of his work, that it had been the opinion of the great navigators, Dampier and King, that there must be some large river or water inlet (that grand desideratum for colonists) on the western or south-western side of Australia. Up to the year 1836, very little of the western coast and interior of that vast continent was known; but upon Messrs. Grey and Lushington proposing to Lord Glenelg (then Secretary for the Colonies) to "conduct an exploration from Swan River to the northward," with the view of ascertaining the existence or otherwise of any such body of water, their offer was accepted, and the result was the series of discoveries, of which we propose to set the outlines before our readers.

On the 5th of July, 1837, the two gentlemen above mentioned, with Mr. Walker, a surgeon and naturalist, and corporals Coles and Auger, of the Sappers and Miners, who had volunteered their services, sailed from Plymouth in her Majesty's sloop of war the *Beagle*, commanded by Captain Wickham, then about to proceed on a survey of the coasts and seas of Australia. Touching at Teneriffe and Bahia, our voyagers arrived, on September 21, at the Cape of Good Hope, where Mr. Grey (finding that a vessel for the expedition could be procured more readily and economically than at Swan River,) engaged the *Lynher*, a schooner of 140 tons. Here, likewise, he increased his party by a few additional hands of good character, and among them one Thomas Ruston, a seaman who had already served on the Australian coast under Captain King. On the 13th of October, they hove anchor for the land, " which," adds Captain Grey, " I so long to see, and to which I was now bound, with the ardent hope of opening the way for the conversion of a barren wilderness into a fertile garden." And this was no metaphorical expression on the Captain's part, for his plan was not only to introduce all the useful animals that he possibly could into this part of Australia, but also the most valuable plants of every description.

It had been arranged before leaving England, that the expedition, instead of beginning its operations from the Swan River, and so proceeding northward, should commence exploring in the vicinity of Prince Regent's River, and work its way southward to the Swan,— a plan of proceeding deemed more advisable, since the travellers would then proceed in a direction parallel to the unknown coast, and which would therefore necessarily compel them to cross every large river flowing from the interior to that side of the continent.

On the 2d of December the *Lynher* anchored off Entrance Island, (Port George the Fourth,) on the north-west coast of Australia.

" At the first streak of dawn, I leant over the vessel's side, to gaze upon those shores I had so longed to see. I had not anticipated that they would present any appearance of inviting fertility; but I was not altogether prepared to behold so arid and barren a surface as that which now met my view. In front of me stood a line of lofty cliffs, occasionally broken by sandy beaches; on the summits of these cliffs, and behind the beaches, rose rocky sandstone hills, very thinly wooded. Whilst I mused on this prospect, all hands were busied in getting the vessel under weigh, which was soon accomplished; but there was little or no wind, and the ship lay almost motionless upon the waters.

" By ten o'clock, however, we were abreast of High Bluff Point, and as there appeared to be little chance of our having even a gentle breeze for some time, I determined to land with a party at the Point, and to walk from thence to Hanover Bay, where, on our arrival, we could make a signal to the vessel for a boat to reconvey us on board. By the adoption of this course, I hoped to be able at once to select a spot affording water and forage, in the neighbourhood of which the sheep and stores might be landed; the vessel could then proceed without delay to the Island of Timor, to procure the requisite number of ponies for our expedition, and if she made a quick passage there and back, I trusted, notwithstanding the numerous unforeseen delays that had arisen, we might yet be able to start for the interior, before the rainy season set in.

" The necessary orders were soon given : the boat was lowered, and whilst the party prepared themselves, I went below to arrange with the master the precise spot at which the vessel was to anchor, in order that no mistake might occur upon so vital a point. This done, I returned once more on deck, and found all ready for departure.

" The party to land consisted of Mr. Lushington, Mr. Walker, and three men who were selected to accompany us. I also brought away three of the dogs, to whom I was anxious to give a run after their long confinement on board.

" The shore for which we pulled was not more than half a mile distant, and we soon gained the edge of a sandy beach, on which I sprung, eagerly followed by the rest; every eye beaming with delight and hope, unconscious as we were how soon our trials were to commence.

" I soon found that we had landed under very unfavourable circumstances. The sun was intensely hot. The long and close confinement, on board a small vessel, had unfitted us all for taking any violent or continued exercise, without some previous training, and the country in which we had landed, was of a more rocky and precipitous character than any I had ever before seen; indeed I could not more accurately describe the hills, than by saying, that they appeared to be the ruins of hills; composed as they were of huge blocks of red sand-stone, confusedly piled together in loose disorder, and so overgrown with spinifex and scrub, that the interstices were completely hidden, and into these one or other of the party was continually slipping and falling.

" The trees were small, and their foliage so scant and slight, that they afforded no shelter whatever from the burning rays of the sun; which appeared to strike up again from the sand-stone with redoubled heat, so that it was really painful to touch, or to stand upon a bare rock : we therefore kept moving onwards, in the hope of meeting with some spot favourable for a halting-place; but the difficult nature of the ground which we had to cross, rendered our progress slow and oppressively laborious.

" A feeling of thirst and lassitude, such as I had never before experienced, soon began to overcome all of us; for such a state of things we had unfortunately landed quite unprepared, having only two pints of water with us, a portion of which it was necessary to give to the dogs, who apparently suffered from the heat in an equal degree with ourselves. These distressing symptoms I can only ascribe to the extreme heat of the sun reflected from the sand-stone rocks, and our previous long confinement on board.

" Our small supply of water, although but sparingly used, was soon exhausted; and the symptoms of lassitude, before so excessive, now became far worse. As usual, the endurance of the animals gave way before that of the men. We had not completed more than a mile of our route (although it was far more, if the ascents and descents were taken into account), when Ranger, a very fine young dog, dropped behind some rocks, and although we turned back to look for him directly he was missed, he could not be found.

" The next to give way was Ringhalz, a fine Cape buckhound; he fell amongst the rocks, and died almost instantly. The only dog now left was a greyhound, who manifested his extreme distress by constantly lying down. For some time we dragged him along, but he was at last, from necessity, abandoned. The cry of water was at length raised by one of the party, and immediately afterwards we found ourselves on the edge of a deep ravine, the precipitous sides of which were composed of nearly horizontal layers of red sandstone. Down these some of us contrived to scramble, although not without difficulty; but on reaching the bottom, we had the mortification to find the water salt; and as it would have been very laborious to follow its course along the bottom of the ravine over the mud, mangroves, and rocks which filled it, we had the pleasure of scrambling up again as we best could.

"For some short time we remained seated on the edge of the cliffs above the ravine; but as there was no shelter here from the sun's rays, and the pangs of thirst were pressing, I roused the men at last, and moved on again, following the course of the ravine upwards—we had not walked more than half a mile when the salt water inlet terminated, and the bed of the ravine became thickly wooded. At the moment we gained this point, some white cockatoos came soaring upwards from beneath our feet; and, as we knew that this was an infallible sign of the presence of water, we descended again to renew our search for it."—Pp. 67—71.

Accordingly, in a few minutes they found a pool of water, which, brackish as it was, afforded a most delicious draught to the weary, thirsty travellers. Meanwhile the day was wearing on, and the nature of the country was so rocky and difficult, that a night-march was impossible. It became desirable, therefore, to make the sea-coast before sunset; it was easy to walk along the shore after dark, and the firing of a gun would serve as a signal to the schooner to send off a boat.

"With this view," says Mr. Grey, "I moved onwards towards the sea, requesting Mr. Lushington, when I fired, to follow my course with the men. As I walked a-head, I found the country very rocky, with lofty bare pinnacles standing up every here and there in the forest, one or two of which I climbed, but could see nothing of the vessel." Eventually, however, the shore was reached, and Mr. Grey's first act was to strip off his clothes and plunge into the water; the quantity of moisture taken into the system by absorption, as he lay in the sea, soon relieved his burning thirst, and by the time the rest of the party came up, he was quite recovered. Still there were no signs of the schooner, and Mr. Grey therefore proceeded onwards in hopes of finding her, but he had hardly proceeded half a mile before his progress was arrested by an arm of the sea, some four or five hundred yards across, from which the tide was running out with fearful rapidity. What was to be done? Night was closing in; the guns had been repeatedly fired as a signal, without any answer from the ship; the beach afforded no wood wherewith to make a fire; the cliffs were too precipitous to be climbed; and it was evident that but very few of the party could swim so broad a space of water. Mr. Grey, therefore, like a gallant fellow, as he is, determined to run all risks alone, and swim the arm of the sea which stopped his way.

"I directed Coles to wait until the others came up, and then to remain with them, until I returned in a boat. From the rugged nature of the shore I could not have walked a yard without shoes, so I kept them on, as well as my shirt and military cap, and I took a pistol in one hand, as a means of defence against the natives, or else to fire it when I reached a spot where it could be seen or heard from the vessel.

"I plunged in, and very soon found myself caught in a tideway so violent, that resistance to its force, so as either to get on or return, appeared at the moment hopeless. My left hand, in which I held the pistol, was called into requisition to save my life; for the stream washed the cap from my head, and the cap then filling with water, and being carried down by the strong current, the chin-strap caught round my neck and nearly throttled me, as I dragged it after me through the water; whilst the loose folds of my shirt, being washed out to seawards by the tide, kept getting entangled with my arm. I grew weak and faint, but still swam my best, and at last I providentially reached a reef of rocks, which projected from the opposite shore, and to which I clung until I had somewhat regained my strength.

"I then clambered up on the rocks, and from thence made my way to the beach; but no sooner had I gained it, than I heard a native call from the top of the cliffs, and the answering cries of his comrades rang through the wood, as they followed me along; my pistol was so thoroughly soaked in my passage across the inlet, that it was quite useless, except as a club. To attempt to swim back again, after the narrow escape I had just had, would have been madness; besides which, if I had succeeded, I should have lost the object for which I had put my life at hazard. Nothing therefore was left, but to walk along shore to the schooner, trusting, in my defenceless state, that I might not fall in with any natives. It was now dark, and the shore was so broken and rocky that I got terribly cut and bruised, and was, moreover, so weak from my exertions in swimming, that when I arrived opposite the vessel, I could scarcely hail. Some of those on board, however, heard me (as I found afterwards), and shouted in reply; but their voices never reached my ears, and I imagined they were too far, for I could not now see the vessel.

"I made one or two more efforts to hail the *Lynher*, but the noise I made had now attracted the notice of the natives, and I heard their cries in several directions round me; this rendered my situation an unpleasant one, for I was worn out, naked, and defenceless: at first I thought to return and rejoin my party, and even turned back for a short distance with this intention, but I found myself too weak for such an undertaking, and changed my plans; resolving to remain nearly opposite to the vessel until the morning, and resting my chance of safety upon being discovered from it before the natives found me.

"With this intent I returned to the position from which I had lately hailed, and crept into a hole in the rocks, whence I could still occasionally hear the calls of the natives; but being thoroughly worn out, I soon forgot my toils and dangers in a very sound and comfortable sleep. I might have slept for some two hours, when I was roused by hearing a voice shout, 'Mr. Grey;' still, however, feeling rather distrustful of the truth of my mental impressions, and unwilling to betray my whereabouts to the natives, I returned no answer, but putting out my head from my secret place of rest, I waited patiently for a solution of my doubts. But again I certainly heard the same voice shout, 'Mr. Grey,' and I moreover now distinctly recognised the noise of oars working in the rullocks; I therefore hailed '*Lynher*, ahoy,' and all my doubts were completely put at rest by the hearty cheers which greeted my ear, as Mr. Smith, the mate of the schooner, called out, 'Where shall we pull in, Sir?'

"In a few minutes more I was in the boat, and rejoiced to find all the party safely there before me. My next question was, 'Have you a little water here?' 'Plenty, Sir,' answered Corporal Coles, 'as he handed me a little, which I greedily swallowed.'"—Pp. 76—78.

Such was the perilous commencement of Mr. Grey's expedition, and such it continued throughout; and nothing, humanly speaking, could have saved this band of adventurers from destruction over and over again, but the prompt decision, self-possession, and fortitude of their admirable commander.

Early in the following January, the *Lynher*, which in the interim had been despatched to Timor for ponies for the service of the proposed expedition into the interior, appeared off Hanover Bay, and on the 29th the march commenced; but Mr. Grey was destined to what the sailors call "a run of bad luck." The ponies were unmanageable, the sheep drooped under the influence of the climate, the rains were incessant, the rivers were swollen, the nature of the ground became more and more inaccessible, and to crown all, when their misfortunes were apparently at their height, an incident occurred which we must leave Mr. Grey to tell in his own simple and affecting words.

"It was the duty of the Cape man who accompanied me, to mark a tree every here and there by chipping the bark, so that the party might the next day easily recognise the route which they had to pursue; upon looking back I now perceived that he had neglected a very remarkable tree about twenty or thirty yards behind us, and which stood close to the spot where I had fired at the kangaroo. I desired him to go back and chip it, and then to rejoin us; in the mean time I stood musing as to the best means of avoiding the little rocky ravine in our front.

"Finding that the man remained absent longer than I had expected, I called loudly to him, but received no answer, and therefore passed round some rocks which hid the tree from my view to look after him. Suddenly I saw him close to me breathless, and speechless with terror, and a native with his spear fixed in a throwing-stick, in full pursuit of him; immediately numbers of other natives burst upon my sight; each tree, each rock, seemed to give forth its black denizen, as if by enchantment.

"A moment before, the most solemn silence pervaded these woods, we deemed that not a human being moved within miles of us, and now they rang with savage and ferocious yells, and fierce armed men crowded round us on every side, bent on our destruction.

"There was something very terrible in so complete and sudden a surprise. Certain death appeared to stare us in the face: and from the determined and resolute air of our opponents. I immediately guessed that the man who had first seen them, instead of boldly standing his ground, and calling to Coles and myself for assistance, had at once, like a coward, run away; thus giving the natives confidence in themselves, and a contempt for us: and this conjecture I afterwards ascertained was perfectly true.

"We were now fairly engaged for our lives; escape was impossible, and surrender to such enemies out of the question.

"As soon as I saw the natives around me, I fired one barrel of my gun over the head of him who was pursuing my dismayed attendant, hoping the report would have checked his further career. He proved to be the tall man seen at the camp, painted with white. My shot stopped him not: he still closed on us, and his spear whistled by my head; but whilst he was fixing another in his throwing-stick, a ball from my second barrel struck him in the arm, and it fell powerless by his side. He now retired behind a rock, but the others still pressed on.

"I now made the two men retire behind some neighbouring rocks, which formed a kind of protecting parapet along our front and right flank, whilst I took post on the left. Both my barrels were now exhausted; and I desired the other two to fire separately, whilst I was reloading; but to my horror, Coles, who was armed with my rifle, reported hurriedly, that the cloth case with which he had covered it for protection against rain, had become entangled. His services were thus lost at a most critical moment, whilst trying to tear off the lock cover; and the other man was so paralyzed with fear, that he could do nothing but cry out, ' Oh, God! Sir, look at them! look at them!'

"In the meantime, our opponents pressed more closely round; their spears kept whistling by us, and our fate seemed inevitable. The light-coloured man, spoken of at the camp, now appeared to direct their movements. He sprang forward to a rock not more than thirty yards from us, and posting himself behind it, threw a spear with such deadly force and aim, that had I not drawn myself forward by a sudden jerk, it must have gone through my body, and as it was, it touched my back in flying by. Another well-directed spear, from a different hand, would have pierced me in the breast, but, in the motion I made to avoid it, it struck upon the stock of my gun, of which it carried away a portion by its force.

"All this took place in a few seconds of time, and no shot had been fired, but by me. I now recognised in the light-coloured man an old enemy, who had led on the former attack against me on the 22d of December. By his cries and gestures, he now appeared to be urging the others to surround and press on us, which they were rapidly doing.

"I saw now that but one thing could be done to save our lives, so I gave Coles my gun to complete the reloading, and took the rifle which he had not yet disengaged from the cover. I tore it off, and stepping out from behind our parapet, advanced to the rock which covered my light-coloured opponent. I had not made two steps in advance when three spears struck me nearly at the same moment, one of which was thrown by him. I felt severely wounded in the hip, but knew not exactly where the others had struck me. The force of all knocked me down, and made me very giddy and faint, but as I fell, I heard the savage yells of the natives' delight and triumph; these recalled me to myself, and, roused by momentary rage and indignation, I made a strong effort, rallied, and in a moment was on my legs; the spear was wrenched from my wound, and my havresack drawn closely over it, that neither my own party nor the natives might see it, and I advanced again steadily to the rock. The man became alarmed, and threatened me with his club, yelling most furiously; but as I neared the rock, behind which all but his head and arm was covered, he fled towards an adjoining one, dodging dexterously, according to the native manner of confusing an assailant and avoiding the cast of his spear; but he was scarcely uncovered in his flight, when my rifle ball pierced him through the back, between the shoulders, and he fell heavily on his face with a deep groan.

"The effect was electrical. The tumult of the combat had ceased: not another spear was thrown, not another yell was uttered. Native after native dropped away, and noiselessly disappeared. I stood alone with the wretched savage dying before me, and my two men close to me behind the rocks, in the attitude of deep attention; and as I looked round upon the dark rocks and forests, now suddenly silent and lifeless, but for the sight of the unhappy being who lay on the ground before me, I could have thought that the whole affair had been a horrid dream.

"For a second or two I gazed on the scene, and then returned to my former position. I took my gun from Coles, which he had not yet finished loading, and gave him the rifle. I then went up to the other man, and gave him two balls to hold, but when I placed them in his hands they rolled upon the earth,—he could not hold them, for he was completely paralyzed with terror, and they fell through his fingers; the perspiration streamed from every pore; he was ghastly pale, and trembled from head to foot; his limbs refused their functions; his eyes were so fixed in the direction in which the natives had disappeared that I could draw his attention to nothing else; and he still continued repeating, ' Good God, Sir! look at them,—look at them!'

"The natives had all now concealed themselves, but they were not far off. Presently the wounded man made an effort to raise himself slowly from the ground: some of them instantly came from behind the rocks and trees, without their spears, crowding round him with the greatest tenderness and solicitude; two passed their arms round him, his head drooped senselessly upon his chest, and with hurried steps, the whole party wound their way through the forest, their black forms being scarcely distinguishable from the charred trunks of the trees, as they receded in the distance.

" To have fired upon the other natives, when they returned for the wounded man, would, in my belief, have been an unnecessary piece of barbarity. I already felt deeply the death of him I had been compelled to shoot: and I believe that when a fellow-creature falls by one's hand, even in a single combat rendered unavoidable in self-defence, it is impossible not sincerely to regret the force of so cruel a necessity.

" I had now time to attend to my own state and that of my men, and found that they were uninjured. I had been severely wounded in the hip; another spear had just cut my right arm, and a third had deeply indented my powder-flask, whilst lying in a havresack, immediately over my stomach. The men were not, up to this moment, aware of my being wounded, as I had thought it better to conceal this circumstance from them as long as I could. The natives had gone off in the direction of the tents; and as I felt doubtful whether they might seize upon a favourable opportunity to surprise the party there, and thus revenge their defeat, I was anxious to reach the encampment as soon as possible. We, therefore, bound up my wound as well as we could, picked up the spear which I had drawn out from my hip, and started homewards.

" We did not take with us any of the other spears or native weapons, which were lying about in abundance; for I still wished to shew this people that I was actuated by no ill will towards them. They did not, however, deal so generously with us; for Coles, unfortunately, forgot a note-book which he was carrying for me, containing many observations of great value; and I sent back a party to look for it, but the natives had returned to the place, and carried off all their own spears, and other weapons, and my notebook likewise.

" The first part of our march homewards was managed tolerably well; we saw the tracks of the natives, as if they were still retiring in the direction of the tents; and at one place, close to a group of detached rocks, were several tame native dogs, near which, I have no doubt, a party of men or women were concealed, as these animals seldom wander far from their masters. We did not, however, see any natives, and continued our route unmolested.

" My wound began, by degrees, to get very stiff and painful, and I was, moreover, excessively weak and faint from loss of blood; indeed, I grew so dizzy that I could scarcely see, and neither of the others were capable of leading the party back to the tents; yet I was afraid to halt and rest, for I imagined that if I allowed my wound to grow cold and benumbed I should then be unable to move; leaning, therefore, on Coles's arm, I walked on as rapidly as I could, directing the men which way to go. Unfortunately, however, we lost our track, and after walking for nearly two hours, I found that we were far from the encampment, whilst my sight and strength were momentarily failing. Under these circumstances, I told Coles to walk in a direction which I gave him, and which led directly across the beaten track of the party; having reached which, he could easily make out the encampment, and, leaning on his arm more heavily than before, we again moved on.

" Having reached the track of the party, and turned southward to follow it, I still pushed on until we were within two miles of the tent, when, as I tried to cross a stream, I strained my wounded hip severely, just reached the opposite shore, and fell utterly unable to rise again. Coles, with his usual courage and devotion to me, volunteered to go on alone to the party and send assistance; the other man was to remain with me, and keep a look-out for the natives, and had they again attacked us, I should still have had strength enough to have shot two of them, and thus have sold my life dearly. I desired Coles to say that a tent, stores, the surgeon, and two men were to be sent to me, for that I was not well enough to be moved.

"The water of the stream revived me considerably. My wound, however, was very painful, and the interim between Corporal Coles leaving me, and assistance arriving from the tent, was spent in meditations, arising naturally from my present circumstances. I sat upon the rocky edge of a cool clear brook, supported by a small tree. The sun shone out brightly, the dark forest was alive with birds and insects,—on such scenery I had loved to meditate when a boy, but now how changed I was;—wounded, fatigued, and wandering in an unknown land! In momentary expectation of being attacked, my finger was on the trigger, my gun ready to be raised, my eyes and ears busily engaged in detecting the slightest sounds, that I might defend a life which I at that moment believed was ebbing with my blood away; the loveliness of nature was around me, the sun rejoicing in his cloudless career, the birds were filling the woods with their songs, and my friends far away and unapprehensive of my condition,—whilst I felt that I was dying there."—Pp. 147—155.

Our extracts have been already so long that we can only find space to say that the grand result of this expedition was the discovery of the Glenelg River, which at the spot where Mr. Grey first saw it was three or four miles across, and which flows through a country admirably adapted both for commerce and agriculture.

The remainder of the first volume, and the whole of the second, (with the exception of an Appendix by Mr. Gray, of the British Museum, on the Natural History of Australia,) are filled with "hair-breadth 'scapes" of a similar description, each one making the reader shudder as he peruses it, and filling him with more and more admiration of Captain Grey. Into the details of these various expeditions we cannot enter, and we would not spoil our readers' pleasure by letting them know beforehand all that they are likely to find in these most interesting volumes. But we cannot take leave of Captain Grey without adverting to the humble, gentle, unobtrusive manner, in which he speaks of the comfort which he derived from religion in all his perils and necessities, and of the proof he gives us that it is indeed equal to support men in all dangers and carry them through all temptations.

"It may be asked," says he, when recounting the circumstances of a time when their situation was most gloomy and desolate,—

"It may be asked, if, during such a trying period, I did not seek from religion that consolation which it is sure to afford? My answer is,—Yes; and I farther feel assured that but for the support I derived from prayer, and frequent perusal and meditation of the Scriptures, I should never have been able to have borne myself in such a manner as to have maintained discipline and confidence amongst the rest of the party: nor in all my sufferings did I ever lose the consolation derived from a firm reliance upon the goodness of Providence. It is only those who go forth into perils and dangers, amidst which human foresight and strength can but little avail, and who find themselves, day after day, protected by an unseen influence, and ever and again snatched from the very jaws of destruction, by a power which is not of this world, who can at all estimate the knowledge of one's own weakness and littleness, and the firm reliance and trust upon the goodness of the Creator which the human breast is capable of feeling. Like all other lessons which are of great and lasting benefit to man, this one must be learnt amid much sorrowing and woe; but, having learnt it, it is but the sweeter from the pain and toil which are undergone in the acquisition."—P. 381.

But perhaps the most affecting instance of the practical faith and patience of this good man, is to be found in the narrative of the expedition from the Gascoyne River to Gantheaume Bay. The party were at this time half-starved, and their object was to reach a depôt of provisions which they had some time previously buried in Bernier Island, a wretched spot, which the reader will find in the maps a degree or so north of Dirk Hartog's Island. In leaky boats, and in a heavy sea, set forth; and thus the narrative continues:—

"Bernier island at last rose in sight, and amidst the giant waves we occasionally caught a peep of its rocky shores; but we were so tossed to and fro, that it was only now and then that from the summit of some lofty sea we could sight a high shore, which was not more than four or five miles from us. We had made the island about five miles from its northern extremity, and I ran along the shore until I found a convenient landing place, about a mile and a half to the south of our old one. It was perfectly sheltered by reefs and an island, but it surprised me that I had not remarked this cove in my previous visit to the island, and I was still farther astonished to see now three new small rocky islands, of which I had no recollection whatever. Indeed, the men all for a long time stoutly denied that this was Bernier Island, and had we now sighted Kok's Island, I should have doubted my skill in navigation, and made up my mind that I had fallen into some strange error; but as it was, forebodings shot across my mind as to what pranks the hurricane might have been playing upon the island, which consisted of nothing but loose sand, heaped upon a bed of limestone rock of very unequal elevation.

"I ran in my own boat upon a convenient point of the beach, and the other boat followed in safety, for I did not like, in such foul weather, to leave them at anchor on a lee shore, which had previously proved so unsafe a position. A most awkward question now presented itself to my consideration: from the altered appearance of the coast, I felt very considerable doubts as to the state in which the depôt might be found; supposing anything had occurred to it, I felt it would be unadvisable that such a discovery should be made in the presence of too many persons; as future discipline would in a great measure depend upon the first impression that was given. Who, then, had I better select for the purpose of visiting the depôt, in the first instance? After some deliberation, I made choice of Mr. Smith, and Corporal Coles; in the courage, disinterestedness, and self-possession of both of whom I placed great confidence. I directed Mr. Walker to see certain little alterations made in the boats before the men were allowed to straggle; these I knew would occupy them for some time, and leave me, therefore, during this interval, free to think and act according to circumstances. I now called Mr. Smith and Corporal Coles to accompany me, and told Coles to bring a spade with him.

"Before we had gone very far, alarming symptoms met my eyes, in the form of staves of flour casks scattered about amongst the rocks, and even high up on the sand hills. Coles, however, persisted that these were so far inland, that they could only have come from the flour cask which we had emptied before starting. I knew they were far too numerous for such to be the case, but I suppressed my opinion, and made no remarks. We next came to a cask of salt provisions, washed high and dry, at least twenty feet above the usual high water mark : the sea had evidently not been near this for a long period, as it was half covered with drift sand, which must have taken some time to accumulate. This Coles easily accounted for, it was merely the cask which had been lost from the wreck of the Paul Pry. I still thought otherwise, but said nothing.

"At length we reached the spot where the depôt had been made : so changed was it, that both Mr. Smith and Coles persisted it was not the place; but on going to the shore, there were some very remarkable rocks, on the top of which lay a flour cask more than half empty, with the head knocked out, but not otherwise injured; this also was washed up at least twenty feet of perpendicular elevation beyond high water mark. The dreadful certainty now flashed upon the minds of Mr. Smith and Coles, and I waited to see what effect it would have upon them. Coles did not bear the surprise so well as I had expected; he dashed the spade upon the ground with almost ferocious violence, and looking up to me, he said—'All lost, Sir! we are all lost, Sir!' Mr. Smith stood utterly calm and unmoved; I had not calculated wrongly upon his courage and firmness. His answer to Coles was—'Nonsense, Coles, we shall do very well yet; why there is a cask of salt provisions, and half a cask of flour still left.'

"I now rallied Coles upon his conduct; compared it with that of Mr. Smith, and told him that when I had taken him on to the depôt, in preference to the other men, it had been in the expectation, that if any disaster had happened, he would, by his coolness and courage, have given such an example as would have exercised a salutary influence upon the others. This had the desired effect upon him; he became perfectly cool and collected, and promised to make light of the misfortune to the rest, and to observe the strictest discipline. I then requested Mr. Smith to see the little flour that was left in the barrel and on the rocks carefully collected by Coles, and, leaving them thus engaged, I turned back along the sea-shore towards the party; glad of the opportunity of being alone, as I could now commune freely with my own thoughts.

"The safety of the whole party now depended upon my forming a prompt and efficient plan of operations, and seeing it carried out with energy and perseverance. As soon as I was out of sight of Mr. Smith and Coles, I sat down upon a rock on the shore, to reflect upon our present position. The view seawards was discouraging; the gale blew fiercely in my face, and the spray of the breakers was dashed over me; nothing could be more gloomy and drear. I turned inland, and could see only a bed of rock, covered with drifting sand, on which grew a stunted vegetation, and former experience had taught me that we could not hope to find water in this island; our position here was, therefore, untenable, and but three plans presented themselves to me : first, to leave a notice of my intentions on the island, then to make for some known point on the main, and there endeavour to subsist ourselves until we should be found and taken off by the Colonial schooner; secondly, to start for Timor or Port Essington; thirdly, to try to make Swan River in the boats. I determined not to decide hastily between these plans, and in order more fully to compose my mind, I sat down and read a few chapters in the Bible.

"By the influence these imparted, I became perfectly contented and resigned to our apparently wretched condition, and, again rising up, pursued my way along the beach to the party. It may be here remarked by some, that these statements of my attending to religious duties are irrelevant to the subject, but in such an opinion I cannot at all coincide. In detailing the sufferings we underwent, it is necessary to relate the means by which those sufferings were alleviated; and after having, in the midst of perils and misfortunes, received the greatest consolation from religion, I should be ungrateful to my Maker not to acknowledge this, and should ill perform my duty to my fellow-men, did I not bear testimony to the fact, that under all the weightier sorrows and sufferings that our frail nature is liable to, a perfect reliance upon the goodness of God, and the merits of our Redeemer, will be found a sure refuge and a certain source of consolation."—Pp. 389—394.

We must now bring our observations to a conclusion, without having laid before our readers a tenth part of the passages which we could have wished to extract; but there are other and abler contributors to the Christian Remembrancer upon whose space we must not trench, and we therefore lay down our pen, cordially thanking Mr. Grey for the instruction and amusement he has afforded us, and strongly urging all who have the opportunity to peruse his most valuable work.

The Liber Landavensis. Edited by Rev. W. J. REES, M.A. F.S.A. Published for the Welsh MSS. Society.

HISTORY teems with examples of the firm and tenacious hold retained upon the minds of men, from generation to generation, by positions which have been advanced in favour of the party to which they are attached, or by the opinions in which they have been brought up. It is indeed the consequence of the providential constitution of our moral and mental nature, according to which it is, in its healthy state, slow of admitting that which is inconsistent with its general frame of thought and feeling, reluctant to part with that which is entwined with its associations, and apt to regard with distrust every appearance of novelty; thus it is enabled to maintain some stability amid the fleeting scenes of slippery change by which it is surrounded. But, at the same time, this conservative principle may be exercised too much in exclusion to others, and the more so, inasmuch as it favours both our indolence and our wilfulness. It may often be a positive duty to contend with it, just as in the body we have often to combat with our natural attachment to spots where we have long dwelt; and as these spots may have no beauty or anything else but long familiarity to recommend them, so those positions may be destitute of truth. But from long familiarity they have assumed such an appearance of reality, that they stand for first principles, or indubitable facts; and a cry of indignation is immediately raised at every attempt to shake, or even question, their authority. Thus they go on from age to age acquiring strength, and rooting themselves deeper in conviction.

Circumstances, however, occasionally happen which compel the mind to some investigation. For example, a controversy arises, which in its course gives a rude shake, even to a question which seemed most settled ground. Immediately an alarm is given, there is a run to repair the damage, and if the workmen but fill up the chinks and smoothe again the swells of the surface, the general feeling of security returns. Thus, the champion of a party, which relies upon some historical position whose basis has been so shaken, is applauded as a mighty conqueror, if he but go so far as to look out the detached passages on which the presumed fact is built, in the original authors, without reading any further, and having satisfied them that they are there, replaces them to their eyes in the same view in which their leaders first represented them. There is not a sect in this country which is not thus resting in perfect security upon some unsubstantial ground, which will not bear examination. Good reason has it indeed to believe with all its heart and mind; otherwise it loses the distinguishing articles of its creed, and dissolves into the general mass. Presbyterianism, with all its manifold brood, is seated upon a heap of such traditionary misrepresentation, which as yet it has wanted both the learning and candour to investigate. The same isolated passages are produced; the original context remains unread.

Equally sectarian will be the views of any member in our Church who shall decline for her the most searching investigation into the facts on which she rests or resists any claim. And yet it cannot be but that there are too many whose minds have become so prepossessed with the notion that our palmary argument against the usurpation of Rome, is our derivation from the ancient British Church, that they are impatient of any doubt which may shake such a position. They see no end of ruinous concessions, leading to ultimate submission, if we abandon it. But surely the first object of the true Churchman is truth, lead whithersoever it will; and the true Anglicanist has been taught, from his youth up, to look antiquity in the face, like a generous and dutiful pupil, and not to skulk away like a truant. Her learned men have been used to expatiate without misgiving, to the utmost extent of ecclesiastical and historical record, and not inured to dare to shut up a volume because they dare look no further. If, therefore, any ground which has been generally presumed on as secure, be found slippery, is it not the part not only of truth, but even of self-preservation, to remove the scene of our struggle to a more stable support of our feet. Is it wise in any warfare obstinately to maintain a post which is not tenable, and on the loss of which our own cannon may be turned against us? Truly we must not rail at popery, laughing at her slavish submission to all that has been once admitted, if we deal in the same spirit. However emancipated from her yoke, we shall have but changed the master, and not the man.

It was under the impression, we trust, of some such feelings as these, that, in the number for February last, we undertook, not only to question, but flatly to deny any derivation of our Anglican church from the Ancient British; which we attempted to show had been long extinct, without leaving any succession. We gave but a very brief and general sketch, and lay therefore open to objections. We now propose to go into detail; and will show that not only the ancient British, but even the Augustinian succession has long been utterly extinct. So far from entertaining any fear of the consequences, as to the independent attitude of our Church, we are confident that she will stand more unassailable by Rome than ever. The deep importance and interest of the subject is our excuse for recurring to it.

We must begin by recalling to the reader's mind the fact, that it was a ruling principle, steadily inculcated by Rome on the Anglo-Saxon church, to have no communion with the British, on account of certain of its usages, which she pronounced uncanonical. This appears from the instructions of Gregory to Augustine, (Bede, i. 27, 64,) according to which he was to make no use of assistance in his consecrations, (unless he could perchance obtain it from Gaul.) As a canonical consecration required at least one assisting Bishop, according to the very first of the apostolical canons, this departure from rule supposes an overwhelming necessity, and places the estrangement of the churches from the first in a very strong light.

This principle was acted upon most uncompromisingly in the case of the church of South Britain. The exception made by Wini, Bishop of the West Saxons, when he called in the assistance of two of its Bishops to the consecration of Chad, only serves to prove the rule more remarkably. Theodore pronounced that consecration null; so that he reconsecrated him.

It was not, however, maintained for a long time against the church of North Britain, Bishops of whose successions filled, for several successions together, the sees of Northumberland and Mercia, where the influence of Rome was for a while too distant for interference; and they even, in the person of Cedd, obtained that of the East Saxons, or London. The effect of the council of Whitby, however, held A.D. 664, was to draw the line of separation; so that Jaruman was the last of this succession, dying Bishop of Mercia, before the arrival of Theodore.

The arrival of this able prelate forms the critical juncture in the history of the succession of our Church, which we are now prepared to discuss. It took place in the spring of A.D. 669, in the second year after his consecration by Pope Vitelieu. He found the sees in the following situation, which will show how motley up to that time had been the succession.

Canterbury, waiting for the successor to Deusdedit, of Augustinian succession, who died A.D. 664.

London, filled by Wini, of Gallic succession, who, having been expelled from the see of Wessex, A.D. 666, purchased this from Wulfhere, king of Mercia.

Rochester, *vacant* by death of Damian, of Augustinian succession, A.D. 664.

East Angles, *vacant* by death of Boniface, of Augustinian succession.

West Angles, *vacant* by the expulsion of Wini.

Mercia, *vacant* by death of Jaruman, of North British succession, A.D. 667.

Northumberland, held by Chad, who was consecrated by Wini, assisted by two South British Bishops.

Thus only two sees, out of the seven which England then contained, had Bishops; and of those two Bishops,* Chad only could transmit a British succession; the question is, did he transmit it? Now there is no mention of his assisting at any consecration whatever. British succession therefore cannot possibly be proved, and therefore any presumption upon it is unfounded. But we will go further, and show that it is very improbable that he should ever have assisted.

We will refer to that part of Bede's history which begins thus:—

"Itaque Theodorus, perlustrans universa, ordinabat locis opportunis Episcopos, et ea quæ minus perfecta reperit, his quoque juvantibus, corrigebat. In quibus et Ceadda Episcopum cum argueret non fuisse ritè consecratum," &c: iv. 2. s. 258.

From this we may presume that Theodore, in his progress from Canterbury, took first of all the five dioceses which lay comparatively close at hand; consecrating Bishops in them, perhaps with the assistance of Wilfrid, who had arrived before him in England, consecrated by the Bishop of Paris for the see of York, and was on the spot in Kent, ordaining priests and deacons until Theodore came: and that he reserved the distant sees of Mercia and Northumberland to the last. All his consecrations, therefore, except that to Mercia, were finished before he came to Chad. And there, as in Wini's case, he found the see indeed full, but irregularities to be corrected. He reconsecrated Chad, either now, or towards autumn, when he sent him to the see of Mercia: at present, however, Chad resigned the see of Northumberland to Wilfrid, and retired to the monastery of Lastingham. Hence, even had Theodore left any of those Bishops unconsecrated, and reconsecrated Chad when he came to him, there would have been no opportunity for Chad's assistance, before he was called forth to go to Mercia. And it is exceedingly improbable that any consecration should have been delayed until he was bishop of Mercia. Indeed Bede's account tells us just what we should have expected; namely, that he first filled the sees, and then looked into the irregularities of those that were already full. And supposing the vacancies which Theodore found at his arrival to be filled up by the time that Chad became Bishop of Mercia, there was no possible opportunity for Chad assisting at any consecration; for the very first

---

* Though not a matter of importance, in this question, it is one of interest, to know whether Wini's assistance was required. But Bede seems remarkably shy of mentioning Wini. On several occasions where we might have expected his name to appear, as for instance in mentioning the appointment of his successor Earconwald, he avoids, as if industriously, the mention of it. Very probably his simony, to say nothing of his irregularity in communicating with British Bishops in the consecration of Chad, highly incensed Theodore against him; and his business would undoubtedly have been included with Chad's, when, "ea, quæ minus perfecta reperit, corrigebat," (Bede, iv. 3. 258,) had he not been shielded by the strong arm of Wulfhere, who had too good reason to protect him. But he was alive at the time of the council of Hertford, and yet he does not appear there, even by legate, as Wilfrid was allowed to do. This looks as if he were not admitted. From these considerations we may presume that Theodore did not use his assistance at his consecrations; and went upon the privilege which (as we have mentioned) Gregory conferred upon Augustine, if at least he was not assisted by Wilfrid.

vacancy that occurred on the bench was by his own death, which was in two years and a half from his appointment.

We may add that, even supposing one or even two of the southern sees to have remained vacant after Chad's accession to Mercia, Chad, distant as his situation was, and incessantly as he was occupied, would be the last person to be called in by Theodore to assist at consecrations. There were Bishops enough at hand.

Thus the notion of a British succession transmitted through Chad is not only unsupported by any evidence of fact, but opposed to all reasonable probability. The only channel remaining is the remnant of the British church which survived in Wales. But we showed, in the article before alluded to, how vain it was to look to this quarter. We will now state our reasons somewhat more in detail.

That church had its own metropolitan in the Bishop of St. David's; but as the kings of England were intent on wresting the supreme civil power from the princes of the country, so had the Archbishops of Canterbury no less set their hearts upon supplanting its metropolitan in the supreme ecclesiastical power. So early as A.D. 982, Dunstan added Llandaff to the suffragan sees of Canterbury, and consecrated Gwgan at Canterbury, with the assistance of four Anglican Bishops. In progress of time, St. Asaph and Bangor were added, and their Bishops similarly consecrated, as we might *a priori* conclude; since, from the very nature of the case, the Archbishop would not call in the assistance of any suffragan of his rival of St. David's. Thus, by the end of the eleventh century at latest, the Anglican succession, in all its purity, had displaced the British in three of the sees, and St. David's stood alone, bereft of her daughters. Early, however, in the twelfth century her day also was come. After having a pure uninterrupted British succession from David, she was at last compelled to receive an Anglican prelate in Bernard, A.D. 1115. Thus expired the succession of the British church, after a duration of at least eight hundred years. We may take a specimen of the utter revolution in the succession of the church of Wales, by exhibiting two consecrations:—

A.D. 1176. Peter, consecrated Bishop of St. David's, at Canterbury, by Gilbert, Bishop of London, assisted by the Bishops Walter of Rochester, and Roger of Worcester.

A.D. 1256. William de Radnor, consecrated Bishop of Llandaff, at St. Paul's, London, by Archbishop Boniface, assisted by Walter, Bishop of Worcester, and Walter, Bishop of Norwich.

So utterly vain is it to seek any channel of British succession in this direction. It has been utterly, irrecoverably lost, for these last seven hundred years and more.

Perhaps some one may say, that there still survives a presbyterian succession; and, undoubtedly, had there been no Anglican priests introduced, after that the sees in Northumberland, Mercia, and Wales, had fallen under Anglican Bishops, the presbyters in those sees might, at this day, have traced a line in the mere presbyterian direction up to the British Church. But since nothing is more common than the transference of presbyters from other dioceses into these, (to say nothing of letters dismissory,) and since ordinations must have taken place in them over and over again, at which the assisting presbyters as well as the Bishops had their orders conferred in a purely Anglican (so to say) diocese, all trace, (however such a line may possibly exist,) is quite lost; and therefore, practically speaking, the succession is gone. Our present motley English population of Britons, Saxons, Danes, Normans, have as much reason to make any claim on account of the ancient Britons as the present generation of presbyters in any of those sees, due as it is to British, Gallican, Roman succession, to refer to the ancient British Church. But supposing such a line could be proved, what has a catholic and apostolic church to do with a line which is not traced through Bishops as such?

The Augustinian line we see is also quite extinct. It may be important to keep this in view on several occasions of discussion.

We will now return to consider the crisis of the Church in this island, under Theodore.

We may assign this period as the commencement of our *national* Church. Hitherto there had not been that unity which is essential to its existence. Bede especially remarks that Theodore " Primus erat in Archiepiscopis cui omnis Anglorum Ecclesia manus dare consentiret." iv. 2. § 256. It had had no succession prevailing and permanent in itself, but had borrowed where it could, whether from the line of Augustine, or from Iona, or from Gaul, or from Rome. Neither had it ever met in council, for what is commonly called the Council of Whitby was merely a conference between the British and the Romish parties. But now in A.D. 673, Theodore assembles a council, at which too every Bishop present had been consecrated by himself. And all the Bishops of the Church were present except Wini and Wilfrid; the latter of whom, however, sent his legates. Its professed object was to cement the unity of the Church, thus for the first time so happily assembled under one head, and, as it turned out, with one mind.

Here, then, is the ground to which we are to come with the Romanist. The claim of Rome, founded upon the mission of Augustine, is refuted by her own practice in the case of Bulgaria, which our readers may see extracted from Mr. Palmer's Reply to Dr. Wiseman, in our late series, in the number for October 1840. But she founds a claim also on the derivation of our orders; in answer to which we have seen that it will argue either ignorance, or dishonesty, to deny the fact. But we have the best reason in the world to deny the conclusion which she would draw from it. Such a claim was never dreamed of at the time when this succession was permanently derived through Theodore. Only let us study the whole transaction in Bede, peruse the pope's own letter to King Oswy, read Theodore's own words at the opening of his council, and mark Bede's narrative of its proceedings, bearing also in mind the style of such letters, speeches, and narratives, after Rome had set up her claims; and it is impossible not to perceive that neither the pope, nor Theodore, nor Bede, had any other notion than that the Anglican church was entirely independent of Rome, and no further bound to her, than in that filial love and desire of unity, which the American church for the same reason at this day entertains towards the Anglican. In fact, we see at this day, on the same soil of America, examples of the practice of Rome in her better days of the seventh century, and in her worst since. There is the American church, deriving her orders from consecration at Lambeth, completely organized within itself, and in that sense a national church: and there is a branch of the Romish church, which cannot stir without continual reference to Rome. Indeed, ever since Rome has so taken upon her that whosoever asks a favour from her, must from that moment be regarded as a slave or a rebel; the derivation of national churches from her has become impossible. In every spot where the planting of Christianity over the newly-discovered countries of the East and West can be at all referred to her, she has planted a mission rather than a church; a branch which cannot live without her, not a tree which has life and the power of propagation in itself. No wonder, therefore, that the advocates of her claims are so prepossessed with this her spirit, that they cannot help carrying it into their perusal of the history of our early Church, and see things there which have no existence but in their own wilfulness or prejudice. Thus they falsify every fact that they touch. Baronius (if we remember right) in mentioning the above council, cannot help *inserting*, that it was called by order of the pope. Should the Romish argument be allowed, there could never exist any church, properly such, which had not had an apostle for its immediate founder. There could have been no independent churches, like Carthage, or Constantinople, or even Alexandria.

We earnestly hope that henceforward our controversy with Rome will be fought on this stable ground of historic fact; and that our advocates will not, by indulging in mere speculation, give Rome the advantage of answering them with speculation equally true. But the mischief is, that the most forward in this conflict on our side are too often the least qualified to conduct it. They are like the old Germans, who were flourishing in the air with their broad sword, while the Roman pointed sword was thrust into their body. They are slashing, now here, and now there, with all the vague and indecisive aim of second-hand information, affording an easy triumph to the wary foe who has his eye fixed upon one point; and the worst is, that they know not that they are dead.

"The times have been
That when the brains were out the man would die,
And there an end. But now they rise again,
With twenty mortal murders on their crowns."

And so we shall go on, giving the advantage to the enemy, if our Clergy shall be unable, for want of proper information, to decide where the victory really lies; for it is at least as important to have a body of spectators on our side acquainted with the rules of the fight, as it is to have a champion at all. Let them not then be frightened from the study of antiquity by the cry now raised against it. Oh, how delightful is the sound of that cry in Romish ears! Nor let them think it of such inferior consequence compared with that of Scripture, that it may be safely laid aside. We presume that they are not come to that pitch that they starve the body, because it is so very inferior to the soul. But let them remember that they owe a duty to their Church as well as to their flocks, and that the circumstances of the times imperatively demand the exercise of this duty. The Church desires a hearing, demands an audience that can understand her arguments, appreciate her claims, examine her authorities. Does such an audience exist, even amidst her own ministry, to that fulness which is required? We fear not. We state with sorrow our belief, that many zealous but ill-instructed champions of the platform are more in the eyes and ears of her Clergy, than such as the truly learned author of the Reply to Dr. Wiseman. Rome would indeed gladly keep our eyes confined to the platform, as she has proved by the stir which she made upon a late occasion. She knows that she has nothing to dread there; but finds there, on the contrary, an useful diversion of public attention from much more formidable antagonists.

It is, therefore, not only most desirable, but most necessary, that the ecclesiastical antiquities of our country should engage the interest of the body of our Clergy much more than they now do. Many have abundant leisure for it, and may be said to be retained by her as her advocates. If only our cathedral and university Clergy would do their duty in this respect, we should have a body sufficiently large and respectable to direct public opinion aright, and it might not only send forth well appointed controversialists into the field, but would form an audience which would at once deter such as now venture forth utterly unacquainted with the true bearings of the controversy, and, like all irregular troops, expose the common cause to danger, and would encourage all such as were truly qualified to enter the lists. The facilities of acquiring such knowledge have been wonderfully increased of late. For instance, Bede's ecclesiastical history has now been brought within reach of every clergyman, by the edition published by the English Historical Society; and as the style of this author is easy, and the work of a moderate compass, it may not be too much to hope that it will, with many, supersede the usual books of second-hand information. Then we may hope, at length, to be rid of a heap of modern false tradition, which at present so much encumbers the subject of the early period of our ecclesiastical history. Then will feelings be awakened of a far deeper tone, affections moved of a far more healthy nature, knowledge acquired of a far more exact and truth-telling character, than the excitement of novelty, the gratification of party spirit, the conceit attending second-hand information. Then we shall not have a body which will dispute orders through ignorance, and wherein, from the general want of knowledge and discipline, any one may set up to be an officer; but a well-disciplined army, which will put an effectual stop to the aggressions of Rome.

Among the joyful signs of this improving spirit among us, may be reckoned the volume, the title of which has been prefixed to this article. It is the ancient chartulory of the cathedral of Llandaff; containing the lives of its more ancient and eminent prelates, which were read in the church, as of S. Dubricius, S. Teilo, S. Oudoceus, and giving an account of the endowments and estates of that church. It therefore contains a body of information highly interesting to the lovers of our ecclesiastical history; and consequently, although hitherto confined to the less accessible form of MS., has been so frequently and diligently consulted by our antiquaries, Usher, Godwin, Wharton, that almost all its direct historical information has been extracted. It requires, however, some critical powers for its proper use. The lives above mentioned are quite in the legendary style of the twelfth century, and seem to have come from much such a hand as that of the celebrated Geoffry of Monmouth. There is the usual quantity of miraculously-obedient stags, of dragons the terror of kingdoms, and other prodigies. Indeed, nothing can be more different than the Welch and Latin documents concerning Wales. The former are sober and trustworthy, and generally cotemporary: the latter, being the work of monks, fabulous, and treating of times long gone by. It is much to be desired that the latter should be made accessible, through translation, to the students of the antiquities of our Church and State.

---

1. *Histoire de Saint François d'Assise.* Par E. C. de Malan. Paris. 1841.

2. *Letter from the Earl of Shrewsbury to Ambrose Lisle Phillipps, Esq., descriptive of the Estatica of Caldaro, and the Addolorata of Capriana.* London: Dolman. 1841.

THE great christian hero of the middle ages, was undoubtedly St. Francis d'Assisi. Thrown on the world at a time when the secular grandeur of the Church, the avarice and pride of the hierarchy, and the licentiousness of the laity, had nearly reached their greatest height, he undertook to restore and react the humility, the poverty, and self-abnegation of the great Captain of the faithful, and his immediate followers. This was his mission; in this his heroism consisted. He had the hardihood, under every possible discouragement, to attempt to combat, single-handed, the spirit of worldliness and luxury, that every where reigned predominant, and had, to all appearance, supplanted the crucified life of Christ in the Church; to rekindle the flame of divine love, that had been well nigh extinguished by the love of the world; to convert, in short, the Church of the middle ages from the carnal to the spiritual.

The era of St. Francis was one doubtless of unbounded zeal for the interests of Christendom;—on every side the prince and the peasant were found willing to peril their lives, and to sacrifice the dearest ties of social life, for the good of the Church. But it was rather for her temporal than for her spiritual advancement, that the magnificent efforts of the middle ages were undertaken. All tended to the aggrandizement of the Clergy, and to secularize, in a bad sense, the bond of union between the Clergy and the people. The spiritual enemies of the great European family of Christ, ceased to be fought against with spiritual weapons. "Jews, Turks, infidels, heretics," came to be regarded as the natural foes of Christendom, and fire and the sword accordingly took the place of the pulpit and the pen in the work of their extermination.

There was, it is true, something novel and admirable in a zeal which could induce the confederated kings of Europe to lay their treasures in the lap of the Church, and to expend with reckless courage their own and the best blood of their subjects, in the assertion and maintenance of what were supposed to be her rights and privileges; but it was after all a delusion,—a wide-spreading, fearful delusion of the arch-enemy of Christ, having its source in opinions and practices that tended to sap the very foundations of his spiritual kingdom. The worldly and vain-glorious spirit of the Crusades operated within its degree, in all the relations and duties of the christian life. Religion became a thing purely external; the sacrifices which the Church absolutely required of her children, were only such as carried with them a present reward and renown, and these were too generally accepted as a substitute for the real sacrifice of heart and affections, to which, if there be a present reward, it is not in the glory of the world. In few words, at the time St. Francis appeared, the Church had forgotten her origin and her destiny; she had succeeded in erecting the fabric of a magnificent earthly dominion, and in her pride had become ashamed to wear her native garments of mortification and self-denial; his mission, therefore, was to exhibit in himself and his followers, the attributes of the spiritual life of primitive Christianity.

We are not going to defend the mode in which he set about this. There may have been much that was extravagant, fanatical, and superstitious, in his proceedings. If any of our readers wear spectacles through which these characteristics appear in frightful magnitude, we are not going to show them that their optics are distorted, or that their visions of middle-age superstition and grossness are phantoms, not realities. We are not going to insinuate that their spectacles are begrimed with the dirt of prejudice, or to endeavour to hide from them or ourselves the bad realities of religion in the thirteenth century. There are, we fully admit, many drawbacks to an appreciation of the merits of St. Francis as a reformer; but still we think they may be appreciated. The exterior may be unpromising; but that need not hinder us from penetrating beyond the surface. There may have been all the fanaticism, extravagance, and superstition, that seem to stare us in the face; but we are quite sure that in the case of St. Francis they were but the covering of a design from which we cannot withhold our admiration.

Neither are we going to pick a quarrel with those who, perhaps with good reason, have been accustomed to regard with delicate horror the numerous progeny of St. Francis, associating with the very name of "Begging Friar," all that is disgusting, dirty, lazy, and obnoxious; at the same time we think it quite possible to contemplate the original *idea* of the Franciscan order, apart from its degraded condition at any after period, when the spirit of its founder had ceased to animate it, or when the character of the age, being changed, it had ceased to be necessary, and may have become a useless burden on society. More than this; we see no difficulty in regarding the foundation of an order as an accident, rather than a necessary fruit of the work and mission of St. Francis. It arose from the custom of his time; and for our parts, we think the custom was, in its intention at least, a manly, straightforward, and honest one. If in these days any of us become deeply sensible of defects and practical errors in the Church, we address ourselves to the business of reform, by preaching, if we are preachers; or by writing books and printing them, if we are authors; or by making speeches, if we be orators. We are accustomed to rest our hopes of a reformation (of clerical discipline, for example), on the co-operation of the whole body of the Clergy; and hence it is that each one looks on another, to see who will take the first step; each hangs back, as if matters might be brought into such a condition that a reformation would come of itself unnoticed and unhated. We talk about it and write about it, and are convinced of its necessity, but we do nothing—because we wait to see what others will do. Not so in the middle ages. A reformer began the work of reform in his own person; he commenced by doing that which he was desirous that others should imitate. Taking, for his object, the counteraction of particular defects or errors in the religious life or temper of his age, he framed for himself a rule or pattern of christian conduct, expressly intended to bring out, in strong relief, the characteristics of piety, which he felt to be wanting. Men of like dispositions or sentiments associated themselves together in the work; the originator gained followers and imitators; and so confraternities were instituted that, after the fashion of the times, assumed the form of monasticism. And there was, in fact, this difference between the orders of monks founded in primitive ages and those which sprung up in the times of which we are writing, that the former were, in a great measure, devoid of any peculiar or individual character, while the latter rested their claims to utility on the maintenance of some specific obligation and purpose. Without this, indeed, we can hardly imagine any necessity for their institution. The Franciscan vow of poverty was not new; it was common to the Benedictines and Augustinians. Preaching, the peculiar business of the Dominicans, was also the business of the more ancient orders. But the times of St. Francis required that a more positive and striking testimony should be made against the prevailing love of the world, than the general purpose of the ancient orders permitted; and so on analogous grounds there seemed to be occasion for the services of men more exclusively devoted to preaching and the instruction of the poor than was compatible with the monastic obligations of Benedictines or Augustinians. The same view may be taken of institutions of a more recent date. We are not, indeed, aware of any of these that, like the primitive orders, have been founded merely for the general purposes of retirement and holy living. Each has had some definite and specific use; as, for instance, the "congregation of the Mission," established in France by St. Vincent de Paul, about the beginning of the seventeenth century, whose business was the assistance of the parochial clergy, in preaching, and in visiting and catechizing the poor; or his foundation of "spiritual retreats," to afford to young men the means of engaging in exercises of piety, preparatory to their entrance into holy orders; or his inimitable institution of the "Daughters of Charity,"* for attendance on the sick poor in the hospitals and in their houses. Nor are the Jesuits altogether an exception to the rule we have laid down; at least in their original condition, and before they had begun to assume the privileges and characteristics of all other orders. But admitting that they did form an exception, the early history of the society shows the correctness of the rule. When Ignatius first submitted his draft of its laws and constitutions to the papal see, he could scarcely obtain a hearing, on the ground that his plan embraced no new purpose, or at least no purpose that could not be fully accomplished by orders already established; and it was only on the offer of Ignatius and his followers, to take, in addition to the usual vows of poverty, chastity, and monastic obedience, a special vow of absolute obedience to the Roman see, to be binding wherever they might be placed, that the pope was induced to give his sanction to the scheme.

But to return to St. Francis. The result of his early struggles with the world and its allurements, was a conviction that his only chance of victory rested on absolute compliance with the conditions under which the first preachers of the New Testament commenced their labours. When the apostles were sent to " preach the kingdom of God and to heal the sick," Christ said," Take nothing for your journey, neither staves nor scrip, neither bread nor money, neither have two coats apiece;"—they were to depend, in short, on alms. St. Francis believed that this rule was binding on him, and he determined accordingly to reduce himself to a condition of absolute poverty.

---

* This seems to be their proper title, and not "Sisters of Charity," as they are usually termed. In all formal documents relating to the order, they are named "Filles de la Charité," and by this appellation they were distinguished from an association which bore the name of " Dames de la Charité."

Till this period he had been the idol of his young companions, and their leader in every kind of gaiety and dissipation, having all the advantages that a handsome person and command of his father's wealth could bestow. But now his conduct and appearance underwent an entire change. He gave his fine clothes and money to the poor, and sometimes begged with them, and for them, at the doors of the churches where they were wont to assemble. His body became emaciated with fasting, and his whole aspect so cadaverous and unusual, that the people of the town and his former gay companions believed he had gone mad, or was playing the fool, and ridiculed him, and loaded him with every kind of opprobrium. His father, too, accusing him of having stolen his goods and money, threw him into prison, in hopes of either recovering the property which he supposed his son had made away with, or of converting him by severe treatment from his absurd course. This not having the desired effect, an appeal was made to the Bishop of Assisi, who summoned Francis before him, and desired him to comply with his father's demand; but the young saint, having nothing about him that could be supposed to belong to his father but the clothes he wore, stripped himself naked, and delivering up his clothes to his father, said, "Now I may safely say, that I have no father or treasure but in heaven."*

After this, it appears that he fled from the city of Assisi, and lived for a time in solitude, wandering about from place to place, and begging his bread at the doors of the houses or monasteries he happened to pass; and having now, as he imagined, brought himself into obedience to the evangelical rule of life, he began to increase the severity of his mortifications and self-denial, by applying himself to such occupations as he had formerly deemed the most revolting,—in particular to the care and relief of those who were afflicted with leprosy. His biographers inform us, that " one day he heard a voice from heaven," saying, " Francis, if thou wilt know my will, hate and despise the things that according to the flesh thou hast most loved and desired. Fear not this trial, for those offices which have hitherto seemed disgusting and painful, will soon become sweet and agreeable." Immediately he perceived a leper coming towards him, and overcoming with a strong effort his horror and disgust, he gave him such assistance as he could, and kissed his hand. The leper, continues the legend, instantly disappeared; for it was Christ who presented himself in that form, in order to try the faith of the saint.

In the middle ages it was impossible to have adopted any greater form of self-abasement than to become the associate and servant of poor lepers. The disease of itself was a fearful infliction, even when the sufferer had every means that wealth could supply to alleviate his

---

* St. Bonaventura's account of this scene is the following :—" Insuper ex admirando fervore, spiritu ebrius, totus coram omnibus denudatus dixit ad patrem, ' Usque nunc vocavi te patrem in terris, amodo autem securè dicere possum ;' Pater noster qui es in cœlis, apud quem omnem thesaurum reposui, et omnem spei fiduciam collocavi."—*S. Bon.* cap. 2.

pains. But when to the malady poverty added its evils, we can hardly, taking into account the kind of quarantine to which the afflicted were subject, conceive any more dreadful condition of suffering humanity. Lepers were prohibited under the severest penalties from entering a church, a tavern, a fair, a mill, a market, or any crowded place. They were obliged to wear a particular dress. They were prohibited from touching any article till they had paid for it, from washing in any river or fountain, and from drinking except from a vessel they were obliged to carry. They were prevented from walking on the public roads; if they met any one, they were obliged to take the *leeward* side. They were entirely prohibited from speaking, and ordered to carry a little bell, by which they were to give notice of their approach, or make known their wants. The food which they received in the basket they carried, was to be eaten apart from all society, except that of their fellow-sufferers. In short, they were completely cut off from intercourse with mankind, and supposed to be dead. So entirely was this idea carried out, that in the ceremonial of the " separation of the leprous," the priest took in his hand some earth from the cemetery of the church, and sprinkling it on the head of the diseased, pronounced him " dead to the world."[*] It may be easily imagined that this fearful excommunication from society often produced the most aggravated forms of misery, want, and actual starvation. To the rich, the privations endured were sufficiently painful; but the poor had no alleviation in their sufferings. If beggars, they had to solicit charity from people who fled at their approach; if of devout minds, they were to a great extent deprived of the consolations of religion, and it too often happened that they were driven to despair and perished of want. Such was the class to whose welfare St. Francis for a time devoted himself, for the purpose of completing his self-abasement.

Our limits do not permit us, nor would it be consistent with the purpose of these remarks, to trace the history of the saint through all its vicissitudes; we pass on, therefore, to the termination of his career, with which at present we have chiefly to do. We cannot help, however, recommending to our readers the perusal of the work which stands first in the list at the head of this article; or if they have opportunity, the original memoirs from which the modern work is compiled; being persuaded that there is no set of documents in existence more replete with interesting details of the personal religion of the middle ages.

The ruling idea in the work of St. Francis was, we have observed, to oppose, by a life of continual poverty and mortification, the love of riches, worldly grandeur, and self-indulgence, by which the Church of his day had been overcome; and having done this, to set up the love of Christ as the only true principle of action and legitimate source of happiness. With this idea, his whole career was perfectly con-

---

[*] D. Martène, tom. iii. De Antiquis Ecclesiæ Ritibus.

sistent;—it began with an excess of mortification never, perhaps, previously equalled, and it terminated in an ecstasy of divine love. Were the history of his life but a mere fable, we must admit its consistency. Call it, if you will, a fiction of christian poesy,—call it the portraiture of an imaginary christian hero; still you must allow its beauty, its perfect arrangement and harmonious glow of colouring. You may be disposed to reckon the *ideal* of the life of St. Francis imperfect, or his notion of evangelical obedience one-sided (though, indeed, in judging truly of this we must take into account the specific object he had in view, and the character of his times); but you cannot help wondering at the precision with which every action of his life, every incident in his history, whether important or trivial, served to develop the ideal perfection at which he aimed. It is this unity and completeness in his character as a saint that has, we think, gained him so many passionate admirers and imitators in the Roman Church, especially among her imaginative children. He has long been, and is still, the model and measure of excellence to the ascetic devotee; but in former days, when art lent its creative powers to the Church, the life of St. Francis was its most universal theme of inspiration,—the locality of his birthplace and tomb, the altar on which its richest treasures were placed.* And perhaps this very fact has greatly contributed, in more recent times, to brighten the kind of poetical halo which seems to surround the memory of the saint, and to render him an especial object of admiration to the multitudes of imaginative Christians of these days, whose religion consists so much more in sympathy with

---

* M. C. de Malan has given the following list of painters, occupying places in the history of art, from the 13th to the 17th century, who have illustrated the life of St. Francis:—

Giunta Pisano,	Sinibaldo Ibi,
Margaritone,	F. Morone,
Cimabue,	Vincenzo Catena,
Giotto,	Ercole Grandé,
Bonaventura Berlinghieri,	Sebastiano d'Udine,
Taddeo Gaddi,	Francesco Francia,
B. Angelico da Fiesole,	Giovanni Carotto,
Pesellino,	A. Buonvicini,
Benozzo Gozzoli,	F. Mino da Turrita,
Domenico Ghirlandaio,	Adone d'Assisi,
Ridolfo Ghirlandaio,	Cæsare d'Assisi,
Giovanni Bellini,	L. Cigoli,

and ten or twelve Spanish and Italian painters of the 16th and 17th centuries. Of the poets who have sung the praises of St. Francis, there is also a goodly list, commencing with the very fathers of Italian poesy, Guitton d'Arezzo and Dante. The former thus addresses the saint:—

"Cieco era il mondo; tu failo visare
Lebroso; hailo mondato
Morto; l'hai suscitato
Sceso ad inferno; failo al ciel montare."

St. Francis was himself a poet. Three "cantici" are extant, in the Italian language, which are attributed to him: two of them in verse, and the third in measured prose. The one commencing, "In foco l'amor mi mise," has great beauty.

the past, and regret that the former glories of the Church are gone, than in the present reality of a mortified and spiritual life.

The ecstatic termination of the career of St. Francis is thus described by St. Bonaventura:—" Francis, the servant and truly faithful minister of Christ Jesus, being in prayer on Monte Laverna, lifting himself to God by the seraphic fervour of his desires, and transforming himself by the movements of a tender and affectionate sympathy with Him who, in the excess of his love, was willing to be crucified for us, saw, as it were, a seraphim, having six shining wings of fire, descend from heaven. This seraphim came with a very rapid flight towards Francis; and then he beheld among the wings the figure of a man crucified, who had his hands and feet extended and attached to a cross. Two of the wings covered the head, two were extended for flight, and two veiled the body. Francis seeing this was greatly surprised, and a joy mingled with sadness and grief filled his soul. The presence of Christ, who showed himself under the figure of a seraph in a manner so marvellous, so familiar, caused him an excess of pleasure, but at the grievous spectacle of his crucifixion, his soul was pierced with grief as by a sword. He profoundly wondered that the infirmity of suffering should have appeared under the figure of a seraph, knowing well that it agreed not with his condition of immortality; and he could not comprehend this vision until God made him understand interiorly, that it had been presented to his eyes, to let him know that it was not by the martyrdom of the flesh, but by the quickening of the soul, that he could be entirely transformed into the perfect image and resemblance of Christ crucified. The vision disappearing, left in his soul a seraphic ardour, and marked his body with a figure conformed to that of the crucified, as if his body, like wax, had received the impression of a seal; for soon the marks of the nails began to appear in his hands and feet, such as he had seen in the image of the God-man crucified. His hands and feet were pierced with nails in the middle: *the heads of the nails, round and black, were on the palms of the hands and fore part of the feet. The points of the nails, which were a little long, and which appeared on the other side, were bent backwards on the wound which they made. He also had on his right side a red wound, as if he had been pierced with a lance, which often shed sacred blood on his tunic.*" The same account is repeated by Friar Elias in 1226, in a circular letter, on the occasion of the death of St. Francis;—and in 1227, Luc de Tuy, in a treatise against the Albigenses, wishing to prove that Christ was really crucified, quotes the fact, that St. Francis received the marks described by St. Bonaventura, and which, he says, " were seen by many religious and seculars, clergy and laity, who enjoyed that happiness five years ago. They were not," he says, " mere openings made by nails, but nails themselves formed, of the substance of his flesh, and which, with the wound on his side, made him appear at his death, as if he were just taken down from the cross." The same facts are related in three bulls of Gregory IX. in 1237; and in 1254, Alexander IV., preaching publicly, and in presence of many Franciscans and Bonaventura, affirmed, that during the life of St. Francis, he had seen the *stigmata* with his own eyes. In 1255, in a bull addressed to all Bishops, on the life and miracles of St. Francis, the same pope says, that " attentive eyes had seen, and assured hands had touched his hands, and that there were certainly in them nails well formed, either of his own flesh, or of some material newly produced. We are not," continues Pope Alexander, " resting on fables or chimeras, when we assure you of the truth of the *stigmata* of St. Francis, for long time since we were perfectly acquainted with him, God having given us the grace to form with the holy man a strict intimacy, while we were of the household of Gregory IX., our predecessor." The evidence, in short, seems to be perfectly conclusive as to the fact that St. Francis, for two years previously to his death, bore the marks which have just been described.

Nevertheless, many who lived at the time were incredulous. It appears that a Bishop of Olmutz considered the miracle to be derogatory to the peculiar prerogative of Christ, and if even it were not so, to be irrational and unnecessary; and in 1237 he addressed " letters to all the faithful," in which he asserted that " neither St. Francis nor any other saint ought to be painted in the church with the *stigmata;* and that whosoever maintained the contrary, sinned, and was undeserving of credence, as an enemy of the faith; because the Son of the Eternal Father having been crucified for the salvation of mankind, his wounds alone were to be revered, according to the christian religion." To these letters, Gregory IX. replied in one of the bulls already referred to. " We wish," says he, " to examine well the reasons which you may have in support of your opinions, to show you that they are bad, and to induce you to abandon them; you found your sentiments perhaps on this—' It is not lawful in the mystical body to attribute to a member the marks of honour that appertain to the head.' But you forget to add— ' unless by a special grace these marks be accorded to a saint for his merits.' On which we observe, that God, whose wisdom is infinite, not having disdained to form man of the slime of the earth after his own image and resemblance, and to take to himself by the mystery of the incarnation the fashion of a man, that he might redeem him from death, may have wished to honour a saint whom he loved by the impression of the *stigmata*. What rashness or sin then is there in representing by pictures, to the eyes of the faithful, this singular privilege, to the glory of Him who is its author? Not to speak of other pictures, do they not represent the prince of the apostles attached to the cross, though in a manner differing from that of Jesus Christ? ' It is,' you will reply, ' because He, who is the truth itself, having predicted that which would happen to the apostle, and his prediction having been accomplished, one has good reason for saying that he was crucified, and for representing him on the cross.' But have we not every proof that St. Francis, after having assumed the habit of penitence, crucified his flesh by the continual practice of virtue, and that the *stigmata* were truly impressed on his body?"

Another class of disbelievers in the miracle were still more obstinate; for they affirmed that the whole affair was an imposture, the invention of the new order of Franciscans, to raise their credit in the Church. It must be admitted, however, that as these objectors were Dominicans, themselves a newly-founded and rival order, there is every likelihood that jealousy had something to do with their incredulity.

There is one circumstance in the account which we have given of the *stigmata* of St. Francis, to which we beg the especial attention of our readers. All ancient authorities agree in stating, that the hands and feet were not merely pierced as if by nails, but that there were actually remaining in them the appearance of nails, either "formed of the flesh, or of some matter newly produced." No writers affirm that blood ever flowed from the hands and feet, but only from the side. Now this is at variance with the popular belief, based, we suppose, on the representations of painters, who probably wishing to increase the importance of the miracle, have departed from the truth of the legend, and, by a pictorial license, painted the stigmata as bleeding wounds. We call the attention of our readers to this fact for two reasons:—in the first place, because in the case of St. Francis himself, mere wounds were more likely to have been self-inflicted than the kind of formation which has been described; or rather, we should say, that the fleshy formation could not have been produced artificially, while nothing was easier than to inflict the wounds; and in the second place, because, in the two cases described by Lord Shrewsbury, the wounds are made according to the popular version of the legend, and are solely of a kind which may be self-inflicted.

Let us, however, turn to his lordship's pamphlet. The subjects of the supposed or real miracles are two young women, named Maria Mörl and Domenica Lazzari, the former aged 29, and the latter 25; both of whom are labouring under maladies, the nature of which is not stated, but which are supposed to be incurable. Maria is termed the *Estatica of Caldaro* (her native place), on account of the state of ecstasy in which greater part of her time is spent; and Domenica, the *Addolorata of Capriana* (her native town), because of the long and excruciating diseases to which she has been subject. Of the Estatica, Lord Shrewsbury relates, on the authority of Görres, that during her early years she suffered various attacks of illness, "which she bore always with the most exemplary patience, and ever ending in increased piety and devotion, and in a still more frequent approach to the sacraments, notwithstanding her other avocations; for her mother being dead, the affairs of the family fell principally upon her. When, in 1822, she had attained her twentieth year, she evinced the first symptoms of ecstasy, falling into that state each time that she received the Holy Communion. But it suddenly took a more decided character on the festival of Corpus Christi of that year in Caldaro, as is thus related by Görres:—

"As her confessor was aware that she always after communion remained six or eight hours, sometimes longer, in a state of ecstacy, he thought it expedient that she should receive it early, in order to be at rest the remainder of the day. Accordingly he carried the blessed sacrament to her at three o'clock in the morning, after which she fell immediately into a state of ecstacy. Her confessor left her; and being much occupied that day and the next morning, he did not return to her till three o'clock in the afternoon of the following day, when he found her kneeling in the exact position in which he had left her thirty-six hours before. In great surprise he questioned the people of the house, and learnt from them that her ecstacy had continued uninterrupted during the whole of this time. He perceived from this how deeply the ecstatic state had penetrated her whole being, since it was already a state of second nature to her; and that it must in future be her habitual condition, unless he should bring it within limits by recalling her to herself; he therefore undertook to regulate this state by virtue of that holy obedience which she had vowed upon entering the third order of St. Francis...... So early as the autumn of 1833, her confessor observed accidentally that the part of the hands, where the wounds afterwards appeared, began to sink in, as if under the pressure of some external body, and also that they became painful, and frequently attacked with cramps. He conjectured from these appearances, that the *stigmata* would eventually appear; and the result fulfilled his expectations. On the Purification, on the 2d of February, 1834, he found her holding a cloth, with which, from time to time, she wiped her hands, frightened, like a child, at what she saw there. Perceiving blood upon the cloth, he asked her what it meant. She replied, that she did not know herself; that she must have hurt herself so as to draw blood. But, in fact, these were the *stigmata*, which thenceforward continued upon her hands, and shortly afterwards made their appearance upon her feet, and to these, at the same time, was added the wound upon the heart. . . . . They (the wounds) are nearly round, but a little extending lengthwise, from three to four lines in diameter, and are stationary on both the hands and the feet. Drops of clear blood frequently flow from these wounds on Thursday evenings and Fridays; on other days they seem covered with a sort of crust of dry blood, without the least appearance of inflammation, ulceration, or any vestige of lymph."

Of Domenica, the *Addolorata*, Lord Shrewsbury says,

"Her sufferings were so great that her screams were often heard to a great distance: still her patience was inexhaustible, and her resignation so perfect, that in the midst of her torments she continually expressed her gratitude and her love to God, and her sense of his mercy and goodness to her. The holy communion alone relieved her, *after which she frequently lay entranced for a considerable time. It was under these circumstances, that during one night* her whole head was encircled by small wounds, fifty-three in number, which opened and bled profusely every Friday. Fourteen days after the crown of thorns, she received the stigmata in the hands and feet, and the wound in the side."

It is also related of Domenica, that for eight years she had neither eaten nor drank any thing but the holy sacrament, and that during this period she had never slept! At the conclusion of the pamphlet, Lord Shrewsbury quotes, from a recent life of Catherine Emmerich, who died in 1824 (and who herself received the stigmata), accounts of several persons who are supposed to have enjoyed the same privilege.

"'There have existed,' says the biographer, 'in the Catholic church, since St. Francis of Assisium, a considerable number of pious personages, who have attained to this degree of the contemplative love of Jesus, this most sublime expression of identification with his sufferings, known to theologians by the name of *vulnus divinum, plaga amoris viva*: there have been at least fifty persons thus favoured. *Veronica Giuliani*, of the order of the Capuchines (Franciscans), who died at Citta di Castello in 1727, was the last of the number who was canonized (May 26, 1831)...... Those best known in our days have been the Dominicans; *Colombe Schanolt*, who died at Bamberg in 1787; *Madeline Lorger*, who died at Hadamar in 1806; and *Rose Serra*, a Capuchiness at Ozieri in Sardinia, stigmatized in 1801: *Josephine Humi* of Wollrau, of the convent of Wesen, near the lake of Wallenstein in Switzerland, who was living in 1815; she belonged to this class of persons, but we do not remember whether she had received the stigmata.'"

Now, what are we to say to these things? Are such miraculous gifts, in their own nature, impossible? That we cannot affirm:— no one is able to say in what variety of forms it may please God to exemplify the death of Christ in the members of his body. "I am crucified with Christ, nevertheless I live," says St. Paul; and so, in his degree, must every faithful man be able to respond. In the early ages of the Church, the sufferings and death of the persecuted were reckoned the highest and most honourable forms of participation in Christ's passion. Might we not say, then, that when persecution ceased, and Christians were exposed to the temptations of ease, riches, and the honours of the world, it was necessary by some new means to crown the victory of those who had been the foremost in resisting and overcoming perils to which the primitive believers were not exposed? This seems to have been an opinion current in the middle ages; but whether or no the theory be probable, we do not pretend to decide; we can only deal with facts. Can we, then, deny the facts testified by witnesses such as Lord Shrewsbury, and the other persons of honour and credit whose concurrent evidence he adduces? That is impossible; no one can doubt that the appearances described by his Lordship are real and true—that the young women are exactly affected as he has related.

But, giving every credit to the truth of the relation, so far as it goes, the great question still remains,—" Are the appearances miraculous?" On this point, we fear there is no evidence whatever. It does not appear that any one was present (as in the case of St. Francis there was) while the stigmata were received. The subjects themselves are described to have been in a state of unconsciousness at the time; the one, Maria Mörl, being ecstatic, and unaware, after the wounds appeared, how or when they had been inflicted; and the other, Domenica Lazzari, *being entranced during the night* of their production. The one was unable to give any account of the origin of the wounds, and the other has (for all we know) never uttered on the subject. In the absence, then, of evidence to the contrary, we are bound to assume that the wounds are natural wounds, and not miraculous. But if so, how have they been produced or inflicted—by the parties themselves, or by others? If by themselves, was it with their own consent and knowledge? This we cannot say; for the Estatica was not aware how the wounds arose, and the piety of both her and the Addolorata is obviously too sincere to allow us to suppose them capable of imposture. In charity, we cannot suppose this; but is it not possible that the wounds should have been self-inflicted while the subject was unconscious or entranced, or, being in that state, that they should have been produced by others from piously fraudulent motives? Physiological facts demonstrate that neither of these cases is impossible. Our readers who have looked into the history of Mesmerism, must be aware that cases have occurred in which the patients, after being thrown by artificial means into an entranced state, have undergone, without any symptom of suffering, the most painful operations in surgery. But we do not insist on such cases, though, so far as evidence goes, they are quite on a par with those of the Addolorata and Estatica; we rather turn to records of medicine or physiology, which, having been penned as matter of simple history, lie under no suspicion of having been invented or exaggerated in support of a preconceived system. These records inform us that *women** are liable, from constitutional or other causes, to a peculiar and very inexplicable derangement of their mental and physical powers. Under the influence of this deranged state, various manifestations of intellect and of the powers of the senses take place, which wholly disappear when the patient is restored to her ordinary condition. Sometimes we have the phenomenon which has been termed *double* or *divided consciousness* or *personality;* " which exhibits two separate and independent trains of thought and general mental capabilities in the same individual: each train of thought and each capability being wholly dissevered from the other, and the two states in which they respectively predominate subject to frequent interchanges and alternations."† Sometimes, apart from any increase or double action of the mental powers, we find the perceptions of sense exercised with a degree of acuteness altogether incomprehensible and truly wonderful. These facts are sufficiently well known to those who are conversant with the annals of physiology; and we believe that, supposing the Estatica and Addolorata to be labouring under some form of the malady just described, there is no medical man who would not admit the possibility of referring to natural causes most, if not all, the phenomena in their cases which are supposed to be miraculous.

Let us take the instance of the young woman whose case is described in the Transactions (1822) of the Royal Society of Edinburgh. Her malady commenced with a propensity to sleep, during which " she repeated the occurrences of the day, and sang musical airs, both sacred and profane. One evening, in the house of an acquaintance of her mistress, where she seems to have come for the purpose of seeing her home, she fell asleep in this manner, *imagined herself an episcopal clergyman,* went through the ceremony of baptizing three children,

---

* It cannot have escaped the notice of our readers, that all the modern subjects of the stigmata have been women.

† Report of Dr. Dewar, on a case submitted to the Royal Society of Edinburgh. Transact. R. S. E. vol. ix. p. 365.

and gave an appropriate *extempore* prayer. Her mistress shook her by the shoulders, on which she awoke, and *appeared unconscious of everything*, except that she had fallen asleep, of which she showed herself ashamed." .... " In the mean time a still more singular and interesting symptom began to make its appearance. The circumstances *which occurred during the paroxysm were completely forgotten by her when the paroxysm was over, but were perfectly remembered during subsequent paroxysms.* Her mistress says that when in this stupor on subsequent occasions, she told her what was said to her on the evening on which she *baptized* the children." When she was brought to the physician for medical advice, "she appeared as if in a state of stupor. Her eyes were half open; but when desired she could open them completely." .... " When desired to turn her eyes to the direct rays of the sun, she readily obeyed, *but there was no perceptible contraction of the iris.*" When desired to sing, " she sang a hymn delightfully," which appeared to those about her to be " incomparably better sung than she could sing the same tune when well." Shortly after this, while under the influence of her complaint, she became the victim of an infamous design, of which " next day she had not the slightest recollection, nor did any one interested in her welfare know of it for several days, till she was in one of her paroxysms, when she related the whole facts to her mother." One day she was taken to church while the paroxysm was on her. "She shed tears during the sermon, particularly during an account given of the execution of three young men at Edinburgh, who had described in their dying declarations the dangerous steps with which their career of vice and infamy commenced. When she returned home, she recovered in a quarter of an hour, was quite amazed at the questions put to her about the church and the sermon, and denied that she had been in any such place; but next night, on being taken ill, she mentioned that she had been at church, repeated the words of the text, and gave an accurate account of the tragical narrative of the three young men, by which her feelings had been so powerfully affected." Other cases are alluded to in the paper from which these extracts have been made. " One of them," says Dr. Dewar, " was an apparently simple girl, in the neighbourhood of Stirling, who in her sleep talked like a profound philosopher, solved geographical problems, and enlarged on the principles of astronomy, detailing the workings of ideas which had been suggested to her mind by overhearing the lessons which were given by a tutor to the children of the family in which she lived. .... Another case was mentioned in the newspapers, two, or perhaps three years ago, of a more marked instance of double consciousness. The individual was liable to two states, each of which, if I rightly recollect, continued for two or more years. In one state, when it first came on, there was an oblivion of all former education, but no deficiency of mental vigour, as applied to ideas or pursuits subsequently presenting themselves. It was necessary for this woman to recommence the studies of reading and the art of writing. A separate set of notions and separate accomplishments were now formed. In one of the states, an exquisite talent for music, and some others which implied refinement, were displayed. When another mental revolution arrived, these utterly disappeared, and the individual was reduced to a level with the rest of mankind, displaying a sufficient portion of common sense, but nothing brilliant."

The most remarkable case that has recently occurred of increased power of the senses, unaccompanied with the phenomenon of divided consciousness, is that of a lady now, we believe, living and residing in the neighbourhood of Plymouth. The facts of this case have not yet been given to the public in an attested form, but they are pretty generally known, and the particulars we are about to relate have been received from a gentleman who is acquainted with the parties, and with the physician who attended the subject of this most extraordinary form of disease.

It was during her recovery from a lingering malady, induced by a violent shock her nerves had received in consequence of her having unexpectedly witnessed the death of a near relative, that the phenomena appeared which excited so much wonder. At the time we speak of, she had recovered so far as to be free from any other complaint but that of weakness, an inability to walk, and extreme excitability of the nervous system. She generally lay on a sofa; and it was while in this confined position that her senses acquired an acuteness and a range of perception which, but for the testimony of witnesses of undoubted veracity, must appear to be altogether incredible. It seemed, at times, as if the several senses had lost their individual uses, and merged in one marvellous and universal faculty of almost boundless perception. One day, when lying in her usual posture, at a distance from the windows of the room, she suddenly said, "There is a man coming with rats." One of the family went to the window, but could see no one. On her still persisting that he was coming nearer, some one went out, and after a few minutes, observed a man " at the distance of several fields " (so went the words of the narrator) coming towards the house, and who proved to be a rat-catcher. When Miss B. first was sensible of his approach, he must have been from a quarter to half a mile distant from the house. On another occasion, a gentleman, a friend of the family, called, and after he had been a few minutes in the room, Miss B. exclaimed, " You have brought some chestnuts with you." " No," said he, " I have not;" but on searching the pockets of his great coat, he found a couple of chestnuts, which he remembered to have picked up some time before. But the most incredible fact of all, was the power she possessed of *reading by her hands.* A letter containing some family matters, of which Miss B. could not by any possibility have heard, was received by a friend who was residing with her family. The letter was placed between her hands, and on her feeling all over the writing, she related every particular of its contents. It must be remembered, in explanation of the possibility of this apparent miracle, that blind people have been taught to read by means of letters formed in high relief, and that even common writing with ink is actually raised above the surface of the paper, though in a degree so minute as to be scarcely perceptible to the ordinary sense of touch. But the power of feeling in Miss B. was so acute that, as we have said, she could trace the forms of the letters above the surface of the paper. Nor was this all. Her sense of touch seemed to operate, in reading, very much like the ordinary cultivated sense of sight. A practised reader is not obliged to follow by the eye successively the form of every letter, and thus to spell, as it were, every word, but by a single glance he discovers the import of a sentence. And so it was in the case we are describing. Miss B. seemed at once, and without practice, to have gained the same power of instantaneously feeling, by the hand, the import of a piece of writing as she had before possessed by seeing. It was only necessary for her to pass her fingers over the lines as rapidly as she had been accustomed to run her eye, to tell what they contained. Many other anecdotes are current respecting this interesting and extraordinary case; but enough has been related for our present purpose. Return we, therefore, to the Estatica and the Addolorata.

Our readers will already have seen the application we propose to make of the cases which have been adduced, to the supposed miracles described by Lord Shrewsbury. If the Estatica be afflicted similarly to the young woman of whom we read in the Transactions of the Royal Society of Edinburgh, it is obvious that her wounds may have been inflicted by herself during some mental aberration similar to that related of the girl who imagined herself an episcopal clergyman. Who knows what her thoughts may have been? What if her fervent piety, her admiration of St. Francis (for it must be remembered that she is a Franciscan), may have led her to imagine herself the saint himself? What if she have imagined herself to have been actually crucified, and to have done that to herself which she supposed to be the work of others? And if we remember the phenomena of dreams, this is neither an impossible nor an improbable supposition. If it be said that the pain of such wounds must have restored her to consciousness, we point at the case of the girl who was not awakened from her stupor even by an atrocious attack on her virtue, of the occurrence of which, though it is proved that she offered a vigorous and successful resistance, she was not aware after the stupor had passed away. On the other hand, supposing the devout Franciscan to have been tutored, as no doubt she has been, to look upon *stigmatisation* as the crowning mark of her love to Christ, and to have ardently desired its infliction, might not the wounds have been the work of some other hand than her own, without any collusion on her part? her previously excited state of mind, her aspirations after this supposed identification with the sufferings of Christ, serving not only to prevent her being aware that the wounds, at the time of their infliction, were real and not imaginary, but to make the pain itself a desirable feeling, or, at least, a form of suffering to which she would be inclined to offer no resistance. We should be sorry to think that this supposition had any foundation in fact; but nevertheless, if the ecstatic condition of Maria Mörl be a form of the malady, of which various aspects are seen in the cases we have quoted, the supposition is perfectly tenable.

Again; one great peculiarity in the malady of the young woman whose case is reported on by Dr. Dewar, was her partial consciousness of what was going on about her. When spoken to, she answered, though not always coherently, but she always did as she was desired. The same happened in the case of the Estatica. Lord Shrewsbury says (page 4),

"She might have remained in this (ecstatic) state and posture for several hours, had not her confessor, by a slight touch or a word, we could not exactly say which, so quiet and imperceptible it was, caused her to fall back on her pillow, which she did with the most perfect ease, placing herself in a sitting posture, with her legs extended under the counterpane, without the slightest effort, *and without awaking from her ecstasy, remaining with her eyes shut and her hands joined as before, in the attitude of prayer*, her lips motionless, and her soul transfixed in the same profound meditation. After again contemplating her for a few moments in this new position, her confessor *proposed to us that he should awaken her entirely from her trance*. We had no sooner assented than he addressed her in a mild gentle tone, as did the assistant priest from the other side of the bed, which was placed with its head against the centre of one side of the room, we standing close at her feet, *when in an instant the most perfect animation was restored to her*. She let fall her hands and opened her eyes, ... looking first to one side, then to the other, as if it was the unexpected meeting of friends whom she had not seen for years."*

Then, again, we are told that† "when M. de la Bouillerie visited her on his way to Rome, whither he was going to receive ordination, he found her kneeling in a state of ecstasy, when he *saw a fly walk quietly across the pupil of her eye, when wide open, without producing the slightest sensation upon her.*" To this we oppose the statement of the physician who attended the young woman already noticed; "when desired to turn her eyes to the direct rays of the sun, she readily obeyed, *but there was no perceptible contraction of the iris.*" Lastly; Lord Shrewsbury says, "Prince Licknowsky, whom we met here the other day, told us that he also visited her in October 1839. While kneeling in ecstasy on her bed, to his great surprise, he observed her moving round towards the window; neither he nor any of those present knew what it meant, till looking out, they saw the *viaticum* passing on its way to the sick, without bell, or chanting, or any sound that could indicate its presence." Here

---

* The account given by Görres seems even more distinctly to evince the existence of the phenomenon of divided or double consciousness in the case of the Estatica. Speaking of her awakening from her entranced state, he says, "It takes but the necessary time to recollect herself and open her eyes, and *she is as if her ecstasy had never existed;* the expression of her face changes." ... And of her again becoming entranced: "In the midst of conversation ... at once *her eyes become heavy*, and in a second, without further hesitation, she is in an ecstasy."

† Page 15. Foot-note.

again we oppose the case of Miss B.; and may not the Estatica have known and heard the peculiar tramp of the priests' feet, though unknown to and unheard by the bystanders? May she not (and we must not be thought to speak profanely), have detected by the sense of smell, that which, however changed by the mystical operation of the Holy Spirit, remains the same to sense?

We should sincerely regret if these remarks were supposed to proceed from the infidel rationalism that now-a-days seeks to deny, if not the possibility, at least the actual occurrence of miracles,—not only in these times, but in the more gifted ages of the Church. Far be it from us to forget, that a mystery hangs over all that relates to the spiritual life; or that in itself, in its origin, its continuance, and its consummation, it is a greater miracle than any that can be supposed to accompany it in demonstration of its existence and its power. Equally sorry should we be were it likely that any observations of ours should tend to weaken the moral influence, which, it is affirmed by Lord Shrewsbury, the piety of the two Tyrolese women has exerted. "The good," says his Lordship, "which they have already done is great—the conversion of many reprobates, and the edification of thousands. None have ever visited them without returning better than they went." But nevertheless, we are sure that the discovery of a mistake or deception, we will not say imposture, in these cases, would do more harm to the cause of religion, in the long-run, than would be counterbalanced by any present, and apparently good effect; and therefore it is, that we think a rigorous inquiry into the facts, to be a duty of the first moment. Nor let any Roman Catholic, in whose way these observations may fall, imagine that we treat the inquiry as a party one; that we have any interested motives for wishing to show that the miraculous appearances are deceptions. Either way, the cases can make nothing for the questions between the Churches. We do not require miracles to convince us that the Catholic church in the Tyrol is the true church; that the Gallican church is the Catholic church in France; or that the Anglican church is the Catholic church in England. Supposing the cases of the Estatica and Addolorata to be really miraculous, they have no bearing whatever, as Lord Shrewsbury imagines, on the question, whether we in England ought to conform to all the practices and customs of the church of Rome. Nor, on the other hand, if the miracles be false, do we gain any thing; while the Roman church, if they be so, is certainly a loser. Nay, we should rather say that we were interested in believing, than in denying the truth of the miracles; for those who in sincerity pray daily for "the whole estate of Christ's church militant here on earth" can hardly be supposed to regard with willing indifference, or mistrust, any relation that seems to make us acquainted with activity of spiritual life, in any quarter of the church catholic, however obscure or remote. If it were proved to a demonstration, in the case of Maria Mörl, that all the miraculous appearances were traceable to the influence of an ardent piety, misdirected and exaggerated by a deranged state of the nervous system, we should still wonder at a fervency of devotion, which is able to make even disease assume a religious character.

And in truth this is the impression left on our minds, after an attentive perusal of the letter of Lord Shrewsbury, and the most careful consideration we can bestow on the facts he has related. The accounts furnished of the Addolorata, are too scanty to enable us to form an adequate opinion on her case; but with respect to the Estatica, we are constrained to believe that she labours under some nervous affection, giving rise to a double consciousness or personality, under one of which her piety takes a form for which she is not responsible, and of which, on her restoration to her natural state, she retains no recollection, and can give no account. Other facts may be yet in store, the relation of which might induce us to change our minds; but if the view which we have taken of her malady be a just one, neither her long-continued ecstasy nor her wounds need be reckoned miraculous, unless we are to suppose every phenomenon to be so, the immediate causes of which we are unable to trace. Physiologists, we believe, have not the remotest notion of the nature or causes of divided consciousness; nor can they tell why it sometimes is accompanied with the temporary annihilation of certain of the operations of sense, sometimes with the acquisition of incredible acuteness of one or more of the senses, sometimes with the development of talents and powers of mind, which disappear in the healthy state. That a human being should be conscious of what is passing around, should answer questions, obey directions given, be affected as other people, and the moment afterwards, awaken to an utter oblivion of the questions, the directions, the feelings, which had been asked, given, or entertained, is a puzzle which we cannot unravel. But this puzzle is every whit more perplexing in the case of the young woman described by Dr. Dewar, as it is in that of the Estatica. In one respect, indeed, it is less so; for in the former we look upon the phenomenon as a merely inexplicable disorder; whereas, in the latter we have not only the physiological difficulty to contend with, but a moral one. We have to comprehend how the continuance of an ecstatic state is consistent with the interruption occasioned by the command of a superior. Görres relates in explanation of this, that the ready obedience of the Estatica, is due to her vow, taken on entering the third order of St. Francis; but the explanation is not satisfactory. We can understand the entire discontinuance of an ecstasy in obedience to a command, or indeed its discontinuance from any kind of interruption whatever; but without upsetting all our notions of ecstasy, we fear it is impossible to comprehend the concomitancy of a state of mind and feeling, which supposes entire abstraction from visible objects, with an acuteness of sense and a sympathy with the external world, which only needs "a word or a touch," or something between the two, to ensure obedience as to a change of posture, *without interrupting the state of ecstasy.* This we conceive is a moral impossibility; but we imagine that the term "ecstasy" is misapplied to the habitual paroxysms of Maria Mörl. The accounts given by Görres show that, at certain periodical times, while under the influence of her malady, she is filled with rapturous thoughts, or borne down by the most agonizing sympathy with the passion of Christ; but in general she seems to be in a passive state; possibly one of happy oblivion and freedom from the bodily sufferings to which, in her ordinary condition, she is liable.* And if this be the case, our moral difficulty vanishes; for her ecstasy, except at the periods specified by Görres, is not real, but apparent; she is in a state of stupor analogous to that of the young woman already so often alluded to, the only difference being—and it is an important difference as to its results—that, in the one case, there was little or no preoccupation with religious feeling, whereas, in the other, the whole existence is one of devotion —a devotion which evinces its sincerity by its overpowering influence on the workings of a deranged nervous system, and which gives the appearance of a miracle to that which, after all, is only a disease.

---

1. *Masterman Ready; or, the Wreck of the Pacific.* By Captain MARRYAT. London: Longman and Co. 1841.
2. *Leila; or, the Island.* By ANN FRASER TYTLER. Second Edition. London: Hatchards. 1841.
3. *The Forest of Arden. A Tale, illustrative of the English Reformation.* By the Rev. W. GRESLEY, M.A. London: Burns. 1841.
4. *Tales of the Village.* 1st, 2d, and 3d Series. By the Rev. F. E. PAGET, M.A. London: Burns. 1841.
5. *The Fairy Bower; or, the History of a Month.* London: Burns. 1841.
6. *The Lost Brooch; or, the History of another Month.* London: Burns. 1841.
7. *Rutilius and Lucius; or, Stories of the Third Age.* By ROBERT I. WILBERFORCE, M.A. London: Burns. 1842.
8. *Conversations with Cousin Rachel.* 3 Pts. London: Burns. 1841.
9. *Sintram and his Companions.* Translated from the German of De la Motte Fouque. London: Burns. 1842.

THE works now before us are, in one respect, sufficiently various. Some of them are professedly, and we may add very skilfully, adapted to the wants and likings of the young; while others are as suitable for grown-up readers as any books they could possibly open. Still they all may be said to fall under the designation with which we have headed this article, of "Didactic Fiction;" and they all, therefore, may be considered as more or less addressed to the young, who have still their tastes to form, their convictions to rectify or to mature, and

---

* The remark of the assistant priest, on her being awakened in presence of Lord Shrewsbury, seems to hint at this. "Maria," he said, "this is an easy life:" to which she replied, "Yes;" with her usual sweetness.—P. 6.

their principles to strengthen and settle. It will consequently be no disparagement to some of them, as books of intrinsic value for all readers, if we view them now mainly in reference to youthful ones (comprehending within the term all whose education is still uncompleted), and compare them with by-gone tales of the same class.

No man accustomed to anything like a comprehensive survey of human nature, will deny the educational importance of Fiction, and its bearing on the intellectual development for good or for evil. The ridiculous scruples which have sometimes been raised on the subject have, in scarcely any quarters, succeeded in proscribing it; indeed, we are by no means sure that we have not yet to see the man or woman whose mind has, from infancy, been fed on nothing but the bare reality of things. One of the first truths children unconsciously proclaim of themselves is, that their thoughts and feelings have a wider span than the actual circumstances around them. Pursue what course with them we like, we cannot annihilate the imagination—it will put forth its powers—it will take a terrible revenge if its legitimate claims be slighted—it will make slaves of those who have not been helped to use it as a servant—and instead of being the bright minister of cheerfulness, hope, and energy, for which God designed it, it will become a dark and portentous fiend, the inflicter of torture untold.*

Our ancestors, encumbered with few theories on the subject, and being guiltless of all reforming designs in this department, treated their children to older fictions than are, perhaps, to be found in the whole compass of literature besides. If anything be the common property of the race, it is those fairy tales which have come to us from beyond the Caucasus, and in which man's yearnings after the beautiful and the spiritual expressed themselves in most intelligible accents. Yet, forsooth, this was not the diet, in the estimation of enlightened men and women, for childhood to thrive on. There are no fairies, it seems, in the actual world; and therefore children, not dreaming that there are, nor happening to be thinking at the moment of the actual world, ought to hear of none. We own ourselves somewhat sceptical as to the gain secured, when "Beauty and the Beast," and "The Sleeping Beauty," and "Cinderella," and even the lively "Tom Thumb," were dismissed, to make way for "Harry and Lucy," with their barometers, and their measurements of bricks, and all the medley of sciences which thenceforth were to be studied in the nursery and the school-room. The old class of tales were more valuable, we think, both in an intellectual and a moral point of view: in an intellectual, as being in themselves often very lovely creations, and always appealing to the fresh, unalloyed and undiseased imagination; in a moral, as being of distant time, free from particular theories (which are often but particular perversities), and having commended themselves to the hearts and the consciences of all ages. We may have, perhaps, exaggerated to ourselves the degree to which the treasures we are speaking of have been allowed to melt away. Possi-

---

* See the late Mr. Lamb's beautiful essay on Witches and Night-fears, in "Elia."

bly they may be still transmitted by means of that oral tradition which stood them in such stead for many a day; and the parent, too enlightened an advocate of modern reforms to select them in print for the nursery or the school-room, may nevertheless indulge himself after dinner in retracing his own early impressions to the child on each knee, whom he wisely holds to be as yet unsusceptible of that discernment between good and evil which paper and print bring along with them. But we do not now see some of the pleasant volumes which, pretending to no wonderful illumination, and professing no new or profound wisdom, beguiled the leisure hours of our own childhood.

Even, however, at the time we speak of, their reign was drawing to a close, and young and rational gods were usurping their cloudy throne. The sway of Dr. Aikin and Miss Edgeworth was becoming universal and undisputed. Indeed, we may perhaps be post-dating the revolution. We have dim recollections of older books on the rational model, in which both text and prints indicated a state of manners with which we could claim no fellowship—dress and allusions being equally mysterious to us—" Elements of Morality," "Children's Friends," and such like. Whether the most diligent antiquarian could now lay hold on an entire copy of them we cannot say; but their names seem to have been blotted out of men's memories.

Such can hardly, however, be the fate of the works to which we now allude, and which were considered at the time of their appearance as creating quite an epoch in education. Their intellectual power is unquestionable, their ingenuity very great, and the amount of interest they excite, beyond all doubt, very lively. They stand, however, as representatives of the fallacies which prevailed at the time of their publication, one or two of which it will be worth while to mark and consider.

1stly. That the presumption is, that our ancestors were all wrong in their notions of education. On this fallacy we need say no more at present than that it was probably the root of the others.

2dly. That the heart can be cultivated independently of the conscience, and that a boy is more likely to learn to avoid sin from having pointed out to him the inconveniences which will probably before long arise from it any how, than from being straightway punished for it; and so led to connect it with the just displeasure of those who are above him, and through this with the displeasure of God.

3dly. That the imagination is of very little use; though how truth is likely to be conveyed by means of fiction, supposing we were without imaginations; or how, if in that predicament, we could take any lively interest in history, does not appear.

4thly. That learning by heart is unprofitable to the young, either the memory requiring no cultivation, or its cultivation being a thing of no consequence. Of all wretched and ridiculous mistakes this is one of the worst. No one ever had a well-trained memory without having afterwards deep reason to be grateful towards those who secured him the boon. No one ever thought or studied in after life without perceiving how indispensable is a retentive memory to all vigorous and successful exertion of the intellect. No man of fine mind but must rejoice in the power of knowing things by heart—a power, however, which will hardly come afterwards to those in whom it has not been early instilled.

5thly. That a child should never be presented with anything he cannot altogether understand: a maxim which was the parent of two others—that a habit of asking questions upon every subject is to be encouraged, and that nothing is to be done on the mere principle of obedience. Of course, this necessity for understanding at every step was and is extended to religion, though, if followed out, it would as much preclude adults from entering into their heritage of faith as little children, for—

"—— what are all prayers beneath,
But cries of babes that cannot know
Half the deep thought they breathe?"

Such maxims make no appeal to faith, and cultivate no sentiment of reverence. The learner is reminded of nothing greater or deeper than himself. His own mind is to be the measure of every thing, and at the very age to which faith and reverence are most congenial he is discouraged in the exhibition of them.*

These and a few other fallacies partly caused, and were partly aided in their ascendency by, the works in question. Enough has ere now been said on a greater evil than all—that both Dr. Aikin's and Miss Edgeworth's tales recognise no birth from above—no heavenly provision—no armour of God, in the struggle against infirmity and sin. The child, according to them, is to learn by what he sees, instead of walking by what he does not see. Any approach to religion that does happen to be introduced is something worse than the surrounding silence and neglect. Dr. Aikin treats us to a Sunday morning, in which a boy is represented as going to church along with his father, through the streets of a large town. As the crowd passes along, the doors of church, mass-house, conventicle and Quakers' meeting, all standing open, engulph each its own share of the motley stream. The boy, thinking not unnaturally that if his own destination be right, some at least of the others must perforce be wrong, asks his father the cause of all this diversity of worship, and receives the satisfactory answer that religion was one of the things in which *men were meant to differ*. He goes, if we recollect aright, to church—whether the second lesson was John xvii. is not said. Coming home they encounter a man who has broken his leg, or met with some other bad accident, and is assisted in the various needful ways by a Churchman, a Romanist, a Dissenter, and a Quaker. "Behold, my son," says the liberal parent, "one of the things in which men were meant to agree." Now, what is the inference from this in logic not more strict than obvious? Why, sheer infidelity. Place the incident on the shores of the Levant, and a Mussulman would have been one of the be-

---

* There are some excellent remarks on this subject in Archdeacon Hare's "Victory of Faith."

frienders of the hurt man, and the remark of the father would have been as natural and as called for. Yet this setting at nought of the worthy name whereby we are called, and making the cross of Christ of none effect, was the food of our childhood, in so far as we were encouraged to read, and taught to respect the "Evenings at Home;" and harmonized beautifully, to be sure, with the "Essay on Man" and the "Universal Prayer." In the same way, Miss Edgeworth's mention of religion is worse than her silence concerning it. Does she describe a slave of fashion, who is yet decent in a few notions? We read that "she had good principles, moral and religious."* Are we presented with a pattern governess? She is a French refugee, and if of any religion at all, is a Papist. It is *commendably* arranged between her and a gay mother who is always in company, and therefore commits her children entirely into the governess's hands, that while she is to form their minds and attend to their morals, on the subject of religion she is not to interfere.† Is the scene laid in Ireland? Then we may count on being warned against Papist and Protestant treating their differences as of any the slightest moment. Such is the religion of Miss Edgeworth's tales, and by its fruits may it be known. *Moral*, as a whole section of them is formally designated, and *moral* as they all profess to be, yet how immoral they often are! In "Helen," truth, the groundwork of all possible virtue, is so lightly treated, that a young woman is made very amiable, in whom it is more than commonly absent; and suddenly reformed by the force of incidents at the last,—a tendency to lying being the only unfortunate item in her character—one solitary fault remaining for her to correct. Belinda *conditionally* betroths herself to one man, about whose character she is not sure enough to do so absolutely, her affections being all the while another's. As to the taste in subordinate points, think what the heroes and heroines would be if we met them in real life, unset in Miss Edgeworth's sparkling writing,—how intolerable the young man, recollecting at the moment to have read some ridiculously isolated fact, and receiving a smile of approval from the great man in company, who thenceforth becomes his own and his families' most powerful friend; or the intelligent lady, "coolly questioning" the original distinctions of mind in the presence of a learned doctor, who *warmly maintains* it; ‡ or young ladies in company analyzing the passions? § These violations of congruity and good taste would hardly have been committed by one of Miss Edgeworth's quick wit, had she not made from the first a false start. Men and women she takes for granted were created mainly for the purpose of being literary and scientific. Had she begun by recognising their immortal destiny, and the heavenly citizenship to which they are admitted by baptism, she would have learned how to keep the sexes and the different ages of life each in its own place; she would have seen, for example, both the fact and the reason of it,

---

* The Absentees.   † The Good French Governess.
‡ The Good Aunt.   § Manœuvring.

—that even the most gifted and intellectual of women are unfitted for logical or metaphysical discussion; and that all really wise and modest women, therefore, decline such. She would have seen, too, the importance of unity of aim; of individual pursuit, instead of encyclopædic knowledge; and would therefore have given a very different impression of what intellectual pursuits should be, than can be derived from the farrago of detached facts in which her heroes shine, and with which her novels abound.

Having spoken thus much of Miss Edgeworth's faults, it will be unfair not to dwell for a moment on the mass of merit and utility which remains behind in her works. In the first place, viewing them merely as fictions, their ingenuity, their liveliness, their intellectual strength, and at the same time their refinement, are such as must always charm, and, so long as we remedy their errors from some other source, must always beneficially charm us. It would be an insult to the sex of the writer to speak of their purity. But we must praise the manliness of her young men—the stress laid on their honour—the importance attached to early habits, (for, except in her last novel, Miss Edgeworth presents us, as far as we remember, with no sudden reformations,) and the gentlemanly character with which they are all invested. This is peculiarly apparent in the school-boys. In spite, therefore, of the immense deductions from it which we have been constrained to make, much value remains in Miss Edgeworth's tales: and so long as parents keep their great leading fallacies steadily in view, and provide suitable counteractions, we shall rejoice to hear of their continued popularity.

A more earnest and serious spirit has since prevailed; and however inadequate and distorted may be their view of some of the peculiarities of the New Testament, the evangelical school deserve our thanks for the testimony they have borne to the universal importance of those peculiarities. They have taught us not to descend *in any case* from a vantage ground, on which we have been placed by the Gospel—they have shown that if heathen ethics were inadequate for man's renewal, and the revealed grace of God is adequate, education ought to be based on the latter—they have proclaimed the great principle, that all moral lessons are best learned from the Cross of Jesus Christ. With whatever errors this testimony was accompanied (and many and serious we think they were), it contained in it too much truth, and was too much needed, not to make a great impression. Indeed, the truth that there was in the evangelical movement may be said to have, by this time, won its victory. In its course, it developed itself in fiction, having for its chief writers in this department, Mrs. Sherwood and Miss Grace Kennedy. The clever fictions of the former are designed for a younger class of readers than those of the latter. Both are tainted by the same theological errors,—though the vastly superior refinement and eloquence of Miss Kennedy renders them more dangerous. Before considering those dangers, let us protest against a fallacy which we sometimes encounter in conversation. When we point out the unsound doctrine of any production intended for the young or the untaught, we are occasionally met by the answer—that they do not observe it,—that they are stirred by it to goodness, and do not mark its deviations from doctrinal accuracy. A stranger fallacy never prevailed. He who marks such deviations, has it in his power to see the remedy; it is the stealthy impression that is made on readers who do not appear to have arrived at any doctrinal conclusions, which is most of all to be deprecated. And certainly Miss Kennedy's tales are full of precisely the sort of error which is likely to be most detrimental to the young. They nearly all turn on *conversion*, in the modern sense of the word, the dating christian privileges from which, instead of from baptism, we look upon as injurious in any case, but peculiarly so to the young. A few words will explain our reason for thinking so.

What is meant by conversion, as the word is used by the evangelical party, is a fact of which we have frequent experience, and as such, interesting and important; but it is not, as they are apt to view it, an elementary feature in the covenant of grace, and a part of the revealed scheme of our deliverance. We say, it is a fact we experience. We do see persons who have long lived in seeming neglect of baptismal privilege, being, at some definite period of their lives, graciously turned in the right direction. And though on St. Paul's principle of judging nothing, not even our ownselves, before the time, it may admit of doubt whether previously to such an epoch they were so far, and after it, are straightway so near the christian mark, as is for the most part imagined, it cannot be denied that the change in such cases must be very great. But how ought we to view it? As an ascertainable fact, certainly; and therefore one of which we were meant to take cognisance, and on which we were meant to reflect. And when we do so, it certainly presents us with abundant matter for musing and praise. But when,—instead of adding to our sense of the benefit of baptism, by being represented as, what in truth it is, one among the many indications of the power of that regenerating Sacrament,—it is used to disparage the blessed laver; and considered as being more the law of deliverance,—the divine plan of imparting Christ to the sons of men, than that other—then serious mischief ensues. Instead of being the exception,* it is made the general rule, that baptism should be powerless, and a subsequent conversion, supposed to be independent of it, should do every thing for a man. Hence those who have experienced no such conversion are taught to regard themselves as out of the pale of the christian covenant. And to a child, this, as we have said, is peculiarly prejudicial. He is seldom at all likely to conceive himself the subject of such a conversion. Every thing in his own consciousness testifies to him that he is even as his fellows. The victory over impulse— the occupation with heavenly things—the solemnity of spirit which

---

* Even if the cases in question could be proved to be numerically the majority, they must remain *ideally* the exception.

do belong to the matured saint, are unsuitable to his age. He does not know this; but he knows that they are in no way descriptive of himself, and therefore thinks himself unconverted, and without the pale of the christian covenant. It would be a curious statistical inquiry, were we to go the round of evangelical households, and ascertain in how many the younger members consider themselves in a state of practical heathenism. If we found this common in the Church, we might conclude that it was nearly universal among the sects. To this perverted state of feeling such tales as Miss Kennedy's powerfully minister, in which the young are described as going on throughout a certain period of their lives, amiably and happily, but "strangers to the power of the Gospel," which comes upon them at last in some way or other.

There is a further mischief in all this. It is no doubt true, and it is very important to teach the lesson—that generosity and honour and amiability are not enough, that they may be very signally displayed in hearts where God has not His right place, and where, therefore, much renewal and change must have been accomplished before we can look on their condition as satisfactory or even hopeful. But when such excellent qualities are spoken of as the mere growth of the natural man, we must either deny their goodness, and so bewilder and stun the conscience which in the first instance affirms it; or else we must contravene the position of St. Paul, that in our flesh dwelleth no good thing.

The best known of Miss Kennedy's tales are, "Dunallan;" "The Decision;" "Profession is not Principle;" "Harriet and her Cousin;" and "Father Clement." The first is not, we believe, a very great favourite with any class, nor does it deserve to be. The plot is not only wildly improbable, but absolutely offensive. The others, however, are exceedingly interesting and pleasing as tales, though all nullified for practical purposes by the pervading error of which we have spoken. The best known of all, is the one which, in a literary point of view, is really an uncommon work, "Father Clement." We know few things in modern fiction more interesting than the noble-minded hero, or more natural than the state of feeling which all the parties respectively exhibit. Dormer's death-bed, too, is most eloquent and touching; and it is *like a* death-bed. He makes no long speeches, within an hour of his last breath,* and displays no rapturous exultation. Instead, we have that awe with which every thoughtful mind, and, not less surely, every saintly one, draws near to the unseen world. Beyond this our praise of "Father Clement" must end. Its subject is the Romish controversy, and not even in Exeter Hall is that controversy entered on in more blissful ignorance of its difficulties and its dangers, than it seems to have been by Miss Kennedy, when she commenced "Father Clement." Such books must really be a high entertainment to Dr. Wiseman and his

---

* We wonder that so judicious a writer as Mr. Paget, should have fallen into this error in the first series of his admirable "Tales of the Village."

coadjutors; nor do we see how a devout Romanist is likely to be attracted to us by the *note of holiness*, when he finds all bodily discipline treated as a badge of Antichrist.

Such was the educational fiction of the days immediately preceding the present; first cold and latitudinarian, next zealous and full of unction, but untaught, jejune, and shallow. And as it was defective in the higher, so was it in the lower regions of thought. Miss Kennedy is an improvement on Miss Edgeworth, as regards warmth and impulse : but she shares with her a radical deficiency in the deeper energies of imagination. She is equally distant with her from the world and the sympathies of poetry. Neither writer will ever bring the young out of their own sphere, or shew them that there is something larger and deeper than themselves, with which, notwithstanding, they may themselves claim fellowship. Neither will help them to "see into the life of things;" or reveal to them any pure unclouded glimpses of the " beauty in which all things work and move."

A great improvement has now, however, taken place. As the evangelical movement told upon fiction, so has the nobler and truer catholic one,—with all the advantage that belongs to universality over sectarianism,—to that which has been from the beginning over that which is but of yesterday,—to the changeless faith, rules, constitution, and sentiment of the holy Church over the evanescent prejudices and ephemeral fashions of one age. Indeed, if we are but sure that we are Catholics, we may also feel sure that the intellectual development is, in virtue of that one consideration, a stronger and a healthier one than it would otherwise have been. We do not, of course, mean that we are to predicate uncatholicity of an age or a people in which and in whom we find little or no literature. But we do mean, that if literature be pursued under the influence of a catholic spirit, it is sure to be successfully pursued. No catholic literature was ever weak,—no catholic art was ever vicious or false in essentials. In a catholic community the imagination may, from circumstances, not happen to be cognisably developed or exercised ; but if it should, it will be found to be the healthy, creative, religious imagination. For the catholic thinker knows the relative position and true bearings of every thing with which he comes in contact. Time and space are viewed by him each in its sublime totality, wherein every object finds its proper place and suitable adjustment. And accordingly, with the progress of catholic sentiment has appeared, if we mistake not, a livelier imagination, a juster taste, and a more vigorous intellect, on every subject to which they may happen to be applied, than were previously manifested among us.

Any how, the improvement in the region of literature we have now been considering is very marked indeed. For children, we have the Archdeacon of Surrey's beautiful Parables, and the tales in Mr. Burns' smaller series, among which, the "Conversations with Cousin Rachel" are on all hands allowed to hold the foremost and a most worthy place. Then we have Capt. Marryatt's most suitable, pleasant, healthy, and well-principled little book, "Masterman Ready." This will probably supplant the "Swiss Family Robinson." The cravings of the youthful heart to have represented a Crusoe life, which shall yet not be a lonely one, ought to be gratified. The "Family Robinson" is amusing enough, but it is *unreal*. It appears from Capt. Marryatt's preface, that the seamanship with which it begins is all wrong, a charge which we are quite willing to believe. The productions found in the island, moreover, belong not, it seems, to one climate. A still deeper falsity pervades the book: the religion is but sickly sentiment: indeed, where the father is a Swiss Protestant pastor, our hopes cannot be very high in that direction. Capt. Marryatt's book is one on which we can bestow all but unqualified praise. The incidents have every air of reality: the party are not, as in the case of the "Family Robinson," surrounded with comforts too soon or too easily after reaching the island. The character of old Ready is a most wholesome object of contemplation; and his religion, and indeed all that is expressed in the book, has a tone of manly reverence and modesty about it, which is just what we want in a book of this sort. There is no reason why a tale professedly written for amusement should enter into the doctrines of the faith. Let other seasons and more suitable methods convey direct religious instruction. But it is most important that children should find in their books of amusement that habit of reference to religious considerations which belongs to the truly christian character, and which they must acquire; that use of the material world and of the common accidents of life, as suggestive of the presence, wisdom, and goodness of God; and that respect for all the ordinances of religion and means of grace which are put in our power, which consistent Christians will always exhibit. It is not necessary that the characters should develope all their religious views, but most important that they should be represented as acting on all occasions like persons who have such. This merit belongs to Capt. Marryat's little tale, for the second volume of which we shall wait with some impatience, having as yet only seen our friends somewhat comfortably housed in their new island abode. As we are speaking of a book certain to come to another edition, we think it worth while to extract a passage for censure, commending what we have to say to the author's serious reflection.

"'Now, father, answer me another question. You said that nations rise and fall; and you have mentioned the Portuguese as a proof. Will England ever fall, and be of no more importance than Portugal is now?'

"'We can only decide that question by looking into history; and history tells us that such is the fate of all nations. We must, therefore, expect that it will one day be the fate of our dear country. At present we see no appearance of it, any more than we perceive the latent seeds of death in our own bodies; but still the time arrives when man must die, and so it must be with nations. Did the Portuguese, in the height of their prosperity, ever think that they would be reduced to what they are now? Would they have believed it? Yes, my dear boy, the English nation must in time meet with the fate of all others. There are various causes which may hasten or protract the period; but, sooner or later, England will no more be mistress of the seas, or boast of her possessions all over the world."—Pp. 271, 272.

Now, if like Mr. Seagrave, we had nothing but history to consult on the question here discussed, we should probably have no conclusion to arrive at but his. But we have holier oracles to inquire at; and they tell us, that "if that nation against whom God has pronounced, turn from their evil, he will repent of the evil that he thought to do unto them." Holy Scripture, in more places than one, promises prosperity to the nation that preserves the fear of God within its borders; and though history may present us with no example of such a nation, we may feel sure that our own land has but to persevere in a religious course, and it will afford one. We have paused on this point, because we think it one on which it is of great consequence that the thoughts of the young should not be perverted.

Another "Family Robinson" has just appeared, bearing the inauspicious title of "Leila." A good taste in names may be a very subordinate part, but it is still a part of the minor moralities; and in real life, our esteem for new acquaintances would not be enhanced by finding them select Leila as a *christian* name for one of their children. This fault is, we regret to say, somewhat symbolical of the whole book. It is full of a false sentimentality, full of mere prettinesses and *luxuries*, when the scene and the circumstances ought rather to suggest the moral of learning to *rough it*. Miss Tytler probably has powers that may produce much better things; but she has wandered from the spheres and circumstances which could alone have come within her observation, and accordingly her shipwreck and desert island have not that air of reality which is indispensable to the enjoyment of this sort of fiction. All is fantastic and uninstructive.

We will now ascend a little, and come to the fictions for those of riper age, with which we have lately been favoured. Here the improvement on Miss Edgeworth and Miss Kennedy is very marked indeed. First, we have Mr. Gresley's tales, which are *sui generis*. Perhaps no writer has succeeded in giving at once so much and so little fiction. When the subject is historical, we have a lively ingenious tale, and sound accurate history all the while. When the scene is laid in our own day, our fancies are interested in imaginary characters, and all the while important truths are brought out clearly, and fully, and well defended as in any essay. There is one advantage in Mr. Gresley's books, which is perhaps more his than any other writer's of the present day. There is *just enough* of fiction. The interest in the subject is sufficiently promoted by it, without the disquisition coming in as something extraneous or disturbing, and without day-dreams of sentiment or of earthly happiness being made to dance before us. Our attention is kept fully awake, and, being so, cannot well miss the grave practical truths which the author sets before us. Another merit of Mr. Gresley consists in the impressive passing reflections which he introduces on common occurrences, and the combination of causes which he brings before us. Thus, in

"Charles Lever," when the stupid mayor has been induced to grant the use of the town-hall for a Socialist meeting, by self-interested motives which have just been explained, Mr. Gresley begs us to pause and—

" observe the concatenation of events. It was owing to the good offices of the mayor that the Socialist obtained the use of the town-hall for his meeting. The good offices of the mayor were afforded in consequence of the appointment of his friend, Mr. Hare, to the registrarship at A——. The appointment of Mr. Hare to the registrarship was made by the Right Hon. Fox Wigley, member of her Majesty's most honourable privy council, that gentleman having determined to make another attempt to secure the representation of A——, and being anxious to obtain the support of so influential a man as the president of the Socialist lodge.

"Thus unconsciously was the thoughtless Liberal doing the work of Satan, and prostituting his talent and station to the vilest uses. And thus, in the selfish pursuit of power, was he spreading abroad the most pestilent doctrines of anarchy and atheism, and contributing to ruin the souls of hundreds of his fellow-men."—*Charles Lever*, pp. 104, 105.

Again, in one of the books at the head of this article, "The Forest of Arden," the workings of a mob are thus strikingly pondered, analyzed, and referred to the real principles of operation.

" It may be questioned why Friar John should interest himself in any movement in favour of the Abbot of Merevale; but though active amongst the people, he was only the tool of others more designing even than himself, who kept aloof in the background, themselves partly abetting the designs of the Pope, and partly using the Pope's name and authority to forward their own schemes and interests. Thus always in politics there are a multitude of wheels within wheels, counter-checking and cooperating with each other; while the prime mover is no individual human agent, but the combination of human power and feeling, either guided by the direct providence of God, or permitted for his good purposes to exercise an influence in the affairs of men."—*Forest of Arden*, p. 136.

This "Forest of Arden," from which we have just been quoting, is Mr. Gresley's last, but certainly not his *least*, contribution to our stock of *didactic fiction*. Viewed as a tale, it is a most pleasing one—the characters and the incidents being selected with admirable judgment. As far as it presents us with a picture of the manners of the time in which the scene is laid, we can vouch for its liveliness, and see no reason to doubt its accuracy. Let our readers judge of the following description of a dinner-party in the reign of the bluff King Harry.

" While the domestics are employed in serving up the dinner, we will take the opportunity of briefly describing the apartment in which it was spread, with its accompaniments and decoration. Dame Margaret Neville, like many other widow ladies, was a little fastidious with regard to the proprieties of social life; and, as her entertainments were not frequent, she made a point of having every thing in the best order; so that we must take her household and establishment as a favourable specimen of the style of the day.

"The hall in which the table was spread was tolerably spacious, and rather long in proportion to its width; one end of it was occupied by a staircase, which led into the upper parts of the house, and was guarded, not by open balusters, but by solid walls or parapets. The roof was open-work of carved oak, the beams being arched, and resting on sculptured corbels. The end opposite to the staircase was adorned by a piece of handsome tapestry, representing a stag at bay, which had cost the good lady of Bentley many years of diligent labour: other portions of the walls were ornamented with pieces of old armour, and swords, and bucklers, bows and arrows, tastefully arranged in various devices; and in the centre was a magnificent pair of antlers, from one of the branches of which hung the silver bugle which on the preceding day had been presented to Maurice by the queen of the forest. But the greater portion of the wall was covered with hangings of green say or baize, which the taste of the good lady had relieved, according to the custom of the day, with stripes of red—giving the hangings, one would think, something of the appearance of a horse-cloth.

"The sombre furniture, though in winter it must have looked gloomy, was not unpleasing to the eye, on entering from the glare of summer noon-day. The length of the side opposite the door was relieved also by the spacious chimney, occupied, as there was no fire, by shining andirons, or dogs, on which in winter rested the blazing wood, but which were now adorned with a profusion of green boughs and flowers. On the opposite side of the room was a projecting bay-window, in which was a carved table of cypress wood. In one respect the care of Dame Margaret was conspicuous; for whereas in many houses of that age the halls were strewed with grass or rushes, which were suffered to remain so long that they became little better than the litter in a stable, the floor of the hall in Bentley Manor was laid with tiles of different colours, beautifully polished; and the part occupied by the table was spread with clean mats of rushes.

"The descent of Dame Neville and Mistress Alice from the upper apartments into the hall was the signal for dinner to commence.

"The dinner-table itself, or as it might most properly be called the hospitable *board*, was literally a long narrow tablet formed of oak-planks, and placed on tressels, or movable legs. This was the ordinary dinner-table of the day. But the mistress of Bentley was more fortunate than her neighbours, in possessing some pieces of damask naperie, which her eldest son had brought with him as a present from Flanders. These being spread on the table, served to cover the bare boards, and conceal the homely nature of the table itself,—a fashion which it has been found convenient to revive in more modern days. We must not forget to mention the seats which were placed for the guests. There were two richly carved Flemish chairs; one of which was occupied by the good dame, who sat at the top of the table; the other, placed at her right hand, was appropriated to Hugh Latimer, as the most dignified person in company. The rest of the party sat on very plain oaken chairs, with straight backs, which, inconvenient as they may appear to us, were at that time a luxurious substitute for the joint-stools of former generations.

"The repast itself was such as might have satisfied even a modern gourmand. There was a dish of very fine carp, stewed with black sauce; a prime haunch of venison, with frumenty; capons, quails; and divers smaller dishes, such as jellies, and various preparations of cream and milk; all these, garnished with rosemary and other sweet herbs, were placed in a single row down the middle of the table, which was much too narrow for side or corner dishes,—so narrow, indeed, that the guests could not sit exactly opposite each other without the danger of treading on one another's toes.

"Dame Margaret had brought out for the occasion her richest plate, which consisted of several massive pots and flagons. These were filled with various beverages, as metheglin; bracket, a preparation of ale with honey; and, instead of the ippocras, or mulled wine, which was the favourite beverage, the good lady had judiciously chosen, on account of the heat of the weather, to substitute a cool preparation of mortified claret. The ladies, when they required to drink, received a portion from the pots or flagons in small silver cups, while the male portion of the company drank from the pots themselves. On the whole, my readers will be disposed to think that Dame Margaret's dinner was not to be despised. There was, however, one serious drawback, which, to modern ears, will sound extraordinary—*they had no forks.* Perhaps it will be supposed that we mean, no silver forks; a deficiency which (till within the last century) might perhaps have been not unfrequently met with in the houses of country gentlemen. But, no—they had no forks at all; knives they had, with tolerably broad points, and spoons; but forks were not then invented. How Maurice Neville managed to carve that delicate slice of venison which he is just sending to the fair Alice, or how the young lady is to convey it to her mouth, I can no more explain, than I could tell how a Chinese can eat his dinner of rice with two little sticks about the size of knitting-pins. If my readers draw the conclusion that Alice Fitzherbert must have eaten her dinner in a very ungenteel manner, I can only assure them that she did no worse than the accomplished Anne Boleyn, or the stately Catherine of Arragon herself.

"Dame Margaret did not think it necessary to have a second course served up—it was not customary; but as a sort of substitute (or perhaps rather it may have been the origin of second courses,) when the venison was removed, a serving-man brought up from the kitchen a broach, or spit, on which were a brace of partridges, hot from the fire. These were handed round on the spit to the company in succession, who helped themselves as they felt disposed."—Pp. 104—108.

Again, take the following, as we doubt not, most characteristic scene.

" On entering the church, a scene presented itself which to his eyes was rather unusual. In the side-aisle, near the door, stood a desk, on a slight elevation, and on this a massive Bible was fixed by an iron chain: a good number of people were gathered around, one of whom was engaged in reading with an audible voice, the rest listening with attention. Master Arnold (for so we must now call the ex-abbot) immediately took his seat amongst the group, not at all displeased with their occupation, though he observed with dissatisfaction a certain irreverence in the tone in which the holy book was read, and the careless postures in which the listeners were disposed. After a while the reader was tired, and resigned his place to a sour-featured man, who began to read in a still more irreverent and disagreeable tone.

" He had not proceeded far, before a single bell rang for the daily prayers, and the officiating priest entered the church from the vestry; but perceiving the reader still continuing his occupation, he said with courtesy, as he passed, 'I must now beg of you, good master, to desist for a while from your reading, since the hour is arrived for the service of prayer; and I rejoice to see so goodly a congregation.'

" 'Why, how now, Master Mumble-matins?' said the reader, in a contemptuous tone; ' thinkest thou we have come here to listen to thy canting service, when we can draw for ourselves from the cistern of living water?'

" ' My friend,' said the priest calmly, ' let every thing be done in due order. Thou hast done a good work in reading God's word to the people; and now is the time to offer up prayers, in order to beseech God's blessing upon ourselves and His word.'

" ' I tell thee, Sir Priest,' said the other, with a dogged air, ' the king hath given orders that the Bible shall be read in all churches; and I will read it, in spite of thee or any of thy brother shavelings. They who choose to listen to thy anti-christian mummery may do as they please; and I shall do as I please.'

" So saying, this *humble-minded* Christian continued to read in even a louder voice than before; while Master Arnold, much wondering in his mind, accompanied the priest towards the altar, to join in the service of prayer. The church being but a small one, the greatest inconvenience arose from the sound of the two voices occupied in different ways; and the good ex-abbot was much scandalized by the irreverent exhibition, so different from the solemn unison with which the choir at Merevale had been used to chant the sacred service.

"The prayers being over, Arnold departed immediately from the church, and returned to the hostelry, in order to take some refreshment before proceeding on his journey: but here his feelings were destined to undergo another severe shock. On entering the guests'-room, which was tolerably filled, he found two persons engaged in a violent and angry altercation. One, who had the stronger voice and firmer nerve, was laying down his opinion in a dogmatical tone; while the other, with the vexed and petulant air of a disputant who has the worst of the argument, from his own unskilfulness, was unsuccessfully seeking opportunity to retort the biting words of his opponent. On the table before them were cups and flagons; and it was evident, from their flushed cheeks and heated brows, that both had been drinking more than enough. Several of the other guests were gathered round them, listening to their eager dispute, and taking part with one or the other, according to their respective views and sentiments.

"'Talk not to me,' said the one, 'of thy consecrated fonts and holy water. I tell thee, thou mightest just as well christen thy child in a tub of water at home, or in a ditch by the way, as a font at the church. What is a font but a vessel to hold water? And, for the matter of that, what is a church but a building to keep folks from rain while they listen to the preaching of the word? And all your singing of masses, and matins, and evensong, what is it but roaring, howling, whistling, conjuring, mumming, and juggling?'

"The poor man to whom all this was addressed, in vain endeavoured to put in a word of rejoinder.

"'And what is she whom you papists call the Holy Virgin Mary? why no better than another woman: and if she was once, she is now dead and gone, and like a bag of saffron or pepper when the spice is out. And the mass itself, what is it but'——

"Here the speaker went on to utter words respecting the holy sacrament which we will not venture to transcribe. Deeply indeed was the worthy abbot moved when he heard the holiest mysteries of the christian faith—mysteries which lie hid in the bottomless depth of the wisdom and glory of God, and to which our human imbecility cannot attain—handled thus irreverently; names uttered in angry invective at which every knee should bow; and the sacred word of God quoted by men whose spirit was full of strife and bitterness.

"'Sirs, sirs,' said he, unable to restrain his feelings, 'let me beseech you to cease this altercation. Such holy mysteries were not revealed to be the subjects of angry strife, but to be thought on and spoken of with becoming reverence. Let me intreat you, in the name of Him whose servants we all are, to cease to speak of them thus rudely.'

"This was said in a tone which arrested the attention of the disputants; but they were not in a mood to benefit by the pious counsel.

"'Ha,' said one of them, 'who art thou? Who made thee a ruler and a judge over us? Some shaveling monk, I warrant, turned out of his nest to get an honest livelihood, instead of battening in idleness.'

"'And if he be a monk,' said the other, availing himself of the momentary pause, 'I doubt not he is an honest man—better, anyhow, than a heretic like thee.'

"'Heretic, forsooth!' said the first; 'I'll teach thee to call one of thy betters a heretic:' and with that he took up an empty flagon by the handle, and would have hurled it at his opponent's head, had not Arnold arrested his arm, and perhaps saved the other from some serious injury."—Pp. 144—148.

Our readers may perhaps have gathered, from this last extract,— what they will find pervading the whole book, and what gives it much of its value,—that Mr. Gresley takes a temperate and well-balanced view of the Reformation. He is too learned and accurate a thinker to fall into the common error, which indeed is incompatible with his principles, of regarding that event as the foundation of our Church. He is too well aware of the imperfection of all with which man is permitted to mingle, to look on it with idolatry, and to set it up as a perfect standard for the church in all ages. At the same time, he is too practical a man—has too much reverence for that which his immediate fathers have delivered to, and which has the first authority over him, and has too scriptural a turn of mind,—not to see the putting forth of God's power and glory which were apparent in our Reformation. Because the leading Reformers, called by the great Head of the Church to one great and holy work, were not mentally and morally qualified for every other, he neither disparages what, by the grace of God, they were permitted to do, nor enters, otherwise than most thankfully, upon the harvest of their labours. He cannot bring himself to think it a light matter that the Word should have been unsealed—that the exceeding spirituality of God's law should have been proclaimed from the housetops—that hewers of wood and drawers of water should have been raised (as eventually they have been) so far above the level of their former conceptions—that the leaven of paganism should have been expelled (as we trust for ever) from our Church—that her majestic services should be performed in a tongue that is understood—that the volume of eternal life should be put into the hands of the poor and the heavy-laden. These things, he feels to be of God, and he looks on them with holy thankfulness, though as fully aware as any decrier of the Reformation, that man's rebellious will often perverted and profaned it—that sin made that which was good the minister of evil—that the purification of the church became the occasion of schisms, and the offering men their rightful heritage tempted many to hideous sacrilege. Thus nobly free, as it is, from one-sidedness, we should be glad to recommend the "Forest of Arden" to our readers — supposing it had no other merit—as exhibiting the best and completest view of the English Reformation we ever fell in with.

Mr. Paget's excellent Tales of the Village, "The Fairy Bower," and "The Lost Brooch," two delightful tales—"Sintram," a most exquisite northern romance—and "Rutilius and Lucius," admirable Roman tales, are lying before us; but they open too large and diversified a field to be entered on now; and our readers must wait for our detailed opinion of them till next month.

The Kingdom of Christ delineated, in Two Essays, on our Lord's own Account of His Person, and of the Nature of His Kingdom, and on the Constitution, Powers, and Ministry of a Christian Church, as appointed by Himself. By RICHARD WHATELY, D.D. *Archbishop of Dublin.* 1 vol. 8vo. London: Fellowes, 1841.

WE are aware, painfully so, of the difficulties of the task which we are undertaking. Feelings of reverence and respect, the impossibility of disconnecting altogether the office from the man, and yet more, the scandal of making ourselves personal opponents of a Bishop of the Church,—if these, and kindred associations, stood alone, we would be content to remain silent, even at the hazard of being thought incapable of a reply by one towards whom to employ criticism, and controversy, and rebuke, seems as unnatural as invective against a parent. We do not say that in a healthier state of the Church there is no remedy and no court of appeal in such a case; but although we find ourselves in a false position, we ought to pause before we snatch up the first weapon of offence which offers, even though every rivet be unclasped, and each plate unsound, of the mail which covers an episcopal breast. Come what may of it, for ourselves, and in the long run perhaps for the Church, as a rule it is well for us to " hold our tongue, and speak nothing ; to keep silence, yea, *even from good words;* though it be pain and grief to us." It may be in us dutiful to submit to almost anything from the Bishops of the Church. Reverence unnerves the arm, as did love that of the gallant Cid —:

" Je cours à mon supplice, et non pas au combat ;
Et ma fidèle ardeur sait bien m'ôter l'envie,
Quand *vous* cherchez ma mort, de défendre ma vie."

This is, we take it, the true Church principle; and this is probably the reason why so little public notice has been taken of Archbishop Whately's theological works. But this shrinking from the controversy on our part has been misunderstood; because no answer has been given to his Grace, it is concluded that no answer can be given ; and we are posted for cowards, when it may be that it has cost a greater struggle not to fight than to fight with such an opponent.

" I may appeal to the strongest of all external confirmations—the testimony of opponents—who have never, to the best of my knowledge, ever attempted any refutation of the reasons I have adduced. I have never seen even an attempted refutation of any of those arguments. It cannot be alleged that they are not worth noticing; since, whether intrinsically weak or strong, the reception they have met with from the public indicates their having had some influence. . . . These arguments, though it is not for me to say that they are unanswerable, have certainly been hitherto, as far as I know, wholly unanswered, even by those who continue to advocate opposite conclusions. Should it be asked why they do not abandon those conclusions, or else attempt a refutation of the reasons urged against them? *that* is evidently not a question for me, but for them to answer. . . . All that I wish to invite notice to is, the confirmation that is afforded to the conclusiveness of arguments to which no answer is attempted, even by those who continue to maintain doctrines at variance with them."—*Preface*, pp. vi.—xi.

This note of defiance scarcely leaves the Church an alternative: willingly, as heretofore, would we have refused to accept the taunt: and it is with the most sincere pain that we allude in any other way than with respectful deference and ready obedience, or if not this, with silent sorrow, to the words of those who sit in Moses' seat.

Now of the two indirect evidences of the truth of his arguments, which the Archbishop produces, we have disposed of one; the silence of those whom he opposes may arise from an intensity of grief which is speechless, and unwillingness is not always the same as incapacity, either in worldly or in religious polemics. And of the second topic of self-gratulation to which allusion is made, "the reception they have met with from the public," we need only remind the writer of a certain treatise on Logic:—

"The applause of *one's own party* is a very unsafe ground for judging of the real force of an argumentative work, and consequently of its real utility."—*Elements of Logic*, p. 175, 4th edit.

There is nothing so consolatory to an earnest spirit as the treatment which, for the most part, the great revival of catholic truth has met at the hands of the rulers of the Church. We know that in some quarters it is usual to account for this upon grounds of policy; as though it were the highest virtue in a Bishop, if not to have, at least to express, no definite views at all; and that his chief excellence were cleverly to trim the balance between existing controversies, without committing himself by risking an opinion either way. Such a view is as unworthy of the sacred order of Bishops as it is thankless to Him who will "guide us into all truth." All things considered, it is a matter of wonder, if we may so say, that God has ruled circumstances hitherto so peaceably, that His Church has "joyfully served Him in all godly quietness." The true reason is very deep and solemn: the unruly wills and affections of sinful men we see constantly calmed, and soothed, and sanctified, by the grace of ordination; careless boys are mellowed down into thoughtful and improving deacons; and if this be so with the lower ranks of the Church, and if, in general, the sense of privilege and responsibility bring its own blessing and unearthly strength with it, we might, by strong faith in Christ's abiding presence, reckon with confidence upon what we have hitherto been largely, of course not entirely, blessed with—an orthodox synod of Bishops. And in the "unhappy divisions" which are among us, let us do justice to the Bishops personally. Let us recall the state of things in which we found ourselves ten years ago. We were all pupils, to express it with the least possible offence, of an indifferent school—

"Ætas parentum pejor avis tulit
Nos nequiores"—

doctrine was perilled—discipline scouted—the whole tone of the Church lowered—ourselves ignorant of our position, our resources, our strength—careless of our duties, either in preserving or transmitting the deposit of our inheritance, the great heir-looms which reminded us of apostolic ancestors: while the wild boar was gnashing his teeth, it was not so much that we were incapable as ignorant of the means of defence. And then came the change. We know, from the experience of the Reformation period, what the breaking up of men's minds involves; and it is useless to deny that the chief object of the catholic movement was to unsettle and stir deeply the popular religionism of the times. Change for good, as well as for evil, so far as it is change, has in it doubtful tendencies. Strange plants grow upon ground when it is first exposed to light and air after being buried for centuries. It requires time for the mind to become acclimatized. One temper will be too forward, and with unnatural rapidity run to seed—immature seed; and another is overtaken by autumn frosts before it has flowered. The chief husbandmen have no easy task in this state of transition. Their duty is to pause. Accusations of party feeling are so easily made, and with so great difficulty refuted, that what common and shallow minds mistake for timidity, is often in our rulers the truest caution. It were not to be wished, as a rule, that any individual, not even a Bishop, should set himself at the head of a great movement. It is one of the surest notes of truth that, as in our own case in these times, the energies of a Church are developed not by individual teaching or example, not by the eloquence or influence of this or of that man; but rather in a simultaneous and unaccountable change; the movement is *ab intra.* It is a certain mark of spiritual influence that " we hear the sound thereof, *but cannot tell whence it cometh.*" Heresies are always individualized; without Arius or Paul of Antioch—without Calvin or Knox—without Wesley or Irving—the whole system falls in ruins: not so with catholic truth; it has a deeper, firmer foundation than any one doctor or scribe. This is the true sense in which we are to " call no man master upon earth." Rather than repine that the Bishops have not distinctly taken a side, we ought to rejoice at it. Hitherto to have done so, might have looked like partizanship, and we have at least this most cordial satisfaction, that their condemnations have been rather of misconceptions of catholic truth than of that truth itself.*

But in the midst of all our thankfulness for this thoughtful reserve on the part of our spiritual rulers, now, as ever, will occur some especial contrariety, which ought to make us prize more reverentially not only the meekness, but the orthodoxy of the majority. We bring ourselves to discuss this matter with great difficulty and serious pain; yet if it be a duty, we trust, while protesting against the mistakes, or if need be (*quod Deus avertat*), the heresy of one Bishop, to preserve the most dutiful respect for the holy office itself, and yet more, with implicit

---

* While we are writing, a remarkable illustration of this point occurs in Mr. Williams's " Remarks on the Charge of the Bishop of Gloucester and Bristol, on the subjects of Nos. 80 and 87 of Tracts for the Times," which, as we understand, his Lordship has most cheerfully acknowledged.

deference " to follow with a glad mind and will their godly admonitions, submitting ourselves to their godly judgments."

Archbishop Whately has been known as a writer on subjects of theology and science for many years. We believe him to be thoroughly in earnest; he writes honestly, and from the heart: he has done good service to the cause of serious religion; and even his great fault, indifference to authority, imparts to all his works the charm of freshness and reality, which are very striking. He is always sincere. Of his doctrinal authority, some of our readers may not be prepared for the following evidence. It is, we know, an ungracious task to unearth errors which may be partially disavowed; but when we find writers, even though they be Bishops, representing the (supposed) failure of the appeal to catholic decisions, as " recalling to one's mind the case of Haman (! l) and the result of his jealousy of Mordecai "—(*Essay* ii. *on the Kingdom of Christ*, p. 145)—it may not be indecent to inquire into the character of one who can thus, with something like chuckling, place his own brethren in the place of Haman, and can compare the unexpected success of the enemies of that Church of which he is himself a Bishop, with the triumph of Mordecai. To meet the charge of schism (" they are the immediate authors of schism,"—(*Ibid.* p. 118, note t,)—it is fair to oppose something not very different from heresy; and if the Archbishop summarily describes what he calls " the system" of his opponents, as "radically wrong throughout; based on false assumptions, supported by none but utterly fallacious reasoning, and leading to the most pernicious consequences" (*Ibid.* pref. p. x.); it will not be reckoned intrusive to examine the qualifications of one who, from his office alone, is, by God's permission, suffered to pronounce censure upon truths, to understand which spiritually, he seemed, at least during his presbyterate, to have been incapacitated. We may be permitted, by simple juxtaposition, to show either that the Archbishop holds, or has held, opinions, which have been condemned by general councils; or which, in this division of the Western Church, he entertains in common with a writer on whom the brand of censure has burned to a memorable depth.

Elements of Logic, p. 291, 1st edit.

" Person—has a peculiar theological sense, more closely connected with its etymology. It is well known that the Latin word *persona* signified, originally, a *mask*, which actors wore on the stage; each of which being painted in each instance suitably to the character to be represented, and worn by every one who acted the part, the word came to signify the character itself, which the actor played; and afterwards, any character, proper or assumed, which any one sustained; as *e. g.* in a passage of Cicero :—' Tres personas unus suscipio — meam, adversarii, judicis "— *Persona*, in its classical sense, was na-

" Neither CONFOUNDING THE PERSONS, nor dividing the substance."— Confession of our Christian faith, commonly called the *Creed of St. Athanasius.*

" The three creeds ought thoroughly to be received and believed," &c.— *Art.* viii.

" Personam sine essentiâ concipi non posset; nisi statueris personam in divinis nihil aliud esse, quam merum

turally adopted by theologians to distinguish the Father, the Son, and Holy Spirit, in the Blessed Trinity, so as to imply the Unity of the Divine Being, who is all and each of them; and the word Person was adopted by our divines in the same sense as a literal, or rather an etymological, translation of the Latin word *persona*. . . . In the Catechism, our Church sets before us the relations in which the Most High stands towards us, of Maker, Redeemer, and Sanctifier."

Elements of Logic, p. 325, 4th edit.

" —— notion of the word Person in common use, wherein the same man may be said to sustain divers capacities—the same man may at once sustain the person of a king and a father, if he be invested both with *regal* and *paternal* authority."—*Adopted from Wallis.*

Ibid. p. 330.

" Scripture teaches us (and our Church Catechism directs our attention to these points) to believe in God, who, *as* the Father, *hath made* us and all the world,—*as* the Son, *hath redeemed* us and all mankind,—*as* the Holy Ghost, *sanctifieth* us, and all the elect people of God."—*Adopted from Hawkins' Manual.*

Sermons by R. Whately, Archbishop of Dublin. 1835. p. 203.

" The belief of God's being revealed to us in these characters (which was anciently the ordinary sense in our language of the word Person) —as standing in three relations to us,— there can be no doubt that this is what was conveyed, and therefore must have been intended to be conveyed, to ordinary, unphilosophical Christians," &c.

Essay ii. *sect*. 15, *On the Constitution of a Christian Church*, (*Kingdom of Christ,*) p. 100.

" Among the things excluded from the christian system, we are fully authorized to include all subjection of the christian world, permanently and from generation to generation, to some one spiritual ruler (whether an individual man or a Church), the delegate, representation, and vicegerent of Christ ; whose authority should be binding on the conscience of all, and decisive on

τρόπον ὑπάρξεως, quod plane Sabellianum est."—*Bull. Def. Fid. Nic.* iv. 1, 7, p. 696, vol. v.

" Theodoret describes the Sabellians as professing one person, ἐν μὲν τῇ παλαιᾷ ῾ΩΣ πατέρα νομοθετῆσαι, ἐν δὲ τῇ καινῇ ῾ΩΣ υἱὸν ἐνανθρωπῆσαι."— *Pearson on the Creed*, Art. iii. note (c), vol. ii. p. 194.

—δογματίζει οὗτος (Sabellius) καὶ οἱ ἀπ᾽ αὐτοῦ Σαβελλιανοὶ τὸν αὐτὸν εἶναι Πατέρα, τὸν αὐτὸν Υἱὸν, τὸν αὐτὸν εἶναι ἅγιον Πνεῦμα· ὡς εἶναι ἐν μιᾷ ὑποστάσει τρεῖς ὀνομασίας. — *Epiphan. Hæres.* lxii. 1.

Quin et varius, et a seipso discrepans videtur Sabellius fuisse, ut interdum tres personas tres quasi partes totius alicujus esse diceret: aliàs unam et eandem personam pro divinis functionibus (ἐνεργείαις) diversa vocabula sortitam. —*Petavius. Dogm. Theol.* tom. ii. l. i. c. vi. s. 6.

—ἐπεὶ τόν γε ἀνυπόστατον τῶν προσώπων ἀναπλασμὸν οὐδὲ ὁ Σαβέλλιος παρῃτήσατο, εἰπὼν τὸν αὐτὸν θεὸν ἕνα τῷ ὑποκειμένῳ ὄντα, πρὸς τὰς ἑκάστοτε παραπιπτούσας χρείας μεταμορφούμενον, νῦν μὲν ὡς Πατέρα, νῦν δὲ ὡς Υἱὸν, νῦν δὲ ὡς Πνεῦμα ἅγιον διαλέγεσθαι.—*Basil. Ep.* ccx.

The general council of Constantinople, can. vii. A.D. 381, decreed that the Sabellians were to be received as pagans.

Μοντανιστὰς καὶ Σαβελλιανοὺς— ὡς ῞Ελληνας δεχόμεθα."—*Labbe*, ii. p. 951.

Hoadly—Sermon before the King, p. 11.

" As the Church of Christ is the kingdom of Christ, He Himself is King ; and in this it is implied that He is Himself the sole lawgiver to his subjects, and Himself the sole Judge of their behaviour in the affairs of conscience and eternal salvation, and in this sense, therefore, His kingdom is not of this world ; that He hath in those points left behind Him no visible every point of faith. Jesus himself, who told his disciples 'that it was expedient for them that he should go away, that he might send them another Comforter who should abide with them for ever,' could not possibly have failed, had such been his design, to refer them to the man, or *body of men*, who should, in perpetual succession, be the depositary of this divine consolation and supremacy. And it is wholly incredible that He Himself should be perpetually spoken of and alluded to as the Head of his Church, without any reference to any supreme Head on Earth, as fully representing Him and bearing universal rule in his name,—whether Peter or any other Apostle, or any successor of one of these,—this, I say, is utterly incredible, supposing the Apostles or their Master had really designed that there should be for the universal Church any institution answering to the oracle of God under the Old Dispensation, at the Tabernacle or the Temple.

"The Apostle Paul, in speaking of miracles as 'the signs of an Apostle,' evidently implies that no one NOT possessing such miraculous gifts as his, much less without possessing any at all,—could be entitled to be regarded as even on a level with the Apostles; yet he does not, by virtue of that his high office, claim for himself, or allow to Peter or any other, supreme rule over all the Churches. And while he claims and exercises the right to decide authoritatively on points of faith and of practice on which he had received express revelations, he does not leave his converts any injunction to apply, hereafter, when he shall be removed from them, to the Bishop or Rulers of any other Church, for such decisions; or to any kind of permanent living oracle to dictate to all Christians in all ages. Nor does he ever hint at any subjection of one Church to another, singly, or to any number of others collectively;—to that of Jerusalem, for instance, or of Rome; or to any kind of General Council.

"It appears plainly from the sacred narrative, that though the many Churches which the Apostles founded were branches of one *Spiritual* Brotherhood, of which the Lord Jesus Christ is the Heavenly Head,—though human authority, no vicegerents, who can be said properly to supply His place; no interpreters upon whom His subjects are absolutely to depend; no judges over the consciences or religion of His people."

Hoadly—Sermon before the King,
p. 16.

"If, therefore, the Church of Christ be the kingdom of Christ, it is essential to it, that Christ Himself be the sole lawgiver and sole judge of His subjects, in all points relating to the favour or displeasure of Almighty God; and that all His subjects, in what station soever they may be, are equally subjects to Him; and that no one of them, any more than another, has authority either to make new laws for Christ's subjects, or to impose a sense upon the old ones, which is the same thing; or to judge, censure, or punish the servants of another master in matters relating purely to conscience, or eternal salvation. If any person has any other notion, either through a long use of words with inconsistent meanings, or through a negligence of thought, let him but ask himself, whether the Church of Christ be the kingdom of Christ, or not? And if it be, whether this notion of it doth not absolutely exclude all other legislators or judges in matters relating to conscience, or the favour of God; or whether it can be His kingdom, if any mortal man have such a power of legislation and judgment in it?

Ibid. p. 26.

"No one of Christ's subjects is lawgiver and judge over others of them in matters relating to salvation, but He alone."

Ibid. p. 14.

"When any men upon earth make any of their own declarations, or decisions, to concern and affect the state of Christ's subjects with regard to the favour of God; this is so far taking Christ's kingdom out of His hands, and placing it in their own. Nor is this matter at all made better by their declaring themselves to be vicegerents, or law-makers, or judges under Christ, in order to carry on the ends of His kingdom."

there was 'one Lord, one Faith, one Baptism,' for all of them, yet they were each a distinct, independent community *on Earth*, united by the common principles on which they were founded, and by their mutual agreement, affection and respect; but not having any one recognised Head on Earth, or acknowledging any sovereignty of one of these Societies over others.

"And as for—so-called—General Councils, we find not even any mention of them, or allusion to any such expedient. The pretended first Council, at Jerusalem, does seem to me a most extraordinary chimera, without any warrant whatever from Sacred History.

P. 105. "On the whole, then, considering in addition to all these circumstances, the number and the variety of the Epistles of Paul, (to say nothing of those of the other Apostles) and the deep anxiety he manifests for the continuance of his converts in the right faith, and his earnest warnings of them against the dangers of their faith, which he foresaw; and considering also the incalculable importance of such an institution (supposing it to exist) as a permanent living oracle and supreme Ruler of the Church, on Earth; and the necessity of pointing it out so clearly that no one could possibly, except through wilful blindness and obstinacy, be in any doubt as to the place and persons whom the Lord should have thus 'chosen to cause his name to dwell' therein—especially, as a plain reference to this infallible judge, guide, and governor, would have been so obvious, easy, short, and decisive a mode of guarding against the doubts, errors, and dissensions which he so anxiously apprehended;—considering, I say, all this, it does seem to me a perfect moral impossibility, that Paul and the other sacred writers should have written, as they have done, without any mention or allusion to any thing of the kind, if it had been a part (and it must have been a most *essential* part, if it were any) of the Christian System. They do not merely omit all reference to any supreme and infallible Head and Oracle of the Universal Church,—to any Man or Body, as the representative and vicegerent of Christ, but they omit it in such a manner, and under such circumstances, as plainly to amount to an exclusion.

"It may be added that the circumstance of our Lord's having *deferred* the Commencement of his Church till after his own *departure* in bodily person, from the Earth, seems to have been designed as a further safeguard against the notion I have been alluding to. Had He publicly presided in bodily person subsequently to the completion of the Redemption by his death, over a Church in Jerusalem or elsewhere, there would have been more plausibility in the claim to *supremacy* which might have been set up and admitted on behalf of that Church, and of his own successors in the Government of it. His previously withdrawing, made it the more easily to be understood that He was to remain the spiritual Head in Heaven, of the spiritual Church-universal; and consequently of all particular Churches, equally, in all parts of the world."

These are the four propositions on which the celebrated Committee of Convocation drew up their representation "on the dangerous positions and doctrines contained in the Bishop of Bangor's Preservative and Sermon." But the whole matter seems so curious, that we are tempted to pursue the parallel, and contrast the Archbishop of 1841 with the Bishop of 1717 a little more closely. How far the Church may derive instruction from the example of our fathers, it is for us to lay to heart seriously.

Archbishop Whately's first Position, p. 3.

"1. The most obvious course would be, to appeal, in the first instance, to that founder himself, and to consider what account He gave of his own character, and that of his kingdom. He (Christ) must have understood the principles of the religion He was divinely commissioned to introduce."

And after applying this principle to our Lord's declaration that "He was the Son of God," the Archbishop, p. 28, proceeds:—

"2. So now, before Pilate, He asserts His claim to be a king, but declares, that 'His kingdom is not of this world.' The result was, that Pilate acquitted him. It is plain, therefore, that he must have believed, or at least professed to believe, both that the declarations of Jesus were true, and that they amounted to a total disavowal of all interference with the

Hoadly. Sermon, p. 23.

"1. The question with you ought to be, whether He (Christ) did not know the nature of His own kingdom or Church, better than any since His time? Whether you can suppose He left any such matters to be decided against Himself and His own express professions?"

Hoadly. Serm. pp. 10, 11.

"2. Since the image of His kingdom is that under which our Lord himself chose to represent it, we may be sure that if we sincerely examine our notion of His Church by what He saith of His kingdom, 'that it is not of this world,' we shall exclude out of it every thing that He would have excluded."

P. 29. "When you read nothing in

secular government by Himself or his followers, as such."

P. 29. "The declaration that 'Christ's kingdom is not of this world,' amounts to a renunciation of all secular coercion,—all forcible measures in behalf of his religion."

P. 40. "The civil magistrates would *cease* to act on Christian principles,—if they should employ the *coercive power* of civil magistrates *in the cause of Christianity*; [*sic*]—if they should not only take a part in civil affairs, but claim *as* Christians, or as members of a particular church, a *monopoly* of civil rights. It is this, and this only, that tends to make Christ's kingdom "a kingdom of this world."

"This is a distinction which is readily perceived. For instance, there are many well-known societies which no one would, in any degree, call political societies, such as academies for the cultivation of mathematical and other sciences,—agricultural societies,—antiquarian societies, and the like; it would be reckoned silly to ask, respecting any one of these societies, whether the members of it were excluded from taking any part in civil affairs, and whether a magistrate or a legislator could be admitted as a member of it? It would at once be answered, that the society itself, and the members of it *as such*, had nothing to do with political, but only scientific matters;—the provinces of the two societies, *as* societies, are altogether distinct.

"Now, this is just the non-interference in political affairs which Christ and his apostles professed, and taught, and carried into practice, in respect of the religion of the Gospel."

3. Pp. 136—140. "No shadow of proof can be offered, that the Church, —the universal Church,—can possibly give any decision at all;—that it has any constituted authorities, as the organs by which such decisions could be framed or promulgated:—or, in short, that there is, or ever was, any *one community on earth* recognised, or bearing any claim to be recognised, as the universal Church, bearing rule over and comprehending all particular Churches. The Church is undoubtedly one; but not as a society. In short,

His doctrine about His own kingdom, of taking in the concerns of this world and mixing them with those of eternity: no commands that the frowns and discouragements of this present state should in any case attend upon conscience and religion: no orders for the kind and charitable force of penalties, or capital punishment, to make men think and choose aright: no calling upon the secular arm, whenever the magistrate should become Christian, to impose His doctrines, or to back His spiritual authority: but, on the contrary, as plain a declaration as a few words can make, that 'His kingdom is not of this world.'"

Hoadly. Answer to Committee of Convocation, p. 176.
"The office of a civil magistrate respected the good of human society as such only;—as to religion, properly so called, particularly the Christian Religion, it was left by its great Author to other hands, and other arguments than those employed by magistrates."

Id. Sermon, p. 18.
"The sanctions of Christ's law are not the rewards of this world,— not the offices and glories of this state,—not the pains of prisons, banishments, fines, or any lesser or more moderate penalties, — nay, not the much lesser negative discouragements that belong to human society. He was far from thinking that these could be the instruments of such a persuasion, as He thought acceptable to God."

Id. Sermon, p. 12.
3. "Whoever hath an absolute authority to interpret any written or spoken laws, he it is who is truly the lawgiver, and not the person who first wrote or spoke them. He, Christ, never interposes to assert the true interpretation of His law, amidst the various and contradictory opinions of men about it. As He doth not; if such an absolute authority be once lodged with men, under the notion of interpreters, they then become the legislators, and not Christ, and they rule in their own kingdom and not His."

the foundation of the Church by the Apostles was not, properly, the foundation of Christian societies, which occupied them, but the establishment of the principles on which Christians, in all ages, might form societies for themselves."

"The above account is sufficiently established by the mere negative circumstance of the absence of all mention in the sacred writings of any *one* society on earth, having a government and officers of its own, and recognised as the Catholic or universal Church."

P. 17. "The Church of Christ is the number of men, whether small or great, whether dispersed or united, who truly and sincerely are subject to Jesus Christ alone."

P. 24. "The grossest mistakes in judgment about the nature of Christ's kingdom or Church, have arisen from hence, that men have argued from other visible societies, and other visible kingdoms. I speak of the universal invisible Church."

We are far from intending, by these parallel extracts, to say that Archbishop Whately is conscientiously a Sabellian, or an Hoadleian; not he: very likely he knows not what Sabellianism is, nor cares what Hoadly wrote: but this is his very fault; he calls "no man master" but himself, and a worse he could not have chosen. We mean this in no figure of speech, but he absolutely seems fettered to the decisions of himself and his own school. Scornful of the wide domain of catholic truth, he submits implicitly to the " traditions" of his three or four friends: and, jealously anxious that his readers should in all its largeness avail themselves of the " right and duty of judging ultimately for themselves," he overwhelms them with quotations from himself. In fact, in his own opinion, Archbishop Whately is more than two to one better than the whole Church for fifteen hundred years. In the book before us occur sixty-one quotations, of which thirty-one are from his own numerous works, seventeen from Drs. Hinds and Dickinson, his own chaplains, the " Encyclopædia Metropolitana," probably also his own writing; Dr Arnold, Dean Waddington, Bishop Stanley, Professor Powell, [1] Dean Hoare, and Dr. Hawkins; and the thirteen remaining (" one halfpenny-worth of bread to this intolerable deal of sack,") are from such high authorities as Burnet, and Warburton, D'Aubigné, Luther, and Cruden's Concordance! The sad truth is, that the Archbishop is very ignorant; and, like all other ignorant persons, very proud of his own talents; not of his reading, but of what he thinks much better than reading, a clear head, and a sound unprejudiced judgment, and great common sense, as he would call them. And this temper is not only a very unhappy one, but one very difficult to analyze, because his doctrine would be negative, rather than positive. The book before us teaches us-not what to believe, but what to disbelieve: it is not so much " the kingdom of Christ delineated," as " what I think not the kingdom of Christ caricatured." To describe the Church by negatives is not to convey a very vivid picture of it; and yet to represent his Grace faithfully we must do this.'

The kingdom of Christ, according to the Archbishop, then, is not—

1. One, in any real sense: the Church is one society "only when considered as to its *future existence*." p. 13.;—the Apostles did not

found any Christian society upon one invariable model, they contemplated the existence of future societies " formed on similar principles," p. 139 ;—the duty of every Christian " is to submit to the ordinances of the *particular* church of which he is a member," p. 141.

2. Nor is it Catholic; " There is no shadow of proof that the universal Church can possibly give any decision at all: that it has any constituted authorities as the organs by which such decision could be framed or promulged :—or, in short, that there is, or ever was, any *one community on earth* recognised, or having any claim to be recognised as the universal Church," p. 136.

3. Nor is it Apostolic ;—The true " apostolical succession is not of individuals, but of uncorrupted gospel principles," p. 204. " Compliance with the profession of a particular creed, or conformity to a particular mode of worship, must not be *absolutely enforced*," p. 189. Circumstances may arise when "pious laymen, having no regularly-consecrated priest among them, were to agree to choose for that office one of their number, this man would be as truly a priest as if he had been consecrated by all the bishops in the world," p. 265, quoted from Luther. " Such men are not to be shut out from christian ordinances for ever: their circumstances would constitute them a christian community : to make regulations for the Church thus constituted, and to appoint as its ministers the fittest persons that could be found among them, and to celebrate the christian rites, would be productive of union. Ministers thus appointed are, to all intents and purposes, real, legitimate christian ministers: the ordinances of such a Church are valid and efficacious: it is a real christian Church," pp. 190, 191. The ministers of such a Church would rightly claim "apostolical succession, because they would *rightfully hold the same office* which the Apostles conferred on those 'elders whom they ordained in every city,'" p. 192. "A certain Church may, suppose, have originated in a rash separation from another Church on insufficient grounds : but for an individual to separate from it *merely for that reason*, would be not escaping, but incurring, the guilt of schism," p. 195.—What the apostolical "*principles*" are which it is necessary for reformers or seceders to carry with them when they separate from what they consider a corrupt Church we are not told, but we are taught : " If they have among their number christian ministers of several orders, or of one order—if they can obtain a supply of such from some other sound Church—if they can unite themselves to such a Church, these are advantages not to be lightly thrown away. But the unavoidable absence of any of these advantages, not only is not to be imputed to them as a matter of blame, but, by imposing the *necessity*, creates the *right*, and the *duty*, of supplying their deficiencies AS THEY BEST CAN," p. 204. "Reformers have an undoubted right to appoint such orders of christian ministers, and to allow to each such functions as they judge most conducive to the great ends of the society: they may assign to the *whole*, or to a *portion* of them, the office of ordaining others as their successors ; they may appoint *one* superintendent of the rest,

or *several*; under the title of Patriarch, Archbishop, Bishop, Moderator, or any other they may prefer; they may make the appointment of them for life, or for a limited period,—by election, or by rotation,—with a greater, or a less extensive jurisdiction; and they have a similar discretionary power with respect to liturgies, festivals, ceremonies, and whatever else is left discretionary in the Scriptures," p. 205. " It follows from these principles, that the bodies of Christians we have been speaking of, viz.—the Presbyterian Churches —had full power to retain, or to restore, or to originate, whatever form of church-government they, in their deliberate and cautious judgment, might deem best for the time, and country, and persons, they had to deal with, whether exactly similar, or not, to those introduced by the Apostles; provided nothing were done contrary to Gospel-precepts and principles. They were, therefore, perfectly at liberty to appoint Bishops, *even if they had none* that had joined in the Reformation; or to discontinue the appointment, *even if they had*; [*sic*] whichever they were convinced was the most conducive, under existing circumstances, to the great objects of all church-government," p. 208. " They had no reason to hold themselves *absolutely bound* to adhere, always and everywhere, to those original models," p. 209.

In plain words, then, His Grace the Archbishop of Dublin believes in a Church, which is neither 1, ONE, 2, nor CATHOLIC, 3, nor APOSTOLIC. Of the Athanasian Creed we can surmise His Grace's sentiments by the significant marginal note, p. 12. " Metaphysical disquisitions, on abstruse scholastic terms (such as ' consubstantiality,' ' personality,' ' hypostatic union,' ' eternal filiation,') unnecessary;" and we presume that certain clauses of the Apostles' and Nicene Creeds, which speak of the Church as One, Catholic and Apostolic, if not the symbols themselves, stand on no higher authority; since we are told, (p. 75,) " that a systematic creed, or confession of faith, not being found in our Scriptures, was *on purpose* withheld by the Apostles, that other churches, in other ages and regions, might not be led to consider themselves bound to adhere to several formularies that were of local and temporary appointment, but might be left to their own discretion." (!!)

Our readers may perhaps think that we have done enough, and they may now estimate, at his right value, one who, whatever his dignity of office by God's inscrutable purpose, has published flat Sabellianism—has followed the only Bishop of our own Church, who was all but degraded for heresy—thinks the three creeds dispensable matters,—and sneers at the eternal Sonship of the Blessed Word. It may be deemed superfluous, therefore, to mention by way of recapitulation; 1. (what has already been shewn, that) Episcopacy is an accident to, not of the essence of, the Church. 2. The power of the keys is, not " the knowledge of the Scriptures, as St. Chrysostom calls it; nor the interpretation of the law, with Tertullian; nor with Eusebius, the Word of God," to use the " *consensus patrum* " of

Jewell's Apology; not " doctrinally to teach what is bound or loose, or lawful and unlawful," as Lightfoot has it; but, " authority to make, from time to time, to alter, abrogate, or to restore, regulations respecting matters of detail, not expressly mentioned in Scripture," (p. 65;)—or, for choice, " to baptize or not to baptize converts," (p. 66.) 3. "Christianity is a religion without sacrifice, altar, or temple," (p. 95.) 4. " The claims of ministers rest, not on some supposed sacramental virtue, transmitted, from hand to hand, in unbroken succession from the Apostles, but on the fact of those ministers being *regularly-appointed officers of a regular christian community*," (p. 116.) The regular appointment being recognition by a number of individuals " combining themselves into a Christian Society, regulated and conducted, in the best way they can, on Gospel principles," (p. 192.) 5. The necessity of separation from a Church is " our conviction" (upon what, or if upon any grounds, is not stated) that its " doctrines or practice are unscriptural," (p. 193.) 6. " Catholic tradition is the same tradition which our Lord condemned in the Jews," (p. 155.) 7. The foundation of the Reformation was the right to test all doctrines by the Scriptures, *passim.* 8. " Appeals to Catholic decisions superfluous and unsound," (p. 143.) 9. " The appeal to the early Church leads to disquiet, and danger of ultimate infidelity; it is obscure,—uncertain,—disputable,—unstable," (p. 134-5.) 10. The notion of the Church in the XIXth Article, is not of " THE Church, the universal Church," but of " A Church,"* (pp. 114, 150.) 11. The Thirty-nine Articles are " the authoritative confession of the FAITH of our Church," (p. 153,) and this in spite of the title in every prayer book, which calls them " Articles of Religion."

The fundamental defect of Archbishop Whately's mind is pride. We regret to say it, but here is a tolerably-sized volume, the original matter of which formed ordination and visitation charges, and a consecration sermon; on this very sacred occasion could not his Grace have found a more edifying theme? Were it not possible to furnish the novices of the Church's army with more substantial armour? Have they but to defend a Church of shadows, to preach a creed of negations, to minister in " a society" which " circumstances constituted a Christian community?" (p. 190.) A public newspaper just informs us, that the candidates for the ministry in the diocese of Dublin, who were ordained December 3rd,† in addition to the ordinary books, were examined in his Grace's " own

---

* The Archbishop has a strange fancy, that the Articles were first written in Latin, and the English is a translation,—" in some few places, a careless translation, from the Latin." Be it so—how then can his Grace defend his denial of the Christian priesthood, by the title of the *original* Thirty-second Article—De Conjugio SACERDOTUM? or what can his Lordship of Chester make of translating " renatis" by " baptized" in the Ninth Article? The argument was perplexing enough the other way, to the Protestant party, while the English was considered, as it is, the original; when they got over it by denying the authority of the Latin version: how stands it with them, if the Latin is the original?

† What wilful and useless " private judgment " is it to hold ordinations precisely a fortnight before the Church prescribes them! it is easy enough to shew, that you

works on the Christian ministry," and were addressed for two hours on the day of ordination,—after "dining with his Grace,"—of course, on the one subject. Is there no holier preparation for the work of the ministry, than " see my Logic," and " consult my Essay on Omissions," and " see my Sermon," and "listen to me in the Encyclopædia Metropolitana," " refer to my Notions of the Peculiarities of the Christian Religion," and " examine my Disquisition on the Difficulties of the Writings of St. Paul?" Can his Grace find no better list of subjects for a deacon's examination than a " catalogue raisonnée" of Mr. Fellowes' publications: Dr. Hinds, Dr. Hampden, Dr. Arnold, *et id genus omne?* Are the rich pastures of the Church to be neglected for these husks and chips of neology? Would not solemn prayer, and affectionate counsel, and grave encouragement, and paternal advice, have been to the full as edifying, and twice as heartening—to coin a word—as his flippant advertisement of all that the Archbishop of Dublin has written? Could not even the " after dinner" charge ring a holier and a less polemical note?

Truth to say, this book contains no novelty. It is but the *crambe recocta* of what his Grace has said before: the oft-repeated distinction between ἱερεὺς and πρεσβύτερος, of which he is as proud as was Coleridge in marking out " reason " from understanding, is repeated again and again. Dr. Arnold, too, is so fond of it, that he places it in the front of the introduction to his Sermons. What does it amount to? that, strictly speaking, Christ is the only Hiereus in the Church; granted to the full in the sense that the ministers of the Church are not personally Christ Himself; but to say this is not to say that their actions are not His actions: " They do not the same in their own name, but in *Christ's*, and do minister by His commission and authority; the effect of *Christ's* ordinances is not taken away; the sacraments be effectual because of *Christ's* institution and promise." (Acts xxvi.) This is the one great fallacy upon which are founded all the misconceptions of catholic truth. When Catholics speak of the Church, of the sacraments, of the ministry, mere Protestants draw a distinction between the Church and Christ, where Catholics make none; and on this principle, if the Church could be without Christ, if the ministry could be without Him, if the sacraments could be, and yet not be Christ's; then, to speak, as we do, of the Church's voice being God's voice, the absolutions of the Church being the keys of the kingdom of heaven, the sacraments of the Church being the direct conveyance of spiritual life, and the rest, would indeed be, as has been said, " to usurp His place, to perform His acts, to receive His homage, to depose Him from His throne." Truly, if the Church were nothing more than the Archbishop of Dublin represents it, there is indeed in it neither sacrifice nor priest. But if the Church be the society of the faithful, founded by our Lord and Saviour, with promise of

---

can scorn the provision of the Ember days: is it dutiful? is it wise? is it not rather the petulance of a froward child, who does a thing for no other reason than because he is told not to do it?

permanence, "even unto the end of the world," we shall find in the Church, by a perpetual succession, the everlasting continuance, not repetition, of the very same works by which He worked our redemption in the flesh.

(1.) We say, then, if there was "the one sacrifice" on Calvary, that sacrifice will be perpetuated; if "the Word became flesh and dwelt with man," the Church will also dwell among men, in a visible, tangible, accessible form also; and, to use the forcible phrase of a foreign writer (Moehler, Symbolik, vol. ii.), "The Church is Jesus Christ everlastingly renewing Himself, reappearing continually under sensible forms; it is the permanent incarnation of the Son of God. 'The Church, which is His body, the fulness of Him that filleth all in all.'" (Ephes. i. 23.)

Psilo-Protestants admit the one sacrifice; we plead for its continuance. St. Paul—or, as the Archbishop of Dublin and Bishop of Chester delight to style the apostle, Paul—expressly declares (Heb. xiii. 10), "We have an *altar*;" the Lord Jesus Himself intimates that His followers would have an altar,—"If thou bring thy gift to the altar," —and yet we are told, "Christianity is a religion without an altar!"— and surely "altar," as all admit, has "priest and sacrifice" for its correlatives. Besides, St. Peter speaks of our "spiritual sacrifices." In the church at Antioch, we read (Acts xiii. 2), that " they ministered unto the Lord," λειτουργούντων τῷ Κυρίῳ; the very same phrase is used of the Levitical priests, "every priest standeth daily ministering," λειτουργῶν (Heb. x. 11), [which daily ministration, in the case of Zacharias, is called ἱερατεύειν]; the very same phrase is used also of our blessed Lord's own priesthood, "We have such an High Priest—a minister of the sanctuary," τῶν ἁγίων λειτουργὸς, (Heb. viii. 1, 2.) Whatever "the ministering" in the church of Antioch was, we have it now, "Jesus Christ, the same yesterday, to-day, and for ever;" that ministering was a liturgy, or sacrifice; the same liturgy or sacrifice which the temple priests daily ministered; the same liturgy or sacrifice, in kind, which Jesus Christ, "our High Priest," offers. Nor is this all: the prophets, as has been repeatedly shown, spoke of the times of the gospel dispensation, as when "in every place incense unto His name and a pure *offering* should be offered," (Mal. i. 11.) Sacrificial terms, ἀνάμνησις, ἐπιτελεῖν (1 Cor. viii. 6), and, above all, ποιεῖν ("this *do*," in the sense of offer, as is said, "after sacrifice *done*"), are always used in connexion with the Eucharist, which is a proper sacrifice, though a spiritual sacrifice; in which not His substantial, but His sacramental, and therefore in its highest sense, real body and blood, are offered; in which the oblations of bread and wine represent, and therefore continue, though they do not repeat, the one sacrifice on the cross. If, therefore, there be a sacrifice in the Christian Church, there must be priests to offer, and an altar on which to offer it. On this head, we would gladly enlarge, but we trust soon to follow it up by a distinct view of the Christian Priesthood and Sacrifice. So also in other things, this identification of the Saviour with His Church will at once disperse all the Archbishop's false views of the other great points of the christian system, which rest upon the single assumption that they are made channels of grace separate from the Saviour, the sole giver of all grace.

(2.) As " the Word became flesh, and dwelt among us," so we may expect that the gospel is objective still. The incarnation once, and the visible Church since, are alike one and the same prolonged manifestation of the Eternal Son; as the miracles were sensible proofs of His divinity, so the authority of the Church continues the proof of Christ's authority to His people and to the heathen. Miracles ceased when authority was confirmed; and the *historical fact* proves that the result of miracles was thenceforth to be attained by another, and yet the same, way. When, therefore, the Church is slightingly asked to "show her pretensions to divine authority, to produce the 'signs of an apostle,'" (p. 225,) the answer is, The true faith—the unity of the Church—that life which is inseparable from Christ, and if inseparable from Christ, inseparable from His Church,* because He is in his Church, and His Church in Him—the apostolate, which is His presence—the teaching of His word—the communication of His Spirit; these are the perpetual miracles and signs of divinity —these the permanent credentials, the signs and living witnesses of the Indwelling Presence—these the proofs of the certainty of the decisions of the Church—the attestations of the need of a succession to which the promise of everlasting continuance was made, and of an unity which is itself but an essential form of truth. What the Lord and His personal teaching was to His own immediate disciples, the Church and her authoritative teaching are to the baptized Christians; the miracles which He wrought physically, while on earth, He now works spiritually for conviction and for confirmation; there can be as little doubt about the one as about the other. And this is an infallibility, not of individuals, as is pretended by the Archbishop,—nor of the Pope, as the exponent of unity, as the Romanist would urge,—but of the diffused faith of the Church. The "newly-constituted christian communities" of the Archbishop—the "private judgment"—the "right of forming a society under what regulations men thought might best suit the emergencies of the time"—"the irregular formations"—the "temporary expedients" —"the things altogether indifferent, or non-essential," how contradictory are they to the true idea of the Christian Church!

(3.) We may now ascertain what catholic tradition is. The great question is, How do we obtain the true teaching which is able to make us wise unto salvation? How am I to know that I have built upon the true foundation? The common protestant answer is, The infal-

---

* " That they all may be one in Us: *that the world may* believe that Thou hast sent Me: and the glory which Thou gavest Me I have given them; that they may be one, even as We are one. *I in them*, and Thou in Me, that they may be made perfect in one." St. John xvii. 21—23.

libility of holy Scripture; the catholic replies, Holy Scripture as interpreted by the Church. For Scripture in itself is nothing; it is but so many words and sentences: what is its sense? who is to interpret it? what is its meaning? If the church be the body of Christ, His everlasting manifestation, His continual presence on earth, the tabernacle of His Spirit, then the voice of the Church is His voice, dwelling in the hearts of His faithful people, and expressed by the whole body; and in this sense "hath authority in controversies of faith, is a witness and keeper of holy writ," and is possessed of "the RULE" of faith.

(4.) And so also of the Christian ministry—as a divine institution, not as operative in the individual bishop, priest, or deacon: for the very presence of this book of the Archbishop of Dublin, if nothing else, were a sufficient proof that the authority, dignity, power and privilege which we claim for the Christian hierarchy is in the Church's diffused capacity, not in individuals. As before, we said that the visible Church—the one Church—the Church possessed of the authority of teaching, are but conditions of His perpetual presence, as they serve but to realize the great promise, that "He is with us always, even unto the end of the world,"—so this same truth implies a succession, unfolding itself from the original manifestation of the Saviour. Be it that the Church is thus "one with Christ," then it follows that the power of ordination and the priesthood of the sacraments are as inseparable from her, as was the first mission of the twelve from our Lord Himself. As well might the adherents of Theudas have pretended to be apostles of Christ, as they who have neither commission nor succession from Him. Hence it is that "Bishop and Moderator" do not stand on the same ground of expediency: unless the Divine will and man's choice be the same. We do not enter on the Archbishop's hackneyed objection to the Apostolical succession, that flaws *may* have occurred. His Grace is unaware of the fact, but it has been produced and refuted *usque ad nauseam*, and we really have not the heart to reiterate such stale arguments.

And here we pause, and in his Grace's own words, (p. 113,) we say, that, instead of this very simple doctrine, which we have sketched, viz.: that *the Church is the Lord's prolonged spiritual presence upon earth*, which we take the liberty of calling a "clearly-intelligible, well-established, and *accessible* proof of Divine sanction for the claims of our Church," his Grace has "substituted one that is not only obscure, disputable, and out of the reach of the mass of mankind, but even self-contradictory, subversive of our own and every Church's claims, and leading to all the evils of doubt and schismatical division:"—than which sentence there could not be a more just description of the Archbishop's "Kingdom of Christ delineated."

All that we have said has been extorted from us: we have spoken, we repeat it, with great pain. But the times are ominous: we shall soon be called upon to entertain that most fearful question, how far must our duty be strained in accepting, upon questions of *faith*, the decisions of a single bishop?* In the case of the Archbishop of Dublin, does the teaching which we have produced differ from Sabellianism? does this sentence, " that threefold manifestation of God, which we express by the word Trinity," (*Sermons*, p. 190,) fall short of that heresy? is not the prayer, with which the book concludes, (p. 230,) " May all be enabled, under the Divine blessing, to carry into effect more and more fully, and to bring to completion, all the holy desires, all the good counsels, and all the just works *of our reformers*," a reckless adaptation of the liturgical formula? do not his principles open the door of our Zion, or even challenge a more forcible entry from every schismatic? Is it not perfectly appalling to see a Bishop of the Church, which the Lord purchased with His own blood, denying His Master's presence—scorning His ordinances—making light of the only claim, that of office, upon which he can secure a moment's attention—throwing away his own holy unction—selling his birthright of apostolical descent for a mess of pottage, the hollow applause for false liberality, from dissenters of " every denomination," and Socinians, who always, (we assert this from our personal knowledge,) consider him a model of a Christian Bishop? Let every prelate remember the warning,

" Neu *matris* validas in viscera vertite vires."

One word more. In addition to a very proper admonition on the restoration of the order of Deacons, note y, p. 216, (by the bye, Dr. Arnold urges the same thing admirably and forcibly), Archbishop Whately has one observation (p. 268,) in which we cordially concur, " deploring the many evils resulting from the want of a legislative government for the Church." The evils are very great—grievously so. How long it is since the Irish Church met in synod, we do not just now remember; nor can we call to mind the termination of their deliberations; but if the convocation of the province of Dublin are in doubt where to begin, let them commence just where the English convocation left off; their proceedings would form an admirable supplement to Wilkins's Concilia, the last pages of which we earnestly commit to the meditation of Archbishop Whately. That sun would rise with happy auspices in censuring the Archbishop of Dublin,—to adopt a well-known image of the late Mr. Froude,—which set so gloriously in a vain endeavour to condemn Hoadly.† It is but to re-write the notorious Bangorian controversy.

---

* " The highest authorities of the Church cease to exist when they put forth any thing uncatholic. Bishops derive whatever authority they possess from the Church; when therefore they lift up their voices against it, they speak without authority. The Catholic Church gave them authority to enforce her truths, she never empowered them to teach heresy."—*Doctrine of the Catholic Church, on the Holy Eucharist*, p. 5.

† We have taken little notice of the first essay in this volume: it is but an attempt to say again what this same Hoadly said long ago, and said better. Under the colour of showing that our Lord claimed, neither for Himself nor followers, a kingdom like Cæsar's, when He said, " My kingdom is not of this world," the Archbishop draws the conclusion, that if " magistrates should employ the *coercive power* of the civil authority *in the cause of Christianity;* if they should not only take a part

Vox Stellarum; or, A Loyal Almanac for the Year of Human Redemption 1842. *With Astrological Observations on the four Quarters of the Year; and a Hieroglyphic adapted to the Times.* By FRANCIS MOORE, *Physician.* Printed for the Company of Stationers.

The Churchman's Almanac for the Year of our Lord 1842. Published under the Direction of the Committee of General Literature and Education appointed by the Society for Promoting Christian Knowledge.

WE who live in this century of inventions, are very apt to congratulate ourselves, not so much in excelling our ancestors in steaming against wind and tide, floating in iron ships, communicating signals by electricity, increasing the horrors of war by the aid of science, and drawing our features with the pencils of light; as in the nonexistence of superstition and prejudice among us. We congratulate ourselves, because we have no High Commission Court for the trial of witches; because our Queen does not keep an alchemist among her household, or have the nativities of our prince and princess cast by the court astrologer. It is no doubt very comfortable to console ourselves with these reflections as we expend our shillings and sixpences in the purchase of a "Moore's Almanac," a "Murphy's Weather Table," or a "Raphael's Astrological Ephemeris" for the year 1842. The immense circulation of such works as these is an awkward fact in the history of the progress of civilization, when combined with the infinitesimals of Homœopathy, and the manipulations of Mesmerism. Buying is, indeed, one thing, and believing another; but it too often happens that the predisposition to believe preceded the intention of purchasing. Our fathers did so before us.

Without tracing almanacs to the Arabs, through one derivation of the word, or to the ancient Germans, through another, we must admit their existence from very early times. Indeed, if M. Delambre's account of the commentary of Theon on the Almagest be correct, the Alexandrian Greeks in the days of Ptolemy had reduced the formation of almanacs to a science. But to confine ourselves to our

---

in civil affairs, but claim, *as* Christians, or as Members of a particular Church, a *monopoly* of civil rights, they would *cease* to act on Christian principles," p. 40. "The possession and monopoly of civil rights and privileges," p. 34, he declares to be unchristian; and, Note A, p. 234, he protests against "the employment of secular coercion in religious matters, with a view to compel men to conform to that faith and mode of worship prescribed by the civil government, or to give more or less ascendancy and monopoly of civil rights and power to those of a particular persuasion;" and thinks that is making Christ's kingdom "a kingdom of this world," "to exclude Dissenters from all, or from some of the rights of citizens, and reduce, more or less, to the condition of Helots, those who do not profess the religion which the State, as such, enjoins:" in other words, his Grace wishes us to believe that our Lord's declaration sanctioned by anticipation the Roman-Catholic Relief Act: the Test and Corporation Acts; the Jew Bill; the Dissenters' Marriage Act; the tooemphatically *Irish* scheme of Education without Religion; and the admission of Dissenters into the Universities; all of which are mixed up with the "monopoly of civil rights."

Almanacs.

own isle. Our Anglo-Saxon ancestors had their rude and simple records of the good or bad fortune of the different days of the year. They had their tablets, which told them of the weekly feast, the Saint's day, and the lucky and unlucky portions of the month. On one day it was good to buy, on another, to be let blood—a proceeding (as we shall see to a very late date) under the especial direction of the moon ; on a third, to tame cattle ; on a fourth, to do nothing. Of these, the tradition alone exists. No relics of almanacs date further back than 1150; and in this country our earliest specimen is in the year 1386, wherein astrology is discussed as an approved and certain science, rules given for raising spirits, and calculating to a nicety the influence of the stars and the nativities of children on the most approved principles. The almanacs of the next century present a different aspect. The astrological prefaces and disquisitions disappear, together with the rules for the calculation of nativities; and in their places we have tables of the eclipses for several years, and others for finding the place of the moon and the price of corn and bread. Sufficient, however, remains to mark the existence of the belief in sidereal influences. Among the Harleian MSS. of the British Museum, is a beautiful copy of an almanac of the year 1406, which may be considered a good specimen of the almanacs of the time ;—a short account of it may be interesting.

The MS. itself is of vellum, about the size of a square 32mo. book, of forty-four pages, neatly written on both sides, and highly emblazoned. Each month has two pages, containing an ecclesiastical calendar, with the proper dominical letter, the saints' days, and other information to us incomprehensible. In the left corner of the first page of each month is a figure emblematical of the season : a man in gauntlets, warming his hands over a fire, being the sign for January; one bearing a tree, for April; and another with a sickle, for August. Beneath this figure is the zodiacal sign for the month ; whilst along the top of both leaves, across which the days are arranged, are certain emblems of the various saints whose days happen in the month ; as in February, a female bust pierced with a sword, for St. Agatha ; a bishop's mitre, with a bird on it, for St. Valentine ; in March, a harp for St. David, showing how the writer had confounded the Psalmist with the Welsh saint ; and a vase of alabaster for Mary Magdalen. After the twenty-four pages of calendar, are two tables of eclipses of the sun and moon, the former extending to 1449, the latter to 1443. In these tables the months are indicated by the implements carried by the several emblematical figures, at the head of each month's calendar; as a gauntlet for January, a sickle for August, a flail for September. We then have an astronomical diagram, for some purpose now unknown, a plate of a man covered with the signs of the zodiac, indicating the influence of each sign on a certain portion of the body, such as is now perpetuated in Moore's column of head, arms, and legs. Besides this is a Tabula sciendum in quo signo fuerit luna in omni die; a list of lucky and unlucky days ;

a table of the price of bread and corn; portraits of all the kings, from the Conqueror to Richard II., all very ugly and much alike; and lastly, a diagram for calculating the moon's motion, with a moveable hour index. Such was an almanac of the beginning of the fifteenth century.

In the year 1463 the astrological portion had shrunk to a very short table of the lunar influences under the different signs of the zodiac. During the latter part of the fifteenth, and the entire sixteenth century, the English almanacs seem to have been very harmless in their predictions; not so, however, in France, where, in 1579, Henry III. was obliged to promulgate an edict, forbidding the insertion of any more predictions, about either private or public affairs, in future almanacs. Towards the close of the sixteenth century English prophets seem to have confined their powers to the weather, and allowed the world and its troubles to go on unheeded. When we read the following quotation from our old dramatist of that time, we might fancy we were overhearing some old woman, or foolish farmer of the present day, as he dilates on the promises of a Moore, or a Murphy.

" *The* 20, 21, 22, *days, rain and wind;* O, good, good! *The* 23 *and* 24, *rain and some wind,* good! *The* 25, *rain,* good still! 26, 27, 28, *wind and some rain;* would it had been rain and some wind! well, 'tis good, when it can be no better. 29, *inclining to rain;* inclining to rain; that's not so good now. 30 *and* 31, *wind and no rain;* no rain! slid, stay; this is worse and worse. What says he of St. Swithin's? turn back, look, *Saint Swithin's,* no rain!"*

In the year 1604, the University of Oxford, in their Almanack printed at the Theatre, perpetuated their belief in lunar influences, informing the world, "that it is not convenient to let bloud whilst the Moone passeth by Taurus, Capricorn, Gemini, Leo, and Scorpio; or the Moone be neere the change, the full, or the quarter; or being affected by Saturne or Mars:" and also, that, "the Moone in Aries, well affected, is fit tyme to let bloud, for such as be of a sanguine complexion or phlegmatick. When the Moone in Cancere, let bloud the cholerick complexion; and when the Moone in Aquarius or Libra, it fitteth yᵉ melancholy." Such were the opinions of that learned body on those matters at the commencement of the seventeenth century. As the evil days of the civil wars came on, the predictions became more political, and the probable state of the weather was a mere secondary part of the work. Now was the time of Lilly and his bold prophecies, his hard words and bad Latin. During the heat of the Rebellion, the almanacs became mere political pamphlets; each party having its prophets, who foretold the victory of their own friends and the downfall of their wicked opponents, and wielded the prophecies of the Bible now on one side and now on another. In the year 1645, the author of the New Bloody Almanack informs his readers that, "the eclipse that year doth threaten great calamities, as bloody wars, famine, pestilence, and the like." It wanted no

---

* Ben Jonson. Every Man out of his Humour, Act I. Scene 1.

prophet to predict ill of those times. After the year '88, the weather seems to re-assert its claims, whilst the political predictions become excessively vague, and quite as applicable to one month as to another. And yet it did not take over much to satisfy the credulity of those times. W. Andrews, in his News from the Stars, in 1689, a work of great favour at that day, is quite content to tell his friends, that, "As unto the weather, in January, it will be pretty cold, now and then; and some snow and cold storms may be expected therein." The Speculum Uranicum, and the Syderum Secreta, were not more communicative. The Nuncius Sydereus, however, of the same year, tells us a little more. "The year begins," he tells us, "with snow, or cold rain blown up, but continues not long; however 'tis moderately seasonable, and the greatest alteration should be about the New Moon; then it is strange if the Apertroportarium of the Sun and Saturn do not make considerable alteration in the air, which may continue." Whilst the author of the Olympia Domata informs us that, "the year will begin with a troubled air, and wet producing bad weather for many days together, if he be not greatly mistaken." However, the City and Countrie Almanack promises better weather, and the Angelus Britannicus leaves his readers in doubt. We might collate a curious account of these days, did space permit, only to be equalled by placing the promises of the weather-breeders and event-mongers of 1842 in parallel columns.

Now is it not a considerable disgrace, that at the present day there are several thousands of old women, and good Protestants, who believe that because in some one month five conjunctions happen in the ascendant of Rome, ergo, something must happen to the Romish church—perhaps, as Moore saith—"the death of his Holiness;" that as many are firm believers in Mr. Raphael's pictures of burning cities, coffins and crowns, mitres volant, and thumb-screws regardant; and no despisers of the hieroglyphic of that hearty Protestant, Francis Moore, wherein the Pope is always getting the worst of the affray: and that there are nearly half a million in this isle, in the nineteenth century, who purchase and believe in the weather-table of Moore, and the fair, rain, and changeable of Mr. Murphy!

That we are not one whit less credulous than our forefathers, Moore's Almanac for 1842 is a standing evidence. We have the old column of zodiacal influences on the body; the old vague promises of "snow somewhere about this time, or perhaps rain;" the Rythmical prophecies, wherein we are told,

"Now Jove meets Saturn—and in Leo's ire,
 The Moon's eclipsed:—some great events transpire;"

and how in February—

"The great conjunction works—which Mexico,
 Greece, India, Russia, Saxony will show."

The Pope, indeed, has departed from his usual corner of the Hieroglyphic, having given place to a Mahometan mosque; but his loss is admirably supplied by a bit of second sight in October, where he tells us, that "the quartile aspect of the Sun and Jupiter indicates disputes and dissensions on religious subjects. Some sticklers for Puseyism are busy; they seem as though they would kiss the Pope's toe! but Popery, as well as Mahometanism, must ultimately wither and die beneath the powerful rays of truth." When we first lost sight of our old friend from his accustomed corner, we feared that the Roman Catholic Institute had condescended to tamper with Francis Moore. The Protestant Association may be happy; such has not been the case. And yet Francis Moore, with his prophecies, his zodiacal influences, and his unintelligible hieroglyphic, has a greater circulation than any other almanac, and almost as great as all the rest combined! How far the Stationers' Company felt themselves justified in printing what will sell rather than what will instruct, we will not stay to consider. Perhaps they console themselves, as they did in 1624, by issuing in one almanac the approved predictions, and in another casting undisguised contempt on them; or, it may be, that the return of nearly all the copies of Moore, when they did endeavour to reconcile the physician with common sense, by omitting the table of zodiacal influences, read them a lesson not to be forgotten.

With these remarks on the first of the works prefixed to our notice, we in conclusion strenuously recommend the second almanac to all classes of persons.

ON EPISCOPAL VISITATIONS.
No. IV.

In some former articles on the subject of Episcopal Visitations, it was endeavoured to trace their origin and history in the eastern and western church generally, up to the period of the reformation. It was also shown, that the practice of visitation is essentially connected with the spiritual nature of the episcopal office; and that it is a necessary consequence of the pastoral relation which exists between a bishop and the people of his diocese. We are now to examine more particularly the history of episcopal visitations in England.

I must again observe, that the notion of a visitation is now very different from that which prevailed for at least twelve centuries in the church. We understand by it at present, an assembly of clergy and churchwardens, who meet at the bishop's direction, to hear an episcopal charge; to pay certain fees; and to produce letters of orders, &c. In ancient times a visitation meant what the term implies—an actual repairing to the place visited, and an examination instituted on the spot, into the doctrines and conduct of the clergy and people; combined with the exercise of such discipline as might be called for by the circumstances of the case. Such was the system of visitation which originally prevailed in our churches, as well as in all other churches of the East and West; and in proof of this assertion I shall first produce the words of Bishop Gibson, who, in commenting on the 60th canon of 1603, which ordains that bishops shall confirm during their visitations every third year, makes the following remarks:—

"EVERY THIRD YEAR.—The ancient law of visitation was *once a year.* 'Decrevimus, ut antiquæ consuetudinis ordo servetur, et annuis vicibus ab episcopis diœceses visitentur (10. q. 1. c. 10).' And 'Episcopum per cunctas diœceses parochiasque suas per singulos annos ire oportet (c. 11).' The same was the law particularly of the English church, in the council of Cloveshoe, Ann. 747, 'Unusquisque episcopus parochiam suam pertranseundo et circumeundo speculandoque, visitare non cesset.' And afterwards Ann. 787, 'Unusquisque episcopus parochiam suam omni anno semel circumeat.'

"But it is to be noted, that these and the like canons are all meant of *parochial visitations,* or a general repairing to every church; as appears not only from the assignment of procurations (originally in provisions, afterwards in money), for the reception of the bishop; but also by the *indulgence* which the law grants in *special cases;* when any church cannot be conveniently repaired to. 'Et si commode vel absque difficultate accedere ad unamquamque non poterit; de pluribus locis ad unum congruum clericos et laicos studeat convocare, ne in illis visitatio postponatur.' From this indulgence, and *the great extent of dioceses beyond what they anciently were,* grew the custom of citing clergy and people to *attend* visitations at particular places, the times of which visitations, as they are now annually fixed about Easter and Michaelmas, have evidently sprung from the two yearly synods of the clergy, which the canons of the church required to be held by every bishop about these two seasons, to consider of the state of the church and religion within their respective dioceses: an end that is now also answered by the *presentments* that are there made concerning the manners of the people; as they used to be made to the bishop, at his visitation of every particular church.

"But as to *parochial visitations,* or the inspection into the fabric, mansions, utensils and ornaments of the church, that care hath been long devolved upon the archdeacons, who, at their first institution in the ancient church, were only to attend the bishops at ordinations, and other public services in the cathedral: but being afterwards employed by them in the exercise of jurisdiction, not only the work of *parochial visitation,* but also *the holding of general synods or visitations* when the bishop did not visit, came by degrees to be known and established branches of the archdeaconal office, as such; which, by this means, attained to the dignity of ordinary instead of delegated jurisdiction.

"By these degrees came on the present law and practice of *triennial visitations* by bishops, so as the bishop is not obliged by law to visit annually, but (which is more) is restrained from it. Which restraint, being itself unreasonable, and having grown merely from the *profits* which attend the act of visitation, is thus moderated by the Reformatio Legum: 'Diœcesim totam, tam in locis exemptis quam non, tertio quosque anno visitet, et consuetas procurationes accipiat: ut verò aliis temporibus, quoties visum fuerit, visitet propter novos casus qui incidere possint, ei liberum esto, modo suis impensis id faciat, et nova onera stipendiorum aut procurationum ab ecclesiis non exigat.'"—*Bp. Gibson, Codex,* vol. ii. p. 998.

This statement seems to be generally correct: and it is now intended to produce some of the principal evidences which ecclesiastical history furnishes in attestation of its truth.

We possess so few authentic records of the state of the church of England during the first six centuries, that it cannot be a matter of surprise that no traces of the practice of Episcopal Visitations amongst us can be pointed out in that time. The labours of Augustine and his successors, and of the venerable bishops from Ireland, who in the sixth and seventh centuries brought the Anglo-Saxons to the profession of the Gospel, were essentially of a missionary character; and therefore cannot be adduced in proof of the ordinary discipline by which the English church meant to guide herself. It was not till the time of archbishop Theodore, in the latter part of the seventh century, that Christianity took firm root, and any considerable number of bishops were ordained. Without doubt, the English bishops at that time followed the practice of the whole church, and made continual local visitations of their dioceses; but this discipline seems to have become in some degree relaxed, or to have been neglected by some of the prelates in the course of the eighth century, for in the year 747, a council assembled at Cloveshoe, under Cuthbert, Archbishop of Canterbury, (probably in consequence of the epistle of Boniface, Archbishop of Mayence, which was cited in the last article,) enacted the following canon, on the subject of episcopal visitations.

"In the third place, they ordained, that *every year*, each bishop should not omit to *visit his parish* (diocese), *by passing throughout, going round, and examining it;* and should assemble the people of divers conditions and sexes in suitable places, and teach them openly, since they rarely hear the word of God; forbidding, amongst other crimes, all pagan observances, such as diviners, sorcerers, auguries, omens, charms, incantations, and all the filth of the wicked, and the errors of the gentiles."*

At this time very few lesser or parochial churches had been founded; and the country had not yet been divided into what we call parishes. The diocese was still called "the parish" of the bishop, and the sacraments were administered, and instruction imparted by the bishops and presbyters in the course of visitations or perambulations.

The same rule which had been made in the synod of Cloveshoe was renewed and enforced in the synod of Calcuith, A.D. 785, in the following terms:—

"Thirdly, we have enacted . . . that every bishop perambulate his parish once in every year, diligently holding assemblies in proper places, where all may come together to hear the word, lest any one, through the negligence of his pastor, should wander through the devious ways of ignorance, and be devoured by the raging lion; and that he preach with vigilant care to the flock committed to him; that he confirm; and excommunicate the wicked; and restrain soothsayers, fortune-tellers, enchanters, diviners, wizards; and take away all vices. And that no one seek to feed the flock committed to his care for the sake of filthy lucre, but in the hope of an eternal reward;

---

* Tertio sanxerunt loco: ut singulis annis unusquisque episcopus parochiam suam pertranseundo et circumeundo speculandoque visitare non prætermittat; populumque diversæ conditionis ac sexus per competentia in se convocet loca, aperteque doceat; utpote eos qui raro audiunt verbum Dei, prohibens et inter cetera peccamina, &c. *Concilium Cloveshoviense*, can. iii. *Wilkins, Concilia,* t. i. p. 95.

and that he study to give freely to all what he has freely received, as the apostle testifies, saying, 'I charge thee therefore before God, and the Lord Jesus Christ, who shall judge the quick and the dead at his appearing and his kingdom: Preach the word; be instant in season, and out of season; reprove, rebuke, exhort with all long-suffering and doctrine.' As the prophet saith: 'Get thee up into the high mountain, thou that bringest good tidings to Zion.' That is, let him be as eminent in merit as he is in rank.

"And lest any one should be restrained by fear from preaching, let him hear those words, 'Lift up thy voice with strength; lift it up, be not afraid.' Jeremiah also says, 'Gird up thy loins, and arise, and speak unto them: be not afraid of their face, for I will cause thee not to fear their countenance.' Alas, what sorrow! what lamentable lukewarmness! which many beholding say: 'Why are ye involved in secular cares, or are afraid to open the word of truth, through terror, at some crime?' If the rulers of churches are silent through fear, or worldly friendship, and do not reprove sinners, like evil shepherds taking no care for the sheep, and fly when they behold the wolf; why do they not rather fear the Prince of princes, the King of kings, the Lord of lords, who by his prophet rebukes the shepherds, saying, 'Ye have not gone up into the gaps, neither made up the hedge for the house of Israel to stand in the battle in the day of the Lord?'

" Finally, as a watchful shepherd is accustomed to guard his sheep against beasts of prey, so the priest of God ought to be anxious for the flock of Christ, lest the enemy scatter them, lest the persecutor assail them, lest the cupidity of some great man disturb the life of the poor; for the prophet saith, 'If thou dost not speak to warn the wicked from his way, that wicked man shall die in his iniquity; but his blood will I require at thine hand. Nevertheless, if thou warn the wicked of his way to turn from it; if he do not turn from his way, he shall die in his iniquity; but thou hast delivered thy soul.' For 'a good shepherd giveth his life for the sheep.' Bearing this in memory, fathers and brethren, labour that it be not said of you, as it was to the shepherds of Israel: 'who feed *themselves*,' &c.; but that you may deserve to hear, 'Well done, good and faithful servant, enter thou into the joy of thy Lord.'"*

We find the following amongst the constitutions of Odo, Archbishop of Canterbury, A.D. 943.

" Thirdly, bishops are to be admonished that, with all propriety and modesty, and in the piety of our holy religion, they preach, and set forth a good example to all people. That they *perambulate their parishes every year*, with all vigilance, preaching the word of God, lest any one, through his pastor's negligence, wander through the devious paths of ignorance, and be devoured by wolves; and that no one, for the sake of filthy lucre, but in the hope of an eternal reward, study to feed the flock committed to him; (for what we have freely received, we should not delay to impart freely;) [and also] to preach the word of truth without fear or adulation, but with all boldness, to the king, the princes of his people, and all dignities, and never to conceal the truth; to condemn no one unjustly; to communicate no one except lawfully; and to show unto all the way of salvation." †

---

* Tertio sermone perstrinximus omni anno, secundum canonicas institutiones, duo concilia ... ut unusquisque episcopus parochiam suam omni anno semel circumeat, diligenter conventicula per loca congrua constituendo, quo cuncti convenire possint ad audiendum verbum Dei; ne aliquis per incuriam pastoris per devia cujuslibet ignorantiæ errans, rugientis leonis morsibus invadatur: et vigilanti cura gregem sibi commissum prædicet, confirmat, &c.—*Concil. Calcuth.* can. iii. *Wilkins,* t. i. p.146.

† Tertio anno monendi sunt episcopi, quatenus cum omni honestate et modestia in sanctæ religionis pietate prædicent et ostendant exempla bona omnibus. Ut suas parochias omni anno cum omni vigilantia prædicando verbum Dei circumeant, &c."
—*Const. Odonis,* cap. iii. *Wilkins,* t. i. p. 213.

This constitution represents the discipline which was in force in England up to the period of the Norman conquest, and which continued until the Roman canon law was introduced into this country, in the twelfth century, by the compilation of Gratian. The introduction of this law, however, did not make any alteration in the practice of Episcopal Visitations, for its rules on this subject were exactly in accordance with those which had been previously in force in England. The canons of several councils of Toledo and Braga, which are contained in that compilation, strictly enforced the ancient practice of *annual and parochial visitations* on the bishops. (See vol. i. p. 46.)

It has been shown in a former article (vol. i. p. 47) that in 1179 the council of Lateran made regulations as to the number of attendants whom bishops and others might bring on their visitations, which plainly show that the practice of parochial visitations was still universal. The church of England, in A.D. 1200, adopted the rules of the Lateran council, and thus testified her continued adhesion to the ancient custom of the Church. The following occurs amongst the canons of the synod of London in 1200:—

"Since amongst the statutes of the fathers in recent times, the Lateran council is very celebrated, and most worthy, in all ways, to be observed; we, following its directions with humility and devotedness, decree:—that an archbishop visiting his parish shall by no means exceed a train of forty or fifty attendants, a bishop not more than twenty or thirty; that archdeacons be content with five or seven horses : deans, constituted under the bishops, with two. Nor let them go with hounds or hawks, but so that they may seem to seek, not their own things, but the things of Jesus Christ. We forbid the bishops also to presume to burden their subjects with charges and exactions. We permit them, however, for their many necessities which sometimes occur, that if the cause be manifest and reasonable, they may, with charity, ask from them a small assistance. For, since the apostle saith, 'Children ought not to lay up for the parents, but the parents for the children,' it seems far remote from paternal love, if rulers are burdensome to those who are subject to them, whom they ought to cherish, like fathers, in all their necessities.

"Let no archdeacons or deans presume to make any exactions or charges on the presbyters or clergy. Indeed, what has been said of the aforesaid number of attendants (by way of toleration) should be observed in those places in which the ecclesiastical incomes and means are more ample. But in poor places we wish such a measure to be held, that the inferiors be not burdened by the visits of their superiors, lest, under such a permission, those who have hitherto used a smaller number of horses, should believe themselves invested with greater powers.

"It pertains to the office of visitation, *to see with all diligence, in the first place, to what concerns the cure of souls;* and that every church has a silver chalice, and sufficient and proper clerical vestments, and the necessary books, utensils, and other things which relate to divine worship and reverence of the sacrament. Moreover, to cut off the vices of avarice and negligence, we enjoin, resting on the authority of the council of Toledo, that no visitor presume to exact any procuration, or redemption of a procuration, from any church in which he does not perform the office of visitation in the lawful manner."*

---

* Concilium Londinum, can. v. Wilkins, t. i. p. 505.

This canon not only establishes the fact, that parochial visitations were at this time made by the bishops of England; but also shows that the principal object of that visitation was held in view, namely, *its connexion with the care of souls*. It was at this time the duty of the bishop to preach the Gospel in his parochial visitation; to teach, admonish, and reprove the clergy and people; and to institute an examination into the state of religion, and inflict spiritual penalties on evil-doers.

The next canon which I shall adduce as bearing on this subject, occurs amongst the constitutions of Cardinal Otho, made in the synod of London, A.D. 1237.

" What pertains to the office of the venerable fathers, the archbishops and bishops, is evidently expressed by the title of their dignity (which is 'episcopus,' that is, 'superintendent'): for it is their peculiar duty to oversee, and, according to the language of the Gospel, to 'keep watch over their flocks by night.' Since, therefore, they ought to be an example to the flock, after which their subjects should regulate themselves, which cannot be, except they show forth themselves an example to all, we exhort and admonish them in the Lord, that, residing at their cathedral churches, they fitly celebrate divine service there, at least on the principal festivals and Sundays, and in Lent and Advent. *Moreover, let them perambulate their dioceses at convenient times, correcting, and reforming, and consecrating churches, and sowing the word of life in the Lord's field.* Which, that they may the better perform, let them cause the profession which they made in their ordination to be read to them at least twice in the year, that is, in Advent and Lent." *

It may be remarked on the above, that the office of visitation was still regarded as a perambulation of the diocese, and that it comprised amongst its duties the exercise of discipline, and preaching the word of God. Thus the *pastoral* character of the episcopate was still fully recognised and acted on. But it may seem, perhaps, from the vagueness of the term "opportunis," employed to designate the *times* at which visitations were to be made, that the rule of the canons which prescribed *annual* visitations, was not at this time generally attended to. At what period the visitations became triennial instead of annual, I have not been able as yet to discover; but I should think it probable that this relaxation took place gradually during the thirteenth and fourteenth centuries, when the dioceses of England became very extensive by the erection of new parishes. The size of our dioceses even then was such that bishops could not personally visit the whole of their dioceses parochially each year; but as the canons permitted them to appoint deputies for the purpose of visitation, there was not any absolute necessity to relinquish the custom of annual visitation.

The next document which I shall adduce, in reference to this subject, is one of the constitutions of Cardinal Othobon in the synod of London, A.D. 1268.

" Whereas we are given to understand, that many prelates exact procura-

---

* Wilkins, t. i. p. 654.

tions from their subjects, although they do not perform the office of visitation; we, looking advisedly, as well to the indemnities of churches, as to the salvation of the prelates, strictly inhibit any of them to receive from any church the procuration which is due on account of visitation, except when he performs the duty of visiting the same; and that whoever should receive such, shall be suspended from entering any church until he return it. Bishops and other inferior prelates are not to presume to burden their subjects in their visitations with superfluous companies or numbers of attendants, or by any other expense."*

Joannes de Athon, canon of Lincoln, who lived about A.D. 1290, in his comment on the above canon, says, in reference to the inhibition against receiving procurations without visiting—

" This reason, perhaps, wisely moves the bishops of this kingdom, who, in their visitations commonly do not exact procurations from the church, because they *do not turn aside to each particular church for the purpose of visitation, although they fully visit the persons, as well clergy as laity, assembling them together in various convenient places.*" †

Here, then, we have evidence that the rule of the ancient canons was no longer attended to, and that visitations had, to a certain extent, assumed their present shape. Still, however, the visitation was a serious and important business. The bishop, indeed, no longer went to each church, and preached the gospel, and exercised his apostolical authority there; but still the clergy and laity were assembled in some neighbouring place, and the same forms of inquiry and discipline were observed in these meetings.

I have observed in a former article (vol. i. p. 273), that this alteration in discipline was sanctioned, if not introduced, by a decree of Pope Innocent IV., between A.D. 1243 and 1254, by which metropolitans were permitted, in their metropolitan visitations, to assemble the clergy and laity of several parishes in one place, if they could not conveniently and without difficulty go to each particular parish church. It was also remarked, that it seems very doubtful, from the wording of the decree, whether *bishops* were intended to have the same privilege of relief from the strict injunctions of the canons. It was, however, so interpreted; and we accordingly find, from the testimony of Athon, that in 1290 the bishops of England thought themselves at liberty to relinquish, in a great degree, the practice of *parochial* visitation.

Still, however, it would seem that the practice alluded to was viewed only as a matter of *indulgence*, and that the church of England continued to expect her prelates to make parochial visitations when they could do so without inconvenience. This may be collected from a constitution of Archbishop Stratford, in a provincial synod, A.D. 1341.

" Some archdeacons, and other *superior* and inferior ordinaries of our province, grasping at temporal gains, and casting behind them the things of God, in the progress of their visitations, indulge in hunting and other inso-

---

* Wilkins, t. ii. p. 7.
† Joannes de Athon, Annot. in Constitutiones Legatin. p. 114. Ed. Oxon. 1679.

lencies, and frequently send persons to visit places, by whose exhortations or information the clergy and people receive no instruction; and do not fear to exact in money, contrary to the canons, the customary procurations from churches, *which they do not enter or inspect on the day of visitation;* and from some which have not been visited at all by themselves or others; and from many which they cause to be perfunctorily visited by others in one day, each of which would have been sufficient for the customary procuration of one day for the archdeacons and their servants. . . . We strictly inhibit, by authority of this present council, any one to presume to receive a procuration on account of visitation, from any church, *unless he has diligently performed the office of visitation thereto, having personally examined and inspected effectually whatever was to be investigated.* But if any one wishes *to visit many churches in one day,* let him be content with one procuration, in victuals or in money, to which he may cause all and every one of those visited in one day to contribute in proportion, according to the canons."*

From this canon it would appear that the Church still required her ordinaries to visit parochially, though she permitted them to visit several churches in one day; so that the practice which Athon mentions seems to have been rather tolerated than authorized as yet.

The *archdeacons* were always supposed to visit parochially. Of this we find plain proofs in the preceding canons, and also in the canons of the synod of Oxford, held by Archbishop Langton, in 1222;† in the synodal constitutions of the diocese of Sodor, in 1291;‡ and in the constitutions of Walter Reynolds, archbishop of Canterbury, A.D. 1322.§ Even in the time of Lyndwood, *i. e.* in the fifteenth century, the archdeacon's visitations are always spoken of as parochial and local, and it was held that he might visit a church several times in the course of a year, if necessity so required.‖

Visitations, however, whether held by bishops or archdeacons, were always of the nature of a judicial inquiry and examination. Thus we find Archbishop Stratford, on occasion of his visitation of the chapter of Canterbury in 1334, going to the chapter-house of the cathedral, and there formally examining the lives and conduct of the monks of Canterbury, and determining disputes amongst them.¶ In 1376, Archbishop Sudbury issued his mandate to the archdeacon's official at Canterbury, commanding the archdeacon and the clergy of the deanery of Canterbury to appear before him at his visitation, together with six or four parishioners from every parish which was to be visited, and to answer such inquiries as the archbishop or his commissioners might address to them.**

The articles concerning the Reformation of the Church, which the University of Oxford published in 1414, show that very great abuses had arisen in the practice of visitation.

"Although all judicial visitations are appointed for the correction of crimes, and not to obtain money, nevertheless some ordinaries in these days exercise their visitations not merely to correct faults, but to make col-

---

* Wilkins, t. ii. p. 676.   † Wilkins, t. i. p. 588.   ‡ T. ii. p. 179.
§ T. ii. p. 513.   ‖ Lyndwood, Provinciale Angliæ, p. 34, ed. Oxon. 1679.
¶ Wilkins, t. ii. p. 577.   ** Ib. t. iii. p. 109.

lections, and, contrary to the intention of the written law, ride with very great trains, which is burdensome to their subjects, and causes some of them to obtain privileges of exemption (from visitation); and some of the archdeacons receive procurations from the clergy to forbear their visitations, which they are officially bound to exercise." *

We now come to the period of the Reformation of the church of England, and the reign of Edward the Sixth, when we find the following regulations made concerning visitations, in the "Reformatio Legum," which may, in some degree, aid us to determine the practice which was at that time approved in the Church. It may be remarked that the practice of *triennial* visitation seems to have been, for the first time, recognised in these regulations.

"OF VISITATIONS.
"*Wherefore a Church is to be visited.*—Cap. 1.

"Let archbishops, bishops, archdeacons, and all others whose duty it is, and who possess ecclesiastical jurisdiction, visit and heedfully view their churches, and hold the appointed and customary meetings in them, that the people committed to their care may be wholesomely and rightly governed by their pastors, and that, by the assiduous and pious labours of their ministers, the condition of the churches themselves may be preserved aright.

"*What inquiries are to be made in Visitations.*—Cap. 2.

"These things should form the chief subjects of inquiry in such stated meetings:—Whether the holy Scripture be handled with diligence and sincerity; whether the administration of the sacraments be fitting and right; then, what is the discipline of the church, and of how much vigour it is possessed; and finally, whether the form of public prayers be correctly, and at the proper times, observed; and whether all other matters comprised in the care of the churches be rightly discharged.

"*The form of Visitation.*—Cap. 3.

"In order that these things may proceed with more care, let the whole multitude, as is customary, and as seems very convenient, be assembled in some one place; and after oaths have been administered to the syndics and other customary witnesses, let the crimes of persons of all degree, which pertain to the ecclesiastical law, be most diligently inquired into; and where they are fully understood, let them suffer the just penalty of the law, and a severe punishment be inflicted on them."

After this follow directions as to the repairs of ecclesiastical buildings and cemeteries, and the duty of churchwardens, which seem to have been subjects of inquiry in visitations. The next chapter refers to the procurations due for visitation.

"*That a reasonable allowance be paid for Visitations.*—Cap. 6.

"Since labour ought not to be unaccompanied by reward, if an archbishop *visit and survey* his province, or a bishop his diocese, or an archdeacon the churches of his jurisdiction, or any other ecclesiastical ordinaries whatever their churches, and there hold the usual and customary assemblies, and perform the other lawful rites of visitation, let them enjoy all the emoluments which pertain to the common administration of this business."†

In fine, we have it distinctly stated that the bishop's visitation was *triennial*, in the following regulation defining the duties of bishops:—

---

* Wilkins, t. iii. p. 363.   † Reformatio Legum, p. 63, &c.   Ed. Lond. 1571.

"Let the bishop especially teach the sound doctrine of the word of God in his church, as well personally as through others, with the greatest possible diligence and carefulness. . . . . . Let him also visit his whole diocese, as well in exempt places as in non-exempt, every third year, and receive the customary procurations; and let it be also lawful for him at other times, whenever it may seem fit, to visit on account of new causes which may occur, provided he perform it at his own expense, and exacts no new burdens of stipends or procurations from the churches."*

The canons of the synod of London, in 1573, contain a provision for holding confirmations during the bishop's triennial visitations, which was repeated in the canons made in 1603, in the following terms:—

"Forasmuch as it hath been a solemn, ancient, and laudable custom in the church of God, continued from the apostles' times, that all bishops should lay their hands upon children baptized and instructed in the catechism of christian religion, praying over them and blessing them, which we commonly call *confirmation;* and that this holy action *hath been accustomed in the Church in former ages, to be performed in the bishop's visitation every third year;* we will and appoint, that every bishop, or his suffragan, *in his accustomed visitation,* do in his own person carefully observe the said custom."†

It appears from this, that the practice of triennial visitation had been long established, and that it still consisted in a sort of progress of the bishop throughout his diocese, for he was to confirm "*in* his accustomed visitation," which implies that he was to go throughout his diocese. But it is plain that at this time, the practice of parochial visitation had become superseded, to a considerable extent, by the present plan of synodical visitation. Still, however, the ancient notion was not entirely relinquished, for, in a synod held under Archbishop Laud, in 1640, a form of articles of inquiry was prepared for the use of all those who had the right to make parochial visitations; and it would seem that there is nothing whatever at this moment to prevent any bishop from visiting parochially instead of synodically, provided that his visitation be not made more frequently than once in three years. The practice of our present synodical visitations seems only permitted by custom, while that of parochial visitations still remains sanctioned by law as well as by custom.

I cannot but think, with deference, that it would be highly desirable to revive the ancient practice of parochial visitation, especially in the case of bishops. Putting out of view the antiquity of this custom, and its sanction and enforcement by the laws of the Church, it would surely seem most desirable in itself, that all bishops should, as the chief pastors of every soul within their dioceses, have frequent opportunities of fulfilling those solemn duties in relation to the care of souls, which their ordination vows impose on them. And does it not seem that *parochial* visitations would exactly harmonize with the wishes and intentions of the Church of England in this respect, by enabling the bishops to preach the word of God *personally* to the people of their jurisdiction? Under the existing arrangements, the

---

* Reformatio Legum, p. 50. † Canon lx.

great mass of the people never can have an opportunity of receiving spiritual instructions or admonitions from the successors of the apostles; and they are, thus far, placed in less advantageous circumstances than the Church desires. They are, to a certain extent, deprived of privileges which were intended to contribute to their salvation. For if we believe, as we do, that a bishop is really a successor of the apostles, that he is the immediate pastor of the laity of the diocese, and that the parochial clergy are only his assistants and coadjutors in this great spiritual work, we cannot think it a matter of indifference whether the episcopal office is or is not in a state of full efficiency. The result of the disuse of parochial visitations is, that our people are less alive to the importance of the episcopal office than they might be. They are, in various cases, hardly aware of its essential characteristics; and are not impressed with any practical sense of its benefits. However the educated classes may be able to appreciate such points, the illiterate, who form the great mass of the community, almost forget that such a being as the bishop is in existence; or, at least, imagine that his duties are connected only with the clergy. The parochial clergyman is too generally viewed as the sole pastor of each parish; while the bishop is regarded as the superintendent of the clergy, and the minister of confirmation, and nothing more.

It seems to me impossible to revive the feelings of affection and attachment which ought to subsist between the successors of the apostles and their people, except by a recurrence to the ancient, lawful, and truly apostolical practice of parochial visitation. Let that visitation be what the Church intends it to be—directed chiefly to the *spiritual edification of the people*—to their instruction in the gospel—to examination into their doctrine and morals—to administration of the sacraments and rites of the Church by episcopal hands, to lend greater dignity and impressiveness to those solemn duties— to exercise of discipline on offenders by censures, excommunications, and absolutions. Let visitations, in short, be what they were in all the best ages of the Church, or even be, in any degree, or with any modifications, restored to their real objects; and I cannot but think that more would be done for the discipline and unity of the Church, more for the regularity of the clergy, more for the attachment of the people to their bishops, more for the strengthening of the Church, and for its defence against its enemies, than by any other regulation that could be enacted. Is it desirable to restore church discipline? I believe that if the *existing* powers of bishops in their visitations were *acted on* with discretion, and with a due regard to the temper and feelings of the present age, much, very much, might be accomplished.

But I am well aware, that with dioceses of such large dimensions as those which now exist, it would be in vain to urge the restoration of parochial visitations. This, however, furnishes a strong reason for desiring a *large increase* in their number. The very first step, if we desire to render the Church really efficient, if we are anxious to put the theory of the Church into full and energetic practice, should be to multiply the bishoprics to three-fold their present number at least. The addition of a few sees would be, in this point of view, wholly and entirely useless. Nothing but an increase *on a very large scale*, could possibly enable the episcopal office to resume the full exercise of its spiritual functions, and disengage it from the enormous load of matters relating to the temporalities of the Church, by which it is at present burdened and oppressed.

Several plans, on a large scale, have lately been proposed for the erection of new sees. It would seem that in any such measure, it ought, at least, to be an essential feature to make each bishop a *real* bishop—*the head of his own diocese, the centre of unity to that diocese*, and exercising his powers without any *delegation*, or in the light of the *deputy* of another bishop. It would seem that the plan of making the existing bishops metropolitans, and placing the additional sees under them as suffragan, though really distinct sees, involves less difficulty than any other. We have heard it objected to this plan, that, were it carried into effect, metropolitans might be found with only one suffragan see, or even with none at all. But there is no very material weight in such an objection, for it is certain that in various parts of the Eastern and Western Church, similar instances may be pointed out. Pope Benedict XIV., in his Treatise on Diocesan Synods, informs us that in Italy there are four metropolitan sees with only one suffragan each, and four others without any suffragan.

" Aliqui sunt in Italia Archiepiscopi, unicum habentes suffraganeum, Theatinus videlicet, Brundusinus, Cosentinus, et Sipontinus. Aliqui suffraganeis omnino carentes; Rossanensis nimirum, Lancianensis, Lucensis, et Ferrariensis."[*]

It also appears from Thomassinus, De Veteri et Nova Ecclesiæ Disciplinæ, that in the Eastern Church there are many archbishops who are honorary metropolitans, and have no suffragans.[†] Smith, in his account of the Greek Church, furnishes us with a catalogue of the sees subject to the Patriarch of Constantinople, in which occur the names of many metropolitan sees with one or two suffragans, or even with none at all. These last continue to be called metropolitans, though, having lost their suffragan sees, they are in fact only honorary metropolitans.[‡] The see of Cambray has just been made metropolitan, with one suffragan, the Bishop of Arras.

The next article will contain some more particular accounts of the mode of proceeding in the ancient parochial visitations.

W. P.

---

[*] Benedict XIV. De Synod. Diœcesana, lib. ii. c. iv.
[†] Thomassinus, pars i. lib. i. cap. xxxix. n. 10; xliii. n. 12.
[‡] Smith's Account of the Greek Church, p. 85, &c.

NOTICES OF BOOKS.

1. *The Authenticity, Uncorrupted Preservation, and Credibility of the New Testament.* By GODFREY LESS, *late Professor in the University of Göttingen. Published in the Series of "Christian Literature."* Edinburgh: Black.
2. *Christian Theology.* By G. C. KNAPP, *Professor of Theology in the University of Halle. Published in "Ward's Standard Library of Divinity."* London: Ward & Co.
3. *Biblical Geography of Asia Minor, &c.* By E. F. C. ROSENMÜLLER, *Professor at Leipsic. Published in "The Biblical Cabinet."* Edinburgh: Clark.
4. *The Life of Christians during the Three First Centuries. Being a Series of Sermons, by Dr.* C. L. CONARD, *of Berlin. Also published in "The Biblical Cabinet."*

BEFORE we give a separate notice to these different works, we are anxious to call attention to the phenomenon of their existence as parts of a system. Here we have Nos. 35, 29, and 34, in three separate series of theological publications. And what is the nature of them? The first, which is the most innocuous, consists of reprints of works, whose chief fault is that they are out of date. It is the speculation of a bookseller, and not the well-digested scheme of a theologian. The "Library of Standard Divinity" is a medley of heresies gathered from every country under the sun. The frontispiece most accurately bespeaks its character. Let the reader fancy a Grecian portico, designed, doubtless, to be a symbol of the church of Christ, according to the well-known scriptural figure. He will doubtless expect to see it resting upon the foundation of the apostles and prophets, Jesus Christ himself being the chief corner-stone. Alas! for the simplicity of his mind. Mr. Ward's Grecian portico—fit type of Dissent—is built upon the foundation of Matthew Henry and Scott; while Owen and Howe enjoy that distinguished place which the Divine Author of our religion has reserved for himself! "The Biblical Cabinet" seems to have confined its favours to German writers, which, to say nothing of their theological views, have not even the merit of being well selected; for several of them (Rosenmüller amongst the rest) have long since been superseded in their own country. But meanwhile *we* are Englishmen, and we must most vigorously protest against such a theological Babel as these publications are calculated to establish. But we must not altogether throw the blame on these respectable booksellers. People are crying out for food; and we, the authorized dispensers of the word, have nothing to give them. Of books on the Evidences, there is certainly no lack among us; nor is a treatise on Scriptural Geography, perhaps, any great desideratum. But it is a fact, we believe, though it will scarcely be credited, that there is no such work as a "Systema Theologicum" in the English language. It is now nearly three hundred years since our formularies have been changed, and many meanwhile have been the generations of professors in our universities and dignitaries in our chapters; and yet, strange to say, not one has cared to put forth a systematic work (the miserable comments on the Thirty-nine Articles are no exception) which the student may take as his text-book in theology. The natural result is, that those who cater for the religious appetite are obliged to go to Germany, or Switzerland, or America, for what their own country does not yield.

A few words concerning the books specified at the head of this notice. The works of Less and Rosenmüller were respectable in their day. The former, however, as well as Knapp's "Christian Theology," has been considerably tampered with by the translator, even though there is a pledge given in the prospectus that "in no instance is the slightest abridgement or alteration of the author's text ventured upon." The volume of Rosenmüller is part of a large cumbrous work. Moreover the facts and statistics have long since become obsolete. Knapp's is a laborious work, but radically unsound. Conard's Sermons are also unsound; neither do they present any very favourable model for the pulpit. We are at a loss to see, in fact, who is to be benefited by any of these publications.

Conformity; a Tale. By CHARLOTTE ELIZABETH. London: Dalton. 12mo. 1841.

CHARLOTTE ELIZABETH is the type of another phenomenon, to which we are anxious to direct attention. We are told that she is one of the most popular, certainly of the most prolific writers of the day, and that a large proportion of her readers are to be found among Churchmen; at the same time it is manifest from every page of her writings that she is in spirit a Dissenter. We think it necessary, first of all, to prove this charge from the little volume before us, for probably the intention of this *nom de guerre* is to conceal such inauspicious facts, and shall then inquire, how it happens that Church-people encourage such publications? Multiform as is dissent, all the sects, if we except Popery and Unitarianism, *leave* the Church at *one* point. They assume that the business of religion is to do, what the Scriptures expressly state it may not do, viz. to separate between the sheep and the goats—between the nominal and the real Christian. Hence each sect sets up a new test, and invents a new machinery. The Baptist immerses his disciple afresh in the river. The Wesleyan, taking a scriptural term, requires an unscriptural "conversion." The Independent decides the question by a jury of voices, among his own community. And so on with the rest, *ad infinitum;* for there is no limit, save that which limits the inventive faculties of man.

The Church's system, as derived from the Bible, is altogether diverse; and being a diversity which forms the readiest method of distinction, it is one well worth noting. The Church receives the infant from the hands of its parents at the font, to "nurse it" for them, and educate it; and henceforward never does she lose sight of it. Through the medium of god-parents, by the rite of confirmation, by a commissioned ministry, by the distribution of the bread of life, by the power of the keys, she seeks to carry on the work of God, till the infant shall gradually grow in grace to the measure of the stature of the fulness of Christ. A church within a church is not recognised by the Catholic system—least of all may any private individual presume to predicate concerning the condition of any other. Nor has this system any, the smallest, tendency to encourage a false security in the careless liver. For what is his baptismal vow? To fight and to serve under Christ; and he is pledged especially to resist the evil influences of the world, the flesh, and the devil. But as the two last are not visible and tangible, so neither is the former. It is that remnant of corrupt practice and principle, which Christianity has failed to overcome, and which is still working by a sort of counter-leaven in the hearts of the regenerate, and not unfrequently taking the very guise of religion. As well may we expect to *see* the devil, when he tempts us, as to be able to point with the finger to " the world."

By this ready test, which we again recommend as *the* true proper criterion by which to judge, the writer before us stands convicted of having departed from the Catholic system; indeed, the very object of the tale is to illustrate this fundamental fallacy, or rather, we must say, heresy. The dialogue which follows is a key to the whole.

"*J*. You admit that all mankind are divided into two classes—the children of light and the children of darkness?

"*L*. Yes.

"*J*. The former you allow to be those exclusively to whom we apply the apostle's words, ' But ye are washed, but ye are sanctified, but ye are justified in the name of the Lord Jesus, and by the Spirit of our God.'

"*L*. Precisely those, and none other.

"*J*. The children of darkness you comprehend under that term from every class of human beings: as heathens who never heard of Christ; Jews and infidels who reject him; nominal Christians, who have a form of godliness, but deny the power thereof. And this great bulk of mankind you allow to be those who, in the language of inspiration, are called ' the world,' in contradistinction to those of whom Christ says, ' I have chosen you out of the world.'

"*L*. To all this I fully assent."

To none of this, of course, do *we* assent. When is not regeneration, and sanctification, and justification, to be predicated as universally of the Church of England as of that of Corinth? Nor can we admit that there were any "nominal Christians" in that " world" from which Matthew the publican and the fishermen of Galilee were " chosen."

The least of the mischief which flows from this kind of teaching is that which is *intended* in the present tale; viz. that all general society, "from the thronged ball-room and sumptuous feast to the small tea-party and plain dinner," are all evil. We certainly should not trouble ourselves to argue with any person who chose to act on such principles—least of all with those whose unfortunate experience has caused them to believe, as does Charlotte Elizabeth, that in all society God and good men are ridiculed. In truth, we think that those who hold such opinions of the majority of their fellow-Christians do wisely to shun all intercourse with them; for, if true to their principles, the world will certainly " hate them," and recrimination and dislike will be mutually engendered. But, as has been already shown, this fallacy lies at the bottom of all dissent; and we are, therefore, particularly anxious to unmask it. If we have seemed to our learned readers to be confining ourselves too much to "first principles," we can only appeal to the universal ignorance concerning theological systems which prevails among all classes. There is need that men should "be taught again which be the first principles of the oracles of God," or writings of this nature would not be found upon our drawing-room tables and in our lending libraries. Either people are ignorant that the doctrine in question is the great fount of all dissent and heresy, or they forget the apostolic injunctions for the treatment of those who depart in the smallest particular from the faith "once delivered to the saints." A dissertation upon the meaning of "the world," as the term is used in Scripture, would at the present time be very seasonable.

The History of the Knights Templars, Temple Church, and the Temple. By CHAS. G. ADDISON, *Esq., of the Inner Temple.* London: Longman and Co. 1842. Small 4to. Pp. 395.

THE public have great cause to be indebted to Mr. Addison for this very interesting volume. The history and exploits of the Knights Templars are well known to every student: but with the circumstances attending the dissolution of the Order we are much less generally familiar. And yet, perhaps, few more touching narratives can be met with. The fall of Acre, the last stronghold of the Christians in Palestine, took place in the year 1291. From that moment a universal conspiracy appears to have been organized against them throughout Europe. Whether it is to be attributed to a natural reaction of the popular mind; whether they were made the scape-goats of the disgrace of Christendom; or whether it be true, as old Fuller says, that "the chief cause of their ruin was their extraordinary wealth;" or lastly, whether, however unjustly treated, some at least of the accusations laid to their charge were not too true, is not easy to determine. The facts of the case, however, were as follows:

France was the first to lead the way. On the 13th of October, 1307, Philip the Fair, in concert with Pope Clement V., caused all the Templars in his dominions to be arrested. The most horrible crimes were laid to their charge; but when we find part of the accusation to be that "*in order to conceal the iniquity of their lives* they made much almsgiving, constantly frequented church, comported themselves with edification, frequently partook of the Holy Sacrament, and manifested always much modesty and gentleness of deportment in the house as well as in public," we cannot but suspect the accusers. Be that as it may, however, "on the 19th day of the same month, after they had remained constant in the denial of the horrible crimes imputed to them, the grand inquisitor proceeded with his myrmidons to the Temple at Paris, and 140 Templars were, one after another, put to the torture. Days and weeks were consumed in the examination, and 36 Templars perished in the hands of their tormentors, maintaining, with unshaken constancy, to the very last, the entire innocency of their Order. Many of them lost the use of their feet from the application of the torture of fire, which was inflicted in the following manner: their legs were fastened in an iron frame, and the soles of their feet were greased over with fat or butter; they were then placed before the fire, and a screen was drawn backwards and forwards so as to moderate and regulate the heat. Such was the agony often produced by this roasting operation, that the victims often went raving mad." The Grand Master and the Grand Preceptor were both burnt to death.

In England, matters did not quite proceed to such extremities. The Order was dissolved, their estates confiscated, and William de la More, the last Master, died of a broken heart in his solitary dungeon in the Tower. But what aggravates the sinfulness of these measures is, that Edward had previously testified to the exemplary conduct of the English Templars.

We cannot resist making one observation upon this history. There appears to be a tendency in the minds of some, almost to renounce the Reformation, in consequence of the sacrilegious rapacity of Henry VIII. with which it was attended. Let these persons consider, that such acts are not peculiar to a Protestant monarch. The Papist may be safely challenged to produce any fact in the dissolution of the monasteries by Henry, which can parallel the atrocities committed in the suppression of the Knights Templars. Moreover, these shameful proceedings actually emanated from the Pope himself. He it was who roused the sovereigns of Europe against this unhappy Order; and thereby set a fatal precedent, which Henry and his courtiers were too glad to follow. It is most important that the character of Romanism, both past and present, should at this time be fully understood: as regards the latter, we shall find, that imperfect as may be the condition of our own Church, the Roman is certainly much farther removed from perfection: as regards the former, the history which has just been given will show, that the worst excesses of the Reformation can appeal to a too faithful precedent in earlier times.

The Life of Beethoven, including his Correspondence with his Friends, and numerous characteristic Traits and Remarks on his Musical Works. Edited by IGNACE MOSCHELES, *Esq. Pianist to H. R. H. Prince Albert.* In two vols. 8vo. Pp. 674. London: Colburn. 1841.

THIS is a disagreeable memoir of a singularly disagreeable man, which has been edited by M. Moscheles for Mr. Colburn, with the unpleasant proviso, that the work should be given to the public in its English dress, as originally written by Schindler, " without omission or alteration." Had M. Moscheles been left unshackled, we think, (to judge from his editorial notes) that he might have produced a very readable book; and although he could never have made the subject of his biography an interesting character, he might have told the truth faithfully, and yet judiciously.

We never fell in with a biographer who has shown so little judgment in the selection of his materials as M. Schindler. Love-letters are proverbially absurd compositions, and no one, with a spark of delicacy, would *publish* such extracts from a friend's correspondence:

but M. Schindler has printed all he could lay his hands upon; and that the reader may judge of the quality of what the German biographer has chosen to expose to the public eye, we will extract one of these amatory epistles:—

"Monday Evening, July 6, 1806.

"Thou grievest, my dearest! I have just learned that letters must be put into the post very early. Thou grievest! Ah! where I am, there art thou with me; with me and thee, I will find means to live with thee. What a life!!!! SO!!!"—[*sic.*]—"Without thee, persecuted by the kindness of people here and yonder, which, methinks; I no more wish to deserve than I really do deserve it,—humility of man towards men,—it pains me,—and when I consider myself in connexion with the universe, what am I, and what is he who is called the greatest? And yet herein lies the divine in man! Love me as thou wilt, my love for thee is more ardent,—but never disguise thyself from me. Good night! As an invalid who has come for the benefit of the baths, I must go to rest. Ah! . . . . . So near!—So distant! Is not our love a truly heavenly structure, but firm as the vault of heaven!"—(Vol. i. p. 104.)

Our readers will agree with us in thinking that this is as fine an example as need be, of what the authors of the Rejected Addresses describe as the

"—— Sentimentalibus lacrymæ roar 'em,
With pathos and bathos delightful to see."

And the best of the joke is, that this man, who talks of his affection being "firm as the vault of heaven," confessed that "the love which enthralled him longer and more powerfully than any," lasted "*full seven months!*" (Vol. i. p. 107.)

Having given a specimen of M. Schindler's treatment of his friend's correspondence, we shall add an extract which he has no less judiciously made from poor Beethoven's journal, with the twofold object of shewing the great musician's "interior life" and domestic distresses:—

"1819.
" Jan. 31.—Given warning to the housekeeper.
" Feb. 15.—The kitchen-maid came.
" Mar. 8 —The kitchen-maid gave a fortnight's warning.
" 22d of this month, the new housekeeper came.
" May 12.—Arrived at Mödling. Miser et pauper sum.
" May 14.—The housemaid came; to have six florins per month.
" July 20.—Given warning to the housekeeper.

"1820.
" April 17.—The kitchen-maid came.
" May 16.—Given warning to the kitchen-maid.
" May 19.—The kitchen-maid left.
" May 30.—The woman came.
" July 1.—The kitchen-maid arrived.
" July 28.—*At night, the kitchen-maid ran away.*
" July 30.—The woman from Unter-Döbling came.
" Aug. 28.—The woman's month expires.
" Sep. 6.—The girl came.
" Oct. 22.—The girl left.
" Dec. 12.—The kitchen-maid came.
" Dec. 18.—Given warning to the kitchen-maid.
" Dec. 27.—The new housemaid came."

A pleasant household this must have been, both for master and servants! But the chief fault must have lain in the head of the family.

The fact is, that, great and (in some respects) unrivalled as were Beethoven's musical talents, it is as a composer only that he has any claim on our admiration. We have very little sympathy with, or respect for, what are called "the eccentricities of genius." We cannot make allowance for rudeness because a man is a "great lexicographer." We cannot conceive why pre-eminence in music or painting should be permitted to afford an excuse for an unwashed body, or an ill-disciplined mind; we cannot see the necessary connexion between dirt and cleverness, or why a man should set at defiance the conventional forms of civilized society, so soon as he can play a sonata upon one string of his fiddle.

Of Beethoven's personal history, we know nothing beyond what we find in the work under review; but if, as we take for granted, his biographer has told us all that he deems worth preserving, we confess that we are disposed to think that M. Schindler would have done his friend's memory more service by condensing his facts into a paragraph of twenty lines, and getting them inserted in the next edition of the Biographical Dictionary, than by publishing a long trashy memoir. People will always desire to know the chief events of Beethoven's life, and the respective dates of his works; but nobody cares to dwell upon the foibles and unamiable propensities of an ill-tempered and miserable infidel.* A lengthened and elaborate biography is in such cases unadvisable on all grounds, and, in the hands of such a writer as M. Schindler, quite intolerable.

The Contest and the Armour. By the Author of *Think on these Things, &c.* London: Longman & Co. 18mo. Pp. 51.

WHEN we say that this little book is by Dr. Abercrombie, the author of a Treatise on the Moral Feelings, and other respectable works, it will be seen that we have taken more than an average specimen of a class of writers, who have no little influence in "the religious world," of the day. We have done this, because we desire to propose the inquiry to the good sense of Churchmen, whether the tone of religious belief and sentiment is likely to be improved by encouraging such writers. Dr. Abercrombie is a Scotchman, a Presbyterian, and a Layman; each of which "accidents" (we desire to say it without offence) is, in our view, sufficient to disqualify him for the office which he here undertakes. 1. As a Scotchman, (both by birth and education,) his language is full of latinisms, and abstract metaphysical terms, very far removed from a commendable *simplicity:* as "evolvement of imagination," "*moral* perceptions of the mind," "*moral* emotions of the heart," &c. &c. Whether Dr. A. uses this word "moral" in the sense assigned to it by a witty person, as signifying something which the writer or speaker is unable to describe, we

---

* It will appear surprising, to those who have heard the sacred compositions of Beethoven, that he should have been an unbeliever. "It my observation," says M. Schindler, " entitles me to form an opinion on the subject, I should say he inclined to Deism; in so far as that term may be understood to imply natural religion." (Vol. ii. p. 163.) And in another passage, (vol. ii. p. 72,) M. Schindler, in a letter written to Moscheles, while Beethoven was dying, says, "He is conscious of his approaching end, for yesterday he said to me and Brewning, 'Plaudite amici, comœdia finita est.' He sees the approach of death with the most perfect tranquillity of soul, and *real Socratic wisdom.*"

will not undertake to say: but he employs it more unsparingly than any one with whom we are acquainted. It is to be found on almost every one of these little pages, and sometimes it recurs as many as three and even four times. 2. As a Presbyterian, our author " divides " his text in the extreme of tediousness and unnaturalness. 3. As a Layman, it is not his province to preach and publish sermons: in his proper sphere, we have respect for him. It is much to be wished, at the same time, that some competent person would supply a series of solid practical treatises upon moral and religious duties.

Letter to a Friend, on the Evidences and Theory of Christianity. By LORD LINDSAY. London: Hatchards. Pp. 120.

IT is impossible to read this letter without a feeling of sincere respect to the writer. It proves not only that he is an amiable man, but that he possesses very respectable theological attainments, and is acquainted with many of our best authors. We say this without meaning to guarantee the exact accuracy of every theological statement; still less do we think that the letter is at all of a nature to convince the sceptic. Those, however, who merely wish to " stir up pure minds by way of remembrance," will read it with pleasure. The following is a favourable but fair specimen:—

" The style in which the narrative [of the New Testament] is delivered, is a strong corroborative argument. Throughout the Old Testament, as long as the notes of preparation had to be sounded, the utmost beauty of language, the highest flights and flourishes of poetry, were employed to do honour to the approach of the Deliverer. But when He appears on the scene, all is hushed before the majesty of his presence. Except when used by our Saviour himself, not a trope or metaphor is to be found in the Gospels. There is no poetical embellishment—no attempt to work on the passions—no specific character is even drawn of him. Awe-stricken, and conscious that human speech falls far short of their high argument, the evangelists give a plain simple matter-of-fact statement of what they have heard and seen, and leave the reader to draw his own conclusion."

The great Duty of frequenting the Christian Sacrifice, and the Nature of the Preparation required, with suitable Devotions. By ROBERT NELSON, Esq. *A new Edition, with Memoir of the Author. By the* REV. W. B. HAWKINS, M.A. London: Burns. 1841. 8vo. Pp. 183.

THIS is an elegant specimen of typography, profusely adorned with wood-cut illustrations of sacred emblems, being like the old devotional works, ruled (or rather printed throughout) with red lines round the margin; and having the rubrics of the proper colour.

It is certainly a matter of no great consequence whether a man says his prayers out of an ill-printed or well-printed volume; and in an age so luxurious as our own, there may be danger lest our devotional books be made to minister to our self-indulgence, pleasing our eyes, instead of exercising a salutary influence over our hearts, and becoming toys instead of objects of reverence. Still, when we call to mind the appearance of the more popular religious books, which, till recently, held undisputed possession of the market, we are glad that the change, which has produced a sounder tone of theology, has been accompanied by a corresponding improvement in the medium through which it is conveyed.

Mr. Pickering of London, and Messrs. Combe of Leicester, were among the first, we believe, who adopted the ornamental style of printing to which we allude; and some of the earlier volumes of Mr. Parker's Oxford series of reprints issued from the press of the latter firm. The Gothic ornaments (engraved by Jewitt) which have been inserted in the later volumes of the same publisher, are, for the most part, of great beauty, and very happily introduced; but some of these books (Laud's Auto-biography, for instance) are very awkward, thick-set, *dumpy-looking* tomes.

We do not think that the wood-cuts introduced into Mr. Burns' publications have as yet equalled those in the Oxford series; the reason of this is that Jewitt's engravings are almost invariably correct copies from pure Gothic ornaments; whereas Mr. Burns' artist seems to have followed his own inventions, and has occasionally jumbled trefoils and quatrefoils among scrolls and foliage, till he has produced something like the dazzles before a sick head-ache, but as unlike the ancient style as can be conceived. There is a great improvement, however, in this respect of late, and we greatly prefer the size of Mr. Burns' volumes to those of Mr. Parker.

The reprint before us is beautifully executed. Of the value of the work itself it is quite unnecessary for us to express an opinion; but Mr. Hawkins has given an additional interest to the edition before us, by adding a brief but admirable memoir of the saint-like author.

The Careless Christian reminded of his Privileges, warned of his Danger, and urged to Repent without Delay. By the REV. G. W. WOODHOUSE, M.A. *Vicar of Albrighton.* Pp. 181. Rivingtons.

IT is very rare, in so small a space, to find so much excellence as is contained in this little book of Mr. Woodhouse's. The deep convictions, and clearly-defined notions of the writer, are conveyed with a simplicity of language, and earnestness of purpose, that can hardly fail to make a powerful impression upon even the most reckless of the class to whom the work is inscribed, if only they would read it. The careless Christian is met upon his own ground; and the wisdom of his indifference tested by the application of principles universally admitted, but not so generally recognised, as bearing upon matters of religion. Mr. Woodhouse uses, with much skill, the dread of pain and misery ineradicably inherent in our nature, as a means of stimulating attention to his warnings; and then, from the perilous condition of the unawakened sinner, he leads his reader to a distinct view of the conditions of escape from the great condemnation. He rests not here, however, but sets in prominent light the startling truth, that "*those who seek for salvation, and for nothing more, are not likely to be saved;*" shatters the futile devices and bubble excuses with which men seek to palliate to themselves their fatal carelessness in the most important of all concerns; and, demonstrating that " without holiness no man shall see the Lord," clearly establishes the position of the truthful but ill-appreciated poet, that

" without breathing, man as well might hope
For life; as, without piety, for peace."

Such is the aim and tenor of the work. We heartily recommend it as a valuable book. A brief extract will hardly suffice to show its excellence as a whole, but the selection of a passage or two may serve to give an idea of his manner. Speaking of the delusive comfort of a so-called creditable life, the author thus writes:—

"For in what consists the sin of idolatry, that evil and bitter thing which has drawn down upon mankind so much of God's displeasure? Does it not consist in this, that it draws away the heart from God? And if this be so, what real difference is there between the sin of idolatry, and the sin of that man whose only ambition is to pass creditably through life? However different the idolater and the man of the world may be in other respects, they clearly agree in this,—that they both alike are guilty of forsaking God, and ruling their conduct by the maxims of men, instead of being guided by a reference to His will. Oh! miserably is that man deceived, who deems it sufficient to live honestly and quietly, instead of walking before God in holiness, and living to shew forth His praise. For who shall ascend into the hill of the Lord, but such as are renewed after the image of Christ?—and who are renewed after the image of Christ, but such as delight to glorify God?"—Chap. viii.

In another part, speaking of delay, he says:—

"But further, remember that your delaying to turn to God, is contrary to your solemn vows. It was promised for you, when you were baptized, that you should keep the commandments of God. At your confirmation, you yourself confirmed this promise. And was this a mere ceremony? Was it nothing more than a customary compliance with an unmeaning form? Or was it indeed, what it is called in terms, a solemn vow made to Almighty God? Oh! look back to your confirmation vow, and see if it were not a serious thing. Look back to it, and ask your own heart, how far you have ever fulfilled it; yea, consider how far you have ever honestly endeavoured to fulfil it. If you were fairly to view the matter, you would see that you are living in just the same way, as if, instead of having solemnly engaged to live as the child of God, you had entered into a covenant to devote yourself to the world. . . . You have lived to indulge the flesh, instead of studying to subdue it. You have thrust aside the word of God, instead of striving to obey it. Will not, then, your own vow rise up in the judgment and condemn you, if you still delay to give glory to the Lord your God? Having promised to be His servant for ever, is not this promise forgotten, if you are only thinking of doing His will towards the end of your days? You indeed may pay no respect to those vows and promises, which were first made by others in your behalf, and afterwards ratified by yourself with your own lips; but remember that the God you have to do with, is one who will not admit any loose interpretation of so strict and solemn an engagement. 'Be not deceived. God is not mocked!'"

Our table is covered with children's books, new for the season, the prevailing characteristic of which is mediocrity. They may be classed, as regards subjects, under three heads—natural history, history, and religious and moral conduct. 1. Lady Callcott's "Little Bracken-burners," (Parker, London;) Mrs. Loudon's "Young Naturalist's Journey," (Smith, London;) and Miss Taylor's "The Ball I Live On," (Green, London;) are all respectable publications. The second is the most captivating, by means of external decoration and the novelty of some of the subjects treated; but the first is more to our taste, for it is altogether a domestic story. 2. The historical batch are, "Evenings with the

Chroniclers," and "The Story of Joan of Arc," both published by Mr. Smith, of Fleet-street, and compiled by the same editor as the "True Tales of Olden Time," which we noticed some months since. The same fault also still adheres —the absence of a natural and earnest tone. The writer seems afraid of saying something which he ought not to say, and which he thinks would damage the sale of his books. 3. "Look Forward," by Catherine Irene Finch, and "The Well-spent Hour," by the Rev. S. Wood, (London, Green,) are religious, or rather, we should say, moral tales; for the language of the writers seems to us to be studiously constrained upon the great doctrine of redeeming grace. The former, moreover, contains some very objectionable American politics.

A writer, under the title of "A Commoner," has put forth an answer to Lord Alvanley ("The State of Ireland re-considered," Hatchard), in the preface to which he states that "it is perfectly understood, as a general question, that a pamphlet, no matter upon what subject, or how the subject may be treated, has just as little chance of doing good *or evil*, if left to the ordinary course of events, as if it had never seen the light." We cannot agree with him. Of the merits of the controversy we say nothing, having never read Lord Alvanley's Letter. Such pamphlets as this author's must infallibly do harm to the cause which they are meant to support.

The author of "Essays written in the Intervals of Business," (Pickering,) is evidently a man of good feeling and principle. Indeed we are disposed to think that he has been induced to sacrifice himself with the view of alleviating the present distress of the printers. At least, we cannot conceive any other motive which can have led to the embalming of such very vapid thoughts in the beautiful typography of the Chiswick Press.

Many of our readers will be glad to hear that Mr. Sewell has collected into a volume the various articles on Plato which he wrote for the "British Critic" and the "Quarterly Review." The title of the volume is "Horæ Platonicæ." It is published by Rivingtons.

Every true lover of poetry—all, that is, who can appreciate harmony of versification and purity of sentiment,—will rejoice to learn that the works of Spenser are now made accessible in a single elegantly-printed volume. We sincerely hope that the publisher (Spiers, London) may be rewarded with a rapid sale.

"Modern Flirtations; or, A Month at Harrowgate," in 3 vols, by Miss Catherine Sinclair, is preceded by a Preface, enforcing high moral principle. Now, a preface to a novel we hold to be altogether out of place; and morality, in connexion with Harrowgate and "Flirtations," appears to be scarcely more consistent. It will not, therefore, surprise our readers that this book should have the faults of its class; nor do we think that even the acknowledged powers of the authoress have succeeded in giving it the tendency which she wishes and claims for it.

We have not lately encountered anything more interesting than "A Letter to a Medical Student on some Moral Difficulties in his Studies, &c., addressed to the Rev. J. H. North, M.A., Chaplain to St. George's Hospital,".(Rivingtons, 1841.) Without discussing schemes for the better education of the class to which this author belongs, we will say that their best chance consists in the example of men like him.

"Recollections of Clutha," (Smith, Elder, and Co. 1842,) is the somewhat sentimental title given to a little record of a visit to that wonderful stream, termed by ordinary mortals the Clyde. The authoress has a feeling for the beauties of nature, and a hearty habit of enjoyment, which we cannot but welcome. She has a youthful *efflorescence* of style, which we trust she will see the importance of remedying. From what we have seen of her pencil, we feel convinced that the scanty space she has allotted to her engravings do anything but justice to its powers.

"The Canadas," by Wollaston, (Colburn, 1841,) will be acceptable in many respects to those who are interested in British America. The accounts of the Indians and of the coast of Labrador are striking.

We call attention to Mr. Poole's important pamphlet on "The State of Parties in the Church of England," (Green, Leeds; Burns, London, 1841.) Also to Mr. Perceval's Letter to the Bishop of Chester, on that Prelate's recent Charge (Rivingtons, 1841.) The author has given a beautiful example of the tone in which a Bishop ought to be addressed by a presbyter or layman of another diocese, who finds himself in the painful necessity of differing from him on such points as are at issue here. We wish the appendix had been spared, which, entering as it does on questions, a full harmonious view of which cannot be developed in such short space, seems likely to mar the usefulness of the whole.

We have alluded elsewhere to Mr. Williams's short pamphlet, entitled, "A Few Remarks on the Charge of the Lord Bishop of Gloucester and Bristol, on the subject of Reserve in communicating Religious Knowledge," &c. (Parker and Rivingtons, 1841), which, report says, has removed the Bishop's uneasiness as to Mr. Williams's opinions on that subject.

In our last, we noticed the "Christian Magazine." We have great satisfaction in announcing the publication of the first number of one of a similar class, entitled "Burns's Magazine for the Young." When we mention that it is in the hands of such writers as the contributors to Mr. Burns's Juvenile Series, we have said enough to recommend it to our readers.

From the same publisher there has also appeared the commencement of a series of Select Homilies for Holy Days and Seasons, translated from the writings of the Saints, each to come out shortly before the time to which it refers.

Mr. Gresley has just published a volume of Parochial Sermons, (Burns, 1841,) to which he has appended a preface, stating the object for which he has done so—that of procuring funds for a new country church, near Lichfield—and containing some important remarks on the true spirit and purposes of church building. The volume is embellished with a frontispiece, giving a view of the new church; the design, it seems, of a country architect, but worthy of the best we at present possess in the metropolis, or elsewhere.

We must also notice a volume of Whitehall Sermons, by the Rev. C. Merivale, B.D. (Deighton, Cambridge; Parker, London; 1841.) The former specimen this author gave the world of his pulpit powers is such as leads us to welcome his present volume.

We have to announce, moreover, and really we have seldom been able to wind up with so many pieces of good news, a volume of Miscellaneous Sermons by Dr. Hook. (Rivingtons, 1841.)

Among single Sermons, one by Dr. Pusey, entitled, "The Preaching of the Gospel a Preparation for our Lord's Coming," (Parker, Oxford: Rivingtons, London, 1841); and another by Mr. Dodsworth, "Allegiance to the Church," (Burns, 1841;) must command attention.

List of Books recommended to Students in Theology.

It will be observed that this list is divided into three classes, according to the order in which it is thought desirable that the student should prosecute his reading. With the principal portion of those books in the first class he should be acquainted, before he offers himself as a candidate for Holy Orders; in addition to which, he should have studied some sermons by our best divines, as

Andrewes, Barrow, Lowth, Wilson; and made himself acquainted with the Hebrew language.

Bloomfield's Greek Testament.
Horne's Introduction to the Scriptures.
Barrow's Summary of Christian Faith and Practice.
Hooker's Works.
Bingham's Christian Antiquities.
Pearson on the Creed.
Wheatley on the Common Prayer.
Soames' Mosheim.
Apostolical Fathers.
Palmer on the Church.

Mant's Notes to the Bible.
Beveridge on the Articles.
The Clergyman's Instructor.
Burton's Testimony of the Ante-Nicene Fathers.
Routh's Opuscula.
Homilies.
Walton's Lives.
Lectures on Antichrist (in " Tracts for the Times").

Bishop Bull's Works.
Collier's History.
Palmer's Origines Liturgicæ.
Waterland's Works.
Lawrence on the Articles.
St. Cyril's Catechetical Lectures.

Graves on the Pentateuch.
Bishop Taylor's Works.
Barrow.
Wall on Infant Baptism.
Bishop Butler's Works.

Bishop Wilson's Works.
Controversy between Laud and Fisher.
South's Sermons.
Magee on the Atonement.
Stanhope on the Epistles and Gospels.
Cardwell's Conferences, &c.
Bethel on Regeneration.
Chrysostom's Homilies.

Berriman on the Trinity.
Bishop Horsley's Works.
Bishop Andrewes' Sermons.
Some of St. Augustine.
St. Basil de Spiritu Sancto.
Atterbury's Sermons.
Sherlock's   Do.
Leighton's Works.

CHRIST CHURCH, STREATHAM.

(With an Engraving.)

THE interest excited by this remarkable building, has led us to offer to our readers some description of it, illustrated by two engravings. The view of the west front forms the frontispiece to our present number: we intended a view of the interior to accompany it, but it is not ready; it will appear in our next.

The architect (Mr. J. W. Wild) has evidently attempted in this building the one great requisite of art—unity. Nothing has been sacrificed to a principal front; every side, and every detail on all sides, is finished with equal richness and care. The general effect of the exterior is that of severe simplicity and massiveness. The depth of the doors and windows, the generally unbroken mass of the basement, and the inclination or slope of the external angles of the building, contribute to this effect, which is continued every where, uninjured by any trifling projections or details. Every part of the exterior is executed in brick. The general colour is a pleasing warm yellow; but the details are enriched by the contrast of coloured bricks, inlaid in different patterns. This coloured ornament, or polychromy, as it is called, was common to many ancient styles, and is now much studied by architects. Some of the new buildings at Munich are enriched in this manner. The chief value of colour seems to us to be, that richness and variety are gained without impairing the simplicity of the general outline by unmeaning breaks. In Streatham Church the effect is rich without the least gaudiness. These details, and especially the large cornice, deserve particular attention, as they develop some peculiar architectural resources in our most usual building material. It appears to us that when we use stone dressings to brick buildings, we at once strongly mark the inferiority of the brickwork, which then seems a coarse material, used, not from choice, but for economy only; on the contrary, when the enrichments are also in brick, they give a dignity to the whole material of the building.*

The arrangement of the galleries is one leading feature of the design: it explains equally the exterior and the interior. They are supported on a sub-arcade, between the piers of the main arches of the building; they are lighted by long ranges or arcades of small windows, and, by their constant repetition, add to the effect of length in the building. Externally, these gallery ranges express the object they are applied to, and are the principal ornament of the side elevations.

On whatever grounds we may object to galleries, they are, in consequence of the necessities of the present time, unavoidable; and as in most of our larger new churches, they are a part of the original building, they should be designed in harmony with the rest of the architecture. This is seldom attempted; and unless we conceive, in the excess of our admiration of "styles," that the galleries which cut across the piers and windows, are, by some convention, unseen, we have no excuse in ancient buildings for the use we make of them in our imitation.

We defer the description of the arrangements of the interior until our next number, when they will be illustrated by the accompanying engraving.

The greatest dimension of the church, from the outside of the west front, to the outside of the apsis, is one hundred and three feet. The size of the body of the church within the walls and staircase is seventy-six feet, by fifty-two feet six inches. The diameter of the apsis is eighteen feet within the walls; its plan is rather more than the semicircle. The campanile, which is attached to the church at its south-east angle, is fifteen feet square. The height to the apex of the spire or pyramid, is one hundred and thirteen feet. The height from the floor line to the apex of the roof is fifty feet. The tie-beams of the trusses of the centre roof are curved, as it is intended, when the decorations of the interior are proceeded with, to make these arches a panelled vault; by this mode of construction, very little height is lost in the roof.

The number of persons accommodated in the church is twelve hundred—one half the sittings are free.

It was originally intended to expend only 4,000*l*.; this amount was then increased to 4,250*l*., but since the contract and the commencement of the building, the architect has been enabled by the committee, and principally by the indefatigable exertions of the Rev. W. Raven, to improve the building in every detail. The amount is now 6,000*l*. including also the expense of the boundary walls.

It is evident that this design has been the result of much thought. The usual unfortunate affectations of styles and dates have been avoided, and the very simplicity and plainness of the church appears the effect of choice, in the rejection of all trifling ornament, and not a mere matter of economy, or a compromise between the "style" and the money.

The name of the "style," as well as the merits of this design, have been the subjects of discussion. Some call it Byzantine—a name most conveniently inclusive; others, Turko-Greek, Egypto-Gothic, Moorish, &c. Notwithstanding names, and the inquiry of the Commission Office, "Whether the church is Grecian, and of what order, or Gothic, and of what century?" design and style ought to be regulated by the arrangements to be provided for, the cost, and the materials used; as these belong to the present time, so does the date of this church. The great merit of it consists in the example it has set, of avoiding pedantry, and discarding *style*. As far as it goes, it is what all real architecture has ever been, an *utterance* of something,—a combination, in harmonious and reverential form, of the materials the architect had to use and to put together; and its success has been such as may well encourage others to imitate his independence.

---

* These details are beautifully executed; indeed the whole work does great credit to the builder, who, we understand, is Mr. Thompson, of Camberwell-green.

ECCLESIASTICAL INTELLIGENCE.

ORDINATIONS.

By Bp. of Ely, at Cath. Church of Ely, Nov. 28.

DEACONS.

Of Cambridge.—H. L. Guillebaud, B.A. Trin.; F. L. Lloyd, B.A., N. M. Manley, M.A., F. Jackson, B.A., J. A. Coombe, B.A. St. John's; T. C. Peake, B.A. Sid. Sussex; W. H. Guillemard, M.A. Pemb.; W. Keane, B.A. Emman.; W. Harries (*l.d. Llandaff*); G. Halls, B.A. Queen's, H. King, B.A. Jesus, (*l. d. Ripon.*)

PRIESTS.

Of Cambridge.—W. S. Parish, M.A. St. Pet.; T. Clarkson, M.A., B. M. Cowie, B.A., G. Currey, M.A., J. Woolley, B.A. St. John's; T. R. Birks, M.A., F. C. A. Clifford, B.A. Trin.; J. Bell, M.A. Clare; W. Young, B.A. King's; A. J. Hanmer, B.A. St. John's; W. B. Hole, B.A. Exet. (*l. d. Exeter.*)

By Bp. of Winchester, at Farnham, Dec. 12.

DEACONS.

Of Oxford.—J. C. Ryle, B.A. Ch. Ch.; J. Meyrick, B.A., T. Coulthard, B.A. Queen's; J. H. Janvoin, B.A. Oriel; S. Clarke, B.A. St. John's; R. Cooper, B.A. Wad. (*l. d. Sarum*); H. E. Pettman, B.A. Trin.

Of Cambridge.—E. T. Smith, B.A. St. John's; R. C. Hales, B.A. Magd.; G. E. Tate, B.A. St. John's; C. H. G. Butson, B.A. Magd.; H. H. Molesworth, B.A. St. John's (*l. d. Exeter.*)

PRIESTS.

Of Oxford.— G. Hadow, B. A. Ball.; J. D. Durell, B.A. New Inn H.; C. S. Grueber, B.A., W. H. Cope. M.A. Magd.; G. W. Cockerell, M.A. Queen's; J. Compton, B. A. Mert.; T. G. Hatchard, B.A. Brasen.; W. H. Le Marchant, M.A. Exet.; C. D. Kebbel, B. A. Univ.; G. De Carteret Guille, B.A. Pemb.; J. Hawksley, B.A. St. Edm. H.

Of Cambridge. — C. Heath, B. A. Jesus; F. Fisher, B.A. Magd.; S. S. Gower, B.A. St. John's.

By Bp. of Peterborough, at Cath., Peterborough, Dec. 19.

DEACONS.

Of Oxford.—T. Bourne, B.A. St. Edm.; W. Renaud, B.A. Exet.; E. Steed, B.A. Pem.; A. R. Webster, B.A. St. Mary.

Of Cambridge.—H. J. Bolland, B.A. Trin.; S. W. Hinckson, B.A. Cath.

ORDINATIONS APPOINTED.

Bp. of Ripon, *Jan.* 9.
Bp. of Norwich, *Jan.* 16.

Bp. of Salisbury, *Feb* 20.
Bp. of Peterborough, *Feb.* 20.

PREFERMENTS.

Name.	Preferment.	County.	Diocese.	Patron.	Val.	Pop.
Allen, E.	Barton St. David.	Somerset	B. & W.	Preb. of Barton	38	410
Atkinson, R. M.	Gt. Cheverill, R.	Wilts	Sarum	Rev. R. M. Atkinson	*353	576
Barlow, H. M.	Ch. Ch. St. Clement's, Norwich, P.C.	Norfolk	Norwich	Rec. of St. Clement's		
Barnett, J. C.	Berrow, V.	Somerset	B. & W.	Archdn. of Wells	*186	496
Brock, O.	Dengie, R.	Essex	London	W. R. Stephenson	754	249
Darnell, W.	Bambrough, P.C.	Northumb.	Durham	Lord Crewe's Trust	*121	3949
Dowell, T.	Wellington Heath, P.C.	Hereford	Hereford			
Edmonds, G.	L. Wenlock, R.	Salop	Hereford	Lord Forester	550	1057
Edouart, A. G.	St. Paul's, Blackburn, P.C.	Lanc.	Chester	Vicar of Blackburn		
Frobisher, J. J.	Halse, V.	Somerset	B. & W.	Mrs. Frobisher	*174	444
Garrow, G. B.	Chiselborough, R.	Somerset	B. & W.	Earl of Egremont	*449	1006
Gibbs, M.	Ch. Ch., Newgate-street, V.	Middlesex	London	Gov. of Bartholomew's Hospital	537	2842
Guyon, C. L.	Lamyat, R.	Somerset	B. & W.	Bp. of Llandaff	*266	204
Gwyther, G. H. A.	Madeley, V.	Salop	Hereford	Sir R. Phillips	*241	5822
Harden, J. W.	Condover, V.	Salop		E. Owen, Esq.	258	1455
Hill, R.	Timsbury, R.	Somerset	B. & W.	Balliol Coll.	*389	1367
Hole, W. B.	Woolfardisworthy.	Devon	Exeter	Rev. J. Hall	258	226
Jones. H. W. W.	New Ch., Denbigh.		St. Asaph	Rev. of Denbigh		
Marindin, S.	Penselwood, R.	Somerset	B. & W.	Earl of Egremont	*140	361
Mickle, J.	Apesthorpe, P.C.	Notts.	Lincoln		81	95
Newnham, G. W.	Coombe-Down, P.C.	Somerset	B. & W.	Trustees		
Owen, O.	St. Edmund, Exet. R.	Devon	Exeter	G. Hyde, Esq.	187	1523
Platt, G.	Sedbergh, V.	York	Ripon	Trin. Coll. Camb.	*184	4711
Powell, M.	Clapton (New Ch.)	Middlesex	London			
Prodges, E.	Upton Lovell, V.	Wilts	Sarum	Lord Chancellor	*325	249
Rigg, G.	St. Peter's, Eastgate. Lincoln.	Lincoln	Lincoln		147	496
Skipper, J. B	Ashchurch, P.C.	Gloucester	G. & B.	Rev. H. Fruen.	48	649
Stephenson, J. H.	Corringham, B.	Essex	London	Rev. W. R. Stephenson	723	234
Tartly, E.	Grimston.	York	York		160	158
Tillard, J.	Connington, R.	Cambridge	Ely	Bp. of Ely	*238	203

Intelligence.

PREFERMENTS,—continued.

Name.	Preferment.	County.	Diocese.	Patron.	Val.	Pop.
Tripp, R. H.	Alternoun, V.	Cornwall	Exeter	D. & C. of Exet.	*320	1069
Uwins, J. G.	St. Matthew's, Stroud			T. C. Croome, Esq.		
Vallance, H.	St. John's, Southw.	Surrey	Winchester			
Voules, F. P.	Middle Chinnock.	Somerset	B. & W.	Earl of Ilchester	189	216
Waites, J. B.	So. Stainley, V.	York		R. Reynard, Esq.	75	243
Walpole, T.	Limpsfield, R.	Surrey	Winchester		595	1042
Watman, P.	Barnley - on - Don, P.C.	York		T. Gresham, Esq.		
Wood, J. R.	St. John's, Bedward			D. & C. of Worc.	639	2661

*** *The Asterisk denotes a Residence House.*

APPOINTMENTS.

Abbott, P. .... { Head Master of Qu. Mary's School, Clitheroe.
Anderson, P. ...... Chap. E. I. Comp., Bombay.
Bankes, E. .... { Official of Peculiar of Wimborne.
Burrow, C. U...... Chap. to Mayor of Camb.
Evans, T. .... Hd. Mas. Coll. Sch., Glouces.
Gabbett, J. .... Economist Cath., Limerick.
Green, T. S. ...... { Chap. to Ashby-de-la-Zouch Union.
Jones, R. J. ...... Dom. Chap. to Earl Cawdor.
Maude, J. B. ...... { Dom. Chap. to Earl of Lonsdale.
Moore, T. B. G... Chap. to Bromsgrove Union.
Steveley, R. ...... { Preb. in Cath. of St. Patrick's, Dublin.
Thomas, D. T. ... Rur. Dn. Up. Carmarthen.
Whiting, — ...... Chap. to H. M. S. Cambria.
Whytehead, J. ... { Chaplain to Bishop of New Zealand.

CLERGYMEN DECEASED.

Birmingham, R., Preb. of Mora of Lismore.
Cresswell, F., Rector of Gt. Waddingfield, Suffolk.
Chichester, R., Vic. of Chettlehampton.
Davis, J., Rec. of Melcombe, Horsey, Dorset, '68.
Evans, G., Vic. of Pathers Pusey, Northamptonshire, 72.
Eyre, W., Mast. and Librarian of Archbp. Tenison's School and Library.
Hamer, H., Rec. Pointington, Somerset., 30.
Irwin, T., Per. Cur. of Hackness and Harwood-dale, Yorkshire.
Langton, G. T., Rec. of Barton, Norfolk, 63.
Lee, L. C., Rec. of Wootton, Woodstock, 74.
Richardson, F., at Iron Acton, 46.
Rowlands, W., Per. Cur. of Longtown and Llanveyno, Herefordshire, 66.
Vivian, J., Rec. Hatton Hall, Wellingboro'
White, J., Per. Cur. of Woodland, Devon, 85.
Ward, M., Rector of Stiffkey and Marston, Norfolk, 72.

UNIVERSITIES.

OXFORD.

Degrees conferred, November 25.

D.M.

W. A. Greenhill, Trin., one of the Physicians to the Radcliffe Infirmary.

M.A.

W. Powell, Exet.; Rev. T. B. Croome, Trin.

B.A.

S. B. Harper, New Inn; R. M. Martin, Edm.; C. Cripps, Mag.; J. H. Crowder, Postmaster of Merton; P. S. Ashworth, St. Alb.; J. Forbes, Exet.; G. G. Hayter, Scholar of Oriel; D. P. Chase, Scholar of Oriel; L. C. Wood, Jesus; C. D. Hamilton, St. M. Hall; B. Belcher, Wadh.; J. G. Brine, Fell. of John's; C. Beswick, John's; C. E. Prichard, Scholar of Ball.; H. Foot, Ball.

December 2.

M.A.

R. H. Bentley, New Inn, Grand Compounder; Rev. G. W. Cockerell, Queen's; M. I. Brickdale, Student of Ch. Ch.; W. H. Hughes, Ch. Ch.; Rev. A. O. Fitz-Gerald, Ball.

B.A.

J. P. Marriott, Ball., Grand Compounder; E. LeVien, Ball.; R. Sumner, Ball.; C. S. P. Parish, Edm.; R. Walker, Linc.; M. Webster, Scholar of Linc.; A. R. Webster, St. M.; E. Ellis, St. M.; W. M. E. Milner, Ch. Ch.; P. C. Kidd, Ch. Ch.; J. Macintosh, Ch. Ch.; J. G. Mountain, Postmaster of Merton; A. N. C. Maclachlan, Exet.; J. Townend, Oriel; J. Kitcat, Oriel; W. D. Bathurst, Fell. of New Coll.; F. E. Thurland, New Coll.; C. W. Heaton, Jesus; J. Addams, St. John's; T. H. Roper, St. John's; T. H. House, Worc.; W. T. Hutchins, Worc.; H. J. Torre, Univ.

B.D.

Rev. J. Williams, Fell. of Jesus; Rev. W. Mallock, Ball.

B.A.

L. Carden, Univ.; H. H. Cornish, Mag.; C. R. Clifton, Merton; E. L. Sandys-Lumsdaine, Oriel.

November 18.

Rev. W. R. Wardale, M.A., and Rev. M. Harrison, M.A., Scholars of C. C. C., admitted Probationer Fellows of that Society.

November 23.

Mr. C. J. Dawson, Captain of the Charter House School, and Mr. A. Taylor, of St. John's College, elected Exhibitioners of the Michel Foundation at Queen's.

J. H. Latham, Commoner of Brasennose Coll., elected a Craven Scholar.

C. J. P. Foster, Esq., B.A. of Oriel Coll., admitted *ad eundem* at Durham University.

November 25.

R. R. W. Lingen, B.A., and Scholar of Trin. Coll., and E. K. Karslake, B.A. and Student of

Ch. Ch., elected Fellows of Ball. Coll. E. Walford, late of the Charter-house, and Commoner of Balliol, and E. Palmer, of the Charter-house, elected Scholars of Ball.

R. P. Williams, B.A., L. C. Wood, B.A., and J. Morgan, Commoners of Jesus Coll., elected Scholars of that Society.

December 2.

Rev. C. Clapham, M.A., of Trin. Coll., Cambridge, was admitted *ad eundem.*

December 1.

Mr. A. Bathurst, Scholar of New Coll., admitted actual Fellow of the same.

December 4.

Rev. T. Whytehead, M.A. Fell. of St. John's, Camb., and Chaplain to the Bp. of New Zealand, admitted *ad eundem.*

Select Preachers, to succeed those who go out of office at Michaelmas, 1842:— The Rev. D. Williams, D.C.L. Ward. of New Coll.; the Rev. F. K. Leighton, M.A. Fell. of All Souls; the Rev. H. E. Manning, M.A. Mert.; the Rev. T. L. Claughton, M.A. Fell. of Trin.; and the Rev. H. Kynaston, M.A. Ch.Ch.

The Vice-Chancellor nominated the Rev. B. P. Symons, D.D. Ward. of Wad. Coll., to be a Pro-Vice-Chancellor, in the room of the Rev. the President of Corpus, who has resigned that office.

December 9.

Rev. E. R. Jones, B.A. of Brasen., admitted a Fellow on Michel's Foundation at Queen's.

CLASS LISTS.

The names of those candidates who, at the examination in Michaelmas Term, were admitted by the Public Examiners according to the alphabetical arrangement prescribed by the statute, are as follows:—

In Literis Humanioribus.

CLASS I.

Chase, D. P. Alban. | Prichard, C. E. Ball.
Hutchins, W. T. Worc. | Rawstone, W.E.Ch.Ch.

CLASS II.

Ashworth, P. S. Oriel. | Maclachlan, A.N.C.Ex.
Beswick, C. St. John's. | Marshall, J. Ch. Ch.
Blackett, J.P.B.Ch.Ch. | Mountain, J. G. Mert.
Brine, J. G. St. John. | Pocock, I. J. J. Mert.
Butler, P. Ch. Ch. | Prat, R. Mert.
Harrison, C.R.AllSouls | Sumner, R. Ball.
Hayter, G. G. Oriel. | Webster, A.R.St.Mary
Langhorne, C.H. Exet. | Webster, M. Linc.
Lea, W. Bras.

CLASS III.

Carden, L. Univ. | Phillimore, G. Ch. Ch.
Crowder, J. H. Mert. | Soper, J. Mag.
Jones, T. Mag. | Townsend, J. Oriel.
Lempriere, C. St. Joh. | Wilson, T. P. Bras.
Macintosh, J. Ch. Ch.

CLASS IV.

Belcher, B. Wad. | Kennicott, B. C. Oriel.
Chapman, E. J. Wad. | LeVien, E. Ball.
Collier, C. J. Mag. | Milner, W. Ch. Ch.
Cripps, C. Mag. | Round, E. Ball.
Ellis, E. St. Mary. | Smith, C. J. Ch. Ch.
Fort, H. Ball. | Stroud, R. A. H. Wad.
Heaton, C. W. Jesus. | Thurland, F.E. NwCol.
Hemsted, J. Mag. | Walker, R. Linc.
Jemmitt, G. E. Trin. | Warneford, J. H. Worc.
Jenkins, W. J. Ball.

EDW. ARTHUR DAYMAN,
CHAS. PAGE EDEN,   } Examiners.
WM. EDWARD JELF,
ARCH. CAMPBELL TAIT,

In Disciplinis Mathematicis et Physicis.

CLASS II.

Battersby, J. H. Ball.

CLASS III.

Brine, J. G. St. Joh. | Twiss, E. R. Univ.
Lempriere, C. St. Joh. | Wilson, W. D. Wad.
Marshall, J. Ch. Ch.

CLASS IV.

Allen, W. Mag. | Richards, R. M. Mert.
Jackson, W. Queen's. | Shand, G. Queen's.
Macfarlane, W. Linc.

The number in the fifth class was 84.

ROBERT WALKER,
WM. F. DONKIN,   } Examiners.
JOHN A. ASHWORTH,

CAMBRIDGE.

Number of resident members of the several colleges of the University, according to the latest returns:—

	In College.	In Ldgngs.	1841. Total Resdt.	1840. Total Resdt.
St. Peter's Coll.	60	25	85	75
Clare Hall	52	4	56	59
Pembroke	45	15	60	60
Gonville & Caius	55	33	88	96
Trinity Hall	28	4	32	33
Corpus Christi	85	22	107	113
King's	34	—	34	34
Queen's	48	54	102	111
Catharine Hall	34	50	84	83
Jesus	57	7	64	60
Christ's	72	12	84	72
St. John's	248	102	350	342
Magdalene	53	3	56	50
Trinity	220	227	447	448
Emmanuel	70	5	75	73
Sidney Sussex	38	2	40	34
Downing	10	3	13	11
	1209	568	1777	1754

Degrees conferred, Dec. 1.

D.M.

T. Willis, Caius Coll.

M.A.

S. R. Carver, Cath.; J. N. Wilkins, Trin.; J. F. Stanford, Christ's.

B.A.

C. Richson, Cath.

December 15.

M.A.

E. Cusack, Cath.

B.P.

J. Simpson, Caius.

B.A.

W. E. Tauuton, Trin.; E. M. S. Sandys, St. John's.

December 1.

The following Graces passed the Senate:—
That, in addition to the sum of 1878*l*. allowed by Grace of the Senate, July 3, 1841, for certain contracts therein specified, there be allowed a further sum of 110*l*. for the same purpose, in consideration of a proposed enlargement of the dimensions of the frieze of the ceiling, in accordance with the recommendation of the Fitzwilliam Syndicate.

To add the name of Mr. Robinson, of St. Peter's College, to the Fitzwilliam Museum Syndicate.

To appoint the Vice-Chancellor, the Rev. Dr. French, Master of Jesus College, the Rev. Dr. Tatham, Master of St. John's College, the Rev. Professor Whewell, Master of Trin. College, the Regius Professor of Divinity, the Norrisian Professor of Divinity, the Margaret Professor of Divinity, the Regius Professor of the Civil Law, and the Regius Professor of Greek, a Syndicate to consider whether any and what steps should be taken, to provide a more efficient system of Theological Instruction in the University—and, to report to the Senate before the end of the ensuing Lent Term.

This proposition was received without opposition in the Senior, or *Black Hood*, House; and, though *non placeted* in the Junior, or *White Hood*, House, was carried by a majority of 23 to 3.

In the examination held at Gonville and Caius College, on the second and two following days, the first places in Mathematics were assigned to the following:—

Freshmen.

Hopkins, 1st prize. | Watson, jun.
Woodhouse, 2d prize. | Brooke.

Senior Sophs.

Suffield. | Ottley } æq.
          | Eastwood

No prize was given to the Junior Sophs. The first place in Moral Philosophy for the Junior Sophs, to Gould.

There will be Congregations on the following days of the ensuing Lent Term:—
Saturday, Jan. 22, (B.A. Com.) at 10.
Wednesday, Feb. 2, at 11.
Wednesday, Feb. 9 (Ash Wednesday), at 11.
Wednesday, Feb. 23, at 11.
Friday, March 11 (M.A Inceptors), at 10.
Friday, March 18 (end of Term), at 10.

The Bishop of Ely's Fellowship at St. John's College, to which his lordship resigned his right to nominate, leaving it open to public competition, has been conferred upon A. M. Hopper, of Trin. Coll. (B.A. 1839), now a tutor of Eton. There were six candidates.

J. M. Croker, B.A. has been elected a Fellow of Gonville and Caius College, on the foundation of Dr. Perse.

CLARE HALL PRIZE MEN.

Declamation—Haskoll.
Theme—Sells.
Reading in Chapel—Haskoll.
Divinity—None adjudged.

COMBINATION PAPER—1842.

PRIOR COMB.

Jan. 2. Mr. Fisher, Ch.
     9. Mr. Burgess, Regin.
Jan. 16. Mr. Hodgson, Sid.
     23. Mr. Browne, Emm.
     30. Coll. Regal.
Feb. 6. Coll. Trin.
     13. Coll. Joh.
     20. Mr. Tate, Magd.
     27. Mr. Richmond, Regin.
Mar. 6. Mr. Myers, Clare.
     13. Mr. Holmes, Emm.
     20. Coll. Regal.
     27. FEST. PASCH.
Apr. 3. Coll. Joh.
     10. Mr. Proctor, Chr.
     17. Mr. Biscoe, Regin.
     24. Mr. Grigson, Corp.
May 1. Mr. Bourne, Cai.
     8. Coll. Regal.
     15. FEST. PENTEC.
     22. Coll. Joh.
     29. Mr. Hasted, Magd.
June 5. Mr. Sandys, jun. Regin.
     12. Mr. Bolton, Clar.
     19. Mr. Daniel, Cai.
     26. Coll. Regal.
July 3. COMMEM. BENEFACT.
     10. Coll. Trin.
     17. Coll. Joh.
     24. Mr. Webb. Chr.
     31. Mr. Frost, Cath.

POSTER COMB.

Jan. 1. FEST. CIRCUM. Mr. Evans, sen. Regin.
     2. Mr. Martin, Regin.
     6. FEST. EPIPH. Mr. Hayworth, Regin.
     9. Mr. Forster, Cath.
     16. Mr. Dawson, Cath.
     23. Mr. Barker, Cath.
     25. CONVER. S. PAUL. Mr. Cotton, Cath.
     30. Mr. Camson, Cath.
Feb. 2. FEST. PURIF. Mr. Dawkins, Cath.
     6. Mr. Prosser, Cath.
     9. DIES CINERUM. CONCIO AD CLERUM.
     13. Mr. Heaton, Cath.
     20. Mr. Kenrick, Jes.
     24. FEST. S. MAT. Mr. Clarkson, Chr.
     27. Mr. Morris, Chr.
Mar. 6. Mr. Whitmore, Chr.
     13. Mr. Wilkinson, Chr.
     20. Mr. Oldknowe, Chr.
     25. PASSIO DOMINI. Mr. Robertson, Chr.
     27. FEST. PASCH. Coll. Trin.
     28. *Fer.* 1*ma.* Mr. Wharton, Ch.
     29. *Fer.* 2*da.* Mr. Browne, Emm.
Apr. 3. Mr. Holmes, Emm.
     10. Mr. Barlow, Sid.
     17. Mr. Roe, Sid.
     24. Mr. Simpson. Sid.
     25. FEST. S. MARC. Mr. Hodgson, Sid.
May 1. FEST. SS. PHIL. ET JAC. Mr. Cartmell, Chr.
     5. FEST. ASCEN. { Mr. Harvey, Regal.
                     { Mr. Hand, Regal.
     8. Mr. Brooke, Regal.
     15. FEST. PENTEC. Coll. Trin.
     16. *Fer.* 1*ma.* Mr. J. H. Brown, Trin.
     17. *Fer.* 2*da.* Mr. A. Chatfield, Trin.
     22. Mr. Brooking, Trin.
     29. Mr. J. W. Campbell, Trin.
June 5. Mr. Tatham, Mag.
     11. FEST. S. BARNAB. Mr. Read, Mag.
     12. Mr. Williams, Corp.
     19. Mr. Greaves, Trin.
     24. FEST. S. JOH. BAPT. Mr. Hubbard, Trin.
     26. Mr. Lamb, Trin.
     29. FEST. S. PET. Mr. Monk, Trin.
July 3. COMMEM. BENEFACT.
     10. Mr. Marshall, Trin.
     17. Mr. Tindal, Trin.
     24. Mr. Bovell, Trin.

July 25. FEST. S. JAC. Mr. Brookfield, Trin.
31. Mr. Fitzroy, Trin.

RESP. IN JUR. CIV.	OPPON.
Mr. Moody, Trin.	{ Mr. Hodges, Emm. Mr. Bennett, Emm.
RESP. IN MEDIC.	OPPON.
Mr. Burman, Cai.	{ Mr. Price, Emm. Mr. Jarvis, Trin.
RESP. IN THLOLOG.	OPPON.
Mr. Reeve, Clar.	{ Coll. Regal. Coll. Trin. Coll. Joh.
Mr. Ferrand, Trin.	{ Mr. Owen, Mag. Mr. Grffiths, Regin. Mr. Molineux, Clar.

RESP. IN THEOLOG.	OPPON.
Mr. Reymond, Trin. ...	{ Mr. Eade, Cai. Coll. Regal. Coll. Trin.
Mr. Mason, Clar.	{ Coll. John. Mr. Russell, Pet. Mr. Marcus, Regin.
Mr. Armstrong, Joh. ...	{ Mr. Baily, Clar. Mr. Howarth, Cai. Coll. Regal.
Mr. G. L. Thompson, Trin.	{ Coll. Trin. Coll. Joh. Mr. Potter, Pet.

The Crosse Scholarship has been adjudged to H. Lovell, B.A. of St. John's College.

H. M. Birch, Scholar of King's College, has been elected a Fellow of that Society.

DURHAM.

November 23.

J. Thomas, M.A. made the requisite declaration, on being admitted to the office of Junior Proctor.

The Rev. J. Cundill was nominated by the Junior Proctor to the office of Pro-Proctor, and made the requisite declaration.

Addresses of Congratulation to the Queen and to Prince Albert, on the birth of a son, the heir-apparent to the throne, were proposed by the Senate, and approved by Convocation.

C. J. P. Forster, B.A. of Oriel College, Oxford, was presented and admitted *ad eundem*.

The Rev. G. Reeke, M.A. of Merton College, Oxford, was admitted *ad eundem* by vote of the House.

A Statute was proposed by the Senate, and approved by Convocation, for the management of the estates lately assigned to the University by an order of the Queen in Council.

A Grace was passed for making some changes in the regulations relating to the Observatory.

Colonel J. A. Hodgson, of the Hon. East India Company's Service, was nominated by the Warden, and approved by Convocation, to be a Curator of the Observatory.

PROCEEDINGS OF SOCIETIES.

INCORPORATED SOCIETY FOR PROMOTING THE ENLARGEMENT, BUILDING, AND REPAIRING OF CHURCHES AND CHAPELS.

A meeting of the Committee of this Society was held at their chambers, St. Martin's Place, on Monday, the 20th December, 1841. N. Connop, jun. Esq. in the chair. Among the members present were the Reverends Dr. D'Oyley, Dr. Shepherd, J. Jennings, and Benj. Harrison; J. W. Bowden, Esq., S. F. Wood, Esq., &c. &c.

Grants were voted towards building a church at Yeadon, in the parish of Guiseley, York; building a church at Nepicar, in the parish of Wrotham, Kent; repewing and erecting galleries in the church at Snitterfield, Warwick; repewing the church at Great Chesterford, Essex; repewing and erecting galleries in the church at Holme, Norfolk; enlarging the chapel at Stonnall, Stafford; enlarging and repewing the church at Stony Stanton, Leicester; enlarging gallery and extending pews in the chapel at Flockton, York; enlarging the church at Ashelworth, Gloucester; building galleries in the church at Sunderland; enlarging by rebuilding the church at Countesthorpe, Leicester; building a chapel at Cambo, in the parish of Hartburn, Northumberland; enlarging by rebuilding the church at Shipham, Somerset; and other business was transacted.

MISCELLANEOUS INTELLIGENCE.

CANTERBURY.—*Roehampton*.—On Sunday, Nov. 21, collections were made at the proprietary chapel of Roehampton, Surrey, for the purpose of erecting in that hamlet a handsome and capacious chapel for consecration. The contributions of communicants were offered at the altar. Those of non-communicants received at the door, both at morning and evening service.

The sum offered at the altar
amounted to £614 19 8
That taken at the doors 16 13 2

Total £631 12 10

Nearly 1000*l.* more has been put into the hands of the Committee, who have undertaken to superintend the work, which is to be effected entirely by voluntary contributions, and without application for pecuniary aid to any society. The nomination of the curate will be vested in his Grace the Archbishop of Canterbury, the diocesan.

DURHAM.—Dr. Waddington, Dean of Durham, presided the other day at a meeting of some thirty clergymen, including Archdeacon Thorp and the Rev. Dr. Gilly, to establish a training school in Durham, for the purpose of teaching and sending into the diocese a superior class of teachers. Four hundred pounds had been subscribed, and it was confidently believed that in a very short time a hopeful and permanent establishment would be formed.

The Dean and Chapter of Durham have given a donation of 100*l.* towards the fund for the restoration of Hexham Abbey.

ELY.—*Cambridge.*—The Provost and Fellows of King's College have resolved to restore, as far as possible, the beautiful stained windows of their noble chapel to their original splendour. For this purpose, they have engaged the able services of Mr. Hedgland, of London. Mr. H., a short time since, superintended the cleaning and repairing of a compartment of the window at the west end of the chapel, an improvement which has gained the approbation of all observers. He has now taken down the whole of the window on the south side of the altar, and we believe that, should he succeed in restoring this window, the restoration of the others will be committed to his care. There are twenty-four painted windows, exclusive of the east window, and it is computed that each window will cost about 400*l.*, and that Mr. H. will require about twelve years to complete the work.

Camden Society.—Twenty-second Meeting. Twenty-one new members were balloted for and elected, and the Right Rev. the Bishop of the Anglican Church in Jerusalem was admitted a patron of the society.

A list of presents received since the last meeting having been read, a short report was next given from the Committee. From this it appeared that 25*l.* had been granted by the Society to St. Sepulchre's, and 5*l.* to the restoration of Meldreth Church: that applications had been received from Leicester, St. Margaret's, and Stapleford Abbots, Essex: that, after much discussion as to the roof of St. Sepulchre's, it had been resolved to vault it, if sufficient funds could be raised, in stone, otherwise the conical roof would be left open, and in no case a lath and plaster imitation allowed: that 5*l.* had been voted for the purpose of obtaining working drawings of the wood seats in Whittlesford Church: that the first number of the Society's periodical report, the Ecclesiologist, was lying on the table; and that the fourth number of the Illustrations of Monumental Brasses would appear in about ten days.

A paper on the History of Pews was then read by the Rev. J. M. Neale, B.A., chaplain of Downing, in which, after proving that in the present sense of the word they did not exist before the Reformation, he proceeded to bring forward various passages containing allusions to them, in pamphlets of the 17th century; and concluded by pointing out several reasons why they were always supported by Puritans.

A paper was then read by S. Nicholls, Esq., of Trinity College, on the Round Towers of Ireland; illustrated by several sketches.

After a few words from the Right Hon. W. E. Gladstone, M.P. (who was introduced to the Society by the President,) which he expressed his sympathy with, and interest in its proceedings, the meeting adjourned at a little before ten.

LONDON.—*Rishop's Stortford.*—We are glad to be able to record the revival of the primitive mode of collecting at the offertory in this church. Here as elsewhere, we believe, it has been found that this is not only the right way, but that it is also the most effectual in procuring liberal contributions.—*From a Correspondent.*

OXFORD.—*Architectural Society.*—A meeting was held on December 1, Dr. Buckland in the chair.

New Members admitted:—J. R. Fletcher, Esq., Worc.; J. D. Mereweather, Esq., St. Edm.; R. S. Sutton, Esq., Exet.; W. B. Lott, Esq., Ball.; E. Hobhouse, Esq., Mert.; S. H. Cooke, Esq., Ch. Ch.; W. G. Gibson, Esq., Worc.; B. Drury, Esq. Linc.; H. Pigott, Esq., Brasen.; J. Dawson, Esq., Exet.; E. B. Smith, Esq., Queen's.

A collection of specimens of Gothic Tiles, from the manufactory of Mr. Minton, were presented by Mr. Theodore Jewitt.

A new Tile, of a large size, having the royal arms for the pattern, from the manufactory of Messrs. Chamberlain, was also exhibited.

A paper was read by the Rev. W. Sewell, of Exeter College, on the characteristics of the various styles of Architecture, more particularly the Gothic, which is to be printed.

Hungerford.—We mentioned, not many months since, that Rd. Compton, Esq., of Eddington House, had given to the clergymen and churchwardens of Hungerford a freehold site and a large quantity of materials towards building a schoolroom at New Town, in that parish. We have great pleasure in learning that the good gift has been fully profited by, and that the new room was opened on Monday last for daily use. The entire cost of it will be little more than 100*l.*, nearly the whole of which has been subscribed. The Dowager Lady Cooper has given 50*l.*; the Misses Compton 10*l.* (in addition to supplying the benches, books, &c.); Wm. Honywood, Esq. 10*l.*; the Rev. Dr. Gaisford (Dean of Ch. Ch.), 10*l.*; the Rev. C. B. Coxe, 5*l.*; the Hon. Miss Harley, 5*l.*; the Rev. Wm. C. Edgell (Curate of Hungerford), 5*l.*; Mr. Robt. Pitt, 5*s.*—*Berks Chronicle.*

SODOR AND MANN.—On Sunday, the 21st of November, the New Schoolhouse, built at Cronk-y-Voddy, in the parish of German (aided by a grant from her Majesty's government) was opened with Divine service by the Bishop of this diocese, who preached on the occasion; and Divine service was again performed and a sermon preached in the afternoon. The schoolroom is about four and a half miles from the parish church of German, and three and a half miles from the parish church of Michael. It is purposed to have Divine service performed in the said schoolroom every Lord's day, every afternoon, and also, if possible, every morning.

On Thursday, the 25th November, the new chapel of St. Jude, in the parish of Andreas, in this diocese, was consecrated by the Right Rev. the Lord Bishop, who preached on the occasion, and administered the Sacrament of the Lord's Supper; several of the clergy were present. The collections amounted to about 12*l.* Dr. Carpenter, of St. Barnabas, Douglas, preached in the evening. The desk service was read by the Rev. William Drury, Curate of Andreas, who on the following day received his presentation to St. Jude's from the Venerable Archdeacon Hall, Rector of Andreas, and Mr. Drury was instituted to the chapelry, at Bishop's Court, by the Bishop on the same day. The chapel is built in a remote district of the parish of Andreas, on the lands of Close-E-Kee, the property of W. W. Christian, Esq., who made a present of the ground on which the chapel is built, and also for burial-ground when required for that purpose. The chapel of St. Jude was built by an Act of Tynwald, passed at Castle Rushen, Jan. 4, 1839, and by an Act of Tynwald, passed in the second year of her present Majesty, intituled "An Act for the Commutation of Tithes in the Isle of Man," the sum of 101*l.* is to be paid annually to the Chaplain of St. Jude. The patronage is in the Rector of the parish of Andreas. The plate for the Communion Service was presented by Dr. Pepys, Bishop of Worcester. The chapel contains thirty-four seats or pews, twelve of which are free.

WALES.

LAMPETER.—The College of Lampeter, South Wales, founded through the exertions and benevolence of the late Bishop Burgess, is in a very prosperous state, and contains, at this time, about sixty students preparing for the work of the ministry. A legacy of 500*l.* has just accrued to the college, by the decease of a clergyman in Essex.

CHURCH IN SCOTLAND.

NEW THEOLOGICAL SEMINARY.

To all faithful Members of the Reformed Catholic Church, the Bishops in Scotland, greeting.

Grace be with you, mercy and peace, from God the Father, and our Lord Jesus Christ.

Whereas certain lay members of the Church, moved by a pious desire to promote the glory of God, and the welfare of the flock over which he hath made us overseers, have represented unto us that our Church, having been long depressed, hath suffered the total loss of temporal endowments; and that hence great difficulty hath been found in maintaining the decent administration of God's word and sacraments, more especially in so far as the same depends upon the due education of candidates for holy orders; that the sense of this deficiency hath been frequently declared by various pious but inadequate bequests for this purpose, and more recently by the Church herself in her XLth Canon, and that the same still exists in almost undiminished magnitude:

And whereas they have represented unto us their desire, under God's blessing, to attempt a remedy for this want, and, in pursuance of such design, have proposed to us the foundation of a School and Theological Seminary, to be devoted to the training, under collegiate discipline, of candidates for holy orders, and at the same time of such other persons as may desire the benefit of a liberal, in conjunction with a religious, education:

And whereas they have represented unto us, that sufficient pecuniary support hath been secured to warrant their perseverance in the design, and that they are now desirous, under our sanction, to make a public appeal to the members of the Church in its behalf:

Now we, the Bishops of the Reformed Catholic Church in Scotland, in Synod assembled, desire to express our warmest gratitude to those with whom this proposal hath originated, and above all to God, who hath put it into their hearts to attempt the supply of wants, the reality and urgency of which we have long painfully experienced; and having maturely considered the said design, we do hereby formally approve the same, and recommend it to you, our brethren in Christ, as a fitting object for your prayers and alms.

We have farther, for the promotion of this good work, requested certain discreet persons to act in Committee, and, in concert with ourselves, to prepare a scheme for its execution, to be submitted to the members of the Church.

In thus endeavouring to awaken your zeal and charity in behalf of that portion of the Church committed to our charge, we deem it fitting to state solemnly and explicitly, that we are moved by no feelings of rivalry towards any religious community, but by a desire to supply the wants of our own communion, and thereby to fulfil a duty implied in the first principles of the christian church.

Brethren, the grace of our Lord Jesus Christ be with your spirits. Amen.

W. SKINNER, D.D. *Bishop of Aberdeen, and Primus.*
PATRICK TORRY, D.D. *Bishop of Dunkeld, Dunblane, and Fife.*
DAVID LOW, LL.D. *Bishop of Moray, Ross, and Argyll.*
MICHAEL RUSSELL, LL.D. *Bishop of Glasgow.*
DAVID MOIR, D.D. *Bishop of Brechin.*
C. H. TERROT, D.D. *Bishop of Edinburgh.*

Edinburgh, 2d Sept. 1841.

For further particulars respecting this important measure we refer our readers to the paper appended to the present number.

CHURCHES CONSECRATED.

New Catton	Christ Church	Bishop of Norwich	Nov. 16.
Bradford, Wilts	Christ Church	Bishop of Sarum	Nov. 17.
Cornute Hall End, Essex	Chapel	Bishop of London	Nov. 23.
Liverpool	Wannell Street New Church	Bishop of Chester	Dec. 1.
Yatton, Ledbury	New Chapel	Bishop of Hereford	

We gladly correct an error in our November number. It appears that the Messrs. Haldane have never held the heresy of denying our Lord's eternal Sonship, which we had been led to attribute to them.

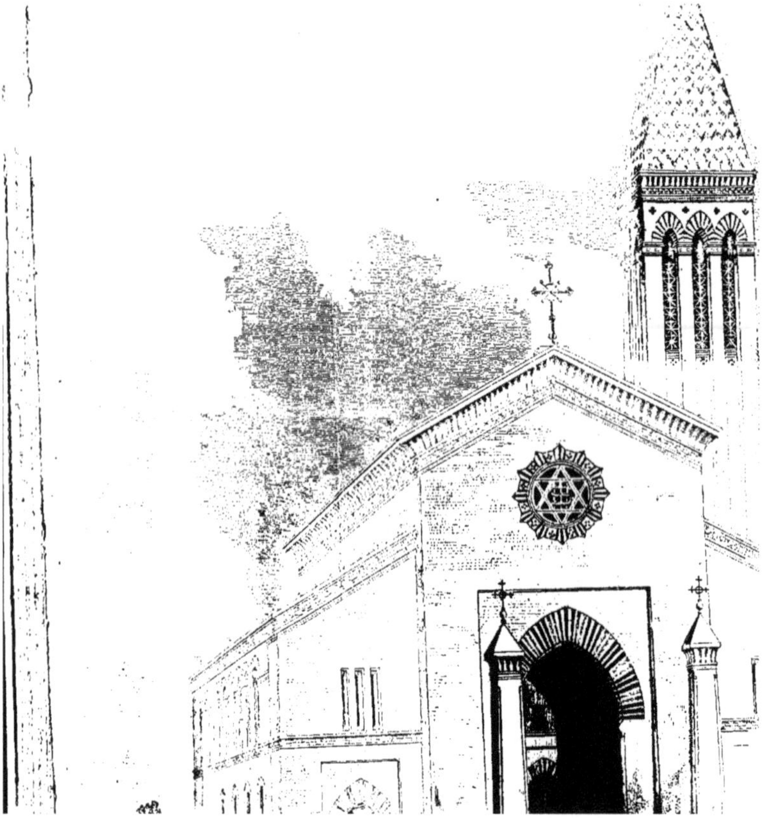

Interior of Christchurch Cheltenham.

THE CHRISTIAN REMEMBRANCER.

FEBRUARY, 1842.

1. *Masterman Ready; or, the Wreck of the Pacific.* By Captain MARRYAT. London: Longman and Co. 1841.
2. *Leila; or, the Island.* By ANN FRASER TYTLER. Second Edition, London: Hatchards. 1841.
3. *The Forest of Arden; a Tale, illustrative of the English Reformation.* By the Rev. W. GRESLEY, M.A. London: Burns. 1841.
4. *Tales of the Village.* 1st, 2d, and 3d Series. By the Rev. F. E. PAGET, M.A. London: Burns. 1841.
5. *The Fairy Bower; or, the History of a Month.* London: Burns. 1841.
6. *The Lost Brooch; or, the History of another Month.* London: Burns. 1841.
7. *Rutilius and Lucius; or, Stories of the Third Age.* By ROBERT I. WILBERFORCE, M.A. London: Burns. 1842.
8. *Conversations with Cousin Rachel.* 3 Pts. London: Burns. 1841.
9. *Sintram and his Companions.* Translated from the German of De la Motte Fouque. London: Burns. 1842.
10. *Abdiel: a Tale of Ammon.* London: Burns. 1842.

(Continued from page 89.)

WE will resume the subject of "Didactic Fiction" with Mr. Paget's Tales of the Village. His St. Antholin's is perhaps still better known, but hardly falls within our present scope, having a particular purpose, and that not immediately connected with education. As we have already dealt largely in comparisons, we will commence with a new one, and entreat our readers to remember the celebrated Death-bed Scenes. The plan of that work is very similar to Mr. Paget's, the main difference beyond what is produced by the respective minds of the two authors, consisting in Dr. Warton laying his scene in a populous, and seemingly suburban district; and Mr. Paget in an entirely rural one. This is a circumstance which it is but fair to keep in mind, as it must be one cause of the greatly pleasanter impression produced by the latter. But even after this allowance, the difference is in this respect so greatly in Mr. Paget's favour, that we must look about for other causes. His book is altogether a much more amiable one than Dr. Warton's.* It is impossible not to feel that the Death-bed Scenes were written for party

---

* In the following remarks we must be understood as referring only to the first volume of the Death-bed Scenes, being unacquainted with the others.

purposes, and that the orthodox principles contained in them are brought out rather as weapons against a hostile party than as if valued for their own sakes and at all times. From Dr. Warton and the school which he represents we should never hear of the apostolical succession, were there no unauthorized teachers, who at once want and gainsay it. Mr. Paget would fain there were none, that he might all the more undisturbedly dwell on, and believe, and rejoice in it, without being put to the pain of defending it. In brief, Dr. Warton's high churchmanship is negative, Mr. Paget's is positive. We encounter next to nothing of the evangelical party in the Tales of the Village; we have far too much of them in the Death-bed Scenes. And one most important result from this difference between negative and positive churchmanship is fully manifested in the two works. In the Death-bed Scenes, the Church is but one separate item in the writer's creed, and the rest of the doctrine is seemingly independent of it; in the Tales of the Village, whatever subject the writer brings before us, we feel at once that we have to do with a man of catholic mind. As long as the doctrine of the Church is supposed to be independent of the rest of the christian scheme, it may be accurately (though certainly not adequately) stated, and ably and satisfactorily vindicated; but it will remain unattractive and inoperative. Whilst it is viewed merely as a mean to an end, men of sectarian tendencies will turn a deaf ear to arguments proving it to be the only legitimate mean; however unable to answer such arguments, they will content themselves with the persuasion that they have attained or are attaining the end, so long as we concede them that. Represent the Church as itself an end, yea, as God's eternal purpose in Christ Jesus, as that to produce which all other things, the whole visible creation, and all the energies of the universe, are but means; tell men that their whole being is a riddle and a monstrosity except as members of the Holy Catholic Church; that to the Church, and not to individuals, (except as belonging to the Church,) are all the promises made; tell them that it is because the Church is God's holy constitution in Christ Jesus, that relationship to Christ, justification and sanctification, are possible for any creature; tell them all this, and such as have honest and true hearts will listen to you; they will feel this to be living truth; they will then see, that to assert and uphold an apostolical ministry, is to assert and uphold no cold notion of mere authority, but a vital channel of derivation from their Lord and Saviour; that it must needs be a great thing to ascertain who are God's Jeshurun, and to join their ranks; that it must needs be a great thing to cease to regard ourselves as individuals, and to feel that we belong to the true Israel of God. Accordingly, when a man has once learned to look upon the Church in this light, an all-penetrating element has been introduced into his theology; every doctrine gets coloured by this pervading idea; and of whatever he is speaking, be it pardon or justification, or holiness, or the sacraments or death, or the unseen world, his churchmanship must at once be apparent.

Now, this living and pervading high churchmanship is just what we think the Death-bed Scenes are without. We are told not to go to dissenting meetings, because their ministers have no commission from Christ. We are told not to agitate ourselves with the question whether we be regenerate or no, because regeneration is the benefit of holy baptism—two important truths undoubtedly; but then we are told of them in a way that stirs up all the antagonism of our nature; they are spoken to us *at* others, or to hush the aspirations of our better being; we are not presented with them in such a way as to find in them a refuge from our own naked and shivering individuality, a fellowship with all the blessed in Christ, a participation of Him who is one with the Father.

Again, Dr. Warton deals largely in matter which we think ought to be wholly excluded from '*didactic fiction*,'— the question of Calvinism. It is a question of which we trust churchmen are now heartily sick. But few of them (none of them indeed who are in any measure conformed to the spirit of the Prayer-book) are likely to present us with the full and frightful symmetry of Genevan doctrine. And in regard to those Calvinistic and Arminian questions of which churchmen certainly take different views, which indeed men's minds will entertain more or less variously to the end of time, and the diversity of judgment concerning which is probably to be ascribed more to the different sides from which they are approached than to anything else, we have been taught, we think, to deprecate the discussion. What the eloquence of Horsley could not instil into us, we have learned from the progress of events; we have been made to feel that we *must* have union; that the Church and the sacraments give us all needful ground of union; and that questions of fixed decrees and election ought not to put asunder those whom God, by means of the Church and the sacraments, has made one. Mr. Paget's Tales of the Village, as compared with the Death-bed Scenes, represent, we think, this salutary change. To introduce the Calvinistic and Arminian controversy in a fiction about almshouses, would be only less abhorrent to his feelings, we should think, than introducing it within the walls of real ones; he does not, we hope and believe, so greatly waste his time.

One merit he and Dr. Warton have in common—the liveliness and verisimilitude of their incidents. Neither introduces anything that might not very well have occurred. Each, though perhaps more especially Dr. Warton, writes from experience, the creditable experience of an active and conscientious parish priest; each laudably refrains from doing what the powers of each might have tempted him to do, working up exciting scenes in connexion with holy things.

Dr. Warton is free from an error which we greatly wish Mr. Paget would correct, that of giving significant names to his characters, a practice which is a favourite one with many writers and no readers. It is more tolerable in a satire like St. Antholin's, than amid the calm, rural, English scenes and personages of the Tales of the Village. Its disturbing influence on illusion is too obvious to require explanation; but it has also, we think, an injurious and fettering effect on the writer himself, which it may be worth while to point out. When he introduces us to a Miss Prowle and a Miss Burr, not only are we balked of the pleasure of gradually finding out their characters for ourselves, studying them as we should other new acquaintance, and comparing subsequent with first impressions, but he incapacitates himself from any progressive evolution; he fixes himself to his first announcement, and gains nothing by his own labours. Moreover, he almost inevitably presents us with characters all one or all another quality—all malignity or all gossip. We do not get that distinct individual whole of which the several features and colours are confusedly blended, and in which each sometimes baffles detection just where we expect to find it, yet is never far off, and never suffers itself to be long forgotten, which real characters are, and in compounding which the great masters of fiction have excelled.* Hamlet is not always musing and always overmastered by sensibility in the hour of action; Lear is not always a vain silly old man; Macbeth is not a ruffian, nor Falstaff a self-indulgent coward in all things. There goes more than one quality to the composition of any man or woman, and the action and counteraction of many elements often produce results inconsistent with the leading ones.

We have dwelt the longer on this fault, because it is nearly the only one we have observed in Mr. Paget, and because it can so easily be avoided another time. We will now give our readers a short account of the "Tales of the Village," and shall be happy if our recommendation have the effect of leading any to become acquainted with them, who were not so before. We assure parents they can find no books of the sort more useful for the school-room or the drawing-room table.

Each series of the three which have appeared has a leading subject of its own; in consequence of which, in the Tales of the Village we have three prevalent evils illustrated, Romanism, Dissent, and Infidelity. In the first the heroine, Magdalen Fernley, is a Papist; and on coming into Mr. Warlingham's (the fictitious author's) parish is doomed for a while to an ultra-protestant course of treatment at the hands of a certain Mrs. Hopkins, which only binds her to the Roman communion faster than ever. Subsequently, however, Mr. Warlingham gets her to see what the Church of England really holds, and what she is; in consequence of which she abandons the Romish errors, and joins the apostolic communion of this country. The whole tale is pleasingly told, and the theology most unexceptionable. The claims of our Church as the apostolical and ancient one of the land are well set forth. That of Rome is not ignorantly taxed with faults that do not belong to her; our differences with her are not over-stated, neither are they, we assure sensitive Protestants, understated. If any of our alarmist friends fear lest Mr. Paget draw the line between ourselves and Rome too faintly; or if, like the news-

---

* This makes Mr. Paget much too frequently a caricaturist, in consequence of which the parties portrayed will naturally exclaim against his injustice, and lose the benefit he designs for them.

papers, they consider Messrs. Sibthorp and Wackerbarth real representatives of high Anglican theology, and their desertion to the Pope its legitimate fruit; we commend to their perusal pp. 168, 169, with the adjoining passages of the first series of the Tales of the Village. They will there find that Mr. Paget sees more than a slight difference between the churches; and that so long as he continues in his present way of thinking, it is absolutely inconceivable that he should either be enticed himself, or be the means of enticing others, into the popish errors. In the present sensitive state of the public mind, it seems necessary to point out what otherwise would hardly require explanation on this point.

We alluded last month to a defect in this First Series, the long speeches put into the mouth of Mr. Lee in the very article of death. Should it come to another edition, we hope Mr. Paget will correct this. The awfulness of death, the sublime isolation expressed in the words "je mourrai seul," seem to us tampered with, by representing it with a feature for the most part physically impossible, the dying man *conversing* with those around him.

The Second and Third Series seem to us a good deal more powerful than the first. In the second, the character of Mark Fullerton, the nature of his dissent, and his downward progress, are admirably sketched.* They are manifested throughout the book, but the reader may gain some insight from the following passage, in which the whole state of the case is condensed:—

> Thus I argued with myself, and for a while succeeded in quieting my misgivings; but it would not do; the more I thought over the evening's conversation the less I was satisfied. I could not be sure that I had gained any ground; and I remembered with pain that (though, for the reader's sake, I have not thought it necessary to give evidence of the fact) Mark reverted again and again to arguments which had been already answered, and that he brought forward his old objections as if unconscious that they had been refuted.
>
> He did not appear to wish to inquire fairly or candidly. When beaten from one position, he directly took up another of perhaps a directly opposite nature. He seemed disposed to maintain any notion, no matter how untenable, sooner than give in. He argued, indeed, good-humouredly, and in a gentlemanlike manner, but defeat made no impression on him. "You may very possibly be right," he more than once exclaimed, "and I may be wrong; but I do think it, and always shall think it."—*Tales of the Village*, Second Series, p. 126.

How often does one encounter all this in real life! How common is it for *getters up of* reasons for any thing they do not like to return to an argument in this way, however often it has been refuted; and how astonished they would be to hear themselves taxed with dishonesty! It is one of the perversities of human nature, that slight and shallow persons of this sort tempt one to discussion oftener than any other; whereas, at once the truest friendship and the justest treatment would be, to decline argument with them, on serious subjects, on the express ground of their dishonesty.

We commend the following to the consideration of ultra-Protes-

---

* Even here, however, dissenters *generally* will not consider themselves fairly aimed at.

tants. Mr. Warlingham's reasoning is both ingenious and unanswerable :—

"This may be all very well," said Mark, "but, to my simple apprehension, the end of your system is, and must be, the admission of mere human authorities."

"Do you mean," I asked, "that we are not to admit human explanations of Scripture? If you do, you will soon find yourself in an extraordinary difficulty."

"How so?" said Mark.

"Because if (casting aside all external aid) you take your Bible in your hand, and explain it to yourself, that explanation will be human to you, or else it would not be human to those who receive it from you."

"Do you mean, then, to tell me that human explanations of Scripture are Scripture?"

"I will answer you," I replied, "in the words of Waterland: we receive the evidence of tradition; and if we thus preserve the true sense of Scripture, and upon that sense build our faith, *we then build upon Scripture only; for the sense of Scripture is Scripture.*"—Pp. 117, 118.

We have not left ourselves space for more notice of the Third Series than is involved in presenting our readers with the following extract, which every man who has reached the years of discretion and discussion in the course of the last twenty or fourteen years, must admit is most true to nature :—

I had no time for further reflection, for the door had scarcely closed upon Mr. Mandevyl, when it opened again: a young man hastily entered, and, without noticing me, (who happened to be concealed from his view by the folds of a screen,) exclaimed, "Why, hey-day, Flint! what's the matter now? Martin Gale stops me in the stable-yard, to tell me you have turned him off at a moment's warning; and Bob Mandevyl meets me in the passage, looking black as night and fierce as ten furies, and says you have got a parson into the house on purpose to insult him."

Mr Flint, who was a very good-natured man, looked quite distressed at this untoward speech; but I suppose an involuntary smile on my part reassured him, and he introduced me to Sir Luke Warme.

"Why, I'll tell you, Luke," he continued, "how the case stands. I find that Martin Gale, besides laming the chestnut filly, has been cockfighting on a Sunday under Mr. Warlingham's windows—both of them pretty strong measures on his part, I think;—so the sooner he's off the better. And as for Mandevyl, he is old enough and impudent enough to fight his own battles; but a poorer figure than he cut in the last I never saw. And, mark you, it was *he* who commenced the attack, not Mr. Warlingham."

"Well then," said Sir Luke, "I hope he got a good 'blowing-up' for his pains. I'm for every man holding his own opinions, without let or hinderance; but that's no reason why he should obtrude them upon other people; and I know of old that master Mandevyl is apt to go rather too far."

"Especially when he questions the truth of revelation," said I.

"To be sure—to be sure," replied the baronet, in a somewhat patronizing tone,—"I really don't see what people would be at, or what they gain by trying to disbelieve the Bible. I trust I am as free from intolerance and bigotry as most people; but still I own I have not much respect for your deists: they are too fond of their own opinions, think nobody knows any thing but themselves. With our fellow-Christians, indeed, of all sects and opinions, I think we are bound to hold communion. Sink all the minor differences, say I. I am a Churchman myself; but I live as much with Dissenters as Churchmen.

' For modes of faith let graceless zealots fight;
 His can't be wrong whose life is in the right.'

That's my doctrine, Mr. Warlingham."

"I am sorry to hear it, sir," I replied; "for it is not the doctrine of that Bible which exborts us earnestly to contend for the faith which was once delivered unto the saints; otherwise the Church of England would not in her articles pronounce those '*accursed*' who 'presume to say that every man shall be saved by the law or sect which he professeth, so that he be diligent to frame his life according to that law and the light of nature.'"

"Sir, I protest I never heard of such an article before ; and I think it the height of illiberality."

"Surely, sir, as a Churchman, and a man of education, you must know what are the articles of faith prescribed by that Church with which you profess to hold communion?",

"Why, upon my word, Mr. Warlingham, I don't think I have read the articles since I left Brasennose; and to confess the honest truth, I don't believe I read much of them there; for the divinity lecture often fell on a hunting morning; and I was more apt to go to cover than to the lecture-room."

"But you studied them eventually for your degree?"

"Why, Mr. Warlingham, my Oxford studies came to their close rather abruptly. Marry, how and why, the proctors knew better than I did: but if, as you say, the articles are so intolerant, I wish they would reform them, or get rid of them. I have long thought that we should get on much better without them."

"But as you admit, Sir Luke, that you have not studied the articles, is it not just possible that you may be rather indiscreet in thus condemning them?"

"Oh, upon my word, sir," replied the baronet, in a tone of indifference, "I cannot pretend to discuss the matter theologically,—indeed, I make it a rule to avoid polemics ; independently of their being exciting, and irritating, and all that, they only tend to fill one's mind with prejudice, and bigotry, and partybias, and so cramp the charities of life. I am a citizen of the world, I flatter myself; and as such, Mr. Warlingham, I should think it shame to brand a fellow-citizen with the name either of hireling or heretic. I would be well with all parties; and where I can harmonize in principles, I will not differ for punctilios."

"And you would so designate the points insisted on in the articles?" said I.

"I don't know for that exactly; because, as I told you, I am not very well read in them; but I belong to the Protestant religion——"

"What is that?" I asked, feeling that the profession was of the vaguest, and scarcely anticipating the extent of his liberality.

Sir Luke did not heed the question, but proceeded—" I belong to the Protestant religion ; and I therefore look on Protestants of all denominations as so nearly united with me in sentiment, that I do not stop to inquire into minor points of difference. And further, Mr. Warlingham, I am a Christian ; and so, although a Protestant, I do not forget that Roman Catholics are Christians too; and therefore, why should I bother myself with the petty controversies which have been the cause of disunion between the adherents of one common Christianity?"

"Well put, Luke!" cried Mr. Flint triumphantly; "I love to hear such liberal, generous sentiments as these."

"Indeed," said I, interposing, "I must confess that Sir Luke has disappointed me; he has stopped short just where I expected him to go forward. He has spoken of himself as a Protestant and a Christian ; but after all, what are these but party-names, and petty distinctions? Is he not a member of a yet larger family? Has he forgotten that he is a *man*? Has he forgotten that

'One touch of nature makes the whole world kin?'

that the same sun which shines on him shines likewise on the Buddhist, the Mahometan, and the worshipper of Fo? Why should he enter upon the immaterial question, whether Mahomet was an impostor, or Fo or Buddha are mere idols? why should controversies on such points as these disunite and divide the human race?"

Sir Luke stared for a moment, as if puzzled, for hitherto I had spoken with much gravity; but when I saw the expression of his face, I could keep my countenance no longer, and thereupon the baronet burst into a hearty laugh.

"Eh? what, you are quizzing me, are you, Mr. Warlingham?" he said: "well well, it is better to laugh than to fight about such matters. But for all your laughing, you may rely upon it I am not far wrong. I don't mean that there are not many worthy, respectable people of your way of thinking—(we *must* make allowance for prejudice and early impressions);—but the world is arriving at true principles; illiberality and bigotry are on their death-beds; and it will soon be universally acknowledged among philanthropists, that all opinions are true to those who think them true."

"And that therefore in state-policy, all are to be equally encouraged?" said I.

"Exactly so," replied Sir Luke; "this is the sentiment of men of the most enlightened minds among us. It is a great moral truth, the discovery of which is worthy of an age like ours."

"Indeed, I think so," I answered; "for we live in an age which is ready to adopt any opinion that has plausibility or expediency to recommend it; but as a *discovery*, your philanthropical sentiment is by no means new: the opinions you advocate are precisely those of the king of Siam, who, when Louis XIV. sent ambassadors and a band of missionaries to his territories, and invited him to embrace Christianity, replied, that since unity in religion depended absolutely on Providence, who could as easily have introduced that, as the diversity of sects that prevail in the world, his conclusion was, that the true God takes as much pleasure in being served one way as another; and therefore, while his Siamese majesty permitted the Jesuits to preach any thing they liked, he and his people begged to remain idolaters. This was a very easy, comfortable way of going on, and one which, by his own showing, Sir Luke Warme would most thoroughly approve: the only objection to it that I can see is, that the Bible declares that it is by no means immaterial what men believe, and that God is not indifferent whether he is addressed as

'Jehovah, Jove, or Lord.'

But perhaps you find no difficulty in this, Sir Luke."

The nonchalant baronet could not but perceive the absurdity of his position; but what cared he? he had a fund of imperturbable good humour, and was quite ready to laugh at himself.

"Ah, I see you want to drive me into a corner, Mr. Warlingham, by putting an extreme case," said he; "I may not be a good hand at an argument, and, indeed, I started by reminding you that I was unprepared to enter on a polemical discussion. People will differ; but let me hold my opinions, and I shan't quarrel with yours. Every man for himself, say I. Mr. Warlingham, sooner or later you will come to be of my way of thinking: you will find liberal opinions are to you as the air you breathe; you will say, ' I must have them, or die.' Flint, my good fellow, who made those boots? they are a very good fit."

Of course it was vain to attempt to pursue the conversation further; and even if I had had the opportunity, I should have only elicited a few more of Sir Luke's common-place plausibilities. He was one of those people who seem hardly to be aware when they have got the worst of an argument. Cool, calm, thoroughly well satisfied with himself, never put out of temper, neither troubled with any great acuteness of feeling, of fixedness of principle, he was considered a very rising man among the liberal party of the day in the House of Commons. Year after year, as member for the borough of Blackswhite, he used to get up, and with the greatest professions of kindly feeling towards the Church, endeavour to do her all the harm he could. His fallacies, indeed, were continually answered, and his misstatements exposed; but having apologized for them one day, he revived them in some other shape the next, still insisting on his regard for the Church, and his desire for her purity and peace, but never failing to lend his vote to those measures respecting her which were rather based on expediency than justice, and ever maintaining the opinion that it was her duty to yield till her opponents should be satisfied.

The conversation being now turned to Mr. Flint's boots, I saw no further necessity for prolonging my visit; and, having shaken hands with my host, took my leave, and departed.

I returned home sad and sick at heart with all I had seen and heard. If these, and such as these, were to be the chosen inmates of Baggesden Hall, the death of Gideon Bagges was a misfortune, instead of a blessing. To be sure, I had no great fault to find personally with Mr. Flint; but it was evident that he was worldly and unprincipled; and how could I hope to gain an influence with him, while his stay among us was so short, and he was surrounded with such companions? He seemed to have many good points; was kind-hearted, gentlemanlike, and too refined not to be disgusted with the glaring impropriety of Mr. Mandevyl's conduct. Above all he had submitted to hear the truth without losing his temper. There were at least therefore *some* grounds of hope that I might sooner or later be of service to him. But " evil communications corrupt good manners."—*Tales of the Village*, pp. 34—42.

We must now turn to two works in a very different style from those which have been occupying our attention,—works belonging more distinctly to the genus novel, and as such, admitting of a more obvious comparison with the tales of Miss Edgeworth and Miss Kennedy; we mean the "Fairy Bower" and "The Lost Brooch." We have no hesitation in placing them at the very head of their class. The authoress (for we do not stand in need of universal rumour to decide the writer's sex, seeing that every page testifies to it) has a power of drawing characters equal to that of Miss Austen. Indeed, as she views them in higher relations, and introduces higher as well as more complicating elements, we may call it in some sense superior: and her characters answer to those of real life in the way we spoke of some time back. They are not all one thing or another,—we do not make them out quite at first,—they sometimes perplex us, and often reveal unexpected elements. We feel the distinctness of each individual; but, unless we put ourselves to some pain, we only *feel* it; it costs some labour and thought to analyze it, and trace it to its sources. What has been remarked of Shakspeare's characters, too, applies to them. They resemble real ones in being estimated differently by different people. One likes one, one another. People differ as to whether such a one is amiable or attractive or not.

Our readers must content themselves with a very brief sketch of the works in question. The heroine, Grace Leslie, has been brought up alone by a widowed mother. The companions to whom she is introduced, are two families, the Wards and the Duffs; the former brought up according to average worldly, and the latter according to serious but sectarian notions. Miss Newmarsh, the governess of the Duffs, educates on all manner of reforming plans, has discarded punishments as not calculated to *touch the heart*, makes her pupils keep religious diaries, which are shown every week, and perpetrates many other innovations. They are, of course, kept out of what is arbitrarily termed *the world*, and taught to believe that there is inherent sin in cards and dancing. Grace does not seem to have been educated on any particular plan, except in so far as she has been taught to look out for the right and the wrong on every the smallest occasion. She is emphatically a doer of small duties. In other respects, her gifts are such as to impose upon the teacher little work beyond that of guiding. Ellen Ward is educated differently from the rest of her family, residing with her grandmother, to whom, neither in "The Lost Brooch" nor the "Fairy Bower," are we personally introduced; but of whom it is easy to gather that she is an old-fashioned high churchwoman. Such are the respective starts in life afforded to the leading characters of our two tales. In "The Fairy Bower" we see the different kinds of education in progress. In "The Lost Brooch" we have the beginning of the harvest. Taken as a whole, the two books, glancing as they do at many things, have sundry morals; but the following are the leading ones:—

First. That nothing is gained by attempting to be very much ahead of all mankind in education. Do what we like, we cannot make this otherwise than an imperfect state of matters—we cannot get rid of the possibility of evil. Every plan of education, as every other step in life, small or great, has its attendant danger. Among the acquaintances to whom we are introduced in the tales in question, is a Mrs. Newton Grey, a widow lady left with an only son, over whom she watches with too much anxiety to allow him to encounter the dangers and temptations of a public school. What the success of the safe home education he receives may amount to, the reader is very soon enabled to judge. As yet, we have only got him expelled from Oxford; but judging from what we have seen of him, the worst is yet to come.

Secondly. The importance of formal and minute obedience, as seen in Grace and Ellen Ward, compared with (in their own estimation) the more spiritual Duffs. This, indeed, is but one feature of the general comparison between the Church and the sectarian temper which is insinuated throughout.

Thirdly. That some sense of the absurd is desirable. Of this the Duffs (and we think the school to which they belong) are quite devoid. But let us listen to our wise and good Ellen on the subject.

"Oh! there can be no harm in laughing at people for wickedness of some sorts, I am sure," cried Emily; "it is just a fit punishment, and must tell in the world."

"Well, perhaps so," said Ellen, "if the wrold were in other respects what it should be."

"I cannot think it right to give over laughing at follies," continued Emily.

"Well, I believe I do agree with you, Emily, in the principle," said Ellen; "I know I think the Duffs injure their sense of right and wrong, by destroying in themselves the feeling of the absurd;—what unsuitable, and even wrong things, they think and do, by not allowing themselves to perceive absurdities in their friends."—*Lost Brooch*, vol. ii. p. 321.

On the whole we agree. It is doctrine, indeed, which requires to be well guarded in statement; and the putting it in practice demands continual watchfulness. Still we may say that a sense of propriety involves a sense of the absurd, and *vice versa;* that such a sense is the tact by which we instinctively see our way in the minor moralities; that the subdued expression of it is often the gentlest way of announcing disapproval which we must announce. And these remarks apply to our authoress's tales altogether. A quiet sense of the ludicrous runs through them at all times, even when we do not light, as oftentimes we do, on something irresistibly droll. Many, indeed, would call the authoress a satirical writer; but on the whole she is not so, or not so to any unloving extent. Neither is her satire or humour (whichever we like to call it) misplaced. It is reserved for violations of those minor moralities of which we have been speaking. In regard to the greater vices, she writes like one who knows that

> "——Leviathan is not so tamed;
> Laughed at, he laughs again; and stricken hard,
> Turns to the stroke his adamantine scales,
> That fear no discipline of human hands."

Finally, though she has to do with religious errors, our authoress exhibits no levity in connexion with holy things.

One word more, to prevent misapprehension. The aim of the two books might seem to be directed against the evangelical party, and in a certain sense perhaps it is so. But, unless the authoress has a totally different experience of that party from ours, she cannot be understood as wishing us to take the Duffs as a sample of it in its present state, either as regards opinion or practice. In the first place, it must be remembered that we are carried back some eventful years, during which much silent transformation has been effected on the Church, and, in spite of certain painful differences of late, we may say her really earnest and devout members have come to understand each other much better than they did. The party in question is, as a whole, much more orthodox than it was; and very few of the Clergy now belonging to it would approve of Constance Duff setting off to a dissenting meeting on the ground of the gospel, as she alleged, not being preached in any of the churches where she was. And at any time, we cannot but think such a family as the Duffs must have been an extreme case. Still their ways and sentiments are specimens of what exists more or less; and all who are in the habit of swearing by certain popular preachers, or by the canons of *the religious world*, or of taking for granted that certain persons are *spiritual*, and what they do and patronize must be right, and certain others unspiritual, and what they do and patronize must be wrong; may learn much from the powerful picture here drawn of the natural result of such and kindred errors. If they compare it with their own experience, they will find that a vague notion of spirituality often covers the want of hourly self-denial, and masks many an unchristian sentiment; that, instead of being raised, the standard of christian holiness is assuredly lowered by the adoption of fashions and the cherishing of sentiments which are uncongenial to the Prayer Book, and that the habit of believing that true religion resides only in certain coteries, must, in addition to its other evils, keep those who are enslaved by it from much valuable experience. How much might not Constance have learned from Mrs. Leslie, from Grace, from Ellen, and from her own brother, from which she debars herself by considering them as hardly within the favoured pale! For instance, how completely did she act the part of the self-blinded Jew, in the following conversation with Ellen, on the subject of her having gone to the meeting:—

Constance wished to continue with Ellen her conversation which occurred in the streets on Sunday. As she thought it important, she sought out an opportunity the following day; but, during the short time Constance was at liberty, she found every body in such an unsettled state owing to Fanny's illness, that she was obliged to submit to the general weakness of mind, and it was not till Wednesday evening, when all the party took tea at the Wards, after their walk in the gardens, that she actually effected her purpose. Music and singing were going on, and Ellen was entranced in silent enjoyment, when Constance drew her aside, and said, she wished to explain and defend her conduct on the foregoing Sunday. The truth was, that Constance was taken so by surprise at Ellen's treatment and method of argument, that she hardly knew what to say, and she felt conscious that she had not done justice to her cause. She was accustomed to quote texts against opposers; but it was quite a new thing to her to have texts quoted by others against her views; and it was even more disagreeable, than new, to feel she had not properly replied to them. Of this she was sufficiently conscious, to wish for a further discussion. Nothing could be fairer than this; it is what every one should do, who would arrive at the truth. The common error in those who are accustomed to interpret the text of scripture entirely for themselves, is to listen only to one set of interpreters, to receive only one set of texts, and to discard all but these as unnecessary to be attended to at all, which must be altogether the same as making a religion for ourselves, and then seeing what the Bible has to say in its favour.

"You took me so by surprise the other day," said Constance to Ellen, as soon as they were sufficiently withdrawn from the piano, "that in my haste to fulfil my appointment, I did not say half I wished, and I want now to explain to you my views; I hope you will always find me willing to give a reason for the hope that is in me, as well as acknowledge me a consistent Christian."

"I cannot, Constance, think you a consistent Christian, if you are not a consistent churchwoman," said Ellen, who had had to force her mind suddenly into a new position, as it was the moment before utterly absorbed in the tones of Mrs. Leslie's magnificent voice.

"We talk a different language," said Constance; "I speak only of those who love the Lord Jesus, while you are for ever dwelling on the Church."

"I must keep to the Church if I believe that our Lord founded it, and commanded all who love Him to belong to it, and not to separate from it."

"But I do not see that, Ellen."

"But I do, dear Constance," replied Ellen; "where is the use of talking of it? I shall not convince you, while you remain in your present state of mind, and I am sure you will not convince me."

"What do you mean by my present state of mind?" asked Constance.

"I mean that you are not inclined at present to submit to any body, and that while you are in that state you cannot see the truth."

"I do not see what right you have to say that," replied Constance; "I submit myself to all who teach and preach the gospel, but certainly not to those who do not."

"You have no rule of any sort or kind to go by, Constance," said Ellen; "your religion, I think, must sink you lower and lower, till at last you have no ground at all to stand upon; but *I* cannot make you feel the truth of this."

"Ellen," said Constance, "I am not one of those timid weak-minded professors who are frightened by words. I dare say you would frighten me, as Mr. Taylor and Miss Newmarsh do, by Socinianism. I look to things and realities. I take the spirit and the kernel of scripture, and leave others to dispute over its chaff and its dross. To all who can thus apply its precious testimony to their souls, I give the right hand of fellowship, without regard to sect or creed, while to the pharisee and to the bigot, I can only repeat the warnings of scripture."

"This is all your own opinion, Constance," replied Ellen; "we find nothing in the Bible about its chaff and its dross; on the contrary, we are told that all scripture is given by inspiration, and is profitable."

"I confess that chaff and dross are my own words," said Constance, "and that many good Christians would startle at them; but this is one of the things I allude to when I talk of timid professors, they strain at a gnat, but swallow a camel; they are afraid of the words, but not of the things they represent; and their whole system is hollow and unsound; they never can keep up the Church establishment by the means they pretend. They are under a delusion, and they will see it some day; the fact is, many of them are blinded by mammon, and they will sacrifice all to this god. Depend upon it a church is a church only so long as it is bound together by the tie of love; when that tie is broken, the sooner it falls to pieces the better."

"But the Bible says we are to make but one body, and your plan would divide it constantly into a thousand pieces," said Ellen.

"Better be divided than bound together by its present hollow tie," replied Constance.

"We cannot tell what is better and what is worse on such a subject, Constance; those far beyond us in age and scriptural learning find it a most difficult subject. All we can do is to try and follow the Bible and the Church, and not to be making schemes of our own."

"I make no schemes of my own," answered Constance, "nor do I follow human teachers; I look only to the guidance of the Spirit, who is promised to lead those who trust Him into all truth."

"But, Constance, if we mean to be led into all truth, we must take the Bible as we find it, and not put aside some parts and take others, just to please ourselves."

"What parts do I put aside?" asked Constance.

"I judge from what you say yourself of the chaff and the dross," replied Ellen; "and from what you say of other persons you esteem, who do the same indeed, though not in word; besides you have never answered the text I gave you on Sunday by your own request, and till you do that, I cannot think you are really seeking the truth."

"I hope I have not the truth yet to seek," said Constance; "I hope I am not to be judged of men's judgment. We live under the gospel, under a law of liberty, and are no longer under bondage to the elements of the world: your doctrine of the Church would be as slavery, and a harder service than the Jewish law of ceremonies. We worship in spirit and in truth; ye know not what you worship."

"You should remember that those words were said to those who considered themselves the spiritual party in the Jewish nation;* those who separated from the worship that was commanded by God himself; and I do not see how you can in common fairness use them, and apply them to my side of the argument."

"Certainly, Ellen," replied Constance, you have not the clearest of heads for argument. First, you accuse me of not going enough to scripture, and then, when I quote texts, you say I have no right to them. Are you to be the judge of the texts I may or may not appeal to?"

"You must remember, Constance," returned Ellen, "that you forced me into argument; I told you it was of no use, and I wished to avoid it, if you would let me."

"Because you felt yourself unable to maintain your cause, I suppose?" asked Constance.

"No, Constance, I have told you; not exactly that," returned Ellen.

"Well, then, you force me to say you are the proud pharisee, looking down upon the publican."

---

* The authoress must correct this extraordinary blunder in the next edition. The words in question were spoken to the woman of Samaria.

"I am sure, Constance," replied Ellen, with a sincerity and quietness which few could have possessed at such a moment, "you can have no reason to complain, if you feel satisfied you are in the publican's place."

Constance was more thrown back by Ellen's manner and remark than she had been before by her texts and arguments. She had accurate enough memory of the following words of the parable, and sense enough beside, to pause for a moment before answering. Oh, that in that pause she would have followed up the thoughts and feelings which, for the moment, impelled her to silence! or that she would afterwards have really and truly examined the motives of her anxiety for not replying hastily! Alas! she was too satisfied with her own state of heart to admit of this; and she thought it the best way, as well as the easiest, to class Ellen with that set of formalists who were scarcely raised above the heathen. Ellen saw her cousin's hesitation, and by no means wished her to reply. Both therefore gladly took advantage of a movement of change that was made in the party, and the conversation between them ended, as such often do, without any conclusion. Thus, both the sisters, Constance and Fanny, though such different characters, and pursuing such different lines of action, seem to shrink from seeking truth in her full beauty and perfection. Both smother matters of fact presented to them; in the one case, in daily incidents; in the other, in scripture words. If we do not accustom our minds to seek truth in detail, and in the small occurrences of life, it is in vain to expect we shall be so favoured as to attain it on a grand scale, or in deep religious views.—*Lost Brooch*, vol. i. pp. 257—262.

In short, the tales before us may teach the important lesson thus admirably expressed :—

"Oh, Ellen," cried Grace, a little startled, "where are we to look for religion, if not in the religious world!"

"I think," replied Ellen,—" because grandmamma always says so,—if we look for religion, that is, pure religion, in any world at all, we shall find ourselves some day grievously deceived or undeceived."—*Lost Brooch*, vol. i. p. 218.

We have found so much to say of these two delightful tales, that we have not left ourselves space to quote from them as we could wish. What we have extracted has borne on our argument, but not given the reader any sample of the powers of the authoress; of her keen-edged and finely-tempered wit, or her skilful portraying of character; but our readers need not complain. They can go and find it out far better for themselves, while they afford us the benevolent satisfaction of imagining them laughing over and at Fanny and Mr. Guppy, or delighted with the brilliant Emily, the gifted Grace, and the "sage, serious" Ellen.

We must, in parting, have a small quarrel with our authoress. She has no right, in works of this sort, to insinuate a derogatory estimate of Milton's poetry; if she will believe us, it is inconsistent with her own principles to do so. We need not, indeed, style him, "holiest of men," who made so fatal a progress through schism to heresy; but it really is, in its way, flying in the face of consent and authority, to decry his transcendent greatness as a poet : and it is teaching bad morality to the young. Their idleness will be too apt, at any rate, to lead them to decline the arduous task of climbing as he bids them—of following his severe guidance—of purging their ear for his high harmonies, without such encouragement as the example of a Grace Leslie.

If the taste for Milton—a taste not surely natural to the corrupted, the giddy, or the affected—is one which ought to be unlearned, instead of studiously attained to, let us have the case carefully argued. But it is surely an insult, not to the popular opinion or fashion of any one time, but to the deliberate, ratified, authoritative judgment of the English mind, thus to indulge in chance decrials of her divine poet. Better far, surely, to learn from that other mighty one, who has twice supplied our authoress with a motto, and who has shown but little sympathy with his errors, but who has yet taught his numerous and ever-multiplying scholars to " gaze upon that mighty orb of song, the divine Milton."

We have exceeded our limits, and must very briefly despatch three books, which are worthy of a much more lengthened notice. "Sintram," a translation from La Motte Fouque, is one of the finest romances we ever read. A beautiful mist of allegory sometimes passes across the picture of *the heroic age* of modern Christendom, for such we may deem the days of the Norsemen. It is a book which there is no laying down till we have reached the end, and from the perusal of which a man may well rise

"A sadder and a wiser man."

" Rutilius and Lucius" are two Roman tales by Archdeacon R. Wilberforce, and are most worthy companions to that masterly sketch of his, the Five Empires. The period of both is the latter part of the third century, when the stone cut out without hands was indeed smiting the idol kingdoms of the world. The difficulty of writing tales about such a period is much greater, we think, than most would imagine. Its leading features are, no doubt, vast and impressive, as became their deep significance and momentous results; but its details and personages are pale abstractions, or dry bones, which it is most difficult for the breath of art at least to make live. Our author has done all that could be done. In the wide field of his reading, he has seized on the salient points: he has taken the best features, and combined them into two tales of very great interest. Those for whom Bingham or Augusti must have but small attractions, will here find a very masterly, and at the same time, accurate sketch of the early Church, such as can hardly fail to attract them. They will find interestingly exhibited what was the real secret of her persuasive power—not argument, though of argument she had no lack when wanted,—not miracles, though in the fulness of her glory she, perhaps, often broke out into preternatural manifestations,—not earthly bribes of any sort, for contempt and persecution were her portion, and the rewards and honours she held out to her members; but the consistent development of her principles, the majestic unearthly spectacle of the christian life, making men feel that the kingdom of God had indeed come nigh them. This was more powerful than all argument, or than any possible bribe; and a deep lesson is to be learned from it. The way in which the Church won her early triumphs is surely the way in which she is most likely to win fresh ones. Now, she won the world once not by argument, but by example. She persuaded it into her ranks, not by propitiating it, not by assimilating herself to it, but by manifesting her difference from it. And this is the only way. We are learning to conduct missionary operations on the old plan. We hope to do more with the heathen, by sending out among them the complete Church, bishops, priests, deacons in full organization, than has ever been done by the stray efforts and arguments of individual teachers, however zealous, holy, and accomplished. Let us do the like also at home. We shall never, we think, make a permanent impression on our dissenting brethren, except we show them what the Church is—except we manifest her dissimilarity, not her resemblance, to themselves. An orthodox and acute incumbent of a parish may argue most soundly and unanswerably that he has a commission which the dissenting teacher has not. But arguments, however valid, are for the schools, not for the masses. As long as his people see, as they think, the same thing done in church and at meeting, only in different ways—as long as their notion of the affairs transacted in both is confined to each being open twice every Sunday, in order that in each may be preached a sermon, prefaced, in the one place, by prayer split into short fragments, and in the other by one long one, they will never learn to view it as of any vital consequence to which they betake themselves. But let them see that the Church is altogether different from the conventicle; that it is the scene of quite dissimilar occupations, and harbours a class of sentiments all unknown to the other; let them see, that not on Sundays only, but throughout the week, it is open for the prayers and praises, even of one or two poor members, if no others will join;—let them see that within its walls there are cherished high associations with a distant past—stated observances linking us with the stages and instruments of salvation,—commemorations of the leading events in our Saviour's life, and of those whom He bequeathed to follow out His work;—let them see all this, and the kindred manifestations of the Church's temper and sentiment; and the elect spirits among them will feel that she has something to give to which no sect pretends; that she is, indeed, the harbour for their world-wearied souls—the shrine of heavenly influences—the home for their yearning affections, —the communion of saints, for which they are panting.

Abdiel, a tale of Ammon, has but just reached us. We cannot, therefore, notice it at length; but we name it now, because, hastily as we have read it, we see that it is worthy of the companions we have assigned it, and like them, a valuable gain to our stock of *didactic fiction.*

Principles of Geology; or, the Modern Changes of the Earth and its Inhabitants, considered as illustrative of Geology. By CHARLES LYELL, Esq. F.R.S. 3 vols. Sixth Edition. London: Murray. 1840.

" GEOLOGY," says Sir John Herschell, "in the magnitude and sublimity of objects of which it treats, undoubtedly ranks in the scale of the sciences next to astronomy." The latter presents to our contemplation objects the most sublime, and invites us to speculations of overwhelming grandeur and unlimited extent. And yet it must be confessed that there is a remoteness in its objects, and a vagueness in its speculations, that tend to weary the mind, which pants to alight on some place of rest, and relieve its exhausted wing. We soon lose ourselves when we attempt to traverse the intricate and dazzling paths of the starry heavens. Our most vigorous powers of realization quickly fail us, and we are glad to summon to our aid the resources of mathematical analysis, which, when the unsupported intellect begins to reel, conduct it in safety along the dizzy heights of abstract speculation. In geological researches, on the contrary, we tread the earth, and seem to gather strength, like Anteus, as we embrace our ancient mother. The noblest objects of nature, her most striking and beautiful phenomena, display themselves to the geologist. Her glorious and exciting panorama presents to the enraptured eye of the geologist the stern alpine height, whose venerable head is wrapped in perpetual snows; the life-like river, which now madly rushes through a narrow gorge, now calmly winds through low alluvial plains, until its waters mingle with those of the eternal ocean; the profound ravine, the waving forest, the desolate cliff, the fruitful field, the dreadful glacier, the thundering waterfall, the earthquake and the deluge, the volcano and the avalanche. The scale traversed by the facts included in geology is immense. The same agency which is now busied in rounding a pebble, once exerted all its powers in the production of a continent. One unbroken chain of causation extends through both space and time, stretches from the lowest depths of the ocean to the highest point of the cloud-capt mountain, binds together periods the most remote, and attaches "the great globe" to the throne of the infinite and eternal GOD.

" Præsentiorem conspicimus Deum,
Per invias rupes, fera per juga,
Clivosque præruptos, sonantes
Inter aquas, nemorumque noctem."

The work whose title stands at the head of our article having passed through six editions, we feel ourselves to be exempted from the necessity of submitting it to a formal review; and we shall content ourselves with drawing from its copious resources for the entertainment and instruction of our readers. Its professed object is to explain the former changes of the earth's surface by reference to causes now in operation. We shall not, however, enter upon the consideration of Mr. Lyell's arguments under this head, but will rapidly survey, under his guidance, the general history of this fascinating science, from the period when all philosophy was included in " the wisdom of the Egyptians," down to our own day.

Fifty years ago the science of geology was comparatively unknown; and yet it is a remarkable fact, that the ancients were acquainted with the immense antiquity of the earth, and with the successive destructions and renovations of its surface.

" The earliest doctrines of the Indian and Egyptian schools of philosophy agreed in ascribing the first creation of the world to an omnipotent and infinite Being. They concurred also in representing this Being, who had existed from all eternity, as having repeatedly destroyed and reproduced the world and all its inhabitants."—Vol. i. p. 6.

We find this doctrine in the Institutes of Menu, the sacred volume of the Hindoos, which, according to Sir William Jones, could not have been compiled less than eight hundred and eighty years before Christ. Even at that early period philosophers had begun to observe the traces, so deeply engraven upon the face of nature, of those alternate periods of violence and repose which are now recognised in every sound geological theory. "There are creations and destructions of worlds innumerable; the Being, supremely exalted, performs all this with as much ease as if in sport, again and again, for the sake of conferring happiness." *

In the Hymns of Orpheus, which derived many of their tenets from the sages who taught on the banks of the Nile, a definite period is assigned, as in the Indian systems, to the duration of each successive world. According to one of these hymns, as we learn from Plutarch, the period of the *Annus Magnus*,—or cycle composed of the time occupied by the revolutions of the sun, moon, and planets, from some given point of conjunction, round to the same point again,—was 120,000 years.

" We learn, particularly from the Timæus of Plato, that the Egyptians believed the world to be subject to occasional conflagrations and deluges, whereby the gods arrested the career of human wickedness, and purified the earth from guilt. After each regeneration mankind were in a state of virtue and happiness, from which they gradually degenerated again into vice and immorality. From this Egyptian doctrine the poets derived the fable of the decline from the golden to the iron age. The sect of Stoics adopted most fully the system of catastrophes destined at certain intervals to destroy the world. These, they taught, were of two kinds—the Cataclysm, or destruction by deluge, which sweeps away the whole human race, and annihilates all the animal and vegetable productions of nature; and the Ecpyrosis, or conflagration, which dissolves the globe itself. From the Egyptians also they derived the doctrine of the gradual debasement of man from a state of innocence. Towards the termination of each era the gods could no longer bear with the wickedness of men, and a shock of the elements, or a deluge, overwhelmed them; after which calamity, Astrea again descended on the earth to renew the golden age."—Vol. i. p. 13.

---

* Institutes of Hindoo Law, or the Ordinances of Menù, from the Sanscrit, translated by Sir William Jones, 1796.

We must here interrupt the course of our historical sketch for the purpose of offering a brief comment on the above passage, with regard to a subject of too much importance to be passed over silently, although nothing is further from our intention than to enter into the painful controversies, in connexion with this subject, which have been engendered by the imperfection of men's knowledge, and the infirmities of their tempers, to the hindrance of science, and the scandal of religion. We observe, with sincere regret, a disposition on the part of Mr. Lyell to ignore the book of Genesis. As for Mosaical cosmogonies, scriptural geologies, and all the other fanciful, impertinent, and irreverent speculations of the schools of Whiston, Burnett, Hutchinson, *et id genus omne*, we leave them to the contempt they deserve. Neither religion nor science have been benefited by these unbecoming attempts to foist a mass of crude *private* interpretations upon Holy Scripture. But surely the book of Genesis, which is the portion of Holy Scripture that just now more immediately concerns us, loses nothing of its interest or its value as an ancient historical document, through the circumstance of its being also an *inspired* document. Unless Mr. Lyell is prepared to disprove, or to throw reasonable doubt upon its authenticity, genuineness, or veracity,—and we do not think he is either competent or desirous to do any thing of the kind,—he is bound, simply in his capacity of an historian of science, to assign its due place to that information on the subject he is treating of, which is derived from one of the writings of Moses, as much as to information derived from the Hymns of Orpheus, the Timæus of Plato, or the Institutes of Menù. But to return.

The doctrines of the Egyptian sages became generally disseminated through the civilized world by means of those inquirers who visited the banks of the Nile; and among these Pythagoras holds a distinguished place. We are indebted to Ovid for a view of the cosmogonical theories of the philosopher of Samos. Mr. Lyell has given a translation of those celebrated passages in the *Metamorphoses* which exhibit the Pythagorean doctrines, but it is too long for extraction. The resemblance of the doctrines contained in these passages to some of the most approved doctrines of modern geology is so striking, that it is hardly to be wondered at that persons imperfectly acquainted with the real nature of scientific discovery and inductive reasoning, have regarded these poetic veins in the mines of ancient learning as rich in physical philosophy. But we must refuse to class together the lively speculations of the ancient Grecian schools, and the patient inductions of the modern geologist. If it be true, in any subject, that he only discovers who proves, it is true with regard to the science under consideration. A guess, however happy, is nothing more than a happy guess; and is nothing worth until it has been verified. All the natural probabilities of the case are opposed to the idea that Pythagoras or Ovid were acquainted with those truths which the painful labours of the powerful philosophy of recent periods have only just begun to realize.

In the assertions under review, fable and truth are so intimately blended, that we cannot but believe that they presented themselves to the minds of those who held them as an homogeneous whole; that is, that the portions which have since been verified were to their minds as conjectural as those which are now rejected as fabulous. The various Hindoo, Egyptian, and Grecian theories respecting the creations and destructions of worlds without number, alternating throughout cycles of almost immeasurable duration, do not rise to a higher rank than that of mythological fictions. They are fanciful dreams, which have made their escape through the shining, but delusive, " gate of ivory."*

Aristotle appears to have held the same doctrine as Pythagoras respecting the conversion of sea into land, and of land into sea; the excavation of valleys by rivers and floods; the growth of deltas, and the effects of earthquakes and volcanoes in convulsing and elevating the dry land.

" When we consider the acquaintance displayed by Aristotle, in his various works, with the destroying and renovating powers of nature, the introductory and concluding passages of the twelfth chapter of his 'Meteorics' are certainly very remarkable. In the first sentence he says, ' The distribution of land and sea in particular regions does not endure throughout all time, but it becomes sea in those parts where it was land, and again it becomes land where it was sea; and there is reason for thinking that these changes take place according to a certain system, and within a certain period.' The concluding observation is as follows:—' As time never fails, and the universe is eternal, neither the Tanais nor the Nile can have flowed for ever. The places where they rise were once dry, and there is a limit to their operations; but there is none to time. So also of all other rivers; they spring up, and they perish; and the sea also continually deserts some lands and invades others. The same tracts, therefore, of the earth are not, some always sea, and others always continents; but every thing changes in the course of time.' "—Vol. i. p. 22.

In the theory of Strabo,—who enters largely, in the second book of his Geography, into the opinions of Eratosthenes and other Greeks, on one of the most difficult problems in geology, namely, by what causes marine shells came to be so plentifully buried in the earth at such great elevations, and at such distances from the sea,— Mr. Lyell finds one that remarkably accords with his own; which looks to TIME, rather than to FORCE, as the agent which has brought about the present condition of the surface and crust of the earth. " It is proper," observes this early geographer,† " to derive our explanations from things which are obvious, and, in some measure, of daily occurrence, such as deluges, earthquakes, and volcanic eruptions (ἀναφυσήματα), and sudden swellings of the land beneath the sea."

After the decline of the Roman empire, the dormant and languishing physical sciences first gave signs of returning life and vigour among the Saracens, about the middle of the eighth century of the christian era; but, unhappily, almost all the works of the early

---

* Virg. Æn. vi. *fin.*
† Strabo, Geog. Edit. Almelov. Amat. 1707, lib. i. p. 93.

Arabian writers are lost. A fragment by Avicenna, however, remains; and, in a treatise on the formation and classification of minerals, he has offered some remarkable observations on the cause of mountains.

"A manuscript work, entitled the 'Wonders of Nature,' is preserved in the Royal Library at Paris, by an Arabian writer, Mohammed Kazwini, who flourished in the seventh century of the Hejira, or at the close of the thirteenth century of our era. Besides several curious remarks on aerolites, earthquakes, and the successive changes of position which the land and sea have undergone, we meet with the following beautiful passage, which is given as the narrative of Kidhz, an allegorical personage:—' I passed one day by a very ancient and wonderfully-populous city, and I asked one of its inhabitants how long it had been founded.' 'It is indeed a mighty city,' replied he; 'we know not how long it has existed; and our ancestors were on this subject as ignorant as ourselves.' Five centuries afterwards, as I passed by the same place, I could not perceive the slightest vestige of the city. I demanded of a peasant, who was gathering herbs upon its former site, how long it had been destroyed. 'In sooth, a strange question!' replied he; 'the ground here has never been different from what you now behold it.' 'Was there not of old,' said I, 'a splendid city here?' 'Never,' answered he, 'so far as we have seen, and never did our fathers speak to us of any such.' On my return there, five hundred years afterwards, I found the sea in the same place, and on its shores were a party of fishermen, of whom I inquired how long the land had been covered by the waters. 'Is this a question,' said they, 'for a man like you? This spot has always been what it is now.' I again returned, five hundred years afterwards, and the sea had disappeared. I inquired of a man who stood alone upon the spot, how long ago this change had taken place, and he gave me the same answer as I had received before. Lastly, on coming back again, after an equal lapse of time, I found there a flourishing city, more populous and more rich in beautiful buildings than the city I had seen the first time; and when I would fain have informed myself concerning its origin, the inhabitants answered me, 'Its rise is lost in remote antiquity; we are ignorant how long it has existed; and our fathers were on this subject as ignorant as ourselves.'"—Vol. i. pp. 32, 33.

It was not until the commencement of the sixteenth century that the spirit of geological inquiry sprang up in Christendom. About this time a very animated controversy arose in Italy, as to the nature and origin of marine shells, and other organized fossils.

"The celebrated painter, Leonardo da Vinci, who in his youth had planned and executed some navigable canals in the north of Italy, was one of the first who applied sound reasoning to these subjects. The mud of rivers, he said, had covered and penetrated into the interior of fossil shells at a time when these were still at the bottom of the sea, near the coast. 'They tell us that these shells were formed in the hills, by the influence of the stars; but I ask, where in the hills are the stars now forming shells of distinct ages and species? and how can the stars explain the origin of gravel, occurring at different heights, and composed of pebbles rounded as if by the motion of running water; or in what manner can such a cause account for the petrifaction in the same places of various leaves, sea-weeds, and marine crabs?'"—Vol. i. p. 34.

Similar enlightened views were held by Fracastoro, who maintained that fossil shells had all belonged to living animals, which had formerly lived and multiplied in the places where their exuviæ have been found in modern times; and exposed the absurdity of having recourse to a certain " plastic force," to which imaginary agent it was the fashion at that time to attribute the power of moulding inorganic substances into organic forms. But, on the other hand, there were not wanting those who denied the organic nature of these fossils. Andrea Mattioli, for instance, an eminent botanist, and the illustrator of Dioscorides, embraced the notion of Agricola, a skilful German miner, that a certain *materia pinguis*, or "fatty matter," set into fermentation by heat, gave birth to fossil organic shapes. Falloppio of Padua attributed these results to "the tumultuous movements of terrestrial exhalations;" Mercati, to "the influence of the heavenly bodies;" while Olivi of Cremona was satisfied with considering them as mere *lusus naturæ*. The sounder doctrines were, however, destined to prevail; and accordingly we find a return to the principles held by Leonardo da Vinci, Cardano, Cesalpino, and Majoli, in the writings, among others, of Steno, a Dane, who published a remarkable work, in 1669, under the quaint title of *De Solido intra Solidum naturaliter contento*. Inferior to Steno, but in advance of his age, Hooke, in his Discourse on Earthquakes, put forth philosophical views in regard to the causes of former changes in the organic and inorganic kingdoms of nature. "However trivial a thing," says Hooke, "a rotten shell may appear to some, yet these monuments of nature are more certain tokens of antiquity than coins or medals; since the best of those may be counterfeited, or made by art and design, as may also books, manuscripts, and inscriptions; as all the learned are now sufficiently satisfied has often been actually practised; . . . . . . and though it must be granted that it is very difficult to read them (the records of nature), and to raise a chronology out of them, and to state the intervals of the time wherein such or such catastrophes and mutations have happened, yet it is not impossible."* Hooke's principal object was to account for the existence of shells on the Alps, Apennines, and Pyrenees, and in the interior of continents generally. These and other geological facts might, he said, have been brought about by earthquakes, "which have turned plains into mountains, and mountains into plains; seas into land, and land into seas; made rivers where there were none before, and swallowed up others that formerly were; . . . and which, since the creation of the world, have wrought many great changes on the superficial parts of the earth, and have been the instruments of placing shells, bones, plants, fishes, and the like, in those places where, with much astonishment, we find them."†

"This doctrine," observes Mr. Lyell, "had been laid down in terms almost equally explicit by Strabo, to explain the occurrence of fossil shells in the interior of continents, and to that geographer, and other writers of antiquity, Hooke frequently refers; but the revival and development of the system was an important step in the progress of modern science."— Vol. i. p. 51.

Ray was a contemporary of Hooke; and was one of the first

---

* Posth. Works, Lecture, Feb. 29, 1688. † Posth. Works, p. 312.

English writers who dwelt upon the encroachment of the sea upon its shores. Woodward was also one of Hooke's contemporaries: he examined many parts of the British strata with minute attention; and his systematic collection of geological specimens, bequeathed by him to the University of Cambridge, shows how far he had advanced in ascertaining the order of superposition. He also deserves honourable mention as the founder of that professorship, which is now adorned by the genius and attainments of Mr. Sedgwick. About this time, the cosmogonical speculations of Burnett, Whiston, and Hutchinson, were published: but they are unworthy of any detailed consideration. Meanwhile the Italian geologists continued to enrich their favourite science with numerous original observations. Mr. Lyell has given a rapid sketch of the researches of Vallisneri, Moro, Generelli, Marsilli, and Donati; extending from 1721 to 1750. This sketch is too concise to admit of further condensation, yet too long to be extracted entire; nor would it be of sufficient interest to the general reader. For the same reason, we pass over Mr. Lyell's equally concise view of the contributions to geology made by Targioni in 1751; Lehman in 1756; Gesner in 1758; our own countryman, Michell, Woodwardian Professor of Mineralogy at Cambridge, in 1760; Raspe in 1763; and various Italian naturalists, down to the end of the eighteenth century. We now arrive at the name of Werner, the celebrated professor of mineralogy at Freyberg. Mr. Lyell has given an interesting sketch of his labours.

"Werner was named, in 1775, professor of mineralogy in the 'School of Mines,' at Freyberg, in Saxony. He directed his attention not merely to the composition and external characters of minerals, but also to what he termed 'geognosy,' or the natural position of minerals in particular rocks, together with the grouping of those rocks, their geographical distribution, and various relations. The phenomena observed in the structure of the globe had hitherto served for little else than to furnish interesting topics for philosophical discussion; but when Werner pointed out their application to the practical purposes of mining, they were instantly regarded by a large class of men as an essential part of their professional education, and from that time the science was cultivated in Europe more ardently and systematically. Werner's mind was at once imaginative and richly stored with miscellaneous knowledge. He associated every thing with his favourite science, and in his excursive lectures he pointed out all the economical uses of minerals, and their application to medicine: the influence of the mineral composition of rocks upon the soil, and of the soil upon the resources, wealth, and civilization of man. The vast sandy plains of Tartary and Africa, he would say, retained their inhabitants in the shape of wandering shepherds; the granitic mountains and the low calcareous and alluvial plains gave rise to different manners, degrees of wealth, and intelligence. The history even of languages, the migrations of tribes, had been determined by the direction of particular strata. The qualities of certain stones used in building would lead him to descant on the architecture of different ages and nations; and the physical geography of a country frequently invited him to treat of military tactics. The charm of his manner and his eloquence kindled enthusiasm in the minds of his pupils; and many, who had attended at first only to acquire a slight knowledge of mineralogy, when they had once heard him, devoted themselves to it as the business of their lives. In a few years, a small school of mines, before unheard of in Europe, was raised to the rank of a great university; and men already distinguished in science studied the German language, and came from the most distant countries to hear the great oracle of geology....

"The principal merit of Werner's system of instruction consisted in steadily directing the attention of his scholars to the constant relations of superposition of certain mineral groups; but he had been anticipated in the discovery of this general law, by several geologists in Italy and elsewhere; and his leading divisions of the secondary strata, were, at the same time, and independently, made the basis of an arrangement of the British strata by our countryman, William Smith."—Vol. i. pp. 82—86.

Werner's distinguishing theory, as we need hardly inform our readers, was that of the chemical precipitation of universal formations from *an aqueous menstruum*, or "chaotic fluid:" which theory he pushed to such extreme lengths as to deny the existence of volcanoes in the primeval ages of the world, and to refer the origin even of such rocks as basalt and pumice (to which his followers, in the excess of their zeal, added obsidian) to the agency of *water*. This theory was a retrograde step in the great geological movement, inasmuch as the *igneous* origin of the ancient trap-rocks had been taught in Europe for twenty years before the rise of the mineralogical school at Freyberg.

"So early as 1768, before Werner had commenced his mineralogical studies, Raspe had truly characterised the basalts of Hesse as of igneous origin. Arduino had pointed out numerous varieties of trap-rock in the Vicentin as analogous to volcanic products, and as distinctly referable to ancient submarine eruptions. Desmarest had, in company with Fortis, examined the Vicentin in 1766, and confirmed Arduino's views. In 1772, Banks, Solander, and Troil, compared the columnar basalt of Hecla with that of the Hebrides. Collini, in 1774, recognised the true nature of the igneous rocks on the Rhine, between Andernach and Bonn. In 1775, Guettard visited the Vivarais, and established the relation of basaltic currents to lavas. Lastly, in 1779, Faujas published his description of the volcanoes of the Vivarais and Velay, and showed how the streams of basalt had poured out from craters which still remain in a perfect state.

"When sound opinions had thus for twenty years prevailed in Europe concerning the true nature of the ancient trap-rocks, Werner, by his simple dictum, caused a retrograde movement, and not only overturned the true theory, but substituted for it one of the most unphilosophical that can well be imagined. The continued ascendency of his dogmas on this subject was the more astonishing, because a variety of new and striking facts were daily accumulated in favour of the correct opinions previously entertained. Desmarest, after a careful examination of Auvergne, pointed out, first, the most recent volcanoes which had their craters still entire, and their streams of lava conforming to the level of the present river-courses. He then showed that there were others of an intermediate epoch, whose craters were nearly effaced, and whose lavas were less intimately connected with the present valleys; and lastly, that there were volcanic rocks, still more ancient, without any discernible craters or scoriæ, and bearing the closest analogy to rocks in other parts of Europe, the igneous origin of which was denied by the school of Freyberg."—Vol. i. pp. 86—88.

A furious controversy now arose on the continent between the Neptunists and Vulcanists. It soon spread to our own country, and Hutton entered the field as the champion of the second of these rival factions. "Hot" and "Moist," two "champions fierce," led on their hosts from the heights of Edinburgh and the mines of Freyberg. "The ruins of an older world," said Hutton, "are visible in the present structure of our planet; and the strata which now compose our continents have been once beneath the sea, and were formed out of the waste of pre-existing continents. The same forces are still destroying, by chemical decomposition or mechanical violence, even the hardest rocks, and transporting the materials to the sea, where they are spread out, and form strata analogous to those of more ancient date. Although loosely deposited along the bottom of the ocean, they become afterwards altered and consolidated by volcanic heat, and then heaved up, fractured, and contorted."

"The absence of stratification in granite, and its analogy, in mineral character, to rocks which he deemed of igneous origin, led Hutton to conclude that granite also must have been formed from matter in fusion; and this inference he felt could not be fully confirmed, unless he discovered at the contact of granite and other strata a repetition of the phenomena exhibited so constantly by the trap-rocks. Resolved to try his theory by this test, he went to the Grampians, and surveyed the line of junction of the granite and superincumbent stratified masses, until he found in Glen Tilt, in 1785, the most clear and unequivocal proofs in support of his views. Veins of red granite are there seen branching out from the principal mass, and traversing the black micaceous schist and primary limestone. The intersected stratified rocks are so distinct in colour and appearance as to render the example in that locality most striking, and the alteration of the limestone in contact was very analogous to that produced by trap veins on calcareous strata. This verification of his system filled him with delight, and called forth such marks of joy and exultation, that the guides who accompanied him, says his biographer, Playfair, were convinced that he must have discovered a vein of silver or gold."—Vol. i. p. 92.

While the scientific world was agitated and engrossed by the contests between the devoted partisans of the rival schools of Freyberg and Edinburgh, a single individual, armed neither with wealth nor station, was unostentatiously and successfully prosecuting researches which have since gained for him the honourable and just designation of "the father of English geology."

"Mr. William Smith, an English surveyor, published his 'Tabular View of the British Strata,' in 1790; wherein he proposed a classification of the secondary formations in the west of England. Although he had not communicated with Werner, it appeared, by this work, that he had arrived at the same views respecting the laws of superposition of stratified rocks; that he was aware that the order of succession of different groups was never inverted; and that they might be identified at very distant points by their peculiar organized fossils.

"From the time of the appearance of the 'Tabular View,' the author laboured to construct a geological map of the whole of England; and, with the greatest disinterestedness of mind, communicated the results of his investigations to all who desired information, giving such publicity to his original views, as to enable his contemporaries almost to compete with him in the race. The execution of his map was completed in 1815, and remains a lasting monument of original talent and extraordinary perseverance: for he had explored the whole country, on foot, without the guidance of previous observers, or the aid of fellow-labourers, and had succeeded in throwing into natural divisions the whole complicated series of British rocks. D'Aubuisson, a distinguished pupil of Werner, paid a just tribute of praise to this remarkable performance, observing, that 'what many celebrated mineralogists had only accomplished for a small part of Germany, in the course of half a century, had been effected by a single individual for the whole of England.'"—Vol. i. pp. 103, 104.

The Geological Society of London, which was founded in 1807, contributed largely to the carrying on of the great work which Mr. Smith had commenced. Men of science were beginning to weary of contests at once so bitter and so barren, as those which had been maintained between the Neptunists and Vulcanists; and there was a general disposition to suspend all attempts to form so-called "theories of the earth." It was acknowledged that data were wanting; and it became a favourite maxim among the influential members of the Geological Society, that the time was not yet come for any general theory upon the subject. The professed object of the Society was, accordingly, to multiply and record observations which should furnish materials for future generalizations. This object it has steadily and successfully pursued; and the prospects of geology are, in consequence, of the most encouraging kind. Geology may be considered to have now entered upon the third stage of its course. The first stage was that to which it was advanced by the labours of Werner; for although valuable contributions to the nascent science were made by those Italian naturalists of whom we have spoken above, yet their discoveries do not possess sufficient unity to entitle them to be regarded as forming a distinct and positive step in scientific geology. Germany, accordingly, must be held to have the honour of giving shape and life to geological research; which, again, owes its advancement to its second stage to England. The classification of the secondary formations, each marked by its peculiar fossils, was the main characteristic of this stage. The foundation of the third stage, which is that relating to tertiary formations, was laid in France, by the splendid work of Cuvier and Brongniart, published in 1808, "On the Mineral Geography and Organic Remains of the Neighbourhood of Paris." The labours of Cuvier in comparative osteology, and of Lamarck in recent and fossil shells, have contributed greatly to the advancement of this last stage.

The great and increasing importance of the natural history of organic remains is the characteristic feature of the progress and condition of geology during the nineteenth century. This branch of physical knowledge has already become an instrument of great utility in geological classification, and daily furnishes the geologist with new data for grand and enlarged views respecting the former changes of the earth.

"When we compare the result of observations in the last forty years with those of the three preceding centuries, we cannot but look forward with the most sanguine expectations to the degree of excellence to which geology may be carried, even by the labours of the present generation. Never, perhaps, did any science, with the exception of astronomy, unfold, in an equally brief period, so many novel and unexpected truths, and overturn so many preconceived opinions. The senses had for ages declared the earth to be at rest, until the astronomer taught that it was carried through space with inconceivable rapidity. In like manner was the surface of this planet regarded as having remained unaltered since its creation, until the geologist proved that it had been the theatre of reiterated change, and was still the subject of slow but never-ending fluctuations. The discovery of other systems in the boundless regions of space was the triumph of astronomy: to trace the same system through various transformations—to behold it, at successive eras, adorned with different hills and valleys, lakes and seas, and peopled with new inhabitants, was the delightful meed of geological research. By the geometer were measured the regions of space, and the relative distances of the heavenly bodies; by the geologist, myriads of ages were reckoned, not by arithmetical computation, but by a train of physical events—a succession of phenomena in the animate and inanimate worlds—signs which convey to our minds more definite ideas than figures can do of the immensity of time."—Vol. i. pp. 108, 109.

Here Mr. Lyell closes his history of geological inquiry; and here, accordingly, we close ours. But the science itself still remains untouched. It is not improbable, therefore, that we shall take an early opportunity of exhibiting to our readers some of the treasures and wonders that are stored up in its vast museum.

History of Scotland. By PATRICK FRASER TYTLER, Esq. Vol. V. from 1497 to 1546. Edinburgh: W. Tait, 1841.

IN this volume of the new edition of his voluminous History of Scotland, the able and accurate historian treats of the events of the reign of the chivalric James IV., from the departure of the imposter Warbeck from the Scottish court to its close on the field of Flodden; of the troubles during the minority and reign of James's hardly less romantic and ill-fated son; and of the intrigues of the French and English factions during the minority of Mary, under the regencies of Beaton and Arran. The cotemporary events in the religious politics of England and Germany during the reign of James V. and the childhood of the queen, naturally lead us to the consideration of the state of religious feeling in Scotland during the same periods.

The reformation in Scotland has many epochs; the murder of Beaton in 1546 forms one; the year 1560 presents another, when the reforming party, at that time a clear majority, petitioned the estates for relief against persecution, until the disputes in point should be settled by *a lawful general council.* The sanction of the reformed confession of faith, the abolition of the spiritual courts, and the proscription of the office of the mass, which was thus obtained from the majority of the convention of the estates, is the first step in the nationality of the Church in Scotland. The accession of the four bishops to the views of the reformers, and the silence or flight of the rest of the prelates, whereby those four were made a majority, is another important period. The era of the actual nationality of the Scots Church in 1572 is another epoch in that reformation, which cannot be considered to have been completed until, in the reign of James I., the Scotch bishops elect received from the English Church that apostolical commission which was necessary to the completion of their disorganized Church. That the Church in Scotland had forfeited her character of a Church of Christ, by her conduct during these periods, we do not mean to assert: though it cannot be concealed that her disorganized state, and the awful prevalence of schismatic principles in her communion, rendered the consecration of 1612 advisable, if not absolutely necessary.*

The period we would now speak of is that antecedent to the year 1560;—the period of the progress of the opinions of the foreign reformers, not only without the sanction, but against the commands of the Church; the period of the assertion of Protestantism, by some few of the clergy, in despite of the injunctions and punishments issued against them by the Church; the time when many of the nobles,—some for the sake of political power, some for the sake of the Church property which they hoped to gain for themselves,—openly professed the reformed opinions; and when such of the laity as deemed the intervention of human authority unnecessary for authoritative preaching, witnessed, by their sermons and their writings, against the immoralities of the clergy and the corruptions of the faith, and endeavoured to remedy the defect by destroying the use with the abuse. The Church, on the other hand, strong in her own position,—and politically strong as the master-spirit of that popular faction whose watchwords were "Independence," "Hatred to England," "Love to France,"—preferred to award the dungeon and the stake to her opponents, rather than to commune with her own self, and of her own hand cast out the corruptions that had crept in. It was with such feelings and on such principles as these, that the youthful abbot of Ferne and the schoolmaster of Montrose went readily and willingly to their deaths; that the lords of Cassilis, Glencairn, and Maxwell, and the lairds of Brunston and Grange, openly professed the new doctrines, and protected their preachers by force of arms, whilst, as the paid servants of England, they plotted for the destruction of their fatherland; and that the proud prelate, and his nephew and successor, the wily intriguer and licentious cardinal of St. Andrew's, sent Hamilton, Kennedy, Keillor and Wishart to the stake.

Towards the latter part of the minority of James V., when the daily feuds of the English and French factions (then in their infancy, when compared with their progress during the minority of Mary) permitted and encouraged a general spirit of insubordination to all authority, the opinions of the foreign reformers began to find favour with many, especially with that party who sided with England against

---

* That the Scottish Church was considered a true Church by ours, see the form of prayer for the Holy Catholic Church, in the Canons of 1605, and Palmer, Church of Christ; vol. i. 571.

the clergy and the French influence. By degrees, books of Luther's—some of his treatises against the corruptions of the papacy—began to find their way into Scotland, and to have their influence on the minds of the educated. It was one of these treatises which induced the young and enthusiastic Hamilton, the youthful abbot of Ferne, so far to admit the principles of the reformers as to fear to face the ecclesiastical council which summoned him to answer for his opinions. He fled to the continent, where the friendship of Luther and Melancthon, and the learned scholarship of Lambert, the head of the University of Marpurg, confirmed the opinions of the fugitive abbot.

"No sooner," says Mr. Tytler, "did a full conviction of the errors of the Church of Rome take possession of his mind, than a change seemed to be wrought in his character; he that before had been sceptical and timid, became courageous almost to rashness; and, resisting the tears and entreaties of his affectionate master, declared his resolution of returning to Scotland, and preaching the faith in his native country. He embarked, arrived in 1527 at St. Andrew's, publicly addressed the people, and, after a brief and zealous career, was arrested by the ecclesiastical arm and thrown into prison. His youth, (he was then only twenty-eight,) his talents, his amiable and gentle manners, interested all in his favour, and many attempts were made to induce him to retract his opinions, or at least to cease to disturb the tranquillity of the Church by their promulgation to the people. But all was in vain; he considered this tranquillity not the stillness of peace, but the sleep of ignorance; he defended his doctrines with such earnestness and acquaintance with Scripture, that Aless, a Catholic priest, who had visited him in his cell with a desire to shake his resolution, became himself a convert to the captive, and he was at last condemned as an obstinate heretic, and led to the stake. On the scaffold he turned affectionately to his servant, who had long attended him, and taking off his gown, coat, and cap, bade him receive all the worldly goods now left him to bestow, and with them the example of his death. 'What I am about to suffer, my dear friend,' said he, 'appears fearful and bitter to the flesh; but, remember, it is the entrance to everlasting life, which none shall possess who deny their Lord.' In the midst of his torments, which, from the awkwardness of the executioner, were protracted and excruciating, he ceased not to exhort those who stood near, exhibiting a meekness and unaffected courage which made a deep impression. Lifting up his eyes to heaven, he exclaimed, 'How long, O God, shall darkness cover this kingdom? How long wilt thou suffer this tyranny of men?' And when death at last came to his relief, he expired with these blessed words on his lips, 'Lord Jesus, receive my spirit.'"—Vol. v. pp. 177-8.

Thus died the first Protestant martyr in Scotland; the cruel circumstances of whose death, while they for a time threw a cloud over the opinions for which he had been sacrificed, eventually tended to strengthen the party for whose intimidation and discomfiture the tragedy had been enacted. The small tract which Hamilton has left, in which he professes to give his opinions, and which is to be found in Foxe, authorizes us in classing him with the Protestants of Germany, and not with the reformers of our own country.

The troublous times that succeeded the temporary reconciliation of Beaton and Angus, and the events consequent on the sudden assumption of the sovereign power by the young king in 1528, so fully engrossed the attention of the leading authorities of the Government, both in Church and State, as greatly to permit and encourage the spread of the new opinions. For six years, the new religion was allowed to go on spreading wider and wider over the country, without any interference from the ecclesiastical power. And until the year 1534 James, though staunch to the Roman faith, and firm in refusing the proffered friendship of his uncle, was unable to do more than express his sorrow at the double divorce of Catherine and the See of Rome, and his own determination to support, at all hazards, the religion of his fathers, and resist the opponents of the Church. This resolution he soon after fulfilled, by instituting an ecclesiastical court at Holyrood, over which Hay, bishop of Ross, presided; and at whose meetings he himself, in judicial robes, took his seat on the bench, and added to the solemnity of the tribunal. Before this tribunal many were summoned to answer as to their opinions: some publicly abjured; others, amongst whom were the brother and sister of Patrick Hamilton, fled from the country; whilst two alone, David Straiton, brother of the Baron of Laurieston, and Norman Gourlay, a priest, appeared to the summons, and defended their opinions. Among those who fled were Aless, the canon of St. Andrew's, who had been influenced by Hamilton; and John Macbee, the favourite of Christiern of Denmark, who returned in after years as active instruments in the Reformation.

"Straiton," says our historian, "had engaged in a quarrel with the Bishop of Moray on the subject of his tithes; and, in a fit of indignation, had commanded his servants, when challenged by the collectors, to throw every tenth fish they caught into the sea, bidding them seek the tax where he found the stock. From these violent courses he had softened down into a more quiet inquiry into the grounds of the right claimed by churchmen; and frequenting much the company of Erskine of Dun, one of the earliest and most eminent of the reformers, became at length a sincere convert to their opinions. It is related that, listening to the Scriptures, which were read to him by the laird of Laurieston, he came upon that passage in which our Saviour declares that he will deny before his Father and the holy angels any one who hath denied him before men; on which he was greatly moved, and, falling down on his knees, implored God that, although he had been a great sinner, he would never permit him, from fear of any bodily torment, to deny him or his truth. And the trial soon came, and was most courageously encountered. Death, in one of its most terrible forms, was before him; he was earnestly exhorted to escape by abjuring his belief; but he steadily refused to purchase his pardon by retracting a single tenet, and encouraged his fellow-sufferer, Gourlay, in the same resolution. Both were burnt on the 27th of August, 1534."—Vol. v. pp. 206-7.

An act of robbery and insult was David Straiton's first step towards Protestantism; and yet he died with as much firmness of soul and sincerity of mind as the self-denying and humble-minded Abbot of Ferne. With these executions the court of Holyrood were satisfied, and Henry once more attempted to bribe his nephew into supporting his views, and establishing the Reformation in Scotland. But, although Barlow and Lord William Howard offered the hand of the Princess Mary, foreign possessions, and the glory of a continental war,—and attempted to open the eyes of the king, according to their instructions, to the crimes of the Roman hierarchy,—the keenness of Barlow and the haughtiness of Lord William failed in the management of their negotiation. The conference at York and at Calais was excused, the hand of the princess courteously declined, and, whilst James sent back by the hands of the ambassadors the " Treatise on the Doctrine of a Christian Man," his embassy departed to France for the purpose of concluding a matrimonial alliance with that crown.

Clement's successor in the papal chair, rightly deeming that England was lost to him, at least during the life of Henry,—and no doubt aware that it wanted but the adhesion of James to the new doctrines to cause the Scottish nation to cast off the allegiance of Rome,—left the executioner of Fisher and Moore to his own courses, and turned his attention to James and his people, if that he might preserve the spiritual allegiance of his yet remaining children in Britain. To Campegio the delicate mission of securing the attachment of James was wisely entrusted.

" To James," says Mr. Tytler, " Campegio addressed an exposition of the scandalous conduct of the English king, in making his religious scruples and his separation from the Church of Rome a cloak for the gratification of his lust and ambition ; he drew a flattering contrast between the tyranny and hypocrisy which had guided his conduct, and the attachment of his youthful nephew of Scotland to the holy see, addressing him by that title of Defender of the Faith, which had been unworthily bestowed on its worst enemy; and he laid at his feet a cap and sword which had been consecrated by the pope upon the anniversary of the Nativity. We are to measure the effects of such gifts by the feelings of the times, and there can be little doubt that their influence was considerable; but a permission from his holiness to levy an additional contribution on his clergy was, in the present distressed state of the royal finances, not the least efficacious of his arguments."—Vol. v. pp. 209-10.

With this last dictum we do entirely disagree, firmly persuaded that there is no trait in the character of the chivalric and enthusiastic James to warrant such a deduction ; in order to arrive at which, it is necessary entirely to forget the conduct of the youthful king at the ecclesiastical council of Holyrood, his rejection of the offers of his uncle of England, and the alliance which his ambassadors were then endeavouring to negotiate for their sovereign at the court of France, in despite of the machinations of Henry with Sir Adam Otterbourn, the ambassador of James.

Henry, baffled in his attempts on the king himself, turned his attention to those factious nobles of the clan of Douglas whom the stern commands of James had exiled from Scotland ; leagued with them and their adherents in Scotland, he hoped to effect by revolution and rebellion that which the firmness of James prevented his doing by open measures. The successive marriages of the young king had bound him more firmly than ever to the French party and the cause of Rome, and Henry felt that he must strive by every measure to prevent the dreaded alliance of the emperor, Francis, and James, against the common enemy of the papacy. But a great opponent had now risen at the court of James, neither to be swayed by the threats nor the bribes of Henry. Beaton, the famous cardinal, had succeeded his uncle in the primacy of St. Andrew's, and in the influence he had exercised over the affairs of Scotland. His hatred to the new doctrines he had already proved by the burning of Keillor, Forret, Kennedy, and Russell; his hatred to Henry had long been established. With the hope of evicting the cardinal from the court of James, Sir Ralph Sadler proceeded, in 1539, as ambassador to the king from his uncle of England.

"His" [Sadler's] "instructions directed him to discover, if possible, James's real intentions with regard to the league by the emperor and Francis against England; to ascertain in what manner the monarch was affected towards the reformed opinions, and, by an exposure of the tyranny of the papal power, the scandalous lives of the majority of the clergy, and the enormous wealth which had been engrossed by the Church, to awaken the royal mind to the necessity and *advantage* of a suppression of the monasteries and a rupture with the supreme pontiff. To accomplish this more effectually, the ambassador carried with him certain letters of Cardinal Beaton, addressed to Rome, which had accidentally fallen into Henry's hands, and the contents of which it was expected would awaken the jealousy of his master, and lead to the disgrace of the cardinal. Whilst Sadler was to renew the proposal for a personal conference between the two princes, and to hold out to his ambition the hope of his succession to the crown of England, in the event of the death of Henry's infant and only son, Prince Edward."—Vol. v. pp. 227-8.

The embassy failed as far as the rejection of the Pope and the disgrace of the cardinal was concerned. And James, whilst he declared that nothing should induce him, if his uncle's conduct corresponded to his professions, to join in a league against him, yet steadily refused to follow his example in throwing off the allegiance of the head of the Church, dissolving the monasteries, or abjuring his religion. As for the letters of the cardinal, he smiled as he received those letters which he had seen before they were sent from Scotland; and whilst he admitted the immoralities of his clergy, and swore to enforce a moral reformation among them, he pronounced a merited eulogium on them for their superior knowledge, talents, loyalty to their king and country, and readiness to assist him with their wealth and their abilities. In the parliament which assembled in the March of the following year the power of Beaton and the clergy enabled the king to act up to his resolutions through the medium of legislative enactments against the new doctrines. To argue against the supremacy or infallibility of the pope was rendered a capital offence; the mere suspicion of heretical opinions was a disqualification for office in the state; whilst flight from judicial examination was a confession of heresy in its worst form. Private meetings and religious conventicles were declared illegal, and the revealer of such was highly rewarded; and no good churchman was henceforward to hold converse with any one who had ever held the new views, although he might have recanted and been absolved from his sin. The progress of the iconoclastic spirit of the Protestants is evidenced by the Acts against the defacing and casting down the images of the Saints; whilst the truth of the charges of licentiousness and immorality against the clergy is equally substantiated by the strong exhortations of the parliament, that all churchmen, both high and low, should reform their lives and conversations, and labour to restore that respect for the services of the Church, which, said the parliament, had of late been lost, through the dishonesty and misrule of the clergy, proceeding from their ignorance in divine and human learning and licentiousness of manners. These proceedings, equally with the cruel executions of such as Hamilton, Straiton, or Kennedy, tended to encourage that very doctrine which it was thus hoped to destroy; so that, notwithstanding the wishes of the king and the labours of the clergy, the new doctrines continued to progress in secret during the life of the king, in no slight degree supported by the dealings of Henry with the Douglas faction and that party of the nobles whom the disastrous rout at the Solway Moss threw into his power.

On the death of the young king, Beaton, unable to contend, for the time, against the intrigues of Henry and the Douglasses, was soon after his dismissal confined in the castle of Blackness, under the charge of Lord Seton.

"The seizure of the cardinal," says Mr. Tytler, "was attended with effects which his opponents had not anticipated. The public services of religion were suspended; the priests refused to administer the sacraments of baptism and burial; the churches were closed; an universal gloom overspread the countenances of the people; and the country presented the melancholy appearance of a land excommunicated for some awful crime. The days, indeed, were passed, when the full terrors of such a state of spiritual proscription could be felt, yet the Catholic party were still strong in Scotland; they loudly exclaimed against their opponents for so daring an act of sacrilege and injustice; and the people began, in some degree, to identify the cause of Beaton with the independence of the country, exclaiming against the Douglasses and the Scottish prisoners as the pensioners of England."—Vol. v. p. 264.

Those who may have read the correspondence contained in the Sadler state papers are fully aware how much ground the Catholic party had for their suspicions, and which were greatly increased on the refusal of Arran and his allies the Douglasses to permit the release of the cardinal on the surety of the earls of Huntley, Bothwell, and Moray. In consequence of this refusal, the earls who had rendered themselves as sureties for the cardinal, supported by Argyle and a powerful body of bishops, abbots, barons and landed gentry, assembled at Perth and avowed their determination of resisting Arran the regent, and his friends and the maintainers of the new doctrines. Reid, Bishop of Orkney, as their ambassador, demanded of the regent and his haughty councillors the release of the cardinal, the forbidding the reading of the Testament in the vulgar tongue by the people, the dismissal of the ambassadors to whom had been entrusted the negotiation of a marriage between Mary and Edward of England, and their right of being consulted by the regent in all affairs of importance. Arran knew well that by acceding to the release of Beaton he let loose one powerful in opposition, and doubtful in friendship, for the temporary support of a party who hated him bitterly, and at the certain expense of the loss of Henry's support. He therefore rejected their demands, following up his rejection by a summons to disperse their assembly under the pains of treason, and to depart to their homes until the meeting of the estates. Conscious of their weakness, the Catholics acquiesced in the command, and before the day of the meeting of the parliament gave in their nominal adherence to the government, determined to follow the motto of the Lords of Ravenswood, and "bide their time."

The parliament, which met on the twelfth of March, 1543, after having determined the matter of the matrimonial alliance between the two crowns, reversed the attainder of Angus and the Douglasses, and selected the keepers of the Queen's person, was prorogued, whilst the all-powerful lords of the articles continued sitting for the introduction of such statutes as the general interests of the kingdom required. Previous to our next quotation from Mr. Tytler, it may be advisable to remark that, as far back as the reign of David II. certain committees had been elected from the three estates, to whom, with the king, was committed the legislative power of the parliament; and that these committees had been reformed and remodelled by James the First, under the title of Lords of the Articles. With this explanation we proceed.

"Lord Maxwell, when a prisoner in England, had become a convert to its" [the Reformation] "doctrines, and proposed that all might have the liberty to read the Bible in an approved Scots or English translation, provided none disputed on the controverted opinions. Against this the Archbishop of Glasgow solemnly protested for himself and the ecclesiastical estate in parliament till the matter should be debated in a provincial council; but the proposition obtained the consent of the lords of the articles, and was publicly ratified by the governor. Arran, indeed, was at this time esteemed, to use the words of Knox, one of the most fervent Protestants in Europe. He entertained in his service two celebrated preachers, Friar Williams and John Rough, who inveighed with much severity against the corruptions of the Romish Church; and under his protection the Holy Scripture began to be studied very generally throughout the country."—Vol. v. p. 271.

In this enactment, we have, under protest from the ecclesiastical estate, the first recognition by the authorities of the realm of one of the principles of the Reformation. At this period the demands of Henry rendered the present success of the new doctrines entirely nugatory. Arran had too much honour to submit to the placing of his country under the sway of England, or to make the marriage Henry's first step to the crown of Scotland. Before the year was ended, the demands of the king of England, seconded by the management of Hamilton, abbot of Paisley, the negotiator of the cardinal's party, had had their effect. Beaton had escaped to his own castle, with the sanction, if not the connivance, of Arran; Lennox, supported by the cardinal and the entire Catholic party, was raised up as a rival to Arran; and the governor preferred sealing a peace with Beaton, to siding with Angus and those renegade lords who were preparing to support the army which Henry now threatened to pour across the borders. On the third of September the cardinal and Arran met as friends at Callander House; a letter of Lord W. Paris to the duke of Suffolk, dated ten days after, relates how Arran had already publicly abjured the new religion, received absolution for his having wandered from the faith, renounced the treaties with England, and delivered his eldest son to the cardinal as a pledge of his sincerity. So soon had the wily prelate obtained a complete command over the mind of the pliant Arran. During the period that Arran had openly professed the Protestant views, many were induced openly to declare their adherence to those doctrines, and eagerly to read and circulate the works of the English and foreign reformers throughout the country. By such methods these principles were very generally disseminated, and a large party existed at once unfavourable to the designs of the English faction, and favourable to the progress of the Reformation. From the unauthoritative mode in which these new principles had been disseminated, we are not surprised at the extreme ultra-Protestantism and schismatic tendency of their opinions. Beaton now followed up his advantage, by inducing the parliament, by which the treaties with England were annulled, to pass an act against the multiplying of heresies, enjoining the Bishops to make inquisition in their dioceses for heretics, and to proceed against them according to the laws of the Church. At this juncture the meanness and dishonesty of the English party showed itself. Lennox, Cassilis, Angus, and Glencairn, for fear of incurring forfeiture, bound themselves to Arran and the cardinal " to remain true and faithful servants to the Queen, to assist the lord governor for defence of the realm against the old enemies of England, to support the liberties of the Church, and maintain the true religion." In less than two months these nobles, so highly praised by Protestant writers, were in correspondence with Henry and using their utmost endeavours to induce him to invade their country. Indeed, from that time they became the more bitter and secret enemies of Scotland, using their utmost endeavours to overthrow the government, destroy the Cardinal, and obtain as Henry's deputies the supreme power of the realm.

Events now succeed each other with great rapidity. About the middle of the year 1544, Beaton made his ecclesiastical progress to Perth, and commenced against the Reformers a persecution so cruel as to defeat its object. The interrupting a friar during his sermon, and denying the efficacy of prayer to the saints, brought death to Lamb; whilst ridicule of an image of St. Francis, and breaking his fast in Lent, sent his three companions to the gallows. A refusal to address her prayers, during her labour, to the Virgin, involved the wife of one of these sufferers in the same condemnation. Such cruelty only strengthened the convictions it was intended to extinguish. Whilst Beaton was thus employed, Henry found time, amid his preparations for the invasion of Scotland, to mature a plot for the destruction of his wily enemy.

"The history of this plot," says our author, "presents an extraordinary picture of the times, and demands more than common attention. On the 17th of April Crichton, laird of Brunston, who, since the coalition between Beaton and the governor, had been employed by Sadler, the ambassador, as a spy on their movements, despatched to the earl of Hertford, then at Newcastle, a Scottish gentleman named Wishart, who communicated to Hertford the particulars of the plot. He stated that Kirkaldy, the laird of Grange, the master of Rothes, eldest son to the earl of that name, and John Charteris, were willing to apprehend or slay the cardinal, if assured of proper support from England. Wishart, who brought this offer, was instantly despatched by post to the English court, and in a personal interview with the king, informed him of the services which Kirkaldy and Rothes were ready to perform. Henry received the letters of Brunston, and listened to the report of his messenger with much satisfaction, approved of the plot, and in the event of its being successful, promised the conspirators his royal protection, should they be constrained to take refuge in his dominions. But Beaton had either received secret information of the project for his destruction, or the design was, for the present, interrupted by some unforeseen occurrence. Succeeding events, however, demonstrated that it was delayed only, not abandoned, and that the same unscrupulous agents who now intrigued with the English monarch were at last induced by Henry to accomplish their atrocious purpose."—Vol. v. pp. 299, 300.

All these men were protestants, and ready and willing to defend its preachers by force of arms: the laird of Brunston, the originator of the plot, was that confidential servant of the cardinal's from whom those letters were taken by Henry's orders, with which he endeavoured, through the means of Sadler, to render Beaton suspected in the eyes of his royal master James. Such was the prime agent of our great Harry in this plot, which so redounds to his honour.

It were impossible to give any short account of the disasters of the English invasion under Lord Hertford, or the intrigues to which it gave rise. Suffice it to say, that, as an whole it failed, and only brought on the northern counties of England a severe retaliation. Politically speaking it was a most grievous blow to Henry, breaking as it did the Anglo-Scottish party; and though for a time it environed Arran with enemies, it eventually rendered his and the cardinal's party more than a match for the open violence of their opponents. In the following year, the earl of Cassilis, Henry's firmest friend, and Scotland's most constant enemy, clearly perceiving that inroad and invasion did but unite more firmly all parties in favour of the government, persuaded Henry to send him as his ambassador with offers of peace, while at the same time he relaxed not his preparations for a fresh invasion. Although backed by the support of his old comrades in treason, the earls of Glencairn, Marshal, and the Douglases, Henry's envoy could not prevail against the influence of the Cardinal, increased to the utmost by the prospect of auxiliaries from France and Denmark, and the dignity of Legate à Latere, which he had lately received from the papal court. Foiled in their purpose, the noble earl and his royal master returned to their plan of assassination. We cannot give a more clear and explicit account than that of Mr. Tytler, in the following rather lengthy extract:—

" Mortified to be thus repulsed, Henry's animosity against Beaton became more vehement than before. To his energy and political talent he justly ascribed his defeat; and whilst he urged his preparations for war, he encouraged the earl of Cassilis in organizing a conspiracy for his assassination. The plot is entirely unknown, either to our Scottish or English historians; and now, after the lapse of nearly three centuries, has been discovered in the secret correspondence of the State-paper office. It appears that Cassilis had addressed a letter to Sadler, in which he made an offer '*for the killing of the cardinal, if his majesty would have it done, a promise, when it was done, a reward.*" [Truly our earl is a respectable bravo, for a protestant noble.] " Sadler showed the letter to the earl of Hertford and the council of the North, and by them it was transmitted to the king. Cassilis' associates, to whom he communicated his purpose, were the earls of Angus, Glencairn, Marshal, and Sir George Douglas; and these persons requested that Forster, an English prisoner of some note, who could visit Scotland without suspicion, should be sent to Edinburgh to communicate with them on the design of cutting off Beaton. Hertford accordingly consulted the privy-council upon his majesty's wishes in this affair, requiring to be informed whether Cassilis's plan for the assassination of his powerful enemy was agreeable to the king, and whether Forster should be despatched into Scotland. Henry, conveying his wishes through the privy council, replied, that he desired Forster to set off immediately; to the other part of the query, the answer of the privy council was in these words:—' His majesty hath willed us to signify unto your lordship, that, his highness reputing the fact not meet to be set forward expressly by his majesty, will not seem to have to do in it, *and yet not misliking the offer, thinking good,* that Mr. Sadler, to whom that letter was addressed, should write to the earl of the receipt of his letter containing such an offer, which he thinketh not convenient to be communicated to the king's majesty. Marry, to write to him what he thinketh of the matter; *he shall say, that if he were in the earl of Cassilis' place, and were as able to do his majesty good service there, as he knoweth him to be, and thinketh a right good will in him to do it, he would surely do what he could for the execution of it, believing verily to do thereby not only an acceptable service to the king's majesty, but also a special benefit to the realm of Scotland, and would trust verily the king's majesty would consider his service in the same; as you doubt not of his accustomed goodness to those who serve him, but he would do the same to him.*"—Vol. v. pp. 321-2.

The advice was followed. Sadler wrote a letter in which he made it to appear that the notion of assassination came from him, and that he had not communicated the project to the king. Forster met the earls, who were silent on the subject, and confined themselves to other matters.

" Sir George Douglas, however, was less timorous, and sent by Forster a message to the earl of Hertford in very explicit terms. '*He willed me,*' says the envoy, '*to tell my lord lieutenant, that if the king would have the cardinal dead, if his grace would promise a good reward for the doing thereof, so that the reward were known what it should be, the country being lawless as it is, he thinketh that that adventure would be proved; for he saith, the common saying is, the cardinal is the only occasion of the war, and is usually beloved in Scotland; and then, if he were dead, by that means how that reward should be paid.*' Such was the simple proposal of Sir G. Douglas for the removal of his arch-enemy; but though the English king had no objection to give the utmost secret encouragement to the conspiracy, he hesitated to offer such an outrage to the common feelings of Christendom, as to set a price upon the head of the cardinal, and to offer a reward and indemnity to those who should slay him. For the moment, therefore, the scheme seemed to be abandoned by the earls, but it was only to be afterwards resumed by Brunston."—Vol. v. pp. 323-4.

Though we must admit that the royal hirer and his noble bravos tend to lower the party which they led in the eyes of right-thinking persons, yet we cannot but be grateful to the royal Defender of the Faith, at the time that he recognised the principle of discovery being the test of crime, that he had so great a respect for the prejudices of Christendom as to forbear from setting a price on the cardinal's head, as his Norman predecessors did on that of the ravening wolf.

To these events succeeded the invasion of Scotland by the English army under Hertford; the condemnation of Lennox for his many treasons, and the confiscation of his estates; the renewal of the attempt against Beaton by the laird of Brunston and the earls of Cassilis and Angus; and the proposal of the discontented Lord of the Isles to join his forces with those of the rebel Lennox, to the army of Henry, and to ensure the destruction of Arran, the cardinal, and Scotland, by a concocted scheme of simultaneous invasion on the northern and southern parts of the country. These latter offers in all probability never reached the English king; and if they did, they found him too deeply engaged with important affairs which that year brought forth, connected with the murders of Wishart and Beaton. Two years before this, though the reformed doctrines had received a severe blow in the recantation of Arran, and had suffered much from the persecutions of Beaton, yet the principles and works of the English and foreign reformers had been gradually progressing, amid dangers and difficulties, and were now very generally professed, and even openly supported, as well by conscientious believers in the truth inculcated by them, as by that large party among the nobility and lairds, to whom the desire of reforming the Church was an excuse in the eyes of some for their intrigues with Henry against the liberties of their country. The lax discipline, the immoralities, the worldly-mindedness of the clergy, when combined with the spectacles exhibited by the Scotch protestants, in their last hours under the pains of a cruel death, compelled even the most indifferent spectator to some inquiry. And when those inquiries were discountenanced, or rather forbidden by the Church, with ruthless cruelty, instead of being directed by the teaching and the conduct of the clergy, these enquiries led many to renounce the entire system of Church doctrine and discipline, with a portion of which they were disgusted, since the Church would not direct their crude and hardly-formed views. Fearful indeed were the two great parties at that time. On the one side were wild enthusiasts, ever ready to pour forth vials of wrath against every abuse of the Church, and while they argued against innovations which had crept in, paving the way (the greater part intentionally) to the ultimate destruction of the holy edifice. To support these were those nobles who hoped to reap political and territorial advantages from the ruin of the party of the cardinal, and the confiscation of the Church property. On the other side, the Church in Scotland had fallen greatly from her high estate; and the example of its head and leader, cardinal Beaton, a prelate stained with open profligacy, and remarkable alone for his ability in intrigue, was fitted to produce the worst effects upon the great body of the inferior clergy. Some few indeed there may have been on both sides who were willing, in a pure catholic spirit, to have aided, as clerics or as laymen, in the work of self-reformation. But enthusiasm on the one hand, and persecution on the other, prevented their appeal from being heard.

Among those over whom the Anglo-Scottish nobles cast their protection was George Wishart, the martyr, as he is commonly called, a schoolmaster at Montrose, who, instructed in the principles of the reformers by Erskine, the then provost, had been obliged to flee to England, for attempting to introduce the reading of the New Testament in Greek among his pupils. In England, Bristol was a witness to his sermons against the offering of prayers to the Virgin; of his open recantation and faggot burning in the church of St. Nicholas; whilst in less than five years he might be heard in the towns of Montrose, Dundee, Perth, and Ayr, inveighing against the errors of popery, and the profligate lives of churchmen, (for, like others, his text was, *Ex uno disce omnes*,) with sufficient eloquence and truth to make many converts, and sufficient severity and want of caution to give rise to acts of violence, wherein, as at Dundee, the monasteries became the prey of an infuriated and plunder-seeking mob. During the two years after his arrival in Scotland, that he was enabled, under the protection of the barons, to defy persecution, Wishart was in confidential intimacy with Cassilis, Glencairn, Brunston, and Maxwell, the advisers of Henry's invasions, and the concocters of the plots for assassinating the cardinal. Of this Beaton was aware, and with his wonted unscrupulousness counterplotted against the reformer, each, perhaps, consoling himself that he was doing God service, in laying wait for the life of his opponent. For a time his mailed attendants and the two-handed sword which some tried follower bore before him to his preachings, preserved him from Beaton's power. At last, however, a tempting message from his friend Cassilis, calling him to Edinburgh, in order to, if possible, have a public disputation with the bishops, placed him within Beaton's reach. The cardinal was not one to neglect his opportunities. The preacher was now in the immediate neighbourhood of Edinburgh, waiting for the coming of Cassilis, who had before offered to slay the cardinal, and harbouring, with another volunteer in the same plot, the laird of Brunston. Against Wishart and Brunston the cardinal made his attempt; and when, on the return of the earl of Bothwell from the house of Ormistown, he found he had only one prisoner, though it was indeed the preacher, the disappointment of Beaton was shown in the eagerness with which he pursued and endeavoured to seize his companions who had escaped. Bothwell, who had induced Wishart to surrender by a promise of safety for life and person, appeared for some time resolved to be honest. At length money had its effect, and Wishart was consigned to the custody of the cardinal.

"Having secured him," says Mr. Tytler, "Beaton was not of a temper to hesitate in his measures, or adopt a middle course. He summoned a council of bishops and dignified clergy to meet at St. Andrew's; requested the governor to nominate a judge, whose presence might give a civil sanction to their proceedings; and being refused by the timidity or humanity of Arran, determined to proceed on his own authority. The alleged heretic was immediately arraigned before the spiritual tribunal, and defended his opinions *meekly, but firmly,* with a profound knowledge of Scripture. He appealed to the word of God as the *sole rule* by which he was guided in the doctrines he had taught the people. As he was ready to admit all its precepts, so was he bound, he declared, to refuse and deny every thing which it condemned; *whilst he deemed of little consequence such points as it left in obscurity.* He maintained his right to preach, notwithstanding his excommunication by the Church, and contended that any man, with fervent faith, and a sufficient knowledge of Scripture, might be a teacher of the word of life. He declared the insufficiency of outward ceremonies to salvation, when the heart was unaffected, derided auricular confession, and admitted only such sacraments as were recorded in Scripture. Of fasting he warmly approved; upheld the Lord's Supper as a divine and comfortable institution; maintained the necessity of our fully understanding the vows taken for us in our baptism; condemned the invocation of saints, and the doctrine of purgatory as unscriptural; and asserted his belief that immediately after death the soul would pass into a state of immortal life and unfading felicity; whilst he defended his own creed," [*meekly,* but firmly?] "supporting it by a constant reference to Scripture, he did not hesitate to stigmatize the doctrine of his opponents in unmeasured terms, pronouncing it 'pestilential, blasphemous, and abominable; not proceeding from the inspiration of God, but the suggestions of the devil.' The result of all this was easy to be anticipated; Wishart was found guilty of heresy, and sentenced to be burned. The trial took place at St. Andrew's, and no time was lost in carrying the sentence into effect."—Vol. v. p. 346, 347.

In this quotation we have the received creed for which Wishart died at the stake, the deliberate opinions of the Scotch reformer. The courage, meekness, and patience with which he bore his sufferings, have gone far to shroud his errors in the eyes of churchmen in after ages; whilst at the time of his execution they produced a deep effect on those who believed his doctrines to be true, or wished for their establishment, for the sake of private profit or public aggrandizement.

It had ever been a favourite point among protestant writers to consider the murder of Beaton, which followed so soon on the death of Wishart, to have been entirely caused by a spirit of revenge for their favourite preacher. That whispers of revenge were circulated among the people, and hints thrown out that God would not suffer such cruelty to go unpunished, is not to be denied. But our readers are by this time fully aware of how old a date the intended assassination of the cardinal was, and that though fostered by royalty, and volunteered by nobility, *for a consideration,* it had already failed thrice. In one way these feelings of revenge, now so prevalent, were the occasion of the murder; namely, as enabling the conspirators to talk boldly against their victim, now no longer popular among the people, and to organize, with better prospects, a fourth conspiracy against the cardinal. And it cannot be doubted that the death of Wishart induced many persons, who would have spurned to unite with such men as Brunston, the Leslies, and Kirkaldy, in their mercenary motives, to applaud, and even join in the attempt against the life of Beaton. After the marriage of one of his natural daughters, Margaret Bethune, to David Lindsay, the master of Crawford, which was celebrated with gorgeous pomp soon after the execution of Wishart, Beaton retired to his castle of St. Andrew's, with the intention of fortifying it against the now expected inroad of the English forces, and providing for the defence of the country in the event of the invasion.

"In the midst of these exertions, Beaton seems to have forgotten the secret enemies by whom he was surrounded, whilst they continued more warily than before to hold correspondence with England. In his last letters, the laird of Brunston, whose mortal enmity to Beaton has been amply shown, complained to lord Wharton, *that the king of England was neither sufficiently definite in his commands, nor explicit in his promises,* [no doubt out of respect to the prejudices of Christendom;] but he expressed, at the same time, *the readiness of his friends* to serve the king, his wish to have a meeting with lord Wharton in *the most secret manner, as a discovery might cost him both life and heritage, and his fervent expectation, that, although Beaton now intended a voyage to France, it would be cut short.*"—*Tytler,* vol. viii. p. 352, 353.

The laird of Brunston was as safe in his expectation as his friend Wishart had been in his prophecies of impending invasion and burning from the forces of the English, and with equal reason. Brunston was aware of the readiness of those of his friends who had years ago offered to be the paid murderers of the cardinal, to renew the attempt, and ensure the cutting short of the intended voyage by the sword of assassination; whilst Wishart, associating with those rebellious lords, whose constant endeavour it was to persuade Henry to invade their country, living in habits of intimacy with those who knew too well that a visitation of fire and sword was already determined on Scotland, could not err very far in his predictions of famine, fire, and slaughter. Anxious, however, as Brunston and his friends were to effect their black purpose, on purely mercenary motives, a private quarrel between Beaton and Norman Lesley, the master of Rothes, about interchanging of an estate in Fife, matured, or rather precipitated, the accomplishment of the design. High words passed between the master and Beaton, when the former came to claim his promised equivalent for the estate he had surrendered to the latter. Mutual threats concluded the meeting; and Lesley, repairing to his uncle John, was soon persuaded by one so eager to slay the cardinal, that his own safety depended on Beaton's instant death. The master of Rothes agreed, summoned Melville and Kirkaldy of Grange, whose wishes were known to agree with those of the Leslies, and arranged for the immediate committal of the murder.

"On the evening of the twenty-eighth of May, Norman Lesley came with only five followers, to St. Andrew's, and rode, without exciting suspicion, to his usual inn. William Kirkaldy of Grange, was there already, and they were soon joined by John Lesley, who took the precaution of entering the town after night-fall, as his appearance, from his known enmity to Beaton, might have raised alarm. Next morning at day-break the conspirators assembled in small detached knots, in the vicinity of the castle; and the porter having lowered the drawbridge, to admit the masons employed in the new works, Norman Lesley, and three men with him, passed the gates, and inquired whether the cardinal was yet awake. This was done without suspicion; and as they were occupied in conversation, James Melville, Kirkaldy of Grange, and their followers, entered unnoticed; but, on perceiving John Lesley, who followed, the porter instantly suspected treason, and springing to the drawbridge, had unloosed its iron fastening, when the conspirator Lesley anticipated his purpose by leaping across the gap. To despatch him with their daggers, cast the body into the fosse, and seize the keys of the castle, employed but a few minutes, and all was done with such silence, as well as rapidity, that no alarm had been given. With equal quietness the workmen who laboured on the ramparts were led to the gate and dismissed. Kirkaldy, who was acquainted with the castle, then took his station at a private postern, through which alone any escape could be made, and the rest of the conspirators, going successively to the apartments of the different gentlemen who formed the prelate's household, awoke them, and threatening instant death if they spoke, led them, one by one, to the outer wicket, and dismissed them unhurt. In this manner a hundred workmen and fifty household servants were disposed of by a handful of men, who, closing the gates and dropping the portcullis, were complete masters of the castle. Meanwhile Beaton, the unfortunate victim against whom all this hazard had been encountered, was still asleep; but awakening and hearing an unusual bustle, he threw on his night-gown, and drawing up the window of his bed-chamber, inquired what it meant. Being answered that Norman Lesley had taken the castle, he rushed to the private postern, but seeing it already guarded, returned speedily to his apartment, seized his sword, and with the assistance of his page barricaded the door on the inside with his heaviest furniture. John Lesley now coming up demanded admittance. 'Who are you?' said the cardinal. 'My name,' he replied, 'is Lesley.' 'Is it Norman?' asked the unhappy man, remembering probably the bond of Maurent; 'I must have Norman, he is my friend.' 'Nay, I am not Norman,' answered the ruffian, 'but John, and with me ye must be contented.' Upon which he called for fire, and was about to apply it to the door, when it was unlocked from within. The conspirators now rushed in, and Lesley and Carmichael throwing themselves furiously on their victim, who earnestly implored mercy, stabbed him repeatedly. But, meanwhile, *a milder fanatic*, [rather, a more cold-blooded villain,] who professed to murder, not from passion, but religious duty, reproved their violence. 'This judgment of God,' said he, 'ought to be executed with gravity, although in secret;' and presenting the point of his sword to the bleeding prelate, he called on him to repent of his wicked courses, and especially of the death of the holy Wishart, to avenge whose innocent blood they were now sent by God. 'Remember,' he said, 'that the mortal blow I am now about to deal is not the mercenary blow of a hired assassin, [perhaps he thought those dealt by the others were, and with reason,] but the just vengeance which hath fallen on an obstinate and cruel enemy of Christ and the holy gospel.' On his saying this, he repeatedly passed his sword through the body of his unresisting victim, who sunk down from the chair to which he had retreated, and instantly expired."—*Tytler*, vol. v. 353, 354, 355.

The conspirators were now interrupted by the cries of the citizens of St. Andrew's, who standing gathered round the fosse, loudly demanded speech with the cardinal. They were answered from the battlements that he could not come to them. Still they cried out the more furiously. Whereupon Norman Lesley, reproving them as fools for desiring speech of a dead man, dragging the body to the walls, hung it over the parapet, naked, ghastly, and bleeding. "There," said the murderer, "there is your god, and now that ye are satisfied, get you home." The people obeyed his orders.

Thus fell Cardinal Beaton, accomplishing that plot, which, two years before, Brunston and Henry the Eighth had concocted against him. The leaders of the assassins, Kirkaldy and Norman Lesley, were still in the pay of England, and still styled by Henry as his good friends. And though Brunston himself and Cassilis do not appear either in the actual murder, or in communication with the murderers immediately before-hand, yet when we consider how intimately these men had been connected together now for two years and more, in their plots against Beaton, and their intrigues with England, we can hardly help believing that the good wishes, if not the secret aid, of Cassilis was with the murderers, and that the daring and unscrupulous Brunston was as much implicated with the last plot, as with that by which the same men, Kirkaldy and Lesley, were to have slain the cardinal two years before in Fife. Thus fell Cardinal Beaton, the clever and unprincipled opponent of the new doctrines, by a foul and bloody murder; a murder which we are now enabled to pronounce, without fear of contradiction, not to have arisen simply out of indignation for the fate of Wishart, but to have been years before projected by Cassilis, Douglas, and Brunston, and to have been encouraged, as openly as he dared, by the English monarch; and which murder was committed by the principal conspirators from private and mercenary considerations. Until Mr. Tytler's laborious investigations in the State-paper Office, we had little, if any, certain evidence to rebut the common account originated by the writers of the same principles as Wishart, that revenge for his death was the sole reason of the assassination. But now we hardly believe the most determined hater of Beaton and admirer of Wishart will, in the face of Mr. Tytler's revelations, dare to question the correctness of the views advanced by that historian, and with which we have endeavoured to make our readers acquainted. The vituperation and inconclusive argument which the deed elicited from protestant and Roman catholic writers may now be laid aside, and the exultation and unseasonable pleasantry of Knox give place to historical truth. We had hoped in this paper to have carried on the account to 1560, but the space we have already occupied forbids it.

1. *Du Vandalisme et du Catholicisme dans l'Art.* *Par le* Comte de Montalembert. Paris. 1839.

2. *Etat du Catholicisme en France,* 1830-40. *Par* Alphonse Pepin. Paris. 1841.

The depressed state of catholic feeling in this country, for many years past, has in no way, we think, been evinced more significantly than by an entire cessation (at least till very recently) of the interest that used to be taken in the affairs of foreign Churches. A long and gloomy interval has now passed, during which we seemed to have forgotten not merely the obligations and duties, but the very feelings that are implied in our professed belief in the " holy catholic Church, the communion of saints." For all that we have long appeared to care, the catholic Church might have ceased to exist. If our sympathies have extended at all beyond the limits of Anglican communion, they have unfortunately been raised on behalf of the sects that, under one guise or another, have been constant and uniform in their efforts to undermine the foundations of the Church; we have been more willing to symbolize with them, than desirous of regaining the esteem of our catholic neighbours on the continent.

At one period the case was far otherwise. We can point at a time when English theologians were congratulated by their brethren of the Gallican Church on their success in combating the very sectarian errors which, during the recent dark age of our history, have come to be overlooked, palliated, and even to a great extent tacitly adopted. The time was when the mutual claims of the neighbouring churches were fully recognised. Even though estranged, each regarded the other as a sister, in whose welfare it was impossible not to take a continued and anxious interest. The intercourse, it is true, between the prelates and clergy of the two Churches was not always friendly; but it was maintained in a spirit of charity, and long cherished by ardent desires and strenuous efforts on both sides for the restoration of catholic communion.

The unsuccessful issue of the many negotiations that were set afoot had, no doubt, much to do with the gradual breach of intercourse. Each party, vexed and discouraged by continual misunderstandings, and the apparent hopelessness of accommodation, was driven back upon itself; and on our side, perhaps, this had the effect of giving currency to the unfortunate sentiment, that the isolated position of the Church of England being without remedy, it was but in justice to herself and to the goodness of her cause, that she assumed the tone of independence and exclusiveness by which she has been characterised for a century past. We say unfortunate sentiment,—not that we are in the smallest degree inimical to the just independence of national Churches, or that we overlook the noble stand which the

Church of England has made for her rights in that respect; but because, in our case, the isolated position, in the first instance forced upon us, has, through the gradual decay of catholic piety, brought about the substitution of a proud indifference for an independence in most respects constrained—a sort of self-gratulatory and holiday contentment with our lot—instead of the sackcloth of continual mourning and heaviness for the unrepaired rents in the "garment of Christ." It is matter of great thankfulness, however, that such a state of things may now be contemplated, if not as passed, at least as rapidly passing away. A series of unforeseen events, travelling in speedy succession before our eyes, has conspired, not only to throw the Church of England back upon her long-forgotten first principles, but to force her out of the false security and self-seclusion in which she had entrenched herself. The revival of Church principles,—not in theory but in practice,—not as matters to be discussed in argument, but as the living springs, motives, and forms of christian life, has begun every where to exhibit its effects,—principles that, in spite of all the calumny, the malice, and ignorance by which they are assailed, are, beyond any question, with wonderful rapidity and power, making their way to the hearts of the people, and shaking to its very centre the old sluggish and inanimate fabric of religion. On every side the clergy have been stirred up to an activity that has long been foreign to their habits.

The events, on the other hand, connected with the consecration of a Prussian Bishop in communion with the Church of England for the strangers at Jerusalem (forming, as it is acknowledged to be, a preliminary step to the establishment of Episcopacy in the Prussian states*) seem to bear in them the seeds of changes so vastly momentous in the relations and interests, not only of the Church of England, but of the Church catholic, that one cannot help wondering whether by this the way has not been opened that will in the end lead to a consummation we had almost ceased to hope for,—the restoration of catholic unity on a healthy footing. At all events, in the prospect of the enlarged sphere of action thus appearing to be providentially forced upon the Church of England, and the new and unexpected position about to be assigned her of confronting the unreformed catholicism of the continent on its own field, it is but natural that we should desire to learn something of the actual condition, moral and religious, of the foreign Churches with which she is to be brought in contact. More especially, as it seems to us, we are drawn again towards the Gallican Church, for whom we must always have a preeminent regard, not only on account of neighbourhood, but from the fact that of all Churches adhering to the Roman see,

---

* We understand that two individuals, MM. Neander and Strauss (not the Strauss of whom we have heard most) have accompanied the King of Prussia, for the purpose of being consecrated bishops. Before this is printed, however, our readers will have learned the facts. The King of Prussia *created* M. Neander a bishop in the same way as he creates a baron; but he finds that this is not quite enough.

she has been the only one that has continued, by the assertion of her national independence, to set bounds to papal usurpation.*

What is the real state of catholicism in the various parts of the continent? Is it still in the same miserable condition that brought about the religious revolution of the sixteenth century? Do idolatry and superstition still reign so paramount as people would force us, for a point of faith and duty, to believe? Or, with respect to France, in particular, has the revolution of 1789 had no effect on the Church? How has she come forth from that sore trial?—as gold tried by the fire? or has she been consumed like stubble? What hold does she retain in the affections of the people? These are questions which seem to us of the greatest interest; and on which we hope to have a good deal to say from time to time, according as we are able to obtain materials. For the present we offer a few rambling and desultory observations on the actual position of the Gallican Church, which may serve as a sort of introduction to the subject until we can furnish our readers with more minute details.

Looking merely at the outward aspect of religious affairs in France, there is no sight that meets the eye of a traveller, at the present moment, more surprising than the activity that prevails in the restoration and re-opening of ruined and desecrated churches. We are not alone in our zeal for church building; our French neighbours all of a sudden have begun to rival us in that particular, and bid fair to outstrip us, at least in the splendour and costliness of their labours. A wonderful change, in truth, has " come o'er the spirit of their dream." But a very few years ago, the few devout souls who seemed to rise above the sweeping tide of desolating infidelity and religious ignorance that overspread the land, had no voice but that of unmingled sorrow. Day after day, year after year, some new tale was told of ruin;— some beautiful and cherished fabric, reared by the pious hands of former times, had been levelled, its ornaments sold, its tombs violated, and the ashes of the faithful departed scattered to the winds. Monument after monument, which, if destroyed, no human power could ever replace, perished; and it seemed as if the universal appetite of demolition would only be satiated by the utter effacement of every relic of ancient Gallican piety and skill.

Nor has this sad work of destruction been solely carried on by the misguided and blind fury of republican and revolutionary mobs. The revolution of 1792, it is true, bringing with it the denial of Christ, the abolition of his service, the proscription of his ministers, and the

---

* The catholic Church of the Austrian states is *practically* less dependent on the Roman see than the Gallican Church is. But the latter maintains her liberties as a matter of principle, whereas the former is forced, whether she will or no, to be independent, by a government too jealous of its own authority to allow any foreign interference with its affairs, whether ecclesiastical or secular. All correspondence of the Austrian clergy with Rome, accordingly must pass through the hands of the government. Before the passing of the Roman Catholic Relief Bill, this expedient was recommended to our government by Count Dal Pozzo.

desecration of his altars, had the first and greatest share in laying prostrate the external fabric of religion;—the injuries it inflicted can never be altogether repaired. But when the empire came, and with it the concordat of 1801, by which the churches were re-opened, one might have hoped that the work of demolition had ceased. If nowhere else, it might have been expected that at least among the Clergy the utmost alacrity and zeal would have been found to repair the defaced beauty of the sanctuary. One might have imagined them led by an affectionate love of their old haunts,—a love heightened in proportion as it had been outraged, to preserve with the fondest regard every relic of old piety that the demoniac fury of the revolution had spared; and even where the spoiler's hand had fallen the heaviest, to cherish and deem consecrate the very ruins that were irreparable, hallowed as they were by so many associations, and forming the sorely-tried, but still unsevered, link and bond of communion between the present and the past.

But it was not so. The revolution had obliterated all the ancient land-marks of society, and broken up every association either with the religion or the religious art of catholic times. The new empire of reason had proscribed and abolished all reverence for any but pagan antiquity; there were, in short, no elements in the spirit of the times of the empire that were not antagonist to Christianity itself; no sympathies that could be excited by the glories of ancient christian art. However firm an attitude of resistance, therefore, might have been assumed by the clergy, there was little likelihood of their being able to oppose successfully the domineering spirit of impiety and irreverence that formed an oppressive atmosphere around them, from whose influence there was no escape.

But there was not even attempt at resistance on their part; nor is this surprising. Before the revolution, the taste that prevailed in the externals of religion was of the most wretchedly-degraded and meretricious description. The clergy, on whom the evils of the revolution fell, had been educated in a school that inculcated no reverence for the sacred art of their forefathers; they never had learned to appreciate its beauties. They might venerate a church of the middle ages for its antiquity, or because it was the house of God; but it never entered their imaginations that its architecture was other than the barbarous invention of rude and uncivilised times. When, therefore, the work commenced of rendering the violated churches serviceable, the clergy had no regrets for the entire demolition of the most beautiful monuments of antiquity, so that some habitable erection, no matter what, and the more modern looking the better, were substituted. The most exquisitely carved tabernacle work of the choirs was thrown out or sold, because the hatchet or the torch had been at work upon it, to make way for clumsy benches of deal. Chancel screens, partially broken down, were removed to make way for rows of Greek columns, or more generally were swept away without an attempt at repair. The painted glass of the windows, because broken and mutilated, was given in exchange for the commonest glazing that would keep out the wind or rain.

Many, no doubt, of these now irreparable misfortunes were due to the necessities of the clergy, who, having to struggle for the very existence of Christianity itself, might be justified in postponing for a time every consideration to the importance of restoring its rites by the speediest means that occurred to them. But under the Restoration they could plead no such apology. The Church was then, in one sense, placed at comparative ease; she had leisure to repair after her own fashion and inclination the damages inflicted under the reign of infidel reason; yet we find the destruction of the christian architecture of France proceeding as before, not only unresisted by the clergy, but even under their guidance. Count Montalembert, who has written on this subject with all the bitterness and mortification that every lover of religious art must experience at the bare thought of the systematic demolition of christian remains, that has been going on in France for the last half century, has furnished us with details of the most provoking description. He says, that it is a mistake to suppose that the work of destruction is merely revolutionary; for there is a *vandalism* that attempts to restore, even more pernicious than the *vandalism* that merely pulls down.* The *destructive vandals*, he says, have been:—
   1. The Government.
   2. The Mayors and Provincial Authorities.
   3. The Proprietors.
   4. The Building Committees and the Clergy.
   And 5th (but at a great distance from the others) *L'Emeute*.

Of his *restoring vandals*, we have:—
   1. The Clergy and Building Committees.
   2. The Government.
   3. The Municipal Authorities.
   4. The Proprietors.

"The mob has, at least," he says, "the advantage of making no attempt at restoration; it only pulls down." "There is no where," continues he, "except in France, that *vandalism* reigns without restraint . . . . . . One trembles at the very thought, that every day some destruction is going forward. The whole soil of the country, surcharged, as it was, with the most marvellous creations of imagination and of the faith, becomes every day more naked, more uniform, more bald. Nothing is spared; the devastating hatchet overthrows equally the forests and the churches, the chateaux and the hôtels-de-ville; one might suppose it to be a conquered land, from which the barbarian invaders wished to efface even to the last traces the generations who have inhabited it. It would seem, that they wished to persuade themselves that the world was born yesterday, and will come tomorrow to an end, so much do they hasten to annihilate every thing that seems to have lasted longer than the life of a man. They do

---
* Du Vandalisme et du Catholicisme dans l'Art. Paris, 1839.

not even respect the ruins they have made.....'' " If you could make them believe that a church had once been consecrated to some Roman god, they would immediately promise it protection and open their purses.... There would be no end to the enumeration of Romanesque churches that owe their preservation to this ingenious belief. I need only cite the cathedral of Angoulême, the beautiful façade of which has only been preserved, because the bas-relief of God the Father, figured among the symbols of the four evangelists, was taken for a representation of Jupiter. There is still on the frieze over the portal of this cathedral The Temple of Reason." " Do not, however," continues the Count, " suppose that it is religion merely that is repudiated. Do not imagine that our monuments purely historical, our *souvenirs* of poetry or of love, have escaped the outrages of vandalism—all is confounded in the proscription. At Limoges, they have had the barbarity to destroy the monument celebrated under the name of *Le bon mariage* ;* not a single voice was raised to save it. At Avignon, the church of St. Clara, where Petrarch first saw Laura, in 1328..... has perished with a hundred others. It is now transformed into a manufactory of madder. The church of the Cordeliers, where reposed the ashes of the chaste and beautiful Laura, near those of the brave Crillon, has been razed to make way for the *atelier* of a dyer; there only remain a few arches : the place of the tombs is marked by an ignoble column raised by order of an ENGLISHMAN (!)..... The Goths themselves—the Ostrogoths acted not thus...."

The most recent popular outrage has been the partial destruction of the beautiful church of St. Germain L'Auxerrois, in Paris, and the total demolition, with all its archives and monuments, of the archiepiscopal palace adjoining the cathedral of Nôtre Dame. This was done, as our readers are probably aware, during the riots that took place on the occasion of a legitimist attempt, in 1831, to celebrate the anniversary obsequies of the assassinated Duc de Berri. There is no reasoning, however, as Count M. has observed, about the doings of a mob; we receive tidings of the havoc it has made with simple regrets. Not so, when we are told that the authorities, the clergy, or the proprietors inflict on us the very same injuries in cold blood. " Figure to yourself," he writes to M. Victor Cousin; " Fontevrault, the celebrated, the royal, the historical abbey of Fontevrault—the name of which is found in almost every page of our chronicles of the eleventh and twelfth centuries—Fontevrault, that had fourteen princesses of royal blood for its abbesses, and where so many kings were entombed that it has been called the 'cemetery of kings'—Fontevrault, a marvel of architecture, with its five churches

---

* The tomb of two newly-married young people, who vowed a pilgrimage to S*t*. James of Compostella. The bride died at Limoges during the journey, and the poor husband fulfilled his vow, but on his return to Limoges died of grief. On opening the tomb, the bride, as the story goes, moved herself to one side to make way for her husband.

and its cloisters, is now dishonoured by the name of '*Central Prison!*' But this was not enough: to render it worthy of its new destiny, its cloisters have been blocked up; its immense dormitories, refectories, parlours, rendered undistinguishable; its five churches destroyed; the first and principal one, beautiful and lofty as a cathedral, has not even been respected, the entire nave has been divided into three or four stories, and metamorphosed into workshops and prison cells. The choir, it is true, has been left to its pristine use, but the painted glass has all been removed or destroyed, and the interior stone-work actually plastered so thickly, that the groining of the roof is scarcely traceable. The *debris* of the cemetery of kings, the four invaluable statues of Henry the Second of England, and his wife Eleanor of Guienne, of Richard Cœur de Lion, and of Isabella, wife of John Lackland, lie in a sort of ditch near the place. *All this took place under the Restoration.*" Under the same *régime*, in 1820, a similar fate befel the gigantic and marvellous palace of the popes at Avignon: it was converted into a *barrack for soldiers, and a magazine of military stores.* "At present," says M. de Montalembert, " all is consummated; there remains no longer any one of those immense halls which certainly had no rivals in the Vatican. Each has been divided into three stories."

The abbey of Cadouïn, in Perigord, one of the most beautiful of the ancient Cistercian houses of France, and said to have been founded by St. Bernard himself, was sold at the revolution. Some years ago several catholics of the neighbourhood determined to form an establishment of Trappists on this spot, not only on account of its sacred associations, but to preserve from further demolition the venerable remains of the ancient abbey. They made the most advantageous offers to the proprietors, who, however, would not consent on any account to a "movement so retrograde." "They preferred," says Count M. "to destroy, piece by piece, the whole monastery, with the exception of a little cloister in the interior. At the time I was there, a hexagonal tower highly ornamented was under the pickaxe. . . . . With respect to the interior cloister, which had been used by the monks for recreation after the offices of the choir, having no communication with the external courts, but only with the church and the cells, the proprietors actually claimed *a right of passage to it through the church,*" to convey to and fro the herd of swine which are littered in the cloister.

M. de Montalembert is evidently under the greatest distress with his first category of *Vandales restaurateurs*, viz. the clergy. He is quite at a loss to reconcile their supposed feelings as ministers of the temple with the deliberate barbarism of their conduct towards it. Their sole aim, for the last twenty years, seems to have been to efface every mark of antiquity from the churches. Wherever they have put their hands all has been modernised in the vilest taste. If any part of a church required rebuilding, the remains of the old work have been uniformly demolished, to make way for constructions in the newest style of the Rue de Rivoli or the Boulevard des Italiens. If the church had merely the soil of age on it, it was certain to be white-washed, or painted in streaks of yellow, green, blue, or any other tint that happened to be most economical. Outside and inside were served after the same fashion. The cathedral of Valence, for example, an extremely ancient church in the Byzantine manner, has been painted *in imitation of marble, outside and inside*. The cathedral of Avignon has been white-washed, the brush of the *vandal* actually obliterating an invaluable fresco, attributed to Simone Memmi, representing Petrarch and Laura. At Foix, the principal church, though one of great beauty, built in the pointed style, was not sufficiently admired by the clergy and municipal authorities, and they have accordingly substituted Ionic pilasters, adorned with porcelain cherubs, for the shafts that supported the vault of the choir. At another place M. de Montalembert found painted on the wall over an altar dedicated to the "sacred heart of Jesus," a colossal scarlet heart on a white ground, transfixed by a sabre, exactly copied from one of those worn by sub-lieutenants.

Such has been the state of matters till within the last two or three years, when the hand of the destroyer and obliterator seems to have been arrested as if by magic. A reaction has taken place, with a suddenness and strength that would be impossible among any but a volatile people like the French. When M. de Montalembert published his book, in 1839, he was able only to cite one exception to the barbarous usage of churches and monastic buildings that obtained all over France; here are we, only in 1842, and we see all the churches of Paris undergoing repairs in the most admirable style, and the work proceeding with a vigour and rapidity that is surprising. The church of St. Germain l'Auxerrois has recently been opened, and we find all the old whitewash removed, the stonework rechiselled, the ornaments restored, with a beauty of workmanship we fear it would be impossible, at any cost, to equal in this country; the lancet windows of the choir and apse filled with stained glass designed very accurately in the style of the thirteenth century; the chapels behind the altar filled with new sculpture, of a kind that harmonizes perfectly with the date of that part of the building; and the ceilings of these chapels, and of the whole circular aisle of the apse painted blue and studded with gold stars, in the old manner, with angels here and there, bearing scrolls, censers, musical instruments, &c. Whenever it is practicable, the barbarous rubbish of the last century, in what is shrewdly called the *Pompadour* style, has been removed. The cathedral of St. Denis, near Paris, has undergone the same kind of repair; and though the decorations are not quite completed, it has been opened to the public. The old stained glass, of the date of the Abbot Suger, has been repaired; and all the windows of which the stained glass had been destroyed (or which had never been so ornamented) have been filled with excellent imitations of the old glass. The whitewash has been removed from the interior, and the stonework chiselled and repaired, or replaced by exact restorations of the old ornaments. Where colour was found under the whitewash, it has been again laid on. Altogether, this church, in its present state, reminds one forcibly of Canterbury Cathedral, which has lately undergone the same kind of repair. The chapel of the Palais de Justice, in Paris, called La Sainte Chapelle, built by St. Louis, and corresponding in date and style to our Salisbury, is also undergoing a complete restoration. It has remained unoccupied since the first revolution; and, singular to relate, only three of its magnificent windows of stained glass (the finest in France) were destroyed. These will be replaced, and the whole of the interior repainted and regilt, in the original manner, which, for the most part, is still quite apparent. Much more, however, than mere repairs are now being carried on. A vast deal of original architecture, sculpture, and painting, is everywhere appearing in the churches.

One naturally inquires, whether this sudden reaction be really a religious movement, in which the Church herself participates, or if it be only the caprice of a passing fashion, that, having gratified itself, will straight run after some other novelty. No doubt fashion must always be a large ingredient in every popular bias of the French people; but that the bias should be a religious one can hardly be an accident. French fashions are always expressive of some political, social, or artistical feeling of the day; and in this case also, there must have been some predisposition, some preparation, some undercurrent of religious thought, that has gradually gathered strength enough to ruffle the surface; and which, having got to the surface, has immediately created for itself a form or fashion to which all at once conform themselves without hesitation, whether they participate in the sentiment in which the fashion originated or no. We do not think there is any doubt that in France the Church has been making rapid advances in the esteem and affection of the people; or that, primarily, the movement towards early christian art is due to an increase of real religion. At the same time the present enthusiasm for it is, with the majority, a mere fashion, that will soon expend itself, and leave the maintenance of a right taste in the externals of religion to the few whose devotion to the Church is based on something deeper than the transient artistic and poetical associations of a day.

The same movement, in truth, has been going on in France that we see progressing among ourselves. It is a movement that may be termed *romantico-religious*,—a grafting of religious feeling on the already existing romantic sentiment of the age. Like ourselves, the French have had their romantic school of poets and novelists, who taught the people to admire the secular life of the middle ages in the pictures which they drew of its heroes. What Walter Scott and his followers did for us, a host of French novelists have been accomplishing for their own nation; they have treated the middle ages as the very romance of human existence in all its social relations. The sympathies once excited, a transition became comparatively easy from the romance of the secular to the romance of the ecclesiastical; and that transition has been effected in France, just as we believe it has been among ourselves, by an increase of religion. We have brought our devout feelings to bear on our romantic; and thus we have passed from the *chivalry* to the *church* of olden time. We before felt the poetry of the old secular life; becoming more devout, we are now sensible of the poetry of middle age religion and its accessories.

Now, all men are artists more or less. We are not content with mere admiration of a loved object; what we admire we straight fall to imitating. When Walter Scott's wizard power held its sway, what myriads of gimcrac baronial castles started up all over the country! Not a retired shopkeeper but must invest himself with the semblance of lordly greatness in the olden time; men, who " never had grand-fathers," hung their walls with ready-made ancestors; men, who never went to the wars, adorned their halls with spear and bill-hook, matchlock and target! Then was the harvest of Jew-brokers and old furniture dealers. But the spirit of the age changes; we have become admirers of the piety, instead of the chivalry and social magnificence, of our ancestors; and being admirers, we have become imitators; each one of us striving to invest himself with some characteristics of the persons, the things, or the circumstances that make up his ideal of the old religion. Now the same solemn farce is being enacted that we witnessed when we were mad on the baronial magnificence of old England. Alas! alas! that we are not aware how much identity there is between the gimcrack castles of the Scott-inspired shopkeepers and our imitation churches and their furniture. The exquisite folly of the former consisted in their attempt to realize romantic ideas that were totally at variance with the habits and feelings of time present, and that, if realized to the fullest extent, must have been a useless annoyance. And is there not much of this folly in the conduct of our ecclesiastico-romantic Clergymen, who issue dogmatical orders for the adoption of certain forms and fashions of church-building, for no other reason than because they were in use at the times which they are pleased by way of eminence to term Catholic; and in such a tone that one would suppose obedience to their behests to be a matter of salvation? Preposterous absurdity! as if there were any such thing as catholicity in architecture!

We do not underrate the services of those Clergymen who are now so busy with the externals of religion; but we entreat them to remember, that they are dealing with matters that lie within the province of artists,—who, if left to themselves, would never fall into the absurd inconsistencies that are likely to be perpetrated by the enthusiasm and half-knowledge of amateurs. Our Clergy must beware, lest, while they imagine themselves to be advancing the cause of catholic piety, they are in reality hindering it, by wasting their strength on that which would be better done by others;— while they believe that they are reforming the Church, they are but giving way to the influence of a change in the artistic sentiment of the age, to the neglect of weightier matters, for the want of which no external decorum can make amends; but which, being obtained, the outward order would speedily follow. There is a severe proverb to the effect, that "when a man is his own lawyer, he hath a fool for his client," which, we fear, has been verified in the recent encroaches of our Clergy on the business of architects. Every one knows that, in the history of the arts, your mere imitator has always been found to be practically an advocate, not only for the beauties in the works of his model, but for the very forms and characteristic subjects on which the beauties have been engrafted. This is always the mark of a little genius. This is always the feeling of your amateur. He cannot conceive any other use of the charms of art displayed in some particular work than that which the artist has made of them. So our clerical architects, unable to distinguish between art and the use made of it, prescribe to us the adoption of the fashions of past times, not because of their present necessity, fitness, or utility, but because, being used formerly, the artists added beauty to utility; as if, forsooth, had these fashions never existed, the art would not have discovered other means and forms of displaying itself. If these good Clergymen would busy themselves about the holiness of men's lives,— if they would preach sermons to architects, and make them good Churchmen—the architects would soon discover the secret of building them beautiful churches. The works of the middle ages were works of creative genius; they were the offspring of imagination, fettered only by its subjection to the spirit of Christianity; and if the productions of this age in the same kind are to possess any merit as works of art, they must originate thus; otherwise, in a very few years, they will appear just as grotesque, in comparison with the ancient, as the modern mock-heroic castles of pseudo-country gentlemen do, when compared with the real fortresses of our warlike ancestors. We cannot, in short, revive an age that has served its purpose and passed away. So long as artistic genius exists, it must be to itself its law. Its very nature is to create; if this liberty be denied, you stifle, you annihilate it. True, it will make use of the inspirations of former ages, but the use must be a new one. You may force it to exert its creative power on christian sentiment; but you must leave it to discover the form in which the sentiment is to be expressed. The character of the age may make that form poor, feeble, earthly, sensual, compared with the works of better times; yet, if we are to have genius exhibited in its freshness, we must take it with all its faults; it must have, it always has had, the character of its age stamped upon its forehead.

The justice of these observations has been fully borne out and exemplified by the recent revival of a taste for ecclesiastical art in Paris. The Clergy have had no share in it; (at least no apparent share; for we shall have occasion to see in a future paper how much their admirable zeal and piety has silently and quietly had to do with the reaction that has been brought about towards the Church;) they have not been students of architecture; they have not established societies, and gone wandering about the country, measuring every little church, and moulding every morsel of ornament they met with; they have not troubled themselves with the identity of this crocket or that finial, with this or that variety of style. No: they have given themselves to the care of men's souls, well knowing that if they could gain for the Church the hearts of those whom Providence has endowed with artist power, these would soon enough bring their powers an offering to the Church. And so it has fallen out. All that our architectural busybodies among the Clergy are hunting after on a wrong scent, has come of itself, as if by magic, in France; ay, and come in a way that, until our system is changed, can never come among us. The works that are now produced in Paris, though inspired by the spirit of past ages, are nevertheless stamped with a character of freshness that identifies them with the present, and that alone. The Clergy do not pretend to know any thing of these artistic matters; but they are willing and glad to be taught by those whom Providence has fitted for the task. They imagined that the churches were beautified by whitewashing;—the artists tell them that it is an abomination. There is no reply; the whitewash is removed. The Clergy had no objection to gigantic *Pompadour* altars;—the artists exclaim against their monstrous deformity, and the Pompadour altars are swept away. Had the Clergy then in bodies set out to measure and take models of all the stone altars throughout France, and laden with portfolios of measurements, sketches, and plans, prescribed not merely the kind of altars they wanted, but the identical ones they wished to be copied, the artists would have felt that their vocation was at an end. "No, Messieurs," they would have said, "we are not copyists or stone-masons; if you desire our services, you must tell us merely how high or how low, within a little, your altar must be, and leave its beauty of form and decoration to us." Here, in short, is the grand difference between the state of matters in England and France. In the latter, the Clergy have contrived to enlist the arts in the service of the Church; with us the Clergy have themselves become artists. In the one case, artists have with hearty enthusiasm brought all their skill in aid of the decorum of church service; in the other, the artists stand aloof, disgusted with the ignorant self-conceit of men half artists half amateurs; men who, if they are good artists, must be bad Clergymen; who, armed with the dangerous acquirement of half-learning, attempt to carry the dogmatical method of councils in the matter of faith into the free domain of sentiment in matters of art.

Perhaps in all this we shall be thought to have used very severe language towards our own countrymen; but we write solemnly and earnestly, because we are persuaded that there is a spirit at work labouring hard to counteract and pervert the influence of a real increase of piety in the Church, by identifying catholicity in religion with what was, after all, its merely external fashion at a particular period in the north-western half of Europe. Our real want of catholicity does not lie in a lack of beautiful churches, but in the manners and habits of the Clergy, and 'in the reverent affection of the people to the Church. Go into any of our ancient cathedrals, and prove the truth of this. Take any parish you will in the metropolis, and inquire whether the priest keeps an exact reckoning of the number of communicants, knows their names and their condition, physically and spiritually; has a record of all who keep aloof from the church, of the causes that deter them, and who is ever found going about pressing men into the kingdom of heaven. All this is done by the Parisian clergy. Each parish priest has his return of communicants to make to the archbishop; each has it in his power to say, on an increase of the number, " These are the souls I have gained back into the fold of Christ during the last year." It is all very well to build gew-gaw churches to gratify a taste in the arts, if we remember that the catholicity of a building consists not in its form, but in the catholic use that is made of it. But if the profanity, indifference, and indecorum, to which one is so much accustomed in the places of worship that have all the supposed advantages of catholic architecture to recommend them, are suffered (as, alas! they are) to continue without remonstrance, we are committing a fatal error in applying all our energies to the ornament of the outside, while the inside is falling to pieces with disease and decay.

In our next, we propose, in continuation, to give some account of the internal condition of the Gallican Church.

CHAPTERS ON ECCLESIASTICAL LAW.
No. II.
RESIDENCE OF THE CLERGY.

OUR ancestors were wont to believe that obedience to the precepts of the law was fostered by the hand of religious education, rather than enforced by the terrors of additional statutes. We moderns are pleased to entertain far different views, and, in that respect, at least, consistent, to pursue a far different method. Legislation is the panacea of the nineteenth century. Enact, say our modern philosophers,—enact; pass statute after statute; regulate with exquisite minuteness the cries of the baby in the cradle, the laughter of the hoop-trundling boy, the murmurings of the toothless old man. Enforce temperance, chastity, and honesty, by station-houses, model prisons, black masks, and police acts; extinguish the evil passions, by dark lanterns, solitary cells, and police staves; regulate the morals of society, by commissioners, annual reports, decimal fractions, and registration acts. "Let not the law err," as Lord Coke says, "through its universality, but rather be minute even to the smallest trifle;" distance the Chinese legislator in levying so much per grain on the quantum of hair appropriated in a court scuffle, and run a neck-and-neck race with his Hindoo rival in distinguishing between the heinousness of throwing the wax of the ears or the pairings of the nails at a neighbour's head. In consequence of the prevalence of this legislative epidemic, how few there are, and of necessity must be, who are not ignorant of the many laws with which our statute book is crowded, and which, by yearly additions, have now grown to the enormous number of ten thousand, the solid contents of some eighty thick octavo volumes, averaging five hundred pages of close type. And yet the law kindly presupposes to every one a knowledge, not of this or that act, but of every one of those acts "to amend an act to repeal an act" for the regulating of chimney-sweepers—the abolition of the constitution—or the discipline of the clergy. With respect to one branch alone of the statutes, that which relates to the Church, any one who looks at the outside of the many stout volumes professing to be compendiums of ecclesiastical law, must forthwith be convinced of the utter impossibility of any one, therein legislated for, being acquainted with one tithe of the contents. But still, to continue ignorant of every one of the contents, because we cannot know them all, is to whip one's own hide to spite another. This, then, has been our inducement for calling the attention of our clerical friends to the provisions of the act passed in August, 1838, relating to the residence of the clergy, and for analyzing the solid contents of this statute, in order that we may present to our readers, in a somewhat less repulsive form than nature has given them, the meaning of the many words and phrases of the lengthy clauses of this lengthy act.

If we are to believe the title of this act,* its objects are the abridgement of the holding of benefices in plurality, and the better provision for compulsory residence of the clergy. If we are to believe its three preambles and one hundred and thirty-three clauses, not only does it provide for these deficiencies, but also for the union and disunion of benefices, the severing and alienation of tithes, glebe, and demesne lands from one benefice to another; the raising—compulsory raising—of residence houses, and the consequent mortgaging of the benefices, the compulsory imposition of curates on vicars and rectors, the non-farming and non-trading of the clergy, and the enforcing of all these hundred and more clauses, by penalties, monitions, sequestrations, and deprivation. The first fourteen clauses treat of pluralities; from thence to the twenty-seventh, benefices are united and disunited, glebes, tithes, and lands cut, carved, severed, and joined; by the three following, clerical farming and trading is legislated upon; from the thirty-second to the fifty-third clause, the question of residence is considered, and the many penalties, for neglect of that duty, enforced by the seven consecutive clauses; by the next dozen, houses are built, money raised, and mortgages created;

---

* 1 & 2 Vict. c. 106.

then come about two dozen and a half about curates, obstinate incumbents, and Welsh parishes; and lastly, the act concludes with seven and twenty clauses, " de omnibus rebus et quibusdam aliis," a kind of legal lazy, where stray enactments and out-of-the-way clauses are thrown, for want of any more convenient residences.

And first, as to pluralities. Strong as is the temptation, we must not here delay in inquiring what was the state of the law respecting pluralities before the passing of this act, or how far *in foro conscientiæ* even now every cleric is bound by the statute of Lateran, recognised by the constitutions of Archbishop Peckham, and embodied into our common law, "forbidding all plurality of benefices to one man, and requiring a single priest to every church."

The provisions henceforth are of this nature:—Should any spiritual person, holding any cathedral preferment or benefice, accept any other cathedral preferment or benefice, not within the dispensatory limits of the act, and be admitted, instituted, or licensed to the same, then his previous preferment becomes *ipso facto* void. And any cleric who now holds more than one cathedral preferment or benefice, or one cathedral preferment and one benefice, will render his former preferments and benefices void by the acceptance of any other benefice or cathedral preferment, unless he shall, previous to his institution, deliver to his Diocesan his written option as to which of the benefices or preferments (being within the limits of the act) he proposes to hold together. And it deserves especial remembrance, that as these voidances are as well *absolute* as against patrons, unless the patron present in time, the presentation will lapse for that turn."*

From these enactments two classes are excepted. Archdeacons—who may hold two livings, together with their archdeaconry, if situated within the limits of the act, so that one living be within the diocese of the archdeaconry; or may hold one benefice and one cathedral preferment, besides their archdeaconry, so that the latter be within the cathedral church and the former within the limits of the diocese to which the archdeaconry belongs: and, secondly, spiritual persons holding cathedral preferment, with or without a benefice, who may hold therewith any office in their cathedral or collegiate church, statutably and accustomably performed by the holders of such preferments.†

The dispensatory limits of the act are these:—Two benefices may be held together, if distant by the nearest road, or usual footpath or ferry, not more than ten miles, from church to church, or to the nearest church, if more than one, or if no church, to such place as the diocesan of the second preferment shall appoint. But this cannot be allowed: if the population of the one benefice being more than three thousand, that of the other should exceed five hundred, or *vice versa*, or if the united income of the two should exceed a

---

* Sections 2, 11. † Sec. 2.

thousand a year, and unless—for we have here an exception to an exception—unless one of the benefices situated within ten miles of each other, should contain more than two thousand persons, and have an income of less than 150*l.* per annum; the bishop having it in his power to compel residence for three-fourths of the year on the larger parish.* To take advantage of these permissions, considerable difficulty and trouble must be undergone. The incumbent who applies for the requisite license—for be it remembered, without a license none of the benefits can be obtained—must make a statement to his diocesan of the yearly income of each benefice, the sources of that income, his annual rates, taxes, and outgoings, the population of the benefices according to the last parliamentary returns, and lastly, the distance between the livings. Then the bishop is to forward all these papers to the archbishop, who may then, if satisfied, issue his license to the petitioner; should he refuse, an appeal lies to the queen in council. All the expenses consequent on, and incidental to, these transactions, are to be paid by the incumbent who applies for the permission.†

The act, having thus persuaded itself that it has done its work as to pluralities, and henceforth taken out of the power of any satirist to describe the journeys of some person who desired to have an interview with a great pluralist, and pursued him from one end of England to the other, in vain, exclaiming—

" 'Twas——here, 'twas——there,
'Twas——nowhere,—everywhere,"

proceeds to repeal two acts passed by Henry VIII. and Charles II. concerning the union of benefices, and to re-arrange the system.‡

To this end, the act proceeds to vest in the archbishop for his own diocese, or when it shall be represented to him by the bishop of any diocese, that the union of two or more benefices would be desirable, the power of recommending such union under certain restrictions. And these are, the benefices being either in the same or a contiguous parish—the aggregate population being not above 1,500—the aggregate income not more than 500*l.*—the consent of the patrons—a public notice of six weeks' duration—and no sufficient cause to the contrary being shown by any person interested therein, previous to the expiration of the six weeks; on these conditions being complied with, the queen in council may, on such recommendation, order the union to be effected, and decide as to the succession of the nomination between the patrons, and all *other necessary matters.*§ Should it, however, be represented to the archbishop that the income of the proposed united benefice will be *larger than sufficient* to provide for the due maintenance and support of the incumbent, and that any

---

* Sec. 3, 4, 5.   † Sec. 6, 7, 8, 9, 10.
‡ 37 Hen. VIII. c. 21; 17 Chas. II. c. 3.   § Sec. 16.

part of the glebe lands, tithes, rent charges, tenements, and hereditaments, belonging to the benefice, can be separated from such union; then he has power to recommend to the queen in council such separation, and the addition of the same to some other poor adjoining benefice, at his discretion, by an exchange in such manner that the proposed augmentation shall be situated within the limits of the poor benefice.* These exchanges must be made by deed, and all parties interested must join. To ensure their validity, they must be enrolled in the Court of Chancery within six months after their execution.† By the same act, benefices already united, or to be united under the provisions of the act, may, within sixty years after the passing of the act, that is, before the year 1898, be disunited in a similar manner, the patronage and the glebe severed, and separate residences provided on each part of the benefice. Should, however, the benefice be full at the time of the disunion, the incumbent is permitted to choose which of the benefices he will retain, and the patron to appoint to the one or more so vacated.‡ We cannot but consider this a good provision, and capable of producing great benefit to the Church, if rightly used. Take, for instance, an example—we allude to a real case—of four small parishes lying contiguous to one another, not in a clump, but in a long line; each parish has its residence-house, its church, and its small school; they are united into one, the vicar receives an income of about 800*l.* a year, and having established himself in one parish, the furthest of the line to the north, and placed his curate in the furthest to the south, considers his duty rightly performed. But what is the case? each parish obtains one service a Sunday, and no more; distance and bad roads preventing any further services: the two parishes at the extremes, where the vicar and the curate reside, are well managed; those in the interior get what attendance they can. Now, were these livings divided into two of 400*l.* a year each, each vicar would keep a curate, and each parish would have the advantage of a resident minister. Few vicars with an income of 800*l.* a year, can be expected to afford three curates; few vicars of half that income would delay in appointing one. The Bishop of Norwich would find many parishes in his diocese where the provisions of the 21st, 22d, 23d, 24th, and 25th clauses of this act might beneficially be carried into effect.

By another clause, isolated places may be annexed to contiguous parishes, or made into separate benefices, at the discretion of the same authority, and then all disputes—not a few, if the world be not changed—arising out of any of these alterations, are to be settled by a supplemental order of her majesty in council. This part of the act concludes with a proviso, that none of these alterations are to affect in any way the secular rates, taxes, charges, duties, or privileges of the parish.§

---

* Sec. 17.   † Sec. 18.   ‡ Sec. 21, 22, 23, 24, 25.   § Sec. 26, 27.

Squeezed in between the union and disunion of benefices and licenses for non-residence, are four clauses, relating entirely to farming and trading, which were mainly occasioned by certain proceedings at law, against a clergyman as a partner in a joint-stock bank. From the passing of this act, no spiritual person holding any cathedral preferment, benefice, curacy, or lectureship, may farm more than eighty acres of land, without the written permission of his diocesan, which permission can be for no more than seven years, and not renewable; a fine of forty shillings per acre, for every acre above eighty, may be yearly exacted from any clergyman who may infringe this rule.* Those who see little of the clergy in the out-of-the-way portions of dioceses, might readily suppose that any such enactment as this would be perfectly superfluous; those who have resided in a purely agricultural diocese can testify to the contrary. In some counties it is the exception for a clergyman not to farm large portions of land; in some cases five hundred, and even twelve hundred acres, the care of which must effectually prevent his due attendance on his flock; the more so, as it is not uncommon for the farm to extend very far beyond, or to lie entirely away from the parish where his presence is required. Surely it is now the duty of every ordinary to make strict inquiry as to the state of the dioceses in this particular. The act further provides that " no such person shall by himself, or by any other for him, or to his use, engage in or carry on any trade or dealing for gain or profit, or deal in any goods, wares, or merchandise, unless in such cases where such trading or dealing shall have been or shall be carried on by or on behalf of any number of partners exceeding six," or where it may have devolved on the clergyman by way of devise, bequest, inheritance, intestasy, settlement, marriage, bankruptcy or insolvency, provided he does not act as manager, or carry on the trade in person.† The exceptions to these clauses include tutors and schoolmasters, as to buying or selling in such employment, or selling any thing *bonâ fide* purchased for the use of the family; managers, directors, partners or shareholders in any benefit or life assurance society; buyers and sellers of corn or cattle necessary or convenient to be kept, sold, bought, or maintained by the buyer or seller; and, lastly, holders of mines situated in their own land, except in all cases as to personal sale, which is strictly prohibited. The penalties are severe: for the first offence, suspension for any time under one year, at the discretion of the judge; for the second offence, if proved to have been committed after previous suspension, the judge shall suspend the offending person for such time as he shall deem fit; whilst for a repetition of the offence again, the offender is to be deprived *ab officio et beneficio*, and the profits of his living sequestered, until the patron choose to present again; unless, by refraining for twelve months, he permit the benefice to lapse.‡

---

* Sec. 28. † Sec. 29. ‡ Sec. 29.

As we are now about to proceed to the chief provisions of the act, relating to residence, we have placed, in a note, the legal meaning of certain terms which we have already used occasionally, and which we shall now meet with at every page. *

Residence in the parsonage-house of any benefice rightly belonging to the spiritual person, is a legal residence under this act; or in a house purchased by the governors of Queen Anne's Bounty, if previously approved of by the diocesan, by writing under his hand and seal, and duly registered; or, by license, in any other house, either within or without the parish, if the parsonage is unfit for residence.† An absence of three months in one or more periods within one year, except whilst residing on any other benefice, will subject the absentee to the penalties and forfeitures imposed by this act,‡ unless he can reckon himself among any of those four classes, who, by the 37, 38, 39, and 40 clauses of the act, are either entirely, or in a qualified degree, exempted from the penalties of non-residence.

1. Those whose office renders them absolutely exempt from all the penalties for non-residence.

2. Those who are exempt during the actual discharge of the duties of those offices in behalf of which they claim exemption.

3. Those who, having been in possession of their benefice before the act was passed, were exempt under the previous statute of the 57th Geo. III. c. 99.

4. Officers of cathedrals and fellows of Eton and Winchester, who are allowed to count their residence for cathedral and collegiate duties, under certain restrictions, as residence on their livings.

For facility of reference, the four classes are shown under the four following tables, with the nature of their respective exemptions.

Class I.

Having but one benefice, with cure of souls:
1. The head of any college or hall at Oxford or Cambridge.
2. The warden of the university of Durham.
3. Head master of Eton, Winchester, or Westminster.
4. Principal or professor of the East India College, if appointed before the passing of the act.

Absolutely exempt from all penalties for non-residence.

---

* *Benefice—Benefice with cure of souls*—includes all parishes, perpetual curacies, donatives, endowed public chapels, parochial chapelries, and chapelries and districts belonging or annexed, or reputed to belong or to be annexed to any church or chapel. *Cathedral Preferment*—includes every dignity or office in any cathedral or collegiate church. *Annual Value*—is to be computed by deducting from the gross yearly income, rates, taxes, tenths, dues, and other permanent charges and outgoings; but not stipends to curates, tenants' or occupants' rates or taxes, for house or glebe, nor expenses of repairing or improving the buildings, house, or fences. *Time.*—The year is to commence on the 1st of January, and end on the 31st of December; months are to be reckoned according to the calendar, unless made up of different periods less than a calendar month, when 30 days is to complete a month.

† Sec. 33, 34, 35.   ‡ Sec. 32.

Class II.

Having but one benefice with cure of souls.

1. Dean of any cathedral or collegiate church.
2. Professor or public reader in either university.
3. Chaplain to the sovereign, queen dowager, king or queen's children, brethren, or sisters.
4. Chaplain to any archbishop or bishop.
5. Chaplain to the House of Commons.
6. Clerk, or deputy clerk, to the sovereign's closet.
7. Chancellor, vicar-general, commissary of any diocese, or archdeacon.
8. Dean, sub-dean, priest, or reader, in any of the sovereign's public or private chapels.
9. Preacher in any of the inns of court or rolls.
10. Provost of Eton, warden of Winchester, master of the Charterhouse, principal of St. David's, and King's College, London.

Exempt whilst actually discharging the duties of such offices respectively.

Class III.

If in possession of the benefice previous to the passing of this act, and entitled to exemptions or licenses by any previous acts,

1. Chancellor or vice-chancellor, or commissary, of either university.
2. Scholars under thirty years of age, abiding at either university for the purpose of study, without fraud.
3. Chaplains to authorized persons, during abidance and daily attendance on their duties.
4. Chaplain, clerk, or deputy-clerk of the closet, to the heir apparent.
5. Chaplain-general of the forces, by sea or land, or dockyards, during attendance on duty.
6. Chaplain to any ambassador.
7. Bursar, treasurer, dean, vice-president, sub-dean, public tutor, chaplain, or other such public officer in any college in either university.
8. Public librarian, registrar, proctor, and public orator, of either university, Sion College, or British Museum, during actual official residence.
9. Any fellow of a college, during residence required by statutes, and masters of Eton, Winchester, and Westminster.
10. Deans, prebendaries, and canons, and others holding any dignity in any cathedral or collegiate church, during their legal residence therein.

Are still entitled to the same exemption or license, after the passing of this act.

Class IV.

Residing and performing the duties of their office during the period required by the statutes or charter,

Any prebendary, canon, priest, vicar, vicar choral, or minor canon, in any cathedral or collegiate church, or fellow of one of the colleges of Eton or Winchester.

Proviso 1. Not to be absent from his benefice for such performance of his duty, for more than five months in any one year.

Proviso 2. That it shall be lawful for any of the aforesaid spiritual persons, in any cathedral or collegiate church, or college, where the year for the purposes of residence is accounted to commence at some other period than the 1st of January, who may keep the periods of residence required for two successive years, in whole or in part in one year, to account such residence, though exceeding five months, as if he had resided on his benefice.*

Shall be allowed to count such residence as if he had resided on some benefice.

---

* Sec. 40.

The privileges and exemptions of these four classes do not require any license from the diocesan previous to the enjoyment of them.

We now come to those incumbents to any one of whom licenses of non-residence may be granted by their diocesan, on his presenting his petition to the bishop, containing his reason for the application, the proof he can offer of the truth of his statement, and the time during which he desires to be permitted to be absent from his benefice. To the petition, his own signature, or that of some person duly authorized by the bishop, must be appended. On the facts of one of the five reasons following being proved to the satisfaction of the bishop, he may grant the petitioner license of non-residence for such time (so that it do not extend beyond the last day of December in the quarter next after the year in which the license is granted,) and out of such limits as he may consider expedient.* It is also necessary that every petition should specify the four particulars which will be found in the third column of the next table ;† for the omission of any one of these will subject the petition to certain rejection. Should the bishop refuse to grant the license, an appeal lies to the archbishop of the province, and there is also a discretionary power vested in the diocesan of granting licenses of non-residence for any other reasons, after proper notice to the archbishop, and the addition of his signature to the license.‡

REASONS TO BE STATED.	PROOFS REQUIRED.	PARTICULARS TO BE SPECIFIED.
	In every Petition for Non-residence.§	
1. Incapacity of mind or body.	Medical certificate.	1. Whether the petitioner intends to perform the duty himself, and if yea, at what distance from the church or chapel he desires to reside.
2. Dangerous illness of wife or child, making part of his family, and resident with him as such.‖	Ditto.	2. If he intends to have a curate, and at what salary, and whether resident, and whether in the residence-house, or in what other.
3. No house of residence, or house unfit for residence, unless such unfitness has been caused by wilful neglect of the petitioner.	Proof of unfitness, and certificate of two neighbouring clergymen, countersigned by the rural dean, that no convenient house in the parish or prescribed limits.	3. If the latter, at what distance, and where, and whether such curate serves any other and what cure, and in what capacity, or has any other preferment.
4. Occupying in the same parish a mansion, whereof the petitioner is owner.	Proof of the good and sufficient repair of the parsonage house.	4. The annual value and population of the benefice, number of chapels or churches, and date of the admission of the petitioner.

After the petitioner has by the above means obtained his license, " if there appear good cause for revoking the same," the bishop who granted it may do so by a writing under his hand, having previously given a sufficient opportunity to the licensee to show cause in favour of the license, subject to an appeal to the archbishop against the revocation. Every petition must be registered, and every license or revocation of license filed by copy in the registry of the diocese, within one month of the grant or revocation, and a copy of the license forwarded by the petitioner to the churchwardens of his parish, and

---

* Sec. 43.   † Sec. 42.   ‡ Sec. 44.   § Sec. 42, 43.
‖ License for six months renewable by archbishop alone.

of the revocation, by the person by whom it has been revoked, within the same time.* It seems doubtful, under the registration clauses, whether a license of revocation for a benefice in an archbishop's peculiar, need be registered in the registry of the diocese in which it lies. Under former acts, registration in the registry of the archbishop was sufficient. From the uncertainty of the act, it will be safer and worth the expense to register in both offices. It is also provided, that in case of a vacancy, the guardian of the spiritualities of the diocese, or any one lawfully authorized to exercise general authority, has the same power of licensing and revocation, with the consent of the archbishop, as the bishop of the diocese. And now passing over some minor and unimportant clauses, we proceed to the pains and penalties of this discipline bill.

The penalties, for non-residence, imposed by this act, rise gradually the forfeiture of a regulated portion of the proceeds of the benefice, to monition, and from thence to sequestration, and eventually deprivation. Any clergyman absent from his benefice without license or exemption, under this or the former acts, or not resident on any other benefice belonging to him, for any period of time together, or to be accounted at several times, in one year, exceeding

Three months, and under six, is to forfeit one-third of the annual value of the benefice.
Six months, and under eight   „   one-half.
Eight months, and under twelve   „   two-thirds.
For one entire year   „   three-fourths.†

We have already seen how all forfeitures under this act are to be estimated, or rather how the annual income of a benefice is to be accounted; let us now see how this scale of duties is to be levied; for that purpose we must skip from the thirty-second clause to that legal olio with which the act concludes, where, among a variety of clauses, we shall discover three or four very much to our purpose.

All penalties and forfeitures incurred under this act, say these clauses, by spiritual persons holding a benefice, are to be recovered in the court of the diocesan. From all spiritual persons not holding a benefice, by the common action for debt, in any of the courts at Westminster. Monition and sequestration may also be used in enforcing the forfeitures, and the money recovered applied to the augmentation of the living, at the discretion of the bishop, or paid over to the treasurer of Queen Anne's bounty.‡ No penalty or forfeiture, however, can be recovered against any spiritual person under this act which he may have incurred previous to the first of January in the year immediately preceding that in which the proceedings against him, for the infringement of the act, not for the payment of the penalty, were commenced.§

Instead, however, of proceeding under the 32d section, or indeed

---

* Sec. 43, 50.   † Sec. 32.   ‡ Sec. 114, 115, 117, 119.   § Sec. 118.

after such proceeding, the bishop, should it appear to him that any clergyman in his diocese does not reside sufficiently according to the meaning of the act, may issue a monition to the offending person, ordering him to make his return to the monition within thirty days of its date, or to return and reside on his benefice, and pay the costs of the proceedings. The bishop may also require proof of any facts stated in the return to the monition, and on such proof appearing to be unsatisfactory, he may then *peremptorily* order the clergyman to return to residence within thirty days after the service of the order; and in case of non-compliance, sequestration may follow until the order is complied with, or sufficient reasons for non-compliance stated and proved to the satisfaction of the diocesan. The proceeds of such a sequestration are to be applied, first, for the costs and expenses of serving the cure, then to the payment of the penalties, the costs of the proceedings, repair of chancel, house of residence, glebe and demesne lands. Should the benefice be under a previous sequestration for debt, then the creditor under that proceeding is to come in for payment, and after all these charges have been paid and satisfied, the bishop may apply the *surplus* to the augmentation of the benefice, or pay the same to the treasurer of Queen Anne's bounty.* He possesses also a discretionary power of paying any portion of the profits of the sequestration to the incumbent, within six months after the date of the order. Where the bishop's discretion in this case is to come in the act does not inform us: it first gives him power to sequester, if he pleases; then of ordering the profits to be distributed in a certain way, by which they must all be consumed, as the last provision is for the disposal of the surplus, and then comes this discretionary power of paying any portion thereof, " whether it remain in the hands of the sequestrator, or have been paid to the treasurer of the bounty," to the clergyman. From the terms of the clause just quoted, it seems that the discretion cannot take effect until after the debt, if any, on the living has been cleared off, and that the bishop has only the choice of augmenting the living or the bounty fund, or paying the surplus, or such part as he thinks fit, to the incumbent. However, the point is open to argument. The appeal to the archbishop, which of course lies in this case, is confined within one month of the service of the order. There is also a power in the bishop of remitting the penalties, provided that in every case where the offence is more than six months' non-residence, the nature and special circumstances of such case shall be presented to the queen in council, in whom the allowance, alteration, or disallowance of such remission is vested.†
The act then goes on to provide, that in case any unlicensed or unexempted cleric, after he has obeyed the monition or suffered from sequestration, shall wilfully and within twelve months after the commencement of such residence, absent himself for *one month*, either together or to be accounted at separate times within the year, his

---

* Sec. 54, 55. † Sec. 54, 57.

bishop may proceed to sequestrate without any monition, in the same way as by the former section, unless the incumbent can protect himself by an appeal to the archbishop. And see the results. If any benefice should remain under sequestration for non-residence *for one whole year,* or *(be it for any time)* a benefice be sequestrated *twice,* during two years, (for the offence of the same incumbent,) without relief or appeal, then such benefice shall be *void, as if such spiritual person were dead.**

The great reason, in modern times, of non-residence being the inadequate provision of residence houses, this act takes this point into consideration; of these details a short summary must suffice. Immediately on the avoidance of any benefice, the bishop may issue a communication to the rural dean of the district, and any other three clergymen of the diocese, to inquire and report to him the value of the living, the state of the parsonage or its non-existence, and the probable expense of erecting a new one, or repairing the old. Then a professional estimate is to be made, and with the report to be forwarded to the patron, and unless within two months he objects and obtains some alteration, or the entire setting aside of the report, the sum required is to be raised by mortgaging the glebe, tithes, &c., for thirty-five years, to any one who will lend money on them, at any legal interest. If the living is under a hundred a year, it may remain without a residence, otherwise four years of the net income may be raised, one-thirtieth part to be repaid annually with the interest. Instead, however, of raising an entirely new house, any house in the limits of the benefice, deemed suitable, may be purchased and conveyed to the patron as a trustee for the incumbent. All the practical part of the business is to be vested in the person appointed by the bishop, who may receive five per cent. on the expenditure for his trouble. And Queen Anne's bounty, and any colleges at either university, may lend their money, the former at four per cent., and the latter without any interest, for the purposes of the act.†

No doubt the provisions of previous acts, and of this one too, are very useful in providing residence houses in benefices; but still their provisions should be used with great caution and much discrimination. How many livings do we find overbuilt, overburdened with a parsonage, well adapted to the private fortune, perhaps, of the person who raised it, and who mortgaged the tithes to their utmost to complete his house, but little suited for a succeeding incumbent, whose only dependence is the income of his benefice, already lessened by the mortgage of his predecessor. Again, taking for instance a living of two hundred a year. By this act 800*l.* can be raised on such a benefice, and that without the consent of the incoming cleric, on whom will be entailed a payment in its first year of 32*l.*, or perhaps 36*l.* for interest, besides 26*l.* 13*s.* as the portion of the principal to be paid off yearly. His interest will decrease yearly by some five and twenty shillings, by which process it will require more

---

* Sec. 58.   † Secs. 62—74.

than seven years, should he succeed in raising the money at 4*l*. per cent, and more than ten years otherwise, before his annual payments will be reduced to one-fourth of his income. Surely this would be a high rent for an eight hundred pound house in the country.

We must now conclude our analysis of the last enactments respecting plurality—clerical farming—residence and residence houses, reserving until another opportunity those clauses which relate to curates; and that with less regret, as we hope to be able to make a general *resumé* of the law respecting curacies, in our next article on Ecclesiastical Law.

APPENDIX TO THE ARTICLE ON BENNETT'S THEOLOGY OF THE EARLY CHRISTIAN CHURCH.

THE evidence for episcopacy in St. Clement of Rome is so interesting as well as important a subject, that there is no need, it is trusted, to apologize for referring to it, in connexion with the review of Dr. Bennett's book, in the last Number of the CHRISTIAN REMEMBRANCER.

The question was there argued on grounds narrowed by two remarkable concessions:—1. that the Corinthians were without a bishop: 2. that St. Clement does not bear testimony to episcopacy.

These were of course only made for argument's sake. But when we find even a writer like the Provost of Oriel, (in his Bampton Lectures,) so far carried astray by a spirit of extreme candour, as to make these concessions *simpliciter*, it is time to re-consider the matter.

Perhaps, therefore, it will not be useless to state briefly some conclusions from the Epistle of St. Clement :—

I. The first "proof" of non-episcopal government at Corinth is sought from the salutation. "Had there been a bishop, would he not have been named as the head of the Church?"

Now, inasmuch as St. Clement makes no more mention of a bishop of Rome, than of a bishop of Corinth, this proves a little too much. His words are,

Ἡ ἐκκλησία τοῦ Θεοῦ ἡ παροικοῦσα Ῥώμην, τῇ ἐκκλησίᾳ τοῦ Θεοῦ τῇ παροικούσῃ Κόρινθον, κ. τ. ἑ.

It is not necessary to demonstrate the existence of a bishop of Rome, and therefore the argument is reversed. The two churches are spoken of in the same terms: therefore, on probable grounds, we say that their constitution was the same.

II. Proceeding to the first section, we find these words: ἀπροσωπολήπτως πάντα ἐποιεῖτε, καὶ τοῖς νόμοις τοῦ Θεοῦ ἐπορεύεσθε, ὑποτασσόμενοι τοῖς ἡγουμένοις ὑμῶν, καὶ τιμὴν τὴν καθήκουσαν ἀπονέμοντες τοῖς παρ' ὑμῖν πρεσβυτέροις· νέοις τε μέτρια καὶ σεμνὰ νοεῖν ἐπετρέπετε.

Here are mentioned, 1. ἡγούμενοι, 2. πρεσβύτεροι, 3. νέοι: clearly three separate classes, with the proper line of conduct to be adopted towards each; ὑποταγὴ to the first, τιμὴ to the second, ἐπιτροπὴ τοῦ νοεῖν σεμνά, κ. τ. ἑ. to the third.

It is admitted that the words may mean, 1. "any rulers," 2. "any seniors," 3. "any juniors." But let us consider, whether there is no probability of their meaning something more definite. In section thirty-seven, ἡγούμενος is used for "*a general.*" In ecclesiastical language we find it the technical name of the head of a monastery: Chrysostom is quoted by Sucier, who also gives passages where *Hegumenus* occurs in Latin, in the same sense. In the Greek church it is so to this day. Does the language of the New Testament help us?

Matt. ii. 6, in the prophecy of the Messiah, we have ἐκ σοῦ γὰρ ἐξελεύσεται ἡγούμενος, ὅστις ποιμανεῖ τὸν λαόν μου τὸν Ἰσράηλ. Let us mark the words, ἡγούμενος and ποιμανεῖ, remembering how immediately "*the pastorate*" was assigned (by the use of the latter word) to bishops, and them alone, under the Chief Shepherd.

Acts xiv. 12, St. Paul is called ἡγούμενος τοῦ λόγου.

——— xv. 22, Judas Barsabas, and Silas are ἄνδρες ἡγούμενοι ἐν τοῖς ἀδελφοῖς.

Of this Judas we know nothing which can throw doubt on my interpretation of ἡγούμενος: and of Silas, all that we know would confirm us in taking it as denoting high ecclesiastical office. We have ancient authority (it is not meant, however, to discuss Hippolytus's Catalogue of the Seventy) for calling him *Bishop of* CORINTH.

In Luke xxii. 26, we read the words of our blessed Lord, ὁ μείζων ἐν ὑμῖν γενέσθω ὡς ὁ νεώτερος, καὶ ὁ ἡγούμενος ὡς ὁ διακονῶν. To this we shall return.

In Heb. xiii. 7, μνημονεύετε τῶν ἡγουμένων ὑμῶν, οἵτινες ἐλάλησαν ὑμῖν τὸν λόγον τοῦ Θεοῦ, κ.τ.ἑ.; and ibid. 17, πείθεσθε τοῖς ἡγουμένοις ὑμῶν καὶ ὑπείκετε· αὐτοὶ γὰρ ἀγρυπνοῦσιν ὡς λόγον ἀποδώσοντες ὑπὲρ τῶν ψυχῶν ὑμῶν.

The word Ἡγούμενος clearly is used of the holders of an office, (1.) supreme, (2.) in spiritual things, (3.) distinct from that implied in πρεσβύτερος. Moreover, its use as opposed to ὁ διακονῶν, by our Lord himself, makes it more than probable that as διάκονος became the name of a specific "ministry," so ἡγούμενος of a specific "primacy," in the Church. And this is confirmed by the word ὑποτασσόμενοι, which (except in Ephes. v. 21,) seems always to be used of duty to a *supreme* power: compare Luke ii. 51; x. 17, 20; Rom. xiii. 1; 1 Cor. xiv. 34, &c.: and ὑποταγὴ, in Gal. ii. 5, 1 Tim. ii. 11, iii. 4. The technical use of πρεσβύτερος is of course admitted. That it is so used here is probable from the fact, that while ὑποταγὴ is mentioned as the duty to ἡγούμενοι, that to πρεσβύτεροι is ἡ καθήκουσα τιμή: compare 1 Tim. v. 17, οἱ καλῶς προεστῶτες πρεσβύτεροι διπλῆς τιμῆς ἀξιούσθωσαν, μάλιστα οἱ κοπιῶντες ἐν λόγῳ καὶ διδασκαλίᾳ. The case of the νέοι is more difficult; yet, if we adhere to our rule of weighing the scriptural use of St. Clement's words, there will seem to be reason to identify them with the διάκονοι, and to suspect that their insubordination had something to do with the miserable state of the Corinthian Church.

Luke xxii. 26, ὁ μείζων ἐν ὑμῖν γενέσθω ὡς ὁ νεώτερος, καὶ ὁ ἡγούμενος ὡς ὁ διακονῶν.

Here μείζων is to νεώτερος as ἡγούμενος to διακονῶν.

Acts v., of Ananias and Sapphira:—ver. 6. ἀναστάντες οἱ νεώτεροι συνέστειλαν αὐτὸν, καὶ ἐξενέγκαντες ἔθαψαν; ver. 10. εἰσελθόντες οἱ νεανίσκοι εὗρον αὐτὴν νεκρὰν καὶ ἐξενέγκαντες ἔθαψαν. This was before the ordination of *the Seven*: and the men who carried Stephen to his burial, have not the same epithet.

1 Tim. iii. 6, (δεῖ ἐπίσκοπον εἶναι) μὴ νεόφυτον.

It must be noticed that σεμνὰ νοεῖν ἐπετρέπετε is exactly in accordance with St. Paul's pastoral injunctions, wherein σεμνότης is the characteristic most inculcated,—διακόνους ὡσαύτως σεμνούς· γυναῖκας ὡσαύτως σεμνάς, etc. Lastly, we have to consider the use of ἐπιτρέπειν, in 1 Cor. xiv. 33, αἱ γυναῖκες ἐν ταῖς ἐκκλησίαις σιγάτωσαν, οὐ γὰρ ἐπιτρέπεται αὐταῖς λαλεῖν. 1 Tim. ii. 12, διδάσκειν γυναικὶ οὐκ ἐπιτρέπω, οὐδὲ αὐθεντεῖν ἀνδρός.

Bearing in mind the delicacy with which St. Clement plainly felt that he must suggest his admonitions, suppressing even his own name and authority at Rome, is there not something very striking in the peculiar, specific meaning of which all his words in this passage are at least capable? To understand this fully, we must try to throw ourselves back to a time when such words were becoming only half technical, (that is, when the technical sense had not excluded the general one,) and consider the way in which *Elder* and *Minister* might then have been used: and it will be difficult to escape the conclusion that St. Clement, with his heart full of the "new things and old" of both Testaments, was applying scriptural words in their fullest scriptural sense; albeit, to those who were blinded among the Corinthians, as in later times, he may have spoken in parables.

III. Section Forty, we have, πάντα τάξει ποιεῖν ὀφείλομεν, ὅσα ὁ Δεσπότης ἐκέλευσεν ἐπιτελεῖν ..... τῷ γὰρ ἀρχιερεῖ ἰδίαι λειτουργίαι δεδομέναι εἰσὶν, καὶ τοῖς ἱερεῦσιν ἴδιος ὁ τόπος προστέτακται, καὶ λευΐταις ἴδιαι διακονίαι ἐπίκεινται· ὁ λαϊκὸς ἄνθρωπος τοῖς λαϊκοῖς προστάγμασι δέδεται.

This passage is so important that Neander coolly says, it *must be* interpolated, because it transfers Jewish notions to the Christian Church. He therefore confesses the meaning; and we are not afraid of what any reasonable man may say of the "vicious circle," by which he gets rid of it.

Others, less ingenuously, say that it is only a comparison *drawn from* the Jewish Church. True; but a comparison which requires a similarity. There is nothing implying, "The Jews were so and so."

It is, "*We* have each his office;" and three distinct *clerical* offices are named, along with the duties of the *laity*. The verbs all imply a present sense :—ὀφείλομεν, ποιοῦντες, οὐ διαμαρτάνουσι, δεδομέναι εἰσὶ, προστέτακται, ἐπίκεινται, δέδεται. Every scholar knows the force of these tenses. Only *the names* of God's priesthood under the older dispensation are applied. It is therefore a plain metaphor, and there are three orders of the Christian ministry, which so correspond to these Jewish ones, that they may be called by their names. The words too must be noticed: λειτουργία is given to the ἀρχιερεὺς, διακονίαι to the λευῖται. That the deacons were in ecclesiastical language called Levites, is well known: see Suicer *in voce*.

IV. Section Forty-two. But, say the enemies, here is a distinct statement of what the apostles did,—κατὰ χώρας καὶ πόλεις κηρύσσοντες, καθέστανον τὰς ἀπαρχὰς αὐτῶν, δοκιμάσαντες τῷ Πνεύματι, εἰς ἐπισκόπους καὶ διακόνους τῶν μελλόντων πιστεύειν.

Our answer is—

1st, These ἐπίσκοποι being confessedly identical with *presbyters*, as always in the New Testament, (for we fight for *things*, not *names*,) this is a distinct statement that the apostles constituted their first converts *priests* and *deacons*, in the Churches of which they retained the apostolical charge. Had they ordained *three* orders at that time, there would have been now *four* in the Church.

2d, He goes on to say, Καὶ οἱ ἀπόστολοι ἡμῶν, (the apostles, which stood in this relation to the churches which they founded,) ἔγνωσαν . . . . . ὅτι ἔρις ἔσται ἐπὶ τοῦ ὀνόματος τῆς ἐπισκοπῆς· διὰ ταύτην οὖν τὴν αἰτίαν . . . . . κατέστησαν τοὺς προειρημένους, καὶ μεταξὺ (*after them*) ἐπινομὴν δεδώκασιν, ὅπως ἐὰν κοιμηθῶσιν, διαδέξωνται ἕτεροι δεδοκιμασμένοι ἄνδρες τὴν λειτουργίαν αὐτῶν. Is it not the natural interpretation of this passage, that the apostles, towards the end of their lives, made a second appointment, from among the subordinate ministers, of those who were to succeed them in the apostolate?

The word ἐπινομὴ is indeed a doubtful one: see the note in Mr. Jacobson's invaluable edition. But a sense, certainly as agreeable to analogy and appropriate to the passage as any there mentioned, would be *the place of first shepherd to the flock*, equal to ἐπισκοπή.

3d, St. Clement is here arguing from Isai. lx, 17; where he read the words, ἐπισκόπους and διακόνους, and these only.

NOTICES OF BOOKS.

Sacred Hymns from the German. Translated by FRANCES ELIZABETH COX. London: Pickering. 1841.

THIS beautiful little volume consists of translations of Hymns from the German, varying in the date of their composition from the era of the Reformation to the present day. It is a valuable addition to our collections of sacred poetry; and we have no hesitation in pronouncing it to be one of the most successful attempts at translation which it has been our good fortune to meet with, whether we regard the faithfulness of the translator to the sentiment and metre of the original hymns, or the spirit and life which she has contrived to transfuse from them into her own translation. Take the following hymns as samples of the whole:—

EPIPHANIASLIED.

" Ich bin die Wurzel des Geschlechts Davids:
Ein heller Morgenstern."

IM Abend blinkt der Morgenstern,
Die Weisen nahen sich von fern;
Im Niedergang entsteht ein Licht,
Das kennet keinen Aufgang nicht.

Es strahlet aus der Ewigkeit,
Und senket sich hier in die Zeit;
Sein heller Glanz vertreibt die Nacht,
Aus Finsterniss wird Tag gemacht.

O Jesu, heller Morgenstern,
Leucht in die Näh und in die Fern,
Dass du auch seist zu unsrer Zeit
Von uns erkannt und benedeit.
ERNST LANGE (1650—1727.)

HYMN FOR THE EPIPHANY.

" I am the root and the offspring of David, and the bright and Morning Star."—Rev. xxii. 16.

THE wondering sages trace from far,
Bright in the west, the Morning-star;
A light illumes the western skies,
Seen never in the east to rise.

Eternity produced its blaze;
Time's fulness hails its nearer rays;
Its brightness chases night away,
And kindles darkness into day.

O Jesu! brightest Morning-star!
Shed forth thy beams both near and far,
That all, in these our later days,
May know Thee, and proclaim thy praise.

TAUFLIED.

" Lasset die Kindlein zu mir kommen, und wehret ihnen nicht; denn solcher ist das Reich Gottes."

LIEBSTER Jesu, hier sind wir,
Deinem Worte nachzuleben:
Dieses Kindlein kommt zu dir,
Weil du den Befehl gegeben,
Dass man sie zu Christo führe,
Denn das Himmelreich ist ihre.

Ja, es schallet allermeist
Dieses Wort in unsern Ohren:
Wer durch Wasser und durch Geist
Nicht zuvor ist neu geboren,
Wird von dir nicht aufgenommen,
Wird in Gottes Reich nicht kommen.

Darum eilen wir zu dir,
Nimm das Pfand von unsern Armen;
Tritt mit deinem Glanz herfür
Und erzeige dein Erbarmen,
Dass es dein Kind hier auf Erden
Und im Himmel möge werden.

Mache Licht aus Finsterniss,
Setz es aus dem Zorn zur Gnade;
Heil den tiefen Schlangenbiss,
Durch die Kraft im Wunderbade;
Vor des heilgen Geistes Wehen
Lass den Sündenwust vergehen.

FOR THE SACRAMENT OF BAPTISM.

" Suffer the little children to come unto me, and forbid them not: for of such is the kingdom of God."—St. Mark, x. 14.

JESUS, Lord, thy servants see
Offering here obedience willing;
Lo! this infant comes to Thee,
Thus thy mandate blest fulfilling:
'Tis for such thyself declarest
That the kingdom Thou preparest.

Loudly sounds thy warning plain,
Us with holy fear imbuing,
" He must here be born again,
Heart and mind and life renewing,
Born of water and the Spirit,
Who my kingdom will inherit."

Take the pledge we offer now,
To the font baptismal hastening;
Make him, Lord, thy child below,
Let him feel thy tender chastening;
That he here may love and fear Thee,
And in heaven dwell ever near Thee.

Let thy light from darkness shine,
Grace instead of wrath revealing,
Through the water's power divine,
Satan's venomed death-sting healing;
Make his soul thy Spirit's dwelling,
By its breath all sin expelling.

Hirte, nimm dein Schäflein an,
Haupt, mach es zu deinem Gliede;
Himmelsweg, zeig ihm die Bahn,
Friedefürst, schenk ihm den Friede,
Weinstock, hilf, dass diese Rebe
Auch im Glauben dich umgebe.

Nun wir legen an dein Herz
Was von Herzen ist gegangen;
Führ die Seufzer himmelwärts,
Und erfülle das Verlangen:
Ja, den Namen, den wir geben,
Schreib ins Lebensbuch zum Leben.
BENJAMIN SCHMOLCK (1672—1737.)

Prince of Peace, thy peace bestow;
Shepherd, to thy sheep-folk take him
Way of life, his pathway shew;
Head, thy living member make him;
Vine, abundant fruit providing,
Keep this branch in Thee abiding.

Lord of grace! to Thee we cry,
Filled our hearts to overflowing;
Heavenward take the burdened sigh,
Blessings on the babe bestowing:
Write the name we now have given,
Write it in the book of heaven.

TRAUUNGSLIED.

"Der Herr segne dich und behüte dich:
Er erleuchte sein Angesicht über dich und
gebe dir Frieden."

ERHEBT euch, frohe Jubellieder,
Zu Gottes lichtem Thron empor;
Es hört, es neigdt zu uns hernieder
Der Weltenherr sein Vaterohr:
Gott, der da ist, sein wird und war,
Gott, segne dieses neue Paar.

Ja möge, Gott euch beide segnen;
Mög er, ohn den kein Haupthaar fällt,
Mit Licht und Kraft euch stets begegnen,
Beim Gang durch diese dunkle Welt:
Gott, segne dieses neue Paar,
Sei mit ihm heut, seis immerdar.

Lasst euch vom Worte Gottes leiten,
Nach Christus bildet euren Sinn,
Stets eingedenk der Ewigkeiten;
Dort führt das Pilgerleben hin:
Gott, segne dieses neue Paar,
Sei mit ihm heut, seis immerdar.

Schämt euch nicht, Gott um Gnad zu flehen,
Ohn den euch keine Freude blüht;
Seid nicht zu träg vor Gott zu stehen,
Bis ihr in Liebe zu ihm glüht:
Gott, segne dieses neue Paar,
Sei mit ihm heut und immerdar.

Wohlan, ergreift mit Gottes Freude
Und voll Vertraun den Pilgerstab,
Dass euch nichts von einander scheide,
Von Gott nichts bis ins stille Grab:
Gott, segne dieses neue Paar,
Sei mit ihm heut und immerdar.

Wohlan, es sei mit euch der Friede,
Die treuste Liebe Lebenslang;
Beim Morgen—und beim Abendliede
Stärkt täglich euch im Christengang:
Gott, segne dieses neue Paar,
Sei mit ihm heut und immerdar.

Wohlan, sprecht nun: Her, wir geloben
Dir ewge Treue, Hand in Hand!
Bis wir dich schauen einst dort oben
In jenem selgen Heimathland:
Gott der da ist, sein wird und war,
Sei mit euch heut, seis immerdar.

HYMN FOR A MARRIAGE.

"The Lord bless thee, and keep thee; the
Lord make his face shine upon thee, and give
thee peace."—Numb. vi. 24—26.

RAISE high the note of exultation
To God's bright throne with voices clear;
The mighty Lord of all Creation
Lends to our song a Father's ear;
Eternal Lord of heaven above,
Look down and bless their plighted love.

O'er each event of life presiding,
May God rich gifts on both bestow,
With heavenly light your footsteps guiding,
As through the world's dark wild ye go;
Eternal Lord of heaven above,
Look down and bless their plighted love.

By God's own word each action measure,
Let Christ your great exemplar be;
Still fix your hearts on heavenly treasure,
We hasten towards eternity;
Eternal Lord of heaven above,
Look down and bless their plighted love.

Together bend, God's grace imploring,
Or no true joy your love will know;
Your voices blend, his name adoring,
Till love to God each heart o'erflow;
Eternal Lord of heaven above,
Look down and bless their plighted love.

With cheerful faith in God confide ye,
The pilgrim's staff with courage take,
And, till the silent grave divide ye,
God and each other ne'er forsake;
Eternal Lord of heaven above,
Look down and bless their plighted love.

May peace and love, your lives adorning,
Attend you all your course along;
Your Christian walk, each night and morning,
Oh! strengthen still with prayer and song;
Eternal Lord of heaven above,
Look down and bless their plighted love.

Together now your voices raising,
Vow truth to God, hand join'd in hand,
Till, on his glories ever gazing,
Ye meet in heaven's own happy land;
Eternal Lord of heaven above,
Look down and bless their plighted love.

After conceding this due meed of praise to the fidelity, skill, and taste displayed in these translations, we feel compelled to state, however reluctantly, that the accomplished authoress has not been quite so happy in her selection of hymns for translation as in the execution of the translations themselves. We greatly prefer to hymns so comparatively modern, as the majority contained in the present volume, those of a date coeval with the dawn of the Reformation, many of which, we believe, are themselves nothing more than translations from the Latin of hymns previously used in the churches on the continent. If inferior as poetical compositions, their disparity is, in this respect, more than supplied by the advantage which they possess, of embodying more of the objective than of the subjective system of religious truth—a distinction that will be found to pervade, more or less, all the compositions of the earlier, as contrasted with the later period. We have not Chevalier Bunsen's collection at hand (from which the present selection was made), and are therefore unable to state whether or not it contains any of the hymns to which we refer; but we beg to call the attention of the authoress of the work before us to the hymns, "Christ ist Erstanden," "Der Tag der ist so freudenreich," "Ein feste Burg ist unser Gott," as examples of what we mean, because we know of no greater service she could render to the lovers of the poetry, and we may add of the music, of the Church, (for some of the most beautiful of the old German Chorals were set to these metrical hymns,) than by presenting the public with a second volume of hymns, translated with the same talent and spirit as those contained in the present volume, and, like them, retaining the same metres as the originals, but selected on the principle suggested in the above remarks. We shall be the first to hail with pleasure the announcement of such a volume.

The Seven Sermons preached at the Consecration and Re-opening of the Parish Church of Leeds; with an Introduction. Leeds: T. W. Green, 1842. Small 8vo.

IN this very elegant volume, the Seven Sermons preached at the Consecration and Re-opening of the Parish Church of Leeds, are accompanied with a view and description of the church, with a list of the several benefactors to the church, and with a full account of the circumstances attending the consecration, and of whatever else can satisfy the curiosity of those who looked with the feelings of churchmen upon the dedication of so splendid a sanctuary, under circumstances replete with more than ordinary interest.

In the Introduction, the editor (Rev. W. H. Teale) has found room for some important matter on the subject of the consecration of churches in general; and he has afforded proofs, never unimportant, and at the present season peculiarly valuable, of the comparative neglect of the consecration of churches previous to the Reformation.

But we will not suffer the general question to detain us from some of the more remarkable features which distinguished the particular instance before us. At the head of the list of the Clergy present, we find the following names:—His Grace, the Lord Archbishop of York; the Lord Bishop of Ripon; the Right Rev. the Bishop of Ross and Argyll; and the Right Rev. the Bishop of New Jersey; and all these illustrious prelates took their part in the solemn service. The presence of the two latter prelates, (representatives, as it were, of the Church in Scotland and in America,) engaged in the service of the same altar with an English metropolitan and Bishop, exemplifying as it did the harmony between three several branches of the Church, so widely separated in local situation and in circumstances, was an incident involving some important principles.

It is only within a short time that the Clergy of the sister-churches have been permitted to officiate among us;* the laws of the State, (we need not say for bad reasons, yet for reasons which we are glad to see overruled,) having hitherto prevented this interchange of ecclesiastical courtesy. It was almost immediately upon the modification of the law, that Dr. Low, the venerable Bishop of Ross and Argyll, and the senior member of the College of Bishops in Scotland; and Bishop Doane, the much-venerated Bishop of New Jersey, U. S.; were enabled to meet in token of their perfect communion with us, in this splendid ceremony; and this embodying of a high ecclesiastical principle to the eye of churchmen cannot have been uninstructive. We cannot do better than borrow the words of Bishop Doane, in the eloquent sermon which stands first in this volume. " Most Rev. Brother, and Right Rev. Brethren," says he, addressing the Archbishop of York, and the Bishop of Ross and Argyle:—

" Most reverend brother, and right reverend brethren, it is no ordinary providence of God that brings us here together. In other days, solemnities like this were the occasion when the Bishops of Christ's Church were wont to come together from distant provinces, for the confirmation of the faith, and the increase of charity, and to renew their solemn vows to God, and pledge themselves, each to the other, to new service, and, if need should be, new sufferings, in his name. Is it not so again? Shall it not be so now? From the far-distant west, a Bishop of that Church, which, as the youngest daughter of the Saviour's household, has so much to acknowledge, and so gratefully acknowledges it, of " first foundation," under God, and " long continuance of nursing care and protection," I come, to pay my vows here in my fathers' Church, and to my fathers' God."—Pp. 22, 23.

The quotation might have been much longer without failing in interest. Sure we are, that the readers of his sermon will sympathise with the American prelate, in the intense feeling with which he describes himself to have visited several places in England which seemed marked out as connected by successive important incidents, with the existence and purity of the apostolical succession in a new world.

But the person on whom all eyes were most necessarily turned, and with whom all hearts must have been in unison, on that day of religious festival, was the Vicar of Leeds himself. To him, directly or indirectly, whatever was peculiar in the solemnity and interest of the occasion, was due. To him, and to his influence, we must refer as well the splendour of the edifice, as the eminence and importance of the illustrious congregation of ecclesiastics assembled at the dedication of that noble church to the Most High. Here was the visible fruit of many years' labour, by a man of greater power in exciting worthy emotions, and instilling high principles, than almost any one of the present day. His noble church embodies a principle and a feeling which he has successfully excited and fostered. There were thousands indeed ready to

---

* The first church in England, in which an American divine preached, was St. James', Leeds.

respond to his appeal. He would have a sanctuary worthy of the worshippers, and the worshippers would have one too: he was ready beyond his proportion, yet not alone, to supply the means: the spirit of pious and intelligent Churchmanship, which would have the house of God not merely large and fine, but appropriate and christian, was touched to good effect in many hearts: and when the *visible building* was provided, and the strength, beauty, and unity of the *spiritual church* also was to be exemplified; when the opportunity presented itself of affording the most important and intelligible signs of that christian fellowship which binds the whole body together; many there were, even fathers in the Church, ready at his appeal to their kindred feelings, to join heart and hand in the inculcation of so important a lesson. If we can collect any thing of the character of the Vicar of Leeds from his works, he would be the first person gratefully to acknowledge the sympathy he has found in others, and the great alacrity with which his wishes have been met; yet we must confess also that it was under his auspices that the effect was produced. The strings which were to be touched to elicit a full harmony of principles, of feeling, and of action, were there; but who else could have *so* touched them as he has done?

Dr. Hook's own sermon, on the text, "The palace is not for man, but for the Lord God," asserts the principles on which he has laboured effectually to erect a noble church in his wealthy and extensive parish. It would be doing him injustice to represent any particular passage as giving a summary of his views; but we must extract the following, with the remark that, the moment at which he could so speak must have been to him a happy moment indeed; and in whatever sense it might be consistently with pure religion, a *proud* one. Canopied by the lofty roof which had risen under his auspices, and surrounded by thousands of worshippers, whose minds had been elevated by the solemn service, and the noble fabric, he might well say—

"It has been to enable us thus to serve God according to the ceremonial, not of the middle ages, but of the existing Church of England, that this our 'beautiful house' has been erected, a palace for the King of kings. We admit that there may be circumstances under which the lowly hovel may be a fit place for christian worship, as well as for the preaching of the gospel; but then of the hovels that surround it, it ought to be the best. The tabernacle was but a tent; but then among the tents of wandering Israel it stood pre-eminent and conspicuous. We would not have the palace of our heavenly King inferior in magnificence to the palace of our earthly sovereign. But then our ideas of magnificence are relative. Heaven alone is magnificent. When we shall be in heaven, how insignificant will the most magnificent of earthly things appear to be! What is requisite is only that we should offer at all times of our best. If the sovereign of this land were led by circumstances to sojourn for a time in some poor village, the poor inhabitants of that village could not erect a sumptuous palace for their queen, nor would she expect it; but she *would* expect what loyal hearts would be proud to render, the very best accommodation the humble village could afford. And so in a retired hamlet, if we do feel shame to see a ruined church beside a princely mansion, or, still more disgraceful—(oh! disgrace of the Church that ever it should so be!) beside a decorated parsonage, yet we do not there expect a magnificent sanctuary. We merely desire to see it neat and cleanly, and so arranged that the services may in it be properly performed. But in a wealthy town, where our merchants, the princes of the earth, dwell in their ceiled houses, we should expect to behold a pious people lavishing their money in order to decorate the palace of their God; and they would feel shame to see his house alone unadorned by those arts in which He has inspired our Bezaleels and Aholiabs to excel. So have felt the Churchmen of Leeds. Nobly, generously, piously have they come forward, the rich with their gold, and the poor with their brass, all desirous, before they erect, as I trust they will do, a multitude of humbler oratories, as aisles to this church, in the poorer districts of the parish,—all desirous to see their parish church what the palace of their heavenly King ought in this great and generous town to be."—Pp. 102—104.

On the Sufficiency of the Parochial System, without a Poor Rate for the right Management of the Poor. By THOS. CHALMERS, D.D., *Professor of Theology in the University of Edinburgh.* Glasgow: Collins. 1841. Pp. 335. 12mo.

THIS little book labours under the usual disadvantages of Dr. Chalmers' style. He possesses, however, as all allow, an earnestness of mind, to which, when he happens to take a right view, the reader yields himself with no little degree of pleasure. And here we think our author's views are, in the main, right. To a certain extent, he adopts the principles of the late Mr. Malthus; *i. e.* he believes that pauperism may almost indefinitely be reduced; and that real charity consists rather in teaching a man how to be independent, than in relieving his present necessities. The dangerous tendencies of this theory meanwhile are corrected by his strong religious feelings, and by the fundamental hypothesis on which he rests the working of it; viz. that it is to be under the immediate control of the christian minister, and should avail itself of all those ties of responsibility on the one hand, and protection on the other, which the notion of parochial association necessarily engenders.

But the chief value of the book consists in the details of a trial to which his system was subjected at Glasgow some years since. We shall endeavour briefly to explain his proceedings, and to state the result, as far at least as, from the unfortunate defects of his style, and the patchwork nature of the volume before us, we are able to understand them. In Glasgow, it appears that there is a fund raised by compulsory assessment for the general support of the poor, which is administered by the united "elders"[*] of the various congregations, and of which a "town-hospital" is the type and impersonation. A portion of the collections made weekly at the doors of the several places of worship is also devoted to this object. In the year 1819 Dr. Chalmers became minister of the parish of St. John's, in Glasgow, numbering a population of 10,000 people. He does not tell us what the annual cost of maintaining the poor had up to this time

---

[*] We cannot forbear to quote, for the instruction of our readers, a bit of Scotch theology, with which Dr. Chalmers favours us, from "the Second Book of Discipline." "The whole policy of the Kirk consisteth in three things—doctrine, discipline, and distribution. Hence ariseth a sort of threefold office-bearers in the Kirk: viz., of ministers, preachers; elders, governors; and deacons, distributors. There is, in the New-Testament times of the Evangel, the ministry of the apostles, prophets, evangelists, pastors, and doctors, in the administration of the word; the eldership for the order and administration of the discipline; the deaconship to have the care of the ecclesiastical goods of the Church." We really should like to know where any authority may be found for the existence of our second office named as superior to the order of the sacred ministry; for we presume that is superior which controls the other.

been; but with a noble exercise of faith he at once undertook the whole charge. The poor already on the list were still to be supported out of the old funds, and through the town-hospital; but all future pauperism was to be provided for by the weekly alms of the congregation. The parish was portioned out among active district visitors; and incredible as it may seem, the average expenditure required during the first four years amounted only to 66*l*. 6*s*. The number of paupers taken on was thirteen!

To our mind, this statement manifestly proves too much; for supposing that by the activity and skill of the person administering the system, work was found for every able-bodied individual, it is quite impossible that so small a sum could have adequately provided for the bare casualties that must have occurred in so dense a population. Nevertheless the system certainly worked wonders; for it was carried on in spite of a most vigorous and persevering opposition. However, Dr. Chalmers avers that it was very popular among the poor. It has now, however, been suffered to drop, after a successful experiment, says its projector, of eighteen years, because of the ingratitude of the people of Glasgow, who still continued to tax the inhabitants of St. John's, to the fund which they never used, and who broke through other of the covenants into which they had entered with Dr. Chalmers. Into the merits of these disputes we cannot enter. Dr. Chalmers was certainly viewed as an enthusiast and a visionary; and no doubt had his share of misrepresentation. We confess, however, that we do not see what right he had to claim a total exemption for St. John's from the general assessment, so long as the original paupers of the parish continued to receive any assistance from that quarter, as by the terms of the engagement they were to do. But here again Dr. Chalmers' feelings are so strong, and his book is so overloaded with words, that we do not feel sure that we have caught his meaning. Nevertheless, we strongly advise those who are interested in the matter to examine for themselves.

Notes of a Half-Pay in search of Health; or, Russia, Circassia, and the Crimea in 1839-40. *By* CAPT. JESSE. London: Madden & Co. 2 vols. 8vo.

THE chief fault of these volumes is, that they are written without making due allowance for the circumstances of the writer in the country through which he was travelling. A dyspeptic valetudinarian is not the person to encounter the discomforts of the Russian provinces. We are not surprised, therefore, that he takes a very jaundiced view of affairs. Nevertheless, his "Notes" are interesting; —how could they be otherwise upon such countries?—and some of his reflections, as we shall show immediately, just; but to apply Guizot's definition of civilization to an empire like that of Russia appears to us absurd. We will now quote a passage or two from the book; and first upon the much litigated subject of the corn-laws:—

"What is to happen in the event of a continental war [supposing the present protection removed]? Has the policy of Russia in Persia and Central Asia been so honest that we should be justified in trusting her even *in peace?* She is quite as likely to form an alliance with any enemy we might have to-morrow as to keep her faith with us. In either of these cases, where is the cheap loaf? When I hear it stated that Russia is one of the countries on which we may in future possibly depend for bread, which, having been much on the continent, I invariably eat *à discretion,* the inward man exclaims loudly against a measure so likely to be short!

"With regard to the advantages we are to gain by her taking an increased quantity of manufactures, the idea is altogether a delusion: she will not alter her prohibitive tariff, nor is the mass of the people sufficiently advanced in their social system to require any even of the most ordinary comforts of civilization; and if they were so, they have no money to go to market with. Let the working classes in England, whose expectations have been so much raised on this subject, be clearly made to understand the state of the poor in Russia, in times of *plenty*, and not be misled by the false idea that where corn is cheap there can be no distress; nor take it for granted that their wages will remain high, when the price of bread is low, supposing, which it is evident still remains quite a chance, the loaf is a cheap loaf after all. The low price of wheat in Russia, and the high price of wheat in England, are constantly compared; and it is asserted that the poorer classes in the former country are better off than those in the latter;—that the condition of a Russian serf is better than that of a poor man in England; when, in fact, there is perhaps no country in which more squalid poverty exists than in the great corn districts of Russia, where, in an average harvest, rye (not wheat), the staple article of food, is only five shillings the quarter."

We were much pleased with Capt. Jesse's Strictures upon the Foundling Hospital of St. Petersburgh; an enormous institution, which receives all infants that are brought there, without inquiry:—

"It is monstrous to set up to admiration as one of the public charities of which a country should be proud, an establishment like this, offering as its boasted recommendation every facility for severing the tie between parent, nay, mother and child; the effect of which is, to keep up a perpetual canker in the morals of the people. From the manner and the scale on which it is conducted, it can be looked upon as nothing better than a premium upon vice; and, as such, is taken wholesale advantage of by those who live within reach of it."

A Pilgrimage to Auvergne from Picardy to Le Velay. By LOUISA STUART COSTELLO, *Author of "A Summer among the Bocages,"* &c. 2 vols. 8vo. London: Bentley, 1842.

IT appears that Miss Costello was attracted to this country as well by the reported beauty of its scenery—she calls it the Switzerland of France—as by the associations by which it was connected in her mind with the tales of Froissart. She was also naturally not unmindful of the success which attended the publication of her previous tour along the banks of the Loire.

Miss Costello, both in style and information, is certainly superior to the mass of travellers and bookmakers. The following passages are quoted solely in regard of the testimony which they bear to an impotent but melancholy fact:—

"To an eye accustomed, as we are in England, to see a crowd composed of all ranks [in the public walks of our towns] it is dreary and unpleasant to meet with no figures but those of peasants, in places where their manners are unsuitable; and the knowledge of the reasons for this exclusiveness makes the fact less pleasant still. It cannot be concealed from the observer of the present state of France, that the superior orders live in a state of *constant fear* of those beneath them. The arrogance and purse-proud insolence of the latter, when circumstances bring forth an expression of their opinions, explains this feeling; their envy and hatred of all those above them, and their ignorant assumption, is too apparent to escape comment; and the only way to prevent unpleasant collision seems, to be by retiring and leaving the coast clear for the all-powerful and all-engrossing people; who, in proportion as their wealth has increased, have lost all the respect and deference for others; and though not a whit superior to their former selves, they are always looking forward to the time when an equal division of property shall make them superior to those who are not yet altogether degraded from a rank to which they were born."

"The manufacturers never dream of these things [she is speaking of the ancient glories of the town of Soissons], content with their new and comfortable houses built upon the site of edifices where such strange doings abounded. ' Tout ça ce sont des choses de la religion, qu'on ne connait pas maintenant,' is the reply to any inquiry on these *auld warld* subjects."

Such are the fruits of revolution!

A Search into the Old Testament. By JOSEPH HUME, *Translator into English Verse of " Dante's Inferno."* London: Longman & Co. 8vo. Pp. 304.

TRADITION speaks of a certain man who boasted that his horse had but two faults; and upon our conscience we believe that Mr. Hume's book has not more. The faults in the quadruped, to be sure, were considerable—amounting to this: first, that it was almost impossible to catch him when loose; and secondly, that he was not worth having when caught. Of this " Search," we would say, first, that we are quite unable to discover what the object sought for is; and we believe that the discovery, if possible, would not be worth the making. The author tells us, indeed, what he has not " searched" for, viz.: " the doctrines which have collected mankind into separate masses, designated by different churches or congregations;" and, above all, he protests that he has not searched for Him of whom the Apostle tells us that " all the Scriptures testify." But, we repeat, he nowhere tells us what *is* the object of his " search."

There transpire, however, by the way, a few incidental discoveries which appear to have rewarded Mr. Hume's search; and a specimen or two we think it right not to withhold from our readers. 1. He has " searched" and discovered that " mankind in connexion with religion may be divided into three classes—the Atheist, the Theist, the Revelationist." 2. Again, our author has searched very diligently into the narrative of the deception practised by Jacob upon his father, because he tells us the " pious mind cannot observe without a regret, and even an astonishment, that the functionaries holding authority of the various established Churches of Christendom, have so long allowed these passages to have been unexplained;" especially has he " searched" to ascertain why " Rebekah should have instructed Jacob to obtain *two kids* for his father's eating—this exuberance of meat for such a purpose seeming inconceivable; or why she should have attired her son in *goodly raiment*, to present his venison to his parent, then blind." We regret to say that his search after all proves unavailing; though he thinks that he is more successful in discovering how it happened that Esau should not have known from the appearance of the kitchen that his brother had anticipated him in the preparation of venison; for he conjectures that Isaac had provided his sons with " separate establishments ;" and indeed he considers that their standing in society was so respectable, that the " culinary operations would not have been performed by either of the sons in person." Incidental discoveries of this sort abound, *passim*—but we must not poach further on Mr. Hume's manor. We shall already have sufficiently excited our reader's curiosity—or disgust.

Episcopacy and Presbytery. By the Rev. Archibald Boyd, A.M. *Curate of the Cathedral of Derry.* London : Seeley & Co. 1841. 8vo. pp. 436.

It has been a principle held and acted upon very generally of late years in our Church, that the fact of a doctrine having been once established against opposition is a sufficient discharge for all future generations from noticing any subsequent, especially weaker, attacks that may hereafter be renewed. Of this principle we are most decided opponents, and on several grounds. 1. The folios of our ancient divines are inaccessible to the great mass of modern readers. 2. By lapse of time their language is often unintelligible. 3. They were written exclusively for persons possessing a learned education. 4. Controversy (in minor points, at least) is constantly changing its ground. But further, we consider that there is a necessity imposed upon the Church not to decline the labour; for if the providence of God still declares that " there must need be heresies," it is for the trial of our faith, and in order to call forth our active christian energies in behalf of the truth. Moreover, it often happens that in peaceful times admissions are made by the adversary, which it may be useful to recall and to collect.

Upon these *general* grounds we have pleasure in noticing the present volume,—the result, it would seem, of a revival of the presbyterian controversy in the north of Ireland. We hail it also as an omen [for this we have to thank the dissenters] that the unrighteous compromise which recently existed in that quarter, reminding us too forcibly of the league with the Gibeonites, is at an end : we do not expect to hear again (for example) of the cathedral of Derry being lent to the presbyterians.

And now a few words as to the intrinsic merits of Mr. Boyd's volume. It seems to be laboriously and skilfully prepared; and we think may do good service in that portion of the Church to which he belongs. The author is what a short time since would have been called a low-Churchman; and therefore, along with a very encouraging acquaintance with ecclesiastical antiquity, we are not surprised to find a lurking remnant of inconsistency. It is possible that this circumstance may recommend his book in certain quarters. We are tempted to notice one of these points, simply because it may be corrected in a very few words. Mr. Boyd, after an evident struggle, admits the doctrine of baptismal regeneration; but he qualifies it with two most untenable corollaries; first, that there are other means of regeneration besides baptism recognised by our Church; and secondly, that *after regeneration we are to look for "conversion."* The first corollary he grounds on the use of the indefinite article in the Catechism, which speaks of a sacrament as "*a* means of grace." How singular that it should never have occurred to Mr. Boyd that the indefiniteness of the expression is altogether done away with by the previous answer, which states that there are "two *only*" sacraments, *i. e.* two only means by which regeneration and the grace peculiar to the other sacrament are to be obtained!

"Confessions of an Apostate," by the Author of "Felix de Lisle," (London, Seeley and Burnside,) is really the most wicked book we ever met with. It is the imaginary history of a person who had been successively a Protestant,—a "Puseyite" (as this abominable book would call it), and a Papist. The ground of his present despair, *of course*, is the fact of having once delighted in the "Tracts for the Times." We really are surprised that any respectable publisher should allow his name to appear upon the title-page of so unchristian and libellous a book.

"The Country Parson's Wife," (Hatchard,) as the author tells us, is intended as a continuation of, and companion for, Herbert's "Country Parson." We cannot think that it is a very successful attempt;—least of all do we think that Herbert himself would have fallen in love with the prototype of this description, as it is well known he did with his own wife from the description given of her by a common friend.

We have several times taken occasion to recommend Archdeacon Wilberforce's "Scripture Stories;" but we really now become alarmed in contemplating the number of unsound and injudicious tales which appear to have been written in imitation of his very successful little books. "The History of Job," (by the Author of "Peep of Day,"—itself a most objectionable book,) is lying before us, which, besides doctrinal errors, has travestied Scripture in a way certainly not calculated to create reverence in the youthful mind. One specimen will suffice: "Job had a wife, seven sons and three daughters. I believe his children were grown up, for his sons had houses of their own. There was a custom among Job's sons which showed that they loved each other, They used to give a feast to each other by turns, upon particular days that they fixed upon; and they always invited their sisters to come and dine with them. I do not know whether they invited their friends to come also, but I suppose that they did. I think that Job did not go to these feasts, for he was a man that spent his time chiefly in doing good to the poor, and in judging the people and in prayer; and he had not much time for feasting." Indeed we are almost disposed to think that these supplemental illustrations of Scripture can only come with effect, or even safety, from the sacred mouth of the parent.

Some of our readers may perhaps not be aware that a new edition of "Warton's History of English Poetry" was lately published by Mr. Tegg, in three volumes. It contains a large accession of notes by several of the best scholars and antiquarians of the day. The historian of our poetry, like the biographer of our poets, lived in a degenerate age; nevertheless, his work is still the best introduction to a very interesting study.

From the same quarter has also just proceeded a reprint of "Wheatley on the Common Prayer," which sells at nearly one-third less than the edition published at Oxford. For ourselves, we certainly prefer giving a few shillings extra in order to *secure* correctness and accuracy, which cannot always be depended on in cheap editions; but there are many for whose sake it is desirable to have our standard works at as low a price as possible; and it is certainly encouraging to find that books of this character are beginning to supersede less sound productions.

It is our painful duty to announce that Mr. Howitt has published a second series of "Visits to Remarkable Places." Those who are at all acquainted with the man or his writings will not need to be warned that the book abounds with all sorts of inaccuracies. We must, however, give one specimen of the beautiful taste with which he illustrates his subjects:—Near to Seaton Delaval, in the county of Durham, is found "The Monk's Stone," a memorial of the penitence of an ancestor of the house of Delaval, who sought to atone for the crime of manslaughter by the surrender of a large estate to a religious house. The person murdered was a monk of the said house; and the ground of offence was that he had made free with a pig which was roasting in the squire's kitchen. The inscription on the stone is—

"Oh! horrid dede!
To kill a man for a pigge's hede!"

and Mr. Howitt's comment is as follows:—"How the pious rogues must have laughed in their sleeves as they solaced themselves over the tragedy of the 'pigge's hede!' By the bye, this notable verse should be repeated with a hollow voice, a slow tone, and a solemn look, and it has quite *a swinish sublime* about it."

The "Letters of the Rev. Henry James Prince to his Christian Brethren at St. David's College, Lampeter," are more nearly profane than any professedly religious publication we have lately met with. We had heard much of the lax proceedings at Lampeter; but these letters betoken a state of things which seems to call imperatively for the interference of the visitor. As for a person who illustrates the theory of spiritual communion by mathematical diagrams, so far from being fit to "teach others," we really think that he should be placed under restraint.

Mr. Jameson's "New Zealand, South Australia, and New South Wales," (London, Smith and Elder,) gives, in the compass of one moderate volume, just such information as a person meditating emigration to one of those colonies would require. We have seen nothing before so complete or (apparently) so impartial.

"Discursive Remarks on Modern Education, by E. L." (London, Cadell, 8vo. pp. 102,) belongs to that class of respectable publications whose fate it is, in these stirring times, to fall almost still-born from the press. The authoress is evidently a person of sound principles, and of some experience in teaching; but her voice will not be heard amid the turmoil of the elements.

Some books, like other "coming events," "cast their shadows so far before them," that their characters are fixed and established before they come into the hands of the general reader. Such has been the case with two volumes of very interesting "Letters from the Baltic," lately published by Mr. Murray, and which therefore we have forborne to notice at length, as altogether a work of supererogation. One exception only do we feel it necessary to make to our otherwise unlimited commendation, and that is as regards a habit of irreverently and unnecessarily (irreverently *because* unnecessarily) quoting Scripture.

Of another book, also, Stephens' "Incidents of Travel in Central America," 3 vols., we find that our praise would come too late. It is the record of some very extensive and able researches, which testify to the existence of ruined cities of great splendour, hitherto unknown to fame; and which are now only to be discovered by a most laborious use of the woodman's axe. What may be the date of these remains can at present only be guessed. Mr. Stephens thinks that four or five centuries in those tropical climates may account for the wilderness of vegetation in which they are enveloped; and he is disposed to assign them to a period not very long anterior to the Spanish invasion. Sketches are given of some of the most interesting architectural objects, as idols, temples, &c. In one day Mr. Stephens met also with ruins of seven gigantic churches,—a problem which the antiquarian, we may safely say, will never be required to solve in any country colonized by the English. For further information, we refer the reader to the volumes themselves, which, together with "Grey's Australia" and the work mentioned above, we consider to be *the* books of the season.

"The Christian Diary," &c. (Hastings, 1842,) is a series of religious reflections for every day in the year. Being dedicated to, and of course meant for "The Christian Public of all Denominations," it is not suitable, as a whole, for those who think a variety of denominations wrong. The author seems a well-intentioned person, and can now and then write so pleasingly, that we wish he knew better what Christ's Church and what Catholic Theology are.

"Twelve Sonnets on Colyton Church," &c. by John Farmer, (Wertheim, 1842,) are the productions seemingly of an amiable and well-principled man. His whole tone is so modest, and he appears so little to have intended, in the first instance, that they should obtrude themselves beyond the locality to which they relate, that criticism is in some measure disarmed. Nevertheless, we are bound to say that they are not good sonnets. As the author is a young man, and as sonnets are a very difficult form of art, (in regard to which our readers know we are peculiarly fastidious,) we say this with the less pain; inasmuch as the two circumstances in question render our adverse sentence less final. Mr. Farmer may improve, but before he undertakes sonnets again, he must be a far more practised versifier than he is at present. They are nothing, unless they are perfect.

"Part the First of a Defence of the Church of England, in a Series of Essays," by a Clergyman, (Priest, Thetford; Simpkin and Marshall, London, 1841,) is both well-informed and well-principled.

"Notes on the Book of Genesis," &c. by one of the Professors of the British College, (Hamilton, 1841,) embrace, of necessity, too many varied matters for us to have an opinion of their merits without careful examination.

We hope shortly to take much more particular notice than we can at present of one of the most admirable and delightful books which has lately appeared, "Remarks on Church Architecture, with Illustrations," by the Rev. J. L. Petit, M.A. (Burns, 1841.) In the meantime, we heartily recommend to the lovers of architecture these two volumes, in which they will find much knowledge combined with much thought.

We ought long before now to have noticed an elegant work, which has been coming out in parts, ten of which are expected to complete it, (if they have not already done so,)—"A History of British Forest Trees," &c. by P. J. Selby, F.L.S. &c. (Van Voorst.) The subject is one which precludes our passing any opinion on the text; but we may say that it is very attractive.

Mr. Maitland has just given to the world two pamphlets,—one a re-publication from the *British Magazine*, entitled "Six more Letters on Foxe's Acts and Monuments," &c. (Rivingtons, 1841;) the other, "Remarks on the Rev. S. R. Cattley's Defence of his Edition of Foxe's Martyrology," (Rivingtons, 1842.) Mr. M.'s learning and shrewdness stand in no need of eulogium from us. Those interested in the controversy must possess themselves of the two pamphlets.

We regret to perceive that the Camden Society of Cambridge are suffering their publications to be characterised by a flippancy of tone and a sort of conceit which is not only contrary to all good taste, and specially out of place in those who would "build the waste places of Jerusalem," but which must inevitably excite the jealousy of a large portion of their brethren. The "wise-hearted" alone among the people were permitted by Moses to have any share in rearing the tabernacle: the same qualification will God look for in the restorers of his Church. These remarks have been extorted from us by a paper on the "History of Pews," which, while it displays very laborious research, is the product of an unchastened, and therefore we must say, uncatholic mind. We do hope that this spirit will not be allowed to mar the usefulness of a very promising Society.

Since writing the above, Mr. Paget's "Milford Malvoisin," a tale illustrating the evils and absurdities of the pew system, has reached us. It is marked by the same humour, good taste, and feeling, as the author's previous volumes, in all these respects affording a remarkable contrast to the production just named; and no one, we are sure, who has read "St. Antholin's" will be satisfied to leave "Milford Malvoisin" unread. There is one point, however, (to which we have already alluded in this number,) in which we think even Mr. Paget offends, and that is in the selection of his names, which are more fitted for a pantomime or farce than for a book illustrated with engravings of churches. We allude to such names as Dr. Fustiefowl and Miss Wrinkletrap. We must say, also, that we think it unfair to throw all the blame of architectural monstrosities upon churchwardens, when rectors and vicars were much more in fault. And should it not be considered that much of the evil, as far as it rests at all with churchwardens, is to be attributed to an indisposition to change, a habit which in these days ought certainly not be dealt hardly with?

"Corn-Law Opposition detected and exposed, and its real nature laid bare; a Few Words addressed to People of Common Sense, by a Plain Man;" (J. Ollivier, 1842,)—is an excellent pamphlet. It fully redeems the promise of its title, and gives a complete view of the artful and delusive schemes adopted by many of the opponents of the present corn-laws. It displays in every page a thoroughly English spirit. The comparison between the respective advantages derived by the country from the manufactories and the landholders is well worthy of attention.

"The true Difference betwixt the Principles and the Practices of the Kirk and the Church of Scotland," &c., by the Rev. R. Calder, (Moffat, 1841.) This is a reprint, under the auspices, we believe, of the able and orthodox Mr. Stephen, of a pamphlet of other days, by one of the Scottish clergy, ejected, for conscience sake, from his preferment, and afterwards subjected to the cruel persecution of the Presbyterians. It is very interesting and important.

From Mr. Stephen, too, has just proceeded "A Companion to the Fasts and Festivals," (Moffat, 1842.) We have great pleasure in recommending it.

The Society for Promoting Christian Knowledge has recently issued two useful tracts:—"Debt; its Peril, Pains, and Penalties;" and "The Parish Church" (by Dr. Molesworth). The latter is illustrated by several neat wood-cuts.

"Practical Suggestions on Church Reform, by the Rev. Thomas Spencer, M.A., Perpetual Curate of Hinton Charter-house, &c." is the title given to a tract, which for shallowness and heresy resembles those with which the press was deluged nine years ago. The influence under which it was so, is so much by-gone, that we should not be apt to dread much from the present pamphlet, were it not that we know that error and treason are never harmless, and that we see the words "eighth thousand" on the title-page. Wherever it is circulated, the clergy must *descend* to the task of counteracting this utterance of the trash and disloyalty with which the author's mind is filled.

After a suspension of some duration, Winkle's "Cathedrals of England and Wales" (Tilt and Bogue) are again in progress. This third volume will complete the work; and, as the numbers are double ones, that event does not seem very distant. *Hereford*, which is lying before us, is a great improvement on *Gloucester*, the beautiful tower of which was most unworthily represented in Mr. Winkle's engravings.

We call attention to the Report of the Scottish Episcopal Church Society for 1841, which we hope to have appended (if not to the present) to our next number. The formation of the London Committee is a very important new feature in the Society's proceedings.

Similar interest belongs to a "Pastoral Letter to the Clergy, and other Members of the Protestant Episcopal Church of America, from their Bishops." (New York, 1841.)

"Thoughts on the Christening of the Prince of Wales," (Burns, 1842,) a cheap tract for distribution, will be found very interesting. The author gives an account of the conversion of our Anglo-Saxon ancestors, and of the baptism of several of our early princes.

"A new Tract for the Times," attributed generally to the Rev. Miles Jackson, for many years the leader of low-Churchmen in Leeds, has issued from the press. It contains 120 pages of misrepresentations, personalities, and antichristian spirit; and it has been answered by the Rev. G. A. Poole, in a pamphlet of six pages, with that gentleman's usual ability, and in a tone and spirit which would be in themselves a sufficient reply. Mr. Poole's pamphlet is entitled "A Letter to the Churchmen of Leeds," &c. (Green, Leeds; Burns, London, 1842;) and it deserves a wide circulation. As the causes which called for it at Leeds exist elsewhere, the remedy which is suitable in one case, may well be in another.

We ought sooner to have noticed Mr. Bird's beautiful and orthodox "Lent Lectures," (Seeley and Burnside, 1841.) They have given us much gratification.

"A Tract on Regeneration," by the Rev. R. Anderson, of Brighton, (Hatchards, and Burns, 1842,) is, like every thing else of the author's, orthodox and useful. We may also mention that the second volume of his Exposition of St. John's Gospel has come out, completing the work.

The Bishop of Barbados' Sermon, preached at the consecration of the Bishop of New Zealand, (Rivingtons, 1841,) must, for every reason, command attention; and so we trust will one by Archdeacon Manning, entitled, "The Mind of Christ the Perfection and Bond of the Church," preached at a meeting of the diocese of Calcutta, before its late Bishop. (Mason, Chichester, 1841.)

"Preaching Christ," by the Rev. E. Auriol, (Seeley, 1841;) "The Prospects of Africa," by the Rev. F. D. Morgan, (Seeley, 1841;) "The Lord's House," by the Rev. G. E. Biber, LL.D.; "The Standard of Faith," by the Rev. J. Davies, B.D. (Hatchards, 1841;) are the titles of sermons which we have to acknowledge. Some of the clergy who feel tempted to controversy on occasion of having to preach at Visitations, must remember that there is a Canon which bears on the subject.

"A Sermon preached at the Opening of Christ Church, Bolton," by the Rev. J. Slade, M.A. &c., will be found very interesting, as having welcomed into the unity of the Church a late Wesleyan minister, along with six of the local preachers, and some of the leading members of the congregation.

CHRIST CHURCH, STREATHAM.

WE trust that our friends will accept the highly-finished steel engraving of the exterior of this church, prefixed to our present number, as our best apology for the delay in its appearance. The interior view, which accompanies it,* represents the building as it is intended to be finished, with the ceiling pannelled, and the decorations painted. The only decorations yet executed, are three very richly painted glass windows in the apsis, representing the Transfiguration, presented by — Fuller, Esq., of Streatham. In this view, also, the pulpit (to which we have adverted in a former number) is placed where it was originally intended to be. The present position, in the centre of the church, is both indecorous and unsightly. It is a blot on the design, which we trust speedily to see removed.

MISCELLANEOUS.

[*The Editor is not responsible for the opinions expressed in this department.*]

A PLAN FOR THE FORMATION OF COLLEGES OF "BISHOPS' FELLOWS," IN THE SEVERAL DIOCESES OF ENGLAND AND WALES.

A Letter addressed to the Lord Bishop of Oxford.

[THIS letter, of course, is not published without the permission of the prelate to whom it is addressed: I am anxious, however, to state that the Bishop is not pledged to any one of the details. The most that he can fairly be considered to sanction, in allowing the publication, is the general principle, that *something* is wanted, in order to render the Church adequate to the performance of the duties required of her; and that it is well that a variety of plans should be proposed and discussed, in order to the selection of that which may appear best suited. Whatever practical measures may be adopted must proceed from the Bishops themselves.]

MY LORD,—I am aware that the announcement of a new "Plan," involving, as will be anticipated, new machinery and a large expenditure, will be received by many persons with great jealousy and distrust. So many expedients have been promulgated of late years for the extension and confirmation of the Church, and so many experiments have absolutely been set on foot, of the ultimate success

---

* We regret that the size of our page does not admit of the showing these plates to the best advantage. Separate copies, however, printed in a folio size, may be had of the publisher, at a small cost.

and permanency of which it is impossible yet to predicate, that a fresh proposal could only expect a very cold reception. I am anxious, therefore, to assure your Lordship that my object is to promote the union and consolidation of existing machinery, rather than to originate a fresh agency.

That "the staff" of the Church,—using that term to express either the collective bench of Bishops, with their various officials; or taking the Bishops as the representative of the body of Clergy, in each separate diocesan church,—is unable to meet all the demands that are being made upon it, might, I conceive, almost be assumed; or, if proof be needed, it will be found in the various expedients or experiments proposed or undertaken within the last few years. It may be well to enumerate some few principal ones.

1. The earliest attempt at increasing the ministerial agency of the Church was embodied in the Church Building Society, of which branches have more recently been organized in most dioceses. And, in point of fact, the Diocesan Associations alone fall within the proper scope of our inquiries; for they differ (at least many of them) in this very important respect from the parent from which they proceeded, that they embrace not only the building, but also the endowment or supply of churches.

2. But more recently two distinct* societies—the Additional Curates Fund and the Pastoral Aid Society, have devoted themselves to the supply of an increased number of labourers in the vineyard, and are now straining every nerve to gather in the plentiful harvest.

3. More lately, various Bishops have delegated a portion of their office to Diocesan Boards of Education: viz. for the training and sending forth fit and accredited schoolmasters, according to the 77th canon; and for the inspection of schools, which was ever considered to be a work inherent in the Episcopal office.

4. In addition to these measures, and still more recently, Diocesan Colleges have in more instances than one been opened, for improving clerical education; and a very strong feeling is spread throughout the country that such a step is imperatively called for.

And besides these wants, which as many associations have been framed to supply, attention has been drawn to many other crying evils in our system—as the inadequacy of the number of Bishops; the want of a college for missionaries; cheap places for the education of orphan and other sons of poor Clergy; the lack of bodies of men devoted either to literature as a profession, or to intercessory prayer; also of a lower order in the ministry, and of a sort of "unattached corps," who shall be ready to follow the disposal of their diocesan, moving from station to station as he should see fit.

Having enumerated so large a catalogue of wants, I almost fear, my Lord, that I may seem to be "proving too much," if I say that the plan I have to propose is calculated to meet them all. Yet so it appears to me; and I must now beg your Lordship's attention while

---

* Some few years before, a society had been formed in your Lordship's diocese, "in aid of Queen Anne's Bounty,"—the objects of which are to assist in maintaining additional Clergymen and in building parsonage houses.

I develop the principal details of it. I propose, then, that there should be in each diocese, what I venture to call a "College of Bishops' Fellows," immediately attached to the residence of the Bishop—where he has two residences, to the one in the country, in preference to a town residence. The "fellows," who should vary in number according to the wants of the diocese, would be elected by the Bishop, and be at his sole and entire disposal. Marriage of course would exclude from the society; and it would be desirable that the Bishop should be invested with power to remove them at any time from the college, when they ceased to be serviceable to the ends of the institution; though, as will presently be seen, the variety of occupation will be so great, as to render such a step scarcely ever, if ever, necessary.

In order to explain the nature of the plan more precisely, I will suppose the college to consist of twelve fellows; of these, two should be devoted to study, one of whom at least should always be upon the spot. It is obvious that these would be of great service as counsellors to their diocesan: they would examine candidates for holy orders; and under them might be placed a theological library, which, subject to certain regulations, should be available to the general use of the Clergy. Three others should be employed in superintending education: one in directing the studies of candidates for orders, for whom accommodation would be provided in the building; a second should preside over the school for training masters, which should likewise be under the same roof; and the third be employed in inspecting schools in various parts of the diocese. Among these five would be distributed the duty of celebrating the daily service, which, I believe, in some Bishops' palaces is neglected. One (if required) might be appointed domestic chaplain and secretary; and the six (or seven) remaining would be at the disposal of the Bishop, as the service of the diocese might seem to demand. I have not spoken of any superior of the college, because the office might be held by any one of the fellows in residence, whom the Bishop should please, from time to time, to appoint.

Each fellow would possess a small sitting-room and bed-room. There would be a common dining hall for all the inmates of the college, distributed at separate tables; the fare at each table being of the plainest description.

The funds of the college should constitute a common stock; from whence the expenses of those fellows who are absent from home on service would be defrayed. A very small sum would suffice for the private income of each fellow. Into the question of pecuniary means, I do not feel called upon to enter, further than presently to show that the expense would not be so great as might be supposed. The first point to decide is the expediency of the measure proposed; if that be decided in the affirmative, I shall not despair of means being found. Something might be expected from the voluntary offerings of the fellows. But I shall return to this subject.

It is now time to enumerate some of the principal instances in which the beneficial results of the plan under consideration would be felt.

1. It may seem scarcely necessary to point out the great variety of cases in which such a disposable force would be of the greatest possible service. Your Lordship will know, for example, how frequently the building of a church is postponed beyond the right season, in consequence of the difficulty of procuring an endowment; whereas upon the falling in of some life or lives, there will be ample funds. How desirable, then, that the Bishop should have it in his power to supply the temporary want from his own college! Or again, take the case of a Clergyman worn out with age or other infirmity: the Bishop, partly from the State having unfortunately made laws upon the subject, which he is apprehensive will not support him in interfering, and partly also from the poverty of the benefice, is unwilling to require the maintenance of a curate: how gladly, under these circumstances, would he have it in his power to send a curate at little or no cost to the incumbent! The ordinary cases of an additional Clergyman being required in consequence of an increase of duty need not be specified. It would not be designed, however, save in peculiar cases, to afford *permanent* relief from the body of fellows. Nor would it be a slight advantage that the command of such a body of men would materially strengthen the hands of the Bishop, and enable him to make his influence felt in a more directly practical way than it is at present.

2. Something is manifestly wanting in order to the more ecclesiastical working of our different societies; and I do not see how that improvement is to be effected save by one of two expedients; either by an increase of Bishops, or by an increase of their officers: and in the way of the former, regard being had to the present relations of Church and State, I apprehend that insurmountable[*] objections will be found. Your Lordship, I am sure, cannot be satisfied with the way in which even our best constituted societies are necessarily conducted—both at head-quarters and in the several dioceses. Everything is left to Mr. Secretary So-and-So: he has no one with whom to consult upon important questions; and the only clumsy expedient which occurs to him in assuming what he feels to be an unwarrantable authority, is to personify a board or a committee which exists only in theory. A most inconvenient diversity of practice is the necessary result. The societies begin indeed to taunt one another with the want of ecclesiastical order; but it would be difficult to point out one, which, both practically and theoretically, acts up to the Church's system. But did such a body as that of Bishops' Fellows exist, the various diocesan societies might at once fall under their management, and thus acquire a unity, and consequently a vigour of action, from which they are at present very far removed. Or rather, one might hope that they would all be merged in one general Diocesan Church Fund, which should be applied, without restriction of purpose, to the service of the Church, at the discretion of the Bishop.

3. As another very valuable result of this measure, we might look, I think, for an authoritative statement from each Bishop of the spiritual

---

[*] This (*as were all the main parts of this letter*) was *written* some time before the appearance of Mr. Gresley's or Mr. Palmer's pamphlet.

wants of the several dioceses. Attention has recently been drawn to the destitution of portions of the metropolis, of Manchester, Birmingham, and other of the larger towns; but, as respects the general face and circumstances of the country, we are still in the dark. Nor do I think that we know the worst. It sounds of course very deplorable, and is, nationally, most disgraceful, that thousands of poor persons in our manufacturing towns, are, in the matter of spiritual supervision, by us, wholly unprovided for—as sheep without shepherds. But these crying evils happily contain a remedy within themselves. There is that whereon to rest an appeal, which no christian heart can refuse; and along with great poverty is found usually abundance of riches. But I apprehend, if we were to have the smaller and non-manufacturing towns thoroughly examined, and accurately reported on, there would appear an amount of destitution, not equal of course in degree to that which prevails elsewhere, nor perhaps so demonstrable in figures and statistical tables, but fully as much calculated to engage the sympathies of one who knows the value of souls.

In a large city or town, consisting of several parishes, it will generally happen that in one or more there is a deficiency of church accommodation; which, for persons whose calculations are based solely upon figures, may make a case: but the experience of every one will suggest, that it is no uncommon thing for the parish next adjoining to have a superfluity of room in their church; and thus the abundance of one supplies what is lacking to the other. Besides, it is notorious that in these large towns masses of persons are congregated, who are by birth and education aliens to our faith.

But contrast, my Lord, with this the condition of the small market town, which, with a population of three thousand, a vicarage of 120*l.*, without any parsonage-house, has accommodation for about seven hundred in the church; which, however, being parcelled out into pews, is not really available to that extent. The only persons above the rank of tradesmen in the town, besides the half-famished Clergyman (who is probably obliged to take pupils, in order to eke out a scanty maintenance for his family), are two apothecaries, three attorneys, one land-surveyor, and two persons, who having made enough in business to secure to themselves a decent competency, have adopted the motto, "Live while you live;" interpreting the said motto to mean, that as they have none to whom they care to leave their money, and, moreover, are indebted solely, as they think, to their industry for procuring it, they are resolved to spend it in that way which promises to minister most largely to their personal comforts and enjoyments. In a town so circumstanced, the two or three hundred families excluded from the parish church, have no neighbouring place of worship of which to avail themselves. The Clergyman and churchwardens shrug their shoulders when asked for seats; the retired tradesmen above-named have no thought of relinquishing an inch of their square, well-cushioned pews; that a Bishop and Archdeacon possessing jurisdiction exist, is a fact barely known, certainly not understood, in the town. And the sole alternative for the unprovided families *seems* to be, either wholly to abstain from all acts of social worship, or to become partakers in the schism of some dissenters.

Your experience, my Lord, will, I am sure, bear me out in what I have stated. Would it not then be a great advantage, if each diocese had its authoritative "Notitia" at hand, in order that the many charitable and wealthy members of our Church might know the extent of the evil under which we are labouring; and where assistance is most needed? Indeed, were the matter placed in the proper light, and by the proper authorities, even before the two retired tradesmen above mentioned, I should not despair of, at least, a legacy on their decease.

It may appear at first sight that I am wandering from the matter in hand; but in point of fact every thing that tends to awaken us to a consciousness of the magnitude of the evil under which we labour, is, in so far, a justification of any proposed remedial measures: and this I must beg your Lordship to accept as my excuse, while I venture a little more into detail upon this point—the spiritual statistics (if I may so speak) of the agricultural districts. Let a *bonâ fide* survey be made of every diocese, which, without exaggerating or extenuating aught, should boldly and faithfully make known what is wanting in every parish, for the full and effectual preaching of the gospel, both to young and old, poor and rich, in a manner, as far as may be, not unbecoming the Lord of hosts; and I feel confident that the people would "willingly offer themselves." A single specimen would almost be enough to rouse the whole Church; for let even the best conditioned diocese be taken, and we should find a state of things that would quite appal us. For example, let the inquiry embrace the following heads:—1. Churches; 2. Schools; 3. Clergy. Concerning the first, let it be inquired, If there are churches enough in the parish? (2.) If the church (or churches) is capable, according to its present arrangement, of accommodating all the *families* in the place? (3.) If the church (or churches) is in a state of good repair, and decent order? 2. Concerning schools, let it be inquired, If the different classes of society—the middle as well as the lower—are provided with suitable means for the education of their children? 3. Lastly, let it be ascertained, If there is a sufficient number of Clergy? If they are well and sufficiently paid for their services? and are capable, as respects age and health, and other causes (as well moral as physical), of exercising[*] an efficient pastoral superintendence over the flock? Various minor points of inquiry might also, at the same time, be embraced; as, *e.g.* the amount contributed by the various parishes to the Church fund, or the sum of money raised annually as sacramental alms, and other matters which the Bishops might think it desirable to ascertain. With documentary evidence of this sort in their possession, they would be able to put forth an appeal that could not be resisted; and it may, perhaps, be allowed a simple Presbyter to express his opinion, that no effectual remedy can be applied to the present evil, disorganized state in which we are circumstanced, till the heads of the Church vindicate for themselves, more generally, their high place and station, as the responsible pastors of *every* parish in their respective dioceses. I know that their hands are most inconveniently tied by acts of parliament; and I am aware, also, that some Clergymen are to be found,

---

[*] It would not be necessary publicly to expose the names of the inefficients: it would be enough to give their aggregate number.

who will stand to the utmost upon their presbyteral rights. Still, it appears to me, that the Bishops have themselves very much to blame for the existence of this disposition. They have leaned hitherto too much upon acts of parliament; but let them try a moral and spiritual appeal to the consciences of their Clergy, and I verily believe that they will be met by no unwilling or tardy obedience. Both Clergy and laity are waiting to be led. There is, throughout the land, a vast amount of religious energy pent up, which desires only a safe channel in which to pour itself forth. The vast numbers of unauthorized schemes, which are rife in the Church, testify to this fact. But people have for some time observed, with regret, that the good which they do is not unmixed with evil; the condition of conscientious Churchmen is beginning to be something like that of the Egyptians, during the plague of darkness: "they saw not one another; neither rose any from their place." How great a boon, then, would they consider it, if the Bishops, in their several dioceses, might be induced to set themselves boldly forward, and direct how the Lord's work may best be done!

The great extent of the English dioceses has, at present, rendered this almost impossible. Would not the Bishops then, my Lord, find Colleges of Fellows a most useful institution in this respect also? An officer appointed immediately by the Bishop, from his college, would be able to report more impartially and fearlessly than could the rural dean, who, being commonly a neighbour, is restrained by personal feelings from exposing very rigorously the imperfections of his brethren. The complement of diocesan officers is, at present, so inadequate, that it is difficult for a Bishop to acquire anything like an individual knowledge of the several parishes committed to his care; and yet, without such a minute and familiar knowledge, it is obvious that the affairs of the Church cannot be satisfactorily conducted. Bishops have not been able to become personally acquainted even with their Clergy; and it is owing to the want of accurate and authentic information that they have of late years confined the exercise of the Episcopal authority to cases of public scandal; leaving each Clergyman to manage the affairs of his parish as may suit his own views of ministerial responsibility. Your Lordship, I am sure, has sincerely regretted this apparent necessity. The office of a Bishop, we know, is to set in order *whatever* (without exception) "is wanting," in every parish throughout his diocese; a commission which must not only justify, but require him, in the sight of God (independently of human, and especially civil laws) habitually to inquire of each individual Clergyman, whether aught is "wanting" in that sphere in which he is set to labour, for the full and effectual building up of his people in the faith and fear of God. For example, not only, I would humbly submit, can there be no impropriety or want of delicacy in the Bishop informing Mr. A. that a school, or second service, or sermon (as it may be) is grievously wanted in his parish; or that his curate, Mr. B. would be better suited for a different sphere of duty; that the singing is improperly conducted, or the house of God not well cared for, although the matter has not been formally presented by the churchwardens: but I am sure that every thoughtful person will admit, that we should not rest satisfied till we have placed our Bishops in a condition fearlessly and effectually to exercise such interference. We, the Church at large that is, have tied the hands of our Bishops, and it behoves us (and therefore, my Lord, it is that I venture to address you) to do what we can, each in his own sphere, to release them. And, further, I would desire by all means to strengthen their position. The object of this letter is to suggest a plan by which that end may be promoted; and should it fail in its immediate aim, it will not be without use, if it shall have the slightest influence in increasing the moral weight which shall be accorded them by willing Clergy and congregations: for I repeat, my Lord, what is indeed most obvious, that it is upon the inherent authority of his office, rather than upon legal privileges, that the successor of the apostles must ever rely. I say that this is obvious, partly because the law *can* only contemplate extreme cases, and cannot possibly provide for the innumerable contingencies and combinations of circumstances which are ever occurring in the world; and partly because (as painful experience in the Dean of York's case proves) legal authority is not unfrequently purchased at the expense of a much more valuable and earlier right, inherent in the office by divine appointment, not given by man, and therefore only revocable by him, when the holders have consented to receive it as *his* gift, and to exercise it in *his* name.

4. The bearing which the proposed plan would have upon the education of Clergy, is a subject of such extreme importance, as to demand particular notice. The colleges which have been opened in some dioceses, contemplate the giving a professional education to candidates for the ministry, who have already taken a degree at one of the universities. It would be difficult to over-rate the value of such institutions: they would be included, as has been already stated, in the foundation of colleges of Bishops' Fellows; and the end attained with much greater economy. But it appears to me, that the wants of the Church are much more extensive than what these institutions propose to supply. Their object is to improve clerical education, but in improving it, they necessarily increase the expense of it; while what we require is a facility for educating *more* Clergy, and *at a less cost*, as well as the improvement of existing means; and one of the most difficult problems to solve (as the experiments at Durham and Lampeter testify) is, how this object can be secured. Do I say too much, my Lord, in asserting that the retired situation, the strict discipline, and the holy character imparted to the place, by the residence of the Bishop and his fellows, would afford the best possible opportunities for accomplishing this great object, equally with the former? The formation of the character would here proceed concurrently with the needful instruction of the mind; and in lieu of the previous academical course, it might be required, as a condition of receiving testimonials from the Bishop, that the diaconate of a person, so prepared for the ministry, should extend over a certain defined period (say seven or ten years), during which period he might be at the entire disposal of the Bishop who ordained him. The annual expenses of a pupil need not exceed 40*l.*; and two or three years' uninterrupted residence (provided that care be taken in the first selection) would serve both to test the

habits and dispositions, and to communicate an education by no means despicable.

The proposed colleges might likewise afford an asylum for superannuated Clergy. I believe that many an aged Clergyman, who was free from domestic ties, would willingly make way for a more efficient successor, provided that he could enjoy such a dignified retirement for his declining years. Institutions designed for this express purpose are common in Roman-catholic countries.

In estimating the cost of establishing colleges of Bishops' Fellows, it must be remembered that they would be the means of superseding the clerical college, the training school, and (partially, at least,) the Diocesan Association for providing Additional Curates: a considerable saving would thus be effected. But what really appears now to be called for at the hands of an Administration professing to be favourable to the Church, is the repeal, or at least a modification of the Mortmain statutes. The intention of these statutes, it is well known, was to restrain lands from falling into the hands of monasteries, or other clerical corporations, either sole or aggregate, which, as regarded the military defence of the country—a matter at the date of their enactment of capital importance—were "as good as dead." With the extinction of the feudal system ceased the custom of requiring every holder of land to attend the summons of the lord under whom he held; and with it ceased the justice and policy of the Mortmain statutes, as the very name was no longer applicable. It is surely, then, not too much to ask, in this hour of the Church's need, that these statutes should be either permanently modified, or, at least for a time, repealed. Let every possible opening for abuse be rigidly guarded against, for the sake, not of heirs expectant, but of the Church, which is the real sufferer in all proceedings that are not upright and straightforward. For instance, let it be required that notice should be sent of any intended bequest of land or monies to the Church, to the office of one of the masters in chancery, whose business it should be to acquaint the nearest of kin how the property in question is disposed of, or any equivalent measure which the necessities of the case may seem to require. But let not so unjust a law as the 9 Geo. II. c. 36, stain our statute-book: it is contrary to common sense that the same number of Clergy who were sufficient when the population of England did not exceed four millions, can be adequate to the pastoral charge of sixteen millions; and with what conscience can the State, so long as this inadequacy lasts, forbid the free-will offerings of pious Christians? It is no necessary consequence that this boon should be extended to the institutions of dissenters, or even to ordinary charitable foundations. It rests with those who would advocate such an extension to show that the cases possess equal claims. The very name of an "Established" Church implies that it should enjoy some preference at the hands of those who establish it.

It is characteristic of the present plan that it admits either of larger or smaller application. In its full development it would require the exemplification of the whole church system around the person of the Bishop; but it might be commenced on a much smaller scale: the Bishop might commence with gathering around him all the existing societies which are at present engaged in supplying any of the wants which the College of his Fellows would hereafter meet. For this purpose a small building fund would alone be necessary; and, according as fresh objects are attempted in the diocese, might the college be enlarged. Here would be a nucleus for perfecting and carrying out the diocesan system; and no great number of years, I am satisfied, would elapse, ere the liberality of Churchmen would furnish the means for its full completion.

In this persuasion, though at the risk of some repetition, I shall conclude with briefly summing up the entire advantages which might be expected to result from the plan, if fully carried out.

1. First must be placed the strength that would accrue to the Bishop, from thus surrounding him with learned men and laborious and faithful officers, and making him more conspicuously the centre of light and charity to the whole diocese.

2. The more orderly and effectual organization and working of the various diocesan* societies.

3. A diocesan library would be among the first-fruits of this plan, of which branches might shortly be established in the several archdeaconries or deaneries.

4. A hall or room would be afforded for synodical meetings of the Clergy.

[Nos. 3 and 4 are wants very severely felt by the Clergy; the former increasingly in proportion as clerical education is improved. Periodical meetings of neighbouring Clergy are becoming general; and there is a growing wish to make them partake more of a catholic and ecclesiastical character. A tavern is certainly not the proper place for such solemn convocations; nor are private houses, where the courtesies of society are apt to interrupt the order of the Church. I would hope that the central hall or chamber might shortly act as a model for such buildings in every deanery; and an annual diocesan synod lead the way to authorized quarterly decanal chapters.]

5. The Bishop would have it in his power to afford temporary supplies of Clergy to overgrown parishes and distant and neglected hamlets.

6. The number of Clergy might be materially increased.

[A learned Clergy is indispensable; and few persons would dispute the wisdom of the rule which requires a candidate for holy orders to produce not only testimonials of good conduct, but also a certificate of having satisfied the examiners in the schools of one of our universities, and of having attended a course of theological lectures in the same place. But the wants of the Church, at the present time, are so manifold, and the variety of stations to be filled, both at home and abroad, so great, that it appears absolutely necessary both to increase the number of candidates, and to extend the range from which they are taken. At the same time an efficient check is required as to the character of persons admitted. Now, what could be so proper a place for breeding up a body of devout and useful associates in the ministry as "the Bishop's school?" None should

---

* This would be especially necessary in the case of weekly collections being made at the offertory, as recommended by Mr. Gresley and Mr. Palmer.

be admitted but young men of earnest piety and good natural abilities; and with the strict discipline, and unintermitted application, which persons so circumstanced would gladly adopt, a three years' residence, even if they came ignorant both of Latin and Greek, would, I am sure, turn them out as good proficients in classical learning and theology as some who pass in the examinations at Cambridge. The whole expense need not exceed 120*l*.]

7. A clerical college, in the ordinary sense of that term, for the benefit of those who have already graduated at one of the universities, would be an essential element of the plan.

8. A very cheap school for orphans and others duly recommended, might be an addition. The Jesuits opened schools for gratuitous education; and how could the charity of a christian Bishop be more usefully or appropriately displayed?

9. Next comes the school for training masters. As these already exist in most dioceses, the transfer of the site is all that would be required. The rent of house and salary of master would then be entirely saved; and I need scarcely observe that there would be other indirect savings, to a considerable amount, in conducting the various branches of education upon the same spot. For instance, the training-masters would assist in the orphan school, and the theological graduate-students would aid in superintending the studies of those candidates for the ministry who had enjoyed less advantage than themselves. One Fellow might probably overlook more than one school.

10. The inspection of parochial schools, a matter which promises to be of much difficulty as well as importance, would be provided for.

11. There would be a refuge for worn-out Clergy, being unencumbered with families.

Such, my Lord, is an outline of the plan which I venture to propose to your consideration, and (if you permit) to that of the rulers and members of the English Church. That it must suffer much from the feebleness and humble station of its present advocate, no one is more feelingly conscious than myself. God, however, will not allow even the single talent to be buried in the ground. In this conviction, I am emboldened to contribute[*] my mite towards building up "the old waste places" of Jerusalem. I feel sure that nothing which I have recommended is, in point of principle, an innovation. The present plan contemplates no alienation of funds from the bequest of donors—no disruption of ancient associations; and should it fail in producing the immediate end which it proposes, even in a single instance, it may yet strengthen the conviction that something is required to be done; and that this will be most satisfactorily accomplished by rigidly observing the order, discipline, and unity of the Church, and by more strongly developing the Episcopal system.

But perhaps it may be said, "Your plan has been anticipated many centuries ago. It was the object of cathedral institutions to furnish bodies of men who should at once be a council to the Bishop, preside

---

[*] The total disuse of the Ecclesiastical Synod affords, perhaps, a better justification of such a step in a presbyter than some persons imagine.

over education, and be frequent in preachings, 'as well in other churches as in their own cathedral;'* and if they have ceased to answer the ends for which they were founded, let the visitors see to their restoration." I admit, my Lord, that in some at least of our cathedrals, all the objects proposed in the present plan do really fall within the meaning of their statutes and charters of incorporation. I admit that where the Bishop really presides in his own church, and the chapter includes his archdeacons, his two chancellors (as the statutes of Canterbury cathedral provide),—the one to defend the legal rights of the Church, the other to preside over "all sorts of literature,"—together with a scholarchus; where the grammar-school flourishes in the precincts, exhibitioners are maintained at the universities, and the " Prælector Theologicus" efficiently discharges his duties; a college of "Bishops' Fellows" might be superfluous: provided there be a willingness on the part of those whom it may concern, acting upon the *spirit* of their charters and statutes, to accommodate themselves to the altered circumstances of the present day. I admit all this, and claim it as a remarkable illustration that what I have ventured to recommend is strictly in harmony with the best precedents of the Church. But no one will know better than your Lordship, that though it is possible, in the statutes of one or other of our cathedrals, to find specified all the objects for which I contend, it would be very unfair, by a sort of cumulative argument, to make any one, still less all those institutions, responsible for carrying them into operation. Moreover, there are other causes which render it impossible:—1. The chapters are so reduced in the numbers of their members as to be almost inadequate even to the due celebration of divine worship in their respective churches. Any increase of duties is altogether out of the question.—2. But, further, it is matter of notoriety that the connexion between the Bishops and the chapters over which they nominally preside is not of that nature as to warrant the hope of any very harmonious co-operation, in fields which, if not new, have at least for a long space of time been unoccupied. Such a state of things, your Lordship is well aware, is of no recent origin. It may be traced to the times when popes endeavoured too successfully to detach the regular clergy from allegiance to their diocesans, in order to make them the more ready instruments of the see of Rome. Bishops and chapters have never worked cordially together; and a want of harmony, which was originally the result of jealousy, is now, as it were, necessarily perpetuated upon the conscientious principle of maintaining inviolate, privileges which have descended by prescription. In the ancient possessions and the proper constitution of the Church, there were abundant means for effecting all the objects we desire, and in the best way; but of the former she has long since been robbed by regal violence and grasping lay impropriation; and the latter has been more recently impaired by the well-meant but questionable† measures of the Ecclesiastical Commissioners. Under these circumstances, it

---

* See Statutes of the Cathedral Church of Ely, chapter ix., quoted in Mr. Selwyn's pamphlet, "Are Cathedral Institutions Useless?"

† By a sort of fatality, one of their *very few* confessedly good recommendations has been suffered to drop: I mean that for the extinction of peculiars.

behoves the true friends of the Church to restore the breaches that have been made, both in the one and in the other, as much as possible in the spirit of those first architects who, under *the* " Great Master Builder," carried out the system of her policy; and I repeat, my Lord, it is my earnest hope that nothing will be found in these pages contrary to that spirit.

My Lord, with great respect, I beg to submit them to your consideration, and to that of your brethren in the Episcopal College; and am,

My Lord,
Your Lordship's very obedient humble servant,
THOMAS CHAMBERLAIN.

CHRIST CHURCH, OXFORD,
Jan. 1, 1842.

THE DIVINE RIGHT OF TITHES THE TRUE PRINCIPLE, THE OFFERTORY THE REAL INSTRUMENT, OF CHURCH EXTENSION.

No. V.

THE celebrated Mr. Fox suggested a whimsical reason why " *Concordiâ res parvæ crescunt* " was adopted as a motto by a celebrated school in London. The motto in question would seem to belong, *vi terminorum,* to the Shilling Fund (miscalled Church) Society, and perhaps some appropriate vignette, illustrative of its meaning, might adorn the circulars. Certainly a given number of shillings would constitute a sufficient fund to build a church; but I cannot think that *nine,* or *ninety-nine,* or any multiple of *nine,* shilling subscribers, can make the *ninth* part of a churchman. The following letters are, I must think, " christian or churchman remembrancers:" they will tell their own story :—

" *October* 20, 1841.

" REV. SIR,—I beg to acknowledge the receipt of your circular, applying for a trifle towards the building a church. I trust, however, you will not think me backward, in the promotion of so good a work as that of church building, if I decline to contribute towards the one you have in contemplation.

" My reasons for so doing are these :—

" 1stly. I consider my own parish has the first claim on all my abundance. Property has, in my opinion, a local responsibility attached to it, binding every one to make a proportionate provision for the services of God in the place where his property is situate. Of course I do not mean to say that if any one has really more than is wanted for his own parish, he is not to give elsewhere. I think, however, if such be the case, his diocese has the next claim.

" 2dly. I have a strong objection to your plan of collecting money. I consider it one of those temporary expedients which aid in continuing a narrow system, already too unfortunately prevalent ;—a system which has no regard to the proportion with which God has blest us, and which we must get rid of, for one more wholesome, if we would see good fully done.

" Perhaps you will say, 'What would you do?' My answer is, Turn to the Bible and the Church, and see what is there taught—taught by the Bible as to proportion; and by the Church as to the manner of collecting. In the Bible we find this rule of proportion—the tithing of property. It is a rule of divine origin, and the one, therefore, we should follow. It may, perhaps, be difficult, in these anti-tithe, and therefore, I fear, anti-Bible days, to teach people this doctrine; but better notions will, I hope, some day again find their way into men's minds and hearts, and then we may look for more good. In the mean time, however, we—the Clergy—should teach, with proper courage, this divine rule of proportion in giving to the Church, while we teach the responsibility which every man lies under for the right use of his property to God's honour and glory. That every man ought to contribute some part of his property for the services of religion, few, I willingly believe, will deny. The question is, what part? Now, as all men are not blest alike, they ought not all to give alike, but each according as God has prospered him. There must, therefore, be some general rule of proportion between property and gifts. This rule we can find in the Bible. Tithing is the rule of that book. It may be that, for a time, men will not understand this principle, and that an appeal to them on it will not at first appear to answer. The principle is new to the minds of many of our days, though, in fact, it is at least as old as Melchisedek; and men do not understand it, because they have sought out inventions of their own, instead of going to the Bible to be taught. We must, however, work in faith, believing that the right principle, properly persevered in, will assuredly do the most good. So persuaded am I of this, that I feel certain if any one would begin, and give a tithe of his property to help in building and endowing a church where such property was situate, the example would soon be followed, and, having the blessing of God, because according to the Bible, be gradually effectual to the relief of those spiritual necessities so many places now labour under in the want of churches and Church ministration. Such is the rule of proportion in giving to be found in the Bible—a rule, not the invention of man, but the appointment of God. Such is the rule we should follow, never reducing it, except through absolute necessity; but, of course, exceeding it when we can, as the lesser duty alway implies the greater.

"Let us now see what the Church teaches, I may say, commands, as to the manner of collecting. Her rule is also in the Bible. We have in the Communion Service the offertory sentences; and a direction in the Rubric that they be read from the altar whenever that service is used, and that, at every time of such reading, a collection be made 'for pious and charitable uses.' These sentences regularly read through, and regularly impressed upon the people, and a collection made, will be sure to answer in the long run, though to modern minds the practice may be strange at first. They are Scripture, and those that value Scripture will both hear and take heed how they hear them. Such people, too, will desire to have their gifts blest by the prayers of the Church to the service of God, and have a greater faith in their efficacy, when so offered and blest, than if given in a common worldly way. The Rubric, too, which directs these sentences to be read, for the purpose of making a weekly collection, is in strict conformity with Scripture and apostolical practice. 'Upon the first day of the week, let every one of you lay by him in store as God has prospered him.' (1 Cor. xvi. 2.) To give in this way is to give in faith, and with good security of having our gifts sanctified unto efficacy. Here, then, in the practice of the Church throughout all ages we have a rule; one I believe, as well as hope, will be again restored. It is not dead, for it cannot die. It sleeps, I lament, though I rejoice it gives symptoms of awaking. If we will but awaken it, we shall find it still strong. These ways of the Bible and the Church are the old ways, the good ways, which have been from the beginning, and will be to the end. They are the only ways by which we can hope effectually to do the great work now required to be done in this country. Narrow systems and temporary expedients will fail us; 'they have been weighed in the balance and found wanting;' but these ways will never fail us, if we will but follow them, not doubting but believing.

"May I then take the liberty of suggesting to you to follow my plan for collecting money, and try and provide for the building and endowment of your new church upon these principles. You possibly might find some pious churchman in your parish who would be glad to give the tithe of one year's income at least, whether derived from real property or profits in trade, in this scriptural way; and rejoice also at the opportunity of having his offering sanctified to the service of God at the altar of the church. This is possible; I cannot but believe such men are to be found. It is next, however, to certain, that collections at the altar from the faithful (and I want them from no other) will answer your end, in a little time. Some perseverance will be necessary: but, in the end, I feel convinced you would succeed, because you would be working, not in a worldly, but in a religious way.

"Being an entire stranger, I feel I ought to make my humble apologies for the liberty I have taken of making these remarks. I feel assured, however, you will grant me your pardon, when I say that these remarks are the result of much thought on the subject of church building and church ministration, and, of course, of much desire for the increase of our Saviour's kingdom, and the honour of Almighty God.

"I beg also to add that, though I do not approve your plan for raising the necessary sum for your undertaking, I admire the zeal which has led you to try and raise another temple for the service of the Almighty.

"I subscribe myself, Rev. Sir, with many apologies,
"Your faithful and humble servant,
"T. L."

"REV. SIR,—I thank you for your kindness in answering my letter, and in sending me your report and your sermon. By your answer you seem to think I intimated that 'the splendid edifices which cover our country and Europe were erected exclusively by the means my letter suggested.' I do not find my letter to be so exclusive in its opinions. Great munificence may have been exercised without adherence to the letter of the divine law of tithes, and without a positive eucharistic blessing upon it; but that munificence was exercised when tithes and eucharistic blessing were recognised and appreciated, and it was of the same spirit with them. Since these divine ways have been despised or forgotten, the offerings to the Church have lamentably diminished, the dissenting voluntary principle, against which your sermon contends, has become more general, has infected all, and the 'land perisheth for lack of knowledge.' Little things have taken the place of great ones, shillings are given instead of £50 or £100, and £10 instead of £10,000. I wish to see the munificent principle brought into operation again; but I do not think we ever shall see it, so long as we keep to systems whose tendency is to make men satisfied with giving trifles. If we can teach men the divine right of tithes, we may hope to see them with truer notions touching the duty of giving, in proportion as they are blessed of God: and if we can teach them the beauty of having their offerings sanctified at the altar, whenever they can, according to the primitive way, we may hope to see them come forward more cheerfully and more munificently with their free-will and their thank offerings. Then we may look for more churches and more endowments. We should teach men to do, as your sermon describes the Jewish and early Christian churches to have done. But if the Clergy leave the divine right of tithes and eucharistic offerings untaught, and satisfy ourselves with asking for shillings, and selling trifles at Bazaars, we cannot expect men to have either right knowledge or real munificence. Real munificence is occasionally found in men of the present day, but I believe it is confined to those who are alive to the principles I have asserted. "T. L."

How sad it is that we should be contracting this miserable habit of sewing jack-daw's feathers on the majestic plumage of the Church!

"At the conclusion of the Nicene Creed, a Rubric gives the following directions:—'Then shall follow the sermon,' &c. 'Then' (that is, after the sermon is concluded) 'shall the priest return to the Lord's Table and begin the Offertory.' Another Rubric directs, that whilst the sentences of Scripture are reading, the deacon, churchwardens, or other fit person appointed for that purpose, shall receive the alms for the poor, and *other devotions* of the people, in a decent bason provided for that purpose, and reverently bring it to the priest, who shall humbly PRESENT and place it upon the Holy Table.

" Now these Rubrics have been for the most part disregarded, and our congregations have been but seldom reminded of the duty, or permitted to enjoy the privilege, of making their contributions for charitable and religious purposes an offering to God. Other ways of making collections of our own devising* have been substituted for this wholesome and pious ordinance of the Church, and they have proved lamentably deficient;† as (not to cite other instances) the notorious want of church room and clergymen in populous districts amply testifies. A reflecting mind would be apt to consider that this state of things had some connexion with the prevailing neglect, and would feel persuaded that Almighty God would withhold His blessing from the irregular exertions of His servants; and would only then ‡ bestow it in all its fulness, when, according to the directions of the Rubric, *continual* appeals were made to the people in the words of Scripture from the altar. Should any one doubt the possibility of reviving this all but forgotten ordinance, the answer is obvious, ' what has been done, may be done again,' and ' to faith all things are possible.' Only then let the Clergy, according to their solemn engagements, obey the Church in the spirit of faith, and God will stir up the wills of His people to supply all our need."—*See a Sermon preached at Harlow Church, by the Rev. J. C. Stafford, B.D.* (Rivingtons, 1840.)

The following is extracted from a recent publication:—

" ' Perhaps,' says Judge Blackstone, ' considering *the degenerate state of the world* in general, it may be more beneficial to the English Clergy to found their title on the law of the land, than upon any divine right whatsoever, unacknowledged and unsupported by temporal sanctions.'—*Commentaries*, book ii. c. 3.

---

* It has been a very common practice of late to make collections from pew to pew during the singing a psalm or hymn appointed for the occasion. It is surprising that many who have done this should not have thought of returning to the use of the Offertory, as the proper way.

† We need only refer to the second Report of the Metropolis Church Fund for confirmation of this assertion. "The Committee are constrained to confess their disappointment that it (the object in view) should not have received a more liberal measure of assistance in quarters where they were fully entitled to look for large contributions." (Pp. 9, 10, &c.) They at the same time speak of the decrease of subscriptions during the last year, a painful consideration, when they also state that, "presuming the population will increase in the ratio it has done in the last ten years, by the time the churches at present provided for are completed, there will be a greater number of persons destitute of the means of worship than there were when this fund was first established." While noticing this, it is pleasing to observe, in the list of subscriptions following the Report, several instances of a better principle of giving, and such as it is one design of this sermon to encourage; though it is to be hoped that the time will come when such and all other gifts will be mostly made in obedience to the directions of the Church in the Rubric.

	£	s.	d.
A cheerful giver, by the Bishop of London	5	0	0
First fruits of increase	16	10	0
One very grateful for religious instruction, by Rev. W. Bennett	5	0	0
Jewels of a Clergyman's wife	51	0	0
Produce of the sale of a pair of diamond earrings	35	0	0
Spe gaudentes	5	5	0
An humble offering of gratitude from a woman	100	0	0
H. W. " Lay not up for thyself treasure on earth"	100	0	0
Money, the right to which seemed questionable	30	0	0
&c. &c.			

‡ 2 Chron. xxxi. 20, 21. "And thus did Hezekiah throughout all Judah, and wrought that which was good and right and truth before the Lord his God. And in every work that he began in the service of the house of God, and in the law, and in the commandments, to seek his God, he did it with all his heart, AND PROSPERED."

As if Christianity could be said to be propagated in that heart or country where this *degenerate* spirit was allowed to exist. But

'Ætas parentum, pejor avis, tulit
Nos nequiores.'

The tithe system, as established by law, has in these days been denounced in no measured terms by Dr. Chalmers, in his 'Bridgewater Treatise.' I will here place his sentiments in contrast with those of our Hooker.

HOOKER.

"We might somewhat marvel what the apostle Paul should mean to say that *covetousness is idolatry*, if the daily practice of men did not show that, whereas nature requireth God to be honoured with wealth, we honour for the most part wealth as God. . . . Unless, by a kind of continual tribute, we did acknowledge God's dominion, it may be doubted that in a short time men would learn to forget whose tenants they are, and imagine that the world is their own absolute, free, and independent inheritance. . . . . And as Abraham gave voluntarily, as Jacob vowed to give God tithes, so the law of Moses did require at the hands of all men the self-same kind of tribute, the tenth of their corn, wine, oil, fruit, cattle, and whatsoever increase His Heavenly Providence should send. Insomuch, that Painims being herein followers of their steps, paid tithes likewise. I imagine we that this was for no cause done, or that there was not some special inducement, to judge the tenth of our worldly profits the most convenient for God's portion? . . . . The Jews were accustomed to name their tithes the *hedge* of their riches. Albeit a hedge do only fence and preserve that which is contained, whereas their tithes and offerings did more, because they procured increase of the heap out of which they were taken. God demanded no such debt for his own need, but for their only benefit that owe it; wherefore, detaining the same, they hurt not him whom they wrong; and themselves, whom they think they relieve, they wound; except men will haply affirm that God did, by fair speeches and large promises, delude the world in saying (Mal. iii.), *Bring ye all the tithes into the storehouse, that there may be meat in mine house* (deal truly, defraud not God of his due, but bring all), *and prove if I will not open unto you the windows of heaven, and*

CHALMERS.

"Of the two instances that we are now to produce, in which law hath made a deviation from nature, and done in consequence a tremendous quantity of evil, the first is the tithe system of England. . . . . There are few reformations that would do more to sweeten the breath of English society, than the removal of this sore annoyance—the brooding fountain of so many heartburnings and so many festerments, by which the elements of an unappeasable warfare are ever at work between the landed interest of the country and far the most important class of its *public functionaries!* and, what is the saddest perversity of all, those whose office it is, by the mild persuasions of Christianity, to train the population of our land in the lessons of love, and peace, and righteousness—they are forced by the necessities of a system which many of them deplore into the attitude of extortioners; and placed in that very current, along which a people's hatred and a people's obloquy are wholly unavoidable. Even under the theocracy of the Jews, the system of tithes was with difficulty upholden; and many are the remonstrances which the gifted seers of Israel held with its people, for having brought of the lame and the diseased as offerings. Such, in fact, is the violence done by this system to the possessory feelings, that a *conscientious submission to its exactions may be regarded as a most decisive test of religious obedience:* such an obedience, indeed, as was but ill maintained even in the days of Hebrew polity, although it had the force of temporal sanctions, with the miracles and manifestations of a presiding Deity to sustain it." (And have not we too a presiding Deity, though he be as a God that hideth himself?) "Unless by the express appointment of heaven," (will a dutiful and affectionate child be guided by nothing but *express* appointment?)

pour down upon you an immeasurable blessing."—Book v. 79.

" this yoke of Judaism, unaccompanied as it now is by the peculiar and preternatural enforcement of that dispensation, ought never to have been perpetuated in the days of Christianity."— Vol. ii. c. 7.

"It will be seen that the two foregoing views coincide with each other as to the *test of religious obedience;* they differ, in that the one gets rid of the duty and the blessing, the other retains both. Let the reader judge by the Bible, and the Bible only, which system savours most of the Spirit of God, and which of the spirit of the world, and let him make his choice accordingly."

Would that it had been put into the heart of her Majesty to have made her offering of gratitude, on a recent occasion, at the altar in St. Paul's cathedral! *Thanksgiving*, in the strict and proper sense of the word, means the *offering* of a real gift, whereas the thanksgiving of women after child-birth is now commonly nothing more than thanks *saying*, with or without the accompaniment of a FEE! The gift (offered, of course, in the right manner and upon the right principle) would seem to be the essential part of the service. Mere words are not adequate means of expressing a real spirit of thankfulness. Naaman's history will tell us this, as assuredly it will rise up in judgment against us, and condemn our present practice. Here I will illustrate the Church principle by an extract from the works of an author whom I have quoted on a former occasion:—

" Indeed 'he that *giveth alms he sacrifices praise*,' says the son of Sirach, (Ecclus. xxxv. 2.) And praise is a blessing. But to bless is to *honour* too. And '*honour the Lord with thy substance*,' says a wiser than the son of Sirach, (Prov. iv.) Something must be done to his *own* honour. Something given or offered to support that here among us. For to bless is to *give* thanks, and that intimates something to be *given* to him, as well as said or spoken to him. It will else be *verba dare* and not *gratias*, a mere cheating him of our thanks. As soon as *Naaman* the *Syrian* was cured of his leprosy, he begs of the prophet to accept a blessing for it. Nature had taught him God was to be blest so. (2 Kings v. 15.) When the captains of Israel had found, by their whole numbers, how God delivered them, they came with a *blessing* in their hands, *sixteen thousand seven hundred and fifty shekels of gold for the house of God.* (Numb. xxxi. 52.) David, and his people, the story tells us, *blest* him *so* too, (Prov. xxix. 20, 21,) *offered* incredible sums of gold and silver for the service of the house of God. And let me tell you, without *begging* for it, that the house of God being now by this visit in the text (Luke i. 68, 69,) made the very *office* of salvation, where he daily visits us, and entertains us with his body and blood, with holy conference and discourses, where he seals us every day till the day of redemption, and offers us all the means of salvation, there can be no way of blessing God, so answerable and proportionable to his thus blessing us, as *thus* blessing him again."—*Sermons by Dr. Mark Frank.* London: 1672.

"'Of offerings there are two kinds,' says Mede, 'accepted under the law and required under the gospel, *eucharistical* and *euctical* or *votal*. Eucharistical offerings are such whose end is thanksgiving to God for benefits received. Euctical, such as are made to God when we come to pray before him, that he might accept our supplications, and we find favour in his sight.'"

Why do we hear nothing of vows in these days? Is not the practice sanctioned by Scripture? Why then do we make the word of God of none effect by our traditions? Why are not vows now to be made and to be paid upon our receiving any blessing which we may innocently desire? Are we not casuists enough to distinguish between a promised gift and a bribe? We do not put edge tools into children's hands! But are we never to throw away our childish principles, and learn in this case to be in nature children, and in understanding men? But this subject requires much consideration, though I treat it only in a cursory way; it being the object of these papers, not so much to discuss the subjects to which they relate, but to induce my readers to discuss them, and I endeavour to do this either by calling attention to Church rules or to what others have said, or by throwing out a few hints or suggestions, which occur to my own mind.

ON THE PROSPECTS OF THE CHURCH OF ENGLAND.
No. III.

THAT the real dangers of the Church arise, not so much from the principles or tendencies of political parties, as from her own utter inadequacy to meet the wants of the population of this country, has been shown in the preceding articles. The existence of so vast a mass of people without any religious instruction, or at least without any instruction which is calculated to make them friendly to the Established Church, and to attach them to the existing frame of society—this is the deep, the permanent, the overwhelming evil under which we are labouring, and which, if not remedied in time, can have but one issue—the destruction of all our institutions, and the overthrow of society itself. Unless we go to the root of the evil—unless measures are taken without delay to probe and to heal thoroughly this wound of the body politic—we may prepare to bid farewell to all that we value and love best on earth. What we want is, some remedy that shall not produce a momentary feeling of satisfaction and relief, while it leaves the evil to multiply in silence, and only to break forth with renewed vehemence at some future time. We require some large and comprehensive measure of relief, based on a full view of the real facts of the case—some measure which shall provide not only for the present but for the future necessities of the Church.

It appears to be the common fault of plans for Church extension, that they are not based on any calculations of the actual wants of the country; and that they propose schemes which are either utterly inadequate, or in a great degree chimerical. There seems to be no notion of what the extent of our wants really is; and therefore it is very natural that people should satisfy themselves that this or that plan would be sufficient, and that it is very right and necessary to oppose some other plan which involves certain inconveniences. But were they fully aware of the extent of our wants, they would see that it is only by the combination of *every possible resource* that any impression can be made on the evil before us. They would feel that not one single channel of relief should be left untried; and that the *danger* of the Church ought to make us accept measures which may, perhaps, have some inconveniences—some evils; but which are essential to our preservation.

I have placed this question on comparatively low ground, because I am appealing to those who are, perhaps, accustomed to hear arguments referring chiefly to the preservation of the temporalities of the Church, and its connexion with the established framework of society in this country; but I would not limit my argument and my appeal to such motives. I would ask the moralist and the Christian to look on the millions of our countrymen to whom the blessings of pure religion, and the consolations which it imparts, are denied. I would appeal on behalf of ONE-THIRD of our population, and would ask, fearlessly, whether any interests, or objects whatever, can be put in comparison with the grand object of preaching the Gospel to so vast a multitude of *heathen* at our own doors, and united to us by so many ties? I have no hesitation in asserting, that this necessity exceeds, in every point of view, all others that can be alleged. This duty outweighs all other duties; and the danger which arises from its neglect or imperfect discharge is incalculably greater, both in reference to God and man, than any inconveniences, or any evils, which may be unavoidably caused in the attempt to perform it. I cannot but think that the supply of this deficiency is the first and leading question before the Church, and that nothing but positive *unlawfulness* in the means proposed for its remedy, should justify us in rejecting them. We are in the condition of one who is, with his family, starving for want of the necessaries of life, and who is obliged to assume the attitude of a suppliant for the charity of others, or if he possesses ornaments and luxuries, to part with them, however reluctantly, to supply his extreme necessities. In the hour of pressing want, we must be content for a time to part with much that we value, and look forward to some future period, when the sacrifices which we make to God may be more than repaired.

I have said that the necessitities of the Church are so overwhelming that we cannot dispense with aid from any quarter. Let us for a little space contemplate those wants, and see how far any of the sources of relief commonly looked to can be expected to assist us. Mr. Palmer has recently estimated the amount of population unprovided with instruction by the Church of England at SIX MILLIONS. His calculation proceeds on the assumption that the care of 1000 souls is, on an average, as much as each clergyman can well manage. It may, perhaps, admit of question, whether two clergymen by their united labours in a parish may not be able to attend efficiently to a population of more than 2000. I am inclined to think that they might instruct a population of 3000. In this point of view the above estimate may seem too high; but on the other hand, it decidedly falls short of the truth, in assuming that all clergymen whose parishes contain more than 300 souls, may be supposed to have 1000 souls under their care. There can be no doubt, that there are several thousands of parishes in which the population averages 500, or 600, instead of 1000; so that the calculation to which we allude, seems, on the whole, rather to fall short of the truth than to exceed it. We may therefore assume, that about six millions of our people are at present unprovided by the Church of England with spiritual aid and instruction.

Assuming that one-third of this population should be provided with sittings in church, and that those sittings might be obtained at the expense of not more than 5*l.* each (which is too low an estimate), we should require 10,000,000*l.* for additional churches *at this moment*. And if we suppose that 4000 clergy would be sufficient for the spiritual instruction of the above number of people, and place their salaries at not more than 150*l.* a-year each, on an average, there would be a permanent income of 600,000*l.* per annum requisite. If this income were to be produced by endowments, about 18,000,000*l.* would be necessary for that purpose. In addition to this, we may reckon the expense of clerical residences at three or four millions: so that, on the whole, we want about *thirty-two millions of money* to place the Church at this moment in the position which she ought to occupy!

But in addition to this, it should be observed, that the population of England and Wales is increasing at the rate of more than 200,000 annually. Supposing church-room to be provided for one-third of this number, at the same rate as above, it would require a sum of 350,000*l.* The salaries of 150 clergymen at 150*l.* each, would amount to 8000*l.*, and if arising from endowments, would require a sum of 200,000*l.* and upwards; to which we may add about 70,000*l.* for clerical residences. So that, on the whole, to provide for the increase of population would require upwards of 620,000*l.* per annum.

Let us take the expense of the next twenty years, supposing that it is wished to render the Church efficient by that time. The annual expense, just mentioned, would in the course of twenty years amount to a total of 12,400,000*l.*; and this, added to the sum which is requisite to supply our *existing* deficiency, would make, on the whole, nearly *forty-five millions* of money.

I have left out of view in this calculation any provision for new bishoprics, which would be obviously necessary if so large an addition were made to the clergy. Suppose only forty new sees erected (a number which would be greatly below our wants) and endowed with not more than 2000*l.* per annum each; the endowment of these sees alone would require a sum of more than two millions, and the erection of see-houses would amount to near half a million in addition.

On the whole, then, it appears that, to provide for the religious destitution of our people, even on the most moderate scale, in the next twenty years, would require an outlay of near *fifty millions of money, or an annual expense of about two millions and a half.*

I have entered into these details, 'because they are essentially necessary to every one who has to make up his mind on the question of Church extension. Were our wants *limited* in their extent—could they be met by an outlay of a few millions of money, the remedy might be comparatively easy. We might make our choice between various plans of Church extension, and reject all that involved inconveniences and disadvantages. We might rely entirely on the assistance of the State, or we might look to private liberality. But when the demand amounts to fifty millions of money, the question assumes altogether a different aspect. It presents itself in the light of a fearful and overwhelming necessity, which will exhaust every resource within our reach, and be after all to a great extent unsatisfied.

(1.) There are very many friends of the Church, who, acknowledging and deploring the extent of our spiritual necessities, are satisfied that the State is bound to supply the means of relief, and that there would be little difficulty in obtaining sufficient means, if the government were alive to the duty which it owes to religion and morality. They refer to the grant of twenty millions for the extinction of West Indian slavery, and are of opinion that nothing would be easier than the adoption of some similar measure in relief of our religious necessities. Now, in the first place, it may be observed, that the sum required for Church extension is *fifty* millions instead of *twenty*. It may be next remarked, that the above grant was carried by a *combination* of all political parties in the House of Commons, and that it was a positive *compensation* for injury done to property— a mere act of common honesty; and therefore stands on altogether different grounds, and experienced a reception altogether different from that which would await any proposition for making large grants for Church extension. In the latter case we should have large and powerful parties in parliament violently opposed to any grant. We should see them backed and supported by all the various classes of dissenters, Romanists, infidels, liberals, and economists in the country. If a conservative government were to make such a proposition, they would expose themselves to the imputation of extravagance in the use of the public money. Under present circumstances, it is needless to say, that it would be altogether out of the question. With a deficiency of near three millions in our income, and a debt of ten millions accumulated within the last three or four years, it is, of course, the first duty of government to bring the expenditure of the country to a level with its income, and therefore to avoid every expense which is not strictly essential. While the country is thus circumstanced, it is wholly impossible to enter on any schemes of amelioration and improvement which would involve expense. It may be years before our income and expenditure can be equalized, and it will be years more before the debt incurred by our present deficiency can be discharged. When that has been accomplished, it will remain to be seen what sort of relief parliament may be disposed to grant. When the finances of the country were in a comparatively flourishing state; and when a Tory minister, in a Tory House of Commons, proposed grants for Church extension; what was their amount? On one occasion, *a million* of money, doled out gradually: some years after, *half a million* in addition! This was the full extent of parliamentary bounty from 1818 to 1830, when the Tory government came to an end. It was at the rate of about 120,000*l*. per annum.

Let us again contemplate the case of the Church of Ireland. With what unwillingness did parliament grant *a million* for the relief of the starving Irish clergy, and the payment of a miserable per centage of the incomes which had been illegally withheld from them. How frequently was this act of most imperfect justice made the theme of angry declamation; and how rigidly were the unfortunate recipients of parliamentary bounty called to account for the loans which had been made them in the hour of their bitterest poverty. In the colonies we see the same disposition to refuse pecuniary aid to the Church. The grants to the Church in Canada have been materially reduced. There is not, apparently, in any political party a disposition to adopt large and liberal measures of relief towards the Church: even those individuals who may be considered, and who undoubtedly are, most friendly to her interests, have repeatedly declared, that she must not look to parliamentary aid until her own resources have been first made fully available.

If we contemplate the measures of parliament in reference to *education*, the same conclusions will be forced still more strongly upon us. Education is to parliament an object of first-rate importance: it is one in which all political parties unite. No one disputes that a very large proportion of the population in England and Ireland are without the means of education: and yet the sums granted annually for this most important and *most generally popular object*, have not, I believe, in any year exceeded 60,000*l*.—*i. e.* about 30,000*l*. for Ireland, and 25,000*l*. for England. I believe the Reports of the Commissioners for Education in Ireland alone have estimated their wants at more than ten times the income which has been voted to them by the House of Commons. Such is the disposition of the legislature with reference to pecuniary grants, even for objects on which there is comparatively little difference of opinion!

Now, with all these facts staring us in the face, it does seem most strange, that people will continue to lean on this broken reed. Parliament *cannot* do any thing for us for many years to come; and when it can, the relief will almost certainly be of so limited a nature, that it will be of comparatively little moment. Suppose parliament to commence eight or ten years hence with annual grants of 120,000*l*., as formerly; or even suppose it to *double* its former grants; what would this avail us, when, as has been shown, we want two millions and a half per annum, *from the present time*, to meet our wants in twenty years? We could not, at the most, look for the supply of more than a *tenth* of the income requisite, from parliamentary aid: and we could not expect even *that* aid, until our destitute population had increased from *six* to *eight* millions.

But, besides this: Is there not some reason for apprehending that parliamentary grants will not be made without some equivalent which may not be altogether palatable to the Church? We know that many churchmen look with no inconsiderable jealousy to such grants as tending to invest the State with greater powers over the Church than it already possesses—powers of scrutiny, of redistribution, of inspection in various forms. I have no very serious apprehensions that evil consequences must necessarily arise from such grants, but it is only right that the fact of the existence of such apprehensions should be known, and that their foundation should be maturely weighed and considered.

(2.) It seems to be the opinion of many persons, that the voluntary liberality of the well-disposed members of the Church would, if properly appealed to, produce funds amply sufficient for the supply of all our existing necessities; and in proof of this they refer to the great exertions which have been lately made in the way of building new churches. That much has been done in this respect is indeed most true, and it presents one of the most cheering features of the times in which we live. But how very small is the amount of what has been accomplished in comparison with what remains to be done! In the course of twenty-three years, which have elapsed since the Society for Building Churches was instituted, it has succeeded, *with the aid of a million and a half of public money,* in providing church accommodation *for less than a quarter* of the increase of our population. Let us suppose, that the various diocesan church building societies instituted within the last few years, have done *as much;* and we have then *one-half* of the increase of our population provided for. This is very well in itself: but we must remember, that independently of the public money already mentioned, there have been collections in church under the Queen's Letters for the above purpose, and also that the subscriptions for church building have been so liberal, that it is rather a question whether they can be kept up at their present amount, than whether they can be materially extended. If we suppose no more parliamentary grants to be made for some years, the utmost that voluntary subscriptions can do, will probably not provide for *half the increase of our population each year.*

It is very easy to talk of raising some hundreds of thousands of pounds in the year; but when we come to the point of actually raising such sums, is it quite so easily accomplished? An appeal was made some years since to the public to provide funds for the erection of churches in London. It appeared, that about 380 new churches were requisite in the metropolis; but the Bishop of London limited his claim to the very moderate number of 50; and it has been with the *greatest difficulty,* that in the course of four or five years the sum of 180,000*l.* has been raised for this purpose, leaving a considerable deficiency, which is still to be made good. Now, if there ever was a case which would have drawn forth public liberality on a large scale, it was surely this. Individuals felt the call, and even impoverished themselves to meet it; but on the whole, it was near proving a failure. An appeal was made to supply only *an eighth part* of the spiritual destitution of London; and that appeal has scarcely succeeded. In the mean time the population of that vast metropolis has been annually increasing at a rate which will probably render its destitution as great as ever, when the above plan has been fully carried into effect. We may, from this instance, form some notion of the effectiveness of the system of voluntary contribution in meeting the wants of the Church. By gigantic efforts we might possibly provide for the increase of population; but we should not touch that wide waste of desolation—the permanent destitution of SIX MILLIONS of our people, who are at present cut off from the Church of England.

But, besides this, *how* has provision been made for the wants of our population hitherto by voluntary contributions? Have *endowments* been provided for the churches which have been erected? No: churches have been built, and in some instances have received nominal endowments; but, in the generality of cases, their clergy have been left to depend wholly on the uncertain and most unsatisfactory resource of pew-rents. They have thus been subjected to some of the worst evils of the voluntary system, and the Church has suffered accordingly. If we are to depend on mere voluntary subscriptions in future, we can only expect, *at the utmost,* to provide churches for our increase of population: we cannot hope for endowments or satisfactory incomes from the same source.

To take another instance: Every one knows the immense and fearful deficiency in the amount of clerical aid in many districts. Two societies have been instituted for the purpose of obtaining funds for the payment of additional curates and assistants. The reports of these societies abound in the most appalling pictures of distress: every effort is made to rouse the feelings of the public, and of the religious world, by details of the most touching and lamentable destitution. These societies are patronized by the heads of the Church, and by many of the most eminent persons in the country, and they have succeeded, or perhaps *will* succeed, in raising about 20,000*l.* per annum. There seems little prospect of augmentation to their funds; and yet this is the result of voluntary contributions, at a time when *four thousand* additional clergy are imperatively requisite, and when our population is increasing at the rate of more than 200,000 per annum!

Another example of the inadequacy of the system of voluntary subscription is, we fear, to be afforded by the results of the noble plan for the endowment of new sees in the colonies. The subscriptions to this splendid design have fallen very far short of what might have been expected on such an occasion. It is said that they do not much exceed 40,000*l.*, and it is obvious that unless they are raised to something like ten times that amount, the pressing wants of the colonies, in respect of Bishops, cannot be supplied. This subject leads us to remark further, that when we rely on voluntary contributions as the means of Church extension in *England,* we should take into our account the continual supplications for aid which come from Ireland, Scotland, the various colonial Churches, and even from the United States. These claims are continually on the increase, and therefore they tend to diminish the means applicable to Church extension in England. On the whole, we cannot think that there is any reasonable ground for expecting that, in future, the system of voluntary subscription for church building will produce much greater effects than has hitherto been the case.

It has been represented lately, that if the principle of contributing *a tenth of our incomes* to religious purposes were generally adopted, the Church would possess ample funds for the purposes of Church extension. Undoubtedly it would: but can we in fact expect that such a view will generally be acted on, especially when there is no positive direction in the New Testament imposing on Christians that rate of contribution? We think it would be difficult to obtain the practical recognition of such a principle. At present many persons doubtless contribute more than a tenth of their incomes to religious purposes; but, at all events, such notions, being only advocated by *argument,* can only be expected to make very slow and gradual progress; and in the mean time our wants are unsupplied.

(3.) It generally happens that people are satisfied, that if parliamentary grants and voluntary subscriptions would be each singly insufficient to meet the wants of the Church, yet their *combination* would, without doubt, be fully adequate to all she can require. Let us consider for a little, the correctness of this opinion. Now, in the first place, it has been shown, that voluntary contributions would not, at the utmost, do more than build churches for the *increase* of population every year. We have then to look to the State for their *endowment*, or the payment of their clergy. Parliamentary relief may be afforded in either of two ways—by granting sums with a view to provide permanent incomes, or by voting incomes from year to year. Suppose the former plan adopted. I have already shown that the endowment of so many churches, even on the most moderate scale, would involve an annual expense of 200,000*l*. and upwards. Is the liberality of parliament likely at any time to exceed this? I think not: I think that there is no precedent which should induce us, under any circumstances, to hope for larger grants. But suppose the other alternative—suppose the incomes of the additional clergy provided for, from year to year, by votes of the House of Commons, and sums also voted for the endowment or erection of churches. Without doubt greater relief would be experienced by the Church in this case than by the former plan; but it would have this most serious disadvantage—that the incomes of a very important part of the clergy would be dependent on votes of the House of Commons. The Church would therefore be much more in the power of government than she now is. She might receive the most fatal injury by the withdrawal of such grants or their diminution. We may therefore put out of view this notion of receiving *salaries* for our clergy from the State: it is fraught with danger and humiliation.

On the whole, then, it is pretty clear, that parliamentary aid, combined with the system of voluntary contributions, would probably not enable us to do more than meet the *increase* of our population with the means of religious instruction. I say this on the supposition that parliament could *now* commence its grants to the Church, but it is plain, as I have already said, that we cannot look to any immediate aid from this source; and thus the means at our disposal would, in fact, *fall considerably short* of the wants of our increase each year; and besides this, we have still permanently unprovided for, a mass of SIX MILLIONS of people in this country—more than a third of our population—given up to influences hostile to religion and the Established Church; and left to be the prey of dissent, immorality, popery, atheism, and democracy.

Such, then, is the condition in which we should be left by the operation of prevalent notions. And as nothing can be more fatal than the application of inadequate remedies to serious disorders, I have felt it a duty—a most solemn duty—to expose to public view the utter inefficiency of the plans which are commonly proposed for Church extension. I am most deeply anxious that the friends of Church extension should take a practical view of the question, and that they should not place their whole dependence on means which will, at the best, leave the Church in her present position, exposed to her present dangers, and always most fearfully inadequate to the high and holy object for which she exists in this country. Under a deep sense of the vital importance of the interests involved in this question, I would invite the friends of church extension to consider calmly and dispassionately whether we can, in fact, look for any adequate relief from parliamentary grants and from voluntary contributions; and whether, in our extremity, we ought not, and must not, look to other resources, in addition to those which we may derive from those above mentioned.

One resource would certainly be found in the measure which Mr. Gresley and Mr. Palmer have recently recommended—the revival of the Sunday Offertory, or of Sunday collections in the churches, as still practised in Ireland. It appears that, if each church and chapel in England and Wales should, on an average, produce a collection of five shilling per Sunday, we should have upwards of 150,000*l*. a year available for Church extension. Now, we think that this is a low average to take: we have no doubt that, in very many churches, the subscriptions would amount to several pounds each Sunday. How many persons in our London churches would give their shillings and sixpences each Sunday without reluctance! It may be that in many of the small country churches, it would not be possible to raise more than two or three shillings each Sunday; but the average would be made up by the large collections in other churches.

Supposing this system to produce 150,000*l*. per annum, according to Mr. Palmer's calculation, it would be much more valuable than a grant to the same amount from parliament; for, as it would not be liable to be withdrawn by a vote of the House of Commons, it might be employed in paying *salaries* to additional curates, who would then be dependent, not on the government, or their own congregations, but on the Church at large. It is also very probable, that, as the supply of clergy would for several years not be so rapid as to exhaust the whole of this fund, a considerable surplus would remain each year, which might be applied to the erection of additional churches. Mr. Palmer estimates the whole amount of the surplus which might be derived from this fund before it became entirely applied to payment of curates' salaries, at 1,000,000*l*. and upwards. This would, unquestionably, be no inconsiderable relief to the Church: it would perhaps enable us to provide churches for about 600,000 people, and would thus reduce our destitute population to less than five millions and a half. I will even suppose that the collections are very much larger than has been above estimated, and that their surplus would enable us to provide church room for a million of people. Still we have a population remaining of full *five millions* without the means of religious instruction in the national Church.

Now, I put it to the friends of the establishment; to the friends of the Church; and to its ministers—to the commissioned ambassadors of Jesus Christ—to those whose duty it is to carry the Gospel into all the benighted parts of the earth—whether they can be content to view this most fearful deficiency without availing themselves of every lawful means for its remedy. Is not the existence of this deficiency a crime in the nation which permits it, and in the Church which stands contemplating it without making efforts commensurate to the exigency? Is it not enough to bring down the Divine vengeance upon us; and to punish us, by the destruction of all those interests which withhold us from accomplishing this vast work? And if the nation is involved in the most awful responsibilities by its past and present neglect, how far greater is the responsibility of the Church herself! We have been looking jealously to the security and preservation of our temporalities, and to a variety of other objects more or less connected with our temporal interests, and with questions of expediency; when unnumbered millions have been passing on their way around us, unenlightened by the truths of the Gospel, ungathered into the fold of Christ. And can it be a matter of surprise—does it not seem rather a sort of retribution—that the very interests which have prevented us from meeting the spiritual wants of the country, have been most deeply endangered by the very population which they have left destitute? Had we been less careful of our temporalities, less jealous of every principle which concerns them—less indisposed to alterations, even of a *beneficial* character, our temporal interests would at this moment have been more secure than they are. Important as it is to maintain and defend the temporalities of the Church, yet we think that her first duty is to seek for the promotion "of the kingdom of God;"—that this should be her single object, in comparison with which all others ought to sink into nothingness; and that if, in the promotion of this object, the security of her temporalities may seem to be in some degree affected, or her position in the eye of the world be rendered less brilliant; she ought to throw herself in faith on the promises of the Redeemer, and to believe that "all these things shall be added unto her." She should believe that the sacrifices which she makes to Jesus Christ will be more than repaid even in this present world.

I am fully aware that much sound and valuable *principle* is enlisted against any appropriation of ecclesiastical property to church extension. I most fully admit the purity of the motives which dictate opposition to any proposition for applying any part of our endowments to spiritual purposes different from those to which they are at present devoted. I readily admit that *change* in itself is undesirable; and should regret to see further precedents established which might be hereafter applied by the enemies of the Church, to a dangerous extent. I should be sorry to see the respectability of the clergy diminished, and I admit the *possibility* of some such diminution as a result of any plan of re-distributing Church property. And I am also most fully aware, that the parties who have advocated that principle have been in various instances hostile to the Church; and that some persons have even urged it with a view to unsettle Church property; to lower the respectability of the clergy; and to injure Church and State. This and much more I admit; and yet am still driven, though very reluctantly, to the conclusion, that the Church is bound to adopt or support some measures for rendering

Church property more available than it now is to the supply of the spiritual wants of the community.

Let us consider the objections which are raised to any plan for endowing new parishes from the wealthier benefices now existing.

(1.) In the first place it is alleged, that such a diversion of ecclesiastical property from its present uses is an innovation; a change; which *may* be followed by *other* changes highly injurious to the Church. "You are opening the flood-gates of innovation," it is said, " and know not when they may be closed again." Now, in reply to this, I should say, that innovations *have already commenced :* the acts in reference to the Church of Ireland, the Tithes Act, and the Cathedral Act, have fully established the principle and practice. If, therefore, parliament is inclined at any time to make innovations, it has precedents enough ready at hand. I do not now consider the question whether it is or is not desirable to *interfere* with Church property : that question has been settled. In the next place, it may be remarked, that if a parliament was at any time really desirous of injuring the Church, it would easily find the way to do so *without precedent.* The Spanish legislature has confiscated the property of the Church, though the history of that country furnished no precedents. France did the same in its revolution. Thirdly, admitting that even beneficial changes *may* furnish precedents for bad ones, is this always a sufficient reason to prevent them? Fourthly, supposing that these innovations may possibly be followed by others, is there no danger in letting things remain as they are? Does not the existence of a mass of *five millions* of people alienated from the Established Church, threaten still greater and more vital changes than any which might possibly arise from a moderate scheme of re-distribution of church property? Are not the dangers in the one case certain—in the other speculative? Fifthly, admitting the evil of change in its fullest extent, is not the Church bound to disregard and put aside that consideration, when the question is, whether she shall or shall not evangelize millions of immortal souls placed under her immediate care? Is she not bound to throw herself for protection on the good providence of God, in the discharge of the holy and sublime commission which has been given to her?

(2.) I come next to the objection, "that it is unlawful to apply funds given by those who endowed benefices to purposes different from those which their founders contemplated." It is asserted, "that we are bound rigidly, under all circumstances, to apply funds left by founders, to the precise objects originally in their contemplation." Now, I fully admit that the intentions of founders ought, as a general rule, to be attended to as far as possible; but I certainly can see that circumstances may, in the course of ages, be so changed, as that it may become necessary to depart in some degree from the exact letter of the founder's intentions, or rather to modify his directions in such a manner as may be conceived to harmonize best with his intentions under an altered state of things.

For example, the endowments of various minor benefices, which were given originally with a view to the moderate support of an incumbent, have, in the course of ages, become so valuable, that they exceed the revenues of the bishoprics. The prebendal stall of Finsbury, to which is annexed the duty of preaching a sermon once in the year, will, in some years, enjoy a revenue of twenty or thirty thousand per annum. It was surely never the intention of the founder of that stall, that its incumbent should possess larger revenues than the Archbishop of Canterbury. Its enormous value arises from accidental circumstances, which the founder could never have contemplated.

The tithes of certain tracts of land were originally given to support a parish priest; and, when they were thus appropriated, they were barely sufficient for this purpose. They were covered with forests and intersected with marshes. In the course of ages they have been brought into cultivation, and the income of the clergyman becomes vastly greater than the founder contemplated. We have heard that the tithes of a parish in Cambridgeshire have been lately commuted for about 12,000*l.* per annum. Several others might be mentioned, in which the incomes vary from from 3000*l.* to 5000*l.* per annum. Nor are these parishes remarkable for large populations: they are of tolerably manageable dimensions.

I believe that founders of parishes never *intended* to endow their clergy with large incomes, or to make them *wealthy*. Sufficient support was all that they could have lawfully intended to afford, *and all that the Church could lawfully have permitted them to give*. If there be now, in any case, more than sufficiency, it is certainly not in accordance with the intention of the founder; and under these circumstances it seems that those intentions would be best carried out, by dividing richly-endowed parishes, where the population requires it, or by applying a part of their revenues to the endowment of new parishes in some neighbouring district, or to some other strictly spiritual purpose. I maintain, that such an application of the surplus revenues would be exactly what founders ought to have made, and would have made, had they witnessed the present state of things. Their wishes should be always adhered to as regards the sufficient supply of clerical aid in the particular places which they provided for; but after that has been attended to, their intentions may be fairly supposed to extend to the relief of religious destitution elsewhere.

I might go further, and prove from history and from the canon law, that the Church has never held herself bound, under all circumstances, to continue the appropriation of her property strictly to the purposes for which it was originally given. I might point to the powers reserved by the canon law to bishops and chapters to alienate their property for some reasonable cause of piety, charity, or necessity. I might mention bishops who had sold all, even to the ornaments and vessels of the Church, in order to redeem Christians from captivity. I might point to the innumerable monasteries which were endowed with lands and tithes alienated from the purposes to which they were originally given. Nay, I might point to the whole existing parochial system as a convincing proof, that it is sometimes lawful to change the original destination and arrangement of ecclesiastical property; for the tithes now applied to the support of the parochial clergy were for centuries paid to the *bishops*, and employed by them in the support of religion generally throughout their dioceses. It was only by an alteration of this universal system, that parishes were gra a founded in the eleventh, twelfth, and thirteenth centuries; and it might have been argued in those ages, that it was unlawful to alienate this property from its original and canonical uses, confirmed for ages by the laws of the land, had it not been perfectly understood, that a power existed in the Church which could, for good and sufficient reasons, alter the arrangement of ecclesiastical property.

But here I may, perhaps, be met by an admission, that there is indeed, *some* power in the Church to make such alterations; but it is strenuously denied, that the *State* can interfere in the matter. It is alleged, that *convocation* alone is competent to such measures, and that parliament has nothing whatever to do with them. Now, this objection might have come with some force in ages when the Church had acquired absolute control over her temporalities, and when the clergy were only taxed by convocation; but for several centuries the parliaments of England have regulated not only the temporalities of the Church, but even matters of discipline. They have been for a long period of time more or less sanctioned by the Church in the exercise of those legislative powers in Church matters which belong primarily and originally to the Church herself. The Church has, in fact, *for the time*, devolved her power of enacting laws on matters relating to temporalities on the State, which, however, is bound, in policy and discretion at least, to act in accordance with the advice and wishes of the rulers of the Church. So that, as things now are, the State seems fully competent, with the advice of the heads of the Church, to effect alterations in the distribution of ecclesiastical property. And, in fact, this power has been lately acted on in several instances, more especially in the Ecclesiastical Duties and Revenues Bill. It seems, therefore, too late to stand on the above objection, when the contrary principle has been recognised not only by the legislature, but by the votes of at least half the episcopacy, and the acquiescence of the remainder, and of the whole body of the clergy.

(3.) Another objection which may be raised to any scheme for dividing rich benefices, or endowing other churches from them, is, that in proportion as we diminish the number of rich endowments in the Church, we furnish fewer inducements to the aristocracy to devote their children to the sacred ministry. On the same principle, objections have been raised to measures for diminishing pluralities and non-residence. Now let us consider this point for a little. I admit, then, in the amplest manner, that it is desirable that a portion of our clergy should be taken from the higher classes, because they are thus better adapted to influence and instruct those classes; but I cannot admit that it is any part of the duty of the Church to support the younger branches of the aristocracy in the splendour suitable to their birth. Were the Church possessed of funds adequate to the supply of clergy to the whole population—were her means ever so ample—still it would neither be right or expedient to devote them to support any of her clergy (however distinguished by birth) in luxury and splendour. If the aristocracy enter the ecclesiastical profession, they ought to moderate their wishes and habits, and to place themselves on a level with the great body of the clergy. It would be any thing but desirable for the Church, that a portion of her parochial clergy should live in a style of splendour which should tempt the remainder to expenses beyond their means, or diminish their respectability by comparison. If the aristocracy must continue their habits of expense as clergy, the Church, at least, is not to furnish the means. All that the Church can afford—all that she *ought* to afford to any of her priests—is, *sufficiency*. I believe this to be the principle of scripture and of the primitive Church.

There is another objection of the same sort, which is often deduced when any suggestions for the re-distribution of ecclesiastical property are made,—That it would tend to introduce a lower class into the Church than at present; that the clerical profession might not be so exclusively filled by *gentlemen* as it now is,—and consequently that its influence on society at large would be diminished. It seems to me that rather too much importance is attached to this argument. It is very true that polished manners and habits are, in very many cases, essential to the success of a clergyman. In the metropolis, and in many country towns and rural districts, our congregations would be offended by any want of elegance and of good breeding in their clergy. But there are various situations where refined manners and habits would not only be thrown away, but would rather impede the success of the ministry. They would frequently be only a source of pain to their possessors, and would perhaps unfit them, in some degree, from entering into the feelings and views of the population by whom they were surrounded. I am of opinion that in many of our manufacturing and rural districts, where there is nothing of refinement, it would be positively *desirable* to have the clergy generally drawn from a class below that which contributes the mass of our clergy at present. A deficiency in birth, however, does not necessarily imply a defective education. I would have those clergy thoroughly educated in their profession, and trained under an effective discipline for the discharge of their sacred office; and I have no doubt that any want of polish and elegance in their manners, would not render them less efficient ministers of God's word, amongst a coarse though intellectual population.

But, in conclusion, I must repeat my conviction, that be the inconveniences which attend on plans for Church-extension what they may, they are of no weight in comparison with the duty of endeavouring to provide for the spiritual instruction of FIVE MILLIONS of our countrymen. It may be—it is indeed pretty certain—that, after every effort, a vast mass of the population must still remain beyond the reach of the Church. But would this be any excuse for not attempting the salvation of the remainder? I am satisfied that the Church was never, since her foundation, subjected to a stronger call, or bound to make greater exertions, in reliance on Divine protection, than at this moment.

W.

ECCLESIASTICAL INTELLIGENCE.

ORDINATIONS.

BP. OF GLOUCESTER AND BRISTOL, *at Cath. Church of Gloucester, Dec.* 19.

DEACONS.

Of Oxford.—W. G. S. Addison, M.A., Mag.; R. Champernowne, B.A. Ch. Ch.; T. Debary, B.A. Linc.; R. Inchbald, B.A. St. John's, Cam.; T. P. Little, B.A. Trin.; N. A. Howard, B.A. Exet. (*l. d. Exeter.*)
Of Cambridge.—M. Cockin, B.A. Queen's; J. B. Gisborne, B.A., and R. M. Hutchings, Trin.; J. S. Money, B.A. Emm.; F. Palmer, B.A., and J. C. Turnbull, B.A. Trin.

PRIESTS.

Of Oxford.—W. H. Biedermann, B.A., H. Bubb, M.A. Pem.; C. Ross de Havilland, M.A.; Oriel; J. B. Gabriel, B.A. St. Edm.; O. F. Owen, B.A. Ch. Ch.; A. Reeve, B.A. Wad.; F. Stonhouse, B.A. Oriel; J. S. Woodman, B.A. Worc.; H. W. Steel, B.A. Jesus, (*l. d. Llandaff.*)
Of Cambridge.—R. T. Budd, B.A. Mag.; A. Grant, B.A., W. P. Haslewood, B.A., H. H. Jones, M.A., W. Spearman, B.A. Trin.; W. N. Griffin, M.A. St. John's.
Literate.—J. Davis.

BP. OF WORCESTER, *at Cath. Church, Worcester, Dec.* 19.

DEACONS.

Of Oxford.—C. T. Arnold, B.A. Mag.; H. P. S. Ashworth, B.A. St. Alb.; A. Clifton, B.A., J. R. Crawford, M.A. Linc.; C. Dolben, B.A. Trin.; E. L. Howell, B.A. Queen's; J. M. Mottram, B.A. Mag.; T. C. B. Stretch, B.A. Wor.; J. B. Winckworth, B.A. St. Edm.
Of Cambridge.—W. B. Budd, B.A., J. King, B.A. Queen's; G. Elton, S.C.L. Gonville and Caius; C. H. Foster, B.A. Mag.; A. Rawson, B.A. Trin.; W. S. Symonds, B.A. Christ's; F. Taunton, B.A. St. John's.
Literate.—W. Croone.

PRIESTS.

Of Oxford.—H. W. A. Cookes, B.A. Worc.; W. Dowding, B.A. Mert.; E. Garbett, B.A. Brasen.; G. W. Garrow, B.A. Worc.; J. H. Moor, M.A. Mag.; P. P. Myddelton, B.A. Queen's; A. K. Thompson, B.A. Queen's.
Of Cambridge.—E. Male, B.A. Gonville and Caius; C. Meyer, M.A. Trin.; T. W. Richards, B.A. Sid.

BP. of BATH AND WELLS, *Dec.* 19.

DEACONS.

Of Oxford.—J. Acres, B.A. Linc.; J. Crokat, B.A. Mag. H.; M. W. James, B.A. Oriel; H. J. Marshall, B.A. C.C.; G. F. Master, B.A. Univ.; W. A. Napier, B.A. Ch. Ch.; W. E. Smith, B.A. Exet. (*l. d. Llandaff.*)
Of Cambridge.—W. F. Neville, B.A. Mag.; H. P. Wright, B.A. Pet.
Of Lampeter.—T. Brown, G. Griffiths, W. D. Rees. (*l. d. Llandaff.*)

PRIESTS.

Of Oxford.—T. Fox, B.A. Wadham; O. R. Knight, B.A. Wad. (*l. d. Llandaff*); H. Malpas, B.A. Ed. H.; C. Penny, B.A. Worc.

BP. of LICHFIELD, *Dec.* 19.

DEACONS.

Of Oxford.—H. E. Devey, B.A. Pem.; W. C. Dowding, B.A. Exet.; T. S. Hewett, B.A. Worc.; A. T. G. Manson, B.C.L. Mag.; F. J. Rooke, B.A. Oriel; C. J. Sale, B.A. Linc.; E. Tew, B.A. Mag. H.; F. C. Twemlow, B.A. Oriel.
Of Cambridge.—J. L. Allan, B.A. Trin.; W. Bell. B.A. C. C.; S. F. Bolton, B.A. St. John's; J. Manners, B.A. C.C.; H. Pearson, B.A. Cath.; T. M. Pyke, B.A. C. C.; T. G. Ragland, B.A.; C. C.; W. Rushton, B.A. Trin.

PRIESTS.

Of Oxford.—P. H. Dod, B.A. Worc.; C. A. Fowler, B.A. Oriel; J. Isaacson, B.A. New Inn H.; W. R. Ogle, B.A. Trin.; G. F. S. Weideman, B.A. Ch. Ch., C. Whittaker, B.A. Brasennose.
Of Cambridge.—A. A. Bagshaw, B.A. C.C.; W. J. Conybeare, B.A. Trin.; D. Cooke, B.A. Queen's; F. Day, B.A. Pem.; R. S. Drayton, B.A. Trin.; T. P. Ferguson, B.A. Trin.; J. W. Hall, B.A. Trin.; H. B. Harvey, B.A. Clare; G. B. A. Lloyd, B.A. Emm.; J. M. Lowe, B.A. St. John's; E. H. L. Noot, B.A. C.C.; A. B. Strettell, B.A. Trin.; F. Williams, B.A. C. C.
Of Dublin.—J. Wilkin, B.A.

BP. of HEREFORD, *Dec.* 19.

DEACONS.

Of Oxford.—E. B. Hawkshaw, B.A. Oriel; A. H. Ingram, B.A. Ch. Ch.; J. Roe, B.A. Worc.; W. Thorn, B.A. Univ.; J. G. Watts, B.A. Ball.

PRIESTS.

Of Oxford.—E. Bather, B.A. Mert.; E. F. Coke, B.A. L. E. G. Clarke, B.A. Brasen.; J. W. Davis, B.A. Worc.; J. L. Hoskyns, B.A. Mag.; J. M. Lakin, B.A. Worc.; J. J. Trollope, B.A. Pem.
Of Cambridge.—K. E. A. Money, C. C.; R. Potter, B.A. Pet.; W. F. Rawes, B.A. Caius; J. Rogers, B.A. St. John's; L. Spencer, B.A. Christ's; J. L. Sisson, B.A. Jesus.
Of Durham.—S. Dupre, L.D.

BP. of LONDON, *Dec.* 19.

DEACONS.

Of Oxford.—S. Holmes, B.A. Mag. H.; H. W. Tylden, B.A. Balliol.
Of Cambridge.—T. Boggis, B.A. Emm.; R. Bradley, B.A. Queen's (*l. d. Canterbury*); G. M. Gould, B.A. St. John's; J. Hitchcock, B.A. Christ's; E. H. Hunter, B.A. Trin.; H. Porter, B.A. Pem.; J. R. Stock, B.A. St. John's; F. Vigers, B.A. Trin.; T. C. Whitehead, B.A. St. John's; W. Wigson, B.A. St. John's.
Of King's College, London.—W. Hayes, jun.
Of Church Missionary College, Islington.—G. P. Badger; I. Brittain; S. Franklin.
Lit.—G. L. Allen; J. C. H. West.

PRIESTS.

Of Oxford.—R. Gee, B.A. Wad.; N. Germon, B.A. Oriel; W. D. Jackson, B.A. St. John's; F. Poynder, M.A. Wad.; C. Torkington, B.A. Brasen.; T. H. Woodroffe, B.A. Edm. H.
Of Cambridge.—C. Baldock, B.A. St. John's; R. Bull, B.A. St. John's; J. W. Harris, B.A.

J. J. B. Marriott, B.A. C. C.; J. H. Rowlatt, M.A. St. John's.
Lit. F. A. Hildner; C. W. H. Pauli; J. C Reichardt.

BP. of DURHAM, *Dec.* 19.
DEACONS.
Of Cambridge.—J. P. Parry, B.A., J. Romney, B.A. St. John's.
Lit.—J. Marshall.

PRIESTS.
Of Oxford.—E. H. Adamson, M.A. Linc.; H. R. Ridley, B.A. Univ.
Of Cambridge.—W. Mackenzie, B.A. Trin. H.
Of Dublin.—E. Edmunds, B.A.; J. Elliott, B.A.
Of Durham.—B. E. Dwarris; J. Stevenson; H. Stoker, M.A.; M. Thompson, M.A.
Of St. Bees.—T. J. Steele.
Of Lampeter.—A. A. Rees.

BP. of LINCOLN, *Dec.* 19.
DEACONS.
Of Oxford.—J. B. N. Heard, M.A. St. Mary H.; A. G. Newbold. B.A. Mag. H.
Of Cambridge.—G. Bryan, M.A. St. Pet.; R. E. Harrisson, B.A. Christ's; L. D. Kennedy, B.A. Christ's; J. E. S. Legh, M.A. King's; C. W. D. More, B.A. St. John's.

PRIESTS.
† *Of Oxford.*—J. Emeris, B.A. Univ.; M. T. Latham. B.A., G. Sandbach, B.A., Brasen.; W. Toms, B.A. Worc.; E. Trollope, B.A. St. Mary H.
Of Cambridge.— T. B. Bensted, B.A. St. John's; C. Bernal, B.A. Clare; J. H. Browne, B.A. St. John's; W. Burnside, B.A. St. John's; W. Harker, B.A. Cath.; C. W. Lowndes, B.A., J. Spence, B.A. Christ's; R. Tindall, B.A. St. John's.

BP. of CHICHESTER, *Dec.* 19.
DEACONS.
Of Oxford.—W. H. Anderdon, B.A. Univ.; G. Braithwaite. B.A. Queen's; H. Sockett, B.A. Exet.; J. White, B.A. Linc.
Of Dublin.—F. A. Golding, A.M.; W. St. G. Patterson, B.A.

PRIESTS.
Of Oxford.—H. Smith, B.A. Queen's; T. R. Smyth, M.A. Brasen.
Of Cambridge.—F. Brown, B.A. Mag.; H. G. Vigne, B.A. Pet.

ARCHBP. of YORK, *Dec.* 19.
DEACONS.
Of Oxford.—R. O. Walker, B.A., B. Wake, B.A. St. John's.
Of Cambridge.—H. Deck, B.A. C. C.; J. Robinson, B.A. Jesus.
Of St. Bees.—H. F. Hewgill.

PRIESTS.
Of Oxford.—R. Hale, M.A. Brasen.; St. John Mitchell, B.A. Ed. Hall.
Of Cambridge.—G. Edmundson, B.A. Sid.; C. W. Woodhouse, B.A. Caius.
Of Durham.—M. E. Wilson.
Of Dublin.—S. B. Brasher, B.A.; T. Carmichael, B A.
Lit.—W. S. Gatterill.

BP. of OXFORD, *Dec.* 19.
DEACONS.
Of Oxford.—J. E. Bode, M.A. Ch. Ch.; R. N. Buckmaster, B.A. Ch. Ch.; W. Burnett, M.A. New; E. K. Burney, B.A. Magd.; C. J. Collier, S.C.L. Magd.; R. Congreve, B.A. Wad.; T. B. Cornish, B.A. Wad.; J. B. Fawkes, B.A. Ch.Ch.; J. Hannah, B. A. Linc.; J. Hemsted, B.A. Magd.; E. Hobhouse, B.A. Mert.; J. M. Holland, B.A. New; J. B. Hughes, M.A. Magd.; P. C. Kidd, B.A. Ch. Ch.; R. W. Mason, Jesus; E. W. Pears, M.A. Magd.; B. Price, B.A. Pemb.; H. Randall, B.A. Brasen; H. M. Richards, B.A. Ch. Ch.; W. P. Walsh, B.A. Worc.
Of Cambridge.—C. Wood, B.A. Clare.

PRIESTS.
Of Oxford.—R. A. Bathurst, B.A. New; S. E. Bathurst, B.A. Mert.; H. Bennett, B.A. Worc.; G. F. Childe, B.A. Ch. Ch.; R. H. Gray, B.A. Ch. Ch.; Hon. H. Grimston, M.A. All Souls; M. Harrison, M.A. C. C.; S. Lee, B.A. Queen's; H. W. Lloyd, M.A., P. H. Morgan, B.A. Jesus; H. Pearson, M.A. Ball.; J.W. Routh, M.A. Magd.; W. J. Wise, B.A. St. John's; E. C. Woollcombe, M.A. Balliol.

BP. OF CHESTER, *Dec.* 19.
DEACONS.
Of Oxford.—S. B. Arnott, M. A. St. John's; E. Pigot, B.A. Brasen.
Of Cambridge.—J. F. Coates, B.A. Cath. H.; G. W. Goodchild, B.A. Sid.; E. Witley, B. A. Queen's.
Of Durham.—A. Peyton.
Of Dublin.—W. Blake, B.A.; R. Butler, B.A.; T. Eager, M.A.; J. Hebden, M.A.
Of St. Bees.—J. Bonwell; C. M. Christie; J. M. Crockett; E. B. Squire; R. Thomson; W. Wells.

PRIESTS.
Of Oxford.—J. R. Alsop, B.A. Brasen.; H. Branker, B.A. Wad.; J. Gregson, M.A. Brasen.; R. Tomlins, B.A. St. Mary's H.; J. M. Twist, B.A. Queen's.
Of Cambridge.—H. B. Birks, B.A. Cath.; G. C. Bowles, B.A. St. John's; C. W. Cahusac, B.A. St. John's; A. Chirol, B.A. Clare; J. Jackson, B.A. St. John's; C. James, B.A. St. John's; G. Y. Osborne, B.A. Sid.; R. N. Prettyman, B.A. Caius; H. C. Seller, B.A. St. John's; C. F. Smith, B.A. Queen's; B. Wills, B.A. C. C.
Of Dublin.—J. E. Armstrong, M.A.; A. C. Cary, B.A.; J. S. Dodd, B.A.; J. Elliott. B.A.; C. Mangmiss, B.A.; C. Mitchell, B.A.; J. Sheffield, M.A.
Of St. Bees.—B. S. Clarke.

BP. OF RIPON, *Jan.* 9.
DEACONS.
Of Oxford.—G. Antrobus, B.A. Brasen. (*l. d.* York); W. Baldwin, B.A. Ed. H.; S. B. Harper, B.A. New Inn H.; R. J. Mapleton, B.A. St. John's; R. M. Martin, B.A. Ed. H.
Of Cambridge.—C. Grenside, B.A. Pet.; A. B. Hill, Jesus; J. S. Oxley, B.A. Queen's.
Of Dublin.—I. L. Lloyd, B.A.; T. H. Manning, B.A.
Lit.—C. H. S. Nicholls.

PRIESTS.
. *Of Oxford.*—F. E. Lott, B.A. Alb. Hall (*l. d. Exeter.*)
Of Cambridge.—H. Baily, B.A. St. John's; T. Hervey, B.A. Clare; S. Pagan, B.A. St. John's.
Of Dublin.—T. B. Browne, B A.; L. B. Poyntz, B.A.

BP. OF LLANDAFF, *in the Church of St. Gregory, London, Jan.* 9.
DEACONS.
Of Cambridge.—E. S. Stanley, B.A. Jesus.
Lit.—J. Hughes.

BP. OF NORWICH, *Jan.* 9.

DEACONS.

Of Oxford.—R. Frith, B.A. New Coll.; G. F. Turner, B.A. Trin.
Of Cambridge.—W. P. Borrett, M.D. Caius; C. D. Gibson, B.A. John's; A. W. Hall, B.A. St. Peter's.

PRIESTS.

Of Oxford.—R. C. Denny, B.A. Trin.; W. W. Dickinson, B.A. Brasen.; J. W. Doligrion, B.A. Ball.; W. Ewing, B.A. Linc.; T. L. Fellowes, B.A. Ch. Ch.; J. E. L. Schreiber, B.A. Ball.
Of Cambridge.—J. A. Ashley. B.A. Jesus; J. B. Bumpton, B.A. Christ's; T. H. Deacle, B.A. John's; J. H. Jerrard, D.C.L. Fell. of Caius; T. Reynolds, B.A. Pem.; W. C. Snooke, B.A. St. Peter's; J. W. Spencer, B.A. Pem.; F. Sugden, B.A. Trin.; F. W. Wilson, B.A. Christ's.
Of Durham.—G. F. Hill.
Of Dublin.—H. M'Master, B.A.

ORDINATIONS APPOINTED.

BP. OF SALISBURY, *Feb.* 20.
BP. OF LINCOLN, *Feb.* 20.
BP. OF PETERBOROUGH, *Feb.* 20.
BP. OF BATH AND WELLS, *Feb.* 20.

BP. OF LICHFIELD, *March* 20.
BP. OF OXFORD, *May* 22.
BP. OF WINCHESTER, *July* 10.

PREFERMENTS.

Name.	Preferment.	County.	Diocese.	Patron.	Val.	Pop.
Alexander, D.	Bickleigh, V.	Devon	Exeter	Sir R. Lopez, Bart.	£253	466
Alford, C. R.	St. Matthew, Rugby, P.C.	Warwick	Worcester	Bp. of Worcester		
Bates, T. E.	Christ Church, Litherland	Lancaster	Chester	Trustees		
Bayne, T. V.	St. John's, Broughton, P.C.	Lancaster	Chester	Trustees		
Beechy, S. V.	St. Peter's, Fleetwood, P.C.	Lancaster	Chester	Sir Hesketh Fleetwood		
Boyd, A.	Christ Church, Cheltenham, P.C.	Gloucester	G. & B.	Trustees		
Buxton, H.	Britford, V.	Wilts	Sarum	D. & C. of Sarum	281	838
Cann, P.	Virginstow, R.	Devon	Exeter	Crown	103	136
Chapman, J.	Milton, R.	Cambridge	Ely	King's Coll. Camb.	390	377
Chichester, R. H.	Chittlehampton, V.	Devon	Exeter	Lord Rolle	*413	1897
Chudleigh, R. F.	St. Columb Minor, P.C.	Cornwall	Exeter	Sir J. Y. Buller	117	1406
Clayton, J.	Weston-on-Avon, V.	Gloucester	G. & B.	Earl Amherst	84	108
Corbett, S.	Orsdall, R.	Nottingham	Lincoln	Lord Wharncliffe	424	809
Courtenay, C. L.	Broadclist, V.	Devon	Exeter	Sir T. Acland		
Edwards, J.	Trinity Church, Southport, P.C.	Lancaster	Chester		107	2855
Forester, O.W.W.	Broseley, R.	Salop	Hereford	Lord Forester	*432	4410
Garfit, E.	Saxilby, V.	Lincoln	Lincoln	Bp. of Lincoln	167	719
Godfrey, —	Bredicot, R.	Worcester	Worcester	D. & C. of Worcester	120	52
Gregson, J.	Upton Overchurch, P.C.	Chester	Chester	W. Webster, Esq.	52	191
Harris, J.	All Saints, P.C. Stepney	Middlesex	London	Bp. of London		
Heming, S. B.	Caldecote, R.	Warwick	Worcester	D. Heming, Esq.	149	106
Hendrickson, W.	CottonChapel, Alton	Hants	Winchester	T. Gilbert, Esq.		
Hepworth, W.	Finningham, R.	Suffolk	Norwich	J. H. Frere	*350	497
Hodges, R.	Little Barrington	Gloucester	G. & B.	Lord Chancellor	100	162
Homes, H.	BartonSt.Andrew, R.	Norfolk	Norwich	Lord Chancellor	163	459
Hutchinson, C. G.	Batsford, R.	Gloucester	G. & B.	Christ Church, Oxf.	*370	107
James, E.	Llangurig	Montgomery	Bangor	Bp. of Bangor	175	1847
Langton, A. W.	Kempstone, R.	Norfolk	Norwich	Earl of Leicester	167	59
Lloyd, G.	Willesley, P.C.	Derby	Lichfield	Sir C. A. Hastings, Bt.	62	63
Mayne, J.	Hanslope w. Castlethorpe, V.	Bucks	Lincoln	G. Hyde, Esq.	*90	1989
Moore, R.	Wetheringsett cum Brockford	Suffolk	Norfolk	Rev. R. Moore	*604	1001
Nelson, J.	Peterstow, R.	Hereford	Hereford	Gov. of Guy's Hosp.	*290	261
Nicholson. M. A.	Ch. Ch. Acrington	Lanc.	Chester	Trustees.		
Pearson, H.	Sonning, V.	Berks	Oxford	D. & C, of Sarum	*451	2558
Peers, J. W.	Tetsworth, V.	Oxon	Oxford	R. B. Slater, Esq.		530
Procter, W.	Bp. Burton, V.	York	York	D. & C. of York	100	539
Pym, F.	Plymstock, P.C.	Devon	Exeter	D. & C. of Windsor	188	3088
Richards, C. W.	St. Chad, Lichfield, P.C.	Stafford	Lichfield	Vicar of St. Mary's	90	
Salmon, T. W.	Hopton, P.C.	Suffolk	Norwich	D. & C. of Norwich	102	260
Thompson, R.	Shotley, P.C.	Northumb.	Durham		*139	1104
Trollope, E.	Ranceby, V.	Lincoln	Lincoln	Sir J. H. Thorold, Bt.	*165	262
Trollope, J. J.	Wigmore, V.	Hereford	Hereford	Bp. of Hereford	120	429
Williams, H.	Llangavelach, V.	Glamorgan	St. David's	Bp. of St. David's	159	7753

⁎ *The Asterisk denotes a Residence House.*

APPOINTMENTS.

Bentinck, W.H.E. {Rur. Dn. North Halderness, York.
Burrows, N. ...... {Head Mast. Prop. Gram. Sch. Gt. Yarmouth.
Burton, R. L...... Surrogate Dioc. of Hereford.
Bramah, A. T. ... {Sec. Mast. Went. Gram. Sch. Brompton
Cox, J. .... Runcorn, Sur. Dioc. of Chest.
Cornish, Dr. ...... Sur. Archdeaconry of Exeter.
Dodsworth, G. ... Chap. Eton & Windsor Union.
Davies, N.......... Preb. of St. David's.
Drury, C........... Preb. of Hereford.
Fentrell, C......... H. Mas.Gr. Sch., Rotherham
Green, T. S. ...... Chap. Ashby-de-la-Zouch Un.
Hughes, T. W. ... {Head Mas. of Gram. School, Woodbridge.
Melvill, E.......... Preb. of St. David's.
Sharpe, J. .... Chap. E.I.C. Bengal Station.
Sutton, T. .... Vic. of Sheffield, Rural Dean.
Sydney, E.......... Acle, Surrogate.
Thornton, W. J.. Preb. of Hereford.
Venables, J........ Preb. of Sarum.

CLERGYMEN DECEASED.

Barker, G. A., Rec. of Kevenlleece, Radnor, 70.
Barker, W. Vic. of Broadclist, Devon, 36.
Bowles, H., at Frampton House, Boston.
Bowen, J. G. Rec. of Stawley, Somerset.
Champneys, T. W. Rec. of Fulmer, Bucks, 69.
Colmer, J. Rec. of Askerswell, Dorset.
Fisher, P. Master of Charterhouse.
Fosbrooke, T. D., Vic. of Walford, Herefordshire, 72.
Grant, C., Vic. of West Barsham, Norfolk.
Grylls, R. G., at Helston, 84.
Garratt, T. Vic. of Audley, Staffordshire, 46.
Jones, W., at Bleadington, Gloucester, 87.
Kubff, H., Fell. of Cath. Hall, Camb., 38.
Lade, W. Rec. of Wickhambreux, Kent, 81.
Marsden, W. Rec. of Everingham, Yorks., 32.
Messenger, J., Per. Cur. of Shotley, Northum.
Marwood, G., at Busby Hall, Cleveland.
Manley, G. P., Cur. of Petton and Raddington, Somerset, 40.
Myers, W. J., Cur. of Eltham, Kent, 46.
Press, E., Norwich.
Pyemont, J., Cur. of Eyke, Ipswich, 35.
Roberts, J., Rec. of Withenley, Leicesters., 75.
Saunders, G. E., Rec. of Tarrant Rushton, and Hinton, Dorset, 57.
South, T. H., Cur. of Fittleton, &c., Warwickshire, 81.
Stranger, R., Rec. of Zeal Monach, 34.
Usko, J. F., Rec. of Orsett, Essex, 81.
Wagstaffe, D., at Scalby, 74.
Wallas, E., late Vic. of Rampton Retford, 92.
Wait, W., formerly Min. of St. Mary-le-Port, Bristol, 78.
Watts, R., Preb. of St. Paul's, and Librarian of Sion College, London, 92.

UNIVERSITIES.

OXFORD.

Dec. 17.

In Convocation the nomination of the Rev. J. Griffith, M.A. Sub-Warden of Wadham Coll. to be a Delegate of Accounts, was unanimously approved.

Degrees conferred.

B.D.

Rev. J. Williams, Fellow of Jesus; Rev. W. Mallock, Ball.

B.A.

L. Carden, Univ.; H. H. Cornish, Magd. H.; C. R. Clifton, Mert.; E. L. S. Lumsdane, Oriel.

CLASS LIST.—MICHAELMAS EXAMINATION.

In Disciplinis Mathematicis et Physicis.

CLASS II.

Battersby, J. H. Com. of Ball.

CLASS III.

Brine, J. G. Fell. of John's.
Lempriere, C. Fell. of John's.
Marshall, J. Com. of Ch. Ch.
Twiss, E. R. Com. of Univ.
Wilson, W. D. Com. of Wad.

CLASS IV.

Allen, W. Magd. H.
Jackson, W. Com. of Queen's.
Macfurlane, W. Com. of Linc.
Richards, R. M. Com. of Mert.
Shand, G. Com. of Queen's.

The number in the Fifth Class was 84.

Robert Walker, }
William F. Donkin, } Examiners.
John A. Ashworth, }

Dec. 24.

Congregations will be holden for the purpose of granting graces and conferring degrees, on the following days in the ensuing term, viz.—

Jan.	Friday, 14	Mar.	Thursday, 3
——	Thursday, 27	——	Thursday, 10
Feb.	Thursday, 3	——	Saturday, 19
——	Thursday, 17		

No person will, on any account, be admitted as a candidate for the degree of B.A. or M.A., or for that of B.C.L. or B.M., without proceeding through Arts, whose name is not entered in the book, kept for that purpose, at the Vice-Chancellor's house, on or before the day preceding the day of congregation.

On Tuesday, Feb. 8th, a Congregation will be holden, as provided in the Dispensation, for intermitting the Forms and Exercises of Determination, *solely* for the purpose of receiving from the Deans, or other officers of their respective colleges or halls, the names of such Bachelors of Arts as have not yet determined: and their names having been so signified to the House, and thereupon inserted in the Register of Congregation, they may at any time in the same, or in any future Term, be admitted to all the rights and privileges to which they would have been entitled by the intermitted Forms and Exercises.

And every Bachelor of Arts is desired to take notice, that unless he has proceeded to that Degree on or before Thursday, February 3d, his name cannot be inserted in the Register of Congregation during the present year.

Jan. 1.

The Rev. John B. Fawkes, B.A. and the Rev. Philip C. Kidd, B.A. have been appointed Chaplains of Christ Church.

The following gentlemen have been elected actual Students of Christ Church:—G. R. H. Somerset, H. T. Glyn, H. E. Cramer, from Westminster; T. O. Blackall, W. E. Rawstorne, C. Lloyd, Commoners.

Jan. 8.

H. M. White, and J. W. Goodenough, have been admitted actual Fellows of New College, the former after two years of probation, the latter as of kin to the Founder.

Jan. 14.

Vaughan Exhibition.—The examination of Candidates for this Exhibition will commence at Oxford on Thursday, the 24th of Feb. next.

Candidates are required to be "the sons of freeholders of the county of Merioneth, in North Wales, or natives of that county, or natives of any other county in England or Wales, one of whose parents shall be a native of the said county of Merioneth."

They must not exceed nineteen years of age, nor, if already members of the University of Oxford, must they have passed the third term from matriculation.

Candidates are requested to transmit to Mr. Walsh, Secretary, on or before Wednesday, the 16th of February next, a declaration in writing of the nature of their qualification, with a certificate of baptism, and testimonial from the senior Master of their respective schools, or last private Tutors; or, if members of the University, from the Head or Tutor of their respective Colleges.

Degrees conferred.

M.A.

S. Waldegrave, Fell. of All Souls; H. W. Cripps, Fell. of New Coll.; Rev. G. T. Driffield, Fell. of Brasen.; W. E. Buckley, Fell. of Brasen.; A. J. Christie, Fell. of Oriel; Rev. T. R. Branfoot, Trin.

B.A.

N. T. Travers, Scholar of Linc.; W. F. Everest, Magd. H.; J. W. Kirkham, Jesus.

The Poetry Professorship.—The following circulars will inform our readers that the contest for the above Professorship is at an end:—

Brasennose College, Jan. 20, 1842.

Sir,—A comparison has this morning been made of the number of promises given in behalf of each Candidate for the Professorship of Poetry, when they were found to be for Mr. Garbett, 921, Mr. Williams, 623. Mr. Williams has in consequence withdrawn. We beg you to accept our thanks for the intention expressed by you of supporting Mr. Garbett, and to congratulate you on this termination of the contest.

I am, Sir, for the Fellows of this College and myself, your obedient faithful servant,

A. T. GILBERT, *Principal.*

Common Room, Trin. Coll. Jan. 20, 1842.

Dear Sir,—At a Meeting held this morning before the Vice-Chancellor, for the purpose of comparing the number of Votes respectively promised to both Candidates for the Poetry Professorship, it appeared that there were for Mr. Garbett, 921, for Mr. Williams, 623. Under these circumstances Mr. Williams withdraws from the contest. With our best thanks for the interest which you have taken, and with the desire to save you farther and unnecessary trouble,

I am, dear Sir, on behalf of the College, yours faithfully,

JAMES INGRAM, *President.*

[We are informed that a large proportion of Voters, (especially among the residents,) remained neuter; thinking Mr. Williams the fittest candidate, and, in the main, approving his views; but not wishing, in the present posture of affairs, to give unqualified support to the party to which he belongs.]

CAMBRIDGE.

PRIZE SUBJECTS.

The Vice-Chancellor has issued the following notice:—

I. His Grace the Duke of Northumberland, Chancellor of the University, being pleased to give annually a Gold Medal, for the encouragement of English Poetry, to such resident Undergraduates as shall compose the best Ode or the best Poem in heroic Verse; the Vice-Chancellor gives notice that the subject for the present year is—

The Birth of the Prince of Wales.

N.B. The Exercises are to be sent in to the Vice-Chancellor on or before March 31, 1842; and are not to exceed 200 lines in length.

II. The Most Noble the Marquess Camden, being pleased to give annually a Gold Medal, as a prize for the best Exercise in Latin Hexameter Verse; the Vice-Chancellor gives notice that the subject for the present year is—

Cæsar ad Rubiconem constitit.

N.B. The Exercises are to be sent in to the Vice-Chancellor on or before March 31, 1842; and are not to exceed 100 lines in length.

All Undergraduates who shall have resided not less than two terms before the day on which the Exercises must be sent in, or who shall, at least, be then in the course of their second term of Residence, may be Candidates for this Medal.

III. The Representatives in Parliament for this University being pleased to give annually (1) Two prizes of fifteen guineas each, for the encouragement of Latin Prose Composition, to be open to all Bachelors of Arts, without distinction of years, who are not of sufficient standing to take the degree of Master of Arts;

(2) And two other prizes of fifteen guineas each, to be open to all Undergraduates, who shall have resided not less than seven Terms, at the time when the Exercises are to be sent in;

The subjects for the present year are—

(1) For the Bachelors,

Sanctiusque ac reverentius visum de Actis Deorum credere quàm scire.

(2) For the Undergraduates,

Argentum et Aurum propitii an irati Dii negaverint dubito.

N.B. The Exercises are to be sent in on or before April 30, 1842.

IV. Sir William Browne having bequeathed three Gold Medals, of the value of five guineas each, to such resident Undergraduates as shall compose—

(1) The best Greek Ode in imitation of Sappho.
(2) The best Latin Ode in imitation of Horace.
(3) { The best Greek Epigram after the model of the Anthologia; and
The best Latin Epigram after the model of Martial.

The subjects for the present year are—

(1) For the Greek Ode—*Ad dextram de viâ declinavi, ut ad Periclis Sepulchrum accederem.*
(2) For the Latin Ode—*Navis ornata atque armata in aquam deducitur.*
(3) For the Greek Epigram—*Is solus nescit omnia.*
(4) For the Latin Epigram—*Pari incepto eventus dispar.*

N.B. The Exercises are to be sent in on or before April 30, 1842. The Greek Ode is not to exceed twenty-five, and the Latin Ode thirty stanzas.

The Greek Ode must be accompanied by a literal Latin Prose Version.

V. The Porson Prize is the interest of 400*l.* stock, to be annually employed in the purchase of one or more Greek books, to be given to such resident Undergraduate as shall make the best translation of a proposed passage in Shakspeare, Ben Jonson, Massinger, or Beaumont and Fletcher, into Greek Verse.

The subject for the present year is,

Shakspeare.—Hen. V. Act IV. Scene 1.

Beginning—"*O Ceremony!*"
And ending—"*Whose hours the peasant best advantage.*"

N.B.—The metre to be *Tragicum Iambicum Trimetrum Acatalecticum.* These exercises are to be accentuated, and accompanied by a literal Latin Prose Version, and are to be sent in on or before April 30, 1842.

N.B.—All the above Exercises are to be sent in to the Vice-Chancellor privately; each is to have some motto prefixed; and to be accompanied by a paper sealed up, with the same motto on the outside; which paper is to enclose another, folded up, having the Candidate's Name and College written within.

The papers containing the Names of those Candidates, who may not succeed, will be destroyed unopened.

Any Candidate is at liberty to send in his Exercise *printed* or *lithographed.*

No prize will be given to any Candidate who has not, at the time of sending in the Exercises, resided one term at the least.

The subject of the Seatonian Prize Poem for the present year is, "The Cross planted on the Himalaya Mountains." Each candidate for this prize is to send his performance, without his name, to the Vice-Chancellor (fairly written, or it will not be attended to,) on or before the 29th of September next, with some Latin Verse upon it: and he is at the same time to send a paper sealed up, with his name written within, and the same Latin Verse on the outside. The papers containing the names of the unsuccessful candidates will be destroyed unopened; by which regulation the delicacy of those, who might otherwise fear a repulse, is, it is hoped, effectually consulted.

ST. JOHN'S COLLEGE EXAMINATIONS.

Third Year.—First Class.

Adams	Gifford	Babington ⎫
Gruggen		Bulmer
Bashforth !	Drew	Boteler ⎬
Brown	Babb	Alston
Campbell	Christian	Burbury
Foggo	Symons	J. Cole
Goodeve	Barnicoat ⎬	Slater
Spencer	Jowett	Watherstone
		Cockle

Second Year.—First Class.

Hemming	Wright	Tatham
Hiley	Stewart	Lawson
Dixon	Gorham	Smith
Stephen	———	O'Reilly
Waddingham		Walker
Gutch	Snowball	Murton
Wall	Wilkinson	Field
Underwood	Frewer	Wilson
Mason	Curtis	Chawner
Barrett	Hoare	Greensmith
Whittaker	Leeding	

January 1.

The Hulsean Prize has been awarded to the Rev. Charles Wright Woodhouse, B.A. of Gonville and Caius College. Subject—"The Use and Value of the Writings of the Ancient Fathers, considered as auxiliary to the Proof of the Truth of the Christian Religion, and to the Elucidation of its Doctrines."

The Trustees of the Hulsean Prize have given notice that a premium of about one hundred pounds will this year be given for the best dissertation on the following subject:—"What is the relation in which the Moral Precepts of the New and of the Old Testament stand to each other?" The dissertations are to be sent to one of the Trustees (the Vice-Chancellor, the Master of Trinity College, or the Master of St. John's College), on or before the 20th of October, 1842, with the names of the respective authors sealed up. The author of the essay best approved is to print it at his own expense, and is not to be a second time a candidate for the premium.

On Saturday, the 18th ult. Henry Annesley Woodham, B.A. was elected a Foundation Fellow of Jesus Coll.

January 8.

John Parker Birkett, B.A. of Jesus College, in this university, has been appointed to the Mathematical Mastership at Harrow, vacated by the Rev. J. W. Colenso, M.A.

BACHELOR'S COMMENCEMENT, *January* 22, 1842.

MODERATORS.
Thomas Gaskin, M.A. Jesus College.
Duncan Farquharson Gregory, M.A. Trinity College.

EXAMINERS.
Alexander Thurtell, M.A. Caius College.
Richard Potter, M.A. Queen's College.

WRANGLERS.

Cayley,	Trin.	Frost,	Joh.	Westmorland,	Jesus	Penny,	Joh.
Simpson,	Joh.	Parnell,	Joh.	Dumergue,	Corpus	Davies, H.	Joh.
Mayor, R. B.	Joh.	Johnstone,	Joh.	Bryan,	Trin.	Eastwood,	Caius
Fuller,	Pet.	Castlehow,	Emm.	Shears,	Joh.	Venables,	Pem.
Bird,	Joh.	Carter,	Emm.	Greenwell,	Joh.	Baily,	Chr.
Jarvis,	Corpus	Wilson,	Joh.	Suffield,	Caius	Light,	Joh.
Shortland,	Pem.	Smith, B. F.	Trin.	Middlemist,	Chr.	Walker,	Sid.
Austin,	Pet.	Fenn,	Trin.	Davies,	Qu.	Tandy,	Joh.
Fenwick,	Corpus	Ainger,	Joh.	Cook,	Joh.	Kinder,	Trin.
Jones,	Clare	Goode,	Pem.				

SENIOR OPTIMES.

Vidal, J. H.	Joh.	Walpole,	Caius	Litle,	Chr.	Lloyd,	Jesus
Fitz Gerald,	Chr.	Rowton,	Joh.	Green,	Caius	Postle,	Corpus
Hey,	Joh.	Wolfe,	Joh.	Hughes, J.	Qu.	Woodford,	Pem.
Parkinson,	Qu.	Morse,	Joh.	Cobb,	Corp.	Thurnall,	Sid.
Ottley,	Caius	Clubbe,	Joh.	Shaw,	Trin.	Blake,	Jesus
Allen,	Trin.	Ommaney,	Trin.	Fowell,	Chr.	Montagu,	Caius
Metcalfe,	Sid.	Ridley,	Jesus	Parr,	Cath.	Balderstone,	Joh.
Vidal, O. E.	Joh.	Douglass,	Trin.	Sharples,	Joh.	Boyce,	Sid.
Inchbald,	Cath.	Hogg,	Emm.	Hopwood,	Pet.	Rothery,	Joh.
Penrose,	Mag.	Marie,	Qu.	Buckham,	Joh.	Salkeld,	Pet.
Riley,	Trin.	Tabor,	Trin.	Thrupp,	Trin.	Gordon,	Pet.
Brooks,	Joh.	Swann,	Chr.	Atkinson,	Clare	Stansfeld,	Joh.
Gillett,	Emm.	Hazlehurst,	Trin.	Kingsley,	Mag.	Munro,	Trin.

JUNIOR OPTIMES.

Twisady,	Joh.	Sheringham,	Joh.	Pratt,	Joh.	Hough,	Caius
Maul,	Joh.	Nugée,	Trin.	Ramsay,	Trin.	Sheepshanks,	Trin.
Vaughan,	Chr.	Peter,	Jesus	Hutchins,	Trin.	Shackleton,	Cath.
Wilkinson,	Joh.	Webster,	Emm.	Slade,	Joh.	Firman,	Qu.
Teague,	Emm.	Smythies,	Emm.	Conybeare,	Pet.	Worlledge,	Clare
Kerry,	Joh.			Yeoman,	Trin.	Barstow,	Trin.

ÆGROTAT.
Onslow, Emm.

DEGREES ALLOWED.

Bishop,	Corpus	Hamilton,	Trin.	McNiven,	Trin.	Parry,	Chr.
Fowler,	Clare	Knipe,	Pem.	Parminter,	Trin.	Wyer,	Joh.

QUESTIONISTS, NOT CANDIDATES FOR HONOURS.

Denman,	Trin.	Broadwood,	Trin.	Langdon,	Joh.	Boucher,	Pet.
Maskew,	Sid.	Brown, S. C.	Joh.	Smelt,	Caius	Hull,	Joh.
Collett,	Pet.	Metcalfe,	Joh.	Plomer,	Joh.	Chase,	Qu.
Briant,	Qu.	Luscombe,	Joh.	Daman,	Qu.	Corbett,	Trin.
Jukes,	Trin.	Wilshere,	Joh.	Griffith,	Jesus	Hibbit,	Cath.
Beresford,	Joh.	Blakiston,	Em.	Morice,	Trin.	Phillips,	Qu.
Browne,	Corpus	Finch,	Cath.	Mayor, C.	Joh.	Nash,	Pem.
Felgate,	Trin.	Crompton,	Trin.	Bulwer,	Trin.	Pell,	Trin.
Hewett,	Sid.	Burnett,	Joh.	Green,	Joh.	Marsden,	Trin.
Webb,	Trin.	Gilpin,	Trin.	Hilton,	Jesus	Koe,	Chr.
Dawes,	Trin.	Hutton,	Cath.	Robinson,	Clare	Anson,	Jesus
Francis,	Trin.H.	Milne,	Trin.	Williamson,	Trin.	Morris,	Cath.
Dowding,	Caius	White,	Mag.	Biddulph,	Em.	Allen,	Cath.
Williams,	Clare	Chase,	Emm.	Mansfield,	Trin.	Creyke,	Cath.
Wagner,	Trin.	Crabbe,	Qu.	Mott,	Joh.	Foster,	Corp.
Holligan,	Trin.	Fleming,	Joh.	Lewis, D. P.	Joh.	Sandford,	Trin.
Brimley,	Trin.	Burke,	Qu.	Hartopp,	Trin.	Ambrose,	Joh.
Snape,	Chr.	Bingham,	Jesus	Burgess,	Chr.	Mathews,	Clare
Norman,	Qu.	Stanton,	Joh.	Tomlins,	Joh.	Croft,	Trin.
Dew,	Jesus	Ridout,	Emm.	Campbell,	Trin.	Laing,	Qu.
Clarke,	Down	Suckling,	Joh.	Howell,	Emm.	Turner,	Caius
Fenwick,	Joh.	Cole, A. W.	Joh.	Crouch,	Trin.	Parker,	Corpus
Sheldon,	Trin.	Goldham,	Corpus	Richardson,	Jesus	De St. Croix,	Joh.
Marston,	Trin.	Neville Rolfe,	Trin.	Spong,	Caius	Fowler,	Mag.

Newbould,	Trin.	Call,	Joh.	Rogers,	Trin.	Bell,	Joh.
Bellman,	Pet.	Lush,	Corp.	Williams,	Trin.	Dry,	Caius
Dutton,	Trin.	Caulfeild, H. C.	Trin.	Gream,	Mag.	Wright,	Pet.
Millman,	Joh.	Hewit,	Trin.	Pane,	Joh.	Farr,	Joh.
Whitelock,	Joh.	Franks,	Trin.	Monk,	Joh.	Charles,	Trin.
Willis,	Trin.	Day,	Joh.	Mills,	Trin.	Lee Warner,	Joh.
Lighton,	Trin.	Burman,	Caius	Dennis,	Trin.	Hill,	Jesus
Harriott,	Trin.	Burr,	Joh.	Hughes, sen.	Qu.	Hewson,	Joh.

DEGREES ALLOWED.

Bunce,	Clare	Haggitt,	Pet.	Newnham,	Trin.	Steel,	Joh.
Calvert,	Pem.	Henderson,	Trin.	Raven,	Mag.	Vincent,	Joh.
Featherston,	Jesus	Killick,	Qu.				

ÆGROTAT.

Headley, Joh.

NOT PLACED.

Chalk, Caius.

DURHAM.

VAN MILDERT SCHOLARSHIPS.—In consideration of two several sums of money given to the University by the subscribers to a scholarship and the subscribers to a monument, in memory of the late Bishop Van Mildert, two scholarships shall be founded of the annual value of £50 each, to be called the Van Mildert Scholarships. The first scholar on this foundation shall be elected in June, 1842; and there shall be no further elections on the old foundation. Regulations were passed for the election to the Van Mildert scholarships.

GISBORNE SCHOLARSHIP.—The Rev. Thomas Gisborne, M.A., Canon of Durham, having placed £500 at the disposal of the Dean and Chapter for the benefit of the University, and the Dean and Chapter having determined that this sum should be applied to the foundation of a scholarship: It is agreed—That £100 previously given to the University by Mr. Gisborne shall be added to the above sum, and that, in consideration of these gifts, a scholarship shall be founded of the annual value of £30, to be called the Gisborne Scholarship. That the warden and senate shall have authority to make regulations respecting the Gisborne Scholarship.

REGULATIONS FOR UNIVERSITY FELLOWSHIPS.—1. The University fellows shall be elected by the warden and senate in the Michaelmas term in each year. 2. No one shall be eligible unless he has been placed by the examiners in the third class, at least, at the public examination for the degree of B.A., or in the second class, at least, at the public examination for the degree of M.A., or has been recommended by the said examiners as eligible. 3. No one shall be eligible unless he has produced satisfactory testimonials of character from his college, hall, or house. 4. No one shall be eligible for more than three elections after he is admissible to the degree of B.A. The warden and senate shall have authority to dispense with the last regulation in the case of those students who have been admitted to the degree of B.A. in or before Michaelmas Term, 1841. 5. The warden and senate in making their election shall have due regard for the candidate's place on the class list. But they shall have authority, if they think fit, to subject the candidates to further examination, either by themselves or by persons whom they may appoint. 6. The warden and senate shall have authority to settle the form of admission to a fellowship. 7. The fellows shall be under the government of the warden; but in graver cases the warden shall consult the senate; and, with their concurrence, he shall have full power to forbid residence, to suspend the payment of stipend, or to remove from the fellowship altogether. 8. Every fellow shall proceed regularly to the degree of M.A., unless he shall obtain the consent of the warden to proceed to a degree in another faculty. If he neglects to proceed to the required degree within a reasonable time, the warden shall have authority to declare the fellowship vacant. 9. A fellowship shall not be tenable with a foundation studentship.

THE BISHOP OF DURHAM'S PRIZES.

HEBREW LITERATURE AND HELLENISTIC GREEK.—A prize of ten guineas to the Student who shall pass the best examination in the Book of Genesis, in Hebrew, and in the Septuagint Version, and in the Gospel according to St. Mark, in Greek, with special reference to Hellenistic phraseology and expression.

CLASSICAL LITERATURE.—For Students in Arts who have not completed their ninth term of residence:—

A prize of five guineas for the best translation into Latin prose of No. 133 of the "Spectator."

A prize of five guineas for the best translation into Latin hexameter Verse of Milton's Paradise Lost, Book vii. 387—446: beginning, "And God said, let the waters generate," and ending, "coloured with the florid hue of rainbows and starry eyes."

MATHEMATICAL AND PHYSICAL SCIENCE.—A prize of ten guineas to be given to the student who shall pass the examination in Mathematical and Physical Science, at the final examination for the degree of B.A., or at the final examination of Engineer Students in the year 1842, and shall be recommended by the Examiners.

PROCEEDINGS OF SOCIETIES.

INCORPORATED SOCIETY FOR PROMOTING THE ENLARGEMENT, BUILDING, AND REPAIRING OF CHURCHES AND CHAPELS.

A meeting of the Committee of this Society was held at their chambers, St. Martin's Place, on Monday, the 17th of January, 1842; the Lord Bishop of London in the chair. Among the members present were the Reverends T. Bowdler, and B. Harrison; H. J. Barchard, J. Cocks, B. Harrison, S. F. Wood, T. D. Acland, M.P., A. Powell, and E. Badeley, Esqs.

Grants were voted towards enlarging the church at Blackpool, in the parish of Bispham, Lancashire; erecting a gallery in and repewing the church at Ebbesborne Wake, Wilts; enlarging and repewing the church at Brotherton, Yorkshire; rebuilding the church at Honley, in the parish of Almondbury, Yorkshire; building a gallery in and repewing the church at Brodsworth, Yorkshire; building a gallery in and repewing the church at Stoke Holy Cross, Norwich; repewing the church at Pembridge, Herefordshire; enlarging by rebuilding the church at Rodborough, Gloucestershire; repewing the church at Alwalton, Huntingdonshire; building a church at Newcastle-on-Tyne; and other business was transacted.

MISCELLANEOUS INTELLIGENCE.

HEREFORD CATHEDRAL. — Earl Somers, Lord Bateman, and Mr. E.T. Foley, have respectively given the munificent donation of £200. for the restoration of Hereford Cathedral. Mr. J. Bailey, M.P., has subscribed £150, and the Hon. T. H. Rodney and Sir J. G. Cotterell, bart. are donors of £100 each. The fund to liquidate the expenses of that necessary undertaking has already reached nearly £5000.

RECENT DONATIONS.—The Earl of Harewood has given the handsome donation of £3000 to the Ripon Diocesan Board of Education. Mrs. Burgess, widow of the late Lord Bishop of Salisbury, has given £50 towards rebuilding the parish church of Abergwilly, in the diocese of St. David's, of which the late bishop was heretofore the diocesan.

The Right Hon. William Yates Peel has given the liberal sum of £50, and Sir Edward Scott £100, in aid of the funds of the Lichfield Diocesan Church Extension Society.

The Right Hon. Mrs. Berkeley Noel has presented a service of communion plate for the use of the new church at Wishaw, Warwickshire.

BIBLE SOCIETY.—The *Dorset County Chronicle* publishes a letter from the Bishop of Salisbury requesting that his name may not be announced as connected with the Bible Society, or as patronizing any of its meetings. The right rev. prelate intimates that he has withdrawn from all connexion with that body.

EMBARKATION OF THE BISHOP OF NEW ZEALAND.

The Bishop of New Zealand embarked for the scene of his apostolic labours at Plymouth, on the day following Christmas-day. For the following interesting letter, descriptive of the embarkation, we are indebted to our contemporary, the *Exeter Gazette*.

"My dear Sir,—Feeling assured as I do, that you will be glad to receive from me a few lines on the subject of our dear and honoured friend's departure from this place, I take up my pen, though in great haste, to send you a very brief account of what has taken place here since Thursday last.

"Immediately after the morning service at St. Andrew's Church on that day, we repaired to the bishop's lodgings; whence, after a short delay, he set out, accompanied by a few of his most intimate friends, in the barge of the *Caledonia* for the *Tomatin*, while the greater part of his followers, with the luggage, sailed from the Barbican in the Trinity-house Cutter. We passed two or three hours on board; but the wind being adverse, and there being no chance of sailing, we came off again to shore. The rest of the day was passed in cheerful, yet serious, conversation, and we ended, as usual, with prayer; our number being now very much diminished by the loss of those who were on board, and of those friends who had been obliged to return to their several homes. On Friday we again went on board soon after breakfast, taking Mrs. Selwyn and her little child with us; but the wind being still adverse, and Mrs. S. not being well, it was thought advisable to bring her ashore again, until the signal should be made for sailing. The bishop remained on board, where Divine service was duly performed on Christmas-day. The bishop came on shore for an hour on that same evening, and returned again to the ship to sleep.

"The wind having come round to the N.N.W. during the night, we were summoned by nine o'clock on Sunday morning to go on board. This we did without any delay. At 11 o'clock Divine service was performed, and the Sacrament of the Lord's Supper announced for the following Sabbath. This done, the bishop wrote a few lines to his mother, and a few words of affection in my Bible, while they were weighing anchor. At half-past twelve we embraced each other fervently, as those who did not expect to see each other again in this world, and descended into the boat amid the prayers and affectionate good wishes of many on board; and in a moment the vessel, with her goodly freight, was on her way. The bishop, Mrs. Selwyn, Whytehead, Cotton, and others, all dear to us, remained on the poop waving their hands to us, and exchanging with us short prayers for God's blessing each on the other. Our last words were, 'God bless you; Floreat Etona! Floret Ecclesia!' To which they all responded by a cheer of heartfelt acquiescence. And then I felt the full force of those words of St. Luke, Acts xxi.6, which the bishop had a few moments before inscribed in my Bible, 'When we had taken leave one of another, *we* took ship, and *they* returned home again.'

"It will, I am sure, do your heart good to know that they maintained their wonted cheerfulness and well-grounded fixedness of purpose to the end. Indeed I may say of all going forth on this holy mission, that they seemed with one accord to have resolved to put all things behind them for the sake of Christ, and to seek the glory and love of God with *all* their heart, with *all* their mind, with *all* their souls, and with *all* their strength. O may the presence of God go with them, leading them safely through the pathless waste of ocean, into the haven where they would be, and guiding their feet hereafter in the arduous course they will have to run.

"Let us in our daily prayers remember the last words uttered by our dear and devoted friend from the Cathedral pulpit, 'Brethren, pray, pray for us.'

"I am, my dear Sir, yours very heartily,
"EDWARD COLERIDGE."

"*Plymouth, Dec.* 26, 1841. *St. Stephen's Day.*"

WALES.

LAMPETER.—The Rev. G. F. Bates, Vicar of West Malling, Kent, has bequeathed to St. David's College, Lampeter, £500 three per cent. Consols. It has been determined that the dividends arising from this legacy shall be given in two prizes; one to be awarded at the commencement of each term to such candidate for admission, being a native of the Principality, as shall pass the best classical examination, such candidate bringing a certificate of good conduct, during two years at least, at some classical school, previous to his application for admission.

CHURCHES CONSECRATED.

Llangorwen, Cardiganshire		Bishop of St. David's	Dec. 16.
Weston Point, Runcorn		Bishop of Chester	Dec. 24.
East Peckham		Opened on Christmas Day.	
Deptford, Sunderland	St. Andrew	Bishop of Durham	Dec. 21.
Bethnal Green	St. Andrew	Bishop of London	Dec. 20.

THE CHURCH IN AMERICA.

The American Church Almanack for 1842, gives the following account of the Church in the United States:—

Diocese.	Bishops.	Clergy.
Maine	A. V. Griswold, D.D.	7
New Hampshire		9
Vermont	J. H. Hopkins, D.D.	26
Massachussetts	A. V. Griswold, D.D.	52
Rhode Island		18
Connecticut	T. C. Brownell, D.D. LL.D.	92
New York	B. T. Onderkonk, D.D.	193
Western N. York	W. H. De Lancy, D.D.	90
New Jersey	G. W. Doane, D.D. LL.D.	43
Pennsylvania	H. U. Onderkonk, D.D.	105
Delaware	Alfred Lee, D.D.	10
Maryland	W. R. Whittingham, D.D.	80
Virginia	{R. C. Moore, D.D. W. Mead, DD. Assist. Bp.	98
North Carolina	L. S. Ives, D.D. LL.D.	25
South Carolina	C. E. Gadsden, D.D.	45
Georgia	S. Elliott, D.D.	10
Kentucky	B. B. Smith, D.D.	20
Ohio	C. P. M'Ilvaine, D.D.	58
Tenesse	J. H. Otey, D.D.	11
Mississippi		9
Louisiana	L. Polk, D.D.	6
Michigan	S. A. M'Coskrey, D.D.	19
Alabama	L. Polk, D.D.	12
Illinois	Philander Chase, D.D.	11
Florida	(No Bishop)	7
Indiana	J. Kemper, D.D.	15
Missouri		10
Wisconsin		9
Iowa		3
Arkansas	L. Polk, D.D.	4

Clergy	1097
Bishops	21

Total number of Clergy.. 1118

Including the Bishops, the total number of Clergy appears to be 1118, and counting 100 for Western New York, which Dr. Rould states to be the correct number for that diocese, we have the still higher total of 1218. It will be observed that there are more dioceses than Bishops. Bishop Griswold, of Massachussetts, administers, in addition, the dioceses of Rhode Island, New Hampshire, and Maine. Bishop Otey, of Tenesse, presides all over the diocese of Mississippi; Bishop Kemper of Missouri, over Iowa, Wisconsin, and Indiana; and Bishop Polk, of Arkansas, over Louisiana and Alabama.

TO CORRESPONDENTS.

We are much obliged by the following communication:—

"*Burton Agnes, Driffield, Jan.* 8, 1842.

"Sir,—A mistake in my country bookseller has prevented me from seeing your December number till to-day. But on looking over the article on Archbishop Laud's Letters, I see that you have published one (at p. 390) which had already appeared in the Introduction to Cotelerius's Apost. Fathers. It is the first in the Syllabus Epist. (edit. 1698). The person addressed was the learned Benedictine Menard. It was communicated by Archbishop Sancroft.

"I remain, Sir, your obedient servant,
"*The Editor of the Christian Remembrancer.*" "ROBT. I. WILBERFORCE."

ST. NICHOLAS, CAEN.

FONTAINE, NEAR DIJON.

From Petit's "Remarks on Ecclesiastical Architecture." See p. 353.

THE CHRISTIAN REMEMBRANCER.

MARCH, 1842.

History of Scotland. By PATRICK FRASER TYTLER, *Esq.* Vol. VI. 1546—1565. Edinburgh: William Tait, 1842.

(*Continued from p.* 187.)

WHEN the first volume of Mr. Tytler's elaborate history of his own country appeared, now many years since, Sir Walter Scott honoured it by a full and careful notice in the leading review of the day, expressing, at the same time, his intention of analyzing with equal care every successive volume, as it might appear. Circumstances, however, prevented Sir Walter from fulfilling his intention; but the record of that his wish still remains as an evidence of the high opinion he had of the value and interest of the historian's labours. It must be our excuse for attempting to follow one of the ablest of historical reviewers, (haud passibus æquis,) in discussing *seriatim* those volumes of the work in which the events of the Scottish Reformation are treated on. In this sixth volume, the Reformation bursts on us in all its fulness of confusion, rapine, and bloodshed, affording us one example, among many, of that mysterious Providence which turns the worst actions and the worst motives of the worst of men to the best of purposes. The bigotry of Mary of Guise—the ambition of France—the vacillating temper of the Lord James—the cruelty of the border wars—the cowardice of Knox—the intrigues and falsehoods of Elizabeth and Cecil, all seem to be working to one great and mysterious end. But to return to our history.

The murder of Beaton, the head and heart of the government and of the party that looked to France for assistance, was for the moment a great blow to the professors of the ancient faith, who almost alone cherished the freedom and independence of their native land. To the English faction it came as a long-expected boon, and afforded a crisis in the affairs of Scotland which it wanted but the immediate exertion of the monarch, who had encouraged the conspiracy, to turn to his own advantage, by the marriage of his son with the youthfu queen, the establishment of the Reformation, and the subjugation o the country through those nobles who sold themselves to his wishes. Delay on the part of Henry permitted the government to rally from the shock. And eventually, that murder, which was planned and executed for the destruction of the French party, through its head, became the means of increasing its power. The assassins, who had seized the almost impregnable castle of St. Andrew's, were soon joined by many adherents, who, well aware that suspicion must attach to them through those of their party who had committed the deed, preferred throwing themselves into the fortress, where peradventure they might exact good terms, to trusting to the tender mercies of their opponents. Among those who thus joined themselves to the murderers, and made common cause with the bloody crew, was the great advocate and promoter of the Reformation, John Knox.

"This extraordinary man, whose future career was connected with so many great events, was now forty years old. Born, in 1505, of parents in the middle rank of rural life, and wealthy enough to give him a learned education, he had been sent in 1521 to the university of Glasgow, where he distinguished himself in philosophy and scholastic theology, and took priest's orders previous to his having attained the canonical age, as it is said. It is difficult to fix the time when his mind became unsettled on the grounds of his adherence to the communion of the Roman catholic church; and it is remarkable, that the labours of his numerous biographers have left his history from birth to middle age almost a blank. The fact asserted by Beza, of his having been condemned as a heretic, and degraded from the priesthood, rests on no certain evidence. It has been stated, also, by Dr. Maine, that he publicly professed himself a Protestant in 1542. But this learned author has given no satisfactory authority for this fact; and I have found no trace of such a public declaration of his belief previous to the capture and execution of George Wishart in 1545. But the step which he now took was decisive By casting in his lot with the assassins of the cardinal, he openly declared his approval of the principles on which they acted; and they, as we may well believe, warmly welcomed such an accession to their party."—*Tytler*, vol. vi. pp. 2, 3.

The first act of David Straiton in the cause of protestantism was to refuse, with insult, a rightful demand of his bishop. The first public act of Knox in the same cause was openly to sanction a mercenary and cold-blooded murder. The temporary union of the more moderate men on both sides, and the acceptance by Scotland of that clause in the late treaty between England and France, by which the Scots might claim to be comprehended in the benefits and terms of the treaty, enabled the government to proceed with vigour against Beaton's murderers. After an ineffectual attempt at negotiation, the Parliament, in July 1546, declared them guilty of treason; and proclamation having been made, interdicting all persons from rendering them any assistance, the governor Arran assembled the forces of the kingdom, and sat down before the castle, with the determination of speedily reducing the fortress. The great strength, however, of the defences of the castle, and the imperfect and ill-served artillery of the Scottish army, enabled the castilians, as they were called, to defy the attacks of the governor's host; whilst the immense stock of provisions stored up by the cardinal, provided them with a defence against starvation, even should they not be assisted by supplies thrown in by the English fleet. At last Arran agreed to obtain for them absolution from the pope, and to grant a free pardon to the conspirators, who were to hold the castle until both had been obtained. And whilst Arran laboured to obtain the one from the pope, by the influence of the king of France, of whom he besought an immediate supply of arms and artillery, and men learned in the attack and defence of fortified places, the castilians sent an envoy to Henry of England, to request him to throw every impediment in the way of the absolution, as it was but a feint, in order to obtain time for revictualling the castle.

" In the mean time," says Mr. Tytler, "an extraordinary and interesting scene took place within the fortress. Knox, as we have seen, had retreated into the castle and joined the conspirators. He was accompanied by the barons of Ormistown and Lang Niddry and their sons, whose education he conducted. In the chapel within the fort he catechised his pupils, and delivered lectures on the Scriptures, where a little congregation was soon assembled, who earnestly entreated him to preach publicly to the people. This, however, he at first peremptorily declined, observing, 'that he would not run where God had not called him;' but they who were deeply interested in his assuming the office of the ministry, for which they believed him to be eminently qualified, determined to overcome his reluctance. John Rough, whom we have seen dismissed, on account of his zeal for the Reformation, from the situation of chaplain to Arran, the governor, had taken refuge with the rest in the fortress; and on a certain day which had been agreed upon, having selected as the subject of his discourse the power resident in a congregation to elect their minister, and the danger of rejecting their call, he, on the conclusion of the sermon, turned abruptly to Knox, who was present—'Brother,' said he, 'I charge you in the name of God, in the name of his Son, and in the name of this congregation, who now call you by my mouth, that you take upon you the office of preaching, and refuse not this holy vocation as you would avoid God's heavy displeasure.' The address was solemn, and totally unexpected by Knox, who, confused and agitated, in vain attempted to reply, but bursting into tears retired from the assembly. After a few days of great conflict and distress of mind, he accepted the invitation; and without any further ceremony or ordination than that already received previous to his adoption of the reformed opinions, he assumed the office of public preacher."—*Tytler*, vol. vi. 9, 10.

Admitting this event to have been unexpected by Knox, and not a pre-arranged scene on the part of all the actors, could the reluctance of Knox have originated from any doubt on his part as to the validity of his ordination having been affected by his adoption of views deemed heretical by his Church? Or did he ponder on the awful nature of that call in which the names of his Creator and his Redeemer were associated with that of a congregation, of whose members, many had plotted, many had effected, and all had by their entry within the walls of the castle given in their approval of, the cardinal's murder, and their adherence to the perpetrators of the deed? or did he, with his usual timidity, fear to assume that position among the reformers which he had already seen to lead, by no circuitous path, to prison and to death?

.The death of Henry, at this period, threw the power of England into the hands of one who was a determined enemy of Scotland, and an earnest and active friend to every one who would wage war with Rome, and therefore of the conspirators; whilst the decease of Francis threw the entire power of the realm of France into the hands of the Guises, who soon showed how earnest they were in their opposition to England and their support of the Roman Catholic faith. The one event caused a border war of a short duration; the other brought Leo Strozzi, the knight of Rhodes, and his well-armed fleet, into the Firth of Forth, to assist in the reduction of the castle of St. Andrew's. The rejection of the pope's absolution, the excesses and debauched conduct of the traitors, and the cruelties they had exercised on all around, during the armistice, notwithstanding the remonstrances of Knox, had deeply incensed Arran against them. Hastening back from the borders, he soon commenced his attack, and with the aid of the heavy artillery and skill of the knightly prior of Capua, soon forced the conspirators to surrender to Strozzi, as the representative of France, (for they would not recognise any lawful authority in Scotland,) on the condition of their lives, should such terms be afterwards approved by the king his master. On their arrival in France, some were consigned to the dungeons of the various castles in Brittany; whilst others, amongst whom was Knox, worked in chains on board the galleys.

The destruction of the castle of St. Andrew's brought to light the register book of the conspirators, in which the autographs of two hundred Scottish nobles, the chief leaders of the protestant party, appeared as bound,—some by bribes of matrimonial alliances, others by pensions,—to support the king of England in the enforcement of his marriage with Mary, and the establishment of the Reformation at the sacrifice of the independence of the country. In September 1547, the protector Somerset, well aware how little resistance he should meet with, in consequence of the adherence of so many barons to his side, broke across the borders with his powerful army; and in less than a week, the thousands of Scots whom the fiery cross had summoned to the defence of their country had melted away, and the rout at Faside Hill and Pinkie had laid the land of Scotland at the feet of the protector. The secret plotting in England, and the firmness of the queen-mother, saved the country. The defeat of Lord Wharton, and the threat of forthwith providing for the safety of the young queen in France, had their effects on Somerset; and though the Lord Wharton held some sway over the west marches of the country, and had tampered to an alarming extent with the nobility of the land, yet affairs were hardly so disastrous as the fatal field of Pinkie might have led them to expect. The escape of Mary to France, the strong auxiliary force sent by that country, and the failure of pensions from England, eventually restored the power of Scotland; and after nine years of unceasing and most cruel warfare, peace was proclaimed at Edinburgh in 1550, and France and Scotland united more closely than before as the opponents of England and the Reformation.

A few years now brought about many important events. Mary of Guise, by the diligent and unscrupulous use of those means which circumstances placed at her command, contrived to deprive Arran of his governorship, and to assume to herself the protectorate of her daughter's kingdom. The death of our Edward, and the accession of Mary, contributed to the success of the plans of the queen-mother.

"Mary of Guise," says Mr. Tytler, "who now assumed the supreme authority, was in many respects well qualified for her high situation. She possessed a calm judgment; good, though not brilliant, natural parts; manners which, without losing their dignity, were feminine and engaging; and so intimate a knowledge of the character of the people over whom she ruled, that, if left to herself, there was every prospect of her managing affairs with wisdom and success. Her abilities, indeed, were sufficiently apparent in the quiet and triumphant manner in which she had brought about the revolution which placed her at the head of affairs. Although of a different religion, she had so entirely gained the affections of the Protestant party, that their support was one chief cause of her success. Nor by the prudent concessions she made to their opponents, had she alienated from herself the hearts of the adherents of the ancient faith, whose leaders she attached to her interest by gifts of the vacant benefices, and the exertion of her influence at the papal court. It was chiefly by her management that the fierce and sanguinary feuds, which for a long period had distracted the Scottish aristocracy, were composed; and her assumption of the regency was viewed with equal satisfaction by the clergy, the nobility, and the people. But the possession of power is fraught with danger to the best. She had incurred many obligations to the court of France, which her gratitude impelled her to repay by intruding foreigners into the offices hitherto filled by natives; and, unmindful of the extraordinary jealousy with which the Scottish people were disposed to regard all interference of this kind, she lent herself to measures dictated more by the ambition of the house of Guise, than by a desire to promote the happiness of her daughter's kingdom."—*Tytler*, vol. vi. pp. 59, 60.

Under the influence of the new regent, not only the French interest, but the actual numbers of that nation, rapidly increased in Scotland, and in one way or other assumed to themselves the chief offices in the realm. The marriage of Mary with the dauphin was hastened, and the power of France thus established in Scotland; and when the commissioners, who had been sent by the estates to be present at the ceremony of the marriage, and confirm the agreements under which it had been made, remained firm against the seductions and intrigues of the Guises, it is worthy of remark, when we remember the unscrupulous character of the age, that not one of them who was most opposed to the encroachments of France left that country alive. No infectious disease was at that time prevalent in France. Yet when they reached Dieppe, those of the commissioners who had throughout been most opposed to the wishes of the Guises, and who from their station and rank would exercise the greatest influence over their countrymen, died suddenly one after the other. On the 6th of September, 1558, Reid, bishop of Orkney, one of the wisest and most upright men in Scotland, died suddenly on reaching Dieppe, and was followed, within a few days, by the earl of Rothes, the Lord Treasurer Cassilis, and the Lord Fleming. During these events, Mary died, and Elizabeth ascended the throne of England, with the determination of uniting the whole nation into one way of religion; and whilst she protested against the errors of Rome, was equally opposed to the iconoclastic fury of the puritanical party. According to Neal, she affected a middle way between popery and puritanism, disliking the secular pretensions of Rome, yet attached to the splendour of her worship,—approving the christian doctrines of the Reformed Churches, yet at the same time thinking that they had stripped religion too much of its ornaments. Such was the sovereign with whom Mary of Guise contracted peace in the beginning of the year, after the solemnization of the marriage between her daughter and the dauphin.

Having thus made a general summary of events, from the death of Beaton to the accession of Elizabeth, let us now turn to the more immediate actors in the Reformation. Knox, the head of the reforming party, remained a prisoner at the galleys until his release was obtained in 1550, by the intercession of Edward the Sixth. The opinions of the young king and his advisers made him a welcome guest at the court, where he remained, until the accession of Mary drove him into exile, and he assumed the place of minister to the brethren at Francfort. His attachment to the doctrines of Calvin, and his opposition to the service-book of Edward VI. soon drove him from thence. He again visited Calvin, and became more and more a convert to all his views; and having learnt, no doubt, that the cautious policy of Mary of Guise offered security to Protestants, as well as Catholics, he determined to return to Scotland, and, now that times seemed less dangerous, " to abide at his post," as he said, and sacrifice every thing to the establishment of his views of what the Reformation ought to be. During Knox's absence, little had been done in favour of the Reformation in Scotland; the preaching of refugees from the tyranny of our Mary had spirited away some few images, and kept alive the hatred to superstition; but, on the other hand, the conduct of the queen regent, and her perfect system of toleration, had gone much further in persuading the Protestants not only to conform outwardly to the national Church, but to have some conscientious doubts as to their duty of openly separating from Rome. The arrival of Knox, in 1555, soon changed the face of affairs; and in obedience to his commands, the practice of conformity was renounced, and a public and formal separation from the national Church determined upon, by the hearers of his sermons. At length, the clergy were roused from their lethargy, and the preacher was summoued to appear before an ecclesiastical convention in the capital. Perhaps well assured of the extent to which the queen regent was prepared to extend her toleration, he repaired to the meeting,—found the diet deserted, and remained in Edinburgh, the denouncer of his opponents. As long as he confined his attacks to the pulpit, Mary of Guise did not interfere; but when he boldly addressed a letter to her, demanding the encouragement of the protestant preachers, he soon learnt that he had overstepped the bounds of the regent's toleration; he soon became aware that persecution was coming on, and he acted according to his interpretation of " sacrificing every thing for the Reformation"—he fled from the country, and left his hearers and his brethren to abide the storm. Although Mr. Tytler is too good a Scot not to call Knox, " *the uncompromising and intrepid advocate of the Reformation*," he is too honest an historian to attempt to conceal the awkward coincidence of his accepting the Genevan invitation at this time.

" At this critical period," says Mr. Tytler, " when rejoicing in the success of his preaching, and congratulating himself that the time of the Church's deliverance was drawing nigh, Knox received an invitation to become pastor of the Reformed Church at Geneva; *and the readiness with which he obeyed the summons is an inexplicable circumstance in his life.* Although his labours had been singularly rewarded, the infant congregation which he had gathered round him still required his nurture and protection. During his last journey into Angus, the threatenings of the friars and bishops had increased, and the clouds of persecution were gathering around him. The state of the reformation at Geneva, on the contrary, was prosperous. He had before bitterly upbraided himself for deserting his (self?)-appointed charge in the hour of peril; yet he now repeated the same conduct, left his native country, and settled with his family on the continent. It was in vain to tell his followers, as he did, that if they continued in godliness, whenever they pleased they might command his return. They were continuing in the truth, as he has himself informed us; and they earnestly but unsuccessfully endeavoured to detain him. The rage, indeed, of his opponents was at this time about to assume a deadly aspect. They had delated him as an enemy to the magistrates, as well as a seducer of the people, and possibly by retiring he saved his life: but, judging with all charity, it must be admitted, that, whilst his writings at this season had all the impassioned zeal, his conduct betrays some want of the ardent courage, of the martyr."—*Tytler*, vol. vi. pp. 80, 81.

Knox, no doubt, had a great respect for his own opinions on Church government and religion in general, but he had a far greater respect for his own life; and though he might be ready to admit that great benefits had resulted to the Protestants from the murder of Wishart, as well as of Beaton, yet he hardly recognised the necessity of his being burnt, in order that the natural revulsion of men's minds might work out good to the cause of the Reformation, and some few nobles might immediately lay hands on the property and lands of their nearest convents.

As soon as Knox was gone, he was condemned by his opponents and burnt in effigy, and an attempt was made by the queen regent to intimidate the preachers, who had not received invitations to foreign congregations, by issuing a proclamation, in which certain of them were summoned to answer for their conduct. The multitude of armed barons who attended the preachers to the capital, and the bold defiance given to the queen regent by one of their number—

Chalmers of Gathgirth — when commanded to leave the capital and repair to the borders, compelled the regent to revoke her proclamation, and promise to judge of the controversy herself. The success of this demonstration on the part of the protestant nobles, and the tranquillity with which it was followed, induced the leaders to commission the prior of St. Andrew's, afterwards the great regent Murray, to inform the runaway Knox, " how they thirsted for his presence, and were ready to jeopard their lives for the glory of God :" adding, what they knew was far more effective, that " little cruelty had been used against them; the influence of the friars was decreasing, and they had good hopes that God would augment his flock." Knox accepted the invitation ; and on his arrival at Dieppe, on his return, learnt from letters that met him there, that his presence was now hardly desired, as too many preferred the toleration they now enjoyed to the peril of a public reformation. Such symptoms of cowardice the reformer could not tolerate, except in his own case, and, consequently, by a series of impassioned letters and addresses, recalled the nobles to his own views, and so far encouraged them, as to obtain the signing of the covenant, by which open war was declared with the national Church, and toleration and compromise were ended.

" The Lords deplored their weakness; a new impulse was given to the cause; zeal and resolution animated their repentant followers; and on the third of December, 1557, that memorable bond or covenant was drawn up, which henceforth united the Protestants under one great association, which was subscribed immediately by their principal supporters, and could not be deserted without something like apostasy. It described, in no mild or measured terms, the bishops and ministers of the Roman Catholic church, as members of Satan, who sought to destroy the gospel of Christ and his followers; and declared, that they felt it to be their duty to strive in their Master's cause even unto death, certain as they were of victory in him. For this purpose it declared, that they had entered into a solemn promise, in the presence of ' the Majesty of God and his Congregation,' to set forward and establish, with their whole power and substance, his blessed word—to labour to have faithful ministers, to defend them, at the peril of their lives and goods, against all tyranny; and it concluded by anathematizing their adversaries, and denouncing vengeance against all the superstition, idolatry, and abominations of the Roman Church."—*Tytler*, vol. vi. pp. 83, 84.

This new authority in the state soon proceeded to action. The Congregation, as they styled themselves, having resolved that the service-book of Edward VI. should be henceforth used in every parish church on Sundays and week-days, and such curates as could not read, should be displaced by the most qualified in their parish ; the earl of Argyle and the rest of the Lords of the Congregation proceeded to put these resolutions into practice wherever their power extended. Knox, however, still remained abroad, whilst he continued to excite his party by letters and remonstrances. The Roman Catholics, seized with a deep alarm at the new feature presented in the contest by the formation of the Congregation, presented to the queen regent the treasonable nature of its declaration and subsequent acts, in openly attacking the national religion, and assuming a power of legislation and execution vested in parliament and its officers alone. The regent endeavoured to temporize, and expressed her disinclination to all extreme measures against the Congregation, encouraging by her leniency the views of the Protestants, which it only required the cruel execution of Walter Miln to fix immoveably. The horror and indignation which the execution of that octogenarian Protestant excited amongst the people, and the denial of her sanction to such proceedings by Mary of Guise, enabled the unwearying agents of the Reformers to unite the majority of all classes in favour of their opinions. The address which was presented to the queen regent against the " tyranny of the state ecclesiastical," embodies the views of the leaders of the Reformation at this period.

" ' Your grace,' said the petitioners, ' cannot be ignorant what controversy hath been, and yet is, concerning the true religion and right worshipping of God, and how the clergy (as they will be called) usurp to themselves such empire over the consciences of men, that whatsoever they command must be obeyed, and whatsoever they forbid, avoided, without respect to God's pleasure revealed in his Word, or else there abideth for us but fagot, fire, and sword.' They then noted the cruel executions of their brethren, and declared that, although at the time they had neither defended these martyrs, nor demanded a redress of their wrongs, they were now convinced that, as a part of that power which God had established in the realm, it was their duty either to have protected them from such extremity, or to have borne with them open testimony to their faith. It was evident, they said, that abuses had grown to such a head that a public reformation was necessary, as well in religion as in the temporal government of the state; and they therefore implored her Grace and her grave council, whom they willingly acknowledged as the only authority placed in the realm for the correction of ecclesiastical and civil disorders, that she would listen to their requests, unless by God's Word it could be shown that they were unjust, and ought to be denied."—*Tytler*, vol. vi. pp. 87, 88.

To this supplication, which seems to prove that the Congregation had begun to perceive that their former proceedings had been far from legal, certain requisitions of reformation were attached. The first demanded leave for the Congregation to hear common prayers, in public or private. The second prayed that it might be lawful for any one present, sufficiently well qualified, to expound the Scriptures. Thirdly, they demanded the administration of the sacraments in the vulgar tongue, and the Eucharist in both kinds: and, lastly, such a reformation of the lives of the clergy as was in obedience to the New Testament, the writings of the Fathers, and the godly laws of the Emperor Justinian—the three standards of their disputes with the Roman Catholics. Had we no other evidence, we could not fail of tracing in the first and second requisitions the opposing influences of the English and the Genevan schools: the one supported by the followers of Knox, the other by those of our own countrymen whom the persecution of Mary had driven into Scotland some years before. To the petitioners, Mary of Guise extended her protection, without either admitting or refusing their requisitions;—a proceeding which called forth the grateful forbearance of the Protestants and the bitter reproaches of their opponents. An offer, however, was at last made from the latter, to allow prayers and baptism in the vulgar tongue in their private assemblies, on the admission of the mass, purgatory, and prayers to the saints, by the Protestants. The terms were of course rejected, and the Congregation became petitioners to the Parliament of December 1558.

In the supplication which the leaders of the Congregation then presented, some important requests were annexed. They desired the suspension of the acts against heretics until the determination of the points in dispute by a general council; praying that all Churchmen should in the mean time be confined to accusing, and not allowed to judge; and that all so accused should be carried before a temporal judge, by whom, after a full defence and exposition of their views, they should not be condemned unless proved by the Word of God to have erred from the faith necessary to salvation. The remonstrances of the queen regent, as to the danger of raising such points at that time, obtained the withdrawal of the petition; and the Lords of the Congregation remained contented with the presentation of a protest to the parliament. In this instrument, after alluding to the controversies of the time, and their frequent complaints of the unprofitableness and idolatry of many ceremonies, they stated their intention of seeking redress in this parliament, and the withdrawal of their petition in consequence of the troubles of the time. But fearful of this act being misrepresented, they protested the lawfulness of continuing in the scriptural faith, without incurring danger of life or lands for the neglect of the acts of parliament in favour of their adversaries; and, in conclusion, they declared that no blame ought to attach to them should any tumults arise in consequence of the delay of the necessary reformation. This returning boldness in the Congregation was due to two events: the one, the evident proximity of danger from the side of the regent, which they could not but perceive must be met by force; the other, the sudden revulsion of feeling in favour of their views in England, occasioned by the accession of Elizabeth to the English throne.

The ascendency of the Guises over the mind of the queen regent soon manifested itself. A blow was to be struck at Elizabeth, and through the side of Scotland, as one link in a great chain extending from Madrid to Rome, by which the Roman faith was to be reunited. For a time, Mary remained firm; but at last her brothers, the cardinal and the duke, aided by the clergy in Scotland, overcame her better resolution, and bent her to their plans. When the Lords of the Congregation renewed their petition, in the spring of the year 1559, and at the same time required the election of the bishops by the votes of the gentry, and of the priests by the parishioners, they not only met with a decided refusal, but the Synod, at the same time, issued an injunction against the use of any other language than the Latin in the public services. This the regent followed up with a proclamation of general conformity and daily resort to the mass, and a summons to the most distinguished of the preachers to appear before the Parliament at Stirling, and abide their trials.

The temporary moderation on the part of the regent, which the bold language of Glencairn and Campbell produced, was soon destroyed by the conduct of the men of Perth and the malapert reply of lord Ruthven; and May having been assigned for the trials of the preachers, Knox returned to take his stand with his brethren. This may seem a bold step on his part: much, however, of the danger disappears, when we consider by what powerful nobles, and large masses of the people, the reformed faith was now embraced, and with what confidence it could look to the effectual support of England in the case of attack.

The treachery of the regent towards the leaders of the Congregation who had accompanied their preachers to Stirling, went far towards occasioning the sacrilegious outbreak which followed Knox's sermon in the cathedral of Perth, and in precipitating that war between the Congregation and the Crown, by which the French were eventually expelled from the land, and the party of the Reformation firmly established. That war was begun by the march of the queen regent on Perth, about the middle of May, with the ostensible purpose of punishing the sacrilege of the men of that city, and avenging the destruction of the shrines in the cathedral, and the spoiling of the monasteries of the Grey and Black Friars and the royal foundation of the Carthusians. The bold remonstrances, addresses, and anathemas of the Congregation brought to their aid the troops of the earl of Glencairn, and enabled them to obtain from the Regent the terms of the Convention of Perth. No one, it was agreed, was to suffer for the late doings; toleration was guaranteed; and the French garrison were to depart the city with the queen. The violation of these terms by the regent, by the means of a disgraceful quibble, detached the Lord James and the duke of Argyle from her party, and brought on that powerful meeting at St. Andrew's, in June, where, for the first time, we discover a new principle in the conduct of the Reformers—the defence of Scotland against the dominations of the French troops, by which the regent wielded her tyrannical power. The duty, too, of destruction had been now fully recognised by the preachers and their adherents; and hardly a sermon ensued but with scenes of violence. Altars, shrines, painted glass, and images, went down before the eloquence of Knox, Douglas, and Willock; and every little town in Fife had already had its purgation from idolatry. Knox's greatest effort was reserved for St. Andrew's, where, in defiance of the threats of the archbishop, and the remonstrances of his own party, he hounded on the people, from the pulpit, to the work of demolition, who, nothing loath, and encouraged by their chief magistrates, soon levelled the wealthy monasteries of the Dominicans and Franciscans to the ground. Again the forces of the regent and the Congregation were drawn up in battle array, and again a hollow truce obtained for the former that delay in which she trusted. No sooner, however, were the latter assured that the regent had no intentions of redeeming her promises, than, influenced by the accession of Sir W. Kirkaldy, a brave and experienced soldier, they laid siege to Perth; and within twenty-four hours of the opening of the batteries, Lord Ruthven planted the standard of the Congregation on the walls of the city.

"The Lords of the Congregation were now to discover that it was infinitely more easy to excite than to direct or check the fury of the people. In the immediate vicinity of Perth was the abbey church of Scone, regarded with peculiar reverence, as the spot in which, for many centuries, the Scottish monarchs had held the ceremony of their coronation. Beside it stood the palace of the Bishop of Moray, a prelate of profligate life, and hated by the men of Dundee (who had assisted in the capture of Perth) as a chief instrument in the martyrdom of Walter Miln. It was thought proper, therefore, that some 'order' should be taken with him; and a message was sent by the leaders of the Congregation, requiring him to join them, with his servants, otherwise they would neither spare nor save his abbey. He consented to this, and added, that not only would he meet them with all his force, but vote with them against the clergy in Parliament. But before his answer arrived, the citizens of Dundee had seized their weapons, and rushed forward to the abbey, followed by Knox and their chief magistrates, who in vain attempted to restrain them. It was the earnest wish of the Reformer and the leaders of the Protestants to save both the palace and the abbey, and in this they so far succeeded, that nothing but the images were pulled down. Argyle and Moray then drew off the multitude, and receiving intelligence, in the evening, that the queen regent meditated to garrison Stirling, and pre-occupy the passes of the Forth, so as to prevent a junction between the northern Reformers and their lowland brethren, these two leaders made a rapid night march to, took possession of, the town, and, according to the expression then commonly used, purged it of idolatry. Their absence was fatal to Scone. Some of the poor, in the hope of spoil, and others with a lingering wish of vengeance, returned on the morrow, and began to prowl about the abbey. The prelate, in the interval, had barricaded his mansion; his servants had armed themselves; and a citizen of Dundee approaching near the 'giruel,' or granary, was thrust through with a rapier, by one reported to be the son of the prelate. In a moment, all was tumult: the air rang with shouts and cries of vengeance—the story flew to Perth—a multitude, which no power could control, attacked the ecclesiastical palace and the abbey—and within a few hours both were in flames. Many even of the most zealous leaders lamented this destruction, and Knox appears personally to have exerted himself to prevent it."—*Tytler*, vol. vi. pp. 113, 114.

The well known predisposition on the part of Elizabeth, with whom Knox and the other leaders were now in correspondence, induced the regent to retreat to Dunbar, and not to attempt either to drive the Lord James out of Stirling, small as was his army, or to defend the capital. Onward, therefore, went the army of the Congregation, and having purged Linlithgow of its idolatries, entered Edinburgh in triumph, on the twenty-ninth of June, 1559.

According to the letters of Kirkaldy and Knox to Sir Henry Percy, the Congregation at this time meant neither sedition, nor yet rebellion against any constituted authority; but sought the legal establishment of the reformed religion, the expulsion of the French troops from Scotland, and a league, offensive and defensive, with Elizabeth. They had indeed aided in destroying many ecclesiastical buildings, and permitted the destruction of many more; but as yet their hands were clean from the appropriation of Church property, which, in imitation of the English Parliament, they were ready to make over to the crown, on its consent being given to a general Reformation. The regent, on the other hand, publicly charged them with sedition and treason under a religious pretence, and with a desire of raising their leader, the Lord James, to the throne, which caused some to fall away from them, and among these, the late governor, the duke of Chastelherault. These desertions, added to the cautiousness of Cecil, gave courage to the party of the regent, and so far influenced the Protestants, that, when Mary of Guise advanced against the capital, they surrendered it to her, on the condition of toleration to its inhabitants.

It is very clear that neither party intended to keep the terms of the convention of Edinburgh; but regarded them merely as opportunities for strengthening their respective positions. And, whilst the regent renewed her solicitations for aid from her brothers in France, Knox and his friends were in constant communication with the agents of Elizabeth, and endeavouring, by every means in their power, to obtain from her, not only assistance of men, arms, and horses, but the grant of pensions to the leading nobles. The instructions of Knox, in his visit to Sir James Crofts, which Mr. Tytler has given at some length, prove this assertion. Cecil, however, was not to be hurried; the time had not arrived for an open outbreak with the queen regent; but yet much good might come of the disturbances: therefore, whilst Elizabeth wrote letters to Mary of Guise, beseeching her to promote the peace of her kingdom, she sent, at the same time, other letters to the Lords of the Congregation, advising open rebellion against the regent, and expressing her astonishment that they had not more vigorously exerted themselves for the great objects they had in view. What Elizabeth aimed at was to distress France, through Scotland, and to destroy the influences of the Guises in that country. She by no means desired the establishment of the Reformation on the principles of the Congregation, well assured of the too great prevalence of Calvinistic opinions among the leaders and preachers of that body. By degrees, the Congregation began to entertain Elizabeth's views regarding a change of the government; and it was not long before they established a council, and waited only for a full agreement with England to depose the queen regent, and place one of their own friends in her stead. The Congregation favoured the son of the late governor, Arran, a man unsuited and wanting in every respect.

"But Elizabeth" [says Mr. Tytler], "and still more, her able minister, Cecil, had their eyes upon another and very different person—the Lord James, natural son of James V., afterwards the noted regent, Murray, and regarded even at this time, when he had not completed his twenty-sixth year, as the most influential leader in the Congregation. There is every reason to believe that his attachment to the principles of the Reformation was sincere, and that at first he proposed no other end in taking so prominent a lead than to procure liberty of conscience, and the free exercise of his religion for himself and his adherents. But personal ambition and the love of power were deeply planted in his character; his mind was one of no ordinary cast; and when he began to busy himself in public life, a very short period sufficed to make him feel his talents, and take pleasure in the eminence they conferred upon him. Educated for the Church, at first in his own country, and afterwards at the schools in France, he acquired habits of study and a cultivation of mind superior to the barons by whom he was surrounded. He had early attached to himself some of those able and unscrupulous men who at that time were to be found in the profession of the law or in the Church—men who combined the craft and intrigue of civilized life with the ferocity of a still feudal age. But whilst he used their assistance, his own powers of application were so great as scarcely to require it: his acquaintance with European politics, superior to most of those with whom he acted, enabled him to transact business, and conduct his correspondence with uncommon clearness, brevity, and precision. His knowledge of human nature was profound: he possessed that rapid intuitive insight into the dispositions of those with whom he acted, which taught him to select with readiness, and to employ with success, those best calculated to carry forward his designs: and it was his peculiar art to appear to do nothing, whilst in truth he did it all. There was a bluntness, openness, and honesty about his manner which disarmed suspicion, and disposed men to unbosom themselves to him with equal readiness and sincerity; yet when the conference was ended, they were often surprised to find that the confidence had been altogether on one side: they had revealed their own purposes—Murray, with all his apparent frankness, had betrayed none of his secrets. There is, perhaps, no kind of man more dangerous in public life than he who conceals matured purposes under a negligent and careless exterior; and if to this we add, that his talents in war were of a superior order,—that he was brave almost to rashness,—that his address was dignified, and his countenance noble and kingly,—we shall be at no loss to comprehend the extraordinary influence which such a man acquired, not only over his own party, but in England and on the continent."—Vol. vi. pp. 135, 136.

Long as is this extract, we believe few will find fault with us for giving in full this perfect and elaborate character of the famous Murray, the man whom Cecil and our queen had already marked out as the future governor of Scotland.

The Congregation having now determined on deposing Mary the regent, Elizabeth advanced her money for their assistance in time to counterbalance the support which the queen regent had lately received from France, in men, arms, and money. And now the duke of Chastelherault having been brought over to the Protestants, the Congregation assembled their forces, and, fifteen thousand strong, marched on Edinburgh; and having, on the retreat of Mary to Leith, occupied the city, erected two councils, the one for civil, the other for religious matters. The former council forthwith sent a message to the regent, bidding her send away all foreigners and men-at-arms from Leith, and leave the town free to her subjects. The demand was of course rejected, and the Congregation were bidden by the mouth of the lion herald to depart from their assembling together. All clearly perceived that the scabbard was now thrown away, and that force must be met by force alone. In full congregation, they debated the question of the deposition of the regent; and when Willock and Knox had given their opinions, as their teachers of religion, in favour of the motion, a message was sent by the herald, who had been detained for the purpose, commanding Mary to resign her authority by virtue of an act of suspension which the Congregation had publicly proclaimed.

Misfortunes began to gather round the Congregation, and notwithstanding the money which Elizabeth now advanced with great alacrity, dissensions crept in among their troops, and the discipline of the French auxiliaries turned the scale in the regent's favour. In less than twenty days from the act for suspending the powers of the regent, the Congregation had retreated from the capital, and the regent entered Edinburgh in triumph.

Their present distresses subjected the Protestants to the demands of, Elizabeth; and Knox and Balnaves having consented to omit all mention of the intended reformation in religion in their supplications to the queen for aid, and to request her assistance, in the name of the Congregation, on the sole ground of the tyranny of the French troops, and the supposed scheme of subjugating Scotland and afterwards England to France, Cecil assured them that orders had now been given for the immediate advance of an English fleet and army to cooperate with the reduced forces of the Congregation. In the beginning of January, 1560, the treaty between Elizabeth and the confederate lords was signed, by which she took them under her protection, so long as they recognised Mary of Scotland for their queen, and retained inviolate the rights of the crown. In April, Lord Grey led the auxiliary army into Scotland, and the siege of Leith was commenced. But success did not attend their efforts, and it is difficult to conjecture what might have been the results of the defection of Huntley and the coldness of several of the leading nobles with whom the regent had now expressed her wish to negotiate, had not death suddenly removed the leader of the French party. Anxiety and fatigue had worn out her constitution, and though in a situation to have exacted good for her party, as she saw death approaching, Mary of Guise sought to compose the troubles of her kingdom: at her request, the leaders of the Congregation were sent for.

"The duke, the earls of Argyle, Marshal, and Glencairn, and the Lord James, immediately repaired to the castle, and, entering her bed chamber, were welcomed by the dying queen with a kindness and cordiality which deeply moved them. She expressed her grief for the distracted state of the nation, and advised them to send both the French and English forces out of the kingdom; she declared her unfeigned concern that matters had been pushed to such extremities; ascribed it to the perverse counsels of the French cabinet, which she found herself obliged to obey, and denounced the crafty and interested policy of Huntley, who had interrupted the conference at Preston, when she herself was ready to have agreed to their proposals.

She recommended to them a faithful adherence to their league with France, which was in no degree inconsistent with, but rather necessarily arose out of, the obedience they owed to their lawful sovereign and the maintenance of their national liberty. To these advices she added many endearing expressions, and with tears asked pardon of all whom she had in any way offended, declaring that she herself freely forgave the injuries she might have received, and trusted they should all meet with the same forgiveness at the bar of God. She then, with an expression full of sweetness, though her countenance was pallid and emaciated, embraced and kissed the nobles one by one, extending her hand to those of inferior rank who stood by, as a token of dying charity. The hardy barons, who had so lately opposed her with the bitterest rancour, were dissolved in tears; they earnestly requested her to send for some godly man from whom she might receive not only consolation, but instruction; and on the succeeding day she willingly admitted a visit from Willock. Mild in his manner, yet faithful to his belief, the minister spoke to the dying princess of the efficacy of the death of Christ, and the abomination of the mass as a relic of idolatry. To the first point, she assured him that she looked for salvation in no other way than in and through the death of our Saviour; to the second, she quietly declined to give an answer; and on the succeeding day expired, full of faith and hope."—*Tytler*, vi. 163, 164.

Thus died Mary of Guise, whose sound and clear intellect, good heart, and forgiving temper, would have composed the differences of her kingdom, had she not been compelled by circumstances in other countries to adopt the violent principles of the house of Guise, and allowed her councils to be swayed by the intrigues of that family. Forgiving as she had been on her death-bed, her enemies were not equally generous; the intolerant rancour of the preachers followed even to her burial, and they who claimed toleration for themselves, and cried out for freedom from persecution, would not allow the clergy of that faith in which she had died to perform their accustomed ceremonies over the tomb of their deceased queen. After some delay, her corpse was carried to France, where it obtained that christian burial which had been denied to it in Scotland. With the queen regent the power and the religion of the Roman Catholics fell.

Within a few days after the death of the regent,—all parties being completely averse from the continuance of the war,—the commissioners of England and France met at Edinburgh for the conclusion of a treaty of peace. Treat with the Congregation as a recognised authority the queen of Scotland could not; nor could she recognise the treaty of Berwick, between Elizabeth and them, without a serious compromise of her dignity. After many angry meetings and discussions, the superior diplomacy of Cecil obtained the required terms for the Congregation, and at the same time the queen preserved her dignity by the omission of any formal declaration of the reasons of the concessions. An act of oblivion was to cover all acts for the last two years, and a general peace and reconciliation between the nobles of both faiths was to ensue. Those amongst the lords who had lands in France were to be restored to their possessions, and redress was to be given by parliament to those ecclesiastics who had suffered injury; for the future, no foreign troops were to abide in the land, and the government was to be committed to a council during the absence of the queen in France ; the last clause provided for the assembling of a parliament in the succeeding month, for which a commission was to be sent from France ; but it was added, that this meeting of the Estates should be as lawful as if the same had been convoked by the command of the king and queen of France. Such were the main terms of the treaty of Edinburgh, which occasioned the first national recognition of the Reformation in Scotland.

Although there were no express provisions in favour of the Protestants, but, on the other hand, a protection and restoration of property for the professors of the ancient faith, yet the Lords of the Congregation could not fail of perceiving the advantage, both personally and politically, which Cecil had secured for them, in the universality of the act of oblivion, and the provision for the immediate meeting of the Estates, whilst as yet the cause of the Reformers was encircled with the glory of their late successes.

On the tenth of August the Estates assembled, greatly augmented in their numbers by the presence and admission of above a hundred of the lesser barons, who for some time had ceased to claim their privilege, but who now petitioned for and obtained their right of sitting and voting in parliament. On the admission of these barons, among whom the principles of the Reformation had made the greatest progress, the Church party raised the objection of the want of the commission from France, without which they argued the meeting of the Estates was invalid. After a week's debate, it was declared, by a large majority, that the clause in the late treaty rendered this meeting as valid without the commission as with it. On this many departed from the parliament, and very few of the spiritual estate attended at the succeeding meetings.

The Reformers knew their strength, and were prepared to use the opportunity now accorded to them. Having chosen the lords of the articles almost exclusively from their own body, and denied redress to the spiritual estate, when it was declared that many whom they had chosen as spiritual lords of the articles were mere laymen, they followed up their work by the presentation of their petition to the parliament. Those who bear in mind the intimate connexion between Knox and Geneva, and his eager adoption of the principles of Calvin, and call to mind the persecution of Servetus, and the tyrannical edicts which Calvin enforced on the unfortunate citizens of Geneva, will be in no great degree astonished at the persecuting spirit which the petition demonstrates to have been prevalent amongst the leaders of the Scottish Reformation.

" It prayed," says Mr. Tytler, " that the doctrines professed by the Roman Catholic Church, *and tyrannically maintained by the clergy*, should be condemned and abolished ; and, amongst the errors, it particularly enumerated transubstantiation, the adoration of Christ's body under the form of bread, the merit of good works, purgatory, pilgrimages, and prayers to departed *saints*. It declared that God, of his great mercy, by the light of his Word, had demonstrated to no small number within the realm, the pestiferous errors of the Romish Church ; errors which the ministers of that Church had maintained by fire and sword, and which brought damnation on the souls that embraced them. It stated, in strong and coarse language, that the sacraments of our Lord were shamefully abused by that Roman harlot, by whom the true discipline of the Church was extinguished; and proceeded to give an appalling picture of the corrupt lives of those who called themselves the clergy. Embracing the whole Papal Church in one sweeping anathema, the petitioners offered to prove that, in '*all the rabble of the clergy,*' there was not one lawful minister of the Word of God, and the practices of the Apostles and the primitive Church were to be taken as authority upon this point. *It denominated them thieves and murderers, rebels, traitors, and adulterers, living in all manner of abominations, and unworthy to be suffered in any reformed commonwealth.* Lastly, using that blessed name which ought to be the bond of love and charity, as an incitement to railing and persecution, *it called upon parliament, in the bowels of Jesus Christ, to employ the victory which it had obtained with wholesome vigour; to compel the body of the Romish Clergy to answer these accusations now brought against them; to pronounce them unworthy of authority in the Church of God, and expel them for ever from having a voice or vote in the great council of the nation;—in conclusion, it virtually declared that this petition was not theirs, but God's, who craved this by his servants; and it prayed Him to give them an upright heart and a right understanding of the request made through them.*"—Vol. vi. p. 180.

Violent and impious as this petition was, there can be little doubt that it would have received the sanction of the majority of the Estates, had it not contained a clause, calling upon the nobles to restore the patrimony of the Church to the uses to which it had been originally designed—the support of ministers, the restoration of godly learning, and the assistance of the poor. This was an unpalatable doctrine to the lords, who, according to the exclamation of Lethington, were not prepared "now to forget themselves, and bear the barrow to build the house of God." Not but what they recognised the precept of Scripture, that the " labourer was worthy of his hire ;" they only differed in their interpretation of the word labourer; and took the liberty of considering, that as the Reformation—as far as men were concerned—had been promoted and sustained by the arms of the nobles and their retainers, more than by the preaching of godly ministers or the education of pious men, they were entitled to so much of the wealth of the Church as was equivalent to their services. And then, as they were their own judges in this point, and admitted to the fullest extent their right of private judgment, each noble adjudged his services to be equal to the wealth of the abbey which lay nearest to his castle.

Leaving, therefore, the practical part of the question, and retaining the wealth they had stolen, the majority of the Estates commanded the ministers to draw up a confession of their faith, or a brief summary of the doctrines they considered wholesome, true, and necessary to be believed and received within the realm. Within four days the godly ministers had decided what they ought to believe, and presented to the parliament that volume of articles called the Confession of Faith. As articles of faith were matters of little moment, if not of perfect indifference, to the majority of the nobles, and as it was of the utmost consequence to them to quiet the people, lest the cry for the restoration of the Church property should become too powerful to be resisted, they were most eager for the immediate adoption of the Confession of Faith. And when those among their own body and some few of the bishops complained of the length of the book, and the abstruse nature of many of the doctrines which it contained, and which they were now to approve or condemn without a day's consideration, they were cried down by their opponents; and some among the Protestants hesitated not to threaten their relations with death, if they persisted in their opposition. Finding opposition fruitless, some few of the nobles and the clergy gave in their protests, and the Confession of Faith was immediately sanctioned by the Estates.

The Reformers having thus obtained legal sanction for their doctrines, proceeded to exact a similar sanction for a Protestant persecution, by an act by which they abolished the mass, and inflicted the punishments of confiscation, banishment, and death, on any one who *should dare* to attend that service; thus proving how natural it is to man, when resting on his own private judgment, to complain of persecution when in dependance, and to enforce the same practice against others when endowed with power to do good or evil.

It was not, however, against the prelates and professors of the Roman Catholic faith that this intolerance, except in action, was confined. Our own hierarchy was constantly denounced as hardly one remove from and nearly as corrupt as that of Rome herself.

"In a letter addressed by Goodman, originally a minister of the English Church, but now one of the most active preachers of the Congregation, to Cecil, he exhorted that powerful statesman to '*abolish all the relics of superstition and idolatry which, to the grief and scandal of the godly, were still retained in England, and* (alluding probably to Bonner and Gardiner) *not to suffer the bloody bishops and known murderers of God's people and your dear brethren to live, upon whom God hath expressly pronounced sentence of death, for the execution of which he hath committed the sword into your hands, who are now placed in authority.*' '*It was this delay, this leniency in Cecil, that sticketh,*' so he declared, '*most in the hearts of many.*'"—*Tytler*, vi. p. 186.

Influenced by such a spirit as this, the ministers proceeded to draw up the famous Book of Discipline, by which the election of ministers was committed to the people; and all other ceremonies of ordination were abolished "as not necessary," save an examination of the candidate by certain ministers and elders, mainly on the controversy with Rome, and generally upon the whole extent of sound Christian doctrine. The same book appointed readers in various parishes, simply to read the Common Prayers and the Scriptures; and having divided the country into ten dioceses, appointed ten superintendants over them—a kind of ambulatory bishops, who were to preach three times a week, to inquire into the life of ministers, the manners of the people, the provision for the poor, and the instruction of the youth; in which latter duty they were to be assisted by the erection of public grammar schools in every parish throughout the country, in which the Catechism of Geneva was to be taught. This Book of Discipline, involving matters of practice, was as vigorously and bitterly opposed by the nobles, as the Confession of Faith had been eagerly supported.

> " Some of the nobles and barons positively refused to subscribe it; others, who dreaded the punishment of their vices, or the curtailing of their revenues, mocked at its provisions, and pronounced them devout imaginations. 'The cause,' says Knox, 'we have before declared; some were licentious, some had greedily gripped the possessions of the Church, and others thought that they would not lack their part of Christ's coat. . . . . . The chief great man,' he continues, 'that professed Christ and refused to subscribe the Book of Discipline, was the Lord Erskine. And no wonder; for. besides that he had a very evil woman to his wife, if the poor, the schools, and the ministry of the Church had their own, his kitchen would lack two parts and more of that he now unjustly possesseth.' . . . . *There were none within the realm more unmerciful to the poor ministers than those which had the greatest rents of the churches."—Tytler*, vi. 188-9.

This characteristic letter of Knox enables us fully to comprehend the spirit in which this parliament acted, and with what a harmony of purpose the majority rapturously admitted and sanctioned the Confession of Faith, the acts against the pope and the mass, and the ordinances against those leases by which the clergy endeavoured to save the Church lands and revenues from spoliation, and equally rejected the remonstrances of the clergy and the Book of Discipline of the ministers.

Such were the principal proceedings of that parliament, by which the Reformation received its first national sanction; a parliament which was called by virtue, indeed, of a treaty which provided for its legality in the absence of a commission from France, but called before that treaty, under which that legality was to be granted, had received the sanction of one of the contracting parties. We have now fulfilled our first intention of bringing down the history of the Scottish Reformation to the parliamentary sanction in the year 1560, and conclude, for the present, our remarks on the sixth volume of Mr. Tytler's valuable and interesting history.

The Sunday Service of the Methodists, with other Occasional Services.
London: Mason.

WE have not chosen the Wesleyan Prayer Book as the heading of this article, that we may pronounce upon its merits, or compare its contents with those of "*The Book of Common Prayer and Administration of the Sacraments, and other Rites and Ceremonies of the Church, according to the use of the United Church of England and Ireland; together with the Psalter or Psalms of David, pointed as they are to be sung or said in Churches; and the form and manner of making, ordaining, and consecrating of Bishops, Priests, and Deacons;*" or that we may minutely point out the variations between the two, and enlarge upon the differences between Wesleyan Methodism and the Church, as they are thus exhibited. So far is all this from our purpose, that we propose to consider the history and system of methodism, not as militating against the Church, but as testifying, however unwillingly, in her favour: and we know not how we could find, or well hope to find, a stronger example of this indirect and unwilling testimony than the adoption, in good part, of the solemn services of the Church, by which they have declared it to be a privilege to approach the Almighty in the same terms that the Church does; and to repeat, now they have arrived at their perfection, and at the stature of a self-supported society, the lessons of devotion which they learned while yet they lisped their tender prayers at the bidding of the Church. Far superior must they be to us, of course, by this time; for, beginning with the assumption of great superiority, and dwelling much on their own " perfection," while they were yet but an infant society, they must by this time have grown into a giant strength and an angelic purity: yet still, in their solemn addresses to the throne of majesty and of grace, they can find nothing better than we are privileged to use: nothing better certainly, because nothing else; and it may be something far inferior, because much is omitted that at least seems to us both beautiful and important. But, we repeat it, we omit for the present our differences, and only speak of the truths to which that form of dissent which is properly called methodism bears a powerful testimony.

We must first state the principle on which we proceed. We conceive, then, that wherever any great religious movement has taken *much*, and especially when it has taken *lasting hold* of society, it has been rather from the exaggeration of some striking and important truth, than from the bare inculcation of error. Every heresy has its bright as well as its dark side; and often we find it witnessing, directly or indirectly, of truths which were perhaps beginning for a season to drop out of men's minds, and to cease to influence their conduct. In short, heresy is often rather exaggerated truth, than bare positive error. Thus, for instance, the Arian heresy grew out of the jealousy of some individuals for the honour of God the Father; and it was by the stress which it laid on the first article of the creed, that it commended itself to the reception of many, and maintained its hold by argument, even before it had imperial influence on its side; and though nothing can justify the denial of the proper divinity of the Son, yet the heresy of the Arians has certainly a fairer aspect than that of mere God-denying blasphemy. So again the Sabellians did not simply and at once deny the Trinity of persons in the Godhead, but they were surprised into this error by that jealousy for the honour of the Son, which they thought best served by making Him one with the Father; a better aspect, surely, of their erroneous theology than that in which catholic Christians are obliged to present it, when they refute it polemically, or dogmatically denounce it.

Not that heresiarchs of these or any other sects are justified by such considerations. Their matured systems are still the offspring of wilfulness and pride, and not of mistaken but venial jealousy for the truth. They begin, perhaps, by too violent or unguarded a statement of what they think is catholic theology. If their minds are rather acute than impetuous, they refine too far, or illustrate too nearly, still believing that they are holding and illustrating the truth: but their error in morals is this, that they would thrust their services on the Church, instead of humbly offering them; and when they are rebuked by authority, they become disputatious instead of compliant; confirmed in error, instead of humbled for their fall; more exceedingly pertinacious, instead of simply earnest and sincere. The zeal and acuteness which the Church has rebuked, because of their false application, they employ thereafter, not nominally, but actually against her; that is, in the pertinacious maintenance of their own positions. Thenceforth they are not merely mistaken, but criminally engaged in the propagation of error; and, according to their influence and power to carry others with them, they are leaders of a cabal within the Church, or heresiarchs, giving a name and distinctive dogmas to a new sect.

Still, bad as this result is, it were foolish not to see in it this much at least of good: that wherever there is a heresy thus originating in the disproportionate inculcation of a catholic doctrine, there is a witness for the truth which that heresy exaggerates; and that too with this additional circumstance, that it evinces also a craving of the human mind, and proves the aptitude of a certain phase of divine truth to satisfy it. It is thus with the contending doctrines of free-grace and of free-will, both true in their measure, but still exaggerated,—the one by the Calvinist, the other by the Pelagian,—and both taking very strong hold on multitudes, because each has a responsive chord in the heart of man. Each, then, has its strenuous witness in the several parties who make it their watchword; and each is displayed in its experimental power, for the warning of those who would too readily adopt it alone, and for the instruction of those who would keep the right way, the middle path, in sobriety and truth.

Much the same process is observable in those separations from the Church which arise, in the first instance, rather from differences in practice than from error in doctrine. Persons with ardent and enthusiastic minds (we use the word enthusiastic in its good sense) are struck with the inherent beauty and moral excellence of some course of life or other, and with the nobleness of a higher flight of virtue than most members of the Church attain to; and in the working out of their own system of perfection, they clash, at first unawares, with some ecclesiastical rule, or even with some essential doctrine of the Church. The greatest stumbling-block of such men has been the doctrine which our blessed Lord, as if anticipating the arguments of such sectaries, has so often and so strongly inculcated,—the mixture of evil with the good in the Church, of good and bad fishes in the net, of tares among the wheat in the field. Now, we need by no means hesitate to admit the integrity of a man who is shocked at the visible condition of the Church in this respect, nor believe that he is at once and without premeditation a sectarian, if he seeks some new and untried method of purifying that portion at least of the corrupt body which Providence seems to have placed within his influence; and if he becomes something extravagant in his plans, something fanatical in his conduct, we may freely admit his integrity, though we doubt his wisdom. We may rejoice in the witness which he affords of the necessity of holiness, and may even go along with him with unmixed admiration, until he begins to anathematize others, as well as to stimulate his companions in the same zealous conduct. He may be as energetic *within rule* as he will; but if he steps beyond rule, then wilfulness and disobedience are as the dead fly in the apothecary's ointment. He may labour all that he can *within the Church;* for, so doing, he is still a labourer in the vineyard; and he may and should strive to be the best in the vineyard: but out of the vineyard he must not step, under the pretence of being better than the rest of the labourers, for whosoever gathereth not with the Lord's servants scattereth. If, however, he have done so, and become a leader of sectaries, rather than a subordinate centre of life and energy within the Church, still there is a view of his character that we may take better than that of a mere apostate, and there is a use which we may make of that very development of his principles which we deprecate: for if it does not *excuse him,* it at least *condemns the laxity from which the offence first came;* if it does not prove the perfection of his own character, it does at least prove how mighty is that claim upon man's reverence and love, of a high tone of moral and religious excellence; and if it does not establish the lawfulness of schism, it may suggest an expedient by which the Church may moderate the fanaticism, and retain the service and allegiance of her zealous sons.

Now the party which John Wesley gathered around him, and which has grown into the sect of methodists, partakes somewhat of the character both of separatists for differences of conduct, and of disturbers of the harmony of christian religion, by the exaggeration of particular articles of belief. In other words, they appear in the double character of heretics and of schismatics: yet wherein they *differ* from the Church and wherein they *agree;* nay more, wherein they *retain* and wherein they have *deserted* their own early principles and conduct, they still, directly or indirectly, afford a very strong witness to catholic truth, to catholic communion, and to a sound ecclesiastical polity. John Wesley himself, (who was so far from being a methodist according to the present form of methodism, that he protested against it again and again,) exaggerated certain truths, till they became errors as he taught them; but these very truths he was led to make so disproportionately prominent from the obscurity into which they had fallen, so that he may be accounted almost as much a witness of the truth as an originator of false doctrine. Taking into consideration the state of religion, even in the Church, at the time at which he commenced his erratic course, his doctrines of *conversion*, of *assurance*, and of *perfection* will scarcely surprise us. Indifference of the lowest kind had crept over the whole fabric of the Church; orthodoxy was little better, in the aspect which it wore in the world, than desiccated theology; christian ethics were as little understood almost as they were practised;* and mysteries were, as they were set before the people, of a wretchedly cold and heathenish complexion. Men scarcely dreamed of aspiring at a high order of character, either in religion or in morals; and to appear visibly to protest against the laxity and immorality, against the coldness and indifference which reigned on all sides, was to brave the sneers of the world, and to earn the character of an ascetical fanatic. Man's *capability of holiness,* (or shall we rather express it his *susceptibility of grace,*) and his capacity of living to God's glory, were not tried. To be " good sort of people" was considered praise enough; and to be *separate from sinners,* to be *lights in the world,* was beyond all aspiration. The scriptural precepts and expressions which spoke of being *perfect* and *holy,* of Christ *being formed in us,* of *putting on Christ,* of *going on unto perfection,* and the like, must have been accounted *mere* figures of speech; and in consequence none strove to realize them in their own conduct. The necessary result of feelings, opinions, and practices so very cold and low, was the absence of the appointed reward of a high christian character; the absence of that *comfortable assurance* and *good hope* of the Christian in his Saviour, which makes him in humble, yet in no vague confidence, feel that he is *a child of God,* and *an inheritor of the kingdom of heaven.*

Now, we do not mean that this is really a fair view of the Church, even then, in her better aspect, or that there were not here and there a few who would be examples at any time of sound fervid theology, and of true christian holiness of heart and life; but there was an aspect of the Church (and it was that which presented itself to John Wesley's mind) of which this is no exaggerated portrait. No wonder, then, that, seizing upon the doctrine of CONVERSION, he made it swallow up almost every other preparation. No wonder that, in rebuking the meagre religion and morality of his day, he fell upon the doctrine of PERFECTION, which is not a false doctrine, if held reverently, and that he pressed it beyond the proportion of faith. No wonder that he somewhat exaggerated, or rather somewhat distorted, the Christian's ASSURANCE; since, as the true doctrine follows on a sound view of conversion and holiness, the perversion of these naturally issued in a distorted view of assurance also. Yet, if we could suppose it possible that such a slumber had fallen on the Church, that the true doctrines of *conversion,* of *perfection,* and of *assurance* were really lost, but for the startling voice of Wesley, surely we might rather rejoice in the witness that he bore to their reality, than follow his memory with unmitigated dislike; and rather hail the resuscitated

---

* Compare Paley's Moral Philosophy with Sewell's Christian Morals.

verities, than despise them for the incongruous robes with which they were invested, when he presented them again in the light of day.

Hitherto the testimony of Wesley, and of his system, to catholic truth, has been direct, and we have been able to speak of him in almost unqualified praise. The same may be said of his powerful and influential testimony against ultra-Calvinism and antinomianism, in which Fletcher was his very able supporter. The power with which Wesley maintained a position in which he was right was marvellous, and his aggressive movements against error were extremely powerful; and we know not where we can find a better opportunity of observing, that he is not to be dealt with, in any part of his religious career, as a mere wild enthusiast, or to be laughed down as a deluded fanatic. If the *result* of his labours had not taught us a more respectful appreciation of his power and importance, anything like a just view of the man, his acuteness, his eloquence, his energy, his self-devotion, his high mind—wherever it was not overborne by the recoil of his own principles; and the apparently unexpected results of his own proceedings,—would force us to view John Wesley with respect. We have not time to enter into the very interesting and instructive details; but the character, and earnestness, and piety developed by him and his first associates in methodism at Oxford, give the promise of a career which can never be treated merely with derision; while the labours which he and his friends endured in America, before the actual development of the system of methodism in England, only affords an additional earnest of proceedings which we must in some sense respect, though we cannot always approve them.

We *must* at last proceed from the instances of direct witness to the truth, in Wesley's teaching, to his indirect and involuntary testimony to the Church and her polity. The most prominent difference of the Wesleyans from the Church arose, by slow and regular degrees, out of an arrangement by which John Wesley sought to secure to his followers greater edification. Besides the services of the Church, and supplementary to them, (not as in any case or degree, in fact or in theory, superseding them,) he provided sermons to be preached wherever and whenever he or his emissaries could find hearers, with the single and most significant proviso, that it was not to be during the ordinary hours of church service. That men should so meet together for mutual edification, after divine worship was concluded; or that those who have much knowledge themselves, and much facility in conveying it to others, should take that means to do good, cannot be thought, *in itself*, sinful: but unless we strangely misread the indications of opinion and feeling, both in Wesley himself, and in his earliest companions in itineracy, lay or clerical, they were as much influenced by the vain-glorious assumption of superiority over the appointed pastors of the Church, as by an humble, patient, and ardent desire to labour *with* them, *for* them, and *under* them, in the work of teaching and of edifying one.

another. Soon, therefore, we find them forgetting that the very word "edification," if its use be gathered from the sacred Scriptures, can be applied only to the Church, and can exist only in the Church; and forgetting this, they began to talk of separation from the Church, as if the temple of God could be built up by separating its parts from each other.* This ardent desire in his preachers to separate from the communion of the Church, seems to have been one of the greatest troubles that Wesley himself experienced; for he had a keener perception of its consequences than his followers in general; and probably, also, a deeper feeling of its positive sinfulness. We find him setting forth "Reasons against a separation from the Church of England," wherein, mostly on the very lowest ground of expediency, yet such, in all likelihood, as he knew to be best adapted to those for whom he wrote, he deprecates any such step. We will give a specimen or two of his reasons:—

"Whether it be *lawful* or no (which itself may be disputed, being not so clear a point as some may imagine) it is by no means *expedient* for us to separate from the established Church:

"Because it would be a contradiction to the solemn and repeated declarations which we have made in all manner of ways, in preaching, in print, and in private conversation:

"Because it would be throwing balls of wild-fire among them that are now quiet in the land. We are now sweetly united together in love. We mostly think and speak the same thing. But this would occasion inconceivable strife and contention, between those who left, and those who remained in the Church, as well as between those who left us, and those who remained with us; nay, and between those very persons who remained, as they were variously inclined one way or the other:

"Because to form the plan of a new Church would require infinite time and care, (which might be far more profitably bestowed,) with much more wisdom and greater depth and extensiveness of thought, than any of us are master of."

Charles Wesley, in his adoption of the document from which these extracts are made, speaks out far more boldly than his brother, and takes higher ground:—

"I think myself bound in duty, to add my testimony to my brother's. His twelve reasons against our ever separating from the Church of England, are mine also. I subscribe to them with all my heart. Only with regard to the first, I am quite clear, that it is neither expedient nor LAWFUL for me to separate. And I never had the least inclination or temptation so to do.

"CHARLES WESLEY.†"

One instance, out of many, shall serve for the scenes which John Wesley describes as arising out of the growth of avowed schismatical tendencies:—

"1787, January 2d.—I went over to Deptford; but it seemed I was got into a den of lions. Most of the leading men of the society were mad for separating from the Church. I endeavoured to reason with them, but in vain—they had neither sense nor even good manners left—at length, after meeting

---

* See London Cases, vol. i. p. 84. Ed. 1718.
† John Wesley's "*Reasons Against a Separation from the Church of England*" have been reprinted in a cheap form for distribution; and for the same purpose we may mention, "*John Wesley Vindicated by Himself; an Allegory.*" Burns, and Houlston and Stoneman, London: Harrison, Leeds.

the whole society, I told them, if you are resolved, you may have your service in Church hours; but remember, from that time you will see my face no more. This struck deep, and from that hour I have heard no more of separating from the Church."

Thus do we find the originator of the most unjustifiable schism that has ever distracted the Church of England, and the head of the largest sect at present in existence within this kingdom, contending for the great catholic doctrine and practice of unity with the Church,—giving his solemn testimony to its importance, and labouring to neutralise the effects of his own rash and wilful proceedings, which were tending violently and rapidly to open and avowed defection.

We must not suppose that the society of methodists could stop short at this point; and, in fact, even before John Wesley's death, and by his own acts, they had assumed a more manifestly schismatical character. The particular act of their founder which most savours of formal schism, is also a powerful testimony to another grand catholic doctrine,—the necessity of an order of men set apart by a solemn consecration to minister in holy things. The monstrous assumption of Wesley, in arrogating to himself the right of ordaining, which he must have known was only granted to bishops, gives extraordinary force to his involuntary testimony to the necessity of holy orders.

This fundamental change in the constitution of the Wesleyan connexion, which has deprived them of the benefit of being judged as a party within the Church, and has obliged us to account them in formal schism, was forced upon Wesley by external pressure; nor was it fully effected until after his death. It was not to be expected that a set of lay preachers, the heads of separate classes or assemblies, or the itinerating propagators of imposing religious dogmas, would long be contented to remain mere class leaders, dependent upon the Church for those ministerial offices which John Wesley constantly enjoined them to frequent themselves, and to press upon their followers. They were in general very ignorant men in ecclesiastical matters, though not unknowing in the system which they had adopted; and they could not be expected to know what they asked, when they sought permission from John Wesley to administer baptism and the Lord's Supper. His declaration that this was unlawful, except to those who have a commission from a bishop,[*] must have puzzled them; and his refusal to ordain them himself (so long as he did refuse) must have seemed to them a great bar to the growth of their society. It is certain, however, that his followers (whether or no they saw the connexion between orders and the sacraments, and whether or no they had yet got an inkling of the extraordinary mission of John Wesley himself, which might justify his assuming such authority) soon desired him to permit the administration of the sacraments in his preaching houses, and to ordain some from among his

---

[*] "We believe it would not be right for us (himself and his brother) to administer either baptism or the Lord's Supper, unless we had a commission so to do from those bishops whom we apprehend to be in succession from the Apostles."

itinerant preachers. These latter would earnestly second the demand, from their jealousy of the episcopally-ordained clergymen who had condescended to place themselves under the guidance of Wesley, and who carried with them greater weight and respect than their unordained, and comparatively uneducated, associates. The first irregular ordination among the methodists was that of some of the lay-preachers, which Wesley, thus prevailed upon, procured of one Erasmus, a Greek, calling himself Bishop of Arcadia, who at least acted a part unworthy of a bishop, whether or no his episcopate was, as some suspected, merely assumed; for no act could be more glaringly schismatical than the ordination by a foreign bishop of men to act against the authority of the Church.

In commencing the history of Wesleyan ordination we have been obliged to confuse it with that of the administration of the sacraments in their societies; they are, indeed, inseparably and essentially connected. We shall, however, sketch the progress of Wesley's opinions and practice in the mission and ordaining of ministers, as separated from the question of the sacraments.

In his inclination to episcopize, we find Wesley advancing, from a strong conviction that any assumption of a power of mission or ordination in a presbyter was sinful, to the actual usurpation of those offices in a most exaggerated form—the pretended consecration and mission of a bishop, though he himself was a simple presbyter. At first it was with reluctance, and even with disingenuous equivocations, that he sanctioned even lay-teachers; and so tender was he upon this point, that "to touch it was to touch the apple of his eye."[*] It was an evasion to employ the ministry of a Greek bishop; but it showed that he was not delivered from his doubt whether it was lawful "for presbyters in his situation to appoint or ordain others." This mist was cleared away by the help of Lord Chancellor King, who had convinced him, he says, (in 1784,[†]) many years ago, that bishops and presbyters are the same order, and consequently have the same right to ordain.[‡] It is very strange that the laws of a human polity should have restrained him for many years after he had learned to despise the constitution of the Church of Christ.

---

[*] Southey's Life of Wesley, ii. 74. A clergyman, who would gladly have co-operated with him, but that he saw through this and the like subterfuges, and dreaded the coming schism, thus wrote to John Wesley on this subject: "I fear, Sir," said he, "that your saying you do not appoint, but only approve of the lay-preachers from a persuasion of their call and fitness, savours of disingenuity. Where is the difference? Under whose sanction do they act? Would they generally think their call a sufficient warrant for commencing preachers, or be received in that capacity by your people, without your approbation, tacit or express? And what is their preaching upon this call, but a manifest breach upon the order of the Church, and an inlet to confusion, which, in all probability, will follow upon your death, and if I mistake not, you are upon the point of knowing by your own experience."

[†] In his letter "*to Dr. Coke, Mr. Asbury, and our brethren in North America.*"

[‡] This is the heresy of Aerius, who came to this conclusion, as natural to one under his circumstances, as it was to John Wesley, when he had himself been disappointed of a bishoprick.

The fact is, that Wesley's wisdom (and for wisdom, in one sense, few have been more remarkable) saw the danger of interfering with an order of men established by positive human laws; he continues, therefore, in his letter to Dr. Coke:—

"For many years I have been importuned, from time to time, to exercise this right, by ordaining part of our travelling preachers; but I have still refused, not only for peace sake, but because I was determined, as little as possible, to violate the established order of the national Church to which I belonged.

"But the case is widely different between England and North America. Here there are bishops who have a legal jurisdiction. In America there are none, neither any parish ministers; so that for some hundreds of miles together there is none either to baptize or administer the Lord's Supper. Here, therefore, my scruples are at an end; and I conceive myself at full liberty, as I violate no order, and invade no man's right, by appointing and sending labourers into the harvest.

"I have accordingly appointed Dr. Coke and Mr. Francis Asbury to be joint superintendents over our brethren in North America; as also Richard Whatcoat and Thomas Vasey to act as elders among them, by baptizing and administering the Lord's Supper."

Thus we see that it was Wesley's Erastianism that kept him for a long while from assuming episcopal functions; and we have again to wonder at the combination of Erastian principles and of actual non-conformity.

The Dr. Coke whom Wesley addressed as above had been eight days before ordained bishop by him. We give the doctor's letter of ordination, under Wesley's hand and seal: and we cannot but wonder at the contradictions implied in the ordination of a bishop by a presbyter; at the facility with which Wesley deceives himself by substituting the names *superintendent* and *elder* for the names *bishop* and *presbyter*, while he assigns to the newly-ordained person a *bishop's* office; and at the coolness with which he speaks of this as a boon to those who would *still adhere to the doctrine and discipline of the Church of England*. And we must also draw the attention of the reader to the marvellous incongruity of the apology before mentioned from Lord King's proof that the bishop and the presbyter are the same, with the declaration that he *thought*[*] *himself to be providentially called at that time to set apart some persons for the work of the ministry;* a call which would surely take away the necessity of any apology, and supersede any reasoning from Lord King or any one else, seeing that it makes Wesley more than either bishop or presbyter,—that is, *an apostle!* Add to these glaring inconsistencies and self-contradictions, the amusing combination of a desire to episcopize in substance, and to avoid such a step in appearance; and we really think there is but this one way of accounting for such a singular exhibition:

---

[*] "*Know* all men, that I, John Wesley, *think myself* to be called," &c.: suppose some one were to open a commission of Oyer and Terminer, "*Know* all men, that I, A. B. *think myself* to be commissioned," &c.

"Ὅταν γὰρ ἐργῇ δαιμόνων βλάπτῃ τινὰ
Τοῦτ᾽ αὐτὸ πρῶτον ἐξαφειρεῖται φρενῶν
Τὸν νοῦν τὸν ἐσθλὸν, εἰς δὲ τὴν χείρω τρέπει
Γνώμην, ἵν᾽ εἴδῃ μηδὲν ὧν ἁμαρτάνει.

And the sentence of Æschylus, quoted by Plato in the second book of his Republic, may well express the ultimate result of such inauspicious mistakes.

— Θεὸς μὲν αἰτίαν φύει βροτοῖς
Ὅταν κακῶσαι δῶμα παμπήδην θέλῃ.

But we detain the reader too long from Dr. Coke's letters of orders.

"To all to whom these presents shall come, John Wesley, late fellow of Lincoln College, in Oxford, Presbyter of the Church of England, sendeth greeting:—Whereas, many of the people in the southern provinces of North America, who desire to continue under my care, and still adhere to the doctrine and discipline of the Church of England, are greatly distressed for want of ministers to administer the sacraments of Baptism and the Lord's Supper, according to the usage of the same Church; and whereas, there does not appear to be any other way of supplying them with ministers,—know all men, that I, John Wesley, think myself to be providentially called, at this time, to set apart some persons for the work of the ministry in America. And, therefore, under the protection of Almighty God, and with a single eye to his glory, I have this day set apart, as a superintendent, by the imposition of my hands and prayer, (being assisted by other ordained ministers,) Thomas Coke, Doctor of Civil Law, a Presbyter of the Church of England, and a man whom I judge to be well qualified for that great work: and I do hereby recommend him, to all whom it may concern, as a fit person to preside over the flock of Christ. In testimony whereof, I have hereunto set my hand and seal, this second day of September, in the year of our Lord one thousand seven hundred and eighty-four. "JOHN WESLEY."*

The extremely Erastian views of Wesley were exemplified by his extending the same benevolence to the Wesleyans in Scotland that he had done to those in America; for though it was clearly wrong for a presbyter to ordain any one, to minister any where, yet for Scotland there was not the same shadow of an excuse. When Dr. Coke was appointed "superintendent" for America, there was no bishop on that continent in communion with any Protestant Church, Bishop Seabury being consecrated in Scotland about a month after; but while the Churchmen of America were supplicating orders from the Church in Scotland, (a pure and apostolic branch of the Church Catholic, and, though obscure, yet not so entirely hidden as to escape the eye willing to see an ordinance of God wherever it exists,) John Wesley was exercising his assumed right of ordination for that country.

We are now prepared for the total abandonment of all principle in the matter of ordination, and for the avowed assumption of the privilege to ordain *bishops*, *priests*, and *deacons*, by the Wesleyan

---

* It is not perhaps generally known that Dr. Coke himself afterwards shewed that he was not satisfied with Wesley's apostolical powers, by seeking orders and mission from the American Bishop White.

ministers themselves:—*superintendents, elders,* and *deacons,* the methodists call them; but, of course, the name cannot alter the question. It can only suggest a suspicion, that if the very names are so displeasing to them, the offices themselves would not have been assumed, except for some overwhelming necessity; and it gives, therefore, an additional emphasis to the witness of the methodists to the apostolic orders.

We must not, however, suppose that no intervening changes in the assumed position of the methodists had taken place between the death of John Wesley, who himself, as an *extraordinary minister*, as an *apostle,* assumed the right to ordain, and the fancied and allowed exercise of the same right, according to an appointed ordinal, of the Wesleyan bishops or superintendents. Which should come first, a bishop or a Church, no primitive christian, no well instructed son of the Church of England, can hesitate to declare; but in methodism the order was inverted. A Church came first; and then, because a Church cannot exist without sacraments, and sacraments cannot be administered without clergy, orders were added.* It would puzzle a divine, however, (though not a methodist, we presume,) to say how methodist assemblies became Churches, or how the whole connexion was transformed into a Church. If it was the largeness of the body which occasioned the change, this is singular enough, because it would seem self-evident that the distinction between a conventicle and a church is one, not of degree but of kind. If, according to the 19th Article, (which the Wesleyans retain,)†

"The visible Church of Christ is a congregation of faithful men, in the which the pure word of God is preached, and the sacraments be duly ministered according to Christ's ordinance in all those things that of necessity are requisite to the same,"

then, in fact, methodism is no Church even now; and even on their own principles, it would be impossible to show how and when it became so. Before the assumed right of ordination it clearly was not: afterwards how could it be, since, unless it was first a Church, which they cannot pretend, there was no *such* society as could exercise such powers?

But, however, the history of these changes is something of this kind.

The united societies instituted by John Wesley himself he has thus defined:—

"Such a society is no other than a company of men having the form, and seeking the power of godliness, united in order to pray together, to receive the word of exhortation, and to watch over one another in love, that they may help each other to work out their salvation." ‡

Nothing can be more abundantly manifest than that such societies

---

* We need not always repeat that the Church was but a pretended Church, and the orders only pretended orders.
† It is the 13th with them.   ‡ Works, vol. viii. p. 269.

"were *not* independent Churches;"* and yet so overwhelming is the necessity to assume the name—since, if Churches they were not, nothing else among the methodists ever was a Church,—that they, or parallel institutions, are often called Churches by methodist writers. Thus, Adam Clarke says, " It was by this means, (the institution of united societies,) that we have been enabled to establish permanent and holy *Churches* over the world." † And the same Mr. Jackson, who says so plainly that these societies were *not* independent Churches, says afterwards of an attempt to separate certain " chapels" from the connexion : " Had it succeeded, the methodist societies would at once have been converted into independent *Churches*." ‡ Such is the omnipotence of the voluntary principle!

And yet another minister declares, that it was *an act of pacification*, which did what *an act of separation* would have necessarily effected ; for, at the Conference in 1836, Mr. Galland said, that "the Conference, *by the plan of pacification*, invested our societies with the privilege *of becoming* christian *Churches*."

As if he dreaded this effect of *quarrelling*, or of *pacification*, whichever it was, John Wesley had ever protested against the assumption of the title, " The Church," by his people, and against the name " church" or " chapel," as applied to the meeting places of his ministers. " Warn them," said he, " against calling our societies *a Church*, or *the Church* ; against calling our preachers *ministers*, our houses *meeting-houses*—call them *plain preaching-houses* ;"§ and of the preachers in these houses he says, " They no more take upon themselves to be priests than to be kings. They take not upon them to administer the sacraments, an honour peculiar to the priests of God."|| We need not say how entirely this takes the societies, and the whole body of Wesleyans, from the character of Churches or a Church, according to the definition of a Church, in which we and they are agreed.

One thing is clear, that the Wesleyans had proceeded so far, that they must either go backward or forward. To return to the Church was their clear duty, as every one but themselves must perceive : to arrogate to themselves the name of a Church was easier, and more consistent with their predilections; and without accusing them of greater self-deception than falls to the lot of most men, we may affirm, that with good intentions, they followed the worse course. We can only note the more marked steps of their progress to

---

* THE CENTENARY OF WESLEYAN METHODISM: *a Brief Sketch of the Rise, Progress, and Present State of the Wesleyan-Methodist Societies throughout the World.* By THOMAS JACKSON, *President of the Conference*, p. 80. We have quoted this work largely, because being published by the president, at the request of the Conference, it has as much authority as it could have, as a Wesleyan view of the matters of which it treats. We must observe, however, that it is not a fair history of methodism.

† Miscellaneous Works, vol. xiii. p. 527, quoted from Jackson.
‡ Jackson's Wesleyan's Centenary, p. 225.
§ See Jackson's Life of Wesley, vol. ii. p. 306. || Works, vol. xii. p. 253.

avowed separation. One of the most important had been anticipated by individual ministers; but it was afterwards allowed by Conference, that " under certain regulations, the sacraments of Baptism and the Lord's Supper should be administered in the methodist chapels."* This was a formal recognition of schism which cannot be mistaken.

After this comes the first formal ordination of which we have any notice, by imposition of hands, the report of the proceedings at which is contained in *The Watchman* for August 10, 1836, reprinted in some late numbers of *The Church Intelligencer*. There is much and amusing inconsistency in the reasons which seem to have weighed with the Conference in formally admitting this rite. How, for instance, do we reconcile the two sentences of the following paragraph of the speech in which the president (Dr. Bunting) opened the proceedings:—

" He believed that it was a practice of *divine authority*, of great antiquity, and was *observed by the universal Church;* and that *it tended* also *to raise the character of the christian ministry*. He had been taunted that he had not been ordained himself by the imposition of hands : but his answer was, that *as to the essence of the thing*, he had been *as truly ordained* as if any bishop, or even John Wesley himself (!) had laid hands on him."

"Mr. Davis ' had scarcely considered his own ordination valid for want of it'—imposition of hands."

But few seem to have looked so deeply into the matter. The general impression seems to have been that imposition is a scriptural circumstance, a primitive usage, a thing practised by the Apostles, and never omitted by the whole Church; yet of so slight importance, that whether it was to be adopted, was a mere question of popularity, of expediency, of time.

One member of Conference seems to have considered it a note of catholicity. After speaking of the unequivocal meaning of the sacred Scriptures, of the present practice of the Churches of Christ at large, of the universal practice of the christian Church, in its purest and best portions, Mr. Buchan concludes that " *there ought to be a oneness in the body*." What a reason for adding an additional circumstance to a formal act of schism !

However, for these and the like reasons, the resolution was adopted, that for the future imposition of hands should be a part of the ceremony of methodist ordinations.

Accordingly, into " *the form and manner of making and ordaining of superintendents, elders, and deacons,*" which forms a part of the Wesleyan Prayer Book before us, this ceremony is in its due place admitted.

This ordinal needs not to be farther described, than by saying that it is almost identical with ours, only that the names of two of the orders of ministers are changed, *superintendent* being placed every where for *bishop*, and *elders* for *priests*. We find nothing retrenched even in those very parts of our own service for which we bear the

---

* Jackson's Centenary, p. 226.

opprobrium of *sacramentarianism* from dissenters "at large." Thus we have the words of the "superintendent" in the ordination of "a superintendent," just as strong as the words of the archbishop in our Ordering of Bishops; the *superintendents* also and *elders laying their hands upon the elected person,* just as the archbishop and bishops lay their hands on the bishop elect:—

"Receive the Holy Ghost, for the office and work of a superintendent in the Church of God, now committed unto thee by the imposition of our hands, in the name of the Father, and of the Son, and of the Holy Ghost. Amen. And remember that thou stir up the grace of God which is given thee by this imposition of our hands; for God hath not given us the spirit of fear, but of power, and love, and soberness."

When it is remembered that we are speaking of the ritual of a body of men who claim a filial relation to John Wesley, who himself for a long while protested against anything like an ordination out of the Church, who always deprecated a separation from the Church, who died with a prayer for the Church on his lips, we shall not be expected to go further in adducing proofs of their inconsistency with their professed allegiance to his authority; and when we add that they have even echoed as precious words, his warning: "Do not mend our rules, but keep them, and that for conscience' sake;" we shall at once admit that the Wesleyan methodists are "*in some respects* a peculiar people,"* and that their peculiarities are only to be reconciled with anything like a fair share of integrity and common sense, by the wonderful solution of Mr. Leech, which is certainly unparalleled in the history of acute inconsistencies:—

"In reading Mr. Wesley's writings, he was confirmed more than ever in his admiration of the doctrine and discipline which were distinguished by his name. One thing after another rose before him, as he pursued his way. Methodism, piece by piece, as it was wanted, came down from heaven. He (Mr. L.) was one who wished methodism to remain as it is. Some years ago he should, on this question, have spoken differently. The Lord had given them one thing after another. Methodism was now a far better thing than when he first knew it—the plans which had been adopted had mended it."

Here we close the notice of Wesleyan methodism as witnessing to catholic truth; not as having exhausted the subject, but rather as having suggested a train of thought which will lead to profitable meditation, and as having said enough to sustain a very important conclusion.

We have found John Wesley and his society directly, powerfully, and justly witnessing to the vital doctrines of *conversion,* of *perfection,* of *assurance;* we have found them entering a worthy protest against that part of *Calvinism* which is conversant with the *divine decrees,* and its natural progeny *antinomianism;* and thus far we have admitted that we should rather rejoice in the good done, and join in the praise, than follow those who can coldly sneer at such a movement in "the religious world," originating with such a man, and commencing, and for a while carried on with such integrity and zeal.

---

* Mr. Keeling, at Conference, in 1836.

But we have gone on, and have found worse passions in play, and worse principles broached, and a conduct which we cannot but condemn, and eventually a system evolved which in almost all its parts is monstrous, and in its very essence and form is a schism: still we have found a witness to catholic truth equally strong, though indirect, and now no longer voluntary; we have found a witness to the necessity of a three-fold ministry, and of a solemn consecration, and of an apostolical derivation, in order to the administration of the holy sacraments, and to the very being of a Church: not that we have found these things contended for *nominatim*, and as if in harmony with us; but that we have seen the inconsistencies in which the want of them at first involved the methodist body, and the still greater inconsistencies which the irregular attempt to supply them has occasioned: and we can think of no possible inducement, but the sense of their absolute necessity, that could move them to involve themselves in such strange contradictions. We have found them for a long while declaring most energetically the duty and privilege of maintaining the unity of the Church; and at last, when this was no longer within even their sense of consistency, (which we have seen is not very delicate,) assuming the only position which can seemingly indemnify them for their loss, that of a Church in themselves, forgetting that this does, in fact, more nearly approach to an avowal that they have *divided the Church of Christ*, than any one step besides that they could take. But the necessity they see, and we may thank them for avowing it; the inconsistency they do not see *yet*. When they do see it, what course ought they to pursue?

If inconsistency were all, we might allow their plea of expediency; we might allow them to address those who would call upon them to retrace their steps: "Do you wish us to burn our hymn-books; turn our chapels into warehouses; trample on the bones of our fathers, who sleep around our places of worship; scatter our societies and congregations; recall our missionaries; break up our negro schools and congregations, and the schools and congregations of converted savages in Southern Africa and in the South Seas, and let them relapse into heathenism?"* But in truth, something more than *consistency* is at stake, even *duty;* and we cannot but see that duty cries aloud, "There is but one Church to which men ought to belong, and that one is the Church which Jesus Christ founded." The Church is eighteen hundred years old; methodism has just celebrated its centenary. Can it then be THE *Church* of Christ? No. If they will restore unity to the body, if they will obey the solemn warnings of John Wesley himself, if they will act on a plain consistent plan of duty,—they will certainly return to the Church of their fathers: and they would do this, even though all the evils deprecated above should follow; for *duty* is ever before *apparent expediency:*—but in fact not one of them need follow. A right view of the VOLUNTARY PRINCIPLE, which is really a sacred prin-

---

* Jackson's Wesleyan Centenary, p. 268.

ciple in its proper application, would lead them to retain all, and to sanctify all, by still doing the good that they do, but in communion with the Church of Christ; making a *voluntary* sacrifice of all their feelings and prepossessions, as well as of their alms and energies, to the Lord; instead of sacrificing duty and allegiance to *self-will*, which is really the original of every VOLUNTARY SYSTEM, in its usual sense. This Wesley was quick to see, when it led some of his followers to seek ordination of Erasmus *without his knowledge*. Would that he had seen it when he was setting up a society *against the Church!*

The Wesleyan puts another question, which suggests one or two reflections: " Does he wish us to avow our conviction, that the Church meets all the religious and moral wants of the community?"* Clearly, no: but as clearly, with the additional energies that are now engaged against her by the Wesleyans, she might, if they were directed as they ought to be, do more than both together, or rather both separately, do at present. But one lesson there is which the Church may gather from the origin and progress of methodism. We want two things: we want an aptitude to direct the energies of zealous men in an useful, though sometimes it may be an unaccustomed, channel; and we want a more popular ministry for certain forms and habits of society. Had we been able to find them occupation, the Wesleyan preachers themselves, and John Wesley at their head, might have been instrumental in carrying the Church and its high doctrines and privileges among those very people who are now separated from her by their stirring and popular ministry. It would be absurd in this place to attempt the evolution of a plan of ecclesiastical proceedings which would meet the case; but just to suggest something tangible for the mind to work on, these two expedients would be catholic in principle, and surely not despicable in probable results: The ordination of a considerable number of persons, as deacons, whose circumstances would give them a readier access to the poorer orders, and who should not consider the diaconate a mere step to the priesthood; and The licensing of fit persons to preach wherever congregations could be assembled, though it were in the fields and lanes, or in the streets of our cities. The spirit of such a commission is surely, in the words of our blessed Lord,—" Go out into the highways and hedges, and compel them to come in, that my house may be filled."†

An Inaugural Lecture on the Study of Modern History, delivered in the Theatre, Oxford, December 2d, 1841, *by* THOMAS ARNOLD, D.D. *Professor of Modern History.* Pp. 45. Parker, Oxford.

WE are inclined to believe that the active part of mankind may be roughly divided into two great classes: those who find time to do everything, and those who can never find time to do anything

---

* Jackson's Wesleyan Centenary, p. 268.   † Luke xiv. 23.

There are some men to be seen amongst us, whose whole existence is one continual hurry; they are always to be found bustling through their present employment to get to something beyond; which again in its turn is despatched with the same unsatisfactory haste to make way for a third. While these men are thus laboriously doing nothing, we meet now and then a man who has the happy art of doing much, while he seems to casual observers to be busy about nothing; one who, without ever being in a hurry, or ever being idle, is quietly getting through as much work as seems enough to occupy three or four men fully, and would certainly keep half-a-dozen of the former class in a perpetual round of wearying and unprofitable irritation.

There can be no doubt in which of the two classes Dr. Arnold must be placed. Any one of his different employments seems enough to fill the whole time of a man of no common activity. To be head-master of one of our largest public schools;—to be the writer of four thick volumes of Sermons;—to edit and comment upon Thucydides;—to become the historian of Rome;—to give lectures as professor of modern history at Oxford;—any one or two certainly of these various undertakings would seem likely to give full employment to the best informed and most fertile mind. Yet all of them together have not overwhelmed Dr. Arnold's energies: and long may it be before their joint pressure compels him to abandon any one of them! For we verily believe that no one of his pursuits suffers materially by the time and thought devoted to the rest; while in most of them he has shown powers such as belong to few men in our time and country. We do not mean, of course, that Dr. Arnold can possibly be either so profound and accurate a scholar, or so patient and accomplished an historian, or so calmly and learnedly wise a divine, as some other men are, and as he himself might perhaps be, were his powers concentrated on a single object. We would protest most earnestly against many of his conclusions on perhaps nearly every subject which he has handled: we think him often mistaken; sometimes, especially on theological subjects, radically and dangerously wrong. But every man is really *most* useful when he is doing the work for which he himself is best fitted, even though it be not in itself the best; and the work for which Dr. Arnold seems best fitted is rather to rough-hew many things, than to perfect one. And we do not hesitate to avow, with unfeigned thankfulness for much pleasure and much instruction received from his writings, that we believe him to be gifted with a native vigour and originality of mind, applied always with singular honesty and nobleness of intention, which makes even his mistakes instructive, and has enabled him, wherever he has laboured, to do something which few men could have done equally well. Of course this applies less to his theological writings (if indeed the name of theological can properly be applied to what consists almost wholly of sermons, most of them practical) than to his other publications. Yet even these, so far as they are intended to meet the wants of boys at school, (their primary purpose,) are in their own kind most admirable. Many, we believe, owe even their own selves to impressions first made by them.

The Lecture which we now proceed to notice is the first-fruits of the author's appointment to the chair of modern history at Oxford. It was delivered before a large audience in the theatre, near the end of the last October term. It contains an exposition of the nature and purpose of history in general, and of modern history in particular, intended primarily to show the importance and interest of the study, and secondarily to prepare the way for a course of lectures on the best manner of studying modern history. A discussion by Dr. Arnold of matters so interesting in themselves as the nature and value of history, the characteristics and real limits of modern history, and the reasons for thinking that the period in which we live is the *last* in the history of the world, cannot be otherwise than interesting. But on these points we must leave our readers to judge for themselves. Indeed we might have been disposed to pass the Lecture by with a general expression of interest and acquiesence, but for Dr. Arnold's determination of one question (closely though perhaps not obviously connected with the primary subject of the Lecture,*) which is raised near its beginning, as to which we think his reasoning unsound, and his conclusion erroneous. The question is that so often agitated, upon the answer to which turn so many important political controversies in our own time: What is the great purpose for which the State exists? Does it exist as such simply for some *material* object, such as security of life and property, or has its existence some higher object, and if so, what is the precise nature of that object? We need not point out how much a man's answer to this question must influence (perhaps in practice we might rather say, *how much it will be influenced by*) the course which he takes as to all matters which affect the relations of the Church and the State; *e. g.* test-laws, church endowments and immunities, grants of money for church extension and popular instruction, &c. &c. &c. All these are naturally held to be at least questionable measures by those who take the lowest view of the functions of a State; while those who, like Dr. Arnold, take higher views, sometimes jeopardy their results, by basing them on theoretic principles rashly assumed. Dr. Arnold's doctrine on this subject has the better claim to be examined, because it has some points of coincidence with that maintained in Mr. Gladstone's very remarkable, and, in so many respects, most admirable book on Church and State; though on so large a part both of their principles and results the two authors are directly at issue.

We give, in his own words, Dr. Arnold's answer to the fundamental question,—What is the great end for which the nation or state exists, as such?

The nation's highest object or end "appears to be *the promoting and se-*

---

* "For, history being defined as 'the record of the life of a nation,' its nature cannot be rightly understood without a clear conception previously gained of the end or which a nation is meant to live."—See pp. 6-13.

curing a nation's highest happiness; so we must express it in its most general formula; but under the most favourable combination of circumstances, this same end is conceived and expressed more purely, as *the setting forth God's glory by doing His appointed work. And that work for a nation seems to imply not only the greatest possible perfecting of the natures of its individual members, but also the perfecting of all those acts which are done by the nation collectively, or by the government standing in its place, and faithfully representing it.*"—P. 19.

The first object, then, if we understand Dr. Arnold rightly, for which a state exists, is *an educational one;* it exists to promote and secure the highest possible perfecting of its members, first individually, and then collectively. *The moral training of its individual members is the primary purpose to which all its actions and institutions are meant to be directed.* We need not say one word to show how entirely different this statement of the end for which a nation exists is from those which have been long current amongst us; nor yet to show with what important results such a principle, once supposed to be established, may be pregnant.

We do not think the reasoning by which Dr. Arnold attempts to establish his proposition by any means satisfactory. His mind appears to be one of those which first reaches its conclusion by a sort of *divination,* and only afterwards looks for arguments in support of it. His first guess at truth is always vigorous, and often happy; his subsequent reasoning is apt not to be precise or cogent. We could easily point out some of the ambiguities and arbitrary assumptions by which we think that his reasoning on the present matter is vitiated, and shall attempt to do so presently.* But as we are persuaded that good and able men are not led to a theory like Dr. Arnold's so much by any process of reasoning, as by an unwillingness to accept what is often presented as the only alternative—a theory substantially the same with what is called Warburton's,—we will, before examining that part of the Lecture, attempt to sketch an account of the objects of a state's existence, which may, perhaps, satisfy the wish for something loftier than the one theory, without being open to the objections which lie against the other.

We must first beg the patience of our readers for a moment, while we point out a distinction seemingly obvious, but often forgotten in particular cases, between the *immediate* purpose to effect which a certain thing exists, and the *ulterior* uses of its existence; or, in other words, between its *proper work* or *business,* and the *ulterior ends to which the doing of that work is subservient.*—To illustrate the distinction by an example or two. The proper work or business of the piston of a steam-engine is simply to slide in a certain tube; an ulterior end of its work is to give a certain motion to a particular rod and crank; a still further end, to expedite travelling, or to raise coal from a mine. The proper

---

* We would instance the indistinctness in the use of the words "moral ends," (pp. 14, 15,) "*sovereignty* of the state," (pp. 16, 17,) which seems to us to cover at least one arbitrary assumption.

work of the compositor in a printing-office is simply to arrange the types in his composing-stick, in the reverse order of that in which the corresponding letters stand in a given manuscript; an ulterior object of his work is (what is itself the proper work of the whole society of the printing-office) to print certain books; a still ulterior object, to spread knowledge more easily and rapidly; and so on. Or, to take rather a less homely illustration; the proper work to do which the Bible Society has been established, is simply to procure the printing and circulation of a particular book in different languages; an ulterior end to which this work is meant to be subservient is to extend the knowledge of the contents of the Bible as widely as possible; the ultimate end contemplated by its founders, we suppose, was to glorify God by forwarding the salvation of men. It may be well to remark, by the way, that it is by no means necessary that the ulterior ends should be consciously kept in view by the agent in the immediate work; nay, even that the immediate work is often likely to be best done, and to promote those ends most effectually when the eye of the doer is fixed most steadily upon his own work alone. Should the compositor, for instance, begin to think of the diffusion of useful knowledge, and contrive his own means for this end, books would certainly be more slowly and worse printed, and useful knowledge in the end less advanced, than now, when he keeps close to his types and his manuscript, and thinks perhaps of nothing beyond.

Applying this distinction, then, to the matter in hand. It is plain that there are two different questions which might be comprehended in the same words—" What is the highest object of a nation?" (the words in which Dr. Arnold states the question now under consideration,) but which ought to be considered separately; the one being, what is the *proper work* or *business* of a state? the other, what are the *ulterior ends* which the doing of that work is meant to promote, consciously or unconsciously?* Were the latter question really the one meant to be answered by Dr. Arnold's statement of the "highest object of the nation, as such," we might be little disposed to object to it. Unquestionably the *ultimate* end of the state's existence is, in Dr. Arnold's words, " the setting forth God's glory." Unquestionably also, whatever be the exact definition of a state's proper work, still, since it must be one which implies a divine commission to make and administer laws; and since the laws under which men live must have a most important bearing upon their moral condition, either advancing or retarding the " highest perfecting of their natures;" and since this educational effect of the state's work must have been foreseen and intended by Him who has constituted it; the moral training of men may well be the greatest of the ulterior purposes of its existence :—" *ulterior purposes*," we say, as distinct on the one hand from the *immediate business,* and on

---

* Had Dr. Arnold attended carefully to this distinction, we are inclined to think that he would have modified considerably, perhaps his whole theory, certainly his argument in support of it.

the other from the *ultimate end of all.* But this is not what Dr. Arnold means by the question, unless we completely misunderstand the drift of his argument. *He* appears to make the educational effect of laws and institutions, and the moral training which it involves, not an ulterior purpose which the state's work is designed by God to subserve, but actually in itself the proper business which has been given it to do, and with a direct view to which it is to order all things. Here it is that we are at issue with him. Our theory, if we must dignify it with the name,—let us not be understood to claim any right in it as inventors; we believe it to be a very old one, nay, to be that which most men in most former ages have felt instinctively to give the true idea of the state, and according to which they have, though it may be unconsciously, spoken and acted;—our theory would make the *proper work or business of the state,* as such, to be *the maintenance amongst men, in its application to their outward actions, of the law of God revealed to man by conscience;*—of that primal law which is briefly comprehended, when *positively* expressed, in the two great commandments, "Thou shalt love the Lord thy God with all thy heart;" and "Thou shalt love thy neighbour as thyself;" and, when expressed *negatively,* (in which shape most properly the state is concerned with it,) forbidding impiety towards God, and the doing of wrong to man. The business of the state therefore, if we are right, is *primarily* to secure its subjects from injury by their fellow-citizens and all others, (*injury* we mean as distinguished from mere *harm,*) and to keep them from crime; and *secondarily,* as means to this end, to see that the material concerns of its subjects are so arranged, that the laws affecting the distribution of property and political power are such, as to secure permanently, so far as may be, that the principles of the divine law are correctly drawn out in detail, impartially applied, duly enforced by a system of retribution, and unhesitatingly obeyed by all. Whatever laws, then, and whatever institutions, dealing directly with the material concerns of men, are best fitted to uphold veracity and justice in permanent and unquestioned supremacy amongst the members of the nation, these the nation is empowered by the God of truth and righteousness to establish and maintain; and by so doing, to bear witness of Him to men, and train them to acknowledge Him. To Him, as "the Judge of all the earth," the nation is answerable for the fulfilment of this its office; and accordingly as it is faithful or unfaithful to the charge, so will it prosper or be brought low; dwell long in the land, or perish from amongst the nations.

We agree, then, with Dr. Arnold, in so far as we explicitly acknowledge that the great ulterior end of a nation's being is strictly an educational one: we differ from him in so far as we deny, that to educate men is the exact business of the nation, as such. Nay, we would strenuously deny that to address itself *directly* to the work of education belongs, *in idea,* to the state at all;—if the word education be used in its only adequate meaning of *moulding the will and affections of man in conformity with the relations in which he* stands, as a spiritual creature, to God and to other men.* We are not denying, be it observed, but would confess and proclaim, that it is absolutely necessary for the permanent well-being of a state to *have its citizens educated*: nor are we affirming that there are no conceivable circumstances in which, the appointed means not being available, it might become the duty of the state, at least for a time, to contrive its own means of cultivating,† so far as possible, its own citizens. But we maintain that real education is peculiarly a *spiritual* work,— one begun and carried on in the spirit of man by the Holy Spirit alone, through means, indeed, but those means both appointed and made efficacious by Him; and that, when those means are available, men sin if they devise others for themselves. We believe further that there is a society distinct from the state, and co-ordinate with it, which has been divinely constituted and perpetuated for the express purpose of educating mankind;—a society endued with the promise of the unfailing presence of the Holy Spirit for this very work, and entrusted with the dispensation of that word and those ordinances of God, in and by which the Holy Spirit has engaged to work upon the hearts of men, that so He may train them for heaven by disposing and enabling them to fill up rightly their own place on earth, as men, as members of families, as subjects of the state: and we believe that to this body, and not to the state, it has been committed to educate men truly for this world and for the world to come. To furnish the Church in some measure with the *material* means of making its educational powers available, and, above all, to prepare the way for the Church's ministry of grace, by disciplining men through the maintenance of law amongst them; this we believe to be the state's real business in the education of men. He must judge strangely who can think otherwise than most highly of its dignity and importance.

We have sketched our own theory but slightly, and are compelled to leave it open, we fear, to some misunderstanding.‡ But we must proceed to notice some of the points in which we think that Dr. Arnold's reasoning in support of his theory is unsound. The proposition which he undertakes to prove, it will be remembered, is, that the highest object of the state is, in the first instance, the moral training, or the "highest possible perfecting," of its members. The first step of the proof is, to show (see pp. 14, 15) that the state must be "cognizant of moral ends;" and, being cognizant of them,

---

* This is what we should understand by the "highest possible perfecting of the natures of men:" we do not imagine that Dr. Arnold, or any other religious man, would desire to assign a lower meaning to the words.

† We need scarcely say that we adopt the word with allusion to Coleridge's use of it in "Church and State."

‡ We beg to refer for a fuller development of a theory substantially, we believe, the same, to Mr. Maurice's Letters to a Member of the Society of Friends, Nos. IX. and X., and to the same author's Lectures on National Education. To the former, especially, of these works we desire to acknowledge a deep debt of gratitude for much most valuable instruction.

cannot "prefer others to them." We have already complained of an ambiguity here. If Dr. Arnold means only that the state cannot have been intended to pursue any other end in a degree or manner subversive of the highest moral end, we agree with him. Indeed, we do not require a proof so elaborate as his to satisfy us of this; for, since every act of the state, or nation, is the act of individual men, acting in a certain capacity, and since men are equally bound by the law of God, whatever be the capacity in which they are acting, the nation, as such, must be bound by that law. Or if, by saying that the state's ends must be moral, Dr. Arnold means that they must be ends the pursuit of which is *essentially and universally right*; not, like that of power or wealth, only *accidentally so*; then, however we may question the validity of his reasoning, we are not concerned to dispute his result; since the end which we have assigned as the immediate one of the state's existence, fully satisfies this condition; but if, as we imagine, Dr. Arnold really means that the state, being cognizant of moral ends, must necessarily therefore have for its supreme object, as a state, to pursue the highest possible moral end as its own immediate end; then we answer, that the conclusion does not appear to us to be at all connected with the premises, except upon the assumption that the state has no particular work assigned to it by its Author, but is left to choose for itself what its own work or immediate end shall be. If God, in constituting the state, has assigned to it a certain work to do for Him, its duty is simply to do that work, without considering whether it be or be not the highest possible; or, if it be replied, as we gather from certain passages, (see pp. 16, 17,) that Dr. Arnold would reply, that it is not conceivable that God can have meant to assign any but the highest possible work to the supreme earthly society; or, that to assign to the state any other work, is to trench upon its "sovereignty;" we answer by demanding to have this proved. We do not know how to attach any other meaning to the "sovereignty" of an agent confessedly subject to the one Lord of all, than simply his exemption from being controlled in the doing of his work by any but its supreme Prescriber himself; and, if this be so, we are unable to see that there is any necessary and universal connexion between the agent's sovereignty in the doing of his work, and the dignity of the particular work assigned to him. What is to hinder that the Arch-Workman should assign distinct portions of his great work to different agents; making each, whether his work be complete in itself, or have respect to something beyond itself, sovereign (under Himself alone) in the doing of his own peculiar portion?

We must be content with stating very shortly, in conclusion, three main objections which appear to us to lie against Dr. Arnold's theory.

The first is that *his doctrine makes the business of the State identical with that of the Church;*—since it would be hard to describe the latter except in terms substantially equivalent to those in which he has expressed the former;—and that *it thus leads to the conclusion that the societies themselves are identical.* Dr. Arnold would, we believe, accept this conclusion, pleading in support of it the often-alleged authority of Hooker; indeed, he has formerly maintained one scarcely, if at all, distinguishable from it. In this he has been misled, we think, by an illegitimate inference from the admitted truth, that the Church in each country is, *in idea, co-extensive with the nation;* which is almost as if it were to be supposed that the Society for the Propagation of the Gospel was identical with the Christian Knowledge Society, because every member of each ought to be also a member of the other. With our readers, however, as with most men who have written and thought upon the subject, we may assume at present the distinctness of Church and State to be a first principle; and we then ask whether, if so, our first objection is not fatal to Dr. Arnold's theory?

Our second objection is of a more directly practical character. It is, that *the proper work of the state being defined simply as, in the first instance, the perfecting of its individual subjects, without further limitation*, the end to be sought in government and legislation is made so large, and admits of so much difference of judgment, both as to its own nature, and as to the best means of pursuing it, that *it becomes impossible to govern rightly with reference to it.* Fancy a king in the thirteenth century, or a parliament in the nineteenth, endeavouring to legislate with no more intelligible guide than such a principle.

Our third and last objection is, that *Dr. Arnold's theory would authorize something, at least, very like persecution.* The state is to enjoin and enforce (for the state does not work by persuasion) whatever is necessary for the perfecting of its citizens as moral beings. Is not religious worship necessary for this end? Why then not compel men by civil punishment to observe it? Is not the reception of revealed truth necessary, according to God's appointment, for the same end? Why then not punish men for unbelief? or, at least, for avowing unbelief? or for arguing, however reverently and honestly, against belief? The argument might be pushed much further, but our limits compel us to forbear.

We have freely attacked the doctrine which Dr. Arnold maintains as to the proper function of a state. Having done so, let us repeat that we have found much interesting and instructive matter even in this first Lecture, and shall look with much interest for those which are to follow.

1. *Hints to Teachers in National Schools: selected from Modern Works on Practical Education.* Edited by the REV. HENRY HOPWOOD, Inspector of Schools. Burns. 1841.
2. *Home Education.* By the AUTHOR OF NATURAL HISTORY OF ENTHUSIASM. Jackson and Walford. 1838.
3. *Education for the People.* By MRS. HIPPISLEY TUCKFIELD. Taylor and Walton. 1839.
4. *Account of the Edinburgh Sessional School.* By JOHN WOOD, Esq. Oliver and Boyd. 1840.
5. *Training System, Established in the Glasgow Normal Seminary.* By DAVID STOW, Esq. Blackie and Son. 1840.
6. *Practical Remarks on Infant Education.* By the REV. DR. MAYO and MISS MAYO. Seeley. 1838.
7. *What De Fellenberg has done for Education.* Saunders and Otley. 1839.
8. *Reports on the Training of Pauper Children.* London: Hansard. 1841.
9. *The Schoolmaster.* 2 vols. C. Knight. 1836.
10. *Report to the Trustees of the Bequest of the late James Dick, Esq.* By ALLAN MENZIES. Oliver and Boyd. 1838.
11. *Principles of Teaching.* By HENRY DUNN. 1839.
12. *On the Management and Education of Children.* Published under the Direction of the Committee of General Literature and Education, appointed by the Society for Promoting Christian Knowledge. J. W. Parker. 1841.
13. *Letters to a Clergyman.* By MRS. TUCKFIELD. Taylor and Walton. 1840.
14. *The Schoolmistress.* By EMILY TAYLOR.
15. *Hints for School-Keeping.* By the REV. T. VOWLER SHORT, D.D. (Now Bishop of Sodor and Mann.) J. W. Parker. 1839.
16. *Practical Hints on the Formation and Management of Sunday Schools.* By the REV. J. C. WIGRAM. J. W. Parker. 1840.
17. *Lectures on National Education.* By the REV. F. D. MAURICE. Rivingtons. 1839.

WE could easily extend this list to a much greater length; but our readers will probably agree with us in thinking that we shall find in the works lying before us abundant matter for a single article. We reserve to some future number an account of the *official* publications on the subject; namely, the Minutes of the Committee of Council on Education, and the Reports of the National Society.

The work which stands at the head of our list consists chiefly of selections, of a practical nature, from those which succeed it, from " Home Education," to " Report on Training of Pauper Children," inclusive; together with passages from an abridged translation of Madame Neckar de Saussure's " L'Education Progressive; ou Etude du Cours de la Vie." We hope to have some future opportunity of reviewing this and some other French works on education. Our notice of the other books from which the " Hints" are selected will be brief.

The author of " Home Education" has endeavoured to construct—

"A comprehensive system, specifically applicable to the peculiar circumstances of a *home* course of instruction."

And he informs us that the leading characteristic of his system is, that it affords peculiar facilities—

" For bestowing a well-considered culture upon each of the separate faculties of the mind, in the order of their natural development."

Mr. Taylor thus draws the distinction between home and school :—

" A HOME, whether its inmates be related by the ties of consanguinity or not, is a place where the stress of government rests much rather upon affection and sentiment, than upon rules and penalties, or the mechanism of external order. SCHOOL, on the contrary, is a little world, where, as in the great world, if delicate sentiments exist at all, they must be kept out of view; or at least must neither be allowed to interfere with the movements of the general body, nor must be mainly relied on. On this point of distinction much will be found to hinge;—one might say, every thing, more or less immediately, within the two systems respectively; and especially so in relation to whatever affects moral training."

This distinction may be expressed in a very few words. LOVE is the characteristic principle of home; JUSTICE of the school. From this distinction we draw two practical conclusions; first, that the discipline of schools for *young children* and for *girls* ought to be assimilated as much as possible to that of home; and, secondly, that *all* schools ought to be constructed upon Church principles; for in the Church system, and in that alone, " mercy and truth are met together; righteousness and peace have kissed each other;" justice and love unite in perfect harmony. Mr. Maurice, whose admirable " Lectures" ought to be in the possession of every school-manager, has brought forward some valuable truths with regard to the education of girls and young children :—

" As the universities and grammar-schools make up what I have called our national education, it is obvious that there is no provision for the instruction of females or of infants. Modern commentators will have no difficulty in explaining this deficiency; they will say, of course, that it arose from the low opinion which our barbarous ancestors formed of the female intellect, and from their believing that children who were not yet able to study school-logic, or take part in martial exercises, had no souls which it was possible to cultivate. This solution is very easy and plausible; but I am afraid that facts show it to be untenable.... I should find it hard to believe that the old knights made such accurate and scientific distinctions between moral, intellectual, and external qualities; that no homage to wit and wisdom ever mingled with their admiration for goodness and beauty.... Is the exquisite portrait of a princess of the house of D'Este, the friend and inspirer of Tasso, which a modern poet has drawn, solely the creation of his genius? Were not the materials for it supplied by authentic records of herself, her mother, her sisters, and of many other ladies of the court of Italy?... Did not the brave and humble-minded daughter of Sir Thomas More assist Erasmus with her criticisms? Was not Lady Jane Grey a student of Plato?

"Equally unfortunate is the suggestion that either in the middle ages or in the period which followed them, INFANCY could have been regarded with contempt, as only the shell of a substance hereafter to come into being. Every thing that we know about the opinions of those times would lead to directly the opposite conclusion; that a more awful recognition of a mysterious presence in the child than is at all common in these days characterized them. But they had learnt from the discipline of old Rome, which was surely not disposed to undervalue the authority of the state, or the hold which it had upon its citizens, that it is much safer for the interest of this very state that it should, in the first place, maintain the parental authority; and should not, for some years, claim any rights of its own, distinct from that. It seemed to the wise men of this old republic, that great as was the risk of leaving children to the chance prudence of particular parents, it was a far greater and more terrible risk not to recognise the FAMILY PRINCIPLE, not to assert the parental responsibility..... Rome felt herself more indebted, and was more indebted, to her WOMEN, for the firm and manly character of her citizens, than to any other cause whatsoever... It seemed to the Romans that a nation, in order to be perfect, supposes something besides itself; that in the domestic character of woman, continually brought into contact with those who (properly speaking) form the nation, it possesses this blessing.... And so among our ancestors, the women grew up as members of the great and universal society;... under the condition, that their life should be *domestic;* that they should sustain the nation by standing, in a manner, apart from it."

We do not think it worth while to discuss the theory upon which Mr. Taylor's "system" is constructed. He thinks that every thing, in method and in matter, ought to be exactly adapted to the *individual* capacities and tastes of the learner, and the utmost advantage secured for every special talent; indulges in a senseless tirade against what he is pleased to call "the incumbrance and despotism of statutes, of immemorial but perhaps irrational usages, and of prevalent notions;" and magnifies "home education" on the ground of its engendering a "decisive *individuality* of temper." We, for our part, are of opinion that that system of education cannot be too severely condemned whose chief tendency it is to create and foster self-will and self-conceit.

In writing on so glorious a theme as education, even Mr. Taylor cannot avoid saying some things that are worth listening to; and we turn to the more grateful task of bringing these under the notice of our readers. The following observations relate to a subject of great importance in the conduct of dame and infant schools :—

"The *natural felicity of childhood* may be assumed as the guiding principle of all education. . . . : The happy characteristic of infancy, and, in a modified form, of childhood, is that . . . whereas the *pains* of the infant are scarcely, if at all, extended beyond the limit of animal uneasiness, its *pleasures* are expanded, and compounded, and enhanced, incalculably beyond the simple organic gratification.

"The recollection of a thoroughly happy childhood (other advantages not wanting) is the very best preparation, moral and intellectual, with which to encounter the duties and cares of real life. . . . To have known nothing but misery, is the most portentous condition under which human nature can start on its course."

One of the most valuable endowments of a teacher is that combination of intuitive good sense and innate kindness of disposition, which enables her—for this is one of those "gems rich and rare" which belong chiefly to *women*—to place herself in the inmost shrine of a young child's heart. Such a teacher may be comparatively untaught, untrained: but she will far excel those who have been formed by external teaching and training only in the art of securing obedience, of diffusing enjoyment, and even of imparting knowledge. Where this is wanting, there may be observed—

"A something *too much* in the modes of treatment—too much talking and preaching, and a too frequent bringing in of ultimate motives; until the natural sensibility and 'delicacy of children's minds are, if the phrase may be allowed, worn threadbare; for all the gloss of the feelings is gone, and the warp and substance are going."

Many a village dame, observes the author of "Home Education," plies the machinery of human nature well; but never has a professor of philosophy told those to whom Nature has not granted this tact, either how to acquire it, or how to manage without it. But if those to whom GOD—according to Mr. Taylor, "Nature"—has given this talent, would use it aright, although they will not ask philosophy to teach them, they will seek counsel and aid of the "wisdom from above," which has been entrusted to the Church's accredited ministers. Let us hear Mr. Maurice on this point. He, a living guide, conducts us to the practical measures to which Mr. Taylor, a mere finger-post, can only point.

"It is this machinery," [says Mr. Maurice, speaking of the mechanical arrangements of the 'mutual method' of instruction,] "which has overshadowed our ecclesiastical education, and prevented it from coming forth in its fulness and power. . . . We have been worshipping our own net, and burning incense to our own drag; looking at our system, and forgetting the beings upon whom the system was to act. . . . Once let us believe this,— that in every poor child there dwells a human spirit which *we* can speak to, which *we* have a commission from above to speak to, and to call forth, and to instruct in all its divine and human relations;—once let us begin to act upon this conviction, and all the instruments we want will speedily gather themselves about us. . . . The country parson may find, in many cases, that the revival of the old-dame-school system for girls, or at least for infants, may save him the expense of building a school-room, and do the work more effectually. For looking upon himself as the head schoolmaster of the parish, he may put the dame upon such a method of appealing to the heart and understanding of her pupils as may give new life, both to herself and them. In every case he will care more for the teacher than for the lesson: him he will try, by every means, to inform and cultivate. In the hands of a living teacher, the CATECHISM, he knows, will be no dead book; it will unfold mysteries to the heart of a child which will surround him, and possess him, and give him a sense of his nothingness and of his greatness, through infancy, and youth, and manhood. In the hands of a living teacher, the BIBLE will be a revelation, not on those subjects only which are technically called religious; but it will be the awakener and satisfier of innumerable puzzles about himself in the heart of the boy; the teacher of political wisdom to the youth in whose heart the social impulses are beginning to stir."

We have carefully examined the course of instruction pursued in a large number of schools, but we have seldom found in them any fixed principle of progression. The only guide that appears to be followed, and that in but a blind way, is the ability of the boy with regard to *reading;* that is, his ability to go through a merely mechanical process, as *at present* practised, and involving no exercise of the spirit of the child whatever. Now, we may divide the intellectual occupations of a child into *literary* and *scientific;*—and our readers must not be startled at our using the same terms in reference to the education of the lower orders that are used in reference to the education of the higher; for, in this matter, " the rich and poor meet together—the LORD is the maker of both." With regard to the former and more important of these two heads of intellectual instruction and discipline, we believe that a course of POETICAL reading, not in a dead, but a living way, will be found to involve the best principle for classifying children, and of arranging the course of their lessons and exercises. We have been led to this subject by the following passage from " Home Education: "—

"There can be no doubt that POETRY is to be employed as a principal means of intellectual and moral culture, during the first period of education; and by poetry, as adapted to infancy and early childhood, I intend, severally—rhyme, rhythm, ornamented description of familiar objects, and condensed moral sentiment. . . .

" Verse for children should always embrace some substantial element of poetry;—it should present what is really poetic of its kind, however familiar. Contrary to what the inexperienced would suppose, and to what many writers of verses for children appear to have taken for granted, it is by no means the most prosaic, or the most nakedly intelligible pieces that are chosen and delighted in by children, when left to make their own selection. . . . Children, in almost all cases, are most delighted with that which most immediately quickens the conceptive faculty, and which leaves **much** to be done by the imagination; while that which is frigidly exact and merely true, does not arouse the mind; and, on the other hand, that which is gorgeously descriptive and highly-coloured, fails entirely to attract a child's ear. ... The poetry which children choose, is that which, with a light descriptive brevity, brings the familiar aspects of the visible world before the fancy; and that also which is simply and briskly narrative, and which is enlivened by turns of humour, and deepened by just moral sentiments, and especially by touches of pity."

The next book on our list is Mrs. Tuckfield's " Education for the People." This little book contains so much that would be useful to the teachers of small village schools, that we greatly regret to find in it some very unnecessary discussions and some uncalled-for strictures, which we should decidedly object to bring under the notice of teachers, by placing the book in their hands. We should like to see a Manual or Guide-Book for Village Dame Schools from Mrs. Tuckfield's pen; it might contain the letters between " Mrs. Barlow" and " John and Sarah Roberts;" portions of the correspondence between " Dr. Benson," " Mrs. Barlow," " Miss Baker;" and the more practical passages of " Letters to a Clergyman;" together with some further matters of a more technical nature. Mrs. Tuckfield has herself described the kind of book we mean.

" It has often occurred to me, that, if the grand leading principles of education could be put forth in a very simple familiar manner, and that to such an *exposé* extremely simplified and minutely detailed directions could be added on the elementary teaching of infant boys and girls, such a work might be found to supply a desideratum. ... Our mistresses would be selected from the most simple-hearted, respectable, and pious, of our own neighbourhood; and we might raise the tone of their minds and manners, without altering their simple frugal habits of living. Finer clothes and more luxurious diet would not be thought necessarily connected with the power of imparting knowledge, and training the young to habits of self-denying temperance and industry, instilling virtuous and religious feelings and principles."

The following passages from one of " Mrs. Barlow's " letters to " John and Sarah Roberts " is a favourable specimen of Mrs. Tuckfield's familiar and pleasant manner of dealing with her subject.

" My dear Sarah,—I hope, though I am obliged to be absent from home, that I may be able to give some advice to you and John, and that, when I return next year, I shall find you surrounded by a large family of affectionate, industrious, intelligent children.

" You say that you and John feel ignorant, and fear that you may not be able to give the little ones much learning. Never fear; only give your whole hearts to your business. These children are committed to you as if they were your own; love them, watch over them, as if they really were your own; remember, their happiness throughout their whole existence depends on your love and care. Be firm, steady, patient; be always gentle; remembering the direction St. Paul gives to parents,—' Fathers, provoke not your children to wrath, but bring them up in the nurture and admonition of the Lord.' ...

" I must add a few words to John about the garden. John, Mr. Barlow wishes you not to begin to trench the acre of land till the school opens. We have determined to admit only six boys and six girls the first week. Mrs. Benson will kindly select from the applicants the six best boys and six best girls between ten and twelve years old. Direct them to be at the school a quarter before nine, and each to bring twopence. If any come without their weekly payment, you will send them home, and not admit them till another week. You must insist on punctual attendance, and let the parents feel that no rule of the school can be broken. You will read the rules we gave you respecting attendance, cleanliness, &c. to the parents, when you inform them that their children are elected. The first week we wish the boys to be chiefly engaged in trenching the ground, and the girls in needle-work. One hour in the morning, and one in the afternoon, will be sufficient at first for reading and writing. . . .

"You may admit six more boys and six girls the second week, till we have filled up the number, twenty-four of each. You remember, we are to admit only these twenty-four boys and twenty-four girls, above seven years old, the first month. The second month, with Betsy's assistance, your wife may open the little infant school in her inner room, for twelve little ones under seven, boys and girls; and by that time she will be able to choose out two or three of her elder girls who can, by turns, assist with the infants. . . .

"When you take little ones into your school, who have not yet learned any thing, let your rule from the first be, *little and well*. Be in no haste to bring them forward; in this case it is certain that 'more haste is worse, speed.' You will be convinced of this, by the difficulty you will find in getting rid of the bad habits your elder scholars have acquired. You cannot hope to do this at once: attack these bad habits one by one. If your elder boys read in a loud drawling tone, missing half their words, running their words into one another with little attention to stops or pauses, holding their books awry, standing with their heads down, on one leg, &c.; if, when they write, they hold their pens or slate pencils the wrong way, twist their slates or copy-books on one side, and hang their heads down over their shoulder, while they scribble mis-shapen letters and figures,—it will be of no use to stand by, calling out, 'Read better; mind your stops; speak plain; hold up your heads; hold your pens well,' &c. &c.; and then, when none of these things are done, calling out louder, 'Why don't you mind?— you are very idle boys,' &c.: the poor fellows are all the time, perhaps, doing their best to fulfil very irksome, unintelligible tasks, and by no means deserving of any censure. Instead of this, I should stop the whole proceed-ing, and merely say, 'We will try a new way, my boys, of reading. We will read three or four lines to-day; I will speak each word distinctly and sepa-rately, and you shall speak it after me, in a gentle voice.' The next day, a few more lines might be read, in a similar way. I would at first not attempt pauses or stops, but only attend to distinct pronunciation, and to a subdued tone of voice. Then I would add a proper attitude of body; and the books should all be held straight. In a few days more, I would begin the same sentences again, writing the words, and attending to the stops; afterwards, I would read the same sentences, taking care to lay the emphasis, or stress, on the proper words. . . .

"Now, John, by doing all this patiently and carefully, you will not only improve the boys' reading, but you will improve their characters. You will teach them, by experience, that there is a right and wrong way of doing every thing; that whatever is worth doing at all, is worth doing well; that it requires some pains to do things well; that in all things they will find— 'no pains, no gains.' Then, when they begin to succeed and to improve, you will just say, you are glad they have the pleasure of improving, when pains are taken. Do not dwell on these remarks, as if you were giving lessons they must learn or remember; but rather let it all pass as a little friendly conversation, as if you were entering into their feelings, and rejoicing with them when they had taken pains and were improving."

We must conclude our notice of Mrs. Tuckfield's little book with one more short extract, which we take from one of the letters to " Sarah Roberts."

" I am pleased to hear that your lessons on your black board answer so well. I advise you, now your girls can tell you how to spell so many simple words, to let them invent little sentences. While they sit at their knitting, do you go to the board, and take one word to begin with; suppose you write the names of the colours, black, blue, &c.; and then let each girl in turn mention all the things they can think of, which are black, blue, green, &c. They will say, 'The grass is green; the trees are green; my frock is green; my lips are red; ink is black; the sky is blue; my shoes are black,' &c. &c. . . . . Another day, you may write down all that is sweet, sour, bitter; all they can think of that is hard, soft, rough, smooth, round, square, heavy, light; and so you may go on day after day, inventing many a pretty lesson to write down, while your girls work or knit. . . .

" It is a good exercise sometimes to ask children to recollect all the objects they observed in the woods, fields, or lanes, as they walked to or from school, and let them bring the leaves of different trees, the wild flowers, &c., and then let them tell you how to spell the words.

" Now, some people may tell you that it is of no use to teach these children these common easy things, and that all you should do is to give them what they call book-learning; but I assure you, that if you do not allow them to write, from their own heads, little sentences about easy matters they can think and tell about, they will never know how to express themselves properly or clearly; and if they can tell you in writing what they now know, and think, and understand about, when they have read and learned more, they will be able to write down their thoughts and recollections on other and more difficult subjects. . . .

" I dare say you have noticed that there is nothing infants like so much as to *fetch* and *carry;* well, put the bricks I gave you in a heap at one end of the room, and allow each of your little infant class to go to fetch one at a time, and to place it on the table, and then for each brick which is fetched, make a stroke on the black board, and say, ' One brick, one stroke;' and then when another is fetched, say, ' One brick and one brick make two bricks; look here, I must make another stroke; now, one stroke and one stroke make two strokes.' In this way go on till you have had five bricks fetched, then make them hold up one hand, stretching out the fingers and thumb, and show them four fingers and one thumb make five; and make them fully sensible there are the same number of strokes and the same number of bricks; then let the bricks be taken back, one by one, and say, ' Take one brick away from five bricks, four are left;' and at the same time, let them double down the thumb and fingers, one by one, leaving only the same number stretched out as the number of bricks remaining on the table, and of strokes remaining on the board: and after they have done this some time, accustom them often to count different things as far as five, in this way; put three, two, or four pebbles, flowers, or letters, on the table, and let them hold up the same number of fingers: when they can count clearly as far as five, go on just in the same way to ten; both hands, with fingers extended, must be held up for ten.

" Now, pray be satisfied for a good while not to go further than ten; and after they can add and take away the bricks readily, and can tell you that two bricks and two bricks are four bricks, and two bricks and three bricks five bricks, three bricks and three bricks six bricks, and that if you take three bricks away from six, three will be left, &c., you may then proceed to put your ten bricks all close together in one row, and say, 'Those altogether make ten; one ten:' and then you may add a one again, and say, 'Ten bricks and one brick make eleven,' and make ten strokes on the board, and at a little distance one stroke, and say, 'Ten strokes and one stroke make eleven strokes; ten bricks and two bricks are twelve bricks; ten strokes and two strokes are twelve strokes;' and when you have got as far as fifteen, then hold up the two hands for ten, and one hand afterwards for the five; and go on in the same gradual manner till you get on to twenty, when, of course, you will arrange your bricks in two rows, and say, 'Two tens are twenty,' and hold up the hands twice, and make the two sets of ten strokes on the board. When they are a little older, you will show them how different figures stand for and represent these numbers; which I advise you to do in this manner on the board.

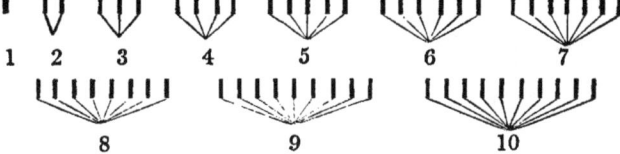

" When you show the ten strokes, tell them you put the figure 1 to stand for one ten, and that the 0 you put after it is a sign that no ones are added to this one ten, and that the figure means all together one ten and no more: then go on in this manner, and say, ' One ten and one one make eleven,'

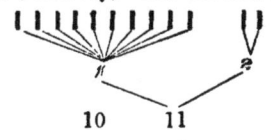

and explain that, of the two ones you have made underneath, the first stands for one *ten*, the second for one *one;* in the same way go on to twelve, thirteen, &c. till you get to twenty,

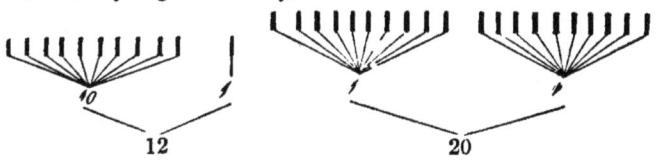

when you will draw two bunches of the ten strokes, and join them together in this manner, and then explain that the figure 2 placed below these bunches stands for two tens, the nought means that no ones are added to the two tens, and that two tens are called twenty. This may seem to you a very long round-about way of teaching children to count twenty; but the longest way about, you know, the old proverb says, is sometimes the shortest way home. . . . Besides, this way I have been describing will be very pleasant to your little ones; it will make them look and think before they speak; and they will know that when they say, 'Two and two are four; take three from five, two will remain,' and so on, *they are really speaking the truth, and a truth which they can really understand.*"

The "Account of the Edinburgh Sessional School" was much

in advance of the average condition of popular education in this country, when it was first published; but in consequence of the progress made and making in this great national work, it is dropping into the rear. Its advocacy of the method of mutual instruction, or as it is sometimes called " the monitorial system," to which it was originally indebted for much of its popularity, is now becoming prejudicial to its claims to occupy a place in the schoolmaster's library. In one department, however, of instruction, and that an important one, it is still considerably in advance of the majority of English schools: we mean the etymological analysis of words. We commend our next extract to the careful consideration of all such of our readers as are engaged in the management or government of schools for the lower and middle classes.

" As the pupils advance in this book, (the 'Sessional School Collection,') each passage, besides being fully explained in all its bearings upon the subject in question, is subjected to a still more minute analysis than had been practised in the former stages, with the view formerly explained of giving them *the full command of their own language,* and such general information as the passage may suggest.

" Take, for example, the following passage extracted from ' Wakefield's Juvenile Travellers,' which, as well as the ' Family Tour,' by the same authoress, we would recommend for introduction into all libraries for schools or young families.

SWITZERLAND.

" ' How shall I describe to you the vast variety of wonderful and romantic prospects that we have seen since we came into Switzerland? These charming views are varied with mountains, whose snowy heads seem to reach the skies; craggy rocks and steep precipices, with foaming torrents gushing from the crevices in their sides, delightfully intermixed with beautiful valleys, adorned with groves of fir, beech, and chestnut; clear lakes, rapid rivers, cataracts, and bridges of one arch, extending a surprising width from rock to rock. The cultivated parts of the mountains are covered with villages and scattered cottages; and then the insides of the cottages are so very neat, and look so comfortable, that I should like to live in some of them that are situate in the most delightful spots, were it not for the dread of being swallowed up in one of those enormous masses of snow that frequently roll from the tops of the mountains, and destroy every thing in their way. In going to the tops of the high mountains of Switzerland, you may enjoy all the seasons of the year in the same day,' &c.

" After reading the passage, the children are required to recapitulate, in their own language, the substance of what they have read, and describe the peculiar character of the Swiss scenery,—the internal appearance of the dwellings of the peasantry,—the particular dangers to which they are exposed,—the variety of climate and its cause,—and to mention any other scenery of a similar kind, which is nearer home; such, for example, as the Highlands of Scotland. But, as the passage is read in school, not merely for the purpose of communicating to them the direct information which it contains, however interesting in itself, but, like all the other passages which they read, *to render them familiar with their own language,*—to act as a vehicle for the communication of general knowledge, and as a field for examination on that which has formerly been communicated,—they are also called upon to answer some such questions as the following, or, at least, as many of them as the pupil is not already sufficiently acquainted with, or the time specially set apart for such examination will permit.

"What is Switzerland? Name its boundaries. What is the literal meaning of the word 'describe?' What does the termination *scribe* denote? Mention some of its other compounds with their various meanings. [Here the pupil will give and explain the words *inscribe, prescribe, subscribe, superscribe, transcribe, circumscribe, proscribe, ascribe.*] Do you know any word from the same root which signifies a writing? [Here he will mention *Scripture.*] In what sense is this word now generally used? Do you know a word which signifies that which is *written by the hand*? [*manuscript.*] Do you know any other part of a word besides *scribe* which signifies to *write* or *describe*? [*graph.*] Give and explain to me some of its derivatives and compounds [such as *graphic, paragraph, telegraph, chirography, geography.*] What is meant by *variety*? From what verb does it come? Mention some of the other words derived from this verb. Does the word *wonderful* take any other form? [*wondrous.*] Could you give me any other word varied in the same manner? [such as *plentiful, plenteous; bountiful, bounteous.*] What then does the termination *ous* denote? Could you give me any word meaning *wonderful* which is applied only to anything out of the course of nature? [*miraculous.*] Can you give me any verb from the same root? [*admire.*] What is the meaning of 'romantic?' From what noun does it come? What is a prospect? What does the syllable *pro* signify? Give some other examples of this [such as *progress, project.*] What does the termination *spect* denote? Mention some other words from this root [such as *spectator, spectacle, aspect, expect, inspect, circumspect, retrospect, suspect.*] With reference to the word 'seen,' can you tell me any word which signifies 'that can be seen?' [*visible*] and the opposite? Can you give me any word from the same root with these which signifies *sight*? [*vision*] or *to go to see*? [*visit*] or *to go to see again?* [*revisit.*] Do you know any word which originally signifies *to see forward*, but is used figuratively? [*provide.*] What adjectives come from that root? What is the difference between *provident* and *providential*? What word is formed by contraction from *provident*? [*prudent.*] What then does a *prudent man* properly mean? With reference to the word 'came,' can you tell me any termination that signifies *to come* [*vene* or *vent.*] Give me examples [*convene, intervene, advent, adventure, event, invent, prevent.*] Mention some of the principal 'mountains' of Switzerland. What is the difference between a 'mountain' and a hill? What is the adjective from *mountain*? What is *an inhabitant of a mountainous district* called? What does the verb 'mount' signify? Has it any compounds? [*surmount, amount.*] What does a mountebank mean? Why? What are 'craggy rocks?' What are 'precipices?' Why are they so called? Do you know any other words from the same root? What are 'torrents,' and 'crevices?' With reference to the word 'sides,' can you give me any word that signifies *belonging to the side*? [*lateral.*] Mention any other words from the same root [*collateral, equilateral, multilateral.*] What is meant by *intermixed*? What does the former part of that word signify? Give some other examples of its application [such as *interval, intermediate, intercede.*] What does the first syllable of the word 'beautiful' mean in our language? What is the corresponding feminine word? What is the verb from it? [*embellish.*] Does 'beautiful' ever take any other termination? What are 'valleys?' What are 'lakes?' What are they called in Scotland? and in Ireland? Mention the principal lakes in Switzerland, describing at the same time their respective situations. Mention also in like manner some of its principal 'rivers.' Can you give any diminutive from the word 'river?' What are 'cataracts?' Can you give any other words for them? [*waterfalls, cascades.*] What parts of words in composition signify 'one?' [*uni, mono.*] Give examples [such as *uniform, unicorn, monotony, monosyllable.*] What is the literal meaning of the word 'extending?' What does the first syllable signify? Can you give any other example of its application? [such as *extract, expel.*] What does the syllable *tend* signify? Mention some other of its compounds [such as *distend, pretend.*] Do you know any noun from the simple root? [*tent.*] Why is a tent so called? What do you mean by 'cultivated?' What word expresses *the cultivation of fields?* or *the cultivation of gardens?* What is the meaning of the word *occult?* Whence does it derive this meaning? [From seeds covered over in tillage.] What are 'villages?' What name is given to *a smaller collection of houses?* What is an inhabitant of a village called? What do you mean by 'scattered cottages?' What is the name given to *the inhabitant of a cottage?* What is the difference between a 'cottage' and a 'hut?' Could you substitute any other word for 'insides?' What is the opposite of *interior?* What does 'very' literally mean? [Truly.] Can you mention any other words from the same root? [*Verily, verity, veracity, verify, aver.*] What do you mean by 'dread?' What adjective comes from this root? What other words denote *dreadful?* [*frightful, terrible, formidable.*] What do you mean by 'enormous?' What name is given to 'enormous masses of snow rolling from the tops of the mountains?' [*avalanches.*] Could you give any other word employed to signify 'tops of mountains?' [*summits.*] or any other words from the same root? [such as *consummate, sum.*] What are 'all the seasons of the year?' What occasions the diversity of seasons? How can they all be anywhere enjoyed on the same day? Can you give me any part of a word which expresses 'all' in composition? [*omni.*] Give examples [*omnipotent, omniscient, omnipresent, omnivorous.*] What is the adjective from 'year?' Give another word for 'yearly?' Express a *yearly payment* in one word? and the *receiver* of this payment? also *a book detailing the events of a year?* and *the writer* of this book? Is the word 'same' ever compounded with any other to make it emphatical? [*selfsame.*] Is there any other word which expresses "same" emphatically? [*identical.*] Mention some other parts of speech from the same root [*identity, identify.*] Can you give any word which means *belonging to the "day?"* [*diurnal,*] *lasting for a day?* [*ephemeral,*] *a book containing a day's transactions?* [*diary* or *journal,*] any other words from the same root with *journal?* [such as *journey, adjourn, sojourn, journeyman.*] Such is a specimen of our mode of examination in its fullest form."—Pp. 216—221.

We now pass on to the work which stands as ninth on our list; namely; "The Schoolmaster: or, Essays on Practical Education, selected from the works of Ascham, Milton, Locke, and Butler; from the Quarterly Journal of Education; and from Lectures delivered before the American Institute of Instruction." Some useful information may be gleaned from this work; but its principles are unsettled, its views are defective, its tone is low; and it is therefore far from being a safe book to put into the hands of a schoolmaster.

It begins with an analytical account of Ascham's "Schoolmaster:" Ascham well describes the general manner and temper in which instruction ought to be given, and school-discipline administered.

"If your scholar do miss sometimes, chide not hastily: for that shall both dull his wit and discourage his diligence; but monish him gently, which shall make him both willing to amend, and glad to go forward in love and hope of learning. . . .

"I have now wished twice or thrice this gentle nature to be in a schoolmaster. And that I have done so, neither by chance nor without some reason, I will now declare at large why in mine opinion love is fitter than fear, gentleness better than beating, to bring up a child rightly in learning. . . .

"I do gladly agree with all good schoolmasters in these points following; to have children brought to good perfectness in learning; to all honesty in manners; to have all faults rightly amended; to have every vice severely corrected. But for the order and way that leadeth to these points we somewhat differ; for commonly many schoolmasters, some as I have seen, more as I have heard tell, be of so crooked a nature, as when they meet with a hard-witted scholar, they rather break him than bow him, rather mar him than mend him. For when the schoolmaster is angry with some other matter, then he will soonest fall to beat his scholar; and though he himself should be punished for his folly, yet must he beat some scholar for his pleasure, though there be no cause for him to do so, nor yet fault in the scholar to deserve so.

" These, ye will say, be fond schoolmasters, and few they be that be found to be such. They be fond, indeed, but surely over many such be found everywhere. But this will I say, that even the wisest of your great beaters do as oft punish *nature*, as they do correct *faults*. Yea, many times the better nature is sorer punished. For, if one by quickness of wit take his lesson readily, another by hardness of wit taketh it not so speedily; the first is always commended; the other is commonly punished: when a wise schoolmaster should rather discreetly consider the right disposition of both their natures, and not so much weigh what either of them is able to do now, as what either of them is likely to do hereafter. For this I know, not only by reading of books in my study, but also by experience of life abroad in the world, that those which be commonly the wisest, the best learned, and best men also, when they be old, were never commonly the quickest of wit when they were young."

We now pass to an entirely different department of the subject. We account it one of the happiest omens of our times, that there is a settled conviction on the minds of the most influential English educationists, that the great object for which our schools are established, is not to push forward the children of the working classes to some extreme point in the scale of intellectual advancement inconsistent with their future social position; but,—to use the words of the Baptismal Office, and of that profound educational formulary, the Church Catechism,—" virtuously to bring them up to lead godly and christian lives;" to teach and train them "to learn and labour truly to get their own living, and to do their duty in that state of life unto which it shall please God to call them." We are of opinion that too much importance cannot be attached to the *political* bearings of education; using that much-abused word "political" in its true sense, as embracing whatever relates to the organization of the State, and the social condition of its individual members. For this reason, we would have MORAL instruction and discipline take precedence of intellectual instruction; and, indeed, determine, from first to last, its nature and amount.

M. de Saintville, one of the writers in the publication under review, has some just observations on this subject.

" The course of instruction followed in schools, which generally has for its sole object the cultivation of the intellectual powers, is essentially defective and incomplete. And yet we see in all countries honourably and generous men uniting to extend knowledge, instruction, and useful information throughout society; and in England we see enormous [?] sums annually expended with the professed, and, we may fairly admit, the real object of diminishing human suffering, and improving human character. . . .

" Instruction by itself is an instrument of which either a good or a bad use may be made. That which is learned in elementary schools, and which consists in knowing how to read, write, and cipher, cannot exercise much influence on morals. In fact, we shall be puzzled to understand how it would be possible to give a man regular habits and just moral sentiments, by merely teaching him to perform certain operations almost mechanical, such as reading and writing are..... We will admit that the cultivation of the intellect alone has some effect, in so far as it tends to make immediate impulse yield to reason, and tends also to form some habits of order and industry..... It is true, that neither our minds nor our bodies can be educated without the concurrence of our will, and, consequently, not without accustoming this faculty to desire that which the others ought to do, and without labouring more or less to give it instruction. Our education, such as it is, by compelling us to perform a certain work, necessarily inculcates certain virtues. Every kind of labour requires us to have a certain command over ourselves; every kind of labour exercises our patience, in a greater or less degree, and makes us acquire habits of activity, application, and a sort of regularity. Besides, education cannot develop our sensitive and intellectual faculties, without at the same time acting indirectly upon our will: it cannot awaken good feelings in us without exciting us to do good; it induces us in some degree to practise it, simply because it makes us know what it is, and shows us the advantages we may derive from it..... The result of our present course of education is to render our habits more or less moral, though it does not directly keep that object in view. But what we condemn in it is precisely that it does not make the formation of our moral habits a special object, because it does not subject the will, as it does the understanding, to regular exercise.

"This absence in education of exercises suited to form our moral character has been growing more striking ever since those changes in our social life which have deprived the Church of much of its former influence in Europe. While men were entirely under the influence of the Church, we observe that exercises were enjoined analogous to what is, in our opinion, now required. To the observance of duties purely religious, there were united certain usages, which might be considered as exercises suited to correct our evil inclinations, and make us acquire good habits. The exercise of prayer, the being obliged to retire and present ourselves frequently before God, good resolutions taken in the morning, self-examination in the evening, the confession of our faults to God, or to our spiritual guide, whom we consulted on the mode of correcting our moral imperfections,—all these things had undoubtedly this object in view. We shall not enter into a particular examination of these practices; we simply state that they did exist, that their aim was to correct our morals, and that, under this system, to know how to live was generally the object of a formal labour and an express and positive study."

This system still exists in our colleges, and is, indeed, the characteristic principle of collegiate life. The student at the university is not an independent person, living where he pleases, and how he pleases, merely attending certain lectures, reading certain books, paying certain fees, and passing a certain examination; but first, as a member of the university, Oxford or Cambridge, he is bound by its disciplinary statutes; and as a member of some particular college, he belongs to a distinct society, a *domus;* dining in a common hall, sharing in a common worship, dwelling beneath an appointed roof, and furnished with a scheme of life.

It would lead us into too wide a field of inquiry to enter upon a consideration of the question, by what practical measures can this disciplinary system be adapted to schools of the class we are just now more especially concerned with; but we must be allowed to express our deep conviction that unless some better understanding is established between school-regulations and the claims of family life, the measures now so actively employed for imparting primary instruction to the future " masses " of England's population, are likely to issue in a curse rather than a blessing.

We have been led to these reflections by Ascham's vigorous description of those " quick wits," whom it ought to be one of the great objects of education to correct and restrain, not to develop and encourage ; but whose evil tendencies, we firmly believe, would be fostered and matured by that *individual* education which finds advocates in certain " philosophical " writers on this subject.

" Quick wits be apt to take, unapt to keep; soon hot, and desirous of this and that; as soon cold and weary of the same again ; more quick to enter speedily, than able to pierce far; even like our sharp tools, whose edges be very soon turned. .... Also, for manners and life, quick wits commonly be, in desire, new-fangled; in purpose, inconstant; light to promise anything; ready to forget everything, both benefit and injury ; and thereby neither fast to friend, nor fearful to foe ; inquisitive of every trifle, not secret in the greatest affairs; bold with any person; busy in every manner; soothing such as be present, nipping any that is absent; of nature, always flattering their betters, envying their equals, despising their inferiors; and by quickness of wit, very quick and ready to like none so well as themselves.

" Moreover, commonly, men very quick of wit be also very light of conditions ; and thereby very ready of disposition to be carried over quickly by any light company to any riot and unthriftiness when they be young: therefore seldom either honest of life, or rich in living, when they be old. .... In youth, also, they be ready scoffers, privy mockers, and ever over light and merry ; in age, soon testy, very waspish, and always over-miserable. And few of them come to any great age, by reason of their misordered life when they were young; but a great deal fewer of them come to show any great countenance, or bear any great authority abroad in the world; but either live obscurely, men know not how, or die obscurely, men mark not when. ....

" Contrariwise, a wit in youth that is not over dull, heavy, knotty, and lumpish; but hard, tough, and though somewhat staffish, (as Tully wisheth, *otium quietum non languidum*, and *negotium cum labore, non cum periculo ;*) such a wit, I say, if it be at the first well handled by the mother, and rightly smoothed and wrought by the schoolmaster, both for learning and whole course of living, proveth always the best. For wood and stone,—not the softest, but hardest,—be always aptest for portraiture; both fairest for pleasure and most durable for profit. Hard wits be hard to receive, but sure to keep; painful without weariness, heedful without wavering, constant without new-fangledness ; bearing heavy things, though not lightly, yet willingly; entering hard things, though not easily, yet deeply ; and so come to that perfectness of learning in the end that quick wits seem in hope, but do not indeed ever attain unto.

" Also, for manners and life, hard wits commonly are hardly carried, either to desire every new thing, or to marvel at every strange thing; and therefore they be careful and diligent in their own matters, not curious and busy in other men's affairs; and so they become wise themselves, and also are counted honest by others. They be grave, steadfast, silent of tongue, secret of heart; not hasty in making, but constant in keeping, any promise; not rash in uttering, but wary in considering, every matter; and thereby not quick in speaking, but deep of judgment, whether they write or give counsel in weighty affairs. And these be the men that become in the end both most happy for themselves, and also most esteemed abroad in the world."

Milton's Letter on Education " to Master Samuel Hartlib," containing " the burnishing of many contemplative years altogether spent in the search of religious and civil knowledge," which comes next in order in " The Schoolmaster," will always be read with interest. Milton resolved " learning" into its two great elements —*religious* and *moral*. Of the first he says,—

" The end of learning is to repair the ruins of our first parents, by regaining to know GOD aright; and out of that knowledge, to love him, to imitate Him, to be like Him, as we may the nearest, by possessing our souls of true virtue, which being united to the heavenly grace of faith, makes up the highest perfection."

And of the second, he says in words that have been often quoted, but that will well bear to be quoted again,—

" I call a complete and generous education that which fits a man to perform justly, skilfully, and magnanimously, all the offices, both private and public, of peace and war."

The next article is an analysis of Locke's " Thoughts concerning Education." Locke adopts the Spartan idea,

" As the strength of the body lies chiefly in being able to endure hardships, so also does that of the mind. And the great principle and foundation of all virtue and worth lies in this, that a man is able to deny himself his own desires, cross his own inclinations, and purely follow what reason directs as best, though the appetite lean the other way."

So reasoned the Spartan legislator of old; whose aim it was to build up a consistent and powerful nation, by subjecting the faculties of its individual members to a stern, unyielding discipline and restraint. All individual affections and desires, nay, even tastes and relishes, were proscribed. All individual feelings, dispositions, and habits, were beaten down and trodden under foot. The nation was hardened into one homogeneous mass, and moulded to one purpose. Physical unity supplanted moral unity. The temple of national life rose upon the sepulchres of personal will, energy, and virtue. One sacrifice only, during upwards of four centuries, was offered upon its altars; when the Three Hundred died as one man, in obedience to the laws of their country. But it is not by a single sacrifice, however costly, that the character of a nation is redeemed; nor the virtue of the principle that leads to it, established. The Spartan knew better how to die, than how to live. " Strict as was the Spartan discipline at home, its citizens were no sooner sent to command in foreign countries, than they forgot not only their own severer rules, but even those common principles of duty which were regarded by the other Greeks."

The principle of *restraint* is however false, so far as it is exclusive; and its position is false only when it is made primary and fundamental. In Locke's opinion, the first principle to be implanted in a child's mind is awe of the parent; for this being acquired, obedience and respect, he says, will follow of themselves, and then affection will easily be added to the rest, without endangering authority; but on the other hand, authority, he contends, cannot with the same ease be raised on a groundwork of love. The christian principle of education is just the reverse of this:—LOVE takes precedence; love is the living stem of all the virtues, and obedience is its choicest fruit.

Bishop Butler's "Sermon on Charity Schools," A.D. 1745, contains a valuable note, (it does not amount to a definition,) on the nature of education generally.

"Solomon might probably intend the text, '*Train up a child in the way he should go, and when he is old he will not depart from it,*' for a particular admonition to educate children in a manner suitable to their respective ranks and future employments; but certainly he intended it for a general admonition to educate them in virtue and religion, and good conduct of themselves in their temporal concerns. And all this together in which they are to be educated, he calls '*the way they should go;*' *i.e.* he mentions it not as a matter of speculation, but of practice. And conformably to this description of the things in which children are to be educated, he describes education itself; for he calls it '*training them up*,' which is a very different thing from merely teaching them some truths necessary to be known or believed: it is endeavouring to form such truths into practical principles in the mind, so as to render them of habitual good influence upon the temper and actions, in all the various occurrences of life. And this is not done by bare instruction; but also by restraining them from what is evil, and exercising them in what is good."

Those of our readers who are interested in practical education, and we hope we have few who are not, are probably acquainted with what has been designated "the *training* system," as pursued in certain schools at Glasgow. We agree with Mr. Hopwood, who has made one or two selections from Mr. Stow's work on the subject, that there is nothing original or new in the *principle* on which "the Glasgow training system" professes to rest: and we more than doubt the usefulness of that "elliptical" mode of giving instruction, which occupies so prominent a place in the Glasgow system; except as an occasional and subordinate instrument in summing up a catechetical exercise, or in dealing with those secondary particulars which may arise in the course of it; particulars necessary for the purpose of keeping up the connexion of its several parts, but not of sufficient importance to occupy that prominent place which direct questions would tend to give them. As the selections given in the "Hints," relate chiefly to the elliptical mode, we will, in justice to Mr. Stow, allow him to expound those principles upon which the schools under his active directorship are conducted; principles which in their essence have, as the foregoing passage from Bishop Butler shows, the sanction of one of the profoundest thinkers of the English Church.

"Moral training is of course practical throughout, and is the main end and object of the whole system in every department. It comprehends the restraining of all the evil propensities of our nature, and a cultivation of all that is noble and virtuous, founded on Bible training: in other words, on the principles of the immutable standard of revealed truth, and stimulated by its high sanction and motives.

" We must here notice a fundamental error in education, which is the confounding of two things essentially distinct. Moral instruction and moral training are generally imagined to mean the same thing; whereas the former is merely imparting knowledge, the latter is the cultivation of the practical habit. On this clear and practical distinction hangs one chief peculiarity of our system.

" Habits are so important a part of education, and so influential on individuals, as well as nations, that we may almost be said to be the children of habit. Proceeding then on this idea, how important must early training be before *habits* are formed, and when we have only evil *propensities* to contend with.

" A few of the evil propensities and habits may be mentioned, which it is the duty of the trainer to restrain and suppress as they are developed; whether mental, in the school gallery, or practical, in the school play-ground; viz. rudeness, selfishness, deceit, indecency, disorder, evil-speaking, cruelty, want of courtesy, anger, revenge, injustice, impatience, covetousness, and dishonesty, so fearfully general in society.

" On the contrary, all the amiable feelings and christian virtues must be cultivated, such as speaking truth, obedience to parents and all in lawful authority, honesty, justice, forbearance, generosity, gentleness, kindness, fidelity to promises, courteousness, habits of attention, docility, disinterestedness, kindness to inferior animals, pity for the lame, and the distressed, and the weak in intellect; and in general, doing to others as we would wish to be done by.

" Such evil propensities must be subdued, and moral habits formed, not by teaching, but by training. We cannot lecture a child into good manners, or change habits of any kind by the longest speech. The physical, intellectual, or moral habit, is only changed by a succession, or rather by a repetition of *doings*.

" This department requires a *play-ground*, for moral development and sympathy, as the intellectual department does a gallery for mental sympathy.

" Nor is there any dread here of too much being done. An over-working of the intellect is, indeed, frequently fatal to health; but the fullest exercise of the moral powers only improves the health."

The remaining articles in the first volume of " the Schoolmaster" possess neither interest nor value, with the exception of a " Lecture on the means which may be employed to stimulate the student without the aid of emulation." We shall endeavour to embody the substance of this in a few sentences.

The mind is naturally active, and delights in exercise; but delight may be changed into indifference, and even disgust, and this by various causes. Mental exertion may be continued too long. One faculty only, say memory, that Gibeonite of the faculties, may be exercised, while the others are suffered to lie dormant. One set of objects may be exclusively presented to the mind. Again, between mind and body there is, as we all know, a most intimate connexion. The pleasure naturally arising from intellectual effort may be destroyed by bodily weariness.

" If, for want of exercise, or from a confined posture, the blood does not circulate freely, and all the vital functions go on briskly, the intellectual operations will be impeded. When the bones begin to ache, or the blood to stagnate, the mind becomes dull; and that which otherwise would be very interesting, now loses its power to charm. Let, then, the parent or teacher carefully guard against all these counteracting influences, and he will find that the pupil will *voluntarily, and with pleasure*, exercise his mental faculties and his bodily senses on such subjects and such objects as are suited to his age and capacity. . . . He will love to learn. The exercise of the faculties, and the acquisition of new ideas, are both *naturally* sources of pleasure to the mind. This pleasure, once tasted, will be again desired. This desire, which gains strength by fruition, is a stimulus pure in its nature, safe in its operation, salutary in its influence, and powerful in its effects."

Mr. Parkhurst's observations in the next paragraph relate to a matter of great practical importance.

" There are many teachers who do not afford their pupils a proper opportunity to exert their faculties. Instead of setting their pupils to *thinking* and *investigating*, they, as far as possible, do all the thinking for them: thus making them almost entirely *passive* in the acquisition of ideas. The teacher who wishes to stimulate his pupils to the highest degree of exertion, should guard against this course. He should never do for his pupils what they can do for themselves. He should never tell them a thing which they can find out for themselves. And when they must be assisted, he should afford them only so much assistance that they can do the rest themselves. In a word, he should, as far as possible, in all the branches, pursue that *inductive method* which, we hope, will effect a greater advance in the intellectual improvement of the rising generation than can be effected by any other course."

Mr. Parkhurst's observations on the art of *questioning* are judicious and practical.

" Questions should be so managed, that individuals cannot answer unless their attention be unremitted. This may be done, partly by expressing questions in such language that the pupils cannot understand them without having attended to the previous questions and answers;—partly when one pupil has failed to answer a question, or has answered it wrong, by calling on another to answer, without repeating the question;—partly, by analyzing the ideas, and making each question and answer as short as possible, so as to pass rapidly round the class;—partly, when one pupil has committed an error in some part of his answer or performance, by calling on another to specify the error, and to show why it is an error;—and partly, by calling on individuals to answer questions, or to correct one another's errors, not in the order in which they stand or sit, but promiscuously. In many cases, the teacher will find it useful to announce a question previously to calling the individual by name who is desired to answer. The putting of questions promiscuously, and refusing to repeat a question which has been once distinctly announced, may be made a powerful means of keeping alive the attention of a class." . . . .

" Questions should be asked in the language of the instructor, and answered in that of the pupil, instead of using printed questions, and giving answers verbatim, as they have been marked with a pencil. If the pupil does not know precisely what questions will be asked, or in what form they will be put, and finds it necessary to answer more by an exercise of understanding than by an act of memory, he will exert himself to understand the subject; and by so doing, he will acquire more knowledge, will cultivate his mental faculties in a higher degree, and will become far more deeply interested in his studies, than by pursuing a different course."

These means for awakening and maintaining the interests of a learner may be classed under the common head of a skilful mode of teaching. To these may be added the inducements to learn which arise out of the sympathy of numbers, ever a powerful instrument for good or for evil; the approbation of teachers and parents, not cheerlessly distilled through the artificial channels of tickets, and badges, and place-taking, but gushing fresh from the heart; the association of pleasing ideas with that of school—and to be pleasing they have only to be just; and, most of all, the appeal to a sense of duty.

The second volume of "The Schoolmaster" opens with an interesting article, "On Teaching Reading," by Mr. Charles Baker, the intelligent head-master of the Yorkshire Institution for the Deaf and Dumb, at Doncaster. The following observations are worthy of attention.

"The present mode of teaching the art of reading is not more defective as an instrument for unfolding the capacities of the intellect, than for communicating the knowledge and pronunciation of words.... A child's manner of speaking is too much disregarded; if it be intelligible, it is deemed sufficiently correct. The imperfection being no great obstacle to the child's progress in knowledge, it is thought that as the child grows older the evil will correct itself. Like other errors, which, from being unnoticed at first, settle into vices, this evil sometimes produces a faulty habit of speaking which can never be eradicated... If there is a possibility of preventing this by early attention to a child's pronunciation, it is surely better to attain this certain good, which may be attained without trouble or annoyance to the child, than to force it to utter words above its comprehension, and to dole out sounds which nobody can understand."

Lessons on objects ought to precede lessons in reading, much less artificial, however, than those which have been published for infant schools. We have witnessed object lessons in many infant schools, but we have not yet seen one that was not a decided failure.

" For children from three to six years of age, we know of no lesson so good as oral exercises on the names and properties of objects. The worlds of nature and art will furnish a never-failing supply of examples. Pictures will materially assist in such exercises; a slate and pencil will also help to amuse and instruct. Books, reading, and spelling should not, in our opinion, be introduced at this early stage. Careful pronunciation, and correct oral language, should always accompany these primary lessons. Form, magnitude, weight, colour, number, sound, are the chief developments to be made during the infancy of the mind. Instruction in these may be imparted without books. Few situations are unfavourable to the growth and expansion of the youthful intellect by the analysis of objects: the rooms of a house, the garden, field, wood, road, will also supply materials well adapted for this purpose....

" To explain the kind of lessons which it is proposed to substitute for the present very unsatisfactory modes of commencing a young child's education, the following examples are given; from which it will be seen that a person of very moderate attainments may both amuse and instruct a child of three or four years old.

" *Teacher.* What covers the floor of the parlour? *Child.* A carpet. *T.* What colours do you observe on the carpet? *C.* Red, blue, brown, yellow, green, &c. *T.* Bring me your slate. What shape do you call this? *(drawing a circle) C.* Round. *(Other figures are drawn and their names told to the child) T.* Now tell me the shape of the carpet? *C.* It is oblong. *T.* What else in the room is oblong? *C.* The windows, that table, &c. *T.* Which is the larger, the carpet or the floor? Now look round every part of the floor. *C.* The carpet covers the whole floor—the carpet is the same size as the floor. *T.* What is the small carpet called which lies before the fire-place? *C.* A hearth-rug. *T.* Yes. Are its colours like those of the carpet? *C.* No. *T.* No: they are brighter and deeper. Now, look well at the carpet—feel it—and tell me of what it is made. Is it made of wood? *C.* No; it is not hard like wood.

T. Is it made of leather? *C.* No; it is not at all like my shoes. *T.* Of what are your warm socks made? *C.* Of worsted. *T.* Yes; and the carpet is also made of worsted—blankets also: and worsted is made of wool. And you know we get wool from— *C.* Sheep. *T.* I must tell you about the mode of making carpets when you are older."

The next example is of the same simple kind. But we must pass on to Mr. Baker's observations on the method of teaching reading. When we come to treat of the recent official publications on practical education, we shall endeavour to give our readers some idea of Prinsen's Phonic mode of teaching reading, which has lately been adopted in this country by the authority of the Committee of Council. Mr. Baker's mode is that of beginning at once with *words;* a mode which has in many cases been very successful. Mr. Baker has, in our opinion, though it would appear not in his own, described the course he recommends more fully in the third publication of the (defunct) " Central Society of Education " than in " The Schoolmaster." We shall, therefore, take our next extract from the former work.

" It is not our wish that children should any longer conquer this ' most difficult of human attainments,' the art of reading, through the medium of A, B, C; a, b, ab; b, a, ba, &c.; neither would we encounter with them any system of syllabic classifications, on which several meritorious elementary reading-books have been recently published; and the naming of the letters, as in spelling, we would altogether discard. Neither the individual nor the mutual-instruction systems are necessary in teaching the mother-tongue, or any other living language. Simultaneous instruction to acquire the art of reading, and conversation for the acquisition of popular grammar, are all that is needed. A modification of the system of Jacotot, with a series of interesting lessons printed so large that all the children could see them, would be found to be the only needful auxiliaries to be employed. The lessons must be graduated, and every sentence in them must possess a meaning level to the comprehension of the children. *Monosyllabic* lessons, though almost universally employed in early teaching, are not of the value generally attached to them; indeed, such lessons are so filled with *particles,*—words which only possess a meaning in connexion with others,—and so deficient of the language of ordinary life, that they have less interest for children than exercises apparently more difficult, but less cramped and more natural. The best plan in the constructions of reading-lessons is to follow nature,—to use those words of which children may early obtain an accurate acquaintance. Many long words are called ' hard words,' but it will be found that some of the hardest words in the language are the shortest. No word is ' hard ' to a child if he can pronounce it, and attaches to it a correct idea. We do not begin to talk to our children in monosyllables; and it will be found that most children understand pollysyllabic words before they can utter them. The first lessons for reading should convey simple facts to them, without reference to the length of the words, but a progression in the subject-matter of the lesson. A few sentences read by the teacher, who is to point to them, and simultaneously repeated by the children, will be enough for the first lesson; after frequent repetitions, it will be seen that the children will name any words pointed to in those sentences. The difference in the length of the words is an advantage not to be found in lessons confined to two, three, four, five, &c., letters. Children soon perceive that words are arbitrary pictures; they express different things, qualities, and motions, &c.; and children naturally expect them to have a different appearance, as much so as they expect to see a lion of a different figure to a horse, after hearing facts which show their different habits and modes of life: the very dissimilarity of the words assists in their acquisition. The children have to remember the entire combinations,—

not the letters, nor the syllables, but the words,—so that they may at once recognise them whenever they see them. Their eyes are engaged on the forms of the words, their ears on the sounds, their voices on the utterance."

And in " The Schoolmaster," Mr. Baker adds—

" To give facility and strength to this exercise, *writing* must accompany the reading of the words."

And he goes on to recommend that one of the walls of the school-room or nursery be painted of a dark slate colour,* as an enduring tablet for writing lessons upon, and for drawing any necessary illustrations connected with them.

" And thus," he continues, " the exercises of the pupil may be made to assume all the interest of oral and written language combined with delineation. . . . .

" Under ordinary circumstances, in families and in private schools, about a quarter of a year will be found sufficient for the instruction of a child in reading, spelling (acquired by copying the reading lessons), and plain writing. . . . . The characteristics of the proposed method are :—*the education of the ear and voice*, by which a perfect pronunciation may be recognised and produced; *the education of the eye*, by means of which minute objects shall be discovered and discerned, preparatory to its being exercised on types and writing; and the preliminary *education of the mind* on a variety of subjects, by which it may be prepared to enter the wider fields of knowledge, as soon as the teacher has recourse to the assistance of books."

We must not carry our notice of The Schoolmaster any further; indeed the remaining articles, with the exception of some by Mr. De Morgan, are of inferior interest, and we shall have subsequent opportunities of considering the subjects of which Mr. De Morgan treats.

We are compelled to bring our article to an earlier conclusion than we had anticipated, by a brief notice of the "Report to the Trustees of the Bequest of James Dick, Esq., &c., by Allan Menzies." This is one of the best reports on the state of education that has been published. We will not occupy our readers by any account of the merely local circumstances connected with it, but proceed at once to present to them a few of its more important practical notes and suggestions for the improvement of schools. The first we shall give, relates to a subject which all who are practically conversant with schools for the labouring classes find to be one of the most painful and difficult they have to encounter; namely, irregularity in the attendance of scholars.

---

* The following directions for preparing the painted walls are given by Mrs. Tuckfield, in the introduction to her " Evening Readings."

" The black walls cost about 7*s*. the square yard. The material is *mastic*, well known to all builders and plasterers. Mastic is a kind of cement, which is laid on a common brick or stone wall, like mortar, and, when dry, painted with three or four coats of paint, either very dark blue or black. When well done, the walls will last a century. Two bands of hard oak should be laid on the walls, one at the bottom of the mastic, the other about fifteen inches above it. The upper band is intended for the insertion of the points of the compasses, to describe curved lines, without injury to the wall; and from the bands, which are painted white, being parallel to each other, they serve as a guide to straight writing.

" When this plan for painted walls is thought too expensive, *stucco*, though much less durable, may be used; it costs 1*s*. a square yard. Mastic resists damp. Slates may be introduced between the wall and the stucco, to prevent damp, when stucco is used."

"There is no disadvantage under which country parochial schools more generally or more grievously labour, than irregularity in the attendance of the scholars. This is an evil which must no doubt always prevail more or less in rural districts, where the service of their children is, at certain seasons, valuable, and frequently indispensable to parents in the labours of the field. The urgency of this call has every where been acknowledged, and provision has been made for it in some German states, where public education is subjected to a very exact legislative control, by limiting the hours of attendance during the busy seasons of seed-time and harvest. A similar regulation might, with great advantage, be introduced in this country (Scotland); and indeed the practice prevails partially in many schools.

"Various causes conduce to generate and perpetuate this evil; . . . . but it appears attributable, in a very large degree, to a prevailing laxity on the part of . . . . the parents in paying school-fees. . . . .

"There is much reason to regret that such causes are allowed to operate. Of the fee paid for instruction it may truly be said, that, like mercy,

"It is twice blest—
It blesseth him that gives, and him that takes."

To the giver the blessing is,—1. That it prevents the commission of a moral wrong in withholding a just debt, and thus, in one instance, tends to maintain a higher tone of character. The influence of such a feeling is important in a community of whatever rank. Its effect upon the minds of the pupils, who are always aware of the facts, the payment being made through them, must be in the highest degree beneficial. 2. It gives a sensible value to that which, in one sense, is indeed beyond price, viz. the culture of the mind, but the worth of which, for that very reason, is apt to be forgotten, unless there be some material token to remind us of it. 3. It bestows upon the parent a title, and creates in him a desire and feeling of duty, to ascertain and be satisfied, from time to time, that justice is done to his child......

"To these important advantages is to be added, that the regular payment of fees has a direct tendency to secure and invariably produces a more regular attendance of scholars than otherwise exists. Here there is an evident benefit to the scholars. The teacher derives one equally certain and important. He has no longer to contend with that distraction and derangement and disorganization, to which an irregular and fluctuating attendance necessarily gives birth, and which has a most discouraging effect; and he is thus enabled to exert his powers in the most favourable circumstances, and instead of giving his lessons piecemeal, and at detached intervals, to institute a steady systematic course of instruction."

We would earnestly call the attention of all who may have a voice in the appointment of teachers, to the following observations of Mr. Menzies, on the requisite qualifications of a candidate for this responsible office.

"Literary and scientific acquirements form, no doubt, a great and a very important part of the necessary qualifications of a teacher; but no truth is now better established, than that the faculty of *acquiring* knowledge is different from, and may exist without, the faculty of *communicating* it. The latter exists among different individuals in various degrees. In some it develops itself spontaneously, as occasion demands; in others it requires to be excited, directed, and matured. But there is no doubt that, in whatever degree it may have been bestowed by nature, the power may be improved by training and exercise. This ability to communicate instruction ..... converts what is otherwise problematical into certainty. The teacher who is equipped with learning merely, is but half provided for his undertaking. He is a husbandman who has laid up stores of seed, but is destitute of those implements, and of that knowledge of the capability of the ground, and its culture, which alone can enable him to sow with judgment and profit. He, on the other hand, who has the faculty of teaching, is furnished with the power of descending in imagination to the ideas and feelings of boyhood, and by picturing to himself the exact image of his pupil's mind, he finds the precise mode through which that mind is capable of receiving the impression he desires to make. Enabled to sympathize in the feelings of oppression from difficulty, and of conscious joy in acquirement, he knows when to cheer and encourage, and when to temper commendation with warning of trials yet to be surmounted."

The next passages that we lay before our readers relate to that "intellectual system," as it is somewhat too proudly called, which originated, in a great measure, in the Sessional Schools in Edinburgh.

"It could not but happen, especially in such a period as the present, when the public mind is, in most quarters of the world, under the influence of a great and energetic power of inquiry and activity, which has not applied itself to any subject with more zeal and earnestness than to that of education, that considerable discrepancy of manner and success should be found among parochial schools, according to the various degrees in which the spirit which is abroad has penetrated or been admitted.

"It does not admit of serious dispute, that great progress has, of late years, been made both in the philosophy and practice of teaching. Doubtless here, as in all similar cases, the impulse, in some instances, has taken a wrong direction. It is the inevitable lot of improvement to advance amidst errors—many of them, it may be, called into being by herself; and notwithstanding the partial evil of these, they serve the great end of illustrating, by contrast, the truth with which they are at variance. But no one who has attended to the recent history of education, can doubt that the prevalent spirit of inquiry and experiment has been eminently successful in ascertaining, 1. The manner in which instruction may be most successfully conveyed to the youthful mind; and that by observing the nature and extent of its faculties and susceptibilities, and the mode and direction in which these may be most effectually excited and impressed. 2. The correlative faculties and dispositions on the part of the teacher—the existence and cultivation of which are requisite to secure his success; and 3. As a necessary consequence of these, the nature of the moral and intellectual food, which the teacher must prepare and communicate, as best adapted to the powers and exigences of the pupil's mind.

"It is not too much to say, that if these principles were not disregarded in our systems of education until of late years, they did not, at all events, receive an express and practical recognition. When knowledge and learning alone were demanded in a teacher, without reference to powers of communication, it is obvious that the importance of these powers was not acknowledged. When the acquirements of the pupils were limited to a knowledge of words, and the ability to read with fluency, and the understanding was not instructed, or, at all events, no effort was made designedly and avowedly to inform the understanding, or ascertain that it was informed, it is no less clear that the latter branch of tuition was in abeyance. It is indeed unquestionable, that the human mind will, in a greater or less degree, derive instruction from almost any mode of discipline; and it may be said, in behalf of that which is now becoming and receiving the name of the 'old system,' that although intellectual instruction was not given professedly or nominally, yet it was virtually instilled by the necessary mental action of the pupil. This is to a certain extent true, but it points out the precise nature of the deficiency. The mental progress of the pupil was not ascertained—no test of its existence was applied—it was left to be matter of vague and unsatisfactory inference.

. . . .

"It is in the teaching of ENGLISH that the adoption of the improved methods has produced the most striking satisfactory results. The test of the full operation of the intellectual system is its application to the youngest scholars. These are taught, from the first, to explain the meaning of the words in their lesson;

and the benefit of the practice is incalculable. It shows, from the outset, that there is something more to be learned than the sounds of words. It challenges the exercise of the higher faculties of the mind; and above all, it forms the invaluable habit of mastering the sense of whatever is read. This is, indeed, the criterion of all good teaching; viz., making the understanding keep pace with the external organs, and habituating the mind not to rest satisfied without a thorough apprehension of the meaning of what is got. The forming of this habit is, no doubt, a work requiring patience and skill, but that it is practicable is shown by ample experience; and whatever labour it may cost, may truly be said to be bread cast upon the waters, lost, in the eye of ignorance, for a time, but yielding, in the appointed season, an abundant harvest. Powers of attention and of mental exertion are thus formed, and these are implements which unspeakably facilitate and expedite the labours of the teacher, and the pupil's progress.

"The benefits of this thorough method of tuition are found, 1. In the superior intelligence of the pupil, indicated even in the tones of his voice in reading, which are felt to express a finer perception of the sense of the passage. 2. In the rapid progress consequent upon the interest and excitement invariably produced by the successful cultivation of the mental powers. 3. In the hilarity and cheerfulness which are diffused wherever a willing and active spirit is excited. These attributes are peculiarly characteristic of the intellectual school, to which drowsiness and lethargic indifference are strangers; and this effect is mainly produced by that community of feeling between master and pupil, produced by the former letting himself down, as it were, mentally; and by the exertions of the latter gradually to elevate his intellectual standard: this effort of approximation producing, in every sense, a good understanding between the parties."

We must not allow ourselves to dwell any longer on this interesting Report. We shall take an early opportunity of enabling those of our readers who are practical educationists to judge how far the remaining books on our list, together with several others we have yet to submit to them, are calculated to assist them in training up the future "millions" of England's people to do their duty to GOD and their neighbour.

On Heroes, Hero-worship, and the Heroic in History. Six Lectures, reported, with Emendations and Additions. By THOMAS CARLYLE. London: Fraser. 1841.

MR. CARLYLE at all times, more particularly and professedly in this his last work, is fond of contemplating, and bidding us contemplate, individual men. We mean, at present, so far to apply his lessons, as to bestow a little of such contemplation on himself; holding him to be well worthy of it,—a man of mark, whose speech, to use words of his own, " is wild and wondrous, such as men long remember."

His literary history is somewhat remarkable. To the majority, perhaps, his existence has been but recently known—the last novelty that has hit the public fancy. But for these fourteen or fifteen years his pen has been busy, translating Goëthe, writing in the Edinburgh Review, in Fraser's Magazine, and elsewhere. Though, however, he was then, as now, both diligent and powerful, Fame did not seem to "mark him for her own." Suddenly he published his "History of the French Revolution," and made one spring to celebrity. He is now the most popular writer in the region of pure literature that we possess; and so *piquant* is his style, so interesting the subjects of which he treats, and so unwonted his way of treating them, that we do not foresee a very speedy decline of his popularity. Let us, therefore, as is our part, while he continues speaking to us in such wise that we cannot refrain from listening to him, examine what manner of man he is, and how we may best turn him to account.

On whichever side of the Tweed he had happened to be born, there is small question that he must have been held something unusual and novel. But being a Scotchman, the novelty is considerably enhanced. There are, no doubt, many national traits hanging obstinately around him; so many that, putting his frequent Scotticisms out of the question, we imagine few readers would remain long in doubt of his country. But withal, his style of thought is not Scottish in the main. It is an exception to Charles Lamb's inimitable, though severe, delineation of the Caledonian brain. " His Minerva is born in panoply. You are never admitted to see his ideas in their growth—if, indeed, they do grow, and are not rather put together upon principles of clock-work. You never catch his mind in an undress. He never hints or suggests any thing, but unlades his stock of ideas in perfect order and completeness. He brings his total wealth into company, and gravely unpacks it. His riches are always about him. He never stoops to catch a glittering something in your presence to share it with you, before he quite knows whether it be true touch or not. You cannot cry *halves* to anything that he finds. He does not find but bring. You never witness his first apprehension of a thing. His understanding is always at its meridian; you never see the first dawn, the early streaks. He has no falterings of self-suspicion. Surmises, guesses, misgivings, half-intentions, semi-consciousnesses, partial illuminations, dim instincts, embryo conceptions, have no place in his brain or vocabulary. The twilight of dubiety never falls upon him. Is he orthodox? he has no doubts. Is he an infidel? he has none either."* So is it written by Elia, with much besides, that we do not quote at present, of a tendency uncomplimentary to Scotsmen, but such as Scotsmen can well afford to listen to with good humour. Any how, Mr. Carlyle can, for never was a writer to whom it less applied. He is altogether different from any previous Scotch writer. His rugged, lawless style is not more unlike the formal periods of a Blair, a Robertson, or a Stewart, than his wandering, straining, amorphous thoughts are unlike their easy, comfortable, unlaborious, unpuzzled sets of opinions. Just as little does he resemble the noisy Scottish writers of the present day. They, too, are people who encounter no difficulties,

---

* Elia's Essays—"Imperfect Sympathies."

have no perplexities, to whom nothing can be clearer than—their own opinions. Mr. Carlyle is suggestive, and merely suggestive enough to have pleased Charles Lamb. His thoughts are but *guesses at truth.* It would be unfair to speak of them as his *opinions.* They seem to be his yearnings—feelings after something, which he is sure is, or is to be, and on which he is satisfied that no homage of reverence or admiration will be mispent. They are such as we neither adopt, nor reject, nor neglect. He sets us a thinking, in company with himself, and is satisfied if he get us to acknowledge that there are more things in heaven and in earth than were dreamt of in our philosophy.

A writer such as we have described is sure to have great merit, even if possessed of far inferior powers to Mr. Carlyle's. In a world where we know and prophesy only in part, *hints* are the very things we most want. Not to be saved the trouble of thinking for himself, but to be set a thinking, is the result a man ought to ask for from a book. And besides, a suggestive, glimmering, wondering writer, is of necessity a reverent one. His whole state of mind is an acknowledgment of greatness—an acknowledgment that he cannot take the measure of the things around him. Accordingly, with all his faults, (and very serious we think them,) Mr. Carlyle's works have this advantage, that they are generous and admiring. He pulls down no reputations, and exalts a great many that have been unjustly depressed. He is loth to believe that any man of note was altogether unworthy. He makes much of any ray of light which he observes in the very darkest region. That unmixed evil should ever have a large or long enduring triumph is to him the most incredible of opinions. All this is very healthy and admirable, and we heartily thank Mr. Carlyle for the tendency of his works in this respect.

There is another and a cognate advantage in all this. A writer of this wondering and admiring kind cannot escape observing, and can hardly ever fail to keep in mind the mystery of life, whether discernible in the phenomena of external nature, or of our own individual and social condition. He is thereby preserved himself from the shallow creed of *liberalism,* and can cure those of his audience or readers who may have been infected with it. Such a man cannot but know and feel, in regard to all questions of national greatness or well-being, that—

" There's on earth a yet auguster thing,
    Veiled though it be, than parliament or king;"

that—

" There is a mystery in the soul of state,
    Which hath an operation more divine
    Than our mere chroniclers dare meddle with."

He must see the emptiness of all theories, as applied to the whole condition of a nation, founded on the advantages to be derived from some one or more definite legislative changes—of all mere constitution making—of all definitions of Liberty, restrained to some one or two fashions taken up by Liberty at some one particular time. He knows that—

> "The sensual and the dark rebel in vain,
> Slaves by their own compulsion; in mad game
> They burst their manacles, and wear the name
> Of Freedom graven on a heavier chain."

If we were asked what was the prominent result likely to be produced by Mr. Carlyle's French Revolution among his admirers, we should say, it was a death-blow to any remnants of liberalism that might be still lingering among them. Never was more powerfully exhibited the vanity of all mere tamperings with institutions, of all mere reform bills; the necessity of remembering how deep are the springs of national well-being; how little superficial workings can do when they are neglected, or placed by the providence of God beyond our reach. Above all, does that book, with its deep insight and far-reaching sarcasms, lay bare a delusion under which most parties in England are labouring—that there is an intrinsic substantial force in respectability; that if the *respectable* classes are of one way of thinking, or are sure at a particular emergency to become so, they must carry all before them; and that, in consequence, neither Chartism nor any thing else from which respectability stands aloof need be dreaded? The answer to this, spoken in thunder by the French revolution, and recorded in living and winged words by Mr. Carlyle, is, that respectability is but a relative and accidental thing; that it presumes quiet, orderly, social existence, and the ordinary routine of life; that as long as these are preserved the word has a meaning, but none at all should they have been broken up and taken away; that then, respectability being out of the question, inasmuch as there are neither its materials for exercising and displaying itself, nor any to look at and value it, we need some deeper wisdom and some higher virtue to preserve us and those around us; and that they who at a great crisis lean on respectability, may fearfully be made to learn that they are leaning on a broken reed. This is the moral of the history and fate of the Girondins. Very respectable men they would all have been held in a quiet community, that was prone to respect, we doubt not. But they had themselves taken all this out of the way; they had broken up the coherence of French existence, and then came forward with a claim on men's allegiance, that had no meaning except during that coherence.

If to the advantages we have been speaking of, we add a reconciling of his readers to the existence of mystery, we shall have enumerated the higher advantages likely to result from the study of Mr. Carlyle's works.

Their literary merit is too obvious to require much eulogium; far the most of it is combined in the History of the French Revolution. Never, surely, did an author undertake a work more entirely suited to his genius and powers. His eloquence, (and the vast sweep and tremendous rapidity of the events he treats of surely justify eloquence,) his flashing descriptions, his profound sarcasm; the novelty of his plan, of his designations,—all these, along with the general eccentricity of the writer, rendered it, on its first appearance, a book to which all others of necessity gave place. And though Mr. Carlyle's other works have not all the same advantages in respect of subject, they are all characterised in their degree by the display of the same powers.

We must now speak of this author's faults. Of these, the style lies on the surface. We need not say that it is un-English—a strange mixture of Germanisms and Scotticisms. This can be no news to those who have read a couple of pages of any of the author's works, but all may not be alive to the evil that is involved in it. Style and thought are closely connected, when either is in any way real or characteristic. It would be paying a bad compliment to Mr. Carlyle to say that his style was not indicative of his thoughts. He himself is well aware of this connexion, as appears from the following passage: " Coleridge remarks very pertinently somewhere, that whenever you find a sentence musically worded, of true rhythm and melody in the words, there is something deep and good in the meaning too; for body and soul, word and idea, go strangely together, here as everywhere."—(*Lectures on Heroes*, p. 146.) The converse of this seems almost necessarily to follow—that whenever we find a want of such music and true rhythm in the words, there is something crude and inharmonious in the meaning. No very great thinker was ever a bad writer, the state of the language with which he had to work being considered. This last qualification arms us against those who might object to our proposition—the sacred writers of the New Testament or the Fathers. Should Bishop Butler be alleged as one who cannot come within the benefit of it, we beg leave to deny the fact of his style being a bad one. With all due respect to Sir J. Mackintosh, who has laid it down of Butler that " never was so great a thinker so bad a writer," we own the style of our illustrious philosopher and divine seems to us one of his great merits. It would be rather difficult to express all the thoughts and all the shades of thought in the Analogy otherwise than Butler has done, without making a change for the worse: and if this be so, the style must be a good, nay, a first-rate one. Of its power and flexibility there can, we think, be no question.

Now, Mr. Carlyle's style being harsh, disrupted, and ill-formed, presents, we cannot but consider, the indication of an ill-joined, unformed mind. Indeed, at times, it is a style hardly amounting to composition at all; proceeding rather like the headings of a chapter, or the clauses of an index, than by a succession of regularly-constructed sentences. This must not only impede the due development of thoughts in the writer, but its influence must be injurious on the admiring reader. We do not indeed fear that Mr. Carlyle will have many direct imitators, though we have come across a portent in this way. On the whole, his peculiarities are so broad, that the mimicry would at once be detected and laughed at. But insidious corruption of a language is of all things in the world the most rapidly propagated by example; and every one who reads Mr. Carlyle with admiring interest, and whose ears are ringing and whose mind is filled with *Carlylisms*, ought to give good heed, and replenish himself with copious draughts of " the well of English undefiled."

But, further: it is a great disadvantage to a writer if he can never be quiet, never like other people, never seemingly common-place; for no subject will of itself supply the writer with materials for unfailing grandeur. Ordinarily, be it or be he what you will, there must be intervals when all that we want is to go quietly on—when we are glad to pass for awhile into the shade. No writer can avoid this, nor need any writer wish to avoid it; but if unhappily he does,—if he can never write a quiet page or passage, he cannot escape the evil of disguising what is really common-place in a veil of verbal originality—a mist of grand sounding words, signifying nothing. Mr. Carlyle, we think, does this oftener than would be possible for such a man were he not blinded by the pretensions of his style. Much, we fear, of his philosophy could be so expressed as to provoke the remark that there needed no ghost to come and tell us that. His whole doctrine of a progressive spirit casting away the forms which have ceased to be its fit receptacles is, *when innocent*, such as no man in his senses would gainsay; and, generally speaking, the moment the author leaves off exposing the vanity of other people's schemes, and attempts giving us something positive, we find the case to be so with him. For instance, in his Essay on Chartism, we wish nothing more powerful or serviceable than his exposure of the slight way in which many would attempt to heal the hurt of England; but when he comes to his own remedy, how are we off? Let our readers judge.

" From which we for our part conclude, that the method of teaching religion to the English people is still far behind hand; that the wise and pious may well ask themselves in silence wistfully, 'How is that last priceless element by which education becomes perfect, to be superadded?' And the unwise, who think themselves pious, answering aloud, 'By this method,' 'by that method,' long argue of it to small purpose.

" But now, in the meantime, could not, by some fit official person, some fit announcement be made, in words well weighed, in plan well schemed, adequately representing the facts of the thing, that after thirteen centuries of writing, he, the official person, and England with him, was minded now to have the mystery of the alphabetic letters imparted to all human souls in this realm? Teaching of religion was a thing he could not undertake to settle this day, it would be work for a day after this. The work of this day was teaching of the alphabet to all people, the miraculous art of reading and writing. Such seemed to him the needful preliminary of all teaching, the first corner-stone of what foundation soever could be laid for what edifice soever in the teaching kind. Let pious Churchism make haste—let pious Dissenterism make haste—let all pious preachers and missionaries make haste—bestir themselves, according to their zeal and skill; but the official person stood up for the alphabet, and was even impatient for it, having waited thirteen centuries now. He insisted, and would take no denial, postponement, promise, excuse, or subterfuge, that all English persons should be taught to read. He appealed to all rational Englishmen of all creeds, classes, and colours, whether this was not a fair demand; nay, whether it was not an indispensable one in these days. Swing and Chartism have risen. For a choice of inoffensive horn-books, and schoolmasters able to teach reading, he trusted the mere secular sagacity of a national collective wisdom, in proper committee, might be found sufficient. He purposed to appoint such schoolmasters, to venture on the choice of such hornbooks, to send a schoolmaster and horn-book into every township, parish, and hamlet of England; so that in ten years hence an Englishman who could not read might be acknowledged as a monster."—*Chartism,* pp. 104, 105.

Was ever such a disguise as this? Here we have merely the shallow prate of the whig and radical newspapers made to sound very original and profound. For in this plan of his has Mr. Carlyle added any thing to what at the time he wrote they were dinning in his ears? What symptom, when we come to think of his meaning, does he show of having gone deeper into the question than they? Why, he does not seem even to have guessed at the preliminary difficulties which must be disposed of before we can even approach his scheme.

Here is a still more notable instance of what we mean:—

"And now, how teach religion? So asks the indignant ultra-radical cited above—an ultra-radical seemingly not of the Benthamic species, with whom, though his dialect is far different, there are sound churchmen, we hope, who have some fellow-feeling. How teach religion? By plying with liturgies, catechisms, and credos? Dinning thirty-nine or other articles incessantly into the infant ear? Friends, in that case, why not apply to Birmingham, and have machines made and set up at all street corners, in highways and byeways, to repeat and vociferate the same, not ceasing night or day? The genius of Birmingham is adequate to that. Albertus Magnus had a leather man, that could articulate. Not to speak of Martinus Scriblerus' Nürnberg man, that could reason as well as we know who. Depend upon it, Birmingham can make machines to repeat liturgies and articles, or to do whatever feat is mechanical. And what were all schoolmasters, nay all priests and churches, compared with this Birmingham iron church. Votes of two millions in aid of the Church were then something. You order, at so many pounds a head, so many thousand iron parsons as your grant covers, and fix them by satisfactory masonry in all quarters wheresoever wanted, to preach there, independent of the world. In large thoroughfares, still more in unawakened districts, troubled with argumentative infidelity, you make the windpipes wider, strengthen the main steam cylinder,—your parson preaches to the due pitch, while you give him coal, and fears no man or thing. Here were a church extension to which I with my last penny, did I believe in it, would subscribe. Ye blind leaders of the blind, are we Calmucks, that pray by turning of a rotatory calebash with written prayers in it? Is Mammon and machinery the means of converting souls as of spinning cotton?"—*Chartism,* pp. 102, 103.

This is amusing enough, but it is sad nonsense—nonsense through which, we think, the author would have seen, had he written it in plain, humdrum diction. Who on earth ever advocated a merely mechanical religion? Who ever dreamt that church-extension alone would supply our need, unless the spirit of the Church went along with her form? We strongly suspect that if there be any subjects of which Mr. Carlyle knows less than others, they are the Church of England and the sentiments of her clergy. Had either awakened in his mind the respectful notice to which they are entitled, he would have seen how utterly aimless is the satire we have just quoted.

We must now, however, betake ourselves to Mr. Carlyle's last work, which has given occasion to these remarks, and in which all his faults have, we think, come to a head. What we have yet to say upon them will therefore be best done mainly with reference to it. Indeed he could hardly have chosen a subject more indicative of himself than that which has inspired it. *Hero-worship* seems to us the predominant principle of his character. His whole search in history is for great men. Great men, according to him, regulate the world's destinies, and he all but says, such can do no wrong. Let us consider for awhile this same principle of hero-worship so dominant in the mind of Mr. Carlyle, and so congenial, we venture to say, in spite of his opinion to the contrary, to the temper of the age in which we live.

Is it a good or a bad principle? Whichever it be, we confess we should not much like a person—above all, a young person—who had no tendency to it. A mind destitute of a sense of greatness must be destitute of "imagination, honourable aims, free commune with the choir that cannot die." And of all sublunary greatness, none certainly is so mysterious, so captivating, at times so overwhelming, as that which resides in our fellow-man. It is surely a generous and purifying feeling that we have towards the names of Dante, Shakspeare, Bacon, Newton, and Burke—the feeling which every young Englishman of the present day, who is worth anything, has towards the names of Wordsworth and Coleridge—the feeling which all Englishmen whatever have towards that of Wellington. God did not create such excellent works as those great men without meaning them to be contemplated and admired. The thought of a fellow-mortal, alike us in so many things, being at the same time so different in others,—having powers not only in another degree, but quite another kind from our own,—the perception in him of that indefinable but most real gift of genius, whereby he is not merely abler than his fellows, but placed beyond the reach of comparison, whereby he is not so properly styled *able* as *creative*,—seeing by intuition more than others can by any process of observation or induction,—capable at the thrilling moment of uttering the thrilling word, and daring the one unlooked for and decisive deed; this, as we have said, is the most fascinating and ennobling of earthly thoughts. We should have no objection to as much of it being expressed as is felt by Mr. Carlyle, provided he would take pains to guard it from taking a false direction.

But, unfortunately, he takes no such pains. The sense of greatness, unless the mind's homage be carefully given where alone it is fully due, is too sure to become the worship of greatness. In such a result Mr. Carlyle apparently sees nothing wrong, nothing to be dreaded. His only fear is lest great men be not exalted enough. Idolatry would seem in his eyes to be no sin. The gift of greatness, according to him, can hardly be considered too much bound up with the man in whom we find it residing. Now, we cannot but think that, like every other leading sentiment of our nature, this enthusiasm for great men requires to be exercised with continual self-mistrust. We must always remember that the greatness we are contemplating is God's work, and only great for that reason—that the true use of it, therefore, must be to lead our thoughts to Him, instead of permitting them to repose on anything short of Him; that the whole ought to be viewed as His gift, continually bestowed by his good pleasure, and liable, at the same good pleasure, to be withdrawn. With this primary limitation, our *Hero-worship*, if we are to designate our reverence for greatness by that name, will be preserved from its chief danger—that of becoming idolatry.

And next, a strong sense of the brotherhood into which baptism admits us, which the eucharist cements, and for which the Church witnesses in all her appointments, is desirable. We fear that, in saying this, we are as barbarians to Mr. Carlyle. But we feel sure that were his mind livelily and habitually impressed with these things, his way of speaking of great men would deserve less suspicion than it incurs at present. For then the union, not the chasms, between individual men and their fellows, would occupy most of his attention. He would see that all really good things must be done by those who feel that no individual should be more than one among many brethren—that in no great matter can a man be a law to himself. He would write no more such painful sentences as that the ethics do not yet exist by which we are to measure the conduct of a Mirabeau. Great men would not take more than their appointed place in that greater vision, the brotherhood of redeemed and regenerate men, which would then rise before him; they would rank among the details—the comparative accidents, however ornamental, of the stately temple. He would set up no separate shrines for them by the way; but, on the contrary, would follow their pointing to the one true altar.

There are other, and perhaps greater, objections to Mr. Carlyle's tone of thought. What his formal religious opinions are we know not; and must beg, in at present characterising much of his writing as infidel, not for a moment to be understood as calling the author an infidel. It is quite possible for a man who considers himself a believer, to cherish, unknown to himself, an unbelieving temper; and all the more is this the case with one who writes and thinks, like Mr. Carlyle, in a mystical and reverential tone. This latter circumstance makes it imperatively our duty to put his readers on their guard. He says many things so eloquently religious, that they may fancy all is safe; or, at least, they may not be alive to the extent of their danger. Once more, therefore, protesting against being supposed to represent Mr. Carlyle's formal and conscious opinions, we must make the following sketch of what we think is the practical creed to be found in his works.

That all things are tending to a vast and as yet unimagined spiritual perfection; and that every thing, be it creed, or be it rite, which has had any extensive sway, has done or is doing its part in bringing about this result: that each of these, however, is of necessity partial and transient; that when it has done its work, it of necessity passes away, and ought to pass away. Accordingly, Mr. Carlyle sees much that is true and divine in Paganism and Mahommedanism. His notions of Odin and Scandinavian mythology are, many of them, just and striking and profitable in this way, though vitiated by a fallacy that runs throughout,—we mean the assumption, that man has had to start from imperfect and false religions, and gradually to rise to nobler and truer ones. But holy Scripture tells us of an original revelation made to the sons of men, and, consequently, views idolatry as apostasy, and condemns it as " without excuse." Modifying, however, Mr. Carlyle's teaching by these momentous considerations, we may derive much instruction from his lecture on Odin. The following paragraph suggests solemn thoughts indeed :—

" And now, if worship of a star had some meaning in it, how much more might that of a hero! Worship of a hero is transcendent admiration of a great man. I say great men are still admirable; I say, there is at bottom nothing else admirable! No nobler feeling than this of admiration, for one higher than himself, dwells in the breast of man. It is to this hour and at all hours, the vivifying influence in man's life. Religion I find stand upon it; not Paganism only, but far higher and truer religions—all religion hitherto known. Hero-worship, heartfelt prostrate admiration, submission, burning, boundless, for a noblest godlike Form of Man,—is not that the germ of Christianity itself? The greatest of all heroes is One—Whom we do not name here. Let sacred silence meditate that sacred matter; you will find it the ultimate perfection of a principle extant throughout man's whole history on earth." — *Lectures on Heroes*, pp. 17, 18.

The ultimate perfection, indeed! Would that Mr. Carlyle would oftener write as if keeping in mind that it is so! For our complaint against him is, that he too frequently leaves the impression, that he ranks the everlasting Gospel among the stages of man's progress, itself in the course of that progress to be transmuted into something higher. What we desiderate in him is an abiding sense of some one enduring authority, among all the changes through which we have to pass—a faith and a rule, " the same yesterday, to-day, and for ever,"—something that will remain true and obligatory, into whatever " varieties of untried being" society may have to pass. We want in him not merely reverence for the christian ideas, of which he has abundance, but the signs of a distinct objective faith in the christian creed. He too much reminds us of the following impressive picture : " No one can trace the progress of this silent revolution in philosophy (that from mechanical necessity to transcendental spiritualism) without perceiving that it must affect men's theological views and apprehensions much more remarkably than any which has occurred since the time of Lord Bacon. A person who maintains that our understanding is not a court of ultimate appeal,—that the very constitution of our being involves that of which it can take no cognizance, will not, of course, speak of mysteries as essentially impossible or worthy of contempt. The tone in which the writers of last century treated them will seem to him not profane, but ridiculous. He will smile, with great exultation and self-complacency, at those who thought themselves privileged to smile at every one else. But it may be pretty surely conjectured, by those who know any thing of themselves, that with a tone of considerable contempt for certain kinds of philosophical infidelity, and of occasional compliment to the grand ideas of Christianity, there will be mixed in such thinkers no slight infusion of self-idolatry,—no slight dislike of any thing that savours of humiliation. For all that he stands proclaiming that the reason lifts a man out of himself, and demands the infinite for its satisfaction,—for all that he looks into the dark abyss of the will, and feels that it requires the ground of a Supreme Will to rest on,—you will find that he is very apt to make this necessarily self-dissatisfied reason, this necessarily dependent will, the real objects of his wonder and his worship. Still more apt will you find him to believe that these conclusions and discoveries respecting the reason and the will, are the highest and most amazing developments of the religious principle; that Judaism and Christianity were but vestibules to the inner shrine of the temple; that all the facts of both were well contrived to embody so much of those principles as man could apprehend (being important possibly, as facts, till an age of greater illumination,) and that their mysteries are exceedingly interesting studies for a person who has investigated the laws of his own being." *

We have already expressed our ignorance of what Mr. Carlyle's religious opinions may be; we are not entitled, therefore, to apply this description to him personally, but we do to his works. If it is not like himself, it is like what he would render his followers.

Persons of the tone of thought in question, will perhaps object to our enforcement of the creed and the sacraments as obligatory always, and on all—that we are seeking to imprison the universal and infinite, under conditions of time and sense, conditions which their philosophy tells them are but laws of our own minds; unfit, therefore, to measure the great reality of things. Historical facts, they will say, cannot be more than phenomenal and accidental. We admit the truth of this: we admit that what is manifested to us under the conditions of our finite being, cannot be manifested in all its transcendent reality; and we remain where we were notwithstanding. We did not require to wait for German philosophers, or for Mr. Carlyle, to tell us this. St. Paul has told us so long since. He has

---

* Maurice's Kingdom of Christ, vol. i. pp. 325, 327.

reminded us that we but "know in part, and prophesy in part," and taught us to wait for the time when that which is perfect shall have come; and that which is in part shall have been done away: that "now we see through a glass darkly;" but that a day is coming, when we shall see things, as Coleridge sublimely expresses it, "in the depths of real being"—see "face to face, and know even as also we are known." The most dogmatic creed which the Church employs solemnly and with reiteration declares it. St. Augustine eloquently preaches it. Thus he enters on the task of expounding the opening words of St. John's Gospel—"Aderit misericordia Dei, fortasse ut omnibus satis fiat, et capiat quisque quod potest: quia et qui loquitur dicit quod potest: *Nam dicere ut est quis potest? Audeo dicere, Fratres mei, forsitan nec ipse Johannes dixit ut est, sed et ipse quod potuit, quia de Deo homo dixit:* et quidem inspiratus a Deo, *sed tamen homo.* Quia inspiratus dixit aliquid; si non inspiratus esset, dixisset nihil: quia vero *homo* inspiratus, *non totum quod est, dixit:* sed quod potuit homo, dixit." *

In truth, the objection might as well shake our faith in ourselves, or in the world around us, as in the Church or the creed, for it applies no less to the one than to the other. No man knows the commonest things around him as they really are. He apprehends them, as he does the truths of the creed, under the conditions of his own finite being, and therefore inadequately—in a particular perspective, as it were. While we are here our justest apprehensions of any thing must be but *approximations.* By the phenomena of the material world we apprehend the realities of external existence and the "action of being upon being" sufficiently for practical impression and guidance. By the revealed word and the sacraments we apprehend the realities of spiritual existence, and the relationships which hold among them in the same sufficiency. Both guide us aright, both are true, both make up all the truth which, in their respective provinces, we can at present attain. For all that a man learns to regard the outward world of phenomena and facts as but a set of forms to teach him truth, which he cannot otherwise apprehend, and which he cannot thus *comprehend,* his practical faith in them is never for one moment shaken. He never expects whilst here to rise above these forms, to be able to get at the truth except by them. Men require no reasoning to persuade them that there is not any conceivable progress of science, or improvement of our social condition, which shall enable mankind to learn the truth that is in the external world, except through the phenomena and facts of that world. Nor shall we ever, while here below, learn the truth that is in the spiritual world, except through what we may call its phenomena and facts—the history of redemption, the confessions of the creed, and the sacraments of the Church. We do not ask men to place these on any other footing, relatively to the truth of things, than

---

* Augustin. in Johann. Evang. Tract i.

they place their own bodies,—the apprehensions they have of their friends,—the facts which they discover around them. They apprehend both truly, though both inadequately. At their utmost height of wisdom, they must, during their mortal condition, acquiesce in the only conditions of thought and knowledge which have been vouchsafed to them. We must cleave to our creed, then, as teaching us the eternal truth of God to be as much received by the philosopher as the peasant in every age of the world. We must continue in the communion of the Church, and use her sacraments as the one way by which philosophers and peasants in every age of the world are to maintain their union with the eternal Word—the Son of God and the Son of Man. We must, while here, choose between knowing only in part and prophesying only in part, and not knowing and not truly prophesying at all. The day is coming when this knowledge in part shall give way to that which is perfect—when we shall not unlearn, but fully learn, the lessons of the Gospel and the Church—seeing the eternal realities to which they shall have brought us in their full glory and unclouded splendour.

1. *Remarks on Church Architecture.* By the Rev. J. L. PETIT, M.A. Burns. 1841.
2. *Hints to Church Builders.* By the CAMBRIDGE CAMDEN SOCIETY. 1841-2.
3. *The Principles of Pointed or Christian Architecture.* By A. W. PUGIN, Esq. Weale. 1841.
4. *Sermons on Church Building.* By the Rev. J. A. EMERTON, M.A. Hatchard & Son. 1842.
5. *Parochial Sermons.* By the Rev. W. GRESLEY, M.A. Burns. 1842.

IN a recent article we had occasion to quote an old and quaint writer of the time of Charles the First, who affirmed that the age in which he lived was more forward than any previous one had been in zeal for church building; but it would now appear that we of these days are about to outstrip our predecessors, if not in fact, at least in willingness,—and if not in willingness, at least in the fuss we make about our doings. If we go on at our present rate, the library tables of reviewers will break down under the sheer weight of the paper and print that, in the cause of architectural inquiry, issues forth from the press and the bookbinder's shop in a daily accelerated ratio. Instead of the five works at the head of these observations, which (with the exception perhaps of the first and third) were the ones that we happened soonest to lay our hands upon, we might have set down the titles of twenty; and certainly, if our zeal in church building is now-a-days often abortive, it is not for lack of counsellors; if there still seems to be something wanting in the works that are built, it is not for lack of attempts at inquiry into the various methods on which our sacred structures might be contrived and erected. The ecclesiastico-architectural world is, in truth, driving very hard at something, though it scarcely as yet, we fear, knows precisely what, either of principle or fact. For the present, the confusion of ideas, buzzing about in all directions, falls little short of an artistical Babel. True, we must have a chaos before a world,—a rude and undigested mass before an adorned structure; and therefore one may hope, that, all in good time, the principles which are now in a mist may unbidden raise their heads above the surface, and draw towards them, like magnetic poles, and arrange in due order, the heaps of facts, and surmises, and hypotheses that are now drifting about without benefit of rudder or compass. Or it may be, that a future age (if the world lasts so long) will look back upon the present, and recognise in its medley works of sacred art a distinctive character,—a something that, for all our endeavours to the contrary, is not the mere *tale quale* repetition of the labours of our ancestors at some bygone period or other.

But, on the other hand, the principles may *not* come of themselves; we may have heaped such a mountain of facts upon them as to smother them quite; or, instead of admiring us, our posterity (if we have any) may possibly reckon us the offspring of a foolish and doting old time, who, having arrived at second childhood, clutched with feeble hands whatever toy pleased most for the moment. "What!" exclaims Mr. Pugin, "no principles d'ye say? Why I have written a book upon the 'Principles of Pointed or Christian Architecture.'" True, so you have; but let us analyse for a moment the title of your book, and we shall see how far you have penetrated into the matter of principle. On the first glance we recognise two elements which, it is to be feared, are not so identical as they are assumed to be. That pointed architecture is Christian we concede; that all Christian architecture is pointed we deny. Supposing, therefore, that Mr. Pugin has given us the "true principles" of *pointed architecture,* we have only advanced a single step towards discovering the principles of *Christian architecture;* the history of the pointed style is only a single class of facts in the history of the architecture of the Church,—a class of facts traceable during, at the most, three out of the eighteen hundred years of her existence.

Before the pointed style came into use, there were a good many churches built, as we learn from history, some of them pretty large ones and costly too; many of them still standing, and likely to last our day : are we to reckon these to be specimens of Christian architecture? According to Mr.

Pugin we suppose not. "Oh! but," he may say, "there are principles which are common to both the pointed and the previous styles." True, but in your book you never told us so. On the contrary, you assume that the pointed style is not only the *Christian*, but the *Catholic, par excellence.*

When Mr. O'Connell undertook, some time since, to advocate the cause of an ill-used individual, whom he termed a *Catholic* cook, all the world wondered what that might be in which the *catholicity* of cookery consisted; and when, not long after, an advertisement appeared in the newspapers, to the effect that a Catholic dinner or breakfast (we forget which) would take place on some grand occasion or other, the exact meaning of the announcement was involved in the same obscurity. Did the catholicity refer to the people who were invited, or to the dishes that were served up? There was the puzzle. If it referred to the ladies and gentlemen who had the good fortune to partake of the dinner, we imagine that nothing more was meant than that they should say grace (which we hope they did) in a Catholic manner, and so eat their victuals like good Christians. But if reference was made to the *viands*, we are in a perplexity of doubt,—unless indeed it happened to be a Friday or a fast-day, when the absence of beef and mutton, or other lusty eatables, might be supposed to indicate a compliance with Catholic usage. Now we are just as much perplexed when we hear about *Catholic* architecture. Does it mean the architecture used by the Catholic Church? We suppose it must. But if so, where does the catholicity reside,—in the architecture itself, in the people who use it, or in the use they put it to? If in either of the two latter, our minds are greatly relieved. The "upper room" where the apostles met then becomes a *Catholic room;* but if in the first, we are in a "sea of troubles." We have to find out that in which the catholicity of architecture consists apart from and beyond its mere adaptation to the uses of Christian worship; for this, it must be kept in view, has very little direct bearing on the style or taste or design of the architecture. The Roman Basilica, the Byzantine Cathedral, the English Cathedral of the thirteenth century, the Palladian Church of the sixteenth and seventeenth, nay, the conventicle-looking affair of the days of our youth,—all are adapted to the necessities of the same worship; but which of them is Catholic? To solve this problem, we have endeavoured with all our might to apply the ancient rule by which our forefathers determined the catholicity of a rite, a custom, or a doctrine; but without success. The *quod semper et ubique et ab omnibus* sets us sorely at defiance.

If Catholic architecture be that which the Catholic Church has ever used since the era of Christ commenced, we must include every possible variety of taste, from the Greek and Roman down to the newest conventicle fashion of these days. By this rule the chapel of the Palace of Versailles, which would make a handsome ball-room, or a saloon for private theatricals, has as good a right to the title of Catholic as the Sainte Chapelle of Louis IX. in the Palais de Justice of Paris; or, to come nearer home, our own St. Paul's possesses the same claim as the cathedrals of Salisbury or York. This is what we get by the *quod semper*. Does the *quod ubique et ab omnibus* help us? Yes, if we leave out the *quod semper*. There certainly has been a style of Church architecture that prevailed everywhere, and was practised by all; but not always. It went out when its day declined, like a thing of fashion. In its room another style arose, that lasted less than half the time of its predecessor, and that was neither practised by all nor everywhere. This also disappeared by a fresh touch from the wand of the sorceress novelty. In other words, the earliest style of ecclesiastical architecture that might be looked upon as being exclusively christian, was practised, with comparatively little variation, from one extremity of Christendom to the other down to the beginning of the thirteenth century. We recognise it in Constantinople by the name of Byzantine; in Italy we term it Lombard or Romanesque; Carlomagnian or Rhenish in Germany; Norman in France; and Saxon or Norman in England;—from Jerusalem to St. Kilda, the *round-arch manner* was orthodox and catholic for the long period of eight centuries. After this, for three ages, we have all the varieties of the pointed-arch style; and then, in its turn rejected, we revert to the long repudiated inventions of paganism, and with these we have delighted ourselves for the last three hundred years.

Now, if catholicity " admits of more or less," as the schoolmen were wont to speak, we may conclude that the *Lombard* or *Romanesque* (or give it any other name if you will) is the most catholic style of church building;* the *pointed* next in degree; and, last in order, the *revived antique.*

We fear that in saying all this we are stirring a nest of hornets, but we cannot help it; the ground we take cannot be impugned, and we have good reason for assuming it at this time. It is utterly preposterous to assert, as Mr. Pugin has done, and as

---

* The following specimen of critical acumen and knowledge is so rich that we cannot refrain from quoting it. " Streatham Church," says the " Ecclesiologist," (published by the Cambridge Camden Society,) " is so utterly unlike every other ecclesiastical building (1) that it is by no means easy to describe it. The style is *Moorish*, and the building consists of a nave and two aisles, with a long thin tower at the south-west angle; this latter is 113 feet in height, and 15 feet square, and being pannelled in three enormously lofty lancets, presents an appearance *perfectly indescribable.* . . . Why were our own styles deserted for forms, which, if they express any thing, express only the *spirit of a false religion*, and are adapted to the *necessities of a burning climate?*" Admirable critic! Profound architect! So profound, that he despises such small matters as historical facts. What is it to him that the *Moorish* style was actually derived from the Italian ecclesiastical style of the ninth, tenth, eleventh, and twelfth centuries; or that the Alhambra itself was built by Italian architects? What

the Camden Society have reechoed, that a style of architecture is exclusively christian and catholic which was not introduced till twelve long ages of Christianity had lapsed, and with which not more than a half of Christendom was ever acquainted; which was neither uniformly nor simultaneously practised among those who adopted it; and which, to say nothing of the incessant changes it underwent from its origin to its extinction, lasted at the most for three centuries.

It may suit Mr. Pugin's purpose, as a Romanist, to assume, and to endeavour to persuade those who do not know better, that this kind of architecture is alone worthy of the name of catholic, because he is desirous of making us believe its discontinuance was owing to the interruption of communion between the Churches of England and Rome. He acts on a principle the reverse of that of John Knox, the *deformer*. Knox said, "Let us destroy the nests, and we shall soon get rid of the rooks." Mr. Pugin says, or would say if he dared, "Let us rebuild the nests; let us persuade people of the beauty of the old strongholds of popish catholicity, and the popery will come of itself; let us get the members of the Anglican Church, who are now yearning after catholic communion, heartily in love with the forms of past ages; let us once get them to sympathise with and admire the consistent beauty and harmony of the forms and furniture of a well-ordered church of the thirteenth or fourteenth century; let us *wheedle them into a belief that unless a church contains all the parts and ornaments that were then used it is incomplete and uncatholic;* and we shall soon persuade them to apply their churches to a *Roman* Catholic use."

The Camden Society of Cambridge has fallen into this snare. What, in the name of all that is honest, do they mean by telling us, in their "Hints to Church Builders," that a rood screen is "a catholic appendage to a church which never ought to be wanting?" It cannot be proved that in England they were used earlier than the twelfth, or later than the middle of the sixteenth century; and the very authority quoted by the writer of the "Hints" for their present use certainly makes against him. Everybody knows that the rood screen was only the lower *story* (if we may so speak) of the rood loft, or narrow platform, on which the huge crucifix and other statues were erected, which we still see

---

is it to him that the "long thin tower," whose appearance is "perfectly indescribable," has its prototype in nearly every ancient city of Italy? The towers of St. Zeno and of St. Anastasia, in Verona; those of St. Antonio, of Padua: St. Francesco d'Assisi, or of St. Mark of Venice; and a hundred others, are of course "perfectly indescribable," because they are pannelled in enormously lofty lancets, like the tower of Streatham; and, moreover, they "express the spirit of a false religion,"—so we had better say nothing about them. But if the Italian brick churches, with round or pointed arches, expressed the spirit of a false religion, what did our own cotemporary buildings express? We had always a notion that during the periods we allude to the religions of Italy and England were not very different.

in some of the German churches;* and though we may admit that the screen had been introduced before it was used to sustain a crucifix, yet the screen itself was not a "catholic appendage to a church," if it is intended by this expression to signify that chancel screens were either used at any period everywhere through Christendom, or that at the time of their actual use they were common to all churches. They were undoubtedly monastic and conventual appendages to a church,—partitions, in fact, by which the choir, occupied solely by the monks, was shut off from the rest of the church. But even this is a departure from the practice of more primitive times; for the place of the regular clergy was behind, not in front of the altar, as may be seen in innumerable conventual churches of great antiquity in Italy.

The assertion, again, that "altar rails were not known to our ancestors any more than to the Romish Church at the present day," made by the writer of the "Hints," at p. 20, is purely gratuitous. We can only suppose that he has never seen a "modern Romish church," either in this country or in France and Italy, where, in fact, they are never wanting. In cathedrals, the altar rails are properly the *cancella*, or low rails to the choir; but if there is no choir, as in many parish churches or chapels, they are identical with our altar rails. If he should ever visit Lombardy, we will undertake that he will find plenty of them of a workmanship that he must refer to the tenth and eleventh centuries.

What, again we ask, is meant by the dogmatical assumption of the writer, that "on each side of the chancel there is (*i. e.* ought) to be a double, or, if needed, a triple row of *misereres;*" which, he says, afford "scope for an almost unlimited extent of carving?" *Cui bono?* For what purpose are these *misereres?* To exhibit the powers of the carver? He might just as well have said, "All round the nave there ought to be three tiers of niches; these would afford admirable and unlimited scope for stone-masonry." People would naturally think this a very expensive kind of decoration, and very unnecessary, unless it could be shown that the niches were for some use, practical or mystical; and so we say in the case of *misereres:* we ask what they are intended for? The Camdenite will reply, "Oh! our *ancestors* had them, they are part and parcel of *Catholic* architecture, and we, if we are Catholics, must have them too." Yes, my good friend; but our ancestors had monks to fill these seats, which afforded such unlimited scope for carving, (and beastly things to be sure, vide Henry VII.'s Chapel, they carved upon

---

* In the Laurenz Kirche, and St. Sebalds, of Nuremberg, these frightful deformities still exist; we say deformities, because we have felt, not through any mawkish feeling of delicacy, but from, as we believe, a true conception of the right use of art in religion, that a crucifix, large as life, and painted *ad vivum*, is a revolting object, and debasing in its effect on the feelings.

them;) but we have no monks. Except in cathedral and collegiate churches, we have no supernumerary clergy; our *hare* therefore *must first be caught before we can cook him.* First provide your choristers in parish churches, and then we may listen to your injunctions about *the miserere seats* for the antiphonal chanting of the psalms; which, as every body knows, were contrivances for the double purpose of preventing the monks or canons from falling asleep, and of allowing them after a sort to sit during the long recitations of the psalms; contrivances which, now that the daily service, especially in psalmody, is so much shortened, are absolutely unnecessary.

But to return to the question of principle,—Are there any principles of christian architecture? Is there any *ideal* of a church? What ought it to be considered ecclesiastically or æsthetically,—as a matter of ecclesiastical fitness, or as a matter of taste and artistic beauty? It is obviously vain to look for any light on these points in the lucubrations of the Camden Society, or of Mr. Pugin. Both have made up their minds that the pointed style is the christian style, that certain old churches are built in the best possible manner, and that nothing remains for us but to copy them as exactly as we can. Mr. Pugin's "principles" amount to nothing more than a description of the methods of building at certain times, and his practice shows that he only aims at the exact copying of some model or other.* We leave Mr. Pugin, then, and his patrons, the Camdenites, to their crotchets, and turn to sober-minded people, like Mr. Petit, who, looking upon a church of whatever date, *as a church*, set themselves, according to the best of their ability, to inquire how far, taken as it is, and as a work of art, it comes up to their ideal of a christian temple. We confess that, though disagreeing with Mr. Petit in many of his views, and unable to follow him through the multiplicity of unconnected facts which he has brought forward, the tone of his book has given us great pleasure. There is a candour and frankness about it, and a freedom from prejudice, which contrasts most favourably with the productions of his fellow-labourers in the same field. He assumes nothing, but is willing to acknowledge, and obviously feels, that the whole history of ecclesiastical architecture presents a series of attempts to develop the idea of a christian temple; and hence that we ought rather to regard the works of past ages as experiments than as conclusions,—as facts to judge of, rather than as models for exact imitation. This is the right tone; and we gladly recognise in it a return to a more healthy feeling on the subject of

---

* Stay! we forgot his affirmation, that steeples were made very high to signify the resurrection. This, at least, looks like a hint of the mystical principles of church-building:—but is it a fact? Can he quote any ancient writer who says so? What if the tower were an imitation of that built by King Solomon over the porch of the temple, and which was 180 feet high?

church building as a matter of art than has been prevalent for some time past. The various styles of church architecture in the middle ages were, in truth, merely the fashions of the day, varying with the ever-changing desires, tastes, sentiments, and aspirations of the artists; hence each successive production has about it the freshness and truthful character that original genius alone can impress on its creations. This freshness is wanting in all our attempts to copy the beauties of ancient art; and it is wanting just because we are imitators. Apply, in short, the rule of the Camden Society to the art of painting or sculpture, and its absurdity is manifest. It is the old story: "necesse enim semper sit posterior qui sequitur;" and inferior too, Quintilian might have said. (By the way, we recommend the Camden Society to take another sentence of Quintilian for their motto, "Pigri est ingenii contentum esse iis quæ ab aliis sunt inventa.") "If it were asked which of the buildings of the present day," writes Mr. Petit, vol. ii. p. 151, "bid fairest to command the admiration of posterity, I should answer, without hesitation, those connected with the railways. I do not speak of the ornamental, but the essential parts, as the bridges and viaducts; many of which may be pronounced the very perfection of mechanical beauty. And the same may be said of other structures of public utility and convenience,—as that noble range of bridges which connects our metropolis with its opposite suburb. Can any of our modern ecclesiastical buildings compare with them? And where is the deficiency? Is it in skill, or is it in spirit?" Mr. Petit does not answer his question, but the reply is obvious:—the railway is the offspring of the talent and genius of our day, just as the gothic cathedral was of days by-gone. In both there is the freshness and novelty of creation;—the spirit of the age breathes out vigorously in each. In our imitation churches, on the other hand, we attempt to restore,—what? not the spirit, but the mere form of the art of past ages; we are mechanically setting up a sort of skeleton, into which we have no power to breathe the breath of life; we are stifling and crippling, by the trammels of blind imitation, the genius and inspiration of the artist, without which, do as we will, no work of art can ever please; and yet we expect success.

We cannot conclude without expressing our regret that Mr. Petit, who evidently has considerable artistic power, has not made his profusion of illustrations more valuable than they are. Some of the sketches are so slight as scarcely to give a notion even of the "general effect" (as artists say) of the buildings represented. We regret this, because the specimens which we have been enabled to give in the present number, show that it was in Mr. Petit's power to have taken more pains. Still, even such as they are, the memoranda are very desirable acquisitions.

SCHERTZLINGEN—LAKE OF THUN.

LLANBADERN VAWR NEAR ABERYSTWITH.

NEAR MANTES, ON THE SEINE.

TONG, SHROPSHIRE.

The Egyptian Bondage; or, a Second Call to Union, on the Principles of the Holy Catholic Church, and the everlasting Gospel of Christ. By the Rev. F. D. WACKERBARTH, A.B., of Queen's Coll. Camb. &c. &c. London: Dolman; Bohn. 1841.

IN placing this pamphlet at the head of our article, we have no intention whatever of reviewing it; but we feel constrained to say a few words on a part of the great question of Church and State, from a sense of its being at the bottom of most of our present religious embarrassments.

The subject is so large and difficult a one, and has been so carefully entertained by so many of the greatest men of whom modern England can boast, that we feel some apology to be due to our readers for thus cursorily entering on it. But it seems to us far from exhausted. It is the second greatest question for every serious mind in the present age. To nearly every one, therefore, whatever be his post in the world of thought, is assigned the task of considering it. We are not aware that precisely what we are about to say on it has ever been said hitherto; and we feel bold, moreover, to place it before others in the light in which it is mainly seen by ourselves for this reason amongst many, that, whilst if that light be a just it is an important one, it need not exclude other ones which may be both just and important also.

The relation between Church and State, whatever it be, is an existing fact which we are to discover, not a plan which we are to form and carry into execution. However we like to regard it, and whatever terms we may prefer by which to denote it, it seems to have been something naturally resulting from the position in which both Church and State found themselves in the beginning of modern Europe. This is a solemn consideration. It does not seem as if we had the arrangement yet to choose; he who objects to it, seems almost to quarrel with the providence of God. Let him find any nation where the Church and State have come together as they did in ours without nearly the same result, and we will admit that it is a question for us to entertain and decide upon. But if that cannot be, we think it one to be approached with reverence and restraint, as larger and deeper than ourselves,—larger and deeper than any individual mind,—larger and deeper than any set of minds at any one period.

It is not, however, with the *voluntary* (to use the barbarous slang of the day) that we have to do at present. The parties of whom we are now thinking, have no objection to Church and State coming to some terms, but they are dissatisfied with the English adjustment of the question, as having in their judgment been effected by too large a surrender of her prerogatives on the part of the Church, and as tending to her enslavement.

On the other hand, there are many who see that there are prerogatives in the State which she has no right to surrender, and who strongly object to the Romish and presbyterian views, as necessarily tending to her enslavement.

This, then, is the problem to be solved,—how to place the union between Church and State on such terms as that neither shall destroy the other. If, with the Erastian, we make the State the fountain of all authority within its limits, then there is, say what we like, no such thing as the Church, and the words *spiritual power* are but a deception. If, on the other hand, we exalt Church authority, what place is left for the magistrate? For it is easy to speak of each keeping to its own province; of the ecclesiastical authority being left unfettered in matters ecclesiastical, and the civil having undisturbed jurisdiction over civil affairs. Why, in three-fourths of the questions that arise, the grand point to be determined is, whether the case be ecclesiastical or civil. It is often a preliminary discussion in our Church courts, whether they are competent to entertain the case in hand at all; and however satisfactorily they may determine it, according to their own apprehensions of things, they cannot enjoy a moment's security against the common lawyers taking a different view of the matter, and coming down on them with that well-known extinguisher hight *prohibition*. Are things better in Scotland? There the sovereign is not considered, as here in the south, an ecclesiastic. There the temporal and ecclesiastical authorities are co-ordinate; there the rule is recognised by both, that neither is to meddle with what comes properly under the jurisdiction of the other. But do they work harmoniously? Is not this the very question which they cannot settle,—what matters are solely ecclesiastical, and what civil? and the unsettlement of which is bringing the affairs of the Scottish establishment to a dead lock?

In truth, two co-ordinate jurisdictions, talk as men like, are an impossibility. Unless religion can be separated altogether from the affairs of this life, we cannot settle the question thus. The Clergy, and we believe we may add the christian laity, must absolutely resolve to have no civil rights, properties, or immunities whatsoever, or they must come in contact with the secular power. And as we have already said, co-ordinate jurisdiction is impossible. Whilst the two authorities are liable to be occupied with the same matter, they must also be liable to clash. One must in the long run overpower the other. Neither can we get out of the difficulty by making one superior to the other; for, as we have already said, this must be for one to annihilate the other. *Qui facit per alium, facit per se;* and the jurisdiction of a subordinate is but one development of the jurisdiction of the governing authority. If the temporal authority governs the spiritual, then the State is really every thing. If the spiritual courts can overrule the temporal, then the Church is the only governing power; the monarch and the magistrates are but her officials, acting for themselves only by her permission.

Now, of course, if, looking the matter in the face, any man is prepared for either of these alternatives, and means to abide by it as desirable and right, there is no further difficulty awaiting him, except in the choice of a residence such as shall satisfy his views.

That residence cannot be England, for neither Dr. Arnold nor Thomas à Becket can now find the state of affairs which either might be supposed to desire. And though at present it may be easy to find in several countries much realization of the Erastian alternative, it is questionable whether there be any in which a legitimate branch of the Church is recognised and established, in which it does not every now and then manifest something of its independent character; in which it does not every now and then throw out a hint what powers it might put forth in time of need. On the other hand, nowhere, unless in the papal state, does the Church appear as the dominant power.

Is there, then, no settlement of this question?—It has been the great European one since European states were: above all, it has been the great English one since England was. Has all been in vain? Have no results been arrived at? We think there have; we think that as it was the peculiar calling of England, to entertain, so it has been the peculiar honour of England to answer this question; not prematurely, not under any partial influence, not at any one excited moment; but calmly, in the fulness of time, by the mysterious leadings of God's Providence through "ways that we had not known," by the combined operation of the passions of bad and the aspirations of good men, by the mixture of earthly influences and heavenly strivings, by the contact of a political position and the necessity of the Church—by all this complication of human elements under Divine guidance.

Let us look at this a little more closely. In the very idea of a State, truly such, is involved that of integral independence. One of its prime necessities, therefore, must be to secure and maintain free integral action. Our State, like other European states, became early alive to this necessity, and sensible of this craving,—perhaps earlier alive, and more keenly sensible, because of the peculiar character of its population, and because of its island position; but, during the day of its weakness and infancy, there was a powerful enemy to this free integral action in the Church, as having all over Western Europe become prostrate before the chair of Peter, and being as a body but slightly tinged with the quality, or inspired by the sentiment, of nationality anywhere. Hence a struggle, continually reviving, and never more than lulled, between the civil and the spiritual power. Hence a feeling in each that it had something to contend for, something which it could not and should not surrender. Hence the strong sense of right which perhaps animated the partisans of Henry and Becket alike. This was a question which required to be settled at some time or other; it would have proved internecine, if not. It never was properly settled in Austria, in Spain, or in France; but in all these countries, the State, being resolved to assert itself, feeling that it could not be a State if a foreign power (that power, moreover, chancing to be itself a State) could control and govern its members, resolved at different times to assert its own independence, and saw no other way of doing this but by trampling on the Church altogether.

In England the case was quite different. In England, the sentiment of State independence was all along, perhaps, more vigorous and irrepressible; and therefore the question necessarily came to a settlement at an earlier period; and, by the specially favouring providence of God, that period was, as we hold, the right one, and its attendant circumstances the suitable ones. Had the adjustment taken place earlier, it would probably have been either a merely religious or a merely political movement. If the former, (religion viewed in relation to the pretensions of princes being represented by the see of Rome,) the State would have been swamped; if the latter, the Church. As it was, a political emergency conspired with a religious awakening; each acted by means of the other, and so each, under God, was preserved from its own mischievous excess. The politics became sacred—the religious feeling temperate, subdued, considerate, and loyal. Let us, then, fully persuaded as we are that the English settlement of this great question is the true one, devote the conclusion of this article to considering what that settlement is.

The usual English objections to what is rather unfortunately called *establishing* the Church, reduce themselves to two heads, referring respectively to the duties of the State and the duties of the Church. As regards the former, the State is held by some to exceed her commission, if she take any definite step in regard to religion. There is something more than commonly amusing in the cool way in which reasoners on both sides take it for granted that they can ascertain, measure, and limit, the commission of the State. In perhaps nine cases out of ten, no pains have been taken to ascertain what is meant by the State. Waiving this point, however,—taking for granted that people have moulded their notions of it into something like form,—we may demand of them, where they find a charter authorizing it to do some things and not other things. They will hardly pretend to find such in Scripture, though they may well meditate on a few hints to be found there, which, whatever they may teach, are clearly not of a *limiting* character. In truth, the commission of the State is to be gathered from observation—from seeing what the State has received power to do. The phenomenon of a State leads thinking men to the true idea of a State; and to realize that idea is what we mean by the State fulfilling its commission. But let us take what is commonly called a low view. Not on our own parts rejecting, though not for our present purpose entertaining, the high doctrine maintained by Mr. Gladstone and others, that the State has a personality, and therefore a conscience, leading it to use its powers for the direct promotion of true religion,—let us, for argument's sake, accept that explanation of a State's functions, which limits them to the protection of its members, and assisting them, or at least imposing no hindrance on them, in satisfying their wants. Taking up with such an explanation as this, we say that the State's commission will be as the men by whom it is composed, and over whom it rules,— that it will be ample and varied, according as their wants are ample and varied. If they really " live by bread alone," then the State, on this principle, will be conversant only with bread. If they be enterprising and commercial, then the State will be continually kept in mind that they are so, will continually have to occupy itself with questions of enterprise and commerce. And if they be christian men, with christian wants, the State will naturally come in contact with christian matters. If they be disposed to pour their treasures into the lap of the Church, then the State, as guarding all property within its bounds, will take cognizance of that which has been made over to the Church, as appertaining to her. And should it so happen, that such donations have placed in the hands of the Church a large amount of property,—and should the State be of that vital kind, wherein a recognised place is assigned to every large class of the holders of property, according to the nature of its tenure,—then must the Church of necessity become, what in England it is recognised as being, an important " estate of the realm."

Now, this view of the subject, though in no wise excluding other and higher ones, ought to have no great difficulties even to the *liberal* politicians of the present day. They themselves act on the principle of measuring the commission of the State by the character and wants of its members. They do not object to its entertaining the questions of health, of commerce, of education; because it has to do with a people who know the value of all three. And why is it not to entertain (if it profitably can) the question of religion, when it knows its members to be more than earthly beings, to have more than earthly wants, and they themselves more or less know it too?

But our present concern is more with the part to be played by the Church than the State; for the difficulties now felt have reference mainly to her duties. Can she place herself in the position which we have seen that the State has been willing she should occupy without abandoning her essential prerogatives? If she is to have a function in the State at all, must it not be dominant over all others? The State did as we have described by the Church, and found the Church too much for her. The difficulty arose which we stated at an earlier part of this article. Which was to govern? Whichever did really destroyed the other. The State either became the mere creature of the Church, or the Church a mere instrument of the State; and neither could abandon its inherent prerogatives. A king must, within his own realm, be supreme in all outward and visible things; all definite jurisdiction, therefore, must be subject to his control; but there is a Divine fountain of jurisdiction on high unearthly matters, of which the Clergy are in the first instance the depositaries, and which, when exercised, must be exercised in definite acts. Are they to surrender this to the sovereign? If they do, where is Christ's kingdom, and the powers with which he has entrusted them?

The only escape from this difficulty, we are persuaded, is to be found in the continually overlooked distinction which we made last year between spiritual power and spiritual jurisdiction.* By the former, of course, we mean the ability to do preternatural acts, whereby Christ is conveyed to his people—the ability to minister in word and sacrament. This is ordinarily possessed by none but apostolically-ordained men. The latter regulates the exercise of this power,—says who shall be benefited and who excluded from the blessing it brings. Spiritual jurisdiction fixes one particular possessor of spiritual power in one particular place, and tells him to exercise his gift there,—tells him to vouchsafe its exercise to some and not to others, &c. &c. Now this spiritual jurisdiction cannot be validly exercised without *the consent* of the priesthood as represented and comprehended in the episcopal order. But with their consent others may aid in carrying it out. The whole body of christian laity, in early times, were mixed up with its exercise in many important particulars. The State is now. But, in either case, the rule holds good, *Qui facit per alium facit per se;* and if the priesthood consents, the jurisdiction exercised becomes its own act.

All this, however, it may be said, though it may justify the interference, will not justify the supremacy of the Crown in matters ecclesiastical,—will not justify its appellate jurisdiction over the sentence both of bishop and of metropolitan,—will not justify the making Queen Victoria a higher ecclesiastical authority than the Archbishop of Canterbury. Let us see how the case really stands; how the English Reformation has adjusted this question.

No more since the Reformation than before has the English sovereign pretended to *spiritual power* (Art. XXXVII.); and so long as it is exercised as it ought to be, so long is Christ's kingdom flourishing amongst us. And in regard to the jurisdiction exercised by him, we have seen that the consent of the episcopate gives it validity. But if the sovereign, as such, exercise authority, it must be *supreme* authority. The idea of a State, as represented in the crown, requires this. He is therefore " over all persons, and in all causes, ecclesiastical as well as civil, within his dominions, supreme." What does this imply?

It need not imply anywhere, and in England it assuredly does not imply, more than this:—The sovereign knows that his people have spiritual wants, and that neither he nor his generals, nor his lay counsellors, can satisfy those wants; just as he knows that when they are sick they require to be healed, and that neither he, nor his generals, nor his ordinary counsellors, have power to heal them. In the latter case he encourages the physicians, who can; and those physicians exercise those powers of theirs to which he does not pretend, under

---

* Christian Remembrancer, New Series, vol. i. p. 212.

him, as his subjects. In the former case, he goes, in like manner, to the christian Clergy, and says to them, "Here are wants which you have power to satisfy, and I have not. Will you do as the physicians do, exercise those powers under me? I am aware there is more to consider in your case than in theirs; I am aware that you profess to have received a direct commission from a heavenly King, to whom, without doubt, you owe your first allegiance. What I want to know is, whether your allegiance to him will be violated by your also becoming functionaries of mine, and, as one class of my subjects, exercising for the benefit of the rest those powers which you have received from him?" The English Clergy have answered, "No; these two things are not incompatible. So long as you act on our principles, we can fulfil our vocation, not, as before, independently of the realm, but subject to it, and to you, its chief person and representative." Therefore, while viewed simply as priests of the Church, they are the officers of Christ Jesus alone; viewed as a recognised class of functionaries in the realm of England, they are magistrates and officials of the sovereign, acting under him.

By contracting our view we may make the case plainer. The captain of a man of war is the highest authority within its walls. He does not pretend to have the powers of the chaplain, who, nevertheless, is under him. He did not make him a priest, any more than he made the surgeon a surgeon. Each, therefore, traces his right to act to something else than the good pleasure of the captain; each, viewed simply in the light of his own general calling, is irrespective of him. But, as *officers* of the ship, they are under him. He leaves the performance of divine service to the chaplain; but, as he is responsible for the whole ship, the chaplain must obey him as to the when and where, and all matters of that description.

And even so in the greater and more complicated case of Church and State in general; there is nothing Erastian, there is no denial of spiritual power, Christ's kingdom is not lost in one of this world, in putting the sovereign at the head of ecclesiastical jurisdiction. The bishops and priests, viewed in reference to the Church, are Christ's vicegerents; viewed in reference to the State, they exercise their preternatural power as functionaries under the sovereign. The thought is a complicated one, perhaps, but we are sure it is one which anybody may master; and except in mastering it, we see no refuge for a thinking mind from Erastianism on the one hand, or the monstrous doctrine of dominion being founded on grace on the other. In Scotland, we see the result of having no other conception of a Church than its jurisdiction; or of a State than its secularity. There the presbyterians, honourably wishing to be a Church,—to bear testimony to the headship of Jesus Christ,—to have some stamp of spirituality imprinted on them,—to wear some unearthly badge,—but having no lively conception of those spiritual powers conveyed by an apostolical ordination, which they sinfully flung away, see nothing peculiar left to the Church, as such, should she invest her sovereign with the supreme jurisdiction. To do so, they think, and in their case they think rightly, would be to make the State all in all, and the Church as much a creature of hers as any secular commission or board. But as the State guards her rights with equal jealousy, and as on the presbyterian theory, no adjustment is provided, the two are now engaged in mortal combat. We, on the other hand, who feel that the Clergy have spiritual powers, to which no sovereign, as such, ever pretended, and that whilst those powers are on the whole exercised rightly, Christ's sway is being carried on among us, can consistently invest our sovereign with an ecclesiastical character, and make him our supreme ecclesiastic in respect of jurisdiction. Such an arrangement can of course last only while he and the Church are at one in respect of essential principles; and we have a security in reserve. By our apostolical ordination, we keep up the continuity of our own being in the transmission of spiritual power. The existence of that power is of the essence of the Church; jurisdiction, as we have seen, only regulating its exercise; at no time, therefore, have we actually lost ourselves in the State, as the presbyterians of Scotland are in just dread of doing; and should an emergency arise, in which separation from the State shall become necessary, we shall be found to have preserved both our entire organic structure and its permeating life, and shall therefore come out in unimpaired identity. On the continent, we see that, in consequence of Churches refusing to become national, the State has in many places become national without them, in spite of them, and by tyrannizing over them. In England, we have found that the self-emancipation of the State was made available to the purification of the Church, and that, in return, the Church has raised and solemnized the State, investing it with much of a spiritual character, and making its sovereign the head ecclesiastic in matters of discipline.

Thus was the problem solved by England, and we are sure there is no solution so good. It is idle to complain that it involves statements and ideas which were unknown to the first ages. It does so, because the whole state of affairs to which it relates was unknown to them also. The Roman Empire after Constantine had little analogy to the Christian State in modern Europe. The emperor was not the ecclesiastically-anointed king. All the relations into which the Church could enter with him depended of necessity on his personal character. But yet how little she could keep out of his way. Even before Constantine, a difficult, and *solely ecclesiastical* case was decided by the heathen Aurelian. The catechumen, Constantine, was admitted to a place where none but Erastians can approve of his having been, and where we should not admit our baptized sovereign, though we have made the office an ecclesiastical one. So difficult it is either for the temporal power to overlook the spiritual, or the spiritual to keep clear of the temporal, under any circumstances. Even dissenters bring actions into the courts of common law in matters which, could the term be applied to them, are strictly ecclesiastical.

Let those, then, who regard our present perplexities with undue impatience, think well what they are about. Perchance, should they recklessly indulge it, they may be fighting against God. Certainly they are repining at what has resulted from a long, and to us intricate course of Providence. And if the principle, as we have laid it down, be such as they cannot gainsay, and yet many of its results to them unpalatable, let them consider that those results, if sinful, must be such as can be got rid of, though much caution is requisite before we come to such a conclusion. Few thoughtful Churchmen, indeed, profess to be satisfied with every thing in our present condition, or wish to stifle the movement towards something better. And if we have imperfectly apprehended the principle, or if it be new and unfamiliar to us, many of its legitimate results may well perplex us; but let us not seek to be wiser than God; who works in ways that we cannot trace, who assigns to each of us his own part, wherein to do his particular duty, and receive the strength of which he is in need; but who has not bade us have an opinion on every phase of the Church's history and circumstances; has reserved to Himself the prerogative of guiding her throughout the course of time; and who, in the exercise of this prerogative, as in every other, acts with judgments that are unsearchable, and ways that are past finding out.

NOTICES OF BOOKS.

Excursions in Albania: comprising a Description of the Wild Boar, Deer, and Woodcock Shooting in that Country; and a Journey from thence to Thessalonica and Constantinople, and up the Danube to Pest. By Captain J. J. BEST, 34th *Regiment.* London: Allen & Co. 1842. 8vo. Pp. 358.

THAT portion of this volume which contains the Excursions in Albania is sufficiently uninteresting; but we have followed the writer with pleasure in his journey through Greece, and especially along the course of the Peneus, and through the classical vale of Tempe. The interest of the journey, however, we must say, is derived not from the author, but from the country; for it unfortunately happens, that Captain Best is neither a scholar nor an antiquarian; nor is he even what we now so much more often meet with, a geologist, or a statist, or an economist. We shall quote two passages; the first, for the sake of the description; the latter, as containing Captain Best's opinion of the Turks. It is remarkable how much travellers differ in their estimation of this people.

"A ride of about four hours from the snow-enclosed Khan on the top of the Pindus brought us to the open plain; we were descending the banks of the Peneus, and after gradually opening out into a more level country than that we had left behind us, the mountains seemed entirely to have disappeared in our front, and the boundless plain of Thessaly lay open to our view. In this plain, at a short distance, as we imagined, from the spot where we first saw them, but in reality another four hours' ride from us, we observed, rising in a picturesque and remarkable manner to a height of several hundred feet out of the dead level of the plain, some huge, precipitous, and curiously-shaped rocks, all apparently as inaccessible as Shakespeare's Cliff at Dover, but many of them considerably more lofty, the highest, I should say, towering 600 feet above the level of the plain. We continued to follow the course of the Peneus, through a magnificently wooded country, for about four hours more, when we found ourselves in the midst of these huge conglomerate rocks, which seem quite alive with convents. Some are built on the summits of sugar-loaf-like rocks, others about half-way up the faces, but all most carefully constructed in situations apparently inaccessible, and in which they seem to have been placed by enchantment, for it is difficult to conceive how the materials requisite for their construction could have been carried up the sides of almost perpendicular rocks several hundred feet high, or how a sufficient footing could have been gained at the summits of the almost pointed ones, on which some of the convents stand, to place the machinery for raising up the foundation stones. These huge rocks cover a space of about one mile and a half in length, and of a variable width. They are a kind of soft conglomerate with sea pebbles and shells in great quantities, but they show evident marks of the effects of time and weather on a not very solid kind of stone. Besides the convents there are houses in all directions, in and under these rocks, to all of which access is, as to the convents, by a rope-ladder, which can be drawn up at pleasure, or by some most impracticable steps cut in the solid rock. The country in the vicinity belongs mostly to these convents or houses, which have, I conclude, been constructed in these situations of security in consequence of the miserably unsettled state in which this part of the country has always been. . . . . . The convent we were about to visit was the Agios Stephanos, which is one of the highest. Leaving our horses at the foot of the hill, we reached, after about a quarter of an hour's hard climbing, a spot where, on looking up, we saw, about 180 feet perpendicularly over our heads, a projecting wooden building, to which a basket, which was on the ground close to us, was attached by a cord, and which basket appeared to be used as a means of conveyance for provisions, &c. from the spot where we stood to the monks residing in the regions above. We had thus arrived at the back of the rock, on the summit of which the Agios Stephano stands, its height above us being 180 feet, whilst its height above the plain on its front and two side faces must be 300 or 400 feet. On hailing the monks to admit us, they told us to mount by a series of strong, but very disagreeable and rickety ladders, in joints, which ran up one sloping side of the rock, and entered a covered kind of gallery about 100 feet above the ground where we stood, but 200 feet perpendicularly above the nearest point of the ground immediately below it. We considered this mode of ascent as impracticable to any but a sailor, and so declined attempting it. They then called to us to wait, and in a few minutes we saw descending from the building above a sort of strong cabbage-net with very large meshes, and capable of holding two persons at a time. The net is spread open upon the ground, and one or two persons sit down upon it cross-legged; the upper meshes of the net are then collected together over his or their heads, and hung on an iron hook attached to the rope. The monks above then turn a capstan, and in two minutes and a half the traveller finds himself in their exalted abode, about 180 feet above the level of the ground from which he started."

The social condition of the Albanians Captain Best describes as most deplorable; and their misery he attributes entirely to the misrule of the Turks. Nothing indeed can surpass his aversion to the people last named.

"The population (of Greeks and Turks) can never amalgamate: Turkey can never be regenerated entirely; she may remain in her present state for some years, and, propped up by the external influence of the great nations of Europe interested in keeping her together as long as possible for the preservation of the balance of power, and to prevent the far greater evil of endless and bloody contentions amongst themselves for the detached portions, her fall may be gradual; limb after limb may be severed from her without occasioning any great commotion; but come the time must and will when her influence, stability, and strength, dwindled away to a shadow, will become entirely exhausted, and the Ottoman empire will be no more. That her fall may be gradual, is earnestly to be desired; but to prevent her fall is impossible.

We may alleviate the sufferings of the dying patient, and prevent her immediate decease; but to restore her to health is out of the question.

"Great Britain may further the cause of humanity, by exerting her influence to introduce civilization among the Turks; but she ought not to forget that a great portion of their enslaved population professes the same faith with herself—that it is a christian population, oppressed by the tyrannical rule of a heathen despot; and that if it be her policy to keep them under Turkish rule, she is bound to use her influence to render the yoke which they bear less insupportable. Let not Great Britain indulge in the chimerical notion of regenerating Turkey, of endeavouring to make her resume her place in the scale of nations; she may artificially prop up for a time the falling empire, but piece by piece will continue to be detached from it, until it dwindles away to a shadow. The Turkish moon is on the wane, and must ere long set for ever."

An English Grammar for Classical Schools; being a Practical Introduction to English Prose Composition. By THOMAS KERCHEVER ARNOLD, M.A., *Rector of Lyndon, and late Fellow of Trin. Coll. Cambridge. Second Edition, enlarged.* London: Rivingtons. 12mo. Pp. 216.

THE majority of our readers probably have but little acquaintance with the grammars that are now used in English schools. So entirely, indeed, has the science been neglected of late years, that, forgetting the labours of Ben Jonson and Professor Wallis, Englishmen have contentedly resigned themselves to the instruction of certain Scotch schoolmasters, (Lennie, Macculloch, Reid, &c.,) who, being ignorant alike of the general principles of language, and of the genius of the English language in particular, have invented a multitude of such absurd rules as set philosophy, analogy, and common sense most completely at defiance, and have rendered English grammar a very by-word among foreigners. The first person who came forward to retrieve the English language (for Dr. Samuel Johnson was in no condition to perform the task, and Horne Tooke's unsystematic works had but small influence) was Mr. Richardson, who, in the little sketch of etymology prefixed to his admirable dictionary, attempted to bring people back to the simple principles of the earlier grammarians. The present writer, we trust, will do yet much more. Mr. Arnold does not appear to have studied the old grammarians; but he is well acquainted with modern continental works, which have thrown much light upon the general principles of grammar; and being himself a good scholar, we apprehend, has inflicted a serious blow upon the popularity of Messrs. Lindley Murray and Co.

At the same time, we should state, that Mr. Arnold very modestly calls his treatise "the offspring of despair rather than of knowledge;" and we are certainly far from considering it to have attained perfection. Some faults we shall now mention. 1. The classification of the verbs might be considerably simplified. The true formation of the past tense he rightly asserts to be by changing the radical vowel of the present; but, instead of making five varieties of this rule, we would suggest, that two are quite sufficient; one when the participle appears to be made from the present, and the second, when it does not appear to be made from the present, but from the past tense. 2. We think that the whole of Syntax might be greatly compressed; especially we would advise him to get rid of the pedantry of "predicative and objective combination."

Nevertheless, after making deduction for these and other points admitting of improvement, we strongly recommend this grammar as *the best* in existence. And we do not see at all why it should not be introduced in commercial as well as "classical" schools.

Ecclesiastica; or, the Church, her Schools, and her Clergy. By EDWARD MAHON ROOSE, *of Lincoln's Inn, Esq.* London: Hatchards. 1842. 8vo. Pp. 448.

THIS is not a book of which we can find it in our hearts to speak harshly. The intentions of the author are evidently good; and so much of his work as is purely statistical or historical—as the notice of our public schools and universities, and the lists of bishops who have occupied the various sees—is really useful. Those portions, however, which depend more upon the knowledge and principles of the author are lamentably deficient. For instance, Chapter VI., pretending to give a catalogue of "our great theologians," while it finds room for Abbot, Chillingworth, Tillotson, Hooper, S. Clarke, Hoadly, Sherlock, Secker, Paley, Heber,—has no mention of Bull, Waterland, Bingham, Wheatley, Collyer, Wilson, Patrick! Chapter VII., among our great "literary and scientific divines," gives Archbishop Juxon, Archbishop Markham, and Bishop Porteus! and the concluding chapter gravely enumerates Messrs. Wrangham, M'Neile, Croly, Stowell, Stebbing, Close, and Baptist Noel, (with about five other names somewhat more to the purpose) as the "eminent divines of the Church in modern times!" Indeed, this last chapter is in the worst style of that most abominable of books, of most abominable of writers, Grant's "Sketches of Popular Preachers," besides being full of inaccuracies.

Evangelical Repentance: a Sermon preached in the Cathedral Church of Winchester, in aid of the Societies for "Promoting Christian Knowledge" and "the Propagation of the Gospel in Foreign Parts." By the Rev. CHARLES WORDSWORTH, M.A., *Second Master of Winchester College, late Student and Tutor of Christ Church, Oxford.* Oxford: Parker. 8vo. Pp. 70. *Also Appendix to the same.*

WE shall not be surprised to hear that this sermon causes offence to some who read it, as it did to some who heard it preached. Nevertheless, we hesitate not to say that we rejoice in its publication. Does this mean that we are regardless, at this critical moment, of the responsibility of giving offence? Far otherwise. But we are so deeply impressed with the miserable condition of modern theology, that we are willing to run some risk, in the hope of seeing it amended; especially when the correction is offered in the amiable and distrustful tone of the present writer. The object of Mr. Wordsworth is, to discriminate between the two uses of the word repentance; the one as it is sealed in baptism, the other as it is vouchsafed to "sin after baptism;" the types respectively, as he ingeniously shows, of the two Societies in behalf of which he was pleading. In establishing this most scriptural position, he hazards, as we have hinted, some unfortunate suggestions or conjectures (they are nothing more). But while our Clergy are habitually speaking peace where there is no peace, and complacently applying to congregations of backsliding Christians texts (as, " Believe in the Lord Jesus, and thou shalt be saved ;" —" though your sins be as scarlet," &c.) which must be understood with reference mainly to the primary remission of sins in baptism, it is scarcely to be wondered at (though yet we must regret it) that one who has been schooled in a better tone of theology, should make a somewhat too earnest protest against so fatal and treacherous a delusion. Of course, " the grant of repentance is not to be denied to such as fall into sin after baptism;" and if the Church seems to restrict the conditions on which it is offered, she gives (and it is a remarkable proof of the completeness of her system—the divine economy as opposed to man's invention), in the absolving power of her apostolical ministry, *assurance* of pardon, which will commend itself to the wounded conscience far beyond the readiest promises of the sectarian preacher.

The Voice of the Church on the Doctrine of Repentance; a Sermon, extracted from the First and Second Part of the Thirty-second Homily of the Church of England. By the Rev. WILLIAM SINCLAIR, M. A., *Incumbent of St. Georges's Church, Leeds.* Leeds: Harrison. London: Houlston and Stoneman.

THIS is, we suspect, the effusion of a Clergyman, who is labouring under considerable excitement of feeling from late controversies, and who does not duly dread the self-indulgence of his congregation; the season of Lent being, we believe, a season of peculiar gaiety in the religious world. In addressing his congregation in a popular discourse, Mr. Sinclair could not do better than read to them one of the homilies; but he ought to be aware, that it is the mark of a disingenuous mind to quote from only one of the formularies of the Church, and to call *that* the voice of the Church; for i is through *all* of her formularies that the Church speaks; and in the *Commination* service, which Mr. Sinclair ought to have read on Ash-Wednesday, the voice of the Church is heard expressing a wish, that notorious sinners may be put " to open penance and punished in this world, that their souls may be saved in the day of the Lord." This is not inconsistent with the homily, but it is very inconsistent with Mr. Sinclair's introductory remarks. The homilies being popular discourses, require, when quoted on points of doctrine, to be explained by the other formularies of the Church, unless men are prepared to receive the Apocrypha as canonical, and to admit the existence of other sacraments besides the two which are generally necessary to salvation. The notes to this publication are weak, and betray a bitter spirit.

Dr. Croly has just collected into a volume (Seeleys) his "Historical Sketches, Speeches, and Characters;" but in the case of a writer so well known, the reviewer may well be spared a long notice. Dr. Croly has all the characteristic eloquence of his countrymen, and possesses that peculiar vision which also marks modern Irishmen, of seeing but one evil in the world—the existence of Popery.

Sir Henry Ellis has lately published a new and amended edition of Brand's "Observations on Popular Antiquities, chiefly illustrating the Origin of our Vulgar Customs, Ceremonies, and Superstitions." (London, Knight.) The first of the two volumes contains a notice of the several holidays mentioned in the Calendar, from New Year's Eve to "Childermas, or Holy Innocents' Day." The second describes many national customs, games, &c. now fast disappearing from our land.

We cordially recommend "A Clergyman's Address to the Wesleyan Methodists in his Parish," by the Rev. Robert Eden, M.A., Rector of Leigh, Essex. (Rivingtons.) It is chiefly occupied with exposing the departure from their original principles which has taken place in this body.

Dr. Robert Phillimore's "Letter to Lord Ashburton, suggested by the Questions of International Law raised in the Message of the American President," (Hatchards,) we can assure our readers, will well repay perusal. It is a temperate appeal to those principles on which christian nations have consented to act in their intercourse with one another. The conclusions are not those of the writer of the Letter, but of the highest juridical authorities; and we do not envy the American publicists the duty of reply. It should be stated that the Letter is almost entirely confined to the questions arising out of the Canadian rebellion of 1837, of which it gives a most succinct history.

The Rev. John Bentall, M.A., one of the ushers of Westminster School, has published "Remarks" upon the system of education there pursued; upon which *we* would *remark*, that if the author desires parents to send their children to the school, he had much better not write silly pamphlets.

We are glad to announce another number of that must unexceptionable series of publications, called the "Edinburgh Cabinet Library." (Oliver and Boyd.) It contains a complete history of Mesopotamia and Assyria, from the earliest ages to the present time, and proceeds from the experienced pen of Mr. J. Baillie Fraser.

"The History of the Fairchild Family," Part 2, by Mrs. Sherwood (Hatchard and Son), is intended to "show the importance and effects of a religious education." The principal characters are a brother and sister, the types respectively, according to the author's views, of virtue and vice, and the former of whom is instructed nightly to indite prayers for "the conversion" of her scapegrace brother. We only hope for our friends, that they may not have either a "Bernard" or a "Lucinda" in their families; nor yet be obliged to read Mrs. Sherwood's 360 closely-printed 8vo pages.

Archdeacon Todd has just put forth an excellent little pamphlet on "Clerical Societies," (Rivingtons,) tracing their progress in England and showing on what principles they should be conducted. We recommend it to our clerical readers as a very interesting and seasonable publication.

"The Historical Character of St. Luke's First Chapter Vindicated," &c., being the Christian Advocate's Publication for 1841, by W. H. Mill, D.D. &c., Chaplain to his Grace the Archbishop of Canterbury, is a work which can stand in no need of eulogium of ours. Cordially do we congratulate the Church of England on so sound and learned a divine being placed in so conspicuous a position.

"Two New Arguments in Vindication of the Genuineness and Authenticity of the Revelation of St. John," &c. by John Collyer Knight (Rivingtons, 1842), have given us no ordinary satisfaction. They are the productions of a man at once learned, ingenious, intelligent, and seemingly pious. The book deserves very great attention. We have but two faults to find with it; one is, that the author (unintentionally of course) exaggerates, in our judgment, the doubtfulness of the Apocalypse, previous to his arguments; secondly, that his mode of speaking of the high mystery of regeneration (p. 27) almost amounts to a rationalistic explaining away thereof.

Mr. Palmer's (of Magdalen College, Oxford) pamphlets, entitled "A Letter to a Protestant Catholic," and "Aids to Reflection on the double Character of the Anglican Church," are well known. They have produced three letters to him from the Rev. F. D. Maurice, (Rivingtons; Darton and Clarke, 1842,) in which that author's great powers of thought are signally displayed.

Dr. Hook has also published a pamphlet, entitled, "Reasons for Contributing towards the Support of a Protestant Bishoprick at Jerusalem," (Rivingtons, 1842.) Every one must be glad to know Dr. Hook's opinion on any question connected with the Church, and in the present pamphlet they will find it on others besides that announced in the title-page.

"The Swearer's End," and "The Widow's Son," are two excellent tracts lately published by the Christian Knowledge Society, which we recommend for distribution.

A letter has been addressed to us, along with two of our contemporaries, by a writer who signs himself Veles, in reply to Col. Mitchell's Argument for the Abolition of Promotion by Purchase in the Army, (Burns, 1841.) The subject is rather out of our beat, but *Veles* seems a sound thinker and writer, and deserves attention.

The Rev. J. Sinclair has addressed "A Letter to a Member of Parliament on National Education," (Rivingtons, 1842,) on which subject, we need not say, the author ranks among the highest authorities. From the same pen (of course) has just proceeded, "The National Society's Report for 1841." We must call attention too to a paper on the late proceedings of the Society, which will be found appended to our present number, and the dissemination of which is to be desired.

We request our musical readers to notice that a publication has been commenced in Dublin, (Robinson and Bussell,) entitled, "The Choralist," under the patronage of several of the Irish prelates. Its object is the improvement of Church Music. We shall perhaps have occasion to speak more particularly of it and other recent musical works in a little while. At present we shall merely say that there are some obvious advantages in the arrangement, which distinguish it from other publications of the same kind.

A second edition has come out of Mr. Poole's pamphlet on the State of Parties in the Church.

"The Leeds Tracts" are once more being continued, after a long suspension. They are now embellished with a vignette of the parish church of Leeds on the cover.

Archdeacon Wilkins has taken occasion, from the opening of a second Romish Chapel in his parish, to issue an address to his parishioners, (Rivingtons, 1842,) guarding them against the dangers to which they are on every side exposed. A Church Building Society (of which a notice will be found in our Intelligence for this month) has just been instituted for the town and county of Nottingham, which we trust will do much to counteract Popery, as well as every other form of error which may appear.

We must also congratulate the inhabitants of Nottingham in possessing an excellent newspaper, "the Nottingham Journal," and that well-planned institution, "the Englishman's Library," to which we last year called attention.

Apropos of newspapers, "The Church," in Canada, has a worthy kinsman in "The Churchman," at New York. We are very glad to have the privilege of seeing two such sound principled organs of our distant brethren.

We leave the following paragraphs in the hands of our readers. They require no comment.

"Wesleyan Tracts for the Times." Within the last twelve months, the most strenuous efforts have been made, by the distribution of tracts, to unsettle the minds of the members of the Wesleyan societies on the subject of religion. They are told that the ministry which they attend is in every respect invalid; so that they have no sacraments, and, in fact, no scriptural warrant to expect any spiritual blessing from God. They are also vehemently accused of having departed from the principles of their founder, to which they are solemnly pledged. Most of these publications are drawn up with singular unfairness, so far as the views of Mr. Wesley are concerned; the writers making them, by the suppression of truth, vehicles of direct falsehood. Some of these tracts are printed in Oxford; others in London; and the most active agents in their distribution are junior Clergymen, who abet the pernicious errors of Dr. Pusey and his party. It was hoped that this evil would be of short continuance; as it was thought that no men, bearing the sacred name of Christian, and professing to be scholars, and men of honour, would permanently lend themselves to a practice which compromises some of the most sacred principles of morality.

This hope, however, has been disappointed. The nuisance is widely extended, and increases daily. The Wesleyan ministers and societies are therefore informed, that a series of tracts is in a course of preparation, and will be published with all convenient speed, under the general title of "Wesleyan Tracts for the Times," unfolding Mr. Wesley's real views of ecclesiastical order, vindicating the ministers and people who at present bear his honoured name, and supplying an antidote to the ill-disguised popery which has ominously arisen in the heart of the Protestant Establishment of this country. The first of these tracts, it is hoped, will be published on the 23d of February, and the rest will follow at stated intervals, of which due notice will be given. The attention of the Wesleyan connexion in general is respectfully invited to this announcement. The "Wesleyan Tracts for the Times" will not be an attack upon any body of Christians, but an earnest defence of an injured people against a race of intolerant and unscrupulous assailants.

A sixth volume of sermons by Mr. Newman (Rivingtons, 1842,) is an announcement which speaks for itself. We need only say that they are devoted to subjects appropriate to the spring quarter.

"The Union between Christ and his People," is the title given by the Rev. C. A. Heurtley, B.D. Rector of Fenny Compton, Warwickshire, &c., to four Sermons preached before the University of Oxford, which, judging from a very cursory glance, seem to contain valuable matter.

The Rev. T. Ainger, of Hampstead, has published five sermons, (Parker, London; Richardson, Greenwich,) by way of legacy to his flock at St. Mary's, Greenwich. His merits as a preacher have long been known.

"The Unity of the Church," by Archdeacon S. Wilberforce, (Williams, Eton;) "Catholicity and Protestantism," by the Rev. J. W. Blakesley, Fellow and Tutor] of Trin. Coll. Cambridge; and "Christian Forbearance," by the Rev. E. Hawkins, are single sermons which will well repay perusal.

We must also call attention to the following sermons:—"The Profession of the True Faith," by the Rev. W. N. Leger, A. B. "The Prospects of Africa," by the Rev. F. D. Morgan, (Seeley, 1841.) "The Claims of the Church," by the Rev. H. J. Stevenson, M. A. (Rivingtons.) "Against Insubordination, especially in Spiritual Things," by a Clergyman of the Church of England, (Lee, 1842.) "The Church of England and Five of her Societies," by the Rev. R. Parkinson, B.D. (Rivingtons, Burns, 1842.) "The Duty and Doctrine of the Servant of Christ," by the Rev. H. L. Knight Bruce, M. A.; and "The Origin of Death and the Remedy for Death," by the Rev. J. Stoddart, D.D. (Rivingtons, 1841.)

ECCLESIASTICAL INTELLIGENCE.

ORDINATIONS.

BP. OF SODOR AND MANN, at *Bishop's Court, Jan.* 23.

PRIEST.

Of Dublin.—A. Williamson, B.A. Trinity Coll.

BP. of BANGOR, *Feb.* 19.

DEACON.

Of Oxford.—E. Lewis, M.A. Jesus Coll.

BP. OF SALISBURY, (for BP. of BATH AND WELLS,) *Feb.* 20.

DEACONS.

Of Oxford.—E. Machen, B.A. Exeter Coll.
Of Cambridge.—R. Burridge, B.A. John's.

PRIESTS.

Of Oxford.—J. C. Broune, B.A. Wadh.; E. Holland, B.A. Magd. Hall.
Of Cambridge.—J. B. D'Aguilar, B.A. John's; J. R. Watson, B.A. Magd.

BP. of DURHAM, *at Auckland Castle, Feb.* 6.

DEACONS.

Of Cambridge.—C. Thornhill, B.A. Emm.

PRIESTS.

Of Cambridge.—C. A. Raines, B.A. John's. J. Marshall.

BP. of LINCOLN, *Feb.* 20.

DEACONS.

Of Oxford.—H. Neville, B.A. Trin.; E. Shepherd, B.A. Exet.
Of Cambridge.—R. E. Monins, B.A. John's; S. L. Wilson, B.A. St. Peter's; R. Baldock, B.A. John's; J. Teague, B.A. Emm.

PRIESTS.

Of Oxford.—R. Eddie, B.A., N. Morgan, B.A. Brasen.; D. B. Raunsley, B.A. Fell. of Magd.

Of Cambridge.—E. Balston, B.A., W. L. Elliott, M.A., Fellows of King's; H. D. Jones, B.A. Pem.; H. Stockdale, B.A. Cath. Hall.
Of Dublin.—J. D. Hare, LL.B.

BP. OF PETERBOROUGH, *Feb.* 20.

PRIESTS.

Of Oxford.—C. Clarke, B.A. Trin. Coll.; J. W. Deane, B.A. John's; M. W. W. Russell, B.A. Ch. Ch.; A. H. Smith, B.A. Edm.
Of Cambridge.—S. Alford, B.A. Queen's; R. Bickersteth, B.A. Queen's; W. A. Francis, B.A. Christ's; H. Harris, B.A. Cath. Hall; R. M. Sharpe, B.A. John's; D. Pooley, M.A. John's.
Literate.—E. Robinson.

DEACONS.

Of Oxford.—F. W. Cartwright, B.A. St. Mary's.
Of Cambridge.—R. H. Killick, B.A. Queen's.

BP. OF SARUM, *Feb.* 20.

DEACONS.

Of Oxford.—H. B. Mason, B.A.; N. I. Hall; H. Phillips, M.A. Queen's; J. Tyler, B.A. Ball.; R. F. Meredith, M.A. Worc.; P. F. Britton, B.A. Exeter; J. J. Reynolds, B.A. John's.
Of Cambridge.—R. J. Rowton, B.A. John's.
Of Dublin.—W. Badham, B.A.
Of Lampeter.—R. Jones.

PRIESTS.

Of Oxford.—R. Cosens, B.A. Pemb.; C. Forth, S.C.L. Magd. Hall; C. F. Baker, B.A. Exeter; H. J. Dixon, B.A. Mary Hall; E. Stewart, M.A. Oriel; E. Golding, M.A. Brasen.; C. L. Courtenay, M.A. Ch. Ch.
Of Cambridge.—W. C. Lukes, B.A. Trin.; O. P. Vincent, B.A. Magd.
Literate.—F. Langhorne; C. P. Badger, of Ch. Miss. Col. Islington, for her Majesty's Foreign Possessions, by lett. dim. from Bp. of London.

ORDINATIONS APPOINTED.

BP. OF LICHFIELD, *March* 20.
BP. OF HEREFORD, *May* 22.
BP. OF OXFORD, *May* 22.
BP. OF LONDON, *May* 22.

BP. OF PETERBOROUGH, *May* 22.
BP. OF ELY, *June* 5.
BP. OF WINCHESTER, *July* 10.

PREFERMENTS.

The Rev. A. T. Gilbert, D.D. to be Bishop of Chichester.

Name.	Preferment.	County.	Diocese.	Patron.	Val.	Pop.
Allies, T. W.	Launton, R.	Oxford	Oxford	Bp. of London	£*618	570
Arnold, E.	Loudwater, P.C.	Bucks	Linc.		—	592
Baker, F. E.	Allensmore, V.	Heref.	Hereford	Dean of Hereford	—	592
Bennett, W.	Crantock, P.C.	Cornwall	Exeter	Sir J. Y. Buller	78	458
Bloomfield, J.	Orsett, R.	Essex	London	Bp. of London	*577	1274
Bowen, J.	Llandeloy, V.	Pembroke	St. David's	D. & C. of St. David's	120	303
Broughton, H. V.	Wellingborough, V.	Northampt.	Peterboro'	Q. Vivian, Esq.	400	4688
Burr, J. H. S.	Tidenham, V.	Gloucester	G. & B.;	D. H. Burr, Esq.	*441	1180
Butterfield, H.	Fulmer, R.	Bucks	Lincoln	D. & C. of Windsor	*285	391
Calthorpe, H.	Gt. Branded, R.	Essex	London	C. C. Coll. Camb.	*544	471

Intelligence.

PREFERMENTS,—continued.

Name.	Preferment.	County.	Diocese.	Patron.	Val.	Pop.
Compton, J.	Minstead, R.	Hants	Winch.	H. C. Compton, Esq.	*£355	2310
Cox, A.	Askerswell, R.	Dorset	Sarum	Rev. J. Cox	*160	228
Davies, D.	Kevenllys, R.	Radnor	St. David's	Bp. of St. David's	135	367
Forester, O.W.W.	Broseley, R.	Salop	Lichfield	Lord Forester	*432	4400
Gregsan, J.	Upton Overchurch, P.C.	Cheshire	Chester	W. Webster, Esq.	*52	191
Grimston, Hon. & Rev. E. H.	Colne's Wake	Essex	London	Earl of Verulam	*458	442
Haughton, W.	Pattersbury, V.	Northampt.	Peterboro'	Earl Bathurst	*116	1544
Hooper, W. T. H.	St. Paul's, Withington	Lanc.	Chester	Trustees.		
Hopkins, B.	Barban, P.C.	Westmor.	Carlisle	Rev. J. H. Fisher	*66	320
Hughes, I.	Llandyfriog, V.	Cardigan	St. David's	Bp. of St. David's	147	854
Jesson, F.	Spittlegate, P.C. Grantham	Linc.	Linc.	Bp. of Lincoln.		
Kendall, J. H. F.	Hutton Roof, P.C.	Westmor.		Vic. of Kirkby Lonsdale	70	351
Leach, W. C.	Little Stonham, R.	Suffolk	Norwich	W. Haydon, Esq.	*360	329
Lowe, J. M.	Grindleton, P. C.	Yorkshire		Rev. J. A. Addison	85	1103
Morgan, P. H.	Bettws, P.C.	Brecon	St. David's		98	830
North, J. H.	Carbrooke, V.	Norfolk	Norw.	R. Dewing, Esq.	108	789
Nosworthy, S.	Buckland Filleigh	Devon	Exet.	Bp. of Exeter	218	317
O'Donoghue, F.T.	Over Peover, P.C.	Cheshire	Chester	Sir H. Mainwaring	92	561
Orlebar, J. C.	Hockliffe c. Chalgrave, P.C.	Beds	Ely		*393	1206
Paget, T. B.	Evington, V.	Leicester	Linc.	Bp. of London	41	260
Parsons, F. J.	Selborne, V.	Hants	Winch.	Magd. Coll. Oxf.		924
Price, J.	Treddyn, P.C.	Flint	St. Asaph	Bp. of St. Asaph		
Rowlandson, J.	Mardale, P.C.	Westmor.	Carlisle			
Sabine, J.	Thorne Coffin, R.	Somerset	B. & Wells		200	101
Snow, T.	Newton Valence, V.	Hants	Winch.	Rev. E. Auriol	*512	466
Stratton, J.	Graveney & Goodnestane. V.	Kent	Canterbury	Abp. of Canterbury	400	217
Stuart, J. H.	Ampton, R.	Suffolk	Norwich	Lord Calthorpe	*172	110
Thompson, R.	Shotley, P.C.	Northumb.	Durham	Bp. Crewe's Trustees	*139	1104
Tripp, R. H.	Altarnum, V.	Cornwall	Exeter	D. & C. of Exeter	*320	1069
Trollope, J. J.	Wigmore, V.	Hereford	Hereford	Bp. of Hereford	124	429
White, E.	Trin. Ch. P.C. Wray	Lancash.	Chester			
Williams, J.	Llangevelack		St. David's	Bp. of St. David's.		
Williams, T.	Etloughton, v.	Yorks.		Rev. H. S. Markham	97	355

₀ *The Asterisk denotes a Residence House.*

APPOINTMENTS.

Archdall, — ...... Prebend. of Norwich.
Beckett, W. ...... Surrogate Dioc. of Durham.
Churton, H. B. W. { Exam. Chap. to Bp. of Chichester.
Cotton, G. .... Surrogate Lioc. of Lichfield.
Cox, J. .... Surrogate Dioc. of Chester.
Dobson, W. .... { Surrogate of Archdeaconry of Nottingham.
Fessey, G. F. ..... A Rural Dean of Wick.
Frampton, J. ...... Rural Dean of Stonehouse.
Lane, E. .... { Clerical Principal, Gloucester Dioc. School.
Langharne, — ... Dom. Chap. Earl of Warwick.
Layng, T. F. ...... { Head Master Bristol Dioc. & Cathedral Middle School.

Lodge, B. .... Chaplain at Buenos Ayres.
Maunsell, G. E. ... { Dom. Chap. to Earl of Westmoreland.
Morgan, O. .... Chap. to the "Vindictive."
Nevill, W. .... { Chaplain of Borough Gaol, Maldon.
Rushton, W. ..... { Second Master of Brewood Grammar School.
Smith, E. .... { Master and Librarian of Abp. Tenison's School.
Thornton, W. J. ... Prebend. of Hereford.
Wilkin, A. .... Chap. to Lord Lowther.
Willan, W. W. ... { Vice-Princip. Ch. of England Prop. School, Huddersfield.

CLERGYMEN DECEASED.

Bate, H., at Southsea.
Blackley, T., Vic. of Rotherham, Yorksh.
Bewick, T., Cur. of Ilketshall, Bungay.
Bree, R. F., 66.
Boys, R. B., Chap. of Old Ch., Calcutta, 38.
Campbell, A. C., at Canterbury, 68.
De Brett, H. S., Rec. Broughton, Linc. 40.
Denys, T. Vic. of Bourne, Linc.
Hext, F. J., Rec. of Holland, Cornwall.
Hopkins, D., at Cheltenham, 43.
Howels, H., late Cur. of St. Lytham's, Gloucester, 92.

James, T., Rec. Llandevelly, Brecon, 76.
Manners, M., Rector of Thelveton, Norfolk.
Paris, S., at Leamington, 88.
Powys, Honourable & Rev. J., R. Titchmarsh, 81.
Shirley, T. H., Rec. of St. Swithin's, 59.
Thackeray, F., Cur. of Broxbourne.
Threlkeld, P., Per. Cur. of Melburn Chapel, Westmoreland, 43.
Webber, E. Rec. Runnington, Somerset, 78.
Wilkinson, W., Vic. of Glentham, Linc.

UNIVERSITIES.

OXFORD.

Jan. 29.

A letter of thanks from the Bishop of Barbadoes was read in convocation, acknowledging the grant of 150*l.* from the University chest, to be expended in books printed at the University Press, for the use of Codrington College, in the island of Barbados.

The following gentlemen were admitted *ad eundem*:—

Rev. F. D. Gilby, M.A. Clare Hall, Cambridge; J. Fleming, M.A. Trin. Coll. Dub.

Degrees conferred.

B.D.

Rev. T. Evans, Oriel Coll.

M.A.

Rev. E. F. Witts. Magd.Hall; C. E. Thornhill, Ch. Ch.; Rev. E. W. Garrow, Brasen.; Rev. E. Rawnsley, Brasen.; Rev. G. Sandbach, Brasen.; Rev. H. W. Steele, Jes.; Rev. F. A. Iremonger, Scholar of Pemb.; Rev. H. Combs, Fell. John's; Rev. G. A. Blakely, Wor.

B.A.

P. Butler, Stud. Ch. Ch.; G. Philimore, Stud. Ch. Ch.; J. F. B. Blackett, Stud. Ch. Ch.; W. E. Rawstorpe, Stud. Ch. Ch.; C. Simeon, Ch. Ch.; M. Portal, Ch. Ch.; N. Midwinter, Magd. Hall; T. Jones, Magd. Hall; T. P. Wilson, Scholar of Brasen.; C. H. Langhorne, Exet.

D.D.

Rev. T. Evans, of Oriel, and Head Master of the College School at Gloucester.

Feb. 5.

LINCOLN COLLEGE.

Three open Scholarships, and two Exhibitions on Lord Crewe's foundation, will be filled up on Thursday, March 17th. Candidates for the Exhibitions must be natives of the diocese of Durham; and in default of such, of North Allertonshire or Howdenshire, in the county of York; or of the counties of Leicester, Oxford, or Northampton.

The usual testimonials, accompanied, in the case of the Exhibitions, by authentic vouchers for the place of birth, are to be presented, in person, to the Rector on Saturday, March 12th.

The following gentlemen have been admitted *ad eundem*:—

Rev. J. H. Wilding, M.A. Trin. Coll. Camb.; Rev. F. V. Thornton, M.A. Trin. Coll. Camb.; Rev. C. Mayor, M.A. Trin. Coll. Camb.

Degrees conferred.

M.A.

Rev. J. Thompson, Linc.; Rev. J. Carthew, Exet.; Rev. J.Ward, New Coll.; Rev. R.Powell, Worc.; G. J. Bell, Balliol.

B.A.

W. Savage, Queen's Coll.; I. J. I. Pocock, Merton; S. Johnson, Merton; F. Bowles, Oriel; C. C. Clifford, Ch. Ch.; E. A. Ferryman, Univ.

B.M.

Mr. J. K. Pye, Magd. hall.

Feb. 12.

Rev. R M. Dukes, M.A. Linc. Coll. admitted Fellow of Queen's Coll. on Michel's foundation.

Mr. W. E. C. Austin, Scholar of New Coll. admitted Actual Fell. of that society.

Mr. G. W. Pearse, Commoner of Trinity Coll. elected to a Scholarship of Corpus.

Examiners for the Scholarship for the promotion of Latin Literature, usually known as the Hertford Scholarship:—

Rev. F. A. Faber, B.D. Fell. Magd. Coll. Rev. W. Jacobson, M.A. Vice-Principal of Magd. Hall.
Rev. J. A. Hessey, M.A. Fell. St. John's Coll.

Degrees conferred.

B.M. WITH LICENSE TO PRACTISE.

G. J. Bell, Balliol.

M.A.

Rev. C. Davenport, Worc. grand compounder; G. E. H. Vernon, Stud. of Ch. Ch.; Rev. O. J. Humphreys, Jesus; Rev. T. Pearse, Demy of Magd.; Rev. B. H. Adams, Exet.; Rev. H. Crawley, Balliol; Rev. W. Hulme, Balliol.

B.A.

H. Champernowne, Trin. grand compounder. C. S. Slocock. Trin.

C. Reade, Esq. M.A. Fell. of Magd. and Senior Schol. on the Vinerian Foundation, elected Fell. on the same Foundation.

Rev. W. Monkhouse, M.A. Fell. of Queen's College, and Rev. J. S. Pinkerton, M.A. Fell. of St. John's, elected Proctors for the ensuing year.

CAMBRIDGE.

Jan. 29.

Mr. G. Jarvis, B.A. and Mr. J. Fenwicke, B.A. of Corp. Chr. Coll. elected Fellows of that society.

The following gentlemen have been this year elected to the Scholarships at Clare Hall:—

1. Atkinson. 2. Bryans. 3. Mann.
4. Frampton. 5. Jubb. 6. Nelson.

R. Merry, Esq. B.A. Lay Fellow of Jesus Coll. was nominated to a Foundation Fellowship by the Society; the confirmation of this appointment rests with the Bishop of Ely. Both this and the previous election of H. A. Woodham, Esq. were made under the new statutes which have been lately granted to the college.

Mr. G. M. Sykes, of Trinity Coll. has been elected a Fellow of Downing College.

Mr. G. Allen, son of the Bishop of Ely, has been elected Warden of Dulwich College.

Feb. 5.
Degrees conferred.

B.C.L.

R. Coote, Fellow of Trin. Hall.

B.A.

J. Green, Caius; W. S. Chalk, Caius.

Bell Scholarships.—The Vice-Chancellor has given notice, that an election of two Scholars upon this Foundation will take place on Friday, the 11th of March, 1842, and that the Members of any College (except King's College and Trinity Hall) sons or orphans of Clergymen, who were admitted between the commencements of 1840 and 1841, may be candidates. The candidates are required to signify their intention of offering themselves on or before Thursday, the 10th of February, in a Latin Epistle, to be presented to each of the electors, who are — the Vice-Chancellor, Dr. Turton; Regius Professor of Divinity, Dr. Geldart; Regius Professor of the Civil Law, Dr. King; Lucasian Professor, Mr. Crick, Public Orator. The examination will commence on Monday, the 14th February, at ten o'clock in the forenoon, in the Senate-house. Each candidate will be expected to leave with the Vice-Chancellor (together with his Epistle) a certificate from his college of the date of his admission, and of the terms that he has kept.

Rev. J. H. Jerrard, M.A. elected a Senior Fellow, and the Rev. C. Clayton, M.A. a Frankland Fellow of Caius college.

Dr. Smith's prizes of 25*l.* each to the two best proficients in Mathematics, were last Saturday adjudged as follow:—

First Prize.—Ds. Cayley, Trinity Coll. (1st Wrangler). *Second Prize.*—Ds. Simpson, St. John's (2nd Wrangler).

In a Convocation holden at Oxford, the Rev. F. D. Kilby, M.A. of Clare Hall, admitted *ad eundem.*

Degrees conferred.

M.A.

W. H. Simpson, St. John's; C. J. Pearson, Trin. Coll.

B.A.

J. Shelley, St. Peter's; J. Kinder, Trin.Coll.; J. Hallifax, Corp. Chr.; J. F. Harward, John's; H. J. Marshall, John's; A. W. Mactier, Trin.; O. H. Flowers, Queen's.

The prize of books, at Christ's College, for the best composition in Latin Verse, has been adjudged to John Purchas, Esq.

The prize of Christ's College, for the best composition in Latin prose, has been adjudged to Mr. Davenport.

The Pitt Scholarship has been adjudged to Edward Hamilton Gifford, of St.John's College.

At the Lent Term Matriculation, on Tuesday last, one fellow-commoner and twenty-five pensioners were matriculated.

The Professor of Botany has given notice that he will commence his lectures on Wednesday, April 13, in the schools at the Botanic garden, at one o'clock. Herborizing excursions in the neighbourhood will take place as the weather may permit.

Mr. Johnson, K.S. captain of Eton, has been elected to the scholarship of King's College, in this university, vacant by the marriage of the son of Sir John Chapman, of Windsor.

PROCEEDINGS OF SOCIETIES.

INCORPORATED SOCIETY FOR PROMOTING THE ENLARGEMENT, BUILDING, AND REPAIRING OF CHURCHES AND CHAPELS.

A meeting of the Committee of this Society was held at their chambers, St. Martin's Place, on Monday, the 21st of February, 1842; the Lord Bishop of Carlisle in the chair. Among the members present were the Bps. of Hereford and Worcester, the Lord Kenyon, the Very Rev. the Dean of Chichester, the Revs. Dr. Spry, Dr. D'Oyly, Dr. Shepherd, B. Harrison, H. H. Norris, and J. Lonsdale, J. S. Salt, N. Connop, jun., J. Cocks, W. Davis, and J. W. Bowden, Esqs., &c. &c.

Grants were voted towards building a chapel at Worthen, Salop; building a chapel at East Grafton, in the parish of Great Bedwyn, Wilts; building a church at Farsley, in the parish of Calverley, Yorkshire; building a church at Queen's Head, in the parish of Halifax, Yorkshire; rebuilding a church at New Radnor, Radnorshire; enlarging by rebuilding the church at Swallowcliffe, Wilts; enlarging by rebuilding the church at Burghfield, Berks; building a chapel at Llanfair, in the parish of Llantillio Cressenny, Monmouthshire; repewing and erecting a gallery in the church of St. Mary Magdalen, at Taunton, Somersetshire; repewing and rebuilding gallery in the church at Harlington, Middlesex; repewing and building a gallery in the church at East Coker, Somersetshire; erecting a gallery in the church at Creeting, Suffolk; repewing the church at Neston, Cheshire; enlarging the church at High Littleton, Somersetshire; building a gallery in the church at Biggleswade, Bedfordshire; enlarging the church at Camerton, Somerset; repewing the church at Llanviothan, Merionethshire; enlarging by rebuilding the church of St. Nicholas, in the city of Hereford; and other business was transacted.

SOCIETY FOR PROPAGATING THE GOSPEL IN FOREIGN PARTS.

(From a Report of a Visit to Prince Edward Island, by the Ven. Archdeacon Willis.)

* * * * * *

AFTER this we had a full meeting of the Diocesan Church Society, which occupied the remaining part of the day. One leading object of this society has been, to make respectful applications to the principal landed proprietors of the Island for allotments of land for the benefit of the Church. A committee has been formed to carry this desirable object into effect. They are in correspondence with the bishop, who has readily consented to assist them in their good work; and, from answers that have been already received to some of their applications, there is every prospect of complete success attending their labours. I have, in a former part of this report, alluded to the anxious desire of Lord and Lady Westmoreland, and Sir George Seymour, to promote the best interests of the Church, and to the liberal grants which they have already directed to be made. Several others are similarly disposed, and among these I must beg to mention the Hon. Samuel Cunard, who has told me, since my return from the Island, that he is making arrangements for the building of three churches on his estates, and has ordered the allotment of 100 acres of land to each. These movements in favour of the Church, and the appointment at the same time of three valuable missionaries, produced a new and striking era in the ecclesiastical affairs of the Island. A high sense of gratitude to the Society for the Propagation of the Gospel for their Christian liberality, and a steady attachment to the principles of the Established Church generally prevailing, afford at least sufficient ground for encouragement and hope; encouragement to increased exertions for her welfare on the part of her sons—and hope for her future enlargement and prosperity. If the Society, in their anxious and untiring exertions to engage able and well-qualified missionaries, should be as fortunate in their future selections as they have been in their late appointments to this Island, the happy result must be, under the guiding and protecting hand of Providence, that the waste places in our land will be more speedily and effectually brought under the culture of the Christian Church, and more effectually established in the truth as it is in Jesus, than by less qualified agents, or mere lay instructors.

The high and holy authority, " As my Father hath sent me, even so send I you," and " Lo, I am with you always," is the principle and basis on which our venerable Society acts—a principle, I humbly submit, which should, in all its fullest extent, be recognised and acted upon in all our missionary labours and enterprises.

The Church, through the instrumentality of her threefold ministry, holds out the most effectual, because the best—the divinely authorized means of evangelizing the world—means enjoined by the great Head of the Church himself, and on which, if rightly exercised, we hope his blessing may descend.

If men of education, of sound religious principles and enlightened views of Christianity, with zeal for the extension of the Redeemer's kingdom, could be induced to come and help us, we may then hope that our work, being begun on a solid and safe foundation, may end in the promotion of God's glory and the eternal salvation of souls.

DIOCESAN INTELLIGENCE.

LICHFIELD.—Her Majesty the Queen has forwarded the donation of 100*l*. towards the fund now being raised to defray the expense of repairing Hanbury Church, Staffordshire. The Queen Dowager has subscribed 25*l*.

OXFORD.—*Oxford Architectural Society.* A meeting was held at the Society's room on Wednesday evening, Feb. 23; the Rev. the Master of University College in the chair.

Impressions of Brasses, from West Harling Church, Norfolk, were presented by the Rev. C. J. Ridley, of University College.

A communication from the President of Trinity College was read by the chairman, respecting Cassington church, Oxon, which is about to be carefully restored. This interesting little church is principally Norman; its ground plan resembles that of Iffley and Stewkeley, having the tower between the nave and chancel, but no transepts, and the president showed that it never had any, although Warton was of opinion that they had been destroyed. The chancel has a good plain Norman roof of groined stone. The original Norman tower has had a spire added to it in the fourteenth century, of good decorated character. There are some very good Norman corbels, and in the interior some curious paintings, on the walls, of several successive periods, part of them of the twelfth century. A curious paten of brass, or latten, with two figures carrying a bunch of grapes, (in allusion to Numb. xiii. 23,) which, from the costume, appears to be of the early part of the fifteenth century, was handed round the room, with a sketch of the church.

A paper was read by W. Grey, Esq. of Magdalene Hall, on the church of Combe-in-Teignhead, Devon; with some general remarks on the peculiarities of the churches of Devonshire, illustrated by a number of beautiful sketches. This church is in the early English style, with some remarkable features of uncommon occurrence. It appears from the episcopal registers of the diocese of Exeter, that "on the 10th of November, 1259, Walter Bronescombe, Bishop of Exeter, dedicated the high altar and two other altars;" and it is probable that the chancel and transepts are of that date, although some of the features, such as the roll moulding, are not usually met with so early. The arches of the nave are remarkably wide and flat for this style, closely resembling the four-centred arch of the Tudor period, but with early English mouldings. This church possesses several other interesting peculiarities, which were well illustrated by Mr. Grey's sketches, but can hardly be made intelligible without them.

The first peculiarity that a visitor will notice in Devonshire, is the great prevalence of early perpendicular work, to the exclusion of the other styles. This appears to arise from this style having been early introduced into this county, as Kenton church, built a few years before 1379, is of this character, and continued to a late period, with little variation, as the beautiful tower of Cullompton was begun in 1545 and finished in 1549, so that it is probable that this is one of those towers built by the monks of Glastonbury, who, when they found that their revenues were likely to be seized upon by King Henry VIII., spent large sums in building churches, and especially towers, with which Somersetshire abounds. These towers, as is also the case with that at Cullompton, have very bold outlines, and much work that might seem at first sight to be early perpendicular. In Devonshire towers the staircase turret is generally a very prominent object, and placed in front of the tower, as if courting observation, rather than behind for concealment. It forms a very ornamental feature, and adds much to the picturesque effect of these towers. There are few spires in Devon, except in particular districts: generally they are confined to the level country, for which they are best suited, and towers only are found in the hilly districts. These towers are for the most part plain and bald, and their proportions more lofty than is usual in other counties.

The long and narrow churches, without aisles,

so common in Oxfordshire and Berkshire, and other counties, are rarely met with in Devonshire. The chancel arch is a feature generally wanting in the Devonshire churches, the roof being continuous over nave and chancel, and the division made by the rood-loft and screen only. Cradle roofs are continually found; the ribs generally very bold, and the bosses well cut. Four-centred arches, between the nave and aisles, are very common, and the pillars, though formed of several shafts, have one common capital of woven foliage. But what renders the Devonshire churches especially interesting, is the great abundance of carved wood-work, such as benches and bench-ends, of endless variety, rood-lofts and screens, and wooden ceilings, all elaborately carved, and many of them retaining their old painting and gilding, which has a very rich effect, rarely to be found elsewhere.

YORK.—*Appointment of Rural Deans.* The Archbishop of York has recently revived the office of rural dean within his diocese, upon the representation of the archdeacons, for the purpose of aiding those functionaries in the execution of their important duties. The office of rural dean is one of great antiquity, but has long been in abeyance. The duties to be discharged by these officials will be best understood by our publishing a copy of the instructions which have been promulgated. They are as follows :—

"The rural dean is to inquire, and give information to the archdeacon, to be by him made known to the archbishop, of all matters concerning the clergy, churchwardens, and other officers of the church, which it may be necessary or useful that the ordinary should know.

"He is to inquire, and report to the archdeacon, as to the residence of incumbents or licensed curates. Also as to the due performance of divine service every Sunday, with one or more sermons; also, as to the observance and administration of the sacraments of Baptism and the Lord's Supper, together with a return of the annual number of communicants.

"Upon being made acquainted with the avoidance of any benefice within the district, he is to make a return thereof to the archdeacon, in order that due inquiry may be made into the state of the vacant benefice, and sequestration issued out of the ecclesiastical court.

"He is likewise, once in every year, previously to the archdeacon's visitation, and at other times when he shall be required, to inspect such churches and chapels within his district, with their chancels and church-yards, as the archdeacon may appoint, and the books, ornaments, and other articles thereto belonging, as also the houses, buildings, and glebes, belonging to the incumbents, and to make a return thereof to the archdeacon at his next visitation.

"He is also to inspect all parochial and national schools within his district, and to make a particular report yearly on the education of the poor, as connected with the Established Church, and to obtain from time to time such information respecting parochial matters as shall be required of him by the archdeacon, and to make returns thereof to the archdeacon, to be by him transmitted to the archbishop.

"He shall likewise be ready to advise and assist the churchwardens within his district, in framing their presentments of all such things as are amiss within their respective parishes, and are by law presentable.

"He is also to call the clergy of his district together whenever the archdeacon shall appoint, and take care to circulate such orders as shall be sent to him for that purpose.

"He is to inspect, at his annual visitation, and at any other time when he may see occasion, the licenses of all stipendiary and assistant curates officiating within his district, and to give immediate notice to the archdeacon of any who shall officiate as curates without being duly licensed.

"He is to inquire as to the preservation of parish registers, the making due entries therein, and the regular transmission of the annual returns to the registry at York."

The following are the appointments which his Grace the Archbishop has already made :—

In the Archdeaconry of the West Riding.—The Rev. S. Sharpe, D.D., Vicar of Doncaster; the Rev. T. Sutton, Vicar of Sheffield; the Rev. G. Chandler, Rector of Treeton; the Rev. A. B. Wrightson, Rector of Hansworth.

In the Archdeaconry of the East Riding.—The Rev. W. H. E. Bentinck, Rector of Sigglesthorne; the Rev. C. Hotham, Rector of Ross.

In the Archdeaconry of Cleveland (North Riding.)—The Rev. S. Creyke, Rector of Wigginton; the Rev. T. Egerton, Vicar of Dunnington; the Rev. E. Churton, Rector of Creyke; the Rev. G. Dixon, Vicar of Helmsley; the Rev. W. Gooch, Vicar of Stainton; the Rev. F. Lipscombe, Rector of Welbury.

GLOUCESTER AND BRISTOL.—Copy of a circular issued by the Lord Bishop :—

"*Palace, Gloucester, Feb.* 1, 1842.

"Rev. and dear Sir,—You may remember that in the charge delivered to the Clergy at my late visitation, I took occasion to call attention to the deficiency in church-room which still exists in many parts of the diocese,—and to my earnest desire that such deficiency should be supplied, as I trust and believe that by God's blessing may be done through the operation of our Church Building Association.

"Many new churches have already been erected, and several old ones in the Archdeaconry of Gloucester have been enlarged through the assistance of this society. But the means at its disposal are altogether inadequate to the object proposed—which is no less than to make our church accommodation co-extensive with the wants of the diocese.

"It is my intention to address to the parochial Clergy some suggestions upon the methods by which I think that a more general support may be procured for this association, its sphere of usefulness enlarged, and its existence perpetuated. But before doing this, I am desirous to learn, from actual examination, what are the ecclesiastical wants of each parish and district in the diocese, in order that the real nature and extent of the deficiencies may be accurately understood, and that the assistance of the Society in aid of local exertions may be offered upon a systematic and equitable principle. Relying, therefore, upon the disposition which I have always remarked in the rural deans to promote every object which has a tendency to the spiritual benefit of their respective districts and of the Church in general, I request that you, with the assistance of the other incumbents named in this letter, will, at your earliest convenience, inquire into the ecclesiastical condition of every parish in the deanery of ———, and will report to me the result under the following heads :—

1. Population—and how situate in regard to divine worship.

2. Number of persons for whom there is at present church room.
3. How many services on each Lord's day.
4. How often the Holy Communion is administered.—Average number of communicants.
5. If the present church accommodation be inadequate, state whether you recommend that the deficiency should be supplied by enlarging the present building, or by the erection of another church.

"The incumbents whom I wish to be associated with yourself in making this inquiry and report, are—

to each of whom I shall address a copy of this letter.

"Believe me to be, with respect and esteem, reverend and dear Sir, your faithful brother and servant,

"J. H. GLOUCESTER & BRISTOL."
"The Rev. ——, Rural Dean of ——."

LINCOLN.—*Nottingham.*—The Earl of Manvers has presented the munificent donation of 300 guineas to the Church Building Society, for promoting the increase of church accommodation within the county and town of Nottingham. The other noble donors are the Duke of Newcastle, Earl Howe, Archbishop of York, Earl of Stamford and Warrington, Earl of Carnarvon, Earl of Brownlow, Earl of Lincoln, and Sir Richard Sutton, each for 100*l.*; and Earl Bathurst, Lord Wenlock, and Mr. Granville Vernon, M.P., have respectively subscribed 50*l.* The Bishop of Lincoln, and Mr. Galley Knight, M.P., have given 300*l.* each; and Viscount Newark, who is abroad, has forwarded the liberal sum of 200*l.* in aid of the funds of the society.

SALISBURY.—By the decease of Mrs. Burgess, relict of the late Bishop of Salisbury, a reversionary legacy of 3,000*l.* will be added to the funds of that valuable institution, the Church Union Society in the Diocese of Salisbury, founded by the Right Rev. Thomas Burgess, D.D., Bishop of Salisbury, 1827. Next to the great principle of Christian union, the immediate objects of this society are to afford to superannuated or disabled curates, the means of retiring from duties to which they are no longer equal; to enable aged or infirm incumbents, and endowed lecturers of small incomes, to provide clerical assistants; and to promote, as much as possible, the efficiency and *residence* of the parochial clergy. In furtherance of this last object in this immediate neighbourhood, very handsome contributions have been made from the society towards building parsonage houses at Portland, Charminster, and Winterborne St. Martin; and the present addition to its funds will enable it to extend similar assistance to be found in this and the two other archdeaconries of the diocese.—*Dorset Chronicle.*

ELY.—*Cambridge Camden Society.*—The 24th meeting was recently holden, the president in the chair. After a list of presents received since the last meeting had been read, the following report of the committee was also read:—

"The Society was informed during the last term, that with the kind consent of the diocesan, and the archdeacon (our president), circulars had been addressed to every clergyman of the Archdeaconry of Bristol, requesting information upon certain ecclesiological points. We have already received, in answer to these applications, a large number of curious and valuable notices, illustrated in many cases by carefully-drawn ground-plans and sketches of details; for these we take the present opportunity of returning, once for all, our most sincere thanks.

"Since the last meeting of the Society, twenty-two applications have been received for advice, opinions, or assistance.

"The Committee has also been in communication with the Rev. J. Evans, on behalf of the Rev. J. Winder, with respect to a new British Church at Alexandria. Of these cases some have been of the most flattering description; and the Committee believe that in most the suggestions which they have been able to give have been satisfactory to the applicants.

"Among many presents, of which a list has been read to the Society, is a specimen of a beautiful communion-cloth and napkin, presented by the manufacturer, Mr. G. J. French, of Bolton-le-Moors, Lancashire. The Society will view any effort for securing greater reverence in the administration of divine offices with satisfaction; and more particularly so when, as in this case, the effort was suggested by the influence of their own publication.

"The Committee propose publishing a lithographed view of the Holy Sepulchre Church, as it will appear when completely restored. They again solicit increased contributions in aid of the repairs. The architect is preparing for publication the plans of the model parish church for New Zealand: and the Committee confidently anticipate that this work will receive general encouragement. The profits will be devoted to defraying the expense of the models which will be sent out to the bishop."

A series of papers was then read by J. S. Howson, Esq., M.A., of Trinity College. Notice was given that a paper was preparing for the next meeting on the ceremonies formerly observed in the consecration of bells; and one on the crypt and chapel of St. Stephen, Westminster.

LONDON.—*The Charter-House.*—The Right Hon. Lord Wharncliffe was on Saturday last elected a Governor of the Charter-house, in the room of the late Earl of Westmoreland. At the same court the Venerable Archdeacon Hale was elected to the Mastership, in the room of the late Dr. Fisher. By this election the Preachership of the foundation becomes vacant, for which the Rev. Mr. Dicken is a candidate. The election is fixed for the 19th of March.

The Lord Bishop of London will hold his annual confirmation for the metropolitan parishes at the following times and places:—Monday, May 2, in the parish church of St. Marylebone; Tuesday, May 3, St. James's, Westminster; Wednesday, May 4, Christ Church, Newgate-street; Monday, May 9, St. Luke's, Chelsea; Tuesday, May 10, St. Mary's, Whitechapel; Wednesday, May 11, St. Mary's, Islington. Divine service will commence each day at eleven o'clock.

WINCHESTER.—"Sir,—A wish having been expressed that the Ember weeks should be better observed, and the clergy meet sometimes to receive the Holy Communion, it has been agreed that the clergy in the Southampton rural deanery should meet for the above purposes every Friday in the Ember weeks, at one of the churches in Southampton. This they did for the first time on Feb. 18, in Holy Rood Church, where the Vicar, who is also rural dean, preached, and afterwards administered the Holy Communion to thirty clergy and about as many laity. The alms collected at the offertory will be given to the Diocesan Church Building Society.

"Thinking this information may be interesting to the readers of your paper, I send it to you to make it known in any way you think proper.—I remain, Sir, yours sincerely,
"J. E. SHADWELL."
"Southampton, Feb. 21, 1842."
—*Church Intelligencer.*

The Lord Bishop of Winchester purposes to hold Confirmations throughout Surrey, at the latter end of the spring.

EXETER.—*Tithe Commutation.*—The Rev. Prebendary Dennis, at the meeting held on Monday, Jan. 24, for the purpose of commuting the tithes of several parishes, delivered in a written protest, in which the reverend gentleman, upon a retrospect of various ancient statutes relating to the property of the Church—a retrospect which evinces elaborate research upon the subject—denies the legality of commutation for tithe.—*Exeter Gazette.*

IRELAND.

IRISH COLLEGIATE SCHOOL.—We can only here allude to this noble undertaking, of which the prospectus has just been put in circulation. We hope to annex it at length to our next number, by which time we doubt not considerable progress will have been made. Subscriptions are received in London at Messrs. Coutts & Co.'s; and prospectuses may be had of Messrs. Rivington.

MISCELLANEOUS.

COLONIAL BISHOPRICS FUND.—The following is a summary of the Colonial Bishoprics Fund, corrected up to January 1, 1842:—

	Donats.	Ann. Subs.
General Fund	£52,601 3 2	£318 9 6
New Zealand	39 0 0	600 0 0
Malta	472 11 0	—
New Brunswick	40 0 0	—
Cape of Good Hope	10 10 0	—
Ceylon	10 0 0	5 5 0
South Australia	200 0 0	—
Total	£53,373 4 2	£923 14 6

NEW SCOTCH COLLEGE.—The committee of this institution (the success of which is no longer doubtful) have published a list of subscriptions in the *North British Advertiser*, of Saturday, Feb. 19, by which it appears that upwards of 11,000*l.* have been already contributed towards the funds of the college. The standing committee of the Christian Knowledge Society have recommended a grant of 1000*l.* in aid of the undertaking.—*Aberdeen Journal.*

The *Banner of the Cross*, published in Philadelphia, gives the subjoined most welcome evidence of the spread of the Church:—

"*Interesting Ordination.*—We learn, from the *Western Episcopal Observer*, that on the second Sunday in Advent, December 5, the Rt. Rev. Bishop Kemper, in St. Paul's Church, New Albany, admitted to Deacon's orders, Andrew Wylie, D.D. President of the University of Indiana, and for many years a distinguished minister of the Presbyterian denomination.

"In the afternoon and evening Dr. Wylie preached, (in the afternoon also performing the service,) when, in his usual candid and truth-loving spirit, he gave his reasons for seeking the fold of the Episcopal Church.

"As an interesting coincidence, we may also state, that on the same day four students of the Andover Theological [Congregational] Seminary, united themselves with the Protestant Episcopal Church in that place, by receiving the apostolic rite of confirmation. We learn this from *The New England Puritan*, a Congregational paper."

CHURCHES CONSECRATED OR OPENED.

Hop Hill, near Birmingham .... Feb. 21.
Bomling, near Bradford .... St. John's .... Bishop of Ripon .... Feb. 8.

FOUNDATIONS LAID.

Honley, near Huddersfield .... February 10.
Penzance .... St. Paul's Chapel ....

TO CORRESPONDENTS.

If "Mary" will let us know how a letter can reach her, we shall be glad to communicate with her privately.

THE CHRISTIAN REMEMBRANCER.

APRIL, 1842.

Notes of a Traveller, on the Social and Political State of France, Prussia, Switzerland, Italy, and other Parts of Europe, during the present Century. By SAMUEL LAING, Esq., Author of "*A Journal of a Residence in Norway,*" and of "*A Tour in Sweden.*" London: Longman & Co. 1842. Pp. xii. 496.

No doubt of it, Mr. Samuel Laing is a very clever person; shrewd, searching, intelligent, independent of everything like prejudice, as people call it, save a little leaning to the "land of cakes," its presbyterianism, its "Establishment,"—the late ministry,—and "civil and religious liberty all over the world." Of his class this gentleman is a very favourable specimen; he connects principles with results; he sees that there is such a thing as the dependence of the moral and social condition of a people upon abstract truths of religion: he may be, indeed he is, almost invariably wrong in his estimate of these principles, as ideas, or eternal truths; consequently, he is also wrong in his practical conclusions; but his logic is good enough; and if we add to this, that he is competently skilled in metaphysics (Scotch), that he is deep in the corn-law question, quite at home in the German commercial league, well up with the "*management*" of the poor, a desperate Drawcansir in all sorts of political economy, prædial economy, social economy, domestic economy, the economy of "functionarism and centralization," of "reproductive and un-reproductive expenditure," the economy of the olive tree, of maize, and potatoes, and the "coarser kinds of food;" never at a loss with Dr. Chalmers, Mr. Birkbeck, and Miss H. Martineau, on the suppression of mendicity, and "prudential restraints,"—a "good hater" of the fine arts, especially Raffaelle and M. Angelo, (p. 13,) and a great deifier of their natural enemies, the useful ones, especially in the form of "a foundry and cotton mill," (p. 13,)—a sneerer at the old-world notions of primogeniture, and the "interests of kingdoms, territorially or dynastically considered as family estates," (p. 27,)—profound in statistics, tariffs, monopolies, gluts, over-production, and over-population, the rights of conscience, and the "spirit of Protestantism;" very

NO. XVI.—N. S.   3 D

touching and very eloquent on bright visions of the future, and human perfectibility,—on the succession of "new ideas and new principles in every change," conducing " to an evident amelioration of the moral and physical condition of mankind," (p. 408,)—sneering, as of course he should do, at " the bigots in legislation and religious forms, and their inconsistent and fruitless attempts to hold back this mighty movement," (p. 408,)—with a reasonable sprinkling of capital, wages, labour, beneficial investments, rent, barter, liberal views, young France, young Germany, and free-trade,—where, we ask, would you wish for a more accomplished traveller? A better representative of "the age we live in," the said age could not produce; he is a perfect microcosm; the spirit of utilitarianism—the commercial spirit—the useful knowledge and mechanics-institute spirit—that liberalism which is liberal in every thing save charity, alms-deeds, self-denial, and love,—that religious freedom which is free from reverence, submission, faith, the sacramental sense, and the blessedness of ancient truth,—that moral sense which accommodates duty alike and doctrine, truth as well as motives, to expediency and the changeful "tendencies of the times," or " the industrial relations" of this or of that people; he is each and all of these. Oh, age of reform! oh, epoch of universal amelioration! oh, science of social economy! oh, fixed duties! oh, preventive check! oh, Birmingham and Merthyr Tydvil, cotton and steam! these are your comforting and most hopeful results; and is not Mr. Samuel Laing your promising disciple,—nay, your epitome,—the Edinburgh Review in bodily form and substance,—a concrete Wealth of Nations,—Exeter Hall and the first reformed parliament individualized, walking, acting, travelling, publishing?

But, seriously, we have much greater fault to find with the times than with Mr. Laing. And when we find fault with the age, let us remember that "the times" is but the people, and ourselves among them; and let us humbly fear, lest while we condemn others we sentence ourselves; as, more or less we must do. Having premised this, we say that there are many things which we like in Mr. Laing. We believe that he is earnest; we are sure that he is consistent; he has no notion of submission of any sort, either of intellect, or rank, or birth, or religion; but still there is a principle in this, it may be a very false one, but he has the sense and honesty to pursue it; and deals most triumphantly with Dr. Chalmers, for instance, who "thinks the Church a useful thing for supplying younger brothers with a thousand a year." (P. 38.) He tells that learned lecturer in the theological hall of the University of Edinburgh, that this theory of establishmentism, which places " the law, the church, colleges, and other well-appointed institutions, kept up for the good and interest of the nation," upon the same standing, has neither "principle nor justice in it." Then, again, he sees pretty plainly that the once-famous educational system of Prussia, which our school-mongers were raving about a few years ago, is the greatest caricature of the cultivation of moral and religious sentiment and independence of mind, which ever insulted a people. We extract an instructive passage.

"If education, that is, reading, writing, and arithmetic, cannot be brought within the acquirements of the common man's children, but upon the Prussian semi-coercive principle of the state, through its functionaries, intruding upon the parental duties of each individual, stepping in between the father and his family, and enforcing by state regulations, fines, and even imprisonment,* what should be left to the moral sense of duty and natural affection of every parent who is not in a state of pupilage from mental imbecility—then is such education not worth the demoralizing price paid for it—the interference with men as free moral agents, the substitution of government enactments and superintendence in the most sacred domestic affairs for self-guidance by conscience, good principle, and common sense—the reduction, in short, of the population of a country to the social condition of a soldiery off duty roaming about their parade ground, under the eye and at the call of their superiors, without free agency or a sense of moral responsibility. Moral effects in society can only be produced by moral influences. We may drill boys into reading and writing machines; but this is not education. The almost mechanical operations of reading, writing, and reckoning, are unquestionably most valuable acquirements—who can deny, or doubt it?—but they are not education; they are the means only, not the end—the tools, not the work, in the education of man. We are too ready in Britain to consider them as tools which will work of themselves—that if the labouring man is taught to read his Bible, he becomes necessarily a moral, religious man—that to read is to think. This confounding of the means with the end is practically a great error. We see no such effects from the acquisition of much higher branches of school education, and by those far above the social position of the labouring man. Reading and writing are acquirements very widely diffused in Paris, in Italy, in Austria, in Prussia, in Sweden; but the people are not moral, nor religious, nor enlightened, nor free, because they possess the means; they are not of educated mind in any true sense. If the ultimate object of all education and knowledge be to raise man to the feeling of his own moral worth, to a sense of his responsibility to his Creator and to his conscience for every act, to the dignity of a reflecting, self-guiding, virtuous, religious member of society, then the Prussian educational system is a failure. It is only a training from childhood in the conventional discipline and submission of mind which the state exacts from its subjects. It is not a training or education which has raised, but which has lowered, the human character. This system of interference and intrusion into the inmost domestic relations of the people, this educational drill of every family by state means and machinery, supersedes parental tuition. It is a fact not to be denied, that the Prussian population is at this day, when the fruits of this educational system may be appreciated in the generation of the adults, in a remarkably demoralized condition in those branches of moral conduct which cannot be taught in schools, and are not taught by the parents, because parental tuition is broken in upon by governmental interference in Prussia, its efficacy and weight annulled, and the natural dependence of the child upon the words and wisdom of its parent—the delicate threads by which the infant's mind, as its

---

* I asked an intelligent Prussian what could be done if a parent refused to send his child to school? He told me he had lately been at the police-office when a man was brought in for not sending his girl to school. She could not read, although advancing to the age to be confirmed. The man said his girl was earning her bread at a manufactory which he named, and he could not maintain her at school. He was asked why he did not send her to the evening schools established for such cases, and held after working hours, or to the Sunday schools? He said his wife had a large family of young infants, and his girl had to keep them when she came from her work, while her mother was washing for them, and doing other needful family work, which she could not do with a child in her arms. The man was told that he would be committed to prison if he and his wife did not send their girl to school.

body, draws nutriment from its parent—is ruptured. They know little of human nature who know not that more of moral education may be conveyed in a glance of a mother's eye than in a whole course of reading and writing, under educational sergeants in primary schools and gymnasia. Of all the virtues, that which the domestic family education of both the sexes most obviously influences—that which marks more clearly than any other the moral condition of a society, the home state of moral and religious principles, the efficiency of those principles in it, and the amount of that moral restraint upon passions and impulses, which it is the object of education and knowledge to attain—is undoubtedly female chastity. Will any traveller, will any Prussian say, that this index-virtue of the moral condition of a people is not lower in Prussia than in almost any part of Europe?"*—Pp. 165-7.

In a word, he sees pretty plainly that it is not quite consistent to be always prating about free-trade in creeds, non-interference in religion, and such like, and then to advocate compulsory education; dragooning little boys to schools and gymnasia, progymnasia, normal schools, seminaries, real schools, primary and secondary colleges, and the rest of the barrack-master drill of most things in Prussia.

Mr. Laing says the same of the construction of the present Prussian state establishment of religion, "that third thing—the new Prussian Church, neither Lutheran nor Calvinist,—which was set up and imposed by the edict of civil power, upon the Protestant population." (P. 176.) He cannot quite see how this is to be reconciled with the spirit of Protestantism; and as long as he chooses to consider Protestantism the uncontrolled exercise of individual judgment, we partake in his amazement. We can quite understand him characterising this as "a measure not only destructive to the Protestant religion, but the most arbitrary and insulting to freedom of mind and conscience, that has occurred in modern history." (Ibid.) He asks, with some force,

"Who would suppose at the very period Victor Cousin, the Edinburgh Reviewers, and so many other eminent literary men of all countries were extolling the national education and general acquirement of reading in Prussia, this educating government was driving, by religious persecution, from her educated land, upwards of 600 Christians, who went from Silesia to the wilds of America, simply to enjoy the privileges of religious freedom, and of communicating at the altar according to the forms and doctrines of Luther and Calvin, rather than of his late majesty?"—P. 232. "History will have her day of judgment; she will hear the cry of the victims, said to have been 2,966 individuals, suffering for their religious or political opinions, imprisonment, civil disabilities, or other punishments, for this Prussian crime of worshipping God in their own houses, and who were only liberated by the act of amnesty, August 1840, on the death of the late sovereign."—Pp. 219, 232.

"The parish of Hermannsdorf, under its minister the pastor Berger, and the parish of Hoenigern, consisting of ten villages, under its pastor Kellner, refused obedience to the order of the consistory to introduce the new service, and continued to use the old liturgy and service, and to receive the sacrament according to the old Lutheran formulary—*it is* the body and blood of Christ. The

---

* In 1837 the number of females in the Prussian population between the beginning of their sixteenth year and the end of their forty-fifth year—that is, within child-bearing age—was 2,983,146; the number of illegitimate children born in the same year was 39,501, so that 1 in every 75 of the whole of the females of an age to bear children, had been the mother of an illegitimate child.

people flocked from far and near to these genuine old Lutheran preachers. The consistory of Breslau ordered pastor Berger to administer the sacrament alternately according to the new and the old service. He refused any such compromise of conscience, any such *juste milieu* in his religious persuasion and duty, and was consequently suspended. In the great parish of Hoenigern, pastor Kellner adopted measures for a more powerful opposition. Before the arrival of the commissioners of the consistory, he surrendered the church keys and church property into the hands of forty elders chosen from the congregation, who received the commission, with their minister at their head, singing psalms, and who gave a decided No to the question, if they would receive the new liturgy and agenda. The commissioners were not admitted into the church; and when they pronounced a sentence of suspension against Kellner, he protested against their authority as not representing the true Lutheran church by law established in the land. Kellner and his elders were arrested and imprisoned at Breslau; but when the minister appointed as his successor came to perform the church service according to the new agenda, he found the church doors nailed, and a crowd of people obstructing the entrance. On the 20th December, 1834, a body of 400 infantry, 50 hussars, and 50 cuirassiers, marched from Breslau to this recusant parish of Hoenigern. The civil and clerical authorities again tried in vain to induce the people to accept the new service. Their elders and pastor had been twelve weeks in prison, but they continued obstinate; and, at last, on Christmas eve, the military took possession of the church, forced open the door by a petard, and dispersed the people by a charge of cavalry, in which some twenty persons were wounded. The interim minister was thus intruded into the church, and the new service was performed on Christmas day, but it was to a congregation of soldiers only; for not one parishioner was to be seen in the church. It was necessary to resort to other measures to obtain a real congregation for the new service and the stormed parish church. The military were stationed in the villages of the parish, and each recusant householder was punished by having ten or twelve soldiers quartered on him. The soldiers themselves were to exhort their landlords to go to the church, that they might be relieved from the ruinous quartering of men upon them, and those who would not conform were exposed to gross ill usage. These are the peasants, who, ruined by this persecution, sought a refuge in America."—Pp. 224, 225.

At these results of centralization and national education, Mr. Laing marvels much; so do we; but more of this anon. We prefer at present to advert to a kindred topic. Mr. Laing is a pure voluntaryist; he thinks that in politics, religion, education, trade, we have but to create the sense of want, and the want will remedy itself; in other words, make a man feel that he is a rascal, and he and his brethren of Field-lane, will procure a new statute against petty larceny. Leave a nation's religious opinions alone; leave their education alone; the greatest curse to a people is for the "finger of government interfering in all action and opinion, and leaving nothing to free will and uncontrolled individual judgment." This theory he applies, as in other instances, so in a passage not more remarkable for the extraordinary facts which it details, than favourably characteristic of our author's power and style.

" I happened to be at Geneva one Sunday morning as the bells were tolling to church. The very sounds which once called the powerful minds of a Calvin, a Knox, a Zwingli, to religious exercise and meditation, were now summoning the descendants of their contemporaries to the same house of prayer. There are few Scotchmen whose hearts would not respond to such a call. I hastened to the ancient cathedral, the church of St. Peter, to see the pulpit from which

Calvin had preached, to sit possibly in the very seat from which John Knox has listened, to hear the pure doctrines of Christianity from the preachers who now stand where once the great champions of the Reformation stood; to mark, too, the order and observances of the Calvinistic service here in its native church; to revive, too, in my mind, Scotland, and the picturesque Sabbath days of Scotland in a foreign land. But where is the stream of citizens' families in the streets, so remarkable a feature in every Scotch town when the bells are tolling to church, family after family, all so decent and respectable in their Sunday clothes, the fathers and mothers leading the younger children, and all walking silently churchwards? and where the quiet, the repose, the stillness of the Sabbath morning, so remarkable in every Scotch town and house? Geneva, the seat and centre of Calvinism, the fountain-head from which the pure and living waters of our Scottish Zion flow, the earthly source, the pattern, the Rome of our Presbyterian doctrine and practice, has fallen lower from her own original doctrine and practice than ever Rome fell. Rome has still superstition; Geneva has not even that semblance of religion. In the head church of the original seat of Calvinism, in a city of five-and-twenty thousand souls, at the only service on the Sabbath day—*there being no evening service*—I sat down in a congregation of about two hundred females, and three-and-twenty males, mostly elderly men of a former generation, with scarcely a youth, or boy, or working man among them. A meagre liturgy, or printed form of prayer, a sermon, which, as far as religion was concerned, might have figured the evening before at a meeting of some geological society, as an " ingenious essay" on the Mosaic chronology, a couple of psalm tunes on the organ, and a waltz to go out with, were the church service. In the afternoon, the only service in towns or in the country is reading a chapter of the Bible to the children, and hearing them gabble over the Catechism in a way which shows they have not a glimpse of the meaning. A pleasure tour in the steam-boats, which are regularly advertised for a Sunday promenade round the lake, a pic-nic dinner in the country, and overflowing congregations in the evening at the theatre, the equestrian circus, the concert saloons, ball rooms, and coffee houses, are all that distinguish Sunday from Monday in that city in which, three centuries before, Calvin moved the senate and the people to commit to the flames his own early friend Servetus, the discoverer of the circulation of the blood, (?) and one of the first philosophers of that age, for presuming to differ in opinion and strength of argument from his own religious dogma. This is action and reaction in religious spirit with a vengeance. In the village churches, along the Protestant side of the Lake of Geneva—spots upon this earth specially intended, the traveller would say, to elevate the mind of man to his Creator by the glories of the surrounding scenery—the rattling of the billiard balls, the rumbling of the skittle trough, the shout, the laugh, the distant shots of the rifle gun clubs, are heard above the psalm, the sermon, and the barren forms of state-prescribed prayer, during the one brief service on Sundays, delivered to very scanty congregations, in fact, to a few females and a dozen or two old men, in very populous parishes supplied with able and zealous ministers.

" What may be the causes of this remarkable difference in the working of Calvinism in Switzerland and Scotland? The churches of Geneva and Scotland set out together on their Christian pilgrimage, in the days of Calvin and Knox, with the same profession of faith, the same doctrines, and the same forms in congregational worship. We, the vulgar of the kirk of Scotland, have at least always been taught to consider the church of Geneva as the motherchurch of our Presbyterian faith, and established church usages—the model by which both our doctrines and practices were framed and adjusted into their present shape. How widely the two have wandered from each other! The member of the Scotch kirk comes out of the church of Geneva inquiring if it be a Calvinistic or Lutheran service he has been attending—the liturgy, or printed prescribed form of prayer, is there, the organ is there, and the sermon is a neat little moral essay that might do for either, or for any congregation. Scotland is at this day the most religious Protestant country in Europe; and in no country in Europé, Protestant or Catholic, is the church attendance worse, the regard for the ordinary observances of religious worship less, the religious indifference—not entitled to be called infidelity, not so respectable as infidelity, because not arising from any reasoning or thinking, wrong or right, about religion—greater than in Protestant Switzerland, in the district of our Calvinistic mother-church in and about Geneva. Whence is this remarkable difference? The starting point of the human mind was the same in both countries, at the same period, and under the same leaders, Calvin and Knox; and the present divergence of the human mind in its religious direction in Switzerland and Scotland is as striking as was the original coincidence.

"The only obvious cause of this divergence is, that the state and church in Switzerland have from the first engrafted on Calvinism a bastard Lutheranism. It is characteristic of Calvinism as received in Scotland, that it is the only branch of Christianity which flourishes independently of all church establishments, state assistance, or government arrangements, and requires no union of church and state. Spiritual, and unconnected with forms, it is injured by government interference and regulation. In Scotland itself religion is more flourishing in the Secession than in the Established Church, simply because the former is a voluntary, the latter a state church. The doctrine and church observances and education of the ministers are the same in both. The state has—and Calvin himself in conjunction with the state, to prevent probably the excitement of the public mind by the extemporary prayers of fanatic preachers adapting their effusions to the passing feelings of their congregations, or to keep them exclusively Calvinists, and out of the hearing, as far as possible, of other impressions—prescribed a set form of printed prayer, a liturgy, in settling the church discipline and usages of the church of Geneva. The Scotch Calvinistic church, about sixty years after the Reformation, repudiated such interference, even from the church power, with individual freedom of thought and expression in prayer, as being contrary to the genuine spirit of Calvinism. The Scotch were more Calvinistic than Calvin himself. Time has proved that the Scotch kirk was right. In Switzerland, in attempting to guard the people by prescribed forms, against the diseases of fanaticism and erroneous doctrine, the state and Calvinistic church have inoculated the people with the worse disease of indifference."—Pp. 324—328.

Scotch Calvinism, or rather Calvinism-out-Calvinized, then, we are to understand, has not degenerated into heathenism—for we cannot find a milder word—which is the case with Genevan Calvinism, because it has not been polluted by set forms issued by the state; though, to do Mr. Laing justice, he does not say that forms of prayer, as such, have this invariable tendency. He speaks of " the venerated antiquity, the admirable eloquence, and the application to every condition and every mind, of the fine ancient liturgy of the English Church." He says, and says with truth, that " the liturgy in the English Church is the most important part of the pastoral duty," the preaching is but secondary and subsidiary;" but in the Scotch Calvinistic church " the substance of the service is in the sermon." He only says that liturgies and Calvinism are incompatible,—hence the fall or the eradication of all religion in Geneva; to which he bears such melancholy testimony, by the attempt to combine irreconcilable elements. Nor are we prepared to say that there is not *some* truth in this: the Scotch religionism is consistent,—it holds well together,—right or wrong, it is intelligible; there is no egregious illogical process in it: Genevan Calvinism, as described above, is a Mezentian monster; and men's minds soon find out these incongruities; one principle or the other they are not slow to perceive must be utterly false; and when truth and falsehood are mixed in the same cup, what wonder if men reject the unnatural compound! Error itself may pass muster when there is nothing with which to contrast it; but if you wish to pass off a bad shilling do not tender a good one with it, for the chances are, that even if you find a clown who does not know which is the counterfeit, he will be sharp enough to throw them both in your face. But is it wholly so? are there no other causes than this to account for a difference which none can deny? Is the proximity to England, and intercourse with her sounder creed to go for nothing? among the counteracting influences in the sister kingdom, may we not enumerate the state protection, the manses, and parishes, and endowments, which Mr. Laing passes over, *sub silentio*, or rather, if he were consistent, ought to place to the opposite account? and above all, is not the origin of the two connexions essentially different? Calvin was a layman. He and the magistrates of Geneva invented a form of church-government out of their own heads; they pretended no divine appointment; they laid no claim to apostolic descent. Knox and his coadjutors were at least presbyters. We know not how far God has overruled to good what seemed to them but an unimportant accident in the formation of their kirk; but surely presbyterian succession is better than the self-appointed ordinances of mere schismatical laymen; the single grain of the "salt of the earth" alloyed, counteracted, debased though it has been by other elements of evil, may have preserved Scotland from that utter corruption which has banished God's presence from Geneva. If Mr. Cumming and kindred writers are to be relied upon as fair exponents of presbyterianism, they do as a fact prefer authoritative claims to apostolic succession; it is because presbyterianism was the primitive discipline, because the Scotch pastors are the rightful successors, as they tell us, of the Apostles, that they "sit in Moses' seat." Whether the fact be so or not, at least the appeal must go for something; the great Head of the Church may have regarded with favour the attempt, however erroneous and false, to secure incorporation with Him, by means of the Church, which is His body, in preference to the deliberate and wilful slighting of His ordinance, never controverted for 1500 years, which has ruined the self-derived Calvinism of Geneva.

Mr. Laing bears impartial—indeed, in his case, it must be unwilling, and therefore most noticeable—testimony, as do all well-informed writers, to the extraordinary re-action in favour of Catholicism on the continent. Indeed he calls attention to the revival of the Church of Rome, in terms quite as startling to Protestant ears, as Ranke's historical facts.

"Catholicism has certainly a much stronger hold over the human mind than Protestantism. The fact is visible and undeniable, and perhaps not unaccountable. The fervour of devotion among these Catholics, the absence of all worldly feelings in their religious acts, strike every traveller who enters a Roman Catholic church abroad. They seem to have no reserve, no false shame, false pride, or whatever the feeling may be, which, among us Protestants, makes the individual exercise of devotion, private, hidden—an affair of the closet. Here, and everywhere in Catholic countries, you see well-dressed people, persons of the higher as well as of the lower orders, on their knees upon the pavement of the church, totally regardless of and unregarded by the crowd of passengers in the aisles moving to and fro. I have christian charity enough to believe, and I do not envy that man's mind who does not believe, that this is quite sincere devotion, and not hypocrisy, affectation, or attempt at display. It is so common, that none of these motives could derive the slightest gratification from the act—not more than a man's vanity could be gratified by his appearing in shoes, or a hat, where all wear the same. In no Protestant place of worship do we witness the same intense abstraction in prayer, the same unaffected devotion of mind. The beggar woman comes in here and kneels down by the side of the princess, and evidently no feeling of intrusion suggests itself in the mind of either. To the praise of the papists be it said, no worldly distinctions, or human rights of property, much less money-payment for places in a place of worship, appear to enter into their imaginations. Their churches are God's houses, open alike to all his rational creatures, without distinction of high or low, rich or poor. All who have a soul to be saved come freely to worship. They have no family pews, *no seats for genteel souls, and seats for vulgar souls. Their houses of worship are not let out, like theatres, or opera houses, or Edinburgh kirks, for money rents for the sittings.* The public mind is evidently more religionized than in Protestant countries. Why should such strong devotional feeling be more widely diffused and more conspicuous among people holding erroneous doctrines, than among us Protestants holding right doctrines? This question can only be solved by comparing the machinery of each church."—Pp. 430, 431.

And then he goes on to say, that although Protestant doctrine be right, its Church machinery is not so effective as that of the Catholics. The popish priest is, in profession, more of a sacred character; more cut off from worldly affairs than the Protestant clergyman. Knowledge has increased in the flock. The Scotch pastors have not made proportionate advances; they have not kept themselves ahead of the people. Since they cannot challenge a peculiar sanctity for their order,—since there is no sacramental function to constitute them a peculiar class in the eyes and feelings of mankind, by virtue of their ordination,—since the Reformation exploded the papistical pretensions of an order of priesthood,—since "scriptural knowledge, piety, sanctity, and all religious gifts, powers, advantages, and abilities, stand equally open to all men, to be attained through faith and their Bibles,"—(p. 434)—"it is an hopeless claim now, in an educated age, for members of a profession not better educated than men of other professions, not separated by any peculiar exclusive religious function from the ordinary business, interests, modes of living of other well-conducted men, to obtain a separate station in society, analogous to that of the popish clergy."—P. 433.

Persecution has improved the popish clergy.

" The effects of the Revolution have been to reverse the position of the clergy of the two churches; and to place the Catholic, now on the vantage ground in the eye of the vulgar of the continental populations, of being poor and sincere, while the Protestant clergy are, at least, comfortable, and well paid for their sincerity. The sleek, fat, narrow-minded, wealthy drone, is now to be sought for on the episcopal bench, or in the prebendal stall of the Lutheran (?) or Anglican churches; the well-off, comfortable parish minister, yeomanlike in mind, intelligence, and social position, in the manse and glebe of the Calvinistic church. The poverty-stricken, intellectual recluse, never seen abroad, but on his way to or from his studies or church duties, living nobody knows how; but all know in the poorest manner, upon a wretched pittance in his obscure abode—and this is the popish priest of the 19th century—has all the advantage of position with the multitude for giving effect to his teaching."—P. 435.

We have a very erroneous impression of the state of the popish clergy. It is untrue, " injudicious as well as uncharitable," to speak of their luxury and ignorance. In zeal, liberal views, and genuine piety, they are equal to the Scotch clergy; in education "positively higher, and without doubt, comparatively higher."—P. 436. We should " understand better the strength of a formidable adversary, who is evidently gaining ground but too fast upon our Protestant Church," by the " vantage ground of superior education and learning, and consequently of moral influence as teachers."—P. 437.

" It is unfortunate, also, for the influence of the Scotch Calvinistic church, that its service consists exclusively of extemporary effusions or temporary compositions. These, composed in haste by men of moderate education, and often of small abilities, have to undergo the comparison, in the mind of an educated and reading congregation, with similar compositions, prayers, or sermons prepared carefully for the press, by the most able and learned divines. The moral influence resting solely on such a church service cannot be permanent. As a machinery, the English Church is founded on a more lasting and influential bæsis; its established forms of prayer, unobjectionably good in themselves, not placing one minister or his compositions in competition with another, or with other similar compositions, in the public mind—the almost mechanical operation of reading the service well or ill, being all the comparison that can be made between two clergymen in the essential part of the church duty. The competition, also, or comparison of any other compositions of the same kind, however excellent, with the old liturgy, can never occur in the public mind in England; because the liturgy has use and wont, antiquity, repetition from childhood to old age, in its favour, and is interwoven with the habits of the people by these threads, in all their religious exercises."—P. 438.

The comparative education of the Scotch clergy, compared to that of the Scotch people, is unquestionably lower than that of the popish clergy, compared to the education of their people. The Catholic clergy have nothing to lose by the spread of education, because they have the sacerdotal character to fall back upon. But they are not content with this; they make use of general education; they encourage it as a mighty instrument; they use it ably. " In Catholic Germany, in France, Italy, and even Spain, the education of the common people in reading, writing, arithmetic, music, manners and morals, is at least as generally diffused, and as faithfully promoted by the clerical body, as in Scotland."—P. 439. In Rome there are schools in every street; with a population of 158,678, it has 372 public primary schools, with 482 teachers, and 14,099 children attending them; a university with 660 students; and seven universities in the papal states for two millions and a half of people. All this mass of education the clergy direct: "the flocks follow the more readily for being trained, if the leaders only keep ahead of the crowd."—P. 441. The Catholic clergy have adroitly seized on education; they have made use of the great revival of religious feeling, and the reaction consequent upon the reign of French infidelity; they have entered into the spirit of the age; they have exerted the elasticity and flexibility of their Church to " cover with the mantle of Catholicism opinions wide enough to have caused schisms and sects in former ages."—P. 444. Their religion "adapts itself to every degree of intelligence and to every class of intellect; it is a net which adapts its meshes to the minnow and the whale."—P. 445. The general doctrines of Christianity are as ably inculcated as from our own pulpits.

" I strolled one Sunday evening in Prussia into the Roman Catholic church at Bonn, on the Rhine. The priest was catechizing, examining, and instructing the children of the parish, in the same way, and upon the same plan, and with the same care to awaken the intellectual powers of each child by appropriate questions and explanations, as in our well conducted Sunday schools that are taught on the system of the Edinburgh Sessional School. And what of all subjects was the subject this Catholic priest was explaining and inculcating to Catholic children; and by his familiar questions, and their answers, bringing most admirably home to their intelligence?—the total uselessness and inefficacy of mere forms of prayer, or verbal repetitions of prayers, if not understood and accompanied by mental occupation with the subject, and the preference of silent mental prayer to all forms—and this most beautifully brought out to suit the intelligence of the children. I looked around me, to be satisfied that I was really at the altar steps of a popish church, and not in the school-room of Dr. Muir's, or any other well-taught Presbyterian parish in Edinburgh."—P. 446.

The apparent unity of belief in the Romish Church is much in its favour. This unity is only apparent, but it is very engaging.

And the adjustment of " material ideas" to assist the mental energies accounts for "the greater devotional fervour of Catholics than Protestants."—P. 448.

"*Fas est*, &c." Let us ponder these things well. Here is a *précis* of the causes of the success of continental Catholicism, from which we may draw a deep, and if we will, a most instructive lesson. It is drawn up, and with no mean skill, by one who is a friend neither of us nor of Rome: the more valuable then his testimony. What Mr. Laing says is extorted from him; he is, with all sincerity, as little disposed to praise Rome as he must be disinclined to arraign Scotch Calvinism. We may learn equally from the failure of the one as from the advance of the other. The picture may be overcharged, as where he says, that "relic veneration, pilgrimages, penances, and processional mummery* appear to be silently relaxed, or relinquished;" but it is substantially true. Let us dare to look these in the face. Here is a warm friend of the principle at least of the Scotch communion, an admirer and advocate of its theory, admitting that the lack of a priestly and exclusive character of the ministry sinks its influence immeasurably below the authoritative and hierarchical claims of Rome. Are we prepared to give up this claim? Are we ready to

---

* Was the author ever in Sicily? because he would have qualified this expression, had he ever witnessed the painful processions exhibited in Messina, or in Catania: for example, at the feast of the Immaculate Conception.

forego our apostolic credentials? Should we not rather " stir up the gift which is in us from putting on of hands," develop our sacred character, claim from God that grace with which the Holy Spirit, at ordination, has sanctified our ministrations, show the world openly what is the heavenly power of our commission, and what is the danger to souls in neglecting the appointed means of grace? If the **strength** of Rome consists in this,—if we have equal and superior titles **to this** power,—shall souls perish because we fail in telling men of their duties, in manfully displaying those "gifts and powers" which are not our own, but the presence of Christ dwelling in His Church, and in that alone?

Or again, we may bear the taunt, "the Puseyites of the Church of England alone are inconsequent; for if they claim apostolic succession and apostolic reverence for the clerical body, they should lead the apostolic life of celibacy, and repudiate their worldly spouses, interests, and objects."—P. 432. We may bear the taunt, because we can deny the fact, that the celibate of the clergy is an apostolic ordinance, and therefore we escape the charge of a logical inconsequence; but we may profit by this. They that "have wives may be as though they had none:" we may, by purity of life, by self-denial, by walking among men as a holy and separate class, preach by our practice against licentiousness and avarice, evil passions, and worldliness.

If persecution and the neglect of the state has strengthened Rome, it seems as though God's good providence, by providing sharper discipline, were training us to higher duties and more vigorous efforts. No poverty can be much deeper than that to which we are hastening. The multiplication of small benefices, the infinitesimal subdivision of the revenues of the Church, will leave us all poor enough. But our "deep poverty may abound to riches," if we have but grace to be thankful for it, and to use it.

Once more, if, as an alien confesses, our power is in our Church Service, what folly were it not to multiply our prayers; what madness were it to throw away our sole strength! To prize and magnify the blessedness of the Prayer Book, to carry out all its orders, to teach its whole spirit, to exhibit in action the whole system, the heart as well as the form, of our ritual, we are assured, by those who love us not, is that upon which our superior moral influence solely rests. Why, then, should the pulpit take precedence of the altar, as it does?

Has Rome acted with serpentine prudence in cultivating education? Should not "the priest's lips keep knowledge?" Are we to despise a learned clergy, and boast that we have no time to read? Are we prepared, with these startling proofs before us, to give up the education of youth to a government board, to submit to an Irish scheme, from which religion is excluded, or, still worse, taught under a hundred forms? Should we not rather take warning from the success of our enemies, and recur to that oral and catechetical teaching, which, while it cultivates the head, allures, and softens, and engages the heart? If in Rome the clergy " hold the reins, and are the superintendents, if not the actual teachers in all the schools," it is our policy to take a leaf out of the same book: and if it be true, as to some extent it is, that among us "the scholars have outgrown the teachers; and the teachers, instead of advancing with and leading the progress of the age, are in danger of becoming superannuated appendages on the religion of the people, sustained by it, not sustaining it, nor capable of directing it in the vast educational and missionary efforts which the religious sentiments of the people are making by their own agents,"—(p. 444) —we ought to be more than ever cautious how we plunge into the undisciplined chaos of Bible Societies, and Pastoral Aid Societies, and City Missions, and the like, in which "an evangelical laity acts independently, and too frequently in opposition to the Church," to use our author's striking phrase.

Unity, we are told, even though apparent, not real, has a power unknown to Protestantism. "There is," Mr. Laing tells us, "distinct ground for sectarianism and dissent in the very nature of the Protestant Church."—P. 447. If this be its innate tendency, if it be its essence, we must take ourselves to task; seriously, though it be painfully, examine the fact; and if we have not "touched the unclean thing," if we are not committed to this principle, it is our plain duty to deny the charge; to repudiate with scorn the attempt to fasten it upon us; and show forth our Catholic surname in the eyes of foes alike and friends. We repeat, then, that we may profit much by this painfully instructive chapter, the twenty-first, on Catholicism and Protestantism.

But the most interesting portion of Mr. Laing's book remains: we refer to the chapters vii. and viii., on the history and formation of the new Prussian church.

Into the original differences between Calvin and Luther,—how Zwingli endeavoured, at least as far as teaching went, to separate, and Melancthon to reconcile, though by his vacillations he rather disturbed, the discordant elements,—this is not the place to enter. The difficulty and absurdity of confession succeeding confession, and explanation following apology, was soon felt; and as there has always been a vast deal of electoral and imperial influence in religious matters in Germany, the first attempt to promote unity even among the daily diverging elements of the Lutheran body, was by the Formula Concordiæ of 1577, promoted by the Elector Augustus of Saxony; an agreeable appendix of eclecticism this to the Confession of Augsburgh, and Melancthon's defence of it, the Articles of Smalcald, and Luther's two catechisms, all of which were required, in the sixteenth century, as credentials for the ministry. The Lutheran body, never remarkably harmonious in temper, found out in time that this array of fences was not agreeable; beyond them lay the smiling fields of Protestantism in its full development. The symbolical books, too, made a sort of theological hedge, but it was not very uniform; it was weak in some places, and needlessly formidable in others: how were they to escape? Some clever person or other found out a device, unequalled in acuteness; they would not grub up the fence—forbid it the memory of all the Reformers! but they would put a snug little wicket gate, which should always be a-jar, and then, why, " we can get out when we like, and wander as far as we please, and the fence and ditch will look as strong and secure as ever." And, with a vengeance, they did stray pretty far from Luther's stout dogmatism, till rationalism and infidelity found themselves in all but undisturbed possession of nine out of ten pulpits and churches in Germany. What do our readers fancy was this wicket gate?—Only one little clause crept in; just four words were added. Nobody knew how they came there—few stopped to inquire: the ministers swore to all the volumes of articles at which their fathers made such wry faces, and they could with equal safety have sworn to two dozen or two score such confessions; for they qualified it all by the convenient salvo, "*quatenus cum SS. concordant.*" Here was latitude enough—a comprehensive mantle, which included the amiable Stock and the infidel Paulus under the same ample folds; which could reject neither Wegscheider nor Strauss, even while it embraced Neander and Tholuck. We are not desirous of re-writing one of the most painful chapters in religious history; the late Mr. Rose has done it most ably. Indifference and absolute irreligion were the natural results of their qualification. Mosheim describes it complacently in a well-known passage:—

"The Reformed church still carries the same external aspect. For though there.be everywhere extant certain books, creeds, and confessions, by which the wisdom and vigilance of ancient times thought proper to perpetuate the truths of religion, and to preserve them from the contagion of heresy, yet, in most places, no person is obliged to adhere strictly to the doctrines they contain; and those who profess the main and fundamental truths of the christian religion, and take care to avoid *too great an intimacy (nimiam consuetudinem)* with the tenets of Socinianism and Popery, are deemed worthy members of the Reformed church. Hence, in our times, this great and extensive community comprehends in its bosom Arminians, Calvinists, Super-lapsarians, Sub-lapsarians, and Universalists [a few years more would have added Infidels and Pantheists] who live together in charity and friendship, and unite their efforts in healing the breach, and diminishing the weight and importance of those controversies that separate them from each other."—Century xviii.

So much for the stability of Lutheran doctrine.

But what was their discipline? Had they no liturgy, no form of prayer? Yes.

"Several were composed; not one was generally received, nor enforced by authority; and of these different forms, almost all have long fallen into disuse, from the want of a church government, which had either the ability or the will to enforce their use, and from the changes of opinion and entire indifference of the clergy themselves."—*Rose on German Protestantism*, p. 18.

And though we hear of this or that *liturgy*, it must be borne in mind that the phrase is often applied to regulations of the form of worship,—*agenda* seems the German phrase,—and not in the subordinate sense of the office of prayers, still less in its stricter sense of the eucharistic office, to which it ought to be confined.

This was the Lutheran *church* (1) of the present century; we now turn to the other passive party to the marriage, so happily celebrated *auspiciis Regis Serenissimi Frederici Gulielmi, Fidei Paranymphi.*

The Calvinist body, or rather, "the Reformed church," made short work both of confessions and liturgies. They were consistent in so doing.* The Heidelberg Catechism was most in favour, but it was not imperative; the decrees of the synod of Dort were not sufficiently stringent, nor sufficiently liked, to prevent the most fearful intestine differences; the *Formula Consensus Helvetica*, by deciding, but embroiled the fray; besides, its influence was scarcely felt on the "yesty wave" of Calvinistic liberty; and Mosheim speaks of it as "deprived of all authority, and sunk into utter oblivion." Rose thinks it doubtful whether subscription, even at first, was required: it is certain that very early in the history of this communion, the most unbounded liberty of thought and teaching was permitted, if not encouraged; indeed, the bodies composing the complex "Reformed church," rather rejected unity than desired it. If liturgies and forms of administering the sacraments are appointed, yet they are not imperative: though they are used in France, and, as we have seen, at Geneva, the unrebuked and unrebukable pleasure of the German and Scotch ministers has dispensed even with forms; and prayer is abandoned to the enthusiasm or the carelessness, the ignorance or the indecency, of individual teachers.

In France we believe the Reformed service to consist of a portion of Scripture, the Decalogue, a prayer from the Genevan liturgy, a psalm, an extempore prayer and sermon, another prayer from the service book, a hymn, the blessing.

In Germany, as has been shown, some congregations, or rather some teachers, used some liturgy or other, and some used none. And these were the elements of religion which the late king of Prussia found in his dominions; these the sons of the Reformation, celebrating the third centenary of its existence, in the year 1817.

On the Lutheran side there was high doctrine enough. There is consubstantiation, of which Mr. Laing, as was to have been expected, speaks in the most flippant and offensive way (as he does elsewhere of the real presence). "The Puseyite may perhaps understand it; the Calvinist can only wish him joy of his intellect; the doctrine borders on sheer nonsense."—P. 184. He adds that it has been lowered into practical Zwinglianism. This is not the point; it is the doctrine of the body, and as Lutherans have not rejected the Augsburgh Confession, it may be as well to remind our Records and Christian

---

* Mr. Laing (p. 184) has an extraordinary passage:—"The Formula Consensus, and the Resolutions of the synod of Dort, are the only symbolical writings of the Calvinistic church (!) which retain the doctrine of predestination in all its Calvinistic rigidity. The other German confessions of faith softened and modified it from time to time; and, *at last*, the Heidelberg Catechism omitted it." Does he imagine that the Form of Concord of 1675, and the Dordrechtan decrees of 1619, became modified and unused and relaxed in a catechism dated 1563?

Observers, what this same document contains, "De confessione docent quod *absolutio privata* in ecclesiis retinenda sit." " Falso accusantur nostræ ecclesiæ, quod missam aboleant, retinetur enim missa apud nos, et summâ reverentiâ celebratur." "Servatur apud nos una communis missa *singulis feriis, atque aliis etiam diebus.*" "Confessio in ecclesiis apud nos non est abolita. Docentur homines ut absolutionem plurimi faciant, quia sit vox Dei, et mandato Dei pronuncietur. Ornatur potestas clavium." "Sentiunt potestatem clavium seu potestatem episcoporum, juxta evangelium potestatem esse Dei." And there are certain observations which draw a distinction between popular practices (quidam abusus) and the authorized teaching of the Roman church, as in the matter of the mass, where the *mass* itself (*missa*) is retained, while private *masses* and *missæ collatæ ad quæstum* are rejected; and in confession, and in fasting, when occasion is taken to say, "Christianus debeat se corporali disciplinâ aut corporalibus exercitiis et laboribus sic exercere et coercere, ne saturitas aut desidia extimulet ad peccandum;" and in the celibate of the clergy, where the point urged is, "Status monasteriorum qualis fuerat," so many of these observations are there, that we are strongly reminded of a certain No. 90. But the fear of the Record overpowers us, and we pause. We will just dare to ask some of our friends who are loudest in their praises of the "sister churches of the continent," whether they ever saw this sentence:—"Hæc summa est doctrinæ. Et consentaneam esse judicamus et propheticæ ac apostolicæ scripturæ, et catholicæ ecclesiæ; postremo etiam Romanæ ecclesiæ, quatenus ex probatis scriptoribus nota est. Non enim aspernamur consensum catholicæ ecclesiæ, nec est animus nobis ullum novum dogma et ignotum sanctæ ecclesiæ invehere in ecclesiam. Nec patrocinari impiis aut seditiosis opinionibus volumus, quas ecclesia catholica damnavit."— *Confess. Aug. in Epilogo.* We repeat, then, as far as words go, there is catholic doctrine enough on one side of the compact.*

But how stands the Reformed, or Calvinistic, church, for positive doctrine?

Τρὶς μὲν ἐφωρμήθην, ἐλέειν τέ με θυμὸς ἄνωγε,
Τρὶς δέ μοι ἐκ χειρῶν σκιῇ εἴκελον, ἢ καὶ ὀνείρῳ,
Ἔπτατο ———

Definition fails where you must use but negatives. What little of doctrine Calvinism ever possessed had been evaporated; the

---

* We are aware that this is only one side of the Augsburgh Confession: there are very many painful things in it. For example, in the preface, "in hâc religionis causâ nostrorum concionatorum confessionem offerimus." Art. I. "Ecclesiæ apud nos docent." Art. IV. "—docent, quod homines gratis justificentur—*cum credunt se in gratiam recipi.*" Art. VII. "Ad veram unitatem, satis est consentire de doctrinâ evangelii et administratione sacramentorum." Art. X. The significant change of "corpus et sanguis Christi *vere adsint*," of the first edition, to "*vere exhibeantur*," of the second. Art. XIV. The vagueness of the "rite vocatus," the sole qualification of the minister, unexplained by any ordinal or prayer-book, which settles the sense of our 23d Article. Art. VII. Of the supplement, "liceat episcopis, *seu pastoribus* facere ordinationes, ut res ordine gerantur," &c.

dogma of predestination was no longer rigidly taught; the teaching of Calvin, and even of Zwingli, was forgotten on the great sacramental controversy. The Reformed church was emphatically the " barren and dry land, where no water was." What possible element had it in common with Lutheranism? In theory none—in fact it had a most fatal resemblance. There was the same blight of indifference upon both communions: the Lutherans had fallen from the Confession of Augsburgh by the natural steps—enthusiasm, fanaticism, divisions, indifference; 132 liturgies, church services, or agenda, in the first thirty-two years of the Reformation (we quote Mr. Laing, p. 200), were portentous elements from which to expect stability; and during his life-time, like Wesley, even the great Reformer of Geneva began to fear that he had gone too far. (What a bitter moment must that be, when a Reformer finds that he cannot control his own disciples!) The nineteenth century found the different communions of the Reformed at peace; the peace of sleep, almost of death.

The king of Prussia is but a " king of shreds and patches;" his present kingdom is made up of waifs and strays. Good luck and good management have done much for his house; a little by conquering, and a little by stealing, and a little by marriage, and a little by bargains; and thus the margravate of Brandenburgh has been huckstered into the kingdom of Prussia in a hundred years or so; the very counterpart of a chandler's fortune. His people were of the same motley character.

" The Prussian population, in 1837, consisted, according to the official report of Von Hoffman, director of the statistical bureau, of 14,098,125 souls, of whom—

8,604,748	were of the United Evangelical, or new Prussian Church.
5,294,003	were of the Roman Catholic Church.
1,300	were of the Greek Church.
14,495	were Mennonites or Moravians.*
183,579	were Jews, of whom 102,917 had civil rights as Prussian subjects.

14,098,125

" Of the eight and a half millions of the former Protestant, now Evangelical Prussian church, the proportions of those who were Lutheran and Calvinistic are not known, as, after the amalgamation of the two, in 1817, into one church by royal edict, the distinction was considered as abolished in all official acts.

" It appears from the proclamation of his late Majesty, of September 27, 1817, addressed to these eight and a half millions of his Protestant subjects, that the amalgamation of the Lutheran and Calvinistic churches into one Prussian church had been a favourite idea of the royal family for some generations. The political object, probably, was to raise Prussia to the same position with regard to Protestant Germany, in which Austria stands with regard to Catholic Germany—to make the Prussian house the civil head and protector of Protestantism. This proclamation or announcement of the royal will to unite the two branches of the Protestant church into one, is of date September 27, 1817, and in words as follows:—' My illustrious ancestors, the Elector John Sigismund, the Elector George William, the great Elector and King Frederic I.,

---

* Surely Mr. L. does not confound the Mennonites, who are Anabaptists, with the Moravians?

and King Frederic William II., laboured with anxious and pious care, as the history of their lives and government shows, to unite the two divided Protestant churches, the Lutheran and the Reformed (Calvinistic), into one evangelic christian church in their land. Honouring their memory and salutary intentions, I willingly join in this purpose, and pray that a work pleasing to God, which, in their days, met with insurmountable obstacles from an unhappy sectarian spirit, may, under the influence of a better spirit, which sets aside the non-essential, and holds fast by the essential in Christianity, in which both confessions of faith agree, be accomplished in my states, to the honour of God and the welfare of the christian church, at the approaching centenary commemoration of the Reformation. Such a truly religious union of the two Protestant churches, separated as they are only by external differences, accords with the great end of Christianity, fulfils the first intentions of the Reformers, is in the spirit of Protestantism, promotes the public worship, is advantageous to domestic piety, and will be the spring of many useful improvements in schools and churches, which are now prevented by differences of faith. To this wholesome, long wished-for, and often vainly attempted union, in which the Reformed (Calvinistic) church will not have to go over to the Lutheran, nor the Lutheran to the Reformed, but both will form one new created, evangelical christian church, in the spirit of their holy Founder, no obstacle now exists in the nature of things, provided both these parties earnestly, and in true christian spirit, desire it; and on the approaching occasion of returning thanks to Divine Providence for the unspeakable blessing of the Reformation, show that they truly honour the memory of its great founder, by carrying on his immortal work. But much as I wish that the Reformed and Lutheran churches in my dominions may partake with me in these well-considered views, I respect their rights and liberty, and am far from pressing them, on this occasion, to adopt and establish it. This union can only be of real value if neither persuasion nor indifference induce its acceptance, but a real and free conviction; and if its roots and existence be not planted in the inward heart, and not merely in outward forms. As I myself intend in this spirit to commemorate the centenary fast day in celebration of the Reformation, in a union of the two congregations (hitherto called the Reformed and the Lutheran congregations of the garrison and court attendants at Potsdam) into one evangelical christian congregation, and to partake with it of the holy sacrament of the Lord's supper, so I trust this my own example will operate beneficially on all the Protestant congregations in my dominions, and will be generally followed in spirit and in truth. I leave it to the wisdom of the consistories, and the pious zeal of the clergy and their synods, to determine the outward concurring forms of this union, convinced that the congregations will, in true christian spirit, willingly follow them, and that wheresoever the view is directed to what is the essential, and to the great holy subject itself, the forms will be easily adjusted, and the externals will of themselves proceed from the internals, simple, dignified, and true. May the promised period arrive, when all shall form one flock under one shepherd, with one spirit, one love, one hope!'"—Pp. 177—180.

And so the church was made in the Downing-street of Berlin: and in 1822 it was fitted with a liturgy, under the auspices of Bishops*

---

* Among other odd functions, that of making a sort of bishop seems to have belonged to the Prussian sovereigns from the first. "Frederick, the first king of Prussia, found it necessary, for the greater solemnity of his coronation, (!) 1700-1, to give *the title* of bishops to two of the chief of his clergy, the one a Lutheran, the other a Reformed; the former died soon after; the other, Dr. Ursinus, continued without a colleague," &c.—*Abp. Sharp's Life*, vol. i. 403. "These bishops possess merely the name."—*Rose.* We believe that Strauss—not the notorious rationalist,—and this same Neander—not the Church historian,—at present hold this office. Some of the episcopal functions, such as confirmation, are performed by the ordinary ministers putting on a gold chain, and acting bishop, so to say, for the occasion.

Eylert and Neander; and as we have lately been told "from authority," that the "Prussian church has a national liturgy compiled from the ancient liturgies, agreeing in all points of doctrine with the liturgy of the English Church," our readers would like to know what it is like.

"Ten years after the establishment of the new Prussian church, Bishop Eylert, of Potsdam, published a defence (1830) and explanation of its principle and working. According to the reverend author's view, the merit of his new liturgy (he was one of the composers of it) *consists mainly* in the historical presentation of the sacramental elements of the Lord's supper: in the consecration of the elements in the Lutheran and in the Calvinistic church, it is distinctly announced to the communicant in what sense it is presented to him;—in the one, it is as the body and blood; in the other, it is as the symbols of the body and blood. The synod of Berlin evaded the dilemma by not consecrating the elements at all, either in the one or the other sense, but presenting them to the communicant with the historical averment, 'Christ said, This is my body,' &c. 'Christ said, This is my blood,' &c.—that is, in its being so presented that *each denomination of Christians may take it, and apply his own meaning to it.*—Pp. 37, 38. (Ueber den Werth, und die Wirkung des Evangelsche Kirche, &c.)—The reverend bishop forgets that, so taken, it is no sacrament at all: it is only a reference to an historical fact, not to any religious signification of that fact, such as Catholics, Lutherans, and Calvinists attach to it, however widely they may differ from each other as to what that signification is, or ought to be. On his principle, Jew, Gentile, or Mahometan, might receive the Sacrament from him, and remain Jew, Gentile, or Mahometan; for it is only presented to him as figuring an historical fact,—not at all doubted, and not at all connected with any peculiar doctrine attached to that fact. This courtly divinity may suit the meridian of Potsdam, but is not christian divinity."—*Laing*, pp. 188, 189.

Hard words, Mr. Laing, but worse remain; he calls this device of Bishop Eylert a "church trick" (p. 183), "a jesuitical side-door, through which slender consciences, if not the robust, of both Lutherans and Calvinists, could slip in and go to the table, and slip out, and each take the sacrament, and please his Majesty, without offence to his own church doctrines" (p. 185); "a quirk unworthy of the act" (p. 186); "no union of the Calvinistic and Lutheran churches, but a hocus-pocus trick; a knavish way of getting rid of the difficulty; a deception as to doctrine and meaning; a form having no reference to any doctrine; a fiction; a very good cloak." (*Ibid.*) We are quoting Mr. Laing; we say nothing; but it is quite clear that he does not think that the new Prussian liturgy "agrees in all points of doctrine with the English Church;" and it is equally clear that Bishop Eylert cannot think so, for he says distinctly, in his twelve grounds of vindication, that "the new liturgy differs in no essentials of doctrine from the liturgies used in the Lutheran and Calvinistic churches;" unless Bishop Eylert is prepared to say that the Anglican doctrine, and the Lutheran doctrine, and the Calvinistic doctrine, on the Eucharist, are all one and the same thing, a position which we never heard maintained, though, as we have fallen upon strange times, we may live to see it.

This new sacramental form was first used by the late king, 31st October, 1817, and from Mr. Rose's book, p. 252, we learn that the union of the two communities and a similar "historical" administration was introduced into Baden in 1821, and into other parts of Germany at different periods of the century.

But we have not yet done with the new prayer-book of the new church. It was first framed in 1822.

"The ministers of the new church are prohibited in the agenda from occupying more than one hour in the whole service, and the liturgy is to occupy one half hour. The sermon consequently can scarcely have more than twenty or twenty-five minutes, which is totally insufficient, they assert, for conveying christian instruction. They are also prohibited by the new agenda from using any introductory or concluding prayer to the sermon—the most important and effective parts of the old service, both in the Lutheran and Calvinistic church."—P. 201.

"The following is the order of the service in the new Prussian church. There is an altar railed in, and covered with an altar cloth. *Two lighted wax candles and a crucifix stand upon the altar, and behind and around it are pictures of saints and holy subjects, as in a Roman Catholic church.* The only difference observable is, that the priest at the altar is in a plain black gown, instead of the embroidered robes in which the Catholic priest officiates. He reads the new liturgy standing with his back against the altar, and facing the people. The amen to each prayer is finely quavered out by the choristers behind the altar, and the 'Halleluia,' the 'Holy, holy, holy,' the 'Glory to God in the highest,' &c., are delivered with great musical effect, as might be expected in so musical a land."—*Ibid.*

"The *Kurie Eleaison* [sic], and other operatic quaverings in the new service, are, it is said, borrowed from the Greek church, the late king having, when on a visit to Russia, been much pleased with those parts of the Greek service."—Pp. 217, 218.

"So little has it been intended that the congregation should take a part in this new service, that no books of the liturgy equivalent to the English Common Prayer-book are in their hands. The liturgy is for the clergyman only, and is not even to be got at the booksellers' shops.* The only book of public worship in the hands of the congregation, is the Gesang buch. This is a sort of hymn-book, in doggrel verse, which supersedes the Psalms of David and the paraphrases of portions of Scripture used in our church services. It is printed as prose, but each clause of a sentence is a line rhyming to another clause. It is divided into sections and sentences, which are numbered; and the numbers being stuck up in conspicuous parts of the church, the congregation on entering sees what is to be sung without the minister or clerk giving out the place and verse. The whole part that the congregation has to take in the public worship by the new service, is to sing or chaunt a portion of this Gesang buch with the accompaniment of the organ, before the minister comes to the altar to read the liturgy, and again in the interval between the liturgy and the sermon. This Gesang buch is not a collection of versions or paraphrases of any particular passages of the Old and New Testament, nor have its hymns the slightest reference to Scripture, or any biblical allusion or phraseology. It is no doubt

---

* This must be our own apology, for adopting only Mr. L.'s extracts from the Prussian service-book. London cannot produce a copy. We have sent to Berlin for one; and perhaps our readers may see more of it.

distilled from the Scriptures, but it carefully avoids giving any flavour of its origin. . . . . The people have nothing but this Gesang buch as necessary in their public worship, and a meagre childish composition it is, altogether unworthy of being the manual of devotion, and suitable rather for an infant school than for a congregation of grown-up Christians."—Pp. 202, 203.

This we think unfair : some parts of the Gesang buch are simple and beautiful.

"The German language is now so generally studied, that a specimen of the Gesang buch will enable most readers to judge for themselves of this Prussian substitute for the Psalms of David. By giving its exact English synonyme below each German word, the English reader even may be able to form some idea of its style and merits :—

"XXXIV. 1. Jesus wir erscheinen hier deine Sussigkeit zu schmecken!
Jesus we appear here thy sweetness to taste!
deine Gnad erflehen wir Herz und Ohren zu erwecken: dass wir deine
thy grace solicit we heart and ears to awaken: that we thy
Himmelslehren uns zum Trost mit Freuden hören.
heaven-teaching us to comfort with joy may hear.

"2. Oefne deines Dieners Mund, gieb ihm deines Geistes Gaben, dass er
Open thy servant's mouth, give him thy Spirit's gifts, that he
mag aus Herzens-grund, mit des Wortes Kraft uns laben, und dass uns die
may out of heart-ground, with the word's power us refresh, and that us the
Himmels-speise stark auf unser Pilger-reise.
heaven-food may strengthen on our pilgrim-journey.

"3. Dir dem Vater und dem Geist soll das Herz geheiligt werden,
To thee the Father and the Spirit shall the heart dedicated be,
hilf nur dass wir allermeist uns erheben von der Erden, um mit innigen
help only that we most especially us raise from the earth, for with inward
Verlangen deine Gaben zu empfangen.
desire thy gifts to receive."—Pp. 203, 204.

Be it observed, that the above is metrical and in rhyme.

" In the afternoon there is no service at the altar, no liturgical prayers as in the Church of England, but there is a section of the Gesang buch sung, the Lord's prayer, a sermon, the Lord's prayer again, and the blessing, and another portion of the Gesang buch sung, which constitute the evening service. This radical division in the church service appears to have formed a similar division in the religious state of the people. You see some going to church to hear the liturgy, and going out when it is finished, as having gone through all that is essential in religious duties: others, again, are going in when the liturgy is over, or go to the evening service only, as the sermon, and not the ceremonial, is to them the essential. The junction of the two distinct principles in one service is as incongruous as it would be to bind the New Testament and Dr. Strauss' Life of Jesus in one volume."—P. 207.

" In the two distinct services tacked together in this new Prussian church, that which addresses itself to the mind of the congregation, the sermon, is by no means left in free action. It is not only shorn of its introductory and concluding prayers appropriate to the subject preached, and which the twelve ministers consider the most valuable privilege of their former Lutheran church, from its beneficial effect on their congregations, and it is not only confined in time, by church rule given out by the state, to half an hour, but the text on which alone the ministers throughout all the kingdom are allowed to preach, is appointed on all fast days, or particular church days, by government—that is to say, it is given out to the ministers by the consistory of each province, of which consistory the head and president is the high president of the province, the equivalent functionary to the préfet commanding in civil, military, and ecclesiastical affairs, according to his orders from the general government."—Pp. 208, 209.

All this too may be, for aught we know, to agree in all points of doctrine with the English Church, " lighted wax candles, crucifix," and all; but what would the " Marylebone Operative Protestant Association," that power in the church (as somebody said of something behind the throne), greater than the church itself, say to it?

And this is the new Prussian evangelical church, and this its liturgy and *agenda*. The Lutheran and Calvinistic names, and churches, and the term Protestant, are no more; an " order from the Minister of Home Affairs," (like one of Buonaparte's—" The house of Braganza has ceased to reign,") signed their death-warrant. In 1830 the prayer-book was introduced into all the churches; and in 1834 an edict prohibits *any* Protestant religious meetings—the old Lutheran among the rest—which do not use it. But considerable opposition met the new form of worship at first. Some of the tatters of old electorates pieced into the new web of Prussia, had old " Protestant rights," which they scrupled at resigning; the liberals began to think that though political centralization might be a good thing, this ecclesiastical legislation was not only "imposing arbitrary shackles on the human mind," but it was to make every state sovereign a home pope; the old Lutherans looked askance at their new brethren; Schliermacher objected; some magistrates remonstrated; and twelve ministers protested; though, after all, the resistance did not amount to much; rationalism had done its work; indifference was tolerably general; the king's commands were strong; and the barrack and parade obedience of Prussia was ready, in some cases from ignorance, and in most from carelessness, to accept anything and everything from headquarters; and so, out of 8,950 Protestant congregations in Prussia, 7,750 joined the union; and of the rest, the 1,200 recusants, we do not hear much; some, we suppose, were persuaded,—and there was one plan which rather reminded us of another great Head of the Church—Henry VIII.—and the six articles. Good King Frederic William III. had an army to keep, and a church to plant, and dissenters to reclaim, so he wisely contrived to combine all these separate duties; but we prefer Mr. Laing's account of it.

" Forgetting that by his proclamation of 1817 he wants the union to be brought about ' neither by persuasion, nor indifference, but by inward conviction,' the new form of service was introduced with armed force, all objections to it were crushed as treasonable, and on some poor villages in Silesia, which obstinately refused to exchange the old Lutheran service for the new, troops were quartered on the people to be supported at their expense—that is, to live in free quarters, as if they were enemies in the land, until the people conformed. The people were ruined, and a few of these poor martyrs, about six hundred in number, calling themselves old Lutherans, found their way by Hamburgh and Hull to America—the last of the religious martyrs, it is to be hoped, whom the persecution of a despot will drive to her forests."—P. 188.

This scheme of comprehension is by no means new in the annals of the Lutheran and Reformed bodies. The convocation of Torgau, 1574, was designed to unite the Crypto-Calvinists of Saxony with the Lutherans, as well as to heal the divisions among the Lutherans themselves, although its immediate results seem to have been that the churches of Nassau and Hanau, and in 1595 the princes of Anhalt, and in 1604 Maurice, landgrave of Hesse, deserted the Lutheran for the Reformed community. His example was followed, in 1614, by the memorable defection of John Sigismund, elector of Brandenburgh. Through Peter du Moulin our King James, who enjoyed a theological fight with a zest as keen as that of his predecessor for a bear-baiting, interfered to promote an union of the two rival bodies; Sigismund attempted the same; a conference was held at Charenton in 1631, and another at Leipzig in the same year, at the instigation of Sigismund's successor, the elector George William; the King of Poland held a diet at Thorn, in which pacific measure Rome was invited to join, and a conference at Cassel, in 1661, was promoted by the elector Frederic William the Great, son of George William, for the same comprehensive purpose; the learning and piety of Calixtus was expended in vain, and the name of Syncretism is the only memorial of one whose piety and earnestness formed the delightful but visionary scheme—alas! must it ever be so?—of uniting the Reformed, the Lutheran, and Romish communions. The learned Lutheran Pfaff revived the project in 1723; but before this, Frederic, the son of Frederic William the Great, encouraged Ursinus, in 1705, to enter into negotiations with the English Church to promote the comprehension of the two foreign communities by means of the English Church. It was proposed to introduce into Prussia the English liturgy, which was actually translated for the purpose, and communicated to Tennison. The manuscript and proposal seem to have miscarried; the king took affront, and Tennison, who really appears to have been ignorant of the whole matter, bore, though unjustly, the blame of coldness in the affair.* It was renewed afterwards by Jablonski to Sharp, archbishop of York, through Smalridge, afterwards dean of Christ Church and bishop of Bristol. The project was entertained favourably by Sharp, an excellent prelate, in whose life a long and interesting correspondence on the subject is inserted; and it failed finally by the death of the king in 1713, and that of Sharp in 1714.

Jablonski was the father of the well-known author of the "Pantheon Ægyptiacum," and an able and excellent person; he had

---

* It is said that the celebrated Grabe was sent into England by this monarch for consecration. Richardson, the editor of Godwin, tells the story; but this could not have been the case, for Grabe was settled at Oxford in 1697, before Frederic's accession; he left Prussia voluntarily, on account of dissatisfaction with the Lutheran defect of succession: and his unflinching orthodoxy, which he displayed by joining the non-jurors, must have rendered him a very untractable instrument for the pacific measure in question.

personal reasons for recommending the introduction of the episcopate into Prussia, for he was himself senior or bishop of the Polish church, in point of fact of the Moravians, who derive a fancied succession from a certain Catholic bishop who is said to have turned Protestant in the time of J. Huss. This succession was just as false as that of the Swedish bishops (which puzzled even Leslie), though it seems to have satisfied Jablonski, for he adverts to it with great complacency in one of his letters; but it was clearly not sufficient for Frederic, who allowed him to carry it on by consecrating bishops (so called) for Poland, while he never thought of applying to this source for the projected Prussian episcopate. Altogether this scheme promised better than the others; it was countenanced and assisted by the celebrated Leibnitz, whose opinions of the doctrinal orthodoxy of the Roman faith, and his desire for union between her and the Reformed bodies, if it could be accomplished with justice, are a sufficient guarantee for his Catholic views. Frederic William revived the plan of comprehension in 1736, on the one hand proposing to remove the Calvinistic doctrine of predestination; on the other, giving up the Lutheran ceremonial; but without success. Religion seems to have been banished during the reign of Frederic, miscalled the Great; poetry, philosophy, Voltaire, and war, were more congenial to his temper than theological pacification; and it is no wonder that Frederic William II., in 1788, soon after his accession, was obliged to issue the famous religious edict (Rose, p. 183), complaining of Lutheran licentiousness in doctrine, their assumption of a tone contrary to Christianity, and their revival of Socinianism, Deism, &c. Even during the storm of war which desolated his kingdom, the late king of Prussia, Frederic William III., entertained the plan of introducing a general liturgy; his very first act which accompanied the peace of 1814 was to issue a proclamation on the subject, and the result we have already seen in the act of 1817. Of its success, we must once more quote our author.

"The forced amalgamation of the Lutheran and Calvinistic churches into this third thing, neither Lutheran nor Calvinistic, and the abolition of the very name of the Protestant church in Prussia, is undoubtedly the most gratuitous, unhappy, and senseless act of irresponsible despotism ever exercised over, and submitted to, by a christian people in civilized times. There is much in a name. With the abolition of the name of the Protestant religion, this government has effected what emperors and popes could not do—has nearly destroyed the Protestant religion itself in Germany, and with it almost all religion. The ancient liturgy of the Lutheran, the freely out-poured prayer of the Calvinist, being both silenced in the land, the mind of the great mass of the people had nothing Christian to hold by, nothing in religion venerated as doctrines or practices of worship from former times, from respected associations with the sufferings or deeds of their forefathers. Infidelity, Deism, Straussism, and all the other forms and shapes which unbelief in Christianity can assume in the speculative, dreaming, German mind, have had free play. Protestantism as a church, and even as a name, being abolished in Prussia, Christianity was left for its defences to the antiquated bulwark of the Roman Catholic faith. The middle ground between gross superstition and gross infidelity, on which the two Protestant churches were planted, was seized for state purposes to build this new Prussian church upon. The spread, in the same age, of Catholicism on one hand, and of infidelity on the other—the Catholic priest making converts on one side of the street, and Dr. Strauss on the other—shows a religious condition of the German people, which the traveller finds as unaccountable as it is undeniable, until he traces it as a natural consequence of this act of his late Prussian majesty, which cast loose at once all the ties which had held the public mind fast for three centuries to one or other of the two Protestant churches."—Pp. 207, 208.

If our readers are desirous of further details of the persecution which welcomed the new Prussian service-book into the churches, besides what we have supplied at pp. 388, 389, they will find it in a little book, "Persecution of the Lutheran Church," translated by Löwenberg, and published about eighteen months ago. Ministers suspended—dismissed—fined—imprisoned—starved;—the Countess Heukel and other ladies, condemned to imprisonment as rebels;—twenty dollars' fine imposed for a single attendance on the old Lutheran service;—five dollars a month if a peasant has his child confirmed by a Lutheran minister of the old school;—churches stormed;—women beaten and cut down by the sabres of the cavalry;—this is the peaceful birth of the state church of Prussia.

At this moment, when it is generally rumoured that the present king, Frederic William IV., is about to obtain a Prussian episcopate from this church—when he has already, in conjunction with some of our bishops, founded a Pruss-Anglican bishopric at Jerusalem—we trust that these tedious details will not be unacceptable to our readers. It beseems us not to inquire how far political reasons, and the desire, by means of his church, to erect an antagonist power to Russia and Austria, may influence him. Indeed, we have not space for the examination, which we had proposed to extend to these and kindred topics, by means of Messrs. Hope and Palmer, Mr. Maurice, and Dr. Hook. Above all, it behoves us well, before it is too late, *to inquire into the nature of this Prussian liturgy*, and to examine most rigidly the doctrinal purity of the new Prussian establishment. We have ventured to suggest a few hints on this head. We have been told by something like authority, that "the Church of England, by origin and doctrine, is most intimately akin to the German evangelical church;" from Mr. Laing's account, are we prepared to recognise the family likeness; can we say of what it is becoming the fashion to call sister-churches—

" ———— facies non omnibus una,
Nec diversa tamen, qualis decet esse sororum?"

Can we identify the spirit of persecution, which has conduced to the present apparent calm of this religious body, with that peaceful growth in holy things, the earnest of the presence of the Holy Spirit, which would accept the Episcopate as the highest and most heavenly blessing? Are we satisfied with its present results? The whole scheme is of the bureau, not of the altar: it is the court, not the clergy, which is on the move: the people might *accept* bishops as they did the new service; are they praying for them? Above all, *what guarantee have we of Prussian orthodoxy?* Is it the Augsburgh Confession? rating this even higher than we are disposed to do, the faith of a church is to be learned from its ritual, not from polemical confessions. We have already gained some insight into this service-book; and a fact, from which Mr. Laing (p. 205,) deduces a false inference, is to us very significant of its general spirit and soundness. It is this.

The new service approaches much more nearly to the Lutheran doctrines than to those of the Reformed body; and yet the opposition to it is all on the Lutheran side: they alone are dissatisfied, though, as far as externals go, they have it all their own way. How is this, but that there is some principle admitted which offends the more orthodox body, which the Lutheran unquestionably is, and which smooths all difficulties for the Calvinists? How else are we to dispose of the fact, which is a startling one, that the Reformed, who have been accustomed to no preconceived service at all, submit without a murmur to a ceremonial, which to them can differ very little from what they conceive of the Mass—and, on the other hand, the Lutherans object to what, in appearance, they have used since Luther's time? There must be a difference; and if it is the abandonment of any truth to conciliate Genevan doctrine, which we strongly suspect, it is high time for us to look most sharply into the whole matter, unless we are prepared to retrace our steps, and for the first time since the Reformation, commit ourselves to Swiss theology.

And here we dismiss Mr. Laing; accepting with gratitude his facts—estimating very highly his talents—and detesting his principles. We cannot, in parting, but rebuke him very earnestly for introducing a disgusting disquisition on "Checks on over-population," which we cannot trust ourselves to characterise as it deserves. He says, with great truth, that "there are some subjects which it is difficult to treat with decency of expression:" it beseems a Christian then to hold his tongue about them; which Mr. Laing, to his great disgrace, has not done. And we might have been spared some filthy details respecting a flagitious sect, the recent growth of "Evangelical" Prussia, called the Muckers, whose religion consists in sensual lewdness, which, while it finds a parallel in Otaheitan heathenism, too forcibly recalls the abominable history of some ancient heretics. There are things "of which it is a shame even to speak;" and these are of them.

Correspondence between the Foreign Aid Society of London, and the Sociétés Evangéliques of Paris and Geneva. London: Macintosh, Great New-street, 1841.

AMONG many perplexing features in the aspect of our times, it is a consolatory circumstance, that thoughtful members of the Church of England, though differing widely among themselves, are beginning almost universally to feel that our position in the christian world is unsatisfactory. The truth is forcing itself upon many minds, that the existence of divisions and separations, not merely within the limits of a single nation, but in the christian world, is a crying sin; and that every particular church which acquiesces in a state of separation from those whom she acknowledges for brethren, or does not labour (within her sphere) for the conversion and reformation of those whom she holds to have departed from the brotherhood, makes herself a party to the sin. It is beginning to be felt, that no formal diversities, or variations of opinion, which are consistent with the existence of a true church of Christ, can justify any other church in refusing to hold religious communion with those who receive and practise them; and that, on the other hand, no terms may be kept with those who have departed from the faith, but that all true churches are bound to set a mark upon them as heathens and publicans, and bring them back, if possible, by active proselytism, into the fold. It is felt, too, that churches which desire religious communion and reconciliation with other churches from which they are estranged, ought to seek it, or at least do something to promote it; and that if they do not, some responsibility will rest upon them for the continuance of the estrangement, whoever may have been to blame for its commencement.

We do not mean to profess a belief that these principles are now distinctly held by the generality of English churchmen; but we believe them to be acquiring power over many minds at once, and in different directions. It is difficult to see how they should fail to affect all, who use with sincerity the daily prayer, "Thy will be done on earth as it is in heaven," and remember the last words spoken by our Lord Jesus Christ, on the same night that he was betrayed, before he went into the garden where his Passion was to begin:—"Holy Father, keep through Thine own Name those whom Thou hast given Me, that they may be one, as We are.... Neither pray I for these alone, but for them also which shall believe on Me through their word; that they all may be one; as Thou, Father, art in Me, and I in Thee, that they also may be one in Us; that the world may believe that Thou hast sent Me. And the glory which Thou gavest Me, I have given them; that they may be one, even as We are one: I in them, and Thou in Me, that they may be made perfect in one; and that the world may know that Thou hast sent me, and hast loved them, as Thou hast loved Me." Even if love for the Saviour, or fear of the responsibility of counteracting His will, did not furnish sufficient motives, the thought which these words suggest, that the success of christian missions to the heathen (not to say the continuance of a belief in Christ in the nominally christian world) may essentially depend upon the preservation of unity and concord in the Church, ought to kindle zeal for the restoration of unity in every breast.

We are disposed to give credit for such feelings as these to certain gentlemen who have formed a society which they entitle " The Foreign Aid Society, for promoting the objects of the European Sociétés Evangéliques," and who have recently published an " Important Correspondence," which, if it justified their description of it, would be important indeed; for they speak of it as "pointing out a true basis of christian union." We have read this correspondence with interest, and now propose to examine it by those principles of unity which we have already adverted to, practically applied according to the four principal rules of limitation which appear upon the surface of holy Scripture. 1. That we must not unite with those who deliberately disobey the revealed will of God, (John xiv. 21; 1 Cor. xvi. 22.) 2. That we must not unite with those who reject any part of the necessary Faith originally delivered to the Church, (Gal. i. 8, 9; 1 Tim. vi. 3—6; 2 John 10, 11.) 3. That we must not unite with those who reject the Church, or despise the lawful authority of her commissioned ministers, (Matt. xviii. 17; Luke x. 16.) 4. That we must not unite with those who " walk disorderly, contrary to the tradition received from the apostles," or who " cause divisions and offences, contrary to the doctrine which we have learned," (2 Thess. iii. 6; Rom. xvi. 17.)

The object which these gentlemen propose to themselves, is nothing less than the union of the Reformed Churches of the continent with our own, " in one common confession of the truth as it is in Jesus." Having learned that "for more than sixteen months" the Société Evangélique of Geneva had been "anxious to promote a union among those who individually make a good confession of the faith as restored at the Reformation," they addressed, on the 16th of August, 1841, two letters, dated " 10, Exeter Hall," to the Committees of that Society and of the Société Evangélique at Paris. These letters were signed by seven laymen, and by the following priests:—the Rev. R. Burgess, the Rev. J. W. Cunningham, the Rev. E. Bickersteth, and the Rev. H. Hughes. No bishop appears to be a member of the English Society, or to have been consulted about its proceedings. The letters, however, were such in tone and language as might be expected from persons clothed with apostolic authority. That to Geneva began as follows:—

" To the brethren, members of the Committee, &c., the Committee of the Foreign Aid Society in London sends greeting; Grace be unto you, and peace from God our Father and the Lord Jesus Christ.—Beloved brethren, we have heard of the increase of your faith, and hope, and love, for which we cease not to give thanks."

Then, after referring, in terms which we shall presently quote, to the doctrine of the Helvetic Confession and Catechism, it proceeds:—

"We, therefore, having deliberated upon these matters, and heartily desirous of bringing our brethren in England to cooperate with us in aiding your efforts for the furtherance of the gospel, have requested our honorary secretary, who is about to depart for the continent, to solicit your serious attention to matters which he is instructed to lay before you touching Confessions of Faith and the union of Churches. And we have desired him to bring back to us, that we may present the same to the clergy of our beloved Church, a public declaration of your faith, and of your adherence to those great doctrines which were once held by the Church of Geneva."

Their object in seeking for this declaration, the English Committee declare to be, not any design of putting a yoke upon the Genevese Society, but that they may be enabled to "put to silence those who affirm that you do not hold the faith unfeigned."

We shall not stop to inquire whether it is a lawful thing for laymen and priests, living under episcopal authority, to take so much upon them as seems to be assumed in this letter. There is something startling in the tone of this particular document; and to some it may perhaps appear irreverent and presumptuous. It would manifestly be unsuitable to individuals, or a society seeking only to enlarge their own or the common stock of information, or to exchange an expression of sympathy with others like-minded with themselves. But we do not see on what principles it can be objected to, if the act to which it belongs, the opening of a formal negotiation for unity with a foreign religious community, is admitted to be one which it was competent for these gentlemen to undertake; and again, we do not see how it is possible to vindicate the constitution and practice of the greater number of our religious societies, without admitting the competency of any voluntary association of laymen and clergymen to undertake such a work as this, upon the mere suggestion of their own inward sense of duty. So that, if these gentlemen have done what cannot be strictly justified, they have been encouraged to do so by prevailing opinions and practices; and by doing it in a more religious and solemn way than usual, they seem to us only to have shown that they appreciate more clearly than others the character and nature of the office and function which they assume.

It is of importance, (since we are told to look in this correspondence for a "true basis of union,") to inquire on what notion of requisites to unity they have proceeded.

"We have great joy," they say to the Genevese Committee, "in learning that the Lord has raised up among you faithful servants, who are very zealous of restoring the Reformed Churches of the continent to 'the faith once delivered to the saints,' the chief points of which are summed up in the Helvetic Confession of Faith, and the Catechism so long in use in the Church of Geneva. We have compared these formularies with our Thirty-nine Articles of religion, and, with the exception of some minor points relative to ecclesiastical order and discipline, we find a remarkable concord. The Reformers of our Church and the Reformers of your country speak the same thing, and are of one mind with respect to all the essential doctrines of our holy religion; and we feel convinced that no other bond of union would be required to bring us into fraternal communion."

To the same effect, and almost in the same words, they write to their Parisian correspondents, substituting only the general expression, "the doctrines of your Reformers," for the mention of a definite Confession.

In this remarkable declaration there are three things to be observed, on which we shall make no comment beyond simply pointing them out. First, the writers of these letters assume agreement in the confession of a common doctrine to be a sufficient bond of christian union, without taking any notice of that other condition, distinguished from and superadded to orthodoxy of doctrine in Scripture—continuance "in the apostles' fellowship;" as we should interpret it, continuance in the communion of the Apostolic Church. Secondly, they consider that no essential difference from the English Church is involved in such passages of the Helvetic Confession, as those which express the doctrine of Reprobation, or those which state that, as to the Grace conveyed, or the Thing signified, there is absolutely no difference between Circumcision and Baptism, or the Passover and the Lord's Supper, (Helv. Conf. x. xix.) And lastly, they consider that the differences from the English Church expressed by such passages as, (1.) "Data est omnibus in ecclesiâ ministris una et æqualis potestas sive functio;" and (2.) "*Confirmatio* et extrema unctio inventa sunt hominum, quibus nullo cum damno carere potest ecclesia; neque illa nos in nostris ecclesiis habemus; nam habent illa quædam, quæ minimè probare possumus," (Helv. Conf. xviii. xix.); relate merely to "minor points" of "ecclesiastical order and discipline." If this judgment is right, doubtless the conclusion is right too, that such differences ought not to be obstacles to a cordial unity.

We now come to the replies elicited by these letters from the Committees at Geneva and Paris, to which they were addressed; replies so satisfactory to the London Committee, that, after printing them, they conclude with the following appeal :—

"To the above satisfactory and affecting declaration of our foreign brethren, the Committee will add nothing; but will seriously ask all who hold the truth as it is in Jesus, whether those who profess and are contending earnestly for such doctrines, are not entitled to the help and sympathy of our beloved Church established in this country, and of all who love the Lord Jesus Christ in sincerity ?"

Let us examine the reply of the Genevese Committee. Much of it is occupied with generalities and introductory matter, of which we should take no notice, were it not for one remarkable passage, expressing just the view of the Church of England which the communication made to them would naturally suggest.

"To this joy," they say, "is added another, which is, that this appeal comes to us from ministers and members of the Church of England; ...

of that Church, which God has placed in his heritage as one of the most powerful bulwarks against the invasions of the Papacy; of that Church, which, whether by her immediate efforts, *or by those of Christians who have gone forth from her bosom, (and whom, notwithstanding some differences, we please ourselves at our distance in identifying with her,)* has planted the standard of Jesus Christ in vast continents and in the most distant islands; of that Church, the purity of whose doctrine, its power, its constitution, (?) its greatness, and the important sphere which Divine Providence has assigned her, makes us justly regard her as *the elder sister of the Churches of the Reformation;* finally, of *that Church, which, by the Foreign Aid Society especially, manifests towards the other evangelical churches of the continent so cordial an affection,* and such brotherly support."

We agree in the opinion here implied, that, upon the principles of the Foreign Aid Society, a large proportion of the English dissenting communities ought to be included in the contemplated union; and we would suggest to the English Committee, that as natives of Great Britain, they are far more directly called upon to exert themselves for the establishment of intercommunion between the Church of England and those dissenting communities, (together with the Presbyterians of Scotland,) than to procure her reconciliation with the Protestants of Switzerland and France. The maxim, that "charity begins at home," cannot be without its application in religion as well as in other things.

But let us pass from all preliminary matter to the main point, the question of doctrine. The Geneva Committee, (modestly, though we scarcely see on what principle, declining the title of a church, and contenting themselves with that of a school,) declare their belief to be, that "*the fundamental truths of the christian religion,*" "*the capital fundamental doctrines,*" are none other than those "which the Protestant Churches proclaim *with common consent* in their Confessions of Faith," *upon the five following subjects:*—(1.) *The state of man;* (2.) *The grace of God;* (3.) *The nature of the Saviour;* (4.) *The work which he has accomplished;* (5.) *The work which he still carries on for the salvation of his people.* What these doctrines are they proceed to state.

Upon the first head, they express their agreement with "the Protestant Churches, and those of France in particular;" quoting from the French Confession of 1559, to the effect that, by the Fall, the nature of man "is entirely corrupted," and "his will always under subjection to sin." This, therefore, is what they hold to be one of the fundamental Truths of the christian religion, and *the whole fundamental Truth with respect to "the state of Man."* Catholic Christians need not be reminded that, important as the Truth upon this subject unquestionably is, no symbolical expression of it is to be found in any one of the creeds received by the Church.

Upon the second head, they express their agreement with the 17th Article of the Church of England, on Predestination. This, therefore, is, in their judgment, another fundamental Truth, and *the whole fundamental Truth with respect to the "grace of God."* Again, Catholic Christians need not be reminded that there is no article about Predestination or Election in any one of the Three Creeds.

Upon the third head, "the nature of the Saviour," they declare their agreement with "the Protestant Churches, and those of Germany in particular, in the famous Confession of Augsburg," to the following effect :—

> "We hold and teach that there is one only Divine Being, who is truly God; *and that there are, nevertheless, three persons in this one only Divine Being,* equal in power, equal in eternity, God the Father, God the Son, God the Holy Ghost . . . God the Son became man, born of the Virgin Mary, and he united in one person, in a manner inseparable, the two natures, human and divine; so that there is but one Christ, who is truly God and truly Man."

This, upon the most fundamental article of Christianity, is their substitution for the Catholic Creeds. It might have been expected that they would have taken this opportunity of declaring their adhesion to the Nicene Faith. They knew that a multitude of Protestant congregations all around them, in Geneva, in France, in Germany, which originally took their stand upon the Confessions of the sixteenth century, have lapsed into the very heresies which the Nicene and Athanasian Creeds were drawn up to exclude. Yet, so far are they from throwing themselves back upon those bulwarks of orthodoxy, that they even modify the Augsburg statement for the worse; omitting the recognition of the Nicene Creed, which that document contains; excluding the words in which it asserts the consubstantiality of the Three Persons in the Trinity; and introducing an almost Sabellian phraseology, while they dispense with the words by which, in the Confession, that heresy is distinctly guarded against.*

Upon the fourth head, they express their agreement with "the Protestant Churches, the Presbyterian Churches of Scotland and America in particular," referring to chapters 8 and 11 of the "Confession of Faith of the Church of Scotland." The passages intended do not appear in the printed Correspondence; we presume them to include the statements of the Scottish Confession concerning the office of the Saviour, as a "Mediator and Surety," His subjection to and fulfilment of the law, His Passion, Crucifixion, Death, Burial, Resurrection with the same body in which He suffered, Ascension with the same body, Glorification and Intercession at the right hand

---

* The following are the words in the Augsburg Confession (1531). "Ecclesiæ magno consensu apud nos docent, *decretum Nicænæ synodi, de unitate essentiæ Divinæ, et de tribus Personis, verum et sine ullâ dubitatione credendum esse. Videlicet,* quod sit una essentia Divina, quæ appellatur et est Deus, æternus, incorporeus, impartibilis, immensâ potentiâ, sapientiâ, bonitate, creator et conservator omnium rerum visibilium et invisibilum, *et tamen tres sunt Personæ, ejusdem essentiæ* et potentiæ, et coæternæ, Pater, Filius, et Spiritus Sanctus. Et nomine Personæ utuntur eâ significatione, quâ usi sunt in hâc causâ scriptores ecclesiastici, ut significet *non partem aut qualitatem in alio,* sed quod proprie subsistit."

of the Father, thence "to return and judge men and angels at the end of the world;" the statement that "the Lord Jesus, by His perfect obedience, and sacrifice of Himself, which He, through the eternal Spirit, once offered up to God, hath fully satisfied the justice of His Father, and purchased not only reconciliation, but an everlasting inheritance in the kingdom of heaven, for all those whom the Father hath given unto Him," (Westm. Confession, 8;) and the whole of the 11th chapter, which sets forth the doctrines, (1.) of the free justification of "those whom God effectually calleth," "not by infusing righteousness into them," but "by imputing the obedience and satisfaction of Christ unto them, they receiving and resting on Him and His righteousness by Faith, the alone instrument of justification;" "which faith they have not of themselves, it is the gift of God." (2.) The doctrine that "Christ, by His obedience and death, did fully discharge the debt of *all those that are thus justified*, and did make a proper, real, and full satisfaction to His Father's justice in *their* behalf." (3.) The doctrine that "God did, from all eternity, decree to justify all the elect, and Christ did, in the fulness of time, die for their sins, and rise again for their justification; nevertheless, they are not justified until the Holy Spirit doth in due time actually apply Christ unto them." And (4.) The doctrine that "God doth continue to forgive the sins of those that are justified; and," although they may sin from time to time, and have continual occasion for repentance, "*they can never fall from the state of justification.*" This, then, is what the Committee at Geneva hold to be *fundamental doctrine, and the whole of fundamental doctrine*, upon the subject of "the work which the Saviour has accomplished;" and here, as before, though they agree to a certain extent with the Catholic Creeds, they in some respects fall short of them, in others go beyond them, and in some most important particulars (as to the Catholic doctrines, that Christ died and made satisfaction for *all men*, and that we shall be *judged by our works*) contradict their evident meaning.

Upon the fifth and last head, they express their agreement with "the Protestant Churches, and the Reformed Helvetic Church in particular;" to the effect that, "a third state in which we ought to consider man, is that of regeneration;" that "the understanding of regenerate believers is enlightened," and "their will freed, by the Holy Spirit;" that "the regenerate, when they choose the good, *do not only experience the power of God which leads them thereto, but they feel that they act themselves, of their own inclination, and with delight;*" that "there remains always some weakness even in the regenerate," but that "still, *as the passions have no longer sufficient strength to quench the fire of the Divine Spirit, the regenerate are regarded as free*, but in such wise, that they ought unceasingly to feel their weakness." Nothing is here said about baptism. They hold, therefore, that the doctrines of a conscious experience of regeneration, and of the indefectibility of the regenerate, are capital fundamental truths; and that the view above given represents *the whole of fundamental truth*, as to " the work which the Saviour now carries on for the salvation of His People, or the work of Regeneration."

And this is the whole necessary Truth, according to these gentlemen; this is that declaration of Faith, which appears satisfactory to the Committee of the London Foreign Aid Society, and by which they expect to convince gainsayers that the Société Evangélique of Geneva consists of men who hold " the Truth unfeigned;" this is that " true basis of union," which is to reconcile the Church of England to the Protestants of Geneva and France;—we say of France also, for the French Committee, in a more vague and less explicit way, gave an answer which we suppose was intended to convey the same meaning; referring generally for the essence of the Faith to the points *in which all the Protestant Confessions were agreed*. Let us examine this basis of union by the test of the gospel " which we have received;" let us compare this Protestant definition of " fundamentals," with the Apostles', the Nicene, and the Athanasian Creeds.

First, it *adds* to the fundamentals set forth in those Creeds, a variety of modern definitions and dogmas, concerning the effect of the Fall upon human nature, the loss and recovery of Free Will by men, Predestination and Election, Particular Redemption, Justification by imputed righteousness through the Gift of Faith, the indefectibility of the Justified or Regenerate, and the conscious experiences of the Regenerate; none of which are to be found in any symbol of fundamental doctrine ever set forth before the sixteenth century, and some of which apparently contradict the tenor of the Nicene and Athanasian Creeds.

Secondly, it takes away from the category of fundamentals, upon the lowest computation, the following ELEVEN articles of the three Catholic Creeds:—(Apostles') 1. The Descent of our Saviour into Hell. 2. The Holy Catholic Church. 3. The Communion of Saints. 4. The Resurrection of the Body.—(Nicene) 5. That the Son is " Begotten, not made, being of one Substance with the Father." 6. That " by Him all things were made." 7. That the Holy Ghost " proceedeth from the Father and the Son." 8. That the Holy Ghost " spake by the prophets." 9. One Baptism for the remission of sins.—(Athanasian) 10. Judgment according to works. 11. The punishment of " those that have done evil in everlasting fire."

If this is to " hold the Faith unfeigned," then assuredly those depositaries of the Faith which " we have received," contain many unnecessary and omit many necessary things. And as we believe those creeds to contain the Truth as the apostles themselves taught it;—to be summaries of that gospel, of which one apostle has said, " If any man preach unto you any *other gospel*, let him be accursed;" and of which another apostle has said, " If there come any unto you, and *bring not this doctrine*, receive him not into your house, neither bid him God speed; for he that biddeth him God speed, is partaker of his evil deeds;" we must be permitted to think that the correspondence before us has brought out conclusive evidence of the fact, that the Protestant bodies, which these Sociétés Evangéliques represent, have not the orthodoxy of belief indispensable, on scriptural grounds, to a true basis of unity. At the same time, the statement of facts prefixed to the correspondence furnishes to our apprehension decisive proof, that if tried by the other scriptural tests,—whether they do the will of God,—whether they hear His Church,—whether they adhere to the apostolical traditions, or cause division by departing from them, —they will, in all these respects, be found equally wanting.

With a view to make the position of the Sociétés Evangéliques in France understood, the Committee of the Foreign Aid Society have gone into some historical detail. They "inform us, that *the Reformed worship was reorganized by Napoleon* in 1802, (18th of Germinal, an. x.") ; and they explain the organic constitution which the professors of this "Reformed worship" then accepted from the hands of the revolutionary government. The progress of the community thus organized, from the date of " Bonaparte's establishment of Protestantism," to the present time, is then described ; and it is said to consist, at this moment, of " ninety consistorial churches, with 404 pasteurs paid by the state; the number of Lutheran pasteurs in addition being 233."—We are next told with respect to the *faith* of these "churches," that they were originally "reorganized without a creed ;" and that, in the course of time, " it was gradually discovered, that the great body of the salaried pasteurs were infected with the Neologism of Germany, and the infidelity of the age of Louis XV.;" that "*it was hardly possible to find twenty pasteurs who confessed the doctrine of the Trinity and the Atonement;*" that at the present moment, " the *established* (that is, the State-paid) *Protestantism of France is for the most part Socinianism ;*" that there are in all only "an estimated number of 150 pasteurs, who faithfully preach Jesus Christ;" and that "the Lutheran pasteurs, with a few exceptions, are Neologists or Socinians."

We pause to suggest a few reflections upon this state of things. The Protestant communities thus described, whence came they? From what point did they set out upon the journey which has brought them to this end? They begun with the rejection of all ecclesiastical authority, except that which was devised by themselves, or administered in conformity with their judgment;—with the assertion of a principle of independence in matters of religion, and, at the same time, strong professions of what the Foreign Aid Society considers doctrinal orthodoxy—the Helvetic Confession, the Confession of Augsburg, and the rest. They are the spiritual descendants of those who, in the Preface to the Helvetic Confession, wrote as follows: "Attestamur omnibus consensum nostrum unanimem, quem dedit nobis Dominus, ut in nostris ecclesiis, quibus nos ministrare voluit Dominus, idem loquamur omnes, nec sint inter nos dissidia, sed simus integrum corpus, eâdem mente eâdemque sententiâ." Of that consent we now see the result. After the lapse of 274 years, they are admitted by their fellow Protestants to have come from this beginning, to almost a general agreement in Socinianism and infidelity; while the Roman Catholics, against whose errors they began with protesting, in spite of those errors remain where they were, maintaining (as they ever have maintained) the Divinity and the Atonement of their Saviour, and adhering to every article of the Apostles', the Nicene, and the Athanasian Creeds.

This, then, is the state of things which the Sociétés Evangéliques have to deal with in France:—on the one hand, a branch of the Church founded by the Holy Ghost on the day of Pentecost, governed by bishops, priests, and deacons, deriving authority by visible succession from the apostles, and though infected in various points with superstition and error, holding every article of the Faith once delivered to the Saints, so far as it is expressed in the three Catholic Creeds; on the other hand, certain religious communities, founded by Napoleon on the "18th of Germinal, an. x.," governed by pasteurs elected by themselves, and approved by the " Ministre des Cultes" for the time being, and, for the most part, teaching Socinianism or infidelity. Under these circumstances, "several pasteurs, distinguished for their zeal and piety, and lamenting the fallen condition of the Reformed Churches as it regarded their doctrinal system, resolved to form a Society." With what object? the reader will inquire; and will doubtless expect the answer to be, to restore the doctrinal purity of the "Reformed Churches;" to convert the Socinians and infidels of the Napoleonistic persuasion. Nothing of the kind. The first object of this Society was, and is, to evangelize " the *Roman Catholic* population of France!"—to convert them, without asking the consent of their bishops, (for the Society " does not profess to promote an Episcopalian form of church government,") to the same profession of belief which, after the lapse of 274 years, is now everywhere bearing the fruit of Socinianism and Neology. They have also a second object; but even this is not to rescue the unhappy "Reformed" from their Socinian teachers. The respect which is not paid to the institution of Christ,[*] is paid to that of Napoleon; and while the authority of bishops who confess their Saviour is set at nought, that of "pasteurs" who deny Him is recognised. The Society, in this part of its undertaking, proposes only "*to assist and cooperate with any of the pasteurs of the consistorial churches, who may desire* to revive in their congregations,

---

[*] There are persons so ready to pervert every thing which is said in favour of Churches admitted to be infected with superstition and error, that we think it necessary to guard against misinterpretation. We do not, of course, mean that the government, doctrine, and ritual of the Church of France is to be respected as if it were in all points of Christ's institution; but only, that it is to be respected *so far as it is so;* and that the bishops, priests, and deacons of that Church, being legitimately descended from the Apostles, have a true authority, by Christ's institution.

or in the neighbouring districts, the doctrines of the Reformation." And while we are informed, shortly afterwards, that they are now employing sixty agents, at salaries amounting to 2,400*l.* per annum, in their attack upon the Church of France, we learn at the same time that they have not money enough to meet the demands made upon them for the restoration of the Faith among the Protestant heretics. "Last year," say the Foreign Aid Society, "the Committee was under the necessity of *refusing, for want of funds, the application of ninety pasteurs.*" They state also, that very few of those Protestants whom they recognise as orthodox, have in any way separated themselves from the heretical majority.

We leave our readers to judge from these facts, whether it is possible for the Church of England, upon any scriptural principle whatever, to connect herself with the Protestantism which these Societies represent. It is painful for us to think that any four English clergymen could be found, who not only did not see in such facts as these serious obstacles to unity, but who could deliberately put them forward as constituting in themselves *a true basis of union.* A more *unevangelical* basis of union it is certainly difficult to conceive; and the fact that it has been so put forward may perhaps have weight, along with other circumstances, in enabling us to judge of the pretensions of the religious school from which it has emanated. To us, the correspondence which we have been considering appears chiefly valuable, as illustrating two important lessons, which ought to be constantly borne in mind when proposals tending to unity are mooted in the present day. The first is, the very great tendency of religious communities, taught to rely upon private judgment as the foundation of their religion, to undervalue, and virtually abandon, the Catholic objective Faith, while they elevate into its place their own differential opinions; a tendency, of the degree of which they are, for the most part, themselves unconscious. The second is the extreme deficiency of vigilance and theological accuracy in our own prevailing habits of thought. Pious people in England are only too often disposed to accept, as satisfactory evidence of orthodoxy, the most vague and evasive statements, if redeemed by a slight plausibility in their general tone. Professions of belief, which would have been sufficient to convict their authors of heresy in the best ages of the Church, would in many cases require but a very little garnish of peculiar phraseology to give them a perfect odour of sanctity in the eyes of highly respectable people in this country. This consideration ought to make us doubly resolute in adhering to the old Catholic standards, as the indispensable tests of that soundness of Faith, without which any attempt at the reunion of professing Christians could tend only to the corruption of the pure, without purifying the corrupt portions of the nominally believing world.

1. *The Character of the Papacy. Preached for the Reformation Society, by the* Rev. R. W. SIBTHORP, B.D. &c. Nisbet, 1839.
2. *Some Answer to the Inquiry, Why are you become a Catholic?* By R. W. SIBTHORP, B.D. Dolman, 1842.
3. *A Further Answer to the Inquiry, &c. By the same.* Dolman, 1842.
4. *Why have you become a Romanist?* By W. DODSWORTH, M.A. Burns, 1842.
5. *Remarks on the Second Letter of the Rev. R. W. Sibthorp.* By W. DODSWORTH, M.A. Burns, 1842.
6. *Reasons wherefore a Clergyman of the Church of England should not become a Roman Catholic.* By HENRY DRUMMOND, Esq. Hatchard, 1842.
7. *An Examination of the Rev. R. W. Sibthorp's Reasons for Secession.* By the Rev. W. PALMER. Rivingtons, 1842.
8. *A Letter to the Archbishop of Canterbury on some Circumstances connected with the present Crisis.* By the Rev. E. B. PUSEY, D.D. Rivingtons, 1842.

SOMEWHAT less than twelve years ago, a demagogue stood up in a certain popular assembly, and expressed his deep pity for the unhappy young men who still continued to enter into holy orders in the Church of England. "I had hoped," he said, "that these foolish ordinations would terminate. But these young gentlemen must bear in mind, that, though the nation will feel itself bound to make provision for such as in past years have entered into orders; though it would doubtless be unjust that a corporation like the Church, which was set up by parliament nearly three hundred years ago, and is older therefore than either the East or West India Company, should be abolished, without adequate compensation to those who have wasted their youth in its service, yet by them who enter this body now that it is condemned by the country,—when its charter is on the eve of being cancelled by the authority which gave it,—when it is admitted on all hands to be not useless only, but absolutely detrimental,—neither indulgence nor compensation can fairly be expected. They choose to invest their time and property in a condemned building, and can expect no more pity than the man who bought the Borough of Gatton after the publication of schedule A, or a West India estate after Mr. Buxton's motion."

We do not exactly remember which of the

"Spectres wan, and birds of boding cry,"

who flitted about in the tempest of the Reform Bill, the Clergy have to thank for this declaration, though we rather believe it proceeded from the sapient Joseph Hume, a personage whom our readers will perhaps hardly remember, for beings of this sort are forgotten so soon as they sink into their original insignificance. Nor would his words be entitled to longer remembrance than himself, had they not been symptomatic of what for a few moments was the predominant feeling of the British nation. How strong this feeling—how widespread the apprehension—is best shown by the disposition evinced by many of the elder Clergy to make such an alteration in our Church system as might adapt it to the new state of the national mind. We have before us the minutes of a meeting at which a large body of country Clergy in one of the northern districts attended. Besides various changes in the Liturgy,—the adaptation of the baptismal and burial services to the dissenting taste,—we find a grave proposal for disencumbering the Canons of what "may give just occasion of offence;" which is explained to mean those expressions by which "the dissenters complain that they are excommunicated."

What a state of feeling does all this reveal to us! The legislature and people complain that the Church does not answer their expectations; that the national wealth is idly lavished for its support; that various sects have arisen, who are displeased at its exclusive possession of property and power; that its elders must set their houses in order, its youth turn elsewhere for support. And this cry is met on the part of the Clergy by a profession of their willingness to be reduced to the condition of a sect; to abandon those declarations by which our forefathers asserted their belief that the Church was emphatically God's household in this nation,—that baptism received men not merely into an earthly corporation, but into immediate union with the Son of God,—that the very bodies of those who died in the Church's communion were

"The images of God in earthly clay,"—

that children must be instructed respecting the real presence of that Holy Ghost, whereof every child of the Church must be taught to declare, that he "sanctifieth *me*, and all the elect people of God." To abandon those Canons by which "dissenters complain that they are excommunicated," would in fact be to abandon the Church's title. For is Christ divided? Can He have various rival bodies in our land? Is not the Church His body? And therefore, unless those who wilfully separate themselves from our communion are separating themselves also from the communion of Christ, with what show of reason can we call ourselves *the* Church of England?

When such were the dangers from within and without,—such the readiness of our friends to renounce our very name and privileges,— such the internecine war denounced by our opponents,—it was natural that the minds of those who were just entering upon our Church's service should be distracted by various emotions. Many who had been brought up to regard the service of the sanctuary as an honourable and useful occupation, when they heard Mr. Hume's denunciations on the one side, and the admissions of their elder brethren on the other, began to doubt whether they should not devote the years which lay before them to some more promising pursuit. They had been taught, that to minister as the priests of God's service was no degradation even for the greatest families of the earth. But to act as the self-constituted teachers of a sectarian society was a far different employment. This they saw, from their observation of the majority of dissenting teachers, was an office neither beneficial nor ennobling. And however earnest their zeal for the conversion of their brethren, why subject themselves to so useless and vexatious a yoke as was imposed on the Clergy of the Church of England? If the Clergy are only the teachers of one out of various sects, why need they renounce those employments by which other lecturers can employ their leisure and augment their resources? The Rev. Mr. Brotherton lectures in his factory chapel on the Lord's-day, and on the other days of the week in the chapel of St. Stephen's. The pious shoemaker preaches on the Lord's-day to those for whom, during the week, he makes soles and upper-leathers. Why should the Clergy of the Church of England, if they too are but the teachers of a sect, be debarred the profit of the one, or the honours of the other?

We speak from memory as well as observation, when we assert these to have been the thoughts of young men, who twelve years ago were selecting their employment. Thus circumstanced, they looked into the formularies and laws of the English Church, to see whether it was true, as popular belief declared, that the Church was a sectarian corporation, established in the earlier part of the sixteenth century, by King Henry the Eighth and Archbishop Cranmer. Great was their surprise at the result of their inquiries. If they looked at the Church's laws, they found them running back into a far earlier period: they found that Bishop Gibson referred for his authority, not to recent acts of parliament, but to the decrees of councils, which met even in Saxon times. If they looked again at the Liturgy, they found, that, far from being the creation of the Reformers, it was merely a purified exhibition of the worship of primitive times. The early fathers, again, they found set forth by the Church as her standard for the interpretation of disputed passages of Holy Writ,—the first four general councils as her rule for the trial of heresy. Moreover, the authority of her ministers was referred by all her leading divines to a succession derived from the very hands of the apostles.

That these truths have taken hold on the judgment and feelings of the mass of our younger Clergy,—that they have begun, in consequence, to maintain that position from understanding and principle which a few years back was only occupied by prescription and through prejudice,—this is manifest in every part of the land. Everywhere we have young men arising, who declare their willingness to make any sacrifice for the Church of England, so long as she preserves her claim to be the original Church Catholic of this land. The recent willingness on the part of their elder brethren to give up whatever was distinctive in the Church system, is put to shame and forgotten. We can hardly realize the fact that, not ten years ago, it was seriously canvassed whether we should not throw overboard those distinctive portions of our Liturgy and Formularies which are now acknowledged to give our Church the only claim to the confidence of the country.

The revived foliage of spring will ever follow in this manner from winter's tempests, when the tree is sound at heart, and its roots enter into a soil which fears not disturbance. And when men express their surprise at the rapidity of the reaction, and wonder that new views and principles, new subjects of attack, new names and parties, should in so short a period have occupied the field,—we can only declare our conviction, that it is a proof of the vigour of the plant, and of the soundness of the basis which supports it. But we must notice one of the peculiar forms in which this revived energy has exhibited itself.

. The universities could not be expected to escape that excitement which agitated the whole land. At Cambridge, its most marked effect was of a political kind: the Whig members lost their seats, and Tory sentiments became, for the first time, popular in the Debating Society. A religious movement followed; but not of so immediate and striking a kind as in the sister university. It was at Oxford, where Wicliffe had first hoisted the flag of Anglican independence,—where the preposterous excesses of Henry VIII. on the one side, and of James II. on the other, had found their staunchest opponents,—where Wesley had imbibed that spirit which led to an ill-directed but deep-hearted outbreak of zeal in a day of general indifference; it was here that was found the rallying point in this time of danger. The university contained at that time more than its usual number of men detached from the ordinary employments of college life, and able to direct their attention to public interests. Engaged hitherto in moral and metaphysical speculations, they were suddenly recalled from their dreams of science by the threatened downfal of the institutions which they loved. While the heads of the university were satisfied by witnessing the warm-hearted zeal with which Tory sentiments were responded to in the theatre at the Duke of Wellington's installation, these men were pushing their inquiries into the various questions which the overthrow of any existing safeguard made it essential to agitate. They did not, like the mass of the country Clergy, content themselves with realizing their situation as members of Christ's Catholic Church in England; as might be expected perhaps from academics, they took a more general ground, and reverted to more original principles. And this appears to us to be the secret of that divergency which has, in a measure, dissociated the Oxford Tracts—for, of course, we are speaking of their learned authors—from the general mind of the Church of England.

We apprehend that with the earlier numbers of that series the great mass of the Clergy fully agreed. They were glad to find men bold enough to advance opinions which they themselves had always implicitly received, and able enough to vindicate them against their common adversaries. They witnessed with pleasure the total and irretrievable overthrow of the dissenting party in our Church—an overthrow the more remarkable from the surprise and imbecility of the vanquished. In the very moment when they were calling upon the Church to abandon her established principles ; to give up her baptismal formularies, because, after accepting them with the most solemn oaths, they were themselves unable to believe them ; to admit that she was no longer Christ's mystical body, because dissenters did not like to be reminded that they ought to be His living members; at this very moment arose a company of men, strong in knowledge, faith, and self-denial, who proved, in a manner which could not be questioned, that these truths, instead of being abandoned, needed only to be acted upon ; that what we needed was not a new reformation, but to return to the old one ; that, if the Church called herself Christ's mystic bride, it was because she was so in truth ; and that never could she fulfil her high mission till all the great truths which her Prayer-book contained were exemplified in the lives of her children.

If the writers of the Oxford Tracts had persevered in this course, they would, in the full concurrence of the great body of the Clergy, in a hearty assimilation to the ancient divines of the Church of England, have found support enough against any memorials from the Wesleyans of Birmingham, or the lay-elders of Cheltenham. But in the circumstances of the case this could hardly be expected. The leading minds among these writers had not had the advantage of being trained themselves in the Anglo-Catholic school ; they had to grope for their principles, as men suddenly beset by nightly robbers catch at such weapons as the moment allows, while the darkness was as yet broken only by such uncertain glimpses of light as were supplied by the Pietistic or Neological parties with which they were severally connected. Their sentiments, therefore, had not been worked out by a previous development of the English system, but were taken up by persons who came rather as allies than as subjects to the defence of the Church. The just deference which they have shown to the great divines of the seventeenth century was more than, under the circumstances, could be expected from them. And hence arises what appears to us their great defect, as it has been the main detraction from their influence—an indisposition to do justice to our English Reformation.

Were the English Reformation to be viewed as a mere insulated fact, abstracted from the state of circumstances which preceded it, it were a fact as difficult to account for as to defend. That men should be content to be dissociated from a vast body of their fellow-Christians ; that the rulers of a Church originally greatly indebted to the Church of Rome should make a pride of protesting that they owe it no subjection ; that they should be satisfied to be hemmed in by the precincts of this narrow island, unprofited by the prayers of Christ's universal flock, uninterested by its advance, unmoved by its reverses;—all this must seem utterly inexplicable, unless seen in constant juxtaposition with the unjust oppression, the superstition, and impurity of the papacy. Now, the Tracts, though they recognise, yet they can hardly be said to do justice to this truth. When their writers, indeed, have occasion to oppose any popish error, they do so with a force both of learning and logic which renders them, as Mr. Sibthorp confesses, the most successful assailants of Romanism, in this age of theological inquiries. But it is manifest that, while the miseries consequent on the loss of unity throughout the Christian world are continually before them, the countervailing thought of those fearful enormities which were its cause, is a less habitual subject of their cogitations.

This was not an unnatural state of things for men who approached this subject on the side rather of speculation than of action,—not amidst the bustle of life, but in the groves of the academy. But it gives ground for the apprehension, which the Bishop of Oxford some time since expressed, lest a dangerous error, from which the writers themselves, we confidently believe, are free, should display itself among their followers. They should remember for whom they write. They should reflect that the great mass of men have been brought up in the absurd and unphilosophical opinion that out of the mine of Scripture truth they are to shape a set of opinions for themselves, without profiting by the labours or experience of their predecessors. If the great truth of the Church's unity be brought prominently before such persons, while its necessary counterpoise is forgotten, such partial development of truth will be almost as injurious as the maintenance of error. We should feel no surprise, therefore, if some disciples of the Oxford school should fall into schism, as so many clergymen of the Low-Church party have done within our recollection. But it is a curious proof, how much less High Churchmen are in danger of popery than their opponents of dissent, that, while little sensation was occasioned when the Rev. Messrs. Bulteel, Brenton, Philpot, and many others, became separatists, so much importance should be attached to the perversion even of a young layman, by the papists. But as though to show more clearly where the danger of popery really lies, from what quarter its enemies are truly to be expected, we are presented, at this critical moment, with a flagrant case of delinquency, in the instance of a person recently secretary to the Religious Tract Society.

We confess that this appears to us to be a circumstance well worthy of observation. We have long thought, in contradiction to the opinion of many with whom in other points we agreed, that popery was likely to increase. We never quarrelled with Frazer's Magazine for making its stand for *no popery*. We think that for many years every thing was done to favour its advance. For if any truth be clearly written in Holy Scripture, and plainly imprinted upon the history of the Church,—if any thing shines forth more than another in ancient type or primeval prophecy,—it is surely the sacred unity of the Church. Christ's body is one. It was His sublime prayer at that eventful season when He concluded the most heart-thrilling exhortations which were ever given to the sons of men, that His disciples might be one, " as Thou, Father, art in Me and I in Thee, that they may be one in Us, that the world may believe that Thou hast sent Me." And the saying of the departed Saviour found a response in the devotion of generations of men; it spoke in the zeal of missionaries and the agony of martyrs, in the concord which assuaged the hatred of warring nations, in the harmonious institutions which bound together the most distant countries and reduced to order the tangled maze of the history of mankind. Now, it may not be that a truth thus graven in heaven above and earth beneath can for ever be forgotten. The pages of Holy Writ will not always exhibit it in vain. We have ever felt, therefore, that, so soon as men were led to the discovery of this great principle, there would be much risk that ill-informed minds should seek for its realization, however unjustly, in the papacy. The time was, when England presented no such danger; when our national Church stood forth, uniting the whole mind of a great people, who, having received from their forefathers the blessed inheritance of an identity with the one holy society of ancient days, gave promise to hand it on, without diminution or division, to the latest generations. But this blessed prospect has been marred by the growth of dissent. The pillar of western catholicity, " founded on a rock, though standing amidst the sea," no longer presents that fair and united front which can defy the storm. It still indeed abides, but the wreck and sea-weed which defile it make men doubt whether they shall find as firm hold as once for their footsteps,

" Ut pelagi rupes, magno veniente fragore,
  Quæ sese, multis circum latrantibus undis,
  Mole tenet : scopuli nequicquam et spumea circum
  Saxa fremunt, laterique illisa refunditur alga."

Our firm conviction is, that the prevalence of dissent is the certain preparation for popery, and the multitude of divisions the death of the reformed faith.

Here, however, we are met by a contrary system. Unity, it is said, means merely kindness : to agree to unite, means to agree to differ. Let all parties, therefore, but profess themselves satisfied, let them abstain from mutual crimination, let them join in such laudable objects as they can pursue together, and the real end is attained. Charity, not communion, is the unity of the Church.

This principle we need not say is that of the Bible Society; and in the Religious Tract Society it has been still more completely embodied. We hardly know any thing more exact than the manner in which the Religious Tract Society illustrates the great theological error of the day. We refer to the tendency to speak of truth and falsehood, not as having an inherent existence, but only as they are embodied in our own opinions. Men do not feel them to be realities independent of themselves, but regard them only as developed in their own conceptions. Of old, *the faith* meant the eternal realities which were revealed from heaven; now it is supposed to consist only in the acquiescence of man's mind. For an external rule of truth is substituted a mere inward adherence.

Now, to this tendency the Society in question is exactly conformed. It propagates those opinions only, which are held to be essential by orthodox Christians of all parties. The rule by which the importance of opinions is determined is the private feeling of those gentlemen who make up the committee. When the Council of Nice declared what it supposed to be the essential articles of the faith, it rested itself upon the constant belief of the Church in a certain body of external verities. It held " fast the tradition received" from the apostles. It declared those things fundamental which the one body of the faithful had so believed. And therefore did ancient opinion maintain one uniform direction, because guided by the sun and moon which shone in the Church's firmament, so that the change of place and time made no differences in its laws. Not so the time-pieces which, according to the fancy or feeling of individuals, may be altered every hour. The Tract Society's rule of fundamentals varies every year, according as new names are drafted into the committee, or new influences direct its former members. Its late secretary observes with perfect truth, " No two denominations agree in fundamental truths. They would not give you the same list of them. I doubt whether two ministers of any one of these bodies are prepared to say they entirely agree as to what these fundamental truths are, or how many the term comprehends."—*Sibthorp's First Letter*, p. 28.

The person, then, who was to be secretary to an institution in which all the worst features of the time were to be thus fully embodied, must needs have been infected in all its malignity with the epidemic of the day. Of Mr. Sibthorp's preparatory training, we have the following account in a very able letter of Mr. Dodsworth's:—

" You were ordained, I believe, as curate to the Rev. John Scott, of Hull, the son of the Calvinistic commentator of the Bible, who inherited, along with his father's piety, the peculiar doctrines of his school. I remember you at that time an ardent, devoted minister, zealously preaching (so-called) Low Church doctrines, a great favourite with dissenters, and an eloquent speaker at Bible societies, &c. Your associations, therefore, were peculiarly *ultra-Protestant*, and I think that you will not deny that the opinions you generally entertained then were as different from those of the Church of England, as represented in her doctors of highest repute, *e. g.* Hammond, Andrews, Hooker, &c., as are the opinions which you now hold. *I* should say, far more different. Your opinions varied in no essential point from those of dissenters,—Independents, Wesleyans, Baptists, &c., with whom you associated as brethren, and with whom you joined in religious societies, and, if my memory does not deceive me, I think even in social prayer-meetings.

" In a later period of your Protestant life, you became the colleague of Mr. Baptist Noel in the ministry of St. John's Chapel, Bedford Row, whose opinions on " unity" have been put forth in a tract which attempts to show that it consists in a sort of spiritual union of all sects and denominations. As you preached in the evening from the same pulpit which he occupied in the morning, it may be concluded that your views were essentially the same with his. You will scarcely object, therefore, to the inference, that at this time, I believe about nine or ten years ago, you were an extreme Protestant, practically and essentially identified with dissenters in your doctrines and opinions. If any corroboration of these statements were needed, it might be found in the circumstance, that at one time, and, if my recollection does not fail me, at a time *subsequent* to that above named, you were secretary to the 'Religious Tract Society,' a society formed on the express principle, or rather *no principle*, of a community of all sects and denominations holding some fundamental doctrines."—*Dodsworth's First Letter*, p. 8.

With these feelings, then, and this education did Mr. Sibthorp take his place among the leading divines of the Low Church party. His talents gave him an ascendancy which his gentility and generosity increased. Above all, the ardent piety, which evidently shone through his whole character, won for him respect. He took his part in life when those expectations which good men deduced from the religious societies in which he cooperated were in their bloom. The general extension of Christ's kingdom,—the reign of love, peace, purity, and truth,—all that the impassioned students of prophecy brought forth from the ancient stores of revelation,—was anticipated as that which the active spirits of the day were to realize by their exertions. Mr. Sibthorp preached, like others, about "the endeavours now making to extend throughout the British Islands the doctrines and principles which, under the distinctive name of Protestantism, constitute, in fact, the Christianity of the holy Scriptures." (Sibthorp on the Character of the Papacy, p. 28.) Mr. Dodsworth's assertion respecting his disposition to unite with dissenters even in their public worship, would seem to be borne out by the feeling which he himself expresses in his second letter, that on his former principles such union ought to be admitted. If episcopal government be merely, as his friends supposed, an accidental incumbrance of our Church system,—if all other sincere men are equally members of Christ's body with the Church Catholic to which we belong,—to separate men from our communion in consequence of a mere outward formality is indeed a most culpable violation of the great rule of christian love. We do not wonder that dissenting teachers feel that bitterness, which, when occasion arrives, they show with sufficient clearness, at the pedantic stiffness of what they call their *dear evangelical brethren*. Why separate from their society men who agree in fundamentals with themselves? Why exchange a stately bow on the platform, to be followed by a total estrangement in the intercourse of life? There is an unfairness about this from which any observant spectator would gather, that there was only a hollow union. What else could be expected when Clergymen who were most ready at the meeting to hail the presence of their dissenting brethren, were most ready also to make game of them round the dinner table? So it proved. When the dissenters had gained their end, had obtained an unwonted influence and notoriety, had induced a large portion of the Clergy to allow themselves to be regarded by their people as only the teachers of one sect of Christians,—they then threw off the mask, and showed in their Ecclesiastical Knowledge Society at what it was that they were truly aiming. From that time those who give them credence have no right to complain. *Prudens emisti.* Mr. Sibthorp, at all events, escaped from the snare; happy had he known how to use his liberty! His was too christian a temper to be satisfied with a base compromise, in which the mask of interest should shield the reality of hatred. He did not wait till the corn-law meetingers professed that, since religious subjects are so uncertain, they must take refuge in that unity which politics supplied—till they threw overboard the Lord's Prayer, and made their confession of faith out of the Corn-Law Rhymes of Ebenezer Elliot. That this was the secret of his progress he has expressly declared:—

"Could the one body of Christ," he asks, "consist of a mixture of Prussian Lutherans, French Calvinists, and Swiss Socinians; of Independents, Baptists, Quakers, Shakers, and Irvingites, and Plymouth Brethren; of Methodists of the Old and of the New Connexion; of New Jerusalemites, and Primitive Revivalists? Could such discords be the designed fulfilment of a type of such holy order?"—*Sibthorp's First Letter*, p. 12.

Such then were Mr. Sibthorp's expectations, and thus were they disappointed. Now, just when he was under the impulse of such feelings, he came across that other movement, which, in the earlier part of this article, we have slightly delineated. His individual dissatisfaction and disappointment were met by the full tide of public feeling, which was carrying the mass of the Clergy towards the great truths of Catholic union, and of the real and substantive existence of the external Church. Couple with all this the present activity of our Romist separatists, the renewed energy which causes of a public nature have excited among continental Catholics, and it is impossible not to feel how great was the danger.

His old principles, as secretary of the Tract Society, were so far from being a safeguard in this new state of things, that they were the real cause of his danger. We have shown that his aspirations after unity had been called forth only to be blighted by the mortifying conviction that such unity as he had anticipated was hopeless among reformed Christians. On what should he fall back? On the demonstrative certainty of that interpretation of Scripture in which he had been instructed. The Church of England, indeed, appeals to so fixed a rule on this subject, that its controversy with the Romanists, though requiring labour and research, yet admits of final adjudication. Mr. Sibthorp appears to have a suspicion of the impossibility of making good his ground on her principles, when he says, " it was not to be expected that in the second and third centuries there would be found, even if there had been fuller documents, that clear perception of the designed succession to St. Peter, which the ninth and tenth centuries present." (Sibthorp's First Letter, p. 19.) Now, it is evident that, if the writers of the early Church are referred to as witnesses, not as legislators,—if the object be to learn, not what they decreed, but what was delivered to them,—it is precisely to those who are nearest to the fountain that our appeal must be addressed. And we say confidently, that, though Rome was respected as capital of the civil world, and as a signal seat of religious instruction, yet that no vestige can be found in the primitive age of her having possessed an ecclesiastical empire even over the Churches of the West. Her influence was beginning to grow into authority in the days of Leo: Gregory the Great expressed himself, even towards those who were beyond the suburbicarian district, in a manner which persons alive to the usurpations of Rome would rightly suspect; but neither of these prelates spoke of themselves as masters beyond their own patriarchate. Priority, not supremacy, was their claim. And at an earlier period still, even this concession was not demanded; all bishops were as yet equal, and the Roman pontiff had but the advantage of presiding over a wealthier Church. These subjects are well treated by Mr. Sibthorp's various opponents, all of whom take that catholic ground on which only popery can be defeated. Dr. Biber we believe to be a learned German, of great sincerity and singleness of mind, who has taken refuge in our Church, like the excellent Grabe, from dissatisfaction at the want of union among foreign protestants. Mr. Henry Drummond we suspect to have been led to the line which we are glad to see him adopt, by the habit of contemplating the Church under that aspect under which prophecy presents it. The prophetic writings so clearly treat the Church as a visible substantive body, that no one who is imbued with this spirit can be satisfied with the low notions of the present day. With Mr. Drummond's forcible pamphlet we must join the two letters of Mr. Dodsworth, Incumbent of Christ Church, St. Pancras. Mr. Dodsworth writes like a person who is familiar with the errors through which Mr. Sibthorp has made shipwreck, but who has learnt the proper method of avoiding them. His earnestness leads him to inflict a few blows which we clearly see that he is unwilling to deal forth, and by which we suspect that Mr. Sibthorp has been more affected than by the valuable, though somewhat technical, pamphlet of the learned Mr. Palmer.

It is only while we here hold the pen that another pamphlet, of larger dimensions, has reached us; in which Dr. Pusey undertakes to show that it is not to his writings, or those of his friends, that Mr. Sibthorp's defection, or that of any one else, is to be attributed. And this, with the qualification before made, we are quite willing to allow. We wish that our limits enabled us to enter more fully upon Dr. Pusey's letter, which, like whatever he writes, is worthy of attentive consideration. It is eloquent and earnest, yet calm and temperate; and cannot fail, we think, to make a great impression upon those to whom it is more immediately addressed. We are glad to see his explanations on some points on which explanation was especially needed—his own statements on sin after baptism, which he greatly modifies—and the unhappy inadvertence of speaking of *reserve*, where it was designed only to enforce *reverence*. But we can only find time for a very remarkable quotation—the prediction, namely, of an highly esteemed divine of the last age, which seems to be exactly fulfilled in our present situation. The following are said to have been the words which the Rev. T. Sikes, well known as the author of several very valuable publications, addressed to a friend shortly before his death :—

"I seem to think I can tell you something, which you who are young may probably live to see, but which I, who shall soon be called away off the stage, shall not. Wherever I go all about the country, I see amongst the Clergy a number of very amiable and estimable men, many of them much in earnest, and wishing to do good. But I have observed one universal want in their teaching—the uniform suppression of one great truth: there is no account given anywhere, so far as I see, of the one Holy Catholic Church. I think that the causes of this suppression have been mainly two. The Church has been kept out of sight, partly in consequence of the civil establishment of the branch of it which is in this country, and partly out of false charity to dissent. Now, this great truth is an article of the creed; and if so, to teach the rest of the creed to its exclusion must be to destroy 'the analogy or proportion of the faith.' This cannot be done without the most serious consequences. The doctrine is of the last importance; and the principles it involves of immense power; and some day, not far distant, it will judicially have its reprisals. And whereas the other articles of the creed seem now to have thrown it into the shade, it will seem, when it is brought forward, to swallow up the rest. We now hear not a breath about the Church; by and by, those who live to see it, will hear of nothing else; and, just in proportion perhaps to its present suppression, will be its future development. Our confusion now-a-days is chiefly owing to the want of it; and there will be more confusion attending its revival. The effects of it I even dread to contemplate, especially if it come suddenly. And woe betide those, whoever they are, who shall, in the course of Providence, have to bring it forward. It ought, especially of all others, to be matter of catechetical teaching and training. The doctrine of the Church Catholic, and the privileges of Church-membership, cannot be explained from pulpits, and those who will have to explain it will hardly know where they are to turn themselves. They will be endlessly misunderstood and misinterpreted. There will be one great outcry of popery, from one end of the country to the other. It will be thrust upon minds unprepared, and on an uncatechized Church. Some will take it up and admire it as a beautiful picture; others will be frightened, and run away and reject it; and all will want a guidance which one hardly knows where they shall find. How the doctrine may be first thrown forward we know not; but the powers of the world may one day turn their backs upon us, and this will probably lead to those effects I have described."—*Pusey's Letter*, p. 34.

It is difficult to conceive any words more exactly descriptive of what has happened; we would that they might teach a lesson of patience on the one side, and of forbearance on the other.

On the forbearance to which the abettors of High Church opinions are entitled, it is difficult to touch, because they have not always been treated as might be expected by those whose situation should make them value justice above every other virtue. Nothing can be more just, indeed, than that rulers should condemn what is injurious. But it is not just to condemn those who err on one side, and wink at those who err on the other. How many persons openly spurn at so plain a doctrine of the Church as baptismal regeneration! How many scoff at the episcopal office and authority ! Yet these are left almost entirely without censure. Though such heresies are known to exist at the present day, few bishops are careful to reject their abettors from holy orders. Is it fair, then, that those who verge towards the other extreme should be subjected exclusively to the rigour of the law because their principles induce them to suffer without complaint ?*

And yet, if there be one thing more than another which induces impartial spectators to look favourably on the persons of whom we speak, it is that they have borne with exemplary patience what might not unnaturally have been the ground of angry expostulation. We speak not of their conduct towards the majority of their opponents. The virulence and falsehood with which they have been assailed by a great portion of the daily press, especially by that which emanates from dissenting or semi-dissenting parties, it has not been difficult for them to endure. After men have been the victims of a certain amount of calumny, they care little for its repetition. But it must be matter of great patience to have been attacked by several persons of considerable note, who united such harshness of expression with such a perfect ignorance of what they censured. Not that all that has been said of them has been of this kind: they have had fairer opponents, and in writings so various there must needs be much which might be justly questioned. But, assuredly, Mr. Sikes's words have been amply fulfilled—" Woe betide those, who shall, in the course of Providence, have to bring these things forward."

We write while men's passions are at the height, and while it is impossible to predict what shall be the issue. But we have a strong conviction, that, if these writers do not by any false step undo the good which they have achieved,—that, if they gradually qualify the evil which has been its perhaps inseparable concomitant,—that, if they will but pursue the road of submission, meekness, order, and faith, which, notwithstanding all the obloquy poured upon them, they cannot be denied to have walked in,—they will be admitted hereafter to have been in their measure, and like other fallible men, a great and lasting benefit to the Church. It was but a few years back, that, when the celebrated Möhler was nominated to a professorship of divinity at Bonn, his appointment was prevented by the Archbishop of Cologne, in consequence of his admirable work on the Unity of the Church. That which, with certain necessary qualifications, would now pass current among ourselves, was then strange doctrine even to Westphalian ears. A few years, and what a change has come over men's spirits ! Time, the great teacher, has had its effect in that country ; it will have its effect among ourselves.

---

* This subject is well handled in an excellent "Letter to the Bishop of Lincoln," &c., (Rivingtons, 1842,) which has just fallen into our hands.

1. *A Selection of Hymns.* London: Society for Promoting Christian Knowledge. 1841.
2. *The Child's Christian Year: Hymns for every Sunday and Holyday, compiled for the use of Parochial Schools.* Oxford: Parker. London: Rivingtons. 1841.
3. *Hymns for Children on the Lord's Prayer, our Duty towards God, and Scripture History.* Derby: Mozley & Sons. London: Rivingtons. 1839.
4. *Hymns for Childhood.* By FELICIA HEMANS. Dublin: Curry, jun. & Co. Edinburgh: Fraser & Co. 1839.

OF all tasks which combine dignity with pleasure, and importance with cheering encouragement, there is none surely that can be compared to that of awakening in young people the perception and the enjoyment of poetry. It is the only branch of education in which three quarters of the work is done for us already. Yet, though it be at once the easiest and the most delightful of the teacher's duties, it has been, perhaps, the most neglected of all. To many, we have no doubt, the undertaking seems visionary and impracticable. Such will admit that it may be good, in an intellectual point of view, to make a child learn verses by heart, and right, in a moral and religious one, that he should be able to repeat hymns; but to expect from him sympathy or pleasure in poetry as such, is, in their creed, to expect an impossibility. Hence, perhaps, it is that so little attention has been paid to the quality of the verses contained in the elocution and hymn books from which young people are to learn. Till very lately they were all but made up of the very refuse of the English language. What wonder, then, that children should have confirmed the theory which held poetical enjoyment to be impossible at their age? If such were to be their associations with verse,—if, in addition to the natural ingredient of bitterness which there must needs be more or less in *one's lessons*, all that was presented to them in the form of verse was such as no taste could digest,—what wonder that they made wry faces at such *Squeers'* diet? Boys, indeed, have all along had some chance with the classics,—though even they have too often received no great encouragement to associate them with enjoyment, or to connect them in any way with the spontaneous working of their imaginations; but girls have, for the most part, been in a sad predicament as regards poetry. The subject is one on which their teachers have known no more than themselves, with the additional disadvantage of tastes already perverted. All reading of poetry, at their age, beyond what may be contained in the aforesaid elocution and hymn books, has been probably denounced as "filling their heads with nonsense"—the sacred springs of romance have thus been choked at their natural outlets, and left to ooze and disperse themselves in unwholesome swamps.

And yet surely there never was a greater error than this. What condition of being is more susceptible of poetry than that of children? It is better in this respect than that of youth. For in youth, the senses with one sex—false standards of taste and action with the other—sickly feeling with both—disturb the perception and hinder the enjoyment of poetry as such. There may be much impetuous delight in Byron, much languishing over Lalla Rookh, where there is but little relish for actual poetry. But in the case of children, the imagination is lively, without being under the dominion of the senses; it knows not, and would disdain if it knew, the particular fashions which may be dominant,—it is guiltless of all unreality,—it delights in the beauty that is around it. The ear is susceptible of pleasurable impressions, even from infancy. First music and then metre obviously catch and arrest the attention. Such are the results of observation; the facts of the case; and how should they be otherwise? Is not the enjoyment of poetry essentially child-like? Do we not clothe ourselves, intellectually at least, with something of the mind of little children, when we read Shakspeare or Spenser? And if so, must not those in whom this mind is habitual, be even more highly susceptible of poetical influence than ourselves? We do not of course mean that their thoughts can embrace the same range, that they can have the same delight in meditation, or in severe and difficult reflection, that advancing years bring to those who cherish intellectual pursuits. But within their natural range, we say, they have a capacity for enjoying poetry in a way purer and more perfect than ours. Nor is that range so very limited;—their sense of harmony is ordinarily fine; their imagination lively, and fond of the vast, the mysterious, the terrible. Romance is but too easy to those who have had no experience of this dull working-day world. All beyond the precincts of the nursery and the school-room is clothed to their eyes in holiday attire. And be it remembered that the recurring appearances of nature are not the familiar unmarked things to them that they are to us. They return after what in their calendar are long intervals, and so have all the freshness of novelty. This makes imagery striking to them, which to us would be common-place.

It may, however, be objected to all that we have been saying, that, instead of encouraging us to present children with poetry, it rather encourages us to let them do without it, inasmuch as it appears that their imaginations require no stimulant, and are sure to exercise themselves if left alone. But, unless it can be proved that they are sure to exercise themselves in a right and healthy way, the objection must go for nothing. We maintain that, like every other power, and more than any other power, the imagination must be educated and directed from the very first. It will work, no doubt, in any case; but its workings, if left to themselves, may, and will be, irregular, frightful, and disastrous.

A second objection may perhaps come more readily to hand than that with which we have now dealt. There is no good poetry, it will be said, which they can understand. From whatever quarter this objection may come, it will never be from children themselves. They are quite satisfied to admire without understanding. An object is none the less attractive in their eyes for being half-shrouded in mystery. How often do we observe some particular phrase or passage catch their fancy, of the meaning of which they can give no explanation! An eminent poet and first-rate critic of the present day has gone farther than this, has extended the principle to adults, and laid it down that, "in order to enjoy good poetry, it is not at all necessary to understand it." We are not sure whether it is not in the same passage that he instances—

> " The sun to me is dark
> And silent as the moon
> When she deserts the night
> Hid in her vacant interlunar cave."

We honestly confess ourselves to be in the same predicament with this distinguished person. What the moon's vacant interlunar cave in which she hides herself may be we do not venture positively to pronounce; but, notwithstanding, we admire the passage exceedingly. The same divine poet charms both our ear and our soul with a line on which, however, we should be sorry to undergo an examination:—

> " Or hear'st thou rather, pure ethereal stream?"

To pass to more sacred poetry, we delighted in the war-horse of the Book of Job; and more particularly in these words, " Hast thou given the horse strength? hast thou clothed his neck with thunder?" before we had encountered any of the explanations of the latter clause which have been offered; nor do we much trouble ourselves with them now when we are regaling ourselves with that sublime passage. In truth, it is not so much a meaning in actual, as in possible possession that we demand. We cannot enjoy what we know to be sheer nonsense: man and boy turn away alike from that. But if harmonious numbers indicate some deep thought, we are willing to enjoy them in the faith of a meaning being there, though we have seen but glimpses of it—nay, to enjoy them all the more on that account.

If, therefore, there be no valid objection to addressing the minds of children with poetry, let us study to do so, for there is all imaginable argument in its favour. Poetry is the safest, as it is the highest exercise of the imagination. The terrors to which that power so naturally does homage are shorn of their direst and most baleful aspects, when they are brought within the realm of beauty. Thoughts of awe will not so readily act as "night fears," when once they have moved "harmonious numbers." And to enjoy poetry at all, is always an exercise, however unconscious, of the intellect; so that by giving the imagination this its best and noblest outlet, we are making it help to strengthen, instead of, as it otherwise might, enfeeble the mind. Last of all, it is through poetry that religious truth most readily finds its way to the heart of "children and child-like souls;" this divine influence it is which enables us to sympathize with holy men of old. Sacred poetry is, after of course her creed, sacraments, liturgy, and ministry, the brightest possession of the Church—the richest pasturage of her children; eminently fitted, therefore, for her little ones, who, as yet, require none of her stern discipline; whose minds are all open to its gentle and holy inspirations; ready for truth when so presented to them as that they can livingly apprehend it, but incapable of giving it any cordial reception in the forms of logic, or the loveless antagonism of controversy. More delightful to our eyes than the stateliest pageantry,—more grateful to our ears than the fullest harmony,—are the sight and the sound of a young child at the knees of his parents, and amid the family circle, repeating the hymn he has been asked himself to select out of his little stock as his own especial favourite.

For all these reasons, we say, cultivate in children a taste for poetry. It is hardly a labour to do so; and in as far as it is one, it is nearly sure to be richly rewarded. But how is it to be done? This is the question to which we must now address ourselves.

When circumstances do not render it necessary, we confess we are not much disposed to address children with poetry peculiarly meant for them. Sir Walter Scott has one or two important observations bearing on this point, in the Preface to his "Tales of a Grandfather." He mentions that, having begun them in a childish style, he was gradually led to discard it, from remarking how much better pleased children are to be addressed in the language of adults than their own; and from considering how much safer it is to be somewhat above than at all below the level of their understanding. In the former case, we at least command their respect, and if things be well, we set their minds a-working;—in the latter there has been no respect called forth; the intended adaptation to themselves is seen at once; what is presented to them is not supposed to have any intrinsic merit or value, and being understood at a glance is dismissed as readily. *Trying to understand* is our own best and finest intellectual attitude; why may not children be permitted to put themselves in it, with less pride, less reluctance of every sort to stand in their way?

And in truth, experience has shown us that at a very early age children can be interested in the same poetry as their seniors, and all the more because it is the same. *The Pleasures of Hope!* What a burst of melody for the ear, of oratory for the nerves, of visionary rapture for the mind, was contained there when we were young! No cold criticism, no detection of verbosity, no inquisitorial exaction of meaning, no unfeeling discovery of redundance interfered to stop the full enjoyment. We have even known very precocious children delighted with Paradise Lost; nor should we ever doubt the genuine character of their pleasure therein.

Where, therefore, the treasures of English poetry are accessible, we vote for educating a child by means of them, by selections from them, (not in an elocution-book, but in the instructions of a living parent or teacher,) by pointing out their beauties, by awakening inquiry into them. Let the leisure hours of an intelligent and thoughtful child admit him into the family circle, let him be recognised as a participator in his measure in the family tastes, let him be taught to count it a favour to hear good poetry well read, and it will matter little that you go above and beyond his range. Among your scatterings you may count on depositing much precious seed.

Where there is the wish to connect this highest of arts with the highest of all subjects, the means will not be wanting. Among the many privileges of Englishmen, not the least is the amount of religious poetry of which their language is the vehicle, and which is, by consequence, their birthright; and there is a succession downwards from Spenser, which, used in subordination to more direct means of grace, and with prayer to the Giver of grace, might well be turned to far more account, and prove a far more efficacious influence for good on the minds of their offspring, than parents for the most part dream of.

This, however, is not always practicable, and for many schools, especially those designed for the middling and lower classes, it is manifestly out of the question. Even here, however, we ought to beware of visibly condescending. What we offer to our pupils, whether in prose or verse, must be manly and vigorous, such as shall task the mind, and make it mount instead of pulling it down. Selections from our really standard poets seem the most available plan in such cases, as indeed they are in all during the hours of direct learning. Such a compilation as "the Book of Poetry," which we noticed last summer,* will be found most suitable; and there is no reason why it should not have many companions.

For the lower orders, however, we must mainly confine ourselves to religious poetry, and to religious poetry in the form of hymns. And it is here, unluckily, that our language is poorest. We have so little good congregational poetry,—so little that is at once pious, catholic, and poetical, that in all selections the whole of our little wealth should be exhibited. We ought to give, and to give uninjured, the very few really fine hymns we possess. For this reason we must complain that in two of the very excellent books at the head of our article, "The Child's Christian Year," and the "Selection of Hymns" put forth by the Christian Knowledge Society, we look in vain for the truly grand Easter Hymn, "Jesus Christ is risen to-day." Again, in the latter, we have two or three stanzas of Bishop Ken's Morning, two or three of his Evening, and about as many of his Midnight Hymn. Why not, if their length be inconvenient, trust the teacher with the work of selection? As it is, in the Morning Hymn, the stanza, "Wake and lift up thyself, my heart," is omitted; and yet we are sure it is an universal favourite. In that for Midnight we search in vain for the most poetical part, beginning from "All praise to Thee, in light array'd." Again, in that beautiful hymn of Cowper's, "Far from the

---

* Christian Remembrancer, New Series, vol. ii. p. 49.

world, O Lord, I flee," the editor has stopped short at a stanza which we think he can hardly have seen, for we cannot imagine that in that case he could have had the heart to omit it:—

> There like the nightingale she pours
>   Her solitary lays,
> Nor asks a witness of her song,
>   Nor thirsts for human praise.

Had we time, we might carp at one or two other things in this little book; but we gladly forbear, because, on the whole, we can cordially recommend it, as being pretty nearly as good as the design permitted The following Evening Hymns please us much, both for their intrinsic merit, and also because their structure strikes us as advantageous:—

EVENING HYMN.

> Through the day thy love hath spar'd us,
>   Wearied we lie down to rest;
> Through the silent watches guard us,
>   Let no foe our peace molest.
> Saviour, Thou our guardian be,
> Sweet it is to trust in Thee.

EVENING HYMN.

> God of Israel, we adore Thee!
>   Thou hast kept us through the day;
> Thus preserv'd we come before Thee,
>   Ours the new and living way.
> Safely keep us through the night;
> Guard us till the morning light;
>   Nor forsake us,
>   Till Thou take us
> Far from earth to dwell with Thee
> Through a bright eternity.

"The Child's Christian Year," coming out under the superintendence, and partly, we presume, composed by the author of the "Christian Year," will, we are sure, be hailed with delight by numbers. We need hardly say that the faults to which we have been too long accustomed, are not to be met with here. There is no false taste—no irreverent familiarity of address—no intrusive dogmatism. Neither has Mr. Keble fallen into the error which we have already deprecated, of condescending too much. He thus deals with the question in a short supplement to his preface:—

"The first impression on looking over this little book will probably be that the hymns are too difficult, yet it is hoped they will not be thrown aside without a trial, nor without being read in connexion with the services of the day, which will often be found to clear up what otherwise appears obscure.

"It should likewise be considered that such subjects cannot be lowered to the level of childish minds without more or less of irreverence; and if we observe the Church's method of teaching, we shall find that she places in the memories of her young members a form of sound words, the full understanding of which neither they nor their teachers can arrive at.

"In the school for which the hymns were collected, they have been found useful in leading to questions and explanations, and the demand for them is such as to make the supply in manuscript rather troublesome."

We have but two hints to give. Children can enjoy none but *sonorous* verses. The smaller and more delicate melodies which often characterize Mr. Keble's poetry are rather too fine for ears which still require cultivation. Neither should they be presented with anything intricate in the way of versification, with any more than commonly varied metres. Such their ears are quite unable to follow ; just as whilst they can relish tunes, they have no fancy for elaborate pieces of music. Dryden's great Ode for St. Cecilia's Day was in most of the old elocution books ; and a very good exercise it may be in the way of placing accents and emphasis ; but no child, we are sure, ever could tolerate the poem. Its wonderful execution (nearly the only merit that any one ever found in it) is a merit which they are quite unable to perceive. For which reason many excellent little poems, both in "The Child's Christian Year," and in the "Hymns for Children on the Lord's Prayer, &c.," a book which, along with that we have just been noticing, we cordially recommend—seem to us unsuited to their purpose.

One other little volume is on our list, "Hymns for Childhood," by Felicia Hemans. Though new to us, it appears, from the title-page, that it is but a new edition ; consequently it may be known to many of our readers. It seems, to our apprehensions, nearer the mark as regards manner and execution, than any of those we have hitherto noticed ; though it does not embrace such important or such directly christian subjects. We have always admired the genius of Mrs. Hemans. She was a mannerist, perhaps ; but the manner was a very happy one. Her ear was fine, and her verse most musical. In the present little book she wisely adhered to the common metres, such as a child must every where encounter, and such as his ear can easily catch. We cordially recommend our readers to place themselves above the necessity of deriving their notions of any of the books now before us from what we have said ; but by way of samples of the last three, let them now read a hymn from each :—

HYMN V.

"Thy will be done in earth, as it is in heaven."

We dwell with wonders all around:
  Above, below, where'er we turn,
A world of loveliness is found,—
  Sweet flowers that spring, bright stars that burn ;
But there's an unseen world of bliss,
Far, far more beautiful than this.

'Tis there the blessed angels dwell,
  In glorious fields of light above;
They do their Maker's will so well,
  That all is happiness and love.
God thence has sent them now and then,
To bring glad tidings down to men.

Yet little of their forms we know,
   For few their heavenly shape have seen;
And sometimes when they came below,
   They veil'd themselves in mortal mien.
Nor can we tell what joys sublime,
And blissful tasks employ their time.

We only know their faces shine
   With dazzling rays, as lightnings bright;
Their garments, wrought in looms divine,
   Glitter with pure celestial light;
On earth they watch o'er good men's ways,
And sing in heaven high notes of praise.

And may we, sinners frail on earth,
   Hope, pray, and strive as good to be,
As angels pure of heavenly birth,
   Who serve their God so willingly!
Oh, let us prize this precious prayer,
That bids us be what angels are!
Hymns for Children, pp. 12, 13.

EVENING HYMN.

"Thou art about my path, and about my bed, and spiest out all my ways."
PSALM CXXXIX. 2.

Father! by Thy love and power
Comes again the evening hour.
Light has vanish'd, labours cease,
Weary creatures rest in peace.
Thou whose genial dews distil
   On the lowliest weed that grows;
Father! guard our couch from ill,
   Lull Thy creatures to repose.
We to Thee ourselves resign,
Let our latest thoughts be Thine!

Saviour! to Thy Father bear
This our feeble evening prayer;
Thou hast seen how oft to-day
We, like sheep, have gone astray;
Worldly thoughts, and thoughts of pride,
   Wishes to Thy Cross untrue,
Secret faults, and undescried,
   Meet Thy spirit-piercing view:
Blessed Saviour! yet through Thee,
Pray that these may pardon'd be!

Holy Spirit! breath of balm!
Fall on us in evening's calm:
Yet, awhile, before we sleep,
We, with Thee, will vigils keep;
Lead us on our sins to muse,
   Give us truest penitence,
Then the love of God infuse,
   Breathing humble confidence;
Melt our spirits, mould our will,
Soften, strengthen, comfort, still.

Blessed Trinity! be near
Through the hours of darkness drear;
When the help of man is far,
Ye more clearly present are;

Father, Son, and Holy Ghost,
  Watch o'er our defenceless head!
Let your Angels' guardian host
  Keep all evil from our bed,
'Till the flood of morning rays
Wake us to a song of praise!

"I will lay me down in peace, and take my rest; for it is Thou, Lord, only, that makest me dwell in safety."—PSALM iv. 2.

Child's Christian Year, pp. xi. xii.

THE NIGHTINGALE.
Child's Evening Hymn.

When twilight's grey and pensive hour
Brings the low breeze, and shuts the flower,
And bids the solitary star
Shine in pale beauty from afar;

When gathering shades the landscape veil,
And peasants seek their village-dale,
And mists from river-wave arise,
And dew in every blossom lies:

When evening's primrose opes to shed
Soft fragrance round her grassy bed;
When glow-worms in the wood-walk light
Their lamp, to cheer the traveller's sight;

At that calm hour, so still, so pale,
Awakes the lonely Nightingale;
And from a hermitage of shade
Fills with her voice the forest-glade;

And sweeter far that melting voice,
Than all which through the day rejoice;
And still shall bard and wanderer love
The twilight music of the grove.

Father in heaven! oh, thus when day
With all its cares hath pass'd away,
And silent hours waft peace on earth,
And hush the louder strains of mirth;

Thus may sweet songs of praise and prayer
To Thee my spirit's offering bear;
Yon star, my signal, set on high,
For vesper-hymns of piety.

So may Thy mercy and Thy power
Protect me through the midnight hour;
And balmy sleep and visions blest
Smile on Thy servant's bed of rest.

Hymns for Childhood, pp. 37—39.

Since we received the "Child's Christian Year," an illustrated edition has come out, with beautifully executed ornamental headings and tail-pieces, in the outline style of wood-cuts. Should yet another edition be called for, which is likely enough, we recommend, in addition to what we have said, more direct adaptation to the services of each day.

UNPUBLISHED LETTERS RELATING TO ARCHBISHOP BECKET.

I.

WERE we to place as much dependence on the monkish chroniclers of the eleventh and twelfth centuries in respect of motives as we do for facts, our knowledge of the secret springs of action would shrink into a mere nothing. To them, the assassination of a king, the murder of a bishop, the laying waste of a neighbouring province, the sacking of a cathedral or a monastery, are mere acts of murder, sacrilege, or lawless violence, and nothing more. Even if he had the inclination, the chronicler had not, in most cases, the power of accompanying his tale of murder or rapine with an exposition of the motives which had led to the commission of the acts. For the secret motives we must look to the private letters of the actors and their contemporaries,—of the men who perpetrated or consented to the deed of violence. In them, and in them alone, shall we find the kernel of which the chronicler has given us only the shell. Fortunately for us, the collections of letters relating to those centuries are very numerous, and throw a very full light on the state of manners and of feelings in France, Italy, and England, in those troublous times. To confine ourselves to our own country: we have the letters of Anselm, giving us Normandy and England in the days of the Conqueror and his son Rufus; John of Salisbury and the contributors to the Becket Letters continue the sketch to the middle of the reign of Henry the Second, where it is finally and fully illustrated, by the pungent letters of that sovereign's greatest favourite, Peter of Blois, Archdeacon of London.

The Becket Letters, with which our present purpose is, are some four hundred and more epistles written by the leading men in Rome, England, France, and Germany, at the time of the contest between the king and the primate, and collected, according to tradition, by John of Salisbury. It is a matter of little moment who it was who first arranged this mass of letters; their genuineness is unquestionable; of their value there can be no doubt. In the year 1682 Cardinal Lupus, under the direction and with the sanction of the see of Rome, printed the greater portion of these letters from the MS. of them in the Vatican Library; and these it is which the late Mr. Froude so ably translated. Besides those already printed, which we are informed was not, by a hundred, the full contents of the Vatican MS., the various copies of them extant in the MS. collections of this country contain many of interest and importance, especially the copies in the Cottonian and Arundel MSS. in the British Museum; that in the Lumley collection at Lambeth Palace; and that in the collection left by Archbishop Parker to the College of Corpus Christi in Cambridge.

Convinced that it is from such documents alone that we can realize to ourselves the judgment, the feelings, and the social condition of any particular age; well assured that it is they alone that can faithfully convey to us the hopes and fears by which the actors of the time were agitated, and that, as such, they are the most precious records for all who wish to study mankind; it is our intention in this and the following articles to collate and publish such of the letters in the MSS. of our own country as have not as yet been printed, and which serve to illustrate points of varied interest in the eventful history of the contest between Henry and the Archbishop. The writer had doubted whether or not he should present the letters in their original language, or attempt to clothe them with an English dress. After advice and consideration it has been determined to produce them in their native language, and to assist the reader in understanding their import by a moderate preface and running commentary. The difficulty, if not impossibility, of preserving the spirit of the original in a translation; of transforming into English idioms the thoughts and feelings of men, who, for the most part, thought in Latin; and the loss of authority always consequent on the substitution of translations in the place of the original, were the main reasons for this decision.

Passing by the traditions of his Saracenic origin by his mother's side, in the year 1130 we find Becket, as yet a young man, (having received a more than ordinary education at the monastery of Merton, in Surrey, and afterwards at the universities of Paris and Oxford,) employed in some minor capacity in the office of his father's successor in the shrievalty of London. Thence we trace him to the palace of Theobald, his predecessor in the see of Canterbury, where, according to Fitzstephen, he was introduced by his father's friends, Archdeacon Baldwin and his brother Eustace. His urbane manners, his talent for the study of civil law, his aptness for diplomacy, obtained for Becket, even in his early years, several foreign missions, during which he perfected his knowledge of civil law, under the most celebrated professors of Bologna and Auxerre. It was on his return from these missions that Becket received his first preferments from the hand of Theobald. In the year 1158, Henry raised Becket to the chancellorship, then, for the first time since the Conquest, held by an Englishman. What the king's reasons were for raising so young an ecclesiastic to the important place of chancellor the records of those days do not enable us to determine. Be his reasons what they might, Henry did not err in his choice; every writer has testified to the able conduct of Becket during his chancellorship, though it can hardly be doubted, unless the statements of the chroniclers are to be entirely disregarded, that towards his own order he acted rather as a statesman than as an ecclesiastic. On the death of the pious and estimable Theobald, Henry determined on straining every nerve to raise the chancellor to the vacant primacy. The reasons by which the king was actuated, and the manner in which the elevation to the primacy was effected, have ever been questions of dispute among the biographers of Becket. To enter into these discussions now would hardly be relevant; suffice it to say, that in the life and ecclesiastical history of the primate, put forth under the sanction of the see of Rome, the writer assigns as a reason for his election, that "the king, having had manifold trial of him, deemed his magnanimity and fidelity fit for so high a dignity; and also that he would have a care of his people, and govern all things in the Church and the common weal to his good liking." The same expectation on the part of the king of Becket's obsequiousness is admitted by Fitzstephen, Grime, and a MS. life of the date of Henry II., in the library at Lambeth, showing, that, in the opinion of the primate's contemporaries, the king entertained such an expectation from his acts as chancellor. As for the other point, without laying any stress on the admissions of the Lambeth MS., the Life of Grime, and the History of William of Newborough, we have Becket's own admission, that "he did not ascend into the fold of Christ by the true way, not having been called by canonical election, but obtruded by the terror of the secular arm." On the 2d of June, 1162, Becket was ordained a priest, and on the day following consecrated archbishop.

Here arises another question, of late much mooted,—the until lately admitted change of habits and manners, which one party have ever held up as a mark of his hypocrisy, the other as a sign of his sincerity. The late Mr. Froude took up a new line of argument; on the authority of certain passages in the letters, he denied the fact of the change. The matter seems now to stand thus: all sides admit, in accordance with the statements of the chroniclers and biographers, the magnificence and luxury of Becket during his chancellorship. On the authority of three isolated passages in the letters, one of which is contradicted by the sentence which follows it, and the rest of which admit of explanation, Mr. Froude held that no such change took place, as was usually admitted, on Becket's elevation to the primacy. It would be a matter of sorrow, had such really been the case. On the other side, the testimony in favour of the change, even to its greatest extent, is unanimous among the contemporary writers. That he endeavoured, by deeds of charity, and by self-mortification, to atone in some degree for the errors of his former life, is surely no sign of hypocrisy; nay, rather, it is to the honour of the repentant primate.

It was not long before disputes about the possessions of the see of Canterbury, and the right of excommunicating a king's tenant, greatly embittered that hatred which Henry had conceived against his former friend, immediately on his resignation of the chancellorship, as incompatible with his primacy. Peace, however, was made between them, until the disputes at Clarendon once more awoke their feud.

Henry, desirous of compelling the clergy to be tried in criminal cases by the courts of common law, and perhaps stimulated by a laxity of discipline, then too prevalent in the Church in England, of his own authority issued certain orders for the trial and punishment of clerical offenders. These orders, as illegal, the bishops unanimously opposed, and the king, conscious of his error, called them together at Westminster in council, and required of them jurisdiction over clerical offenders. This, they all, save one, denied; and when the king required them to observe the customs of the land, they pleaded their order. In a violent fit of passion, Henry broke up the council. Many of the bishops changed their minds on the breaking up of the council, and endeavoured to persuade the primate to join them in yielding their assent to the king's wishes. Influenced by a message from the pope, Becket went to the king at Woodstock, and promised that he would observe the customs of the land. With this the king was unhappily not content, but determined on having the private promise ratified in parliament. In January, 1164, the king met his parliament at Clarendon, and demanded of his clergy their public acquiescence to the customs of the realm. All agreed, save Becket. The king's anger was unbounded. After much solicitation by his clergy and his friends, the primate yielded. According to Grime he said, "' I yield to the councils of the king, and I bow to his will;' and then before all present, he promised in good faith to observe and keep the laws and customs of the realm." "To avoid disputes," said the king, "let the laws and customs of my grandfather Henry be reduced into writing, and subscribed by us all." The king's commissioners retired for this purpose, and on their return presented the roll of the sixteen constitutions of Clarendon. To affix his seal to these Becket refused; he had promised to observe the laws and customs of the realm, not to confirm them with his hand and seal. Though refused at Clarendon, the otherwise extraordinary proceedings of the king at Northampton, and the statement by Grime of the mission of the bishop of Evreux, would warrant us in concluding that the primate's signature was obtained, though after much delay.

It was not very long after this parliament that the great council of the king was held at Northampton, where a most cruel persecution was commenced against Becket. A charge of constructive treason, in not obeying the king's summons, until then always redeemable on a trifling fine, was punished with the exorbitant mulct of five hundred pounds. This was followed by several demands on the part of the king for balances stated to be due on the old accounts of the chancellorship. That these demands were against all honour and equity no one can doubt; that they were illegal is equally certain, if we may believe Edmund Grime's circumstantial account how the accredited agents of the king, at the council at London, pronounced the chancellor to be free: "*Ex ore regis, ab omni calumpnia et exactione nunc et in omne tempus.*" As difficulties and dangers crowded round the primate; as friend after friend fell away before the violence of the king, the temper of Becket exhibited greater firmness, greater forbearance.

His conduct before the parliament at Northampton was truly that of a martyr for conscience sake. Having appealed to the pope, the primate left the council, and on the day following fled to France, where the abbey of St. Bertin received the fugitive. Soon afterwards he had an interview with Louis at Soissons, and proceeded from thence, under a French escort, to the Roman court at Sens, to plead his cause before the tribunal to which he had appealed.

The pope, weak and vacillating, and too dependent on the support of Louis and Henry to dare to offend either party, refused the request, as well of the king, as of Becket. He would neither bring the cause into his own presence, nor send legates into England to try it there. On this the primate retired to the monastery of Pontigni, leaving John of Salisbury to conduct his matter at Sens: whilst Henry gratified his resentment by driving into exile every one connected with Becket, confiscating their goods, and leaving them to find subsistence from the charity of foreigners. Nothing was done until Henry, perhaps more to frighten Alexander than with the real intention of placing England under the anti-pope, placed himself in communication with the schismatical court of Germany. In consequence of this threat, Alexander required the Bishop of London to command Henry to restore Becket to his see, and make restoration to those whose property he had confiscated, and whose persons he had banished. In the same letter in which these commands are conveyed, Alexander exposes the state of his finances.

"Hereby, therefore, we authorise you to make a faithful collection of Peter's pence throughout all England for the current year, and to transmit the amount to us as soon as possible. We request, moreover, that, before the aforesaid collection is completed, you will furnish us with such a supply of money as your own resources or your credit can procure, and transmit it before the ensuing first of August. You may repay the loan out of the collection."[*]

In reply to this letter, Gilbert, Bishop of London, was commanded to make the king's excuses. At the same time he declined affording the required loan, because, he tells the pope, "no one through the whole kingdom would have paid the slightest attention to us in the matter of Peter's pence, unless the king had backed our applications with his royal mandate."[†] Alexander, unable to risk the loss of the money, declared himself satisfied with the excuses, and requested Gilbert to forward the collection to him by the hands of the abbot of St. Bertin.[‡] Such was his tone in August 1165. In the beginning of the next year, no compliance having taken place with any of his commands, the pope commanded Henry forthwith to receive the primate with the honour due to his station, and to reinstate the exiles in their rights and possessions.

"Furthermore," says the pope, "we wish your discretion (the Bishop of London) to take notice, that we hereby authorise and command you to pay over to the abbot of St. Bertin's the full amount of Peter's pence which is

---

[*] Divi Thomæ, Ep. i. 37.   [†] Ep. i. 38.   [‡] Ep. i. 41.

at present due to us in England. Your discretion should be aware of information we have received from our brother, the venerable Bartholomew, Bishop of Exeter, who tells us that the tax has been generally raised on a defective valuation, but that his diocese has paid in full, and that the sum is now in your hands. We marvel greatly that it has not been forwarded. We will you, moreover, to make good the former deficiencies, and on the present occasion to enforce full payment."*

This letter was the prelude to one to Becket, bidding him remain quiet until Easter, and holding out hopes, that after that time Becket, as well as the pope, might adopt more rigorous measures.† The critical period of Easter, 1166, arrived, without any reconciliation having been effected, and within ten days after the pope commanded the bishops of the province of Canterbury to make restitution, under pain of excommunication; and Becket, free to use all his powers, at first entreated and afterwards commanded the king and the bishops to restore him and his fellow exiles to their rights and possessions. His letter to the king concluded with these words: "otherwise, know for certain that you shall feel the vengeance of God." Well understanding those words, the bishops and the king anticipated the sentence of excommunication by an appeal to the pope, because the primate had suspended the Bishop of Salisbury without the king's consent, and threatened to excommunicate the king. The day for their appeal was Ascension-day, 1167. Before the notice of the appeal could reach Becket, the primate, after a pilgrimage to Soissons, had proceeded to Vezelay, and there, with all due form, excommunicated John of Oxford, for his heresy in communicating with the anti-pope, and for his usurpation of the deanery of Salisbury. He likewise excommunicated the Archdeacon of Poictiers, and several laymen, for interfering with the possessions of the see of Canterbury, and "all others who for the future shall put forth their hands against the goods and property of the Church of Canterbury, or ill use or interfere with those for whose necessities they have been set apart."‡

During the time of this appeal, namely, between July 1166 and June 1169, the following letter is to be placed, in which Gilbert Foliot informs Henry of his having again received the commands of the pope to forward to him as quickly as possible the Peter's pence then due to him from England, and solicits his mandate to the justices, without which, we have before seen, no one in the realm would have listened to the bishop's request, so little power had the papal commands in England in that day. The bishop also reminds the king of the approach of the day on which their appeal was to conclude, and when, unless something was effected in the meantime, the powers of the excommunications of the archbishop could no longer be evaded.

"Henrico, Regi Angliæ, Gillebertus Londoniensis Episcopus.
"Domino suo charissimo, illustri Anglorum Regi, Henrico, frater Gille-

---

* Ep. i. 74.   † Ep. i. 43.   ‡ Ep. i. 140.

bertus, Londoniensis Ecclesiæ Minister, pedibus sanctis conculcato Sathan, in Christo triumphare feliciter.

"Mandatum Domini Papæ nuper accepimus, quo nobis injungitur ut censum Beati Petri a fratribus et coepiscopis nostris suscipiamus, et per nuncios quos direxit ad nos, ipsi cito transmittamus.

"Quod quia de vestrâ totum pendet misericordiâ, nec potest effectu compleri ni per vos, vestræ id notificamus Excellentiæ, ut vestris, si placet, justiciariis superscribatis, et quod vestræ voluntati placuerit id fieri præcipiatis.

"Optamus autem, ut cor vestrum divinitas sancta possideat, et actus vestros sic disponat et dirigat, ut nec in Deum offendatis, nec adversum vos aut regnum vestrum domino Papæ, quem plurimum dilexisse novimus, justam querelæ causam et materiam præbeatis.

"De cætero, dies instat, quem appellationi ad dominum Papam factæ præfiximus; de quâ persequendâ, necesse est nobis, ut voluntatem vestram et consilium animo certius agnoscamus. Nam cum minus lædant jacula quæ pervidentur, timendum nobis est, ne, si ad monitum temporis omnia reserventur, singula quæ præscita minus et minus pertractata fuerint, eo minus commode quam exigat, expediantur. Inscribat cordi vestro digitus Dei quid fieri expediat, et vos manus ejus ubique protegat atque custodiat, Domine in Christo dilectissime."*

In order to conciliate Alexander, the king issued the usual license required, and after writing to the cardinals at Rome for their aid, sent his firm adherent, John of Oxford, one of those on whom Becket had placed the sentence of excommunication, to manage his cause at the papal court. The Roman court, open to corruption, and grossly venal at that date, set on foot a scheme for instituting a legatine commission, for the purpose of examining and deciding the points at issue between the king and the primate; and in the latter part of the year 1166, William, Cardinal of Pavia, and Henry of Pisa, were spoken of for legates. The influence of John of Oxford was distinctly recognised in the obtaining the remission of the cause from the papal court to one of a secondary nature, as well as in the admitted bias of the legates. Becket, warned by his friends of the character of the commissioners,—informed that "one was light and capricious, the other crafty and intriguing, and both greedy and avaricious,"† "whose eyes presents would easily shut, and reconcile to any wickedness,"—expressed his greatest reluctance to submit to the decision of any one, save Alexander himself. These reasons he stated in his remonstrance to his holiness, and to one of the legates, Henry of Pisa; whilst in his private letters to his friends Hyacinth and Boso, he beseeches them to aid him in his difficulties, "as a presbyter cleric of William of Pavia had lately promised the king of England, that his lord, on accepting a legatine commission, would terminate this cause to his liking."‡ The following letter to Conrad, Archbishop of Mayence, expresses similar fears, partly in similar words:—

"Thomas, Cantuariensis Archiepiscopus Conrado Moguntino Archiepiscopo.‖

"Omnia nostra ideo vestra reputamus, quia nos ipsi omnino vestri sumus; sufficere debet hoc ad persuasionem.

---

* Cotton. MS. Claudius B. ii. lib. 1. ep. 121.   † Ep. i. 111.
‡ Ep. i. 135.   ‖ Cott. MS. Claud. B. ii. lib. 1. ep. 130.

"Petimus itaque ut nostræ perspiciatis necessitati, quam ex rescripto literarum quas domino Papæ mittimus advertetis. Illud enim mittimus vobis non minus confidentes de vobis quam de nobis, quia de vestris negotiis æque solicitamur ac nostris.

"Ecce Johannes, ille schismaticus de Oxenfordia, qui perjurio suo nostrum quantum potuit procuravit exilium, sedem apostolicam appetit, ut eam circumveniat et subruat æquitatem. Rogamus ut ei respondeat iniquitas sua, et domi sentiat esse Petrum, qui, quicquid iterato dejeret, eum coram regibus et principibus ausus est impugnare. Discat prophetam esse in Israel, qui tempore accepto justicias judicet.

"Presbiter clericus Domini Willelmi Papiensis, regi Anglorum, nuper promisit, quod dominus suus, legatione acceptâ, causam quæ inter nos et ipsum vertitur ad voluntatem ejus definiet; et de nostrâ depositione tam gloriantur palam hostes ecclesiæ, persecutores nostri, immo Christi.

"Nos autem, nisi inevitabilis necessitas cogat, nullius excipiemus judicium, ni Domini Papæ; magis ecclesiæ subversionem Anglicanæ et Romauæ confusionem, quam nostram, timentes. Vigilate, ergo, apud Dominum Papam et Cardinales; ut saluti suæ perspiciant coram Deo et honori coram hominibus. Nam, quicquid in alterutrâ parte fecerint, memoriale erit in seculum seculi."

The interest of the king at the Roman court outweighed that of Becket and his friends, and by the end of the year the papal letters had been issued, appointing William of Pisa and Cardinal Otho legates for deciding the points under dispute. Leaving the effects of this commission for our next article, let us consider three other letters, which the first book of the Cotton MS. affords us.

The first of these is from Lewis of France to Manuel Comnenus, Emperor of the Romans, by the hands of Theobald, the venerable prior of Crepi, wherein, after more gracious salutations and kindly expressions than are to be met with even in the exordium of epistles of that date, he recommends the venerable bearer, of whose learning, sanctity, and reputation he speaks in the highest terms, to the consideration of his regal brother. Besides the mission which is openly stated in the letter, of collecting supplies for the monastery of Cluny, there were other secret instructions of which he was the bearer, more proper to be committed to the faith of Theobald than to writing. These secret instructions would not arrest the attention, were it not that we find in the following letter the same person introduced to the king of Sicily, with the self-same instructions, and did we not know that among those who received the exiled friends of Becket was William of Sicily, and, that that king, being now firmly fixed on his throne, was one of the most strenuous supporters of the papal cause, whilst at the same time his clergy were ardent in support of Becket, and the personal feelings of the king himself had been clearly demonstrated to be on the side of the exiled primate. It was now more than a century since the churches of the east and west had been divided by the excommunication of Cerularius. The mission of a prior of a Latin convent to the court of Constantinople, under the recommendation of the greatest supporter of the western church, with a commission to solicit alms for another Latin convent, is an interesting proof how far from schismatic the Latin church regarded the separation of their eastern brethren. The desire entertained by Manuel of reuniting the eastern and western empires under his own sceptre, and of overthrowing the Emperor Henry, might be a reason for the mission, as far as the secrets to be communicated were concerned; the ostensible reason, however, was the soliciting the aid of the Greek church for a famous but poor Latin convent. The passage in the letter to Manuel in which Lewis speaks of the kind reception he obtained from the emperor after his ill-fated crusade, would, as we cannot suppose the sentence ironical, go far to refute the popular tradition of the detention, if not imprisonment, of the king of France by the Byzantine; whilst the similar passage in the letter to William of Sicily, in which he speaks of the kindness of his grandfather Roger to him and his fellow-wanderers, warrants us in believing that the Sicilian admiral, when he defied the Greek emperor, assisted in the conveyance of Louis and his defeated host from a land where his stay was all but per force, though he might not, as the Sicilian historians boast, "have liberated the king of France from the dungeons of Constantinople, where he bearded the Greek lion in his den."

"Ludovicus. Rex Franciæ, Manueli, Imperatori Constantinopolitano.[*]

"Manueli, Dei gratiâ illustri et glorioso Romanorum imperatori, semper augusto, venerabili fratri et amico charissimo, Ludovicus eâdem gratiâ rex Francorum, salutem et ei fideliter et feliciter adhærere qui regna largitur et transfert imperia.

"Honor, quem nobis in Domino peregrinantibus apud vos exhibuistis, Deo auctore, a memoriâ nostrâ nunquam excidet; et licet nos maria et intrajectorum regnorum intersticia separent, nulla tamen vis meritis vestris debitam excutiet nobis caritatem. Inde est, quod de vestrâ prosperitate lætamur ut nostrâ; æmulis vestris, quod nostris, optamus evenire; promptum gerentes animum, si Deus oportunitatem dederit, vestram in Domino implere voluntatem et gloriam dilatare.

"Ut autem vos de nostro et nos de vestro statu faciat certiores, latori presentium, Theobaldo, venerabili Priori Crispiacensis ecclesiæ, dedimus in mandatis, ut imperialem adeat majestatem, et ad thronum celsitudinis vestræ secreta perferat, quæ potius fidei ejus quam litteris censuimus imprimenda. Est enim vir litteris eruditus, morum sanctitate conspicuus, præclari nominis, et nobis admodum familiaris. Unde, præ cæteris qui in ordine suo perfecti habebantur, electus est procurare necessitates ecclesiæ Cluniacensis, quæ non modo monasticorum regni nostri capud[†] extitit a diebus antiquis, sed in toto orbo Latino monasticæ religionis præ cæteris obtinuit gloriam.

"Imperatoriam ergo clementiam imploramus, ut tantum virum condeceter admittat, verba nostra quæ posuimus in ore ejus audiat diligenter, et misericorditer exaudiat preces ejus, et respiciat ecclesiæ necessitatem."[‡]

The date of this and the following letter cannot be earlier than 1166, and is most probably in the end of that year or early in the succeeding.

---

[*] Manuel Comnenus, son of John, Emperor from 1143 to 1180, during whose reign the rule of the Normans under Count Roger was established in Sicily, and the Roman Emperors, after fruitless efforts to recover their dominion, were obliged to rest content with hardly a nominal sovereignty.

[†] Sic in manuscripto.

[‡] Cotton. MS. Claud. B. ii. lib. 1. ep. 180.

" Ludovicus Rex, Willemmo, Rex Siciliæ.*

" Ludovicus, Dei gratiâ Rex Francorum, illustri Regi Siciliæ Willemmo, venerabili fratri et amico suo charissimo, salutem, et ei jugiter adhærere qui dat salutem regibus.

" Honor quem nobis, magnificus avus tuus, in obsequio Dei peregrinantibus exhibuit, liberalitas quam in nos et comperegrinantes exercuit, consolatio multiplex, quam fessis et laborantibus, devotus impendit, à memoriâ nostrâ recedere nequeunt; sed animum nostrum indesinenter accendant.

" Utinam devotio quam habemus ad vos possit operis exhibitione clarescem, et effectus meriti conspicuum testimonium reddat affectui promerendi. Gratius enim esset, nec si opportunitas divinitus aperiretur, obsequium vobis rependere, quam tunc fuerit illud a nostris progenitoribus accepisse. Magnique muneris instar erit, si decreveritis imperare, quod desiderio nostro paret materiam obsequendi.

" Licet enim nos interjacentium terrarum spatia separent, et obsequiorum vicissitudines intercludant, ferventissimam tamen a pectore nostro nequeunt excludere caritatem, quin prosperis vestris congaudeamus ut nostris, et adversa quotiens audiuntur feramus ut nostra. Proinde quod honori vestro et gloriæ credimus inservire, secure petimus et sincerâ consulimus caritate, sicut preces vestras admittere prompti sumus, et similiter expedienti consilio obedire.

" Nobilis vir Stephanus,† quem familiaritatis vestræ honore sullimastis, caro et sanguis noster est, et clarissimos proceres regni Francorum cognatione vel affinitate contingit. Qualiter autem, ad ignominiam generis et gentis suæ, dejectus sit et ejectus, prudentia vestra tanto certius recolit, quanto quæ circa eum gesta sunt insidiantium fraude, clarius per præsentiam intellexit. Rogamus ergo affectuosius nobilitatem vestram, ut eum, ad gloriam nominis vestri, et regni Francorum consolationem, curetis maturius revocare, eumque restituatis in integrum amoris, familiaritatis, honoris, et dignitatis.

" Ob hanc causam, et alias quas scripto non duximus committendas, latorem presentium, Theobaldam, venerabilem Crispiacensis ecclesiæ priorem, ad Excellentiam vestram fiducialiter destinavimus, cui, in his quæ vobis ex parte nostrâ dixerit, cedi postulamus ut nobis. Est enim vir fide plenus, reverendus titulo sanctitatis, litterarum eruditione præclarus, nobis admodum familiaris, carus et acceptus regno Francorum. Procurat autem necessitates nobilis ecclesiæ Cluniacensis in Oriente, in quibus eum a vestrâ sublimitate petimur benignius exaudiri, et efficatius promoveri.

" Gloriam vestram, ad honorem suum, in longa tempora promoveat et tueatur Rex regum et dominantium Dominus."‡

The next letter relates to the question of the right of the Archbishop of York to bear his cross before him, " per totam Angliam." Immediately on the election of Alexander (1159) Roger of York had presented his petition to the pope, praying him to confirm the letters of Honorius, by which he claimed the privilege in question. Alexander granted the petition, without hearing the other side, but on Becket's appealing to him in 1163, reversed his confirmation until the cause should be finally settled by the mediation of a " brother of

---

* William the Second, surnamed the Good, grandson of Count Roger, succeeded his father, William the Bad, in 1166. Divi Thomæ, ep. i. iii.

† Stephanus, by birth a Norman, Archbishop elect of Palermo, who with Richard, Bishop elect of Syracuse, an Englishman, was very liberal in providing for the friends and adherents of Becket, when driven from England by the orders of Henry.

‡ Cotton. MS. Claud. B. ii. lib. i. ep. 181.

the Temple" whom he designed to send over "as a mediator between their lordships on the subject of the cross, and to settle any dispute that might arise in the interim." "At all events," says one of Becket's envoys, "the Archbishop of York is not to carry his cross in your diocese. This we obtained by dint of perseverance." The remonstrance of the Archbishop of York, in which he considered this reversal as a prejudging of his cause, seems to have called for the following letter from the pope. As this letter is as late, at least, as the year 1170, if not later, it would not have been introduced had it not been that it relates to that curious and long-pending dispute which was one of the troubles of Becket, as well as of his successors, for many years after.

"Alexander Papa Rogero Eboracensi Archiepiscopo Apostolicæ sedis legato.

"A memoriâ tuâ, non excidit in primo anno nostri promotionis scriptum litterarum felicis memoriæ predecessoris nostri Honorii Papæ nobis feceritis præsentari. In quo continebatur antecessoribus tuis apostolicâ benignitate indultum fuisse, ut tam eis quam successoribus tuis, liberum esse per totam Angliam ante se crucem deferre. Nos vero eisdem antecessoris nostri vestigiis inhærentes transcripti nostri munimine confirmavimus quod antecessoribus tuis fuerat a predecessore nostro clementer indultum. Pmo* dum autem sanctæ et venerandæ memoriæ Thomas quondam Cantuariensis Archiepiscopus existimans hoc in depressionem juris et dignitatis tuæ redundare, exinde cessit questionem morere et propter hoc ad sedem apostolicam appellavit, affirmans si bene meminimus, quod tibi vel prædecessoribus tuis nulla* tenus id licuisset. Sicque factum est quod nos tibi per scripta nostra perhibuimus ne in provincia Cantuariensis Ecclesiæ, donec de causa cognosceretur ante te crucem deferre aliquà ratione auderes. Quare ergo per delectos filios nostros I. et A. clericos tuos, gravem nobis coram querimoniam deposuisti, asserens quod te, possessione hujus rei, quam tu et antecessores tui habueras, absque cognitione judicis spoliassemus."

"Nos volentes tibi tanquam venerabili frater deferre, et jura tua integra, illibata servare, præsentibus litteris statuimus, quod litteræ prohibitionis nostræ nullum tibi prejudicium faciant, quominus tibi et successoribus tuis liberum sit quemadmodum nobis privilegium beneficio indultum apostolicæ sedis, et tu et prædecessores tui id facere consuevistis ante vos per totam Angliam Crucem deferre, quousque deffinitiva sententia decernatur, [he had been at least ten years considering his judgment] an id ecclesia tua debeat de jure habere."

With this, to all appearance, portion of a letter, we close this introductory portion of the Becket letters, the proceeds of the first book of the Cottonian MS. It should not, however, be forgotten, that there is in that book another letter, one from Foliot, bishop of London, to Becket, in which a very different account of the meeting at Clarendon is afforded; an account, exculpatory of the bishops, and condemnatory, in the highest degree, of the primate; and at variance with the testimony of the best contemporary historians and biographers. It was this letter, this ex-parte pamphlet of Foliot's, which led astray Lord Lyttleton in his history of Henry II., and which a late writer, Mr. G. P. R. James, seems to have followed as of undoubted authority, one would almost suppose, without having read the whole of the

---

* Sic in manuscripto.

letter, and certainly without having compared it with the witness of contemporary writers, or read Mr. Berington's reasons against the genuineness of the letter itself. Writers of history ought ever to bear in mind with what caution the witness of a solitary MS. is to be received, even when it does not run contrary to contemporary authority; and in what suspicion it is to be held, when it contradicts every writer on the same subject, and fails even of being consistent with itself. Of Mr. James's view of the contest between Henry and the primate, we shall have occasion to speak in our next article.

ON THE DIVISION OF VERSES IN THE BIBLE.

The invention, as it has been called, of the present division of the Bible into verses, with its numerical notation, is generally attributed to Robert Stephens. This has, in fact, become the received opinion. To ascertain how far the vulgar notion on this subject is borne out by evidence, as well as to examine into the part which this celebrated printer had in this division, is our present object. We shall commence with giving the whole of the proofs on which Robert Stephens's claim is founded to an invention which has been universally received throughout Christendom, and introduced into the printed copies of the Bible in all the dialects into which the Sacred Volume is translated.

The authorities, indeed, in favour of the vulgar opinion are so strong and so numerous, that to some it would probably appear a rash and absurd attempt to call it in question. Among these authorities may be reckoned Stephens himself, and his son Henry; and every subsequent writer seems to have assumed the fact as certain. We shall give an account of the principal of these authorities in chronological order, and then proceed to show the part which Stephens really had in this invention.

Robert Stephens took refuge in Geneva upon his leaving the Church of Rome and embracing Calvinism, in the year 1551,* and published that same year the fourth edition of his Greek Testament, which first contained this division. This edition contains also the Latin Vulgate, and the version of Erasmus, and has in the title the date MDXLI.; but that this is a mistake for MDLI. is evident from the preface, in which he makes reference to the annotations to the New Testament which he had published ten years before.†

---

* Moreri says that this took place in 1547, but this is evidently a mistake, although Maittaire is not fully satisfied that Stephens came to Geneva in 1551.

† "Lectori. Quum nobis in animo esset Novum Testamentum, ut est a veteri interprete Latine redditum, excudere, adjectis tantum brevioribus annotationibus, quales abhinc annos jam decem edideramus in Latinâ editione Novi Testamenti."— *Preface to Edition of* 1551.

Now, as he had published no annotations in the year 1531, nor indeed any edition whatever in that year, and as he makes a special reference in his Preface, to certain annotations which he had published ten years before, and which were attached to his edition of the Latin New Testament published in 1541,* it cannot remain doubtful that this date is an error of the press, unless indeed there was some design in ascribing a false date to the edition. However this may be, the X of the date MDXLI. has been generally erased in all the copies. In the preface to this edition, Stephens observes,—" As to our having marked this work with certain versicles, as they call them, we have herein followed the most ancient Greek and Latin manuscripts of the New Testament, and have imitated them the more willingly, that each translation [viz. that of Erasmus and the Vulgate] may be made the more readily to correspond with the opposite Greek." † In this edition the verses are broken up into short paragraphs, or breaks, each verse commencing the line, with the figures in the inner margin.

This edition was followed, in the year 1555, by one of the Latin Vulgate, containing the whole Bible, in large 8vo. with the present division of verses marked throughout with the Arabic numerals, not placed in the margin, but incorporated into the text, which runs on continuously without being broken up into paragraphs. It contains the following address to the reader from Robert Stephens:—" Here is an edition of the Latin Vulgate, in which each chapter is divided into verses, after the order of the Hebrew verses, with numbers prefixed, which correspond to the numbers of the verses which we have added in our new and complete Concordance, after the marginal letters A, B, C, D, E, F, G, in order that you may be relieved from the labour of searching for what these figures will point out to you as with the finger."‡ The title-page bears Stephens's olive; and the name of the printer, Conrad Badius, at the end of the book, with the date 8 idibus Aprilis, 1555, shows where and when the book was printed. It was the first edition of the entire Latin Bible printed by Stephens since he left the Church of Rome. Of this edition, Le Long observes that it is distinguished from the preceding editions by its external form, in having the division of verses in the Old Testament as well as the New.§

---

* The edition of 1541 bears the following title :—" Novum Testamentum. Breves variorum trälationum annotationes, adjectâ veterum Latinorum exemplarium MSS. diversâ lectione, cum præf. Robert. Steph. 2 vols. 8vo. Paris, ex officinâ Rob. Stephani, 1541."

† " Quod autem per quosdam, ut vocant, versiculos opus distinximus, id, vetustissima Græca Latinaque ipsius Novi Testamenti exemplaria secuti, fecimus, ea autem libentius sumus imitati, quod hâc ratione utraque translatio posset omnino e regione Græco contextui correspondere."—*Preface to Gr. and Lat. Test.*

‡ " Biblia. R. Stephanus Lectori. En tibi Bibliorum Vulgata editio, in quâ, juxta Hebræorum versuum rationem, singula capita versibus distincta sunt, numeris præfixis qui versuum numeris quos in concordantiis nostris novis et integris post literas marginales A, B, C, D. E, F, G, addidimus, respondent, ut quærendi molestiâ leveris, quum tibi tanquam digito quos quæris demonstrabunt."

§ " Distinguitur hæc editio præcedentibus externâ formâ, nimirum distinctione versuum tam in Veteri tam in Novo Testamento."

There are two other editions stated by Le Long to have been published in this and the next year at Lyons, containing the division into verses, the one printed by Frellon, and the other by Anthony Vincent. We shall have some remarks to make on these before we conclude.

The next edition is that called Vatable's Bible, published in 3 vols. folio, 1556—1557. This contains, arranged in parallel columns, the Old and New Testament of the Latin Vulgate, and the version of Pagnini from the Hebrew. The New Testament contains Beza's version, now published for the first time. The notes are those commonly ascribed to Vatable, with those of Claude Badwell on the apocryphal books.* The verses are, as in the edition of the New Testament of 1551, broken up into sentences, and there is a notice to the reader prefixed, apprising him that this edition "contains the text divided into verses as in the Hebrew copies." †

The next authority for ascribing this invention to Robert Stephens is his son, the celebrated Henry Stephens, who records the fact both in his dedication to Sir Philip Sidney, prefixed to his second edition of the Greek Testament, in 1576, and in the preface to his Greek Concordance to the New Testament, published in 1594.

In the former of these he adverts in terms of strong regard to what he calls his "father's idea of the distribution of each chapter of the book into a certain number of verses; and asserts that nearly the whole christian world had borne witness to the great utility of his father's labour in this distribution, in having with one consent embraced his father's invention, in every language into which the New Testament has been translated." ‡

The testimony from the Greek Concordance is thus noticed by the learned Pritius, in his Introduction to the Greek Testament; "This most useful invention (of the distribution of chapters into verses) we owe to Robert Stephens."§ He then gives an extract from the Preface, which we shall cite from the original still more fully than Pritius has done. "Those who think that the last benefit

---

* This is entitled "Biblia utriusque Testamenti; Vetus, juxta editionem vulgatam, et versionem Sanctis Pagnini cum annotationibus quæ dicuntur Vatabli; Novum secundum Vulgatam veterem, et novam Theodori Bezæ, cujus hæc est prima editio, 1556-1557." Dean Prideaux, as well as Chevillier and Maittaire, erroneously supposed that this was the first edition of the Bible by Stephens, which contained the figures prefixed to the verses. The New Testament was published in 1556, and the Old in 1557.

† "Veteris interpretis trālationem in interiori paginæ parte minutioribus literis excusam damus, ad vetustissima exemplaria accuratissime emendatam, versibusque, ut in Hebraicis codicibus, distinctam."

‡ "Pudebat me equidem, quum Pater meus illis toties operam et studium navasset variis Testamenti Novi editionibus .... ac postremo illam singulorum hujus libri capitum in certum versuum numerum distributionem excogitasset, nisi et ipse symbolam meam ... conferrem, ab illo videre degenerare. Sed magnam laboris paterni, id est, illius seu distributionis seu divisionis ab eo excogitatæ, esse utilitatem, universi propemodum christiani orbis in eâ amplectendâ consensus, quâcunque Testamentum Novum excuditur linguâ, satis superque testatur."

§ "Deinde capita rursus in versus distinguuntur. Quod quidem utilissimum inventum Roberto Stephano debemus."

conferred by my father on the Scriptures, or rather on the readers of Scripture, was of no less importance than the former, seem to have exhibited a sound judgment. The benefit of which I now make such honourable mention is this: that as the books of the New Testament had been divided into those sections (tmemata) which we call chapters, he himself divided, or rather subdivided, these sections into those tmematia, or smaller sections, called, by an appellation more approved by others than by him, versicles; for he preferred calling them by the Greek name *Tmematia*, or its Latin *Sectiunculæ*. For he saw that the ancient name for these sections was now restricted to another use. But having said thus much of the name, I shall now speak of the thing itself. I shall set out with two facts, of which you will hesitate which most to admire. One is, that he accomplished the division of each chapter of which we are treating, while on his journey from Paris to Lyons, and indeed the greater part of it *inter equitandum*; the other, that while he thought on the matter, a short time before, almost every one said that he was raving; as if he was about to bestow his time and his labour on a matter altogether unprofitable, and which would not merely procure him no honour, but would come into derision. But, lo and behold, in spite of all their opinions in condemnation of my father's institution, the invention no sooner saw the light, than it met with universal approbation, and at the same time obtained such authority that all other editions of the New Testament, whether in Greek, Latin, or German, or in any other vernacular tongue, which did not follow this invention, were in a manner placed in the rank of unauthorized books."[*]

---

[*] " Robertum Steph. parentem meum literarum bonarum bono natum esse, testati sunt multi, ac testantur quotidie quamplurimi: et omnibus tacentibus, res ipsa id clamet. Sed tam multa in sacras pariter literas (sive Heb. sive Græc. sive Lat. sive Gallico mandatas sermoni) et profanas, præstitit, ut siquis operam ab eo in unas navatam cum eâ quam in alteras navavit conferat, de utris melius meritum dicere oporteat, in dubio fortasse relicturus sit: quum alioqui nulla dubitatio de hoc relinquatur, quin de sacris melius mereri cupiverit. Ultimum autem quod in eas, vel potius in earum lectores, contulit beneficium, minus aliis non fuisse qui judicant, non insagaci 'esse judicio videntur. Id cujus honorificam mentionem facio beneficium, illud est, quod quum Testamenti Novi libri in Tmemata, quæ capita vulgo dicuntur, divisi essent, ipse horum Tmematum unumquodque in Tmematia divisit, vel potius subdivisit; quæ, appellatione ab aliis magis quam ab ipso probata, Versiculi vocata fuerunt.—Nam ipsi vel Græcâ illâ voce Tmematia, vel Latinâ quæ illi respondet, Sectiunculas nominari magis placebat. Illam vero veterem commatum in oratione appellationem (Ciceronis Incisorum) ad alium restringi usum videbat. Verum, ut his paucis de nomine contentus sim, de re ipsâ plura dicam: initium a duobus sumam, quorum utrum magis mirari debeas, dubitabis. Unum est quod Lutetiâ Lugdunum petens, hanc, quâ de re agitur, capitis cujusque catacopen confecit, et quidem magnam ejus inter equitandum partem: alterum quod illum paulo ante de hâc cogitantem, plerique omnes incogitantem esse aiebant, perinde ac si in re prorsus inutili futurâ, adeoque non tantum nullam laudem consequuturâ, sed in derisum etiam venturâ, ponere tempus atque operam vellet. At ecce contra eorum damnatricem instituti patris mei opinionem, inventum illud simul in lucem, simul in omnium gratiam venit: simulque in tantam auctoritatem, ut quasi exautorarentur aliæ Testamenti Novi, sive Græcæ, sive Latinæ, sive Gallicæ, sive Germanicæ, sive in aliâ vernaculâ linguâ editiones, quæ inventum id secutæ non essent. Ut autem aliud ex alio venire illi in mentem solebat, quum et heuretico præditus

Serrarius also, in his Prolegomena, makes the following allusion to this circumstance, which he says that he heard from the mouth of Henry Stephens himself:—" I strongly suspect that it is far from certain who it was in our days who first *restored* the intermitted distinction into verses. Henry Stephens, indeed, having once come to Wurzburg, would fain have persuaded me that his father, Robert, was the inventor of this distinction in the New Testament, and I afterwards saw the same statement published by him in his preface to his Greek Concordance,* with the addition that it was on his way from Paris to Lyons that he made this division, and a great part while riding on horseback (*inter equitandum.*)"

Serrarius seems not at all pleased that the honour of this invention should belong to a Protestant, for he adds, " This may, after all, be an empty boast; but supposing it to be true, as Catholics, who were actuated with the desire of sacred knowledge, have used well, and to the glory of God, the versions of Aquila, Symmachus, and Theodotion, who were either apostates or heretics, so may they use the division of Robert Stephens. 'The most correct notarii, said Seneca,' he significantly observes, ' were frequently to be found among the vilest slaves.' "

That there was nothing particular to boast of in this famous invention will probably occur to the reader before we conclude. Whoever was its author, the boast of its having been done with such post haste expedition as Henry Stephens described it to have been executed by his father, seems no great matter of triumph, however we are to understand the phrase *inter equitandum*. This phrase has been variously understood. According to some, it denotes that Stephens performed this

---

ingenio esset, et magna pars cogitationum ejus non alio intenta foret quam ad excogitandum quidpiam quod sacrosancti voluminis autoribus utilitatem afferret, Concordantiarum Græcarum, vel potius Græco-Latinarum, opus, qua editioni Caput unumquodque in illa Tmematia sectum habenti responderent, prævertendum aliis omnibus existimavit. Neque tamen temporis compendium, quod cum operis illius dispendio non minus quam cum parsimoniâ sordidâ conjunctum esset, quærere voluit, (etiamsi in multis id operibus factitabatur, et hodie multo magis factitatur) quoddam opus, cui autor nomen Concordantiarum imposuerat, interpolatum, et accessione aliquâ accretum edendo: præsertim quum non solum multominus alicubi quam dimidiam locorum partem, sed multos etiam errores haberet ; et quidem aliquos in nonnullis quoque verborum thematibus: qualis est ubi verbo ἠβουλήθην (quod est pro ἐβουλήθην) thema datur ἀβουλέομαι. Quid igitur parens meus? idem nimirum quod de Concordantiis Latinis Universorum Bib. consilium iniit, ut relictâ eâ quæ solum ex rivulis hauserat editione, ad ipsum fontem veniens, non pocillis, ut alii, sed magnis poculis tantum hauserit, quantum ad editionem plenarum Concordantiarum satisforet."— *Preface to Greek Concordance.*

* " Et vero quis nostro isto sæculo intermissam illam distinctionem revocaret primus, quisque suos primus singulis versibus affixit numeros, ignotum etiam suspicor. Mihi sane voluit aliquando, Herbopolim cum venisset, persuadere Henricus Stephanus patrem suum Robertum hujus in Novo Testamento distinctionis auctorem esse, quin et id ipsum ab eo literis Latinis ante Concordantias Græcas mandatum vidi postea. De illo enim ait—'Quum Testamenti Novi libri in Tmemata quæ capita vulgo vocantur divisi essent, ipse horum Tmematum unumquodque in Tmematia divisit, vel potius subdivisit, Lutetiâ Lugdunum petens, hanc quâ de re agitur, capitis cujusque catacopen confecit, et quidem magnam ejus inter equitandum partem.' Vana hæc potest gloriatio esse."—Quæst. xii. Mogunt. 1612.

work while riding on horseback; according to others, riding in his coach. One learned man is of opinion, as we shall presently see, that it was done during the intervals of his journey; and another, that the idea only had suggested itself to Stephens while taking his ride. Pritius adds that Pfaff was of opinion that this phrase could scarcely be understood; but Calmet goes so far as to say that the present punctuation of the New Testament was equally accomplished *inter equitandum* by Robert Stephens.* Pritius gives as a specimen of Stephens's accuracy, Heb. xii. 21, 23, 24, where, he observes, "those parts which should have been *united*, are violently torn asunder." †

"The verses," says Michaelis, "into which the New Testament is divided, are more modern [than the στίχοι], and are an imitation of the division of the Old Testament. Robert Stephens, the first inventor, introduced them in his edition of 1551. He made this division on a journey from Lyons to Paris; and as his son Henry tells us in the preface to the Concordance to the New Testament, he made it *inter equitandum*. I apprehend this must mean that when he was weary of riding, he amused himself with this work at his inn. The wild and indigested invention of the learned printer was soon introduced into all the editions of the New Testament." ‡

The learned Dr. Mill, the celebrated editor of the New Testament, also ascribes this invention to Robert Stephens: speaking of the edition of 1551, he observes, "This edition is remarkable for being the first of all in which the text is divided into the sections or versicles which we now use. Robert Stephens was the author of this division, which happened to *come into his mind* while riding from Paris to Lyons." §

---

* In the Preface to his Commentary on the Bible, vol. i.; Paris, 1715, ed. 2, "The pointing," he observes, "is of uncertain authority." "The ancients," he says, "pointed differently from us. They had but a single point, by placing which at the top, middle, or bottom of a line, they marked a comma, colon, or period. In the good times of the Greek and Latin antiquities, all the words were divided by so many points. When ignorance was spread by the barbarians, punctuation was neglected. At the time of Charlemagne it was reestablished by Alcuin, and Paul son of Warnefrid. Manuscripts, since that period, are pointed with more or less accuracy, according to the abilities of the transcriber. As to printers, the Manutius's are said to be the inventors of points and commas, who inserted them in their beautiful impressions. We are assured that Robert Stephens fixed the punctuation of the New Testament, and that with so much haste, that he laboured at this work in going one day on horseback from Paris to Lyons, according to the relation of his son Henry."—"Henrici Stephani præfatio in Concordantias Græc. Lat. Novi Testamenti, Genevæ, 1594." Calmet has it 1524. The correction of these mistakes has cost us much trouble.

† "Pfaffius loc. cit. hoc vix comprehendi posse arbitratur, at enim quâ ἀκριβείᾳ ejusmodi tmematia distinxerit Robert. Stephanus exemplo esse poterit Heb. xii. 21, 23, 24, ubi ea quæ conjungi debuerant, maximâ vi invicem divelluntur."

‡ Marsh's Michaelis.

§ "Illud vero in hac Edit. palmarium est, quod in ea jam omnium prima textus distinctus sit in tmemata ea seu versiculos, quibus hodieque utimur. Hanc enim divisionem, quæ ipsi forte, cum equitando Lutetia Lugdunum peteret, in mentem venerat, jam perfecit Robertus Stephanus posuitque in hac editione," &c.—Prolegom. p. 127.

The following extracts from Chevillier's "History of Ancient Printing," which are repeated by Maittaire in his "Historia Stephanorum," show that these two learned men were of opinion that Stephens was the author of this division, and that he had introduced it into the New Testament in 1551, and into the Old in his edition of the Latin Bible, published in 1557:—

"En l'année 1551, il réimprima le Nouveau Testament, d'une forme un peu plus grande, en deux vol. où il, &c.; et divisa les chapitres par versets, ainsi qu'il avait vû pratiqué dans les plus anciens manuscrits Grecs et Latins; et mit un chiffre à chaque verset pour une plus grande commodité. Ce qu'il pratiqua ensuite dans l'impression de l'Ancien Test. l'année 1557. C'est là le plus ancien Nouveau Testament, et c'est la plus ancienne Bible Latine, où j'ai vû les versets distinguéz par chiffres; cet exemple fût bientôt suivi. Les Ministres firent imprimer de cette manière leurs Bibles Françoises et leurs Nouveaux Testaments en différentes villes, comme à Genève, à Lyons, à Caen, à Orleans; en 1556, par Phibbert Hamelin; en 1560 et 1562, par Antoine Rébul; en 1563, par Barthelemy Molin, et la même année par Jean Crespin, et par Pierre Philippe; en 1556, par Sebastien Honorati; en 1567, par Louis Rabier, et par pluseurs autres. Les années suivantes, Nicolas Barbie et Thomas Courteau imprimèrent aussi en cette façon, l'année 1564, à Basle, la Bible Latine, selon les traductions de Pagnin et de Vatable; René Benoist fit ainsi paroître à Paris sa Bible Françoise, en fol. 1566. Christ. Plantin, à Anvers, acheva le Pentateuque de sa Polyglotte, en 1569, et les autres tomes en 1570, 71, 72; où se voit la distinction des versets par chiffres. A Rome la Bible de Sixte V., 1590, et celle de Clém. VIII., 1592, furent données au public en cette même manière. Et depuis Clément VIII. la Vulgate a été imprimée ordinairement par versets chiffréz, avec cette différence, que dans les Bibles et Nouveaux Testaments de Robert Estienne, des ministres de Genève et de Basle, tous les versets commencent la ligne; ce que ne se trouvent point observé dans celles de Sixte V. et de Clément VIII. si on excepte Job, les Pseaumes, et les Paraboles de Salomon. Ordinairement les Protestants ont suivis la méthode de Robert Estienne, et quelques-uns parmis les Catholiques, &c. &c. On voit, que depuis le temps de Robert Estienne, l'usage a été d'imprimer la Sainte Bible avec des chiffres Arabes à tous les versets. Jaques Fabry d'Estables les avoit déjà introduits dans son Psalterium Quintuplex, imprimé 1509 et 1513, par Henry père de Robert, &c.

"Sans doute, Robert Estienne avoit vû ces impressions, et il est bien probable, qu'il forma son idée sur ces exemples."

And again,—

"Théodore Jansson d'Almelouë dit dans son livre De Vitâ Stephanorum, imprimé à Amsterdam, 1683, que cet imprimeur imagina le dessein de mettre des chiffres, et de distinguer ainsi les versets du Nouveau Testament, étant à cheval dans un voyage qu'il faisoit de Paris à Lyons. 'Ipsum equitando Lutetiâ Lugdunum dum peteret, tmemata illa seu incisa, vel ut nostri vocant, versus, per Novum Testamentum invenisse.'"

It is needless to multiply proofs of this prevalent idea, which has ascribed the introduction of verses in the New Testament to Stephens. It has been repeated by every subsequent writer who has adverted to the subject.* But the reader will not have failed to observe, that as Stephens asserts that he had introduced this division into the New Testament in imitation of Greek manuscripts, so he had introduced it into the Old in imitation of the Hebrews. The introduction of verses into the Old Testament, as well as the New, is indeed attributed to Stephens by most writers, including Du Pin, Calmet, Father Simon, and Jahn ; the former† observes that "Robert Stephens was the first who followed exactly the distinction of the Masorites in his Latin Bibles;" Calmet‡ asserts that it was in his edition of 1545 that Robert Stephens first introduced this division; while Father Simon,§ in which he is followed by Jahn,|| asserts that this introduction took place in the later edition of 1548.

In Mr. Horne's useful Introduction, into which the inaccuracies, as well as the more correct statements of the learned, have sometimes found their way, the process by which the present verses were introduced into the Bible is thus described:—

"Rabbi Mordecai Nathan undertook a similar concordance for the Hebrew Scriptures ; but, instead of adopting the marginal letters of Hugo, he marked every fifth verse with a Hebrew numeral, thus, אi. ה5, &c., retaining, however, the cardinal's division into chapters. The introduction of verses into the Hebrew Bible was made by Athias, a Jew of Amsterdam [1661], with the figures now in use, except those which had been previously marked by Nathan with Hebrew letters, in the manner in which they at present appear in the Hebrew Bibles. By rejecting these Hebrew numerals, and substituting for them the corresponding figures, all the copies of the Bible in other languages have since been marked." "The verses into which the New Testament is now divided are much more modern, (viz. than the στίχοι) and are an imitation of those invented for the Old Testament by Rabbi Nathan in the fifteenth century. Robert Stephens was their first inventor."

We might infer from these two passages that Rabbi Mordecai Nathan was the first inventor of the present verses in the Old Testa-

---

* Hug, for instance, observes, "The verses came from Robert Stephens, who first introduced them in his edition of the New Testament, in 1551. There is no mention made of the place where it was printed, but it is adorned with Stephens's olive."

† Prolegomena, p. 287.

‡ Preface to the Bible :—"We are assured that it is Robert Stephens, who, in his edition of 1545, has divided the text by verses, numbered as at present. This division passed from the Latins to the Greeks and Hebrews."

§ Simon. Histoire Critique.

|| "Versus in Latinam Vulgatam primum a Rob. Stephano, 1548, inducti et numeris insigniti sunt."—Jahn. Introductio, § 102, p. 121, Ed. 2. emendata. Viennæ, 1814. 8vo.

ment, as well as of their numerical notation, as Stephens was of those in the New; that, however, only every fifth verse was marked with a numeral letter, until the year 1661, when Athias published his edition, introducing the Arabic numerals into the Hebrew Bibles, in the manner in which they are prefixed at present; and that it was not until after this year that the copies of the Bibles in other languages were marked with these figures, in imitation of the Hebrew Bibles. It is true that in another place Mr. Horne says that the Masorites were the inventors of verses, but he does not intimate that they were the same with those now in use.

Notwithstanding the positive assertion that Stephens was the author of these divisions both in the Old and New Testament, we find Elias Levita speaking on this subject as if it were by no means an ascertained fact. "Who," he says, "can name the inventor of the mariner's compass? It is a matter of dispute who was the author of the famous art of printing. The same may be said of the telescope, for Galileo only improved it: and to come nearer to our purpose, who invented the spirits and accents, and who first affixed the points which we call the comma, colon, and period? Who first divided the books of the Old and New Testament into στίχοι? There are even some who entertain doubts respecting a matter but recently come into use, who the person was who first introduced the division of verses into the Greek and Latin Bibles." *

We have already observed that the earliest authority for the received opinion that Stephens was the inventor of these verses, at least in the New Testament, is Robert Stephens himself. But notwithstanding the boastings of his son Henry, it seems to us not quite evident that Robert himself meant to take the credit, such as it was, of this invention; on the contrary, it cannot have failed to strike the attentive reader, that, so far from putting himself forward as the inventor, he even in some degree disclaims it, where he says that in his division of the Old Testament he had "followed the custom of the Hebrews,"† and in that of the New, that he "imitated the most ancient Greek and Latin manuscripts."‡

We shall therefore now proceed with the inquiry, whether any divisions corresponding to our verses existed among the Jews, and

---

* "Quis pyxidis nauticæ primum inventorem certo nominare potest? De arte typographicâ, inventione præclarâ, et vix ante 200 annos in usu, disputant quisnam primus auctor. Tubi optici, sive telescopii, certus auctor ignoratur: Galilæus enim, licet illud multum excoluit, primus tamen ejus non fuit inventor. Et ut propius ad rem, de quâ agimus, accedamus, dicant nobis, quis primus spiritus et accentus libris Græcis apposuit, et tam apud Græcos quam Latinos aliosque comma, colon, et periodum earumque notas, ad distinctionem sententiæ, usurpavit? Quisnam apud antiquos, libros Novi Testamenti et quosdam Veteris in στίχους primo divisit? Quin et de eo, quod nuper in usu cœptum, dubitant nonnulli, quis primus Biblia Latina et Græca per versus primo partitus sit. Videmus in iis, qui paucis abhinc annis inventa sunt, quam difficile sit authores certo designare."—*See* Walton's Prolegomena.
† Preface to the edition of the Latin Vulgate, 1555.
‡ Preface to the edition of the New Testament, Greek and Latin, 1551.

also what divisions of this description are to be found in Greek manuscripts.

But we must take care, in entering on this inquiry, to mark the distinction between divisions into sections or verses, and the enumeration of these divisions, and also between the numbering of these divisions, and the attaching of figures to them, for the sake of arithmetical notation or reference. For instance, there may have been divisions answering to our verses, both in the Hebrew and Greek Scriptures, and yet the number of these divisions may never have been added up; or there may have been divisions, without any figures attached, as in our present Bibles. And again, as our present divisions into verses are not numerical divisions of books, but merely of chapters, and as they are consequently connected intimately with the division into chapters, it will be necessary to recollect when this division into chapters took place, as it is evident that the present numerical divisions of the chapters into verses could not have been introduced, under any circumstances, before the chapters themselves were invented. This, then, must form part of our inquiry and consideration. That there has been a division of the Hebrew Bible into verses from a remote period cannot be contested, but when this division took place must, in all probability, ever remain a mystery. Only it would appear that no division of the kind existed in Jerome's time, or he would scarcely have passed it over in silence, especially as he asserts that he was himself the author of a division, which he introduced into the Latin Vulgate. The probability is, from the close connexion between the vowel points and the סוף פסוק (soph pasuk,) which marks the present division in our Hebrew Bibles, as well as from the fact that the Masoretic copies contain this division into verses, separated from each other by the soph pasuk, that the Masorites were the authors of these, and that they were at least as ancient as the times of the Masorites, whose labours are supposed to have spread over a period from the fifth to the tenth century of our era; but whether these may have been, like the said vowel points, handed down traditionally from an earlier period, is a question which we shall not here stop to examine. We shall only add, that these masoretic verses, called *pesukim*, and separated from each other by the double point called soph pasuk, or termination of the verse, are nearly identical with the verses in our own Bibles.*

The earliest printed edition of the Hebrew Bible, published by Bomberg in 1518, has the present division, marked with the soph pasuk, but without the numeral letters. These are first found in the edition of 1523, in which each fifth verse is marked with the Hebrew numerals, according to the invention of Rabbi Nathan.

There are occasional exceptions, as, for instance, 1 Kings 4, which has in the common copies thirty-four, but in Athias only

---

* See Walton's Prolegomena, viii. § 1—12. Ludov. Capell. Crit. Sac. t. ii. c. 12, also 13 cap. 17, Buxtorf's Tiberias, cap. viii. and Tract. Megilla, c. 3, fol. 22.

twenty verses. Athias says that he followed a very ancient manuscript. Also Gen. vii. 22 is in some MSS. the first verse of the ninth chapter. But "in what way," to use the words of the learned Pareau, "the present division into verses found its way into the Hebrew Bibles it is impossible to say with any certainty."

We now come to the consideration of the Greek manuscripts, which Stephens, in his preface to his edition of 1551, asserts that he followed. It therefore becomes necessary to inquire, what kind of verses were used by the Greeks.

Some division of this kind has been supposed to be of very early date. Eusebius considers it to have been first used by Origen in his Hexapla. Hesychius, who died in the year 433, and is supposed to have been a disciple of Gregory Nazianzen, published a work, which he entitled the Στιχηρεῖς of the Twelve Prophets, or the prophetical books divided into στίχοι, that is, verses, or rather lines. He informs us, at the same time, that this manner of writing was peculiar to the poetical books, that is to say, the book of Job, the Psalms, and the works of Solomon; but at the same time asserts, that he had found a similar division in the apostolical books; and it would appear that this kind of writing by στίχοι was afterwards transferred, for greater perspicuity, to the writings of the Prophets. He* considers this kind of writing at least as ancient as the time of David and Solomon. Eusebius is our authority for asserting, that Origen used this method in his Hexapla, dividing the Greek and other versions into κῶλα.† Jerome acquaints us that the books of Job, Canticles, and Ecclesiastes had been already so written;‡ and there exist Hebrew manuscripts, in which these books, together with the other poetical books, are divided into stanzas and hemistychs. The nature of the subject, and especially the parallelism of the sentences, which forms such a peculiarity of Hebrew poetry, seem to require some such division, which may have proceeded from the original authors, and been transferred from the Hebrew to the Septuagint.

Jerome says that it was to prevent confusion, amid so many proper names, that he introduced this division into the books of Chronicles,§ which he thus distinguished into colons and commas; but it does

---

* ἔστι μὲν ἀρχαῖον τοῦτο τοῖς θεοφόροις τὸ σπούδασμα, στίχηδον ὡς τὰ πολλὰ πρὸς τὴν τῶν μελετωμένων σαφήνειαν, τὰς προφητείας ἐκτίθεσθαι, κ. τ. λ.—*Hesychius.* "It was an ancient invention of the holy fathers, for the sake of greater perspicuity, to divide the prophetical books into colons or members of verses, for they were at 'first written without any distinction. But it was afterwards so introduced by the learned. The books of the Prophets were thus edited by them: also the Psalms of David, the Proverbs, Ecclesiastes, and Solomon's Song. The book of Job is also thus found; and I have myself found the book of the Apostles" (the Acts and Epistles) "divided by some in the same manner."

† Eusebius, Hist. Eccles. b. vi. c. 16. Bishop Christopherson, however, the translator of Eusebius, was of opinion that these κῶλα were the columns into which Origen divided his Hexapla.

‡ See Jerome's Preface to Isaiah and Ezekiel.

§ See his Second Apology to Ruffinus, and his Preface to Joshua, Isaiah, and Ezekiel.

not appear that he introduced a similar division into the other books of Scripture. Martianay is of opinion, that it was in imitation of Jerome, that Hesychius divided the twelve minor prophets into στίχοι, which Hesychius himself says had been previously done in regard to the metrical or poetical books, which are also called στιχηρεῖς by Gregory Nazianzen,* Amphilochius, † Polychronius,‡ (who says that they are metrically written in Hebrew,) and John of Damascus. Epiphanius § also, in his Fourth Catechesis, gives the name of the five στιχηρεῖς, or stichometrical books, to Job, the Psalms, Proverbs, Ecclesiastes, and the Canticles, to which he adds Jesus Sirach.

Hesychius, as we have already seen, asserts that the prophetical books had been originally written without any distinction into verses; but that the holy Fathers had adopted the division for the sake of perspicuity. It is probable that he here alludes not to the Hebrew, but the Greek. It is here observable, that the word used by Hesychius is στίχος; and as it is of importance to our inquiry to examine into the sense of this word, we shall here enter briefly on this consideration. The word στίχος seems to be synonymous with the Latin *versus*, which is used by the Latin writers in exactly the same sense. The word στίχος seems, however, not to have been always used in precisely the same signification. It sometimes seems to denote a short sentence; at other times, one or two words regulated by the sense, but filling only a part of the line, the rest being left blank; a portion, in fact, in which there was any meaning whatever, although imperfect and but commenced. It sometimes signified a whole sentence, as in the following example from Demosthenes's Oratio pro Coronâ, given by Aquila Romanus: οὐκ εἶπον μὲν οὖν ταῦτα, οὐκ ἔγραψα δέ· οὐδὲ ἔγραψα μὲν, οὐκ ἐπρέσβευσα δέ· οὐδὲ ἐπρέσβευσα μὲν, οὐκ ἔπειτα δὲ Θηβαίοις; but it more usually signified a line, consisting generally of the same number of words without any reference to the sense, for the greater facility of counting the number of lines. Most existing manuscripts of the στιχηρεῖς, which are *copies* of stichometrical books, are, however, written in a continued text, with the divisions marked with points, in order to save parchment. The following examples of stichometry will here serve to illustrate our subject.

The verse in Job, " Perish the day," is thus stichometrically divided in the Thecla or Alexandrine MS. (A):

Ἀπόλοιτο ἡ ἡμέρα, ἐν ᾗ ἐγεννήθην ἐν αὐτῇ
καὶ ἡ νὺξ ἐν ᾗ εἶπον Ἰδοὺ ἄρσεν.

So also in the words, which in the Hebrew text make but one verse, it has been found thus:

Ἀπενέγκοιτο αὐτὴν σκότος. Μὴ εἴη εἰς
ἡμέρας ἐνιαυτοῦ, μηδὲ ἀριθμηθείη εἰς ἡμέρας μηνῶν.

---

* Carm. 33.   † Carm. ad Seleucum.   ‡ Prolegomena in Job.
§ Lib. iv. de Orth. Fid.

But in A, it is thus divided:

'Απενέγκοιτο . . . . .
μὴ εἴη . . . . .
μηδὲ ἀριθμηθείη . . . . .

Again, the 13th verse of the fifth chapter is divided into eight verses in the same manuscript.

The following will serve as an example of stichometry, taken from a Greek manuscript of the seventh century. We shall, however, give it in English, according to the authorized version.

Rom. vi. 19—22. . . . . . .

> Because of the infirmity
> of your flesh
> For as ye have yielded
> your members
> servants to uncleanness
> and to iniquity unto iniquity
> Even so now yield
> your members
> servants to righteousness
> unto holiness
> . . . .
> What fruit had ye then in those things
> whereof ye are now ashamed
> For the end of those things
> is death
> But now being made free from sin
> and become servants of God
> Ye have your fruit unto holiness
> and the end everlasting life.

The two first of these lines are said by Montfaucon to belong to the former period. The next period has eight στίχοι or lines. This contains two colons, each having four commas or versicles. This learned writer says that each colon contained two sections. As he informs us that these divisions supply the place of points throughout the manuscript, it would seem more properly to belong to the Euthalian division, which we shall next refer to.

It appears from what Hesychius has said of his seeing a stichometrical copy of the Acts and Epistles, that stichometry had been then some time in use. There was, however, another sort of stichometry invented in the fifth century by Euthalius the deacon (of Alexandria), which was a rude substitute for the art of punctuation. The following example is taken from Wetstein's uncial manuscript, H, Titus ii. 2, 3 :—

πρεσβύτας νηφαλίους εἶναι	That the aged men be sober
σεμνοὺς	grave
σώφρονας	temperate
ὑγιαίνοντας τῇ πίστει	sound in faith
τῇ ἀγάπῃ,	in charity

πρεσβυτιδας ὡσαύτως ἐν καταστήματι ἱεροπρεπεῖς	The aged women likewise that they be in behaviour as becometh holiness
μὴ διαβόλους	not false accusers
μὴ οἴνῳ πολλῷ δεδουλωμένας	not given to much wine
καλοδιδασκάλους.	teachers of good things.

Euthalius thus completed the whole of Paul's Epistles in the year 462, and divided in the same manner the Acts and Catholic Epistles; but his stichometrical edition of the Gospels has not come down to us.* But since his time, we have abundance of stichometrical manuscripts. Some are of opinion, that he took his idea from the stichometrical arrangement of Job, the Psalms, Proverbs, and Ecclesiastes. This mode of writing was, no doubt, of the greatest use to the unlearned, and assisted them in discovering the sense of what they read, in the absence of points. This work came out under the patronage of Nicephorus, patriarch of Constantinople, to whom the work was dedicated.

Although several of the transcripts of these stichometrical manuscripts have not preserved the stichometrical form, they yet continue to enumerate the στίχοι at the end of each book. They sometimes also add the number of ῥήματα; but what this signified is doubtful. It is, however, certain, that there was nearly the same number of ῥήματα as of στίχοι.†

After this, the practice commenced of saving expense, by filling up the entire of the vacant space; and points were used, for the purpose of showing where each separate verse ended. Thus, instead of writing—

> ὁ δὲ ἐγερθεὶς, παρέλαβε τὸ παιδίον·
> καὶ τὴν μητέρα αὐτοῦ· καὶ ἦλθεν εἰς γῆν Ἰσραήλ·
> ἀκούσας δὲ ὅτι Ἀρχέλαος βασιλεύει ἐπὶ τῆς Ἰουδαίας·
> ἀντὶ Ἡρώδου. τοῦ πατρὸς αὐτοῦ·
> ἐφοβήθη ἐκεῖ ἀπελθεῖν·
> χρηματισθεὶς δέ· κ. τ. λ. — Matt. ii. 21, 22.

They wrote thus—

> ὁ δὲ ἐγερθεὶς· παρέλαβε τὸ παιδίον· καὶ τὴν μητέρα αὐτοῦ· καὶ ἦλθεν εἰς γῆν Ἰσραήλ· ἀκούσας δὲ, κ. τ. λ.

The Alexandrian manuscript (A) in the British Museum is a *copy* of a stichometrical MS. in which the close of each στίχος is marked by a point, as—

> καὶ εἶδον τὰ τετράποδα τῆς γῆς . καὶ τὰ θηρία καὶ τὰ ἑρπετὰ . καὶ τὰ πετεινὰ τοῦ οὐρανοῦ : ἤκουσα δὲ φωνῆς λεγούσης μοι· ἀναστὰς Πέτρε· θῦσον καὶ φάγε.

But there are other marks, which prove it to have been altogether independent of Euthalius's invention, and to have been written, together with other uncial manuscripts, including the Codex Ephremi,

---

* Hug seems to think it possible, that Euthalius executed no stichometrical arrangement of the Gospels; and that whoever did, might have called the στίχοι, ῥήματα. Of these στίχοι, it was usual to give the number at the end of each book. They were sometimes also numbered in the margin, as we shall see hereafter.

† Bishop Marsh, no mean authority, seems decidedly of opinion, that στιχοι were lines only, without any reference to the sense, while ῥήματα were short sentences.

and Dr. Barrett's manuscript of St. Matthew's Gospel, (which shall be hereafter referred to,) before the system of stichometry came into repute.

The celebrated Codex Bezæ is a stichometrical manuscript, but the number of verses is not added at the end. Another stichometrical manuscript, the Codex Laudianus E, has preserved the numbers. This contains the stichi both in Greek and Latin, in opposite columns, as does also the uncial MS. D, or the Clermont MS. in the French king's library.

The uncial MS. G, or the Codex Bœrneriananus, a manuscript written by an Irishman in the ninth century, and once in the possession of the famous John Scotus, (or the Irishman,) is also copied from a stichometrical exemplar, and the writing of the present MS. is continuous, and the commencement of each verse merely indicated by a capital initial. The following example is (incorrectly) given by Hug, as a proof that the transcriber was an ignorant man, and incapable of planning a few στίχοι on Euthalius's principles.

> Ταῦτά σοι γράφω ἐλπείζω ἐλθεῖν τάχειον
> Ἐὰν βραδύνω ἵνα ἰδῆς·
> Πῶς δεῖ . ἐν οἴκῳ Θεοῦ ἀναστρέφεσθαι.
> Ἥτις ἐστὶν ἐκκλησία Θεοῦ ζῶντος
> Στύλος καὶ ἑδραίωμα τῆς ἀληθίας
> Καὶ ὁμολογουμένως. μέγα ἐστὶν τὸ τῆς εὐσεβίας. μυστήριον
> Ὃς ἐφανερώθη. ἐν σαρκὶ.
> Ἐδικαιώθη ἐν Πνεύματι
> Ὤφθη ἀγγέλοις
> Ἐκηρύχθη ἐν. ἔθνεσιν
> Πιστεύθη. ἐν κόσμῳ
> Ἀνελήφθη ἐν. δόξῃ.
> Ὁ δὲ πνεῦμα ῥητῶς λέγει
> Ὅτι ἐν ὑστέροις καιροῖς *

The unsatisfactory nature of this kind of stichometrical pause led to attempts at grammatical improvement, which ended in our present system of punctuation, which was introduced probably about the eighth century, and brought to its present state of perfection before the tenth.†

It will be now evident to the reader, that when Stephens said that he had followed ancient Greek manuscripts in his division of the verses, he could not possibly have referred to the ancient system of stichometry:—Stephens has, consequently, been accused of having made this statement to serve a purpose. But as this will form a subsequent part of our inquiry, we shall next give some account of the divisions to be found in the ancient Latin manuscripts.

(*To be continued.*)

---

* The Greek characters are like those in the Psalter of Sedulius the Irishman, in Moutfaucon's Palæog. Græc. l. iii. c. 7,'p. 237, which we shall hereafter notice. The Latin is Antehieronymian. The character is Irish. We have corrected some errors in Hug's stichometrical arrangement of this passage by a comparison with the original.

† Cassiodorus strongly recommends the use of points to those who copy the Sacred Scriptures, urging that they serve, in some respects, the purpose of an explanation. "Istæ siquidem positurae sive puncta, quasi quidem viæ sunt sensuum et lumina dictionum." He attributes them to St. Jerome as the author.

NOTICES OF BOOKS.

Memoir of the Life of Richard Phillips. London: Seeley & Burnside. 1841. 8vo. Pp. 292.

THE subject of this memoir was one of "the persons called Quakers," and his son is his biographer. Mr. Phillips appears to have enjoyed in the religious world of his day a place of some eminence, his claims to which we will not dispute; neither do we doubt that he was a man of earnest piety. At present we content ourselves with quoting a few short passages, which may illustrate the state of religious feeling among "the Friends."

> "Being at one time much tried and distressed by the prevalence of numerous scruples, directed or permitted with the gracious design of reducing and rendering more subservient the obstinate will of man—opposed, as it naturally is, to the real Cross; in a kind of almost despair of obtaining any relief from their pressure and subsequent recurrence, in anguish I hastily exclaimed, 'Why is it thus? I will follow thee even *to the gallows.*' Upon which a sudden flash of light, similar to lightning, passed before me, as into the ground, when these scruples in a very considerable degree ceased. How wonderful and merciful are the ways of the Most High! who thus, by what may be termed things that are not, brings to naught things that are!" . . . . .
>
> "I know an individual who was so dismayed and terrified by an impression on his mind, requiring him to do a particular act, that he hastily resolved that, should such a requisition be repeated, he would, sooner than comply therewith or submit thereto, sacrifice his life: yet, some years later, his mind having been greatly exercised, humbled, and reduced, by the operations of these foolish, despised things, and even by things that are not; on the requiring before alluded to being repeated, he submitted thereto, and had to participate of the sustaining and encouraging fruits of obedience."

These are the words of Phillips the elder; on which his son's comment is as follows: "It now remains for me to raise the veil a little more from these facts, and in so doing, I believe, that I follow my precious father's own advice in the extract which I have just copied. The individual whom he mentions as determining to sacrifice his life rather than comply with the requisition of duty which was impressed upon his mind, was himself. It was at a meeting, in which he felt that he ought to communicate something: and, the effect was so terrific to him, that he eventually resolved, that 'if ever that was repeated, he would *jump into the Thames.*' I believe I quote the expressions which he used in relating the occurrence to me."

It is satisfactory to know, that after all these purposes of self-immolation, the Quaker preserved a whole skin, and died peaceably at a good old age. The reader will not have failed in this passage to observe the singularity of the expression used both by father and son. In part, no doubt, it is the result of sheer affectation, as we shall presently see more at large; but it is to be observed, that there is "method in this madness," and many of the terms which they use are catholic terms, fresh struck in the sectarian mint, in order to conceal their denial of those Christian doctrines which the terms properly denote.

We have also a very peculiar use of the word "Seed," as applied to Christ, as in the following mysterious places:—

"Doubting and discouragement had nearly prevented our going: however we went, and, as yet, have not seen any cause to regret; for although (speaking to a small degree compared with many) bonds and afflictions awaited us, yet when the allotted portion of suffering was borne, the bonds were broken, and the *Seed* reigned in a degree of the Father's strength..... The more the state of our Society opens in these parts [South Wales], the more clearly it appears that the more the living members dwell with the *Royal Seed*, the deeper they will have to dwell, and the more intimate the union, the closer fellowship will they have with suffering."

"While musing one morning in my chamber, after having read the creed of William Cowper, in one of his letters, my mind was very unexpectedly exercised in an unusual manner, which seemed speedily to occupy my whole mind, to the exclusion of all other thoughts, and to possess it under a feeling of solemn, humble silence; when suddenly there appeared, seated before me, at a short distance on my left, my unutterable merciful heavenly Father; and a little further off, on my right, my very precious, beloved Saviour. I then felt urged in my mind to go towards them; and also pressure, as if pushed forward. On approaching to, and when near my merciful, beneficent Father, I felt a reluctance and fear to go forward; but when near to my dear Father, I felt such an increased degree of strength and animation as encouraged and enabled me to look towards him; and at the same time pointing with my right hand (which seemed peculiarly strengthened) towards my dear Saviour, I exclaimed, 'There's my Advocate!' upon which all fear ceased, and the vision immediately vanished; but was very soon succeeded by such a sweet, pure, unmixed feeling of peace (except the consciousness that in this state of being such a feeling could not long continue) that not any language is competent fully to describe it. To the best of my recollection, this state of mind remained for about three quarters of an hour."

We do not extract this passage, or the former one of the same nature, for purposes of ridicule—God forbid; but with a view of illustrating the state of religious feeling among this class of separatists; and we can unfeignedly say, that we rejoice to find that there existed a man amongst them so lately whose mind had so far escaped the general worldly leaven which has pervaded them, as to believe at all in spiritual impressions, however enthusiastic or erroneous. We shall conclude with one more short extract, which *may* allowably create a smile:—

"In the course of his gradual decay, my father's mind recurred with yearning thoughts to sacred music, as a sweet and soothing means of diminishing his sufferings and calming his spirits. He did not, however, permit himself to yield to the wish, *until after diligent examination of the subject, he felt thoroughly persuaded in his own mind that he was permitted, without offending his conscience, to do so.* When my dear father's decision was formed, he procured a large barrel-organ, with only sacred tunes upon it; and very greatly did he enjoy it during the last eight months of his precious life. He frequently expressed his thankfulness, that having made a sacrifice of this gratification in early life, he was now permitted to resume it, in a guarded form, in old age; he did, indeed, often experience it to be,

'Like David's harp of solemn sound,'

of real service to his spirit. At times he liked that those of his little household, who were able, should unite their voices to its swelling notes, in singing a hymn; but not unfrequently he appeared to use the tones of it merely to wing his thoughts to those regions whither his soul stood waiting to depart."

We rejoice that the old man could settle the matter so satisfactorily between his "mind" and his "conscience," as to become reconciled to the proscribed instrument. Concerning the divisions which it is well known are rending the Society of the Quakers to their foundation, this book preserves a prudent silence. Mention is made of a "brightness" which has long since set; we read of Quakers, who both in their "dress and their address" had departed from the pristine rule; and a lax Friend who had made an exchange of hats, is twitted with having "taken his (R. P's.) *umbrella,* and having left his own *mushroom*" in its place. We do not remember any other allusions in the volume, even to laxity of discipline—none as to divisions in doctrine. In these points, the editor has no doubt "exercised himself by silence:" he would "sooner jump into the Thames" than "communicate" anything so injurious to the credit of his Society.

The History of Egypt under the Romans. By SAMUEL SHARPE. London: Moxon. 1842. 8vo. Pp. 276.

MR. Sharpe meets us in the two departments of literature, which we consider most properly to fall within our province—theology and scholarship. In the latter department, the margin of his book shows (we have not had time to consult the originals) a copious list of references; but the theology is decidedly heretical in the most capital of all points, the divinity of Jesus Christ. Whether the author be avowedly a Socinian or Unitarian we know not; the opinion which we have just given is derived solely from the internal evidence contained in this work; and therefore we think it right to show that we are not speaking at random when we bring so grave an accusation against him. His words are these:—

"*Jesus of Nazareth* was acknowledged by Constantine as *a* God or divine person, and in the attempt *then* made by the Alexandrians to arrive at a more exact definition of his nature, while the emperor was willing to be guided by the bishops in his theological opinions, he was able to instruct them all in the *more valuable* lessons of mutual toleration and forbearance. . . . . The schools of Alexandria now gave birth to a quarrel about the nature of Jesus, which has *divided the christian world for fifteen centuries.* Theologians have found it *difficult to determine what the immediate successors of the apostles and early writers thought about the exact nature of the great Founder of our religion.* As it had never been brought to a logical dispute to be settled by argument or authority, the writers had not expressed their opinions in those exact terms which are so carefully used after a controversy has arisen. THE CHRISTIANS WHO HAD BEEN BORN JEWS BELIEVED THAT JESUS WAS A MAN, the Messiah foretold in the Old Testament: with the philosophical Greeks he was the divine Wisdom, the *Platonic* Logos; and with the Egyptians he was one out of several Æons or powers proceeding from the Deity. Clemens Romanus *only* calls him our high priest and master, phrases which Photius, in the ninth century, thought little short of blasphemy: but the philosopher Justin Martyr, and after him Clemens Alexandrinus, speak of Jesus as *a* God in a human form. Dionysius, Bishop of Alexandria, *when arguing against Sabellius,* says, that our Lord was the first-born of *every created being ;* but as Origen writes against the practice of addressing prayers to him, many Christians must have *already* considered him as the disposer or *one of the disposers* of all human events. But these inexact opinions did not satisfy that school which united the superstition of the Egyptians with the more refined speculations of the new Platonists; and as soon as the quarrel with the pagans ceased, we find the Christians of Egypt and Alexandria divided into two parties, on the question whether the Son is of the same substance, or only of a similar substance with the Father."

We have been too long used to the sneers of Gibbon's sceptical school of writers to be much moved by expressions, which, in a spirit contrary to that of Scripture, speak of peace as "more valuable" than truth; and place heresy on a par with "the faith once delivered to the saints." But there are so many positive falsehoods, some very subtilly stated, in this extract, that they demand something of a specific notice. 1. The first falsehood, viz. that it is "difficult to determine" what doctrine the earliest writers held, is only to be refuted by referring the reader to Bishop Bull's triumphant " Defensio Fidei," or to the late Dr Burton's "Testimonies of the Ante-Nicene Fathers to the Divinity of Christ." 2. The assertion that "the Christians who had been born Jews believed that Jesus was a man," can be met more summarily. St. Peter, we believe, has always been considered as "born a Jew;" and *he* said to his Master, "Thou art the Christ, *the Son of the living God.*" 3. Clemens Romanus, so far from "only" calling Jesus his "high priest and master," calls him also "the sceptre of the majesty of God," and "the brightness of his majesty." In the authors already referred to, and in Routh's " Reliquiæ Sacræ," will be found additional testimony from this writer. But why, Mr. Sharpe, leave out Barnabas and Hermas, and especially Ignatius, from your list? The last-named contains expressions not less strong than " Photius in the ninth century." 4. If Mr. Sharpe really thinks, as he insinuates, that Dionysius of Alexandria was led to admit the distinct divine personality of Christ in intemperate zeal against Sabellianism, the following passage will show that he maintained the unity of the divine nature in the three Persons of the Godhead as firmly as the most orthodox Catholic : speaking of the Father's will, which Christ declared that he came upon earth to fulfil, Dionysius writes, that " with respect to the divine nature, it is one will, his own and the Father's." Lastly, in order to make Origen serve his purpose, Mr. Sharpe refers *generally* to his treatise " De Oratione." To this we reply, that the genuineness of this treatise (see Note in " Def. Fid.") has been strongly questioned, amongst other reasons on this very satisfactory one, that it contains *several* doctrines at variance with what is contained in the acknowledged writings of Origen. What his real sentiments are upon this subject will appear by this extract from his book, " Contra Celsum :" " As those who worship the sun, moon, and stars, because of their sensible heavenly light, would not worship a spark of fire or an earthly lamp, as seeing the incomparable excellency of what they thought worthy to be worshipped above that of sparks or lamps; so they who perceive that God is Light,—they who apprehend that the Son of God is the true Light, that lighteth every man that cometh into the world,—they who understand that this Light saith, ' I am the Light of the world,'— cannot rationally worship that small spark of true light, compared to God the Light, which is in the sun, moon, and stars. Nor do we dishonour these so great works of God, or with Anaxagoras call the sun a 'ball of fire, &c.' and therefore speak of them in this manner ; but we speak thus of them, perceiving the unspeakable excellences of God the Supreme, and of the Only-Begotten, who excels every thing else."

To refute the heresy of the Unitarian at this time of day, would be, indeed, a work of supererogation. Had Mr. Sharpe avowed himself such, we should not have noticed his misstatements ; but it is because he appeared to us to be fighting dishonestly, under false colours, that we have been induced to strip off the mask from him. When a man excommunicates himself from the Church of Christ by a voluntary act of deliberate heresy or schism, he is bound, we think, in candour, to advertise all such as are likely to come in contact with him of the circumstance.

---

1. *Letters on the Study of Ancient and Modern History; containing Observations and Reflections on the Causes and Consequences of those Events which have produced conspicuous Changes in the Aspect of the World, and the general State of Human Affairs.* By JOHN BIGLAND. 7th Edition. London: Longman & Co. 1840. 12mo. pp. 450.
2. *Rudiments of Geography.* By W. C. WOODBRIDGE, M. A. London: Whitaker.
3. *Biographical Conversations on the most Eminent and Instructive British Characters.* By the Rev. W. BINGLEY, M.A. F.L.S., late of Peterhouse, Cambridge, Author of " Animal Biography." Designed for the Use of Schools. London: Harvey & Darton.

WE put these three volumes together, as presenting a fair, yet favourable specimen of the class of books which, for the last fifty years, have had undisputed possession of our schools ; and which, being now the property of " the Trade," continue to enjoy a very extensive sale. They are written most of them by members of the Church, and some grace the catalogue of the Society for Promoting Christian Knowledge, but they are marked by so independent and undisciplined a tone, that we wonder how any Churchman can suffer them in his family. They begin uniformly with manifesting a great contempt for all standard historians and writers. "The most uninteresting narratives of battles and sieges, (writes Mr. John Bigland,) of desolation and carnage, a thousand times repeated, and swelled with a long train of ill-authenticated, and often merely ideal circumstances, may amuse vulgar minds, but can afford little entertainment to an intelligent reader, whose ideas are more enlarged, and who desires to form a comprehensive view of things. The inquisitive mind, desirous of drawing from history a true picture of human existence, contemplates the origin and progress of the arts and sciences, of systems and opinions, and of civilization and commerce; in fine, of the whole mass of human improvements, and the progressive advancement of society." Now, who is it that dogmatizes so superciliously ? We shall not err, probably, in stating that this great philosopher never read a word of either of the great historians of Greece. It is certain that he can not have understood them, or he would know that Thucydides is still a model for the philosophical historian, and that the simple narrative of Herodotus conveys a more lively representation of the actual state of manners and society in the several countries which he describes than any subsequent writer has succeeded in doing; and as for weighing the merits of controverted questions, there is not, from the beginning to the end of the " Letters," a single reference to original sources. Or to whom is Mr. Bigland writing when he labours to depreciate all previous authors ? Were he writing to a society of critics there might be some propriety in such remarks—provided they were true; but surely for children a sentiment of contempt for authorities is the very last feeling that a judicious person would desire to implant in their minds. The same tone of self-complacency runs throughout Bingley; who, by the way, commences his catalogue of "Divines" with Wicliffe, and ends with Paley, having included in it Watts and Doddridge.

Theology, indeed, is the great stumbling-block with all writers of this class. Thus Mr. Woodbridge, M.A. describes the state of Christendom at this time:—"There are three great divisions of Christians—Catholic, Greek, and Protestant Christians, each having peculiar doctrines and modes of worship." ... Protestants are divided into various sects, of which the principal are Lutherans, Episcopalians, (or the Established Church of England,) Presbyterians, Independents, Baptists, Methodists, Friends or Quakers." Mr. Bingley states it as the peculiar merit of John Howard, that "his attendance at the church and the meeting-house was equally regular." Mr. Bigland considers the anathemas of the council of Nice no less horrible than the persecutions of the Pagan emperors. The real cause, of course, why writers of this stamp always adopt the latitudinarian view, is that, being used to act themselves on petty, selfish motives, they measure others by that standard. They cannot understand how a man can be zealous for abstract truth; they assume the existence of some private ends, (which, of course, the very title of "catholic" excludes,) and from those premises conclude, logically enough, that no man has a right to control his neighbour's belief. Their conclusion is rightly deduced from the premises; but the premises are false.

We make these remarks with the view of drawing the attention of those whom it may concern—of parents and schoolmasters especially— to the mischievous principles which they are daily sanctioning and propagating; and, till "the Trade" are made to feel that people have some little regard for the truth, they will not care to improve a class of books which affords them a sure and regular income. For example, why does not "the Trade" expunge the modern and unsafe definitions of doctrinal terms which are found in Cruden's "Concordance?" A single uneducated pennyless Scotch dissenting adventurer has been allowed, for about a century, to insult the whole Church with his false doctrine. It is probable that every Clergyman, from the Archbishop of Canterbury downwards, possesses the book; and yet no protest has ever been made against its unsoundness.

The Latin Poems, commonly attributed to Walter Mapes, Collected and Edited by THOMAS WRIGHT, *M.A. F.S.A., &c.* London: Printed for the Camden Society. 1841.

EVERY one who is at all conversant with the relics of the twelfth and thirteenth centuries, is well aware of the existence of a large class of poems in Latin verse, remarkable for their blasphemy, their licentiousness, and their falsehood. In that day, lived one Walter Mapes, a man of extensive learning and high ecclesiastical dignities, of whom his friend Giraldus Cambrensis relates, that he exercised his wit and exhibited his hostility against the encroachments of the Cistercians, in various satirical writings, both in prose and verse. To him, therefore, it has been customary to attribute all the poetical satires of the time, and more especially those which appeared under the name of Golias. The remains of this poetry, the Camden Society's Council have thought of *sufficient interest and importance* to be collected into a volume, and have committed the editorship of it to Mr. Thomas Wright, of Trinity College, Cambridge, one of their own body. In the discharge of his duty, Mr. Wright has endeavoured to show, that not one line which he has published can with any certainty be attributed to Archdeacon Mapes. He might have spared his labour; for we have every reason to believe, that Walter Mapes, with all his satiric effusions against the monks, was a *christian gentleman*, which the writers of these verses could not have been. When this Society wasted a portion of their receipts on the publication of the "Political Songs," several of their members doubted as to the propriety of appearing to sanction by their subscriptions such gross publications under the plea of antiquarian relics. We should humbly conceive, that this last compound of blasphemy, licentiousness, and falsehood, would eradicate all hesitation on the subject. For a proof of its blasphemy, we have only to read the very first poem in the volume, the "Apocalypsis Goliæ Episcopi," one of four hundred and forty lines, and considered by the editor of such importance and interest, as to require two English translations of it of the seventeenth century, so as to render it more intelligible to general readers. This poem is a literal parody on the Revelations, even to words; in which Pythagoras assumes the place of our Saviour, Golias that of the apostle: the seven candlesticks are seven churches of England; the seven stars, seven prelates; the four beasts are the pope, the bishop, the archdeacon, and the dean; whilst from the opening of the seven seals is disclosed the supposed enormities of bishops, archdeacons, deans, officials, priests, pluralists, and abbots. And yet, this poem is, if possible, exceeded by another. Of the licentiousness and grossness of the entire collection, we cannot, of course, give any examples. The Society for the Suppression of Vice might well spend a few pounds in an indictment. It has always been customary for the editors of classical works, where indelicate passages occur, to abstain from all note or comment on them, and to show the utter worthlessness of them by their neglect. Such has not been the practice of Mr. Wright At page 77, he shows the care and trouble he has expended on the poem "De Conjuge non Ducendà," one of the most disgusting in the collection, of which he gives a French and English translation in the appendix, and the text of which, through the kindness of his friend Mr. Halliwell, he has been enabled to collate with four Oxford MSS.; whilst at page 56, where the text of the "Discipulus Goliæ de Grisis Monachis," exhibits the most disgusting allusion to the dress of the monks, Mr. Wright has carefully collated a parallel obscenity from the "Political Songs," (of which he was also the editor,) and a further and most disgusting quotation from the "Speculum Stultorum" of Nigellus Wireker. Such is the spirit in which Mr. Wright has edited these poems.

We cannot here enter into the discussion of the exaggeration and falsehood of the accusations brought in the poems against the Clergy of the twelfth century. The best refutation is contained in the letters of the great men of the day, especially of John of Salisbury and Peter of Blois. To these we refer such of our readers as are not afraid of old Latin letters; to such as are, we recommend an article in a far off *Quarterly*, April 1837, where the state of the Church in that century is illustrated at some length from the letters of cotemporaries. With these remarks, forced from us by the nature of the work, we leave this the last publication of the Camden Society of London.

New Zealand, South Australia, and New South Wales: a Record of Recent Travels in these Colonies, &c. &c. By R. G. JAMESON, Esq., late Surgeon-Superintendent of Emigrants to South Australia. Smith and Elder. 1842.

THIS is an altogether manly and pleasant book. Mr. Jameson has the happiest temperament for a traveller,—sober expectations,—cheerful enjoyment of things present,—and good humour with all around him. His lore seems to lie mainly in the directions most suited to his profession, and to the traveller in uncivilized regions—natural history and the kindred studies. To these he adds a shrewd insight into statistics and business, and sprinkles the whole with many more literary associations than we often find in the votaries of such pursuits. The part of his volume which treats of New Zealand will for every reason excite greater interest than that which is devoted to New Holland; nevertheless, the latter is worthy of a careful reading. In justice to the inhabitants of Sydney, Mr. Jameson's vindication of society there from the charge of moral degradation, so apt to be believed, (in which, be it observed, he is backed by the authority of the Bishop of Australia,) ought to be attended to. Our author writes in a tone of uniform right feeling on moral and religious matters, though ignorant, we suspect, of true Church principles. We cordially recommend this book.

The Martyr of Erromanga; or the Philosophy of Missions. By JOHN CAMPBELL, D.D. London: Snow. 8vo. Pp. 470.

"THE Martyr of Erromanga," be it known unto our readers, is one Mr. John Williams, who, being " deeply convinced by the Rev. Timothy East, in the Tabernacle, Moorfields, of sin, of righteousness, and judgment," sallied forth with great vigour to the conversion of the South-Sea Islanders, and perished in a tumult at the place above named, in the New Hebrides. Concerning one so zealous in his purpose and so single-minded we would not desire to utter a disrespectful word. Our object, indeed, is not to rob him of the glories of martyrdom, but to protest against the more than heathen inhumanity with which Dr. Campbell has disinterred his peaceful remains, in order to embalm them (we suppose, in his ignorance, he conceives) with some of the most senseless and extravagant bombast we ever read. The volume is composed of a series of letters, the first of which is addressed to " the Teachers of British and other Day-Schools ;" the last to " Field-Marshal the Duke of Wellington," whom the author considers to be the last great warrior whom the world will ever witness, since the " missionary character" is now fast superseding the " military!" This is Dr. Campbell's " Philosophy of Missions," (than which there certainly never was a greater misnomer for a book, for there is not so much as a single general principle attempted to be established throughout the volume;) and he concludes, after a lengthened comparison, by showing that Alexander the Great, Cæsar, and Napoleon, were fools to John Williams!

Brief Memorials of the Rev. B. W. Mathias, late minister of Bethesda Chapel, Dublin, (Dublin, Curry, 1842,) will be read with interest by those who remember the unction and eloquence of their subject. He seems to have been a man of deep piety, but deplorably ignorant on many important matters. In all the correspondence given we do not just now recollect a single instance of the Church in Ireland ever receiving that designation. It is throughout styled *the Establishment;* and, indeed, Mr. Mathias and his friends do not seem to have *rejected* the true doctrine of the Church, for there is no indication of its having ever so much as occurred to them.

A Letter has been addressed by the Rev. H. Mackenzie to William Lyall, Esq. suggesting the formation of "A Marine College, for the advancement of Navigation as a Science, and Improvement of the efficiency of the Merchant Marine of Great Britain." (Smith and Elder, 1841.) We cannot pretend to a positive opinion on such a matter, but the suggestion seems an important one.

"The Kings of the East; an Exposition of the Prophecies determining, &c. the Power for whom the Mystical Euphrates is being 'dried up,' &c." (Seeley and Burnside, 1842.) This is a book which, as may be seen from the title-page, treats of subjects on which we pass no opinion. For the same reason we must decline saying anything one way or other about " Israel in China," by Joseph Wright. (Nisbet, 1842.)

"Narrative of a recent Imprisonment in China," &c., by John Lee Scott, (Dalton, 1841,) is sure to be read with interest. The curious in sufferings which they are not themselves compelled to undergo, will here find a more than ordinarily ample and delicate repast. For genuine unalloyed discomfort, commend us to the interior of a Chinese cage.

" Verses by a Poor Man " are now published in one volume. (Painter, 1842.) They are dedicated by permission to Prince Albert, and have received one or two additions. Our readers know the high estimate we have formed of them.

A "Serious Remonstrance" has been addressed to the Rev. R. W. Sibthorp, B.D., on his recent publication, " by those of the Hull Clergy who were personally known to him." (Seeley, 1842.) The pamphlet is marked by a pious spirit and by a good deal of intelligence; but the reverend writers advance one or two opinions which we deeply regret ever to find emanating from any of their order, and which are more likely to fortify Mr. Sibthorp in his present position than their sounder arguments are to dislodge him from it.

"Observations on the Book of Ruth," &c., by the Rev. H. B. Macartney, rector of Creagh. (Dublin, Curry, 1842.) This author is, we doubt not, a man of piety; but either he or the Romanists he describes, p. 27, must be strangely ignorant of the doctrines of the Romish Church, and we suspect the former to be the case. How can an Irish rector justify himself in going without an accurate conception of the enemy by whom he is environed?

"Hope's British Monthly Magazine," &c. (Nisbet & Co. Berners Street,) is the designation of a periodical which has just been started, devoted to the Scottish presbyterian cause of non-intrusion. We have only seen the February number, and wish to see no other. We will not do the leading ministers on that side of the question in Scotland such injustice as to believe them capable of approving of anything so disgraceful. It is due to the respectable publisher to say that he prefixes a disclaimer of any responsibility for the contents. The writers have yet to learn English grammar, good taste, divinity, and a christian spirit.

We rejoice to see that Ireland is at length about to do justice to the greatest of her scholars, in the publication of a complete edition of Archbishop Ussher's works. The editorship is undertaken by Dr. Elrington, who, we are sure, will regard it as a labour of love. Three volumes are out.

Mr. Tegg announces a new and cheap edition of Patrick, Lowth, Arnold, Whitby, and Lowman's most valuable Commentary on the Bible, in 4 vols, imperial 8vo. In this edition the text is given as well as the annotations; and it is said to be "particularly adapted for *family* use." What this means we do not profess to understand, but we hope no harm.

The Rev. W. W. Malet, under the somewhat vague title of "Church Extension," has published a plain and earnest inquiry into our ecclesiastical condition. We agree with him more often as to the remedies proposed, than as to the grounds on which he advocates them, or in the expectations which he builds upon them. As to the great questions of the justice of restoring the impropriated property of the Church, and of the sinfulness of party-spirit among the Clergy, there can be but one opinion; and we thank Mr. Malet for having so boldly broached them. His pamphlet is published by Hatchard.

"The Daughters of England, their Position in Society, Character, and Responsibilities," by Mrs. Ellis, author of the "Women of England," (London, Fisher,) amid a considerable portion of good sense, contains some flagrant violations of taste, and is tainted throughout with the leaven of dissent.

Barr's "Anglican Church Architecture, with some Remarks upon Ecclesiastical Furniture," (Parker, Oxford,) though containing little that is new, either as to letter-press or engravings, appears to us to give much useful information in a comprehensive way on that interesting study.

"Remarks on English Churches," &c. by J. H. Markland, Esq., F.R.S. &c. (Oxford, Parker, 1842,) make a most delightful book, which we cordially recommend, both for its tastes and its principles. The profits "will be given in aid of the funds for completing St. Stephen's Church, in the parish of Walcot, Bath."

We advise such of our readers as are smitten with the works of Neander to read a pamphlet by Dr. Wolff, which has just appeared, with the title of "Mystic Rationalism in Germany," (Hatchards, 1842,) and which consists of a very searching *exposé* of that author's "Life of Jesus Christ." We do not wish that people should either lose sight of the beautiful spirit which pervades so much of Neander's writing, or deprive themselves of the instruction which is to be found so abundantly therein; but it is right for them to know what he really believes and what he disbelieves.

"A Guide to the Holy Eucharist," (Cleaver, 1842,) has just been published by one of the ablest and most exemplary of the London Clergy. It is in two volumes, of which the first consists of meditations to be used at home, and the other is a companion for the service of the Church. We warmly recommend it as, along with the Eucharistica of Archdeacon S. Wilberforce, a valuable gain to our stock of devotional reading.

"Christian Unity," by Henry W. Wilberforce, M.A., (Burns, 1842,) is, as we fully expected, a most excellent tract, which cannot be too widely circulated.

We have also been pleased with some "Catechetical Examinations, &c." (Joscelyne, Braintree, 1842.)

"Charlie Burton," a tale, is a beautiful little tract, which was published last year by the Christian Knowledge Society. It is a shade too sentimental to our taste, but very excellent notwithstanding.

"Memoirs of the distinguished Naval Commanders whose Portraits are exhibited in the Royal Naval Gallery of Greenwich Hospital," (Greenwich, 1842,) will be found an excellent guide to that interesting collection, of which the father of the young gentleman from whose *private* press the book has issued was the founder. It is exceedingly well written, and may, we feel very sure, be depended on for its facts. We believe it is for sale at the hospital.

A weekly newspaper has just been started, with the title of the "Church and State Gazette," (Painter.) It has only reached one or two numbers as yet. The plan is very good, and if worthily carried out, will cause it to supply a desideratum.

We gladly announce a volume of sermons by the Bishop of New Jersey. (Rivingtons, 1842.)

"The Principles that should influence a Christian Student," is the title given by Dr. Ollivant, senior tutor of St. David's, Lampeter, &c. to a very useful sermon preached in the chapel there.

The Cartooons of Raffaelle have been published (Rivingtons, 1842) in a large form, and very cheap, so as to be well suited for schools. For wood-cuts they wonderfully convey the beauty of the originals. We have seen a large map sheet of animals, executed by the same artists (Messrs. Whimper) for the Christian Knowledge Society, which we greatly admire. The engravings now before us are accompanied by short letter-press descriptions.

"The Christian Month," by the Rev. W. Palin, M.A. (Ollivier, 1842,) consists of original hymns, with accompanying music, for each day of the month. The music is pretty enough, but not ecclesiastical.

MISCELLANEOUS.

[*The Editor is not responsible for the opinions expressed in this department.*]

A LETTER ON PROTESTANTISM, BY A PROTESTANT.

TO THE EDITOR OF THE "CHRISTIAN REMEMBRANCER."

MY DEAR SIR,—In common, I believe, with many whose opinion is of much greater consequence than mine, I have delightedly hailed Mr. Maurice's recent pamphlet in answer to Mr. Palmer. I do not, indeed, profess to see my way into every one of his conclusions; nor would he, I am sure, wish me to do so after a single reading of a book which travels over so much ground, and touches on so great a variety of points. I do not even profess to have arrived at a final judgment on the Jerusalem Bishopric, however little perplexity such arguments against it as Mr. Palmer's may occasion me: but in the name of all that is healthy and loyal in England, do I thank him for the general tone and reasoning of his pamphlet;—for, as I conceive, vindicating the catholicism of the Church of England; for showing that our loyalty to that Church is compatible with loyalty to the Church universal; above all, do I thank him, for abiding by the term *Protestant*, as a rallying point of sound principles and most sacred feelings.

It is on this last subject, however, that I am now tempted to say a few words, because it is here that I discover a slight difference between him and myself. He seems to predicate Protestantism of every Christian community that resists the Pope's claim to be universal bishop; and on this principle holds the Greek to be Protestant Churches. Of course, in a case of this sort, all we have to do is to agree in our definitions; and if we find such an one for Protestantism as shall include the Greek Churches, they are included. But I contend that Mr. Palmer on this solitary point has an advantage over him, in that he uses the word Protestant in a sense nearer to that it has always borne, though I am still farther from accepting his definition of it. But I agree with him, that it does not come naturally to us to call the Greek Churches Protestant; that there are qualities usually denoted by the term which we do not perceive existing in them, and which we do find both in our own Church, in her daughters of Scotland and America, and in those Christian communities on the continent, with which we so far have a fellow feeling. I admit the quality to be a modern one in the Church, but I believe it to be a good one notwithstanding; one which, though not in itself sufficient, though no substitute for the higher quality of catholicism, a catholic Church may well rejoice to possess, and which having once possessed, such a Church is most essentially bound to retain and cherish.

Mr. Palmer has some perception of its existence and peculiarity in ourselves and abroad, but he seems to me to have no comprehension of its real character. His definition of it, as a setting up of the individual judgment against the dogmatic teaching of the Church, is one which I altogether refuse to accept. It is true, there have been some who have found such a description of it suit their ends, and accordingly have contended for it; but such have not been generally approved by their fellow-Protestants. The grand majority of plain people, to whom the word is a sacred one, and who are shocked and scandalized when they hear young men repudiating it, attach to it no such notion as this. Neither do I agree with those who condemn it as merely *negative*. With its original sense we have of course nothing do; nor do I think that, as generally used, it is confined to the notion of protesting against Popish corruptions. Even however if it were, it would not therefore be merely negative: terms are often both negative and positive,—negative, if used scientifically; positive, if used descriptively. Cold is in one point of view but the negation of heat; in another it is a word positive enough in all conscience. Strictly speaking, the word *Protestant* denotes, not what a man believes, but what he disbelieves; but it is forgotten that he may disbelieve and protest against what he disbelieves, because of something which he believes—that the negative in him may be the criterion of something very positive; and that when, in ordinary speech, we designate him by the one, we spontaneously include in such designation the other also.

And thus it is that I think the word Protestant is most commonly used by us. People in employing it do not think of *protesting* at all; they are not thinking, or not exclusively, of certain Popish doctrines which they disbelieve. They take the term as denoting a certain temper, spirit, or quality, which resides in the Church to which they belong, which they believe ought to reside in it, and which I do not think they can find in the Greek Churches any more than in that of Rome. There are many things, undoubtedly, in which we resemble those Greek Christians, more than we do the foreign Protestant. Like them, we have retained the apostolical episcopate, and not allowed it to be tampered with by the notion of a bishop of bishops; like them, we retain and reverence the ancient traditions of the Church; like them, we have made the Church's liturgic development the one of most consequence. On the other hand, we are more than tinged with the Protestant hue; and in virtue of that one consideration, there is, as far as it goes, a fellow-feeling between us and unepiscopal Protestants, which we have not with Greeks, however irresponsible we may hold ourselves for the proceedings of the former, and however we may consider our tie with the latter as the stronger and more vital of the two.

I will endeavour to bring out my meaning a little more fully. I suppose every one will admit that there may, not only without offence, but with advantage, be a variety of schools in the Church:—schools, we call them, the apostolical term was "spirits." Every one of these, as it arises, is to be tried and seen whether it be of God; and if approved, is to be received into the Church, there to find its proper place, and do its appointed work. A pious and learned writer of the present day* seems to see indications of this variety of schools even in the sacred writings of the New Testament. In the early ages of the Church it is impossible not to discover several. No one, for example, would hesitate to speak of Chrysostom and Augustine as of different schools. Hardly ever do we expect to find them handling the same passage of Scripture in anything like the same way; and yet we do not consider this divergency as at all amounting to contrariety; we are accustomed to rejoice in it, to believe that the Church has been a gainer by possessing two such explorers of two such different yet fertile regions of thought. Similarly most men, of the least enlargement of mind, rejoice that the British Churches can boast both of a Taylor and a Leighton.

Now, if there may without offence be this variety, not contrariety, in schools of thought at the same time, why may there not be the same at different times? Indeed there must be, whether we like it or not; for each age of civilized history is in itself a school of thought, and none can be precisely the same with any other. And what I contend is, that it is a high, not a low, view of the calling and powers of the Church, to say that she has a capacity for receiving and entertaining every such school or *spirit* that is found to be of God,—that

---

* Newman's Sermons, Vol. II. St. Philip and St. James.

in each successive age she is to draw into herself all that is fair, and pure, and lofty, and aspiring; that she is to harbour, and cherish, and develop, every class of religious thoughts that arises any where and at any time in the world; that to her men of whatever age, country, education, and temperament, are to bring, as to their only true home, the harvest of their struggles and their prayers. If this be so, it becomes no insignificant criterion of a Church's vitality, whether or not she be able to welcome and assimilate into herself such new spirits or schools of thought when God calls them into being. This criterion I find in the Primitive Church; for she was able to absorb and transubstantiate into herself whatever was divine among the men around her, whether the lingering hues of primeval truth in their religion, or the high aims of part of their philosophy, or the deep-based organization of their political existence. I do not think it by any means wanting in the Church of the Middle Ages; though with the progress of corruption, it was of necessity dying away. It was not wanting to the English Church at the Protestant epoch,—when, retaining by the merciful Providence of God her catholic constitution, she was enabled by the same gracious aid to receive into that constitution the new and needful spirit that had been so wonderfully awakened in Europe. And I trust it will not be wanting to her now, when a missionary and a catholic spirit is again called forth; when she is summoned to abandon the merely defensive attitude in which she was compelled to place herself by the events of the Reformation. I trust, that as at that period she could receive and welcome the spirit of Protestantism; so at this present, she may show herself able to meet the spirit of enlargement and union which is now beginning to make itself heard.

But this will not be, if we merely pamper ourselves with ecclesiastical antiquities, and turn away with disgust from every thing in the present time that is, at first sight, uncongenial to such tastes. It will not be, I am sure, if we get ashamed of our Protestantism; for never can we safely part with an advantage we have once gained. The events, indeed, through which the Church passes are fleeting, but the results in and on her are abiding, and never to be forgotten: Protestant it was needful that we should become, and Protestant we must cheerfully continue, would we be Catholic indeed.

But, to come to what is the real subject of this letter, (for who has said what I have hitherto been saying so well as the author who has called it forth?) what is this Protestantism for which I contend? It is here, as I have already said, that I differ from Mr. Maurice. He confines it to a protest against the notion of a visible centre to the Church. Doubtless, such a protest, if devout and earnest, and proceeding from a lively faith in the Unseen Centre, may involve in it all that is good and holy in Protestantism; and if the Eastern Christians be ever led to make it in this way, they may become like us in other things wherein they are not now. But I contend that merely to name this protest and its principle, does not describe what I mean by Protestantism. That word denotes to my ear, not, as I have already said, a rejection or neglect of the Church's dogmatic teaching, nor merely a denial of the Pope's necessary headship, though with one of these things it has been often accidentally associated, and without the other it cannot exist; but a new and peculiar spirit, which arose in the west of Europe in the sixteenth century. New, on the whole, it must be confessed to have been, nor need we be afraid of the admission, if the principles be correct which we have already laid down. Only when an article of faith is propounded, only when the changeless creed is tampered with, need the Church turn away from novelty as such. But new as I confess the Protestant spirit to have been in its full development, prelusive mutterings of it had been heard from of old: it is not too much, I think, to say that the Apostle of the Gentiles largely partook of it. I discern something of it in Augustine; while in Wiclif I find both its merits and defects in good measure. Not, however, till the need for it was at its height was it awakened into any degree of prevalence: then it arose, and made itself heard and felt over Europe; then, many causes, religious and secular, conspiring, was it received into the Church of England, and ever since it has dwelt in her. What is this spirit?

It is easier, perhaps, to feel than to explain what we mean by it; for it does not exercise itself so much in doctrinal statements, as in moulding the temper.* It is something characteristic at once of Luther and Calvin, and of Barrow and Bull. Speaking generally, I think it consists in a greater prevalence of the reflective and disquisitive side of religion,—a greater occupation with questions relating to each individual's condition before God,—a greater reverence for the individual conscience, than were usual before; in a stern sense of the world's manhood, and consequent intolerance of all such dealing with the imagination of the people, as precludes conscious insight into the Christian scheme; an habitual assertion that the whole furniture of the Church is but means to lead the soul to God, and that the moment any part of it is rested in as an end, it becomes worthless and mischievous; a feeling that not here and there, but over the wide face of the Church has this been done,—that man has played the same part with the new as he had done with the old creation—made of it an instrument of apostasy; a grave caution, in consequence, in regard to ritual religion, which they who have once been made alive to this can never again lay aside; and an occupation most natural to men in such circumstances with the Pauline writings. If to these I add much reverence for the liberty of the individual, whose distinct existence is now so strongly asserted; for the integrity of the family, which the Church is not more than is necessary to tamper with; and for that of the nation, which must no longer acknowledge the jurisdiction of foreign ecclesiastics,—I shall have left but one element more to name

---

* It is quite true, as Mr. Maurice observes, that Protestantism has given birth to much dogmatic theology. But this is but an accidental development, not a necessary accompaniment of what I mean by the Protestant spirit. There is a Protestant feeling, e.g. upon justification, which will turn away from the Tridentine decision that it is capable of increase, whether we hold the pure Lutheran theory, or the *Fides formata* of Bishop Bull. When I avow myself an adherent of the latter, an admirer of the Harmonia Apostolica, and of Mr. Newman's Lectures on Justification, I trust that my reverence for Protestantism, will be admitted not to have hindered my reverence for much besides.

in what appears to me to be Protestantism. This remaining element is a very important one:—it is *a sense of broken continuity* in the Church's history. I do not, of course, refer to continuity in essentials, for that were indeed fatal; neither would I deny that those who know that there is such a continuity in essentials, may well cherish an historical temper, and rejoice in a feeling of relationship to churchmen of every country and of every time; but I cannot shut my eyes to the fact, that whereas Greek and Latin Christians look up through an uninterrupted vista to their original, we find a great break in one place. The succession of the ministry indeed, and the faith of the creeds run on, which are the great things; but subordinate associations, rites, customs, and feelings of many sorts, experience a rude interruption in the sixteenth century. We are as men who have received a shock which we can in no wise forget. Do as we like, we cannot resemble the Roman Catholics and the Greeks here,—we cannot have that easy familiarity (so to speak) with the middle and the early ages, which results from the sense of an altogether undisturbed continuity. Do we envy them for this? It is natural for us to do so, for it has much the air of a privilege at first sight. But it is no privilege, nothing but a great calamity, if it proceed from a want of spirituality,—from the Church having got drowsy and never been well awakened again,—from a want of loyalty to God's cause and His truth. If it has happened that the Church herself was well nigh betraying the cause she was ordained to protect, if she was ceasing to witness for that spiritual life of which she was the appointed depository, if she was interposing herself between men and the Divine vision she was commissioned to reveal, then it is good, at nearly any price, to have a lively sense of this. It is good not to forget so new and vast a display of man's tendency to apostasy, good to remember how we have shown that there is in us that which can pervert the very divinest of Divine gifts, good to carry about with us the stern sobered spirit of those who know that they cannot make even a religious development without danger. I have thus attempted to sketch what I mean by the protestant spirit; and if I have failed in my sketch,—if I have not seized on the primary points,—still those who allege this may recognise the same thing as myself when they speak of that spirit, and may form the same estimate of it. Of course, I shall not be supposed to have been eulogizing all its manifestations. I have never meant to speak of it as sufficient by itself; and therefore I am nowise staggered, my faith in its being a spirit sent from God is in no degree shaken, at finding that its operations, without the bounds of apostolical order, have been unsatisfactory and perilous. Neither do I say, that its workings within those bounds have been at all times, and in every respect, such as might be wished. To say this, would be almost tantamount to saying that a particular church was perfect at a particular time. If we have ever cherished the Protestant spirit in any degree at the expense of the Catholic, we have assuredly gone wrong, and the results must in so far have been evil. I believe we have done this, and therefore I am not surprised that our ecclesiastical prospect presents us with so much that is unsightly, and so much more that is perplexing; though I, for one, do not feel called to have an opinion upon every thing in the Church around me, and to measure, weigh, and pronounce on its whole present condition. I never expect, whilst on earth, to live in a state of affairs exactly such as I should have planned myself;. and I am not apt to think it would be well, either for me or that state of affairs, were it possible that I should. We are strangely reluctant to own that the Church is under a guidance that we cannot comprehend.

One word more. I may be asked why I cannot content myself with the name *Reformed*, but must have this other of *Protestant* also. The former, I shall be told, exactly expresses the present position and state of the Church of England, and conveys no untoward impression of alliance with schismatical bodies abroad. I answer, that I am not content with the word *Reformed*, because it does not express what I have been trying to describe, because *it* is merely negative, because it merely tells me that the Church to which I belong made certain changes (as she trusted for the better) at a certain time, but does not convey the slightest hint as to the character of those changes. The word *Reformed* might be applied to the Church of Rome itself. I need not say that the Council of Trent, with all its faults, was in no slight degree a reforming one; that it swept away many an abuse, and that, ever since its assembling, the Churches which obey it have in many things been greatly improved. As to the name Protestant assimilating us, as far as it goes, to the Lutherans and others, I have already expressed my sense that such partial resemblance between us and them is a fact, and being such, I will not shut my eyes to it. Admitting it, commits me to nothing except the duty of candidly pondering it. I am not bound, by admitting it, to justify any departure from apostolical principles, nor to conceal my sense of any grievous deficiencies which I may find in Lutheranism. Seeing, then, that there is a spirit in our branch of the Church for which I must find a name if I wish to describe her present condition,—seeing that the word *Protestant* has long served for that name, seeing that whether it be etymologically fitted for that purpose or not, there is no other at hand,—I, for one, will continue to use it, and will trust to care and consistency to prevent my use of it being misunderstood. If I am right in what I have been laying down, there is no harm in my taking it as one of my religious designations, so long as I do not make it the sole or the chief one; no harm, so long as, on all proper occasions, I produce and glory in the higher name of Catholic, in my now subscribing myself,

Your obedient Servant,
A PROTESTANT.

February 15, 1842.

ECCLESIASTICAL INTELLIGENCE.

ORDINATIONS.

BP. OF CHESTER, *at Chester, Feb. 20.*

DEACONS.

Of Oxford.—F. Hinde, B.A. Lincoln Coll.
Of Cambridge.—H. G. Baily, B.A. Christ's; J. Griffith, B.A. Christ's; H. Briant, B.A. Queen's; H. J. Hindley, B.A. Queen's; D. Shaboe, B.A. Queen's; M. I. Finch, B.A. Cath. Hall; V. Lush, B.A. Corpus Christi; J.W. M'K. Millman, B.A. St. John's; J. H. Sharples, B.A. St. John's.
Of Dublin.—B. Mashiter, B.A.

PRIESTS.

Of Oxford.—A. Boote, B.A. Brasennose; J. Parry, B.A. Jesus; J. D. K. Scott, B.A. Balliol.
Of Cambridge.—W. Bateson, B.A. Queen's; R. Morewood, B.A. Queen's; E. Dean, B.A. St. John's; G. Gibbon, B.A. Cath. Hall; J. Losh, B.A. Jesus; R. P. Jones, B.A. Trin.; B. Crompton, B.A. Trin.; G. B. Norman, B.A. Trin.; E. F. Manley, B.A. Christ's; R. Yerbugh, B.A. Christ's; W. J. Sherly, B.A. St. Peter's; A. Wallace, B.A. Pembroke; F. Stewart, B.A. Pembroke; J. York, B.A. Sid. Sussex.
Of Dublin.—H. F. Beasley, M.A.; W. T. Cust, B.A.; D. Carson, B.A.; F. J. S. Hamilton, B.A.; R Parsons, B.A.; F. T. O'Donoghue, B.A.; R. Townley, B.A.
Of St. Bees.—H. W. Ray.

BP. OF LLANDAFF, *in Church of St. Gregory, London, March 13.*

DEACON.

Literate.—T. Griffith.

PRIEST.

Of Cambridge.—D. W. Williams, B.A. Trin.

BP. OF LICHFIELD AND COVENTRY, *at St. George's, Hanover-square, March 20.*

DEACONS.

Of Oxford.—W. Taylor, B.A. Trinity; G. Bailey, B.A. New Inn Hall; T. C. Griffith, B.A. Wadham.
Of Cambridge.—W. C. Mee, B.A. Christ's; A. F. Boucher, B.A. St. Peter's; J. Thompson, B.A. St. Peter's; J. Morris, B.A. Cath. Hall; J. Fenwick, B.A. Corpus Christi; P. Brown, B.A. Corpus Christi; S. Charles, B.A. Trin.; W. E. Mousley, B.A. Trin.; A. Hibbit, B.A. Cath. Hall; J.W. Hepworth, B.A. St. John's; C. H. Hosken, B.A. Queen's; J. Spurgin, B.A. Corpus Christi; J. Barr, M.D. Emmanuel; R. Goldham, B.A. Corpus Christi; J. A. Beaumont, B.A. Trin.; J. W. Bourke, B.A. Queen's.
Of Dublin.—F. S. Bradshaw, B.A. Trin.
Literate.—J. Lewis, by letters dimissory from the Bishop of Llandaff.

PRIESTS.

Of Oxford.—W. S. Burd, B.A. Christ Church.
Of Cambridge.—W. H. Pillans, B.A. Jesus; R. C. Willey, B.A. Trin.; J. Lees, B.A. Corpus Christi; J. Pulling, B.A. Corpus Christi; J. B. Harrison, B.A. Magdalen.

Messrs. Hoskens, Macfarlane, and Chamberlayne were also ordained on letters dimissory from the Bishops of Exeter, Bath and Wells, and Chester.

ORDINATIONS APPOINTED.

BP. OF LONDON, *May 22.*
BP. OF LINCOLN, *May 22.*
BP. OF HEREFORD, *May 22.*
BP. OF OXFORD, *May 22.*

BP. OF PETERBOROUGH, *May 22.*
BP. OF ELY, *June 5.*
BP. OF WINCHESTER, *June 10.*

PREFERMENTS.

Name.	Preferment.	County.	Diocese.	Patron.	Val.	Pop.
Ashby, E. Q.	Dunton, R.	Bucks	Lincoln	A. Smith, Esq.	*205	116
Brooking, A.	BoVingdon, P.C.	Herts	Lincoln	Hon. G. D. Ryder.		
Cerjat, H. S.	W. Horsley, R.	Surrey	Winch.	Rev. C. Weston	317	702
Courtenay, C. L.	Broadclist, V.	Devon	Exeter		490	2085
Cresswell, J.	Compstall, P.C.	Cheshire	Chester	— Andrew, Esq.		
Dakeyne, J. O.	St. Benedict's, Lincoln, P.C.	Lincoln	Lincoln	Rev.J.H.B.Mountain	90	654
Dean, E. B.	Lewknor, cum Ackhampstead.	Oxford	Oxford	All Souls, Oxford	*320	709
Dene, A.	Rattery, V.	Devon	Exeter	Lady Carew	*215	506
Fidler, I.	Easington, R.	Oxford	Oxford	Bishop of Lincoln	80	13
Gilbert, E.	Hardingstone, V.	Northamp.	Peterboro'	Lord Chancellor	*534	1036
Gilbertson, L.	Llangorwen, P.C. Oberystwith.	Cardigan	St. David's			
Hall, J. H.	Keyworth, R.	Notts	Lincoln	Rev. E. Thompson	*434	552
Heale, J.	Pointington, R.	Somerset	B. & W.	Lord W. de Broke	*247	165
Hughes, J.	Llandyfriog, V.	Cardigan	St. David's	Bp. of St. David's	*147	854
Jenkyns, J.	Wootton, V.	Beds	Ely	Lady Payne	*236	1051
Lloyd, H. W.	Pentre Voelas, P.C.	Denbigh	St. Asaph	C. Wynne, Esq.	200	616
Lowe, F. P.	Saltfleetby, All Saints, R.	Lincoln	Lincoln	Magd. Coll. Oxford	*317	180

PREFERMENTS,—continued.

Name.	Preferment.	County.	Diocese.	Patron.	Val.	Pop.
Mansfield, G......	Trin. Church, P.C. Trowbridge.	Wilts	Sarum	Duke of Rutland.		
Marriott, F. A....	Cotesbach, R.	Leicester	Peterboro'	....	*106	108
Marshall, J.	St. Mary-le-port, Bristol, R.	Gloucester	G. & B.	Duke of Buckingham	150	
Mudge, W.........	Pertenhall, R.	Bedford	Ely	Rev. J. K. Martyn....	*215	373
Roberts, R.	Milton Abbas, V.	Dorset	Sarum	Mrs. E. D. Damer.....	*127	846
Sainsbury, S. L...	Beckington cum Standverwick.	Somerset	B. & W.	Own Pat.	*540	1340
Sandby, G.........	Flixton, St. Mary, v.	Suffolk	Norfolk	Sir R. C. Adair.........	140	206
Smith, T. T.	Whaplode, V.	Lincoln	Lincoln	Lord Chancellor	*309	1998
Sunderland, E....	Glentham, V.	Lincoln	Lincoln	D & C. of Lincoln ...	*90	399
Whitworth, T. ...	Addlethorp, R.	Lincoln	Lincoln	Lord Chancellor	*72	175
Williams, D. A...	St. David's, P.C.	Carmarthen		Rev. D. Rowlands.		
Wordsworth, C...	Audley, V.	Stafford	Lichfield	....	*170	3617

*** *The Asterisk denotes a Residence House.*

APPOINTMENTS.

Allin, T. M. .... { Chap. to Langport Union, Somerset.
Arnold, C. M. ... Chap. to Marquis of Bath.
Bennett, H. ...... Surrog. Pec. of Dn. of Sarum.
Browne, J. F. ... Surrog. Dioc. B. & W.
Capel, S. R. ...... { Chap. to Wareham and Purbeck Union.
Carter, G. .... Chap. to Visct. Canterbury.
Hare, L. D. .... Chap. to Aylesbury Union.
Howell, A. J...... Chap. to Duke of Cleveland.
Larken, E.......... Chap. to Lord Monson.
Lettle, J. .... Chap. to Luton Union.
Lowther, B. ...... Chap. to Lord Lowther.

Murray, J.......... { Ipswich Surrogate Marr. Licenses.
Milcolm, H. J. B. Rur. Dean of St. Alban's.
Nicholson, H.J.B. { Rur. Dean Archdeaconry of St. Alban's.
Parish, W. S...... Chap. to H.M.S. Agincourt.
Quartley, C. J.... Chap. to Bengal Presidency.
Rogers, A. J..... Chap. to Madras Estab.
Turner, G. F. .... Chap. to Duke of Cambridge.
Wayle, — .... Chap. to Giltspur-st. Compt.
Wilberforce, Archdn. R. J... { Chap. to High Sheriff of Yorkshire.
Windham, R. C.. Chap. to Sheriff of Norfolk.

CLERGYMEN DECEASED.

Amphlett, R. H., Rec. of Hadsor, Worc. 60.
Barker, J. C., Chap. to Bp. of Barbadoes, at Tortola.
Bathurst, C., Rec. of Seddington, Glouc.
Braddon, J., Rec. of Merrington, 88.
Blackall, S., Rec. of N. Cadbury, Devon, 71.
Bowman, T., Cur. St. Mary's, Gateshead, 84.
Cantley, R., Rec. of Moulsac, Bucks, 79.
Clarke, J., Vic. of Ilkley, Yorkshire, 85.
Cowe, J., Rec. of Sunbury, 80.
Davenport, E. S., Rec. of Lydham, Salop.
Elton, Rev. Sir E., at Clevedon, near Bristol, 87.
Farrow, T., Per. Cur. Scampston and Knapton, Yorkshire, 78.

Garnett, J., of Trin. Coll. Cambridge.
Herdman, J., at Lesbury, near Alnwick.
Hildyard, W., Rec. Winestead, Yorksh. 80.
James, T., Vic. of Llandeyfulley, Brecon, 73.
Jenkins, S., of Locking, Somerset, 76.
Johnson, A, Vic. of Lit. Baddow, Essex, 93.
Lowthian, J. Vic. of Thatcham, Berks, 83.
Munden, J. M., Rec. of Corscombe, Dorset, 60.
Matthew, J., Rec. of Reepham, Norfolk.
Manhall, J., Per. Cur. of Ireby, Cumb., 92.
Moss, T., Ravenstonedale, 55.
Prowde, R., Per. Cur. Hovingham, Yorksh.
Robinson, J., Rec. Hockliffe, Beds, 74.
Singleton, Dr., Archdn. of Northumb., 58.

UNIVERSITIES.

OXFORD.

MAGDALENE COLLEGE.—A Fellowship is vacant in this College, which will be filled up on the festival of St. James the Apostle next ensuing. Candidates are at liberty to call upon the President on any day before the 21st of July next, bringing with them a copy of their baptismal register, and a testimonial of good conduct from their College. They must be natives of Northamptonshire, and graduates of the University.

March 3.

Degrees conferred.

M.A.

J. H. Mahony, Stud. of Ch. Ch. grand comp.; Rev. G. W. Brameld, Linc.; Rev. H. T. May, Fell. of New Coll.; L. G. Browne, Exet.; Rev. J. Murray, New Inn H. (incorporated from Trin. Coll., Dublin).

Intelligence.

B.A.

C. J. Smith, Ch. Ch.; E. H. Ballard, Wad.; W. Rogers, Ball.

The following have been elected Scholars of Univ. Coll.:—T. Arnold, from Rugby School, to the open Scholarship; and E. Armitage and J. Barmly, Comm. of Univ. Coll., to the Yorkshire Scholarships.

The Examiners of Candidates for the University Scholarship for the encouragement of Latin literature, have awarded it to Mr. Goldwin Smith, Commoner of Christ Church. Messrs. M. Arnold, of Ball., and G. Bradley, of Univ., honourably distinguished themselves in the examination. There were 28 candidates.

March 9.

W. T. Hutchins, B.A., of Worc. Coll., unanimously elected Vinerian Scholar, vacant by the election of Mr. Reade, of Magdalene, to a Fellowship.

March 10.
Degrees conferred.

B.A.

Sir J. E. Harington, Bart., and J. H. Pollen, Ch. Ch.; J. Soper, Magd. Hall; A. E. Whieldon, Trin.

T. Twiss, Esq., D.C.L., and Fell. of Univ., elected Prof. of Pol. Econ., in the room of H. Merivale, Esq.

Granted to the Rev. R. S. Stevens, Vicar of South Petherwin and Trewen in Cornwall, an annual allowance of 50l. during his incumbency, towards the maintenance of an Assistant Curate.

W. B. T. Jones, Scholar of Trinity, elected Ireland Scholar for 1842.

NEW PROFESSORSHIPS.—Whereas her Majesty has graciously intimated her royal will and intention to found two new Theological Professorships in this University, and by an Act of Parliament passed in the session holden in the 3d and 4th years of her Majesty's reign it is provided that the said Professorships shall eventually be endowed with two Canonries of Christ Church; and whereas it is earnestly desired that Letters Patent should be obtained as soon as possible constituting the said Professorships, and enabling the University to make regulations for the due government thereof, and that with a view thereto stipends should be provided *ad interim* for the two Professorships after their nomination by the Crown; it was agreed to grant to each of the said Professors the sum of 300l. per annum, as a stipend *ad interim*, to be paid to each of them by half-yearly payments from the time when he shall be appointed to his office, to the time when he shall succeed to the Canonry assigned to his Professorship by the above-mentioned Act of Parliament; the sum to be provided out of the moneys transferred in the year 1836 to the general purposes of the University from the funds of the University Press.

March 16.

G. Smart, of Exet., and R. T. Davison, elected Lord Crewe's Exhibitioners; W.W. Bradley, of Linc., J. Banks, of St. M. Hall, and J. R. T. Eaton, of Elizabeth Coll., Guernsey, elected Scholars of Linc. C. C. Crakenthorpe, elected Dr. Hutchins's Scholar.

March 19.

This being the last day of term, a congregation was holden, when the following degrees were conferred:—

M.A.

Rev. G. T. Hyatt, of Wad.; Rev. G. Burder, of Magd. Hall; Rev. T. Lowe, of Oriel.

B.A.

T. H. Mynors, of Wad.; S. Newington, of New Inn Hall.

B. C. Price, elected Scholar of Pemb.

The Vice-Chancellor has nominated the Rev. Frederic Charles Plumptre, D.D., Master of University College, to be one of the Pro-Vice-Chancellors for the remainder of the academical year, in the room of the Lord Bishop of Chichester.

Congregations will be holden for the purpose of granting Graces and conferring Degrees on the following days in Easter Term:—Wednesday, April 6; Thursday, April 21; Thursday, April 28; Friday, May 6; Saturday, May 14.

J. W. Knott, Commoner of Wadham College, elected Lusby Scholar.

CAMBRIDGE.

Feb. 14.

Elected Scholars of Magdalen Coll. in this University:— Neville, Sowden, Wigelsworth, Booker.

Feb. 23.

The following graces passed the Senate:— 1. To authorize a grant of 20l. from the University-chest to Mr. Glaisher, as a gratuity for extra services, rendered at the Observatory, in taking observations with the Northumberland telescope during the year 1841. 2. To appoint the Vice-Chancellor, the Master of Jesus Coll., Dr. Paget, Mr. Lodge, and Mr. Philpott, a Syndicate to consider and report to the Senate, on the steps to be taken for the preservation of the Paintings, Books, MSS., &c. in the Fitzwilliam Museum: the Perse Trustees having (in consequence of a decree in Chancery) given notice to the University to quit the premises in Free School-lane at Midsummer next.

Degrees conferred.

B.D.

J. Stoney, St. Peter's.

B.A.

G.A. Dimock, Sid. Sus.; W.A.Waring, John's; J. H. H. Hallett, Caius; J. H. Bastard, Trin.

March 3.

J. Gibson, B.A., Scholar of Jesus, elected a foundation Fellow.

March 7.

The Porteus Medals at Christ's Coll. were adjudged as follows:—*Latin Essay* to J. C. Reynolds; *English Essay* to Thos. Ramsbotham; *Reading Prize* to K. Swann.

B. H. Drury, B.A., elected Fell. of Gonv. and Caius; C. F. Tarver, Schol. of King's, elected Fellow.

March 9.

CAIUS COLLEGE CLASSICAL EXAMINATION.

Freshmen.

Ormerod, 1st prize.	Lewis.
Murphy, 2nd prize.	White, sen.
Collet.	Laborde } æq.
Hutt.	Travers }
White, jun.	Saudham.
Goodwin.	Carver.
Burrows.	Probyn.
Mann.	Ellice.
Dykes.	

Second Year.

R. Barker, 1st prize	Westropp.
Martineau, 2nd prize.	T. Watson.
Brooke.	Suckling.
Trevelyan.	Raven.
Hopkins } æq.	Henery,
Woodhouse }	Hill
Baumgartner,	T. Watson } æq.
Chorley.	Evans.
W. G. Watson.	Hilton.
Robertson.	Dove.
Bromhead.	Kendell.
Loftus.	

March. 12.

Elected Bell's Scholars:—Holden, Trin.; Perowne, C. Ch.

Degrees conferred.

B.D.

Rev. R. W. Evans, Fell. of Trin,; Rev. C. Lenny, John's.

B.C.L.

L. Morison, Trin.; T. G. Stawell, Caius.

An election of a scholar will be held on Friday, the 22d of April next, for C. Ch. Coll.; open to natives of Lancashire, Hampshire, Surrey, Lincolnshire, Gloucestershire, Wiltshire, Kent, Bedfordshire, Oxfordshire, and the dioceses of Bath and Wells, Exeter and Durham.

CLASSICAL TRIPOS, MAR. 12, 1842.

Examiners.

W. H. Bateson, M.A., St. John's.
E. H. Bunbury, M.A., Trinity.
E. Warter, M.A., Magdalene.
J. Hildyard, M.A., Christ's.

CLASS I.

Denman, Hon. G. Trin.	Shaw, B. Trin.
Munro, H. W. J. Trin.	Morse, F. St. John.
Atkinson, E. Clare.	Wilson, W. G. St. John.
Peter, R. G. Jesus.	Kingsley, C. Magd.
Wolfe, A. St. John.	

CLASS II.

Nugée, G. Trin.	Carter, S. R. Emman.
Ainger, G. H. St. John.	Montague, E. W. Caius.
Ommanneny, G. D. W. Trin.	Woodford, J. R. Pemb.
	Vidal, J. H. St. John.
Barstow, T. I. Trin.	Parr, W. Cath.
Venables, E. Pemb.	Sheepshanks, T. Trin.
Vaughan, E. H. Christ's	Sheringham, J. W. St. John.
Vidal, O. E. St. John.	
Powell, R. D. St. John.	

CLASS III.

Walpole, R. Caius.	Thrupp, C. J. Trin.
Yeoman, T. L. Trin.	Light, W. E. St. John.
Slade, J. St. John.	Hogg, L. Emman. } æq.
Conybeare, J. C. Peter.	Ramsey, A. Trin. }
Riley, J. Trinity.	

The two gold medals, value 15 guineas each, given by the Chancellor to commencing Bachelor of Arts, who, having obtained Senior Optimes at least, show themselves the greatest proficients in classical learning, have been adjudged to H. A. J. Munro, B.A. and B. Shaw, B.A., Trinity.

J. P. Birkett, Esq., B.A., Mathem. Master at Harrow, elected Lay Fell. of Jes. Coll., in place of Mr. Merry.

March 14.

The following were elected Found. Fellows of St. John's Coll.:—H. Bailey, B.A.; B. Williams, B.A.; J. Atlay, B.A.; J. Bather, B.A.

E. Atkinson, B.A., Schol. Clare Hall, elected Fellow.

PROCEEDINGS OF SOCIETIES.

INCORPORATED SOCIETY FOR PROMOTING THE ENLARGEMENT, BUILDING, AND REPAIRING OF CHURCHES AND CHAPELS.

A meeting of the Committee of this Society was held at their chambers, St. Martin's-place, on Monday, the 21st of March, 1842; His Grace the Archbishop of York in the chair.

Among the members present were the Bishops of London, Durham, Bangor, Carlisle, Chester, Ely, Salisbury, and Hereford; Sir T. D. Acland, Bart. M.P.; the Revds. Dr. Spry, Dr. D'Oyly, H. H. Norris, and Benj. Harrison; N. Connop, jun., I. S. Salt, Benj. Harrison, James Cocks, and Wm. Cotton, Esqrs.

Grants were voted towards building a chapel in the parish of Holy Trinity, Hull; rebuilding the church at Salcombe, in the parish of Marlborough, Devon; rebuilding the chapel at Firbank, in the parish of Kirkby Lonsdale, Westmoreland; enlarging by rebuilding the church at Barford, Warwickshire; new roofing St. George's church at Manchester; building a new transept to, and erecting a gallery in the church at Ainsworth, Lancashire; extending the north side of the church at Wheatenhurst, Gloucestershire; restoring the body of the church at Aldringham, Suffolk; enlarging the church at Steeple Claydon, Buckinghamshire; repewing the church at Llanbadarnfynydd, Radnorshire; enlarging gallery in the chapel at Sankey, in the parish of Prescot, Lancashire; enlarging by rebuilding the church of St. Lawrence at Southampton; building a church at Nailsea, near Bristol, and other business was transacted.

DIOCESAN INTELLIGENCE.

LONDON.—*Additional Colonial Bishoprics.*—The following is a Pastoral Letter addressed by the Lord Bishop, expressing his wish that a collection should be made in the churches of the diocese, in aid of the Colonial Bishops' Fund, on Palm Sunday.

"*London House, Feb.* 7, 1842.

"REV. SIR,—You are no doubt aware, that a declaration was agreed to by the Archbishops and Bishops of the United Church of England and Ireland, at a meeting held at Lambeth, on the Tuesday in Whitsun week, 1841, setting forth the insufficiency of the provision made for the spiritual care of the members of our Church, in the distant dependencies of the empire, and the great importance of erecting additional bishoprics in the colonies. A copy of the declaration is sent herewith, to which I request your most serious attention.

"I am persuaded that the accomplishment of the object, which we have in view, may be ensured, under the blessing of God, if the Clergy will exert themselves to collect contributions in their respective parishes; and I am desirous of suggesting, to those of my own diocese, the propriety of commencing that exertion on the first day of the approaching holy week, in which we commemorate the death and passion of our blessed Lord, and offer up our special prayers for all estates of men in his holy Church, and for the gathering together in one fold, under one Shepherd, of all those who are not yet within its enclosure.

"It is my wish, that you should have a collection made in your church, in aid of the Colonial Bishops' Fund, on Palm Sunday next, and I would suggest that it might be made in the following manner:

"After the sermon, in which I trust you will explain the object for which the offerings of your people are solicited, let the offertory sentences be read from the communion table, not omitting those which instruct them that are taught in the word to minister unto them that teach in all good things. Whilst these sentences are reading, let the churchwardens, or other persons appointed for that purpose, collect the offerings of the people, and bring them to the minister, to be by him humbly presented and placed upon the holy table. Let him then proceed with the prayer for the Church militant, and with the remainder of the service, according to the Rubric. This revival of the ancient practice of our Church has been attempted in several parishes with great success; but although I would gladly see it become general, I do not wish to interfere with your discretion in the present instance, if you should have good reason for preferring some other mode of making the collection.

"I conclude in the words of the declaration, and 'under a deep sense of the sacredness and importance of this great work, and in the hope that Almighty God may graciously dispose the hearts of his servants to a corresponding measure of liberality, I earnestly commend it to the good will, the assistance, and the prayers of all the members of our Church.'

"I am, Rev. Sir,
"Your faithful friend & brother in Christ,
"C. J. LONDON."

Collections were accordingly made in obedience to his Lordship's letter. Up to this time, the sum of 4,500*l.* has been received from 300 churches; and it is hoped that the whole amount will not be less than 7,000*l.*

Her Majesty the Queen Dowager has sent 300*l.* (in addition to a former donation of 100*l.*) to the treasurer of the Bethnal-green Churches Committee, in aid of the funds for completing the work of supplying ten additional churches, schools, and parsonage-houses, in that parish.

South Hackney Church-Fund.—The following is the result of the third annual collection, made in the parish church of South Hackney, at the offertory, on the first Sunday after the Epiphany, 1842:—

	£	s.	d.
To the Society for Promoting Christian Knowledge	37	0	0
To the Society for the Propagation of the Gospel in Foreign Parts	55	2	0
To the National School Soc.	56	2	0
To the Church-Building Soc.	46	11	6
To the Additional Curates Society	43	5	0
To the Society for the Propagation of the Gospel, as a special contribution in obedience to the Queen's letter	33	17	6
	£271	18	0

"As respects the CHURCH FUND generally, the Committee are anxious to direct particular attention to several interesting features in its plan, convinced that their exhibition will insure to it the continued and cheerful cooperation of every sincere and intelligent member of the Church of England.

"The first feature they would point out is, its setting forth the claims of five Church Societies simultaneously. It is important to do this, not only because no one Society can detach itself from the others, and accomplish its own object by itself; but because it is both proper and expedient to make known at the same time the different wants of the Church, and to set before her members the means by which they may supply them. For it is evident that a number of annual subscriptions, be they large or be they small, if they are *duly apportioned*, are made to minister at once to the edification and the extension of the Church. By the union of single offerings houses of prayer are erected, ministers in poor parishes provided, schools established, Bibles, Prayer-books, and useful tracts dispersed; and not only are the christian principles of individuals strengthened and confirmed, but the condition of various classes of christian brethren, both at home and abroad, is improved, and the Gospel itself propagated in heathen lands. And all this it will be seen is done through the medium of the *Church*, of which each Christian is led to regard himself a living and responsible member. By the same means, too, the unity, extent, and consistency of the Church's design is made apparent, and greater success may be anticipated to her exertions, than if desultory efforts be made for any one of her objects, or for all of them at different and irregular periods.

"A second feature of the plan is, that it recommends itself to the notice of individual members of families, and with great propriety, through the medium of their respective heads. And this, it will be admitted, is a legitimate way of promoting christian feeling and sympathy in the Church. 'If one member suffer, all the members should suffer with it; and if one member be honoured, all the members should rejoice with it.' Children too, taught at the firesides of their parents, or in the nurseries of christian education, and servants encouraged in the houses of their masters to think of and minister, by little sacrifices, to the necessities of others, will, it may be hoped, gradually imbibe the benevolent spirit of the Church's prayers, and be more careful in after life than they perhaps otherwise would be, to exemplify her principles and her prayers *in practice*. It may be hoped, too, that as the centres of other circles in different spheres of society, they will exert a becoming and beneficial influence upon all around them—an influence which shall expand and penetrate to a degree beyond the range of human calculation.

"A third feature of the plan is, that it solicits support from all, whether rich or poor, *in proportion to their ability*. The tendency of this feature is to educe charitable actions from christian motives, and to awaken in the christian mind an abiding sense of its responsibility. It is quite unnecessary to dwell upon the consequences of attending to, or neglecting the working out, this scriptural principle: they are obvious to every sensitive and devout Churchman.

"Another interesting and important feature of the plan is, that it emanates from the parochial Clergy, under the sanction of the Bishop of the diocese. The tendency of this feature is, to keep up a due sense of the pastoral relation, and to aid the development, and promote the recognition of, true Church principles. It serves to remind ministers and people of their mutual obligations, and not only of the duties they owe to each other, but to the whole Church, and the wide world. And it tends withal to promote *Church union*, the benefits and blessings involved in which it is utterly impossible to overrate.

"A fifth, and the most important feature, inasmuch as it forms the groundwork of the plan, is, that it is 'framed in strict accordance with the principles of our ecclesiastical polity,' the Societies it embraces being all, in principle and in practice, whether operating at home or abroad, 'under the efficient superintendence of the Bishops of the Church.' It is this circumstance which gives the great Church Societies so strong and peculiar a claim to the affectionate regards of every member of the Church."

[It is much to be wished that other parishes would follow the good example here set.]

SALISBURY.—*The Bishop of Salisbury and the Bible Society.*—The Lord Bishop of Salisbury has addressed the following letter to the Rev. A. Brandram, in explanation of the motives of his resigning his connexion with the Bible Society:—

"*To the Rev. A. Brandram.*

"MY DEAR SIR,—My attention has been directed to a letter addressed to the editor of the *Record*, and signed by yourself and Mr. Browne, as joint secretaries of the British and Foreign Society, in which you correct an erroneous statement respecting the grounds of my retirement from that Society, which originally appeared in the *Dorset County Chronicle*, and was transferred from that paper to the *Record*. It is hardly necessary for me to say that your statement is quite correct, and that the paragraph in question was altogether erroneous.*

"The mistaken impression, however, on this subject, which has gone abroad, seems to make it necessary for me to remove a misapprehension which may exist, by stating the reasons which did induce me to take a step, in many respects so disagreeable to me, as that of resigning my connexion with the Bible Society.

"In the letter in which I conveyed to you my resignation on the 20th of August in last year, I said, 'I am so unwilling to speak unfavourably of an institution to which I have for some years belonged, and which comprises amongst its supporters so many persons whose opinions have every claim to my respect, that I forbear to state more fully the reasons that have led me to the conclusion that it is my duty to abstain in future from taking part, as I have hitherto done, in the operations of the Society.'

"In accordance with the feeling here expressed, it was my wish to withdraw myself with as little publicity as possible; and not, unless obliged to do so, to state my reasons for taking this step. And even now, though, in order to justify my own course, I am obliged to point out what appear to me the great objections inherent in the constitution and practice of this Society, it is my desire to do full justice to those persons, many of them men whose opinions I am bound highly to respect, who either do not see these defects in the same light in which they appear to me, or think that the advantages attending the operations of the Society in other respects are so great as to outweigh these objections.

"The following, however, are the considerations which were mainly instrumental in leading my mind to the conclusion at which I have arrived:—

"1. The constitution and character of the public meetings by which the business of the Society is carried on. 2. The manner in which its operations frequently interfere with the good order of the Church, and obstruct the ministry of the parochial Clergy. 3. The tendency of the Society to obscure the office of the Church in relation to the word of God.

"I will, as briefly as I can, explain what I mean on each of these points.

"Whoever has been in the habit of attending the meetings of the Bible Society is aware that they are composed of persons belonging to every variety of religious denomination, and holding every shade of opinion which is compatible with the acceptance of the holy Scriptures as a revelation from God. All these persons meet together, and, from the nature of the occasion which assembles them, with an appearance of recognised equality in a matter touching upon the foundation of religious belief. The Independent, the Baptist, the Quaker, the Socinian, assemble on the platform by the side of the member of the Church, on a common understanding that their differences are *pro hâc vice* to be laid aside, and their point of agreement in receiving the Bible as the word of God, and being zealous for its distribution, is to be alone considered. Do not let me be misunderstood as implying that a dishonourable compromise of opinion on the part of any one is required by the constitution of the Society. On the contrary, I know that 'union without compromise' is a sort of watchword in it. But what I do say is, that the necessary tendency of a meeting so composed is to magnify the point of agreement between its members, and to sink, as of comparative insignificance, their respective differences. Whoever has been in the habit of attending meetings of the Bible Society must be familiar with such expressions as that the members of the Society are only separated by 'unimportant differences,' and are joined in 'essential unity;' whereas an examination of what these 'unimportant differences' are, will show that, in one quarter or another, they comprise most of the chief doctrines, and all the ordinances of the Christian religion; and

---

* The statement was to the effect, that the Bishop had relinquished his connexion with the Society because it would not put itself under the Archbishop of Canterbury.

are so clearly recognised in the constitution of the Society, as to make it impossible for a meeting of persons assembled to promote the distribution of God's word, to unite in worshipping him in prayer.

"I have felt, therefore, that the practical tendency of such meetings is to foster a spirit of indifference to the most vital doctrinal truth, as well as yet more clearly to exhibit a disregard of the distinctive character of the Church, as the body to which that truth is entrusted. A member of the Church at such meetings is always liable to hear statements made on those topics which must either be replied to at the risk of very inopportune discussion, or apparently be sanctioned by being passed over in silence.

"The second point on which I proposed to remark is the manner in which the operations of the Society frequently interfere with the good order of the Church, by being obtruded into the parishes of Clergy who do not feel at liberty to take a part in them. A very great proportion of the Clergy are not members of the Bible Society; but from the constitution of that body its operations are necessarily carried on without reference to this, and meetings are holden in the parishes of such Clergy contrary to their wishes.

"It not unfrequently happens, in such a case, that a Clergyman finds that a meeting of the Bible Society is to take place in his parish. The dissenting chapel is perhaps the place of assembly. Of his own parishioners the chief supporters of the cause are the leading dissenters. But members of the Church from other parishes who are supporters of the Society also attend. Perhaps some neighbouring Clergy are induced, even under such circumstances, to take part in the proceedings, which thus practically assume the appearance of giving a sanction and support to the system of dissent; tend to lower the influence of the Clergyman with his parishioners; and to make the very distribution of the Scriptures a means of upholding those 'erroneous and strange doctrines to God's word,' which every Clergyman is bound by his ordination vow, 'with all faithful diligence to banish and drive away.' I have had repeated and painful experience of such cases in the course of the last five years; and I have felt that, while I continue a member of the Society, the sanction of my authority was indirectly given to proceedings which I could not but regard as very detrimental to the good order of the Church, and the influence of the Clergy in their respective parishes. Reflection upon these two great practical evils in the working of the Society will, I think, show that they both proceed from the same fundamental error, that, viz. of forgetting that a body so constituted is not properly capable of performing functions which essentially appertain to the Church in her character of 'witness and keeper of holy writ,' and are capable of being satisfactorily discharged by her alone.

"I mean satisfactorily discharged on the principles which a member of the Church is bound to recognise; because the indifference to positive doctrine, and the unlimited license of private judgment, both in points of faith and discipline, which it is the effect of the system of the Society to foster, are as much at variance with the spirit of the Church as they are agreeable to the views of some of the bodies that are separated from her. And this is the third ground which I mentioned as having influenced my judgment in coming to the decision I have done.

"I have now stated the reasons which brought me to the conclusion that the British and Foreign Bible Society is not so constituted as to enable it to discharge in the best and most satisfactory manner the great office it has undertaken; and that, sensible as I am of the importance of the object proposed, and anxious to promote it, I cannot properly cooperate with this Society in doing so, or continue a member of it, consistently with my duty in other respects.

"I have the honour to remain,
"My dear Sir,
"Your very faithful servant,
"E. SARUM.
"Wilton Crescent, March 2, 1842."

WALES.

CARMARTHEN.—The Lord Bishop of St. David's lately preached an admirable sermon in the Welsh language to a crowded congregation, in St. David's Church, in this town, from James i. 22, "Byddwch wneuthurwyr y gair, ac nid gwrandawwyr yn unig, gan eich twyllo elch hunain." His Lordship took a luminous view of his subject; his style was pure and idiomatic, and his enunciation clear and distinct. It would require close attention to be able to say he was not a native, so perfectly has he mastered the difficulty of pronouncing one of the most difficult of European languages. His Lordship, we believe, is the first Bishop that has preached in the Welsh language since the days of "Rysiart Davies, Esgob Ty Ddewi," the author of the celebrated pastoral letter to the Cymry, more than two centuries ago.—*Ch. Intell.*

SCOTLAND.

EDINBURGH. — *Confirmation.* — This rite was performed on Thursday in St. Paul's Chapel, York-place, by the Right Rev. Bishop Terrot, D.D., to an unusually numerous assemblage of young persons of both sexes; not the least interesting part of the ceremony arose from the circumstance, that about 100 soldiers belonging to the 53d regiment, now in the Castle, attended at the same time with the other candidates, and were confirmed by the Bishop.—*Edin. Paper.*

The Rev. James Marshall, late Presbyterian minister of the Tolbooth Church, Edinburgh, has been presented to the Rectory of St. Mary-le-port, Bristol, vacant by the decease of the Rev. James Neale.

FOREIGN.

ARRIVAL OF THE BISHOP OF THE UNITED CHURCH OF ENGLAND AND IRELAND IN PALESTINE.

(From a Correspondent of The Times.)

Jan. 27.

THE entry of Bishop Alexander into the city of David was marked by as favourable circumstances as could possibly have been anticipated. On the morning of the 20th instant, our little community was much excited by the arrival of a messenger from Jaffa, with the intelligence that the British Consul-General and Bishop Alexander had arrived off that port in a steam frigate, and might be expected in Jerusalem on the following day. Mr. Nicolayson, a highly respectable and talented Holstein Danish gentleman, who is now a Clergyman of the Church of England, and the head of the mission for promoting Christianity among the Jews at Jerusalem, immediately started to meet them. The rencontre took place at Ramleh, the Ramah of Scripture, (still a considerable town,) where the Bishop, the Consul-General, and a numerous suite, halted to pass the night. The Bishop took up his quarters at the house of the American Consul, the wealthiest Christian in the place; and the Consul-General, with several officers of the Devastation steam frigate, alighted at the Armenian convent. On the following day they made their entry into our ancient capital, in a procession which will be remembered by those who saw it to the latest day of their lives. When within five miles of the gates they were joined by the few British and American residents on horseback, headed by Mr. Proconsul Johns, who is architect of the intended church, as well as *locum tenens* of Mr. Young. On approaching the town, the cavalcade, which already consisted of fifty or sixty persons, was swollen by the junction of the Bey, second in command of the troops, who, accompanied by a guard of honour, and the janissaries of the Pasha, had been sent to compliment Colonel Rose on his arrival, while all the loungers of Jerusalem turned out for the occasion. Mrs. Alexander, and the younger portion of her family, were conveyed in a large oriental litter over the rocky and precipitous tracts which lead from Jaffa to Jerusalem. The procession, which consisted of more than one hundred persons on horseback, passed on, and the scene which ensued at the Bethlehem-gate, by which it entered the town, baffles all description: on the one side were the grey massive battlements and picturesque towers of Jerusalem, no mean specimen of the solidity with which Sultan Suleyman fortified the conquests of his predecessor Selim; and on the other, was the vale that leads to Bethlehem, now rugged and now undulated, with all its light and shade softened in the approaching twilight;

while the dark and singularly even and unpeaked line of the mountains of Moab beyond the Dead Sea walled in the prospect. The wildly-accoutred and unearthly-looking Bedouin irregulars, who had been playing the djereed, and gamboling round the procession at the full speed of their desert horses, contented themselves with firing off their muskets, being now hemmed in by the motley throng of citizens and fellaheen,—Mussulmans in their furred pelisses and well-folded turbans, down to the filthy old Polish Jew in the last stage of wilful hydrophobia. After acknowledging the presentation of arms at the Bethlehem-gate, the party moved on towards the house of Mr. Nicolayson, and just as the new-comers turned their heads to admire the Titan-like masonry of the tower of Hippicus, which dates from the days of Herod the Tetrarch, the guns thundered forth the salute for the eve of the Courban Bairam. Thus, by an odd chance, the Protestant Bishop made his public entry into one of the four holy cities of Islam (the others are Mecca, Medina, and Damascus) on the occasion of one of the greatest festivals of the Mahomedan religion. Colonel Rose descended at the Spanish convent of Terra Santa. Dr. Alexander took up his quarters temporarily with Mr. Nicolayson, his own residence, which is upon the Pool of Hezekiah, being as yet unfurnished. On the 22d Colonel Rose, Dr. Alexander, and a large party, inspected the intended site of the new church. It will be built upon the most elevated part of the city; the body of the church will be Gothic, and the towers in the style of mosque minarets, which accords admirably both with the church itself and with the other public edifices of the city; for Gothic and Saracenic are the twin daughters of the Byzantine style. The Bishop's residence will be Elizabethan. The stone necessary for the edifices will be procured from the Mount of Olives. In the afternoon of the same day Colonel Rose presented Dr. Alexander to Tahir Pasha, who, as I have understood, received him with great politeness. Of course, it would be an illusion to suppose that this reception proceeded from any sympathy with the objects of the mission on the part of the Turkish authorities. On the 23d the Bishop preached his introductory sermon, choosing for his text Isaiah, chap. lxv. and ver. 15: "Whereas thou (alluding to Jerusalem and the Jews) hast been forsaken and hated, so that no man went through thee, I will make thee an eternal excellency, a joy of many generations." The tendency of the Right Rev. Prelate's discourse was to show, that although Jerusalem had endured, and might still endure, much suffering in the fulfilment of inspired prophecy, nevertheless brighter days were at hand.

The Completing of the Cathedral of Cologne.—The great energy which has been displayed for several years past in Prussia, to complete that most gorgeous specimen of mediæval German architecture, has now received a new impetus by the formation of an auxiliary committee in Bavaria. It is said, that the idea of having this great edifice completed by the cooperation of all German nations emanated from the king himself, who has increased his annual donation of 10,000 thalers for the completion to 50,000 thalers, about 200,000f. "It is said," says the *Dusseldorff Gazette*, "that the king of Prussia will not lay the first stone for the new works of the cathedral till next autumn."

CHURCHES CONSECRATED OR OPENED.

Kingston-on-Thames.................. St. Peter's..................... Bishop of Winchester......... Feb. 19.
St. Mary's, Spital Square, London, }
(formerly Sir J. Wheler's Chapel) } .... Bishop of London .... Feb. 24.

TO CORRESPONDENTS.

We have to thank a Correspondent (whose letter is not at this moment at hand) for his remarks on the subject of the Sonnet, and also for the very pleasing Poems under that title, with which he has accompanied them. They do not, as he is well aware, quite answer our notion of the Sonnet, but still we think them very beautiful. If our correspondent will re-consider our articles, he will find that we do not advocate unnecessary trammels, but such rules as seem essential as an outward form for the Sonnet, if its peculiar scope and purpose are to be indicated by its structure.

We have sent the letter from St. David's, Lampeter, to the author of the notice, to which it is a reply.

THE
CHRISTIAN REMEMBRANCER.

MAY, 1842.

History of Scotland. By PATRICK FRASER TYTLER, *Esq.* Vol. VII. 1565—1573. Edinburgh: William Tait. 1842.

THE commissioners of the young queen, overreached by the diplomatic craft of Cecil, had been induced, in direct contravention of their mistress's commands, not only to include the Scots in the treaty with Elizabeth, but virtually to recognise their entire conduct. A parliament had been summoned illegally; had refused to wait for the ratification of their sovereign; had, with hurried proceedings, stamped the ancient faith as false, and its professors as blasphemers; had forbidden, under the heaviest penalties, the performance of that service to which their queen looked as the consolation of her religion; had established a regency—of enemies to their sovereign; had entered into new and closer league with England; and, lastly, had shown their contempt for their queen by despatching high and mighty lords to treat with Elizabeth, whilst to their sovereign they sent "ane poor gentleman, whom I disdain to have come in the name of them all to the king and me in such a legation." Is it to be wondered that Mary refused to ratify the proceedings of her subjects? The death of the young king of France made a change in the policy of all parties. It was evident that Mary would return to her country, and it is hard to say whether her expected return was not regarded as a benefit by all her subjects. Each party was now anxious to outstep their opponents in securing the goodwill of their sovereign; and, while Knox and the English party regarded the death of the king as a special judgment on an infidel and stubborn prince, and a mark of God's intervention on the behalf of the Protestants, the Roman party saw in it an opportunity of restoring Mary to her own country, of destroying the power of the Reformer's regency, and of securing the sanction, not of the queen's name alone, but of her presence and her practice in favour of the ancient religion. To the lord James, indeed, the return of his sister might have seemed the breaking down of his hopes of supreme rule, at least until after his visit to Mary in France, his treachery towards her in revealing all his conversations with her to Thockmorton, and his knowledge of Mary's determination, on the discovery of his conduct, to refuse him the office and power of regent. After this, knowing the readiness with which his sister was swayed by an appearance of friendship, her coming into Scotland was to be eagerly desired by him, as it afforded him every means of influencing Mary, and swaying her to his own views. We cannot here delay on the intrigues of the Guises against Elizabeth, of that queen's envoy, Thockmorton, against Mary, or on the unwarrantable attempt of the queen of England to capture her cousin of Scotland as she endeavoured to pass from her husband's to her own land. On the nineteenth of August 1561, the young queen, favoured by a fog, escaped the cruisers of England, and landed at Leith to the joy of her subjects. For a short time, her presence seemed to calm the exasperated feelings of the contending sects; and whilst the rude pomp of her nobles, as they accompanied her to Holyrood, and the lengthy psalms which the citizens substituted for courtly serenades beneath her windows, excited a smile or a sigh, still, as their rude ways of expressing their delight and affection, they for a time enabled her to believe that she had taken too high an estimate of the difficulties and distresses of her situation.

The queen had yet to learn the limits of Protestant toleration. The lord James had guaranteed the celebration of the mass in her own private chapel. Not so, however, Knox; he preferred the rites of the Jews to those of Rome; he had rather welcome ten thousand French soldiers than one mass; and in this spirit stirred up the master of Lindsay to show his valour, his zeal, and his loyalty, by endeavouring to force his way into the chapel, and slay the priests by whom the mass was being celebrated. The lord James turned the advancing tide and shared with his sister the abuse of Knox. Advised by her brother, Mary issued a proclamation, guaranteeing the religion lately established, and prohibiting any innovation upon the then national faith. "The mass, however," cried Knox, "was still in the land, and therefore no peace with antichrist." Still, Mary was unwilling to irritate the passions of her opponents; nay, rather she would have conciliated them, could kindness, combined with dignity, have aroused the good feelings of the Reformers. In despite of his lavish attacks on her conduct, Mary sought an interview with Knox. At first the Reformer remembered in whose presence he stood and tempered his replies; he found, however, in his sovereign no mean adversary, and beaten from several of his points, he had recourse to violent language approaching to menace. Foiled in his endeavour to twist the passive resistance and patient enduring of afflictions of Daniel, Shadrach, and their fellows, into an argument for resistance with the sword, he replied—

"'God hath nowhere commanded higher reverence to be given to kings by their subjects than by children to their parents; and yet if a father or mother be struck with madness, and attempt to slay his children, they may lawfully bind and disarm him till the phrenzy be overpast. It is even so, madam,' continued this stern champion of resistance, fixing his eyes on the young queen, and raising his voice to a tone that almost amounted to a menace, 'it is even so with princes that would murder the children of God, who may be their subjects. Their blind zeal is nothing but a mad phrenzy, and therefore to take the sword from them, to bind them, and to cast them into prison, till they be brought to a sober mind, is no disobedience against princes, but just obedience, because it agreeth with the word of God.' At these words Mary stood for some time silent and amazed; she was terrified by the violence with which they were uttered. She thought of her own youth and weakness, of the fierce zealots by whom she was surrounded; her mind pictured to itself, in gloomy anticipation, the struggles which awaited her, and she burst into tears. On being comforted and soothed by Murray, who alone was present at the interview, she at length collected herself and said, turning to Knox, 'Well then, I perceive that my subjects shall only obey you, and not me; they must do what they list, not what I command; whilst I must learn to be subject unto them, not they unto me.' 'God forbid,' said the Reformer, 'that it should ever be so; far be it from me to command any, or to absolve subjects from their lawful obedience. My only desire is that both princes and subjects should obey God, who has in his word enjoined kings to be nursing fathers and queens nursing mothers to his Church.'"—*Tytler*, vol. vi. p. 240.

The queen pleaded for the Church of Rome, whilst Knox denounced it to her face as the Roman Harlot, polluted with every kind of abomination in doctrine and manners. "My conscience is not so," replied Mary.—"Conscience," replied Knox, "requires knowledge; and I fear that of right knowledge you have but little." The Reformer then denounced the mass, and challenged every Papist in Europe to battle, declaring his earnest wish to meet them before the queen herself. "In that wish," said Mary, "you may be indulged sooner than you expect," and broke up the distressing interview.

The determined and sincere resolution of the queen to support the faith in which she had been brought up, and the bold and violent declaration of Knox of meeting all efforts in its behalf with open resistance as far as his power extended, rendered a collision between the two parties more certain than before. The policy, however, which at this time Mary was persuaded to adopt, of favouring the views of Elizabeth, tended to soften her anger against the Reformers, and even to encourage the more christian and civilized among their leaders, and look askant on the few adherents to the faith of Rome, who endeavoured to sway the queen to a violent imposition of the Roman faith on her subjects. Her recognition of the Protestant confession as the national faith, the great preponderance of its adherents admitted by her to the council, and the implicit dependence placed by her on the lord James, rendered Mary a favourite with the moderate Reformers. This party was able in its leaders, but small in its numbers, and pressed on both sides, by the Purists under Knox, and the Romanists under Huntley. To the leaders of this party the gentleness of the queen was justly contrasted with the rancour and bitterness of Knox.

"'You know,' said Lethington, in a letter to Cecil, 'the vehemency of Mr. Knox's spirit, which cannot be bridled, yet doth sometimes utter such sentences as cannot easily be digested by a weak stomach. I could wish he would deal with her more gently, being a young princess unpersuaded. *For this I am accounted too politic;* but surely in her comporting with him she doth declare a wisdom far exceeding her age.'" —*Tytler*, vol. vi. p. 242.

The encouragement given to the Protestants by the queen's declaration in favour of their faith as that of Scotland, and the cold reception which the Romish clergy experienced from Mary, enabled the Reformers to follow up their measures against the Romanists in the general assembly of the Church. The profits of the Reformation had been divided on border principles. Much booty had been obtained: much, indeed, had been owed to the earnest preaching of the pastors, but more to the sword, the spear, and the jack. Poverty, therefore, was the reward of the preacher, whilst the plunder had gone to enrich the nobles and their armed followers. We have already noticed one attempt, to secure a state provision for the preachers, fail. The scheme was now renewed, and with doubtful success. Lethington, acute and worldly, treated the claim with jeers and scoffs; the rulers of the court party began to draw away from their brethren; the secretary of the lord James ranged himself openly against the preachers; and though after some discussion the legality of the assembly was affirmed, yet the nobles refused to assent to the book of discipline, and thwarted, though they did not openly oppose, the claims of the ministers to support out of the Church revenues. At last it was agreed that one third of the annual revenues of whole benefices was to go to the queen for the support of the preachers, the maintenance of the poor, the endowment of schools, and the increasing the revenues of the crown.

"Before this proposal was made," says Mr. Tytler, "the funds of the Church, previously immense, had been greatly dilapidated. On the overthrow of popery, the bishops and other dignified clergy had entered into transactions with their friends and kinsmen, by which large portions of ecclesiastical property passed into private hands; in some cases sales had been made by the ancient incumbents, or leases had been purchased by strangers, which the pope, zealous to protect his persecuted children, had confirmed; the crown, too, had appointed laymen to be factors or administrators of bishoprics and livings: so that, by these various methods, the property of the Church was so much diffused and curtailed, that the third of all the money collected fell far below the sum necessary to give an adequate support to the clergy. There was much fraud also practised in making up the returns. Many of the Roman Catholic clergy evaded the production of their rentals; some gave in false estimates; and although the persons appointed to fix the rate of provision had been the firm supporters of the Reformation, though the lord James and Maitland of Lethington, with Argyle and Morton, superintended every step, the result disappointed the expectations of the ministers. *It was asserted, that the only effect of the change was to secure a large share for the lay proprietors of Church-lands, to transfer a considerable portion to the crown, and to leave a wretched pittance to the ministers.*"—*Tytler*, vol. vi. p. 252.

It no doubt might be said, that this act recognised the right of the Presbyterian ministers to a state support ; but if that was to be but a mere right, Knox and those others who now looked for more solid rewards, might well assert that the same act equally legalized the private mass of the queen's chapel. In the end no one was pleased. The ministers complained that there were no effects, and that they could not live on " rights ;" the nobles complained that the law deprived them of their hard-earned rewards; the Romanists objected to the legalizing of a heretical profession ; the old clergy thought it hard to support their own opponents and most rancorous enemies; whilst the crown hardly considered the gain equal to the opprobrium and discontent caused by its acquirement. Another source of grief to Knox's friends was the eagerness with which the advisers of the queen endeavoured to cement a union with the English court and the English Church. The pulpit, now the usual place for political harangues, rang with denunciations of the prelatic Elizabeth, the popery of England, and the foundation of her Church in opposition to the word of God, as interpreted by Calvin and Knox. The advice supposed to have been tendered by her cardinal uncle to Mary to embrace the religion of England " made them almost wild, of which they both said and preached that it is little better than when at its worst. Whilst Mr. Knox," continues the more moderate Randolph, " upon Sunday last, gave the cross and the candles such a wipe, that as wise and as learned as himself wished he had held his peace." To the Roman party these negotiations were nearly equally distasteful. The duplicity of Elizabeth prevented their ever being accomplished.

During the intricate negotiations between Murray and Lethington on the one hand and Cecil on the other, involving the entire questions of Mary's succession to the English throne, the proposed meeting with Elizabeth, and the subject of her marriage with Leicester, the Reformers continued to disturb the peace of the kingdom with their violence. With those negotiations the course of these remarks prevents us from interfering, tempting though it be, to go on with our historian in unravelling the dark skein and tangled web of intrigue, duplicity, and falsehood, with which the despatches on both sides abound, and contrasting the free and open heart of the queen of Scotland, and her earnest desire to be her kinswoman's " own dear sister," with the conduct of Elizabeth, always expecting treachery and suspicious of deceit, because ever intending the former and preparing the latter on her own part. It is our task to combine in one view the scattered notices of the Reformation which these volumes afford us.

In the summer of 1562 the arrival of a bishop from Rome, as envoy from the Pope, to strengthen Mary in her religion, and to exhort her to send a representative to the Council of Trent, gave the Protestants another opportunity of illustrating their principles of toleration. He with difficulty escaped with his life ; and had it not been for the peremptory remonstrance of the lord James, the Reformers would have inflicted on the unoffending emissary that death which they had decreed to be his lot, immediately that it was known that a papal envoy had dared to set foot in Protestant Scotland.

The partiality of Mary for her brother,—the fall of the leader of the Roman faction, the overbearing Huntley,—the favour shown by the queen to the Protestants,—evinced a determination on the part of Mary to adopt and succour the national faith, if she might but retain her own opinions unpersecuted. Yet what return did she meet with from the leaders of the Reformation—the Purists—to whom the words of Knox was law? With all our historian's predisposition in favour of the Reformers, the contrast in the following passage is marked.

"It was only to be regretted, that the conduct of Knox, and the more violent of his brethren, *occasionally* excited feelings of resentment, when there was a predisposition to peace; and that his endeavours to secure the triumph of his party, *(conscientious as they undoubtedly were,)* were seldom accompanied by *sound discretion or christian love.* Even Randolph, their partial friend, was shocked by the manner in which the preachers prayed for the queen. 'They pray,' says he, in a letter to Cecil, 'that God will keep us from the bondage of strangers; and for herself, as much in effect as, *that God will either turn her heart or send her a short life.*' . . . . . Although the queen behaved with much forbearance, it seems to have created no impression in her favour. As long as she retained her own faith, and permitted the celebration of mass in her private chapel, *nothing could disarm his suspicions, appease his wrath, or check the personality of his attacks. His natural disposition was sarcastic; he had a strong sense of the ludicrous; and when provoked, his invectives were so minute, coarse, and humorous, that they alternately excited ridicule or indignation.*"—*Tytler*, vol. vi. pp. 269-70.

Conscientiously, doubtless, he railed against the dancing and masques at the palace, because Herodias's daughter was rewarded with the head of John. Doubtless, he was conscientious when he compared his invectives against the court follies to our blessed Saviour's appellation of "Fox" to Herod; accused the courtiers of falsifying the terms in which his attack was couched; declared to the queen that she must be devoid of the Spirit of God, yea of honesty and wisdom, if she disagreed with one word of his sermon; and denounced on the dancers, as their reward, to drink in hell unless they repented. And the queen resented not. Nay, when he to her face denounced her uncles as enemies to God and his Son, "she allowed him to depart as though no offence or slander did arise thereon."

It is curious to remark to what inconsistencies the violence of Knox led him. At the time that he was crying out against the English Church as an offshoot of Popery, and leading his friends to declare rather for a Papist queen, than one a friend to England and of her Church,—at that very moment he was treacherously circulating falsehoods about Mary, and corresponding with Cecil as the friend of Elizabeth, and pretending to warn her of the hollowness of Mary's professions. Knox's own admissions,—the voluminous correspondence of Lethington, Moray, Randolph, and Cecil,—the recorded conversation of Mary with Elizabeth's envoy,—all prove the Reformer inconsistent, false, and treacherous.

Let us note another inconsistency of the Reformers. It will be remembered, that in the parliament of 1558, the Reformers, then a persecuted minority, besought that Churchmen should be confined to accusing,—and the judging and punishing of recusants, which they were, then, should be confined to the civil power. It will also be remembered, that Knox, only the year before the events we are about to relate, renounced for himself even the wish to command any one, or to absolve any from their lawful obedience; this he said in 1561. Two years after, during which time the power of Knox had been greatly increased, his practice showed the altered state of his opinions.

" During the absence of Lethington in England, the papists, encouraged by the bishop of St. Andrew's, and the prior of Whithern, had disregarded the queen's proclamation. Mass was celebrated secretly in many private houses; and when this was found dangerous, the votaries of the Romish faith fled into the woods and mountains, and amidst those silent solitudes they adhered to the worship of their fathers. Upon this, the Presbyterians, despairing, *as they alleged*, of any redress of such abuse from the queen, *took the law into their own hands, pursued and seized some priests, and sent word to the Romish clergy, that henceforth they should neither complain to the queen nor the council, but with their own hands execute upon idolaters the punishment contained in God's word."—Tytler,* vol. vi. p. 279.

And thus, because, as Knox told his sovereign, " Samuel spared not to slay Agag, the fat and delicate king of Amalek, whom Saul had saved, and Elias did not spare Jezebel's prophets and Baal's priests," Knox and his brother preachers were to take into their own hands the power of life and death,—a power which they had deprecated, when by the constitution of the kingdom legally vested in the clergy, but exercised against them, at that time petitioners— a power now by their own enactments taken from the clerical body, and according to their own wishes vested in the civil power, and this because *they despaired, as they alleged*, that the queen would execute the laws she had sanctioned. It is an old, but an over true proverb, that $\dot{\alpha}\rho\chi\dot{\eta}\ \ddot{\alpha}\nu\delta\rho\alpha\ \delta\epsilon\acute{\iota}\xi\epsilon\iota$.

The offenders were summoned and punished by the queen, and Knox, driven from the indulgence of this kind of persecution, soon fell back on another grievance quite as congenial to the disciple of Calvin.

The queen now met her first parliament. Surrounded by a brilliant cavalcade, wherein each noble sought to show his enthusiasm by the costly splendour of his dress, Mary rode in procession to the Tolbooth, where the Estates were sitting. The gorgeous array of the nobles, the glittering dresses of the royal household, the beauty and adornments of the ladies of the court who surrounded the throne and filled the galleries, all tended to heighten the surprise and delight with which the people received their queen. Life seemed to have returned to Scotland, and joy beamed in every eye, as they said with one accord, "God save that sweet face; she speaks as properly as the best orator among them."

All this, however, was gall and wormwood to the preachers. There was too much joyful thankfulness for beauties and benefits of this world to please them as Calvinists, and too great a prospect of the power of the preachers waning before the returning popularity of the crown not to frighten them as members of the assembly of the congregation. The mind of Knox naturally recurred to the rule held by the persecutor of Servetus over the citizens of Geneva; perhaps he had read in the archives of that city, how, in 1537, a married lady having gone out on a Sunday wearing her hair in longer curls than was becoming a Christian, which was a bad example, and contrary to what was taught by the preachers of the gospel, it was ordered that she be committed to prison, together with her attendants and the person that dressed her hair.* It might have been that, at the time he was flying from persecution in Scotland, Knox had witnessed in the city of Geneva the exposure of a card-player in the pillory, the excommunication of a tavern-frequenter, or of the girl that put on boy's clothes, and of her mother that failed to hinder her, or of the imprisonment of the citizen for reading the tales of Poggio, and the swineherd for saying the "devil was in the pigs." Sighing for the inquisition of Geneva, of which their leader could give such enticing accounts, we acknowledge how natural the conduct of Knox appears in the following quotation:—

"Amidst this general enthusiasm, the preachers took great offence at the liberty of the French manners, and the extravagance of the foreign dresses. *They spake boldly,*' says Knox, ' *against the superfluities of their clothes, and affirmed that the vengeance of God would fall not only on the foolish women, but on the whole realm.*' To check the growing licence, an attempt was made to introduce a sumptuary law; articles against apparel were drawn up, and it was proposed to take order with other abuses; but to the extreme mortification of the Reformer, he was arrested in his career of legislation by the hand of the lord James. This powerful minister deemed it impolitic at this moment to introduce these enactments. 'The queen,' he said, 'had kept her promises, the religion was established, the mass-mongers were punished: if they carried things too high, she would hold no parliament at all.' Knox smiled significantly—Mar, he hinted, trembled for his new earldom of Moray, and all must be postponed to have his grant confirmed, lest Mary should repent of her munificence; he denounced in strong terms such selfish motives, reminded him of his solemn engagements to the Church, and accused him of sacrificing truth to convenience, and the service of his God to the interests of his ambition. The proud spirit of Moray could not brook such an attack, and he replied with austerity; the two friends parted in anger, and the Reformer increased the estrangement by addressing a letter in which, in his usual plain and vehement style of reproof [*abuse?*], he exonerated himself from all further care in his lordship's affairs, committing him to the guidance of his own understanding, whose dictates he preferred to the advancement of the truth.

---

* For these acts of persecution under Calvin's new constitution at Geneva, and for many more of a like kind, see the Life of Calvin by M. Audin. Paris: Marson.

'I praise my God,' said he, 'I leave you victor over your enemies, promoted to great honour, and in authority with your sovereign. Should this continue, none will be more glad than I: but if you decay, (as I fear ye shall,) *then call to mind by what means the Most Highest exalted you: it was neither by trifling with impiety, nor maintaining pestilent Papists.*' So incensed was Moray with this remonstrance, that for a year and a half he and Knox scarcely exchanged words together."—*Tytler*, vol. vi. pp. 281, 282.

It is an old adage, that none are so suspicious as those who have most reason to be suspected. Such was the case with Knox. Temporal benefits had before now seduced him from the path of danger: life and the world's rewards had been the reasons of his flight from the storm of persecution to the haven of Geneva, and the profits of the pastorship of its congregation. How natural, therefore, for him to suspect that Moray was actuated by worldly motives in his opposition to a crusade against embroidery, and a persecution of starched ruffs and laced capotes! Though, doubtless, Moray could not but feel enraged at the insolent language of the Reformer's address, and the abuse contained in his letter, a quiet smile must have played over his features as he read the passage in which the preacher refuses to take any further care in his lordship's affairs, and commits him to the guidance of his own understanding. Knox having bearded the lord James, now proceeded to assail the council and the queen. And though he might, as he knew, have ventured to upbraid his sovereign even to her face without personal danger, he felt that, among the proud nobles composing the council, there were some who would not suffer the insolence in their own case, which they permitted in that of their queen's. His sacred character, therefore, as a preacher was to be his shield,—his pulpit his battering-tower, whence to over-top the walls of the fortress of the council. Working himself into a perfect fury, " he was like to ding the pulpit in blads" (tatters), says Melvill, in his diary, " and flee out of it." He ran over the entire progress of the Reformation as a vision; and after he had taunted the nobles with their coldness and want of gratitude to God, he proceeded to attack Mary and her proposed marriage:—

"'And is this to be the thankfulness ye shall render unto your God—to betray his cause, when you have it in your own hands to establish it as you please? The queen says, "Ye will not agree with her." Ask of her that which by God's word ye may justly require; *and if she will not agree with you in God, ye are not bound to agree with her faction in the devil. Let her plainly understand so far your minds;* forsake not your former courage in God's cause, and be assured he will prosper you in your enterprises. And now, my lords,' he concluded, ' *to put an end to all I hear of the queen's marriage: dukes, brethren to emperors and kings, strive all for the best gain. But this, my lords, will I say*—note the day and bear witness hereafter: *whenever the nobility of Scotland, who profess the Lord Jesus, consent that an infidel* (AND ALL PAPISTS ARE INFIDELS) *shall be head to our sovereign, ye do as far as in you lieth to banish Christ Jesus from this realm, and to bring God's vengeance on the country.*"—*Tytler*, vol. vi. p. 283.

In this mass of invective and interference in what, as a preacher, was not within his province, Knox outraged the forbearance not only of the Romanists but of his own friends. This attempt to vilify the queen, and to dictate to the council, called forth the indignation of all parties. He was summoned before Mary, who remonstrated with him on his conduct. Far from feeling sorry for his intemperance, Knox gloried in his attack, proclaiming his purpose to be " to flatter no flesh, but to speak plain, to preach the Gospel." At length, the sufferings of Mary under his continued invectives compelled the nobles who were in her cabinet to command Knox to quit the apartment. The Reformer obeyed, and thus deprived of an opportunity of venting his bitterness on Mary, he poured forth his wrath on the courtiers and ladies that lined the antechamber, and met their averted faces and cold looks with a bold defiance and taunts of cruel bitterness. Advised by Erskine of Dun and the lord James, Mary permitted the officious and intemperate interference of the Reformer to pass over without further notice; and Knox, neither countenanced by the great men, nor raised into a martyr by persecution, began to lose much of his power and influence with the people. The project, however, of the return of Lennox and the marriage of Mary with Darnley recalled him into activity, and consequently into increased power.

As soon as the queen of Scotland, in consequence of the repeated requests of Elizabeth, consented to the return of the exile Lennox, Knox and his friends, firmly convinced that their religion was so slightly built that the coming of one Romanist noble into the land must be its overthrow, intrigued with Cecil in order to stop his coming. Cecil communicated the fears of " Scotland's best friend," as he called his correspondent, to Lethington, whilst Elizabeth took every means to detain Lennox in England, and persuade Mary to recall her permission for his return. The replies of Lethington and the lord James were severe. They did not share in the tergiversation of Elizabeth, or believe in the wondrous intelligence of Cecil's correspondent, and Knox's apprehensions regarding the reformed religion. "The religion here," remarked Lethington, " doth not depend upon my lord of Lennox's return, neither do those of the religion hang upon the sleeves of any one or two that may mislike his coming. For us, whether he doth come or not come, I take it no great matter, either up or down."

"Moray," says Mr. Tytler, " in a letter of the same date with that of Lethington, expressed himself in terms more brief, but still more emphatic. 'As to the faction,' says he, 'that his coming might make for the matters of religion, thanks be to God, our foundation is not so weak, that we have cause to fear if he had the greatest subject of this realm joined to him, seeing we have the favour of our prince, and liberty of our conscience in such abundance as our hearts can wish. It will neither be he nor I, praised be God, can hinder or alter religion hereaway; and his coming or remaining in that cause will be to small purpose.' "—*Tytler*, vol. vi. p. 296.

Let it be borne in mind, that Moray was at this time at enmity with Knox; that he, as his sister's minister, swayed the entire realm of Scotland, and had now gathered round himself honours, wealth, and almost regal power. The religion therefore was *at this time* safe. Ten months after, affairs had altered with the earl of Moray. The English intrigues had been foiled, or rather had so been entangled by their contrivers as to foil themselves; like the army of Xerxes, their very multitude was their ruin. Lennox was now in favour; his son, who had dared to question the power of the earl of Moray, and to expose the danger that must arise from the assumption of so much power by a subject, the accepted suitor of the queen. What were the consequences? The religion was *now* in danger. The earl of Moray had retired from court, and no longer laughed at the fears of Knox. No; *now* Knox was his good friend, and the religion was in danger. Difficulty makes us acquainted with strange bed-fellows.

"Nothing on the part of Moray," says our historian, "could be more futile and unfounded than the pretence that the Protestant religion was in danger, or that the queen at this moment had adopted any measures which threatened its security. It is happy for the truth, that on such a point we have the declaration of Moray and Lethington themselves. [He then quotes the declarations extracted above.] These declarations, indeed, were made a year before this; but during the course of that year, not only had the Scottish queen introduced no one measure which could by any ingenuity be deemed an attack upon the national religion; but she had shown the most decided determination to support it as the religion of the state, and to enforce the cruel and unjust laws against those who adhered to the public exercise of the contrary faith. It is evident, therefore, that the earl of Moray and the party of the nobles who opposed the marriage had raised the cry of 'the Church in danger' merely to cover their own designs."—*Tytler*, vol. vi. p. 345.

Moray, it is evident, was the slave of private ambition, and, as too many have done before him, he masked his selfish projects under a zeal for religion. Does the same remark apply to Knox? Hardly: and yet, though there could not be charged against him the inconsistency of Moray;—though he had from the very beginning characterised the private mass of the queen, and the return of Lennox and Darnley, as measures destructive of the reformed faith; — though no Church plunder had been traced to his hands, and no pensions from England or France secured his services;—was there no pandering to ambition? no wish for personal aggrandizement, for supreme spiritual authority over the Scots, such as his master had exercised over the citizens of Geneva? Was it for the purity of religion that he now allied himself with one of whose worldly intentions he was too well assured; and that, as he had before given his countenance to the murder of Beaton, by casting in his lot with the assassins, he now gave his approval to the scheme for the assassination of Darnley and his father, by joining the barons who had projected it? Be it as it may, with Moray, Lethington, and Argyle, Knox and the preachers now prepared to act in concert. The General Assembly of the Church met at Edinburgh in the June of 1565; and after providing for resistance by arming and organizing the burgesses of the city, after long debates drew up their supplication to the queen.

"It requested," says Mr. Tytler, "that the blasphemous mass, and all popish idolatry, should be abolished, not only throughout the kingdom, but also in her royal person and household; that true religion, as it is founded on the word of God, should be professed, as well by herself as by her subjects; and that it should be made obligatory on all persons to resort to the preaching of the word and to prayers, if not every day, at least every Sunday. It proposed that some sure provision should be made for the support of the ministers of the Gospel; that pluralities should be abolished; a strict examination instituted into the appointment of all teachers of youth in schools and colleges; a fund set apart for the maintenance of the poor out of those lands which of old were destined to hospitality; and some relief devised for the poor labourers of the soil, who were oppressed in the payment of their tithes by unreasonable and illegal exactions."—*Tytler*, vol. vi. 348.

The queen, reminding the commissioners who presented the petition of the liberty of conscience that had been permitted to all her subjects during her reign, respectfully declined being compelled to abjure her faith, asking only that liberty which she had granted to her people. In every thing else she was ready to abide the decision of the Estates of the Parliament. This was not what the discontented petitioners required; they had recourse therefore to rebellion. They plotted to seize Mary and Darnley on their road from Perth to lord Livingstone's house at Callander, intending, according to the assertion of one of the conspirators, to imprison the queen for life, and murder the ill-fated Darnley. The courage and celerity of Mary's movements defeated the treachery of her brother Moray, whilst the discovery of the attempt, added to its failure, rendered the earl and his associates of less reputation among the people. So natural is indignation at unsuccessful villany.

Again the discontented raised the cry, "The Church is in danger!" and whilst they endeavoured to persuade Elizabeth to let loose "some Strapping Elliots" upon Lord Hume, Mary's great partisan, "to keep his hands full at home," they tried to arouse her religious and political jealousy by rumours of intercourse with France and the Papal Court. Elizabeth, however, saw no good reason for moving; promises, indeed, she gave them, but such assistance could not prevent the increasing distrust, lukewarmness, and suspicions of the people, which were not a little increased by Mary's hearing a Protestant sermon whilst at Callander, and renewing her proclamation in favour of the reformed religion and liberty of conscience.

Notwithstanding the assistance given by Randolph to Moray's party, it was evident that the "discontented" were losing their influence, and likely to bring their struggle to a calamitous end. The conduct of Randolph, as his letters prove, deserves the severe remarks of the historian.

"The character of this crafty agent of Cecil," says Mr. Tytler, "was of that accommodating and equivocal kind, which, whilst loving misrepresentation (to use a mild word) for its own sake, did not hesitate to employ it, when he thought it would forward the designs of his royal mistress or her principal minister, as long as all went smoothly in Scotland. The letters of Randolph convey to us a pretty fair picture of the conduct of Mary, and the progress of events; but as soon as she began to act for herself—as soon as her brother, the friend of England, was stripped of his power and lost his influence, this minister transmitted to Cecil, and to the English queen the most false and distorted accounts of the state of the country. His object was to induce Elizabeth to assist the insurgent lords with money and troops, as she had already done in the war of the Reformation; and to accomplish this end, he not only concealed the truth, but did not scruple to employ calumny and falsehood. He represented Mary's proceedings to her nobles as tyrannical, when they were forbearing; he described her as earnestly bent on the destruction of religion, when for five years she had maintained it exactly as she found it on her arrival, and had recently, by a solemn proclamation, declared her determination to preserve the fullest liberty of conscience; he painted her as an object of contempt to her subjects, when she was popular and beloved; and as deserted by her nobles and her people, when, in consequence of the late summons, her barons and vassals were daily crowding into her capital. On the other hand, Moray and his faction were equally falsely depicted as so strong, that the country lay at his mercy, whilst they waited only for the advice and the money of England, to sweep away every opposition, and compel the queen to place herself once more at their disposal."—*Tytler*, vol. vi. 353, 354.

Elizabeth, however, was not to be moved; perhaps she knew the truth of the case; and therefore contenting herself with a formal intercession on behalf of Moray, and a summons to Lennox and Darnley to return to England, she left the conspirators to their own devices, by which they soon convinced the Scots that selfishness and ambition alone prompted their actions. Twenty-nine days after the petition of the Assembly, the marriage of Mary and Darnley was solemnized at Holyrood.

Determined to wander as little as possible from the events of the Reformation in Scotland, and the actions of its chief promoters, we may not now delay over the conduct of Mary, after her marriage, towards her weak and almost imbecile husband, or her vigorous pursuit after the nobles who had banded together with Moray, and the measures by which, in defiance of the secret encouragement of her cousin of England, she drove them from her kingdom, and prepared to punish their rebellion by forfeiture in the estates of the kingdom; though, at the same time, we may not pass over, without mention, the negotiation between Mary and the See of Rome, and the succour afforded to her by the Pope, or her correspondence with Philip the Second, who had expressed to the cardinal Pacheco, the Papal envoy, his determination to assist her in subduing her rebellious subjects, re-establishing the Roman faith, and vindicating her right to the throne of England,—or her accession to the Holy League between France, Spain, and the Emperor, for the destruction of the opponents of the Romish faith throughout Europe. On the signature of that bond hung the fate of Moray and his fellow rebels, and of the unfortunate David Riccio.

"Riccio, who at this moment possessed much influence, and was, on good grounds, suspected to be a pensioner of Rome, seconded these views with all his power. On the other hand, Mary did not want advisers on the side of mercy and wisdom. Sir James Melvil, in Scotland, and Sir N. Thockmorton, one of her most powerful friends in England, earnestly implored her to pardon Moray, and adopt a conciliatory course. Mary was not naturally inclined to harsh or cruel measures, and for some time she vacillated between the adoption of temperate and violent counsels. But now the entreaties of her uncle, the cardinal, the advice of her ambassador, the prejudices of her education, and the intolerance of the Protestants and of Elizabeth, by whom she had been so often deceived, all united to influence her decision, and overmaster her better judgment. In an evil hour she signed the League, and determined to hurry on the parliament for the forfeiture of the rebels. This may, I think, be regarded as one of the most fatal errors of her life; and it proved the source of all her future misfortunes."—*Tytler*, vol. vii. 16.

The instant it was known that Mary had come to this determination, Moray and his friends betook themselves to desperate courses. If the Estates met, they argued, they were ruined; if the Councillors remained unchanged, and the influence of Riccio was not annihilated, the Estates would meet to their utter ruin. If they would be saved, before the Parliament met the queen's advisers must be changed—Riccio murdered. From the day almost of the marriage, the young king had regarded with jealousy the confidence reposed by Mary in her Milanese secretary, and had been led to believe that it was to his influence and advice that he was debarred from the long-promised crown matrimonial. The coldness of the queen increased his jealous fears, and within seven months of his wedding he had determined to rid himself of Riccio, and had sent his cousin, George Douglas, to implore the lord Ruthven to assist him against "the villain David." Ruthven, though hardly able to rise from his bed, eagerly consented to his murder, and the first plot was completed against the life of the secretary. On the 13th of February, 1566, Randolph revealed the plot to Leicester.

"From this letter, which is very long," says Mr. Tytler, "I must give this important passage. 'I know now for certain,' said he, 'that this queen repenteth her marriage; that she hateth him (Darnley) and all his kin. I know that he knoweth himself that he hath a partaker in play and game with him; I know that there are practices in hand, contrived between the father (Lennox) and the son, to come to the crown against her will. I know that if that take effect, which is intended, David, with the consent of the king, shall have his throat cut within these ten days. Many things, grievouser and worse than these, are brought to my ears; yea, of things intended against her own person, which because I think better to keep secret than write to Mr. Secretary, I speak not of them but now unto your lordship.'"— vii. p. 19.

Ruthven, whom the king had called to his aid, assisted by the advice of Morton, who dreaded the assembling of the Estates, lest the report should be true that he was then to be deprived of some lands he had seized unjustly, and lose his chancellorship, grafted on the simple plot for the murder of Riccio a further conspiracy for the return of Moray and his friends, and the seizing of the reins of government by that party. To effect these objects, it was necessary to secure the cooperation of the party of the reformed faith, of Moray, now in exile in England, and the countenance, if not the assistance, of Elizabeth and her ministers.

To such men as Maitland, Grange, Ormistown, and Brunston, to whom murder was as light a matter, as any other piece of crooked policy, it wanted but few words to reconcile them to the plot; it was but a second putting away of a servant of Antichrist; but with less danger and more powerful countenance than the deed of death-doing to Cardinal Beaton. Did any scruple arise in their minds, or trouble for a short space of time the hearts of God's ministers, as their preachers styled themselves, it required merely a moment's thought on the idolatrous worship of Rome,—a moment's reflection on the signature of the Holy League by Mary,—a moment's belief in the reputed correspondence of Riccio with Rome, or in the measures reported to be in preparation for the restoration of the old religion under the sanction of the Estates,—to mislead the little judgment their prejudices had left them, and to harden the few feelings of mercy for Romanists which their fear of idolatry had permitted them to retain. Regarding the plot as a divinely-inspired act for the annihilation of "the accursed faith;"—believing that the end could justify in God's service, as they called their murderous plotting, the most premeditated and barbarous murder;—such men as Knox, and his colleague, Craig, could adopt without hesitation, and support without a fear of God's anger, the desperate designs of Darnley against his wife and queen; and the subsidiary plottings of Morton and Moray against both. The solemn assembly for the General Fast was also moved to account in the matter; and the murder having been fixed for the week in which the Estates had been summoned to meet, the Holy Fast was contrived to be held at that very time, as a further security of Morton and a numerous band of religious partisans.

It has often been denied that Knox was implicated in the murder of Riccio, though at the same time it has been admitted that he expressed his satisfaction at the event, if not his approbation of the conduct of the conspirators; and for this assertion there seemed some ground in the declaration of Morton to the earl of Bedford, that none of the ministers "*were act nor part of that deed, nor were participate thereof;*" and also in the absence of Knox's name in the list of the conspirators, preserved in the Cotton MSS. The labours of our historian in the State-paper Office have set this matter to rest, bringing forward evidence, direct and clear, against Knox, and from those who must be esteemed the best witnesses; evidence sufficient, without the strong corroborating circumstances that may be brought from the position of Knox in the Kirk, his conduct in the case of Beaton, his flight after the death of Riccio, and his admitted opinions on the lawfulness of murder in God's service.

The evidence may be briefly summed up as follows:—On the ninth of March, Riccio was murdered. Eleven days after the event, and about a week after the flight of the conspirators, the Earl of Bedford, then governor of Berwick, in a letter to Cecil, after a tolerably full account of the murder, concludes by informing the secretary, that "he will not trouble him further, as Mr. Randolph was at the very time writing to him, *and would send in his letter the names of the conspirators who had gone abroad.*" In the State-paper Office is the letter from Randolph, and attached to it the list in question; the former in Randolph's hand-writing, the latter in that of a clerk employed by Bedford in his confidential correspondence. The paper is endorsed by Cecil.

"'*Martii*, 1565.

"'Names of such as were consenting to the death of David:

Th' Erle' Murton (Morton).	Haughton.
The L. Ryven (Ruthven).	Loughlyvine (Lochleven).
The L. Lynnesey.	Elvinston.
The Secreatory.	Patrick Murry.
The Mr. of Ryven.	Patrick Ballentyne.
	Andro Car of Fawdonsyde.

Lairds

Ormeston.	John Knox, } Preachers.
Bryanston (Brunston).	John Crag (Craig), }

"'All these were at the death of Davy and (or) privy thereto, and are now in displeasure with the Q, and their houses taken and spoiled.'"—*Tytler*, vol. vii. p. 356, 357.

There was yet another party to be made acquainted with the conspiracy, and to be persuaded either to assist or at least to countenance the attempt—that person was Elizabeth. Three days before the murder, Randolph and Bedford wrote to the queen, informing her of a "matter of no small consequence being intended in Scotland," and referring to a more particular statement transmitted to Cecil by the writers; at the same time naming the day for the event, and stating that its effect would be to bring home the exiled Moray. Nothing can need to be plainer than the letter to Cecil referred to. Our space forbids its being extracted: we must, therefore, supply its place with Mr. Tytler's summary of its effect, and the conduct of Elizabeth.

"It proves that Elizabeth received the most precise intimation of the intended murder of Riccio; that she was made fully acquainted with the determination to secure the person of the Scottish queen, and create a revolution in the Government. Moray's share in the conspiracy, and his consent to the assassination of the foreign secretary, are established by the same letter beyond a doubt; and we see the declared object of the plot was, to put an end to his banishment, to replace him in the power which he had lost, and, by one decided and triumphant blow, to destroy the schemes which were in agitation for the re-establishment of the Roman Catholic religion in Scotland. It is of great moment to attend to the conduct of Elizabeth at this crisis. She knew all that was about to occur: the life of Riccio, the liberty—perhaps, too, the life—of Mary was in her hands; Moray was at her court; the conspirators were at her devotion; they had given the fullest information to Randolph, that he might consult the queen; she might have imprisoned Moray, discomfited the plans of the conspirators, saved the life of the miserable victim who was marked for slaughter, and preserved Mary, to whom she professed a warm attachment, from captivity. All this might have been done; perhaps it is not too much to say, that, even in these dark times, it would have been done by a monarch acutely alive to the common feelings of humanity. But Elizabeth adopted a very different course: she not only allowed Moray to leave her realm,—she dismissed him with marks of the highest confidence and distinction; and this baron, when ready to set out for Scotland, to take his part in those dark transactions which soon after followed, sent his secretary, Wood, to acquaint Cecil with the most secret intentions of the conspirators."—*Tytler*, vol. vii. pp. 26, 27.

On the 3d of March the solemn fast commenced in Edinburgh; on the following day the Estates met. The queen appeared in person; the Lords of the Articles were chosen, and the act of forfeiture against Moray and his associates prepared. In five days the act would be passed. There was little time for deliberation or preparation, but that little was well employed by the ministers, the obedient servants of Knox and Craig, who were privy to the intended death of David.

" Meantime, every thing was in readiness; a large concourse of the friends of the Reformed Church assembled at Edinburgh for the week of fasting and humiliation; directions for prayers and sermons had been *previously drawn up by Knox and the ministers*, and the subjects chosen seemed such as were calculated to prepare the public mind for resistance, violence, and bloodshed. They were selected from the Old Testament alone, and, among other examples, included the slaying of Oreb and Zeeb, the cutting off of the Benjamites, the fast of Esther, the hanging of Haman, inculcating the duty of inflicting swift and summary vengeance on all who persecuted the people of God."—*Tytler*, vol. vii. pp. 27, 28.

On the second day after the meeting of the Estates, the deed of blood was perpetrated, and Mary imprisoned in her chamber, and Darnley *de facto* king. Two more days are passed; the queen has escaped from her rebellious subjects, who were hesitating between death and perpetual imprisonment, should she resist their wishes; the king is alienated from his fellow-conspirators by the persuasion of his wife; the names of the murderers, save *one*, disclosed; Morton, Ruthven, Brunston, and Car, exiles in England; the rest of the gang at hiding in their own country; and Knox, the fiery, zealous, and intrepid conspirator, groaning over his own fortunes and those of the Church in the friendly recesses of Kyle. Before another month had fully waned, the falsehood of the king's declaration before the Council of his innocency of the death of Riccio had been proved to Mary; the covenants and bonds were in her possession; and almost broken-hearted at the discovery, she loudly bewailed the folly and ingratitude of Darnley, and, compelled to place no more confidence in him, determined, in solitary bitterness, to act for herself.

The conduct of Darnley converted this estrangement into hatred; and Mary, grieved and angered at the conduct of the king, and urged onward by the suggestions of Bothwell and his party, could allow the death of her husband to be hinted in her own presence, with a mere declaration, that they were to do nothing to leave a stain on her honour,—could act towards the weak, illfated victim, in a manner strangely coincident with the wishes and plots of the conspirators—strangely coincident, indeed, if innocent of the intended murder,—and when her husband had been slain, permitted the murderers to escape, sanctioned the mock trial of their chief, and within three months of the fatal field of Kirk could unite herself to Bothwell, whom the intrepid Craig dared to his face to denounce as a ravisher, an adulterer, and a murderer. "I take heaven and earth to witness," said Craig, from the pulpit, "that I abhor and detest this marriage, as odious and slanderous to the world; and I would exhort the faithful to pray earnestly, that a union against all good conscience and reason may yet be overruled by God to the comfort of this unhappy realm." We may wish to call Mary innocent: in the face of the evidence the historian has brought, we fear to do so. Innocence never yet had such a likeness to guilt.

Report of a Syndicate, appointed by the University of Cambridge, "to consider whether any and what steps should be taken to provide a more efficient System of Theological Instruction in the University." Reprinted in the Ecclesiastical Gazette for April.

ALL Churchmen will have noticed this document with much interest. To Cambridge men, the perusal will be at once humiliating and gratifying; humiliating, because the Report shows a grievous deficiency in the present system of the university; gratifying, because it shows that the wisest counsellors of the university feel the deficiency, and are endeavouring gradually and cautiously to supply it. The arrangement of the details of any measure intended for this purpose must be left entirely to those on the spot; but we do not think that any Churchman who is a member of either university can be considered to go beyond his place in offering a few remarks upon the outlines of a plan in which the whole Church and nation are so deeply concerned.

We must first observe, that the Report blends together two things essentially distinct; a provision for securing a certain amount of religious knowledge in every candidate for a degree; and a provision for securing a certain amount of theological knowledge in every graduate who intends to offer himself as a candidate for holy orders. Now, it is most important that each of these objects should be attained; and we rejoice that members of the university so influential as those who have subscribed the Report have applied themselves to the work of contriving means. If we are disposed to feel any thing like regret that they have united the two as parts of the same measure, it is only because we fear that possibly in some quarters the whole plan may thus have been rendered less acceptable. Men who are fully prepared to admit the necessity of a better system of theological training, may hesitate to make the proposed changes in the examination for the degree in arts. However good the last measure may be in itself, we do not see why the success of another measure, quite as important and less likely to be excepted against, should be risked in the same bottom with it. We trust, however, that misgivings on this account are causeless. We will not doubt that each measure will be allowed to stand or fall singly, and by its own merits alone.

We have a few words to say of each portion of the proposed plan; and first, since this is placed first by its proposers, of that which concerns the students in arts generally. It is recommended by the Syndicate, that something more of religious knowledge should be required as a qualification for the bachelor's degree. It may be necessary, as more than one change on this point has taken place within the last twenty years, to state shortly what is required at present by the university. A knowledge of Paley's Evidences and of one of the Gospels in the original is required at the Previous Examination. It has also, we believe, been usual to expect men in that examination to answer *vivâ voce* a few easy questions on the outlines of the Old Testament history. This, be it observed, is *the only* examination in which any attempt is made *by the university* to ascertain the amount of religious knowledge possessed by those *who are candidates for honours*. The final examination for those who are *not* candidates for honours requires a knowledge of the Acts of the Apostles in the Greek, of Paley's Evidences, and of his Moral Philosophy. But let a man only have mathematics enough to pass in honours (or even in "the gulph") at the examination for degrees, and the university neither requires, nor ever takes any step to ascertain whether he possesses, any religious knowledge whatever beyond the modicum necessary to carry him through his "Little Go." It should be added, that particular colleges do not for the most part, nor perhaps can they, far outrun the university in this matter. Some give narrower and others larger opportunities of gaining religious knowledge to those who may please to use them. But, *generally speaking*, they cannot *require*, however they may *encourage*, the possession of much more than the university requires.* We write the confession not without something of shame and sorrow. Surely this is not as it should be. Surely it is indeed time, that those who love and reverence the university which has nurtured them should aid her in removing the

---

* We fear that this statement is in the main correct, though not applicable without some qualification to *all* colleges. We fully believe that most would gladly do more than they do, if they were borne out by the example and requirements of the university. We can speak with much thankfulness of what is done, even when it *seems* but little.

reproach. We are most thankful that some of her wisest and most faithful sons are at length striving to do so.

Let us not for a moment seem to forget that religious education and the imparting of religious knowledge are two different things, and that a want of adequate attention to the one does not necessarily imply the absence of the other. If christian education be an education which is fitted to be the means of forming a christian character, no doubt liturgies, and the hearing of the written word of God as read in the course of the Church's year, and sermons, and the many other influences, unseen, perhaps, and scarcely felt, of College life and institutions, hold an equally important place in it with the communication of directly religious knowledge. Let it be confessed, with all humble thankfulness, that a Cambridge education is indeed, as it professes to be, a religious one to those who will receive it. But let it not, on the other hand, be forgotten, that, if the character is to be rightly formed, there must be some due proportion kept between the different ingredients in the portion of knowledge which is furnished to the mind. Those whose minds are scantily informed or imperfectly awakened with regard to all the other parts of the great field of truth, may perhaps be ignorant also of all beyond the first simple elements of religious truth, and yet be comparatively safe. But it is not so with those whom our universities are training as the future leaders and cultivators of the mind of their country. Who shall measure the evil that may and must follow, if, while their minds are keenly awake and richly stored with all other knowledge, they are left unfurnished with that knowledge concerning God and his ways towards man, without which all other truth is seen as disjointed and displaced? They are then almost sure to be the victims of half truths, of specious falsehoods, or, worst of all, of self-satisfied and contemptuous indifference, whenever they come to act, or speak, or think, as all men in this day must, in matters bearing upon religious truth and its consequences. If we would save them from this deadly mischief, their own and their country's bane, let us take care to propose to their mind, and bring home to their conscience, religious truth and its evidence in their great outline at least. We would appeal to the conscience and observation of any Cambridge man, whether he cannot trace, in himself and in others, manifold evil consequences of the want of such instruction. If this is so, we trust that the principle at least of the proposed additions to the undergraduates' courses will be generally received by those who care for the university.

What is proposed is, some may think, after all rather too little than too much. It is recommended to require a complete knowledge of Old Testament history at the " Little Go." And in the final examination, instead of requiring, as at present, the whole book of Acts, to require half of that book,* with one of the longer or two of

---

* The former and the latter half alternately.

the shorter Epistles; and instead of the whole of Paley's Moral Philosophy, to require half, with a small portion of Church history. It is proposed, in the second place, that *all* candidates for the B.A. degree shall be required to pass this part of the examination.—As we have already said, we leave details to be considered by residents. Only we will venture to suggest, (should it be objected to that part of the arrangement which will affect men going out in honours, that it is undesirable to distract and overburden them by adding to the number and variety of the subjects which engage them,) that *possibly* the scriptural subjects need not be made a part of the final B.A. examination, but be taken alone some time previously. But whatever arrangement of the exact time and manner and subjects of examination may be judged best, it is our earnest desire that *some* plan, having the same object with the proposed one, may speedily be sanctioned by the senate. We are of course aware, that the *direct* effect of any such measure in widening the extent and raising the tone of religious knowledge, strictly so called, cannot be great.— Even doctrinal questions will and ought to be introduced but sparingly into any academical examination; and anything having a more directly personal reference we should be first to exclude, if any one could dream of including it. But that all on whom the university is to set her stamp of approval should be required to know thoroughly the History of the Bible, and be made to trace the witness which It bears to the teaching of the Church in her creeds, her services, and her formularies,—even this we hold to be no small gain. And though examinations should not go beyond this, lectures might and would, and wherever lecturers were in earnest (and of such lecturers Cambridge would furnish many) with the happiest effect.

Let us, in leaving this part of the subject, hint at one consideration, which makes the course taken by the university in this matter the object of most anxious interest to ourselves and to many others. All who discern the times are aware of one great danger which impends over educated men. The danger is not yet alarmingly visible, but it is near; and when it comes, woe to us if we are not fore-armed with an antidote. The pantheistic and critical spirit and its workings, will not long be unknown amongst us, except as an object of blind horror and contempt, under the vague name of rationalism. The readers of German have long since trespassed on this forbidden ground, and have brought back with them of the fruits of the land to impart to the less venturesome. Already works most deeply tinctured with the poison are circulated in translations, sometimes under respectable sanction, in England and America; not without effect on the minds of men whom we can ill afford to have perverted. How shall we guard against the danger? By books of evidences Alas! all our standard books of this kind are aimed at objections and a state of mind so different, that against the new enemy they would be useless as some antique engine of war against cannon upon a modern battle-field. What, then, is the antidote? Simply, we believe, to acquaint educated men thoroughly with the Scriptures themselves. Ingenuous minds cannot but feel as they read them the *reality* of what they read. Their conscience will respond to their claim of authority. So habituated, when afterwards Germans, or Germanized Englishmen, (like their models more often in presumptuousness than in learning,) talk to them of myths and idealities, they will *feel* the falsehood of the teaching. Their healthy appetite will loathe and reject the offered drug. We are persuaded that no other mode of treatment can be effectual, and are most anxious that Cambridge should do its part in applying it.

We have now to notice shortly the second part of the proposed scheme—that which concerns the theological instruction of graduates designed for holy orders. We are met here by a preliminary question. Is it desirable that the university should continue to undertake the office of giving theological instruction, or that small theological seminaries, like those at Chichester and at Wells, should be established for this purpose exclusively? Each plan has its advantages. For the latter, it may be urged, that for many men it is most desirable that they should be removed from Cambridge as soon as possible after taking their degree, and have the opportunity of forming in a new place new habits of life and thought; that, generally speaking, some change of scene and associations is almost necessary to bring the mind of a man only just freed from the trammels of undergraduateship into a fit condition to study theology profitably; that, in such an academy, opportunities are given for gaining a practical knowledge of parochial duties such as is unattainable in Cambridge. Other reasons may, doubtless, be alleged, and are well worthy of consideration. On the other hand, it may be urged, that in Cambridge there will be reason to expect a more learned and complete course of theological instruction than any one man (and more than one man duly qualified cannot perhaps be hoped for to preside over each cathedral seminary) having the entire charge of several students can give; while the management of a parish might be better learnt afterwards, during the period of deaconhood, than it can be in any seminary.* On this question, however, we will only remark in passing, that it does seem to us most important for the life and healthiness *even of their theology*, to engage men in some department of the actual work of ministering to others, as soon as possible after they begin to study theology. The plan which we should ourselves perhaps be inclined to prefer would be one which should, after laying for the student the foundation of sound theological knowledge, send him for some time where, under the guidance of an experienced parish priest, he might have a share, but not (as

---

* We beg to refer to Mr. Perry's pamphlet for some remarks on this point, and on the general question.

too often happens now) an engrossing and overwhelming share, of ministerial work, his main employment being study. But we do not think it at all necessary to decide generally between the two plans. Each, doubtless, is good in itself, if well administered. Each, doubtless, will and ought to be considered preferable to the other in some cases. But the university would strangely abandon her duty, and descend from her high station, if she should ever cease to offer the best possible theological instruction to the many who will always seek it from her. Some plan, therefore, having the same end with that proposed ought to be advocated even by those whose preference for the cathedral system is strongest.

For here also much must be done before the actual system of theological instruction administered by the university is worthy of her. True, much is done already; as the abstracts appended to the Report sufficiently prove. The lectures of the Lady Margaret's and Norrisian Professors are, no doubt, in their respective departments, most valuable. Would that infirm health and multiplied other engagements did not deprive the University, so far as *lectures* are concerned, of the deep and accurate learning, the searching penetration, the calm and clear judgment, of her Regius Professor! But then it must be remembered that at present no means whatever are taken to secure that the divinity students shall, or to ascertain whether they do, profit by their opportunities of instruction. Until a very few years ago, the lectures of the Norrisian Professor (often the only professor who gave lectures, and the one whose certificate alone was required as a qualification for ordination) were usually attended by men during their undergraduateship, often by freshmen, who had no thought of beginning to *read* theology for a long time to come; scarcely any one attended more than twenty lectures out of a course of fifty; no means whatever were taken to ascertain whether any one of the twenty heard had been listened to. Attendance upon the lectures of either of the other professors, when such were given, (and occasionally most valuable ones were given,*) was entirely voluntary. What reform may have been effected within the last few years we do not exactly know. We fear that at present some of the worst evils remain, and *will* remain until, as is now proposed, the mere certificate of attendance on the lectures is exchanged for a certificate of having shown a competent acquaintance with their subject. This change, surely, is one which scarcely requires argument to support it. The regulations proposed for the contemplated examination appear to us simple and satisfactory. Above all we are glad to see, that no one appears to think of any plan of classification which could introduce the spirit of competition into theological study. Indeed, as we have already said, we think that this second part of the plan embodied in

---

* A course by the Bishop of Lincoln, when Regius Professor, contained the substance of his valuable works on the writings of the early Fathers. The present Professor gave one short course in continuation in the spring of 1834; but was compelled by ill-health and other hindrances to leave his plan unfinished.

the Report is much less open to doubt in matters of detail than the first. We cordially desire its immediate acceptance.

At the same time we must, with all deference, point out what seems to us a great defect. We are much surprised that it should have been left, and trust that it will be supplied in some way. *The proposed plan does not appear to provide for the delivery of any course of lectures to theological students on the text of Scripture.* The Norrisian Professor gives at present in his lectures, and will continue to do so, a general introduction to Anglican theology. The Lady Margaret's Professor lectures on the history of the early Church, and on parochial ministrations. The Professor of Casuistry will give a survey of *moral* theology. But no mention is made, so far as we can find, of any plan by which the benefit of a thorough course of exegetic instruction can be secured. Now, it seems to us, that this is the very department of theological study in which lectures are most required, and are likely to be most useful. Nothing is so difficult as to find a really satisfactory commentary, at once sound in doctrine, learned in criticism, and hearty in its religious spirit. Indeed we really do not know of any which even attempts to unite these three indispensable requisites, and could scarcely suggest any convenient combination of different commentaries which should possess them in any high degree. Surely, even on this account alone it is most desirable that students should have the opportunity of attending good expository lectures. Nothing, again, could be so likely to give us in due time good commentaries as making it the constant employment of some of our best divines to interpret Scripture in lectures. Let us remember, moreover, that the best conceivable commentary could never command the attention and affect the conscience like the eye and voice of a living man whose heart is in his subject. Nor, again, can any but an authoritative *living* commentary keep men from *neglecting* the scriptural evidence for truths which, without *rejecting* them, they are indisposed to *receive*. The need, therefore, would not cease, though it would be diminished, if commentaries were better than they are, or if it should be granted that we cannot be certain that the spoken commentary would *always* surpass or equal the printed one. It was once hoped, that we might have seen a professor of exegetical theology maintained by the revenues of one of the ravished stalls of Ely. But though this hope has vanished, we trust that we shall yet see the want of such lectures supplied, by the university, if possible; or, if not, by each college for itself. Surely it cannot have been meant by the authors of the Report, that the lectures given in each college to undergraduates on the portions of Scripture required for the B.A. degree should serve also for the theological students.

We write the more earnestly on this point, because we are persuaded that our modern theology fails and is in danger here more than elsewhere. We live in a time when much has been and is talked about Scripture and being scriptural, but not in an age much given to the *study* of the Scriptures. We say it with much shame for ourselves and our brethren, that, whilst the words of Scripture are a familiar sound in the ears of us all, and a certain sort of *reading* of the Bible (not unprofitable even alone; but far less profitable so, than if joined with patient *study*) is perhaps commoner than it ever was amongst men in general, we fear that few of us indeed, whether amongst the priests or the people, are *habitual, thoughtful, submissive* STUDENTS of Scripture. What we hold and what we teach as scriptural truth was for the most part neither at first suggested to our minds in the study of Scripture, (indeed, as to most of the fundamental truths, the Bible was not meant to be the first *suggester* of truth; that office belongs, in the appointment of God, to parents and spiritual pastors, and catechisms and creeds,) nor has it been *verified* by humble and persevering and extensive search into Scripture, with prayer that we might be enabled to discern the truth there. But rather it has been first suggested to us either by some private fancy of our own, or by the words of some self-chosen human guide, and then *countenanced* rather than *confirmed* by a few passages culled often hastily and partially, while all which militates against our own views is explained away or put out of sight. We do not say this in reproach of any one set of men in or out of the Church, but as a humbling truth concerning ourselves and too many on all sides of us. Where shall the remedy be found? Many things might contribute much to diminish the prevalence of the evil. But the grand remedy surely must be, to secure that the foundation of our theological studies shall be laid in a comprehensive and careful examination of the Scriptures under faithful guidance. Let the grand outline of revealed truth be laid before the student in the creeds, which not one age or set of Christians, but the general body of the Church in every age, has accepted and transmitted as embodying it faithfully; let him be accustomed first to trace in the holy volume the scattered lineaments of the form so shadowed to him, and then to search for the true meaning of *every* portion of the Bible from first to last; let him be trained to do this, as a work which he is never to have finished, and to which all he reads and thinks and sees is to be subservient; let this be the discipline to which the minds of our future theologians are subjected, and we shall then trust to see a sounder and riper theology prevail. More than all, we shall see men wiser to win souls, and abler to build them up to perfection. Thus believing, we wish all success to every well-considered scheme for promoting a better knowledge of the Scriptures, whether amongst the private members or the ministers of the Church. We think the proposed scheme defective on this side; but hope to see the defect wisely supplied. Even as it stands, we think it likely to be of much use, and shall watch its progress anxiously.

The Second Book of the Travels of Nicander Nucius, of Corcyra, edited from the Original Greek MS. in the Bodleian Library, with an English Translation, by the Rev. J. A. CRAMER, D.D., *Principal of New Inn Hall, and Public Orator in the University of Oxford. Printed for the Camden Society.* London, 1841.

THE remarks of foreigners on our own country, however unfit the writer may be for the task he has imposed on himself, must always be interesting to us. And although we undoubtedly feel a greater degree of interest in learning how England appears to a stranger in the present day, when all events seem magnified in their importance, still much interest will always attach to such remarks, even of the most insignificant, on the sayings and doings of our ancestors. With some such views as these, the learned member of the Camden Society has sanctioned, by his name and his superintendence, the travels of a Corcyrean in England during the reign of Henry the Eighth. And though Dr. Cramer has been prevented from giving more than a general superintendence to the work, the care which he has shown in the selection of his coadjutor has prevented the recurrence of any of those careless errors, either in the translation or the notes, which have characterized some of the previous productions of this Society. In another respect this small work is superior to many of its predecessors, namely, in the general absence of that grossness which so generally pervades our older writings, and in having an editor who, instead of rendering these defects the more glaring by parallel quotations of a similar nature, has passed them over without comment, and concealed it as far as possible by the delicacy of his translation.

Of the writer of this work we know little or nothing, save that he accidentally met, when at Venice, one Gerardus, a native of Flanders, on his way to Constantinople, as chief of an embassy from Charles the Fifth to the Sultan Solyman; and that, by attaching himself to the train of his friend, he travelled over the greater portion of the Continent, and eventually passed over to England, where Gerardus was commissioned by his royal master to proceed on matters of moment to the English court. His wanderings in Turkey, Germany, and Italy, form the first book of his Travels, and the learned editor would no doubt have endeavoured to supply that deficiency which the Laudian MS. presents, from the more perfect copy in the Ambrosian Library at Venice, had he not been prevented by one of those many instances which the foreigners afford us of the theoretical and by no means practical nature of their politeness.

"It would have been more satisfactory," says Dr. Cramer, "to have inspected myself the Ambrosian MS., and to have completed from its more ample contents the deficiency of the Oxford copy; but my engagements not permitting me to leave England, the Rev. C. Balston, of Corpus Christi

College, in this University, in his way through Milan, in the summer of 1840, obligingly undertook to inspect the MS. and to obtain, if possible, for me a transcript of the portion wanting in ours. Mr. Balston readily obtained a sight of the MS., and ascertained, from a comparison of its contents, that the deficiency of the Oxford copy amounted to about eight or ten pages; and he was enabled also to inform me, which was of consequence, that the second book of Nicander alone related to the history of England. He was, however, unable to obtain the desired transcript; nor was a subsequent application, made through the Laudian Professor of Arabic, more successful, *it being intimated in reply to that gentleman, as a reason for withholding a copy, that there was an intention, on the part of one of the officers of the Ambrosian Library, of publishing the work in question.*"—Introduction, p. 7.

Supposing that when Professor Von Raumer was in England, not so long since, and applied to the government for permission to ransack the stores of our State Paper Office, he had received an intimation that he could not be allowed to transcribe any of the letters, as one of the keepers of the papers was about to publish a work relating to the reign of Elizabeth; what would the foreign journals have said? Suppose, too, that when the same indefatigable transcriber was about to copy out some of the secrets of the Harleian MSS. in our Museum, he had been most politely refused permission, because Sir Henry Ellis or Sir Frederick Madden were about to publish the same materials; what would not the foreigners have said? Or if, when Professor Ewald gathered so much information from the Eastern MSS. in the Bodleian, he had been politely informed by the late librarian that he might look, but not copy, because *he* was about to put forward a work on the same point; would not the learned professor have had a good reason for believing in the "unpolite nation of English?" Dr. Cramer, however, has contrived to afford us some account of the first book of the Travels, and has given, in his introduction, some extracts from the work, relating to Luther, the anabaptists, coal mines, and fire damps. As a literary curiosity we subjoin Nicander's account of the mines at Liege, wherein the phenomenon of the fire-damp, heightened by the superstitious fears of the rude miners, forms a picturesque scene, such as the father of history would have delighted to have sketched:

"In this city, Liege, and all the neighbouring country, they are accustomed to burn a certain black substance, stony and shining, and producing hot embers without smoke. But when the coal has been consumed, it yields no cinders, but a very fine dust is scattered through the air. These stones they dig out of the deepest recesses of the earth, finding certain veins from which they extract them; but a peculiar prodigy takes place when they are being dug out. When they meet with this mineral they form a spacious cavern, but they are unable to throw out the stones immediately, for fire on a sudden bursts forth and encompasses the whole cavern. When the miners are desirous of extracting the coal, they put on a linen garment, which has neither been bleached nor dipped in water. This covers them from head to foot, leaving only certain apertures for the eyes, that they may be able to see through them; they also take a staff in their hands, which serves to guide and direct their steps in the passage leading to the cave. The miner then draws near the fire, and frightens it with his staff.

The fire then flies away, and contracts itself by little and little: having then expended itself, it collects itself together in a surprising manner, and becoming very small remains quite still in a corner. But it behoves the man who wears the linen garment to stand over the flame when at rest, always terrifying it with his staff. Whilst he performs this service, the miners extract the stones. As soon as they have left the cave the dormant fire on a sudden bursts forth, and environs the whole cave. No one then ventures to enter without the above-mentioned garment and staff, for he would inevitably be consumed. . . . . But the most surprising thing is, that when the fire has retired, and the violence of the flame is quenched, instead of being exceedingly hot, it renders the cave of a gentle heat, and capable of being approached. And they call these stones, in the language of the country, '*oulleis.*' And whilst they are burning, no great or bright flame is emitted, but red and blue; and this lasts for about eight hours, and possesses somewhat of a sulphureous nature."—Introduction, p. 20.

Such were the facts from actual experience of this admirer of Nature and of her marvels; and with such a readiness of belief, he came to England, where he seems to have directed his chief attention to ecclesiastical matters; and having in a short stay noted down as many mistakes in history and chronology as the famous Count Smaltork, he dedicated the record to his dear friend, one Nicolaus Cornelius.

About the middle of the year 1545 our Corcyrean traveller embarked at Calais for England, and when within a short distance of our shores, was driven back by a violent storm to the harbour of Newport in Flanders, whence he once more departed with the ambassador, and disembarked at Dover, where he says, " was built a small town, full of inns; and a certain fort stands erected for the protection of the harbour." Greenwich next received them, where they remained for a few days with the court, and then removed to London, where they were lodged near the king's palace. The palaces of London; the houses and turrets on its bridge; the great cities of Antonia, Danebium, Bristol, and Dartenicum; the mansions of the nobles and the merchants; the royal palaces; the gardens; the pavements; the white tower and its unnumbered treasures, equal to those of Midas and Crœsus; and the arsenal at Greenwich—all come in for their meed of applause from Nicander; whilst his eastern habits and feelings are annoyed by the position assumed by our ladies, and the presence of the fair sex as dealers and buyers in the markets. Of the bills of exchange, which were then in use, he gives a curious account, and fails not to note our enmity to our Gallic neighbours, our hospitality among ourselves, and the turbulence of our city mobs.

" The race of men," he says, " are exceeding fair, inclining to a light colour; in their persons they are tall and erect; the hair of their beard and head is of a golden colour; their eyes blue, for the most part, and their cheeks ruddy; they are martial and valorous, and generally tall; flesh eaters, and insatiable of animal food; sottish and unrestrained in their appetites; full of suspicion. But towards their king they are wonderfully well affected; nor would any one of them endure hearing any thing disrespectful of the king, through the honour they bear him; so that the most binding oath that is taken by them is that by which the 'king's life' has been pledged."—P. 16.

The Scotch and their country are next noted by our traveller, who, having given a passing sketch of the barbarous and unsettled state of that country, the general productions of the island, and the breeds of cattle encouraged in it, amongst which he particularises "white horses," passes on to Ireland, the fabled land of Hades and the gates of the infernal regions. The short description which he gives of this country, the savage nature of the life of the people, the fertility of its neglected soil, the rejection by its inhabitants of every political institution or improvement that was not of native growth, and their reckless bravery in battle, is completely borne out by the best contemporary authorities, and by no means exaggerated by the Corcyrean visiter.

We shall not delay our readers over our voyager's wonderful accounts of the Orcades, or the unmanageable sea; nor even of the porpoises which at that day formed a staple dish at our feasts. Nor can we do more than notice the salted fish, that requires to be beaten on an anvil before it is cooked; nor the winged fish with a beak, and feet like a duck, drawn from the recesses of the sea, and whose blood, when killed in the water, becomes of the colour of the element in which it dies, and to which there is no voice, but only a voluble croak. All these, and more veritable facts, which our writer saw with his own eyes, cannot be dilated on now, as we would rather make a few extracts from his notices of the religious state of the country at that time.

Of the monks, Nicander is no admirer; "they hesitated not," he says, "in the plenitude of their power, to domineer over the people, and to treat with contempt their kings. Their retinues were like those rather of nobles and warriors than of God's priests; and when their rights were threatened, or their encroachments attacked, the lives of their kings were endangered." The value of this writer's authority may be fairly judged by the following extracts, in which he relates how the monks deliberately killed Rufus, and gives his account of the contest between Becket and Henry.

"They oftentimes contended even against their own kings. And on one occasion, when one of these sovereigns had devised how to repress these things, and had wished to order them in a more becoming manner, they deprived him of life by a violent death. Now the circumstances of the action were as follows:—The king, then being on a hunting excursion, and having been left alone, as is wont to happen on such occasions, and having obtained some rest from his toils, tied his horse by the bridle to a shady tree; and having stretched himself on the grass, fell asleep. And two of those of the fraternity of such as are called monks, from a certain monastery that happened to be some where close by, accidentally came upon the monarch while asleep. And having discovered who he was, they proceeded to their principal, and made known to him the particulars respecting the king. And he, without hesitation, despatched two of the boldest of the fraternity with bows and arrows, having given them injunctions that they should deprive the king of life by whatever means they were able, as calumniating their mode of life. These, therefore, set off in all haste and despatch, and slew with their arrows the monarch while asleep, and returned to their principal to report to him the issue of the enterprise. No long time having intervened, some of the king's attendants, seeking him, discovered him, still breathing; and being unable to find out who were the perpetrators of this deed, they removed the dead body of the king to London; and having consigned it to the tomb, they appointed his son to reign in his stead."—Pp. 34—35.

It was hardly fair of those courtiers—if they knew better—who were no doubt very ready in instilling in the stranger's mind the enormities and iniquities of the monks, in order to make a fair case in defence of their own and their patron's late spoliations; it was too great a trick on a traveller, to tell him that the son of an unmarried king came to our throne, and to convert a younger brother—but a few years younger—into the son of the victim of the monks. King John, too, according to Nicander, was also another victim of these murderous king-slayers; but as our author has not recorded who his successor was, and had at least a faint tradition in favour of his tale, he has made only an addition to the story, by burning the monastery and all the monks, from whose fraternity the poisoner had come. Surely they must have been joking with the Corcyrean when they told him the following veritable history of Thomas-à-Becket:—

"It is also proper to relate what pertains to Thomas, *formerly bishop of London*, and canonized as a saint by the Roman pontiff, who ordained annual honours to be performed, both rites and sacred orations, as being one of the distinguished saints. *For this Thomas, commonly known by the surname of " Canterbury,"* was said to be nobly descended of the island; and therefore, *having been titled Bishop of London*, he perpetually contended with the *kings* of England; and appeared to favour, as far as he was able, and increase the power of the Roman pontiff; and therefore the then ruling sovereign of England being incensed at his opposition, *beheaded him with the sword*. Wherefore the Roman pontiff, having been greatly offended, conferred honours on Thomas; and by a decree of the Church declared him to be a saint and a hero, and decreed an annual rite and sacred orations should be offered to him. Whence, throughout all his diocese, they venerate this man as a distinguished saint. Henry, therefore, wishing to know in what manner the Roman pontiff had voted him a saint, having investigated all the circumstances of his life, which had occurred *more than 150 years previously* (rather more), and having then thoroughly inquired into the particulars respecting him, he appointed judges; and having instituted commissioners, he commanded that they should investigate the truth, *and should neither seek, by their decision, to gratify the king nor Thomas*, although the greater part regarded him as a saint. Hence, verily, they devoted two years to the inquiry, each one giving his decision as he thought just. But at last those chosen to decide condemned Thomas as having been opposed to the kings of that time, and disloyal and refractory; and they passed a vote of censure against him as a *rebel and a revolutionist*. Wherefore Henry, as being successor to the kings of former ages, condemned Thomas as a rebel and a pest to his country, and gave orders to commit to the fire the coffin which contained his remains. Whence those appointed to this quickly fulfilled the order they had received. Wherefore one might see the remains, formerly honoured as those of a saint, and consecrated, both dragged along the public road, and exposed to the gaze of the populace; and, as one may say, treated with every indignity, and committed to the fire in the middle of the city, and reduced to ashes; *and having put the ashes into a cannon,* they discharged them *into the air.*"—Pp. 73—75.

By our traveller the impostures of the various fraternities of monks are largely and minutely brought forth. The famous Rood of Grace of Boxley becomes the subject of a strange story of a crucifix filled with mechanism, the work of an artificer of Antwerp, buried by the monks, and after a due revelation, by a dream, disinterred amid burning and flashing lights from the earth, and hailed by the prayers of the monks, and the acclamations of the deceived people; and at last discovered by the accidental arrival of the workman from Antwerp, who failed not to recognise his own handiwork, and to acquaint the king of the imposition. The Maid of Kent is changed from a political plot to a mere piece of jugglery for the enriching of a monastery; the monks of which were wont to reveal to the old woman the secrets of the confessional, and then refer every person to her as to a saint. The facts of which she had thus obtained the knowledge, she failed not to declare to each penitent as he came before her, under the form of a heavenly revelation of their sins to her from God; and at the same time, to benefit her patrons, the monks, by replying to the question, " What, then, shall we do?" " Do good to God's most faithful servants, the monks of this monastery, who day and night hold converse with God, and exhibit on earth an angelic mode of life." Such, however, as the friends of the Corcyrean at court no doubt were, did not stop at the charge of pious frauds; offences the most fearful, the most unnatural, are alleged by him against monks, and nuns, without an exemption in favour of any single person or convent. The views of the king's party on this subject, Nicander has collected together in a set speech, which he makes Henry deliver to his council, previous to requiring their aid in the destruction of the monasteries and convents, and the confiscation of the possessions of these religious houses. Were our traveller's information on other points more trustworthy, we might be inclined to believe that the following speech was a relic of the oratory of the reforming king; such as it is we give the report, prefacing it with the words of the father of history, when heralding a respectable wonder, " ἡμῖν οὐ πιστὰ λέγοντες—λέγουσι δέ."

" Councillors and peers of my empire, some of you will, no doubt, wonder at my having thus unwontedly and unexpectedly summoned you, and that I have called you together in the winter season and during such a frost; when, however, ye have heard the reason for which I have summoned you, ye will probably applaud our foresight. In truth, sirs, it is no common stormy season that has fallen upon us; nay, the severest of stormy seasons; for this, which is the object of sense, both by reason of its passing away and changing to spring, transmutes the frostiness and keenness of the air to days of sunshine and calm: but the storm which has befallen us shows no change, either of season or time; but rather increases in winter and spring, and has no thoughts of intermission. For it causes no ordinary inundation; nay, one so great, that the only hope of the kingdom which was left to us, this it hastens to overwhelm. But what then is the storm? and who is he that raises it? No, even to you, perhaps, does he seem unknown. Look, then, O Sirs, at the tribe of them that are called monks; how it having been devised by men of old, in order that men might live upon the earth a mode of life like unto that of angels, on which principles of sublime policy, and divine elevation of the mind, and contempt of the world and the things of the world, and inspired wisdom dwelling in the heart, it has been most excellently ordained, and agreeably with the divine will, and very many persons throughout the world have participated in it; but to so great a degree has it daily declined, through those who abuse things honourable, and to such a depth has it sunk, that it not only gives offence to considerate men, but now also, at times, justly incenses against us the All-seeing Eye, and is leading the multitude into disorders of no ordinary kind."—Pp. 64, 65.

Such is the proemium of bluff King Hal's speech, according to the Corcyrean; to all appearances more like a studied copy one from Xenophon or Procopius, than from our hot-headed and hasty monarch. After a little more figure the king gets to business; accuses the monks wholesale and retail, and in no wise falls below the most approved language of the day; in that particular cautiously letting out that one reason for their downfal was their disobedience to the royal commands; yet, at the same time, mixing this cause among so many more, as to reduce it, in appearance, to a mere trifle in the account. This, however, is not the only speech of the king's with which Nicander favours us, seeing he notes down an equally long and flowery oration from the monarch in defence of the national rejection of the supremacy of the Roman See.

After a rather confused account of the war between Francis and Henry, and the wonders of the cloth of gold, our traveller accompanies the royal forces in their inroad into Scotland, gravely assuring us that certain Argives, from Peloponnese, fought in the king's army; meaning, most probably, some Venetian Stradiotes. Here the present mutilated MS. leaves Nicander, and here we must leave him, until the politeness of the learned librarian of the Ambrosian Library shall enable the world to learn what new wonders the more elaborate MS. in that collection can bring forth. May we hope that the council of the Camden Society have now been well satiated with curious, and will henceforth endeavour to publish useful, antiquities.

The History of the Christian Religion and Church, &c. By Dr. AUGUSTUS NEANDER. *Translated by* HENRY J. ROSE, B.D. &c. Vol. II. Rivingtons. 1841.

History of the Planting and Training of the Christian Church by the Apostles. By Dr. AUGUSTUS NEANDER, &c. &c. *Translated from the Third Edition of the Original German*, by J. E. RYLAND. *In* 2 *vols.* Edinburgh: Clark. 1842.

THERE is hardly any German writer, so many of whose works have been translated into English, or been received among us with so much favour, as Dr. A. Neander. The intellect of the author is so powerful, his learning so varied, and the spirit of his works in many respects so beautiful and good, that it would have been ill done and ungracious in us, not to have given them something like a welcome. To our shame be it said, we had no books of our own that treated in any living way of the manners and condition of the early Christians. Long as our great standard divines had been in the habit of appealing to them, it was new and refreshing to us to find a historian dealing with them in a generous spirit. Moreover, there is a tendency in England to be very indulgent to any Germans who give indications of a spiritual and believing temper, and to make comparatively light of their aberrations from orthodoxy. We feel that what is right in them is too unexpected, and are too thankful for it, to have much to say about what is wrong. Nor ought it to be otherwise with us: their situation claims every allowance we can make; while their superiority in many gifts and graces to ourselves, in spite of all their disadvantages, may well check our tendency to censure. But, though it is right to make every allowance for such a man as Dr. Neander, and to learn from him those lessons which he is so qualified to teach, let us be careful to keep our eyes open. We need not be censorious on one whom we are neither called to judge, nor with whom we have at present any practical relations, but neither on the one hand need we, or should we forget, in how many things he falls short of our standard of orthodoxy, in how many a bold speculation he indulges, such as we cannot approve, how many things he disbelieves, to which we attach (as we think deservedly) a very high importance. Nor is our caution confined to Churchmen. Should these remarks meet the eye of any dissenter, we beg to assure him that we are alluding to other things besides the priesthood and the apostolical succession. Our brethren of the separation are at present hailing, and, as the titles at the head of our article show, translating Neander. They had need to take care what they are doing. He ventures on many a speculation, pursues many a criticism, and disbelieves (in the common form) many an incident of sacred history, all of which exhibitions indicate a temper at which we trust they have not yet arrived. It will come on them, however, unless they give heed beforehand. If they welcome and delight in the works of Dr. Neander, under the previous impression that he comes up, or nearly comes up to *their* standard of orthodoxy, they will soon find that standard to go far down.

We do not mean, however, to enter on any analysis of this author's writings, or to point out the various defects which ought to put his readers on their guard. Our intention, at present, is to resume two subjects, to the further consideration of which we pledged ourselves, when we had occasion to touch upon them in our January number—those of the Christian Priesthood, and Eucharistic Sacrifice. On one of them, as our readers must know, Dr. Neander takes very strong views, which appear continually throughout such of his writings as are read in England. The whole notion of a priesthood in the new covenant is, according to him, a corruption resulting from a confusion of Jewish with christian ideas; nay, he goes so far as to stigmatize the institution of a separate class of clergy, as post-apostolic and unevangelic.

In this latter opinion we do not think he is likely to have many English followers, even among the sects; nor any at all, we should imagine, in the Church. The former, however, has some little prevalence. Not merely the Archbishop of Dublin, and Dr. Arnold, but others less at war with established opinions, are prone to remind us that the clergy are ministers, elders, and overseers, but cannot, consistently with the principles of the New Testament, be *priests*, in the sense which the word priest bears as standing for *sacerdos* and ἱερεύς.

Let us consider the arguments on which this opinion, at variance as it must be admitted to be with ordinary prepossessions, is founded. On the whole, they are the following:—

1st. That the word *priest*, which is used in the Prayer Book to denote the second order of the ministry, comes from πρεσβύτερος, which has no connexion whatever with ἱερεύς,—that it is in fact only an abbreviation of *presbyter*; and that whereas in the New Testament, the ministers of the gospel are styled apostles, bishops, presbyters, as the case may be, none of them is ever called an ἱερεύς.

2d. That in the new covenant there is, and there can be, but one ἱερεύς, our Lord Jesus Christ, who offered the one true sacrifice, and is the anti-type of all previous priesthood; and that, consequently, for any one after Him to pretend to the priesthood is blasphemy against his prerogative.

3d. That in the only sense in which the word priest (as translating ἱερεὺς) can be applied to any besides Him, it belongs to all Christians, who are all "kings and priests unto God," consecrated to offer spiritual sacrifices; and that consequently for one class of Christians to claim a distinction in this respect is to invade the rights of Christ's people, and to lower their standard of living, inasmuch as it leads them to believe that they are not so pledged and consecrated to a holy life as certain others.

We will take these arguments in their order.

I. For the name *Presbyter*, which is distinguished from that of ἱερεύς.—This argument is apt to strike those to whom it is new as a great discovery, which settles the question. But if our readers will duly weigh it, we think they will find it somewhat less cogent than they may have at first been disposed to consider it. From the bold way in which it is stated, one might fancy there was some inherent relationship between the words presbyter and sacerdos, admitting of their being set one against the other; that they were of the same kind, but opposites in that kind, so that the applicability of the one excluded that of the other. It is forgotten that presbyter is merely a title of respect, and in itself by no means descriptive; that it, or one of the same meaning, has been naturally given to office-bearers of various kinds—to certain functionaries among the Jews, among the Christians, among the members of civic corporations in England. One of kindred import denoted the most dignified and venerable branches of the Roman commonwealth. So completely is the meaning of the title elder one merely of respect, that all over Western Europe we employ it whenever we do not feel entitled to use a familiar address, and there is no other especial title to be given.* It is, therefore, a most natural name of honour to confer on any official whose function is one of gravity and dignity; but it describes nothing of that function except such gravity and dignity. It is also beautifully appropriate as a religious title, inasmuch as all the thoughts it awakens are those of relationship and brotherhood. Indeed, out of such, it seems to have had its origin. At present, we must return to that immediately concerning us, that it is not descriptive of office. Among the Jews, we know of at least two kinds of elders,—those associated in council with Moses, and the elders of the synagogue in after-time. In the New Testament we also find indications of two different kinds. So that, whilst all this made it highly natural for the christian community to select such a designation for a class of their gravest functionaries, it remains still to be settled what that function was, which made it natural to give this title of honour to the men who discharged it.

And the force of this consideration will become greater, if we consider that the names usually applied to the two other orders are descriptive of office; while that given to the second is not. Deacons are altogether what their name imports; and so are bishops: the word *episcopus* does describe a part of the bishop's office. But as, besides his duties of oversight, he and the presbyters have a function in common, which is described by neither of their usual titles, (that of *episcopus*, being only partially descriptive, and that of *presbyter* not at all,) we are still to seek for this: and this, whatever it may turn out to be, is what the Fathers meant by the *priesthood*. This is an important circumstance to keep in mind, as inattention to it has caused much confusion. With us, the word *priest* is used to denote one of the orders of the ministry, from whose ancient designation, in fact, it etymologically comes. In the early Church, it designated no one order—being no part of the sentence, *episcopi*, *presbyteri*, and *diaconi*, but was a separate name, given in their measure and degree to the two former of

---

* We suppose, *Sir*, comes from Signor, as that obviously does from *senior*.

these,* in respect of certain functions which they had in common. The ἱερεύς, or *sacerdos*, of the early Church meant either bishop or priest; and, (the former being then the principal minister of the word and sacraments,) if it were used without particular relation, would more naturally be understood of the bishop. It is most futile, therefore, to pit the two names *sacerdos* and *presbyter* against each other, seeing that they are not in sufficient relation together to be opposites, so as that the one shall exclude the other.

But it may be said, although the argument drawn from the distinction between *presbyter* and *sacerdos* must be given up, the applicability of the latter to the two upper orders of the ministry remains yet to be proved; and against such applicability, the silence of Scripture tends very powerfully. Nowhere, in the New Testament, do we find any minister of the new dispensation styled an ἱερεύς. This is certainly true; but the argument drawn from it is nullified by the circumstance to which we alluded in January,—that, although nowhere styled ἱερεῖς, they are described as acting the parts of such. Thus the prophets and teachers at Antioch were engaged in *liturgic* duties, λειτουργούντων δὲ αὐτῶν &c., when the Spirit commanded the separation of Barnabas and Saul, for the especial work to which they were called. And whichever we may prefer of the two interpretations which have been given of Rom. xv. 16, its force, in this respect, will remain unaltered. If, by the προσφορὰ τῶν ἐθνῶν, the eucharist itself be meant, the argument is such as to settle the whole question of the Christian Priesthood and Sacrifice. If the expression be, as is contended, figurative, still the figure can hardly be taken from anything but the liturgy of the Church, to the sacrificial character of which it thus bears decisive testimony; while, in either case, St. Paul's description of himself as ἱερουργῶν τὸν εὐαγγέλιον surely proves that the term ἱερεὺς may, without impropriety, be employed, in some sense, to certain ministers under the New Testament. We forbear, at present, to press arguments that, going to prove the sacrificial character of the eucharist, tend to prove also the priestly character of its ministers; because that subject is so large a one that we must reserve it for separate consideration next month. Neither will we cite the passages in the Prophets that seem to foretel an order of priesthood for the Gentile Church. We trust we have satisfied our readers, that, leaving the peculiar character of the eucharist for awhile out of the question, the argument from the language of the New Testament is, as far as it goes, on our side.

II. We must now approach a yet more solemn consideration. It is alleged that, on all the principles of the New Testament, we must acknowledge but one ἱερεὺς, even the One who discharges his transcendent priesthood within the veil, and offers His own sacrifice at the intellectual altar. We might demur at the outset, on scriptural grounds, the New Testament speaking of our Lord not as Priest, but as High-Priest,—a title which of itself tends to convey

---

* And by some to the third also.

the impression of his having priests under Him. But let that pass. We admit the objection, as it stands, to be a very weighty one, which merits serious consideration; and, contenting ourselves with the title priest instead of high-priest, we fully admit that our Lord is alone in the direct and substantive office which it indicates. But it never seems to occur to the objectors that He is similarly alone in every character which He bears as our Redeemer; He is the One Prophet,—the One King. Yet all who believe that certain are allowed to preach in his name must admit that, in some sense compatible with this, there is an order of prophets under Him; for those who do not see the sacerdotal are alive to the prophetical functions of the Church. And in like manner, compatibly with his royal prerogative, are there kings under Him; for he said to the apostles, " I appoint unto you a kingdom, even as my Father hath appointed unto me." These considerations show that there is no necessary incompatibility between our Lord's one and only priesthood, and others exercising it in a secondary sense under Him. They do more—they supply us with a powerful argument from analogy in favour of its being so. For, if the ministry be apostolical— if it be grounded on the words, " as my Father hath sent me, even so send I you,"—we may naturally look in it for a representation of what Christ is in all his offices as Saviour. These are very generally summed up under the three heads of prophet, priest, and king, which comprehend all the departments of spiritual service and care. Now, though in each of these Christ is alone, the One Prophet raised up like unto Moses, who has concluded God's revelations to mankind (Heb. i. 1),—the One Priest who hath once for all entered into the holy place on our behalf,—the One King who sitteth on the throne of David,—yet, compatibly with this, it is admitted by all who recognise a ministry in any way authoritative, that He has secondary prophets and kings under him. To preach the word of God is to prophesy, to exercise ecclesiastical discipline is to reign, under Christ. If, then, He who is properly alone in all, is yet represented in two of his offices, we are almost irresistibly led to expect that he should be represented in the third also; and that as He who is the One Prophet and the One King has a secondary order of prophets and kings under him, so, though the one true Priest, He has under him a secondary order of priests also.

This principle, indeed, seems to run through the whole constitution of the Church: she is in everything to represent her Lord, and as his body, is to be the organ through which He acts. He only hung on the cross with sacrificial efficacy; but she too must bear the mark of the cross, and " fill up what is behind of his sufferings." He is the one only Mediator; but yet she intercedes for the whole world around her, (1 Tim. ii. 1, 2;) yea, and her members do one for another, (James v. 16.) He only can forgive sins; but yet whose sins she remits, they are remitted; and whose sins she retains, they are retained. He only is the fountain of new birth; but yet she regenerates in her holy laver. He only can feed the hungry soul; but yet she gives immortal food in her heavenly banquet. Paradoxical as all this sounds in the first statement of it, its whole difficulty vanishes before those words of the apostle concerning the Church, that she is "his body, the fulness of Him that filleth all in all." The means we employ to do a thing are not held to derogate from our prerogative as the doer of it: still less do the limbs of the body divide with a man the honour of his physical actions. And, similarly, if the Church be really so joined to Christ as to be his body,—if she indicate and represent the unseen Saviour, even as the body indicates and represents the otherwise hidden human being,—must not her acts be in reality not hers, but Christ's? This is the very privilege of being permitted to believe in Apostolical Ordination, that we may be thereby delivered, if we like, from self-contemplation, self-seeking, and self-glorification; that we may learn to regard our sacerdotal and all other ministerial functions, as discharged only in outward form by ourselves; really by the one Prophet, Priest, and King, of the heavenly world. So can we say with Hooker, that "we have for the least and meanest duties, performed by virtue of ministerial power, that to dignify, grace, and authorize them, which no other offices on earth can challenge. Whether we preach, pray, baptize, communicate, condemn, give absolution, or whatsoever, as disposers of God's mysteries, our words, judgments, acts, and deeds, are not ours, but the Holy Ghost's," (and so of course Christ's, if his Spirit's.)*

It is this identification of the Church with her Head—this seeing Him in her and in all her acts—that we have such need to learn; for this, if it had been well learned and remembered, would have precluded each great corruption that has appeared. The Romish Churches forgot it in regard to their sacerdotal and kingly functions; the Protestant forget it in regard to their prophetical; and hence the unevangelic temper, and the tampering with the conscience in the way of dispensations and the like, of the one, and the idolatry of talent and oratory in the other. This is not the place to touch on the latter of these points. We cannot at present write a treatise on the right way of preaching. Suffice it to observe that, just as we realize the truth that Christ, not ourselves, is the Prophet of the dispensation—that we are but channels through which He imparts his living word,—just as we forget every notion of our own opinion, our own theory, our own views, our own arguments, and feel that we can do nothing but give as we have received,—do we administer the ordinance of preaching rightly. We are no more prophets apart from Christ than we are priests: through Him we are both; the same consideration which shows the possibility of our being the one, showing that of our being the other also.

---

* Eccl. Pol. B. V. cap. lxxvii. 8, p, 589, ed. Keble.

III. But we must now turn to an objection brought from another quarter. To assert that the upper orders of the clergy are priests, is said to be an invasion of the rights of Christ's people, who in a secondary sense are priests by means of his real priesthood. This is the side from which Neander oftenest attacks the position we are maintaining. The following passage occurs in his life of Chrysostom. "In opposition to the mode of thinking which had before prevailed both in religion and philosophy, Christianity had quickened in the hearts of men the principles of a redemption appointed equally for all mankind, and of a unity of godly communion among the redeemed, outweighing human distinctions. Every partition wall which had previously existed among men fell to the ground before the power of this principle; all consecrated to God, the universal Father, through the One Eternal Priest,—all filled, after this common consecration, by the One same Holy Spirit,—are ordained a true priesthood, a spiritual people, all members of which are appointed to fulfil the same higher law of life, and to obey the same calling of a worship spiritual and universal. As this principle of an universal priesthood had been the soul of Christianity from its earliest dispensation, a most essential corruption of the religion arose both in practice and doctrine upon the suppression and falsification of the tenet, by heresies of Jewish and Heathen origin, which drew an unevangelical distinction between priests and laymen, between ecclesiastics and men of the world."* This, as our readers must be well aware, is but a condensation of what runs through much of the earlier part of our author's history of the Church.

The first thing worthy of remark about this objection, founded, like the former, as we cheerfully admit, on a great truth, is, that if admitted, it nullifies that former. If it be true, as it is, that all Christ's people are in some sense priests, then there must be some compatibility between his only Priesthood and that of others under him. Each objection we admit to be weighty, but the same man is not entitled to make use of both. If baptized Christians can with propriety be styled priests, bishops and presbyters may be so also in some peculiar sense.

In truth, the objection may be dealt with in the same way as the last. All Christians, indeed, are priests, but the same passages of Holy Scripture which tell us that they are, tell us that they are kings also, (1 Pet. ii. 9, Rev. i. 6.) Yet the power of ruling Christ's kingdom and of exercising discipline is admitted to belong, under Him, to the clergy. All the people, too, are prophets, (Jer. xxxi. 34, 1 John ii. 27;) but who does not admit a peculiar class of prophets under the Gospel dispensation? It ought to be remembered that the expression "a Royal Priesthood," in 1 Pet. is taken from the Old Testament, (Exod. xix. 6,) and was applied by God himself to the Israelites in general, who are never denied to have had

---

* Neander's Life of Chrysostom. Stapleton's Translation, p. 35.

an authoritative and peculiar priesthood. Whatever right, therefore, a Christian may have to the argument, the same might have been claimed (and, indeed, once was claimed) by the Israelites; so that it clearly proves too much.

And the compatibility between these two things—the priesthood of all the people, and the priesthood of the two upper orders of the ministry—is of the same kind, and is founded on the same consideration, as the compatibility between Christ's only priesthood and the priesthood of his ministry under Him. In either case we have recourse to the declaration that the Church is his body, so that acts distinctively hers are in reality not hers but his. By means of this consideration we can understand how all the baptized exercise a holy priesthood and offer a spiritual sacrifice. By means of this consideration, too, we can understand how bishops and presbyters should be priests also. Should the objection be brought from either prerogative—the inalienable one of our Lord and Saviour, or that inherent in the people at large—we can answer it in the same way. The Church is Christ's body, and she is visibly constituted in the bishops and presbyters; they are her organs. Therefore their priesthood is, on the one hand, but the acting and application of Christ's; on the other, it is but the exercise of the people's, who, constituted in the clergy, offer their " spiritual sacrifices acceptable to God by Jesus Christ." Viewed in reference to the people, they represent their Lord; viewed in reference to God and heaven, they represent the people.

We suspect that, instead of compromising or impairing these two great truths—the efficacious priesthood of Christ, and the acceptable priesthood through Him of his people—the assertion of a priesthood in the clergy will be found to be the best witness for both; and that, wherever the Church's liturgic development, which, as we shall by and by see, implies such a priesthood, has been lost sight of, or in any considerable degree obscured, there, on the one hand, there is little heard or thought of the great Melchisedec offering at the heavenly altar; and on the other, the notion of each baptized man's solemn consecration to God, of his body becoming a shrine of the Eternal Spirit, and himself being admitted into the choir, and summoned to share in the song of the Seraphim,* is nearly unknown. Is it not so? In regard to the first point, let us look northwards; let us take the case of Scotland, where, as we had great satisfaction in remarking in our last number, unepiscopal Protestantism has not been permitted to run the whole dreary length it has traversed on the Continent. Yet

---

* This great truth, of which the scriptural warrant is too copious to be brought forward here, seems to have been nearly the uppermost one in the mind of Chrysostom, whose lips are never so golden as when he launches out on it. Yet Chrysostom's notions concerning the priesthood of bishops and presbyters are too well known to have been as high as they could well be pitched to require citation at present. The standing witness of this truth is the Tersanctus, which is an integral portion of the Communion office in every Apostolical Church, and is altogether unknown, we suspect, to every other. See a letter in the Brit. Mag. for Oct. 1839, pp. 401, 406.

even there, how does the case stand? Let us take the writings (containing so much that is excellent) of Dr. Chalmers or Dr. Gordon, and compare them with those of the venerable Bishop Jolly. In which are we most led to think of a real, now living, High Priest, at this very moment discharging his office on our behalf? In the former we hear much of an atonement made in time past,—little of the sacrifice then offered as being presented within the veil now; and we hear certain doctrines besides connected with this of the atonement, which a man is to receive if he can, and by the *natural* operation of which, if really received, his soul is regenerated and renewed,—little of Jesus Christ as the living Friend and Brother, with whom we can and we must be in living and brotherly communion. We are continually presented with a partial and distorted view of the Epistle to the Romans, the great storehouse of subjective christian sentiment, hardly ever with the general scope of the no less important Epistle to the Hebrews, the great storehouse of objective and liturgic thought. In the writings of Jolly we need scarcely say that the case is far otherwise. To him we may indeed say that the heavens were opened, and that Jesus at the right hand of God was continually before his eye. It would be too large a digression to follow this comparison into details; we shall be glad if we have succeeded in suggesting it. And similarly, in regard to the unction of all the baptized to a holy and spiritual priesthood, it is a doctrine which we often find in the Fathers, who asserted,—not in the modern religious writing, which denies,—an especial priesthood; in the goldenmouthed author of the treatise *de Sacerdotio*, rather than in the sectarian teachers of the present day.

One exception to this remark, indeed, there is—the powerful author whose name stands at the head of our article. He seems most vividly penetrated by the truth, that all Christians under the gospel dispensation are made kings and priests unto God; and it seems to be in great measure from a jealousy over this doctrine in itself most right and befitting, that he is so prepossessed against the position for which we are contending. But we submit that the two positions can be maintained at once, and that each is best maintained by holding fast to the other. All sense of general is best kept up by particular consecration; the consecration of all things by the sight of churches in every direction with their sky-pointing spires, of all time by the recurrence of Sundays and holidays, of all thoughts and words and deeds by holy ordinances and sacraments. Every hour of the Christian's day must be spent in communion with his Saviour, in participation of the flesh broken and the blood shed for the life of the world; but yet, putting Divine appointment out of the question, how few believe that such communion and participation could be continued among us without those definite occasions on which, by the Sacrament of the Lord's Supper, we are enabled to realise and enjoy it in its concentration! And similarly, the holiness of all the people, their solemn consecration to God's service, their spiritual priesthood unto Him, are, we think, best witnessed for by the sight all around us of an especial priesthood—of *personæ exemplares*—of an order of men who not only point but lead the way—of living personal representatives of what the Church at large is meant to be, distinct recurring landmarks of her high and spiritual calling. This seems always to have been the view taken by the Church, and only in the light of it does the designation of the clergy as *the Church* become tolerable. They are not the whole Church,—it consists of the people no less than of them; but they are its formative principle, it is constituted and made visible in them. Therefore they at least must show forth the christian life; they must manifest the unearthly calling of that Church of which they are the representatives; they are to offer her daily sacrifice of prayer, even if none will join them; they, even in times of lax discipline and rare communion, and love waxing cold, are, when assembled in college or chapter, to offer and receive the eucharist weekly as in the beginning of the Gospel. And if they fail in these things, the people will lose sight of them too. If they neglect the daily services of the Church, the people will soon cease to miss them; if they content themselves with rare communion, the people will not cry out for frequent; if they live secularly, the business and the pleasures of this world will gain full victory over the people. Therefore, not to obscure, but to bring out the great principle, that every baptized man is consecrated to a solemn priesthood; not that the people may forget, but that they may ever remember, that they owe spiritual sacrifices to the Majesty of heaven; let there be continually before men's eyes the spectacle of an especial priesthood, offering their time, their talents, the whole tenour of their lives, to the service of Almighty God.

Two more objections remain to be considered before we enter on directer arguments than we have yet employed. First, it is alleged, that the Christian Church comes from the synagogue, not the temple, and is constituted exclusively on the model of the former. Consequently, as the priests, together with the sacrifice which they offered, belonged only to the temple, there can be no place for such in the Christian Church. A more unsupported assertion, we will venture to say, was never advanced than this. That the elements of the synagogue were taken into the Church we will not, indeed, deny; for our position is, that the *whole* Jewish system expanded into the Gospel; and that we have, in consequence, not the synagogue only, but the temple, and the throne also;—none of them, indeed, substantively by themselves, but all in and of Christ. He has summed up in Himself all that had existed separately before; as being both Prophet and Priest, he has for ever united in the apostolate the prophetical and priestly functions, and so made the synagogue and the temple one; and as the antitypal Melchizedec, Priest and King, He has blended all into his kingdom; so that they to whom He has said, "As my Father hath sent me, even so send I you," are as his apostles, prophets, priests, and kings under Him. On this principle we should, no doubt, miss the synagogue, which was one feature of the Jew's prophetical dispensation, could we find nothing answering to it in the Church; but on the very same principle we should miss the temple too; and both, just because Christ is the fulfilment of both, and because we therefore look to find him in respect of both in that Church which is his mystic home.

But let us see how the case stands as regards evidence. That the terms *presbyter* and *episcopus* have come into the Church from the synagogue, is probable enough, and so perhaps may have come that other of *angel*.* But, on the other hand, does not St. Paul (1 Cor. ix. 13, 14) argue the right of the Christian ministry to maintenance from the analogy of the temple? Does not he teach most expressly in the same chapter and elsewhere that the Church is the true temple of God? We forbear to press arguments from Scripture for the Christian Sacrifice, because, as we have already said, that subject stands reserved for separate consideration. To turn to authority which, though not canonical, is of the apostolical age,—Clement, as is well known, enforces the duty of observing Church order, and submission to Church rulers, by referring to the temple. In the place where he does so, he says more things than one which we may have occasion to cite hereafter. It seems superfluous even to allude to Ignatius, whose whole scheme of the Church, as indicated in his writings, is derived from the temple.

If the direct evidence for derivation from the temple which we have now adduced strike some persons as scanty and faint, let them remember that the direct evidence for derivation from the synagogue is still more so; while of *exclusive* derivation from the latter, the only point that could affect our position, we possess not a particle of proof whatever.

Secondly, it may be said, if Christian ministers have a sacerdotal character and sacerdotal functions, how come these to have so little prominence in the New Testament? How comes it that, in defending the position, you are obliged to content yourselves with one or two incidental allusions? How comes it that on the whole we hear so much of labouring in word and doctrine, of apostles, evangelists, and doctors, and that the idea of an hierarchy and a sacerdotal order— an idea which, if well grounded, can never be unimportant— should so seldom seem to have been present to the minds of the sacred writers? In dealing with this objection, we will in the meantime treat it as if founded on fact, having purposely reserved the whole subject of the Eucharist for separate consideration. Even, however, if we embraced that subject at present, we might perhaps concede that the Church's liturgic development is not the one most prominent in a very large part of the New Testament.

The reason, we think, is very apparent. The Church, as we have said, is an expansion of Judaism. Not only did its constitution

---

* See Lightfoot's works, *passim*.

originate in the Jewish polity, but its early members were Jews; nor did they cease to be Jews by becoming Christians. From this, two things seem almost necessarily to follow; first, that the full development of the Church could hardly take place till the destruction of Jerusalem; and, secondly, that, whilst the Jewish temple and priesthood continued, such phrases as *the priests* and *the priesthood* would naturally have been understood of the legal ones; especially as those latter were priests in a substantive independent sense, which, we cheerfully grant, none of Christ's can be. It is always inconvenient and unnatural to give to something new and little known a designation which has long been appropriated to something old and well known. The same difficulty would not have been felt in the case of the title *elder*, which, as we have already seen, has never been exclusively enjoyed by any one class of officials, and designated at least two amongst the Jews.

Now, if any thing like this was the case, it is easy to see that, before the destruction of Jerusalem, we are not so likely to encounter the Church's hierarchical development as after it. Of course, if that development was a right one, its elements must have been in the Church as soon as ever she was duly constituted, and her clergy must, therefore, have been invested with their sacerdotal functions from the time of their ordination. But all this was comparatively latent, both from the cause we have mentioned, and from another equally obvious. The earlier part of the New Testament is mostly taken up with the first formation of the Church, not its internal life when formed and developed,—with the making disciples, rather than with the subsequent occupations assigned to disciples. Now, what function was most required for this? Manifestly the prophetical; manifestly the gifts of utterance, of exposition, and persuasion. Naturally, therefore, we hear much of them,—little of still higher gifts which belonged not to the process of making disciples.

But, surely, after the carnal national polity had been removed, the spiritual and universal one came out in all its features into distincter manifestation than before. There were no longer any Jewish life for disciples to lead, any Jewish observances to keep, which could obscure their position, privileges, and occupations, as denizens of the New Jerusalem, as members of the spiritual Israel. When the earthly city was destroyed, its temple subverted, its children dispersed, its mount of promise and blessing left a scene of desolation and wrath, then must the eyes of believers have turned to Mount Sion and the city of the living God, the heavenly Jerusalem, with its bright and blissful people, now revealed in unclouded majesty and glory. The earthly had passed away, that the heavenly might be distinctly seen.

For these reasons, what learned men have conjectured,[*] seems by

---

[*] Vid. Mede's Christian Sacrifice, and Hickes on the Priesthood.

no means improbable—that the period of the destruction of Jerusalem was the occasion of a fuller hierarchical development of the Church than had been made before; and be it remembered, that such a development would not have been post-apostolic, St. John having survived the event in question. Now, the closing book of the canon comes from him; and, without venturing on any theory as to the drift of its contents, we assert an obvious fact when we say that all its imagery and scenery are of a hierarchical and liturgic character. The fact is, we think, significant; others must judge of it according to their own apprehensions of things.

These considerations may throw light on a well-known passage regarding St. John in the letter of Polycrates to Victor,* wherein he uses of the apostle the remarkable words, ὃς ἐγενήθη ἱερεὺς τὸ πέταλον πεφορεκώς. We are well aware of the difficulties which attend this passage, which we have no intention of discussing. Suffice it to observe, that Polycrates had just before been mentioning, among many others, Philip, simply as apostle and evangelist. How came he, then, to single out John as *priest*? May it not have been because, after the destruction of Jerusalem, John assumed the sacerdotal character more openly than had been done by those apostles who died before that event, and perhaps even arrayed himself accordingly,† as the words in question, if taken literally, must lead us to suppose?

Perhaps, too, the passage before us, and the considerations in which we have been engaged, may in part account for the standing difference between the eastern and western Churches in after time, both as regards the greater copiousness of the liturgies, and the greater prominence of liturgic sentiment in the writers, of the former. We cannot at present digress into the comparison which opens on us here; but the fact must, we think, have struck many; and when it is remembered, that the Latin Churches derived their tradition from St. Peter and St. Paul who died before, and the eastern very much from St. John who died after, the destruction of Jerusalem, we are in possession of at least a probable cause for the diversity.

We have now endeavoured to dispose of the principal arguments against the assertion, that the Christian ministry is of a priestly character. The direct arguments in its favour, along with the consideration of the blessed Eucharist, from which they are mostly drawn, we must reserve for next month. We think we have, meanwhile, shown that no valid argument can be drawn from the language of the New Testament,—that, as far as it goes, being in our favour;—that the two favourite objections derived from Christ's Priesthood and that of his people, if they prove any thing, prove too much for the

---

* Polycrat. ap. Euseb. lib. v. c. 24.
† We of course give this only as one not improbable explanation of the passage; and have not space at present to discuss it either by itself, or in its relation to the similar passages about St. James in Epiphanius, and that about St. Mark, cited from a MS. author by Valesius.

purpose of the objectors;—that the Church's alleged derivation from the synagogue proves nothing, unless such derivation were exclusive, for which there is no argument whatever;—and, lastly, that for the small space occupied in the New Testament by the doctrine we maintain, at first sight so disproportionate to its importance if true, we can conjecture most obvious explanations.

In our next, then, we propose to enter on direct arguments, and we trust to exhibit the doctrine in a light which may remove any lingering distaste to it in the minds of some, as after all unevangelic and unspiritual.

---

1. *Considerations on the State of the Law regarding Marriages with a deceased Wife's Sister.* By H. R. REYNOLDS, Jun. M.A. Barrister at Law. 4th Edition. London: Longman. 1840.
2. *On the present State of the Law as to Marriages abroad between English subjects within the prohibited degrees of affinity.* London: Spettigue. 1840.
3. *A Letter on the proposed Change in the Laws prohibiting Marriage between those near of kin. Reprinted from the British Magazine.* By the Rev. E. B. PUSEY, D.D. Oxford: J. H. Parker.

WERE we of those who faithlessly " seek a sign," not a few things would to a reverent mind serve now to realize the consoling truth of the Lord's presence in this branch of His Church. When things seemed almost desperate, an impressive calm has come over hot and controversial tempers; an unexpected lull has stayed the waves at the very wildest; an earnest, as it were, of that half hour's mysterious " silence in heaven" which prepared for the deeper wonders of the heavenly kingdom. Either some subduing season, like the Lent just past, has calmed into charity those who love the Lord's truth, even though they seem to fight against it or to condemn it; or some exciting topic of mere passing interest, such as a new scheme of politics, or some distressing reverse, like that unrighteous war in which we are engaged in the East,—one or other of these things—has drawn the idle curiosity of mere worldlings into other channels: but so it is, that, if we "seek peace and ensue it," He "stilleth the raging of the sea and the noise of his waves and the madness of the people." There may be something of presumption in alluding to mercies which we so little deserve: but it were altogether to drive Him from us to deny His presence, or to refuse to see His providential care. We can all recall such instances in our own days; but the way in which these gracious dispensations are timed deserves our especial thankfulness. If, humanly speaking, the same trials had occurred a few years or a few months back, we might now be sorrowing for the triumph of evil rather than rejoicing in happy auguries for the future. What, for example, would have been the result had this melancholy proposition for legalizing the incestuous union with a deceased wife's sister been submitted to parliament under the auspices of the late government? Backed as the proposed change now is by the respectable sponsorship of Lord Francis Egerton, all but openly recommended by such a person as Mr. Plumptre,* (and whatever estimate we may entertain of the doctrinal soundness of the party—alas! that we must call it so—which he represents, it would be sad unfairness to impugn its sincerity,) with a portentous array of legal recommendations, and with the still more melancholy sanction of at least two bishops and of a hundred clergymen in the single diocese of Norwich, what could have stood against this combination? Nothing surely in either great party taken at large; and had we only the earnestness of 1832 upon which to rely, *actum esset de ecclesiâ*. But we repeat, the agitation was ill-timed for success; men have taken their side. God has breathed, we trust, into the dry bones; we have suffered too much not to be a sensitive people; and if chastisement has aroused us to a sense of our privileges, it has (may it not be hoped?) awakened us also into a more godly jealousy for His honour.

But, with all this, we cannot but express surprise at the comparative coldness and insensibility with which the Church has been content to await this grievous insult upon her purity. Surely to propose to establish by mere legal enactments what the Church, in all ages, has regarded as *incest*, would, in the ages of faith, have aroused the faithful as one man. With all the unwearied activity and secrecy which, from the days of Arius downwards, have characterized the more perilous assaults upon our faith, all the petitions, and remonstrances, and recommendations have been on one side; most of the speaking, and we fear that we are not understating it when we add, (with the single exception of one, upon whom in the hour of danger we may always confidently repose—Dr. Pusey,) all the publishing. We hate agitation upon principle; but we all know what effect upon the timid or the ignorant a closely-banded array of authorities and precedents, and a compact system of assault, have and perhaps ought to have. It is a humiliating thought, that an indignant remonstrance against the proposed measure was not forwarded from every archdeaconry of the Church; and, as the measure is sure to be renewed, we must review our armour, and select our weapons, before we are again summoned to defend our Zion. God has helped us once. We have escaped, for the time, the threatened danger by the rejection of Lord F. Egerton's motion; but we can no longer avail ourselves of the excuse that we are taken by surprise.

The case we are about to consider is this:—by the law of the

---

* "There could be no doubt but there were many cases in which it might be of essential importance to the fathers and the children, that such a marriage should be permitted."—Debate, as quoted by Reynolds, Considerations, p. 8.

Church, and, as it would seem, by the law of the land, (which, in spite of conflicting enactments, had in this, as in most other cases, made the law of the Church her unwritten law of prescription, superior to mere statute law,) the marriage with a deceased wife's sister is incest, —unholy in the eye of the Church, criminal in the eye of the law.

I. It is well to urge strongly that the *illegality* of such pretended marriages rests, as even the advocates of the change admit, upon "the current of judicial authorities," (Law Magazine, No. xliv. p. 375,) as well as upon acts of parliament. In the confusion incident upon the disputed legitimacy of the successors of Henry VIII., enactment, repeal, and re-enactment followed of course. Henry's pliant commons first excluded Mary, (25 Henry VIII.) and then excluded Elizabeth, (28 Henry VIII.) for the sole benefit of Edward. On the accession of Mary, the act which had illegitimatized her (25 Henry VIII.) was repealed. Now, this act had recited what are called the Levitical degrees of kindred and affinity, and among them the case of the marriage in question. There can be no doubt that this act (25 Henry VIII.) is, in law, repealed. Then comes the act of 28 Henry VIII. c. 7, which, for the benefit of the children of Jane Seymour, illegitimatized both Mary, the child of Queen Catharine, and Elizabeth, the child of Queen Anne Boleyn, repealed the act 25 Henry VIII. but also enumerated again the degrees abovementioned, and repeated the prohibitions against them. On the accession of Mary, as was to be expected, this act in turn was repealed. But the matter does not rest here: what Mary repealed, Elizabeth revived; and how far this particular act, we quote Gibson, Codex, 496.

"In the statute 1 Eliz. c. 10, where many of the statutes repealed by 1 and 2 Mary are revived, it is specially provided, that all others, repealed by the act of Queen Mary, and not revived by that of Queen Elizabeth, shall stand repealed; which seems, therefore, to be the case of the present statute. But it is observed by the Lord Chief Justice Vaughan, that the act 28 Henry VIII. c. 16, being revived by 1 Eliz., and there being in the second section of the said act a special reference to the act 28 Henry VIII. c. 7, as the rule of judging and determining what marriages are or are not against God's law; this act, therefore, [28 Henry VIII. c. 7,] *is virtually revived* by the reviver of 28 Henry VIII. c. 16. Upon which foundation, this statute is alleged *as in force* in the case of Harison and Burwell,[*] and so reported and *taken for granted*, both by himself and by Ventris."

Here, then, as far as the statute law is concerned, there is one express prohibition of the marriage in question, so ruled at least by the chief justice, and his judgment never impugned.

This is not all: there is another statute which seems directly to meet the case; 32 Henry VIII. is the celebrated statute which declares our independence of papal dispensations. It is well to consider the *animus* of this act: it was directed against papal exactions and nothing else; the prohibition of marriages upon the part of Rome,

---

[*] 20 Car. II.

for the mere sake of granting lucrative dispensations, is pointed at; the cases are named. " Further also by reason of other prohibitions then [than] God's law admitteth, *for their lucre* by that court invented, the dispensations whereof they always reserved to themselves, as in kindred or affinity *between cosin-germans, and so to fourth degree*, which else were lawful, and be not prohibited by God's law, *and all because they would get money by it.*" It goes on to enact, "that no reservation or prohibition, God's law except, shall trouble or impeach any marriage without the Levitical degrees." To settle what was God's law is not the bearing of the statute; facts are left precisely where they were. This act enumerates no cases save that of cousins and the fourth degree of affinity. The clear presumption, then, is that it was not intended to decide this or that case; to extend or to restrict the prohibited degrees, except in the cases mentioned by name; in all others to leave the law where it was; only to keep in England the money which was sent to Rome. The whole act is a fiscal arrangement, not, as indeed would be impossible, an ecclesiastical decision. But it is not, what was more usual, even an attempt at it. Mr. Reynolds (Considerations, p. 20,) admits this. The Law Magazine is forced also to confess that " it is by no means so clear [in the writer's favour, of course] as could be wished." An argument is by Mr. Reynolds grounded upon the fact, that this statute does not revive the declaration of the two statutes of Henry already alluded to, that " marriages within certain prohibitions derived from the Levitical law are contrary to the law of God." Of course not; why should the 32 Henry VIII. revive the 28 Henry VIII. *which was then in full force?* The 28 Henry VIII. recited the Levitical degrees which had before been recited in 25 Henry VIII. and why? because the former was passed to repeal the latter, except in this particular matter; but it must be shown that the 32 Henry VIII. stands in the same relation to the 28th or to the 25 Henry VIII. as the 28th does to the 25th, before any arguments can be drawn from the silence of the 32d about the 28th and 25th, as contrasted with the revival of the 25th in the 28th. No, the 32 Henry VIII. has been termed the Magna Charta of Matrimony; this act is still in force; it constitutes the statute law of the realm; under it, until the passing of Lord Lyndhurst's act, the marriage with a deceased wife's sister has been held illegal in the courts; and by it two prohibitions are recited, God's law and the Levitical degrees. It is very remarkable, although the wording of the clause is obscure, that the Levitical degrees and God's law are not considered identical and coextensive: God's law embraces more than the degrees. Mr. Reynolds admits that it is uncertain how widely this phrase must be construed: he enumerates some cases which it must comprehend; some even discoverable by so vague a test as " natural reason;" and among them why should we not include the decisions of the Church? Certainly Henry was not the man to say that the rule of the Church was other than God's law. This is upon one of Mr. Reynolds's assumptions; for he puts the case cleverly, though we are bound to say dishonestly, in the interpretation of this statute:—1st, he says the case of marriage with a deceased wife's sister is not forbidden by 32 Henry VIII. because "it is not prohibited by God's law;" and God's law is *something different* from the Levitical degrees. 2dly, The same case is not forbidden by the same 32 Henry VIII. because (p. 22) "Lord Coke and the judges decide 'that the Levitical degrees *are* the key to the interpretation of the term God's law,'" and then he goes on to argue, either that the Levitical degrees are not binding, or that the case does not come within their restriction.

To which we reply, 1st, that this marriage is forbidden by the statute, because God's law embraces the rule of the Church; and this is our answer upon Mr. Reynolds's first assumption: and 2dly, that the case is embraced in the Levitical degrees, and therefore forbidden by the same statute: and 3dly, that, if the Levitical degrees are not binding, it is forbidden by something higher than them; which is a reply to his second position.

Such being the statute law, how was it administered?

"When this point of marrying the wife's sister came under consideration in the King's Bench, (25 Car. II. Mich. Term. Hill v. Good,) though it was alleged that the precept [of the Mosaic law] *primâ facie* seemed to be only against having two sisters *at the same time*, and prohibition to the spiritual court was granted; yet in Trinity Term, (26 Car. 2,) after hearing civilians, they granted a consultation as in a matter within this statute, 32 Henry VIII. though the former statute, 28 Henry VIII. had never been revived, after the repeal of Queen Mary, which yet it *virtually* was; and there, as in 25 Henry VIII. the wife's sister is *expressly* prohibited."—*Gibson, Codex*, p. 498.

But on this branch of the question, the state of the statute law, Mr. Reynolds wastes his time and our own. Were it not quite certain that the acts are against him, would he and his friends—or shall we say employers—be so anxious to get them altered? We are following Mr. Reynolds's division of the subject, (Considerations, p. 12.) We have settled his first inquiry, "Whether a marriage with the sister of a deceased wife was prohibited by the existing statute law of the realm?"

II. We have to inquire, "Whether, assuming that such a marriage was prohibited by the Levitical law to the Jews, such prohibition is now binding upon us, under the Christian dispensation?" Surely there is something very saddening when we find gentlemen, and scholars, and Christians, arguing as though it were possible that under the Gospel we had gone back; as though, having come to Mount Zion, we had not even reached Sinai; as though the children of Christ were allowed greater license in fleshly things than the seed of Abraham; as though checks and restrictions, which were found necessary even to those for whose hardness of heart much license (as in divorce) was granted, are no longer to be imposed upon us who live under a law of greater strictness and personal holiness. "Christ came not to destroy the law, but to fulfil it;" that is, to make it holier, more heavenly, purer, higher. As sharers in the Lord's most blessed redemption, we are under an unearthly rule; we are required to lead an angel life; "our conversation (πολίτευμα) is in heaven." Admitting, for the sake of argument, that the marriage in question is not forbidden by the Levitical law, it is forbidden by something else—the law of Paradise, to which state of privilege, as Christians, we have returned; that law which determined that a man and his wife were "one flesh." The Jews did not live under this law; they were privileged with but a suspensive dispensation : polygamy was permitted to them ;—Abraham was allowed to marry his sister; Jacob married two sisters at once: it seems the very characteristic of the imperfect covenant, that license in this particular way was permitted to them, as even to David and Solomon, from which a Christian shrinks instinctively. What we mean may be best illustrated by an impressive passage from a recent volume of sermons. " There is one virtue which, of old time, good men especially had not. Indulgences were allowed the Jews on account of the hardness of their hearts. Divorce of marriage was allowed them. More wives than one at once were not denied them. If there is one grace in which Christianity stands in especial contrast to the old religion, it is that of purity. Christ was born of a Virgin; He remained a virgin; His beloved disciple was a virgin; He abolished polygamy and divorce; and He said that there were those who, for the kingdom of heaven's sake, would be even as He."* With the change of a word or two, this is exactly our meaning. Christ re-enacted the law of primeval purity. In Him, as the second Adam, for the first time since the first Adam's sin, did man and wife become one flesh; and, by consequence, the wife's relations became the husband's; and to marry the wife's sister was the same as to marry an own sister. Under the Gospel, marriage is a mystery; a high and "holy estate;" a sacrament in the lower sense, as the Homily teaches; not one of which it was under the law: "the course of God's dealings has been," as Dr. Pusey tells us (p. 5,) "gradually to lay increased restrictions upon this holy union, and fence round marriage more sacredly." At the very first blush there occurs this *à priori* objection to the change, that it places the evangelical state of marriage as low, if not lower, than marriage under the law.

But not only upon the authority of Michaelis and Sir James Mackintosh—valeant quantum—are we told that the Jewish judicial code is abrogated, but to these is added "the venerable name of Hooker." (Considerations, p. 26.) No reference is given; and this is no more than might have been expected from a writer so slippery as Mr. Reynolds: we will endeavour to supply the deficiency. Book iv. c. xi. 7, commenting upon the decree of the Council of Jerusalem, Hooker says, "Did not nature teach the Gentiles to abstain from fornication? No doubt it did. But very marriage within a number of degrees being not only by the law of Moses, but also by the law of the sons of Noah (for so they took it), an unlawful discovery of nakedness; this discovery of nakedness by

---

* Newman's Sermons, vol. vi. p. 203. Judaism of the Present Day.

unlawful marriages, such as Moses in the law reckoneth up (Lev. xviii.); I think it, for mine own part, more probable to have been meant in the words of that canon [of the Council of Jerusalem], than fornication according unto the sense of the law of nature."

If Mr. Reynolds thus ignorantly, we had almost said dishonestly, tampers with the greatest names of the Church, it is well that he should see that so far is Hooker from including this case of marriage in those portions of the ceremonial law which were abrogated in Christ,—and of course there were some, such as circumcision, and the form of the Sabbath,—that he considers its prohibition involved in the very notion of the word πορνεία, and that it was forbidden, not only in the law and gospel, but by the law of nature, which he identifies with the seven precepts given to Noah.

Again, supposing that the prohibition in Leviticus is not binding upon Christians, which of course we do not admit, is marriage merely a part of the ceremonial law? Are we not taught that "no christian man whatsoever is free from the obedience of the commandments which are called moral." Art V.II. Marriage is not a matter of temporary or political convenience; not a thing of climate, or of prejudice, as we are now taught to consider the first covenant; but God's "institution in the time of man's *innocency.*" Let us beware how we lower our notions of christian marriage; let us see to it, lest first the ungodly Act of Registration, which reduced it to a civil contract, and next, this equally scandalous proposition, be not steps towards the revealing of that Antichrist, one of whose signs shall be "forbidding to marry."

We sum up this branch of the inquiry in Dr. Pusey's words; so characteristic of that peculiar habit of mind, which seems fitted, as has been said, only to exhaust every subject which he touches.

"It would be well, too, if they who throw out these hints of the abolition of the Levitical laws of marriage, would consider on what they are prepared to fall back. What authority have they wherewith to supply their place? The Church? But the Church, in its purer days, forbade those unions as peremptorily as the Levitical law. S. Basil appeals to the uniform practice of the Church, to his own time;* the Apostolic Canons, which may be looked upon as the Ante-Nicene code of the Church, forbid it; it was punished by the same sentence of long-continued excommunication as adultery.† This ground then, too, is abandoned, with some common-place remarks on the supposed asceticism of the early Church.‡ Our own Church has, here as elsewhere, followed the ancient. Is the appeal then to natural instinct, which shrinks from certain unions? But natural instinct varies with the moral character. English feeling still, for the most part, we are assured, shrinks from these unions as revolting and incestuous; yet every sort of incest has become habitual in nations highly civilized; as that with mothers and sisters among the Persians§ and Egyptians; and, persons have been already found to contend,|| with no physical deterioration of the nations

* Ep. 160, ad Theodor. [Diodor.] † See Bingham, 16. 11. 3.
‡ Consideration, p. 45, sqq. Observations, p. 57.
§ Tertullian, Apol. c. 9. and other authorities in Brisson de Reg. Pers. ii. 8. and Bishop Taylor, Duct. Dub. b. 2. c. 2. rule 3.
|| Michaelis, quoted as authority in Considerations, p. 12, note.

guilty of it. One of the advocates of these unions has already laid down maxims which go to maintain that there is no such offence as incest. It is stated* that 'the only moral principle of interdicted unions' is that 'clearly laid down by Paley,' viz. that 'in order to preserve chastity in families, and between persons of different sex, *brought up and living together*† in a state of unreserved intimacy, it is necessary, by every method possible, to inculcate an abhorrence of sexual conjunctions; which abhorrence can only be upholden by the absolute reprobation of *all* commerce of the sexes between *near relations*.' In other words, the notion of incest is a fiction, in order to prevent the risk of fornication in persons brought up together; and 'the *only* moral principle of interdicted unions' is one involving no morality in the act itself, but expediency only, to guard against a contingent sin. The writer, indeed, would himself shrink from this conclusion; he declares 'the connexion of marriage between parent and child to be forbidden by a law of universal and eternal obligation,'‡ and that the same 'objections equally apply to all the lineal degrees of consanguinity, (grand-parents and grand-children,) and to most of the lineal degrees of affinity.' He quotes also a saying of Mr. Justice Story, that 'marriages between brother and sister *by blood* are deemed incestuous and void, and indeed repugnant to the first principles of social order and morality; *but beyond this it seems difficult to extend the prohibition upon principle*.' Where, then, is this to end? Of course there are degrees in the violation of nature; but if the first dams be broken down, where is our guarantee that the flood of incest shall be stayed? If persons be found to maintain that the marriage with a wife's sister is not incestuous, will that with the husband's brother be long held to be such? The union of the uncle with the niece, it is held, cannot be prohibited "upon principle." If a man may take to him for a wife his own sister's child, the very substance of his sister, what ground have we for thinking that the union with his sister would be long deemed pollution? If union with a half-sister, the impress of his own father, be tolerated, is that born of his mother also so far removed?"—Pp. 9—11.

III. "Whether such a marriage was, in fact, prohibited by the Levitical law to the Jews?"

We gladly avail ourselves of Bishop Jewel's authority:—

"After my hearty commendations; whereas ye desire to understand my poor advice touching certain words in the xviiith chapter of Leviticus, by which ye think it not unlawful for a man to marry successively his own wife's sister, I would ye had rather taken in hand some other matter to defend. For it is not the best way, in my judgment, neither in these troublesome and doubtful times, to call more matters in doubt without just cause, nor in this intemperance and science§ of life, to open a gate to the breach of laws. I reckon the words in Leviticus, whereupon you ground, are these: 'Uxorem et sororem suam ad lacessendam eam, ne ducas, ut retegas turpitudinem ejus, illâ adhuc vivente.' Which words, I know, have been diversely construed by divers men, and in some men's judgment seem to sound of your side. Pellican, Paul Fagius, and Lyra, with certain others, think such marriage to be lawful; and that God forbad the having of two sisters in matrimony at one time, both of them being together onlyve; and that for the spiteful and continual contention and jealousy, which must needs grow betwixt them, as appeared in the example of Jacob with his two wives, Rachel and Leah, and therefore some think the Jews continue such marriages among them, as lawful, until this day.

"All these things hitherto make on your side; and the same would not greatly mislike me, saving that I find the judgments of the best learned men

---

* Considerations, p. 52, sqq.   † The italics are the author's.
‡ Ibid. p. 40.   § Dr. Pusey conjectures that this should be "license."

now living, and the continual practice of all ages, and in manner very public honesty, to the contrary. There be otherwise women enough to have choice of, so that no man can justly say that necessity drove him to marry her, whom, in our manner of speech, he first called sister.

"The practice of former times appeareth by the canons; whereas it is decreed that only 'carnalis copula cum puellâ septem annorum dirimit matrimonium cum ejus puellæ sorore postea secutum.' But I know you make small stay upon the canons, and sooner rest yourself upon these words in the text, 'illâ adhuc vivente.' And therefore thus you ground your reason; a man may not marry his wife's sister, while she is alive; ergo, he may marry her after she is dead. This reason, *à negativis*, is very weak, and makes no more proof in logic than this doth, 'Corvus non est reversus ad arcam donec exsiccatæ erant aquæ;' ergo, he returned again after the waters were dried up. Or, 'Joseph non cognovit eam, donec peperisset filium suum primogenitum;' ergo, Joseph knew after she was delivered of her first-begotten child; or such other like.

"Yet will you say, although this manner of reason be weak, and the words make little for you, yet thus far the reason is good enough, for these words make not against you; which thing notwithstanding I might grant, yet will not this reason follow of the other side. There are no express words in the Levitical law whereby I am forbidden to marry my wife's sister; ergo, by the Levitical law such marriage is to be accounted lawful. For notwithstanding the statute in that case makes relation unto the xviiith chapter of Leviticus, as unto a place whereunto the degrees of consanguinity and affinity are touched most at large; yet you must remember that certain degrees are there left out untouched, within which, nevertheless, it was never thought lawful for men to marry. For example, there is nothing provided there by express words, but that a man may marry his own grandmother, or his grandfather's second wife, or the wife of his uncle by his mother's side. No, nor is there any express prohibition in all this chapter, but that a man may marry his own daughter. Yet will no man say that any of these degrees may join together in lawful marriage.

"Wherefore we must needs think that God in that chapter hath especially and namely forbidden certain degrees; not as leaving all marriage lawful which he had not there expressly forbidden, but that thereby, as by infallible precedents, we might be able to rule the rest. As when God saith no man shall marry his mother, we understand that under the name of mother is contained both the grandmother and the grandfather's wife, and that such marriage is forbidden. And when God commands that no man shall marry the wife of his uncle by his father's side, we doubt not but in the same is included the wife of the uncle by the mother's side. Thus you see God himself would have us to expound one degree by another.

"So likewise in this case, albeit I be not forbidden by plain words to marry my wife's sister, yet I am forbidden so to do by other words, which by exposition are plain enough; for when God commands me I shall not marry my brother's wife, it follows directly by the same that he forbids me to marry my wife's sister; for between one man and two sisters, and one woman and two brothers, is like analogy or proportion, which is my judgment in this case; and other such like ought to be taken for a rule. And therefore the rabbins of the Jews have expressly forbidden divers degrees by this rule, which God by plain words forbad not.

"And this is one part of the tyranny of the Bishop of Rome, that he will take upon him to rule God's commands at his pleasure, and by dispensation to make that lawful in one man for the time which God hath plainly forbidden as unlawful in all men for ever. He hath dispensed with a man to marry his own brother's wife, as you know; he hath dispensed with the brother to marry his own natural sister,* as ye find in 'Summa Angelica,'

---

* Vid. Pressius. This writ by Archbishop Parker's hand.

in these words:—Papa. And what marvail? He would be omnipotent, and saith he may dispense, contra jus divinum, as you may see 16 q. 1 Quicunq. in Glosa.

"But thus, by the way, you have my mind touching your demand, and I doubt not but, all things well considered, the same mind will be your mind.

"Si quid novisti rectius istis,
Candidus imperti; si non, his utere mecum.

"Thus fare you heartily well.—From Sarum. Calend. Novem. 1561."—(Strype's Parker, App. b. ii. vol. 3. pp. 55—58.)

This "sophism" of the argument *à negativis* is exposed also by S. Basil, Epist. clx.* translated as an Appendix to Dr. Pusey's Letter. The holy Bishop argues, that if we are to be tied to the letter, it might be concluded that if a man could "for passion persuade himself that there would be no 'vexing,' what is to hinder him from taking both wives at once?"

Most of our readers will remember Bishop Pearson's searching detection of the same fallacy, Art. 3, p. 304.

"Many, indeed, have taken the boldness to deny this truth [of the perpetual virginity of St. Mary], because not recorded in the Sacred Writ; and not only so, but to assert the contrary as delivered in the Scriptures; but with no success. For though, as they object, St. Matthew testifieth that 'Joseph knew not Mary until she had brought forth her first-born Son,' from whence they would infer that afterwards he knew her; yet the manner of the Scripture language produceth no such inference. When God said to Jacob, 'I will not leave thee until I have done that which I have spoken to thee of,' it followeth not that when that was done the God of Jacob left him. When the conclusion of Deuteronomy was written, it was said of Moses, 'No man knoweth of his sepulchre until this day;' but it were a weak argument to infer from thence, that the sepulchre of Moses hath been known ever since. When Samuel had delivered a severe prediction unto Saul, he 'came no more to see him until the day of his death;' but it were a strange collection to infer that he therefore gave him a visit after he was dead.' 'Michal the daughter of Saul had no child until the day of her death;' and yet it were a ridiculous stupidity to dream of any midwifery in the grave. Christ promised his presence to the apostles 'until the end of the world;' whoever made so unhappy a construction as to infer from thence, that for ever after he would be absent from them?"

Maldonatus, on Matt. i. 25, refuting the same fallacy, adds, "Sit thou on My right hand until I make Thine enemies Thy footstool;" as though it might be argued that the Saviour's session at the right hand of power were not eternal; and "Till heaven and earth pass, one jot or one tittle shall in no wise pass from the law," for a proof that it would then be destroyed.

It is grievous enough to find our reverenced Bishop, Jeremy Taylor, adopting this loose and random mode of interpretation; to Dr. Dodd, and Adam Clarke, and Mr. (American) Justice Story, and Mr. N. Webster, of Boston, as quoted by the Law Magazine, and to Benjamin Franklin (!) and Milton (!!) who figure among Mr. Reynolds's authorities in "Biblical criticism," we have no hesitation in assigning their proper weight in this question; but it will be well to

---

* Misprinted cxl. in Dr. Pusey's pamphlet.

mark out for our readers the two grounds upon which the Church has settled that the marriage in question comes under the Levitical prohibitions.

1st, The argument from parity of reason.

This is clearly set forth in the Reformatio Legum :—

"Hoc tamen in illis Levitici capitibus diligenter animadvertendum est, minime ibi omnes non legitimas personas nominatim explicari. Nam Spiritus Sanctus illas ibi personas evidenter et expresse posuit, ex quibus similia spatia reliquorum graduum, et differentiæ inter se, facile possint conjectari et inveniri. Quemadmodum, exempli causâ, quum filio non datur uxor mater, consequens est, ut ne filia quidem patri conjux dari potest: et si patrui non licet uxorem in matrimonio habere, nec cum avunculi profecto conjuge nobis nuptiæ concedi possunt."—Cap. 3. De Gradibus in Matrimonio prohibitis, p. 45.

Three rules from the same book fix the interpretation :—

"1. Ut qui loci viris attribuuntur, eosdem sciamus feminis assignari, paribus semper proportionum et propinquitatum gradibus. 2. Ut vir et uxor unam et eandem inter se carnem habere existimentur; et ita quo quisque gradu consanguinitatis quemque contingit, eodem jus uxorem continget affinitatis gradu; quod etiam, in contrariam partem, eâdem ratione, valet. [Cap. 3. ibid.] 3. Non solum istas, maritis adhuc superstitibus, disjungi personas quas diximus, sed etiam illis mortuis idem perpetuo valere. Quemadmodum enim horribile flagitium est in vitâ patris, *fratris*, patrui, aut avunculi, audere illorum uxores violare: sic post mortem illorum matrimonium cum illis contrahere parem turpitudinem habet."—Cap. 6. ibid.

2. From direct precept.

And here we again thankfully avail ourselves of Dr. Pusey :—

"In this case, however, the prohibition does lie so clearly in the words of Scripture that it cannot be called an inference. Scripture prohibits peremptorily all commixtures of those of kin. 'None of you shall approach to any that is near of kin, to uncover their nakedness. I am the Lord.'[*] The solemnity of these last words might well deter any one who knew that he was one day to be judged by that Lord, from tampering with the command to which they are annexed. But if people really wish to know the meaning of that prohibition, not simply to find a plea for passion, it is plain enough. The original is still more expressive; it is literally 'none of you shall approach to the flesh (and hence, near-kin שְׁאֵר) *of his flesh*," (בְּשָׂרוֹ.) Since, then, the wife is 'bone of his bone, and *flesh of his flesh*,' (the very word) and again, 'and they twain shall be *one flesh*,' one sees not on what plea 'the flesh' or 'near-kin' of his wife could be held not to be included in this prohibition. As S. Basil argues, 'What can be more akin to the husband than his own wife, yea, rather than his own flesh?' We need, then, go no further for a distinct prohibition in the very letter of Holy Scripture than this first verse: the more you press the very words of Scripture, the more distinctly does the prohibition appear to be conveyed in those words. And the coincidence certainly is remarkable, that S. Basil does appeal to this verse alone, as in itself containing the prohibition. But, further, in the following verses, instances are given of what is meant by 'near of kin,' and among these is[†] the husband's brother. Since, then, marriage is the same in the two sexes, and purity the same, and breach of purity the same, it can scarcely be called an inference to say that the union with the wife's sister is included in the general prohibition, 'None of you shall approach to any that is near of kin to him, to uncover their nakedness.' Certainly it includes the specific

---

[*] It is upon this text that S. Basil argues against the case of marrying two sisters.
[†] Lev. xviii. 16.

case much more clearly than 'Thou shalt not commit adultery' does fornication or other sins of impurity, or 'Honour thy father and mother,' obedience to kings, and respect for the grey-head. What an undutiful captious spirit is it which pleads for self-indulgence in every thing which the very letter of Scripture does not absolutely in set words prohibit; which will do nothing, give up nothing, unless it 'find it in the bond,' though it be ever so plain, that the whole class of actions to which it belongs is included even in the very letter, and one exactly corresponding is specified. In what way will such arguers prove, on Scripture grounds, 'suicide' to be self-murder? It is plain, then, that all union with the sister of a deceased wife is condemned, in spirit, as defilement; the very words in which it is prohibited imply this; they are such as this age, so refined in words, so carnal in thoughts and actions, does not like to repeat. Will it, then, be pleaded that the 'sister's wife' is not 'near of kin,' although the husband's brother is? And if the one union be pollution, what else can the other be?"—Pp. 6—8.

Mr. Reynolds argues (Considerations, p. 31) that the Levitical prohibition against marriage with a brother's widow cannot be extended to marriage with a deceased wife's sister, because this general rule is set aside by the positive injunction which enjoins marriage with an elder brother's widow, (Deut. xxv. 5,) when that elder brother died childless. It seems significant that this very case was urged by the Sadducees against our Lord's doctrine of the resurrection: our Saviour sets it aside as inapplicable to the heavenly state of the children of the new Kingdom; and it seems difficult to understand how a permission, granted only in the case where there were *no children*, will apply to one of a directly opposite case, in which the same relaxation is sought, expressly for the reason that there *are already children*. To raise up seed to a deceased brother, for the purpose of perpetuating his name and preserving his inheritance, is, in principle, as in fact, very different from finding two mothers to the same family.

IV. It is asked, "under what circumstances and from what causes this prohibition has been introduced into any of the codes of Christian Europe?" We answer at once, from the universal consent of the Church interpreting the Divine Law of Holy Scripture. It is very well for Mr. Reynolds (p. 39) and his friends to quote Chillingworth's hackneyed maxim, " The Bible, and the Bible only;" but Hooker, to whom he avouches so much deference, might have taught him (b. ii. *passim*) " that Scripture is not necessary to be expressly referred to in every action of obedience;" is " not the only law by which God hath made known his will;" is " not the only way of knowing things whereby God is glorified;" and " how unsound their opinion is who think we have no assurance of doing well excepting from Scripture." " For in every action of common life to find out some sentence clearly and infallibly setting before our eyes what we ought to do, (seem we in Scripture never so expert,) would trouble us more than we are aware;—others justly condemning the opinion of the schools of Rome grow likewise into a dangerous extremity, as if Scripture did not only contain all things in that kind necessary, but all things simply, and in such sort, that to do, any thing according to any other law were not only unnecessary, but even opposite unto salvation, unlawful, and sinful." (b. ii. *in fine.*) Supposing, then, that Scripture had not condemned this case of marriage; far from the prohibition of the Church being unlawful, " oppression," or " tyranny," it would be our duty to yield cheerful obedience to it; on the higher ground, because the Church had collected this prohibition from Scripture, or as a lower motive, because the wisdom of past ages had sanctioned it. Universal consent is not only a Catholic rule but a maxim of duty, even upon natural grounds of reason. To the churchman it comes in the reverend guise of unearthly authority; to the philosopher it recommends itself clothed in the robe of seemly propriety. We may be permitted to think the earliest days of the Gospel's youth a better rule of life than times of which it is said, and with too much fearful truth, that " marriage has now become, in the eye of the law, to all intents, a civil rite only," (Present State of the Law, &c. pp. 10, 11 ;) and against the practice of Prussia and Hanover, Hamburgh and Denmark, we may quote the universal law of the Catholic Church; and " what George the Second allowed, or what ex-chancellor Kent pronounced valid by the municipal law of New York ! " (Considerations, p. 58, note,) may be met by the Apostolical Canons, and the decrees of all Christian councils. Mr. Fry and Mr. Alleyne *(quales quantique viri !)* stand but little chance with S. Basil; and we have little reason to fear, even though Mr. Justice Story tell us that " it seems difficult to extend the prohibition of incest beyond the relation of brother and sister upon principle,"—or though Paley make incest a notion of mere expediency, a sort of bugbear to prevent fornication, which in itself has no real existence,—or though Montesquieu regulate truth entirely by the custom of the country. We repeat that we have little reason to fear, while Archbishops Cranmer and Parker, and Bishop Jewel, and Hooker and Hammond, are with us; and as far as the Clergy of our own Church are concerned, we cannot be persuaded that they are ready to exchange the Canons of 1571 and 1603, which to them at least are law, for Lord Brougham and the Examiner newspaper. On this latter head we shall best satisfy our readers by extracting Hammond's summing up of the authority of the Church.

" It is manifest that the Church of Christ, which will bear sway with all humble and sober Christians, and to whose canons none did ever obstinately deny submission without the brand and reward of schism, that great sin of carnality in the apostle's account, most contrary to the unity of members, and to the meekness prescribed by Christ, hath through all ages from the apostolical first and purest times been most strict in prescribing abstinence from such liberties, particularly this which we have now in hand: which appears partly by the infamy which hath attended such marriages, which supposes them to have been reputed unlawful by some former law, partly by the plain words of canons which have forbid them. The apostolic canons (can. 19) forbid the taking of any man into the clergy, making him bishop or deacon, which shall have married two sisters, (one after the death of the other,) or the brother's daughter, Ὁ δύο ἀδελφὰς ἀγαγόμενος, ἢ ἀδελφιδῆν, οὐ δύναται εἶναι κληρικός. And Zonaras styles it there ἀθεμιτογαμίαν, *an incestuous marriage.* Where, if it be thought that this is no mark of the unlawfulness of the thing, but only an interdict to the clergy, that they shall not marry thus, leaving it free to others; this will be the same strange way of arguing, as if from the qualifications of the bishop, set down by St. Paul, that he should be "no drunkard, no covetous person," &c. *i. e.* that such as are so should not be admitted to holy orders, we should conclude that these qualities might be lawful and free for other men, who were not ecclesiastics; or because the bishop must be one that hath not married after such divorces as are forbidden by Christ, and the widow is to be the wife but of one husband, in like manner, it were therefore lawful for all other Christians to use such divorces and marry again, which we know was prohibited by Christ, or that other Christian women might have more husbands, or leave one and marry another, which we know was never lawful among any civil, though heathen, people. The plain of it is, that the only thing conclusible from the interdicts of the Church Canons is the frequency of such practices among unbelievers, which made it necessary to revive and refresh the prohibition to Christians; to whom, under Christ, such marriages were reputed so foul, and the state of such sins, being permanent, did so much enhance them above the nature of single acts of greater sins, that, although for every commission of any known sin a man were not made uncapable of any dignity in the Church, (or rendered irregular, if after the receiving orders he were found guilty,) yet of these sins he that were once guilty should for ever remain under a brand, and be counted uncapable of holy orders, which he that were otherwise worthy would not surely have been, had it not been accounted unlawful before that canon inflicted that punishment on the offender. And then it being acknowledged that Christ hath not descended to the specifying of such particulars, and that the apostle that speaketh of one such sin saith it was not named among the Gentiles, the result will be, that this brand of the apostolical canon is founded in the universal prohibition, obliging all men, and so the Christians of all nations, as well as the Jews, and that not abrogated but confirmed, and, by stricter precepts of continence, and denunciations against the incontinent, continued on the Christian by Christ.

"What was thus punished and marked by the apostolical canon, was after, in the Council of Eliberis, universally interdicted to all under a severe penance, (Can. 61;) or rather a penance of such a quality assigned to it, which presupposed the prohibition and acknowledged unlawfulness of it. Si quis post obitum uxoris suæ sororem ejus duxerit, et ipsa fuerit fidelis, quinquennium a communione placuit abstineri. And the like is so frequent throughout the canons, and so acknowledged to be so, that there is no need of multiplying any more testimonies. They who have disputed this interdict, and against whose doubts this discourse was designed, being the men who express their displeasure against the tyranny of the Church Canons, which have, say they, obtruded these restraints upon men, who have otherwise a richer inheritance of liberty belonging to them.

"To these I shall add but this one thing, that if the authority of the universal Church of Christ be so vile to them, yet the authority of the civil magistrate and municipal laws being not so profestly under their prejudice, it is sufficiently known that thus much of the canon law is received into, and confirmed by, the law of this land, and the marrying the wife's sister expressly prohibited." (See Stat. 25 Henry VIII. c. 22; and 28 Henry VIII. c. 38; and Lord Coke's Magna Charta, p. 683.)—A Letter of Resolutions to Six Quæres of present Use in the Church of England. Second Quære of Marrying the Wife's Sister. Hammond's Works, vol. i. p. 446.*

---

* To these authorities may be added the council of Neocæsarea, A.D. 314, can. 2, quoted by Parker, the council of Agde, A.D. 506, (Labbe, vol. iv. p. 1393,) can. 61. De incestis conjunctionibus nihil prorsus veniæ reservamus, nisi cum adulterium separatione sanaverint. Incestos vero nullo conjugii nomine deputandos, quos etiam designare funestum est, hos esse censemus. Si quis relictam fratris, quæ pene prius soror

It need scarcely be observed that the great case in which the principle of prohibiting marriage with the wife's sister was fully debated is Henry the Eighth's marriage with Queen Catharine, the widow of his brother Prince Arthur. For the affinity is the same: by consanguinity a man may not marry his sister; by affinity he may marry neither his wife's sister nor his brother's widow. The argument, which was fully sifted in the latter case, will help us to a knowledge of the former.

It seems scarcely doubtful that the principle at the period of the Reformation was almost universally settled. The dispensation from Pope Julius, in the first instance, to permit Henry's marriage, at least shows what the natural construction was, viz. that the marriage was bad; for why dispense with what required no dispensation? Several subsidiary points were raised during the controversy, which served to perplex the whole matter; such as the power of the Pope, *in limine*, to dispense with a divine law, or with the Church's rule; the *fact* of the consummation of the marriage with Prince Arthur; and the power of another Pope to annul a marriage which his predecessor had sanctioned. For it is quite obvious that many divines and canonists might be opposed to the divorce, as they settled either of these points, and yet might maintain the unlawfulness *per se* of the marriage as a principle. One might, on the most extravagant Roman theory, hold that the Pope had the power of dispensing with all law, moral, and ceremonial, and divine;—that he was above all fathers and councils; and on this ground he might maintain the validity of the king's marriage, though he was not tied to affirm the same of other such marriages, without the same papal dispensation. Another, again, might

---

exstiterat, carnali conjunctione polluerit: *si quis frater germanam uxoris acceperit*. This canon is repeated at the Council of Epone, A.D. 517, (Labbe, vol. iv. p. 1580,) can. 30. One copy adds, " suæ," and one reads " si quis frater germanam uxorem accipiat;" but, as Sirmond remarks, *male*. And again, at the second council of Tours, A.D. 567, (Labbe, vol. v. p. 862.) can. 21, which recites the decree of Epone, " Si quis insuper germanam uxoris suæ acceperit," and quotes the Theodosian code, B. iii. Tit. xii. Etsi licitum veteres crediderunt, post mortem mulieris contrahere cum ejusdem sorore conjugium: abstineant hujusmodi nuptiis universi: nec æstiment posse legitimos liberos ex hoc consortio procreari: nam spurios esse convenit qui nascentur. So also the first council of Arles, A.D. 314, c. 18, and the first council of Clermont (Arvernense), A.D. 535, c. 12. It is right to say that Bingham seems to have read the canon of Agde, repeated at the councils of Epone, Tours, and Clermont, " Si quis frater uxorem germanam acceperit," which he translates, (vol. vii. p. 283,) " if any one takes to wife his own sister." But with all respect for such authority, it is submitted that the usual reading, " Si quis frater germanam uxoris acceperit," is correct. 1st, From the addition of "suæ" in the subsequent councils; 2d, It may be doubted whether "germanam uxorem acceperit," even supposing that to be the reading, does not mean his wife's sister; 3d, All the cases are of affinity, not of consanguinity; and to mention " his own sister by blood," as Bingham would have it, is inconsistent with that degree (the brother's widow), which in the enumeration precedes it and with those which follow it; and lastly, because the council of Tours, which quotes it, does so for the especial purpose of condemning king Charibert, who married Mèroflede, the sister of his wife Marovefe. (Gregory of Tours.) The prohibition of the Theodosian code was continued throughout the existence of the empire, and engrafted into the canon law of Europe. The penalty inflicted upon parties contracting these incestuous marriages was scourging and banishment.

hold that the queen had never been by consummation Prince Arthur's wife. Catharine herself opposed the divorce upon this ground; the most tenable, and perhaps the most true. If so, the divorce was bad, without debating the original question upon the canon law. Or lastly, from jealousy of any infringements of the authority of Rome, many might hold that a divorce were impossible, where a dispensation was once granted, even though they might hesitate as to the Pope's original power or regularity in granting the dispensation; that is, to defend the validity of a thing when done did not pledge them to the regularity of the proceeding before it was done.

It is but fair to admit, however, that there was at least one good name which may be quoted (which, by the bye, it has not been) by Mr. Reynolds: it is Cardinal Cajetan. Of the Protestants the less said the better. Œcolampadius, Phrygion, Zuingle, and, it is believed, Calvin, maintained the obligation of the law in Leviticus; but Bucer took the opposite ground; so did P. Martyr; while Luther and Melancthon actually declared that they would rather allow the king to have two wives at once than to divorce Catharine. Melancthon, like the notorious Calvinist preacher, Mr. Madan, openly offered to justify polygamy. This difference among the Reformers shows that Mr. Reynolds must have trusted as much to the credulity or ignorance of his readers, as he has drawn hazardously upon his own slender stores of literature or great stock of venturesomeness, when he asserts that what he calls "the Protestant Church of Europe," on the question of Henry's divorce, asserted that marriage with a deceased brother's wife is not forbidden to Christians. When he adds that the English Universities decided in the first instance " that the prohibitions under the Levitical law were not binding under the Gospel," Mr. R. states what is not true: this question never came before them; the point upon which they were divided, and upon which their decision was, we fear, purchased, was whether the divorce was good or not.

We extract from Collier, vol. iv. p. 163, the substance of the arguments on either side.

" Cardinal Cajetan endeavoured to prove the prohibitions in Leviticus were no branches of the moral law. They were not observed, as he reasons, before the law, no, not by the holy seed. For did not Abraham marry his sister, and Jacob two sisters? Thus Judah made no scruple to give his two sons to Tamar; and after their decease married her to the third. To advance to the Mosaic institution, the prohibition in Leviticus is relaxed in Deuteronomy, which proves the law was not moral; for whatsoever is moral must by consequence be immutable. Then, as to the places cited for the divorce, from the New Testament, they would not bear in [on?] the argument. For instance, St. John Baptist's reproof of Herod is foreign to the point: for both Eusebius and Josephus inform us, that his brother Philip was alive, when Herod lived with his wife, and by consequence this prince's crime was adultery, and not incest. . . . . .

" From all which those who wrote against the divorce concluded,—' That the laws touching the degrees of marriage were binding only to the Jews; and that Christians were bound to obey them no farther than they were incorporated with the laws of the Church; and that it was in the Pope's power to dispense with the ecclesiastical custom and constitutions.' . . . . .

"To these arguments, those who wrote for the king's cause replied,—'that they were surprised to find men, who declared against heretical novelties, to argue in so unorthodox a manner! For what is the inlet into all heresy in the opinion of Catholic doctors? Is it not the setting up new interpretations of Scripture? Is it not the preference of private reasoning to the doctrine and tradition of the Church? We have fully made out that the Fathers have unanimously maintained the Levitical prohibitions of marriage to be of a moral and unalterable nature; and that Cajetan was the first that was so hardy as to set up his own exposition against the sense of antiquity. It is true, before the Mosaic law, these prohibited degrees were not observed; but this proves only that the immorality of such a correspondence does not strike full upon the understandings of all men. And therefore, since the thing has not the clearest evidence, nor can be easily discovered by the light of nature; considering this, we need not wonder to find a law in Leviticus for the better direction of practice. And as for the instance of Judah and Tamar, there is so much irregularity in all the circumstances, that it does not seem safe to bring it into precedent. And as to the permission of marrying the brother's wife, we can only infer from hence, that the reason of the law is not altogether unalterable. From whence it follows, that it may be dispensed with by the authority which made it. But though Moses relaxed by divine revelation, it does not follow that the Pope can give this liberty by the privilege of his character.'

"As to the instance of Herod they assert 'it is not clear from Josephus, that Philip was alive when Herod married his wife: for Josephus says no more than that she eloped from her husband, and then divorced herself from him.' . . . . .

"And now, whether those who argued for the divorce disentangled the texts of Leviticus and Deuteronomy may be somewhat a question. For granting, as they affirm, the prohibition in Leviticus was binding on all nations; granting this, why should not the dispensation in Deuteronomy be interpreted to the same extent? Why should the relaxation not be as general as the restraint? It is a received maxim, that laws are to be expounded in favour of liberty. Indeed, were there any limitation in the text to bar this privilege, the case would be altered. But since this cannot be pretended, why may not Christians have the benefit of the Deuteronomy exception as well as the Jews? Since the gospel allows greater liberties in other matters, why must it give less in this? Has not God as great a regard for the public interest and the repose of kingdoms, under the Christian as under the Jewish Church? And if so, how can the provision allowed the one be denied the other?"

To which last inquiry we reply, as Hammond argues in his Practical Catechism on the question of divorce, that the Old Testament economy was an imperfect state; that we as Christians are living not under greater liberty, but under a stricter yoke of purity; that Christ has brought us back to the first institution and law of marriage, viz. that man and wife " shall be one flesh ;" that the prohibition of Leviticus was *a principle*, from which it was not to be expected that the Gospel would retract, rather that it would adopt it and engraft something more upon it; but that the dispensation in Deuteronomy was, like the Jewish divorces, " a precept of permission, or not holding them up to that high pitch of the first institution of marriage— for the hardness of their hearts, a tolerating or permitting, or not forbidding them to do, for some time, till the season of more perfect commands should come."

Cajetan's arguments, however, and Collier's remarks, which tend the same way, are best refuted by Hammond's admirable Resolution of the Six Quæres, from which we have already quoted, and to which we refer our readers. It is too little known. We wish that our space permitted an abstract of this great Doctor's whole argument. But to proceed with the history of the question: after the passing of the act (25 Henry VIII.) above alluded to, and which contains the prohibition in question, Cranmer, two years after, in a letter to Cromwell, takes occasion to mention the principle upon which the restriction was grounded. (Strype's Cranmer, vol. i. p. 66.)

"By the law of God, many persons be prohibited which be not expressed, but be understood, by like prohibition in equal degree. As St. Ambrose saith, that the niece is forbid by the law of God, although it be not expressed in Leviticus, that the uncle shall not marry his niece. But where the nephew is forbid there, that he shall not marry his aunt, by the same is understood that the niece shall not be married unto her uncle. Likewise, as the daughter is not there plainly expressed, yet, when the son is forbid to marry his mother, it is understood that the daughter may not be married to her father; because they be of like degree. As touching the act of Parliament concerning the degrees prohibited by God's law, they be not so plainly set forth as I would wish. Wherein I somewhat spake my mind at the making of the said law, but it was not then accepted. I required then that there must be expressed mother, and mother-in-law; daughter, and daughter-in-law;—also sister, and sister-in-law; aunt, and aunt-in-law; niece, and niece-in-law. And this limitation, in my judgment, would have contained all degrees prohibited by God's laws, expressed and not expressed."

Upon this principle Archbishop Parker's table of the prohibited degrees was drawn up in 1560, and inserted in the Canons of 1603. Strype, (Parker, vol. i. pp. 174-5,) from some notes on a printed copy in the archbishop's own hand, quotes,—

"Mulier si duobus nupserit fratribus, abjiciatur usque in diem mortis.—Conc. Neocæs. Can. 2."

"Henry VIII. 25, c. 22.—This statute repealed, but yet the reason of the law doth remain, which saith, that there be degrees prohibited by God's word."

"Fratris uxorem ducendi, vel duabus sororibus conjungendi, penitus licentiam submovimus, nec dissoluto quocunque modo conjugio."

In the Canons of the Convocation of 1571, this case is especially alluded to.

"Maxime vero, si quis, priore uxore demortuâ, ejus sororem uxorem duxerit; hic enim gradus communi doctorum virorum consensu et judicio putatur in Levitico prohiberi."

Such was the state of the law, both statute and canon, connected, however, with this anomaly, that "such marriages were not void *ab initio*, but voidable only by sentence of separation, and therefore esteemed valid to all civil purposes, unless such separation is actually made during the life of the parties."—(Blackstone, Com. i., as quoted by Cardwell, Documentary Annals, vol. i. p. 283, n.)

A "friendly suit" in the ecclesiastical courts by the parties themselves contracting such a marriage was resorted to as a bar to any hostile suit on the part of others; and this virtually made the marriage impregnable. This absurd state of things was put an end to by Lord Lyndhurst's act of 1835, which enacted " That all marriages which should thereafter be celebrated between persons within the prohibited degrees of affinity or consanguinity should be absolutely null and void to all intents and purposes whatsoever." So far so well: but the real ground of this measure was another clause, which legalized all such incestuous marriages contracted before its introduction; and this, it is usually believed, to meet a particular case in the higher classes of society. Here was the point of the wedge: true, the legislature pronounces marriage within the degrees of affinity null and void, but it does not define what the degrees of affinity are, and it legitimatizes for the past all such marriages as the spiritual courts must, if the matter had been fairly brought before them, have pronounced incestuous. Then commenced the agitation, which began we can all guess where. Lawyers are employed, societies formed, petitions got up, the clergy canvassed, misrepresentation and falsehood do their best; the arguments *ad misericordiam* and *ad verecundiam,* and perhaps *ad crumenam,* are not spared, and why?—because a few persons of uncontrollable passions have contracted, or wish to contract, these sinful connexions, which God's law calls incest, and man's law illegal, and even the world stigmatizes as disgraceful. We do most earnestly and solemnly protest against this unholy attempt to loosen that reverence for the marriage mystery which has already been among us but roughly handled. To give even legal license to incest— for no act of parliament in the world can make it one shade higher than incest in the eye of the Church—would be a heavy national sin; to tempt the clergy to commit perjury by uniting such parties thus closely connected; to hold out the lure of statutory sin to brothers and sisters, —for this is the real relationship,—is what we must not contemplate without horror and loathing. As a Church, we have in this matter to maintain the universal practice of the Catholic body in her best days, sanctioned, too, and enforced in the most emphatic manner not only by the saints of old, but by those Reformers beyond whom some of us are not disposed to look: all parties, then, (if we must mix up even thoughts of our sad divisions in this grave matter,) are interested, if they love the gospel purity at all, in condemning the proposed change. As a nation, we have a duty to maintain those laws which are only assaulted by paid clamour or by men of ill-regulated passions. As a christian people, we have the chaste relations of domestic life and some of our holiest feelings to preserve from a very wanton outrage. It is a sad evidence of a people's morals to be told that persons of opposite sexes cannot preserve purity unless we hold out inducements for them to marry; and woe be to us if we think that we must encourage incest to prevent fornication! To conclude on this, the alleged moral ground of the proposed change, we once more quote Dr. Pusey.

"And what, then, is the great benefit for which all this present evil is to be incurred, and all this future pollution entailed? Passion, of course, never wants a plea: and it is, humanity! It is supposed that, in a certain number of cases, widowers will marry the sisters of their departed wives, and so the mother be provided for them which the departed would most have desired; and for this contingency all our domestic relations are to be broken up! At present, we are by all accounted the most domestic of all nations; the prohibition of such marriages is the safeguard of our domestic relations; the sister of the deceased can be the mother of her children, because she can only be a sister to their father; the father's brother can take his niece for his own child, because she can enter into no nearer relation with him than the child of his own mother's son. All within the prohibited degrees are privileged persons; no bar can be placed to their intercourse, because no security is needed; it is guileless, because no suspicion can be entertained. Take away the restrictions, and the confidence is destroyed. This is sorrowfully confessed by Germans, who have legalized the abuses of modern Rome in the same way as is now sought to be done among ourselves. Their domestic relations are broken up; those who so stand to each other must be every thing, or they can be nothing; those who can be united in marriage, unless they are so, must, by the laws of society every where, be as strangers. There is reason to believe that Germans, who know the happy confidence of our domestic relations, would gladly exchange for it that license which has forfeited theirs.

"And thus, as it will ever be, they who would outstep nature forfeit the privileges and gifts which, by the law of nature, they enjoyed; affection is sacrificed to passion; the very object which they professed to wish to secure is lost; grasping at the shadow, they lose the substance. There are surely, in a Christian land, many who share the feeling which even a heathen could appreciate;

"Ille meos, primus qui me sibi junxit, amores
Abstulit; ille habeat secum, servetque sepulcro.

"There are, surely, many Christians whose hopes being beyond the grave, their love too is beyond the grave; who can love no second with a husband's love, because they still love the first; who, looking to be re-united, though as the angels of God in heaven, after this earth, cannot on this earth displace that union by another; their union continues still, though invisible. Nay, so strong is this feeling, that many of those who contract second marriages merely do so because they have none within that privileged circle who can take the mother's place. All this would be destroyed; the happy confidence with which now the relations of a man's wife are regarded, and are to him as his own, would be at an end; the same rules of society which now prohibit the widower from taking any guardian to his children with whom intermarriage would be likely, would then exclude these now privileged friends; the sister could not be a mother to her sister's children without being their stepmother, or the prospect of children, who must be nearer to her, as being her own; one class of persons would be driven into marriages which they half disapproved, and so a stumbling-block be put in their way and their consciences defiled; another would forfeit the privileges which are a consolation of widowhood."—Pp. 12—14.

ON EPISCOPAL VISITATIONS.

No. V.

I now proceed to redeem the pledge which was given at the conclusion of the last article on the subject of Episcopal Visitations, and to offer some account of the ancient mode of proceeding on those occasions.

The principal object of these visits to each parish was the cure of souls, which was especially incumbent on the bishop, in virtue of his office, as a successor of the apostles. It is the tendency even of the best and holiest institutions, not to improve, but to decay, and fall into disorder; and human nature requires the continual stimulant of the external ministry of God's word, and of the admonitions and discipline of the Church, in order to be restrained from the commission of sins, and encouraged to the practice of virtue. But diseases cannot be cured unless they are known to the physician—unless the sick are visited by their physicians, and their complaints diligently investigated and examined. It was for this reason that the fathers and the canons of the universal Church, so earnestly urged on bishops the duty of continually going throughout their dioceses, visiting every particular church and parish; and we accordingly find that the most holy bishops were almost continually engaged in this apostolical ministry, going from church to church, and strengthening the brethren in all parts.

The objects of episcopal visitations being such, it remains to be seen how those objects were carried into effect, and to this end I shall first examine the proceedings which anciently took place previously to a parochial visitation; secondly, the mode of dealing with the clergy; thirdly, the mode of dealing with the laity; and fourthly, I shall consider the mode of visitation in later ages, and make some general remarks on the subject.

I. In early ages, when the rule of the Church obliged the bishops to visit every parish in their dioceses, either personally or by deputy, every year, or even more frequently when necessity so required, there was no occasion for any long previous notice of the arrival of the visitor. One of the earliest regulations on this subject is found in a canon made by a synod held at Rouen, the date of which is not quite certain, but appears to have been sometime in the ninth century, as it was cited by Regino, Abbot of Prum, about the year 906. It is as follows:—

"When a bishop perambulates his diocese, the archdeacon or archpresbyter ought to precede him by one or two days, in the parishes which he is about to visit; and assembling the people, should announce the coming of their own pastor, and enjoin, by the authority of the holy canons, that all should assemble in his synod on the day fixed, without fail; and declare with threats, that if any one be absent, without urgent necessity, he shall be, without doubt, repelled from christian communion. Then, taking with him the presbyters who in that place are bound to exhibit obedience to the bishop, let him endeavour to amend whatever of the lesser and lighter causes he can correct, that when the bishop comes he may not be wearied with easy questions, or be compelled to make a longer stay than the procurations suffice for. For the Lord says to Moses of such fellow-workmen, 'That they bear with thee the burden of the people, and that thou alone be not burdened.' (Num. xi.) And St. John the Baptist preceded the coming of the Lord, preaching and saying, ' Repent ye,' &c.; and again, ' Prepare ye the way of the Lord.' For the bishop seems to be the representative of Christ; and, therefore, he is to be received with joy, fear, and the greatest reverence by the people subject to him, that it may be said of them with praise, as the apostle said to the disciples, 'I testify unto you, that ye have received me as an angel of God, as the Lord Jesus,' (Gal. iv.)"

According to Barbosa,[*] a learned writer on these subjects, the notice given on such occasions ought to be six or eight days at least, and is to be made in writing, under the episcopal seal, and transmitted by a messenger. The practice of sending the archdeacon or archpriest to give a verbal notice, seems, therefore, not to have been universal, or to have become obsolete by time. Perhaps we may trace in the canon above adduced, one of the modes by which archdeacons gradually came to possess the power of ordinary visitation.

It was generally the custom for the clergy and people to meet the bishop in procession, on his approach towards their parish. This was a usual mark of respect paid, in the primitive Church, to its chief pastors on remarkable occasions. It is recorded, that when St. Epiphanius came to Constantinople, he was met by Chrysostom, bishop of that see, at the head of a procession of all the clergy. When St. Athanasius returned to Alexandria from exile, he was met by all the citizens arranged in different divisions, according to their ranks, ages, and sexes.[†] An ancient life of St. Porphyrius, mentions, that on his return to Constantinople, he was received by a number of Christians, who chanted psalms, and carried the cross in procession.[‡] When Cæsarius, Bishop of Arles, returned from exile to his church, all the inhabitants of both sexes went out to meet him, carrying the cross, and lights, and singing psalms.[§] In later ages, different ceremonies were devised in various churches to add solemnity and splendour to these processions. It is not, indeed, certain, that bishops were always received in this manner in their visitations; though the ancient pontificals of the Roman Church, published previously to the Reformation, all prescribe the practice. Wherever it was customary, however, the ceremony appears to have consisted principally in singing psalms, and accompanying the bishop

---

[*] Augustin Barbosa, De Offic. et Potestat. Episcopi, pars iii. Alleg. 72, art. 19.
[†] Gregor. Naz. Orat. in Laude Athanasii.
[‡] Vita Porphyrii à Marco Diacono, apud Surium, xxvi. Februarii.
[§] Cyprianus, Vita S. Cæsarii, Sur. xxvii. August.

in procession to the church, where, according to the Roman pontifical, he first proceeded to offer his prayers in private, and then gave his blessing to the people.

II. We now proceed to the examination of the clergy.

It will have been observed, that in the canon above cited from the Council of Rouen, the archdeacon or archpriest gives notice of the bishop's "synod." The visitation, then, was in those days regarded as a synod—a *parochial* synod, which all the priests and people of the parish were expected to attend. In the Western Church, at least, the clergy appeared twice in the year before their bishop; first, they came to them before Easter, and gave an account of their ministry.* This regulation was enforced in a synod at which Boniface, Archbishop of Mayence, was present, and is mentioned in his Epistle to Cuthbert, Archbishop of Canterbury. The canon was in the following terms:—"We have decreed, according to the canons of the saints, that every priest dwelling in a diocese be subject to the bishop of that diocese in which he dwells, and that he always give and show unto the bishop, in Lent, an account and order of his ministry, whether concerning baptism, or concerning the catholic faith, or concerning prayers, and the order of divine service." The same custom is also mentioned by Herard, Archbishop of Tours;† but in after ages, the rule was not strictly adhered to.

The other occasion on which an examination of the conduct of the clergy took place, was in the parochial visitation which we are now considering.

The parochial visitation was in some sort a supplement of the diocesan synod. In the latter meeting, the clergy were instructed in their duties by the bishop, and regulations were published for the general direction of the ministers of religion. This custom seems to have been the origin of EPISCOPAL CHARGES, which are usually delivered at the triennial synods of the clergy, now called visitations.

Baluzius, in his notes on Regino, Abbot of Prum, has published from ancient manuscripts a copy of the Admonition which was given to the clergy at diocesan synods, from about the middle of the eighth century.‡ I shall translate some portion of this formulary, because it seems to throw light on the origin of episcopal charges, and because it doubtless represents the discipline which had prevailed on this point for many ages before this particular form was composed.

This Admonition, or Charge, was evidently intended to be delivered by the bishop, but it was frequently read by a deacon, and it commenced thus :—

"Brethren, presbyters and priests of the Lord, ye are fellow-workmen of our order. We, indeed, although unworthy, hold the place of Aaron; ye the place of Eleazar and Ithamar. We are in the place of the twelve apostles; ye are in the form of the seventy disciples. We are your pastors; ye, the pastors of the souls committed to you. We shall render an

---

* Hincmar, Capitula, tit. v. c. v.
† Herardi, Capitula. c. lxxiii.
‡ Reginonis, Abb. Prum. De Eccl. Discipl. à Baluzio edit. pp. 534, 602.

account of you to the chief pastor, our Lord Jesus Christ; ye, of the people entrusted to you. And, therefore, beloved, behold your danger. Shall we then admonish and beseech you, brethren, to commend to your memories the things which we suggest to you, and to labour to put them in practice?

"First, we admonish you that your life and conversation be blameless; that is, that your dwelling be near the church, and that ye have no woman in your house. Rise every night for worship. Sing the psalms in course at certain hours. Religiously celebrate the eucharist. Receive the body and blood of the Lord with fear and reverence.... Let the altar be covered with clean linen, and let nothing be placed on it but relics, or the gospels, or the case containing the sacrament for the sick, &c.... Let none of you be given to drink or to litigiousness, for the servant of the Lord must not be contentious. Let no one bear arms in an affray, for our arms ought to be spiritual. Let no one sport with dogs or birds, or drink in taverns. Let each of you declare unto his people whatever he knoweth of the Gospel or Epistle on Sundays or holy days. Be careful of the poor, of strangers, of orphans, and invite them to your meals, &c.... Let no one leave the church to which he was ordained, and migrate to another for the sake of gain. Let no one hold several churches without the aid of other presbyters. Let not one church be divided amongst several priests, &c."

The above extract will suffice to give a general notion of the Admonition which was given to the clergy at the annual synod, and which informed them fully of the duties expected from them by their bishop. It was impossible for them to plead any ignorance after they had been thus fully and completely reminded of the requirements of their office.

The INQUIRY which was made in the parochial visitation, corresponded to this Admonition. It was intended to ascertain whether the admonition had been attended to, and obeyed. The form which is found in Regino, Abbot of Prum, is thus entitled :—

"AN INQUIRY OF THOSE THINGS WHICH A BISHOP OR HIS MINISTERS OUGHT TO EXAMINE IN HIS DISTRICT OR TERRITORY, THROUGHOUT THE TOWNS, VILLAGES, AND PARISHES OF HIS DIOCESE.

"1. First, it is to be inquired in honour of what saint is the church dedicated, and by whom it was consecrated. After this, let the church itself be examined, whether it be well covered and roofed, and whether no doves or other birds make their nests there.

"2. Of what metal the church bells be made.

"3. If hay, corn, or any such thing be put in the church.

"4. Then the altar should be approached, and it should be seen what are its coverings, how many new and old, and in what state of cleanliness.

"11. It is also to be observed, how many books are there; how many and what sacerdotal vestments, and if they are clean, and put in a clean place.

"13. It is to be inquired, whether the church has lands containing twelve *bonvaria* (a territorial measure) besides a cemetery, and the court wherein are the church and the priest's house, and whether it possesses four servants, &c.

"OF THE PRIEST'S LIFE AND CONVERSATION.

"16. It is to be inquired, whether the presbyter has his dwelling near the church, or if there be a gate in the inclosure, which is suspected.

"18. Whether he visits the sick, &c.

" 20. Whether any infant dies without baptism, through the negligence of the presbyter.

" 22. Whether he be given to drink, or to quarrelling.

" 23. Whether he bears arms in any disturbance.

" 24. Whether he sports with dogs or birds.

" 26. Whether he has a clerk to read the epistle or lesson, and make the responses in divine service, and to sing the psalms with him.

" 32. Whether he preaches the word of God to the people.

" 34. Whether he has care of the poor, of strangers, and orphans, and invites them to dine according to his means.

" 53. Whether he instructs all his parishioners in the Lord's Prayer and Creed.

" 58. Whether he admonishes all the faithful to approach the communion of the body and blood of the Lord three times in the year; that is, at Christmas, Easter, and Pentecost.

" 63. Whether putting aside clerical garments, he uses the dress of laymen.

" 65. Whether, after service, the presbyter himself receives the remainder of the body and blood of the Lord with fear and reverence; and if he has not a deacon or subdeacon, whether he himself, with his own hands, washes and cleans the paten and chalice.

" 72. Whether he instructs those who offer, that they bring their candles, or whatever else they may wish to offer, before the service, or before the gospel is read.

" WHAT IS TO BE REQUIRED OF THE PRESBYTER.

" 74. After all these things have been diligently investigated, then the presbyter himself is to be examined by the bishop or his vicar—

" 75. Whether he was born of noble parents, or of a servile condition.

" 76. Whether he was born or ordained in the same diocese or another.

" 79. If of another diocese, let him show his letters commendatory, which they call *Formatæ*, &c.

" *After this, inquiries are to be made concerning the ministry entrusted to him.*

" 81. Whether he has the exposition of the Creed and the Lord's Prayer in his possession, in writing, and fully understands them, and from thence diligently instructs the people committed to him by preaching.

" 83. Whether he can well read the Epistle and Gospel, and explain its meaning, at least literally.

" 84. Whether he can regularly say by heart the words and divisions of the psalms, with the accustomed hymns.

" 85. Whether he knows by heart the discourse of Athanasius concerning faith in the Holy Trinity, beginning, ' Whosoever will be saved,' &c.

" 94. Whether he has the forty homilies of Gregory, and studiously reads and understands them, &c."[*]

I have merely selected a few of the more interesting points of this examination, with a view to furnish a general notion of the sort of inquiries that were made. The form from which the preceding extracts have been made, represents the discipline in force in France, and other parts of the West, in the eighth and ninth centuries; and of course includes several points which would not have been found in the more ancient visitation inquiries.

It will be observed that the VISITATION ARTICLES which are still used in the Church are derived from these ancient formularies

---

[*] Regino, *ubi supra*, pp. 21—30.

or formed on their model. The only difference is, that these questions are now committed to writing, and transmitted to the clergy for their answers sometime previously to the visitation itself; whereas, the original system was to institute these examinations *vivâ voce*, and on the very spot.

III. We next proceed to the examination which was instituted in reference to the morals and conduct of the laity. It would seem, if we may judge from the formulary preserved by Regino, that this inquiry was conducted in a somewhat different manner from that of the clergy. It had been prescribed by the second synod of Braga, in Spain, that the bishop should on one day "inquire of the clergy how they perform baptism and the eucharist," and the other offices, &c.; and "after the bishop has discoursed with, and instructed his clergy, *on another day* assemble the people of that church, and teach them to avoid the error of idolatry and other crimes, such as homicide, adultery, perjury, &c., and that they believe the resurrection of all men, and the day of judgment," &c.* This inquiry seems to have been conducted with much more formality than that of the clergy. Regino gives the following rules which were observed on these occasions:—

"The bishop being seated in the synod, after a suitable discourse, ought to call out into the midst seven men, the most aged, honest, and veracious of the people of that parish, or more or fewer, as may be expedient; and bringing forth the relics of the saints, should bind each of them by this oath:—

"The Synodal Oath.

"Now, from henceforth, whatever thou knowest, or hearest, or shalt hereafter inquire into, which hath been done against the will of God, and right Christianity in this parish, or which shall be in thy days, provided it cometh to thy knowledge in any wise, if thou knowest it, or it hath been made known to thee to be a synodal cause, and pertaining to the administration of the bishop, thou shalt not by any means conceal from the bishop of Treves, or his vicar, neither for fear, nor for reward, nor for relationship. So God help thee, and these relics of the saints, &c.

"The Address of the Bishop.

"See, brethren, that ye perform unto the Lord your oaths. For ye have not sworn unto man, but unto God your Creator. But we, who are his ministers, do not desire your earthly substance, but the salvation of your souls. Beware lest ye conceal any thing, and your own damnation come from another's sin.

"*After this he shall thus inquire in order:*—

"1. Is there in this parish any homicide, who hath slain a man, either from his own choice, or for the sake of lucre or rapacity, or by chance, or involuntarily and by compulsion, or for revenge of his parents, or in war, or by command of his master, or who hath slain his own servant?

"2. Is there any parricide or fratricide, who hath slain father, mother, sister, uncle, or any other relation?

"3. Is there any one who hath slain or maimed a priest, or deacon, or any clergyman?

---

* Concil. Bracar. ii. c. 1.

"4. Is there any one who hath overlaid or suffocated his or her own infant; and if this was done before or after baptism; or if an infant died naturally by sickness, without receiving baptism, through the negligence of the parent?

"17. Whether any one has put away his lawful wife, and received another in marriage.

"18. Whether any woman has put away her own husband, and joined herself to another.

"19. Whether, through divorce, they are separated from each other, and so remain.

"20. Whether any one, without consent of his wife, forsakes lawful marriage, and enters a monastery.

"38. It is to be inquired, whether any have committed theft or sacrilege, who hath broken into churches, or stolen any thing from the church, or who hath publicly taken by force, or privately plundered; or any who is rapacious, and a robber and spoiler of the Church of God. For although these things ought to be amended and repaid according to human law, yet penance for them belongeth to the bishop.

"39. It is to be inquired, if any one be perjured, or hath committed perjury knowingly, and for earthly cupidity, &c.

"40. It is to be inquired, whether any one has knowingly borne false witness against his neighbour, because this is a capital crime, &c.

"41. It is to be inquired, whether any one hath stolen from a freeman, or the slave of another, or from a stranger and foreigner; or hath seduced him by kind words, and sold him into slavery, or sent him into captivity from his native country; or whether any one hath sold any Christian as a slave to a Jew or a pagan, or whether the Jews themselves sell christian slaves.

"42. It is also to be inquired, whether there is any magician, enchanter, diviner, &c.

"43. If there be any one who makes offerings to trees, wells, or certain stones, as at altars, &c.

"46. It is to be inquired, whether any one eats blood, or what dies naturally, or what is torn by a beast.

"47. If any one, through hatred, does not return to peace, or hath sworn, (what is contrary to God,) that he will never be reconciled to his brother, which is a sin unto death.

"56. Whether there be any Christian who does not communicate three times in the year, *i.e.* at Christmas, Easter, and Pentecost, unless he hath been removed from communion for deadly crimes, by judgment of the bishop or of the priests.

"58. Whether any excommunicated person disregards his excommunication, and whether any one communicates with the excommunicated.

"59. Whether any one does not observe the mode of penance enjoined to him.

"63. Whether any one be so perverse and alienated from God, as not to come to the church on the Lord's day at least.

"67. Whether any one, despising his own presbyter, cometh to another parish to church, and there communicates and pays his tithe.

"69. Whether in every parish, deans are appointed throughout the hamlets, men of truth, and fearing God, who may admonish the rest to go to morning prayer, the eucharist, and evening prayer, and not to do any work on feast-days; and if any one hath transgressed, to tell it immediately to the presbyter, &c.

"88. Whether any one, entering the church, is accustomed to spend his time in idle conversation, and does not diligently listen to the sacred oracles; and whether he departs from church before the service be ended.

"89. Whether men and women offer an oblation, that is, bread and wine, at the eucharist; and if the men do not, whether their wives offer for them, for themselves and all their families, as is contained in the canon."

The object of all these questions was the detection of the crimes and sins committed by the people, with a view to bring them to submit to penance, or else to subject them to the penalty of excommunication. This has been particularly remarked by Morinus, in his Treatise on Penance. He says, that in the above inquiry, an examination was instituted not only with regard to notorious crimes, but even with regard to those which were comparatively secret, or known to few persons. And why, he asks, was there such great diligence in inquiring after public and secret crimes? Those bishops did not examine merely as judges, but as physicians; nor did they deal with sinners as merely wicked persons, but as labouring under sickness. Such was their goodness and mercy towards those sick commended to them by God himself, that they administered the cure of penance to those who were even unwilling and reluctant. They would not have made such laborious and anxious inquiries, and afterwards done nothing. The object was to obtain the confession of sins, and to subject the offenders to the usual course of canonical penances. Morinus remarks, that the collection of Regino, from which the above extracts have been made, evidently implies this; for the inquiries are immediately followed by a large body of canons, derived from various councils, capitulars, and decrees of the fathers, assigning the length and determining the mode of the public penances for each offence.*

After the bishop had imposed penance on such as had expressed contrition by acknowledging their sins, they could only be reconciled to the Church, and admitted to communion by the bishop himself, at the expiration of their assigned period of penance; or at an earlier period, if the bishop should deem it right to extend indulgence to them. It is very probable, that in the course of these parochial visitations, the bishop most generally performed this office of absolution.

With regard to those whose sins had been detected in the abovementioned synodical examination, and who refused to submit to penance from the bishop, there can be no doubt that they were immediately subjected to excommunication in the parochial synod. Regino's collection contains several forms of excommunication adapted for these occasions, of which I shall transcribe the following:—

"A bishop, when he hath determined to excommunicate or anathematize any infidel for certain and manifest crimes, after the Gospel has been read, should thus address the clergy and people:—

"ADDRESS.

"Ye have heard, beloved, what great and horrible works of wickedness and iniquity, (such a man,) at the instigation of the devil, hath not feared to commit; and how he hath profanely departed by apostasy from the whole

---

* Morinus de Pœnitentia, p. 445, ed. Bruxell, 1685.

christian worship. Ye have heard how he hath been canonically invited to satisfaction, but hath refused to come; how, having been frequently admonished to repent from the snares of the devil by which he is held in bondage, he hath despised to hear most salutary admonitions, and closed the ears of his heart. The Lord saith in the Gospel, of such a contumacious brother, who refuses to hear the reproof of the Church, 'If he will not hear the Church, let him be unto thee as a heathen man and a publican:' that is, he is no longer to be counted amongst Christians, but amongst pagans. Hence, Paul, following the doctrine of his Lord and Master, reproved the Corinthians because they held communion with the criminal and wicked, saying, ' Ye are puffed up, and have not rather mourned, that he may be removed from amongst you;' that is, that he who hath committed such a crime, be separated from your communion. And he adds, ' I, indeed, as absent in body, but present in spirit, have judged already as if I were present concerning him who hath done this. In the name of our Lord Jesus Christ, when ye are assembled together, with my spirit, in the name of the Lord Jesus, to deliver such an one to Satan for the destruction of the flesh.' And shortly after, 'I have written to you not to keep company with fornicators.' And immediately he concludes, 'If any be called a brother, that is, a Christian, and be a fornicator or rapacious, with such an one no not to eat.' And elsewhere, 'Take away that evil thing from amongst you.' And, 'The unbeliever, if he departs, let him depart.' For one sheep that is diseased contaminates the whole flock; and a little leaven leaveneth the whole lump; and one putrid member infects the whole body. And therefore let such a pernicious plague be plucked up by the roots out of the Church.

"EXCOMMUNICATION.

"Therefore, being instructed by the precepts of the Lord and his apostles, by the judgment of the Father, and of his Son our Lord Jesus Christ, and of the Holy Spirit; by the authority and power given by God to the apostles, and the successors of the apostles; we, together with you, exclude and separate the aforesaid most wicked man from the threshold of the holy Church, our mother, and from all christian society and communion; and we decree his eternal separation, that is, in the present world, and in that which is to come. Let no Christian presume to say to him, Hail, or to salute him. Let no presbyter dare to celebrate the eucharist in his presence, or to give him the holy body and blood of the Lord. Let no one be united to him in marriage or in other affairs. And if any one unites with him, and communicates in his wicked works, let him know that he is struck by the same anathema—those excepted who unite with him for the sake of recalling him from his error, and bringing him to satisfaction; unless he should repent, and by the inspiration of God's grace be converted to the remedy of penitence, and by fitting amendment, humbly make satisfaction to the Church of God which he hath injured.

"A SHORT EXCOMMUNICATION.

" Following the institutions of the canons and the examples of the holy fathers, we expel these violaters of the churches of God from the bosom of the holy mother Church, and from christian communion, by the authority of God, and the judgment of the Holy Spirit, until they repent, and make satisfaction to the Church of God." *

There can be no doubt that on these occasions the bishops not only excommunicated impenitent offenders, but also restored those who had become penitent to the communion of the Church. Regino supplies a form for the use of bishops in such cases. It is in the following terms:—

---

* Regino, pp. 358—365.

"How a Bishop reconciles or receives an Excommunicated Person.

"When any one who has been excommunicated or anathematized is led by repentance to ask for pardon, and to promise amendment, the bishop who has excommunicated him ought to come before the doors of the church, and twelve presbyters with him, who ought to stand round him at either side, where also should be present those persons who have suffered injury or loss; and there the loss ought to be made good, according to the laws of God and man; or if it has already been made good, it should be proved by their testimony. Then the bishop shall inquire, whether he (the penitent) wishes to receive penance according to the direction of the canons, for the sins he has committed. And if he, prostrate on the ground, seeks for pardon, confesses his guilt, implores penance, and promises a security for his future conduct, then let the bishop, taking him by the right hand, introduce him into the Church, and restore him to christian society and communion. After this, let him enjoin penance to him according to the measure of his guilt, and direct letters throughout the diocese, that all may know that he is received into christian communion. Let him make it known also to other bishops. But let no bishop presume to excommunicate or to reconcile an inhabitant of another's diocese, without the knowledge or consent of his own bishop."*

It is certain that confirmation was generally administered in these parochial visitations; but whether it was before or after the above inquiries and exercise of discipline, is not certain: probably the rules varied in different churches. The same remark may be made as to the celebration of the eucharist, which took place on these occasions.

IV. Having now examined the ancient formularies preserved on these subjects by Regino, it may be interesting to carry on the investigation into later ages, and to ascertain the ceremonial which was observed in parochial visitations in the fifteenth century. I have now before me a manuscript pontifical, written about A.D. 1400, which accords pretty nearly with the earliest *printed* pontificals used in the Western Church, and which comprises the form for parochial visitations as follows:—

"The Order for visiting Parishes.

"A bishop, when he visits his parishes, which he is bound to do by the example of the Lord, who went round the villages teaching (Mark vi.), when he arrives, enters the church-yard, saying, De profundis, &c., with, 'Lord have mercy upon us,' &c. 'Our Father,' &c. [Then follows a collect for the souls of the departed.]

"And let the same be done when he wishes to go away. Then entering the church, he prostrates himself before the altar in prayer; and rising presently, kisses it in the middle of its front, and mass is said.

"Which being ended, and the benediction given, [by the bishop] he takes a surplice, amict, stole, cope, a plain mitre, and a pastoral staff, and propounds to the people the causes for which he is come. That is to say, because the sacred canons and order of the Church require this to be done, for many reasons:

"First, to absolve the souls of the departed; and,

"Secondly, that he may know and see how the same Church is governed in spirituals and temporals; how also it is in respect of ornaments; how the sacraments of the Church are administered there, and the divine offices

---

* Regino, *ubi supra*, pp. 365, 366.

performed; what service is discharged there; what is the life of the clergy and people; in order that if anything is to be corrected in the aforesaid, it be corrected and amended by him, by virtue of his official inquiry; and that he may enjoin books, and other necessary ecclesiastical ornaments to be made.

"Thirdly, to punish adulteries, fornications, fortune-telling, divinations, and like manifest crimes in the people, for which sometimes the rectors of churches are not sufficient: showing diligently to the people how damnable and detestable are those crimes.

"Fourthly, on account of causes which by law or custom belong only to the bishop, which are found in our synodal constitutions; with which no one else can interfere, protesting to the people, that if any person is in need of his advice in any of those cases, he is ready to hear them kindly, and to give them advice and absolution, and to enjoin salutary penance with mercy.

"Fifthly, to give the sacrament of confirmation, which no other but the bishop only can give, by divine and apostolical institution; for the Lord confirmed the apostles, and commanded that the people should be confirmed by the apostles, and their successors, that is, their bishops and superiors. He ought also to teach the people that no one who has been confirmed ought to be confirmed again; that no one who has not been confirmed can be a god-father in confirmation; that no excommunicate person, or any one guilty of grievous sins, present himself to receive this sacrament, or to present any for it; that adults ought first to confess, and afterwards to be confirmed; that in this sacrament, no one present more than one or two at most; that those who are to be confirmed be fasting, not as a matter of necessity, but as a matter of propriety....

"Sixthly, he diligently leads the people to repentance, and instructs them in the sacraments of the Church, and in the articles of the faith, and how they ought to decline from evil and do good, to avoid sin and to follow virtues; and that one should not do to another what he would not wish done to himself, and that he should do to others what he would wish done to him.

"This being concluded, let an indulgence be given, and the people make a general confession, and receive a general absolution.

"After this, taking a cope of a black colour, he goes forth into the cemetery. [Here follow several forms, including prayers for the departed: and the bishop blesses the cemetery, and sprinkles holy water around it. These ceremonies, being probably not very ancient, I do not think it necessary to give in detail.]

"After these things have been concluded, let the bishop lay aside his black cope, and taking a white cope, confirm the children, as has been said before, in the office for confirmation of children.

"Confirmation being finished, and any ornaments which are to be blessed having been so, and his ecclesiastical vestments being put off, the bishop hears confessions, and afterwards complaints, if there be any, and diligently inquires *de plano* concerning the life and conversation of the clergy and people, and how spirituals and temporals be ministered in the said church, and concerning the books and ornaments."

The above form coincides in most respects with that contained in the pontifical printed at Rome in 1497, and another printed at Colle (Collibus) in 1503.

On comparison with the form previously cited from Regino, it will be seen that many of the most stringent parts of the examination had become obsolete. We here find nothing of the synodal witnesses bound by oath to reveal crimes, nor do we hear any thing of the canonical penances, the excommunications, and the reconciliations of penitents, customary in ancient visitations. The inquiry seems not to have been conducted with any of the ancient strictness or solemnity. Still, however, there was much, even in the visitations of the fifteenth century, (when they were made,) which could not fail to have been highly beneficial to the Church. The bishop in effect still preached the word of God, administered the eucharist, held confirmations, and examined into the life and conduct of the clergy and people: he was still the pastor of every soul in his diocese, and the people felt that he was such, and were benefited by his admonitions.

The ancient rule of swearing synodal witnesses to give testimony as to all transgressions amongst the people was abolished by the regulation made by Innocent IV. concerning visitations, which I have cited in a former article, and which will presently be alluded to more particularly. The intention seems to have been, to restrain the proceedings to notorious crimes, and such as did not need any great investigation. The former method of examining by witnesses on oath, probably, may have been productive of inconvenience in disclosing offences that were not notorious and public, and in bringing forward many cases which might demand lengthened investigation, and might, therefore, have been less suitable for discussion in a parochial visitation than in an ecclesiastical court. The parochial visitation had more of a paternal, than of a formal judicial character: it was not conducted with those strict rules of law, or protracted to such a length, as would have been suitable to any causes except those of a very plain and obvious nature.

Van Espen remarks, that bishops and other visitors in their visitations should reform whatever is disordered, *sine strepitu ac formâ ordinariâ judicii, sed summariè, non pœnas ordinarias imponendo sed correctiones;* and that it should not relate to matters of a doubtful nature, and which require deeper investigation, but to matters of notoriety. And he adds, that while bishops do not exceed these limits in their visitations, and are intent only on the correction and improvement of morals, no exemption, appeal, or process can prevent the execution of what is ordained by the visitors. This, he says, was decreed by the Council of Trent, and also by that of Lateran under Innocent III.[*] With reference to matters of a *notorious* nature, Innocent IV., who flourished about A. D. 1250, had decreed that they should be punished at once in the parochial visitations. " In the discharge of this duty of visitation," the bishop was, according to this decree, to " propound the word of God, and examine the lives and conversation of the clergy," and " all other things pertaining to his office, without compulsion or the exaction of any oath, giving diligent heed to their correction." And "if an evil report hath arisen concerning any, he shall (that is, when he is a metro-

---

[*] Van Espen, Jus Eccl. Univers. pars i. tit. xvii. c. iv.

politan, visiting the diocese of another bishop) inform their ordinaries, that they may institute a solemn inquiry; but *notorious crimes*, which need no examination, he may correct at his pleasure, by inflicting due punishment, because the negligence of ordinaries, with respect to them, may be justly marked."*

Barbosa remarks, that a bishop cannot, when he is about to commence his visitation, propound injunctions by which his subjects are commanded to reveal crimes, under penalty of excommunication. A bishop also, according to him, cannot in his visitation impose the ordinary penalties of crime, but only extraordinary, which regard rather the amendment of morals, than the ordinary punishment of crime. His proceeding in the visitation or correction of morals cannot be interrupted by any appeal to a higher jurisdiction, provided the bishop acts without any legal formalities, writings, &c. It may, however, prevent a definitive sentence. The results of the visitation are to be entered in a book, which is a full proof of every thing relating to the visitation of persons, sacraments, and other matters pertaining to the office of the visitor. It is held that the process in visitations is to be made *summariè, et de plano, sine strepitu, et figurâ judicii*, and without citation of those who are to be visited, since they are virtually cited by the general injunction by which they are required to be present.†

Joannes Franciscus de Pavinis published in 1514 a Treatise on Visitations, which contains a great amount of information on this subject, combined with much extraneous matter; I shall merely add to what has been already said, his opinions as to the powers of bishops in visitations. He inquires how visitors ought, and can; exercise jurisdiction in those things which relate to the *forum contentiosum*; and answers, that according to the canon law, archbishops and other superiors may freely exercise jurisdiction in the dioceses of their suffragans, *on crimes of a notorious kind*, on account of the negligence of those suffragans. The notoriety is to be determined by the testimony of the people, or the greater part of them. The bishop may sit in any part of his diocese, and hear ecclesiastical causes, and may call on the civil power to enforce his judgments.‡ It seems plain, from the whole treatise, that the bishop has the power of punishing offences in his visitation, by excommunication, deposition, and the other penalties.

It appears from a statute passed at the beginning of queen Elizabeth's reign, that the bishops of England had always exercised the right of inflicting ecclesiastical censures in their visitations. It is therein provided, "That all and singular archbishops and bishops .. and other ordinaries, having any peculiar ecclesiastical jurisdiction, shall have full power and authority by virtue of this act, as well to

---

* Sextus Decretal. l. iii. tit xx. col. 573. ed. Paris, 1561.
† Barbosa, De Off. et Pot. Episc. pars iii. pp. 433—436.
‡ Joh. Franc. de Pavin. Tract. de Visit. Tractat. Juris Pontif. t. xiv. p. 198. ed. Venet. 1584.

inquire in their visitations, synods, and elsewhere within their jurisdiction, or any other time or place, to take occasions and informations of all and every the things above-mentioned, done, committed, or perpetrated within the limits of their jurisdiction or authority, and to punish the same by admonition, excommunication, sequestration, or deprivation, and other censures and process, in like manner as heretofore hath been used by the queen's ecclesiastical laws."*

That the bishops in England had, previously to the Reformation, the power of inflicting censures in their parochial visitations has been shown in the last article by various canons, constitutions, and examples.

It appears that, according to the canons of the Church of England, made in 1603, the churchwardens, or quest-men, and sidesmen in every parish, may *present* at the bishop's visitation, all those who are guilty of scandalous crimes, and all schismatics, disturbers of divine service, and papists. (See canons 109, 110, 111, 114, 116.)

On the whole, then, it would seem that the bishops of England have, at this present time, the legal power of visiting every parish in their dioceses at least once in three years, and of inquiring into all matters concerning the temporals and spirituals of each parish; and that they have the power of pronouncing ecclesiastical censures in those visitations, without any formal legal process, on such as are guilty of *notorious* crimes; and that they may also absolve from censures, and impose penance. In fine, they are authorized and directed by the canon law, to preach the word of God, and administer confirmation on these occasions; and they are also entitled to examine all pious and religious foundations, schools, &c. With reference to the conduct of the clergy, it would seem, that bishops are now prevented from doing more than instituting an examination, and administering reproofs or commendations; for, by a late act of parliament, the cognizance of all causes concerning the clergy has been restricted to a particular tribunal prescribed in that act. These observations on the present power of bishops are rather thrown out for the purpose of exciting inquiry, than as pretending to any of that accuracy which can only be attained by those who are professionally conversant with the ecclesiastical laws.

---

* Statute 1. El. cap. 2.

ON THE ROMANESQUE STYLE FOR CHURCHES IN LONDON AND LARGE TOWNS.

GREAT preliminary difficulties arise in the path of one who ventures to recommend the adoption, however partial, of a foreign style of architecture, the characteristic features of which have hitherto been unknown amongst us. He must expect that the minds of those who have not attended to the subject, especially if their observation has been confined to the churches of our native country, will be prejudiced against his proposal; and in order to meet this natural prejudice, he must be prepared to show, *first*, the principles (if such there be) on which we at present act in our choice of styles, are not violated by the proposal in question; and *secondly*, that looking at our present wants and condition, the proposed style offers considerable advantages over other modes of building in the same circumstances.

In the following lines, an attempt will be made to prove these two points in favour of the *Romanesque* style, as applicable to ecclesiastical buildings, particularly in the metropolis and large towns. The term Romanesque is employed at the outset, in order to indicate the particular species of the Byzantine style which is here intended. Constantinople being undoubtedly the fountain-head from whence this architecture spread over Europe,* Byzantine may be its most accurate general name; but as in passing into different countries it became more or less modified, so it has in each received a different denomination: in Italy it is called Lombard, in England, Norman; and to the German churches of the same style, Mr. Whewell has affixed the term Romanesque.

It is to those churches which partake more nearly of the Gothic, or pointed character, and sometimes pass into it, as distinguished from those of a more purely oriental type, that this paper is intended to refer; and any one who thinks it worth while to refer to the plates of Hope's Architecture, and compare the *German* churches with those of other countries classed under the common term Lombard, will at once recognise the difference. Many beautiful illustrations of the Lombard style may also be seen in a new work by the Rev. J. L. Petit; † and the present writer is happy to find his idea of the suitability of this style to our own wants confirmed by one so much better qualified to form an opinion on the subject: he refers particularly to a passage from pp. 89 to 92 of the first volume.

1. It would be carrying us too far from our immediate object to discuss at length what *ought* to have been the leading idea, the general principle, in the minds of those who, having professionally studied and discriminated the several styles of Gothic architecture, had more or less the power of recommending the adoption of one or other of them in erecting new churches at the time when these first began to be built. Perhaps the writer may be allowed to suggest that to have taken up

---

* See this shortly and clearly treated by Stieglitz, in the fifth section of his Essay on Architecture.

† Remarks on Church Architecture, with Illustrations, by the Rev. J. L. Petit, 2 vols, 8vo. Burns, 1841.

the *latest* period of Gothic, prior to its acknowledged degeneracy, and to have worked steadily on this model till we became thoroughly masters of its details, and able safely to accommodate them to new circumstances, or to revert here and there to models of a little earlier date, would appear to him to have been the proper and natural course.

There certainly does seem something of caprice and want of diffidence in persons so entirely new to the subject as most of us were a few years ago, attempting to imitate the styles of several different periods *all at once*, and not remembering that inasmuch as it was the wants and character of each age which more or less led to the successive modifications of Gothic architecture, the more nearly the habits of any age resembled our own, the more appropriate its style would be to ourselves; and further, that in reviving it we should be less exposed to the danger of introducing unreal and fantastic details merely for the sake of ornament. Supposing, for instance, that the perpendicular in its earlier stages may be considered as the latest Gothic before its decline commenced, are there not many features in this style which render it more appropriate to the present form of our religious services than the earlier styles? such, I mean, as the greater size of the windows, the lightness of the piers, and loftiness of the arches between the centre and side aisles, and the greater breadth and diminished depth of the chancel, all of these being modifications tending in one direction, and corresponding with the mode in which our new churches are actually built.

But this principle does not seem to have occurred to other minds; and even had it done so, it is obvious how many obstacles would have arisen from private and local circumstances to prevent its general adoption. The consequence is that Norman, early English, and decorated churches, have risen, and are daily rising, side by side amongst us.

This simultaneous imitation of styles, which range over five or six centuries, seeming to the writer to have already involved us in a considerable departure from strict principles, he thinks we have rather debarred ourselves from objecting too rigorously to any deflection in other particulars, such for instance as that of introducing a style not hitherto naturalized amongst us.

But a second consideration to set against the objection to the Romanesque as a foreign style still remains. Let it be borne in mind that, if we would really and truly erect an early English or decorated church, it is not sufficient to copy certain portions and ornaments of it which happen to suit our purpose, omitting other portions which are equally essential characteristics of the style. By thus avoiding all expensive peculiarities, we may build even a cathedral for a sum not exceeding that which a common parish church, built in strict accordance with principle, would require. But is not this precisely what takes place every day amongst us? The Norman loses its massive walls and deeply-receding doorways, the long narrow early English chancels are replaced by a shallow unmeaning adjunct to the east wall, the decorated is supplied with slight buttresses, obviously no support to the walls, and but scantily adorned with crockets and finials, the perpendicular loses its large windows, panelling, and tracery.

Stone vaulting, the essential characteristic of the pointed styles, is not so much as attempted. Nor does there seem a probability of any speedy revival of a strict determination to adhere to ancient models at any cost, nor of pecuniary offerings sufficiently large to carry such determination into effect.

If, then, we shall be able to prove that the Romanesque does not involve the same necessity of curtailment, may we not even assert that a *foreign* style, *completely* and *faithfully* executed, is even preferable to a *defective* imitation of those of our own country?

Let it be remembered, in the last place, that the Romanesque is so nearly allied to the Norman, that it is only in a modified sense that it can fairly be called a foreign style at all. With Norman it harmonizes in most of its features, but there are two or three in which it is different, and these contribute to render it peculiarly adapted to situations in a crowded city, and among lofty buildings; situations for which the Norman, by its low and square outlines, is as remarkably unsuited.

2. In order to prove my second point—the peculiar advantages of the Romanesque style, I now propose to consider shortly the principal parts, exterior and interior, of a church, setting down in each case their proper construction, on the one hand, in the Romanesque, on the other, in the Norman and pointed styles. By this means the superiority of the Romanesque over the Norman, as regards its adaptation to crowded city sites, and over the pointed styles as regards economy, (supposing the proper members of each to be faithfully executed,) will, I think, be evident.

Roofs.—Here we begin at once with a member, the different mode of constructing which presents an essential difference between the two styles. To the Romanesque in its most ancient form, the flat timber roof is exclusively appropriate,[*] and so as regards the centre aisle it continued to the last in England. With one exception, mentioned in a note, Mr. Whewell[†] says, "I know no instance of a large centre aisle of an Anglo-Norman building which possesses, or was intended to possess, a stone roof." And he then proceeds to state, that though stone-vaulting became the practice more early in Germany, many Romanesque churches continued to be built for flat roofs; and that in Italy, this construction is still more common. Subsequently, the simple cylindrical or trunk-shaped vault, which had previously been employed for the side aisles, extended itself likewise to the centre aisle.

Now while the above construction belongs to the Romanesque, that of the groined stone vault is the only legitimate one for the early English,[‡] or decorated, and it was not till the date of the perpendicular that the roofing was resumed. The expense, however, of stone vaulting is so great, that in scarcely a single instance of all the modern churches lately built has it been attempted; and here we have a striking proof of the evil of adopting a style for the sake of one or two of its beautiful features, without considering whether we are able to adopt also what is its essential characteristic. By the employment of the Romanesque, on the other hand, that style of roofing to which our scanty resources at present necessarily confine us, becomes the proper one. If oak

---

[*] Hope's Architecture, p. 269.
[†] Architectural Notes, second edition, p. 50.   [‡] Rickman, p. 67.

timbers can be obtained, so much the better; if not, deal stained in imitation of oak will suffice. In either case, we are able to obtain the proper Romanesque feature; the rafters may be left open, or the spaces between them may be filled up by panelling, thus giving the form of the trunk-shaped roof, employed first for the lesser, and afterwards for the centre aisles of ancient Romanesque churches. This has been the mode adopted in the Byzantine church hereafter alluded to, where the rafters (which are of stained wood) are left open; but means are provided for employing panelling at any future time, if desired.

TOWERS.—Nothing can harmonize more gracefully with the tall buildings of a crowded city, than do the pairs of towers, with pyramidal caps, of the Romanesque style. The larger churches have generally three towers; the larger one in the centre, and a pair at the west end. At S. Castor's, Coblentz, there are two at the west end; and many of the smaller Italian churches have one only at an angle of the building. A reference to Hope's Architecture, or to any set of views on the Rhine, will convey at once the idea of these towers to any one who has not traversed that part of the continent. That they may be erected much more cheaply than plain spires or towers in the other styles is not asserted, for economical advantages I rely rather on other points; but even in regard of economy they have their merit. The decorated, or perpendicular tower, has generally a flat roof, covered with lead, and surrounded by a parapet. These roofs add nothing to the height of the tower, and lead is an expensive covering, more so than either flat bricks, or the peculiar tile with a curled edge, both of which are proper to the Romanesque conical roof, and thus at a slight expense increase the general elevation of the building.

In cases where a single tower would be employed, it should be set on at an angle of the building, instead of being engaged in it, and this—the universal position of the single Lombard tower, would greatly ameliorate the square, barn-like appearance which is presented by most of our new chapels of the smaller size.

The external ornaments too of the towers are of a most simple kind; no windows or large apertures are required; and the faces of the wall are either quite plain, or divided into stories by very simple corbel tables, and round-headed panellings, some of them pierced for light.*

WINDOWS.—The small round-headed windows of the Romanesque are, in several ways, well adapted to our present condition. In the first place, they require no tracery, and hardly any mouldings; considering also our inability to employ any sufficient quantity of painted glass, and the great superfluity of light which consequently flows in upon the meagre interiors of our modern churches, and is obliged to be softened down by such expedients as holland blinds, this small size is a great recommendation. When we come to speak of "galleries," another great advantage they possess will be apparent.

EXTERIOR ORNAMENTS.—For a description of the corbel table,

---

* Whewell, p. 104. Hope, p. 164.

which is always found on the external walls in Romanesque buildings, I will refer to Mr. Whewell's Architectural Notes, p. 101. It is a very simple decoration, and yet it gives a finished look to walls constructed of rough materials: the *apsidal gallery*, however, is the most striking ornament of the Romanesque exterior, and gives to it a distinctive character.* This, consisting of a gallery of open round-headed arches, standing on small shafts two or three feet high, and set two deep, runs round the upper part of the apse, and also occasionally round other sides of the building. Its position on the *upper* part of the external walls seems to render it peculiarly appropriate to city churches. Most of these are built on sites so confined that the neighbouring houses exclude any view of at least the lower half of the exterior. In the part therefore thus obscured, small round-headed windows, of the plainest construction, may be introduced, while the decoration is reserved for that part which remains visible. Any one who will visit the decorated chapel in Berwick-street, or the new church in Wilton-crescent, and observe how greatly the effect of the side windows in both of them is lost, will perceive the advantage of this arrangement.

The very uniform size and shape of the mouldings, shafts, and arches of these galleries, or arcades, as well as of the other ornaments of this style, suggest an idea with reference to the *material* of which they may be composed, which may be conveniently introduced in this place.

Notwithstanding the dislike which is generally expressed to brick as a material for building churches, its use is daily becoming more general, and our only hope seems to lie in improving its shape and quality. On this point **Mr. Hope's** work contains the following remarks:—

"The ancient Romans, whenever they found clay more abundant or easier to work than stone, used it plentifully, both in regular layers throughout the body of walls, as we do, and in an external reticulated coating, from the fineness of its texture and the firmness of its joints as durable as stone itself. Indeed, far from considering brick only as a material fit for the coarsest and most indispensable ground-work of architecture, they regarded it as equally fit for all the elegances of ornamental form, all the details of rich architraves, capitals, friezes, cornices, and other embellishments. *Sometimes it owed to the mould its various forms*, and at others, as in the Amphitheatrum Castrense and the temple of the god Ridiculus, to the chisel.

"In modern Rome, too, very great use was made, until a very late period, of brick. * * * In the plains of Lombardy, where stone is rare, clay has, in buildings of importance, *been moulded into forms so exquisite*, as to have been raised into a material of value and dignity. In the ancient churches of Pavia, &c., it presents itself in all the delicate tracery of the middle ages; in the great hospital, Campo Santo, and Castigliane palace, at Milan, it exhibits the arabesque, medallions, and scroll work of the cinque-cento style. On this side of the Alps, clay has never received forms quite so elaborate; still in the south of France, particularly at Toulouse, remarkable instances exist. Along the Rhine, carved tiles are formed into very elegant cornices and balustrades. Even in England, brick was in former days moulded into forms intended to be handsome. But, whether in consequence of the high duty imposed upon brick, and the consequent limitation as to size and shape, or from the influence of the

---

* Whewell, p. 102.

contracting system of building, the legal English brick has become the least durable and the most unsightly of that used in any country; and has hence produced that dislike to its colour and material, which proceeds, not from its intrinsic ugliness, but from association of the imagination with ideas of coarseness and meanness of construction."—*Hope's Architecture*, p. 297, *note*.

On reading this note, the idea naturally arises,—Why should not *we* employ bricks *moulded in the clay* in building churches, and thus avoid the enormous expense which is entailed by the use of the chisel either upon stone or brick, and which in some cases leads to the paltry substitution of cast-iron for window tracery and mouldings? To this inquiry it would at once be replied—that the form and shape of these ornaments in the pointed style are so various, that moulders in brick could scarcely provide themselves with a sufficient number of moulds for the purpose; and even this would not meet the difficulty unless a stock of every kind of moulded brick was likewise ready in his store. Churches now-a-days are seldom begun to be built till the need of them is so urgent that every moment of delay not absolutely necessary is deprecated; while, on the other hand, building committees defer to the last moment their decision on the details of structure and of ornament. Under these circumstances, we see the advantage of the adoption of the Romanesque style, with its uniform decorations, could it only be effected in a sufficient number of instances to make it worth the brick-moulders' while to have a supply of the proper materials constantly in readiness.

Bricks so moulded as to form the round-headed arch, the roll moulding, and the shaft, would suffice both for the windows and the apsidal gallery, and would in many cases be all that would be required; by two or three more moulds, to execute the external panelling of the walls and the corbel table, a sufficient stock to copy faithfully all the decorations of a large and handsome Romanesque church would be obtained. It has been suggested to the writer, that the vitrified surface of a moulded brick is much more lasting than the porous texture of the interior of a common brick, and which, by the process of cutting, is exposed to the influence of the weather. Patents have also lately been taken out for compressing the clay, and making bricks much heavier and better than formerly; and there can seem no doubt that if ornamental brick-work were encouraged we should succeed as well in it as in the various other articles of manufacture to which the attention of this day is so much devoted.

THE APSE.—This form for the east end of churches, universal in the Romanesque, presents several advantages over the oblong square-ended chancel. A very proper desire not to abandon the chancel altogether, and with it much of those feelings of sanctity which have gathered round it, has led to most of our new churches retaining this appendage: on the other hand, they have been so curtailed in their dimensions, both from motives of economy, and that the services read at the altar may be heard in the body of the church, as to be, within and without, rather a blot than an addition to the beauty of the general outline. But by adopting the semicircular or polygonal apse, we are enabled to avoid this evil, and without increasing the size of our chancels, to obtain a feature which gracefully extends and varies the form of the building instead of being an unmeaning adjunct to it. The adoption of the apse would also naturally lead to the altar being somewhat advanced, thus rendering it the conspicuous object of the interior instead of its being thrust against the wall. The light, too, which, in the square chancel, with the usual large east window, is thrown forward over the altar, and rests upon some less sacred object, would by this disposition fall upon the altar itself, not indeed too glaringly, but chastened and subdued by the height and narrowness of the Romanesque window. The very form of the apse also gives a greater notion of space than is actually the case, by means of the windows being seen less and less as they approach nearer to the side; and not being easily counted, an idea of continuity is thus conveyed.

BUTTRESSES.—Instead of the large projecting buttresses of the later styles, and of which we see such inadequate representatives in modern churches, the Romanesque buttresses hardly project from the wall, and require no ornament in the way of moulding, canopy, or finial. The following is Mr. Hope's description of them:—

"In Lombard buildings, the whole of the strength requisite for support and resistance is sought in the general thickness of the wall, or in the facings that slightly project from it, or in columns leaning against it; seldom we see even solid buttresses very prominent, and I believe the flying buttress to exist no where in this style. The Lombard, or what we call Saxon buttresses, are shallow, broad, shelving upward in regular breaks, and quite unornamented, except by some fillet or other moulding that runs from the intervening panels uninterruptedly across them; from their shallowness, they seem intended rather for mere ornament than for strength and support."*

GALLERIES.—In speaking of the triforium of Romanesque churches, Mr. Whewell says:—

"In England, in our Norman buildings, and almost constantly in the later ones, this space (the triforium) in large churches is filled by a row of openings or panellings of various kinds. It is mostly, however, a merely ornamental member, and I do not know that it was ever applied to any customary use.

"*But in the early German churches the case is different.* In almost all that decidedly belong to this class, we have, instead of the blank wall of the former style, *a large open gallery*, forming a second story to the side aisle: and in most of these instances, or at least in the churches on the Rhine above Bonn, this gallery is still appropriated to a particular part of the congregation, namely, the young men, and is generally called the *Männer chor,* or, as I was told at Sinzig, the *Mannhaus.* This gallery naturally makes it convenient to have the pier-arches somewhat low, which it has been already observed is the case. The openings of this gallery, which of course stand immediately over the pier-arches, are variously arranged. Often there is a large plain semicircular arch, which, however, has frequently shafts at the sides when the pier below is plain.* * * But the more general arrangement is, to have this round-headed opening subdivided into two or three subordinate openings, separated by shafts, which are often in pairs."†

From hence, therefore, it appears that the gallery is a proper part of the Romanesque church. In this style, and *in this alone,* is there ancient precedent for it. Surely with all those who cannot see their way, for several years to come, to the abolition of the gallery, and

---

* Hope, p. 258; see also Whewell, p. 100.   † Whewell, p. 95.

yet deprecate a mutilated imitation of styles, this is a very forcible argument in favour of the Romanesque: and I am fortunately able to refer those who feel the weight of the above consideration to an actual instance of a gallery so constructed, within a few miles of the metropolis; I allude to the beautiful new church lately erected by Mr. Wyld, at Streatham, a notice of which appeared in the February number of this Review, and an exterior and interior view of which was given in the last number. By reference to the latter view, it will be seen that the galleries stand on an arcade of pillars just within the range of the piers of the centre aisle, thus leaving that space entirely unimpeded, and forming (as described by Mr. Whewell), a second story to the side aisles.

The side windows too, in this example, show very successfully another advantage of the Romanesque. They are in *two ranges*; one above the galleries, the other below them; and thus, instead of the long window of the pointed styles, cut in half, and partially blocked up by the galleries, each range has, and is seen to have, its appropriate function. The upper one lights the gallery, the lower lights the body of the church.

I believe I have now enumerated the several members of a church, so far as they differ, in the Romanesque and pointed styles, and I will now give a little summary of them, that we may see at one glance the advantages which, in one or other particular, the Romanesque possesses.

	Early English.	Decorated.	Perpendicular.	Romanesque.
Roofs.	Stone vaulting	Stone vaulting	—	Rafters, or the trunk-shaped vault.
Towers.	—	Have flat leaded roofs — pinnacles, & parapets—large lights	Ditto	Conical tiled roofs, no pinnacles, parapet, or large apertures.
Windows.	In larger churches, foliated.	Large—tracery and mouldings elaborate.	Ditto	Small—roundheaded — no tracery, or mouldings.
Buttresses.	In larger churches, flying buttresses, in several stages.	In stages — much ornamented—projecting	Ditto	Shallow, and without ornament.

These advantages, then, the Romanesque has over the pointed styles; so however has the Norman: I will conclude by summing up the points in which it excels, for the purposes to which this paper points, the Norman also.

	Norman.	Romanesque.
Chancel	Square-ended	Apsis—round or polygonal.
Galleries	None—only blank space, or merely ornamental triforium	A component part of the church.
Towers	Low and flat	Tall, with conical roof.
Ornaments	—	The apsidal gallery, offering a very effective, and (should moulded bricks be employed) cheap decoration.

NOTICES OF BOOKS.

1. *A Ride on Horseback to Florence, through France and Switzerland, in a Series of Letters.* By a LADY. 2 vols. 8vo. London: Murray. 1842.
2. *Excursions along the Shores of the Mediterranean.* By LIEUT.-COL. E. NAPIER, 46*th Regiment.* 2 vols. 8vo. London: Colburn. 1842.
3. *Journal of a Tour in Greece and the Ionian Islands, with Remarks on the recent History, present State, and Classical Antiquities of those countries.* By WILLIAM MURE, *of Caldwell.* 2 vols. 8vo. London and Edinburgh: Blackwood. 1842.

OF these three books of travels, the last only is deserving of notice. The " Lady" is a lively writer; but the highest powers of description, if there be not something more solid at bottom, must fail to interest among scenes familiar to almost every reader. Col. Napier is, in more senses than one, a *loose* writer.

Of Mr. Mure we shall have something more to say. He has evidently endeavoured to make his book as instructive as possible; and for this purpose has studied both the present political and the antiquarian history of the country through which he travelled. Moreover, without pretending to any first-rate scholarship, he evidences a respectable acquaintance with Hesiod and Homer, Pindar, and Aristophanes, and Xenophon. This is refreshing.

In a journey, every mile of which abounds in the richest associations, it is difficult to make any selection which shall fairly represent the whole. To us some of the most interesting pages are those which describe the Cyclopean remains in the centre of the Peloponnese. The discovery which follows, if our author is not deceived in his estimate, would appear to be really valuable:—

" No entire ancient bridge of any kind, still less an arched bridge of a genuine Hellenic period, had hitherto been known to exist within the limits of Greece; and even the ability of the Greek masons to throw an arch had been very generally questioned. Here I saw an arched bridge of considerable size and finished structure, and in a style of masonry which guarantees it a work of the remotest antiquity—probably of the heroic age itself. This monument, therefore, while it tangibly connects us with a period of society separated from our own by so wide a blank in the page of history, realizes to our senses a state of art to all appearance proper and peculiar to itself; and which, but for the existence of this and a few other venerable remains of the same class, might be considered (as the men by whom they were constructed have been by some modern schools of sceptics) to be but the unreal visions of a poetical fancy. The beauty of its situation adds much to its general effect. It is built just where the stream it traverses, a respectable tributary of the Eurotas, issues from one of the deepest and darkest gorges of Taÿgetus. I could learn no other name for this river than that of the neighbouring village on its banks, which is called Xerókampo. The masonry of the arch (of which a view is given), the piers and the portions of wall immediately connected with either, are ancient, and in good preservation. The parapet is modern, of poor rubble work, and where the outer Cyclopean facing of the retaining wall, at the extremity of each flank, has fallen away, traces are also visible of Turkish repairs. The span of the arch is about twenty-seven feet; the breadth of the causeway, between the parapets, from six to seven; each parapet is about one foot three inches in thickness, giving nine or ten feet for the whole breadth of the arch. There are no visible remains of pavement. The largest stones are those of the arch; some of them may be from four to five feet long, from two to three in breadth, and between one and two in thickness. In size and proportions they are nearly similar to those which form the interior lining of the heroic sepulchres of Mycenæ, and the whole character of the work leads to the impression of its being a structure of the same epoch that produced those monuments. Even those who may not be willing to acquiesce in this view, will scarcely venture to dispute its genuine Hellenic or rather Spartan antiquity. Apart from the style of the masonry, it is hardly in a situation to admit of its being a work either of the Macedonian or Roman periods; lying as it does in this remote corner of the peninsula, where in later times it is little likely there could have been a thoroughfare of sufficient importance to warrant such expensive undertakings. Its existence therefore seems sufficient in itself to establish the use of the arch in Greece at a very remote epoch."

Three Discourses on the Divine Will, on Acquaintance with God, on Revelation. By A. J. SCOTT, A.M. Darling. 1842.

MR. SCOTT was not brought up a Churchman, and we believe he is not one as yet; but, judging from his writings, there is no man to whom we are more disposed to apply the hackneyed quotation, "talis cum sis, utinam noster esses." Holding what we do concerning the Church, it is, of course, impossible for any separatist, or any one, even keeping aloof from it, to present us with Divinity in which we shall not find a grievous want. But seldom, indeed, in such cases do we encounter so much important Truth—so much of the necessary groundwork of catholic religion; so much which it behoves him who would be truly catholic diligently to learn and keep in mind, as in the little volume before us. The author is one of powerful and original mind; one of the very few men, Scotch not only by birth but by education, who have been enabled to shake off the fetters of scholastic Calvinism; and looking for reality, life, and love in the Bible, to find them all.* The first of his three discourses, which has been printed several times, draws a distinction between the Will and the Decrees of God, by which the author is enabled to answer a very common Calvinistic argument against the scriptural truth, that God loves every man, and wills the salvation of every man. The conclusion is so beautiful, wise, and, on the whole, true, that we must lay it before our readers :—

" Much of the perplexity on this subject arises from regarding Unbelief as a passive thing, a submitting to the consequences of an unhappy want; and Faith as an active thing, a putting forth of strength to change ourselves, our circumstances, and the relation of God to us. Now, the very reverse is truth. Unbelief is rebellious activity for the attainment of an object, which we cannot leave in the hands of God—our own happiness; and its punishment is the fruit of its own doing; the creature of unbelief, not the creature of God, its worm, *its own* worm,

---

* We are, of course, speaking of men as thinkers and writers; for it would be grievous indeed to believe that the numbers doomed to an education in the Westminster standards, were all as low in spirit as the formal propositions to which they submit.

dieth not, its fire is not quenched. Faith is the cessation of independent activity for objects resigned to God. It is the man, who knows he cannot swim in this flood, ceasing the struggle that must drown him, because he knows his passive body will be borne up safely by the waters. The Will of God is bearing all things that yield to it towards the joy of their Lord. He who knows this, ceases to strive with it, and provide against it, and is borne on unresistingly towards the blessedness to which it presses to carry him."—Pp. 46, 47.

Hints for Meditation on Acquaintance with God is the title of the second discourse, which is written in a strain that is worthy of an Austin or a Leighton.

Of the third, on Revelation, no extracts can give a just notion. It is one of the most vigorous and powerful essays we have fallen in with for many a day, and most cordially do we thank Mr. Scott for it. He must pardon us for expressing our wish and hope that the day may arrive when he shall have discovered that the great and vital truths which have taken such hold on his mind, find their proper place, attain their full significance, and have their standing witness, in the Catholic Church—in her apostolical hierarchy, in her changeless faith, her holy liturgies, her divine sacraments.

A Family Exposition of the Pentateuch. By the REV. HENRY BLUNT, M.A. *Rector of Streatham, &c. Exodus—Leviticus.* London: Hatchard and Son, 1842. 12mo. pp. 299.

THIS volume forms part of a larger work designed after the manner of Mr. Girdlestone's and the Bishop of Chester's Commentaries: to a paragraph of ten or a dozen verses is appended an exposition averaging about three pages. Having mentioned two other well-known works of a similar kind, we may perhaps best express our opinion of this book, by saying, that the composition is more simple than in Mr. Girdlestone, and more lively than in the Bishop: the style of writing, indeed, is altogether pleasing, but there is neither the vigour of the former nor the sober earnestness of the latter. With regard to matter, it will scarcely be thought a fault that there is not much of depth and originality; but it is less excusable when a commentator upon Scripture depends entirely upon his own resources. This, Mr. Blunt appears to us to have done; we do not perceive that he has quoted any author beyond his own contemporaries, who, as soon as they are gathered to their rest, are dignified by the title of "men of old." The necessary consequence is, that the book appears shallow and common-place, and wanting in variety. Neither of course can it be but that a work of this nature should reveal the school of theology from which it emanates, The following view, for example, appears to us to be rather too comfortable to be true:—" *If* God's *word be* TRUE, therefore, **there is not that human being, who** thus deeply and earnestly bewails his sins, **and** is WILLING *to forsake* them, and anxious for pardon only through the blood of Christ, to whom we may not offer it with all the freedom and all the confidence, at the present hour, which the Apostle exhibited, when he said to the Philippian jailor, 'Believe on the Lord Jesus Christ, and thou shalt be saved.' And *there is not that human being* in existence, however widely he may have departed from the vows of his *baptismal* covenant, or however deeply he may have sunk in sin, who by God's grace receives this offer and obeys the Lord who makes it, who does not stand before God at that hour a pardoned sinner, an *adopted son*, an heir of glory, *as certainly and acceptably as if he had never been the fallen denizen of a fallen world.*"

Had not Mr. Blunt been carried away by a desire to "round his period" with so pretty a phrase as "a fallen denizen of a fallen world," he would have seen that the sense required a clause like this, —" as if he had never fallen from grace." And this we presume is the writer's opinion. How is it, then, that St. Paul asserts, " It is IMPOSSIBLE for those who were once enlightened and have tasted of the heavenly gift, and were made partakers of the Holy Ghost, if they fall away, to renew them again unto repentance?" Surely such a passage of Scripture as this ought to be kept in mind, and however we may feel authorised to proclaim the grant of repentance to those who have fallen from grace, we cannot describe such repentance as an easy or instantaneous work.

Memoirs of the Life and Writings of Michael Thomas Sadler, Esq. M.P. F.R.S. &c. London: Seeley and Burnside. 1842. 8vo. pp. 664.

WE have a great respect for the subject of this biography; but none whatever for the biographer. Should the fair fame of Mr. Sadler suffer with posterity, it will certainly be for the opposite reason to that which caused the " many brave men who lived before the time of Agamemnon" to perish " unwept."

Mr. Sadler was born at Snelstone, in Derbyshire, in the year 1780, and there he continued to reside till his removal to Leeds in 1800. His education, though only conducted at a neighbouring private school, was by no means neglected; and to the diligence and ability of his tutor, Mr. Sadler was indebted for a considerable skill and taste in scientific pursuits. The greater part of his life was spent in business, not so however as to prevent his taking a lively interest in local and general politics. In 1828 came out his work on Ireland; and the year following, in consequence of a speech made at Leeds, he was recommended by the Duke of Newcastle to the electors of Newark, and by them returned to Parliament. In the next session he represented Aldborough. Of his upright and consistent conduct during this time it is unnecessary to speak; but we cannot resist quoting one passage from his work already alluded to. It omits, indeed, two alterations which are indispensable for the well-being of Ireland, viz. a vigorous and impartial exercise of law, and the more efficient and adequate working of the Church; but as far as it goes it cannot be improved:—

" Surely Ireland is the last of all countries upon earth that ought to permit its people to starve from want of food, or suffer from want of employment. As to the former, its surplus produce, even now, is probably greater than that of any other country in the world of equal extent; and its surface might, on the very lowest calculations which our practical agriculturists have ever made, sustain in plenty far above ten times the number of inhabitants that it now starves, while ' the wastes of the sea,' to repeat Lord Bacon's expression, by which it is encircled, remain almost untouched. Demand for labour is, however, wanted, in order to accomplish any amelioration in the country; and that can never be obtained while the means of its remuneration are withdrawn, as well as the necessity for it destroyed to so great an extent, by absenteeism. It is this grand evil, and the want of a national provision for the poor, which it renders the more necessary, to which much of the distress and turbulence of Ireland has been distinctly traced. Surely that country presents a noble field for the exertions of the real patriot; there he might build himself an everlasting monument: the imperishable materials are at hand. Its natural capacities are unrivalled; so are those of its people; though both lie uncultured, abandoned, abused! In the character of its inhabitants there are the elements of whatever is elevated and noble; these, however borne down and hidden, are indicated wherever their development is not rendered impossible. Their courage in the field needs no panegyric of mine, and has never been surpassed; their charity, notwithstanding their poverty, never equalled; even while I am thus writing, I will dare to assert that in many a cabin of that country the God-like act of our immortal Alfred, which will be transmitted down to the remotest generations, the dividing his last meal with the beggar, is this instant being repeated. And their gratitude for kindnesses received, equals the ready warmth with which they are ever conferred. In the domestic sphere, according to their means, they are unrivalled in fidelity and affection. I mean not to contend that they have not faults, and grievous ones; but these are mainly attributable to the condition to which they have been reduced, and the manner in which they have been so long treated."

In all this we fully agree; and most heartily do we hope that both Church and State are now prepared, in the proper sense of the term, to do justice to this most grievously mismanaged country.

Gregorian and other Ecclesiastical Chants, adapted to the Psalter and Canticles, as they are pointed to be sung in Churches. 8vo. Burns. 1842.

THE contents of this collection are as follows: 1. The eight Gregorian tones with their several endings, forming twenty-four Single Chants,—intended to be sung in unison according to the ancient practice of the Church, without instrumental accompaniment. 2. A variety of the same Chants harmonized for four voices, but so as to preserve unaltered the original melodies. 3. A miscellaneous collection of Chants,—chiefly *single*, as being most easily learnt by common congregations, as well as most appropriate for antiphonal chanting. To the Chants is added Tallis' music for the Versicles, Responses, &c., in Morning and Evening Prayer. Several of the Gregorian Chants are harmonized by Thomas Morley, (a pupil of the famous Bird;) and as these fine harmonies are little known,[*] we here subjoin two specimens. The first is the fifth Gregorian tone,—the second is the sixth. It will be observed, that the *tenor* voices sing the melody, which is the usual arrangement adopted by the old Masters.

---

[*] They are printed in Morley's "Plain and Easie Introduction to Practical Music," (in conversations between a master and pupil,) 1597,—a book now scarce.

No. 35.   15.

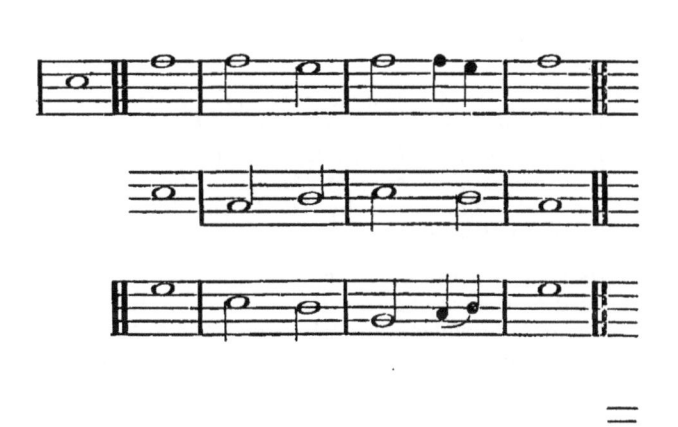

No. 36.   16.

The Bishopric of Souls. By the Rev. R. W. EVANS, M.A. *Vicar of Tarvin, and Fellow of Trinity College, Cambridge.* London: Rivingtons. 1842.

WE trust that few of our readers are unacquainted with the beautiful conclusion of one of the most beautiful books in the English language, "The Rectory of Valehead." The paragraph, it will be remembered, commences thus :—" I think it just possible, as ever so little things often call to recollection what are truly great, as a sparrow-hawk will prompt the thought of an eagle, that this book may remind thee, O reader, in part of its plan, of that holy work, ' The Temple,' of the divine Herbert. I confess that I had him at first in view," &c. A more exact counterpart to the intellectual labours of Herbert is to be found, we think, in the book now before us, which is, indeed, a a very wise and beautiful expansion of "The Country Parson." We find in it Mr. Evans's characteristic merits—the expressive flexibility of his style, the originality and liveliness of his imagery, the depth and accuracy of his thoughts. It is impossible, perhaps, for any human author to write a volume in every word of which another shall coincide, but we have seen few books lately, containing, as we think, more practical truth than this. The parts relating to pastoral visitation are especially valuable, and are obviously the results of much holy experience. We also commend attention to Mr. Evans's remarks on preaching, and on the question of which we have lately heard so much, of Latinisms and Saxonisms. Our only regret is, that so powerful and orthodox a writer should have confined himself so exclusively to the prophetical, and said so little of the liturgic functions which the priest must discharge : unless, indeed, he designs giving us a separate treatise on that branch of the subject, in which case our regret will be turned into joy.

England in 1841 : *being a series of Letters written to Friends in Germany during a Residence in London and Excursions into the Provinces.* By FREDERICK VON RAUMER, *Professor of History at the University of Berlin, Author of " England in* 1835," *&c. &c.* Translated by H. Evans Lloyd. 2 vols. small 8vo. London : Lee, 1842.

THIS book is worth glancing at, just to know the value of a judgment formed by the passing traveller. Mr. Von Raumer we believe to be a person of learning and intelligence; and yet anything more childish than the volumes he has here produced it would be difficult to conceive. They are made up in a way which at first sight seems to give some promise of value, viz. by embodying the remarks of English writers. But this is done so unskilfully, that much of the book reads like a cross-examination, in which, the questions being omitted, there is the most entire apparent inconsequence between the parts. For anything like original or philosophical remark we have looked in vain.

"A History of the English Reformation," by the Rev. F. C. Massingberd, forms the last, but not least, addition to the Englishman's Library. It is written with great care, and develops those impartial and well-considered views of the period which have always characterized the series to which it belongs.

We hope shortly to call our readers' attention, more particularly than we can at present, to the new volumes of poetry which have just appeared; in particular to Mr. Wordsworth's, "The Baptistery" of Mr. Williams, (Parker, Oxford; Rivingtons, London, 1842,) and Mr. Trench's new volume of poems (Moxon, 1842). Meanwhile the mere announcement of their publication will be hailed, we trust, by many.

Dr. Cardwell's two volumes, entitled "Synodalia; a Collection of Articles of Religion, Canons, and Proceedings of Convocations in the Province of Canterbury, from the year 1547 to the year 1717, with Notes Historical and Explanatory," ought to have received earlier notice at our hands. They complete the documentary series proposed by the learned Editor; and embody a mass of information of the highest value to the theological student.

A condensed edition of "Stanhope on the Epistles and Gospels" has just been published by Dr. Kenny, (Rivingtons.) Many persons, no doubt, will still prefer the original work, even at the high price at which it now sells. It must be allowed, however, to be very unequal in execution, and therefore to suffer less by abridgement than the generality of standard books.

We have this month to acknowledge a very great and valuable accession to our stock of books for the young and middle class. 1. In his "Life of William of Wykeham," (which is beautifully illustrated with vignettes,) Mr. Chandler has contrived to convey a sketch of the times in which that great and good man lived, which will be instructive to a very large number of readers. 2. Mr. Burns has likewise published a Second Series of "Fourpenny Books," to be used as rewards in schools. The "Life of Lord Exmouth," the "Gift for Servants," "Two Conversations," by Mr. Gresley, and "Stories from Bede," appear to us the best: but all are good; and the variety of subject is so great as to suit all persons. 3. A "Life of Richard Hooker," compiled, of course, mainly from Izaak Walton, but enhanced in attractiveness by the addition of vignettes of the various scenes with which that illustrious man was connected, and some valuable extracts from his writings.

"Modern Methodism" is the title of a tract (Burns) written in answer to the first of a series just commenced by the Wesleyans. If there are any of this body open to conviction, they cannot, we really think, resist the force of this exposure. It is most triumphant. The Tract should be widely circulated.

"The Martyr of Prusa, or the first and last Prayer, a tale of the early Christians," by the Rev. R. Wood Kyle, (2d edition, Dublin, Curry, 18mo. pp. 141,) appears a respectable production. The first edition was published thirteen years ago, when the taste for ecclesiastical antiquities was not nearly so strong as at the present day. The story contains an account of the destruction of Herculaneum.

Mr. W. D. Cooley has published an inquiry, evincing great research, into the limits of the "Negro-land of the Arabs," (8vo. pp. 150. Arrowsmith.) It is pleasing to see modern science and the learning of the ancients illustrating one another.

The author of "Manasseh, a Tale of the Jews," has surely mistaken his vocation. It is really time that the public should have some protection from writers of this class. We should like to see a law to prevent the publication of all works, which two persons at least would not certify that they believe to be, if not useful, at least readable.

"Robert and Frederick, a Boy's Book," (Seeley and Burnside,) betokens some degree of talent, but we have no sympathy whatever with the writer.

Mr. Poole has expanded the Two Lectures on Churches and their Decorations, which formed the first number of "The Christian's Miscellany," into a very pleasing and instructive volume, entitled "The Appropriate Character of Church Architecture." (Green, Leeds; Rivingtons, Burns, &c. London, 1842.)

Part of the eighth volume of "The Library of the Fathers," (select treatises of St. Athanasius against the Arians,) has just appeared. The prefatory matter, from which great things are to be expected, will appear in the next part.

"Lives of the Evangelists and Apostles, with Conversations upon them," is the title of a very useful book which has just been published by the Christian Knowledge Society, and which we warmly recommend.

We ought to have mentioned some time ago that No. VII. of Mr. Taylor's "Ancient Christianity" has appeared, with the following portentous title, "The Miracles of the Nicene Church in Attestation of its Demonolatry." (Jackson and Walford.) We have not yet examined Mr. Taylor's positions; but even if his facts be more carefully sifted than his previous ones, we should not be led by them to his revolting conclusions. In the advertisement he promises, when his work shall have been finished, to reply to the objections which have been urged against it. Such he will find, on undertaking the task, by no means the "frivolous cavils" he would seem in the same advertisement to insinuate that they are.

The first three numbers of "The Christian Miscellany," (Green, Leeds,) for the present year contain "Reeves' Treatise on the Right Use of the Fathers." The author was a true son of our Anglo-Catholic Church, and we rejoice to see his name rescued from oblivion. One of his sermons has also just been reprinted in the form of a tract; it is entitled "Obedience due to Spiritual Rulers." (Burns.) A subsequent number of Mr. Green's series contains an interesting sketch of the History and Present State of the American Church, from the pen of Mr. Poole.

"A Letter to the Laity of the Church of England, on the subject of recent Misrepresentations of Church Principles," by the Rev. A. Watson, M.A. &c., (Rivingtons; Burns, 1842,) is at once a most able and a deeply important pamphlet. Mr. Watson shows most clearly what true Church principles are, how they have been held by our great divines, and are held now by those who could not have derived them from the Oxford Tracts. His quotations from and his eulogium on the late Mr. Rose are to us most delightful, as they will be to all who know what that good man was, and what the present Church of England owes, under God, to him. Mr. Watson has been compelled to inflict chastisement on a Cheltenham clergyman, who certainly has his theology yet to learn; and who, in the excess of his ignorance, while attacking what he is pleased to term *Puseyism*, has given utterance to deadly heresy. Will this exposure make such persons willing to *think* and to *learn*?

A new edition of Dr. Hook's excellent "Church Dictionary" has just come out, (Harrison, Leeds; Burns, London,) greatly enlarged and much improved. It ought to be in every house of the upper classes, and in every lending library for the benefit of the lower.

We call attention to "The Bishop of Salisbury's Charge," (Rivingtons,) which discusses the relative functions of Scripture and the Church with much accuracy and piety.

We are glad to see that the Rev. H. Alford has not allowed the imaginative literature in which he so greatly excels to hinder his prosecution of graver studies. We allude to the appearance of his "Hulsean Lectures." (Deighton,

Cambridge; Rivingtons, London.) They seem very interesting, and we hope for an agreeable repast when we shall have leisure for a closer study of them.

The Archdeacon of Surrey has published a Volume of Sermons preached before the Queen, (Burns.) This is an announcement we are sure of much interest.

"The Mercies of God to this Church and Nation in the Year that is past," (Rivingtons,) is the title of a sermon preached at Ipswich, by the Rev. Wm. Nassau Leger. We have had no time to read it, but we have every reason to confide in its author's soundness of principle.

. We call attention to "Confirmation and Communion," (Burns, 1842,) a tract which is suitable for distribution at any time, but more especially at present, when many Confirmations, we suppose, are at hand.

Also we recommend, "An Address to the Parents of Children attending the Church School," by the Clergyman of the Parish, (Burns, 1842.)

In our recommendation last month of the Guide to the Holy Eucharist, the author's name (the Rev. W. J. E. Bennett) was accidentally omitted.

We are glad to learn that there is no truth in the rumour of Bishop Alexander having received a rough reception at Jerusalem; but our satisfaction is damped by finding him exchanging civilities with the Armenian Patriarch, whom his lordship's chaplain designates as "the representative of a sister Church," &c. Pray is not this Patriarch a Monophysite? It will surely be most vain that we show an increased reverence for the form, if we grow indifferent to the faith of the Church; and a step more certain to damage us in the eyes both of Greeks and Latins, than this fraternization with deadly heresy we can hardly imagine.

MISCELLANEOUS.

[*The Editor is not responsible for the opinions expressed in this department.*]

THE DIVINE RIGHT OF TITHES THE TRUE PRINCIPLE, THE OFFERTORY THE REAL INSTRUMENT, OF CHURCH EXTENSION.

No. VI.

THE following letter has been addressed to the Editor of the "Christian Remembrancer."* Dr. Chalmers's prejudices upon the subject of tithes were most inveterate, as may be seen from examining the seventh chapter (part 1st) of his Bridgewater Treatise. His change of opinion is a very striking instance of the force of truth on an ingenuous mind. I hope that we shall soon hear of conversions in England as well as Scotland. The University of Oxford has recently

---

* Any further observations relating to the subject of Inquirer's Letter, or other truths connected with it, will be acceptable.

published Comber's Works, in which is contained a Dialogue on the Divine Right of Tithes. Surely the *hiatus valde deflendus* in the "Englishman's Library" might be filled up by a republication of this treatise of Comber, by way of a sequel to the "Early English Church." How strange that Anglo-Catholics should disregard an Anglo-Catholic doctrine of such importance, especially as it is one which the necessities of the Church force so powerfully upon our notice.

Sir,—I have been gratified by your late endeavour to direct the attention of the faithful to the long dormant and lamentably ill understood subject of Tithes. In common with most protestants of our day, I had fancied that the obligation to pay tithes ceased when the law of Moses vanished away; and I was therefore very much surprised when, about a year ago, I learned that "a clergyman of the *Church of Scotland*" was publishing a bulky volume on the divine origin and *perpetual and universal* obligation of *first, second,* and *third,* or triennial tithes. (This author has since declared himself in the person of the Rev. David Thorburn, of South Leith.) It appears that the argument has been thought, in an influential and unlikely quarter, so conclusive, or at least so very strong, that the *Presbyterian Review,* the organ of the major party in that Church, has recommended all her ministers to study the question. And, further, the great divine whose opinions you quoted, with very qualified approval, in your late article on tithes, has written that the proof is irrefragable that tithes *ought* to be paid, though he does not say that he considers the obligation to be in the strict sense *imperative.* In justice to Dr. Chalmers, I shall be glad if you will acquaint your readers with the information; but more particularly in order to obtain the influence of his name in favour of a dispassionate consideration of this very important question. So far as I am aware, there is only one body of Christians who offer to God a tithe of their individual incomes, viz. the followers of the late Mr. Irving; and their peculiarities are so many, that it is doubtful whether their adoption of the principle of consecrating a tithe (which they do in the legitimate way, by the by, of the offertory) is calculated to recommend it to Christians generally. Since the perusal of the elaborate and high-toned work of Mr. Thorburn, I have been led to examine the historical aspect of the question. The result of my investigation is as follows:—

The Scriptures connect together offerings of tithes and first-fruits as cognate duties; and there is therefore ground for conceiving that the offence of Cain, which contrasted so strongly with the "righteous," or just, conduct of Abel, *may* have been his withholding of his first-fruits, or of his tithe.

Among the heathen nations, we frequently read of a tithe being devoted to their false gods; but I am not satisfied that the preponderance of instances recorded where a tenth was offered, is so striking when compared with those where a third, a hundredth, or some other proportion was offered, as to establish incontestably the doctrine that the light of authentic tradition directed them to that particular proportion.

But it is certain that tithes were not *instituted* with the Mosaic dispensation. Holy men gave tithes previously. At least the patriarchs Abraham and Jacob, the spiritual fathers of the whole Christian Church, through whom we mysteriously are brought into the covenant of grace, are mentioned, doubtless by way of example,—the former as giving a tithe of spoil taken after a battle to Melchisedec, that great typical priest and king, after whose order our Lord's everlasting priesthood is constituted,—the latter as vowing a tithe of all that God should give him, and this immediately after the blessing of faithful Abraham, in which was involved the whole of the Christian's hopes, had been renewed in his favour at Bethel.

The law of Moses imposed tithes to an extent which appears not to have been practised previously, the poor being then invested with a right to share in certain of them: and so universal was the obligation made, that even the

Levites were enjoined to give the priests *tithes of the tithes* paid them by the people. The subjects of decimation mentioned in the law were farm produce. That other gains were liable may be inferred from the instances of Abraham and Jacob, and from the boastful declaration of the Pharisee, who gave tithes of all that he possessed.

The Jews were as prone to fall into the offence of robbing God of tithes and offerings as of neglecting to hallow the Sabbath. Accordingly reformation in both respects was strongly, and in this case successfully, urged upon them by Nehemiah; and, at a later period, by Malachi.

Our Lord says nothing in the gospels to annul the precepts of the law regarding tithes; but, on the contrary, he approved of the conduct of the Pharisee for his scrupulous exactness in paying a tithe even of mint and cummin, while rebuking him for his neglect of the weightier matters of the law.

The primitive Christians consecrated much more than a tenth of their substance to religious uses; but whether they acknowledged an *obligation* to consecrate that as the minimum proportion of their income cannot be affirmed. In all probability, *their* love and zeal were so exuberant, that they would have been ashamed of so paltry a quota as an expression of gratitude to God and love to man, and acted solely from the impulse of a heart and conscience enlightened and directed by the Holy Spirit.

The early Fathers have written very decidedly what were the doctrines held in their time on the subject.

After that period, the belief that a tenth part at least of annual produce or income was due to God appears to have been undisputed till the thirteenth or fourteenth century, when some cavils were raised on the subject.

The Reformation produced a great revolution in the minds of men with respect to tithes. Perhaps we are not wrong in assuming that the change from general belief to general rejection of the doctrine was stimulated partly by an excessive desire to escape from the trammels of Rome, and partly by a regard to worldly interest.

In England the change encountered vigorous opposition. Any one who will amuse himself by turning to the word "tithe" in Watt's Bibliotheca Britannica will see the gradual manner in which the public mind has settled down to its present determination, that there ought to be no tithe paid but those which the state demands as burdens upon land. The *earliest* books on tithes were to enforce the obligation; it came to be disputed and denied in *later* books, till, during the *seventeenth* century, works on the negative side *prevailed;* and *latterly* the list contains only the names of treatises on the *law* of tithes and the *civil* questions arising from it!

I hope further elucidation of this subject may induce a more cordial and liberal consecration of substance to the Church and cause of the Redeemer. On the mass of offerings now presented, "shame" might well be imprinted. They are scanty, tiny, despicable. The system of UNSYSTEMATIC "*as you choose*" contributions has been tried and has failed. Let us, by the help of Him who claims the silver and the gold as his own, and in whose hand are the hearts of all men, give fair consideration to the SYSTEMATIC *definite* principle of a FIXED MINIMUM,—which I humbly think is the essence of the *divine* plan of tithes.

I am, &c.

AN INQUIRER INTO TITHES.

ECCLESIASTICAL INTELLIGENCE.

ORDINATIONS.

BP. OF ROCHESTER, *in St. Peter's Church, Pimlico, April* 10.

DEACONS.

Of Cambridge.—H. P. Dawes, B.A. Trin. Coll.; G. Kingsford, B.A. Cor. Chris. Coll. (*l. d.* Bp. of Chester.)

ORDINATIONS APPOINTED.

BP. OF LONDON, *May* 22.
BP. OF LINCOLN, *May* 22.
BP. OF HEREFORD, *May* 22.
BP. OF OXFORD, *May* 22.
BP. OF PETERBOROUGH, *May* 22.

BP. OF GLOUCESTER & BRISTOL, *May* 22.
BP. OF ELY, *June* 5.
BP. OF WINCHESTER, *June* 10.
BP. OF CHICHESTER, *June* 19.

PREFERMENTS.

Name.	Preferment.	County.	Diocese.	Patron.	Val.	Pop.
Alexander, D.	Bickleigh, V.	Devon	Exeter	Sir R. Lopez, Bart.	*253	620
Alsop, J. R.	W. Houghton, P.C.	Lanc.	Chester	Rev. E. Girdlestone.	149	4500
Bell, H.	Long Houghton, V.	Northum.	Durham	Dk.of Northumberld.	*162	690
Bullen, C.	St. George's Chorley, P.C.	Lanc.	Chester	Rector of Chorley.		
Byron, J.	Killingholme, V.	Lincoln.	Lincoln	Earl of Yarborough.	285	793
Cosens, R.	Long Burton, V.	Dorset	Sarum		*275	520
Fox, O.	Stoke Prior, V.	Worcester	Worcester	D. & C. of Worcester	*270	1100
Gilpin, P.	Esdon, R.	Northum.	Durham	Dk.of Northumberld.	*557	1724
Green, J. S.	St. Mary-le-Bow.	Durham	Durham	Archd. of Northumb.	111	
Grey, F. R.	Morpeth, R.	Northum.	Durham	Earl of Carlisle	*1611	5156
Hambleton, G.	Theydon Bois, P.C.	Essex	London		167	648
Hildyard, R.	Winestead, R.	York	York	Mrs. Hildyard	*247	145
Howman, E. J.	W. Dereham, P.C.	Norfolk	Norwich	Rev. G. Jenyns	74	496
Hutchinson, C.G.	Batsford, R.	Gloucester	G. & B.	Ch. Ch. Oxford.	*370	107
Jones, W.	Frisby in Wreak	Leicester	Peterboro'	Lord Chancellor.	*180	442
King, T.	Ordsall, R.	Notts		Lord Wharncliffe.	*424	809
Lee, L.	Broughton, c. Bossington, R.	Hants	Winch.	H. Lee, Esq.	*748	944
Leeder, R.	W. Barsham, V.	Norfolk	Norwich	C.W.M.Balders, Esq.	*155	101
Lloyd, M.	BettwsGarmon,P.C.		Bangor			
Milward, H.	Paulton, P.C.	Somerset	B. & W.	W. Kingsmill, Esq.		
Moody, G.	Gilstone, R.	Herts	London	Bp. of London	*241	233
Mules, F.	Bittadon, R.	Devon	Exeter	W. A. Yeo, Esq.	83	57
Munby, J. P.	Hovingham, P.C.	York	York	Earl of Carlisle	101	1193
Palmer, H.	Crickett Malberby, R.	Somerset	B. & W.	S. Pitt, Esq.	77	28
Quarterly, C. I.	Melcombe Horsey, R.	Dorset	Sarum	Lord Rivers	*342	172
Robinson, R.	Ravenstonedale, P.C.	Westmor.	Carlisle	Earl of Lonsdale	*110	1036
Rowland, W. M.	Bps. Castle, V.	Salop	Hereford	Earl of Powis	*350	2007
Sankey, J.	Stony Stanton, R.	Leicester	Peterboro'	E. Fisher, Esq.	*348	549
Saunders, C. D.	Tarrant Rushton, R.	Dorset	Sarum		*219	226
Serjeant, R.	St. Swithin, R.	Worcester		D. & C. of Worcester	170	833
Shipperdson, T.R.	Woodborn, V.	Northum.	Durham	Bp. of Durham.	*518	1416
Smith, H. C.	Trin. Church, Plymouth, P.C.			Vicar of St. Andrews		
Somerset, G. H.	St. Mabyn.	Cornwall	Exeter	Earl of Falmouth	*712	793
Stone, G.	Bondleigh, R.	Devon	Exeter	Lord Egremont	232	353
Thomas, W. B.	Aberedwy, R.	Radnor	St. David's	Bp. of St. David's.	355	344
Thompson, C.	Kirk Ella, V.	York	York	R. Sykes, Esq.	235	836
Trimmer, K.	St.George Tombland	Norfolk	Norwich	Bishop of Ely	144	710
Tyndale, H. A.	Tatsfield, R.	Surrey	Winchester	W. L. Gower, Esq.	150	166
Vallance, W.	Maidstone, R.	Kent	Canterbury	Abp. of Canterbury.	720	
Webber, F.	St.Michael Penkevil	Cornwall	Exeter	Lord Falmouth	156	176
West, T.	Orchard Portman, R.	Somerset	B. & W.	E. B. Portman, Esq.		112
Wharton, J.	Milburn, R.	Westmor.		Earl of Thanet	85	325
Wordsworth, J.G.	Talk-on-the-Hill.	Stafford	Lichfield		118	1196

*** *The Asterisk denotes a Residence House.*

APPOINTMENTS.

Bowstead, T. S., Preb. of Bobenhall, Lichfield Cath.
Churton, H.B.W. Preacher at Charterhouse.
Cotton, G. .... Chap. to Duke of Cleveland.
Evans, W............ Chap. to Sheriff of County of Radnor.
Germon, N. ...... Head Mast. Free Gram. Sch., Manchester.
Gray, H. F. .... Preb. of Combe, Wells Cath.
May, E. .... Chap. to Earl of Radnor.
Momford, T........ Rec. of Woodbridge, Surrog. for Wells, &c.
Merest, J. W. D.. Dom. Chap. D. of Cleveland.
Morris, F. O....... Ditto ditto.
Raymond, W. F.. Archdn. of Northumb.
Sawbridge, E. H. Chap. H. Sheriff of Devonsh..
Walker, T.......... Master of Clipstone School, Northampton.
Williams, J. ...... Chap. to Cleobury Union.
Wilson, J. .... Sec. Mast. Free Gram. Sch. Manchester.
Woolley, J......... Head Mast. of Hereford Cath. School.

CLERGYMEN DECEASED.

Banks, J., Rec. of Braytoft, Linc., 78.
Bateson, C., P. C. of W. Howton, Lanc., 50.
Blick, F., Vic. of Tamworth, 88.
Brooke, Z., Rec. of Gt. Ormead, Herts.
Brookland, W. J., Vic. of Netherbury.
Catton, R., 38.
Clarke, G. F., Thornton Watlass, Yorkshire, R., 52.
Chichester, C., Prebend of Exeter, 60.
Ekins, F., Rec. of Morpeth, 75.
Getley, M., at Edgbaston, 39.
Gore, W. C., at St. Kitt's.
Hocker, W., Rec. St. Mewan, Cornwall, 70.
Jeans, W., late Chap. at Palermo, 30.
Kennicott, B., Vic. of Woodhorn, Northumberland, 87.
Love, C., Cur. of Iddesleigh, Devon.
Montgomery, J. A., Cur. of Ledbury, 56.
Mayelston, S., Vic. of Brantingham, Yorksh.
Saurin, Dr., Bishop of Dromore.
Serrell, S., Vic. of St. Cuthbert, Wells, 80.
Waceney, W. A., Vic. Bracewell, Yorksh. 74.
Wickens, T., Vaenol, St. Asaph, 75.
Williams, J. H. W., Rec. of Farnham All Saints, Suffolk, 66.
Williams, J. H., Vic. of Marston Magna, Somerset, 86.

UNIVERSITIES.

OXFORD.

April 6.

Mr. D. P. Chase, B.A. of Oriel, and Mr. A. H. Clough, B.A. Schol. of Bal., admitted Probationary Fellows of Oriel Coll.

Degrees conferred.

M.A.
M. J. Johnson, Magd. Hall; R. Observer, grand comp.; H. H. Cornish, Magd. Hall; Rev. S. J. Rigaud, Exet.; Rev. W. Brewster, Trin.; Rev. C. Penny, Worc.

B.A.
G. Shand, Queen's.

MAGDALENE COLLEGE.—A Fellowship is vacant in this College, which will be filled up on the festival of St. James the Apostle next ensuing. Candidates are at liberty to call upon the President on any day before the 21st of July next, bringing with them a copy of their baptismal register, and a testimonial of good conduct from their College. They must be natives of Northamptonshire, and graduates of the University.

The Regius Professor of Hebrew continues his Lectures in the latter chapters of Isaiah, during the present Term, on Mondays, Wednesdays, Thursdays, and Saturdays. The two Elementary classes commenced on Thursday and Friday last: of these, the one is intended for those who are just commencing the language; the other for such as, being acquainted with the rudiments, require instruction in the higher parts of Hebrew grammar. Any members of the University, who need more individual assistance than can be given in the public classes, are recommended by the Regius Professor to apply to the Rev. J. B. Morris, M.A. Exeter College, or the Rev. C. Seager, M.A. Worcester College.

The Rev. Anthony Grant, B.C.L., late Fellow of New College, was chosen Bampton's lecturer for 1843.

W. E. D. Carter, Schol. of New Coll. was admitted Fellow of that Society.

April. 21.

Degrees conferred.

B.D.
Rev. W. J. Irons, Queen's.

M.A.
Rev. E. Clayton; R. C. Price, and E. R. Dukes, Students Ch. Ch.; F. C. Trower, Fell. Exeter; Rev. E. N. Mangin, Wadham; A. Mills, Balliol; Rev. P. W. Brancker, Jesus; Rev. E. Mence, Trinity.

B.A.
J. U. Robson, Magd. Hall, grand comp.: W. Grey and T. Bayley, Magd. Hall; J. Peacock, Lincoln; W. Clayton and C. C. Spencer, Queen's; Hugh St. A. Rogers, Exet.; H. Pigot, and T. Beale, Brasenose; M. J. T. Boys, Wadham; R. Astley, Pembroke; P. P. Newington, and W. C. Clack, Worcester; C. M. Owen, and R. L. Bampfield, Trin.; S. F. Bignold, Balliol.

J. D. B. Pollen, from Harrow School, admitted Scholar of Corpus.

NEW PROFESSORSHIPS.

Her Majesty has been graciously pleased to signify her pleasure that the Rev. Robert Hussey, B.D. and Student of Christ Church, should be the first Professor in Ecclesiastical History; and the Rev. C. Atmore Ogilvie, M.A. late Fellow of Balliol College, the first Professor of Pastoral Theology—these two Professorships being those lately founded by her Majesty's letters patent, and for which the University recently voted a stipend of 300l. a year to each of the Professors, till the Canonries of Christ Church, with which they are eventually to be endowed, should become available.

CAMBRIDGE.

April 9.

On Thursday last the following gentlemen were elected scholars of Trinity College:—

Money	Armitage	Keary
W. Jones	Grignon	
Twining	Walker	Williams
Atkinson	W. G. Clark	Mayne
Coombe	Bowring	Rawlinson
Young	Hedley	*Westmin. Sch.*
	Hotham	

April 12.

Mr. G. F. R. Weidemain, B.A. Scholar of Catherine Hall, elected a Skirne Fellow of that Society.

April 13.

ST. JOHN'S COLLEGE VOLUNTARY CLASSICAL EXAMINATION.

First Class.—Babington, Burbury, T. Field, Gifford, Girling, A.M. Hoare, G. T. Hoare.

Second Class.—Alston, Babb, Darrett, Fellowes, Holcombe, Snowball.

April 20.

Degrees conferred.

M.A.

A. S. Eddis, Trin.; A. J. Rogers, Jesus; G.H. Skelton, Christ's; C. J. Tindal, and H. Baber, Trinity.

B.A.

W. P. Manson, Trin.; W. Collett, St. Peter's; R. Goldham, Corp. Christi; J. Tomlins, John's; W. Miniken, and W. Inchbald, Cath. H.; V. J. Stanton, John's; W. Daman, Queen's; E. Corbett, Trin.; C. E. Parry, and R. Middlemist, Christ's; W. M. W. Call, John's.

PROCEEDINGS OF SOCIETIES.

INCORPORATED SOCIETY FOR PROMOTING THE ENLARGEMENT, BUILDING, AND REPAIRING OF CHURCHES AND CHAPELS.

A meeting of the Committee of this Society was held at their chambers, St. Martin's-place, on Monday, the 18th of April, 1842; His Grace the Archbishop of Canterbury in the chair.

Among the members present were the Lord Bishops of London, Winchester, Bangor, Chester, Ely, Ripon, Hereford, Peterborough, and Worcester; the Lord Kenyon; the Revds. Dr. D'Oyly, Dr. Spry, J. Jennings, Benj. Harrison, H.H. Norris, and J. Lonsdale; H. J. Barchard, J. W. Bowden, I. S. Salt, Wm. Davis, Jas. Cocks, T. D. Acland, M.P., Benj. Harrison, and N. Connop, jun., Esqrs.

Grants were voted towards building a church at Byers Green, in the parish of St. Andrew Auckland, Durham; building a church at Walmley, in the parish of Sutton Coldfield, Warwick; building a chapel at Elmore Green, in the parish of Motcombe, Dorset; building a chapel at Fernall Heath, in the parish of Claines, Worcester; building a chapel at Upper Tean, in the parish of Chickley, Stafford; building a chapel at Newton, in the parish of Clodock, Hereford; repewing the church at Swepstone, Leicester; enlarging by rebuilding the chapel at Boddicott, Oxon; enlarging and repewing the church at Exhall, Warwick; repewing the church at Bruton, Somerset; repewing the church at Measham, Derby; enlarging the church at Davenham, Chester; repewing and erecting a gallery in the church at Riseley, Beds; enlarging by rebuilding the church at Arlingbury, Northampton; rebuilding the chapel at Tibberton, Salop; enlarging the church at Steeple Claydon, Bucks; and other business was transacted.

SOCIETY FOR THE PROPAGATION OF THE GOSPEL IN FOREIGN PARTS.

New South Wales.—We have just received the census of the population of New South Wales, from which it appears that more than half the entire population are members of the Church of England. The numbers being:—

Total population 130,56
Members of the Ch. of England 73,727

South Australia.—Extracts from the Report of the Church Building Committee:—

" The first stone of St. John's Church was laid by his Excellency Colonel Gawler, in Oct. 1839; after some delay, resulting from want of funds, the foundation was laid and raised to a general level of three feet above the surface of the ground, at a cost of 538*l.* A contract has since been taken for the erection of the walls and roof for the sum of 750*l.*, the bricks being procured and conveyed to the site of the church by your Committee, at a further expense of 275*l.*, the requisite supply of lime and sand being also purchased by the Society's funds. The walls are now complete, and it is expected that in two or three weeks the building will be roofed in. Your Committee are very earnestly desirous to be enabled to have the floor laid down, and thus to place the Church in such a condition as to enable the Rev. James Farrell (who has been nominated to the incumbency by his Excellency Col. Gawler, at the request of your Committee) to commence his ministrations therein.

"Until the Committee receive further liberal aid from the friends of the Society, they will not be able to take any steps towards pewing the church, although they feel themselves pledged to the completion of that part of the work as speedily as possible.

"Gladly would the Committee extend their operations to North Adelaide, and erect a church on the site given by John Brown, Esq., which would provide church accommodation not only for the inhabitants of that part of the city, but also for those of the villages of Hindmarsh and Bowden, the population of which is now considerable, if their funds would enable them to do so.

"They feel also that the districts of Mount Barker Gawler, Morphett Vale, and Encounter Bay, stand much in need of a stated ministry, but with their present means it is utterly impossible for your Committee even to make an attempt at providing these rural districts with such a blessing.

"In conclusion, your Committee would earnestly commend the cause of the Society to the zealous and prayerful support of all persons, as well in the Colony as in Great Britain and elsewhere, who feel interested in promoting the true and permanent welfare of the province and its inhabitants."

New Zealand.—An important meeting was held in the course of last year at Government-house, Auckland, for the purpose of taking steps for the erection of a Church in that town. His Excellency Governor Hobson in the chair. The following resolution was unanimously affirmed:—

"That, while it is incumbent on every member of the Christian community to afford assistance in promoting the Christian Religion, it becomes a more paramount and important part of his duty, as a resident in a new colony (the natives of which chiefly remain in ignorance of Christian truth), to provide for and encourage the due observance of public worship."

At the date of the last despatches, the subscriptions had amounted to nearly 500*l.*

Colonial Bishops —The success which has attended the Bishop of London's Pastoral Letter in behalf of the Additional Colonial Bishoprics, is very encouraging. The collections have already produced more than 7,500*l.*; and, as there are still about 150 returns to be made, there can be little doubt that the whole will amount to upwards of 8,000*l.*— *Eccles. Gazette.*

THEOLOGICAL INSTRUCTION IN THE UNIVERSITY OF CAMBRIDGE.

The Syndicate of Cambridge appointed "to consider whether any and what steps should be taken to provide a more efficient system of theological instruction in the University," beg leave to commence their Report with a brief account of the present state of instruction in that department of study.

In the previous examination, and in the ordinary examination for the B.A. degree, the University requires an acquaintance with one of the Gospels and the Acts of the Apostles in the original Greek, with Paley's Evidences and Paley's Moral Philosophy.

The other encouragements and aids to theological studies offered at present by the University (in addition to what is done by lectures, examinations, prizes, &c. in the several colleges) consist of,

The examinations and disputations conducted by the Regius Professor of Divinity in order to divinity degrees: (see Note A.)

The Lectures of the Lady Margaret Professor of Divinity: (see Note B.)

The Lectures of the Norrisian Professor of Divinity: (see Note C.)

The Lectures of the Knightbridge Professor of Moral Theology: (see Note D.)

The Lectures of the Regius Professor of Hebrew.

The three Crosse Theological Scholarships.

The six Tyrwhitt Hebrew Scholarships.

The Prize (occasionally given on the Tyrwhitt bequest) for a Dissertation on some subject connected with Hebrew literature.

The prize for the Hulsean Dissertation: (about 100*l.*)

The Prize for the Norrisian Dissertation: (12*l.*)

NOTE A.

The superintendence of all exercises required for the degrees of Bachelor and Doctor in Divinity is committed to the Regius Professor of Divinity; who also is much engaged in examinations more or less connected with theological studies.

NOTE B.

Memorandum of the lectures delivered by the Lady Margaret Professor since his election in 1839.

I. On the *Early Fathers*:

Introductory lectures, showing, 1st, from her express declarations, and, 2dly from her structure and services, the regard the Church of England pays to early antiquity.

On the Apostolical Fathers (the Lectures on Ignatius, prefaced by an abridgment of Bishop Pearson's Vindiciæ Ignatianæ); on Justin Martyr; Tatian; Athenagoras; Theophilus; and Irenæus; the last now in the course of delivery.

The object of these Lectures is to put the hearers eventually in possession of a knowledge of all the Fathers of the first three centuries. The plan has been to go through each Father in detail; to give the substance of the author, where more than this did not seem necessary; to translate at full and explain, where a passage was remarkable; and lastly, to sum up the whole (with references) under several heads, such as Evidences, Canon of Scripture, Interpretation of Scripture, Sacraments, Ecclesiastical Discipline and Polity, Points of Controversy with Rome, Classical Illustrations, &c.

When the course is completed, it may be adjusted to the period of an undergraduate's residence in the University: meanwhile parts of it are repeated and advances made in it every year.

II. A course of practical Lectures on *the acquirements and principal obligations and duties of the Parish Priest.*

Introductory Lecture, on the ministerial character of St. Paul.

On the Reading of the Parish Priest, advising (1), the study of the Scriptures in the original languages, with examples of the advantage of this, and other hints for reading them; (2) the study of the Fathers of the first three centuries, with illustrations of the benefit to be derived from this study; (3) the study of the English Reformation in the documents set forth seriatim by the Reformers; a list of these given, with remarks on each: the whole intended to put the students on applying themselves to original authorities as the sources of sound knowledge, and to divert them from such as are only secondary and derivative: on the composition of sermons; on schools, Sunday and daily, the method of establishing, maintaining, and conducting them; on parochial ministrations, especially visiting the sick; on ordinary pastoral intercourse; on the observance of Rubric and Canons; on the general rule by which the Parish Priest should be guided.

The Margaret Professor proposes to deliver this latter series of Lectures, with such alterations or additions as may suggest themselves, every second or third year, so that all students intended for Holy Orders may have an opportunity of hearing them.

NOTE C.

Outline of the Lectures delivered by the Norrisian Professor since his election in 1838.

I. The provision made by the Church of England for securing in Candidates for Holy Orders,
 1. Moral fitness.
 2. Literary qualifications.
 3. Soundness in doctrine.

Occasion is taken to explain what is implied in subscription to Articles of Religion generally, and in subscription to the Three Propositions contained in the 36th Canon particularly, references being, at the same time, given to authors who have treated of these several subjects.

II. The course of reading desirable to be pursued by the candidate for Holy Orders is then considered, as embracing—
 a. The Sacred Scriptures in the original languages; and under this head is given a detailed account of some of,
  i. The principal editions of the Hebrew Bible and Greek Testament.

  ii. The Hebrew and Greek Lexicons and Concordances to the Sacred Scriptures.
  iii. The Commentaries on the Old and New Testament.
  iv. Those writers who have treated of the Chronology, Geography, Antiquities, &c. of the Scriptures.

A selection being made in each case for the Biblical Student of such books as seem to the Professor best adapted for the student's use and circumstances.

 β. *The Prayer-Book.*
  Under this head are noticed—
  i. The conformity of the English Liturgy with the Scriptures, and with the best portions of the Liturgies of antiquity.
  ii. The modifications which the Prayer-Book has undergone.
  iii. The importance of an accurate acquaintance with—
   a. The office for the Administration of Baptism.
   b. The office for the Administration of Holy Communion.
   c. The office for the Ordering of Deacons and Priests.
   d. Those of the XXXIX. Articles which treat of the Doctrine of the Sacraments.

In the discussion of these several subjects references are given to such writers as treat of them respectively.

 γ. *The Church of England* as respects her
  A. *History.*
   Comprising under this division notices of
   i. The Ancient British Church.
   ii. The Anglo-Saxon Church.
   iii. The Anglo-Norman Church.
   iv. The Reformed Church.

The more important eras in each being pointed out, and books mentioned in which information respecting the subject-matter may be obtained.

  B. *Polity.*
   Comprising an inquiry into,
   i. The Scriptural Authority for a Threefold Ministry.
   ii. The validity of the Orders of the English Church.

The principal writers on these subjects being referred to as occasion requires.

  C. *Controversies,*
   With
   i. Infidelity.
    The bearing and importance of Natural Religion, as connected with Revelation, being pointed out.
   ii. Romanism.
    Mentioning in detail the chief points in dispute with Romanists, and in the history of the Romish controversy in this country.
   iii. Dissent.
    Marking the peculiarities of dissent, and the different forms it has assumed, both doctrinally and in its workings.

The writers from whom information on these several topics may be obtained being severally referred to.

  D. *Ministrations.*
   i. Preaching.
    Taking occasion under this head to refer to sources from whence instruction may be derived respecting,
    a. The style and composition of Sermons; and then,
    b. Giving a list of some authors whose sermons may be read with advantage.
   ii. Parochial duties.
    In connexion with which such books are referred to as treat of,
    a. The spiritual duties and general conduct of a clergyman.
    b. Or relate to the secular affairs of a parish.
  E. *Endowments.*
   Under this head notice is taken of,
   i. The general principles involved in Establish-

ments, as contrasted with what is called,

ii. The Voluntary Principle.

Then is noticed,

  a. The origin of our Parochial and Cathedral Endowments.
  b. Some of the chief points in their history.

  References being given to writers on these subjects respectively.

Besides the several topics which have been thus recited, it should be borne in mind that the main outlines of the Evidences and Doctrines of Christianity are discussed in such portions of Pearson on the Creed as are read and commented upon in the course of the lectures.

NOTE D.

The Professorship of "Moral Theology or Casuistry," founded by Dr. Knightbridge, is considered by the present holder of it as a Professorship of Moral Philosophy. During the last three years, he has delivered three courses of lectures upon the History of Moral Philosophy, especially its history in England since the Reformation. During the present year he is delivering a course of lectures on the difficulties which attend the formation of a system of morality, and the mode of overcoming them.

Judging from the information received from the professors and examiners, the Syndicate consider that the amount of the attendance at the lectures of the professors, the number of the competitors for the above-mentioned scholarships and prizes, and the proficiency in the theological learning exhibited by those competitors, prove that the existing requirements, together with the encouragements and aids above referred to, are, to a very considerable extent, efficacious towards the end for which they were designed.

The Syndicate, bearing in mind the theological knowledge at present required, and the encouragements and aids to theological studies already afforded both by the university and by the several colleges, and being anxious that whatever may be adopted, with a view to the farther advancement of theological learning amongst the younger students of the university, should be founded on the methods of instruction already established, recommend, in the first place, the following plans, marked No. 1, No. 2, No. 3. It will be observed that those three plans have reference to students before admission *ad respondendum quæstioni*, whether such students be intended for Holy Orders or not. In the first of them, an addition is made to the present previous examination. In the second will be found some additions to the present ordinary examinations for the B.A. degree, together with a few alterations in the same. The object of the third is to afford to questionists, who are candidates for honours, an opportunity of showing that they have paid due attention to theological studies. In the plans marked No. 1 and No. 2, the Syndicate have inserted in the present Report those paragraphs only of the existing regulations, for the previous examination and for the ordinary examination for the B.A. degree, in which any changes are proposed; and all such changes are printed in the *italic* character.

No. 1.

Plan for the Previous Examination.

1. That the subjects of the examination shall be one of the four Gospels in the Original Greek, Paley's Evidences of Christianity, *the Old Testament History*, and one of the Greek and one of the Latin Classics.

2 and 3 to remain unchanged.

4. That every person when examined shall be required (1) to translate some portion of each of the subjects appointed as aforesaid, (2) to construe and explain passages of the same, and (3) to answer printed questions relating to the Evidences of Christianity *and the Old Testament History*.

5, 6, and 7 to remain unchanged.

8. That the persons to be examined each day shall be formed into two divisions; that each of these divisions shall be examined in the Greek subject by two of the examiners, and in the Latin subject by the other two during the morning; and that the Greek Testament, Paley's Evidences, *and the Old Testament History*, be the subjects of examination in the afternoon.

9 to 22 to remain unchanged.

23. *That the first examination, under the regulations now proposed, shall take place in the Lent Term of* 1844.

No. 2.

Plan of Examination for Questionists who are not *Candidates for Honours.*

1. That the subjects of the examination shall be *the first fourteen or the last fourteen chapters of* the Acts of the Apostles,

and one of the longer or two or more of the shorter Epistles of the New Testament, in the original Greek, one of the Greek and one of the Latin Classics, *three of the six Books of* Paley's Moral Philosophy, *the History of the Christian Church from its Origin to the assembling of the Council of Nice, the History of the English Reformation,* and such Mathematical subjects as are prescribed by the Grace of April 19, 1837, at present in force.

2 That in regard to *these* subjects, the appointment *of the Division of the Acts—of the Epistle or Epistles—of the Books of Paley's Moral Philosophy,* and both of the classical authors and of the portions of their Works which it may be expedient to select, shall be with the persons who appoint the classical subjects for the previous examination.

3. That public notice of the *subjects so selected* for any year shall be issued in the last week of the Lent Term of the year next but one preceding.

4 and 5 to remain unchanged.

6. That the distribution of the subjects and times of examination shall be according to the following table:—

Div.		9 to 12.
Wednesday	1	Euclid.
Thursday	1	Greek Subject.
Friday	1	Mechanics and Hydrostatics.
Saturday	1	Latin Subject.
Monday	1	Paley *and Eccles. Hist.*
Tuesday	1	Acts *and Epistle or Epistles.*
Wednesday	1	Arithmetic and Algebra.

Div.		12½ to 3½.
Wednesday	2	Greek Subject.
Thursday	2	Euclid.
Friday	2	Latin Subject.
Saturday	2	Mechanics and Hydrostatics.
Monday	2	Acts *and Epistle or Epistles.*
Tuesday	2	Paley *and Eccles. Hist.*
Wednesday	2	Arithmetic and Algebra.

7 to remain unchanged.

8. That the papers in the classical subjects and in the Acts *and the Epistles* shall consist of passages to be translated, accompanied with such plain questions in Grammar, History, and Geography, as arise immediately out of those passages.

9 to 14 to remain unchanged.

15. That two of these examiners shall confine themselves to the classical subjects, and two to Paley's Moral Philosophy, *Ecclesiastical History,* the Acts of the Apostles, *and the Epistles.*

16, 17, and 18 to remain unchanged.

19. *That the first Examination, under the Regulations now proposed, shall take place in the Lent Term of* 1846.

No. 3.

Plan of Examination for Questionists who are Candidates for Honours.

1. That the questionists who are candidates for honours be required to attend, with the other questionists, the examination in Paley's Moral Philosophy, the New Testament, and Ecclesiastical History, appointed to take place on the first Monday in the Lent Term, and on the following day.

That the names of all such questionists, candidates for honours, as shall, in the judgment of the examiners, have passed their examination in these subjects with credit, be published, in alphabetical order, by the proctors, in the senate-house, upon the day of the bachelor of arts' commencement.

3. That the first examination under the regulations now proposed, shall take place in the Lent Term of 1846.

On proceeding to direct their attention to a plan of examination for persons who, having been admitted *ad respondendum quæstioni,* are intended for Holy Orders, the Syndicate found the subject involved in difficulties; but, after mature consideration, they beg leave to recommend, in the second place, the following plan to the senate.

No. 4.

Plan of Theological Examination for students who shall have been admitted ad respondendum quæstioni *in conformity with the preceding regulations.*

1. In the first or second week of the Michaelmas Term of each year, there shall be an examination in the Greek Testament, assigned portions of the Early Fathers, Ecclesiastical History, the Articles of Religion, and the Liturgy of the Church of England, which examination shall be open to all students who, having at any time been admitted *ad respondendum quæstioni* in conformity with the preceding regulations, shall present themselves to be examined.

2. The examinations shall be conducted by the Regius and Lady Margaret Professors of Divinity; or, in case of the illness or unavoidable absence of either or both of them, by some member or members of the senate, nominated by

either or both of the professors, and confirmed by grace of the Senate.

3. The names of those students who shall have passed their examination to the satisfaction of the examiners shall be published in alphabetical order, and registered in the usual manner.

4. Immediately after each such examination, a portion of the Hebrew Scriptures shall form the subject of a new examination for such students as, having their names published as above-mentioned, shall offer themselves to be examined.

5. The examination in the Hebrew Scriptures shall be conducted by the Regius Professor of Hebrew; or, in case of his illness or absence, by some member of the senate, nominated by him, and confirmed by grace of the Senate.

6. The names of the students who shall have passed their examination in the Hebrew Scriptures, to the satisfaction of the examiner, shall be published and registered in the manner already described.

7. Public notice of the days of examination and also of the portions of the Early Fathers and of the Hebrew Scriptures, assigned for the aforesaid examinatious in the Michaelmas Term of any year, shall be given in the first week of the Lent Term immediately preceding.

8. The first examination under the regulations now proposed shall take place in the Michaelmas Term of 1846.

The Syndicate recommend that the examination marked No. 4, should be open to students in the Civil Law, on producing certificates, from the Regius Professor of the Civil Law, or his deputy, of their having performed the exercises required for the degree of bachelor in that faculty.

G. ARCHDALL, *Vice-Chancellor.*
W. FRENCH.
R. TATHAM.
W. WHEWELL.
T. TURTON.
J. J. BLUNT.
JAMES WILLIAM GELDART.
JAMES SCHOLEFIELD.

The Syndicate are authorized to announce to the Senate, that should the regulations contained in the foregoing Report be adopted, the Regius and Lady Margaret Professors of Divinity and the Regius Professor of Hebrew, in consideration of the length of time which must elapse before the plan marked No. 4 can come into operation, will commence in the Michaelmas Term of 1843, and continue in the corresponding term of each of the two following years, examinations somewhat similar to those proposed in that plan.

A grace to confirm the above Report will be offered to the Senate at the Congregation on Wednesday, May 11.

DIOCESAN INTELLIGENCE.

LONDON.—*Proposed School for Sons of Clergymen, &c.*—The Provisional Committee of this Institution are endeavouring to carry out the plan of it in a manner which they trust will be of much benefit to the Clergy possessed of small livings, with regard to the education of their sons.

It has been agreed, that the nomination payments on the part of Clergymen wishing to nominate their own sons, need not be made in one sum, but by instalments; and that the right to nominate shall commence after payment of half the required sum, the remaining half to be paid by instalments in a similar manner within two years.

In cases of death, and where no privilege has been exercised, either all moneys received will be returned, if required, or the right of nomination be given to legal representatives, acting solely for the benefit of the donor's family.

The sum of 30,000*l.*, mentioned in the first prospectus, will not be required for some length of time; the design of the Committee being to engage in no building expenses, until it shall be shown clearly that the whole scheme is worthy of encouragement; it being easy to obtain the necessary accommodation, and to carry on the business of the school, for a time at least, in some hired house or houses, made fit for such purposes, in some central situation, not too far from London, and accessible by railroad.

The plan of education will embrace, in addition to sound religious teaching, instruction in the Greek and Latin Classics, Mathematics, Modern Languages, and Drawing, under the direction of the best masters that can be obtained; and the character of the whole establishment will be that of a school, and not a college.

The Provisional Committee *do not now, as was first contemplated, consider a public meeting in London necessary.* From information already obtained, they are satisfied, that all that is required might be effected by means of private correspondence, and occasional public advertisements.

Should any of the Clergy or Laity, who have not yet expressed their opinions and wishes, feel disposed to join in this undertaking, the Honorary Secretaries respectfully request that early communications may be made to them, which will be attended to immediately.

The Anniversary Festival of the Sons of the Clergy, will be held on Thursday, May 12th, when the Sermon will be preached by the Rev. Samuel Wilberforce, B.D., Archdeacon of Surrey. The rehearsal takes place on the 10th. (See Advertisement.)

PARISH OF LAMBETH.—Church extension is proceeding successfully in this large and very populous parish. The Rector of the parish proposed about two or three years ago, a plan for erecting three new Churches, in addition to the others before erected, to meet the demands of the still growing population. Two of those new Churches are already built and consecrated. It is now proposed to erect a third Church in the densely peopled district of the Waterloo-road. In that district there now exists only one Church, with a population of 30,000 souls. Funds nearly sufficient for the purpose are already obtained. Her Majesty the Queen made a munificent donation, some time since, of 300*l.* for the three Churches; and Her Majesty the Queen Dowager has recently most liberally made a donation of 50*l.* to the Church now intended, in addition to other donations, from his Grace the Archbishop of Canterbury, the Bishop of Winchester, &c.

BATH AND WELLS.—*Bath United Hospital.*—Collections at the churches, chapels, and meeting-houses in Bath, February and March, 1842:—

	£	s.	d.
Octagon Chapel (Church)	65	8	11
Abbey Church	57	8	7
Argyle meeting-house (Brownist)	50	6	0
Margaret's Chapel	40	15	10
Laura Chapel	38	9	8
Bathwick Church	34	14	11
St. Michael's Church	23	17	4
Walcot Church	20	8	7
All Saints' Chapel	17	8	6
St. Saviour's Church, Walcot	16	18	11
Roman Catholic meeting-house	11	14	0
St. James's Church	11	10	0
Trinity Church	10	6	2
New King-street and Walcot meeting-houses (Wesleyan)	9	5	8
St. Mark's Church, Widcombe	8	5	2
Irvingite meeting-house	7	7	8
Somerset-st. meeting-ho.	5	5	0
Bethesda Chapel	4	13	1
Magdalen Chapel	4	4	0
Dolemeads Episcopal Cha.	3	5	0
St. John's Chapel	3	1	4
Widcombe Church (Old)	3	0	0
Quaker's meeting-house	2	15	0
York-st. meeting-house	2	6	0
St. Mary's Chap., Queen-square	1	13	8
	£454	9	0

From the above accounts it will be seen, that while the meeting-houses only contributed 88*l.* 19*s.* 4*d.*, the Churches contributed 365*l.* 9*s.* 8*d.*! The two Wesleyan meeting-houses are very large indeed, but two of them contributed only the paltry sum of 9*l.* 5*s.* 8*d.*! Surely the poor of Bath will readily see whether Churchmen or Dissenters are their best friends.

YORK MINSTER.—A numerous meeting was lately held at York, Lord Wharncliffe in the chair, at which the Minster Restoration Committee presented the accounts of the expenditure of the subscriptions, with a detail of the works effected. The Rev. W. V. Harcourt submitted the details of a plan, by which the Dean and Chapter proposed to raise 26,000*l.* by a sale of a portion of the Minster estates to complete the restoration, but which would require the passing of an act of parliament to sanction.

DOVER.—About ninety candidates for the vacant incumbency of the Parish of St. Mary's, Dover, have sent in applications to the churchwardens. The following is the advertisement issued by the Churchwardens on the subject, and as it is a curiosity of its kind, we place it upon record:—

"Saint Mary the Virgin, Dover.— Further Advertisement.—The Incumbency of this Church being vacant by the resignation of the Rev. John Maule, M.A., the pulpit will be open, according to ancient custom, to such Clergymen in Holy Orders as may be desirous to offer themselves as candidates to supply the vacancy. Each applicant will be informed on what Sunday he will be expected to take the whole of the duty. The Incumbent, when elected, will be required to perform all the services, except the evening lectures, in his own person, and not to appoint a Curate or Evening Lecturer without the consent of the parishioners, who are the patrons of the living. He will be entitled to receive the surplice fees, amounting to about the sum of 104*l*. per annum. He will have an excellent house to reside in, which is in good repair; and it has been resolved by the parishioners to let 450 sittings (100 at 1*l*. each, 100 at 15*s*. each, 100 at 10*s*. each, and the remaining 150 at 5*s*. each sitting, for the morning and afternoon services), and to apply the proceeds in the following manner:—20*l*. per annum to the parish clerk, 20*l*. per annum to the organist, 30*l*. per annum to the sextons, and the residue to be paid to the Incumbent. In addition to the above it is proposed to let the 450 sittings for the evening service, and to apply the proceeds, after payment of the expenses of lighting, &c., to the remuneration of the Incumbent, or the Minister who shall perform such evening service; the Incumbent being allowed the option of doing so. The parish contains about 10,000 souls, but a district has been assigned to a chapel of ease for pastoral purposes, comprising about one-half of the inhabitants. There are about 1,600 sittings in the parish church. Applications to be made in writing to the Churchwardens or Vestry Clerk on or before the 14th instant (April).—*Church Intelligencer.**

CHURCH EDUCATION SOCIETY FOR IRELAND.

(Extracts from the Report.)

THE third annual meeting of this important society was held at Dublin, April 7.

DR. ELRINGTON read the annual report, which gives a pleasing account of the society's operations. There are at present in connexion with the society, through its diocesan branches, 1,189 schools, having 68,098 children on the rolls, of whom 20,166 are the children of Roman Catholic parents; and in dioceses where no district society has been yet established, 30 schools, with 1,429 children on the roll, of whom 285 are of the Roman Catholic persuasion, making a total of 1,219 schools, and 69,527 children on the roll. The sums contributed to the support of these schools, independent of the subscriptions to the Central Society, amount to 15,112*l*. 4*s*., of which, it is but right to add, a very large proportion is borne by the clergy, the entire support of the schools in their respective parishes, in very many instances, devolving upon them exclusively. The above amount added to the receipts of the Central Society, and of the schools in separate connexion, exhibits a sum of 19,051*l*. 2*s*. 8½*d*. contributed to the support of schools conducted according to the principles of the Church Education Society. From a comparison of these returns with those of the year 1840, it will appear, that although no returns have as yet been received from four diocesan societies, there is, in the number of schools in connexion, an ascertained increase of 191; of children on the roll, an increase of 9,497.

"If the parents of so large a number of children, as already stated, are anxious to have them educated according to the principle of your society, and if so great a proportion of these are members of that religious persuasion which is said to be so averse to the reading of the Holy Scriptures, the conclusion seems irresistible, that those principles are viewed with less suspicion generally than some would have believed they are. Circumstances have, no doubt,

---

* We take this opportunity of acknowledging our obligations to the "Church Intelligencer" for many pieces borrowed from that Journal for the use of our columns. Such of our readers as desire a more detailed view of Church matters than we can profess to give, will find the "Intelligencer" a paper well worthy of their support. It is published weekly by Wertheim.

been in operation of late to prevent their favourable acceptance with the people being so clearly manifested as under a different state of things it might have been; but if, at a time when they are furnished with every facility of receiving secular instruction at schools in which instruction in the Holy Scriptures shall form no essential part, and induced, as they must be by circumstances which it is not necessary here to particularise, to have recourse to those schools alone, any considerable portion of the Roman Catholic population are yet found willing to frequent, in preference, the schools under your society, the inference in favour of the principles upon which it is founded seems as irresistible as it is encouraging. It must not be forgotten, too, that this preference for your society has been manifested at a time when there was little else to attract it than the esteem in which its principles were held. In determining the degree of favour with which these principles are regarded in the country, it should also be borne in mind, there are many schools not in connexion with the society which are, notwithstanding, conducted in strict accordance with its regulations. The schools referred to, being supported exclusively by the patrons of them, do not require assistance from other sources, and are, therefore, not in connexion with any society.

"The last report mentioned the adoption of two important measures—the establishment of a book depository, from whence your schools might be supplied with books of an approved character, and of a central training school, in which the masters might be taught a superior method of conveying instruction, and be further improved in those branches of necessary information in which they should be found most deficient. Beneficial results have followed from both these measures.

"As the character of the books placed in the hands of pupils is of as much importance as the qualifications of the teachers, the committee have not failed to direct attention to the depository with a view to an improvement. They have accordingly made some additions to their catalogue, which experience had shown to be desirable, and supplied the place of certain books that were found unsuitable to your schools with others of a better description. Besides offering these to all schools in connexion at a reduction of 25 per cent., in some cases even to a larger amount, they have issued free grants to the value of 563*l.* 19*s.* 7*d.*, calculated at the reduced rates."

FOREIGN.—SPAIN.

Apostolical Letter of our very Reverend Father in God, Pope Gregory XVI. commanding public prayers to be made on account of the sad state of Religion in the kingdom of Spain, with plenary indulgence in form of Jubilee.

"GREGORY XVI. Sovereign Pontiff, of perpetual memory.

" The situation of the affairs of religion in Spain, and the profound grief with which we have been constrained to weep for many years over the misfortunes of the Church in that kingdom are but too well known.

"The people, indeed, are strongly attached to the Catholic faith; the greater portion of their clergy resist with courage. Nevertheless, in this same country, men of perdition, and the number is not small, bound together by a criminal association, like the waves of an enraged sea, overwhelm their country with their shameful and disorderly proceedings, declaring an unceasing war against Christ and his saints.

. " For ourselves, we have not omitted publicly to deplore the wounds inflicted on the Church by the government of Madrid. All the acts done by the civil power against the rights of the Church we have broken and declared void. Furthermore, we have exclaimed, with every expression of grief, and in vehement accents, against the atrocious injuries and evils they have made our venerable brethren the Bishops of the kingdom to undergo, as likewise the members of the clergy, both regular and secular; also against the abomination established in the holy place, and against the sacrilegious robbery of the ecclesiastical property, sold and applied to the wants of the public treasury.

"We had hoped that our voice would at length have been heard, but we see rather the evil to increase from day to day in these wide-spread countries, insomuch that the Catholic religion is publicly threatened there with complete destruction.

"An execrable law has just been proposed to the supreme assemblies of the nation, principally tending to destroy entirely the legitimate authority of the Church, and to establish the impious opinion that the power of the laity is superior, by its supreme right, to the Church and all that concerns it.

"In fact, this law declares that the Spanish nation is not to pay any attention to the Apostolical See; that all communication with it must be broken off in regard to ecclesiastical favours, grants, and concessions of whatsoever kind; and that it punishes severely those who shall resist such an ordinance. It is also said that apostolical letters and other rescripts emanating from the Holy See, unless they are asked for by Spain, not only must not be observed and shall remain without effect, but even shall be denounced to the civil power without the least delay by those to whom they might have come, and are then to be handed over to the government, a penalty attaching to any one who shall evade this injunction.

"Moreover, it is ordered, that oppositions to marriages shall be submitted to the jurisdiction of the Bishops of the kingdom, until the civil code has established a difference between the contract and the marriage sacrament; that no cause whatsoever relating to religious affairs can be referred to Rome by Spain; and again, that hereafter no Nuncio, nor any Legate of the Holy See, shall be admitted into this kingdom with power to grant favours or dispensations even gratuitously. Finally, the sacred right belonging to the Roman Pontiff to confirm or reject the Bishops elected in Spain is entirely abolished, and those priests who may be chosen by any episcopal church, if they apply to the Holy See for confirmation, shall be punished with exile.

"Therefore, we earnestly implore our venerable brethren to endeavour to soften Divine wrath by mingling their tears with our own, to implore unanimously the mercy of Almighty God for the unfortunate Spanish nation, and *to kindle the zeal of the clergy, and the people* committed to their charge, that they may address fervent prayers to God on this account.

"Consequently, we grant in form of jubilee a plenary indulgence to all faithful servants of Jesus Christ, who, duly purified by sacramental confession, and fed by the most blessed eucharist, shall assist at least thrice at the solemn prayers appointed by the command of each Ordinary, and who shall have thrice prayed to the same purpose, within the space of three days, in the Church assigned by the same Ordinaries.

"Given at Rome, near St. Peter, under the fisherman's seal, this 24th day of February, 1842, and in the twelfth year of our pontificate.

"A. CARD. LAMBRISCHINI."

CHURCHES CONSECRATED OR OPENED.

Southampton	St. Lawrence's	Bishop of Winchester	March 31.
Camberwell	Emmanuel Church	Ditto	April 16.

FOUNDATIONS LAID.

Manchester	St. Barnabas	March 28.
Windsor	Church of the Holy Trinity	April 4.

TO CORRESPONDENTS.

In reply to Dr. Ollivant's second letter, we have no hesitation in declaring that the impression was erroneous, under which, in our February number, St. David's College, Lampeter, was treated as implicated in the disgrace of Mr. Prince's publication. In what was said about "lax proceedings" in that institution, common rumour was *professedly* appealed to, a circumstance which Dr. Ollivant, we think, overlooks. It is one thing to mention having heard such and such reports, and quite another to state their substance without reference to the way one has heard it. Now, that such rumours have existed as those referred to by our contributor, Dr. Ollivant will not deny. We have great pleasure in acknowledging, from what he mentions in his letter, that whatever they may have been in time past, they can hardly be well-grounded now.

One word more. Both Dr. Ollivant and the friend to whom he appeals seem to think that we have been trying to shift the responsibility of the statement in question from ourselves to our contributor. We are well aware of our inability to do that; but surely any one, who considers the state of the case, will admit that our conduct in referring Dr. Ollivant's first letter to him was both right and reasonable. Nobody can suppose that so many books as are noticed in each number of our Magazine can be gone through and pronounced on by one person. We are obliged to avail ourselves of the assistance of our tried contributors in whom we can place confidence. The statement in question came from one to whom this Magazine is under greater obligations than to most. Was it not, therefore, due to him, as well as the best way of satisfying Dr. Ollivant, to ascertain his grounds for what he had written, although we fully recognised our own ultimate responsibility? The only thing for which we blame ourselves is our accidental delay in taking such steps—a fault for which, if we remember aright, we have already apologised to Dr. Ollivant in private.

Will John —— be good enough to furnish us with his address?

THE
CHRISTIAN REMEMBRANCER.

JUNE, 1842.

An Introduction to the Dialogues of Plato. By W. SEWELL, B.D. *late Professor of Moral Philosophy in the University of Oxford.* London: Rivingtons. Oxford: Parker. 1841. Pp. 388.

THIS work, as Mr. Sewell tells us in his preface, contains " the substance of some articles on Plato, which were permitted, by the kindness of the Editor of the British Critic, to appear in that review." It was not, we confess, until their republication in the present form, that we had bestowed upon them the attention which they appear to us to deserve. We are now anxious to atone, as far as may be, for our own neglect, by recommending them to the perusal of those of our readers (not, we hope, an altogether inconsiderable portion of them) who are interested in the study of the Greek philosophy, and of Plato especially. Agreeing, as we do, with Mr. Sewell, (p. 3,) that the University of Oxford has good reason to congratulate herself on the firmness with which she has adhered to the ethics of Aristotle, as "the text-book in her plan of education,"—and disposed, as we are, to think with him, that "no greater mischief could be done than to abandon it for any other less formal treatise,"—we yet hail, with very great satisfaction, every indication, and this among the number, of a reviving taste for the "nobler and more elevated philosophy of Plato," in that one of our English universities to which, according to Mr. Sewell, "the study of the Greek philosophy has been chiefly confined." Various members of that university have, from time to time, favoured us with the results of their Aristotelian studies, in the form of Editions, Commentaries, and Translations; and we are indebted to the Clarendon Press for a very serviceable reprint of Bekker's Edition of Aristotle's whole works. An Oxford bookseller has also had the spirit to publish a translation of Ritter's History of Philosophy, executed by a member of the University of Cambridge. But, so far as our knowledge extends, the present is the first contribution made by Oxford to the study of Plato in particular, that has appeared since the learned edition of the Euthydemus and Gorgias, published by Dr. Routh in the year 1784. Since that time the philosophy of Plato has occupied the attention of some of the profoundest thinkers and acutest critics on the continent. As Mr. Sewell remarks, (p. 32,) " No admirers of Plato can be insensible to the assistance which Schleiermacher, Ritter, Ast, Tennemann, Van Heusde, and many other foreign critics, have rendered to the study of his system." The volume before us furnishes abundant evidence that Mr. Sewell has been careful to avail himself of this assistance. Though differing, as we shall see, from Schleiermacher in some important respects, he is willing to acknowledge that that eminent person has done more than any one to throw the Dialogues into an intelligible order; and though it does not very clearly appear how far Mr. Sewell is disposed to adopt the Schleiermacherian arrangement of them, he is evidently persuaded of the truth of the principle on which that arrangement ultimately rests. He seems convinced that Plato's works do form, and were intended by the author to form, a connected system; and that, if we would know the meaning and estimate the value of any single dialogue, we must view it in its relation to the great organic whole of which it is a constituent portion. And with respect to the two most important of all—the Phædrus and the Republic, he places them, with Schleiermacher, the one at the beginning, the other (of course, with its appendices—the Timæus and Critias) at the end of the connected series of Dialogues. The Phædrus he regards as containing the germ, the Republic as itself the bright consummate flower, of Plato's philosophy. We are happy to find that Mr. Sewell has taken what we consider to be the first and the most important step towards the right understanding of Plato's works; a step which those who refuse to take must be content to remain in hopeless darkness concerning their connexion and purpose. A very large proportion of the volume before us is taken up by the examination of these two dialogues: they are, indeed, the only two that are expressly and systematically treated of.

We could not, without greatly exceeding our due limits, follow Mr. Sewell step by step in this examination; but we feel bound to acknowledge generally that it is conducted with great diligence and ability, and that Mr. Sewell is furnished with many more qualifications of an interpreter of Plato than that first and indispensable one— a true love and heartfelt reverence for the "Father and King of Philosophers." Of these further qualifications, the most striking is his power of vivid and frequently felicitous illustration; a talent, however, which would have been more available in the interpretation of Plato, had it been combined with a larger share of discrimination and judgment. We think the value of the work is very seriously impaired by this unwillingness or inability to draw distinctions, joined as it is to a wanton and almost riotous use of the faculty of comparison. In like manner, Mr. Sewell's natural fluency, and the ease with which he delivers himself of thoughts not always easy to express, are very apt to degenerate into a rhetorical emptiness and mere tumid pomp of solemn phrases, very surprising in so diligent a student of Plato.

We are the more sorry for this, as it will doubtless tend to strengthen those in their error, who hold Platonism and mysticism to be synonymous terms. To a follower of Socrates, δημηγορεῖς was the sharpest rebuke that his master could have administered; and ample as are the folds and gorgeous the embroidery of his greater disciple's rhetoric, language is never used by him as a drapery to conceal the absence of substantial thought and meaning.

We have said that the volume before us presents frequent instances of lively and happy illustration. That which we are about to quote is, we think, as good and as characteristic of its author's manner as any. Mr. Sewell has been describing some of the difficulties which even the warmest admirers of Plato are apt to encounter in the study of his Dialogues, and tracing them, very justly, to the habit of viewing each dialogue in detail, and without reference either to its own particular scope and object, or to its bearing on other dialogues.

" To speak of system, indeed, as applied to the works of Plato, will sound very strange to those who have only seen them bit by bit, and probably from a false position. They seem a collection of fragments—here a line and there a line—hint and hypothesis, doubt and dogmatism, feeling and reason, cold mathematical abstraction and the most gorgeous poetry, the drama and the lecture, the serious and the ridiculous, all thrown together with a hand careless in the profuseness of its riches. They bear no more resemblance to the rigid form, determinate proportion, and sharp clear outline of the treatises of Aristotle, than the rough shapeless splashes of scene-painting, to the finish and precision of a miniature. And yet there is art in each—more art and more system in the scene, than in the miniature. In the one indeed it lies open to every eye; in the other it is concealed in the artist's mind; and not till he places us in the position from which we are intended to see it, and the portions are properly arranged, and the lights are duly thrown, will those rude unsightly daubings shape themselves into life and beauty."—P. 9.

In this view we, for our part, heartily coincide. Long before we were acquainted with the Introductions of Schleiermacher, we had convinced ourselves that, could we once discover the right point of view, much if not all of what perplexed us in Plato would be set right, and fall, as it were spontaneously, into its true position. Whether the arrangement which Schleiermacher has proposed correspond or not to the order of time in which the Dialogues were actually written, is a 'question, we think, still open to discussion; but that, with very few and insignificant exceptions, it is the order in which they may most profitably be read in the present day, is a conviction that gains upon us every time we renew the experiment. The two questions, though Schleiermacher seems to regard them as one, are properly distinct; and we think there is much force and good sense in the reasons which Mr. Sewell adduces (p. 97*) for

---

* In a second edition Mr. Sewell will perhaps vouchsafe to reconcile this passage with what he says on the same subject, p. 36. This is one of the many singular self-contradictions to be found in the Introduction.

disputing the truth of the common tradition, that the Phædrus was the first published of the Dialogues. A similar commendation applies to the following passage:—

"Even if we knew the dates of the publication of each dialogue, it would assist us but little in fixing the order in which they should be read; for any writer with a system ready formed in his mind will throw it out portion by portion, according as the train of thought may happen to present itself. Such a work is not like the erection of a house, in which the foundation must in time precede the walls, and the walls be raised before the roof. It is rather like the planting an estate; and where we begin, and where we end, may depend on the accident of the moment, without any departure from the original plan."—P. 34.

But Mr. Sewell conceives that he has got hold of a better clue to the Platonic labyrinth than Schleiermacher and the Germans. It is in reference, he thinks, to the "*practical object*" of Plato, not "to the artist-like development of the philosophical system" that his Dialogues should be arranged. What this practical object is he tells us in the sentence following:—

"The connexion will be more easy, and the series more natural, and, in particular, (that which constitutes the great difficulty,) the parts of each several dialogue will arrange themselves in greater consistency by bearing in mind throughout that the young men of Athens were the persons to whom they were expressly addressed; that the purification of their morals —the refutation of their corruptors, the Sophists—the elevation of the standard of private and political morality—the laying a firm foundation for a new national character—the cleansing, or endeavouring to cleanse, the Augean stable of the Grecian democracy—and the opening a new world of thought and feeling, as yet hidden behind the veil of a gross sensualistic polytheism,—that these, and not merely the foundation of a metaphysical school, or the development and propagation of barren truth, were constantly before the mind of Plato, guiding his thought and his pen throughout, and offering the only explanation to those innumerable mysteries and anomalies which meet us in every page of his works—which have made many men abandon them in despair, some play with them as a complicated enigma, others ridicule them as an unintelligible chaos, a whole succession of philosophical schools claim him as the champion of their scepticism, and even Cicero himself declare that 'Plato never hazards an assertion, but argues on both sides of the question, and then leaves the reader in his doubt.'"—Pp. 34, 35.

Mr. Sewell admits that "the main outlines of such a plan" as Schleiermacher's "must coincide with that which would be formed in direct reference to the practical object of Plato." He does not, however, give us any reason for so thinking. Schleiermacher would probably say, that it was by means of his philosophy that Plato proposed to accomplish his practical object; that no "truth," in Plato's opinion, was "barren,"—far less those immutable and fundamental truths the contemplation of which, in his mind, formed the best purification of the moral nature. He would maintain that the very distinction into speculative and practical was, in the highest degree, unplatonic; for that Plato knew of no higher practical act than *speculation* (θεώρησις) on the great ethical ideas of the just, the beautiful, and the good. Once bring men to the knowledge and love of the truth, and the truth would make them free, not only from the meshes of sophistry, but from the moral and intellectual fascination of the senses also. And he would probably refer to the parable of the cave in the Republic in confirmation of his views.—So considered, it is true that Mr. Sewell's plan ought to coincide with Schleiermacher's; and in this part of his work he seems to be haunted by a suspicion that something of the kind is the case. But why say that Schleiermacher had "failed in his clue?" Surely the clue is not in his hand who knows whither he would go, but in his who shows him the way.

But if by "practical object" Mr. Sewell means to imply that Plato contemplated any more direct means of working on his countrymen as either practicable or desirable than this moral and intellectual purification, he ought assuredly to have brought forward some more than usually powerful arguments in support of a position so contrary to the tenor of all that Plato ever wrote, and, so far as his biographers can be trusted, of his whole course of life and action. Surely he does foul wrong to the author of the Crito, who should impute to him any wish, by secret societies or otherwise, to tamper with the institutions of his native land. To do evil that good may come was not Plato's maxim, though it may have been Pythagoras's. He who taught that it was better to suffer wrong than to do it, was little likely to make common cause with the unprincipled oligarchal faction, which held both in theory and practice that justice and the interest of the stronger were one.

We should hardly have ventured to impute to Mr. Sewell what we hold to be so gross a misconception of Plato and his writings, but for expressions in the 8th chapter, which are unintelligible on any other hypothesis. For what else can be the meaning of that strange parallel between Plato and Pythagoras and Luther, with which that chapter begins? "We must not, indeed," says Mr. Sewell, "elevate the character of a Plato to a level with that of Pythagoras, so far as existing records enable us to judge. He had not the boldness or decision of character to organize an extensive confederacy, and thus obtain the command of the political movements of his country." Fortunately for his country, himself, and posterity, he had not; nor shall we, without stronger reasons than Mr. Sewell gives us, renounce the belief that higher motives than either fear for his personal safety, or the "catastrophe" of the Pythagorean schools, or "the hopelessness of the case," deterred Plato from cloaking under the mantle of philosophy the designs of a conspirator and a traitor. Any one with the most ordinary aptitude for historical research may convince himself, by a moment's reflection on the wide difference in the age and circumstances of the two men, that the case of Pythagoras forms no parallel to that of Plato; and if the difference in the means they adopted to improve the character of the men among whom their lot was cast be interpreted as a proof that Plato was inferior to

Pythagoras, it is only fair to observe that by the same reasoning he may be shown to fall far short of Mahomet, and many other reformers distinguished for the "energy" of their "measures." How to deal with the case of Luther we know not, it not being easy to draw distinctions in cases where it is difficult to perceive a resemblance. We suspect Mr. Sewell must have come fresh from the perusal of Mr. Carlyle's Heroes and Hero-worship, when he wrote the most unworthy remarks to which we have adverted.* The truth seems to be that the only legitimate engine of political influence in Athens, the eloquence of the *bema*, was an instrument which Plato felt himself debarred from using. He regarded it as an occupation essentially sophistical in its character, and capable of being turned to account by those only who would stoop to flatter the many-headed monster which they sought to rule. This Plato could not do without renouncing that self-consistency, which in theory and practice was the first principle of every true follower of Socrates. And this we take to be the right answer to those who, with Niebuhr, set down Plato as a bad citizen, and those who, with Mr. Sewell, blame him for being too good a one.

The mention of Pythagoras leads us to the consideration of another favourite view of Mr. Sewell, which we feel bound to protest against. Mr. Sewell practises some reserve, apparently, in stating this view; but, by collation of certain passages, we infer it to be the following:— that Platonism is "a revival of the modified doctrine of Pythagoras," (p. 18;) that there were parts of the Pythagorean philosophy which "*stood to his system as the doctrines of religion stand to us,*" (p. 189;) that (p. 30) "the great truths of the Platonic philosophy were connected" (we presume through the Pythagorean) "with an anterior revelation, and especially with the books of Moses." Lastly, we are informed (p. 290) that in Italy "Pythagoras founded a church, and confided to it the mysterious knowledge which he had received from the East, whether doctrines founded on tradition, or dogmas as opinions of men;" and that "to these Plato did undoubtedly look back with a profound reverence and confidence," for (p. 290) "there had been a primitive revelation, and Plato believed it."

Now, that Plato was indebted to the Pythagoreans for the hint of much that was most valuable in his ethical speculations, and that his obligations to them were of a higher kind than those which he confessedly owed to Heraclitus and Parmenides, we are prepared to grant. Let any one compare the discussions on virtue contained in the

---

* Another reason for this comparative disparagement of Plato is his use of irony, and "irony," says Mr. Sewell, "rarely coexists with the highest intensity of feeling." Mr. Sewell does not seem to perceive that this blow tells equally upon Socrates also, (*le modèle du vrai sage*,) into whose character, moral and intellectual, irony entered in far larger proportion than into Plato's. That a man cannot at the same time be intense and ironical may be true; but that an ironical man may be capable not only of earnestness but of the highest intensity of feeling, Mr. Sewell, one would think, might have convinced himself by the perusal of the Theætetus, or, we might almost say, any twenty consecutive pages in any of the Socratic Dialogues.

Charmides and the Protagoras (written in all probability before the death of Socrates) with the comparatively clear and satisfactory description in the Gorgias,* (the first, according to Schleiermacher, of the Dialogues written after his return from travels during which he undoubtedly improved his acquaintance with Pythagorean lore,) and he can hardly doubt that in the picture-writing of Pythagoras Plato had read the solution of problems which had previously exercised him in vain. But, if Pythagoras dreamed the dream, Plato found the interpretation. The formula, "virtue is a harmony," remained an expressive symbol, until † it was raised by Plato into a determination of science. It may also, we think, be admitted, that the doctrine of the immortality of the soul was held by Plato in a form, greatly purified, but still resembling that given to it by the Pythagoreans. Many of the difficulties of the Phædo would probably disappear, were we in possession of the work of the Pythagorean Philolaus, of which that dialogue, among its many higher objects, was apparently designed as a critique. At any rate it is very clearly shown in it,‡ that the doctrine of the transmigration of souls does not imply their immortality; and in another part of the dialogue,§ Philolaus and the Pythagoreans are plainly enough censured for their obscurity. And yet, if there were any part of Pythagoras's system which Plato could regard as standing to him in the same relation "as the doctrines of religion stand to us," it was the doctrine of immortality, which, with the purifying and ascetic discipline connected with it, is the only portion of Pythagorism which there is any pretext for deriving from the east. Of Pythagoras's asceticism Plato retained not a vestige; he alludes to it once in the Republic,|| but in the most cursory manner; and how little store he set by outward observances of this description is abundantly evident from the disrespectful way in which he treats the fanatics of his own day who attempted to revive the similar discipline of the Orphics.¶

The light in which the religious rites of his country were regarded by Plato is a subject of deep interest, and Mr. Sewell has done well, we think, in strongly calling attention to it. Some of his remarks appear to us as important as nearly all of them are ingenious. But that proneness to vague declamation which we have before observed upon, and an impatient anxiety to drag in contemporary allusions, often of the most irritating and merely party description, are faults which seem to haunt him most where their presence is least desirable. Such allusions require the most delicate handling; it is only when

---

* Gorg. p. 506.

† Mr. Sewell (p. 245) very properly points out the coincidence between the fundamental idea of Plato's ethics and that of Bishop Butler's, whose celebrated Preface abounds in language that reads like a translation of passages of Plato. Sir James Macintosh, in his celebrated Dissertation, has strangely misunderstood the whole scope and bearing of Butler's noble attempt to revive the method of the ancients in moral philosophy.

‡ See Schleiermacher's Introduction to the Phædo, (vol. 5. p. 15. of his Plato.)

§ Phæd. p. 61. e. and 62. a. || Book x. p. 600.   ¶ Book ii. p. 364.

magnanimously as well as skilfully used that they escape being absolutely vulgar; nor is it, we confess, without a feeling approaching to disgust, that we see the armoury of Plato pillaged and his glittering shafts flung at random among the very numerous objects of Mr. Sewell's hatred and scorn. The Greeks certainly did well in refusing the arms of Achilles to Ajax.

A subject nearly connected with the foregoing, and one which we do not remember to have seen successfully handled by any German writer,* is the frequent use by Plato of myths in setting forth and enforcing his philosophical views. That these are not to be considered as mere allegories or apologues, like that of the Judgment of Hercules, attributed to Prodicus, is clear at the outset; and to say that Plato adopted the mythical form of enouncing truths which had not yet grown in his mind into perfect scientific clearness, though a true, is not a complete explanation. It would help us, no doubt, in dealing with this subject, could we always pronounce with certainty how much of these mythical narrations comes from previous sources, and how much is the pure and spontaneous product of a philosophical imagination struggling with thoughts too large for ordinary utterance. The writings of the Orphic poets were a rich storehouse of such fictions. For them, in common with the other earliest Greek speculators, images were the only vehicle of truth, and were used by a natural necessity, not of deliberate choice; and in this way, no doubt, the ancient legends of Greece came to be impregnated with a moral and religious meaning far higher than that which they originally possessed. But to assume, as Mr. Sewell appears to do, that the philosophical mythology of the age of Pisistratus was but the publication of the truths of an original revelation, known hitherto only to priests who were interested in concealing them under the garb of mysteries from the eye of the vulgar, is an hypothesis which can hardly be revived with success, after the rough treatment it has encountered at the hands of Lobeck and other critics, the very first of their day for learning, candour, and acuteness. To us this hypothesis appears as pernicious as we think it demonstrably baseless. Where, we would ask, does Mr. Sewell find any traces of an original revelation of "pure deism?" Not, certainly, in any part of the Hebrew Scriptures; and we know of no primeval revelation, in any sense of the word which Mr. Sewell would recognise, the record of which is not contained in them. If the mythology † of Greece leads us up to any revelation, it is to one, not of pure deism, but of pure pantheism,—a somewhat different matter. Mr. Sewell would do well to reconsider a view leading to a result which would be impious, if it were not absurd. A spirit of severe truthfulness is an indispensable requisite in every defender of the truth. In

---

* We have only seen extracts from Eberhard's book on this subject.
† We speak particularly of the mystical mythology. It is somewhat remarkable that Christian divines should be so fond of searching for fragments of an original theism in the secret worship of mother Earth.

handling so very momentous a question as that of God's dealings with mankind, and the extent to which philosophy can advance in its unaided feelings after the Source of all Good, considerations of expediency should be left to those in whose moral creed expediency usurps the place of right and wrong. We would not be understood to apply these remarks to the book before us in any personal or invidious way; but we cannot comprehend how any person so well informed as Mr. Sewell could have attempted to revive so very loose and hazardous a theory as that of the traditional origin of Greek philosophy, unless he had suffered his judgment to be unduly warped by vague apprehensions of danger from the opposite and now all but universally received opinion. We know not how the necessity of a definite historical revelation can be more convincingly shown, or the peculiarities of the Christian revelation more strikingly illustrated, than by that view which represents the whole of Hellenic civilization, in its three branches of art, polity, and philosophy, as the spontaneous and independent growth of Hellenic genius and character. So considered, the history of Grecian development is the record of a great experiment, tried under the most favourable circumstances, of what human reason could accomplish unaided by positive revelation; and surely it is no mean testimony to the truth of Christianity that, both in the form and matter of its communications, it may be shown to be exactly that which was wanting—the "sustaining and completing opposite" to the most elaborate system of pure rationalism which the world ever beheld. The following passage, extracted from a History of Moral and Metaphysical Philosophy which appears at the head of some of the recently published parts of the Encyclopædia Metropolitana, appears to us to come very near the truth in this matter.*

"As the *Republic*, like so many other of the Platonic Dialogues, closes with a mythus, and as the passage in the third book on Lying brings the whole subject of the use which Plato thought it lawful to make of fables and legends directly before us, it may be as well to make one remark on this subject. Throughout this dialogue, even more than in his other writings, it is evident that, dearly as he loved truth for its own sake, and firmly as he believed it could be contemplated in its pure essence, he yet felt that there was no criterion of truth so sure as that it governed practice as well as the law of life. To substitute a pure idealism for the faith of his country was never his object or his dream. He hated such attempts, not more for their hardness and cruelty than for their utter inconsistency with his whole doctrine. He left them to men who did not believe that ideas were substantial,—who thought that they were mere creations of the mind, and had nothing to do with living acts. While, then, he was very jealous of those stories which evidently hindered men from acknowledging goodness and truth as the ultimate ends of their existence, he was equally certain that somehow or other all great principles must have an investiture of *facts*, and cannot be fully or satisfactorily presented to man except in facts. And

---

* We sincerely hope that this Dissertation is destined one day to be published in a form that will make it as widely known as it deserves to be. We by no means express our full sense of its value, when we say that it appears to us by far the most important contribution which England has yet made to the philosophical study of the History of Philosophy.

if no such series of facts embodying and revealing truths were within his reach, rather than leave it to be fancied that his truths are bare naked conceptions of his mind, he will invent a clothing for them; it is the least evil of the two. But it is an evil; it exposed him to fearful contradictions; it often puts his love for truth in the greatest jeopardy. Then what pretence have those to the name of Platonists who *wish* to believe that there is no series of facts containing a revelation of supersensual and transcendant truths,—who think it an *à priori* probability that the deep want of such facts which Plato experienced has not been satisfied,—who are determined, even by the most violent treatment of historical evidence, to prove that, whenever a supposed fact manifests a principle, it must be a fable?"

We now come to a part of the Introduction, which we consider, with some drawbacks, the most valuable part of the work, and to contain many important hints for the students of Plato's philosophy. We allude to the chapters on the Republic, sixteen in number, with which the book closes. Of these, three are devoted to the consideration of the "outward form" of the Dialogue, which, as Mr. Sewell well observes, has always, in Plato, "an essential inherent conformity to the subject-matter." He has accordingly examined very minutely every indication from which the pursuits, circumstances, and character of the *dramatis personæ* can be inferred; and thence deduced, in many cases successfully, in all most ingeniously, the motives which determined Plato in their selection, and the classes of opinions, tempers, or prejudices of which they are severally designed as the exponents. An inquiry of this kind is an essential preliminary to the right understanding of every dialogue Plato ever wrote: his characters are individuals, it is true;—as much so as those of Shakespere; but they are not individuals merely,—they are the representatives of classes also; and we must ascertain this their general or symbolical meaning, if we would penetrate the secret drift of Plato's writings. Something has been done in this way by Ast; and Schleiermacher's Introductions abound in most pregnant hints; but very much still remains to be done by future interpreters, and we should rejoice to see Mr. Sewell pursuing the labours which he has here so well begun. His remarks on the character of Glaucon strike us as not only original, but true; and indicate a very fine and delicate perception of the nicer touches of Plato's pencil. This portion of the work presents a refreshing contrast to the slovenly and, it seems to us, confused chapters on the early[*] sophists. It is, we fear, impossible

---

[*] Particularly chapters vii. xv. and xvi. In the first of these, p. 50, Mr. Sewell has favoured us with an interpretation of the word σοφιστὴς, which appears in no dictionary to which we have access. "The sophists," he tells us, "were persons who professed *to make others wise;*" deriving the word not from σοφίζεσθαι, *to profess wisdom*, but from σοφίζειν, a word of his own imagining. We should not have noticed this *lapsus*, if it had not occurred immediately after an uncalled for, and, it seems to us, pedantic and conceited sarcasm on "a modern sophist" for a blunder not a whit less pardonable (all things considered) than his own. Mr. Sewell's translation of a passage in the Timæus, (p. 87,) is not the only other proof which this volume affords, that his knowledge of Plato would be improved by more accurate study of the language in which he wrote: Mr. Sewell has taken for serious a passage which every scholar must at once perceive to be ironical.

that Mr. Sewell should be brought to perceive, as clearly as his readers must, how very much the forms of antiquity are distorted when beheld through the smoked glass of contemporary passion and prejudice. The names of Mitford and Mitchell ought to be used as warnings, not as examples, in this respect.

The chapters which conclude the work treat of the subject-matter of the Republic. Many of our readers are doubtless aware of the controversies that have agitated and continue to agitate the learned world respecting the true end and scope of this magnificent masterwork of Plato. The seeds of the controversy are involved in its double title: " The Republic, or a Dialogue concerning Justice." Earlier commentators—beginning with Aristotle, the earliest of all—have assumed the former of the two denominations to be the correct one, and have accordingly proceeded to criticise the several parts of the Dialogue in detail, as if its sole object were to furnish practical instruction to legislators in forming or altering constitutions. To such critics it is no wonder that the Republic should appear " visionary and enthusiastic, unpractical and extravagant;" and we can hardly be surprised to find that the manifest irrelevancy and injustice of their censures should have driven men of more genial and candid minds to reject altogether the hypothesis on which they are founded, and to adopt the second title of the Dialogue as containing the only true account of its author's purpose. They have considered the apparently political part of the work as merely subsidiary to the ethical, and they appeal triumphantly to Plato's own language in confirmation of this view. His imaginary polity is but a magnified picture of the constitution of man's inward nature, which it is the design of the Dialogue to unfold. The Republic is a Town of Mansoul; not an Utopia, or Atlantis, far less a Nephelococcygia, or City in the Clouds. This view has been adopted, with more or less exclusiveness, by the majority of German scholars; and if the choice lay between it and the one previously stated, we should not hesitate to give it the preference. Of the two it leaves far less of the Dialogue unexplained. But we own it does not appear to us to explain the whole; nor has it been satisfactorily shown that it was at all necessary for Plato to enter so minutely into the details of his commonwealth, had his only object been to illustrate the constitution of man's inward nature. Still, his own words forbid us, as distinctly as human language can, to imagine for a moment that he thought such a republic as that which he constructs, either an expedient or a possible form of government for human beings as they exist *in rerum naturâ*.* No man knew the actual workings of human nature better than Plato. Aristotle himself is not more eminently practical, where practical knowledge is applicable; and in that deeper knowledge which connects human thoughts and feelings with their outward manifestations, the

---

* See, among other passages, that very remarkable one at the end of the ninth Book.

scholar falls immeasurably short of his master. It would require more space than we can at present command to state our views fully on this subject, more especially as it would be necessary to support them by frequent quotations from Plato himself. We shall content ourselves with observing, that Plato, like Aristotle and all other Greek speculators, undoubtedly considered the science of ethics to be involved in that of politics; the nature of man in the nature of a state; moral in political justice; the inward life of the individual in the life of the nation, or according to Greek notions, the *city*, of which he is an integral portion. So considered, the two titles of the Dialogue presuppose, instead of excluding, each other. Neither title, as Mr. Sewell observes, " can be correct, which should exclude the other." They are linked together by "a very strong and indissoluble chain—the chain, which, in both history and speculation, binds together ethics and politics, the individual and the state; making the man the microcosm of the state, and the state the development of the man." (P. 205.)

We could wish that Mr. Sewell had been as successful in applying this idea, as he is clear in enouncing it; but the part of his work in which this should have been done is dark from excess of illustration, and confused from the very desire to explain. The elaborate comparison of Plato's commonwealth with the constitution of the Christian Church must lead, it appears to us, to hopeless misapprehension of both. Plato's φύλακες are possibly as like the Christian Priesthood as they are to a standing army; but his *ideas* find but a strange counterpart in the creed, the Lord's prayer, and the ten commandments. (P. 283.) Mr. Sewell's ingenuity appears to us to desert him in his attempt to support this most indefensible position. It may be true that Plato would have recognised in the Gospel the actual historical embodiment of that great ideal of humanity which he strove to develope and set forth in his writings; but it can hardly be that in the tablets of stone delivered to Moses he would have seen more than a transcript of those eternal ordinances which, with St. Paul, he held to be written on the heart of humanity.

We recommend the following passage, translated from Plato himself,* to all those who would know what Plato really thought about the nature and value of *positive ordinances.*

" It is assuredly necessary for men to make them laws, and to live according to laws; else are they no better than the most savage animals. The cause of this is, that no man's nature is of itself sufficient at once to understand the true political interests of mankind, and, having this knowledge, to combine with it the power and the will at all times to act up in practice to what is best. . . . . . Were there ever a man to arise, born into the world by express appointment of Heaven, of a nature capable of attaining to this twofold perfection, such a man would need no laws to control him. For there is no law and no ordinance greater or better than knowledge, (ἐπιστήμη); nor is it meet that the reason of any man be a subject or

---

* Laws, B. ix. p. 874.—9, 13, Bekker.

a slave, but contrariwise, lord of all,—if it be but true and genuine, and in its nature essentially free."

With this passage we take our leave of Mr. Sewell. It grieves us that, in a book which contains so much to commend, we should have found so much to protest against. We are not, however, in the slightest degree disposed to retract the recommendation with which our article commenced. We would only urge upon our youthful readers the lesson which none have more strongly inculcated than the author of this Introduction—the absolute necessity of seeking the interpretation of Plato in Plato himself, and the great need there is of caution in applying to his large and perfect intellect the measures and the forms with which his interpreters supply them. If they will set themselves faithfully and diligently to this task, they will be rewarded, not merely by deeper insight into the secret places of their own nature, but, it may be hoped, by increase of high and earnest feeling, and of that true self-reverence, without which zeal becomes fanatical and humility abject.

Sights and Thoughts in Foreign Churches and among Foreign Peoples. By FREDERICK WILLIAM FABER, M.A. *Fellow of University College, Oxford.* London: Rivingtons. 1842. Pp. 645.

NOT one of the least painful effects of the divided state of Christendom is the loneliness which must oppress the christian traveller, or the sojourner among his catholic brethren in other lands, when he is compelled to be absent from his island Church. And it is a healthful sign of the times, that we begin to feel this our isolation as a loss and judgment. Some, perhaps, are too hastily endeavouring to reconcile hearts, which require, perhaps still further than they have yet been visited with such divine mercies, the wholesome discipline of suffering and humiliation. Tears and prayers must go before catholic unity. It would be well were we from our hearts to realize, in all its bitterness, our humiliation. Mr. Hope, in his late able pamphlet, has drawn cheering auguries from the principle which may, under God, have instigated the desire of settling an Anglican Bishop at Jerusalem. We may be comforted by the reflection that our mistakes, if such there be, in this and other schemes, may be overruled to good. The harmony is wild and uncertain which preludes even the noblest strains: but it must be borne in mind that the sins and heart-burnings of centuries are not to be washed out by the first scanty tricklings from the stricken rock. Patience is a stern lesson; but, as we are not to be carried away presumptuously by the first seeming successes, so are we not to be cast down by the first reverses: rather are we to expect such trials as the most blessed steps towards perfect peace. Corunna and defeat trained us for Torres Vedras and victory. The spirit which is at work within us is too tumultuous and heady to reckon much upon; but it may—nay, it must have within it—the earnest, if not the gift, of the blessing, if we are but self-distrusting and full of prayers. We must beware of superciliousness and haste: at once to plunge into such schemes as the entire resuscitation of our domestic Church, by the increase of schools, churches, and clergy, in almost every parish in England; to establish the Colonial Bishoprics; to multiply daily our missions to the heathen; simultaneously to open communication with every Church catholic and heretical body which owns the name of Christ; to expand our relations with the Greek Church, not only in Syria, but in Russia and Chaldea at the same time; to inquire and communicate respecting the Nestorians, Armenians, Copts, and Abyssinians, which efforts towards union are actually in progress; to revive and purify, and, if it may be, to catholicize the foreign reformed societies;—to have all this to do, and to be doing it at once, is a sufficient guarantee of life, but it may be the life of fever. Sedatives, not stimulants, are required at this critical moment. We have said nothing of the unceasing warfare which, in every street and village, we have to maintain against dissent out of the Church; and in almost every family against rationalism—we use the word for want of a better—and disobedience within it. It is well, though very awful, to know all our weaknesses at once; it is better, but still more oppressive, to try to repair every breach at the same moment. Yet some of them are sure " to be daubed with untempered mortar;" and, as we are to look for this, so we are not to be dismayed at it. We are not of those who think that " one false step will throw us back for centuries." God forbid! the way of life is not described as strait and full of offences, for us not to expect many stumbles. And we may say this, not to encourage rash and unsteady minds, but to cheer those who are apt to look at the gloomy side of things. We shall have many a crash, and many a reverse, before we are much better than we are; but from every fall we must renew our confidence and our faith. It is in this spirit that we would have some otherwise alarming checks viewed; such as the recent desertions to Romanism, on the one hand, and the bitter and sectarian spirit, as developed in the late Exeter-Hall display of the Church Missionary Society (to take an instance far from solitary) on the other. It is well in this, as in the walk of human life and the conduct of those we love, not to be too critical of particulars; the spirit is the chief thing; and God may be pleased to set us right in settling details, if we are but faithful to Him in the main object.

That, amidst all this tumult of awakening love, our first yearnings should be towards Rome can excite no wonder. It is only in the spirit of human affection that we naturally turn in our desolation, " as soon as we come to ourselves," like the son in the parable, to the friend from whom we have been last separated. There is a sense in which Rome may be called our spiritual mother; setting this aside, our once intimate relations with that great see,—her nearness,—her members who are mixed up, though schismatically, with our own,—and her legitimate authority on the Continent, with which our connexion is one of daily familiarity,—to say nothing of her services in preserving the one faith,—are reasons, and perhaps higher might be assigned, that our eyes should be first turned to Rome. We say that this is natural; and, though we lay ourselves open to misconstruction, we say that it is right. But we are bound to add, that this spirit is met by no corresponding advances—even if *our* feelings are worthy of this name—on the part of Rome. Where our position is understood, as it is in this country, we see no star in the clouds. Have our readers never seen a portrait of any Roman ecclesiastic which might too forcibly typify Rome's "cruel-hearted" policy? They might have learned to love him, as we had done, by his writings; but on canvass we find him stern, dark, lowering, inflexible, foreign, repulsive. Bland and winning in words, our ideal was faultless—such is Rome on paper and in theory: but we start back from the too faithful picture; in life the controversialist is found to be swart and full of bread—such is Rome in practice. If Rome did not know our position, our gifts, our standing in God's sight, our strivings, our humiliation, and our spirit, we might think better of her; but she does know us, and knowing us reviles us; and while every page of the Dublin Review is filled with unholy insults, with sarcasms, with misrepresentations and scoffings, we have no hope. We must, like our martyred Prelate, "feel that within us which will not let us be at one with Rome, until she be other than she is." She must learn to pour oil, instead of vitriol, into our wounds, before we can learn to respect, much less to love her.

Too many young and ardent minds seem to forget what Rome in action is: we recommend them a few months' continental travel; and the effect we suspect will be the same as it was on the late Mr. Froude—subduing, yet disheartening: "wretched Tridentines everywhere." They will think union a little further off than undergraduates imagine. From these faults Mr. Faber is, for the most part, free: even though he looks at catholicism under its medi-æval, rather than its present character. True, he is too good a poet not to prefer the sunny side of the peach; and we are not of those who are inclined to blame him for this. It is much the most natural thing, especially in the young; and we make this apology for our author, lest some should say he was too neglectful of Rome's most serious errors, and, if so be, sins. His object is to purify and elevate his own feelings, and, through himself, those of his own brethren; and not to find fault. He knows that, if our probation be towards perfection, we lose a good deal of time in running down lanes in order to pelt our neighbour's windows, and he feels that too many among us—

"Put forward the highest possible claims for our Church often in a tone of pharisaical self-conceit, as though the usages and beliefs of the greater part of Christendom were of no account whatever in our eyes; and repeatedly indulge in a very offensive sort of commiseration of Rome; forgetting that Rome's communion is much more extensive than our own, and comprehends wisdom and holiness which must demand the respect of every thoughtful and modest man."—P. 362.

This he would discourage: he would have us respect Rome any how; if we could, unite with her; by all means' profit by her; but never in thought, with all this, to prove unfaithful to our own spiritual mother; he would say—

"Beware of ever doubting her. If you ever begin to doubt her divine commission, increase your fasts and vigils. There is but one thing more wicked than doubting our Church, it is—leaving her."—P. 365.

He says very earnestly and beautifully, though some might think affectedly—

"I have scarcely heard of an apostasy without tears. I have difficulties, but my sins account for them. O dear Mother Church! in whose womb of sanctified water I was regenerated, at whose plain altars I have received my Lord, and made His Body for His people, how should I leave thee the guide of my boyhood! how should I depart from the grave of my father and my earthly mother, who lie in one of thy consecrated yards! Oh, no! It is a better lot than such an one as I have deserved, to walk with thee to my grave these few years that are left, in somewhat of dimness; the threescore furlongs will soon be passed; and, as on the road to Emmaus, it is not that Jesus is not with us, but that our eyes are holden that we should not entirely know Him. Towards evening He will turn in with us, and tarry, and in the breaking of bread we shall some day recognise the Bridegroom, in the east part of the Bride's house. Clouds of controversy may beset our uneasy and forward youth; but holy living will cleanse the air, and the afternoon will be very tranquil, and we shall see to great distances and in a clear landscape."—Pp. 365.

And in a long, and less ambitious passage, he argues, for fiction's sake placing a Greek in the stead of a young Anglican priest, against those who are dissatisfied with our own Church, on the common grounds of the necessity to salvation of communion with Rome, when it can be had; of the alleged want of life among us; of the preference of the Latin ritual; and of the unpopularity and aversion which catholic views and feelings receive among us. The passage (pp. 608—625) is too long to quote, but we gladly refer to it. We extract the practical warning :—

"The Apostle teaches us that where God finds us, where His grace comes to us, there we should remain, not seeking to be freed even from a position disadvantageous, as we deem it, to our religious advancement. You find yourself in a Church, not surely by accident, but by God's Providence; what warrant have you for leaving that Church? Who can authorize you to go away? Is private judgment your ruler? I trust you have not so learned Christ. The presumption—a presumption sufficiently strong to act upon—is always in favour of the circumstances in which you actually find yourself. So long as you do not believe—and you hold no such fearful opinion—that the Greek [Anglican] Church is absolutely apostate and unchurched, her candlestick utterly removed, it is your duty to abide in her. Your allegiance is due to her, and you cannot be free from it without schism and rebellion. You are a member of a Church; explain to me on Church principles, and from the precedents of Church history, what and where the door is by which you have the power to leave her, and who is to open it for you. Let your regrets be ever so vehement, your disapproval ever so strong, men's calumny or persecution ever so hard to bear, your own doubts ever so harassing, foreign claims ever so unanswerable, so long as there remains in your mind a conviction that it is *probable* or *possible* for your Church to be really a true branch of the Church Universal, I am unable to see what can warrant you in leaving it. Oh, beware! beware! This it is which is destroying catholic Unity and catholic Sanctity. Rome's modern doctrine of communion with St. Peter's successor, and modern England's want of realizing the catholic principles of Unity, are plunging the whole world into a depth of spiritual confusion, from which it scarcely appears that anything but a manifest and direct interposition of Providence can save us. Remain, therefore, where you are, for this plain reason—you have found no warrant yet for going away."—Pp. 618—620.

Mr. Faber's very interesting and thoughtful book—and it seems but the portion of a series—consists of detached sketches, thoughts, and impressions originating from an ecclesiastical survey of France, Northern Italy, and the shores and islands of Greece. It is anything but a mere guide-book; it has but little of the description, and none of the wretched details of inns and horses and carriages, and interesting acquaintances picked up in diligences and post-houses, in which consists the so-called spirit of modern books of travels. It is the faithful transcript of the mind of a warm-hearted young ecclesiastic; dutiful to his own branch of the catholic Church, yet with large sympathies for the great christian family of faith. As a composition it seems rather desultory and disjointed; and certain dialogues, in which a nameless stranger impersonates the middle ages, discussing all the vexed questions of this momentous era of the Church, are not very happy in a dramatic view. But with the thoughts maintained we hold very sincere sympathy; and the patient attention which Mr. Faber has given to the less familiar literature connected with the history of the papacy in its various fortunes in France, the Italian states, and the Empire, demands our grateful acknowledgment in proportion to its rarity, even among those who have been privileged with the training and academical fame of our author. Diction, perhaps, less poetic, and imagery and illustration less profuse, would improve the style; and what Mr. Faber lost in attractiveness he would gain in sinew. Subjects so grave seem— though in this writer's hands they only *seem*—unreal, when treated with over-elegance and refinement. Henry the VIIth's chapel has been called a "painfully beautiful" structure, from its elaborate and over-loaded decoration. Ornament and beauty may become fatiguing; and the only fault with which we charge the "Sights and Thoughts" is, that we desiderate a less lofty and humbler flight. But our readers ought to judge for themselves. The following may serve as specimens of Mr. Faber's excellences, and faults—if they exist elsewhere than in our own hyper-critical temper. This seems a very kindly example of what ought to be a traveller's temper:—

"It is an awe-inspiring privilege, if a man would only intelligently use it, to wander up and down the broad Continent, whose very countenance is seamed and furrowed by the lines of God's past providences, and the potent action of His already accomplished decrees, to take up here and there the links of some tremendous chain of mysterious arrangements, to gaze on the fair faces of old cities, whose character and fortunes have been distinct, peculiar, and each subserving, in this or that age, and in this or that manner, the cause of the Catholic Church of Christ. Is there not, to a christian mind, something very solemn and subduing in such spots as Paris, Avignon, Trent, Nice, Rome, Constantinople, Alexandria, and Jerusalem? Are they not all places where steps were taken which gave a peculiar shape and form to the Church? And not only is it a solemn thing to read the face of Christendom, whose cities are each words to be spelled out, telling secrets of the past, and having the foot-marks of the Invisible not yet worn out of their streets, when He passed there with His Church, to guard her and see her through; but it is a solemn thing from books, conversation with strangers, the kindling of thought in stirring localities, which we may hope is sometimes overruled to the discovery of truth, and from other sources of observation, to watch and take the shape and bearings of those huge masses of cloud which are casting here and there such ponderous prophetic shadows upon the Church, in motion here, and there at rest, dipping earthwards here because of sin, and there drawn awhile upwards, because of local prayer and holiness. It is a sight to make such a hush within one's soul, as though a little thought, or a restless thought, or an impure thought, might never inhabit there again, but be for evermore dislodged. Judgment has been done upon Asia: it seems still pausing over Europe. Only at a few epochs has the Church been so awfully, so deeply, with such vivid contrasts, chequered with light and shade as it is now; and oh! how painfully one longs to know what may be the fortunes of our little, separated, tempest-tossed Island-Mother!"—Pp. 121—123.

Our present condition—

"'You think, then,' I asked, 'that our condition is hopeful, even on your principles.' 'Yes,' replied [the man of the middle ages,] 'I do; many obstacles have been overcome which, at the beginning of the century, would have been considered insuperable. But there remains one behind which appears the most difficult of all, and I do not see how you are to get out of it. Yet, often, what seems the prime difficulty in a matter, thaws away, and vanishes no one knows how.' 'What is the difficulty to which you allude?' said I. 'It arises,' he replied, 'from a view of the historical character of your Church and her theology. The modern structure of your Church is revolutionary. It was rebuilt in haste; and, as with the Long Walls at Athens, fragments of tombs, statues, temples, and memorial pillars, were built into it, often upside down; and, when the work was done, you found you had enclosed the besieger's outposts within your city, instead of building him out altogether. You discovered two opposite religious tendencies united in your Church, one prevailing in this formulary, the other prevailing in that, both fettered together by the same tests, and subjected to the same conditions of theological thought, without either having the ability to exorcise the other. The history of your Church, and, indeed, of your country, since that time, has been neither more nor less than the history of those rival tendencies. For English history is peculiarly, and eminently, a theological history. The names of Hooker, Laud, and Ken, only symbolize epochs of the conflict; and Oxford is made now, whether with its good will or not, to typify to the other nations of Europe the old contest, renewed a fourth time under fresh and distinctive banners, a league of many circles, not the mere contingent of a solitary school. Here is the difficulty. One of these tendencies must devour the other, before you can be in any condition, united at home, to work towards a unity abroad. Now, the champions of each tendency have surely an *equal* claim to have their consciences respected, and their interpretations permitted, so long as their subscriptions are honest, and their obedience to the lawful sources of spiritual power and theological interference hearty and consistent. Yet I do not see how any synodical step taken by the English Church now, could be anything but a condemnation of one or other of these tendencies, and its consequent ejection or departure from her pale: and the two tendencies are so evenly balanced in the country, and among the clergy, that the consequences would be tremendous.' 'But,' said I, 'suppose the tendency with which you sympathize were ejected, we might hope that'—— 'Do not suffer yourself to hope anything,' he replied; 'confusion, in such a case, *must* ensue, and in the middle of confusion *might* come ruin. Beware of wishing for persecution. Persecution is, it is true, the best of all things for the interests of a party, once waxed strong; but what is for the interests of a party is never for the interests of the Church. Mark my words: what is for the interests of a party, *as such,* is *never* for the interests of the Church.' "—Pp. 175—177.

The proper estimate of the Roman ceremonial.

"This was the first great Church ceremony we had seen since we came abroad; and I looked in vain for the 'mummery,' disgusting repetition, childish arrangements, and so forth, which one reads of in modern travellers; who, for the most part, know nothing of the Roman service-books, and consequently understand nothing of what is before them. A heathen might say just the same, as the Puritans did say of us, if they entered one of our cathedrals, and saw us sit for the Epistle, stand for the Gospel, turn to the east at the Creed, bow at our Lord's Name, recite the Litany at a faldstool between the porch and the Altar, make Crosses on babies' foreheads, lay hands on small squares of bread; or if they saw men, in strange black dresses, with huge white sleeves, walking up and down the aisles of a country church, touching the heads of boys and girls, or wetting the head and hand of our kings and queens with oil, or consecrating buildings and yards. There *may*, of course, be very sad mummery in Roman services, as there is very sad irreverence oftentimes in English services; such, for instance, as dressing up the Altar in white cloths, with the plate upon it as if for the Holy Communion, when it is not meant there should be one, which is sometimes done in cathedrals, where the clergy themselves are in sufficient number to communicate, and strangers who have wished to stay have been told it will be very inconvenient if they do so. It may be hoped there are few Roman churches where such theatrical mummery as that is practised. However, whatever be the amount of Romish mummery, the gross ignorance of ecclesiastical matters exhibited by many modern travellers, who have spoken the most confidently about it, may make us suspect their competency to be judges on the matter; when we see that precisely the same common-place and offensive epithets might be applied with equal justice to us, by one who was a stranger or an enemy to our services; and, whatever changes people may wish for, the English ritual, characterized by a simplicity of which Christendom for many a century has not seen the like, will hardly be charged with mummery. All ritual acts must, from the nature of the case, be symbolical, being either a reverential imitation of sacred acts, or the sublime inventions of antiquity, whereby the Presence of God and His holy Angels is recognized and preached to the people, or fit and beautiful means for affecting the imagination of the worshipper, and giving intensity to his devotion. All service, not excepting the simple and strict imitation of our Blessed Lord's action at the institution of the most solemn rite in the world, must be dumb-show to a looker-on, who knows nothing of what it sets forth and symbolizes; and this dumb-show such a looker-on, if he were pert and self-sufficient, would call mummery. The existence of Romish mummery is or is not a fact; and must, of course, be so dealt with: and its extent, also, is or is not ascertainable as a fact. But the improbability of its being nearly so extensive as modern travellers represent it, is so monstrous, considering that the Romanists are Christians, and Christians too at worship, that the vague epithets and round sentences, and the received puritan vocabulary of persons ignorant of Breviaries and Missals, cannot be taken as evidence. Indeed, in these days, we may justifiably require beforehand that a traveller shall know so much of what external religion is, and what are its uses, that he can comprehend and subscribe to the simple philosophy comprised in Wordsworth's definition of it:—

> 'Sacred Religion! Mother of *form* and fear,
> Dread arbitress of *mutable respect*.'"

Pp. 302—304.

The purity of the Greek Church. (We altogether dissent, by-the-bye, from what is said of the Nestorians and Armenians. If they are orthodox, why do they still retain their anathemas against the Catholics?)

"This purity is owing, in the first place, to her jealous preservation of the apostolic polity, and a devout clinging to those divine forms to which, as antiquity testified, it had pleased the Lord to tie His grace and promise of indefectibility. It would be easy to show how a humble belief in the supernatural grace of the blessed Sacraments, and a pure holding of the orthodox teaching regarding the Nature and Person of the Saviour, spring from the divine appointment of episcopacy, and are only secured by an adherence to it; but it would be out of place here. Yet it is instructive to note how the only heretical congregations, which have continued to live and abide upon the earth, are those which retained the episcopal succession; and it appears that, by God's blessing upon this humble clinging to this appointment, they have worked themselves clear of heresy. It seems admitted that the Nestorian Christians are now orthodox as to the Lord's unity of Person; and so far as my own experience goes, the Armenians seem equally orthodox as to His two Natures. This is a very singular and providential witness to episcopacy; indeed, the whole case of the Greek Church, whose chief characteristic has been, in her clergy, a jealous adherence to the ancient ecclesiastical forms; and in her laity, a profound submission to spiritual authority, appears to teach us that there is nothing in the Gospel of a merely outward nature, that grace is every where and in every thing, with an exuberance and transcending quickness, peculiar to the Christian covenant. Thus, by holding fast to what we have received, even where our single generation is unable to discern a meaning, or read a promise, or divine a blessing, we receive more than we wot of, and retain a power and life of which we are unconscious. It is impossible to meditate on the history of the Greek Church without being more and more astonished at its purity and completeness, its unblameable polity, its venerable ritual, its orthodox Creeds, its lawful Sacraments. The preservation of these things is owing to God's blessing upon a modest and devout temper, which clung always to forms, whether obviously divine, or so ancient as to be probably divine, or so catholic as that it was unsafe to stir them. The episcopate has been the bundle of myrrh at its bosom, repelling corruption from the heart.

"In the second place, the Greek Church has been kept together and in health by the pious observation of her fasts and feasts. This was observed by an English writer in the seventeenth century, and must be obvious to those who have travelled there. Indeed, there is in our nature so great a tendency to debase and corrupt every thing, that religion, when sundered from external observances, rapidly evaporates into systems of feelings and words, and the concentrated power of faith is dispersed into a mere feeble literary opinion. Where sound words are not laid up within the consecrated precincts of a creed or symbolical hymn, right belief quickly disappears in the dissonance of conflicting sects. Where devout cravings are not gathered up and collected into liturgies, zeal rapidly becomes profaneness, fear degenerates into gloom, and love is lost in sinful familiarity. There is no true liberty of prayer except in this sweet imprisonment. This is one consideration; and another is, that in the very ancient liturgies, the receding waters of antiquity have deposited many a scrap and spar of apostolical usage and tradition, which, embedded in the soil, diffuse fertility around them, and give to the liturgy a power over the soul beyond its own power, and a sacred character which makes it venturesome to shift a single attitude or gesture of worship exhibited therein. And further, to a people like the Greeks, under the Mahometan yoke, without books, or, in most cases, the ability to read, such liturgies, with their significant rites and annual commemorations, represented year by year monumentally, as it were, the great facts and truths of the faith. The symbols of church-worship were the books of the people, and constituted their instruction while young, and their edification when come to mature years. This should be borne in mind whenever we speak of the somewhat dangerous extent to which the use of pictures is allowed in the Greek worship, and with which the porch and partition of the soleas are usually covered."—Pp. 586—589.

There are some things in this book which are over-fanciful, and almost unsafe, speculations; such as that on the Pagan view of Nature, which has an undefined and vague, almost Pantheistic, bias—though this is very far from the amiable author's intention; and one on the animal world: but we recommend it as a whole for one of the most graceful, well-lettered, and well-tempered books which have lately appeared. We augur great things from Mr. Faber when a few years have pruned his luxuriance. A kindly frost may do it: we cannot have much fruit without an over-abundant blossoming. It is much to his credit that he has been almost the first to vindicate the right spirit of a traveller. Unless we voyage in somewhat the spirit of pilgrimage we had better stay at home. Hear one who must be as great a favourite with Mr. Faber as he is with us:—

"In the middle ages the manner even of ordinary travelling had many advantages: young nobles, of high houses, would make their way on foot 'in formâ pauperis' with peasant's shoes, and staff in hand. Thus would they foster habits of simplicity and endurance, and that amiable taste for the beauties of nature, which is so closely allied to many virtues.—The scenes of life, too, with which travelling generally familiarized men, conduced to the formation of a noble and thoughtful character. They were not led by it to associate with the wretched godless crew which, in our own time, is annually discharged upon all the roads of Europe, from the pestilential dens of London and Paris. In general, a modern traveller is only transported from city to city, and from inn to inn; where the same dissipation, the same discourse, the same faces, accompany him: he is escorted frequently by atheists and epicures, as if by demons—

'Ah, fearful company! but in the Church
With saints; with gluttons at the tavern's mess.[*]

---

[*] Dante. Hell, xxii.

A wanderer in the middle ages, like Dante, might be traced, in his devious course, to an assembly in the sacristy of some church, or to some knight's castle among the mountains, or to a chamber in some monastery, in a wild and solitary region, or to a tower of some lord near a river, or to a rock adjoining some castle, on which he used to sit, or to a palace of some splendid patron of learned men, or to some banquet-hall in the house of some illustrious senator. These journeys had even occasionally the character of a pilgrimage. Peruthgarius, son of Theodald, attached to the court of Count Gerald, being despatched on a journey by that nobleman, and coming near the church of the Martyrs, in the town of Kentibrut in Thurgau, was admonished by his page to turn aside a little from the road, for the sake of prayer.* Before setting out the pilgrim provided himself with a commendatory letter, called a letter of communion: these letters were given not only to all clerks, but also to all laymen, in evidence of their being at peace with the Church; for, as Optatus Milevitanus says, 'The whole world was formed into one society and one communion.'† Thus the testimonial of catholic faith answered to the σύμβολα, or *tessera*, of the ancients. Humility, simplicity, and charity characterized the pilgrim's way.— In the old fabliaux of the two rich citizens and the labourer, the former going on a pilgrimage and being joined by a peasant, they all three travel on lovingly together, and join their provisions in a common stock.—St. Gerard set out on his journey with twelve companions of the clerical and monastic order, who with him might continually chant psalms or jubilations: they seemed to make the whole road one Church—the standard of the cross always preceding them.—Many travellers of the modern school feel themselves strangers and aliens as they pass through the nations of the Catholic Church; but the pilgrim of the middle ages had the consolation of finding his home in every church which he passed on the way. Everywhere he found the same holy rites, the same language which had been familiar to him from childhood.—Bounty to the poor was the virtue, more than all others, preeminently to distinguish the pilgrims; who never forgot that it was when travelling the good Samaritan practised that memorable work of charity, and that a hostel was the scene of it.—The hostels, or inns, which have succeeded in most places to the ancient foundations of charity, have, in catholic countries, still retained an aspect which gives them an interest in the estimation of devout or of romantic travellers. The inn-keeper of the middle ages took care to have holy images in the apartments of his hostel. On the bleak wild mountain of Radicoffani there is a solitary inn, in which is a chapel, where mass is said.—As in the primitive days of christian society, if a stranger showed that he professed the orthodox faith, and was in the communion of the Church, he was received with open arms wherever he went: to have refused him entrance would have been thought the same as to have rejected Jesus Christ Himself."—*Mores Catholici*, book iv. ch. 5.

Alas! shall it ever be that these things are other than a pleasant dream?

---

* Mabillon. Acta Ord. S. Bened. sæc. iv. 5.
† *Vid.* Joan. Devoti Institut. Canonic. lib. ii.

1. *A Manual of Electricity, Magnetism, and Meteorology.* By DIONYSIUS LARDNER, D.C.L. F.R.S., &c. Vol. I. Pp. 1—437. Longmans.
2. *Proceedings of the London Electrical Society.* Session 1841-2. Parts I.—IV. Simpkin & Marshall.

THE first of the above treatises proposes to supply that want of a comprehensive and systematic work on the kindred sciences of electricity and magnetism, which has been felt by all those who are desirous of obtaining a general but correct acquaintance with this fascinating department of physical science, without the almost impracticable toil of exploring the memoirs of learned societies, and the scientific periodical works in various languages, to which the mass of original productions, the fruit of philosophic labour for the last fifty years, has been consigned. The greater portion of the present volume is devoted to an Historical Introduction, in which we are furnished with a rapid, but sufficiently minute, narrative of the progressive discoveries which compose the ever-growing mass of electrical science. The subjects to be treated of in the body of the work are arranged under the heads of Electro-Statics, Electrical Machines, Voltaic Electricity, Electro-Chemistry, Magnetism, Electro-Magnetism, Thermo-Electricity, Terrestrial Magnetism, and Meteorology, so far as that part of physics is related to Electricity and Magnetism; and the work will conclude with a notice of the most important applications of these branches of science in the arts of life. In consequence of the length of the Introduction, the present volume contains only a portion of Book I., which is devoted to Electro-Statics, including an account of the construction and phenomena of the principal electrical machines.

"Six centuries before the christian era, Thales was acquainted with that property of amber from which ELECTRICITY derives its name;[*] and Theophrastus and Pliny, as well as other writers, Greek and Roman, mention that property of this and certain other substances, in virtue of which, when submitted to friction, they acquire the power to attract straws and other light bodies, as a magnet attracts iron. . . . . .

"Nor were these the only phenomena which presented themselves to the ancients, and afforded them a clue to the foundation of this part of physics. . . . . The luminous appearance attending the friction of those substances which exhibited electrical effects, was observed. The Roman historians record the frequent appearance of a flame at the points of the soldiers' javelins, at the summits of the masts of ships, and sometimes even on the heads of the seamen.[†] The effects of the torpedo and electrical fishes are referred to by Aristotle, Galen, and Oppian; and at a period less remote, Eustathius, in his Commentary on the Iliad of Homer, mentions the case of Walimer, a Gothic chieftain, the father of Theodoric, who used to eject sparks from his body; and further refers to a certain ancient philosopher,

---

[*] Ἤλεκτρον, amber.
[†] Cæsar, de Bell. Afr. cap. vi. Liv. cap. xxxii. Plut. Vita Lys. Plin. Sec. Hist. Mund. lib. ii.

who relates of himself that on one occasion, when changing his dress, sudden sparks were emitted from his person on drawing off his clothes, and that flames occasionally issued from him, accompanied by a crackling noise."—*Manual of Electricity, &c.*, pp. 3, 4.

It was not until the beginning of the seventeenth century that these and other phenomena were regarded with any other eye than that of vacant and unfruitful wonder. At that time the work of scientific observation, with the still more important work of classification and inductive generalization, was commenced by Gilbert, an English physician; which he did in a treatise entitled *De Magnete*. In this treatise he gives a considerable list of bodies which possess the electric property. "Not only amber and agate attract small bodies, as some think, but diamond, sapphire, carbuncle, opal, amethyst, Bristol gem, beryl, crystal, glass, glass of antimony, spar of various kinds, sulphur, mastic, sealing-wax," and many others. He also mentions several of the circumstances which affect the production of electrical phenomena, such as the hygrometric condition of the atmosphere.

It will have been evident to our readers that the electrical phenomena observed at this early period would appear to be of a mechanical nature only, and analogous to those cosmical phenomena which depend upon the attraction of the several particles of matter for each other. The philosophers of this period were so far from recognising the essential differences between the special attractions which produce magnetic and electrical phenomena and those which are purely mechanical; so far were they also from being able to conceive of the attractive action of one body upon another at a distance, as in cosmical cases, without the intervention of some medium or the active presence of some effluvium; that the only way in which they could account for mechanical attractions was by likening them to that of the magnet upon iron. Magnetic action was taken as the *type* of attractive and repulsive agencies generally. Hence electricity also was regarded as a kind of magnetism. Gilbert, in the book above referred to, has a chapter, *De Coitione Magneticâ, primumque de Succini Attractione, sive verius Corporum ad Succinum Applicatione.* "The magnet and amber," he says, "are called in aid by philosophers as illustrations, when our sense is in the dark in abstruse inquiries, and when our reason can go no further." Gilbert approached these inquiries in the true spirit of philosophical induction, and justly condemns those of his predecessors who had "stuffed the booksellers' shops by copying from one another extravagant stories concerning the attraction of magnets and amber, without giving any reason from experiment." He distinguishes magnetic from electric forces; observing that, while the electric force attracts all light bodies, the magnetic attracts iron only. Gilbert is also the inventor of the name by which the science we are treating of is known; a name derived, as we have already seen, from the Greek name of that substance in which electric attraction was first observed.

Boyle, who verified and extended the experiments of Gilbert, does not appear to have advanced towards the discovery of any general law of these phenomena. The next material step was taken by Otto Guericke, of Magdeburg, (the inventor of the air-pump,) who contrived the first electrical machine.

"This apparatus consisted of a globe of sulphur, mounted upon a horizontal axis, from which it received a motion of rotation, by means of a common handle or winch. The operator turned this handle with one hand, while with the other he applied a cloth to the globe, the friction of which produced the electrical state.

"Aided by such apparatus, this philosopher discovered, that, after a light substance has been attracted by and brought into contact with any electrified body, *it will not be again attracted*, but, on the contrary, *will be repelled by the same body;* but that, after it has been touched by the hand, its primitive condition is restored, and it is again attracted."—*Manual of Electricity, &c.* p. 5.

This fact, namely, that there is an electric force of repulsion as well as of attraction, constituted an important addition to the infant science, when it had been duly verified by a sufficient range of discriminating experiments.

"Otto Guericke also showed that a body becomes electric by being brought near to an electrized body without touching it; but he offered no explanation of this fact, which, as will be seen hereafter, indicated one of the most important principles of electrical science."—*Manual of Electricity, &c.* p. 6.

Hawkesbee, who wrote in 1709, (*Physico-Mechanical Experiments,*) and whose experimental labours are treated too slightly in the *Manual* under review, observed various additional cases of electrical repulsion; more particularly with regard to threads hanging loosely. But the honour of first distinctly grasping the general law of these facts belongs to Dufaye, whose experiments appear in the Memoirs of the French Academy, in 1733, 1734, and 1737. But before we speak respecting the theories of this philosopher, we must notice the experimental labours of his contemporary, Grey.

"About the year 1730 commenced that splendid series of discoveries which has proceeded with accelerated speed to the present day, and now forms the body of electrical science. Mr. Stephen Grey, a pensioner of the Charter-house, impelled by a passionate enthusiasm, engaged in a course of experimental researches, in which were developed some general principles, which produced important effects on subsequent investigations.

"The most considerable discovery of Mr. Grey was, that all material substances might be reduced, in reference to electrical phenomena, to two classes,—*electrics* and *non-electrics;* the former including all bodies then supposed to be capable of electric excitation by friction; and the other, those which were incapable of it. He also discovered that non-electrics were capable of acquiring the electric state by contact with excited electrics. . . . . .

"It was in the prosecution of these experiments,"—namely, those which led to the above results,—" that Grey discovered that when an electrified tube was brought near to any part of a non-electric body, without touching it, the part most remote from the tube became electrified. He thus fell upon the fact which afterwards led to the principle of INDUCTION."—*Manual of Electricity, &c.* pp. 7—11.

We may here observe in passing, that, when a body is rendered electrical by the presence of an electrized body *not in contact with it*, it is said to be electrized by induction; and the electricity developed upon it is called induced electricity.

"The science, however, was not ripe for this great discovery; and Grey accordingly continued to apply the principle of induced electricity, without the most remote suspicion of the rich mine whose treasures lay beneath his feet."—*Manual of Electricity, &c.* p. 11.

Nor was this the only discovery which Grey missed: the history of every physical science being full of instances of a similar nature. In this respect, natural phenomena may be likened to those ingenious contrivances called *anamorphoses*, or rather to Stanfield's exquisite theatrical landscapes, which present to the misplaced eye nothing but a confused picture composed of distorted fragments; but when they are beheld from the true point of view, confusion gives place to order, distortion to symmetry; the unmeaning fragments blend into a significant whole, and the eye rests with satisfaction and delight upon a scene of beauty. But instead of dwelling upon failures, or upon discoveries just coming to the birth but not brought forth, we will proceed to the theories of Dufaye.

"Contemporary with Grey was the celebrated Dufaye; who, though not impelled by the same enthusiasm, nor exhibiting the same unwearied activity in multiplying experiments, was endowed with mental powers of a much higher order, and consequently was not slow to perceive some important consequences flowing from the experiments of Grey, which had eluded the notice of that philosopher.

"Dufaye, in the first place, extended the class of substances called electrics; showing that all substances whatever, except the metals and bodies in the soft or liquid state, were capable of being electrified by friction with any sort of cloth, and that, to secure this result, it was only necessary to warm the body previously. He also showed that the property of receiving electricity by contact with an excited electric was much more general than was supposed by Grey, and that most substances exhibited that property in a greater or less degree, when supported by glass well warmed and dried."
—*Manual of Electricity, &c.* p. 12.

Dufaye also explained several of the phenomena exhibited in those experiments of Grey, on the ground of which he established his doctrine of the difference between electrics and non-electrics. But Dufaye's chief contribution to this department of electrical science was the discovery of the general law of electrical attractions and repulsions. "I discovered," he says, "a very simple principle, which accounts for a great part of the irregularities, and (if I may use the term) the caprices that seem to accompany most of the experiments in electricity. This principle is, that electric bodies attract all those that are not so, and repel them as soon as they become electric by the vicinity or contact of the electric body. . . . Upon applying this principle to various experiments of electricity, any one will be surprised at the number of obscure and puzzling facts which it clears up."

But Dufaye has the merit of a discovery of much higher order than this. " Chance," says he, " threw in my way another principle more universal and remarkable than the preceding one ; and which casts a new light upon the subject of electricity. The principle is, that there are two distinct kinds of electricity, very different from one another; one of which I call *vitreous*, the other *resinous* electricity. The first is that of glass, gems, hair, wool, and many other bodies. The second is that of amber, copal, gum-lac, silk-thread, paper, and a vast number of other substances. The characteristic of these two electricities is, that they repel themselves and attract each other. Thus a body of the vitreous electricity repels all other bodies possessed of the vitreous, and on the contrary, attracts all those of the resinous electricity. The resinous also repels the resinous, and attracts the vitreous. From this principle one may easily deduce the explanation of a great number of other phenomena ; and it is probable that this truth will lead us to the discovery of many other things."

" This was a discovery of the highest order, and in its consequences fully justified the anticipation, that 'it would lead to the discovery of many other things.' It is the basis of the only theory of electricity which has been found sufficient to explain all the phenomena of the science ; and with the subsequent hypothesis of Symmer, and the laws of attraction developed by the researches of Coulomb, it has brought the most subtle and incontrollable of all physical agents under the subjection of the rigorous canons of mathematical calculation."—*Manual of Electricity, &c.* p. 15.

For a considerable time, however, this discovery was comparatively neglected; while the single-fluid theory of Franklin, which was propounded some years later,—Dufaye's experiments and reasonings having been published in the Memoirs of the French Academy for 1733, while Franklin's experiments were made in 1747,—extensively prevailed ; its extreme simplicity, (so long as we keep to the most elementary phenomena,) and the corresponding simplicity of the language in which the American experimentalist published his speculations, giving it a brilliant but a transitory reputation. " Nothing," says Priestley, in his *History of Electricity,* " was ever written upon the subject of electricity, which was more generally read and admired in all parts of Europe than those letters," written between 1747 and 1754, in which Franklin embodied the details of his experiments, and developed the laws which resulted from them. " There is hardly any European language," continues the Birmingham doctor, " into which they have not been translated; and as if this were not sufficient to make them properly known, a translation of them has lately been made into Latin. It is not easy to say whether we are most pleased with the simplicity and perspicuity with which these letters are written, the modesty with which the author proposes every hypothesis of his own, or the noble frankness with which he relates his mistakes when they were corrected by subsequent experiments." The Franklinian hypothesis, in general terms, was this:—The earth is the great reservoir of the electric fluid; all bodies in their natural or unexcited state are charged with a certain definite quantity of this fluid, and this quantity is maintained in equilibrium upon the body by the attraction of the particles of the body for it. But a body may possess more or less electricity than satisfies its attractive force. If it possess more, it is ready to give up the surplus to any body which has less, or to share it with any body in its natural state. If it have less, it is ready to take from any body in its natural state a portion of its natural supply, and from the body surcharged with the fluid a proportionate share of its excess. A body having more than its natural quantity was said by Franklin to be electrified *positively* or *plus;* and one having less was said to be electrified *negatively* or *minus.* This hypothesis enjoyed the additional great advantage of being applied by the principal electricians of the day to the explanation of the very remarkable facts which were shortly after discovered, chiefly by Dufaye, Nollet, and Cunæus.

A luminous spark and a crackling noise not unfrequently accompany electric action. The most striking form of the production of the electric spark was that observed by Dufaye and the Abbé Nollet. "I shall never forget," says the abbé, "the surprise which the first electric spark ever drawn from *the human body* excited both in M. Dufaye and myself." This drawing of a spark from the human body was practised under various forms; the one which made "a principal part," as Priestley relates, "of the diversion of gentlemen and ladies who came to see experiments in electricity," being that familiarly known as "the electrical kiss."

By rendering the sudden actions which gave rise to these phenomena more intense, electricians obtained the electric *shock.* One of the first persons who succeeded in this experiment was Cunæus, a native of Leyden; who being engaged in certain manipulations with a vessel containing water, and in communication with the electrical machine, happened to bring the outside and inside of the vessel into connexion, by touching the outside with one hand, while with the other he touched a chain that communicated with the inside. The consequence was that he received a sudden shock in his arms and breast. The shock was probably not a severe one; but it was so wholly unexpected that Cunæus was filled with terror. Other experimentalists appear to have experienced the same effects under similar circumstances, about this time.

"Professor Muschenbroek and his associates having observed that electrified bodies exposed to the atmosphere speedily lost their electric virtue, which was supposed to be abstracted by the air itself, and by vapour and effluvia suspended in it, imagined that if they could surround them with any insulating substance, so as to exclude the contact of the atmosphere, they could communicate a more intense electrical power, and could preserve that power for a longer time. Water appeared to be one of the most convenient recipients for the electrical influence, and glass the most easy and effectual insulating envelope. It appeared, therefore, very obvious, that water inclosed in a glass bottle must retain the electricity given to it; and that by such means, a greater charge or accumulation of electric force might be obtained than by any expedient before resorted to. In the first experiments made in conformity with these views, no remarkable results were obtained. But it happened on one occasion that the operator held the glass bottle in his right hand, while the water contained in it communicated by a wire with the prime conductor of a powerful machine. When he considered that it had received a sufficient charge, he applied his left hand to the wire to disengage it from the conductor. He was instantly struck with the convulsive shock with which electricians are now so familiar, and which has been since, and is at present, so frequently suffered from motives of curiosity or amusement.

"It is curious to observe how much effects on the organs of sense depend on the previous knowledge of them, which may or may not occupy the minds of those who sustain them. Those who now think so lightly of the shock produced by even a powerful Leyden phial, would be surprised at the letter in which Muschenbroek gave Réaumur an account of the effect produced upon him by the first experiment. He states that 'he felt himself struck in his arms, shoulders, and breast, so that he lost his breath, and was two days before he recovered from the effects of the blow and the terror.' He declared, 'that he would not take a second shock for the whole kingdom of France.'

"Nor was Muschenbroek singular in this extraordinary estimate of the effects of the shock. M. Allamand, who made the experiment with a common beer-glass, stated that he lost the use of his breath for some moments, and then felt so intense a pain along his right arm that he feared permanent injury from it. Professor Winkler, of Leipsic, stated, that the first time he underwent the experiment he suffered great convulsions through his body; that it put his blood into agitation; that he feared an ardent fever, and was obliged to have recourse to cooling medicines! That he also felt a heaviness in his head, as if a stone were laid upon it. Twice it gave him a bleeding at the nose, to which he was not subject. The lady of this professor, who appears to have been as little wanting in the curiosity which is ascribed to her own, as in the courage which is assumed for the other sex, took the shock twice, and was rendered so weak by it, that she could hardly walk. In a week, nevertheless, her curiosity again got the better of her discretion, and she took a third shock, which immediately produced bleeding at the nose."—*Manual of Electricity, &c.* pp. 18—20.

These results excited the utmost surprise among persons of every age, sex, and rank. The electrical shock was everywhere spoken of as "a prodigy of nature and philosophy." The experiment was repeated under a variety of forms; and as the excitement subsided, philosophers set themselves carefully to ascertain the essential circumstances and determining conditions of the electric shock.

"Muschenbroek observed, that if the glass were wet on the outer surface the success of the experiment was impaired; and Dr. Watson proved that the force of the shock was increased by the thinness of the glass of which the bottle containing the water was made. He also observed, that the force of the charge did not depend on the power of the electrical machine by which the phial was charged. Dr. Watson also showed that the shock could be transmitted undiminished through the bodies of several men touching each other.

"By further repeating and varying the experiment, Watson found that the force of the charge depended on the extent of the external surface of the glass in contact with the hand of the operator; and it occurred to Dr. Bevis that the hand might be efficient merely as a conductor of electricity, and in that case the object might be more effectually and conveniently attained by coating the exterior of the phial with sheet-lead or tin-foil. This experiment was completely successful; and the phial, so far as related to its external surface, assumed its present form.

"Another important step in the improvement of the Leyden jar was also due to the suggestion of Dr. Bevis. It appeared that the force of the charge increased with the magnitude of the jar, but not in proportion to the quantity of water it contained. It was conjectured that it might depend on the extent of the surface of glass in contact with water; and that as water was considered to play merely the part of a conductor in the experiment, metal, which was a better conductor, would be at least equally effectual. Three phials were therefore procured and filled to the usual height with shot instead of water. A metallic communication was made between the shot contained in them respectively. The result was a charge of greatly augmented force. This was, in fact, the first electric battery."—*Manual of Electricity, &c.* p. 21.

Similar experiments, all tending to bring to light the theory of the phenomena of the Leyden jar, were made by the Abbé Nollet, M. de Monnier, and others, in France. By Canton, who just touched on the discovery of dissimulated electricity by showing that,

"If a charged phial be insulated, the internal and external coatings would give alternate sparks; and then, by continuing the process, the phial might be gradually discharged."—*Manual of Electricity, &c.* p. 23.

And by Wilson, in Dublin, who observed an almost "glaring instance" of *induction*, (although he failed to discover this great electrical principle,) in the fact that

"A person standing near the circuit through which the shock is transmitted, would sustain a shock if he were only in contact with any part of the circuit, or *even placed very near it.*"—*Manual of Electricity, &c.* p. 23.

But the most striking experiments were those made by Dr. Watson in the presence of Mr. Martin Folkes, then president of the Royal Society, Lord Charles Cavendish, Dr. Bevis, and several other fellows of the Society. The scale on which these experiments were performed excited the admiration of Muschenbroek, who says, in a letter to Watson, "Magnificentissimis tuis experimentis superasti conatus omnium." One of the most remarkable circumstances that was ascertained by means of these experiments was, that the transmission of electricity through a length of 12,000 feet was, to sense, *instantaneous.*

But the greatest discovery which adorns these earlier annals of electrical science, was that of the identity of electricity and lightning. The analogies between these two powers of nature were too obvious and striking to escape the observation of even the earliest speculators.

Dr. Wall, in a paper published in the "Philosophical Transactions," speaking of the electricity of amber, said that he had no doubt, "that by using a longer and a larger piece of amber, both the cracklings and the light would be much greater. *This light and crackling seems, in some degree, to represent thunder and lightning.*"

Mr. Grey, whose experiments have been already referred to, says, speaking of electrical effects,—

"These are at present but 'in minimis.' It is probable that in time there may be found out a way to collect a great quantity of electric fire, and consequently to increase the force of that power, which, by several of these experiments, ('si licet magnis componere parva,') seems to be of *the same nature with that of thunder and lightning.*" — *Manual of Electricity, &c.* pp. 37, 38.

The Abbé Nollet, in his "Leçons de Physique," which was published in the year 1748,—two years before the publication of Franklin's conjectures on the same subject, and four years before the once-famous experiment of the same experimentalist, made by means of a kite,— writes still more explicitly : " If any one," he says, " should undertake to prove, as a clear consequence of the phenomenon, that *thunder* is, in the hands of nature, what *electricity* is in ours,—that those wonders which we dispose at our pleasure are only imitations, on a small scale, of those grand effects which terrify us, and that both depend on the same mechanical agents ; if it were made manifest that a cloud prepared by the effects of the wind, by heat, by a mixture of exhalations, &c. is in relation to a terrestrial object what an electrified body is in relation to a body near it not electrified, I confess that this idea, well supported, would please me much ; and to support it, how numerous and specious are the reasons which present themselves to a mind conversant with electricity ! The universality of the electric matter, the readiness of its action, its instrumentality and its activity in giving fire to other bodies ; its property of striking bodies externally and internally, even to their smallest parts (the remarkable example we have of this effect even in the Leyden jar experiment, the idea which we might truly adopt in supposing a greater degree of electric power) ; —all these points of analogy which I have been for some time meditating, begin to make me believe that one might, *by taking electricity for the model,* form to oneself, *in regard to thunder and lightning,* more perfect and more probable ideas than any hitherto proposed."*

But it was not until Wilke and Æpinus had obtained clear notions of the effect of electric matter at a distance, that the real condition of the clouds could be well understood. In 1752, however, D'Alibard, and other French philosophers, being desirous of verifying Franklin's conjecture as to the analogy of lightning and electricity, erected a pointed iron rod, forty feet high, at Marli. The rod was found to give out electrical sparks when a thunder-cloud passed over the place. This experiment was repeated in various parts of Europe, with similar successful results. Some months afterwards Franklin varied the form of the experiment, by sending up a paper kite during a thunder-storm. He afterwards related the results, and described the methods he pursued, with so much clearness and animation of style, and depicted his various feelings during the progress of the

---

* Nollet, Leçons de Physique, tom. iv. p. 315, 8th edition.

experiment, with so much of that garrulous simplicity and earnestness which impart so peculiar a charm to the writings of Kepler, that he succeeded for a time in attaching his own name to these brilliant discoveries. The writer of the " Manual " under review, labours hard to establish Franklin's exclusive claim to the character of an independent and first discoverer in this department of physical science; but his own dates refute him. The American experimentalist appears to have the same claim to this distinction, which Amerigo Vespuccio had to give his own name to the continent which was discovered by Columbus.

Mr. Whewell, in his admirable " History of the Inductive Sciences," has fairly assigned to Franklin his real merits, and has satisfactorily accounted for his exaggerated fame. " Though, after the first conception of an electrical charge as a disturbance of equilibrium," he observes, "there was nothing in the development or the details of Franklin's views which deserved to win for them any peculiar authority; yet his reputation and his skill as a writer gave a considerable influence to his opinions. . . . . Franklin's real merit as a discoverer was, that he was one of the first who distinctly conceived the electrical charge as a derangement of equilibrium. The great fame which in his day he enjoyed, arose from the clearness and spirit with which he narrated his discoveries; from his dealing with electricity in the imposing form of thunder and lightning; and partly, perhaps, from his character as an American and a politician; for he was already, in 1736, engaged in public affairs as clerk to the General Assembly of Pennsylvania, though it was not till a later period of his life that his admirers had the occasion of saying of him—

" Eripuit cœlis fulmen sceptrumque tyrannis."[*]

Franklin had a strong craving after material utility. This led him to suggest the application of the new discovery to the purpose of preserving buildings from being struck by lightning. We will give this suggestion, and the experiments upon which it rested, in his own characteristic words. " Take a pair of large brass scales, of two or more feet beam, the cords of the scales being silk. Suspend the beam by a packthread from the ceiling, so that the bottom of the scales may be about a foot from the floor; the scales will move round in a circle by the untwisting of the packthread. Let an iron punch (a silversmith's iron punch, an inch thick, is what I use) be put on the end upon the floor, in such a place as that the scales may pass over it in making their circle; then electrify one scale by applying the wire of a charged phial to it. As they move round, you see that scale draw nigher to the floor, and dip more when it comes over the punch; and, if that be placed at a proper distance, the scale will snap and discharge its fire into it. But if a needle be stuck on the end of the punch, its point upwards, the scale, instead of drawing nigh to the

---

[*] Whewell, History of Inductive Sciences, vol. iii. pp. 22, 23.

punch and snapping, discharges its fire silently through the point, and rises higher from the punch. Nay, even if the needle be placed upon the floor near the punch, its point upwards, the end of the punch, though so much higher than the needle, will not attract the scale and receive its fire; for the needle will get it, and convey it away, before it comes nigh enough for the punch to act.

"Now, if electricity and lightning be the same, the conductor and scales may represent electrified clouds. If a tube (conductor) of only ten feet long will strike and discharge its fire on the punch at two or three inches distance, an electrified cloud of perhaps ten thousand acres may strike and discharge on the earth at a proportionally greater distance. The horizontal motion of the scales over the floor may represent the motion of the clouds over the earth, and the erect iron punch a hill or high building; and then we shall see how electrified clouds, passing over hills or high buildings at too great a height to strike, may be attracted lower till within their striking distance. And lastly, if a needle fixed on the punch with its point upright, or even on the floor, below the punch, will draw the fire from the scale silently, at a much greater than the striking distance, and so prevent its descending towards the punch; or if in its course it would have come nigh enough to strike, yet, being first deprived of its fire, it cannot, and the punch is thereby secured from the stroke:—I say, if these things are so, may not the knowledge of this power of points be of use to mankind in preserving houses, churches, ships, &c., from the stroke of lightning, by directing us to fix, on the highest parts of those edifices, upright rods of iron, made sharp as a needle, and gilt, to prevent rusting; and from the foot of these rods, a wire down to the outside of the building into the ground, or down round one of the shrouds of a ship, and down her side till it reaches the water? Would not these pointed rods probably draw the electrical fire silently out of a cloud before it came nigh enough to strike, and thereby secure us from that most sudden and terrible mischief?"*

So completely was Franklin's mind occupied with the idea of the practical application of science, that even his mirth is mechanical. Writing to Mr. Collinson, he says, "Chagrined a little that we have hitherto been able to produce nothing in this way of use to mankind, and the hot weather coming on, when electrical experiments are not so agreeable, it is proposed to put an end to them for this season, somewhat humorously, in a party of pleasure on the banks of the Schuylkill. Spirits, at the same time, are to be fired by a spark sent from side to side through the river, without any other conductor than the water; an experiment which we some time since performed to the amazement of many. A turkey is to be killed for dinner by the *electrical shock*, and roasted by the *electrical jack*, before a fire kindled by the *electrified bottle;* when the healths of all the famous electricians of England, Holland, France, and Germany, are to be drunk in

---

* Letters, p. 235.

electrified bumpers, under a discharge of guns from the *electrical battery.*"*

The subject of atmospheric electricity now began to occupy the attention of the philosophers who were labouring in this department of physical science; the most acute and indefatigable of whom was Beccaria, who, in 1753, published a treatise on electricity, at Turin, and a series of letters on the same subject, at Bologna, in 1758.

" This profound philosopher, and acute and accurate observer, has left in the history of electricity traces of his genius, second only to those with which Franklin and Volta impressed it. Beccaria was the first who diligently studied and recorded the circumstances attending the phenomena of a thunder-storm. He observes, that the first appearance of a thunder-storm (which generally happens when there is little or no wind) is one dense cloud, or more, increasing rapidly in magnitude, and ascending into the higher regions of the atmosphere. The lower edge is black, and nearly horizontal; but the upper is finely arched, and well defined. Many of these clouds often seem piled one upon the other, all arched in the same manner; but they keep constantly uniting, swelling, and extending their arches. When such clouds rise, the firmament is usually sprinkled over with a great number of separate clouds, of odd and bizarre forms, which keep quite motionless. When the thunder-cloud ascends these are drawn towards it; and as they approach they become more uniform and regular in their shapes, till, coming close to the thunder-cloud, their limbs stretch mutually towards one another, finally coalesce, and form one uniform mass. But sometimes the thunder-cloud will swell and increase without the addition of these smaller adscititious clouds. Some of the latter appear like white fringes at the skirts of the thunder-cloud, or under the body of it; but they continually grow darker and darker as they approach it.

" When a thunder-cloud, thus augmented, has attained a great magnitude, its lower surface is often ragged; particular parts being detached towards the earth, but still connected with the rest. Sometimes the lower surface swells into large protuberances, tending uniformly towards the earth; and sometimes one whole side of the cloud will have an inclination to the earth, which the extremity of it will nearly touch. When the observer is under the thunder-cloud, after it has grown large and is well formed, it is seen to sink lower, and to darken prodigiously; and, at the same time, a great number of small clouds are observed in rapid motion, driven about in irregular directions below it. While these clouds are agitated with the most rapid motions, the rain generally falls in abundance; and if the agitation be very great, it hails.

" While the thunder-cloud is swelling and extending itself over a large tract of country, the lightning is seen to dart from one part of it to another, and often to illuminate its whole mass. When the cloud has acquired a sufficient extent, the lightning strikes between the cloud and the earth in two opposite places, the path of the lightning lying through the whole body of the cloud and its branches. The longer this lightning continues, the rarer does the cloud grow, and the less dark in its appearance, till it breaks in different places and shows a clear sky. When the thunder is thus dispersed, those parts which occupy the upper regions of the atmosphere are spread thinly and equally, and those that are beneath are black and thin also, but they vanish gradually without being driven away by the wind."—*Manual of Electricity, &c.* pp. 61—63.

Beccaria also anticipated, with singular sagacity, the fundamental

---

* Letters, p. 210.

principle of electro-magnetism, and terrestrial magnetism; but we reserve this part of the subject to a future article. Contemporaneously with Beccaria, Canton prosecuted similar inquiries in England. The chief discovery due to Canton was, that the electricity developed in the friction of the same substance is not always of the same kind. Thus glass is capable of being electrified *negatively*, to use the language of the Franklinian hypothesis; or in the phraseology of Dufaye, of exhibiting *resinous* electricity.

Lemonnier was another contemporary of Beccaria. By means of an apparatus erected at Germain-en-Laye, he showed that the electricity of the atmosphere undergoes periodical variations in the course of every twenty-four hours.

"Beccaria determined the law of these variations, and was the first who demonstrated that at all seasons, at all heights, and in every state of the wind, the electricity of an *unclouded* atmosphere is positive. He found no indications of electricity in the air in high winds, when the firmament was covered with black and scattered clouds, having a slow motion in a humid state of the air; but in the absence of actual rain, he found that in changeable squally weather, attended with occasional showers of snow, hail, or rain, the electricity was very variable, both as to quantity and quality, being sometimes feeble, and sometimes intense; sometimes positive, and sometimes negative."—*Manual of Electricity, &c.* pp. 68, 69.

We have once or twice had occasion to observe that more than one of the earlier experimentalists touched upon the great principle of *induction*; a principle of great generality, and embracing in its range nearly the whole domain of electrical phenomena. The time was now come for this principle to obtain due recognition, and to be employed as the key-stone to bind into one solid whole, those scattered facts which the experimental labours of electricians, from Gilbert downwards, had brought to light. This result was due chiefly to the patient and able researches pursued at Berlin by Wilke and Æpinus. These researches were carried forward by Volta; of whose remarkable labours we shall speak more in detail when we come to treat of the history of electro-dynamical discovery. It now only remains for us to glance at the labours of Coulomb, as closing our notice of *the history of the discovery of the laws of electrical phenomena*, and as preparatory to a future consideration of *the history of the progress of electrical theory*.

"The year 1785 formed an important epoch in the history of electrical science, marking, as it did, the commencement of those labours by which Coulomb laid the foundations of *electro-statics*. This great experimental philosopher was the first who really brought the phenomena of electricity within the reach of numerical calculation; and thereby prepared the way for his followers in the same field, to reduce this most subtle of all physical agents to the rigorous sway of mathematics. It is to Coulomb we owe it that statical electricity is now a branch of mathematical physics."—*Manual of Electricity, &c.* p. 83.

We have now conducted our readers to the end of the first distinct stage in the history of this brilliant science. We shall shortly resume our labours, by entering upon the history of the closely related sciences of Magnetism and Electro-Magnetism. We shall then be able to consider the subjects of Voltaic Electricity and Electro-Chemistry; concluding all by as full an account of the *theories* which the electricians of our own day are endeavouring to construct by the aid of experiment and mathematical analysis, as will be interesting or intelligible to the general reader.

---

1. *Village Pencillings, in Prose and Verse.* By Elizabeth Pierce. London: Pickering. 1842. Post 8vo. pp. 285.

2. *The Life and Defence of the Conduct and Principles of the venerable and calumniated Edmund Bonner, Bishop of London, in the Reigns of Henry VIII., Edward VI., Mary, and Elizabeth; in which is considered the best Mode of changing the Religion of this Nation.* By a Tractarian British Critic. *Dedicated to the Bishop of London.* London: Seeley and Burnside. 1842. 8vo. pp. xxv. xiv. 382.

We fear that the great fight is over. *Conclamatum est.* There seems to be no remedy for it; we have but to lay down our arms and surrender unconditionally; to march out with the honours of war is now hopeless. Till lately, we had some rather brilliant anticipations for the catholic cause,—we have more than once expressed them; but we find that we sounded the trumpet before the battle was won: with shame and sorrow we humble ourselves in the dust. Alas! for Church theology! For ten dreary years has she stood a fiercer than Trojan siege, and, like her, has she at last been doomed to fall, and in a yet more inglorious way. No Grecian horse, teeming with the secret arms of four, or forty, tutors; nor Mr. Sinon Golightly has betrayed her; in no fairly-foughten field has she been vanquished; neither Argive flames have razed her walls, nor domestic seditions opened her gates. We have experienced the fate of Abimelech; we have been reserved for no warrior's hand; we might not even gain the mercy of a friendly sword; but men "should say, A woman slew him." Alas, our dear and cherished creed!

> "Occidis, Argivæ quam non potuere phalanges
> Sternere, nec Priami regnorum eversor Achilles:
> Hic tibi mortis erunt metæ: *dux fœmina facti.*"

This theological Penthesilea, Camilla, Thomyris, Semiramis, Boadicea, Hippolyta, Clorinda, Britomart—all in one—is, know all men, Mrs. Elizabeth Pierce; wife, we presume, of the Reverend W. M. Pierce, Perpetual Curate of West Ashby, county of Lincoln. We are thus particular, because we are quite sure that such particularity will please the lady, since she has prefixed to her very prettily-bound book a very smart, sharp, steel engraving of the principal street of the said West Ashby, with a square-towered church; also a Parsonage-house, conveniently situated to the west of the said church, from which it is only separated by a very tasty shrubbery and parterre, " pleasure grounds, designed and laid out in excellent style, interspersed with divers American shrubs and flowering evergreens," as our friend George Robins has it: also a portrait of herself, we presume, sauntering up the sunny side of West Ashby street, with a basket—like the celebrated one of Miss Constance Duff—containing, we suppose, the choicest productions of the Religious Tract Society, one of which, in this graceful engraving, she is apparently about to deliver at the white cottage occupying the right hand corner. Her own book is our authority for this " Pencilling."

We are about to do a very naughty thing; to publish a lady's billet. True, it did not reach us redolent of musk, with white wax and lace-bordered envelope; for then we must have held it sacred; we should have laid it up with our choicest κειμήλια; to use her own sweet words, we should have

—— " closed the mine where lies the gem,
And sealed it with a sigh."—P. 32.

But we received it through the prosaic medium of our respectable publisher, in the unpoetical guise of a printed fly-leaf, within the cover of the Pencillings; and here it is:—

" The Reviewer of *Village Pencillings* would confer an obligation, by kindly paying particular attention to its varied contents, and especially to the essay entitled ' The Light of the Parsonage,' which is a defence, by the wife of a Clergyman, of the Lawfulness of Marriage to the Protestant Ministry of the Church of England; a subject now much mooted by the Puseyites, who, in their extreme zeal for the celibacy of the Clergy, with other attempted revivals of Romish peculiarities, have *branded* the domestic condition of the Anglican Priesthood, as a state of profane concubinage."

" 177, PICCADILLY."

And a very modest, delicate, sensible, lady-like note too; we are rather proud of it. By what soft bribery Mrs. Pierce has won us to her own sweet will, we are bound by all the laws of gallantry to conceal; but we have, as she requests, paid " particular attention to the varied contents of Village Pencillings, and especially to the essay entitled " The Light of the Parsonage;" and we are bound to say—and we now speak seriously—that a volume more contemptible in design and execution, in spirit and in diction, we never read. When the wife of an English Clergyman, abetted, of course, by her husband, challenges, in this unexampled way, the attention of the conductors of this Review to her absurd book, we feel it to be the duty of a Christian Remembrancer to remind this lady and gentleman of a certain couple called Ananias and Sapphira, and to recommend them to lay to heart the moral obligation of the ninth commandment, and to ponder what the Catechism—if the Catechism is to be found in the theology of West Ashby—means by " evil speaking, lying, and slandering;" for we need scarcely add, that to say that Dr. Pusey, himself a widower, or one or more of those writers whom she is pleased to call "Puseyites," have "*branded* the domestic condition of the Anglican priesthood as a state of profane concubinage," is a wicked falsehood, maliciously invented, and libellously circulated. We do not charge Mrs. Pierce with this falsehood: she, poor thing, only writes upon hearsay; but it is a lie, nevertheless.*

This immodest *affiche* will have led our readers to anticipate that Village Pencillings is a very unfeminine book: it strikes us as being so. There are weak minds, which, though not yielding to positive indelicacy in words, seem always floating in a hazy atmosphere— half warm and languid, and half pious. We feel that we cannot trust ourselves in describing more fully what we mean; and we are far from saying that Mrs. Pierce intends what she says; but the following may indicate this unsafe sort of writing, which our readers may take, metre, syntax, and meaning, as they find it.

"When roseate rays light the earth-born bower,
And the calm repose of the sunset hour
Bid voiceless thoughts from the heart-cells bring
Incense to bear on seraphic wing,
                           Pensez à moi.

"When the love-glance beams in each gleeful eye,
And the smiles of affection-dance buoyant by,"
                           &c. &c.

These words, we believe, do Mrs. Pierce great injustice; she can have no sort of feeling that this is all very bad; and therefore we deem it right to show her how she injures herself and her own good, we trust, and amiable nature, by wandering from her appointed sphere of duties in writing at all. We speak of her all along as an authoress; and as she adopts writing as a mere mask, to us she is but an εἰδώλον, as unreal and shadowy as her assumed character. She will, we are sure, be as much shocked as ourselves by finding what is the sad tendency of words and sentiments which she uses as vague prettinesses, and nothing more. We charge her rather with no meaning than a bad meaning.

This same fantastic unreality, this *mirage* of unmeaning words, pervades every page of the "Pencillings:" rosy clouds, and sweetest breezes, fevered brows, and yearnings of love, "affection's star-lit cave," "manly beauty, and raven hair drooping in curls over his clear brown forehead" (p. 158), and so forth. This is nonsense, we know, but it may be very mischievous; so we feel it a duty to protest decidedly against it. The christian virgins of England are not to

---

* The fact is, that aspersion of concubinage was cast on the married clergy by that very injudicious person, Mr. Wackerbarth, *after* his secession to the Romish schism in this country. It occurs in his wrong-headed tract "Egyptian Bondage." And it is obvious that this gentleman would, when he used the expression, be as desirous to disclaim any community with Dr. Pusey, as the Oxford school are compelled to disclaim him and his works, as well those written before, as after, his apostasy.

be seduced by this spiritual voluptuousness, though Laura-Matilda and Mrs. Robinson re-appear under the form of a Clergyman's wife. The christian life is not a bower of bliss; the blossoms and scents, the glances and melodies of a Persian heaven, are not the "strait and narrow path;" our daily cross, and the stern strife and contest of good angels and evil spirits about the "world which now is," is far too awful and too personal to be sugared down into ballads and romancettes. "Young men and maidens, old men and children," as we all require, so must we have, in every age and station of life, a more subdued and subduing teaching. The imagination, like the body, must be trained by a lenten discipline.

To urge upon the wife of the incumbent of three cozy livings* in the county of Lincoln, with her avowed horror of celibacy, anything like personal self-denial, sitting at her ease in the drawing-room, or strolling into "the conservatory," and watering "agapanthus," or pacing round "the little Swiss parterre begemmed with the brilliant verbenas and the fuchsia's coralline pendants" (p. 5), is, we fear, Quixotic enough. Somebody, whom she calls an "ascetic," seems to have undertaken the task; he thought Mrs. Pierce

> "A butterfly, thoughtless and gay;
> "He said that her summer was waning,
>   The bloom of her youthfulness past;
> That the world her soul was enchaining,
>   The bliss of hereafter to blast."—P. 191.

Sage counsel too! and if the lady be too self-indulgent to see its wisdom, we recommend her to chasten her fancy, as a fit preparation for some bodily mortification, which would do her much good. It is a sad fate to have all the luxuries and comforts of a snug country parish; and if ladies, be they young or middle-aged, cannot more rigorously control their imagination or their tumultuous feelings than Mrs. Pierce has done, they had better forswear poetry and printing, than write so offensively, alike both to good taste and true plain christian temper, as she has unwittingly done. On the subject of clerical celibacy, we design to speak when we recur to Mr. Gresley's "Bernard Leslie;" and now we must make short work with Mrs. Pierce, promising to renew our acquaintance with this "Light of the Parsonage," on her pet topic, at a future occasion.

1. Her grammar:—

> "Welcome, sweet May! with village pole rear'd,
>   Roses and pinks with woodbine entwine;
> Garden and grove *remorseless are clear'd*,
>   Decking the scene peculiarly thine."—P. 176.

This confusion of adverb and adjective is a license rather common in feminine composition: *ex. grat.*—

---

* See the Clergy List, *sub nomine*.

> " And when the child, to manhood grown,
> Has choked the seed so *careful sown*."—P. 40.
>
> ———— " The languid form of age,
> Whose silvery *locks*, adown the furrow'd cheek,
> Of many a winter *tells* on Time's long page."—P. 243.
>
> " So *yawns* Hade's (!) dark caverns."—P. 271.
>
> " Thy task now fulfill'd, *thou* 'Ariel' May,
> Who the warrior's birth-couch *bare*."—P. 183.

2. Her diction :—

> " The *owlet's* left her rural bower."—P. 150.
>
> " For man, thou'st made in earliest days,"—P. 89,

being an address to " the Sabbath," by which name it is just possible that Mrs. P. may mean to caricature the Lord's Day : otherwise we cannot agree with our authoress that Saturday, which is the only Sabbath spoken of in Scripture, is either " the welcome one," *par excellence*, or " the hallowed one," to parsons, or to parsons' wives.

3. Her prosody :—

> "Welcome, sweet May! thy choral bands sing,
> Carolling high thy praises afar;
> Melody's strains they gleefully bring,
> Heralding forth thy triŭmphăl car."—P. 175.

Sidney tried his hand at hexameters ; so did Southey ; and here is Mrs. P.'s " Harvest," p. 193.

> " August has breath'd her last sigh on the autumnal brow of September,
> Leaving him executor of her wealth in the fruits of her sunny toil :
> And earth, the garden of nature, has spread forth her enamelled robe,
> Inviting the ephemera, who live on her bounty,
> To cull sweets from the flower, bloom from the fruit, and grain for the garner."

The remainder passes our powers of scansion ; and now that Hermann is gone, we leave it as a crux to all metremongers. Talk of Burney's Tentamen ! we offer a prize for the best dissertation De Metris Piercianis ; we venture, with all humility, to suggest the Dactylicus Logaædicus.* The system is certainly asynartetous ; we are not sure that it must not be relegated to the ἀπολελυμένον, or *canticum solutum*. Take a specimen.

> " A faint glimmer in the east—and behold, the golden eye beams o'er the cheek of earth,
> That, radiant in new-born loveliness, blushes beneath its ardent gaze.
> See'st thou the insect weaving the wreathed mist ?
> Mark how she threads the netted gossamer,
> And say, O man ! art thou better than this frail aëronaut ?
> Hast caught no unwary one in thy tangled meshes ?"—P. 195.

---

* Logaædicos versus grammatici vocarunt, qui ob dactylici et trochaici numeri conjunctionem *medii inter cantum et communem sermonem viderentur*.—*Elementa Doctrinæ Metricæ*, lib. ii. c. 30.

"Man talketh of himself, who is a shadow—and keepeth silence of his
 God, who created it—
Of Him who is the substance—the essence—and the life:
But call thou upon Him, for He turns the wheel of destiny;
And thou art blessed by the ruling Sovereign of the skies:
And know that poverty is the blight and the famine of sloth,
While plenty is the golden harvest of industry."—P. 198.

4. This childish nonsense might have passed with only a smile from us, had it not been mixed up with hymns on the holiest festivals of the Church; and, dreadful as it is to say, had not Mrs. Pierce ventured to insinuate that she was inspired by the Holy Ghost Himself, to write this unfortunate book. We know that this charge against a christian woman is so shocking, that we are bound to produce evidence of it; and we do so with no unkindliness to the writer, though with great scruples for our readers; but only to show into what blasphemous profanity and irreverence silly people may fall by using fine words in a trifling, merely literary way, without attaching any meaning to them. The conclusion (p. 280) tells us that when Mrs. Pierce had finished her "Pencillings," she began to reproach herself for her temerity in publishing them. She then feigns that she saw a vision: "a form of surpassing loveliness, glowing in a robe of soft green, spangled with the living fire-stars, appeared," which is made to pass for Virtue; and then "a female form, clothed in purple and fine linen," &c. &c., which appears to be "the Spirit of Earth," whatever that may be:

"Then arose a gentle breeze, that cooled my excited sense; and on the passing gale, rich with the perfume of untold sweets, floated the most thrilling harmony,—music such as only seraphs make. Wrapped in delicious ecstasy, I heard a voice say, 'Arise, and fear not to partake of the passing gifts, for she who presents them is thy mother. Taste, for thy sustenance—abstain but from excess—and blush not to acknowledge thy dependence on her, for thou art a pensioner on her bounty; and, ere it be too late, stretch forth thine hand, for the mirrored boon she offers thee will prove an ægis thou anon mayst need; and if its chord, woven by mortality, may add one note to the celestial choir, the echo of many harps shall resound the melody of blessing and of praise! Stay not thine hand in thy vineyard; it shall be fruitful and multiply, for I have said it; and my words are of those that pass not away. Put a hedge round thy vineyard, and advertise the world thereof; it shall flourish and prosper, for it is planted in the good soil, and the Great Husbandman is not a stranger to it. Thou art as yet but a timid novice; take courage, and know that I will intercede for thee, will help thy infirmities, will sustain thee with my fruits—love, joy, peace, long-suffering, gentleness, goodness; and, above all, I will seal thee with my covenant, written, not with ink, but with the life-stream from the heart; and I will lead thee into the land of uprightness, where fear not to fight the good fight; for I will go with thee, and be thy stay, will put on thee the armour of light, and gird thee with the sword of faith. Then mayest thou conquer, not by might nor by power, but by my Spirit, saith the Lord of hosts.' With that blessed Spirit for my guide, support, and reward, I take comfort to my heart," &c.—P. 285.

We earnestly believe that Mrs. Pierce has not the least notion that all this, as far as it can be said to have any meaning, is downright blasphemy: she only thought that Scripture phrases helped what she took for fine writing, and she uses the most deep and fearful things of the most Blessed Word to make a glittering sentence, or to turn a polished period. But what a dreadful habit of mind! We pray that Mrs. Pierce may be permitted to see, and seeing to repent of it, that this is unreal trifling with sacred things and truths. Reverence is the mother of piety; and we offer these weighty words to her thoughts, if she will but recall sufficient sense and serious humility to think how grievously she errs against propriety by this book-making madness; for we will not attribute any of her errors to a graver cause.

"Words have a meaning, whether we mean that meaning or not; and they are imputed to us in their real meaning, when our not meaning it is our own fault. He who takes God's name in vain, is not counted guiltless because he means nothing by it; he cannot frame a language for himself; and they who make professions, of whatever kind, are heard in the sense of those professions, and are not excused because they themselves attach no sense to it. 'By thy words thou shalt be justified, and by thy words thou shalt be condemned.' Let us aim at meaning what we say, and saying what we mean."—*Newman's Sermons*, " Unreal Words," vol. vi. Sermon III.

And this thought brings us to the second volume named at the head of this article, which is most emphatically an unreal, unscrupulous, and therefore very irreligious, false, and irreverent book. It is not our object to go through it, and explore all its historical inaccuracies and literary falsities; to say the truth, it is not worth it; and we have already wasted too much space on Mrs. Pierce. Writers of this class are to be exposed, not so much for their folly and incapacity, as for their unprincipled style of writing. Ignorance and folly are venial faults; but false sentiment and loose morality, like that which the Clergyman's wife has fallen into, though unintentionally, or such dishonesty, of more kinds than one, as the author of the Life of Bishop Bonner has committed, require open censure.

The so-called Biography of Bonner affects to be the production of "a Tractarian British Critic," we take the phrase as we find it, and under this clumsy fiction, it is an attack upon the present school of catholic writers, by suggesting that their principles and writings would compel them to approve and advocate, both in theory and practice, the acts and sentiments of the Romanist bishop. It is written of course in the fictitious person of Bonner's apologist.

Viewing it merely as a literary production, it is a decided failure. The jest is tedious and expensive in the extreme; 10s. 6d. must be a sore drawback upon the relish of the purchasers of this wearisome attempt at wit. Few people can afford to pay for their laugh; and they who have sufficient spite to enjoy it, must think it dearly purchased. When the pocket sighs, the risible muscles contract; and there is marvellous little sympathy between a good joke and a bookseller's bill. To have been effective it should have been one-fourth the size; and the "Pastoral epistle of the Pope" has twice the point, and mischief too, of Bonner's Life. Risus si aptus est, says Quinctilian, *urbanitatis*, sin aliter, *stultitiæ* nomen assequitur. It happens to this writer, as it did to Demosthenes, according to Longinus, ἔνθα μέντοι γελοῖος εἶναι βιάζεται καὶ ἀστεῖος, οὐ γέλωτα κινεῖ μᾶλλον, ἢ καταγελᾶται.* If brevity be the soul of wit, the length, to say nothing of its malignity, is fatal to this frigid composition. Four hundred pages of irony are anything but sly fun; and a whole volume of cross readings could not be heavier jocoseness. Burke's "Vindication of Natural Society," and the "Argument against Abolishing Christianity," are the best specimens of this experimental argument; in the ablest hands, a perilous one.

Of course we have heavier charges against this book than its mere literary infelicity; the principle of treating grave matters in this unreal random manner is very sad and painful. Controversy in religion is at the best a very awful thing; sorrow and a subdued heart ought to be inseparable from it. Of course it is a duty, but duties are trials; the very existence of controversy implies disunion and schism, or at least a schismatical tendency somewhere; now, schism is a sin, and a grave one, and sin is no laughing matter to a Christian. This we ought all of us to feel; if there were any earnestness in them, the haters of catholicism ought to feel it too; and in their plans of attack they should pause before they gave in to this taunting, goading, exasperating system. Again, fiction is a perilous experiment to try in religious matters for another reason; to say the least of it, exaggeration is all but inseparable from it, and few escape this danger; the sentiment as well as the story is unreal, and we get false and trifling by the hollow affectation of display. There are of course exceptions to the victory of such temptation: Mr. Gresley's little books, for example, seem perhaps more free from this unreality than either Mr. Paget's or Mrs. Mozley's, admirable as they are; but the tendency is fatally strong in all religious storybooks. Once more, this mockery in serious subjects not only galls an adversary into sullenness, and it may be into worse extremes, even when he is wrong, and at the same time leads to a sacrifice or perversion of the truth in those who indulge in it, but as a mode of argument, if it deserve the name, it is unfair for another reason. One of the most hateful characters in real life is the professed wit, who makes use of his character to say rude things to every-body, and then shrinks out of the consequences of his insolence, by pleading the jest, but this only when it suits him, or when he is compelled by circumstances to fall back upon it. He plays off his vulgarity either as jest or earnest only as it is received. So is it in this matter; detect an unfair quotation, a garbled extract, a false inference, or a

---

* De Subl. sect. xxxiv.

downright untruth, and the fiction is pleaded; let it pass, and the book stands for a demonstration.

Our business is now not so much with the book itself, as with its moral turpitude; we do not intend to refute it, for all that it amounts to is a collection of what are supposed to be the most offensive passages in the Tracts for the Times, the British Critic, Froude's Remains, the Works of Dr. Pusey, Mr. Newman, &c.,—such as that saying about " the Reformation being a limb badly set," and "Jewell being an irreverent" (or as the Life of Bonner spells it, irreverend) " dissenter," &c. &c., which have been produced and attacked, and defended and explained, as everybody knows, *ad nauseam*. Some of our readers may have seen an unfair and one-sided collection of scraps, printed by Seeley, on a broad sheet, and headed, " What is Puseyism?": it is to be seen at the office of the Record, and is scattered pretty generally as a tract in ultra-Protestant parishes, such as Islington. This precious *brochure* contains for a penny all the substance of the Life of Bonner; it is quite as fair, and twice as readable.* We will furnish our readers with a few specimens of the dishonesty which this miserable fiction entails upon the pseudo-biographer of Bonner. In the person of " the Tractarian " he writes, p. 73,—

" We must learn to think differently, and to write and speak affectionately of Bonner and Gardiner. This was the result of our dear friend's [the late Mr. Froude's] more extended reading. ' I have been very idle lately,' he says, ' but I have taken up *Strype now and then, and have not increased my admiration of the Reformers. As far as I have gone too, I think better than I was prepared to do of Bonner and Gardiner.*"

We have selected this passage, because, as far as we know, it is the only place in which any of " the Tractarians " speak of Bonner at all; we may therefore assume it to be the peg upon which this life is hung. On turning to Froude's Remains, vol. i. p. 251, we find, between the two sentences quoted from that gentleman's letter, the following inserted, to have quoted which would have spoiled the joke, however its omission affects truth :—

" One must not speak lightly of a martyr, so I do not allow my opinions to pass the verge of scepticism. But I really do feel sceptical whether Latimer, &c. . . . . I will do myself the justice to say, that those doubts give me pain, and that I hope more reading will in some degree dispel them."

For a specimen of positive lies the following may serve : " The reformers whom Froude calls ' snobs,' and ' such a set;'" (p. 301,) and we are referred as authorities for these phrases to Froude's Remains, p. 393 and p. 484. It seems scarcely credible, but p. 393 of the book alluded to contains but two lines, which we reprint accurately.

" Also, why do you praise Ridley? do you know sufficient good about him to counterbalance the fact?"

---

* In connexion with this subject, we desire to call attention, and certainly it scarcely deserves even such notice, to the sermon preached by Mr. Baptist Noel for the Reformation Society during the last religious saturnalia of " the May meetings." It is printed in " the Pulpit," but bears evident marks of authenticity.

The rest of the page 393, consists of a note wholly translated from Pascal, and p. 484 does not exist in any of the four volumes of Froude's Remains, except the last, which consists of the Becket Papers alone! The expressions attributed to Froude, "Snobs, &c." are *invented* by the biographer of Bonner, and the references given for them are *false*.

More than once the historian of Bonner quotes a sentence from Froude: "The Prayer-Book has no greater claim to our deference than the Missal, and the Breviary in a far greater degree;" the inference sought to be established being, that Froude preferred the Roman services to our own Prayer-Book. Let us see this. He is objecting (Remains, vol. i. p. 401) to an expression used by another, which made the teaching of the Church and the teaching of the Prayer-Book equivalent; and he supposes a layman inquiring, why these are represented as identical? If it be replied, because the clergy since its enactment have assented to the Prayer-Book, he thinks that it may be rejoined, " if so, then the Breviary and Missal have an equal claim upon the deference of *those who receive it*, as the Prayer-Book has upon the deference *of those who receive it*, merely upon this alleged ground of the assent of their own teachers, viz. the English clergy." It is obvious that Froude's object was to show that the Prayer-Book was binding upon the laity in doctrine, not because it was compiled by such and such men; not because it is protected by statute law; not because it was sanctioned by convocation; not because it is assented to by the clergy; but because it is the record of apostolic teaching. The Breviary and Missal have assent and authority, and therefore are equal on these grounds to the Prayer-Book; they have superior antiquity, and therefore have claims thus far in a higher degree; but to say all this, is not to say that the Prayer-Book is inferior to the Breviary and Missal, for it would be at once replied, that it exhibits apostolic teaching better than they do, which Froude does not deny. He does not object to the claims of the Prayer-Book *upon us;* he only says, that his correspondent had placed these claims on an insufficient ground.

One of the most revolting passages in this abominable book occurs at p. 298. The writer's object is to argue against prayers for the dead. He feigns himself in sleep, " in deep sleep." " I was in the spirit, methought, with him of Patmos;" and he goes on to travestie the almost unutterable glories of " the heavens opened " in the very words of St. John's vision. We dare not quote it. He and Mrs. Pierce must both parody the splendours of the Apocalyptic vision. Suffice it to say, he pretends to see the throne of God, and "the Lamb that was slain," to hear the voices of the saints, and then to behold the Blessed Virgin " blushing" at the prayers offered to her. He represents himself, under the assumed character of course, as a witness of the Romish saints occupying the throne of the Mediator! The deep disgust with which our readers must receive this passage, warrants us to close this notice of one of the most flagitious books we ever read, with some abruptness; though, in connexion with this atrocious scene, as a specimen of its writer's historical accuracy, (and many such might be adduced,) we may observe that Cardinal Borromeo, the canonized Archbishop of Milan, who died in 1594, is represented as "remaining on the throne of the Mediator," when "the soul of Gardiner appeared among the spirits of the newly dead;" Gardiner having died in 1555.

We had almost omitted to state that an unwarrantable liberty is taken with the name of the present Bishop of London in this book. His lordship will know how to estimate the good taste, as well as reverence for his high office, which could address him in such insolent words as these, supposed to be the dedication of the "Tractarian British Critic."

"It is not probable that your lordship's graver studies have ever been interrupted by the perusal of Lalla Rookh, which I read when I was a young man. There is a person in it named Fadladeen. Some unknown correspondent declares, my lord, that he will denounce me and my brethren, as the Fadladeens of theology and of the Church. 'You are as unable,' he writes, 'to understand and value the greatness of heart of the martyred compilers of the English Prayer-Book, as Fadladeen was to appreciate the poetry of Feramorz. *Your schism shall be Fadladeenery, and your sect shall be the sect of the Fadladeens.*' Here the letter ended. From this fate I trust your lordship will preserve us."—*Dedication*, p. xxii—xxv.

It will be observed, as we have already said, that our business was not with Bishop Bonner; whether his character has been justly or unjustly estimated, is no affair of ours at present; we have no desire to bring him on the stage. Foxe is the chief authority of those who abuse him; and Foxe, thanks to Mr. Maitland, is now estimated at his right value; but it is only fair to suggest that Collier should be read as well as Foxe, by all who desire to know something about one who played no inconsiderable part in that wonderful, and yet inexplicable, drama of the Reformation. Old Antony à Wood preserves one or two odd anecdotes of him, which represent Bonner in a cheerful light under trying circumstances; and as they have been of course studiously concealed by his fictitious biographer, we will relieve the tedium of an unpleasant article by extracting them.

"Afterwards being committed to the Marshalsea, he continued there in a cheerful and contented condition till the time of his death; which therefore made those that did not care for him, say that he was like Dionysius, the tyrant of Syracuse, who being cruel and peremptory in prosperity, was both patient and pleasant in adversity. 'Tis said that Dr. Bonner being sometimes allowed liberty, he would walk, as his occasions served, in the street, and sometimes wearing his tippet; one begged it of him in scoff 'to line a coat;' 'No,' saith he, 'but thou shalt have a fool's head to line thy cap. To another that bid him 'Good morrow, Bishop Quondam,' he straight replied, 'Farewell, Knave Semper.' When another person showed the said Bonner his own picture in the Acts and Monuments of the Church, &c. commonly called the Book of Martyrs, on purpose to vex him, he merrily laughed and said, 'A vengeance on the fool! how could he get my picture drawn so right?'"

Poems, chiefly of Early and Late Years. By W. WORDSWORTH. Moxon. 1842.

The Pilgrim of Glencoe, and other Poems. By THOMAS CAMPBELL. Moxon. 1842.

Poems. By ALFRED TENNYSON. Moxon. 1842.

Poems from Eastern Sources: the Stedfast Prince, &c. By R. C. TRENCH. Moxon. 1842.

The Baptistery. By the Rev. T. WILLIAMS, *Author of " The Cathedral."* Rivingtons. 1841.

Poems. By the Rev. T. WHYTEHEAD, M.A. Rivingtons. 1842.

Luther: a Poem. By the Rev. R. MONTGOMERY, M.A. Baisler. 1842.

Luther, or Rome and the Reformation. Seeley & Burnside. 1841.

The Progress of Religion: a Poem. By Sir A. EDMONSTONE. Burns. 1842.

WHETHER or not the year 1842 be one of fresh hope,—whether or not a spring of promise for England be coming up along with it, one auspicious omen, at least, has marked its earlier half. Our poets have begun to sing, and sweet voices that have been silent long, are making themselves be heard anew. It was not to be expected that the exuberance of poetry truly such which marked the opening of the century, could be continued throughout it. A period of pause seemed the natural alternation from the loud chorus of its first twenty years,—a rest in no way undesirable, for it gave us time to ponder, to select, to measure, and to fathom. But we were never of those who thought that the fountains of poetry were in any danger of being dried up. Such seemed a strange result to anticipate from the everywhere increasing relish for it—from the greater development of the imagination visible everywhere, down even, we think, to fireside talk, from the greater earnestness of men's purposes, and the greater significance of events. We are all, we think, thirsting more than our fathers, for the deep, the spiritual, for order and harmony, for beauty and truth; and, therefore, however arid and barren the soil around us may appear, we feel sure that water will gush even out of the dry rock, in which we may slake that thirst.

Nor let it be forgotten, that during the last twelve years, in which the greater poets have been either all but mute, or, alas! silenced by the stern summons of death, there have every now and then appeared successors to them, not altogether unworthy,—men, on whom we may not say that their mantle has fallen, but who yet have caught a portion of their spirit, and so give us a fair promise for the future. The time seems at hand for them seriously to begin fulfilling that promise. The list at the head of our article, among which are the names of several true poets (and a couple who are only placed in such company for a reason that will appear by and by), is a very remarkable and interesting one. It seems as if it belonged to two different periods. It makes us look both to the past and the future. It unites two separate generations. Wordsworth and Campbell began their poetical career, as we now speak, long ago. Their fame was established considerably before the gentlemen with whom we at present find them had appeared in this nether world. Their reputations were considerable before several had existed, which subsequently have waxed great, and then died off. They were both poets of vigorous growth and firm root, long before the tropical shooting up of Byron; and here we find them having lived to see his fame wither and dwindle—to witness the rarity with which his name is heard around us—and the slight influence he now exercises on the mind of youth, over which he was once almost omnipotent. Here we find them at the head of a list of poets in the third generation from themselves.

We will begin with the name which is first in our list, and we need not say foremost in our minds—a name which is now separated, not only from all ordinary ones, but from all which do not belong to the very first class. It is altogether idle now to indite an eulogium on the genius of Wordsworth. The flippant criticisms with which his works were once assailed, are scarcely remembered; while he himself has become an English classic, of whom no man of ordinary education, none but the redoubtable Coroner for Middlesex, would like to profess himself other than an admirer. Nor need we undertake what has now been made so often—an investigation of his peculiar gifts and character in reference to their broader distinctions. Something yet remains, however, to be done. His later works require some vindication. Such, indeed, is now the sway of his name, that we do not think they have been ever attacked in print; but nevertheless, we doubt much whether his warmest admirers do not feel considerably dissatisfied with them, while not a few, we suspect, proclaim in conversation, that they ought never to have been written—that the great poet (by no fault of his own, but in the mere course of nature) has outlived his powers, and ought now to be contented with the immortality which awaits the works he composed while possessing those powers, instead of seeking to add to their amount.

Now, in answer to this, we will not pretend to attach, by any means, the same value to Mr. Wordsworth's later works that we do to those of his prime. We think that decided symptoms of senility showed themselves even before the publication of Yarrow Revisited; and still more, of course, since. But we do not quarrel with nature. We do not complain that Mr. Wordsworth's ear seems duller,—his power of adapting his words to it less perfect,—his language less clear and flexible, than aforetime, any more than that his joints are stiffer—his limbs less vigorous than they once were. Both decays must come of necessity. He has arrived at old age; and we see old age in his writing, just as we probably should, were we so favoured, in his gait and his limbs, stately and vigorous as they are yet reported to be. What then, if both in body and mind, his be " an old age serene and bright?" His poetry now is not what it was when he and Coleridge stalked over the Quantock hills together; but it is such as we can have from no one else. It is exactly what Wordsworth's should be in his old age. With him, mind (in regard to the highest matters), and heart, and soul, have all been making progress; and we yet hang on his lips for manifestations of wisdom and beauty, which come from him as from the patriarch of our time. The marvel would be greater, but the moral effect, we think, less, could he now write in the pitch of Ruth, or the Song at the Feast of Brougham Castle.

But though we do not think that old age, and its accompanying stiffness of movement, need keep Mr. Wordsworth from writing new poems, it ought to hinder him from tampering with his old ones— a trick to which he has a most unhappy propensity. We would venture respectfully to suggest to him, that, after the lapse of a certain period, a man's compositions become nearly as objective to himself as to others; that he cannot re-produce the original impulse which called them into being, and that their particles, therefore, have got to adhere too closely to be meddled with, or disarranged. The last great edition of Mr. Wordsworth's works teems with new readings, nearly every one of which is deplored by his admirers; whose sentiments we are sure we represent when we entreat him to proclaim authoritatively the restoration of the old ones. Whether he does so or not, that restoration must take place. It is in their original form that many stanzas must remain in men's mouths and hearts.

A few examples will show how little Mr. Wordsworth has done for his verses, by re-touching them at so distant an interval from their original composition. In Ruth, the readers of the last edition will find a stanza, heralding some of the most splendid ones in the English language, which opens thus:—

> "He spake of plants that hourly change
> Their blossoms, through a boundless range
> Of intermingling hues."

Those who possess the earlier editions have the same stanza opening thus:—

> "He spake of plants divine and strange,
> That every hour their blossoms change
> Ten thousand lovely hues."

We think we need not say to which reading they will adhere.

In the same poem, the darling perhaps of all enthusiastic Wordsworthians, we find,

> "It was a fresh and glorious world,
> A banner bright that was unfurled
> Before me suddenly,"

transformed in the last edition into,

> "Before me shone a glorious world,
> Fresh as a banner bright, unfurled
> To music suddenly."

Of these, the former is spirited and impetuous, as like the supposed reality of the youth's impassioned conversation as metre can make it; the latter is more elaborate in its syntax, and therefore less suited to the context and the circumstances.

The following we hold to be a still profaner alteration. In the exquisite " Fountain," who knows not and who loves not this enchanting stanza—

> " Down to the vale this water steers,
> How merrily it goes;
> 'Twill murmur on a thousand years,
> And flow as now it flows?"

But, alas! we have lived to see its first line altered into the following tame one :—

> "No check, no stay, this streamlet fears."

Further down, in the same poem, we have,

> " The blackbird amid leafy trees,"

as a substitution for,

> "The blackbird in the summer breeze."

Again, one of the most wonderful sonnets ever written by Wordsworth, or by any one else, used to open, as with all Wordsworthians, we apprehend, it will continue to open, with a line which is absolutely magical—

> " It is a beauteous evening, calm and free."

This has undergone the following mutations. First it became,

> " Air sleeps, from strife or stir the clouds are free ;"

and then in the edition of 1840, we find it standing as follows :

> " A fairer face of evening cannot be."

Putting rhythm out of the question, either alteration seems to us an injury. Not merely sound, but thought is sacrificed; for how much of the expansive feeling awakened by a summer sunset,—of the emancipation from care, and bustle and confined localization,—of the spirituality of the hour,—and the *sensation*, not of a world, but an universe around one, is suggested in the original reading by the word *free*.

> " A harp is from his shoulder slung;
> He rests the harp upon his knee,
> And there in a forgotten tongue
> He warbles melody."

These have always struck us as most " harmonious numbers ;" but the harmony has been made to disappear by the following change, adopted, we suppose, to avoid what we cannot but consider the imaginary tautology of *warbles* and *melody*.

> " A harp is from his shoulder slung ;
> Resting the harp upon his knee,
> To words of a forgotten tongue
> He suits its melody."

This re-touching his former poems is, as we have said, the only part of his vocation from which we wish Mr. Wordsworth, now that he is old, to abstain. Let him write new ones as much and as abundantly as he will, and we engage to be thankful. We must ever delight in his voice, even although in the course of nature it may have lost a note or two. In him we think has indeed been fulfilled the promise of bearing fruit in old age, as the volume now before us most abundantly testifies.

Before proceeding to give our readers some account of it, we think it well not to enter, as we have already disclaimed doing, on the superfluous task of discussing generally the peculiar genius of a poet so well known and so deeply studied; but to say a few words on the subordinate mutations which his style has undergone. We say the *subordinate* mutations, for, as is sufficiently obvious, none of them ever impaired the identity of that style. The Wordsworth of 1820 had in many things altered his manner from the Wordsworth of 1800; but he was Wordsworth still. Amid all the range and variety of his writings,—up every gradation of his language, from the baldest severity to the most gorgeous decoration,—we know no poet who is always so peculiarly and unmistakeably himself and no one else. Who ever fails to see when a quotation is from him, even if he do not remember the passage? This test of true originality can be applied to Wordsworth more fully than to any one else; for no poet ever undertook such a variety of subjects and styles. The fountain must be far apart, from which such widely diverging streams have manifestly issued.

Consistently, however, with this identity of style, there is not only all the variety we have spoken of in Mr. Wordsworth's poetry, but the style itself, as we have said, has passed through certain mutations. Nor could it have done otherwise. As well might we try to stay the wheel of time altogether, as fasten ourselves down for the rest of our lives to the same precise manner of doing any one thing. Changes take place even in the most obstinately peculiar and unmistakeable hand-writings. But the transitions through which Mr. Wordsworth's style has passed in the course of half a century of active exercise are remarkable in this respect—that they are an epitome of the transitions through which all art must pass. Mr. Wordsworth's peculiar position in the history of poetry, his deep study, and comprehensive range therein, have naturally led to this. He is not only a poet, but he symbolizes poetry in general. A few words more will explain our meaning.

It seems a law in the progress of art, at least of sublime and religious art, that it should pass through three periods: one of severity, boldness, and depth; in which *execution* may be limited, but in which *sentiment* is predominant; in which there are no ornaments, except in so far as the main features are themselves so combined as to furnish such;—a second, in which, altogether obediently to the inspiring sentiment, and with no considerable loss or obscuration of feature and relief, there is a full blow of ornaments, where ornament is needed, and always, more or less, exactly as needed—which period is of course the perfection of the art or style;—lastly comes a time when ornament and execution have gone further perhaps than ever before, but in which they have, to some extent, supplanted depth, feature, and relief; a period in which, with more brilliancy, we have less sentiment than previously—less profound meaning—less that, coming from the depths of one heart, sounds the depths of another. The analogies of art might supply us with divers illustrations of this. Sometimes, as with Raphael and Wordsworth, we can trace the stages in an individual artist; at others, as in the history of Italian literature, and pointed Gothic architecture, in successive ages. Let us take the latter as supplying us with a very pleasing analogy to the progress of Wordsworth's style. His earlier compositions—those written previously and up to the opening of this century—may be compared in respect of pure, severe, and consistent grace, to early English architecture. Then followed a period, of which, in the case of Wordsworth, the limits are somewhat difficult to define, in which his mastery over the English language seemed absolute,—in which he was in such full possession of, and so little possessed by, his various poetical gifts, that ornament of every sort seemed at his command, exactly when, and exactly as, it was needed—ornament that relieved without ever obscuring the features of his work. This period, answering of course to decorated Gothic, may be comprised within the first fifteen years of the present century, and contains what we suppose all admit to be the poet's masterpieces, including the divine Excursion.* Much as has been said about that wonderful poem, we do not know that the exquisite grace and the transparent purity of the style have been noticed as they ought. The story of Ellen singularly illustrates what we mean; and so, above and beyond all, does the whole third book, *Despondency*. Then, to adhere to our analogy, came the period answering to perpendicular or florid Gothic. The first symptoms of Wordsworth's third manner appear in the odes to Lycoris, to Evening, and one or two similar ones. All his subsequent productions are marked by it: and just as he who is penetrated with love for Raphael's earlier works, gives a comparatively small place in his heart to the magnificent Transfiguration; or as he who has reverently paced the solemn aisles of Westminster or Amiens, feels, even amid the manifold beauties of King's or St. George's Chapel, that "there hath passed away a glory" from the art of temple-building; so do Mr. Wordsworth's disciples less delightedly recur to his later works, and less profoundly love them. They are ornate and polished to an extent that would astonish those, if any such yet remain, who imagine that it is a principle with Wordsworth to reject all orna-

---

* We are aware of the difficulty of dating the Excursion, as it must have been the labour of years. There is, however, internal evidence for classing a good deal of it in the period we have assigned.

ment. But the ornaments, while they are elegant, and varied, and delicate, are not, as aforetime, under the guidance of one governing idea; they are not features as well as ornaments; as in Henry VII.'s Chapel, we are distracted by them even while we admire them. This is peculiarly apparent, and the analogy peculiarly perfect, in the case of the Vernal Ode, the Odes to Evening, and Enterprise, and several others in the poet's third manner. The imagery is beautiful and distinct, finely cut, like the Tudor panellings and roses, but the whole is indistinct; we do not readily perceive nor livelily remember its main features, its outline, and scope; nor are we subdued, as in the earlier poems, into reverent love.

The analogy, however, would be incomplete, were not Mr. Wordsworth's third manner full of peculiar grace and beauty; and we have touched upon it now for the purpose of calling attention to that grace and beauty. There are numbers of poems, little known even by his fervent admirers, which alone would have earned fame for another man — poems highly courtly and ornate in their diction, and full of sweet and precious thought. Take the following as a specimen :—

> "Look at the fate of summer flowers,
> Which blow at daybreak, droop ere even song,
> And, griev'd for their brief date, confess that ours
> Measur'd by what we are and ought to be,
> Measur'd by all that trembling we foresee,
>   Is not so long.

> "If human life do pass away,
> Perishing yet more swiftly than the flower,—
> If we are creatures of a *Winter's* day,—
> What space hath virgin's beauty to disclose
> Her sweets, and triumph o'er the breathing rose?
>   Not even an hour!

> "The deepest grove, whose foliage hid
> The happiest lovers Arcady might boast,
> Could not the entrance of this thought forbid:
> Oh! be thou wise as they, soul-gifted maid!
> Nor rate too high what must so quickly fade,
>   So soon be lost.

> "Then shall love teach some virtuous youth
> ' To draw, out of the object of his eyes,'
> The while on thee they gaze in simple truth,
> Hues more exalted, a refined form,
> That dreads not age, nor suffers from the worm,
>   And never dies."

To this manner must be referred the Ecclesiastical Sketches, and the exquisite Triad: these, however, with the Odes to Lycoris, are, we presume, too well known to require notice here, our wish at present being to call attention to some of the beauties of Mr. Wordsworth's florid, which have hitherto, we think, escaped it, amid the broader features and bolder relief of his earlier styles. The ode "Composed upon an Evening of extraordinary

Splendour and Beauty," contains the following exquisitely adorned passages :—

> "Time was when field and watery cove
> With modulated echoes rang;
> While choirs of fervent angels sang
>   Their vespers in the grove;
> Or, crowning star-like each some sovran height,
> Warbled for heaven above, and earth below,
>   Strains suitable to both.
> Such holy rite, methinks, if audibly repeated now
> From hill or valley, could not move
> Sublimer transport, purer love,
> Than doth this silent spectacle—the gleam,
> The shadow, and the peace supreme.
>
> "No sound is utter'd, but a deep
> And solemn harmony pervades
> The hollow vale from steep to steep,
>   And penetrates the glades.
> Far distant images draw nigh,
> Call'd forth by wondrous potency
> Of beamy radiance, that imbues
> Whate'er it strikes with gem-like hues!
> In vision exquisitely clear,
> Herds range along the mountain side,
> And glistening antlers are descried,
>   And gilded flocks appear.
> Thine is the tranquil hour, purpureal eve!
> But long as god-like wish or hope divine
> Informs my spirit, ne'er can I believe
> That this magnificence is wholly thine.
> From worlds not quicken'd by the sun,
> A portion of the gift is won;
> An intermingling of heaven's pomp is spread
> On ground that British shepherds tread."

In the Vernal Ode, a *Bee* is surrounded by an amount of decoration, never lavished, surely, on so small a subject before. Here is a part only of the gleaming mantle of language which the poet has woven for her :—

> "And is she brought within the power
> Of vision? o'er this tempting flower
> Hovering until the petals stay
> Her flight, and take its voice away!
> Observe each wing! a tiny van!
> The structures of her laden thigh,
> How fragile! yet of ancestry
> Mysteriously remote and high—
> High as the imperial front of man;
> The roseate bloom on woman's cheek;
> The soaring eagle's curved beak;
> The white plumes of the floating swan;
> Old as the tiger's paw, the lion's mane
> Ere shaken by that mood of stern disdain,
> At which the desert trembles. Humming bee!
> Thy sting was needless then, perchance unknown;
> The seeds of malice were not sown;
> All creatures met in peace, from fierceness free,
> And no pride blended with their dignity.

> Tears had not broken from their source;
> Nor Anguish stray'd from her Tartarean den.
> The golden years maintain'd a course
> Not undiversified, though smooth and even:
> We were not mock'd with glimpse and shadow then;
> Bright seraphs mixed familiarly with men;
> And earth and stars composed an universal heaven."

We have quoted enough fully to illustrate our meaning, and afford some notion of the peculiar character of Mr. Wordsworth's writing in the third great epoch of his literary life; and if any, who in their admiration of the far superior beauties of his earlier styles, have hitherto overlooked, or perhaps even condemned his later, will read carefully, in addition to the poems from which we have been quoting, the Ode to Enterprise, the exquisite poem entitled Dion, and many others which we cannot name now, they will feel resigned to a change which came in the course of nature, and the necessary progress of art—a change which, indeed, in some degree, obscured much that was glorious, but which brought with it new charm of its own.

We must now proceed to the work more directly before us—that of giving our readers some account of Mr. Wordsworth's just published volume. Its title, "Poems chiefly of Early and Late Years," is one of peculiar interest in reference to the thoughts which have been engaging us; and in accordance with its promise, the collection will be found to span nearly the entire half century of the author's public existence as a poet. The first place in it is occupied by a poem, entitled Guilt and Sorrow, the original whole, as it seems, of which a very cherished favourite of ours, The Female Vagrant, has all along, unknown to us and the public, formed a part. Such a poem (we are speaking just now of the part) could not have borne transplanting or adaptation to anything for which it was not originally meant; but this has happily not been its fate. We have it here in the place which it all along has occupied in the poet's mind, and amid the objects with which he at the first surrounded it; objects, therefore, altogether congruous with itself, and informed by the same spirit. Perhaps it, and the whole poem to which we now find it belonging, forms the finest specimen of the severe graces of our author's earlier style; and it is dated 1793-4, and must therefore have been composed in his extreme youth! What a proof, in this point of view, it affords of the deep-seated originality of his mind! and how innate are the peculiar characteristics of his genius, if thus early in his career, with such vicious models around him as then found favour,—with no severe or deep criticism among men of letters to guide his taste,—with so little of English scholarship in others to aid in forming his style,—before, too, his acquaintance with that other great mind, which was destined afterwards to bring out so much of his own,—he could write a poem so pure from all tinsel and conventionality, so majestic in its simplicity, indicating such confidence in the truth of nature—in the power and the life that reside "in common things that round us lie." The following stanzas may give our readers some sample of those portions of the poem, which have hitherto been withheld from them:—

"The gathering clouds grew red with stormy fire,
   In streaks diverging wide and mounting high;
That inn he long had pass'd; the distant spire,
   Which oft as he look'd back had fix'd his eye,
   Was lost, though still he look'd, in the blank sky.
Perplex'd and comfortless he gaz'd around,
   And scarce could any trace of man descry,
Save corn-fields stretch'd and stretching without bound;
But where the sower dwelt was nowhere to be found.

"No tree was there, no meadow's pleasant green,
   No brook to wet his lip or soothe his ear;
Long files of corn-stacks here and there were seen,
   But not one dwelling-place his heart to cheer.
Some labourer, thought he, may perchance be near;
   And so he sent a feeble shout—in vain;
No voice made answer—he could only hear
Winds rustling over plots of unripe grain,
Or whistling through thin grass along the unfurrow'd plain.

"Long had he fancied each successive slope
   Conceal'd some cottage, whither he might turn
And rest; but now along heaven's darkening cope
   The crows rush'd by in eddies, homeward borne.
Thus warn'd, he sought some shepherd's spreading thorn
   Or hovel from the storm to shield his head,
But sought in vain; for now, all wild, forlorn,
And vacant, a huge waste around him spread;
The wet cold ground, he fear'd, must be his only bed."

* * * * * *

"All, all was cheerless to the horizon's bound;
   The weary eye—which, wheresoe'er it strays,
Marks nothing but the red sun's setting round,
   Or on the earth strange lines, in former days
Left by gigantic arms—at length surveys
   What seems an antique castle spreading wide;
Hoary and naked are its walls, and raise
Their brow sublime: in shelter there to bide
He turn'd, while rain pour'd down smoking on every side.

"Pile of Stone-henge! so proud to hint yet keep
   Thy secrets; thou that lov'st to stand and hear
The Plain resounding to the whirlwind's sweep;
   Inmate of lonesome Nature's endless year;
Even if thou saw'st the giant wicker rear
   For sacrifice its throngs of living men,
Before thy face did ever wretch appear,
Who in his heart had groan'd with deadlier pain
Than he who now at night-fall treads thy bare domain!

" Within that fabric of mysterious form,
  Winds met in conflict, each by turns supreme;
And, from its perilous shelter driven, through storm
And rain he wilder'd on, no moon to stream
From gulf of parting clouds one friendly beam,
Nor any friendly sound his footsteps led;
Once did the lightning's faint disastrous gleam
Disclose a naked guide-post's double head,
Sight which though lost at once a gleam of pleasure shed.

" No swinging sign-board creak'd from cottage elm
To stay his steps with faintness overcome;
'Twas dark and void as ocean's watery realm
Roaring with storms beneath night's starless gloom;
No gipsy cower'd o'er fire of furze or broom;
No labourer watched his red kiln glaring bright,
Nor taper glimmer'd dim from sick man's room;
Along the waste no line of mournful light
From lamp of lonely toll-gate stream'd athwart the night."
                                              Pp. 6, 11—13.

We wish we could quote the whole of the Address to the Clouds, which, we think, belongs to Mr. W.'s latest style. But the following extract is as much as we have room or time for; and, by the way, it is by much the greater part of the poem :—

" Speak, silent creatures.—They are gone, are fled,
Buried together in yon gloomy mass
That loads the middle heaven; and clear and bright
And vacant doth the region which they throng'd
Appear; a calm descent of sky conducting
Down to the unapproachable abyss,
Down to that hidden gulf from which they rose
To vanish—fleet as days and months and years,
Fleet as the generations of mankind,
Power, glory, empire, as the world itself,
The lingering world, when time hath ceased to be.
But the winds roar, shaking the rooted trees;
And see! a bright precursor to a train
Perchance as numerous, overpeers the rock
That sullenly refuses to partake
Of the wild impulse. From a fount of life
Invisible, the long procession moves
Luminous or gloomy, welcome to the vale,
Which they are entering, welcome to mine eye
That sees them, to my soul that owns in them,
And in the bosom of the firmament
O'er which they move, wherein they are contain'd,
A type of her capacious self and all
Her restless progeny.
                       A humble walk
Here is my body doom'd to tread, this path,
A little hoary line and faintly trac'd.
Work, shall we call it, of the shepherd's foot
Or of his flock?—joint vestige of them both.
I pace it unrepining, for my thoughts
Admit no bondage and my words have wings.
Where is the Orphean lyre, or Druid harp,
To accompany the verse? The mountain blast

> Shall be our *hand* of music; he shall sweep
> The rocks, and quivering trees, and billowy lake,
> And search the fibres of the caves, and they
> Shall answer, for our song is of the Clouds,
> And the wind loves them; and the gentle gales—
> Which by their aid re-clothe the naked lawn
> With annual verdure, and revive the woods,
> And moisten the parch'd lips of thirsty flowers—
> Love them; and every idle breeze of air
> Bends to the favourite burthen. Moon and stars
> Keep their most solemn vigils when the Clouds
> Watch also, shifting peaceably their place
> Like bands of ministering spirits, or when they lie,
> As if some Protean art the change had wrought,
> In listless quiet o'er the ethereal deep
> Scatter'd, a Cyclades of various shapes
> And all degrees of beauty. O ye Lightnings!
> Ye are their perilous offspring; and the Sun—
> Source inexhaustible of life and joy,
> And type of man's far-darting reason, therefore
> In old time worshipp'd as the god of verse,
> A blazing intellectual deity—
> Loves his own glory in their looks, and showers
> Upon that unsubstantial brotherhood
> Visions with all but beatific light.
> Enrich'd—too transient were they not renew'd
> From age to age, and did not, while we gaze
> In silent rapture, credulous desire,
> Nourish the hope that memory lacks not power
> To keep the treasure unimpair'd. Vain thought!
> Yet why repine, created as we are
> For joy and rest, albeit to find them only
> Lodg'd in the bossom of eternal things?"—Pp. 86—88.

As usual in Mr. Wordsworth's volumes, we have a considerable sprinkling of sonnets—a branch of art which he has carried further than any other English writer. There is a series to Italy, which we wish all thoughtful Italians could see and deeply ponder. They deserve to be embalmed along with Filicaia's series to the same land. We can only present our readers with one of them.

> " As leaves are to the tree whereon they grow
> And wither, every human generation
> Is to the Being of a mighty nation,
> Lock'd in our world's embrace through weal and woe;
> Thought that should teach the zealot to forego
> Rash schemes, to abjure all selfish agitation,
> And seek through noiseless pains and moderation
> The unblemish'd good they only can bestow.
> Alas! with most, who weigh futurity
> Against time present, passion holds the scales:
> Hence equal ignorance of both prevails,
> And nations sink; or, struggling to be free,
> Are doom'd to flounder on, like wounded whales
> Toss'd on the bosom of a stormy sea."—P. 43.

There is much besides in the volume on which we could say a great deal, but we must hasten to the performance with which it closes—the tragedy of the Borderers. The public have long been aware, through Coleridge and Hazlitt, that in his earlier days, Mr. Wordsworth wrote a tragedy—and three or four lines in it quoted by the latter, are, we doubt not, familiar to many of our readers. It was not generally believed, from a note at the end of this volume, until within the last month or two, that its author had any thoughts of publishing it. There are not many men who could have afforded to allow such a production to lie unknown among their papers; for, with all its faults, of which we dare say no one is more sensible than Mr. Wordsworth himself, who is probably well aware that his genius is not dramatic, it is a most extraordinary production. The plot is, as we expected, defective; the scenery, encumbered by more of the picturesque than suits that branch of art, and in other respects, the action is faulty; but it is full of power and passion,* as the following extracts may serve to show:—

> "OSWALD.   It may be,
> That some there are, squeamish half-thinking cowards,
> Who will turn pale upon you, call you murderer,
> And you will walk in solitude among them.
> A mighty evil for a strong-built mind!
> Join twenty tapers of unequal height,
> And light them joined, and you will see the less
> How 'twill burn down the taller; and they all
> Shall prey upon the tallest. Solitude!
> The eagle lives in solitude!
>   MARMADUKE.   Even so,
> The sparrow so on the house-top, and I,
> The weakest of God's creatures, stand resolved
> To abide the issue of my act, alone.
>   Osw. Now would you? and for ever?—My young friend,
> As time advances, either we become
> The prey or masters of our own past deeds.
> Fellowship we *must* have, willing or no;
> And if good angels fail, slack in their duty,
> Substitutes, turn our faces where we may,
> Are still forthcoming: some which, though they bear
> Ill names, can render no ill services,
> In recompense for what themselves required.
> So meet extremes in this mysterious world,
> And opposites thus melt into each other.
>   MAR. Time, since Man first drew breath, has never moved
> With such a weight upon his wings as now;
> But they will soon be lightened.
>   Osw.   Ay, look up—
> Cast round you your mind's eye, and you will learn
> Fortitude is the child of Enterprise:
> Great actions move our admiration, chiefly

---

* By the way, how much the impassioned character of Mr. Wordsworth's poetry has been overlooked by critics! What is there in Byron to compare with the opening books of the Excursion in this respect?

Because they carry in themselves an earnest
That we can suffer greatly.
  Mar.   Very true.
  Osw. Action is transitory—a step, a blow,
The motion of a muscle—this way or that—
'Tis done, and in the after vacancy
We wonder at ourselves like men betrayed:
Suffering is permanent, obscure and dark,
And shares the nature of infinity.
  Mar. Truth—and I feel it.
  Osw.   What! if you had bid
Eternal farewell to unmingled joy,
And the light dancing of the thoughtless heart;
It is the toy of fools, and little fit
For such a world as this. The wise abjure
All thoughts whose idle composition lives
In the entire forgetfulness of pain.
—I see I have disturbed you.
  Mar.   By no means.
  Osw. Compassion!—pity!—pride can do without them;
And what if you should never know them more!
He is a puny soul who, feeling pain,
Finds ease because another feels it too.
If e'er I open out this heart of mine
It shall be for a nobler—to teach
And not to purchase puling sympathy.
—Nay, you are pale.
  Mar.   It may be so.
  Osw.   Remorse—
It cannot live with thought; think on, think on,
And it will die. What! in this universe,
Where the least things control the greatest, where
The faintest breath that breathes can move a world,
What! feel remorse, where, if a cat had sneezed,
A leaf had fallen, the thing had never been
Whose very shadow gnaws us to the vitals.

   *   *   *   *   *

  Marmaduke (*both returning.*) The dead have but one face.
And such a man—so meek and unoffending— (*To himself.*)
Helpless and harmless as a babe: a man,
By obvious signal to the world's protection,
Solemnly dedicated—to decoy him!—
  Idonea. Oh, had you seen him living!—
  Marm.   I (so filled
With horror is this world) am unto thee
The thing most precious, that it now contains:
Therefore through me alone must be revealed
By whom thy parent was destroyed, Idonea!
I have the proofs!—
  Idon.   O miserable father!
Thou didst command me to bless all mankind;
Nor to this moment, have I ever wished
Evil to any living thing; but hear me,
Hear me, ye Heavens!—(*kneeling*)—may vengeance haunt the fiend
For this most cruel murder: let him live
And move in terror of the elements;
The thunder send him on his knees to prayer
In the open streets, and let him think he sees,

If e'er he entereth the house of God,
The roof, self-moved, unsettling o'er his head;
And let him, when he would lie down at night,
Point to his wife the blood-drops on his pillow!

MARM. My voice was silent, but my heart hath joined thee.

IDON. (*leaning on* MARM.) Left to the mercy of that man!
How could he call upon his child!—O friend! [*Turns to* MARM.
My faithful true and only comforter.

MARM. Ay, come to me and weep. (*He kisses her.*)
(*To* ELDRED) Yes, varlet, look,
The devils at such sights do clap their hands [ELDRED *retires*

IDON. Thy vest is torn, thy cheek is deadly pale; *alarmed.*
Hast thou pursued the monster?

MARM. I have found him.—
Oh! would that thou hadst perished in the flames!

IDON. Here art thou, then can I be desolate?—

MARM. There was a time, when this protecting hand
Availed against the mighty; never more
Shall blessings wait upon a deed of mine.

IDON. Wild words for me to hear, for me, an orphan,
Committed to thy guardianship by Heaven;
And, if thou hast forgiven me, let me hope,
In this deep sorrow, trust, that I am thine
For closer care;—here is no malady. [*Taking his arm.*

MARM. There, *is* a malady—
(*Striking his heart and forehead*) And here, and here,
A mortal malady.—I am accurst:
All nature curses me, and in my heart
Thy curse is fixed; the truth must be laid bare.
It must be told, and borne. I am the man,
(Abused, betrayed, but how it matters not)
Presumptuous above all that ever breathed,
Who, casting as I thought a guilty person
Upon Heaven's righteous judgment, did become
An instument of fiends. Through me, through me,
Thy Father perished.

IDONEA. Perished—by what mischance?"

Pp. 344—347, 386—389.

The next name on our list is that of Campbell, who, like Wordsworth, had achieved greatness before the present generation saw the light, or many of its highest reputations were established. Not that in thus classing him with Wordsworth, we can be understood to treat the two as in any way equal; though a true and most original poet, Campbell impresses us with no sense of the transcendent greatness we have hitherto been contemplating. And in this respect, he fatally differs from Wordsworth, that his old age is not, as regards poetry at least, serene and bright; that the senility of his verses is unredeemed by any great merit; that, in short, we should greatly prefer his abandoning poetry altogether. Though not, as we have already intimated, of the first class, his former writings approved him a true poet, and in the eager and more impetuous ode, he was original and without a rival. With that let him be content. Hohenlinden, and O'Connor's Child, The Mariners of England, and the Battle of the Baltic, must live as long as the English language; and even a more than ordinarily craving ambition might well be content with the immortality thus ensured. Perhaps it is in the very nature of a lyrical genius of the particular kind displayed in those noble songs, quick, impetuous, flashing, and sensuous, to demand a young temperament for its exercise. At all events it seems to have been so in the case of Mr. Campbell, whose verses have exhibited a gradual declension as he has got later into life, till at last we get to this dismal " Pilgrim of Glencoe." Why it ever saw the light, it might puzzle the most acute diver into motives to find out. *Theodric* was a sad falling off from Gertrude of Wyoming; but, after the first burst of disappointment was over, people began to see that the tale was by no means without merit,—that a spirit of sweetness and refinement reigned throughout,—that amid all its feebleness of outline, and slovenliness of execution, the true poet continually appeared; but we cannot fancy that any maturer judgment than our present will enable us to find merit in the Pilgrim of Glencoe. There is hardly a gleam of interest in the tale, though the hero at one time is within an ace of being murdered, and hardly a ray of poetry in the telling it, though its scene is laid in one of the sublimest spots of the earth. But if there be neither interest in the tale, nor poetry in the telling it, why was it published? Possibly to give vent to the author's political feelings, for, be it known to our readers, it is a *Whig* performance. Now, as Mr. Campbell has always been at least a Whig, this circumstance by itself may neither surprise nor pain them, even should they be Tories. But it will surprise and pain them to find the poet, in other days so delicately refined, expressing himself thus of an old Highland savage, who entertains a purpose of murdering his guest :—

> " Yet Norman had fierce virtues; that would *mock*
> Cold-blooded Tories of the modern stock,
> Who starve the breadless poor with fraud and cant,—
> He slew and saved them from the pangs of want."

A pleasant and a courteous way of announcing political disagreement, to be sure!

But we will not part on bad terms with one to whose earlier works we owe such a debt of gratitude. In spite of the utter imbecility of the principal piece in this collection, and the (to us distressingly) Anacreontic character of one of its shorter contents, there are things in it somewhat worthier of Mr. Campbell's fame and his genius. *The Child and Hind* is so sweetly told, that we can even forgive the most portentous piece of bad English we have lately encountered; a party in search of a child being called " the *child-exploring* band;" an expression which conveys to our minds rather the thought of *dissecting*, than of looking for a child. And the verses to Cora Linn are so beautiful, that our readers must share our pleasure in them.

CORA LINN, OR THE FALLS OF THE CLYDE.
Written on revisiting it in 1837.

The time I saw thee, Cora, last,
'Twas with congenial friends;
And calmer hours of pleasure past
My memory seldom sends.

It was as sweet an Autumn day
As ever shone on Clyde,
And Lanark's orchards all the way
Put forth their golden pride;

Ev'n hedges, busk'd in bravery,
Look'd rich that sunny morn;
The scarlet hip and blackberry
So prank'd September's thorn.

In Cora's glen the calm how deep!
That trees on loftiest hill
Like statues stood, or things asleep,
All motionless and still.

The torrent spoke, as if his noise
Bade earth be quiet round,
And give his loud and lonely voice
A more commanding sound.

His foam, beneath the yellow light
Of noon, came down like one
Continuous sheet of jaspers bright,
Broad rolling by the sun.

Dear linn! let loftier falling floods
Have prouder names than thine;
And king of all, enthron'd in woods,
Let Niagara shine.

Barbarian, let him shake his coasts
With reeking thunders far,
Extended like th' array of hosts
In broad, embattled war!

His voice appals the wilderness;—
Approaching thine, we feel
A solemn, deep melodiousness,
That needs no louder peal.

More fury would but disenchant
Thy dream-inspiring din;
Be thou the Scottish Muse's haunt,
Romantic Cora Linn!

The remaining poets in our list must be reserved for next month.

ON THE DIVISION OF VERSES IN THE BIBLE.

(Continued from page 469.)

WE are now come to the consideration of the division of verses which prevailed in early manuscripts of the Latin Bibles. We have already seen that Jerome divided the books of Chronicles into colons, or members, to prevent, as he says, confusion amid so many proper names,* as he had already divided the prophetical books into colons and commas, or greater and lesser sections, which he informs us he did in imitation of a similar custom which prevailed in regard to the Greek and Latin orators.† He further acquaints us that he had found the metrical books already so written; that is, as we have already observed, divided into stanzas and hemistichs. It is quite evident that there was no appearance of the present division into verses in the Hebrew copies in Jerome's time, or he would, doubtless, have noticed it in some way; nor does it appear that this learned father introduced any division whatever into the other books of Scripture.

We must not omit to say, that Leusden goes so far as to maintain that Jerome states elsewhere that he adopted his divisions from the Hebrew; but as we have not been able to discover this in any part of Jerome's writings, we are inclined to think it a hasty assertion of Leusden's, arising from his zeal for the great antiquity and even the inspiration of the present Hebrew division into verses. On the contrary, as Jerome expressly asserts that he was himself the author of this division, it seems almost certain, as we have already observed, that no such distinction existed in his time in the Hebrew copies. It is also evident that the division of Jerome is quite different from the Hebrew. For instance, in the two first Hebrew alphabetical divisions in the book of Lamentations, there is a verse to each letter, while Jerome divides the same sentence with that in the Hebrew into three verses, and sometimes more.

In the fourth alphabetical division the Masorites have one, while Jerome has three verses. Here the verses are somewhat shorter than in the former; but in the third alphabet they both agree, which could not possibly have been otherwise, as they all begin with the same letter.

---

* " Et quod nunc Verba dierum interpretatus sum ; idcirco feci, ut inextricabiles moras et silvam nominum quæ scriptorum confusa sunt vitio, sensuumque labyrinthos, per versuum cola digererem." *Præf. in Paral.*
" Monemusque lectorem, ut silvam Heb. nominum et distinctionem per membra divisas diligens scriptor conservat, ne et noster labor et ipsius studium pereat." Jerome, *Preface to Joshua.*

† "Nemo, cum prophetas versibus videret esse descriptos, metro eos existimet apud Hebræos ligari et aliquid simile habere de Psalmis et operibus Salomonis, sed quod in Demosth. et Tullio fieri solet, ut per cola scribantur et commata, qui utique prosa non versu conscripserunt, nos quoque utilitati legentium providentes, interpretationem novam novâ scribendi genere distinximus."—Jerome's *Preface to Isaiah.*
Jerome herein imitates the Hexapla of Origen. In the Hexapla this plan was adopted for the facility of comparing the different versions.

Again, in the 110th and 111th psalms, the Masorites reckon but half the number of verses that Jerome does. Jerome begins each of his verses with a letter of the alphabet, while the Masorites have condensed the two invariably into one.* They both agree in the 118th psalm, nor could they avoid it, for each letter has eight masoretic verses attached to it, making in the whole psalm one hundred and seventy-six verses. Neither could the Masorites and Jerome disagree in the length of the verses, for each of the eight commences with the same letter as the first. In the 144th psalm, by reason of the length of the verses, the Masorites did not put two of Jerome's into one. Here, besides the soph pasuk, they put the athnac or colon, which they did not find in the 110th and 111th psalms, for the verses in these are short and have but one member.

In the 145th psalm the verse is wanting in the Hebrew which follows the 13th, " Fidelis Dominus . . ." to " suis ;" but that it has been lost from the Hebrew is evident, both from the context and from the Septuagint as well as the Vulgate. Each verse, in fact, of the 145th psalm commences with a letter; but after the 13th verse, which commences with מ, and when the next should of course commence with a נ, it passes over this letter and proceeds with a ס samech.

Jerome has, after the Seventy, divided the third masoretic verse of the first psalm into three. Also the fourth verse of the fifth psalm commences with " Quoniam ad te oraho," but the Masorites refer these words to the third verse. The commencement of the fifth verse, " Nunc astabo tibi et videbo," is the conclusion of the fourth masoretic verse, and so goes on to the ninth. Then Jerome divides the tenth masoretic verse into two, and joins the beginning of the eleventh to the second. In the 12th verse they again agree, but before quitting this they differ, for the greater part of it is attached to the next verse. In the thirteenth, the commencement of the masoretic verse is the end of the twelfth, or the fourteenth of Jerome. Jerome also refers the word " Dominus " to the following verse, the Masorites to the preceding. Finally, the Masorites divide the whole psalm into thirteen, Jerome into fifteen verses. Father Morin observes, that Jerome joined in one the 14th and 15th verses of the book of Genesis, as well as the 17th and 18th, and that he did not separate the 30th from the 29th precisely in the same way as the Masorites did. The divisions of the Septuagint are not only different from the Hebrew, but from the other Greek versions. From all this the inference seems clear, that at this time the Hebrew text was not marked by any divisions. (See Morinus, p. 497.)

It is by no means certain, however, that any manuscripts of the Latin have come down to us written as Jerome left them. Croius † maintains that Jerome used nearly the same division with the He-

---

* Except in the last two verses of each, which form three hemistichs in the Hebrew.

† See Jerome's Commentary on Isaiah and Correspondence with the Virgin Eustochium.

brews, founding his reasons on Jerome's division of the verses in Romans iii. We shall only observe on this point of the argument that the ancient stichometry of the ante-Hieronymian psalms was more copious than that contained in the manuscripts and in the printed editions of the Latin Vulgate. Jerome reckons eight verses of the fourteenth psalm,* as enumerated by St. Paul in his quotation therefrom in the third chapter of the Epistle to the Romans,† while these form but three, according to our present division. Martianay, however, informs us that the remainder is found divided as follows in an ancient St. Germain manuscript of the old Latin:—

> Sepulchrum patens est guttur eorum
> Linguis suis dolose agebant
> Venenum aspidum sub labris eorum
> Quorum os maledictione et amaritudine plenum est
> Veloces pedes eorum ad effundendum sanguinem
> Contritio et infelicitas in viis eorum
> Et viam pacis non cognoverunt
> Non est timor Dei ante oculos eorum.

In the same manner also the thirteenth verse of the eighteenth Psalm formed three verses in the old Latin, which had been formed after the Septuagint version.‡ It may seem probable to some, from Jerome's preface to the Book of Job, where the words cited by him, "Pereat dies," &c. and "Idcirco ipse me reprehendo, et ago penitentiam in favillâ et cinere," form in each instance one of our present verses; that this metrical book was thus divided before his time; and that he followed this division: but in the book of Daniel, iii. 17, he cites a verse according to the more ancient and shorter stichometrical arrangement. He also on one occasion gives the name of *capitulum* to the passage, Genesis xxxvi. 14, which makes exactly one verse in our present Bibles. Martianay labours to prove that Jerome applied the term comma to denote a shorter period than the colon, inasmuch as he speaks of colons and commas together, in describing his division of the prophetical books, but of colons alone in speaking of the larger periods into which he had divided the works written in prose; and they are found thus differently divided in the manuscripts from which Martianay printed his edition of them. He therefore thinks that Jerome used in this instance the word *comma* in a different sense from that in which he afterwards applies it in a more general sense to that portion of scripture which comprises the greater part of the last chapter of the book of Job in our present Bibles. This is also the opinion of Croius, Suicer, Montfaucon, and several others; while

---

* The 14th Psalm has in the ancient Roman psalter twelve verses, but in our division only seven; but twenty-four στίχοι are enumerated in the old vulgar Latin.

† See Jerome's Epistle to Sunnia and Fretela.

‡ Jerome calls " grando et carbones ignis," one verse. He makes mention of this same kind of verses, Ezek. xxi. and Isaiah lxiii. He also observes that there were eight hundred verses wanting in the old Latin version of the Book of Job.—See his Preface to Job.

some, among whom is Jahn, maintain that Jerome invariably uses the word *comma* as including a larger period than the colon.*

Jerome observes, in his Preface to the Book of Job, that this book commences with prose, then glides into verse, and finishes again in prose, in which form the work appears in several Hebrew manuscripts, and might have so existed in manuscripts in Jerome's time. However this may be, we presume that it will be now evident to the reader that from all the information which we can derive from Jerome, the present Hebrew division into verses was unknown to this learned father.

Perhaps there is no work of the ancients from which we can more accurately learn the nature of the ancient verses in the Latin church, than from the Speculum, or Mirror of St. Augustine. It is evident from this work that the whole Bible, both in the Old and New Testament, was in his time divided into a species of verses, corresponding most probably with the στίχοι of the Greeks. We shall now give *all* the examples which bear on this point from the Speculum, by which we shall be enabled to come to a better notion of what Augustine's verses were than by merely adopting the less troublesome plan of taking a specimen from the division of the Psalms, with which former writers have contented themselves.

The first example is from Leviticus, where Augustine having cited chap. xix. first part of ver. 3, " Ye shall fear every man his mother and his father," he adds, " and after *one* verse, Nolite converti ad idola, nec deos conflatiles faciatis nobis," which words form part of our, or the Masoretic, fourth verse. Again, ver. 29, he adds " after one verse, Ego Dominus ; ne declinetis ad magos, nec ab hariolis aliquid sciscitemini, ut polluamini per eos; Ego Dominus vester, &c." to the end of the 37th verse, where he commences with part of chap. xx.

In Psalm xxvi. after citing " Lux mea," &c. (viz. the first and second verses, according to the present notation,) he adds, " and after four verses, Si steterint adversus hæc," &c. viz. the third verse, or according to other enumerations, the fifth.

Psalm xxxiii. after citing the fifteenth verse, he adds, " and after seven verses, Juxta est," or our eighteenth verse.

Psalm xciv. after citing the 6th verse, Augustine adds, " after two verses," citing the present eighth verse.

Psalm xcv. ver. 3, he adds, " and after six verses," and then cites our seventh verse.

Psalm xcvi. after citing the words, " Qui ... malum," (part of

---

* " Porro a verbis Job, in quibus ait, pereat dies in qua natus sum, et nox in qua dictum est conceptus est homo, usque ad eum locum, ubi ante finem voluminis scriptum est; idcirco ipse me reprehendo, et ago penitentiam in favilla et cinere; hexametri versus sunt; dactylo spondeoque currentes, et propter linguæ idioma crebro recipientes et alios pedes non earundem syllabarum sed eorundem temporum. Interdum quoque rythmus ipse dulcis et tinnulus fertur numeris pedum lege solutis: quod metrici magis quam simplex lector intelligunt. A supradicto autem versu usque ad finem libri, parvum coma quod remanet prosa oratione continetur."

verse 10,) he adds, " after three verses," and cites our present twelfth verse.

Psalm xcix. ver. 3, he observes, " after one verse," and then cites our fourth verse, which occurs in the Vulgate in the middle of the fourth section. It is evident that the " one verse" to which he here refers is comprised in the words, " Populus ejus, et oves pascuæ ejus."

Psalm cxi. v. 1, Augustine cites our fifth verse " after five verses."

Psalm cxv. " after three verses" he cites our eighth.

Psalm cxvii. after citing the fifth verse, he adds, " and after five verses," and then gives what constitutes our eighth and ninth verses; and again, " after eight verses" he cites our fourteenth.

Psalm cxviii. (the 119th psalm in the Hebrew) after citing the 48th verse, he adds, " after four verses," and then cites part of our 51st verse, " Yet have I not declined from thy laws."

In the following table of Augustine's quotations, we have, in order to save space, as well as for the convenience of our readers, instead of giving the words quoted by Augustine from the Bible, referred the reader to the text itself, according to the present notation of chapters and verses, neither of which, the reader will bear in mind, were known in Augustine's time.

Ps. cxviii. v. 83 ...	" after two verses "	citing v. 85,* and
again......	" after two verses "	v. 87.
v. 105 ...	" after seven verses ".........	v. 109.
v. 115 ...	" after seven verses".........	v. 119.
v. 129 ...	" after two verses "	part of v. 131, " mandata tua."
v. 141 ...	" after three verses".........	v. 143.
v. 155 ...	" after six verses "	v. 157.
v. 159 ...	" after four verses "	v. 162.
v. 168 ...	" after eight verses".........	v. 173.
v. 174 ...	" after two verses "	v. 176.
Ps. cxxi. v. 6	" after two verses "	v. 8.
cxxxix. v. 9 ...	" after four verses "	v. 12.
cxl. v. 5.........	" after five verses "	v. 8.
cxli. v. 2	" after six verses "............	v. 6.
cxlii. v. 6	" after three verses".........	v. 8.
cxliv. v. 2	" after two verses "	v. 4.
cxlv. v. 7	" after three verses".........	middle of v. 10, "et sancti," &c.
cxlix. v. 3	" after two verses "	middle of v. 4, " exaltabat," &c.

* The following is the exact reading of the Benedictine edition, which will show a slight variation in Augustine's text, and at the same time explain the manner in which the above table is to be understood:—

"Præcepta tua non sum oblitus. Et post duos versus; Foderunt mihi superbi foveas, quæ non erant juxta legem tuam. Et post duos versus; Paulominus consumpserunt me in terrâ, ego autem non dimisi præcepta tua [viz. ver. 92]. Et post quinque versus; Nisi quod lex tua delectatio mea, fortè periissem in pressurâ meâ. In sempiternum non obliviscar præceptorum tuorum, quia per ipsa vivificasti me. Tuus ego sum, salva me, quoniem præcepta tua quæsivi, &c. to "meditatio mea," [viz. end of ver. 99]. " Et paulo post, ab omni semitâ malâ, &c." [ver. 101] to "lux semitæ meæ," [ver. 105]. " Et post quatuor versus, anima mea in manu meâ semper," to " Dei mei," [viz. end of ver. 115].

PROVERBS.

Ch. i. v. 8	" and after fourteen verses,"	citing v. 18, " Ipsi, &c."
v. 19 ...	" and after four verses,"...........	v. 22, " usque quo ... scientiam."
	" and after eleven verses,".......	v. 28, " Tunc, &c."
v. 33 ...	" and after three verses,".........	ch. ii. v. 3, " Si enim."
Ch. ii. v. 18...	" and after thirteen verses,"......	ch. iii. v. 3, " Misericordia."
Ch. iii. v. 7	" and after one verse,".............	v. 9.
	" and after two verses,"	v. 11—15.
	" and after ten verses,"	v. 21.
	" and after nine verses,".........	v. 27—30, to " frustra."
	" and after seven verses,"	v. 34, " Illusores."
	" and after forty-three verses,"	ch. iv. v. 23, " Omni custodia."
Ch. v. v. 5	" and after ninety-seven verses,"	ch. vi. v. 25, " non concupiscat."
Ch. vi. v. 32...	" and after four verses,"	ch. vii. v. 1, " Fili mi."
Ch. vii. v. 2...	" and after fifty-seven verses,"	ch. viii. v. 5, " Intelligite."
Ch. viii. v. 13,	" and after six verses,"............	v. 17—21.
	" and after twenty-three verses,"	v. 34—36.
	" and after nine verses,"	ch. ix. v. 6—10.
	" and after eighteen verses,".....	ch. x. v. 2.
	" and after four verses,"	v. 5.
	" and after four verses,"..........	v. 8—14.
	" and after four verses,"..........	v. 17—24.
	" and after two verses,"	v. 26; ch. xi. v. 7.
	" and after five verses,"	v. 12—15.
	" and after two verses,"	v. 17.
	" and after three verses,".........	v. 20, 21.
	" and after two verses,"	v. 23—28.
	" and after four verses,"...........	v. 31.
Ch. xii. v. 15,	" and after four verses,"	v. 18—24.
	" and after two verses,"	v. 25.
Ch. xiii. v. 25,	" and after two verses,"	ch. xiv. v. 2, 3.
	" and after two verses,"	v. 5—13.
	" and after three verses,".........	v. 16, 17.
	" and after four verses,"	v. 21, 23.
	" and after four verses,"	v. 26, 27.
	" and after two verses,"	v. 29—31.
	" and after seven verses,"	ch. xv. v. 1, 2.
	" and after seventeen verses,"...	v. 12, ending with " graditur."
	" and after twelve verses,"	v. 16, " melius est."
Ch. xv. v. 20,	" and after two verses,"	v. 22—24.
	" and after four verses,"	v. 27; ch. xvi. 21.
	" and after seventeen verses,"...	v. 31.
Ch. xvii. v. 15,	" and after sixteen verses,"......	v. 23, 24.
	" and after three verses,".........	v. 27.
	" and after two verses,"	ch. xviii. v. 1.
	" and after six verses,"	v. 5.
	" and after six verses,"	v. 9, 10.
	" and after two verses,"	v. 12.
	" and after seven verses,"........	v. 17—19.
	" and after two verses,"	v. 21; ch. xix. 8.
	" and after ten verses,"	v. 15. .

Ch. xix. v. 18,	" and after six verses,"	citing ch. xviii. v. 22, 23.
	" and after two verses,"	v. 25.
	" and after two verses,"	v. 13.
	" and after seventeen verses,"...	v. 23.
	" and after twenty-five verses,"	ch. xxi. v. 13—15.
	" and after nine verses,"	v. 23.
Ch. xxi. v. 28,	" and after five verses,"	ch. xxii. v. 1.
	" and after fifteen verses,"	v. 9, 10.
	" and after four verses,"	v. 13.
	" and after three verses,".........	v. 16.
	" and after eight verses,".........	v. 22.
Ch. xxiii. v. 14,	" and after eight verses,".........	v. 20.
	" and after twenty verses,"	v. 31, 32.
	" and after seven verses,".........	ch. xxiv. v. 1, 2.
	" and after sixteen verses,"	v. 11, 12.
	" and after nine verses,"	v. 17—19.
	" and after two verses,"	v. 21.
v. 26,	" and after two verses,"	v. 28.
v. 32,	" and after twenty verses"	ch. xxv. v. 8.
Ch. xxv. v. 12,	" and after seventeen verses," ...	v. 20—32.
	" and after ten verses,"	v. 28.
	" and after two verses,"	ch. xxvi. v. 2—5.
	" and after ten verses,"	v. 11—22.
	" and after three verses,".........	v. 24.
Ch. xxvii. v. 2,	" and after four verses,"	v. 5, 6.
	" and after three verses,".........	v. 10.
Ch. xxviii. v. 6,	" and after two verses,"	v. 8—10.
	" and after four verses,"	v. 13, 14.
	" and after twelve verses,"	v. 20—27.
	" and after ten verses,"	ch. xxix. v. 5.
	" and after twenty-two verses,"	v. 19, 20.
	" and after four verses,"	v. 23—27.
	" and after fourteen verses,"	ch. xxx. v. 7.

ECCLESIASTES.

Ch. v. v. 6	" and after six verses,"	v. 9.*
Ch. vii. v. 7...	" and after four verses,"	v. 9—11.
Ch. viii. v. 18.	" and after two verses,"	chap. x. v. 1.
	" and after thirteen verses,"	v. 8.

CANTICLES.

Ch. viii. v. 6...	" and after one verse,".............	v. 7, " æmulatio" to " aquæ."

JOB.

Ch. xxiv. v. 3,	" and after five verses,"	v. 6, 7.
	" and after two verses,"	v. 9, 10.
	" and after two verses,"	v. 12, 13.
	" and after twenty-one verses,"..	the latter part of v. 20, " sed conteratur quasi lignum infructuosum."
Ch. xxxi. v. 7,	" and after two verses,"	v. 9—13.
	" and after four verses,"	v. 16—21.
	" and after five verses,"	v. 24, 25.
	" and after six verses,"............	v. 29.
	" and after four verses,"	v. 32—39.

---

* This is the 10th verse in the Authorized Version, where the division of chapters is different, the first verse of our fifth chapter forming the seventeenth verse of the fourth chapter in the Vulgate, Pagnini, Stephens, Athias, and Sebastian Munster. The present division of these two chapters was first introduced into the Authorized Version in 1611, probably from Luther's German version.

On the Division of Verses in the Bible.

HOSEA, PART OF.

Ch. iv. v. 2 .... " and after twelve verses,"	citing part of v. 6, " Quia ter."
" and after fifteen verses,"	v. 10, viz. from "fungaris mihi" in v. 6, to " quoniam," &c. (the latter half of v.10,) and from the end of v.11, "cor."
" and after seventeen verses,"...	to the middle of v. 14, " Quoniam ipsi meretricibus," &c.
Ch. v. v. 4 .... " and after sixty-one verses," ...	ch. vi. middle of v. 5, " judicia tua."
Ch. x. v. xii... " and after seventy-eight verses,"	ch. xii. v. 6.
" and after fifty-one verses,"	ch. xiii. v. 4.
" and after thirty-nine verses,"...	ch. xiv. v. 2.

JOEL. (Nil.)

AMOS.

Ch. xi. v. 4 .... " and after two verses,"	v. 6; our fifth verse therefore made two, thus :— " Et mittam ignem in Juda Et devorabit ædes Jerusalem."
v. 7 .... " and after one verse,"............	the latter part of v. 8, " Et vinum damnatorum bibebant in domo Dei sui."
Ch. v. v. 4 .... " and after three verses,"	part of v. 6, " Quærite ..... vivite."
" and after eight verses,".........	v. 10, 11.
" and after three verses,"	v. 12.
" and after two verses,"	v. 14.

MICHA.

Ch. vi. v. 8.... " and after three verses,"	v. 10—12.
" and after twelve verses,".........	ch. vii. v. 1.

ZEPHANIAH.

Ch. i. v. 7 ...... " and after sixteen verses,"	v. 12, (viz. from middle of v. 7, " Dies Domini.")

MALACHI.

Ch. ii. v. 17... " and after fifteen verses,"	ch. iii. v. 5—7.
" and after fifteen verses,"	v. 13.

ISAIAH.

The first portion of this book quoted in the Speculum is the eighteenth verse of the first chapter, " Dicit Dominus:" after this the author proceeds to cite as follows:—

Ch. ii. v. 6 ..... " and after eight verses,"	citing v. 22.
" and after three verses,"	latter part of v. 8, " Repleta est."
Ch. v. .... " exercituum," middle of v. 5.	
" and after three verses,".........	v. 11, 12.
" and after seventeen verses," ...	v. 20.

Ch. xi. v. 5 ... " and after sixty verses," .... citing	ch. xii. v. 2—6.
" and after forty verses,".........	ch. xiii. v. 11, " et quiescere," last member of v. 11.
Ch. xxvi. v. 4, " and after six verses,"............	v. 8.
Ch. xxix. v. 21, to " verbo."	
" and after ten verses,"............	ch. xxx. 1, "Væ filii,"— v. 15.
" and after twenty verses."......	v. 22.
Ch. lv. v. 7.... " and after twenty verses,"	ch. lvi. v. 1.
Ch. lviii. v. 7.. " and after four verses,"...........	middle of v. 9, " Si abstuleritis."
Ch. lxv. v. 3... and half of verse " 4, dormiunt."	
" and after two verses," (viz. "Qui comedant carnem suillam Et jus profanum in vasis eorum.")	v. 5.
v. 7... " and after ten verses,"............	v. 11.
Ch. lxvi. v. 2, " and after six verses,"	v. 4.

JEREMIAH.

Ch. ii. v. 5 .... " and after ten verses,"	v. 7, last clause, " hæreditatem."
Ch. iv. v. 22... " and after thirty verses,"	ch. v. v. 1, " circuite."
v. 5 .... " and after six verses,"	" filii tui," second comma of v. 7.
v. 9 .... " and after forty verses,".........	v. 22, " qui posui," second comma.
v. 31... " and after thirty verses,"	ch. vi. v. 10.
Ch. viii. v. 6... " and after nine verses,"	v. 8.
(viz. to " quid feci," &c.)	
Ch. ix. v. 24... " and after sixteen verses,"......	ch. x. v. 2.
Ch. xxiii. v. 18 after first comma, " Quis ..... domini."	
" and after eleven verses,"	v. 21, 22.
" and after four verses,"	v. 25.

EZEKIEL.

Ch. xxii. v. 26. " and after two verses," .... citing v. 27. viz., to " intellexerant," in leaving two short commas.	
Ch. xxxiii. v. 20. " and after forty-nine verses,"... (In Martianay's edition it is " after forty-two verses,") citing v. 30.	

WISDOM.

Ch. iii. .... middle of verse eleven, " infelix est."	
" and after six verses," .... citing second comma of v. 13, " Quoniam."	

ECCLESIASTICUS.

Ch. i. v. 20.... " and after two verses,"............ citing	v. 22, "corona sapientiæ timor Domini."
" and after four verses,"	v. 25.
Ch. iii. v. 2.... " and after two verses,"............	v. 4—10, "ut supervenerit tibi benedictio a Domino." (Vulg. " ab eo ;" al. " a Deo.")

On the Division of Verses in the Bible. 681

Ch. iii. v. 2 ...	" and after three verses,".........	citing v. 12, to "tui."
	" and after three verses,".........	v. 14, 15, to "virtuti."
	" and after four verses,"	v. 18—23.
	" and after three verses,".........	v. 26—29.
	" and after two verses,"	v. 31.
Ch. vi. v. 2 ...	" and after seven verses,"	v. 6—22.
	" and after two verses,"	"quibus," middle of v. 23—30.
	" and after four verses,"	v. 37.
Ch. vii. v. 15...	to " Presbyterorum."	
	" and after twelve verses,"	v. 22, 23.
	" and after two verses,"	v. 25—33, to "sacerdotes."
	" and after six verses,".............	v. 36.
Ch. viii. v. 4...	" and after two verses,"	v. 6—12.
	" and after sixteen verses,"	v. 20, 21.
	" and after two verses,"	ch. ix. v. 1, "non zeles mulierem sinus tui."
	" and after seven verses,"	v. 5, 6.
	" and after two verses,"	v. 8.
	" and after twelve verses,"	v. 14—17, "non ... injustorum."
	" and after two verses,"	v. 18, 19.
	" and after four verses,"	the latter part of v. 21, " et eum," v. 22.
	" and after forty-three verses,"...	ch. x. v. 23—28.
	" and after five verses,"	v. 31.
	" and after six verses,".............	ch. xi. v. 1—4, to "extollaris."
	" and after six verses,".............	v. 7—10.
	" and after twenty verses,"	v. 22...30, " ante mortem ne laudes hominem quemquam."
	" and after one verse,".............	v. 31.
Ch. xii. v. 7...	" and after four verses,"	v. 10—19.
	" and after sixty-one verses," ...	ch. xiii. v. 30.
	" and after three verses,".........	ch. xiv. v. 1.
	" and after four verses,"	v. 11—13.
	" and after sixteen verses,"	v. 22, 23.
	" and after twenty-five verses,"..	ch. xv. v. 7.
Ch. xvi. 4 ...	" and after twenty-one verses,"..	v. 16.
Ch. xvii. 23...	" and after nine verses,"	v. 28, 29.
	" and after thirty verses,"	ch. xviii. v. 14—23.
	" and after six verses,".............	v. 27.
	" and after five verses,"	v. 30—32.
	" and after five verses,"	ch. xix. 1.
Ch. xix. v. 4...	" and after two verses,"	v. 5.
	" and after eight verses,".........	v. 10—18.
	" and after five verses,"	v. 21.
	" and after sixteen verses,"	ch. xx. v. 1, to "irasci," v. 8.
	" and after eight verses,".........	v. 13, "sapiens ... facit."
	" and after sixteen verses,"......	v. 20—22.
	" and after two verses,"	v. 24—29, first half.
	" and after four verses,"	v. 31.
Ch. xx. 4	" and after four verses,"	v. 7.
	" and after five verses,"	v. 11—20.
	" and after two verses,"	v. 22—24.
	" and after eight verses,".........	v. 29.

NO. XVIII.—N.S.   4 s

Ch. xxii. 1	" and after four verses,"	citing v. 4—13.
	" and after twenty-one verses,"..	v. 25—27.
	" and after ten verses,"	v. 33.
Ch. xxiii. 14...	" and after four verses,"	v. 17—23.
	" and after two verses,"	v. 25.
Ch. xxv. 8 ...	" and after ten verses,"	v. 14, 15.
	" and after twenty verses,"	v. 28.
	" and after thirty-three verses,"	ch. xxvi. v. 11—14.
	" and after four verses,"	v. 16—20.
	" and after eleven verses,"	v. 12—27.
	" and after four verses,"	ch. xxvii. v. 1.
	" and after twelve verses,"	v. 27.
	" and after two verses,"	v. 29—32.
	" and after three verses,".........	ch. xxviii. v. 1.
Ch. xxviii. ...	" and after four verses,"	v. 13.
Ch. xxix. v. 4,	" and after thirteen verses," ...	v. 11—26.
	" and after one verse,".............	v. 27.
	" and after sixteen verses,"	ch. xxx. v. 1.
Ch. xxx. v. 2...	" and after ten verses,"	v. 8—18.
	" and after five verses,"	v. 22—26.
	" and after ten verses,".............	v. 5—30.
	" and after twenty-six verses,"...	ch. xxxii. v. 4—6.
	" and after five verses,"	v. 10—22.
	" and after four verses,"	v. 24.
Ch. xxxiv. v. 8,	" and after five verses,"	v. 12.
Ch. xxxv. v. 18,	" and after four verses,"	v. 21.
Ch. xxxvii. v. 16	" and after five verses,"	v. 10.
	" and after twenty-one verses,"..	v. 30—32.
	" and after four verses,"	ch. xxxviii. v. 1—7.
	" and after four verses,"	v. 9, 10.
	" and after one verse,".............	v. 11, latter half of v. 14.
	" and after one verse,".............	v. 16—19.
	" and after one verse,".............	v. 21.
	" and after nine verses,"	v. 23 to ch. xl. v. 17.
	" and after twelve verses,"	v. 24.

TOBIT.

Ch. iv. v. 4 ...	" and after two verses,"	citing v. 6—17.
	" and after two verses,"	v. 19, 20.
	" and after seven verses,"	v. 23.

MATTHEW.

Ch. xxii. v. 40, " Prophetæ.'
" and after a few verses" .... citing ch. xxiii. v..

MARK.

Ch. x. 12...... " and after four verses," .... citing middle of v. 14, " sinite parvulos."

JOHN.

Ch. xiv. 21 ... " and after three verses," ...... citing second comma of v. 23 " Si quis diligit me."

II. CORINTHIANS.

Ch. iv. v. 13...	" and after six verses,"	citing v. 16, to " faciatis."
Ch. xiii. v. 7...		
	" and after six verses,"	v. 11.

PHILIPPIANS.

Ch. i. v. 24 ... " and after six verses,"............ citing v. 27.
Ch. iii. .... " and after twenty verses," ...... to " in cœlis est."
" and after thirteen verses," ... ch. iv. v. 4, " gaudite.

I. TIMOTHY.

Ch. iii. 13 .... " and after twelve verses," ...... citing ch. iv. v. 1. (3 intervening to make 12.)

II. TIMOTHY.

Ch. ii. 17 ...... to " serpet," middle of the verse.
" and after six verses,"............ citing middle of v. 19, " cognovit Dominus."
Ch. iii. .... " and after eight verses,"........... v. 10.

JOHN.

Ch. v. v. 15... " et scimus quoniam audit nos."
" and after three verses,"......... citing v. 15, " qui scit."

HEBREWS.

Ch. iv. v. 14... " Habentes ergo pontificem magnum," &c., to " confessionem."
" and after three verses,"......... citing v. 16, " adeamus" to " opportuno."
Ch. vi. v. 12... " ut non segnes."
" and after seven verses,".......... citing v. 16, " Homines enim."

We must here observe, that some doubts have existed as to the exact meaning of St. Augustine.* Father Simon is of opinion that the theologians of Louvain, who first edited the Speculum of Augustine, did not comprehend his true meaning in the use of the word *verse*. "They have," he observes, "put throughout this treatise ' et post, tertius versus, et post, secundus versus, et post, quartus versus, et post, quintus versus,' whereas we should read ' post tres versus, post duos versus, post quatuor versus, post quinque versus," &c. "St. Augustine," he proceeds to observe, " did not intend to point out the second, third, fourth, and fifth verses, but that which follows immediately after two, three, four, or five verses, as appears clearly from many other passages in the Speculum." But in whatever manner we are to understand St. Augustine, it is evident that his verses are quite different from those in our present printed editions of the Old and New Testament. These verses are at the same time so intimately connected with the division into chapters, to which alone the numerical notation has any reference, that it will be here the proper place to give some account of these larger divisions.

---

* We may here observe, that in the Benedictine, and other editions of the Speculum, the quotations are from Jerome's Vulgate, which circumstance has, with others, induced those learned men to question its authenticity. Dr. Wiseman has acquainted us, in his Letters on 1 John v. 7, that the ancient MS. of the Speculum, preserved in the monastery of the Holy Cross, wherein the quotations are from the old Latin, and which was some years since about being published, contains the true and genuine Speculum of St. Augustine. The reference to the Psalms, which we have here cited from the Speculum, is according to the numeration of the Septuagint and Vulgate, and not of the Hebrew.

This subject also seems involved in some degree of obscurity. It is not our intention to dwell here on the ancient τίτλοι and κεφάλαια, which have no relation to our present numerical division of chapters, but to proceed at once to the more modern distribution. This has been attributed to various persons: to Theophylact, at the close of the eleventh century;* to the learned Stephen Lanfranc, the first abbot of St. Stephen's, in Caen, afterwards archbishop of Canterbury, where he died in the year 1089; and also,—which is much more probable, as has been shown by the learned antiquarian, Bale,—to his patriotic successor, Stephen Langton, who died in the same see in 1228. But whoever was their author, they were unquestionably first established by Cardinal Hugh de St. Cher, who adapted them to his Latin Concordance, the first work of the kind, and introduced them into the manuscripts of the Latin Vulgate. The cardinal, who died in the year 1263, was the first of the Dominican order who had the honour of being advanced to the purple. He is said to have employed no less than five hundred monks in this laborious undertaking. His division had the honour of being adopted in the fifteenth century, not only by the Greek church, but also into the Syriac version, and was received about the same period by the Jews themselves, Rabbi Isaac Nathan having adapted it to his Hebrew Concordance of all the declinable words in the Bible, which was completed in the year 1448, a few years before the invention of printing. Rabbi Nathan's Concordance was, however, first printed by the learned Reuchlin (better known by his Latin name of Capnio), at the press of Cornelius Bomberg, in Venice, A.D. 1523, shortly before the appearance of the division and enumeration of the chapters in the printed Hebrew Bibles. These were first introduced by

---

* The learned Huet, who favoured this notion, seems to have borrowed it from Croius, who says, "Theophylact, who flourished in the eleventh century, exhibits the same number of chapters in the gospels with us, as appears from his index to each of the gospels. It is, however, certain, that Theophylact was not himself the original author of this division, as we have ourselves seen some ancient manuscripts written before his time, containing these same divisions. The Acts were divided into twenty-eight chapters. Œcumenius afterwards divided them into forty chapters, and two hundred and forty heads." And again, "We have a Latin manuscript, above 800 years old, containing the whole Bible, divided into the very same chapters as at present." He also says, that he has seen several ancient manuscripts, and particularly one of St. John's Gospel, on which the figures are marked in the margin in the same hand and ink with the manuscript. He adds that the *verses* are distinguished also, and marked in the very text. He gives some reasons for conjecturing that in the time of Jerome and Augustine the chapters were divided *nearly* as at present, but his arguments are founded merely on their division of one or two subjects in their comments, in the same way as our present chapters. He also speaks of the probability of their taking the distinctions of chapters and verses from Ezra, and the great synagogue, and transferring them to the New Testament. He does not designate his manuscripts,—we cannot, therefore, sufficiently confide in his assertions; nor does he write with that dispassionateness which becomes a candid critic. See the work of Croius, "Sacræ ac Historicæ in Nov. Fœd. Observationes, &c." part i. p. 55.

In fact, we have ourselves seen several ancient manuscripts, in which the chapters are numbered in the margin, but which did not originally contain this division, the number being added by a later hand, after the chapters had become established.

Daniel Bomberg into his folio edition of 1525. It is true, that for many centuries before the time of the Cardinal de St. Cher, there were certain divisions in the Hebrew, Greek, and Latin Bibles; but it is no less certain, that the *present* division of chapters in both the Old and New Testament was first adopted at the time to which it has been here ascribed, as well as that this was the first attempt at any arithmetical enumeration whatever of chapters, except in the book of Psalms. The nearest division to our present chapters which had previously existed is that of the masoretic *sedarim*, of which there were forty-three in Genesis, where we reckon forty chapters; and the other books are divided nearly in the same proportion.

After the invention of printing, about the year 1450, the present chapters appear both in the editions of the Latin Vulgate, and in the translations of the same into the vulgar tongue; as in the German versions printed in 1466 and 1494, the Flemish version of 1475, the Italian of 1471, and the Spanish of 1478. After the commencement of the Reformation in the sixteenth century, the reformers adopted, from the Vulgate, St. Cher's division of chapters, which was introduced by Luther into his German version, commenced in 1522, and from thence it passed into the French of Olivetan in 1535, and into the English version of Tindale and Coverdale in 1526 and 1535. It passed from these through the Geneva and the Bishops' Bible to our Authorized Version of 1611.

We regret to have to add, that this division is frequently found to be executed with very little judgment, and the reader should ever bear in mind that it possesses no weight whatever in fixing the sense of Scripture, divisions of this kind having been invented, not so much for the sake of distinguishing the subjects, as for facilitating reference, and as convenient accompaniments to a Concordance. We may here observe, that the Cardinal de St. Cher, knowing nothing of a division into verses, marks his references to the concordance in quite a different and a better way, in so far as the sense is concerned. This was by means of Roman capitals applied to the Bible, as they then generally were to all other books furnished with an index. The letters A. B. C. D. E. F. G. were thus placed in the margin, at equal distances from each other, their number being varied according to the length of the several chapters.

We have observed that the book of Psalms was the first book into which any thing like an enumeration of chapters was introduced, viz. by marking each psalm with a number, and designating it accordingly. This mode of designating the psalms has been supposed to have been known among the Jews before the coming of Christ, and is by some ascribed to the authors of the Septuagint version. Thus the *second psalm* is cited by St. Paul, Acts xiii. 33. This point would be still more evident, if we were certain that our copies of the New Testament preserved here the true reading; but this is doubtful, several manuscripts having in this place "the *first* psalm," instead of "the second," while there are strong reasons for supposing that this reference to the number of the psalm is an early interpolation. Under any circumstances, the first psalm, or even the second, might be easily referred to, even on the supposition that the psalms themselves were not then designated by arithmetical enumeration; and the reader will perceive that, in the reference made by St. Paul to the sixteenth psalm in the thirty-fifth verse of the same chapter, he does not designate it by its number, but merely says, "in another psalm," &c. The numeration of the psalms is, however, ancient, as we find it adopted by St. Hilary and some of the Greeks, from whom it passed to the Latin and African fathers.

We now come to the subdivision of each chapter, or the division into verses.

The enumeration of the verses (στίχοι) by figures is not modern. We find ancient manuscripts so marked long before the invention of printing. In a Greek stichometrical manuscript, probably as ancient as the ninth century, now in the Royal Library in Paris, (Cod. Reg. 1892,) the verses—which, however, the reader will perceive are not divided according to the sense—are thus numbered in the margin, reckoning by hundreds, and commencing the enumeration again at the end of each hundred lines. We give it here according to the English version, substituting Arabic figures for the Greek numeral letters.

1. The vision of Isaiah, the son of Amos, which he saw concerning Judah and Jerusalem in the days of Uzziah, Jothan, Ahaz, and Hezekiah, kings of
2. Judah. Hear O heavens and
3. give ear O earth, for the Lord hath spoken.
4. I have nourished and brought up children; and they
5. have rebelled against me. The ox knoweth
6. his owner, and the ass his master's crib.
7. But Israel doth not know, my people
8. doth not consider. O sinful nation
9. a people laden with iniquity. a seed
10. of evil doers. children that are corrupters. they have forsa-
11. ken the Lord. they have provoked the holy one of Israel unto anger. they are gone away backward. Why should ye be stricken any more.
12. Ye will revolt more and more. the whole head is sick, and the whole heart is faint
13. From the sole of the foot even unto the head there is no
14. soundness in it, but wounds
15. and bruises and putrefying sores. They have not been closed. neither bound up, neither mollified with ointment
16. your country is desolate
17. your cities
18. are burned with fire. your land
19. Strangers devour it in your presence
20. and it is desolate as overthrown by strangers*

---

* We have also seen an example from the same library of a manuscript, in which the verses are numbered with Greek cyphers, both in the text and margin; but have

We have also a specimen of the Song of Moses from the psalter of Sedulius Scotus or the Irishman,* who flourished in the beginning of the ninth century. It is written stichometrically, in Greek and Latin, and contains forty-two commas or lines; and has in all seven colons, which are each numbered in the margin with Roman numerals, by Sedulius himself in the opinion of Montfaucon, who observes that this division is not always correct, and that it does not harmonize with other books of Scripture which are divided in the same manner. We give it here from the Latin of Sedulius, which the reader will perceive to be antehieronymian.

I. Cantemus Domino gloriose enim magnificatus est,
equum et ascensorem projecit in mare
Adjutor et protector factus est mihi in salutem.
Iste Deus meus et glorificabo eum,
Deus Patris mei, et exaltabo eum,
Dominus conterens bella, Dominus nomen est ei.
Currus Faraonis et exercitum ejus projecit in mare :
electos ascensores, ternos stantes, demersit in Rubro mari,
Pelago cooperuit eos, devenerunt in profundum tamquam lapis.

II. Dextera tua, Domine, glorificata est in virtute,
dextera manus tua, Domine, confregit inimicos,
et per multitudinem gloriæ tuæ contribulasti adversarios.
Misisti iram tuam et comedit illos tamquam stipulam,
et per spiritum iræ tuæ divisa est aqua.
Gelaverunt tamquam murus aquæ,
Gelaverunt fluctus in medio mari.

III. Dixit inimicus, persequens comprehendam,
Partibor spolia, replebo animam meam :
interficiam gladio meo, dominabitur manus mea;
Misisti spiritum tuum et cooperuit eos mare,
Descenderunt tamquam plumbum in aquam validissimam.

IV. Quis similis tibi in diis, Domine, quis similis tibi?
gloriosus in Sanctis, mirabilis in majestatibus, faciens prodigia :
Extendisti dexteram tuam et devoravit eos terra,
gubernasti populum tuum hunc, quem redemisti
Exhortatus es in virtute tuâ, in requie sancta tua.

V. Audierunt gentes et iratæ sunt,
Dolores comprehenderunt habitantes Philistiim
Tunc festinaverunt Duces Edom
et principes Moabitarum adprehendit illos tremor,
fluxerunt omnes habitantes Chanaan.
Cecidit super eos timor et tremor, magnitudine brachii tui.

VI. Fiant tamquam lapis donec pertranseat populus tuus, Domine,
usque dum transeat populus, Domine, hunc quem adquisisti
Inducens plantato eos in montem hæreditatis tuæ

---

at present no opportunity of giving an extract from the same, having unfortunately lost the note which we had taken of it in France.

* There were two distinguished Irishmen of the name of Sedulius or Shiel, (in Irish, Sidhuil,) the former of whom flourished in the fifth, the latter in the eighth and beginning of the ninth century.

in præparatam habitationem tuam, quam præparasti, Domine.
Sanctificationem, Domine, quam paraverunt manus tuæ.

VII. Domine, qui regnas in æternum et in sæculum et adhuc :
Quia introiit equitatus Faraonis cum curribus et ascensoribus in mare, et adduxit super eos Dominus aquas maris :
Filii autem Israël transierunt per siccum in medio mari.

The following is the Authorized Version of the above :—

I. I will sing unto the Lord, for he hath triumphed gloriously
the horse and his rider hath he thrown into the sea
The Lord is my strength and song, and he is become my salvation.
He is my God and I will prepare him a habitation
My father's God and I will exalt him
The Lord is a man of war, the Lord is his name
Pharaoh's chariots and his host hath he cast into the sea
His chosen captains also are drowned in the Red sea
The depths have covered them, they sank unto the bottom as a stone.

II. Thy right hand, O Lord, hath become glorious in power
thy right hand, O Lord, hath dashed in pieces the enemy.
and in the greatness of thine excellency thou hast overthrown them that rose up against thee.
Thou sentest forth thy wrath which consumeth them as stubble
and with the blast of thy nostrils the waters were gathered together
The floods stood upright as an heap
And the depths were congealed in the heart of the sea.

III. The enemy said, I will pursue, I will overtake
I will divide the spoil, my lust shall be satisfied upon them.
I will draw my sword, my hand shall destroy them.
Thou didst blow with thy wind, the sea covered them
They sank as lead in the mighty waters.

IV. Who is like unto thee, O Lord, among the gods
Who is like thee glorious in holiness, fearful in praises, doing wonders.
Thou stretchedst out thy right hand, the earth swallowed them
Thou in thy haste led forth the people which thou hast redeemed
Thou hast guided them in thy strength unto thy holy habitation.

V. The people shall hear and be afraid
sorrow shall take hold on the inhabitants of Palestine
Then the dukes of Edom shall be amazed
the mighty men of Moab trembling shall take hold upon them.
All the inhabitants of Canaan shall melt away
Fear and dread shall fall upon them.

VI. By the greatness of thine arm they shall be as still as a stone.
Till thy people pass over, O Lord, till the people pass over which thou hast purchased
Thou shalt bring them in, and plant them in the mountain of thine inheritance,
In the place, O Lord, which thou hast made for thee to dwell in
In the sanctuary, O Lord, which thy hands have established.

VII. The Lord shall reign for ever and ever
For the horse of Pharaoh went in with his chariots and with his horsemen into the sea,
And the Lord brought again the waters of the sea upon them.
But the children of Israel went on dry land in the midst of the sea.

The following specimen from the psalter of Sedulius, of his stichometrical arrangement of the Psalms, may be also interesting to the reader, although destitute of numerical notation. We give the first verse in his Greek original, and conclude with his subscription, the original of which is in the autograph of this celebrated Irishman and distinguished Greek scholar, preserved in the monastery of St. Michael, in Lorraine. The Greek original is in uncial letters, and the Latin translation is also in the handwriting of Sedulius. Each Greek word is separated by a point.

Ψαλτήριον. Ψαλμὸς τοῦ Δαυὶδ πρῶτος.
Μακάριος ἀνὴρ ὃς οὐκ ἐπορεύθη ἐν βουλῇ ἀσεβῶν
Καὶ ἐν ὁδῷ ἁμαρτωλῶν οὐκ ἔστη
Καὶ ἐν καθέδρᾳ λοιμῶν οὐκ ἐκάθισε
Ἀλλ' ἢ ἐν τῷ νόμῳ κυρίου τὸ θέλημα αὐτοῦ
Καὶ ἐν τῷ νόμῳ αὐτοῦ μελετήσει ἡμέρας καὶ νυκτὸς
Καὶ ἔσται ὡς τὸ ξύλον τὸ περισσευόμενον
Παρὰ τὰς διεξόδους τῶν ὑδάτων
Ὁ τὸν καρπὸν αὐτοῦ δώσει ἐν καιρῷ αὐτοῦ
Καὶ τὸ φύλλον αὐτοῦ οὐκ ἀποῤῥυήσεται
Καὶ πάντα ὅσα ἂν ποιῇ κατευοδωθήσεται
Οὐκ οὕτως οἱ ἀσεβεῖς, οὐκ οὕτως
Ἀλλ' ἢ ὡς ὁ χνοῦς ὃν ἐκρίπτει ὁ ἄνεμος ἀπὸ προσώπου τῆς γῆς
Διὰ τοῦτο οὐκ ἀναστήσονται ἀσεβεῖς ἐν κρίσει
Οὐδὲ οἱ ἁμαρτωλοὶ ἐν βουλῇ δικαίων
Ὅτι γινώσκει κύριος ὁδὸν δικαίων
Καὶ ὁδὸς ἀσεβῶν ἀπολεῖται

Or thus, according to the Authorized Version:—

Blessed is the man who hath not walked in the counsel of the ungodly
and hath not stood in the way of sinners
and hath not sat in the seat of the scornful
But his delight is in the law of the Lord
and in his law will he meditate day and night
And he will be like a tree planted
by the water side
which will bring forth its fruit in due season
and its leaf will not wither
and all that he does shall prosper
But the wicked are not so
but like the dust which the wind scattereth from
the face of the earth.
Therefore the wicked will not rise in the judgment
nor sinners in the council of the just
For the Lord knoweth the way of the righteous
and the way of the unjust shall perish.

At the end of the Psalter is the subscription of Sedulius:—

. . . . εὐχὰς θεῷ ἐγὼ ἁμαρτωλὸς πράξω
Ἐγὼ Σηδύλιος Σκόττος ἔγραψα.

The first person, however, who applied a system of numbering the verses to the entire Bible was the famous Jew, Rabbi Nathan, in the middle of the fifteenth century, who, at the same time that he intro-

duced Cardinal de St. Cher's chapters into the Hebrew Bible, instead of marking the pages or columns with the first seven letters of the alphabet, marked every *fifth* masoretic verse with a Hebrew numeral.*
By thus employing the masoretic † division into verses which had previously existed, and merely attaching numerals to them, he adopted a better system, so far as the facility of reference was concerned, than that of the Cardinal de St. Cher. We have already observed that this system was introduced into the first printed edition of the Hebrew Bible by Daniel Bomberg at Venice in 1525. This practice has been since continued by the Jews, with this difference, that in the edition of the Hebrew Bible by Athias, in 1661, he introduced the Arabic figures for numbering the intermediate verses between each fifth verse. And this he did in imitation of the editions in all other languages, which had for above a century, viz. after the year 1555, universally adopted this practice. We shall presently see the process by which this custom became gradually introduced into all our Bibles.

(To be continued.)

---

* The following are Rabbi Nathan's words:—" Et quia vidi quod interpres librorum sacrorum Latinus diviserit singulos libros in certum numerum sectionum vel capitum, id quod non fit in libris nostris, ideo notavi versus omnes, juxta numerum ipsorum, pro numero capitum: versuum etiam numerum notavi, prout apud nos extant, quo tanto faciliori negotio in suis locis reperiri possint."

† We have not thought it necessary to discuss the original design of the '*pesukim*,' or masoretic verses, which are retained in all our present Bibles, and which are regulated by the sense. These, it is well known, are separated from each other in the Hebrew by the soph pasuk, an accent marked by two points, placed one over the other like our colon. A current tradition among the Jews attributes these pauses to Moses himself, and considers it as inspired. The Thalmudists attribute them to Ezra; the greater part of the Jewish Rabbins maintain that Ezra added them to the text according to a tradition which had descended from Moses, and that the design of these pauses was to fix the time when the reader in the synagogue was to stop, in order that the Chaldee interpreter might translate each verse into this language for the benefit of the people to whom it had become vernacular since their return from Babylon. They were unknown to St. Jerome, who adopted, in many instances, a much better division as far as the sense is concerned. They cannot be traced beyond the times of the Masorites, and were probably invented at the same time with the vowel points. Father Simon observes, that "it is only some injudicious or ignorant protestants, who prefer this distinction of verses invented by the Masorites, to other divisions supported by good sense, and by the ancient versions."

Referring to this subject, Jahn, with his usual judgment, remarks:—" The protestants, who until the middle of the eighteenth century maintained the perfect clearness of the sense of Scripture, contended that the vowel points were coeval with the consonants, in order, doubtless, to obviate the notion that the Scriptures were at one time less clear than at another. But since their rejection of this dogma, they agree with us [of the church of Rome] that the points are but a commentary of the middle ages, and that it is lawful for the purposes of exegesis to attach other points more agreeable to the context. But the interpreter should not attempt this upon slight grounds, for those points contain within themselves many of the signs of the readings of antiquity; and there have been so many failures in the attempts of the learned at introducing changes into the vowel points, that the errors into which they have fallen ought to render the interpreter extremely cautious and circumspect."

NOTICES OF BOOKS.

Annual Report of the Children's Church Missionary Association.
Annual Reports of the Newington Green Church Missionary Nursery, Islington.

WE remarked, some time ago, that a large division of our fellow-Christians are devoid of all sense of the absurd, to their own considerable moral disadvantage. Since then, we have come across several striking illustrations of the remark. It is not very long since we saw an advertisement informing ladies that it is now happily in their power to purchase reticules and articles of the like description made from the same piece as the robes in which Bishop Alexander was consecrated! We were struck, on reading it, with the dull torpidity of our thoughts and feelings. It appeared that there was in many minds a nimbleness of association—a sensibility awakened by very subtle connexions of thought to which we could make no pretensions. We could in part imagine some value attached or attachable to a reticule made from a canonized person's robes themselves; but one made from the same piece as the robes!—this we must again say is an affinity too remote for our ungenealogical brains. After this, who will laugh at the relics cherished in the church of Rome? There they wait till the object of worship is dead; and, genuine or pretended, the relic at least professes to be connected with him in a way intelligible to dull fancies like ours: it is his head or his toe-nail, or, at farthest, something that he wore or touched. But more magical in his influence than any Romish saint, Bishop Alexander imparts sanctity to what he never saw, touched, nor has himself any conception of—the piece from which his robes were made!

Here follows something that lags not far behind the reticules and the robes:—

"DESCENDANT OF BISHOP JEWELL.
"TO THE EDITOR OF THE RECORD.

"Sir,—I am desirous of laying before the christian public, through the *Record* newspaper, a matter which may be of some interest to them to become acquainted with, and one which appears to others, as well as myself, to be worthy of further inquiry and attention.

"On my appointment to this benefice, I found a family resident, named 'Jewell.' The name naturally brought to my recollection that great and good bishop of our church, 'Bishop Jewell,' whose *Apology* is well known as a master-piece. It occurred to me that possibly the family here might be his descendants; and accordingly, I have held conversations with them from time to time, to ascertain how far my surmises might be correct. I have thus learned that there is a tradition amongst them, of a very distinct character, that they are descended from some great bishop in England; and it is a fact that they are respectable, though much reduced in circumstances. I may mention here that this family have been in the habit of spelling their name with a 'D' instead of a 'J,' but this is evidently a corruption from lapse of time and other circumstances. In the printed list of Irish volunteers, amongst which were enrolled members of the family, the name is spelt 'Jewell.' But, however disposed my mind was to the conviction that this family are descended from Bishop Jewell, from the circumstances already mentioned, I have no doubt of the fact now; for, on lately seeing the print of the Bishop published with the *Apology*, I instantly recognised the most striking likeness between it and 'Matthew,' the boy resident here, who, I am quite satisfied, is the lineal representative of that ever-to-be remembered prelate. Nor am I the only person who thinks so;—the likeness is at once admitted.

"And now, dear Sir, you may probably infer my object in this communication, which is simply this, that, as there are many persons of wealth in England who are anxious to devise means for the spread of the gospel, and who, therefore, at times seek out promising youths to be educated for the ministry, so this opportunity may not be lost. Matthew Jewell is about fifteen years of age, and is a well-conditioned boy. In good hands, I think he would turn out well. He is an orphan, without father or mother, and is at present under the care of his aunt, Miss Jewell, who is much straitened in her circumstances. He has a little sister. Their means are very limited, but they have still some remnant of property. This boy has been instructed in the classics, and is just at that critical period of life when something good might be devised for him, so as ultimately he might become an ornament to the Church, which owes a debt of gratitude to his noble ancestor.

"I remain, Sir, your obedient faithful servant,
"JAMES ANDERSON,
"Rector and Vicar of Ballinrobe, Diocese of Tuam, Ireland.
"The Glebe, Ballinrobe, April 19, 1842."

[*Record*, May 16, 1842.]

But this deadness to all sense of the absurd is never so conspicuous, nor its results so offensive, as in the religious culture of children. We have heard of a school in which the *converted* boys are, or were, allowed to pare apples for puddings, it not being thought safe to trust the ungodly with the privilege. In the same school, rewards were given to such boys as converted their companions!

This, however, was without the Church; but what are we to say to such exhibitions among her members as are recorded in the Reports now before us? In those of the Newington Green Church Missionary Nursery, we have the "Resolutions passed at the formation of the Society." We will not trust ourselves to quote the earlier ones, so our readers must content themselves with the following Resolutions:—

"IX. Resolved, that we do now form a society, which shall be called, 'The Newington Green Church Missionary Nursery.'

"X. Resolved, that this Society consist of twelve or more Fathers and Mothers and other patrons; a Treasurer, a Secretary, a Committee of twelve or more children Collectors.

"XII. Resolved, that by the recommendation of the several Patrons, the following be the Children's Committee, with power to the Patrons to add to their number, and make any alteration of the names which they may find necessary, viz.: Harriett Pitman, Frederick Dugmore, Georgiana Hickman, Hannah Hill, Henry Annesley Voysey, Francis Barnard, Maria Burton, Emma Evans, William Eley.

"XIII. Resolved, that the duties of the Patrons be to attend the meetings of the Committee as often as they can, to speak to the Collectors and Subscribers about the missionary cause; and to encourage them, and guide them on all other occasions in forwarding this good work, and not to forget to train them as plants in the Nursery; so that by and by, if the Lord will, they may be plants of his own right hand planting, and become standard trees in the missionary field.

"XVI. Resolved, that the Committee, and Subscribers, and Patrons, meet together once a month; when the money collected is to be paid, and the collecting books to be signed by the Treasurer.

"The meetings always to be opened with prayer to Almighty God for his blessing."

The Children's Church Missionary Association, St. Paul's, Islington, seems a precisely similar institution, with one remarkable feature, however, which we do not observe in the other. In the list of collectors, certain names have an asterisk prefixed, and a note explains to us that such are infants!

Ridiculous as all this is, it is so much worse than ridiculous, that we feel bound to say a few words further upon it. We can hardly imagine any thing more opposed to nature and to truth, any thing less like reverence for God's appointed bounds and ordinances, than this attempt to make little children *public religious characters,* after the Exeter Hall type. Vulgar and vulgarizing as public meetings assuredly are,* a man of conscience and refinement may feel it his duty, under certain circumstances, to attend and promote them; but what such man would take children out of their appointed spheres and duties, in order to expose them to the snare? Again; we suspect that printed lists of subscribers to any good work make it difficult enough for adults so to give as not to let the left hand know what the right hand doeth; but how on earth are children, with their quick sense of distinction, and their proneness to speedy elation, to be preserved from vanity, if they see their names in print, (itself a circumstance sure to take hold of their minds,) and in so unusual a way as that here presented to our notice?

But we need not dwell on this disgusting absurdity on its own account. We had intended making it the text for some observations on the right religious development of children,—a large subject, on which we cannot enter at present, but to which we may perhaps betake ourselves hereafter.

In concluding, however, we must express our indignation at seeing as presidents of the Church Missionary Nursery, the following names; Rev. J. Sandys, Rev. T. E. Williams. Are these gentlemen clergymen of the Church of England? The title of the institution compels us to believe that they are, improbable as the fact may seem.

Letters and Notes on the Manners, Customs, and Condition of the North American Indians. By GEORGE CATLIN. *Written during eight years travel amongst the wildest tribes, from* 1832 *to* 1839. 2 *vols. large* 8vo., *with* 400 *illustrations carefully engraved from his original paintings.* London: Published by the Author. 1841.

THESE two volumes afford really healthy and instructive reading. The author, whose " Indian Gallery" has been seen probably by many of our readers at the Egyptian Hall, is by birth an American, but is happily free from most of those faults which we are in the habit of imputing to his countrymen; and besides giving us some most valuable and authentic statistical information, evidences a tone of mind which is, alas! too rare in this money-seeking age. For the details of fact we refer to the volumes themselves; to illustrate the spirit of the writer, we shall borrow one short passage, containing, as it were, the result of his experience amongst these tribes, and suggestive of many reflections to ourselves:—

" I have viewed man (he writes) in the artless and innocent simplicity of nature— in the full enjoyment of the luxuries which God had bestowed upon him. I have seen him happier than kings or princes can be; with his wife and little ones about him. I have seen him shrinking from civilized approach, which came, with all its

---

* By the way, we are glad to learn, on the indubitable authority of the *Record*, that the public interest in the May meetings is on the decline. We say we are glad to hear it, for any thing less conducive to true religion than they had become we cannot readily imagine.

vices, like the dead of night upon him. I have seen raised, too, in that darkness, religion's torch, and seen him gaze and then retreat, like the frightened deer that are blinded by the light. I have seen him shrinking from the soil and haunts of his boyhood, bursting the strongest ties which bound him to the earth and its pleasures. I have seen him set fire to his wigwam and smooth over the graves of his fathers. I have seen him (it is the only thing that will bring them) with tears of grief sliding over his cheeks, clap his hands in silence over his mouth, and take the last look over his fair hunting grounds, and turn his face in sadness to the setting sun. All this I have seen performed in nature's silent dignity and grace, which forsook him not in the last extremity of misfortune and despair: and I have seen as often the approach of the bustling, talking, whistling, hopping, elated, and exulting white man, with the first dip of the ploughshare making sacrilegious trespass on the bones of the valiant dead. I have seen the skull, the pipe, and the tomahawk rise from the ground together, in interrogations which the sophistry of the world can never answer. I have seen this in all its forms and features, the grand and irresistible march of civilization, I have seen this splendid Juggernaut trotting on; and beheld its sweeping desolation, and held converse with the happy thousands, living as yet beyond its influence, who have not been crushed, nor yet have dreamed of its approach."

Antiphonal Chants, for the Services of the United Church of England and Ireland. By FREDERICK LINGARD, *of the Durham Cathedral Choir.* London: Novello.

THIS handsomely got up volume contains a complete arrangement of Chants for the daily morning and evening Psalms. When we mention that the whole are original, it will be admitted that the undertaking is a bold one; and it will not create surprise if it should be thought not quite adapted in all points to its intended purpose. The prevailing fault is a want of simplicity; indeed, whatever may be the case with a practised choir of professional singers, such as that of which Mr. Lingard is a member, we cannot but think that common congregations must be quite debarred from the use of a large p opo - tion of these compositions. In this respect the ancient chants, divested as they are of all flourishes and difficult intervals, appear to great advantage; and the more our modern chants approach to their simplicity and severe majesty, the greater the likelihood that we shall get the proper congregational psalmody—the chanting of the psalter— revived in our churches. We are glad to find that Mr. Lingard has very correct ideas on this last head; and we certainly think that, if in the preparation of his volume he had acted in the full spirit of the following words in his own preface, he would have omitted, or greatly altered, many of the compositions which appear in it;*

"The author believes that the practice of singing the chant in alternate parts might be introduced in churches where the formation of a complete choir could not be expected. Even the children of our parochial schools—babes and sucklings, out of whose mouth praise is perfected—might be so arranged and taught as to respond to each other in this 'voice of melody.' And there seems no reason why entire congregations should not be brought to agree in the same edifying method,—from aisle to aisle inciting and encouraging the strain of adoration."—Preface, p. ii.

---

* We are far, of course, from discouraging compositions of the more ornate and skilful kind; only let them be confined to those parts of the service,—*e. g.* the Anthem,—where the choir alone ought to sing. Indeed there cannot be a better field for the enterprise of our young musicians, especially those possessed of talents like the author of the work before us, than the composition of anthems in the ecclesiastical style of Palestrina and Bird. We hope to see this school of genuine church music revived among our cathedralists; and we are glad to learn that the "Motett Society" have it in contemplation to offer prizes for such compositions.

Lives of English Laymen, Lord Falkland, Izaak Walton, Robert Nelson. By the Rev. WILLIAM H. TEALE, M.A. Leeds: Burns, 1842. 12mo. pp. 362.

THIS is the latest addition which has been made to the Englishman's Library; and a more useful undertaking can hardly have been entered on, than to exhibit to lay members of the English Church the bright examples that have been given them by several of their order. We have only had time, since receiving the volume, to read the most important, perhaps, of the biographies which it contains—that of Robert Nelson; but it is executed so admirably, and exhibits such a combination of diligent research, clear discrimination, and sound principle, that we feel bold to pronounce on the book as a whole, and warmly to recommend it. Nelson's is a name fragrant indeed with the odour of sanctity. Thank God! his example is not without imitators at present; and there is a living name which trembles on our lips, and which we are sure only waits for the death of its bearer to be coupled with his.

One word more. The times in which Nelson's lot was cast were times of peculiar division, religious and political; but there is this satisfactory fact to be gathered from the biography now before us—that many of those who felt most strongly in regard to the points at stake, and followed out their principles most uncompromisingly, were most conspicuous for their charity of feeling and conduct. The volume is one of the most beautifully illustrated in the whole series.

The Glorious Things of the City of God; the First Sermon, &c. in St. Mary's Church, Burlington, after a brief Pilgrimage to the Church of England. By the Right Rev. G. W. DOANE, D.D. LLD. *Bishop of New Jersey, &c.* Burlington, 1842.

IT is not generally our practice to bestow very particular notice on single Sermons, but the peculiar circumstances connected with this justify an exception in its favour. Some of our readers may perhaps remember the unfriendly reception which a Sermon of Bishop Hobart's, in exactly parallel circumstances, met with from those among us who seemed to think it right and necessary that an American should see every result of our peculiar constitution in Church and State in exactly the same light as a person bred in regular John Bull principles. An admirable letter on the subject will be found in the eighth volume of the Christian Remembrancer, *Old Series*, p. 543—550, and we think our readers will know the firm Roman hand. Bishop Doane's Sermon will not awaken the same class of feelings, for it contains nearly unmixed eulogy of all that he found among us. Perhaps he was in many respects more favourably circumstanced for judging of us than his illustrious forerunner, and he found us, too, in a more awakened and Catholic condition. At all events, our duty on receiving his Sermon is plain;—to be thankful for the kindly feeling shown by its author; to mourn over our long neglect of those privileges in our situation to which he is so alive; to humble ourselves for our unworthiness of the

Old St. Paul's: a Tale of the Plague and the Fire. By WILLIAM HARRISON AINSWORTH; *Author of* "*The Tower of London,*" &c. 3 vols. London: Cunningham. 1842.

WE remember that it was asserted, contradicted, and re-asserted, that the murderer Courvoisier received the first suggestion of his horrid crime from reading a romance of Mr. Ainsworth's, called "Jack Sheppard." For ourselves, we are happily ignorant of the production referred to; but we are quite sure that, if any one is desirous of corrupting the female mind, he has only to introduce the three volumes before us. They contain nothing but a series of intrigues and adventures, which, being assigned to Lord Rochester and his dissolute companions, suffice, in the parlance of the circulating library, to constitute an "historical novel." There is certainly enough of ability in the writer to make him a favourite in such places; but we repeat, that it is accompanied by such gross violations of propriety, as to render it imperative on every respectable head of a family to keep him without the reach of his household.

When so much more grave offences abound, it may appear but trifling to notice mere historical inaccuracies; but in the present case the representation of the manners of the day is one grand lie. All the contemporary historians relate that the greatest contrition and humiliation characterised the people during the plague; but it suited this writer, who, it appears, can only fish in filthy waters, to portray the greatest conceivable corruption of manners. Why he should have added the gratuitous insult of borrowing the title of one of the Temples of the Most High for his foul publication, it is not easy to conjecture.

Travels and Researches in Asia Minor, Mesopotamia, Chaldæa, and Armenia. By W. F. AINSWORTH, F.G.S. F.R.G.S. *in charge of the Expedition sent by the Royal Geographical Society, and the Society for Promoting Christian Knowledge, to the Christian Tribes in Chaldæa.* In 2 vols. London: Parker, 1842. Post 8vo.

WE have looked into these volumes with very considerable interest. They contain both information and incident. Mr. Ainsworth was accompanied by Mr. Rassam, a native of Chaldæa, who has been some time in this country; and his own qualifications, if not first-rate, were, at least, respectable. The prejudices with which he started, moreover, were not quite so inveterate as in some other recent instances. The following passage, indeed, is candid and sensible. It relates to the custom of engraving a cross at the entrance of their villages by the Chaldæan Christians, which is kissed by the devout on going out and coming in.

"I must confess," he says, adopting the words of Mr. Grant, "that there is something affecting in this simple outward expression, as practised by the Nestorians, who mingle with it none of the image-worship or the other corrupt observances of the Roman Catholic Church. May it not be, that the abuse of such symbols by the votaries of the Roman see, has carried us Protestants to the other extreme, when we utterly condemn the simple memento of the Cross? To how many other little points of Church discipline," he adds, "might not this find an equally strong application!"

It is strange, however, on the other hand, to hear a person who in some sense must be called an emissary of the English Church, speaking of "the schism *occasioned* by the councils of Ephesus and Chalcedon;" as though the blame of the schism rested with the Church, and not with the seceders who went out from her.

Again, one is somewhat startled at reading, that—" It is to the present day very *doubtful* if this *great* man " (Nestorius) " held the doctrines that are imputed to him."—" In all this " (his doctrine) " it may be truly asked, where is there any heresy? And it would be difficult to say in what it differs from the doctrine of the council that condemned him!"

It may not perhaps matter much to the general reader what Mr. Ainsworth's opinion may be upon this question; but it should be a very serious consideration with the Society for Promoting Christian Knowledge, whether they be not compromising the English Church by sending forth emissaries who hold such uncatholic views.

The Great Commission; or, the Christian Church Constituted and Charged to convey the Gospel to the World. By the REV. J. HARRIS, D.D. *President of Cheshunt College, Author of* "*Mammon,*" *&c.* London: Ward and Co. 1842. 8vo. pp. 538.

To enter upon the theology of a book, the very title of which is based upon the fallacy of applying to Christians generally the command which was given to the apostles alone, would be to waste time and words. Our object in noticing it, indeed, is altogether indirect. We are anxious, in the first place, to give an opportunity to Mr. Melvill, of stating how it is that he appears among such strange company. The treatise before us is called a " Prize Essay;" and the judges are stated to have been Dr. Welsh, a preacher of the Established Kirk of Scotland; Dr. Wardlaw, a noted advocate of the voluntary principle; Jabez Bunting, now or lately president of the Wesleyan Conference; and one Mr. Crisp, a Baptist preacher; the Rev. Henry Melvill occupying the centre of this motley group. We think Mr. Melvill will thank us for enabling him to explain the use which is here made of his name. Our other object is, (if our printer can find hyphens enough in his establishment,) to give one specimen of dissenting eloquence:—

"Union is a means of usefulness; and here it is supposed to be universal, visible, divine, as to each individual; here is the union of the whole man,—all his principles and passions combined,—no part of his nature wanting,—no part shedding a counter-influence,—the whole man bound and braced up for one purpose, as if devoted to the grand experiment of ascertaining how much a single human agent can effect in the cause of Christ. Here is the union of a number of these in a particular Church, in which none is inactive;—each has his post,—all act in concert,—the whole blent (*sic*) into a single power, and putting forth an undivided effort to draw the world around them to Christ. Here is the union of all these distinct societies in one collective body, bringing together agencies the most distant,—harmonizing materials once the most discordant,—blending hearts naturally the most selfish in bonds more tender than those of kindred, and so sympathetic that the emotion of one thrills through them all;—a union which economizes and combines all the energies and passions of sanctified humanity, which, collecting all the scattered agencies of good that earth contains, organizes them into a vast engine, whose entire power is to be brought to bear for the conversion of the world. And then, not merely in addition to, but infinitely more than all, here is the union of Divine influence with the whole,—heaven come down to earth,—the powers of the future world imparted to the present,—the Spirit himself, in a sense *incarnate*, pervading *his* (query? whose?) body, the Church,—investing it with unearthly power, and employing it as the organ of an Almighty power for recovering the world to Christ.

" Such, then, is an outline of the Scripture theory of that agency by which Christ proposes to reclaim the world. Can we forbear to admire the simplicity of its principle? It is simply *the law of reciprocal influence, baptized in the blood of the Cross*, and endued with the energy of the Holy Spirit. All in God that can influence is brought to bear, through the Cross, on all in man that can be influenced; and the whole of that is then put into requisition by the Spirit to influence others. If this theory were realized, could we question its efficiency? Of all who are brought within its scope, each of them is prepared to say 'None of us liveth to himself:' and what but the expansion of that sentiment is necessary to fill the world with the influence of the Cross? Would we doubt its ultimate and universal triumph? What when the Spirit himself had come down to work the entire system? What when the Church withheld nothing that could influence, and the Spirit withheld nothing that could crown that influence with success? If even the secret tear of an obscure penitent *creates a sensation* (!!) among the seraphim, the 'travail' of such an agency for the salvation of the world would carry with it the sympathies of the holy universe. God would bless it; and 'all the ends of the earth would fear him.' "

Frederick the Great; his Court and Times. Edited, with an Introduction, by Thos. Campbell, *Esq., Author of* "*The Pleasures of Hope.*" 2 vols. 8vo. Colburn. 1842.

This is a book very little to our taste. Whether we regard the subject, or the writer, or the manner of its publication, we instinctively revolt from it. The character of Frederick, misnamed "the Great" is too well known to need any comment of ours. He may be said, more than any other, perhaps, to have prepared the mind of Europe for the French revolution; and in all points of moral dignity must really be ranked in the lowest possible scale. Of his present biographer we need only say, that he is a person whose highest encomiums are lavished upon the last century, in comparison with which he represents the middle ages as remarkable, not only for "barbarism and brutality," but also for "selfishness!" But more words need not be wasted upon the author. Mr. Colburn—no mean authority in these matters—admits his incompetency for the task of authorship, low as is the bookselling standard; and therefore engages the effete Thomas Campbell, not, we presume, without a consideration, to write about fifteen pages of preface. And now let the reader mark the use which is made of these few trumpery pages. The title-page is so contrived as to make it appear that no other person is concerned in getting up the volumes than the same Thomas Campbell. Once would suppose that he had done just the same in this case that Mr. Tytler did in regard to the volumes illustrative of the "times of Edward VI. and Queen Mary." To "edit" is the usual term applied by writers who avail themselves of historical records to illustrate any particular time, and this is just what has been done in the present case: but then it is not Mr. Campbell who has done it, but some anonymous compiler, employed, probably, by the publisher at so much per sheet. Nor is this all: in the "lettering" of the volumes the authorship is directly assigned to Mr. Campbell. It is evident that "the editor" is not without misgivings as to the part he has taken in the work; but they are of a very singular nature. As to the moral dishonesty of the proceeding he is not in the smallest degree sensitive; but he has some apprehensions as to a possible "degradation" in the *market* which may accrue to him therefrom. But let him not disturb himself. Should any one chance to pass from one of his early poems to this production, there certainly would be a sad feeling of disappointment; but his literary fall has been so gradual, that people have long since ceased to regard him in any other light than as a scribbler for magazines and a disappointed politician.

Rambles and Researches in Thuringian Saxony. By FREDERICK STANFORD, Esq., M. A. London: Parker. 1842. 8vo. pp. 264.

AFTER trying this book in various parts, and wading through many pages, remarkable only for dulness and flippancy, we were about to throw it down in despair, when we stumbled upon two letters which could not be otherwise than interesting to us. They are written in Latin, by Dr. Bretschneider, of Gotha, with a view to publication in this work; and have for their object (in subordination to the primary end of setting forth the greatness of the writer's own achievements) the vindication of the Rationalist School of Germany from the charges brought against them in the well-known work of Mr. Rose. For ourselves, we are satisfied that nothing tends more to the successful propagation of error than that it should be misrepresented by the advocates of truth. We believe that, by one of those happy inconsistencies of which the human mind is capable, individuals in Germany do contrive to hold, theoretically, these opinions, without altogether abandoning practical piety: it is important, therefore, even if it were only to guard against reaction, that persons should not expect to find Rationalism leading, in all instances, to its legitimate fruit of infidelity. But, surely, Dr. Bretschneider must have very strange ideas of English feeling, if he imagines that his letters will be at all calculated to make us think better of Rationalism than we have been used to.

The following articles are altogether excluded from his creed:—
1. The plenary inspiration of Holy Scripture; 2. The doctrine of the Blessed Trinity, as set forth at the council of Nice; 3. The doctrine of original sin; 4. The oneness and completeness of the faith.[*]

[*] 1. "Quod ad scripturam sacram attinet, reprobandam puto veterum theologorum opinionem, Spiritum Sanctum scripsisse literas sacras, et scriptores sacros tantum Spiritus fuisse instrumenta . . . Codex sacer non est ipsa Revelatio, sed revelatio est in codice et ex eo cognoscenda. 2. Subtilissimam illam ecclesiæ

The only satisfactory intelligence which his letters furnish is, that Strauss's views have been very generally disclaimed in Germany, and himself compelled to vacate his chair, and to recant some of his opinions.

"The Churchman's Year, or Liturgical Remarks on the Sundays and Saints' Days, &c," by George Fyler Townsend, M.A., (Rivingtons, 1842,) is a book which we hope, on a more careful inspection than we have yet had time for, to find an excellent *higher step* to Jolly's well-known volume on the Sunday services. It is in every way, both in respect of preparation and dimensions, a much more considerable work.

"Christ our Law," by the author of "Christ our Exampler," &c., (Seeley and Burnside, 1842,) is a book in which the authoress settles matters with some talent and much to her own satisfaction. Unluckily, some of them are matters on which greater minds than hers have felt difficulties which she does not even guess at; and others are points on which she is so plainly ill-instructed that her authority must go for nothing. We wish she would write a book equally devotional and equally powerful with the present, in the spirit of the Prayer Book and the Church Catechism. It would be more in accordance with Holy Scripture than the present.

We have to acknowledge a very beautiful book, in Mr. G. R. Lewis's "Illustrations of Killpeck Church, Herefordshire," to which is prefixed "an Essay on Ecclesiastical Design," by the author. His opinions are not quite the same as our own; for, though we render all homage to the early styles of England and the North of Europe, as fuller of solemn beauty and significance than any other, St. Paul's is not to our eyes the profane looking place that it appears to Mr. Lewis. Farther, though the search after symbolic instruction in our old architecture is a warrantable one, and will, we doubt not, if pursued within bounds, be rewarded with success, it is quite erroneous, we are sure, to speak of such symbolizing as the leading merit—the leading *religious* characteristic of Gothic architecture. A disproportionate exercise of the fancy would have been fatal to the imagination; and symbolic instruction can seldom, at its best, be more than an exercise of, and an appeal to the fancy. But as our old cathedrals are beyond question highly imaginative, it follows that such symbolizing was not the main object before the minds of their architects. Their highest religious merit will be found, not in arbitrary and fanciful connexions between the disposition of parts and the truths of the faith; but in the general sentiment—in the lofty aspiring—in the unworldly and unself-indulgent characters of the whole, in the awful solemnity, and the high harmony of all.

The well-known Mr. Brockedon is now engaged with a work entitled, "Italy, Classical, Historical, and Picturesque," (Duncan and Malcolm, 1842,) which, judging from the numbers that have already appeared, is the most beautiful one of the kind we ever saw.

"The Mother's Help in explaining the Church Catechism, &c.," by the Rev. J. James, D.D., (Rivingtons, 1842,) seems an admirable work in every respect.

Dr. Gilly, of Durham, has published a benevolent appeal on behalf of the Peasantry of the Border. (Murray, 1842.) The facts regarding hinds and

---

doctrinam de Trinitate in Unitate missam facio. 3. Homo nascitur neque bonus neque pravus. 4. Jusjurandum quo doctores in credendo et docendo adstringuntur ad normam librorum symbolicorum per se nullum est. Cujuscunque confessionis vel symboli auctoritas interna nititur eo, quod refert exactam imaginem doctrinæ, quæ viget in ecclesiâ eo tempore, quo confessio facta est."

their cottages in that part of the world may be new to some of our readers, and must be interesting to all.

We are glad to find that the Christian Magazine, (Manchester, Simms and Dunham,) is advancing favourably. The sketch called "Lawyer Lukewarm," in the May number, is a spirited appeal on the necessity of something more than "jogging through life with a good, respectable, appearance." And we believe the concluding remark of Lukewarm must, though scarcely avowed to themselves, have occurred to many of the same stamp: "Well! he's a bigoted ass; but, after all, I cannot say he's very far wrong." In a lighter article, "The Old Church Clock," there are some excellent touches; especially where the old man, being told that the clock is incorrect, says, "It may be so, and perhaps it is. But, sir, I know that clock of old. Five-and-forty years have I gone by it, and it has never led me far wrong yet. And, with God's blessing, so long as I live in Manchester, I will set my watch by that clock, be it right or wrong."

We have received the first number of a little monthly publication, called "Common Sense, or Every Body's Magazine;" edited by the Rev. Dr. Molesworth, and the Rev. W. M. Molesworth. In point of principle, it promises to be such as we should approve; but we much mistake the intellectual standard of our mechanics and artisans if they do not require something very superior to this in ability. We confess also that we are the more surprised at this new attempt, because the editors cannot be unacquainted with the "Christian Magazine," just referred to, which is especially designed for the manufacturing districts, and which is really conducted with first-rate ability. We are not sure, indeed, that Dr. Molesworth may not allude to this periodical in a passage of his address, wherein he condemns the use of fiction, (of which, perhaps, the Christian Magazine *has* too much;) if so, we regret the appearance of rivalry; though it requires no prophet to foresee the result.

The Rev. Mr. Hoare has published a reply to the Bishop of Salisbury's Reasons for withdrawing from the Bible Society. It is interesting both for what it yields to the Bishop, and for what it refuses to yield. For example, the writer gives up as indefensible the habit of Clergymen attending Meetings of the Society in Dissenting Preaching Houses; or of ever holding Meetings when the Clergyman of the place is opposed to them. These are valuable concessions. Mr. Hoare's grand reason for supporting the Society is, because its platforms are the only types of heaven,—being the only places on earth where God's children meet without any intermixture of the wicked. In other words, he believes that to subscribe to the Bible Society, or rather, to attend one of its Meetings, is a sure test of being a child of God! A sufficiently comfortable doctrine! What are Popish good works to this?

"A Tract for Squires, by a Squire," (Burns,) though not free from one or two passages of questionable expediency, deserves our thanks. It is most important that the laity should be reminded of their responsibilities. The abuse of private patronage, for example, both as regards spiritualities and temporalities, is a crying evil. Religion, moreover, as the author of this tract well observes, is often the only subject on which the Conservative politician dares to be "liberal." We are sure that many well-meaning persons only require to have these and such like inconsistencies pointed out to them.

"Thoughts on England's Responsibility," (London, Hamilton and Adams; Hull, Cussons,) proceed, if not from a deep theologian, at least from an earnest mind, which sees that the Church, even upon grounds of temporal expediency, is alone qualified to make this nation a christian people.

"Comments on the Epistles, as appointed to be read at the Communion Table on the Sundays and Holidays throughout the Year; for the Use of

Families," by the Rev. J. F. Hone, Vicar of Tirley, Gloucestershire; (London, Parker, 1842; 12mo, pp. 322.) If this book had been published fifteen years ago, it really would have been useful. At the time of which we speak, theology, as a science, was thought to be an absolute hindrance to the parish priest, or to the popular writer, and scarcely to be consistent with inward piety. Mr. Hone's volume would then have been honoured as at once earnest and orthodox. Now, however, we fear that the public will pronounce a different verdict. They will consider it wanting in doctrinal precision, and depth of practical religion: the thoughts, in fact, bear a very inadequate proportion to the words; and it is in all points immeasurably inferior to the abridged work of Dean Stanhope, which we noticed in our last number.

The Society for the Propagation of the Gospel has just put forth, " a Colonial Church Atlas, arranged in Dioceses : with Geographical and Statistical Tables," which is to be had at the Depository of the Christian Knowledge Society. It will be found most useful.

The Lord Bishop of London's "Three Sermons on the Church," (Fellowes, 1842,) are, we presume, by this time in the hands of most of our readers. In case, however, there should be any who have not seen them, we now take what, in ordinary circumstances, we consider our only becoming course in regard to the Sermons of a Bishop, that of giving some account of their contents. His Lordship holds that a Church was founded by our Lord and set up by his Apostles, to which it is necessary to salvation that we belong; that we are admitted to the fellowship of this Church by baptism, and so regenerated,—that the Church to which we are thus brought is "not merely *instrumental* as a teacher, but *sacramental* as a medium of the believer's personal union with his Saviour, conveying and dispensing spiritual grace." After establishing these points, he proceeds to Episcopacy and the Apostolical Succession, on which his reasoning is most triumphant. Though, however, his Lordship holds Episcopacy to be of Divine right, he deprecates rash judgment of the spiritual condition of such religious communities abroad as unfortunately are without it, and enforces this charitable qualification by the authority of some of our old divines. On dissenters at home he is severer, as reason demands, though even of them his words are wary and tempered. " I would not pronounce, even upon *them*, the sentence of absolute exclusion from the Church of Christ, nor declare that they are beyond the pale of salvation. *I think them in a state of great uncertainty and hazard;* I am sure, *that they want many spiritual privileges which I am thankful for possessing.*"

The Primary Charge delivered to the Clergy of his Diocese, by the Bishop of Edinburgh, (Edinburgh, Grant, 1842,) will amply repay perusal.

"Twenty-one Plain Doctrinal and Practical Sermons," by the Rev. C. J. F. Clinton, M.A., Rector of Cromwell, &c., (Painter, 1842,) are not orthodox, and show the writer to be but a crude divine.

The Rev. Ch. Ch. Bartholomew, M.A., Rector of Lympstone, has published an excellent Sermon, preached at the visitation of the Archdeacon of Exeter, entitled "The Connexion of the Holy Sacraments with the Spiritual Life, and their Influence on the Ministerial Office and Character." (Rivingtons, 1842.)

Several useful Tracts in the form of Cards have lately been printed for distribution, (Burns, London,) among which may be recommended "The Two States;" "The Church of England and the Apostolic Succession;" "The Authority of the Bible and the Church;" "Texts for Meditation," &c. They are sold in hundreds at a cheap rate.

MISCELLANEOUS.

[*The Editor is not responsible for the opinions expressed in this department.*]

THE DIVINE RIGHT OF TITHES THE TRUE PRINCIPLE, THE OFFERTORY THE REAL INSTRUMENT, OF CHURCH EXTENSION.

No. VII.

THE funds for the Society for Promoting Christian Knowledge are less this year than they were last year. The secretaries urged upon the meeting the necessity of exertion to make up the deficiency: they should also, according to my judgment, have called upon the Tract Committee, and have asked whether in the Society's list of publications there were any Tracts which set forth the *true principles* of making contributions to the Church. I would ask, too, whether Bishop Wilson's Sacra Privata is still published in a mutilated form;[*] and then I would suggest in a friendly spirit that, if christian knowledge is to be promoted by Tracts, there should be a *series* of Tracts reminding all Christians, that a guinea subscription to the Society for Promoting Christian Knowledge is quite voluntary, but that it is the *positive duty* of all to contribute a certain portion of their income in the service of the Church. The extracts I have made in former numbers from the writings of Hooker, Bishop Andrews, and Bishop Wilson, would form an auspicious commencement of this new series. It would be a happy circumstance if this deficiency in the funds of the Society for Promoting Christian Knowledge should lead to a removal of the deficiency in its publications.

I will conclude my present number with an extract from a recent publication, and then I would ask my readers, if we are hereafter to be judged by the *law and the prophets*, whether Christians of the present day should not thus examine themselves. Have you not robbed God in tithes and offerings? or his priests in their accustomed dues? *Sherlock's Practical Christian*, part 1st. chapter iv., *quoting Malachi* iii. 8. (This work has been recently republished.)

"We readily and reasonably condemn those who add 'the doctrines of men' to 'the commandments of God,'—but we seem to be falling into the error (no less dangerous) of leaving out in our scheme of duty that part of God's word which does not suit our convenience. We seem to be insensibly adopting the false maxim, that no part of the Bible deserves our attention except positive precepts immediately directed to ourselves. But this is to lay down a very defective rule; it is to have eyes, and not to see; to have ears, and not to hear; to have hearts, and not to understand. In one point of view, the Bible, considered as a whole, is a parable in which the Holy Ghost speaks to us in a language which, with all the powers of our mind, we must 'read, mark, learn, and inwardly digest.' It is pious and prudent to act as if our salvation depended upon observing intimations of our duty; or rather, perhaps, I should say, it is impious and imprudent to disregard them. A faithful servant will not satisfy himself by a bare observance of his master's direct commands, but he will seek to discover his master's wishes,

---

[*] See No. 2, of these papers, in No. VII. of the Christian Remembrancer.

and act in compliance with them, however imperfectly expressed. A dutiful and affectionate child, in the interpretation of his father's will, acts under the impulse of the same generous spirit; he will disdain to take advantage of the absence of any positive instructions; his own interest will be a secondary consideration; he will not retain to his own use any property, however productive, if he only suspects that it was intended for another purpose. Those Testaments, Old and New, which bequeath to us a spiritual and eternal inheritance, must be interpreted with the same dutiful and affectionate spirit. Every book of them, every chapter of them, every verse of them, individually, or, as the case may be, collectively, must be treated with this care and attention.

"There is, I fear, too much reason to stigmatize the Tithe Act as irreligious, inasmuch as it sets aside all the foregoing considerations, as idle fables unworthy of notice. It is hard, I know, to grapple with public feeling; which, in the present instance of tithes, seems to arrogate even more submission to its dictates, and upon no better grounds, than if it were the pope of Rome, or a Romish council. But still, as truth is great, and will ultimately prevail, so, where there are no influences opposed to its reception, it has a force which nothing can withstand.

In a case where the evidence was much less forcible than that before us, I had the satisfaction of observing how much stress was laid upon such intimations of duty as were indirectly conveyed to us in Scripture. Lord Rayleigh, at the meeting at Chelmsford to which I have already alluded, justified his protest against the abolition of Church Rates on these very grounds; and, though he dwelt upon the question with very great minuteness and at considerable length, the breathless attention with which his speech was received, proved most clearly, that that method of applying Scripture finds a home within the human heart, when duly prepared to receive it.

"If, then, in reference to the present question, we will search for evidence of this kind, we shall find much which will deserve our most serious attention. I will here quote the judicious observations of Sir Henry Spelman. 'The first place in Scripture wherein a priest is mentioned, is Gen. xiv. 18. where Melchisedek is said to be the "Priest of the Most High God;" there also are tithes spoken of, and paid to him, ver. 20. "Abraham gave him tithes of all." The first place also where an House of God, or Church, is spoken of, is Gen. xxviii. 18. 22.; there also are "tithes" mentioned and vowed unto God, even by that very name whereby parish churches, upon their first institution in the primitive Church, were also styled, that is, by the name of "Tituli," Gen. xxviii. 22. *Lapis iste quem posui in titulum, erit Domus Dei, et omne quod dederis mihi decimas prorsus tibi dabo;* "and this stone which I have set for a pillar, shall be God's House, and of all that thou shalt give me, I will surely give the tenth unto thee;" thus Church and Tithe went together in their first institution.

"'If there be no mention after of tithes in the Scripture, till the time of Moses, that is no reason to exclude them; for so also is there not of any house of God or priest, yet no man will deny both are necessary; and therefore let them also say, whether they be "ex jure divino;" I mean churches and priests before the Law and the Gospel.'*

"It is certainly very remarkable, that in the very short and concise account of the history of the world, which we have in the book of Genesis, tithes should be so prominently mentioned; and then, that there should be in the New Testament that striking allusion to them, as existing in the patriarchal dispensation. These things are strongly in favour of their divine origin; but the argument for them is very far from being completed. For I must observe, that though, for the sake of perspicuity, I state the arguments under separate heads, yet if we would estimate their full force,

---

* Sir Henry Spelman's larger Work upon Tithes. London, 1647, p. 10.

we must view them both separately and in connexion with each other. To explain my meaning more fully, we have arguments in favour of the divine right of tithes from three sources; from the dispensation before the law, from the law itself, and from the practice of the Christian Church. These three sources of argument tell strongly when taken by themselves; but, beyond this, we have an argument resulting from their combination, for in this point of view they mutually illustrate and enforce each other. The argument drawn from the Jewish law is stronger when viewed in connexion with that derived from the patriarchal dispensation, and *vice versâ;* and again, these two both give and receive additional force when viewed in connexion with the practice of the Church. This circumstance we must bear in mind, and I will now proceed to notice, in the second place,

"2. The argument for the divine right, as supplied by the Levitical dispensation. Here I observe, tithes were neither a typical nor a ceremonial observance. We might, therefore, still appeal to the reason of the case, to the Jewish law as a sanction for them, precisely in the same manner as our Constitution appeals to the Jewish Scriptures as authority for its enactments respecting marriages within the degrees of consanguinity. We have, however, something more to urge in this case than the deductions of human reason, as may be clearly seen by referring to the ninth chapter of St. Paul's Epistle to the Corinthians: ' *Do ye not know that they which minister about holy things live of the things of the temple? and they which wait at the altar are partakers with the altar? Even so hath the Lord ordained that they which preach the Gospel should live of the Gospel.*' vv. 13, 14. The Apostle here plainly supposes (I again quote the words of a layman, the learned Dodwell) 'that our clergy answers the Levitical priesthood, our Churches their Temple, our Communion Table their Altar; and that, what was thought equal in their case in the provisions of the Old Testament is, for that very reason, to be taken for "ordained" in the case of the gospel ministry. There is no other evangelical ordinance so much as pretended for in that whole chapter.' That which was ' ordained' was the ordinance of tithes. The patriarchal dispensation and the practice of the Christian church combine in telling us that this is the true interpretation of the passage. 'EVEN so,' says the Apostle, implying that tithes are the inheritance of the Christian ministry, as they were the portion of the tribe of Levi.

"Moreover, as the ordinance of tithes is an evangelical ordinance, so does it necessarily include us in the blessing or the curse which the prophet Malachi was divinely commissioned to pronounce to the Jews: ' *Will a man rob God? Yet ye have robbed me. But ye say, wherein have we robbed thee? In tithes and offerings. Ye are cursed with a curse, even this whole nation. Bring ye all the tithes into the storehouse, that there may be meat in mine house, and prove me now herewith, saith the Lord of Hosts, if I will not open you the windows of heaven, and pour you out a blessing that there shall not be room enough to receive it.*' Chap. iii. 8—10. Is it possible that the Legislature, in a country whose constitution is based upon religion, can pass enactments in disregard of these solemn warnings, and in neglect of these gracious promises?

"It were better at once to withdraw the legal protection from the property of the Church, than to call upon the clergy, with a threat of compulsion, to carry out a measure which sets at nought inspired words like these. Well, indeed, may those exult, who sneer at the mention of a Providence in the speech of the sovereign, when laws are passed in defiance of that authority, which all but infidels profess to regard as most sacred. Here is a melancholy triumph for those who treat the claims of an apostolical ministry as priestcraft, and the service at the altar as a superstitious delusion. But if it be indeed true, that 'religion as well induceth secular prosperity as everlasting bliss, if godliness has the promise of both lives;' if the blessings of the Jewish law are our birthright also, why disinherit ourselves of so rich a portion? If the evidence of the divine right of tithes be at all such as has been represented, how can we regard this new measure for arranging the property of the Church in any other light but as proceeding from a profane distrust of the Providence of God; especially when we consider in the next place,

"3. The sanction which the system of tithes, as a divine institution, derives from the Christian Church, for this sanction makes the evidence which has been adduced conclusive. Christians, indeed, in the very first period of the Gospel, either brought all their property to the Apostles' feet, or paid much more than their tithes into the Lord's treasury. But as soon as this spirit had subsided, tithes were the appointed means, and that as a divine institution, of maintaining the ministers of Christ. In our own country, tithes have been established by all the authority, both ecclesiastical and civil, that this nation could give. They were dedicated to the service of God for ever with the most solemn vows, and the people were called upon to pay them, by an appeal to their sense of christian duty. That our ancestors applied the words of the prophet Malachi to themselves, and therefore, as a means of averting judgment, enforced the strict payment of tithes, is a circumstance which will never be considered by unprejudiced persons as a sign of a dark age. It is our age that is the age of darkness. We are not amending, as the Act professes, but reversing the laws; we are demolishing that which our ancestors built up, in their piety to God and their zeal for the Church. We are destroying with heedless hands a system which has been consecrated by time, and which traces its origin to Heaven. The charge of irreligion, therefore, attaches itself most strongly to the Tithe Act; and the more so, as it owes its birth to nothing but the covetous spirit of the age. For, notwithstanding the plausible objections which have been urged, tithes are so far from being an oppressive tax, that the payment of them is a natural acknowledgment to God for his blessing on the productions of the earth. One of the present day has said, 'It has always been my boast and pride, that, before I can *spend a single farthing which I receive from the land, a portion of those receipts has gone to the honour of my God. I will say, that if we, as a nation, or as individuals, whether as persons dissenting from the Establishment, or as belonging to the Establishment, do not endeavour to deserve that blessing which I read in my Bible is promised to those who honour God with their substance, and give to his service the first-fruits of their increase, we may expect to receive from Him a curse instead of a blessing.*'"

LATITUDINARIAN HERESY.

Sir,—By their fruits are we to distinguish those who are Christians in deed and in truth from those who *are* what the Jewish Pharisees *were*. And what are the fruits produced by Latitudinarians of the so-called "Evangelical" school? Are they not, amongst others, "hatred, variance, emulations, wrath, strife, seditions, heresies, envyings?" and these are declared, in the 5th chapter to the Galatians, to be works of the flesh. I may refer to what is now occurring in almost every parish in England, and to the articles (greedily devoured) in the Record and the (so called) Christian Observer, &c.; and the truth of my statement, that these works of the flesh are among the fruits of Latitudinarianism, cannot be denied. But I doubt, sir, whether the extent to which *heresy* prevails in this party, where the assertion of heresy gives opportunity to the exercise of the passions to which I have referred, is generally known. I think it proper, therefore, to acquaint the christian public with the following fact. I send you my name, and you are at liberty to make it known to any one who applies to you for the authority on which the statement is made.

During the last month a meeting for a religious purpose was held in Huddersfield. An archdeacon was in the chair. The vicar of a large parish in the neighbourhood came forward with the avowed intention of attacking Catholics, especially those of the Oxford school; and he was very zealous in anathematizing the Romanists. He drew a picture of the horrors which would ensue, if Romanism again prevailed among us; and in the course of his remarks, asserted the Nestorian heresy, ridiculing the idea of speaking of the Virgin as the mother of God, and therefore in effect denying that the LORD JESUS CHRIST is GOD! Except by one respected clergyman who worships the LORD JESUS CHRIST in spirit and in truth, and who trembled to hear his God blasphemed, the heretic was unnoticed and unrebuked; and the catholic clergyman was reviled as intolerant. It was enough; an attack was made on the Oxford divines; and this covered all other sins, and gave opportunity for a manifestation of other feelings which are not certainly the fruits of the spirit. The Latitudinarians, many of them, in conversation afterwards, seemed to treat the subject as one which was of no importance; and a leader among them, said the subject is one of such difficulty, that he did not see any great fault in the conduct pursued by his friend.

Now, sir, these are the men who, because they think that such a man as Mr. Williams would conceal the doctrine of the atonement, are now everywhere preaching it. I am glad that they do so. "Some indeed preach Christ in envy and strife—What then? Notwithstanding, every way, whether in patience or in truth, Christ is preached, and I therefore do rejoice; yea, and will rejoice." But I fear that when they know that Mr. Williams has published the most deeply-interesting and learned lectures on our Lord's passion *in a popular shape*, with reverence, but without what *they* call reserve, they will deny this fundamental verity also. But how they can even now preach the atonement while they forsake its foundation, I cannot guess.

I may add, sir, in conclusion, that the Nestorian heresy, and a refusal to speak of the LORD JESUS CHRIST as God, (one person with two natures,) is not only anathematized in the Athanasian Creed; but is condemned by the ecumenical Council of Ephesus, which council is one of the four, according to the decisions of which the Church of England directs the judges of heretics to form their decisions. Men who are heretics themselves are, at the present time, first and foremost to accuse of heresy all who think not as they do. A Latitudinarian means by heresy, any opinion contrary to his own; but Nestorians are *legally and canonically* heretics, denounced as such by Church and State.

In these days, when in some dioceses a Catholic in the Church of England can expect no justice; when the most cruel persecutions are excited against all who are suspected of holding, with the Catholic

Church, "the truth as it is in Jesus," it is most important to have these facts brought prominently forward.

He who addresses you, as you are yourself well aware, is not a Catholic of the *Oxford* school, but he is, nevertheless, as devoted a Catholic as any of that school can be, and will unite with all Anglican Catholics for the purpose, if not of obtaining justice, at least of vindicating God's truth.

I am, sir, your obedient servant,
A CATHOLIC.

[Diocesan Training School, Chester: Messrs. Buckler, Architects.]

CHESTER DIOCESAN BOARD OF EDUCATION, IN UNION WITH THE NATIONAL SOCIETY.

In the progress of this Board the friends of education in Church principles will find grounds for encouragement and congratulation. Its report for the past year shows that the same principles which it asserted at its formation, in 1838, are boldly avowed in profession, and steadily maintained in practice. It has had to contend with the difficulties which it was prepared to expect, from latitudinarianism on one side, and inconsiderate expectation on the other; yet its uncompromising adherence to a high standard of Church principles seems to have discouraged active opposition on the part of nonconformists, while its persevering zeal has overcome some of the hindrances which spring from lukewarmness or impatience on the part of the Church. It continues to direct its attention to the root of the evil which is universally admitted to prevail, and looks forward to an adequate extension of education as the ultimate product of present improvement in the machinery of tuition. Minute and systematic inspection occupies the whole time of one inspector, the result of whose labours is concisely published and sent to each supporter of the Board in the inspected districts; and an organizing master is continually employed in the formation of model schools (one for each local Board), wherein the system of instruction recommended by the Diocesan Board is exemplified, and to which teachers from neighbouring schools have access at all times for their own improvement. A depository also is established at a central point in the diocese, where schools, which are in union with the Board, may be supplied with every sort of the most approved school apparatus, &c., at a reduced price. Annexed to the report published by the Board, appears an appendix, in which the scheme of instruction which it recommends, with the books which are used in the model schools, is given in detail; and the result of its statistical inquiry is arranged in tables, showing at one view, and for each parish separately, what is the provision therein for scholars; the numbers of pupils on the books, with their average attendance; and what is the amount of parochial contributions to the funds of the Diocesan Board. The form of statistical inquiry, with a letter of instructions, and an appeal to the clergy for their cooperation with the Board, was issued, as heretofore, by the Lord Bishop of the Diocese.

If success had not hitherto attended the labours of this Board, doubts might still be entertained as to the policy of its proceeding with such uncompromising boldness in such a populous and manufacturing district, where all those evils are to be met which naturally abound where a vastly-accumulating population has been left without any adequate provision for their mental or spiritual culture. After four years, however, of steady perseverance in its originally prescribed course, it must be admitted that an honest acknowledgment of the Church, as to her own responsibility in the work of national education, has met with a noble response in the Diocese of Chester; whilst the carelessness of its executive board, in concealing or glossing over any proved and past remissness of the Church in this matter of extending popular instruction, has disarmed opponents, and created hopes of future and successful exertion. And the assertion of a definite and intelligible principle of teaching what the Church defines as the Christian Verity, and prescribes as wholesome discipline, in preference to seeking popularity and support by compromising conciliations in matters of faith, has inspired a confidence in favour of this Board which augurs well for the final result of its labours.

To quote from the report on the points alluded to, the Chester Board announces that it has come to the conclusion, "as evidence of the working of good schools, though on defective systems, that there is no necessity—even were there the justification—for any compromise, either as regards doctrines which are essential to be believed, or in the matter of formularies, which the Church has deemed best adapted for promoting sound and practical piety. It is felt that if any system of education was established which should exclude Church principles, the result would be the rejection of religious culture altogether. If Churchmen consent to be silent respecting any fundamental article of faith, the unobserving will soon disbelieve it. To be neutral about divine truth, is to be an enemy to the truth; an entire suppression of the obligation of any system is the point at which mere secular educationalists are ever aiming. They would for a while probably admit the Bible, in compliance with the spirit of the age, but the rejection of the Bible would soon follow; and the Church, which has been its keeper and witness, would cease to be looked upon as the authorized teacher of God's true religion.

"As regards the machinery of tuition by means of which the Chester Board proposes to extend education, on such principles it expresses its conviction that, in turning its first attention to the improvement of tuition, and to the training of well-principled and soundly-instructed masters, it is employed in that object which the present state of education most requires. All its inquiries have tended to establish the fact, that those who are entrusted with the management of schools, under existing systems of tuition, are, with some honourable exceptions, intellectually incapable of performing the duties of their office, or are personally disqualified for enforcing the proper *influence* of education, from the circumstance, that they are not distinguished as well for their learning and dexterity in teaching, as for sober and honest conversation, and also for a right understanding of God's true religion."

Next to the supply of competent teachers, it has appeared to the Board that there is great need for something like uniformity "in the management of Church schools. Undue reliance, however, will not be placed on the peculiarity of any system, nor is it desirable that the Board should prescribe minute regulations in matters of form. Experience and inspection alike testify that a good teacher will contrive to infuse the spirit of his own mind, and the influence of his own character, into any system, however defective; while, on the contrary, the most approved system, with the most costly apparatus, will be found worthless in the hands of one who is not appointed to teach." The temporary training school is reported to be "quite full—twenty-six students being in residence—of whom six are qualified to take situations;" and that "eleven candidates for admission are entered on the books for the vacancies which will shortly occur."

In the "model schools" established by this Board, and in which its scheme of education is pursued, "*religious* instruction is made more or less dependant, according to circumstances, on the *personal* superintendance of the parochial minister." The Board asserting, that "it is in such schools only where the Church system of pastoral direction and control has been carried out—that satisfactory fruit has been reaped from exertion in the cause of scriptural education."

As the result of its statistical inquiries and of inspection, it is reported that, "taking the diocese throughout, scarcely half of the space actually provided for scholars, is, in fact, occupied during the week;" but that in some old-established schools, "in which improvement has been effected," the attendance of scholars has gradually increased; and that in some "school-rooms, before occupied on Sundays only, a full attendance of week-day scholars has been obtained, by the natural effect of a superior character of masters, and a better mode of tuition." Yet the number of "scholars under education bears no proportion to the number of those who, from their age, ought to be at school; the largest amount in the country districts being "about nine per cent. on the whole population"—whilst in the strictly manufacturing districts "the average number of week-day scholars, of which the Church has any cognizance, does not exceed two per cent. of the whole; and it is only through the Sunday schools, the value and importance of which in such a population is incalculable, that the number is raised to five or six per cent."

The gross amount of parochial contributions for the year ending January 1842, has been 1,813*l*. 0*s*. 5*d*.; and the gross expenditure of the Board, including maintenance of training schools, expense of local boards, grants to model schools, inspection, salaries to assistant secretary, and organizing master, and sundry expenses of printing, &c., has been 1,648*l*. 5*s*. 10*d*. It appears that the building of the Diocesan Training College, which is now erected at Chester (see engraving), will cost the sum of 10,000*l*.; towards which the Committee of Council on Education have voted 2,500*l*., and the balance wanted to complete the undertaking is 1,185*l*. This institution is to be opened for the reception of pupils in the month of September next; and provision is made for the accommodation of fifty pupils training as teachers, and for sixty commercial pupils. Under the same roof will be rooms for the principal and under-master, with kitchen, offices, &c., and two normal schools, one as a model for a middle or commercial school, and the other as a model for national schools. When this establishment is completed, it is estimated that the cost of its maintenance will be considerably less than that of the present temporary institution; and the Diocesan Board will then be enabled to commence making grants towards the extension and improvement of schools in necessitous districts.

This Board presses on the consideration of its supporters the following needful remarks:—The result contemplated "cannot be immediate. We must exercise faith and perseverance. Years will pass before the whole is visible, several years, perhaps, before much appears; but the Board feels confidence that it is working in the right direction. It is instituting no private speculation, following out no personal or party views. It is laying out money in behalf of the Church, and claiming of churchmen their best exertions for the education of her children; and whatever delays may arise, whatever occasional or local difficulties may embarrass "the details of its operation, still the Board looks in humble confidence for the Divine blessing on its work."

We have inserted the above as furnishing a specimen of what *may* be done by Diocesan Education Boards, when managed with the requisite zeal and energy, coupled with a firm adherence to Church principles. It is clear that the members of the Chester Board have not only been talking but *working*, and in this respect they may well be held up as an example to similar associations in other dioceses. Those who desire farther details are referred to the voluminous Report lately printed at Warrington.*

---

* This Report may be had of Mr. Burns.

ECCLESIASTICAL INTELLIGENCE.

ORDINATIONS.

By Bp. of Exeter, *at Exeter, May* 22.

DEACONS.

Of Oxford.—W. T. A. Radford, B.A. Exet.; H. S. Templer, S.C.L. New Inn Hall; R. Bowden, B.A. Wad.; G. Woolcombe, B.A. Ch. Ch.; J. Harris, B.A. Pemb; G. Arden, B.A. Wad.; *Of Cambridge.*—J. V. Vivian, B.A. Trin.; S. Brown, M.A. Jesus.

PRIESTS.

Of Oxford.—B. M. Gane, B.A. Magd.; W. Rogers, B.A. Exet.; H. W. Toms, B.A. Exet.; E. Reynolds, B.A. Wad.; F. J. Taylor, B.A. Christ's; H. J. Drury, B.A. Worc.; C. S. Ross, M.A. St. Mary Magd. (*let. dim.*Bp. of Bath and Wells.)
Of Cambridge.—S. C. Sharpe, B.A. Christ's; E. K. Luscombe, B.A. Trin; S. A. Ellis, M.A. St. John's; J. Symonds, B.A. Clare Hall; J.W.S. Walkin, B.A. St. John's; H. T. Thomson, B.A. Magd.; A. Pope, B.A. Queen's; J. Martin, B.A. St. John's; E. T. May, M.A. Jesus.
Of Dublin.—H. B. Illingworth, B.A. Trin.

By Bp. of Gloucester & Bristol, *in St.Margaret's Church, Westminster, May* 22.

DEACONS.

Of Oxford. — C. B. Garside, B.A. Brasen.; R. W. Hippisley, B.A. Exet.; A. Peache, B.A. Wad.; G.T. Spring,B.A.St. Edm Hall; E. Wood, B.A. Magd. Hall; H. Hill, B.A. Wad. (*let. dim.* Bp. of Worcester.)
Of Cambridge.—B. Blenkiron, B.A., and W. Joy, M.A. Trin; W. Miniken, B.A. Cath. Hall; W. T. Preedy, B.A. St. John's.

PRIESTS.

Of Oxford.—W.T. Beckett, B.A. Trin.; C. R. Davy, B.A. Balliol; R. S. Hunt, B.A. Exet.; J. Lander, B.A. Pembroke; E. Lloyd, B.A. Merton; J. Martin, B.A. Sid. Suss.; J. de la Saux Simmonds, B.A. St. Edm. Hall; H. Skrine,B.A. Wad.; R. Underwood, B.A. St. John's.
Of Cambridge.—J.W. Gunning, B.A. Queen's; J. M. Neale, B.A. Trin.
Of Durham.—G. C. Guise, B.A.

By Bp. of Oxford, *at Oxford, May* 22.

DEACONS.

Of Oxford. — G. R. Brown, M.A. Christ Ch.; H. H. Cornish, M.A Magd.; J. Bellamy, B.A. St. John's; J. G. Brine, B.A. St. John's; R. S. Sutton, Exet.; H.Smith,B.A. Ch.Ch.; S.Waldegrave, M.A. All Souls'; W. Thomson, B.A. Queen's; H. Harris, B.A. Magd.; L. C. Wood, B.A. Jesus; R. P. Williams, B.A. Jesus; J. H. Ashurst, B.A. Exet.; T. K. Chittenden, B.A. St. John's; W. J.Whately, B.A. Ch. Ch.; J. G. Lonsdale, M.A. Ball.; R.Joynes, M.A. Corp. Christi; E. M. Goulburn, B.A. Merton; W. Jackson, B.A. Queen's.

PRIESTS.

Of Oxford.—V. Page, B.A. Ch. Ch.; W.Knight, M.A. Worc.; W. Jackson, B.A. Worc.; T. B. Cornish, M.A. Oriel; S. Buckland, M.A. Ch. Ch.; E. Hill, M.A. St. Edm. Hall; W.S.Newman, B.A. Wad.; E.J.W. H. Rich, B.A. New; E. H. Haskins, B.A. Queen's; E.W. Attwood, B.A. Jesus; J. Marshall, B.A. Worc.; J.D. Collis, M.A. Worc.; T. D. Andrews, M.A. Corp. Christi; T. Garrard, B.A. St. John's; J. J. Plumer, M.A. Ball.
Of Cambridge.—W. C. Sharpe, M.A. St. John's.

ORDINATIONS APPOINTED.

Bp. of Ely, *June* 5.
Bp. of Chichester, *June* 19.
Bp. of Winchester, *July* 10.

Bp. of Worcester, *July* 10.
Bp. of Ripon, *July* 31.

PREFERMENTS.

Name.	Preferment.	County.	Diocese.	Patron.	Val.	Pop.
					£.	
Alston, G.	St. Philip's Bethnal green.	Middlesex	London	Bp. of London		141	177
Austin, A.	Littleton Drew.	Wilts	Sarum	Bp. of Sarum.	141	177
Bazett, A. Y.	Quedgely, P.C.	Gloucester	G. & B.	Mr. Hayward	161	297
Broughton, H. V.	Wellingborough, V.	Northamp.	Peterboro'	Q. Vivian	400	4688
Byron, J.	Killingholme, V.	Lincoln.	Lincoln	Ld. Yarborough	285	793
Chamberlain, T.	St. Thomas, V.	Oxford	Oxford	Ch. Ch. Oxford	105	3277
Corfield, T.	Benthall, P.C.	Salop	Hereford	Vic.of Much Wenlock	93	525
Crowther, H.	St. John's Carisbrook, P.C.		Winchester	Rev. Dr. Worsley		
Payrer, —	EmmanuelCh.Camberwell, P.C.	Surrey	Winchester	Sir E. B. Smith		
Fitzherbert, T.	Marston Magna, V.	Somerset	B. & W.	Mrs. Fitzherbert	324	346
Fynes, W. C.	Maiden Bradley,P.C.	Wilts	Sarum	Ch. Ch. Oxford	111	659
Galland, J.	Laneham, V.	Notts	Lincoln	D. and C. of York.	56	347
Greaves, —	Ch. Ch. Herne Bay.	Kent	Canterbury			
Hayne, J.	Stawley, R.	Somerset	B. & W.	J. Hayne, Esq	150	180
Healey, J.	Scalford, V.	Leicester	Peterboro'	Duke of Rutland	255	467

PREFERMENTS,—continued.

Name.	Preferment.	County.	Diocese.	Patron.	Val.	Pop.
Hodge, C.	Scofton, P.C.	Notts	Lincoln	T. S. Foljambe, Esq.	£.	
Holmes, W.	ThelVeton.	Norfolk	Norwich	The Queen	249	175
Hutton, C. H.	Horsepath, P.C.	Oxon	Oxford	Magd. Coll. Oxford...	91	275
Johnes, T. W	Welton, V.	Northam.	Peterboro'	Lord Chancellor	193	600
Johnstone, J.	Banghurst, R.	Hants	Winch.	Bp. of Winchester		
Kirby, H.	Gt. Waldingfield.	Suffolk	Norwich	Clare Hall	598	679
Lowe, T.	Oldham.	Lanc.	Chester	Rec. of Prestwich	191	
Perrott, T.	Walton-on-Trent, R.	Derby	Lichfield	Ld. Townshend	828	820
Powys, A. L.	Titchmarsh, R.	Northam.	Peterboro'	Ld. Lilford	782	843
Prodgers, E.	Ayot St. Peter.	Herts	London	Ld. Mexborough	300	271
Reynolds, E.	Appledore, P.C.	Devon	Exeter	Rev. J. H. V. Mill		
Rigg, R.	St. Clements-on-Bridge, R. Norw.	Norfolk	Norwich	Caius Coll. Camb.	98	2767
Rogers, W.	Mawnan, R.	Cornwall	Exeter	Rev. J. Rogers	323	578
Russell, M.W.W.	Benefield, R.	Northamp.	Peterboro'		531	519
Sandford, G. B.	Minshull, P.C.	Cheshire	Chester		131	463
Savage, R. C.	Tamworth, P C.	Stafford	Lichfield	Capt. A'Court	170	7182
Shittler, R.	Alton Pancras, V.	Dorset	Sarum	Dean and Chapter	25	210
Stephenson, H.J.	St. Nicholas, R.	Worcester	Worcester	Bishop of Worcester.	260	2210
Stocker, C. W.	Draycott-le-Moors.	Stafford	Lichfield		452	539
Taylor, F. J. E.	Allington, R.	Devon	Exeter	Mrs. Fortescue	510	677
Taylor, R.T. W.	St. Mewan, R.	Cornwall	Exeter	Rich. Taylor, Esq.	284	1306
Toms, H. W.	Combe-martin, R.	Devon	Exeter	Exrs.of H.Toms, Esq.	387	1031
Toyeden, T.	Charleton, R.	Devon	Exeter	Mrs. Twysden	522	644
Webber, E. A.	Bathealton, R.	Somerset	B. & W.	Mrs. E. Webber	226	98
Webber, J.	Thorn St.Marg. P.C.	Somerset	B. & W.			
Wilson, M.	Barrowfold, P.C.	Lanc.	Chester			
Worsley, W.	Braytoft, R.	Lincoln	Lincoln	Lord Chancellor	255	202

APPOINTMENTS.

Aitken, R.......... Chap. to Earl of Caithness.
Coates, P. C....... { Head Mast. of Chatham and Rochester Prop. School.
Hall, E. .... { Chap. to English Residents at Corfu.
Harvey, W. W... Chap. to Earl of Falmouth.
Heathcote, T. H. Chap. to Earl of Macclesfield.
Remington, T.... Chap. to Earl of Burlington.
Symonds, T....... Chap. to Earl of Macclesfield.
Webber, J.......... { Chap. to Wellington Union, Somerset.

CLERGYMEN DECEASED.

Athow, J., Rec. of Halcatt, Bucks, 66.
Barneby, T., Rec. of Stepney, &c., 69.
Bell, E. J., Vic. of Wickham Market, Suffolk.
Blackmore, J., Rec. Combe-martin, Devon, 79.
Bowen, T., Rec. Troedyraur, Cardigan, 88.
Butler, P. E., at Peckham.
Butt, E., Vic. of Taller Fratrum, Dorset, 78.
Cook, H., formerly Rec. of Darfield, Essex, 72.
Drake, T., Rec. Intwood, near Norwich, 84.
Edge, J. W., Rec. Strelley, Notts., 52.
Escott, —, Harborough, near Tainton, 79.
Furness, T., at Hatcliffe Dale Vicarage, Lincolnshire, 64.
Hall, W. R, Cur. of East Cowton.
Hebson, R., Cur. of Tetbury, 27.
Hodges, T. S., Rec. Little Waltham, Essex, 48.
Lamb, J., Rec. Stretton, Rutland, 84.
Lewin, S. J., Vic. of Ifield, Sussex, 76.
Marsh, W., Chap. of Morden College, Blackheath, 64.
Murray, W., Rec. of Lofthouse, Yorkshire, 73.
Nott, E., Rec. of Weeke, Hants.
Peile, B., Cur. of Hatfield, Herts, 44.
Prowett, J. H., of Trin. Hall, Camb.
Rowlands, H., of Plasgwyn, Anglesea, 76.
Sams, J. B., Rec. of Hanington, Suffolk, &c., 79.
Shackleton, J., at Bath, 40.
Thompson, J., Perp. Cur. Matterdale, Cumberland, 53.
Trentham, W. H., at Leamington, 30.
Walter, R., Rec. of Parkham, 79.
Wilson, T., Kingston, Surrey.

UNIVERSITIES.
OXFORD.

April 28.

Degrees conferred.

M.A.

E. W. Rowden, Fellow of New; Rev. W. Pearson, Exet.; Rev. M. Anstis, Exet.; Rev. J. Jones, Jesus; Rev. C. Neville, Trin.; Rev. G.C. Swayne, Schol. of C. C.

B.A.

J. Ruskin, Ch. Ch. grand comp.; C. Vansittart, Oriel, grand comp.; H. O Holmes, Bras., grand comp.; M. Shaw, and J. M. Fletcher, Bras.; W. Ewart, and J. Tonkin, Exet.; J. H. Griffin, H. Hanmer, V. C. Day, and J. L. Harding, New Inn H.; J. A. Froude, Oriel; J. J-Wilkinson, J. Jessop, J. Jameson, and W. B. Turner, Queen's; C. S. Hawkins, A. T. Wilmshurst, and J. T. H. Evans, Magd. H.; J. W. Mason, Jesus; L. S. Dudman, A. C. Rowley, and C. J. S. Bowles, Wad.; J. Harris, S. Shedden, and J. W. Distin, Pemb.; W. Vigor, and J. Lea, Worc.; R. F. Wright, St. John's; L. K. Bruce, Ball.; C. F. Seymour, and R. S. Fox, Univ.; H. C. W. Ekins, Trin.

May 6.
Degrees conferred.
M.A.

Rev. I. H. Gosset, Exet.; H. C. Adams, and E. K. Burney, Dem. of Magd.; Rev. J. Innes, Trin.; R. Mynors, Univ.; Rev. R. O. Walker, John's; Rev. E. Curtis, Magd. H.; J. E. Grubb, Pemb.

B.A.]

H. B. Barry, Schol. of Queen's; E. Pedder, Bras.; G. Lewthwaite, Univ.; F. Fanshawe, Schol. of Ball.; S. W. Wayte, and M. Bernard, Schols. of Trin.; H. D. Heatley, and E. N. Conant, John's; H. Binney, R. W. Bush, and W. Andrew, Schols. of Worc.; J. Collingwood, Schol. of Pemb.

The following have been elected from Westminster School, Students of Christ Church:—T. J. Prout, L. C. Randolph, and J. P. Maud.

May 14.
Degrees conferred.
M.D.
W. Twining, Balliol.

B.C.L.
S. C. Denison, University.

M.A.
Rev. J Mansfield, Trin.; H. A. Bathurst, Merton; Rev. H. Batten, Exet. grand comp.; Rev. R. G. Boodle, Oriel; F. Tate. and S. Burstall, Univ.; Rev. E. Hill, Edmund H.; H. W. Acland, All Souls; Rev. T. W. Robson, Univ.

B.A.
E. A. Tickell, Balliol; L. C. Bathurst, J. Stephens, and G. E. Jemmett, Trin.; S. W. Newbald, R. A. H. Stroud, and R. Henderson, Wad.; H. Ellison, Univ.; M. J. Routh, and P. Le Maistre, Pemb.; J. W. Grane, Exet.; H. F. Inman, and T. R. Green, Linc.; T. A. Falkner, John's, grand comp.; M. L. Lopes, and J. W. Nevill, Oriel; S. Minton, Worc.; R. T. Mills, Magd.; W. E. Rusher, Magd. H.; R. Rolleston, Univ.

May 25.

The following gentlemen were nominated by the Vice-Chancellor and Proctors to be Masters of the Schools for the ensuing year:—Rev. J. W. Richards, M.A. late Fell. of C. C.; Rev. D. Melville, M.A. Bras.; J. F. Boyes, M.A. John's.

Rev. W. L Chafy, M.A. of Sid. Suss. Camb. admitted *ad eundem*.

Degrees conferred.
B.D.
Rev J. Foley, Fell. of Wad.

D C.L. BY COMMUTATION.
W. Robertson, M.A. Fell. of Magd.

M.A.
Rev. D. Hunter, Exet. grand comp.; R. T. Kent, Wad. grand comp.; J. J. Foulkes, Jesus, grand comp.; Rev. T. B. Adair, Exet.; Rev. H. R. Woolley, and Rev. E. J. Wilcocks, Linc.; Rev. W. L. Darell, W. C. Morland, and W. Currer, Ch. Ch.; Rev. J. Fletcher, and Rev. R. Tomlins, Mary H.; R. Joynes, Scholar of C.C.; Rev. W. Knight, Schol. of Worc.; J. Fraser, Fell. of Oriel; Rev. J. B. Sweet, and Rev. J. E. L. Schreiber, Balliol.

B.A.
C. F. Wyatt, Ch. Ch. grand comp.; H. Goodwin, Ch. Ch.; R. Weatherall, C. E. Brewin, and F. E. B. Cole, Edm. H.; J. W. Clapcott, Linc.; F. W. Vaux, A. Gordon, R. Watts, J. Coventry, and C. F. Cook, Magd. Hall; J. C. Paxton, G. Meynell, W. G. Bradley, and R. Stanton, Brasen.; R. G. Swayne, and G. W. Paul, Wad.; A. A. Aylward, S. M. Barkworth, and A. Barrett, Worc.; C. J. Parke, Oriel; H. G. J. Parsons, Demy of Magd.; F. Temble, Schol. of Ball.; H. Robinson, Alban Hall; S. Lucas, W. Jackson, J. Merry, and W. L. Collett, Queen's.

H. W. Norman, Scholar of New Coll. has been admitted Actual Fellow of that Society.

W. Parker has been elected Scholar of Pembroke, on the foundation of Cutler Boulter.

J. Rumsey has been elected Bible Clerk of same College.

J. Freeborn has been elected Bible Clerk of Worc.

OXFORD ARCHITECTURAL SOCIETY.

A meeting was held on Wednesday, May 18, at the Society's room, the Rev. the Rector of Exeter Coll. in the chair. Four new Members were admitted.

Presents received.—An impression of the fine Brass of Bishop Wyvil, from Salisbury Cathedral, presented by W. J. Jenkins, Esq. Balliol College. Lithographic Views of Hereford Cathedral, showing the proposed restorations; presented by the Dean of Hereford. Lithographic Views of Stamford Church, &c. &c.

The chairman informed the meeting that the Society has purchased the entire collection of architectural drawings left by the late Mr. Rickman. The value of these drawings does not consist in their merits as works of art; for they are merely outlines in pen and ink, some of them mere scratches, though generally drawn with great care and accuracy; but in the immense variety of examples here brought together during a long number of years devoted to the study of Gothic architecture. There are altogether upwards of *two thousand* examples, of which the greater part are English, a few Scotch, and about three hundred are foreign, chiefly French, but some from Rotterdam, and other places. The whole of this large collection are drawn from sketches made on the spot, and the greater part are unpublished. Collected by so careful an observer as Mr. Rickman, their value as examples may be relied on, and can hardly be estimated too highly for the use of such a society as this. Mr. Rickman unfortunately died before he had at all completed his design, which evidently was to form a chronological series; and many parts of it are left in a very imperfect state; but other branches of the subject, particularly the variety of the forms of tracery of windows, and of those more especially during the Decorated period, will be found particularly copious and complete. He took this opportunity of urging upon the attention of the members the importance of collecting sketches, and transmitting copies of them to the Society, with the view to carrying out the design of which so noble a foundation is here laid. Let them not be discouraged by the rudeness of their early attempts, but take encouragement from the rudeness of many of Mr. Rickman's drawings; and remember that a rude sketch, if accurate, and accompanied *by measurements*, is more really valuable than a highly finished artist's drawing without them.

CAMBRIDGE.

Degrees conferred.

April 27.

HONORARY M.A.

The Hon. R. H. Dutton, Trin. Coll.

M.A.

E. Walker, King's; C. Colson, St. John's; J. W. Johns, St. John's; C. Thornton, Clare Hall; G. H. Bidwell, Clare Hall; G. R. Lewin, Catharine Hall; E. Hanson, Emm.; R. Baggally, Caius.

B.A.

W. de St. Croix, St. John's; J. C. Chase, Queen's; T. A. Anson, Jesus; T. Richardson, Jesus; J. T. White, Magd.; C. Francis, Trin.; R. G. Creyke, Cath. Hall; R. N. Clarke, Down.; F. J. Biddulph, Emm.

F. Fulford, M.A., Exet., Oxford, admitted *ad eundem.*

May 11.

M.A.

J. L. Fulford, Trin.; W. Joy, Trin.; J. F. Pownall, Trin.; R. H. Tillard, St. John's; R. Ferguson, Pemb.; T. R. Dickinson, Magd.; C. Smith, Magd.

B.A.

H. M. Birch, King's; A. Hume, King's; H. Kirwan, King's; R. B. Collier, Trin.; P. R. Hammond, Trin.; J. H. Henderson, Trin.; M. S. Suckling, Trin.; J. R. Holligan, Trin.; R. G. Maule, St. John's; R. F. Burman, Caius; R. L. Coe, Christ's; Nevill Gream, Magd.

GREAT ST. MARY'S CHURCH.

May 17.

The Tyrwhitt Hebrew Scholarships were adjudged as follows:—

First Class.—C. J. Elliott, B.A., Cath. Hall.

Second Class.—C. Chambers, B.A., Emm.

Mynors Bright, B.A., of Magd., had a gratuity of 20l. awarded to him for the knowledge which he displayed at the examination.

May 18.

TWENTY-SIXTH MEETING OF CAMBRIDGE CAMDEN SOCIETY.

Twelve candidates were balloted for and elected.

A list of nearly one hundred presents was then read by the secretary. This list comprised several books; impressions of many rare and valuable brasses; eight beautifully coloured drawings of decorated windows from Carlisle, Heckington, and Sleaford, made to a scale, and presented by E. Sharpe, Esq., architect; and a large collection of Gothic mouldings, by F. A. Paley, Esq.

The following report was then read from the committee:—

"On again meeting the Society, the Committee beg leave to report the places whence applications have been received since the last meeting:—Alverton, Truro, Cornwall; Aylesbury, St. Mary, Bucks; Bakewell, Derbyshire; Beeston, Nottingham; Bridgerule, Devon; Congleton, Cheshire; Devizes, Wilts; Fairburn, Ferrybridge, York; Lichfield, St. Michael; Madron, Penzance, Cornwall; Mirfield, Dewsbury, Yorkshire; Pauntley, Newent, Gloucestershire; Stonnall, Shenstone, Stafford.

"The Committee for the Restoration of St. Sepulchre's are about to issue a list of additional subscriptions received since the last report, accompanied by a lithographed drawing of the church, and trust to the active exertions of the members of this society in aid of a work in which its credit is so intimately concerned. A very large sum will still be wanting to carry out the repairs in the same church-like and durable manner in which they have so far been conducted. A faculty has been granted for the proposed alterations: the original chancel-arch has been discovered, and will be restored; and rapid progress is making towards the erection of the new aisle.

"The Committee have undertaken to receive subscriptions for a new church at Alexandria, (for which a grant has been made by the Society for Promoting Christian Knowledge,) for which they have also promised to furnish designs.

"The restoration of the font of St. Edward's, under the able superintendence of Mr. Lawrence, clerk of the works at St. Sepulchre's, is highly satisfactory."

A paper was then read from the Rev. W. Airy, M.A., Trinity College, Vicar of Keysoe, near Kimbolton, and rural dean, describing an inscription lately discovered on the font in his church. A model of the font, executed by Mr. Airy, and a full-sized copy of the inscription, were exhibited.

Edmund Sharpe, Esq. M.A. of St. John's College, architect, then proceeded to read a first paper on the Early History of Christian Architecture.

After some discussion on the subjects treated of in this paper, and due acknowledgments to Mr. Sharpe and Mr. Airy for their interesting communications, the meeting adjourned.

TWENTY-SEVENTH ORDINARY AND THIRD ANNIVERSARY MEETING.

The Rev. Dr. Routh, President of Magdalene College, Oxford, and President of the Oxford Society for Promoting the Study of Gothic Architecture, was elected an honorary member by acclamation.

A list of presents received was read; among them was a view of the restoration of Hereford Cathedral, presented by the Very Rev. the Dean, and a view of the chapel of St. Mary, now building at Arley Park, Cheshire, with the copy of the inscription on the foundation stone, presented by R. E. E. Warburton, Esq., the sole founder.

On the recommendation of the Committee, it was next unanimously resolved—

'That the members of the Durham Architectural Society be admitted, in compliance with Law XVIII., to the same privileges as have been granted to the members of the Oxford, Exeter, and Lichfield Association."

The report of the Committee, and that of the Treasurer were then read.

The President then rose and delivered an eloquent address upon the history and prospects of the Society.

PROCEEDINGS OF SOCIETIES.

INCORPORATED SOCIETY FOR PROMOTING THE ENLARGEMENT, BUILDING, AND REPAIRING OF CHURCHES AND CHAPELS.

Report made to the Annual General Court, May 23, 1842.

His Grace the Archbishop of Canterbury in the Chair.

Your Committee, considering it to be unnecessary to occupy the time of the friends of the Society by any statements of its designs, or arguments in their favour, proceed to lay before the meeting a brief account of their proceedings since the last anniversary, and of the means they now possess or may expect to obtain of continuing their operations.

Since their last report, 178 applications have been received, from various parts of England and Wales, for assistance towards the repair, enlargement, or rebuilding of ancient fabrics, or the building of additional churches or chapels in populous parishes.

In consequence of these applications, 143 grants have been voted, of sums varying according to the circumstances of the several cases; and provision has thus been made for the accommodation of 41,554 persons, of whom 30,048 will have the privilege of attending divine service without cost. The sum thus voted amounts to 19,090*l*., being 3,453*l*. less than the votes of the preceding year, while the increase of accommodation given has been in proportion greater; for in the year 1841 accommodation was provided for 45,757 persons by a vote of 22,543*l*., while in the past year the number has been 41,554, and the cost to the Society 19,090*l*.

Your Committee advert to this result with great satisfaction, because they consider it to have been produced by a more skilful arrangement of the space in the several plans which have been brought before them, and not from any sacrifice of the proper character of those sacred edifices merely to save expense. Indeed, they remark with pleasure a growing desire to render churches and chapels, in their general appearance, worthy of the high and holy purposes to which they are devoted, as far as the means of their several founders extend. And they trust that this, as well as the continually increasing call for additional church accommodation from all parts of the kingdom, the retired village as well as the populous town, the manufacturing not less than the agricultural population, may be considered as a convincing proof that the Society, under the Divine blessing, has been the means of cherishing throughout the kingdom a desire of partaking in the benefits of public worship, and an affectionate reverence for the ordinances of our national church.

Deeply impressed with the belief that such has been the effect of their exertions, and desirous of promoting the growing interest in favour of their designs by every means in their power, the Committee have carefully revised the Suggestions and Instructions with regard to the construction and arrangement of churches and chapels which they issue to applicants for aid, and they hope that they may thus more fully meet the wishes of their zealous friends; and, confident that this measure will be duly appreciated, and that this Society will be perseveringly supported by the members of the Church, on whose behalf it is acting, the Committee look without apprehension, though certainly not without concern, to the present state of their finances. They cannot but perceive that, unless speedy efforts are made by their friends to increase the funds of the Society, they will be compelled to restrict their grants, at least for a time, within much narrower limits than has hitherto been their practice, if not to withhold them altogether, in many cases where they would willingly afford assistance if it were in their power.

At the present moment the grants of the Society remaining unpaid, and liable to be called for at varying periods, amount to 50,985*l*., but the sum in its possession is only 47,759*l*., showing a deficiency of 3,226*l*.

The Committee have no doubt of being able, from their accruing means, to pay all their grants as they become due. But when they consider that so large a portion of those means is anticipated, and that more than a twelvemonth must elapse before any proceeds from a royal letter can be realized, should such letter be granted in the ordinary course; they certainly are desirous that some steps should be immediately taken to recruit their funds, and thus relieve them from the painful necessity of withholding aid, on which may mainly depend the success of many an attempt to bestow the full benefit of her communion on the poorer members of the Church, or to recall to her fold those who have strayed from it in search of the spiritual advantages she had no means of affording them.

The Committee cannot conclude their report without thankfully adverting to the munificent donations, amounting to 3,500*l.*, which they have received from various quarters within the past year. They will not occupy the time of the meeting by reading the long list of such benefactions, which will be contained in the yearly statement; but they wish to express their lively gratitude to Her Majesty the Queen Dowager for a donation of 500*l.*, and to Her Royal Highness the Duchess of Gloucester for 100*l.* Nor can they refrain from recording a second donation of 500*l.* from His Grace the Duke of Northumberland. And they trust they may be allowed to mention another sum, not on account of its amount, but as it affords an example of a pious sacrifice to devout and charitable objects, which cannot be too highly esteemed or too earnestly recommended for imitation. It is a donation of 60*l.*, being part of 160*l.*, the tithe of a layman's professional income for 1841, placed at the disposal of the Bishop of London.

With such evidence before them of devoted liberality, the Committee look forward to the future without dismay, humbly trusting that the Great Head of the Church will incline His servants to assist them with their bounty, and that, under His protection, they may still continue with success their zealous endeavours to promote the knowledge of His truth and the extension of His kingdom.

A meeting of the Committee of this Society was held at their chambers, St. Martin's-place, on Monday, the 16th of May, 1842.

Present, The Lord Bishop of Durham in the chair; the Lords Bishops of Winchester, Worcester, Bangor, Chester, Norwich, Salisbury, Llandaff, Gloucester and Bristol, Lincoln, and Ripon; the Revds. Dr. D'Oyly, J. Jennings, J. Lonsdale, and Benj. Harrison; N. Connop, jun., H. J. Barchard, J. Cocks, I. S. Salt, and Benj. Harrison, Esqrs.

Grants were voted towards building a chapel at Westport, in the parish of Curry Rivell, Somerset; building a chapel at Blackgate, in the parish of Kelloe, Durham; building a church at Llanfynydd, in the parish of Hope, Flintshire; building a chapel at Kidderminster, Worcestershire; building a chapel at Dursley, Gloucestershire; building a chapel at Hardway, in the parish of Alverstoke, Southampton; rebuilding the church at Llanarmon Dyffryn Cieriog, Denbighshire; enlarging by rebuilding the church at Arlington, Devon; enlarging by rebuilding the church at Barford, Warwickshire; repewing the church at Holme, Yorkshire; building a gallery in and repewing the church at South Lynn, Norfolk; repewing the church at Bradford Abbas, Dorset; building a chapel at Crook, in the parish of Brancepeth, Durham; enlarging by rebuilding the church at Benghfield, Berks; enlarging the chapel at Newton Heath, Manchester; and other business was transacted.

SOCIETY FOR THE PROPAGATION OF THE GOSPEL IN FOREIGN PARTS.

Extract from the Correspondence of the Society.—Would that our friends in England could have been present at the consecration, last month, of the beautiful church in Vepery, now the church of St. Matthias. I was assisted on the occasion by fourteen clergymen, besides the candidates for holy orders at the approaching ordination. When my present Archdeacon arrived in India, there were scarcely so many clergymen in the whole diocese. We have now sixty-eight actually resident clergymen in the archdeaconry of Madras, twenty-two of whom are maintained by the Gospel Society, and their number likely to be added to at my next ordination.

Having alluded to the consecration of the church at Vepery, I will say a few words about the native confirmation which I held there last month. One hundred and thirty-nine were confirmed; and among them was an old woman of seventy-five, in whose appearance we were all much interested. It was indeed a pleasing sight in this heathen land to see her totter up to the rails of the communion table, and place herself upon her knees to be blessed in the name of God by her Bishop: and I was assured by her minister that she well knew and felt the need of God's blessing. The service being conducted in three languages, lent it, moreover, an interest unknown to it in England; Mr. Taylor interpreting for me in Tamil, and Mr. Howell in Teloogoo, and I myself officiating in Portuguese, as three distinct congregations were brought to me. After Mr. Howell had explained my address to the poor Teloogoos, an old man among them, the chief of his village, stood up and begged hard for a church, be it ever so humble, near to their own homes; and it shall not be long, please God, before they have one.

ADDITIONAL COLONIAL BISHOPRICS.

The following circulars have been drawn up and issued by the several sub-committees appointed to promote the erection of Bishops' Sees in Gibraltar, Van Diemen's Land, New Brunswick, and South Australia.

BISHOPRIC OF GIBRALTAR.—We, the undersigned, having been appointed by the Archbishops and Bishops who have undertaken to arrange measures, in concert with Her Majesty's Government, for the Erection and Endowment of Additional Bishoprics in the Colonies, to act as a sub-committee, with an especial regard to the See of Gibraltar, beg leave to request your assistance and cooperation in furtherance of this most important object.

When it is remembered, that on the shores of the Mediterranean, and within the limits of the proposed episcopal jurisdiction, there are upwards of twenty-five British congregations,— that in the cities thus situated—which are the permanent residence of many of our countrymen, and are frequently visited by still more of the higher and wealthier classes, either in pursuit of health or pleasure—the clergy and their flocks are wholly without efficient ecclesiastical control, and are debarred from the blessing of those ordinances which can be administered only by the episcopal order; when it is remembered, too, that our holy Church is thus placed in humiliating and disadvantageous contrast with the ancient churches of the East, and those of other nations of Europe; few arguments, it is thought, can be needed to impress on the minds of Englishmen the duty of an immediate and effectual exertion to supply this manifest deficiency.

The proposed Bishopric of Gibraltar seems to have peculiar claims on the liberality of English Churchmen. In this case there are not the same local sources of endowment which are to be found in most of our colonies. There are no crown lands, nor colonial revenues, either at Gibraltar, Malta, or in the Ionian Islands, which can be attached as an endowment to the see.

A sum of 20,000*l.*, including the donation of 2,000*l.* given by Her Majesty the Queen Dowager, has been appropriated from the general fund to the establishment of the see, and an annual grant of 500*l.* out of the sums placed at the disposal of the Episcopal Committee has been guaranteed until an income of equal amount shall be provided from some permanent investment. To raise the sum necessary for this purpose, and thereby to ensure, in the only unobjectionable way, an income of 1,200*l.* per annum (the least which can be deemed suitable for a representative of the highest order of the English Church, or adequate to the expenses of his station), a further contribution is absolutely required; for which this appeal, we are confident, will not be made in vain to those who desire to see our Church planted in the perfectness of its constitution, and with all its powers of usefulness, in those regions which witnessed the labours of the Apostles.

(Signed)
    LYTTELTON.
    W. H. COLERIDGE, *late Bishop of Barbados.*
    GEORGE CHANDLER, *Dean of Chichester.*
    JOHN RYLE WOOD, *Canon of Worcester, and Chaplain to Her Majesty the Queen Dowager.*
    GEO. FRERE.

BISHOPRIC OF VAN DIEMEN'S LAND. —We, the undersigned, having been appointed by the Archbishops and Bishops a special committee for raising subscriptions in aid of an endowment for a Bishopric in Van Diemen's Land, take the liberty of applying to you as one interested in that colony, both for your support and cooperation, and also for your advice as to the most eligible mode of investment.

We have the satisfaction of stating that the Government has not only expressed a desire that a see should be founded in Van Diemen's Land, but has consented to endow it in part with the provision hitherto made for an Archdeacon. From this source it is expected that an income of 800*l*. will be derived; but it is obviously indispensable that a further endowment for the Bishopric should be secured from some permanent investment. For this purpose the Trustees of the Colonial Bishoprics Fund have assigned 5,000*l*., in the hope that the remainder may be raised by the exertions of those who are specially concerned in the prosperity of the colony.

Van Diemen's Land at present forms part of the unwieldy diocese of Australia, its capital being distant upwards of 600 miles from the seat of the Bishop. The number of its clergy is twenty-one. With a superficies nearly equal to that of Ireland, and a population of 50,000, rapidly increasing, of whom a large majority are Churchmen—with its insular position and separate civil government—this province has surely the strongest claims to a Bishop of its own.

There is reason to believe, that, should the proposition be liberally met by those interested in the welfare of Van Diemen's Land, there would be no delay in proceeding to the consecration of a Bishop.

(Signed) COURTENAY.
JOSHUA WATSON.
T. D. ACLAND, JUN.
EDWARD COLERIDGE.
W. J. E. BENNETT.
T. W. ALLIES, *Hon. Sec.*

BISHOPRIC OF NEW BRUNSWICK.—We, the undersigned, having been appointed by the Archbishops and Bishops, who are now arranging measures, in concert with Her Majesty's Government, for the Erection and Endowment of Additional Bishoprics in the Colonies, to act as a sub-committee, with an especial regard to the intended See of New Brunswick, beg leave to request your assistance and cooperation in furtherance of this most important design. The Colony of New Brunswick is at present included within the See of Nova Scotia, but the Bishop has long felt, and urged upon the authorities at home, the necessity of dividing the diocese, and placing New Brunswick under a distinct ecclesiastical head. The province in extent is about 26,000 square miles, (nearly the size of Ireland,) and its population, a rapidly increasing one, is now 156,000. But these circumstances, though of great weight in themselves, yet present but inadequately the grounds upon which the necessity for the establishment of the proposed bishopric rests. The distance between place and place, and the difficulty and uncertainty of communication, from the state of the roads, the modes of conveyance, and the severity of the climate during a very considerable portion of the year, contribute to separate the clergy from each other; and will, of course, render their mutual intercourse, even with a resident Bishop, less frequent and regular than would be the case under other circumstances. But the effect of all this is very seriously augmented by the fact that the Bishop of Nova Scotia and New Brunswick resides at Halifax; and that, with the claims which Nova Scotia has on his time, it is impossible for him to visit New Brunswick as frequently, or so thoroughly, as is desirable, and as his lordship most earnestly desires.

The endowment of a bishopric for New Brunswick cannot be estimated at less than 1,200*l*. per annum: and this must arise from a capital invested in permanent securities. We have the satisfaction of stating that the archbishops and bishops have appropriated for this object a sum of 10,000*l*. from the General Fund placed at their disposal; and there is good ground for hoping that from the colony itself some considerable contributions will be transmitted. But there will still remain a large amount to be raised, before the great object which we have in view can be attained.

We now, therefore, earnestly appeal to you for assistance in raising this sum, and we hope and trust that we shall not appeal in vain.

(Signed) HOWARD DOUGLAS.
J. T. COLERIDGE.
JOHN LONSDALE.
H. GOULBURN.
H. TRITTON.

BISHOPRIC OF SOUTH AUSTRALIA.—The Archbishops and Bishops, who, in concurrence with Her Majesty's Government, are now arranging measures for the Erection and Endowment of Additional Bishoprics in the Colonies, have appointed us, the undersigned, to act as sub-committee with especial reference to the intended See of South Australia.

We earnestly request the favour of your influence and cooperation in furtherance of this most important object.

South Australia was created a British province by an Act of Parliament in the year 1834. It contains an area of 300,000 square miles. The colony was founded in December 1836. Its progress has been singularly rapid—the population having, in the course of six years, increased from a very few labourers to the number of 16,000. The healthiness of the climate, and the numerous inducements to emigration, give every reason to expect that the colony will steadily advance in prosperity.

Some churches have been built in Adelaide, the capital of South Australia, and in the neighbourhood, and others are in progress; but the want of episcopal control has been already sensibly felt, and questions have arisen which could only be satisfactorily determined by a Bishop; for although the colony is nominally within Bishop Broughton's diocese, the distance is so great, and the means of transit are so uncertain, that the Church is practically beyond the limits of episcopal superintendence. The churches are not consecrated—the young are not confirmed—the clergy and the community are suffering from the absence of an ecclesiastical superior, to whose decision and counsel they may refer in matters affecting the Church. And as the colony increases, it is difficult to see how disunion on very solemn questions can be prevented, unless measures be taken for planting our Church within it in the perfection of her order and discipline. The history of our North American settlements may teach us the wisdom of anticipating the evil of a colony growing in strength, and in ignorance of the benefits of efficient Church government. And all experience confirms the opinion that no christian community should be left without the counsel and control of a Christian Church in the completeness of her polity.

We are happy to inform you that a proprietor of the land in South Australia has already offered to build, at his own cost, a church at Adelaide, to endow it with land to the amount of 270*l*. per annum, and to furnish plans, &c., for a Bishop's residence. Other individuals have also contributed gifts of land to the amount of 100*l*. per annum. We have no doubt that such examples of christian munificence have only to be known in order to be followed. From the Colonial Bishoprics Fund we have obtained a grant of 5,000*l*., which will yield a further endowment of about 400*l*. per annum. And we trust that, with your kind cooperation and aid, the whole proposed endowment of 1,000*l*. per annum will be provided for the Bishop, who cannot adequately discharge the duties of his station with a less income.

We therefore appeal to you for assistance towards the completion of this work, the benefit and utility of which to the interests of religion, and to the permanent well-being of the colony, can scarcely be exaggerated.

(Signed) H. R. DUKINFIELD.
GEORGE GAWLER.
J. LEYCESTER ADOLPHUS.
WILLIAM LEIGH.
J. G. GIFFORD, *Hon. Sec.*

DIOCESAN INTELLIGENCE.

EXETER.—*Architectural Society.*—At a recent meeting of this Society, Dean Lowe read a paper, one of the objects of which was to show that on each side of the altar in our churches there ought to be a niche, in which the elements of the sacrament might be placed.

LONDON.—*King's College.*—The Annual Meeting of proprietors was lately held in the Theatre of the Institution, to receive the Report of the Council, and for the election of officers for the ensuing year. His Grace the Archbishop of Canterbury, Visitor of the College, presided. The total receipts of the past year amounted to 21,569*l*. 16*s*. 10*d*. The *contra* side, after deducting all expenses, showed a cash balance of 917*l*. 13*s*. 6*d*., besides 4,500*l*. vested in Exchequer bills.

Bethnal Green Churches.—On Monday, 25th April, the consecration of the third of the new Bethnal Green churches, by the Lord Bishop of London, took place. The church is called St. Philip's, and is built in Mount-street, Friars' Mount; one of the most destitute portions of that destitute parish. About 50*l*. were collected at the offertory.

Since the final appeal has been put forth by the committee, as recited in the

Ecclesiastical Gazette for March, the sum of 2000*l.* additional has been raised: consequently 10,000*l.* only remain to be collected, in order to fulfil the design as originally contemplated for the amelioration of the parish. The Bishop stated in his sermon on the occasion of the consecration, that more clergy were still wanted to complete the ecclesiastical organization of the parish, an object which may be beneficially effected before all the churches are built, and which will be necessarily instrumental, through the pastoral efforts of the newly-appointed clergy, in preparing local congregations for the churches about to be erected in those districts, which have been hitherto deficient in clerical superintendence. Another subject of a most interesting character was also touched upon by his Lordship, both in the sermon, and afterwards when he met the clergy at the curate's house. The Bishop pointed out that the pastoral responsibilities of the parish could never be adequately fulfilled while *so large a population as* 6,000 *was left to the ministrations of a single clergyman.* After all the ten new churches are completed, and a minister appointed to each, this will be the case; the population of Bethnal Green being 74,000, while the districts will be only twelve in number. Hence, his Lordship stated plainly, the necessity that would exist for providing assistant curates for all of these large districts, so as to secure the ministrations of *at least* two clergymen for each 6000 of population.

Clergymen desirous of undertaking a part in this work, and desirous to have a separate district assigned to them, wherein a church will ultimately be built (in the mean time to assist the clergymen in the districts already apportioned), may make application by letter to the Secretaries, Rev. Bryan King and Rev. Henry Mackenzie, at the Bethnal Green Churches Office, 3, Crosby-square, Bishopsgate, or personally at their respective residences, 10, Bethnal Green; and St. James's, Bermondsey; and early attention will be paid thereto. A stipend of 100*l.* per annum, and rooms at the curate's house, will be assigned to each of the clergy immediately on appointment, and so soon as the requisite funds can be obtained, additional curates will be appointed to each of the districts.

Statement of Bethnal Green Churches Fund.

1839. Sum wanted to build ten additional churches, schools, and parsonage houses (with partial endowments) 75,000
1842. Sum already collected by donations and annual subscriptions for four years . . . 65,000

—— Sum deficient; yet to be raised in order to complete the work £10,000

NORWICH. — A splendid organ has lately been erected in the **church of** Redenhall, Norfolk, of which a detailed account has been printed, which will doubtless be interesting to the lovers of instrumental music in churches. The builder is Mr. G. W. Holdich, of Greek-street, Soho, whose talents in this line, we believe, cannot be too highly spoken of.

RIPON.—LEEDS.—Dr. Hook begs to acknowledge the receipt of a letter bearing the London post-mark of the 7th instant, enclosing fifty pounds from " A Layman towards the Funds of the Choir of the Parish Church, to be inserted in the Subscription List thus:—
1 Chron. xxv. 6. } £50."
Psalm xcv. 1.

WINCHESTER. — *Diocesan Church-Building Society.*—At the last meeting of the committee, the following grants were made:—For a new church at Hardway, in the parish of Alverstoke, 550*l.* For one at South Hawley, in the parish of Yately, 350*l.* For one in the parish of Chobham, 100*l.*, in addition to a previous grant of 300*l.*

CHURCHES CONSECRATED OR OPENED.

Shaftesbury	Holy Trinity	Bishop of Sarum.
Clapham	St. John's Chapel	Bishop of Winchester.
Hanwell	....	Bishop of London.

FOUNDATIONS LAID.

Redhill, Reigate	....	.... May 11.
Broadway, Westminster	....	.... May 30.

TO CORRESPONDENTS.

Peculiar engagements this month have prevented our paying such attention to the communications with which we have been favoured as we could wish.

INDEX TO VOL. III.

(NEW SERIES.)

ARTICLES AND SUBJECTS.

A.

ALMANACS. [*Vox Stellarum, &c. for* 1842, *by Francis Moore, Physician. Churchman's Almanac for* 1842.] 108—112. Credulity of the present age seemingly considerable, 108. Almanacs in times past, 108—112.

Arnold's Lecture on the Study of Modern History. [*Inaugural Lecture, &c. delivered in the Theatre, Oxford, December* 2, 1841, *by Thomas Arnold, D.D. &c.*] 308—316. Merits of Dr. Arnold, 309. His view of the objects of the State; that object an educational one, 311. Distinction between the immediate purpose and the ulterior uses of anything, 311, 312. Objections to Arnold's theory;—it confuses the State with the Church, would render right government impossible, would almost authorize persecution, 315, 316.

B.

Bagster's Hexapla. [*The English Hexapla, exhibiting the Six Important English Translations of the New Testament Scriptures, Wiclif, Tindal, &c.*] 17—35. History of the Text of the New Testament—Erasmus, Elzevir, Mill, Bengel, Wetstein, Griesbach, 17—19. Alexandrian and Asiatic texts, 20, 21. The latter preferred by Scholz, 21. Texts relating to the divinity of our Lord, 24. Translations of the Bible, 25—34.

Bennett's Theology of the Early Christian Church, 1—16; 212—215. Study of the Fathers spreading even among dissenters, 1. Dr. Bennett's contradictory conclusions; his unworthy estimate of Clement, 2—6. His conceptions of a Church, 8—11. Of its officers, 11—14. Additional argument on St. Clement, 212—215.

British Church. [*The Liber Landavensis, edited by the Rev. W. J. Rees, M.A. &c.*] 47—55. No existing succession from the British Church, 48. Ruling principle of the Anglo-Saxon Church to have no communion with the British; consecration of Chad pronounced null by Theodore; the condition in which Theodore found the English sees, 49. Case of the Welsh Church, 51. Augustinian line extinct as well as the British; national Church of England to be dated from Theodore, 52. Bede's Ecclesiastical History now brought within reach of every clergyman, 54.

C.

Carlyle's Lectures on Heroes. [*On Heroes, Hero-worship, and the Heroic in History, Six Lectures, &c., by Thomas Carlyle.*] 341—353.

Characteristics of Mr. Carlyle as a writer,—different from those of any previous Scotchman—he is suggestive, reverent, and generous, reconciles his readers to mystery, and saves them from liberalism, 342—344. Faults of his style, 345—348. Principle of hero-worship, is it good or bad? 348. 349. Dangerous religious tendency of Mr. Carlyle's writings, 350—353.

Catholic Unity. [*Sights and Thoughts in Foreign Churches, and among Foreign Peoples, by F. W. Faber, M.A. &c.*] 621—630. Isolation of Anglicans; yearnings towards Rome sure to be disappointed, 621—623. Our present condition, 626, 627. The Roman ceremonial, 627, 628. The Greek Church, 628, 629.

Chapters on Ecclesiastical Law. [*No. II. Residence of the Clergy.*] 200—212. Plurality and Residence Act of 1838, 201—212. Residence Houses, 211.

Christian Priesthood and Sacrifice. [*History of the Christian Religion and Church, by Dr. A. Neander, translated by H. J. Rose, B.D. History of the Planting and Training of the Christian Church by the Apostles, by Dr. A. Neander, translated by J. E. Ryland.*] 529—542. Caution requisite in reading Neander, 529. Distinction between the words Πρεσβύτερος and Ἱερεὺς, no valid argument against the priesthood, 530—532. Christ's only Priesthood compatible with a secondary priesthood under him, 532—534. Priesthood of all the baptized compatible with an especial Priesthood of Bishops and Presbyters, 535, 536. Such especial priesthood the best witness both for Christ's and the people's, 536—538. Alleged derivation of the Church from a synagogue, of no value as an argument, 538, 539. Right mention of the priesthood in the New Testament, how accounted for, 539—541. Expression of Polycrates about St. John, 541.

Church and State. [*Wackerbarth's Egyptian Bondage.*] 361—369. Problem to be solved, How to place the union between Church and State on such terms as that neither should destroy the other? Impossibility of two co-ordinate jurisdictions, 362. Idea of a State requires that of integral independence; the Church stood in the way of such independence in the early times of European states, 363. How asserted abroad, and how in England, 364—368. Commission of the State, 364, 365. Distinction between spiritual power and spiritual jurisdiction, 366—368.

Church Architecture. [*Petit's Remarks on Church Architecture. Camden Society's Hints to Church Builders. Pugin's Principles of*

NO. XVIII.— N. S. 4 z

Pointed Architecture. Emerton's Sermons on Church Building. Gresley's Parochial Sermons.] 353—360. What is Catholic Architecture? 354—357. Errors of the Camden Society, 357—359. Moderation and candour of Mr. Petit, 359, 360.

Character of the Papacy. [*Sibthorp's, Dodsworth's, Drummond's, Palmer's, and Pusey's Pamphlets.*] 422—434. Position of the Church of England, and seeming prospects of young men in taking orders twelve years ago, 422—424. Consequent investigation of the history, principles, and constitution of the Church—movements in the universities, at Cambridge how different from that of Oxford, 424, 425. Oxford Tracts, earlier numbers agreed with by the great mass of the clergy, 425, 426. Early training of the writers of, the source of their main defect—depreciation of the English Reformation, 426. Religious unity, the design of God—two very different meanings attached to the phrase by men, 428. Mr. Sibthorp taught to understand it in the sense of the Bible and the Religious Tract Society, finds that sense untenable, 429—431. High Church principles not always treated at present with the same forbearance as avowed heresy, 433, 434.

Chester Diocesan Education Board—Abstract of its proceedings, 708.

Colleges of "Bishops' Fellows." Plan for the formation of 231—243. Advantages of the plan in regard to new unendowed churches, —to the working of our different Societies,—to greater acquaintance of the spiritual wants of the country,—to the education of clergy, 234—239. Further advantages, 240, 241.

Continental Protestantism. [*Laing's Notes of a Traveller on the Social and Political State of France. Prussia, &c.*] 385—410. Characteristics of Mr. Laing, 385, 386. Religious state of Geneva, compared with that of Scotland, 389—392. Revival of the Church of Rome on the Continent; that Church is leading the movement in favour of Education, 392—395. New Prussian Church; Lutheranism and Calvinism; modern rise of the Prussian power, and peculiarity of its territory, 397—402. Prussian Liturgy so called, 403—406.

D.

Didactic Fiction. [*Tales by Marryat, Tytler, Gresley, Paget, &c.*] 74—89, 145—160. Educational importance of fiction,—fairy tales,—their value, 75. Dr. Aikin and Miss Edgeworth, fallacies running through their works, and religious defects, 76—79. Mrs. Sherwood and Miss Grace Kennedy,—Miss Kennedy's tales nearly all turn on conversion in the modern sense of the term—evils of this—Father Clement, 79—82. Catholic movement has told on fiction. Archdeacon of Surrey's Parables, 82. Masterman Ready, 83, 84. Peculiar merits of Mr. Gresley's books. Forest of Arden contains an excellent view of the English Reformation, 84—89. Mr. Paget's Tales of the Village, compared with Warton's Death-bed Scenes,—superiority of the former. Negative and positive high-churchmanship, 145—147. Significant names, their evil, 148. Fairy Bower and Lost Brooch, —power possessed by the authoress of drawing characters, 153. Importance of a sense of the absurd, 154. Rutilius and Lucius—difficulty of writing tales about the period to which they belong. Early Church made progress through consistent development of her principles, 159.

Divine right of Tithes, No. V., 243—249. No. VI., 593—595. Letters on the subject, 243—245. Hooker and Chalmers, 247, 248. Vows, 248, 249. Change of Dr. Chalmers's opinion, 594. No. VII., Christian Knowledge Society. Sherlock's Practical Christian, 703—706.

Division of Verses in the Bible, (Nos. I. and II.) 455—469. Claim of Robert Stephens to the invention, 455—463. Whether any similar divisions existed among the Jews, or are to be found in Greek MSS., 463—469. Early MSS. of the Latin Bibles, 672.

E.

Electricity, History of. [*A Manual of Electricity, &c. by Dionysius Lardner, D.C.L., &c. Proceedings of the London Electrical Society.*] 631—644. Thales, acquainted with the attractive property of amber, 631. Gilbert Otto Guericke, Stephen Grey, 632, 633. Dufaye's discovery concerning vitreous and resinous electricity, 635. The electric shock, 636—638. Identity of electricity and lightning, 638—642.

Episcopal Visitations, Nos. IV. V., 112—123, 562—575. History of episcopal visitations in England. Bishop Gibson on LXXth Canon of 1603, 112, 113. Synod of Cloveshoe and Calcuith, constitutions of Archbishop Odo, 114, 115. Introduction of Roman Canon Law in the 12th century. Adoption of the Lateran rules by the synod of London, 116. Constitutions of Cardinal Otho, 117. Relaxing of the ancient canons, 118. Archidiaconal Visitations, 119. Reformation, and Reformatio legum, triennial visitations, 120, 121. Ancient mode of proceeding at visitations,—notice to be given,—Bishop met by clergy and people, 562, 563. Examination of the clergy, 564—567. Of the laity, 567—571. Legal power in visiting of English Bishops at present, 575.

F.

Foreign Aid Society. [*Correspondence between the Foreign Aid Society of London, and the Sociétés Évangéliques of Paris and Geneva.*] 411, 421. Discontent in the present day with our position in the Christian world, and desire for more extended communion, 411. Attempt of the Foreign Aid Society to establish such communion with Protestants abroad—tried by four tests, and found unwarrantable, 412—419. Tone of its letter to the Genevese Committee, 412, 413. Genevese declaration of faith, 415, 418. Objectionable, and why, 418. Position and State of the Reformed Body in France, 419, 421. Impossible for the Church of England to find a true basis of union with either, 421.

Francis (St.) and his imitators. [*Histoire de St. François d'Assise. Par E. C. de Malam. Letter from the Earl of Shrewsbury to A. L. Phillips, Esq. &c.*] 55—74. Character and times of St. Francis, 55—58. His care of lepers. Their misery in the middle-ages, 59, 60. Ecstasy of Francis and reception of the *stigmata*. Story, how treated at the time. How misrepresented probably by means of pictures. 62—64. The Estatica, the Addolorata, Difference of their *stigmata* from those of St. Francis, and defects in the evidence, 64—74.

G.

Gallican Church. [*Du Vandalisme et du Catholicisme dans l'Art. Par le Comte de Montalambert. Etat du Catholicisme en France, par Alphonse Pepin.*] 188—200. Revival of interest in foreign ecclesiastical affairs, 189, 190. Injury done to churches in France, 190—195. Improvement lately. Banishment of the Pompadour style, 195. Contrast between the revivals of a just taste in England and in France, 198—200.

INDEX.

Geology, Principles of. [*Principles of Geology, &c. By Charles Lyell, Esq.*] 161—171. Antiquity of the earth. Institutes of Menù. Hymns of Orpheus, 162. Pythagoras and Ovid, 163. Aristotle and Strabo, 164. The Saracens, 164, 165. Leonardo da Vinci, Hooke, 166. Werner, 167, 168. Hutton and Smith, 169, 170.

Grey's Australia. [*Journals of two Expeditions of Discovery in North-west and Western Australia, &c. by George Grey, Esq*] 35—47. Peculiarities of Australia, 36. Want of water, 38. Conflict with the natives, 41—43. Excellent spirit of Captain Grey, 44—46.

K.

Kingdom of Christ. [*Delineated in two Essays, &c. by Richard Whately, D.D. Archbishop of Dublin.*] 90—107. Archbishop Whately has courted reply, 90. Unsettlement resulting from Catholic movement. Reserve of the Bishops and its advantages, 91, 92. Archbishop Whately has avowed heresy. Identical with that of Hoadly, 93—99. His views of the Church, 99—101. Christian priesthood, 103—105. Catholic tradition, 105, 106.

L.

Latitudinarian Heresy—Letter on, by a Catholic, 706.

M.

Marriage Laws, proposed changes in. [*Considerations on the state of the Law regarding Marriages with a Deceased Wife's Sister. By H. R. Reynolds, jun. M.A. Present State of the Law as to Marriages Abroad between English Subjects, within the Prohibited Degrees. Pusey's Letter on Proposed Changes in the Laws.*] 542—561. Statute law, 544—546. Levitical law, 546—553. Rule of the Catholic Church, 553—555. Marriage of King Henry VIII. 556—558. Present state of the case in regard to the affinity in question, 559—561.

Methodism, witness of, to catholic truth. [*The Sunday Service of the Methodists, &c.*] 292—308. Probable cause of any great religious movement, 293. Witness borne by heresy to the truth which it exaggerates, 294. State of matters when methodism arose—doctrines of conversion, of perfection, and of assurance, 296. Witness borne by Wesley to the Church and her polity, 297—299. Wesleyan ordination, 300. Lesson to be gathered by the Church from methodism, 308.

P.

Plato, introduction to the Dialogues of. [*An Introduction to the Dialogues of Plato. By W. Sewell, B.D.*] 609—621. Value of Mr. Sewell's work in respect of illustration, 610, 611. Schleiermacher's introductions, 611—613. In what sense Plato had a practical object, 612—614. Whether the Greek philosophy arose from a traditional revelation, 615—618. The republic, 618—620.

Poetry for children. [*Selection of Hymns. Child's Christian Year. Hymns for Children. Hemans's Hymns for Childhood.*] 435—443. Importance of awakening a taste for poetry in children—facilities for doing so, 435—438. Merits of the collections in question, 440—443.

Poetry of the year 1842. [*Wordsworth's Poems of early and late years. Campbell's Pilgrim of Glencoe. Tennyson's Poems. Trench's, Whytehead's ditto. Williams's Baptistery. Montgomery's Luther, &c.*] 655—671. Prospects of poetry at present, 655, 666. Vindication of Mr. Wordsworth's recent poetry, 666, 667—but not of his altering his former verses, 657, 658—three periods of his style, analogous to those of pointed Gothic, 659, 663. Guilt and Sorrow, 663, 664. The Borderers, 667, 669. Falling off of Mr. Campbell's powers, 669, 670.

Practical education, recent English works on. [*Hopwood's, Taylor's, Tuckfield's, Wood's, Maurice's, Short's, &c.*] 317—341. Mr. Taylor's System—his distinction between school and home, 318, 319. Poetry, 321. Mrs. Tuckfield, 322—325. Edinburgh Sessional School, 325—328. The Schoolmaster; or, Essays on Practical Education, 328—338. Ascham's description of "quick wits," 331. Milton's Letter on Education, 332.

Prospects of the Church of England, No. III. 249—262. Overwhelming necessities of the Church of England at present, 250—252. Church of Ireland, 253. Voluntary liberality, 254. Appropriation of ecclesiastical property to church extension, 258—262.

Protestantism, letter on, 480—486. Are the Greek Churches Protestant? 481. A test of catholicism to be able to receive new spirits as they arise. Protestant spirit positive, not merely negative, 482—484.

R.

Romanesque Style for Churches, 576—583. Evil of attempting to imitate several styles at once, 577. Inconsistent adoption of their features—Romanesque not liable to this danger, 578. Peculiar advantages of Romanesque for roofs, towers, windows, exterior ornaments, 578—580. Use of bricks, 580, 581. The apse, buttresses, and galleries, 581—583.

Religious slanderings. [*Village Pencillings, &c. Life and Defence of the Conduct and Principles of Edmund Bonner, &c.*] 644—654. Offensive character of Village Pencillings, 645—649. Its irreverence, 649. Lies in Life of Bonner, 650—653. Impertinent liberty taken with the present Bishop of London.

Reformation in Scotland. [*History of Scotland, by Patrick Fraser Tytler, Esq., vols. 5, 6, 7.*] 171—187, 273—292, 497—514. Church party in Scotland, the French and National, Protestant, the English one, 172, 173. Hamilton, his death, 173. Firmness of James IV., 175. Seizure of Cardinal Beaton, on the death of James IV., 177. Subsequent increase of his influence and his cruelty, 179. Plot against his life—Wishart's connexion with if, 180. Character of Wishart—his death—murder of Beaton, 182—187. John Knox allies himself with the Murderers, 274—275. Mary of Guise, 277. Knox's imprisonment in France, 276—278. His return to Scotland—his accepting the Pastorate of Geneva, 278, 279. Covenant, 280. Address against the tyranny of the State Ecclesiastical, 281. Ascendency of the Guises over the mind of the Queen Regent, 282. Capture of Perth and Stirling by the Protestants, 284. Character of Murray, 286. Death of Mary of Guise, 287, 288. Ascendency of the Reformers, and their persecuting spirit, 289, 290. They obtain legal sanction for their doctrines, 291. Arrival of Mary in Scotland—her treatment by Knox, 498—500. Queen's declaration of Protestant faith as that of Scotland, 500. Double-dealing of Knox, 502, 503. Queen meets her first Parliament, 503, 504. Relations between Murray and Knox—Murder of Rizzio—Whether Knox was concerned therein, 510—512. Death of Darnley, 512—514.

T.

Theological Education at Cambridge. [*Report of a Syndicate, appointed by the University of*

Cambridge, to consider, &c.] 514—521. Two objects to be provided for,—sufficient religious knowledge in candidates for degrees, and sufficient theological knowledge in candidates for orders, 514. Pantheistical critical spirit will come upon us if not guarded against, knowledge of Scripture the true antidote for, 517, 518. Comparative advantages of the university and diocesan seminaries for theological instruction, 518. General absence of study of Scripture, 521.

Travels of Nicander Nucius in England. [*The Second Book of the Travels of Nicander Nucius of Corcyra, edited from the original Greek M.S., with an English translation, by the Rev. J. A. Cramer. D.D. &c.*] 522—528. Fire-damp in the mines at Liege, 523, 524. Nucius' account of the Death of Rufus, and contest between Becket and Henry, 525, 526.

U.

Unpublished Letters relating to Archbishop Becket, 444—455.

NOTICES OF NEW PUBLICATIONS.

A.

Abercrombie's Contest and Armour, 130.
Addison's History of the Knights Templars, &c., 127.
Annual Report (The) of the Children's Church Missionary Association, 691.
Annual Report (The) of the Newington Green Church Missionary Nursery, Islington, 691.
Arnold's English Grammar, 371.

B.

Best's (Captain) Excursions in Albania, 369.
Bigland's Letters on the Study of Ancient and Modern History, 474.
Bingley's Conversations on the most Eminent and Instructive British Characters, 474.
Bishopric of Souls, (The) by R. W. Evans, M.A., 590.

C.

Conard's Life of Christians during the Three First Centuries, 124.
Conformity, by Charlotte Elizabeth, 125.

E.

Ecclesiastica, by Edward Mahon Roose, 372.
Episcopacy, and Presbytery, by the Rev. Archibald Boyd, 225.

F.

Family Exposition of the Pentateuch, 586.
Frederick the Great, with an introduction by Thos. Campbell, Esq., 698.

G.

Glorious Things of the City of God, (The) a Sermon by the Bishop of New Jersey, 695.
Great Commission, (The) by Rev. Dr. Harris, 697.
Gregorian and other Ecclesiastical Chants, 588.

J.

Jameson's Travels in New Zealand, South Australia, and New South Wales, 477.

K.

Knapp's Christian Theology, 124.

L.

Letters and Notes on the Manners, Customs, and Condition of the North American Indians. By George Catlin, 693.
Lingard's Antiphonal Chants, for the Services of the United Church of England and Ireland, 694.
Lives of English Laymen, by the Rev. W. H. Teale, 695.
Lord Lindsay's Letter to a Friend, 131.
Less's Authenticity, Uncorrupted Preservation, and Credibility of the New Testament, 124.

M.

Martyr of Erromanga, (The) by J. Campbell, 477.
Memoirs of the Life and Writings of Michael Thomas Sadler, Esq., 587.
Moscheles' Life of Beethoven, 128.
Memoir of the Life of Richard Phillips, 470.
Mure's Journal of a Tour in Greece and the Ionian Islands, 584.

N.

Napier's Excursions along the Shores of the Mediterranean, 584.
Nelson's Christian Sacrifice, 131.
Notes of a Half-pay in search of Health, 222.

O.

Old St. Paul's, by William Harrison Ainsworth, 696.
On the Sufficiency of the Parochial System, by Rev. Dr. Chalmers, 221.

P.

Pilgrimage to Auvergne from Picardy to Le Velay, 223.

R.

Rambles and Researches in Thuringian Saxony, by Frederick Stanford, Esq., 699.
Raumer's England in 1841, 590.
Rosenmüller's Biblical Geography of Asia Minor, &c., 124.

INDEX.   725

Rudiments of Geography, by W. C. Woodbridge, 474.
Ride on Horseback to Florence, through France and Switzerland, by a Lady, 584.

S.

Sacred Hymns from the German, 216.
Sermon on Evangelical Repentance, by Rev. Charles Wordsworth, 372.
Seven Sermons preached at the Consecration and Re-opening of the Parish Church of Leeds, 218.
Search into the Old Testament, by Joseph Hume, 224.
Sharpe's History of Egypt under the Romans, 472.

T.

Three Discourses on the Divine Will, on Acquaintance with God, on Revelation, by Rev. A. J. Scott, 585.
Travels and Researches in Asia Minor, &c. by W. F. Ainsworth, 696.

V.

Voice of the Church on the Doctrine of Repentance; a Sermon, by the Rev. William Sinclair, 373.

W.

Woodhouse's Careless Christian, 132.
Wright's Edition of Latin Poems, 475.

SHORTER NOTICES OF BOOKS AND PAMPHLETS.

JANUARY.—Children's Books—"Little Bracker-Burners," "Young Naturalist's Journey," &c. &c.—An Answer to Lord Alvanley's "State of Ireland Reconsidered"—Essays written in the Intervals of Business—Sewell's Horæ Platonicæ—New Edition of Spenser—Modern Flirtations—Medical Student's Letter to the Rev. J. H. North, M.A.—Recollections of Clutha—The Canadas, by Wollaston—Poole's State of Parties in the Church of England—Williams's Remarks on the Bishop of Gloucester and Bristol's Charge—Burns' Magazine for the Young—Select Homilies for Holy-days and Seasons—Gresley's Parochial Sermons—Merivale's Whitehall Sermons—Hook's Miscellaneous Sermons—Single Sermons, 133—135.

FEBRUARY.—Confessions of an Apostate—Country Parson's Wife—Books by the Author of "Peep of Day"—Warton's English Poetry—Wheatley on the Common Prayer—Howitt's Visits, Second Series—Prince's Letters—Jameson's New Zealand—Modern Education, by E. L.—Letters from the Baltic—Stephens's Central America—Christian Diary—Farmer's Sonnets—Defence of the Church of England Notes on Genesis—Petit's Church Architecture—Selby's Forest Trees—Maitland's Pamphlets on Foxe—History of Pews—Milford Malvoisin—The Corn Laws—Stephens on the Fasts and Festivals—With a variety of Tracts, Pamphlets, and Sermons, 226—231.

MARCH.—Croly's Historical Sketches, &c.—Brand's Observations on Popular Antiquities—A Clergyman's Address to the Wesleyan Methodists in his Parish—Phillimore's Letter to Lord Ashburton—Bentali's Remarks on Westminster School—Edinburgh Cabinet Library—The History of the Fairchild Family, by Mrs. Sherwood—Archdeacon Todd on Clerical Societies—The Historical Character of St. Luke's First Chapter Vindicated, by Rev. Dr. Mill—Two New Arguments in Vindication of the Genuineness and Authenticity of the Revelation of St. John, by Collyer Knight—Palmer's Letter to a Protestant Catholic, &c.—Maurice's Reply—Dr. Hook's Reasons for Contributing to a Protestant Bishoprick at Jerusalem—The Swearer's End and the Widow's Son—Veles on the Abolition of Promotion by Purchase in the Army—Sinclair's Letter to a Member of Parliament on National Education, &c.—The Choralist—Poole on the State of Parties in the Church—The Leeds Tracts—Archdeacon Wilkins's Address to his Parishioners—Nottingham Journal—The Churchman—Wesleyan Tracts for the Times—Sermons, 374—376.

APRIL.—Brief Memorials of the Rev. W. B. Mathias—Mackenzie's Letter to William Lyall, Esq.—The Kings of the East—Scott's Narrative of a recent Imprisonment in China—Verses by a Poor Man—Serious Remonstrance to the Rev. W. B. Sibthorp—Macartney's Observations on the Book of Ruth—Hope's British Monthly Magazine—Archbishop Ussher's Works—Patrick, Lowth, Arnold, Whitby, and Lowman's Commentary—Malet's Church Extension—Mrs. Ellis's Daughters of England—Barr's Anglican Church Architecture—Markland's Remarks on English Churches—Wolff's Mystic Rationalism in Germany—A Guide to the Holy Eucharist—Wilberforce's Christian Unity—Catechetical Examinations—Charlie Burton—Memoirs of Naval Commanders whose Portraits are exhibited in Greenwich Hospital—Church and State Gazette—Sermons by the Bishop of New Jersey—Ollivant's Christian Student—The Cartoons of Raffaelle—Palin's Christian Month, 478—480.

MAY.—Massingberd's History of the Reformation—New Poems, by Wordsworth and Trench—Williams's Baptistery—Cardwell's Synodalia—Stanhope on the Epistles and Gospels, by Dr. Kenny—Chandler's Life of William of Wykeham—Burns' "Fourpenny Books"—Life of Richard Hooker—Modern Methodism—The Martyr of Prusa, or the First and last Prayer; by Rev. R. W. Kyle—Cooley's Negro-land of the Arabs—Manasseh, a Tale of the Jews—Robert and Frederick—The Appropriate Character of Church Architecture—The Library of the Fathers—Lives of the Evangelists and Apostles—Taylor's Ancient Christianity. No. VII.—The Christian Miscellany—A Letter to the Laity of the Church of England, by Rev. A. Watson—Hook's Church Dictionary—Bishop of Salisbury's Charge—Alford's Hulsean Lectures—

726 INDEX.

Wilberforce's Sermon before the Queen—Leger's Sermon—Confirmation and Communion—Address to the Parents of Children attending the Church School—&c. &c., 591—593.

JUNE.—The Churchman's Year, by Geo. Fyler Townsend, M.A.—Christ our Law—Lewis's Illustrations of Killpeck Church, Herefordshire—Italy, Classical, Historical, and Picturesque, by Mr. Brockedon—The Mother's Help, by the Rev. J. James—Gilly's Appeal on behalf of the Peasantry of the Border—Christian Magazine—Common Sense, or Every Body's Magazine—Hoare's Reply to the Bishop of Salisbury's Reasons for withdrawing from the Bible Society—A Tract for Squires, by a Squire—Thoughts on England's Responsibility—Hone's Comments on the Epistles—Church Atlas—Bishop of London's Three Sermons on the Church—The Bishop of Edinburgh's Primary Charge—Twenty-one Sermons, by the Rev. C. J. F. Clinton—Sermon by the Rev. Ch. Ch. Bartholomew—Cards for Distribution, 700—702.

Christ Church, Streatham (with an Engraving).................................. 136, 231.

ECCLESIASTICAL INTELLIGENCE.

Ordinations—Preferments—Deaths of Clergy—University News—Proceedings of Church Societies—Miscellaneous Diocesan Intelligence—Ireland—Scotland—Foreign, Pp. 138, 263, 377, 487, 596, 711.

N.B.—Copies of the two previous Volumes of the REMEMBRANCER may still be had, price 10s. each, in cloth. Also, a few separate Numbers to complete Sets. The following is a sketch of their Contents:—

Religious Poets of the Day.
Literature and Authorship in England.
Church Architecture, with Plates.
Invalidity of Dissenters' Baptisms.
The Inductive Sciences.
Life and Writings of St. Irenæus.
Chemical Philosophy.
Illustrations of Ballad Poetry.
Christian Almsgiving.
On the Sonnet (2 Nos.)
Episcopal Visitations (3 Nos.)
The Divine Right of Tithes and the Offertory (4 Nos.)

Missions in the East.
The Ancient British Church.
Presbyterianism in Scotland.
Ecclesiastical Music. (4 Nos.)
Astronomy.
Chapters on Ecclesiastical Law.
Convocation.
Original Letters of Archbishop Laud.
The Church in Scotland.
Travels in Palestine.
The Parables of our Lord.
Churches and Churchwardens.

END OF VOL. III.

BIND

BR
1
C637
n.s.
v.3

The Christian remembrancer